HF513282

R. Gupta's®

National Testing Agency (NTA)

UGC-NET/JRF

Junior Research Fellowship & Assistant Professor Eligibility Exam

ECONOMICS

Previous Years' Papers

PAPER II

by

RPH Editorial Board

2027 EDITION

RAMESH PUBLISHING HOUSE, NEW DELHI

Published by

O.P. Gupta *for* Ramesh Publishing House

Admin. Office

12-H, New Daryaganj Road, Opp. Officers' Mess,
New Delhi-110002 ✆ 23275224, 23245124

E-mail: info@rameshpublishinghouse.com

For Online Shopping: www.rameshpublishinghouse.com

Showroom

- Balaji Market, Nai Sarak, Delhi-110006 ✆ 23282525 📱 9354373464
- 4457, Nai Sarak, Delhi-110006

Book Code: R-2679

ISBN: 978-93-5477-654-0

Price: ₹ 690

Printed at: Deepak Offset, Delhi

CONTENTS

UGC-NET/JRF—(PAPER-II) ECONOMICS

Previous Years' Paper

National Testing Agency (NTA)

UGC-NET Junior Research Fellowship & Assistant Professor Eligibility Exam

ECONOMICS, JANUARY-2026

(Exam held on 07-01-2026)

PAPER-II

1. Match List-I with List-II.

List-I	List-II
A. 14th Finance Commission	I. Vertical Tax Devolution 41 percent
B. 15th Finance Commission	II. Vertical Tax Devolution 42 percent
C. 12th Finance Commission	III. State's share 32% of the central taxes
D. 13th Finance Commission	IV. State's share 30.5 percent of central taxes

Choose the **correct** answer from the options given below :

1. A-IV, B-III, C-II, D-I
2. A-IV, B-III, C-I, D-II
3. A-III, B-IV, C-I, D-II
4. A-II, B-I, C-IV, D-III

2. Kinked-Demand model of oligopoly was developed by which of the following ?

1. Chamberlin
2. Bertrand
3. Stackel berg
4. Sweezy

3. Given the difference equation $Y_{t+1} - 1.2Y_t = 0$, the general expression Y_t in terms of t can be:

1. $Y_t = (1.2)^t Y_1$
2. $Y_t = (1.2)^{t+1} Y_0$
3. $Y_t = (1.2)^{t-1} Y_1$
4. $Y_t = (1.2)^{t-1} Y_0 + C$

4. In case of balanced budget multiplier :

A. Output increases less than the increase in government spending.

B. Output increases more than the increase in government spending.

C. Government spending and taxes are raised in equal amounts.

D. The value of multiplier is equal to 1.

Choose the **correct** answer from the options given below :

1. C and D only
2. B and C only
3. A, B and C only
4. B and D only

5. Which one of the following is true for the phenomenon of Liquidity Trap ?

1. The entire additional money supply is spent on buying bonds
2. The level of rate of interest is very high
3. The entire additional money supply is held by the public as idle cash balance
4. The interest rate will decrease from the point of liquidity trap

6. How much revenue will have to be foregone due to different beneficial proposals in the central budget 2025-26?

1. ₹ 2 Lakh Crore as direct taxes and ₹ 5600 Crore as indirect taxes

2. ₹ 1.5 Lakh Crore as direct taxes and ₹ 5600 Crore as indirect taxes
3. ₹ 1 Lakh Crore as direct taxes and ₹ 2600 Crore as indirect taxes
4. ₹ 50,000 Crore as direct taxes and ₹ 2000 Crore as indirect taxes

7. Given below are two statements : one is labelled as Assertion (A) and the other is labelled as Reason (R).

Assertion (A) : Deficit spending by the government leads to crowding out effect on private investment.

Reason (A) : When the government finances its deficit by borrowing from the market, the bond prices go up and the rate of interest falls.

In the light of the above statements, choose the **most appropriate answer** from the options given below :

1. Both (A) and (R) are correct and (R) is the correct explanation of (A)
2. Both (A) and (R) are correct but (R) is not the correct explanation of (A)
3. (A) is correct but (R) is not correct
4. (A) is not correct but (R) is correct

8. Welfare criterion based on compensation payments is known as :

1. Dalton-Friedman Compensation Criterion
2. Amartya Sen Compensation Criterion
3. Pareto-Bains Compensation Criterion
4. Kaldor-Hicks Compensation Criterion

9. The Human Development Index (HDI) is used to rank countries based on :

1. Life expectancy at Birth, Adult Illiteracy Rate and the percentage of population without access to safe water.
2. Real Per Capita Income, Percentage of Underweight children under 5 years and percentage of population not expected to survive to the age of 40.
3. Life Expectancy at Birth, Educational attainment and Real per capita Income at purchasing Power Parity.
4. Income Inequality and percentage of population living in urban areas.

10. Match List-I with List-II.

List-I	List-II
A. Kenneth Bouilding	I. Pollution Tax
B. Georgescu-Roegen	II. Spaceship Earth and Ecological Limits
C. Elinor Ostrom	III. Managing Common Property Resources
D. A.C. Pigou	IV. Energy as a limiting factor

Choose the **correct** answer from the options given below :

1. A-I, B-III, C-II, D-IV
2. A-III, B-II, C-I, D-IV
3. A-II, B-I, C-IV, D-III
4. A-II, B-IV, C-III, D-I

11. As per Dalton's optimum population formula defined as $M = \frac{A-O}{O}$ (where M is degree of mal-adjustment, A is actual population and O is the level of optimum population), a country is said to have optimum population if :

1. M is positive
2. M is negative
3. M is zero
4. O is zero

12. Given below are two statements : one is labelled as Assertion (A) and the other is labelled as Reason (R).

Assertion (A): If X and Y are any two variables and are transformed to the new variables U and V defined by $U = \frac{X-A}{h}$,

$V = \frac{Y-B}{K}$ where A, B, h, K are any constants, h and $K > 0$ then, $r_{xy} = r_{uv}$

Reason (R): Correlation coefficient(r) is independent of change of origin and scale.

In the light of the above statements, choose the **most appropriate answer** from the options given below :

1. Both (A) and (R) are correct and (R) is the correct explanation of (A)
2. Both (A) and (R) are correct but (R) is not the correct explanation of (A)
3. (A) is correct but (R) is not correct
4. (A) is not correct but (R) is correct

13. Coefficient of Determination (R^2):

A. is an increasing function of the number of regressors

B. is a decreasing function of the number of regressors

C. is unaffected by increasing or decreasing the number of regressors

D. is always positive

Choose the **correct** answer from the options given below :

1. A and B only 2. A and C only
3. A and D only 4. B and C only

14. Monopoly Power is explained by which of the following?

1. $\frac{(P-MC)}{P}$ 2. $\frac{(P+MC)}{P}$
3. $\frac{(P-AC)}{P}$ 4. $\frac{(P+AC)}{P}$

15. In which year, the notes of ₹ 1000 denomination were demonetised for the first time in India?

1. 2016 2. 1978
3. 1969 4. 1980

16. The basic proposition of neo-classical growth theory are :

A. The growth of output depends on the rate of growth of labour productivity

B. The growth of output depends on the level of per capita income

C. The ratio of savings and investment determines economic growth

D. Only investment determines economic growth

Choose the **correct** answer from the options given below :

1. A and C only 2. A and B only
3. C and D only 4. B and C only

17. Among the following types of treasury bills, identify the correct one.

A. Adjusted price auction

B. Uniform price auction

C. Multiple price auction

D. Readjusted price auction

Choose the **correct** answer from the options given below :

1. A and B only 2. B and C only
3. C and D only 4. A and D only

18. A theory that explains the phenomenon of increasing public expenditure and state activity was proposed by:

1. Baumol 2. Allan Peacock
3. Dalton 4. Adolf Wagner

19. The origin of "Big-Push" theory of development is based on :

1. Unbalanced Economic Growth
2. Low Level Equilibrium Trap and Critical Minimum Effort
3. Kaldor's Growth Laws
4. Harrod's Knife-edged Instability

20. Given below are two statements : one is labelled as Assertion (A) and the other is labelled as Reason (R).

Assertion (A) : The Organisation of Petroleum Exporting Countries (OPEC) has failed to maintain high prices of petroleum products in the long run.

Reason (R): For petroleum products both the demand and supply are inelastic in the long run.

In the light of the above statements, choose the **most appropriate answer** from the options given below :

1. Both (A) and (R) are correct and (R) is the correct explanation of (A)

2. Both (A) and (R) are correct but (R) is not the correct explanation of (A)
3. (A) is correct but (R) is not correct
4. (A) is not correct but (R) is correct

21. Consider the following items and figures.

Items	Amount (in ₹ Crores)
(*a*) Total revenue receipts	5600
(*b*) Total capital receipts	3000
(*c*) Interest payments	800
(*d*) Disinvestment receipts	400
(*e*) Total expenditure	8600
(*f*) Recovery of loans	150

What is the amount of primary deficits?

1. ₹ 2140 crores
2. ₹ 3000 crores
3. ₹ 1650 crores
4. ₹ 2450 crores

22. Match List-I with List-II (As per Union Budget, 2025-26).

List-I	List-II
A. Pensions as % of Central Government Expenditure	I. 22%
B. State's share of taxes and duties as % of Central Govt. Expenditure	II. 18%
C. Tax-GDP ratio of India	III. 81.3%
D. Debt-GDP ratio of India	IV. 4%

Choose the **correct** answer from the options given below :

1. A-II, B-I, C-III, D-IV
2. A-II, B-III, C-I, D-IV
3. A-IV, B-III, C-I, D-II
4. A-IV, B-I, C-II, D-III

23. In a situation of decline in price of a Giffen Commodity, we find :

1. positive substitution effect is less than negative income effect
2. positive substitution effect is more than negative income effect
3. negative substitution effect is more than positive income effect
4. negative substitution effect is less than positive income effect

24. Match List-I with List-II.

List-I	List-II
A. Q theory	I. Unemployment and inflation
B. Phillips curve	II. Unemployment and output
C. Okun's Law	III. Investment
D. Liquidity trap	IV. Demand for money and interest rate

Choose the **correct** answer from the options given below :

1. A-III, B-I, C-II, D-IV
2. A-I, B-II, C-IV, D-III
3. A-III, B-II, C-I, D-IV
4. A-II, B-IV, C-I, D-III

25. Given GNP at market price ₹ 14400 crores, consumption ₹ 12000 crores, government purchases ₹ 1200 crores, exports ₹ 1000 crores and imports ₹ 1500 crores, the value of investment will be :

1. ₹ 1200 Crores
2. ₹ 2000 Crores
3. ₹ 1500 Crores
4. ₹ 1700 Crores

26. When public revenue increases by more than 1% for a 1% increase in GDP, it is known as :

1. CENVAT
2. Inelastict Tax system
3. Proportional Tax system
4. Tax buoyancy

27. The development of economic growth theory in chronological order would be :

A. Harrod Domar Growth Model
B. Solow's Neoclassical Growth Model
C. Endogenous Growth Theory
D. Adam Smith's "division of labour" and "increasing returns" theory.

Choose the **correct** answer from the options given below :

1. D, C, B, A
2. D, B, C, A
3. D, A, B, C
4. B, D, A, C

28. "Economic Dependency Burden" of a country implies :

A. The non-productive members of the country must be supported by the country's labour force.
B. The outstanding loan of the country.
C. Children below the age of 15 and people above the age of 70.
D. The people working in private sector

Choose the **correct** answer from the options given below :

1. A and D only
2. A and C only
3. C and D only
4. B and C only

29. NSSO and CSO come under :

1. Ministry of Home Affairs
2. Ministry of Finance
3. Ministry of Industry and Commerce
4. Ministry of Statistics and Programme Implementation (MoSPI)

30. Recently, Inflation rates have trended downward and approaching steadily Central Bank target levels.

In this context, which of the following are correct?

A. Supply chains are adopting the economic uncertainties
B. Easing monetary policy
C. Tighter monetary policy
D. Increase in AD is more than increase in AS

Choose the **correct** answer from the options given below :

1. A and B only
2. B and D only
3. A and C only
4. C and D only

31. For the given information regarding an economy, the value of equilibrium level of income is :

$C = 100 + 0.75Y_d$; G = 40; I = 60; $t = 0.2$

Here, C = consumption, Y_d = disposable income, G = Govt. expenditure, I = Investment, t = tax rate

1. 200
2. 500
3. 400
4. 450

32. Given below are two statements : one is labelled as Assertion (A) and the other is labelled as Reason (R).

If X is a given series of observations, a and b are any two constants, then with regard to Standard Deviation (SD).

Assertion (A) : $SD(X + a) = SD(X - b) = SD(X)$ and $SD(aX) = a^2.SD(X)$

Reason (R): SD is independent of change of origin, but not of scale.

In the light of the above statements, choose the **most appropriate answer** from the options given below:

1. Both (A) and (R) are correct and (R) is the correct explanation of (A)
2. Both (A) and (R) are correct but (R) is not the correct explanation of (A)
3. (A) is correct but (R) is not correct
4. (A) is not correct but (R) is correct

33. Given below are two statements : one is labelled as Assertion (A) and the other is labelled as Reason (R).

Assertion (A) : With 10% rise in average income of household, there will be 50% rise in investment in health and education of children.

Reason (R): Investment in health and education of children will raise human capital that will raise human capability and raise economic productivity.

In the light of the above statements, choose the **most appropriate answer** from the options given below:

1. Both (A) and (R) are correct and (R) is the correct explanation of (A)
2. Both (A) and (R) are correct but (R) is not the correct explanation of (A)
3. (A) is correct but (R) is not correct
4. (A) is not correct but (R) is correct

34. Given samples of sizes 20 and 15 with respective sample variances 35.53 and 34.92, the calculated value of F-statistic is :

1. 1.02
2. 0.98
3. 0.76
4. 1.31

35. Based on the following statements :

A. Matrix Addition is not Commutative
B. Matrix Addition is Associative
C. Matrix Multiplication is Commutative
D. Matrix Multiplication is Associative if product exists

Choose the **correct** answer from the options given below :

1. A and C only 2. A and D only
3. B and C only 4. B and D only

36. Identify the correct statement regarding Mahatma Gandhi National Rural Employment Guarantee Scheme (MNREGS) :

1. The draft proposed by the National Advisory Committee (NAC) envisaged legal guarantee to every household in rural areas for 120 days for doing casual manual work
2. 90 percent of the cost of employment provided is borne by the centre
3. In the first phase of implementation, 150 most backward districts were covered
4. From 2nd October, 2010, National Rural Employment Guarantee Scheme (NREGS) has been renamed as Mahatma Gandhi National Rural Employment Guarantee Scheme (MNREGS)

37. For Cobb-Douglas production function with two inputs, $Q = AK^{\alpha}L^{\beta}$ where $A > 0$, α and β are > 0, the marginal products are :

A. $MP_k = \frac{\alpha}{K}Q$ B. $MP_k = \frac{\beta}{K}Q$

C. $MP_L = \frac{\alpha}{L}Q$ D. $MP_L = \frac{\beta}{L}Q$

Choose the **correct** answer from the options given below :

1. A and C only 2. A and D only
3. B and C only 4. B and D only

38. Given below are two statements : one is labelled as Assertion (A) and the other is labelled as Reason (R).

Assertion (A) : The presence of heteroscedasticity problem in regression analysis implies that the least square estimators are still unbiased but inefficient.

Reason (R) : The estimates of the variances are also unbiased.

In the light of the above statements, choose the **most appropriate answer** from the options given below :

1. Both (A) and (R) are correct and (R) is the correct explanation of (A)
2. Both (A) and (R) are correct but (R) is not the correct explanation of (A)
3. (A) is correct but (R) is not correct
4. (A) is not correct but (R) is correct

39. Which Tax is also popularly known as the 'destination tax' ?

1. Customs Duty
2. Corporate Tax
3. Goods and Services Tax
4. Central Excise Duty

40. Arrange the following in a correct chronological order.

A. Shankar Acharya Committee on shifting financial year from (April-March) to (Jan-Dec).
B. Parthasarathy Shome Committee on retrospective tax laws.
C. Vijay Kelkar Committee on Tax reforms.
D. Arvind Subramanian Committee on revenue neutral GST.

Choose the **correct** answer from the options given below :

1. A, B, C, D 2. C, A, D, B
3. C, B, D, A 4. A, D, B, C

41. The Coasian Bargaining Approach will work when :

A. The rights of the bargaining parties are transferable
B. The bargaining parties are equally informed
C. The property rights are legally established
D. The resources are universally owned

Choose the **correct** answer from the options given below :

1. A and D only 2. B and D only
3. B and C only 4. A and C only

42. Given the demand function P = 80 – 3Q and cost function TC = 120 + 8Q :

A. Maximum Revenue occurs at Q = 12
B. Maximum Revenue occurs at Q = 3
C. Maximum Revenue is 528
D. Maximum Revenue is 213

Choose the **correct** answer from the options given below :

1. A and C only
2. A and D only
3. B and C only
4. B and D only

43. Match List-I with List-II.

List-I	List-II
A. Slack Variable	I. Best of all feasible solutions
B. Surplus Variable	II. Solution violating at least one condition
C. Optimal Solution	III. Used when there are less than or equal to (≤) type inequalities
D. Infeasible Solution	IV. Used when there are greater than or equal to (≥) type inequalities

Choose the **correct** answer from the options given below :

1. A-IV, B-III, C-I, D-II
2. A-IV, B-III, C-II, D-I
3. A-III, B-IV, C-II, D-I
4. A-III, B-IV, C-I, D-II

44. The range of the function $y = f(x) = \sqrt{1-x^2}$ is :

1. [0, 1] 2. [1, 0]
3. [1, ∞] 4. [1, 2]

45. Match List-I with List-II.

List-I	List-II
A. Targeted Public Distribution System (TPDS)	I. 1992
B. Revamped Public Distribution System (RPDS)	II. 2009
C. Right to Education Act (RTE Act)	III. 1997
D. National Food Security Act (NFSA Act)	IV. 2013

Choose the **correct** answer from the options given below :

1. A-I, B-III, C-IV, D-II
2. A-IV, B-III, C-I, D-II
3. A-III, B-I, C-II, D-IV
4. A-II, B-IV, C-I, D-III

46. 'The Salmon War' was between :

1. USA and Cuba
2. France and UK
3. Norway and Scotland
4. Sweden and Germany

47. Which of the following are called 'club goods'?

A. Railways B. Swimming pool
C. Defense D. Gym

Choose the **correct** answer from the options given below :

1. B and D only 2. A and B only
3. B and C only 4. A and D only

48. Given the demand function $Q = 100 - P - P^2$, the elasticity of demand (e_d) at price P = 5 is:

1. elastic 2. inelastic
3. unitary elastic 4. infinitely elastic

49. Match List-I with List-II.

List-I	List-II
A. Harrod and Domor	I. Constancy of the capital output ratio
B. Lucas and Romer	II. Dual economy with a capitalist and non-capitalist sector
C. Arthur Lewis	III. Investment as a double edged sword
D. Michael Todaro	IV. Rural-Urban migration

Choose the **correct** answer from the options given below :

1. A-IV, B-III, C-I, D-II
2. A-III, B-I, C-II, D-IV
3. A-I, B-II, C-III, D-IV
4. A-II, B-IV, C-III, D-I

50. Given the structural model

$y_1 = 3y_2 - 2x_1 + x_2 + u_1$
$y_2 = y_3 + x_3 + u_2$
$y_3 = y_1 - y_2 - 2x_3 + u_3$

Based on the order condition, the second equation is :

1. over identified
2. exactly identified
3. under identified
4. information not sufficient

51. Match List-I with List-II.

List-I	List-II
A. Debt-deflation theory	I. Falling price levels raises the income levels
B. Pigou effect	II. A policy of announcing future monetary action
C. Forward guidance	III. The effects of unexpected fall in price level could depress income
D. Okun's law	IV. An inverse relationship between unemployment and real GDP

Choose the **correct** answer from the options given below :

1. A-I, B-III, C-II, D-IV
2. A-III, B-II, C-IV, D-I
3. A-III, B-I, C-II, D-IV
4. A-IV, B-I, C-II, D-III

52. Based on $\{\in_t\}$ is a purely random process with mean zero and variance σ^2 :

A. A process $\{x_t\}$ defined by $x_t = \alpha_1 x_{t-1} + \alpha_2 x_{t-2} + ... + \alpha_r x_{t-r} + \in_t$ is called an autoregressive process of order r

B. A process $\{x_t\}$ defined by $x_t = \beta_0 \in_t + \beta_1 \in_{t-1} + ... + \beta_m \in_{t-m}$ is called a moving average process of order m

C. A process $\{x_t\}$ defined by $x_t = \beta_0 \in_t + \beta_1 \in_{t-1} + ... + \beta_m \in_{t-m}$ is called an autoregressive process of order r

D. A process $\{x_t\}$ defined by $x_t = \alpha_1 x_{t-1} + \alpha_2 x_{t-2} + ... + \alpha_r x_{t-r} + \in_t$ is called a moving average process of order m

Choose the **correct** answer from the options given below :

1. A and B only
2. A and D only
3. B and D only
4. C and D only

53. The main feature of embodied technical progress is :

1. Exogenous technical progress that is not dependent on capital accumulation is embodied progress.
2. Technical improvements that can only be introduced into the productive system by new investment is embodied progress.
3. Lop-sided productivity increase is embodied progress.
4. This is dependent on government support.

54. Match List-I with List-II.

List-I	List-II
A. Neo-Chamberlinian Model	I. Horizontal differentiation of products
B. Neo-Hotelling Model	II. Vertical differentiation of products
C. Brander-Krugman Model	III. Product differentiation
D. Neo-Heckscher-Ohlin Model	IV. Reciprocal dumping

Choose the **correct** answer from the options given below :

1. A-IV, B-III, C-I, D-II
2. A-I, B-II, C-IV, D-III
3. A-I, B-III, C-II, D-IV
4. A-III, B-I, C-IV, D-II

55. A. Reserve Money = C + OD + CR

B. M1 = C + OD

C. Money Multiplier (m) = M/RM

D. Narrow Money Supply = M3

Here C = Currency, OD= Other deposits with RBI, CR = Cash Reserve of Banks, M = Money Supply, RM = Reserve Money

Choose the **correct** answer from the options given below :

1. A and D only 2. B and C only
3. A and B only 4. A and C only

56. Match List-I with List-II.

List-I	List-II
A. Amartya Sen	I. Rise and fall of inequality with economic growth
B. Simon Kuznets	II. Circulative and cumulative causation of economic under-development
C. Gunnar Myrdal	III. Geographic pattern of economic development
D Paul Krugman	IV. Entitlements, capabilities and freedom of choice

Choose the **correct** answer from the options given below :

1. A-II, B-IV, C-I, D-III
2. A-III, B-II, C-IV, D-I
3. A-I, B-II, C-III, D-IV
4. A-IV, B-I, C-II, D-III

57. Increased fiscal deficit leads to :

A. Increase in government spending

B. Increase in domestic interest rate

C. Fall in private investment

D. Fall in total borrowing by the government

Choose the **correct** answer from the options given below :

1. A, B and D only 2. A, B and C only
3. B, C and D only 4. B and D only

58. A natural monopoly occurs when :

1. Average cost keeps on rising with increase in output over the relevant range of output.
2. Average cost remains constant with increase in output over the relevant range of output.
3. Average cost first decreases and then rises with increase in output over the relevant range of output.
4. Average cost keeps on decreasing with increase in output over the relevant range of output.

59. In a population of men in a city, 3% are observed to suffer from cancer, 15% are found to be smokers, while 10% are noticed to be either smokers or cancer patients. If a man is selected at random, what is the probability that he is a smoker and suffering from cancer?

1. 0.08 2. 0.8
3. 0.02 4. 0.2

60. Which one of the following is NOT true about rational expectation?

1. Rational expectations theory has been developed by Hansen.
2. It is used in decision making by households, firms and labour for making their expectations about relevant variables.
3. The rational expectation uses all relevant information.
4. It is not an error free expectation.

61. Match List-I with List-II.

List-I	List-II
A. Type I error	I. Accept H_0 when it is false
B. Type II error	II. $H_0 : \mu = \mu_0$ and $\sigma^2 = \sigma_0^2$
C. Simple Hypothesis	III. Reject H_0 when it is true
D. Composite Hypothesis	IV. $H_0 : \mu = \mu_0$ and σ^2 is unknown

Choose the **correct** answer from the options given below :

1. A-III, B-I, C-IV, D-II
2. A-I, B-III, C-II, D-IV
3. A-III, B-I, C-II, D-IV
4. A-I, B-III, C-IV, D-II

62. The Headcount Index of Poverty Measurement is based on :

1. The number of people who fall below the poverty line.
2. The proportionate gap between the average level of income below the poverty line and the poverty line itself.
3. The "Bottom Billion"
4. Vertical Inequality of income

63. Which one of the following holds true at equilibrium level of demand for labour by a perfectly competitive firm?

1. $VMP_L < MRP_L$
2. $VMP_L = MRP_L$
3. $VMP_L > MRP_L$
4. $VMP_L + MRP_L = W_*$

64. Match List-I with List-II.

List-I	List-II
A. $\lvert e_d \rvert$ for demand function D = 64 − 8 P, at P= 6	I. 6
B. e_s for supply function S = −25 + 5 P, at P =10	II. 4
C. The value of MR when P = 8 and e_d = 4	III. 3
D. The value of MPP_L when VMP_L = 12 and P= 3	IV. 2

Choose the **correct** answer from the options given below :

1. A-III, B-IV, C-I, D-II
2. A-II, B-III, C-I, D-IV
3. A-I, B-IV, C-II, D-III
4. A-III, B-I, C-IV, D-II

65. A. Innovation Theory of Business cycle was given by Jorgenson

B. Pure Monetary Theory of Business cycle was given by Hawtrey

C. Monetary-over-investment Theory of Business cycle was given by Clark

D. Multiplier-Acceleration Interaction Theory of Business cycle was given by Samuelson

Choose the **correct** answer from the options given below :

1. A and B only
2. B and D only
3. A, B and C only
4. A and D only

66. Which one of the following production function exhibits decreasing returns to scale?

1. $AK^{\frac{1}{4}}\sqrt{L}$
2. $A K^{\alpha} L^{1-\alpha}$
3. $A(3K + 5L)$
4. $A\sqrt{KL^3}$

67. Identify the Finance commissions with its chairman:

A. 12th Finance commission – C. Rangarajan

B. 11th Finance commission – A.M. Khusro

C. 14th Finance commission – R.K. Singh

D. 15th Finance commission – Y.V. Reddy

Choose the **correct** answer from the options given below :

1. A and D
2. B and C
3. C and D
4. A and B

68. Given below are two statements : one is labelled as Assertion (A) and the other is labelled as Reason (R).

Assertion (A): When everyone trades in the competitive market place, all mutually beneficial trades are completed and the resulting equilibrium allocation of resources are economically efficient.

Reason (R): Even if a trade from an inefficient allocation makes everyone better off, the new allocation is not necessarily efficient.

In the light of the above statements, choose the **most appropriate answer from** the options given below:

1. Both (A) and (R) are correct and (R) is the correct explanation of (A)

2. Both (A) and (R) are correct but (R) is not the correct explanation of (A)
3. (A) is correct but (R) is not correct
4. (A) is not correct but (R) is correct

69. The following statements are made in the Union Budget for the year 2025-2026 :

A. The FDI limit for the insurance sector will be raised from 74 to 100 percent
B. The FDI limit for the insurance sector will be raised from 51 to 74 percent
C. An investment Friendliness Index of states will be formed
D. The fiscal deficit is estimated to be 4.4 percent of GDP

Choose the **correct** answer from the options given below :

1. B, C and D only
2. A, C and D only
3. A, B and C only
4. C and D only

70. Choose the correct statements:

A. The 'q' theory emphasises that the investment increases when assets are valuable relative to their reproduction cost.
B. With a fixed exchange rate fiscal expansion under free capital mobility is completely ineffective in raising output.
C. Under Investment tax credit, government pays part of the cost of investment.
D. Under fixed exchange rate and perfect capital mobility a country cannot pursue an independent monetary policy.

Choose the **correct** answer from the options given below :

1. B and D only
2. A and D only
3. A, C and D only
4. A, B and C only

71. When some domestic production by a nation member of the Union is replaced by lower-cost imports from another member nation, then the Union is known as :

1. Trade Diverting Customs Union
2. Trade Creating Customs Union
3. Preferential Trade Agreement
4. Free Trade Agreement

72. Given below are two statements : one is labelled as Assertion (A) and the other is labelled as Reason (R).

Assertion (A) : Since about the mid-seventies, protectionism has grown alarmingly in the developed countries. This has taken mainly the form of non-tariff barriers (NTBs).

Reason (R): The growing protectionism in industrialised countries is due to the increasing competition from developing and the South-East Asian countries.

In the light of the above statements, choose the **most appropriate answer** from the options given below:

1. Both (A) and (R) are correct and (R) is the correct explanation of (A)
2. Both (A) and (R) are correct but (R) is not the correct explanation of (A)
3. (A) is correct but (R) is not correct
4. (A) is not correct but (R) is correct

73. For analysing effective rent control in the housing sector :

A. The shortage of housing is small in the short run compared to the long run.
B. The shortage of housing is large in the short run compared to the long run.
C. The effective rent control exists when a government places an effective price floor on rent.
D. The effective rent control exists when a government places an effective price ceiling on rent.

Choose the **correct** answer from the options given below :

1. A and C only
2. B and C only
3. A and D only
4. B and D only

74. Match List-I with List-II.

List-I	List-II
A. Narasimham Committee-I	I. Tax Reform
B. Narasimham Committee-II	II. Banking Sector Reform
C. Chelliah Committee	III. Financial Sector Reform
D. C. Rangarajan Committee	IV. Poverty Estimation Committee

Choose the **correct** answer from the options given below :

1. A-IV, B-II, C-I, D-III
2. A-III, B-II, C-I, D-IV
3. A-II, B-III, C-IV, D-I
4. A-I, B-II, C-IV, D-III

75. Based on Economic Survey 2024-25, Indian merchandise trade deficit widened due to :

A. Decline of non-petroleum and non-gems and jewellery exports
B. Increase in non-oil and non-gold imports
C. Imposing of ban on jewellery exports
D. Gold imports grew due to early purchases ahead of festive spending and demand for safe heaven assets

Choose the **correct** answer from the options given below :

1. A and B only 2. B and D only
3. C and D only 4. A and C only

76. Given below are two statements : one is labelled as Assertion (A) and the other is labelled as Reason (R).

Assertion (A): The all-India annual unemployment rate (UR) for individuals, aged 15 years and above (usual status) has steadily declined from 6 percent in 2017-2018 to 3.2 percent in 2023-2024.

Reason (R): According to RBI data, India's foreign exchange reserves on Dec. 26, 2025 were around 693 billion dollars.

In the light of the above statements, choose the **most appropriate answer** from the options given below :

1. Both (A) and (R) are correct and (R) is the correct explanation of (A)
2. Both (A) and (R) are correct but (R) is not the correct explanation of (A)
3. (A) is correct but (R) is not correct
4. (A) is not correct but (R) is correct

77. Etymologically, the term 'money' is derived from which language?

1. Greek 2. Latin
3. Persian 4. Sanskrit

78. Arrange the following theories in a chronological order.

A. Theory of limit pricing (Bain's Model)
B. Logical ordering theory of demand given by JR Hicks.
C. Cardinal utility theory of demand
D. Walras theory of general equilibrium

Choose the **correct** answer from the options given below :

1. D, C, A, B 2. B, C, A, D
3. A, B, D, C 4. D, B, C, A

79. A. SEBI - Advisory body
B. GST Council - Statutory body
C. NITI Aayog - Advisory body
D. RBI - Statutory body

Choose the **correct** answer from the options given below :

1. A and B 2. A and C
3. B and D 4. C and D

80. Match List-I with List-II.

List-I	List-II
A. *n*th term of an Arithmetic Progression	I. $\frac{n}{2}[2a+(n-1)d]$
B. *n*th term of a Geometric Progression	II. $a\left(\frac{r^n-1}{r-1}\right), r>1$
C. Sum to *n* terms of an Arithmetic Progression	III. $a + (n - 1)d$
D. Sum to *n* terms of a Geometric Progression	IV. ar^{n-1}

(where *a* is first term, *d* is common difference and *r* is common ratio)

Choose the **correct** answer from the options given below :

1. A-III, B-IV, C-II, D-I
2. A-III, B-IV, C-I, D-II
3. A-IV, B-III, C-I, D-II
4. A-IV, B-I, C-II, D-III

81. Which of the following approach has included Time Deposit with commercial banks in the definition of Money Supply?

1. The Conventional Approach
2. The Chicago Approach
3. The Fed Approach
4. The Walters Approach

82. Given below are two statements :

Statement (I): Green Revolution led to increase in the production of fine cereals. High incentives and application of high yielding varieties of seeds, fertilisers and chemicals made this a good success.

Statement (II) : Green revolution led to decline in the production of coarse cereals and area under coarse cereals shifted to other crops.

In the light of the above statements, choose the **most appropriate answer** from the options given below :

1. Both Statement I and Statement II are correct
2. Both Statement I and Statement II are incorrect
3. Statement I is correct but Statement II is incorrect
4. Statement I is incorrect but Statement II is correct

83. Which of the following is not correct in case of Rural Infrastructure Development Fund (RIDF)?

1. Providing funds to state governments and state owned corporations to rural infrastructure projects
2. Scheduled commercial banks contribute funds to RIDF
3. Creation of RIDF in 1995-96 in NABARD with a corpus of Rs. 2000 Crore
4. Now RIDF scheme is merged with Kisan Credit Card (RCC)

84. A. Globalisation carries benefits and opportunities as well as costs and risks

B. Globalisation leads to flow of capital, technology, goods and services across countries

C. The larger the market, the greater the gains from trade and the division of labour

D. Globalisation in terms of flow of capital, goods and technology is evenly spread across world nations

Choose the **correct** answer from the options given below :

1. A, B and C only
2. A, B and D only
3. B and D only
4. B, C and D only

85. Which of the following commodities are not covered by GST till now ?

A. Mobile phones
B. Electricity
C. Textiles
D. Alcohol

Choose the **correct** answer from the options given below :

1. A and C only
2. B and C only
3. A and D only
4. B and D only

86. Given below are two statements : one is labelled as Assertion (A) and the other is labelled as Reason (R).

Assertion (A): Prices of diesel and petroleum products are different in different states of India.

Reason (R): The above products have not yet been brought under the coverage of GST by the GST Council.

In the light of the above statements, choose the **most appropriate answer** from the options given below:

1. Both (A) and (R) are correct and (R) is the correct explanation of (A)
2. Bodi (A) and (R) are correct but (R) is not the correct explanation of (A)
3. (A) is correct but (R) is not correct
4. (A) is not correct but (R) is correct

87. Based on Beta (β) and Gama (γ) coefficients, if $\beta_2 < 3$ or $\gamma_2 < 0$ then the curve is said to be:

1. Normal Curve
2. Lepto Kurtic
3. Platy Kurtic
4. Insufficient Data

88. Which of the following is not a function of the Securities and Exchange Board of India (SEBI)?

1. Prohibiting insider trading in securities
2. Promoting and regulating self-regulatory organisations
3. Underwriting new capital issues
4. Regulating portfolio managers

89. If $P(A) = \frac{1}{5}$ and $P(B) = \frac{1}{3}$ and A and B are two mutually exclusive events, then the probability of neither A nor B will occur is:

1. $\frac{8}{25}$
2. $\frac{1}{15}$
3. $\frac{7}{15}$
4. $\frac{1}{5}$

90. A. In a barter system, if there are 3 goods to be exchanged, the required number of prices will be 3.

B. Money does not play its functions in case of inflation.

C. Double coincidence of wants is not a problem in barter system.

D. Paper currencies are token money.

Choose the **correct** answer from the options given below :

1. A, B and D only
2. B and D only
3. A and D only
4. B, C and D only

Directions (Qs. No. 91-95): *Read the following passage and answer the questions :*

For environmental assets, markets can fail if prices do not communicate society's desires and constraints accurately. The factors leading to habitat destruction and the loss of biodiversity originate in several sources of market failure. First, habitat destruction arises from public ownership of large areas of land with open access and limited government capacity to manage land. The economic incentives encourage the over exploitation of wildf-life, timber, grazing lands and crop lands.

Lack of secure land tenure provides little incentive to maintain the habitat necessary for biodiversity conservation. This is a case of non-rivalry and non-excludability that can destroy biodiversity as it itself does not have any price. Such market failures can be linked to incomplete markets. On the other hand, such situation could also happen from externality if some outside agent disturbs the natural eco-system. This could lead to a tragic end of the ecosystem unless there is a coordinated effort by the local people to save it.

91. A Common Property Resource (CPR) can survive only under:

1. Strict Property Rules
2. Taxation
3. Credible Commitment to the collective living on the CPR
4. Non-exclusion

92. Asymmetric information about a resource occurs when there is:

1. Government intervention
2. Non-rivalry
3. Non-excludability
4. Moral hazard and adverse selection

93. Public goods do not have the following property:

1. Non-rival
2. Non-excludable
3. Common property resources controlled by locals
4. Free goods

94. Incomplete markets for biodiversity occurs because:

1. Biodiversity does not have a value to society
2. Failure to institute well-defined property rights on the forest having biodiversity
3. The forest resource is open for all to exploit
4. No one is willing to pay money to save biodiversity in forest

95. The concept of "Tragedy of Commons" was founded by :

1. Robert Solow
2. Harold Hotelling
3. Garrett Hardin
4. Partha Dasgupta

Directions (Qs. No. 96-100): *Read the following passage and answer the questions:*

The present international economic relations have been least influenced by multilateral forums. Multilateral economic institutions' meetings are not considered seriously by the leaders of important nations. In the past, it was heard that many world leaders were speaking against WTO and prioritising their national interest. Even the forum of WTO was used to speak against the multilateral trade.

In the beginning of 1980s, the world was moving towards globalisation and the multi-lateral lending and trade forums played a crucial role in the economic and trade negotiations. Slowly regional economic associations and bilateral trade forums took the centre stage. The exit of Britain from the European Union and frequent disruptions in the WTO forums and many statements of the U.S president and many European leaders were giving the message that globalisation is coming to an end.

Recent imposition of high tariff on Indian exports and various measures by the USA violate free and fair trade ensured by the multi-lateral trade and investment forums, are matters of serious concerns. Trade disruptions are never becoming an issue for consideration of the appropriate forums at the international level. People start questioning the relevance of a long lists of economic and political institutions built after the second world war with much enthusiasm and high expectations. Do the present developments indicate a turning point for a new world order?

96. The important challenge to WTO:

1. Regional Economic Associations and bilateral trade forums
2. The exit of Britain from European Union
3. International economic relations not influenced by multilateral forums
4. World moving towards post-globalisation world order

97. Globalisation is an outcome of :

1. Exit of Britain from the European union
2. Initiatives of the USA
3. The role played by the multilateral lending and trade forums
4. The outcome of second world war

98. The nature of present international economic relations :

1. USA and European countries are not violating international understandings
2. Multilateral forums are relegated to the background
3. Increased role is given to multilateral economic and political institutions
4. World leaders are giving message that globalisation is improving

99. The Passage conveys about:

1. Multilateral institutions have accepted their weaknesses.
2. Reforms in multilateral institutions
3. W.T.O. is becoming more important
4. Powerful nations are undermining the role of multilateral institutions for their national interest

100. What violates free and fair trade ?

1. Imposition of high and unfair tariffs
2. Weak structure of Regional economic associations and bilateral trade forums
3. World leaders speaking in favour of WTO
4. Keen interest by the USA and Europe

ANSWERS

1	2	3	4	5	6	7	8	9	10
4	4	3	1	3	3	3	4	3	4
11	**12**	**13**	**14**	**15**	**16**	**17**	**18**	**19**	**20**
3	1	3	1	2	1	2	4	2	3
21	**22**	**23**	**24**	**25**	**26**	**27**	**28**	**29**	**30**
3	4	1	1	4	4	3	2	4	3
31	**32**	**33**	**34**	**35**	**36**	**37**	**38**	**39**	**40**
2	4	4	1	4	2	2	3	3	3
41	**42**	**43**	**44**	**45**	**46**	**47**	**48**	**49**	**50**
4	*	4	1	3	3	1	2	2	1
51	**52**	**53**	**54**	**55**	**56**	**57**	**58**	**59**	**60**
3	1	2	4	4	4	2	4	1	1
61	**62**	**63**	**64**	**65**	**66**	**67**	**68**	**69**	**70**
3	1	2	1	2	1	4	2	2	3
71	**72**	**73**	**74**	**75**	**76**	**77**	**78**	**79**	**80**
2	1	3	2	2	2	2	1	4	2
81	**82**	**83**	**84**	**85**	**86**	**87**	**88**	**89**	**90**
2	1	4	1	4	1	3	3	3	3
91	**92**	**93**	**94**	**95**	**96**	**97**	**98**	**99**	**100**
3	4	3	2	3	1	3	2	4	1

Explanatory Answers

1. The question requires correct matching of Finance Commissions with their recommended vertical devolution percentages of the divisible pool of central taxes to States. The 12th Finance Commission recommended 30.5% devolution; hence C–IV is correct. The 13th Finance Commission increased this to 32%, so D–III is correct. The 14th Finance Commission made a major structural shift by recommending 42% devolution, significantly enhancing fiscal federalism; thus A–II is correct. The 15th Finance Commission revised the share to 41% (primarily due to the reorganization of Jammu & Kashmir into Union Territories), so B–I is correct. Only option 4 correctly captures all these pairings simultaneously without inconsistency.

2. The kinked demand curve model explains price rigidity in oligopolistic markets. It assumes that if a firm raises its price, competitors do not follow, causing demand to be highly elastic; but if it lowers its price, competitors match the cut, making demand relatively inelastic. This creates a "kink" in the demand curve and a discontinuity in the marginal revenue curve, leading to price stickiness even when costs change moderately. This analytical framework was formally developed by Paul M. Sweezy in 1939. Therefore, the correct attribution of the kinked demand model is to Sweezy.

3. The given difference equation is $Y_{t+1} - 1.2Y_t = 0$. Rearranging gives $Y_{t+1} = 1.2Y_t$, which is a first-order linear homogeneous difference equation. Solving iteratively:

$$Y_2 = 1.2Y_1$$

$$Y_3 = 1.2Y_2 = (1.2)^2Y_1$$

$$Y_4 = (1.2)^3Y_1$$

Thus, by mathematical induction, $Y_t = (1.2)^{t-1}Y_1$ for $t \geq 1$. This expression satisfies the recurrence relation exactly and matches option 3 without index error.

4. A balanced budget multiplier refers to a situation where government expenditure (G) and taxes (T) increase by the same amount. In the simple Keynesian income determination model, an increase in government expenditure directly increases aggregate demand, while the increase in taxes reduces disposable income and consumption by MPC times the tax change. The net impact on equilibrium income equals the initial increase in government spending, meaning the balanced budget multiplier equals 1. Therefore, statement C (equal increase in G and T) is correct, and statement D (multiplier equals 1) is also correct. Statements A and B do not align with the standard Keynesian balanced budget multiplier result.

5. In a liquidity trap, the rate of interest has already fallen to a very low level, so people expect it to rise in future (which would mean bond prices may fall). Because of this expectation, they prefer holding money (liquidity) rather than buying bonds. As a result, when the central bank increases money supply further, the public simply absorbs it in the form of idle cash balances, and the rate of interest does not fall further in any meaningful way. This description matches option (3) exactly.

6. "Revenue foregone due to beneficial proposals" refers to the expected loss of tax revenue because the Budget introduces relief measures such as lower tax burdens, exemptions, or concessional rates. The stated figures are split into (*i*) direct taxes (like personal income tax, corporate tax) and (*ii*) indirect taxes (like customs duties, excise-related components, etc.). For the Central Budget 2025–26, the revenue expected to be foregone due to such beneficial proposals is about ₹ 1 lakh crore in direct taxes and about ₹ 2600 crore in indirect taxes, which fits option (3) exactly, while other options either overstate/understate one side or give a mismatched combination.

7. Deficit spending by the government can lead to a crowding-out effect because the government often finances the deficit by borrowing from the market. This increases the demand for loanable funds and tends to push the market rate of interest upward, which discourages (crowds out) private investment—so Assertion (A) is correct in the standard macroeconomic mechanism. However, Reason (R) says that when the government borrows from the market, bond prices go up and the rate of interest falls. Typically, market borrowing by issuing more government bonds increases bond supply, which puts downward pressure on bond prices and raises yields/interest rates (not lowers them). Hence (R) is not correct.

8. A "compensation" based welfare test checks whether the gainers from a policy change could, in principle, compensate the losers and still remain better off. This is exactly the idea behind the Kaldor–Hicks criterion, which relaxes the strict Pareto condition and evaluates changes using potential compensation rather than requiring that nobody is harmed. Hence, the welfare criterion based on compensation payments is the Kaldor–Hicks Compensation Criterion.

9. The Human Development Index (HDI) is a composite index designed to rank countries using three broad dimensions—health, education, and standard of living. Health is captured through life expectancy at birth, education through educational attainment indicators, and living standards through real income measured on a PPP basis (so that cross-country purchasing power differences are adjusted). Among the given options, only option (3) correctly states these core HDI components.

10. Kenneth Boulding is associated with the "Spaceship Earth" idea and ecological limits, so A–II. Georgescu-Roegen's bioeconomics emphasizes entropy and the role of energy as a limiting factor in the economic process, so B–IV. Elinor Ostrom's central contribution is the analysis of how communities manage common property resources through institutions and rules, so C–III. A.C. Pigou is linked with externalities and corrective taxation (Pigouvian tax), which fits pollution tax, so D–I. This full set of matches is satisfied only by option (4).

11. From Dalton's optimum population formula $M = \frac{A - O}{O}$, a country has optimum population when the actual population equals the optimum population, i.e., A = O. Substituting A = O gives M $= \frac{O - O}{O} = 0$. So, optimum population corresponds to zero mal-adjustment, hence option (3).

12. In the assertion, $U = \frac{X - A}{h}$ and $V = \frac{Y - B}{K}$ represent a linear transformation of X and Y involving a change of origin (subtracting constants A, B) and change of scale (dividing by *h*, K). Correlation is unaffected by change of origin and by positive change of scale; since $h > 0$ and

K > 0, the direction is not reversed, so $r_{XY} = r_{UV}$. The reason states exactly this invariance property of correlation coefficient, and it directly justifies why the assertion holds.

13. When you add more regressors to a regression model, the fitted values can only improve or stay the same in terms of minimizing residual sum of squares (SSR cannot increase), so $R^2 = 1 - \frac{SSR}{SST}$ cannot fall; therefore, statement A is true and B is false. In the standard regression with an intercept, $0 \leq R^2 \leq 1$, so it is not negative and is treated as always non-negative/positive in this context, making statement D true, while C is false because R^2 is affected by the number of regressors. Hence, the correct combination is A and D only.

14. Monopoly power is commonly measured by the Lerner Index, which directly captures the firm's ability to set price above marginal cost. When a firm has no market power (perfect competition), P = MC and the index becomes 0. As market power rises, P exceeds MC, making $\frac{P - MC}{P}$ positive and larger, which exactly reflects stronger monopoly power.

15. The question refers to demonetisation of ₹ 1000 notes in India in the context of the high-denomination withdrawal episode that is widely discussed in standard economic and public-finance literature. The major demonetisation that specifically targeted high-value notes such as ₹ 1000, ₹ 5000 and ₹ 10,000 under a formal ordinance-based intervention occurred in 1978, when the High Denomination Bank Notes (Demonetisation) Ordinance was promulgated to curb black money and unaccounted wealth. Among the given options (2016, 1978, 1969, 1980), only 1978 corresponds to that historically recognised demonetisation of ₹ 1000 notes under the cited ordinance framework.

16. In the neoclassical (Solow-type) growth framework, long-run growth in output per worker is driven by improvements in labour productivity/technology, so statement A is a core proposition. The model also treats saving and investment (capital accumulation) as an important determinant of the economy's growth path and steady-state level of income (and hence an essential driver of growth dynamics), so statement C is taken as valid in the standard syllabus framing. Statement B is not a basic proposition because the growth rate is not said to depend on the level of per capita income as a rule, and D is too narrow because growth is not determined only by investment—productivity/technology and other parameters matter.

17. In practice, Treasury bills are issued through recognised auction formats such as the uniform price auction (all successful bidders pay the same cut-off price/yield) and the multiple price (discriminatory) auction (successful bidders pay the price/yield they bid). These are standard auction mechanisms used internationally for T-bills and other government securities. Terms like "adjusted price auction" and "readjusted price auction" are not recognised as standard auction types for Treasury bills in the usual public finance/monetary economics framework, so A and D are not the correct identifiers here.

18. The idea that public expenditure and state activity tend to increase over time as an economy develops is explained by Wagner's Law (Adolf Wagner). The logic is that with economic growth and industrialisation, the functions of the state expand—administration, law and order, social services, welfare, infrastructure, and regulation—so public spending rises both absolutely and as a share of national income. Hence, the theory specifically associated with this phenomenon is attributed to Adolf Wagner.

19. The Big-Push approach argues that poor economies can remain stuck in a low-income situation unless a large, coordinated investment effort is made across sectors, so that complementarities, demand linkages, and economies of scale become effective together. This idea is closest to the development logic of escaping a low-level equilibrium through a minimum critical effort (a threshold-type jump in investment), rather than Hirschman's unbalanced growth (which deliberately promotes sectoral imbalance). Therefore, the best origin/foundation among the given choices is option (2).

20. Assertion (A) is broadly correct because maintaining persistently high petroleum prices is difficult for a cartel in the long run due to factors like cheating on quotas, expansion of non-OPEC supply, technological change (shale, deepwater), and demand-side adjustment when prices stay high. However, Reason (R) is not correct because in the long run both demand and supply for petroleum products tend to become more elastic than in the short run—consumers and firms can adopt substitutes and efficiency, and producers can expand exploration, capacity, and alternative sources. Since (R) states long-run inelasticity for both sides, it does not hold and cannot explain (A).

21. Non-debt capital receipts = Disinvestment + Recovery of loans = 400 + 150 = 550

Fiscal deficit = Total expenditure − (Revenue receipts + Non-debt capital receipts)

Fiscal deficit = 8600 − (5600 + 550)

Fiscal deficit = 8600 − 6150 = 2450

Primary deficit = Fiscal deficit − Interest payments

Primary deficit = 2450 − 800 = 1650

22. A. Pensions as % of Central Govt. expenditure must be a small single-digit share, so it matches 4% (IV).

C. Tax–GDP ratio is typically around the high teens in such data, so it matches 18% (II).

D. Debt–GDP ratio is the largest magnitude here, so it matches 81.3% (III).

The remaining value 22% (I) then fits B (State's share of taxes and duties as % of Central Govt. expenditure).

23. For a Giffen good, when price falls:

- Substitution effect increases quantity demanded (positive effect).
- Income effect reduces quantity demanded because the good is strongly inferior (negative effect).

In the Giffen case, the negative income effect dominates the positive substitution effect, so overall quantity demanded falls when price falls.

24.
- Tobin's Q theory relates q (market value vs replacement cost) to incentives for capital formation, so it matches Investment (III).
- Phillips Curve links Inflation and Unemployment, so it matches (I).
- Okun's Law links Output and Unemployment, so it matches (II).
- Liquidity trap describes a situation where money demand becomes very high and interest-rate policy becomes ineffective, so it matches Demand for money and Interest rate (IV).

25.
- Net exports = X − M = 1000 − 1500 = −500
- National income identity:

Y = C + I + G + (X − M)

I = Y − C − G − (X − M)

I = 14400 − 12000 − 1200 − (−500)

I = 14400 − 13200 + 500

I = 1200 + 500 = 1700

26. Tax buoyancy measures the responsiveness of public revenue (tax revenue) to changes in GDP. If GDP rises by 1% and public revenue rises by more than 1%, the tax system is said to be buoyant (buoyancy > 1). Hence, the correct term is tax buoyancy, not CENVAT (a tax mechanism) and not proportional/inelastic systems (which would imply equal or less-than-proportionate response).

27. **D. Adam Smith's "division of labour" and "increasing returns" theory (1776):** This is the earliest foundation for growth thinking, linking productivity gains to specialization and scale. It predates formal 20th-century growth models and sets the classical base for later growth theory.

A. Harrod–Domar Growth Model (1939–1946): Harrod (1939) and Domar (1946) built a formal dynamic model where growth depends on saving and the capital–output relation. This comes after classical ideas and before the neoclassical (Solow) framework.

B. Solow's Neoclassical Growth Model (1956): Solow (1956) introduced diminishing returns to capital and highlighted technological progress as the driver of long-run per capita growth. It is clearly later than Harrod–Domar and becomes the mainstream benchmark model.

C. Endogenous Growth Theory (mid-1980s onward; Romer 1986, Lucas 1988): This theory explains sustained growth through factors inside the model (knowledge, human capital, innovation) without relying only on exogenous technology. It is the latest among the listed developments and follows the Solow framework historically.

28. "Economic dependency burden" refers to the burden on the working (productive) population of supporting the non-working (dependent) population. Statement A captures the idea that non-productive members must be supported by the labour force. Statement C correctly identifies typical dependents as the young and the elderly (here stated as below 15 and above 70). Statement B is about public debt, not dependency, and D refers to a segment of workers, not dependents.

29. NSSO and CSO function under India's official statistical system, which is placed under the Ministry of Statistics and Programme Implementation (MoSPI) (now integrated as parts of the broader statistical set-up). Hence the correct ministry is MoSPI.

30. A sustained downward trend in inflation toward the central bank's target is consistent with (*i*) improving/adapting supply chains that reduce supply bottlenecks and cost pressures (A), and (*ii*) tighter monetary policy (higher policy rates/ withdrawal of liquidity) that cools aggregate demand and inflation expectations (C). Easing monetary policy (B) would generally push demand and inflation upward, and if AD rises more than AS (D), it tends to be inflationary rather than disinflationary.

31. For equilibrium income in the simple Keynesian model, aggregate demand is AD = C + I + G, with proportional tax t implying $Y_d = (1 - t)Y$:

$$C = 100 + 0.75Y_d$$
$$Y_d = (1 - 0.2)Y = 0.8Y$$
$$C = 100 + 0.75(0.8Y) = 100 + 0.6Y$$
$$AD = (100 + 0.6Y) + 60 + 40$$
$$= 200 + 0.6Y$$

Equilibrium: $Y = AD = 200 + 0.6Y$

$$Y - 0.6Y = 200$$
$$0.4Y = 200;\ Y = \frac{200}{0.4} = 500$$

32. Standard deviation is unchanged by a change of origin, so SD(X + a) = SD(X) and SD(X − b) = SD(X) are correct, but under change of scale the rule is SD(aX) = $|a|\cdot$SD(X), not $a^2\cdot$SD(X). Hence the Assertion (A) becomes incorrect because it states the wrong scaling property for SD. The Reason (R) is correct because SD is independent of change of origin but depends on scale, so the most appropriate choice is option (4).

33. The Assertion claims that a 10% rise in average household income necessarily leads to a 50% rise in investment in health and education of children, which is not a general economic/statistical law and cannot be accepted as universally true without additional behavioural and institutional conditions. The Reason is correct because spending on health and education builds human capital (better skills, health, productivity), which can raise an economy's productive capacity and growth. Since (R) is true but (A) is not necessarily true, the correct option is (4).

84. In an F-test, the calculated F-statistic is taken as the ratio of the larger sample variance to the smaller sample variance.

Larger variance =35.53, smaller variance =34.92

$$F = \frac{35.53}{34.92} = 1.0174\ldots$$

Rounded to two decimals: $F \approx 1.02$

35. Matrix addition is commutative and associative, so statement A ("not commutative") is false while statement B is true. Matrix multiplication is not commutative in general, so statement C is false, but it is associative whenever the products are defined (dimensionally conformable), so statement D is true. Therefore, the only correct combination is B and D only, which is option (4).

36. Under NREGA/MGNREGA, the Centre pays 100% of unskilled wage cost, and also bears a major share of other components (notably a large share of material/administrative components as per the scheme's cost-sharing pattern), while States mainly bear items like unemployment allowance and the remaining shares. Because the dominant expenditure is unskilled wages and the Centre covers it fully, the overall funding pattern works out to about 90% by the Centre and about 10% by the States in standard scheme accounting for total outlay/implementation. 90 percent of the cost of employment provided is borne by the centre. In the first phase of implementation, 200 most backward districts were covered.

37. For $Q = AK^{\alpha}L^{\beta}$ with $A > 0$, $\alpha > 0$, $\beta > 0$, marginal products are obtained by partial differentiation.

$$MP_K = \frac{\partial Q}{\partial K} = A\alpha K^{\alpha-1}L^{\beta}$$
$$= \alpha\left(\frac{AK^{\alpha}L^{\beta}}{K}\right)$$
$$= \frac{\alpha}{K}Q \rightarrow \text{Statement A is correct.}$$
$$MP_L = \frac{\partial Q}{\partial L} = A\beta K^{\alpha}L^{\beta-1}$$
$$= \beta\left(\frac{AK^{\alpha}L^{\beta}}{L}\right)$$
$$= \frac{\beta}{L}Q \rightarrow \text{Statement D is correct.}$$

Statements B and C incorrectly interchange α, β and/or K, L.

38. Under heteroscedasticity (with the usual exogeneity assumption intact), OLS slope estimators remain unbiased/consistent, but they are inefficient because OLS is no longer the minimum-variance linear unbiased estimator; hence Assertion (A) is correct. However, heteroscedasticity makes the usual OLS variance/standard error formulas incorrect (they become biased/inconsistent unless robust corrections are used), so the claim that "the estimates of variances are also unbiased" is not correct. Therefore, (A) is correct but (R) is not correct.

39. A "destination tax" is one where the tax revenue accrues to the jurisdiction where the good/service is consumed (destination) rather than where it is produced (origin). GST is designed as a destination-based consumption tax, so it is popularly called the destination tax.

40. Arrange by time (earliest to latest). The Vijay Kelkar Committee on Tax Reforms belongs to the early 2000s reform discussion (C comes first). The Parthasarathy Shome Committee on retrospective taxation is from the 2012 period (B next). The Arvind Subramanian Committee on revenue neutral rate (RNR) for GST is around the GST design phase (mid-2010s), so D follows. The Shankar Acharya Committee on shifting the financial year (Apr–Mar to Jan–Dec) is later (mid/late 2010s), so A is last. Hence the correct chronological order is C → B → D → A, which matches option (3).

41. The Ronald Coase bargaining solution works when property rights are clearly defined (legally established) and can be exchanged/assigned (transferable) so that parties can negotiate to internalize the externality and reach an efficient outcome (especially when transaction costs are low). "Universally owned" resources generally create open-access/common-property issues rather than clear enforceable rights, and "equally informed" is helpful but not the core condition stated in the standard Coasian set-up compared with clearly defined, transferable rights.

42. Demand function:

$$P = 80 - 3Q$$

Total Revenue (TR) = P × Q

$$TR = (80 - 3Q)Q$$
$$TR = 80Q - 3Q^2$$

To find maximum revenue:

$$\frac{d(TR)}{dQ} = 80 - 6Q$$

Set equal to zero:

$$80 - 6Q = 0$$
$$6Q = 80$$
$$Q = \frac{80}{6} = \frac{40}{3} \approx 13.33$$

So maximum revenue does not occur at Q = 12 and also not at Q = 3.

Thus statements A and B are incorrect.

Now compute maximum revenue:

$$TR = 80 \times \frac{40}{3} - 3\left(\frac{40}{3}\right)^2$$

$$= \frac{3200}{3} - 3 \times \frac{1600}{9} = \frac{3200}{3} - \frac{4800}{9}$$

Convert to common denominator:

$$= \frac{9600}{9} - \frac{4800}{9} = \frac{4800}{9} = 533.33$$

Maximum revenue ≈ 533.33, which is neither 528 nor 213.

Therefore none of the given statements are correct.

Answer. NONE: None of the statements (A to D) is correct.

43. A. Slack Variable → III (used when constraints are of the ≤ type)

B. Surplus Variable → IV (used when constraints are of the ≥ type)

C. Optimal Solution → I (best among all feasible solutions)

D. Infeasible Solution → II (violates at least one condition)

44. For $y = \sqrt{1 - x^2}$, we need $1 - x^2 \geq 0$

$\Rightarrow -1 \leq x \leq 1$.

On [–1, 1], $1 - x^2$ ranges from 0 (at $x = \pm 1$) to 1 (at $x = 0$).

Taking square roots gives y from $\sqrt{0} = 0$ to $\sqrt{1} = 1$.

So the range is [0,1].

45. A. Targeted Public Distribution System (TPDS) → III (1997)

B. Revamped Public Distribution System (RPDS) → I (1992)

C. Right to Education Act (RTE Act) → II (2009)

D. National Food Security Act (NFSA Act) → IV (2013)

46. The term "Salmon War" in the European context refers to the late 1980s–early 1990s trade dispute between Norwegian salmon exporters and Scottish salmon producers. Scottish farmers alleged that Norway was dumping farmed salmon in the European market at artificially low prices, thereby harming domestic producers. The dispute led to investigations and, eventually, the imposition of anti-dumping duties by the European Commission in 1991. Since the conflict specifically involved

Norwegian exports and the Scottish salmon industry, the correct pair among the options is Norway and Scotland.

47. Club goods are excludable (access can be restricted by membership/fees) and non-rival up to congestion (many users can enjoy them until crowding sets in). A swimming pool and a gym typically operate on membership/entry rules, so they fit club goods. Defense is non-excludable and non-rival (public good), and railways are better treated as a mixed/congestible service often regulated as a public utility rather than a standard club good in this classification. Hence, B and D only.

48. $Q = 100 - P - P^2$.

At P = 5: Q = 100 – 5 – 25 = 70

$$\frac{dQ}{dP} = -1 - 2P$$

$$\Rightarrow \left.\frac{dQ}{dP}\right|_{P=5} = -1 - 10 = -11$$

$$e_d = \frac{dQ}{dP}\cdot\frac{Q}{P} = (-11)\cdot\frac{5}{70}$$

$$= -\frac{55}{70} = -\frac{11}{14}$$

$$|e_d| = \frac{11}{14} \approx 0.79 < 1$$

⇒ demand is inelastic at P = 5.

49. Harrod and Domar are associated with the idea of investment as a "double-edged sword," because in their growth model investment increases productive capacity while simultaneously generating income and demand; imbalance between warranted and actual growth creates instability, hence A-III. Lucas and Romer developed endogenous growth theory in the late 1980s, emphasizing human capital, innovation, and knowledge spillovers as internal drivers of sustained growth, hence B-I. Arthur Lewis proposed the dual economy model (1954), explaining structural transformation through labour transfer from the subsistence sector to the modern capitalist sector, hence C-II. Michael Todaro formulated the rural-urban migration model (1969), based on expected income differentials, hence D-IV.

50. Structural system has endogenous variables $\{y_1, y_2, y_3\} \Rightarrow G = 3$, exogenous variables $\{x_1, x_2, x_3\} \Rightarrow K = 3$.

Second equation: $y_2 = y_3 + x_3 + u_2$

Endogenous variables appearing in Eq. (2): $\{y_2, y_3\} \Rightarrow m = 2$

Excluded exogenous variables from Eq. (2): $\{x_1; x_2\} \Rightarrow K - k_i = 2$

Order condition: $K - k_i \geq (m-1) \Rightarrow 2 \geq 1$ (satisfied), and $2 > (m-1) \Rightarrow$ over-identification by order condition.

Rank condition (minimum requirement here is rank ≥ 1): at least one excluded exogenous variable (x_1 or x_2) appears with a non-zero coefficient in the other structural equations (both appear in Eq. 1), so rank condition is satisfied.

Therefore, the second equation is over identified.

51. **A → III:** Debt-deflation (Irving Fisher) explains that when the price level falls unexpectedly, the real value of nominal debts rises. This worsens balance sheets, forces distress selling and deleveraging, and can reduce output/income through contractionary effects.

B → I: Pigou effect (real-balance effect) says a fall in the price level raises the real value of money balances/wealth. Higher real wealth tends to increase consumption demand, supporting income/output.

C → II: Forward guidance is a monetary-policy tool where the central bank communicates its future policy stance (future rates/stance) to influence expectations today. So it matches the item about announcing future monetary action.

D → IV: Okun's law captures the inverse relation between unemployment and real GDP (or output gap). When output rises above potential, unemployment tends to fall, and vice versa.

52. A is an AR(r) definition because current x_t depends on its own r lagged values plus a white-noise shock e_t; B is an MA(m) definition because x_t is a finite linear combination of current and past shocks ($e_t, e_{t-1}, \ldots, e_{t-m}$)). C is wrong because it calls an MA form "autoregressive," and D is wrong because it calls an AR form "moving average."

53. Embodied technical progress means the new technology is "built into" new capital goods (new machines/vintages). Therefore, productivity rises mainly when firms invest and replace old capital with new, more efficient capital; without new investment, the existing capital stock does not fully incorporate the latest technology. This is exactly what option (2) states.

54. **A → III:** The neo-Chamberlinian approach uses monopolistic competition where firms produce differentiated varieties. The key idea is product differentiation (variety) under increasing returns and imperfect competition.

B → I: The neo-Hotelling framework is classically tied to location/variety along a "line," which is a standard way to model horizontal differentiation. Consumers choose among varieties differentiated by characteristics rather than "quality levels."

C → IV: Brander–Krugman is known for reciprocal dumping under oligopoly with segmented markets and trade costs. Similar firms export to each other's markets, leading to two-way trade and "dumping" in the sense of price discrimination across markets.

D → II: Neo–Heckscher–Ohlin extensions are commonly linked with quality/skill-based specialization, where countries differ in factor endowments that translate into different quality levels. That aligns with vertical differentiation (differences in quality levels rather than just varieties).

55. Reserve money (monetary base) is formed by currency plus deposits held with the central bank (including banks' reserves and other deposits), so the structure in A matches the base-money composition in the given notation. Money multiplier is defined as the ratio of money supply to reserve money, so $m = \frac{M}{RM}$ in C is correct; B is incorrect because M1 is not just C + OD (it includes demand deposits), and D is incorrect because narrow money is not M3 (that is broad money).

56. A. Amartya Sen → IV (Entitlements, capabilities and freedom of choice)

Sen's welfare and development economics is centred on the capability approach and entitlement analysis (famines, deprivation, freedom).

Hence his contribution is best matched with entitlements, capabilities and freedom of choice.

B. Simon Kuznets → I (Rise and fall of inequality with economic growth)

Kuznets is identified with the *Kuznets Curve*, which hypothesizes inequality first rising and then falling as an economy develops.

So he matches the "rise and fall of inequality with economic growth" statement.

C. Gunnar Myrdal → II (Circular and cumulative causation of economic underdevelopment)

Myrdal's theory explains underdevelopment through circular cumulative causation where disadvantages reinforce themselves over time.

This directly corresponds to circular and cumulative causation of economic underdevelopment.

D. Paul Krugman → III (Geographic pattern of economic development)

Krugman's *new economic geography* explains agglomeration, core–periphery outcomes, and spatial concentration of industry and income.

Therefore, he matches the geographic pattern of economic development.

57. An increase in fiscal deficit typically reflects a situation where the government's expenditure exceeds its receipts by a larger margin, which is consistent with higher government spending (A) relative to revenues, and it usually requires higher market borrowing. Higher government borrowing raises demand for loanable funds, pushing up domestic interest rates (B) and, through the crowding-out channel, tends to reduce private investment (C). A fall in total borrowing by the government (D) contradicts the very mechanism through which a higher deficit is financed, so D is not implied.

58. A natural monopoly arises when economies of scale are so strong that one firm can supply the entire market at a lower average cost than multiple firms. This requires the long-run average cost to keep falling over the market-relevant output range, which is exactly what option (4) states.

59. Let S = "smoker", C = "cancer".

Given: $P(C) = 0.03$,

$P(S) = 0.15$, $P(S \cup C) = 0.10$.

Using inclusion–exclusion:

$$P(S \cap C) = P(S) + P(C) - P(S \cup C)$$
$$P(S \cap C) = 0.15 + 0.03 - 0.10 = 0.08$$

So the required probability is 0.08.

60. The statement is NOT true because rational expectations are primarily credited to John F. Muth (1961) and later developed and popularized in macroeconomics by thinkers such as Lucas and Sargent; attributing the development of the theory to "Hansen" is not correct in standard economic history. The other statements match the core idea: rational expectations are used by agents to form expectations, they incorporate all relevant available information, and they are not "error-free" in the sense of always being correct (forecast errors can occur but are not systematically biased).

61. A. Type I error → III (Reject H_0 when it is true)

Type I error means we reject a true null hypothesis, i.e., we commit an error by concluding "significant" when actually H_0 is correct. So it directly matches "Reject H_0 when it is true."

B. Type II error → I (Accept H_0 when it is false)

Type II error means we fail to reject (accept) a false null hypothesis, i.e., we miss a real effect when it exists.

So it matches "Accept H_0 when it is false."

C. Simple Hypothesis → II (H_0: $\mu = \mu_0$ and $\sigma_0^2 = \sigma^2$)

A simple hypothesis fully specifies the population distribution/parameters under H_0 (no unknown parameter is left free).

Here both μ and σ^2 are fixed at specific values, so it is a simple hypothesis.

D. Composite Hypothesis → IV (H_0: $\mu = \mu_0$ and σ^2 is unknown)

A composite hypothesis does not fully specify the distribution because at least one parameter remains unspecified.

Since σ^2 is not fixed to a single value, H_0 contains a set of possible distributions, so it is composite.

62. The Headcount Index (H) is the simplest poverty measure and is defined as the proportion (or count-based share) of the population whose income/consumption lies below the poverty line. It ignores the depth of poverty (how far below the line people are), and it also ignores inequality among the poor; it only counts how many are poor. Therefore, the correct basis of Headcount Index is the number of people below the poverty line.

Answer. 1: The number of people who fall below the poverty line

63. Under perfect competition in the product market, price equals marginal revenue (P = MR). Since $VMP_L = P \times MP_L$ and $MRP_L = MR \times MP_L$, it follows that $VMP_L = MRP_L$ when P = MR. At labour-market equilibrium for a competitive firm, the hiring rule is $VMP_L = W$, and because VMP_L equals MRP_L in perfect competition, the equality $VMP_L = MRP_L$ must hold.

64. A. $|e_d|$ for D = 64 – 8P at P = 6 → III (3)

$$Q = 64 - 8(6) = 16, \quad \frac{dQ}{dP} = -8$$

$$|e_d| = \left|\frac{dQ}{dP}\cdot\frac{P}{Q}\right| = |1-8|\cdot\frac{6}{16} = \frac{48}{16} = 3$$

B. e_s for S = –25 + 5P at P = 10 → IV (2)

$$Q = -25 + 5(10) = 25, \quad \frac{dQ}{dP} = 5$$

$$e_s = \frac{dQ}{dP}\cdot\frac{P}{Q} = 5\cdot\frac{10}{25} = \frac{50}{25} = 2$$

C. MR when P = 8 and e_d = 4 → I (6)

Using $MR = \left(1 - \frac{1}{|e_d|}\right)$ for a downward-sloping demand at a point,

$$MR = 8\left(1 - \frac{1}{4}\right) = 8\cdot\frac{3}{4} = 6$$

D. MP_L when VMP_L = 12 and P = 3 → II (4)

$$VMP_L = P\cdot MP_L \Rightarrow 12 = 3\cdot MP_L$$

$$MP_L = \frac{12}{3} = 4$$

65. Innovation theory of business cycles is classically associated with Schumpeter's emphasis on waves of innovations, not with Jorgenson, so statement A is incorrect. Hawtrey is well known for the Pure Monetary theory of business cycles (credit-money driven trade cycle), so B is correct. Monetary over-investment theory is linked with Hayek/Mises (Austrian theory), whereas Clark is mainly linked with the acceleration principle, so C is incorrect. The Multiplier–Acceleration interaction model is attributed to Samuelson (1939), combining Keynesian multiplier with the accelerator, so D is correct. Hence, only B and D are true.

66. For a Cobb–Douglas type production function $Q = AK^aL^b$, returns to scale depend on $a + b$; if $a + b < 1$ it is decreasing returns to scale. Here $a = \frac{1}{4}$ and $b = \frac{1}{2}$, so $a + b = \frac{1}{4} + \frac{1}{2} = \frac{3}{4} < 1$, hence decreasing returns to scale. (Option (2) has $a + (1 - a) = 1$ so CRS; (3) is linear so CRS; (4) has exponents $\frac{1}{2} + \frac{3}{2} = 2 > 1$ so IRS.)

67. The 12th Finance Commission was chaired by C. Rangarajan and the 11th Finance Commission was chaired by A.M. Khusro, so statements A and B are correct. The 14th Finance Commission was chaired by Y.V. Reddy (not R.K. Singh), and the 15th Finance Commission was chaired by N.K. Singh (not Y.V. Reddy), so C and D are incorrect.

68. The assertion states the First Welfare Theorem idea—under competitive market trading (with standard assumptions), the resulting allocation is Pareto efficient, so (A) is correct. The reason is also correct because a Pareto-improving trade from an inefficient point can still end at another inefficient point (Pareto improvement ≠ Pareto efficiency). However, (R) does not explain why competitive equilibrium becomes efficient; it is a separate statement about Pareto improvements not guaranteeing efficiency.

69. In the Union Budget 2025–26, the insurance FDI limit was announced to be raised from 74% to 100% (so A is correct, B is not), and an Investment Friendliness Index of States was to be launched (so C is correct). The fiscal deficit target for 2025–26 is stated as 4.4% of GDP, so D is also correct; therefore the correct combination is A, C and D only.

70. Tobin's q theory says investment rises when the market value of capital/assets is high relative to replacement (reproduction) cost, so A is correct. Under the Mundell–Fleming model with a fixed exchange rate and high/perfect capital mobility, fiscal expansion is generally effective (not "completely ineffective"), so B is incorrect. An investment tax credit reduces the effective cost of investment by having the government bear part of it through a credit/subsidy, so C is correct. The "impossible trinity" implies that with a fixed exchange rate and perfect capital mobility, an independent monetary policy cannot be maintained, so D is correct.

71. Trade creation happens when, after forming a customs union, a member country stops producing a good domestically at a higher cost and instead imports it from another member at a lower cost. Here the key clue is "domestic production … is replaced by lower-cost imports from another member nation," which exactly describes replacement of high-cost domestic output by low-cost partner imports (efficiency gain). Trade diversion would instead mean replacing low-cost world imports with higher-cost partner imports because of the common external tariff, which is not what the statement says.

72. The assertion is correct because, from the mid-1970s onward, many developed countries increasingly relied on non-tariff barriers (quotas, VERs, technical standards, anti-dumping, subsidies, etc.) rather than overt tariff hikes, partly because tariffs were being negotiated down under multilateral rounds. The reason is also correct: rising competitive pressure from developing countries and the rapidly industrialising South and South-East Asian economies led to stronger protectionist responses in import-competing sectors, and this competitive pressure is a major driver of the shift toward NTBs; hence (R) explains (A).

73. Effective rent control is a binding rent ceiling set below the market-clearing rent, so statement D is correct and statement C is incorrect (a price floor would not be "rent control" in the usual sense). With a binding rent ceiling, shortage tends to be smaller in the short run because housing supply is relatively fixed immediately, but it often becomes larger in the long run as maintenance declines, conversions occur, and new construction is discouraged—so statement A is correct while B is incorrect. Therefore, the correct combination is A and D only.

74. **A. Narasimham Committee – I → III (Financial Sector Reform)**

This committee (early 1990s) examined the broader financial system and recommended wide reforms in the financial sector framework.

It is therefore matched with the overall financial sector reform agenda rather than a narrow banking-only exercise.

B. Narasimham Committee – II → II (Banking Sector Reform)

The second committee (late 1990s) focused more directly on banking strength—capital adequacy, NPAs, prudential norms, and competitiveness.

Hence it is correctly linked to banking sector reform.

C. Chelliah Committee → I (Tax Reform)

The Chelliah Committee is well known for proposals on restructuring and rationalising India's tax system.

So it directly matches tax reform.

D. C. Rangarajan Committee → IV (Poverty Estimation Committee)

Rangarajan headed a committee that revisited poverty measurement methodology and poverty lines in India.

Hence it matches poverty estimation committee.

75. A widening merchandise trade deficit is most directly explained by higher imports and/or a specific surge in certain import categories. Statement B points to a rise in non-oil and non-gold imports, which increases the import bill beyond petroleum and gold. Statement D points to higher gold imports driven by early purchases ahead of festivities and safe-haven demand—this also raises the import bill and can widen the trade deficit even if other components are stable. Statement C (ban on jewellery exports) is not a standard broad-based driver cited for widening deficit in such summaries, and the option set requires the best-supported pair; thus B and D only is the appropriate combination.

76. The assertion refers to the "usual status" unemployment rate declining over time; this is consistent with recent PLFS-type trends where the usual-status unemployment rate has fallen from around the mid-single digits to nearly low-single digits by 2023–24. The reason statement about India's forex reserves being around 693 billion dollars on Dec. 26, 2025 can also be true as a factual macro indicator, but it does not explain why the unemployment rate declined because unemployment changes are driven by labour-market participation, sectoral job creation, growth composition, and measurement status—forex reserves are not a direct causal explanation for that decline.

77. The word "money" is etymologically linked to Latin through moneta (associated with the Roman temple/mint of Juno Moneta), from which terms for coin/minting evolved and later entered European languages. Hence, among the given language options, Latin is the correct origin.

78. **D. Walras' Theory of General Equilibrium (1874)** – Published in Elements of Pure Economics, it is one of the earliest systematic and mathematical formulations in economics. Hence, it comes first.

C. Cardinal Utility Theory of Demand (1871–1890) – Initiated by Jevons (1871) and later refined by Marshall (1890), it assumes utility can be measured numerically. This follows Walras chronologically.

A. Theory of Limit Pricing (1950s) – Introduced by Joe S. Bain, it explains how existing firms set prices to deter new entrants in oligopolistic markets.

B. Logical Ordering (Ordinal Utility) Theory of Demand (1934) – Given by J.R. Hicks and R.G.D. Allen in *A Reconsideration of the Theory of Value*, it introduced indifference curve analysis and the ordinal approach to utility.

79. SEBI is a statutory regulator (created under the SEBI Act), so calling it an "advisory body" is incorrect. The GST Council is a constitutional body (created under Article 279A), so calling it a "statutory body" is also not accurate in the strict classification used here; however, NITI Aayog is an advisory/think-tank style institution (not created by statute/constitution), and RBI is a statutory body established under the RBI Act. Therefore, only C and D form the correct pair.

80. **A. n^{th} term of an Arithmetic Progression → III** $a + (n-1)d$: In an AP, each term increases by common difference d; after $(n-1)$ steps from the first term a, the nth term becomes $a + (n-1)d$. This is the standard AP term formula used to generate any term directly.

B. n^{th} term of a Geometric Progression → IV ar^{n-1}: In a GP, each term is multiplied by common ratio r; after $(n-1)$ multiplications starting from a, the nth term is ar^{n-1}. This captures exponential growth/decay depending on r.

C. Sum to n terms of an Arithmetic Progression → I $\frac{n}{2}[2a + (n-1)d]$: The AP sum equals number of terms times the average of first and last terms; rewriting the last term as $a + (n-1)d$ yields $\frac{n}{2}[2a + (n-1)d]$. This is the compact closed-form sum formula for AP.

D. Sum to n terms of a Geometric Progression → II $a\left(\frac{r^n-1}{r-1}\right)$, $r > 1$: The GP sum is derived by multiplying the sum by r and subtracting to cancel intermediate terms, giving $S_n(r-1) = a(r^n-1)$. Hence $S_n = a\left(\frac{r^n-1}{r-1}\right)$ for $r \neq 1$ (shown here for $r > 1$).

81. The Chicago School, particularly associated with Milton Friedman and other monetarists, expanded the traditional definition of money beyond currency and demand deposits. They argued that time deposits with commercial banks are close substitutes for money, as they serve as a store of value and can be converted into cash with relatively low cost. Hence, they should be included in the definition of money supply. The Conventional Approach treated money narrowly as currency plus demand deposits only. Therefore, the approach that included time deposits with commercial banks in the definition of money supply is the Chicago Approach.

82. The Green Revolution in India was primarily associated with rapid productivity and output increases in fine cereals, especially wheat and rice, because HYV seeds, irrigation, chemical fertilisers, and plant-protection measures were applied most intensively to these crops. At the same time, policy incentives and profitability shifts encouraged farmers to reallocate land away from many coarse cereals (like jowar, bajra, ragi in several regions) toward wheat/rice and other remunerative crops, which contributed to a relative (and in some areas absolute) decline in coarse-cereal area and production over time. Hence both statements correctly describe the major directional effects.

83. RIDF (Rural Infrastructure Development Fund) was created within NABARD in 1995–96 with an initial corpus of about ₹ 2000 crore, mainly to finance rural infrastructure through state governments and state-owned agencies. Its resources are largely built from contributions linked to scheduled commercial banks, especially when they fall short of priority sector lending targets, and the lending supports projects like rural roads, irrigation, bridges, markets, and similar infrastructure. Kisan Credit Card, however, is a farm credit delivery mechanism for short-term and related agricultural credit; it is not a merger product of RIDF, so the merger claim is the incorrect statement.

84. Statement A is correct because globalisation typically expands opportunities (markets, technology access, efficiency gains) but also brings adjustment costs and risks (inequality pressures, volatility, sectoral displacement). Statement B is correct because globalisation, by definition, intensifies cross-border flows of goods, services, capital, and technology (along with ideas and sometimes labour). Statement C is correct because larger markets deepen specialisation and the division of labour, which can raise productivity and enlarge gains from trade. Statement D is incorrect because these flows are not evenly spread; benefits and integration are highly uneven across countries and within countries due to differences in capabilities, institutions, infrastructure, and comparative advantage.

85. Mobile phones and textiles are clearly within the GST framework and are taxed under GST rates across the supply chain, with input tax credit mechanisms applying. Electricity, however, is generally kept outside GST (states levy electricity duty and related charges), so it is not covered under GST in the standard sense. Alcohol for human consumption is explicitly excluded from GST and continues to be taxed by states through excise/VAT-type levies. Therefore, the commodities not covered by GST are Electricity and Alcohol, i.e., B and D only.

86. Diesel prices vary across States because petroleum products like diesel are not brought under the GST regime. Since diesel is outside GST, individual States levy their own VAT/sales tax rates and additional cesses, leading to variation in tax incidence across States. These differing State-level tax structures directly cause differences in retail diesel prices. Therefore, the reason correctly explains why diesel prices differ across States.

87. β_2 is the coefficient of kurtosis and $\gamma_2 = \beta_2 - 3$ is excess kurtosis. A normal curve has $\beta_2 = 3$ and $\gamma_2 = 0$. If $\beta_2 < 3$, then $\gamma_2 < 0$, meaning the distribution is flatter (less peaked) than normal, which is called platykurtic. Hence, the given condition $\beta_2 < 3$ or $\gamma_2 < 0$ clearly indicates a platykurtic curve.

88. SEBI's core functions are regulatory and supervisory—protecting investors, regulating intermediaries (like portfolio managers), preventing insider trading, and promoting/regulating self-regulatory organisations within securities markets. Underwriting of new issues is an activity performed by market intermediaries (e.g., underwriters/merchant bankers) who may be registered and regulated by SEBI, but SEBI itself does not "underwrite" capital issues as a function. Therefore, "Underwriting new capital issues" is not a function of SEBI.

89. $P(A) = \frac{1}{5}$, $P(B) = \frac{1}{3}$, and A and B are mutually exclusive $\Rightarrow P(A \cap B) = 0$.

$$P(A \cup B) = P(A) + P(B) = \frac{1}{5} + \frac{1}{3} = \frac{3}{15} + \frac{5}{15} = \frac{8}{15}.$$

Probability of neither A nor B $= 1 - P(A \cup B)$

$$= 1 - \frac{8}{15} = \frac{7}{15}.$$

90. A is correct because in a barter system with n goods, the number of exchange ratios (prices) required is $\frac{n(n-1)}{2}$; for $n = 3$, $\frac{3 \cdot 2}{2} = 3$, so 3 prices are needed.

B is not correct as written because inflation weakens money's functions (especially store of value and unit of account), but it does not mean money completely stops functioning. C is incorrect because double coincidence of wants is precisely a major problem in barter (you need a matching of wants between two parties). D is correct because paper currency is token (fiat) money whose value is not equal to the intrinsic value of the paper. Therefore, only A and D are correct.

91. A Common Property Resource survives when the user community can create, accept, and enforce shared rules about access, extraction limits, monitoring, and sanctions. This needs a credible commitment by members to cooperate rather than free-ride, because open-access behaviour leads to overuse and depletion. Strict private property rules convert it away from CPR, taxation is not the core survival condition, and "non-exclusion" would worsen overexploitation instead of sustaining the resource.

92. Asymmetric information exists when one side of a transaction has better information than the other, causing problems like adverse selection (hidden characteristics before agreement) and moral hazard (hidden actions after agreement). Government intervention, non-rivalry, and non-excludability describe policy or public-good characteristics, not the informational imbalance itself. Hence the option that directly represents asymmetric information is moral hazard and adverse selection.

93. Public goods are defined by non-rivalry and non-excludability. "Common property resources controlled by locals" refers to CPRs where exclusion is possible through community rules but rivalry exists due to congestion/limited stock, so it is a different category from public goods. "Free goods" is not a defining property of public goods (many public goods are costly to provide), but the clear "not a property" in the given list is the CPR feature.

94. Incomplete markets arise when a valuable asset/service is not properly priced because property rights are unclear and exclusion/enforcement is weak. Biodiversity often generates benefits that cannot be fully captured by any single owner, so without well-defined and enforceable rights, no proper market for biodiversity services develops and incentives to conserve remain weak. Open access is a symptom of weak rights, but the root institutional cause highlighted is failure to institute well-defined property rights.

95. The "Tragedy of the Commons" is classically associated with Garrett Hardin (1968), who explained how individually rational overuse of a shared resource can lead to collective ruin when exclusion and cooperative governance are absent. Solow is linked with growth theory, Hotelling with exhaustible resources, and Dasgupta with welfare/development/environmental economics, but the specific founding articulation of this concept is Hardin's.

96. The passage repeatedly highlights that multilateral forums (including the WTO platform) are losing influence because important countries are increasingly preferring regional blocs and bilateral arrangements to pursue their national interest. When trade negotiations and dispute-settlement pressures shift away from the multilateral arena toward regional economic associations and bilateral trade forums, the WTO's central role gets directly challenged—its agenda-setting power weakens and rules-based discipline becomes harder to enforce. Hence, the most specific "challenge to WTO" described here is the growing importance of regional and bilateral forums.

97. The passage states that from the early 1980s the world moved toward globalisation and that multilateral lending and trade forums played a crucial role in shaping the negotiation environment and facilitating global integration. This means globalisation is being presented as an outcome driven by the working and influence of multilateral institutions and negotiations rather than being an outcome of one event like Brexit or only a single country's initiatives. Therefore, the correct option is the role played by multilateral lending and trade forums.

98. The passage explicitly conveys that multilateral economic institutions' meetings are "not considered seriously" by leaders and that international economic relations are less influenced by multilateral forums now. It also notes disruptions in WTO forums and a growing focus on bilateral and regional routes, which together imply that multilateral forums are being pushed into the background in current practice. Hence, the nature of present international economic relations, as per the passage, is that multilateral forums are relegated to the background.

99. The passage points to actions like imposing high tariffs and taking measures that violate free and fair trade norms, alongside leaders questioning multilateral institutions and prioritising national interest. Such behaviour indicates that powerful nations are weakening multilateral institutions (including the WTO's influence) by bypassing or violating the multilateral rule-based framework when it conflicts with their domestic priorities. Therefore, the passage conveys that powerful nations are undermining multilateral institutions for national interest.

100. Free and fair trade requires predictable, rules-based market access without arbitrary or discriminatory barriers. The passage specifically mentions the imposition of high tariffs and other measures that violate free and fair trade ensured by multilateral arrangements, making tariffs a direct violation because they restrict trade and distort prices/competition. Therefore, the correct choice is the imposition of high and unfair tariffs.

Previous Years' Paper

National Testing Agency (NTA)

UGC-NET Junior Research Fellowship & Assistant Professor Eligibility Exam

ECONOMICS, JUNE-2025

(Exam held on 29-06-2025)

PAPER-II

1. Match the List-I with List-II:

List-I	List-II
A. Playing each strategy with probability	I. Nash equilibrium
B. Maximum payoff given the strategy of other	II. Grim trigger strategy
C. Long-run behaviour	III. Best response function
D. Period of punishment is infinite	IV. Mixed strategy

Choose the **correct** answer from the options given below:

1. A-II, B-III, C-IV, D-I
2. A-I, B-IV, C-III, D-II
3. A-III, B-II, C-IV, D-I
4. A-IV, B-III, C-I, D-II

2. The null hypothesis that all slope coefficients are simultaneously equal to zero is tested in logit model by.

1. F-test
2. t-test
3. Chi-square test
4. Likelihood ratio statistics

3. Which of the followings is not true?

1. The effect of any tax can be decomposed into an income effect and substitution effect.
2. There is a substitution effect associated with a lump-sum tax, but no income effect.
3. The greater is the substitution effect, the greater is the deadweight loss.
4. There is also a deadweight loss associated with the reduction in prices received by producers as a result of imposition of tax.

4. Which of the following are correct about the foreign trade policy (FTP) 2023 of India?

A. India's FTP 2023 promotes cross border trade in digital economy.

B. FTP 2023 emphasized on creation of E-commerce export hubs (ECEH).

C. It prohibits export and import of arms and related material from/to Iraq.

D. It prohibits import of charcoal from Somalia.

E. It emphasizes strengthening trade with Democratic People's Republic of Korea in combat aircraft, missiles and arms related materials.

Choose the **most appropriate** answer from the options given below:

1. A, D & E Only
2. D & E Only
3. A, B & C Only
4. A, B, C & D Only

5. Which of the followings is true in case of a good i.e., "Crowded City side Walk"?

1. It is non-excludable and non-rivalry in nature.
2. It is excludable but non-rivalry in nature.
3. It is non-excludable but rivalry in nature.
4. It is excludable and rivalry in nature.

6. Which of the followings are not true pertaining to Wagner's Law of increasing state activities?

A. Wagner's Law is classified as positive theory of public expenditure.

B. Public sector in industrializing nations grow as a proportion of total economic activity with the increase in per capita income and output.

C. Proportionate increase in public sector is not constant but increasing with the increase in total economic activity.

D. The law accounts for the effect of war on public expenditure.

E. Public expenditure tends to grow in a stepwise manner.

Choose the **most appropriate** answer from the options given below:

1. A, B & D Only
2. B, C & E Only
3. B & C Only
4. D & E Only

7. Which of the following indicate that country "B" is capital abundant country?

A. $\left(\frac{\text{Total Capital}}{\text{Total Labour}}\right)B > \left(\frac{\text{Total Capital}}{\text{Total Labour}}\right)A$

B. $\left(\frac{\text{Total Capital}}{\text{Total Labour}}\right)B < \left(\frac{\text{Total Capital}}{\text{Total Labour}}\right)A$

C. $\left(\frac{\text{Price of Capital}}{\text{Price of Labour}}\right)B < \left(\frac{\text{Price of Capital}}{\text{Price of Labour}}\right)A$

D. $\left(\frac{\text{Price of Capital}}{\text{Price of Labour}}\right)B > \left(\frac{\text{Price of Capital}}{\text{Price of Labour}}\right)A$

E. $\left(\frac{\text{Total Labour}}{\text{Total Capital}}\right)B > \left(\frac{\text{Price of Capital}}{\text{Price of Labour}}\right)A$

Choose the **correct** answer from the options given below:

1. A & B Only
2. A & C Only
3. B & D Only
4. C & E Only

8. Match List-I with List-II:

List-I (Concepts)	List-II (Given by)
A. Paradox of thrift	I. K. Boulding
B. Water-Diamond paradox	II. A.C. Pigou
C. Wage employment paradox	III. J.M. Keynes
D. Macroeconomic paradox	IV. Adam Smith

Choose the **correct** answer from the options given below:

1. A-II, B-I, C-III, D-IV
2. A-I, B-II, C-III, D-IV
3. A-III, B-IV, C-II, D-I
4. A-III, B-IV, C-I, D-II

9. Which of the followings are true pertaining to the problems of asymmetric information?

A. Sellers can deal with the problem of asymmetric information by sending buyers signals about the quality of product.

B. If a seller of a product has better information about its quality than buyer, then bad products tend to drive good products out of the market.

C. According to the efficiency wage theory, a wage lower than the competitive wage increases worker productivity by discouraging workers from shirking on the job.

D. Adverse selection arises because of asymmetric information in insurance market.

E. Owners can avoid principal agent problem by designing contracts that give their agents incentive to perform better.

Choose the **correct** answer from the options given below:

1. A & B Only
2. A, B & C Only
3. B, C & D Only
4. A, B, D & E Only

10. Integrate $\int \frac{x+3}{x+5} dx$.

1. $\frac{x^2}{2} - 2.\ln|x+5| + c$
2. $\frac{x^2}{2} + 2.\ln|x+5| + c$
3. $x + 2.\ln|x + 5| + c$
4. $x - 2.\ln|x + 5| + c$

11. Arrange the following countries based on the market capitalization to nominal GDP ratio at the end of December 2024 in ascending order (as per the Economic Survey 2024-25).

A. U.K. B. India
C. China D. Brazil
E. Japan

Choose the **correct** answer from the options given below:

1. B, A, C, E, D 2. C, D, B, A, E
3. D, C, A, B, E 4. A, B, D, C, E

12. In which of the following year, the mandate/preamble of RBI has been amended?

1. 2019 2. 2024
3. 2016 4. 2007

13. Which of the following statements best define property rights?

1. Property rights refer only to government ownership of land and capital.
2. Property rights are informal social rules that cannot be enforced by law.
3. Property rights are the legally enforced rights to determine how a resource is used, owned and transferred.
4. Property rights prevent individuals from profiting from private property.

14. Which of the following comprises the current account of the balance of payments?

A. Invisible exports and imports
B. Direct investment
C. Unilateral transfers
D. SDR allocations
E. Borrowings from foreign countries

Choose the **correct** answer from the options given below:

1. A & E Only
2. C & E Only
3. A & C Only
4. A & B Only

15. According to Rostow, any industry can play the role of leading sector in the take-off stage provided following conditions are met.

A. The market for the product is expanding rapidly.
B. The leading sector generates secondary expansion.
C. The sector has an adequate and continual supply of capital from ploughed-back profits.
D. Introduction of new techniques into the sector to increase productivity.
E. Changes in industrial structure should be structural ones.

Choose the **most appropriate** answer from the options given below:

1. B, C, D & E Only
2. A, D & E Only
3. A, C & D Only
4. A, B, C & D Only

16. Match List-I with List-II:

List-I	List-II
A. Inverted "U" hypothesis	I. Herman Daly
B. Sustainable development	II. Garrett Hardin
C. Ecological Economics	III. Simon Kuznets
D. Tragedy of the commons	IV. Gro Harlen Brundtland

Choose the **correct** answer from the options given below:

1. A-IV, B-II, C-III, D-I
2. A-III, B-I, C-IV, D-II
3. A-III, B-IV, C-I, D-II
4. A-III, B-IV, C-II, D-I

17. Lexicographic preference violates which of the following axioms of utility theory?

1. Transitivity Axiom
2. Convexity Axiom
3. Continuity Axiom
4. Independence Axiom

18. According to Lucas Critique.

1. It assumes monetary policy not to be neutral with respect to real variables.
2. Drifting coefficients can make macro econometric models more reliable.
3. Keynesian models correctly consider the impact of policies on future expectations.
4. The stability of coefficients of models are important for policy predictions.

19. Given U = $(x + 2)(y + 1)$ and $P_x = 4$ and $P_y = 6$ and budget (B) =130. Find the optimum levels of purchase of x^* and y^*.

1. $x^* = 11, y^* = 16$
2. $x^* = 15, y^* = 28$
3. $x^* = 18, y^* = 8$
4. $x^* = 16, y^* = 11$

20. Bootstrapping technique is used to ....

1. Tests for specification bias
2. Obtain the sampling distribution of parameters of interest
3. Test for autocorrelation
4. Test for normality of error term

21. Which of the following statements correctly describe the concept of efficiency in environmental economics?

A. All allocation is pareto efficient if no one can be made better off without making someone else worse off.

B. Efficiency ensures a fair and equitable distribution of resources among all individuals.

C. Market allocations are efficient only in the absence of market failures such as externalities.

D. Efficiency is a normative concept concerned with what should be done based on societal value.

E. Environmental policies that internalize externalities can improve efficiency.

Choose the **most appropriate** answer from the options given below:

1. A, B & D Only
2. A, B & E Only
3. A, C & E Only
4. B, C & D Only

22. The management of a manufacturing firm wishes to determine the average time required to complete a certain manual operation. There should be 0.95 confidence that error in the estimate will not exceed 2 minutes. What sample size is estimated by a time and motion study expert as 16 minutes?

1. 96
2. 300
3. 255
4. 246

23. Arrange the following works of J.M. Keynes in chronological order (Starting from the oldest to latest).

A. A Treatise on Money

B. General Theory of Employment, Interest and Money

C. Indian Currency and Finance

D. A Monetary Theory of Production

E. A Tract on Monetary Reform

Choose the **correct** answer from the options given below:

1. E, C, A, D, B
2. C, E, A, D, B
3. C, E, A, B, D
4. A, C, E, B, D

24. Arrange the following rates in ascending order, as decided in 54th meeting of monetary policy committee of RBI.

A. Marginal Standing Facility Rate
B. Standing Deposit Facility Rate
C. CRR
D. Reverse Repo Rate
E. Repo Rate

Choose the **correct** answer from the options given below:

1. C, D, A, B, E
2. B, C, D, A, E
3. D, C, B, E, A
4. C, D, E, B, A

25. Which of the followings are the effects of increase in government spending in IS-LM framework in a closed economy?

A. Increase in income by multiplier times government expenditure.
B. Shift in IS curve to the right leading to disequilibrium in money market at given level of interest rate.
C. Quantity of money demand will be higher.
D. Interest rate will decrease.
E. Private investment will increase leading to increase in aggregate demand.

Choose the **correct** answer from the options given below:

1. B, C & D Only
2. C, D & E Only
3. A, B & C Only
4. B, D & E Only

26. Match List-I with List-II:

List-I (renewable energy sources)	List-II (% of total energy production as on Nov 2024 as per Economic Survey 2024-25)
A. Solar energy	I. 10.50%
B. Hydro energy	II. 20.60%
C. Nuclear energy	III. 10.30%
D. Wind energy	IV. 1.80%

Choose the **correct** answer from the options given below:

1. A-II, B-III, C-IV, D-I
2. A-III, B-I, C-IV, D-II
3. A-II, B-III, C-I, D-IV
4. A-II, B-I, C-III, D-IV

27. Which of the followings are true regarding the outcome of a consumer's optimization process.

A. The marginal utility per rupee spent on each good is the same.
B. The marginal rate of substitution between goods is equal to the ratio of the prices between the goods.
C. The consumer reaches the highest indifference curve in the indifference map.
D. The consumer indifference curve is tangent to his/her budget line.
E. From utility point of view, consumer is indifferent between any two points on his/her budget line.

Choose the **correct** answer from the options given below:

1. A, C & E Only
2. A, D & E Only
3. A, B & D Only
4. A, B, D & E Only

28. Which of the following conditions are required for the set of consumers to exhibit parallel, straight wealth expansion paths at any price vector P?

A. Preferences admit indirect utility function of the Gorman form.
B. Preferences are heterogeneous.
C. Wealth is equally distributed among all consumers.
D. All consumers have identical preferences that are homothetic.

E. All consumers have preferences that are quasilinear with respect to the same good.

Choose the **correct** answer from the options given below:

1. A, B & C Only
2. A, D & E Only
3. B, C & D Only
4. A, B & D Only

29. Arrange the following derivative markets in India in chronological order (starting from oldest to latest).

A. Commencement of trading in options on individual securities

B. Introduction of interest rate futures

C. Commencement of trading in Stock Futures

D. Introduction of Futures trading based on the Index

E. Commencement of trading in Index options

Choose the **correct** answer from the options given below:

1. D, C, E, A, B
2. D, E, A, C, B
3. D, A, E, B, C
4. D, C, E, B, A

30. Which of the followings are true in case of externality?

A. In case of externality, all costs and benefits associated with the goods are not internalized by households and firms involved in buying and productions.

B. Presence of externality results either under production or over production of the good.

C. Market based decision making yields an efficient outcome in the presence of externality.

D. In case of negative externality, the marginal social cost is higher than marginal cost.

E. Well defined property right can solve the problem of externality.

Choose the **most appropriate** answer from the options given below:

1. A, B & D Only
2. B, D & E Only
3. A, B, D & E Only
4. B, C, D & E Only

31. Match List-I with List-II:

List-I	List-II
A. β_2 for Chi-square distribution	I. $(n - 2)$
B. Skewness for Chi-square distribution	II. $48n + 12n^2$
C. Mode for Chi-square distribution	III. $(12/n) + 3$
D. μ_3 for Chi-square distribution	IV. $\sqrt{2/n}$

Choose the **correct** answer from the options given below:

1. A-IV, B-III, C-II, D-I
2. A-III, B-II, C-IV, D-I
3. A-II, B-I, C-IV, D-III
4. A-III, B-IV, C-I, D-II

32. If the marginal propensity to consume is 0.8 and initial increase in tax revenues by the government is ₹ 100, then the impact on national income would be:

1. National Income will increase by ₹ 100
2. National Income will increase by ₹ 500
3. National Income will decrease by ₹ 400
4. National Income will decrease by ₹ 100

33. The Stolper-Samuelson theorem postulates that:

1. An increase in the relative price of a commodity raises the earnings of the factor used intensively in the production of the commodity.
2. An increase in the relative price of a commodity decreases the earnings of the factor used intensively in the production of the commodity.
3. An increase in the relative price of a commodity raises the earnings of the factor used scarcely in the production of the commodity.
4. A decrease in the relative price of a commodity raises the earnings of the factor used intensively in the production of the commodity.

34. Which of the followings are not an assumptions of policy ineffectiveness propositions?

A. Rational expectation
B. Policy changes are not anticipated
C. Economic agents have full information
D. Nominal variables influence economic decision
E. Output and employment are at their natural level

Choose the **most appropriate** answer from the options given below:

1. B & D Only
2. A, C & D Only
3. A, B, D & E Only
4. C, D & E Only

35. Which of the following is the operating target of monetary policy conducted by RBI?

1. Repo rate
2. Reverse Repo rate
3. Weighted Average Call Money rate
4. Marginal Standing Facility rate

36. Match List-I with List-II:

List-I	List-II
A. Specific factors model	I. Prebisch-Singer hypothesis
B. Immiserizing growth	II. Thomas Mun
C. Mercantilism theory of international trade	III. Jagdish Bhagwati
D. Secular deterioration of terms of trade	IV. Paul Samuelson and Ronald Jones

Choose the **correct** answer from the options given below:

1. A-III, B-IV,C-II, D-I
2. A-IV, B-III,C-II, D-I
3. A-IV, B-II, C-III, D-I
4. A-II, B-IV, C-I, D-III

37. Arrange the following Chairman of Finance Commission in order of their appointment starting from the oldest.

A. A.M. Khusro
B. C. Rangarajan
C. N.K.P. Salve
D. K. Bramhananda Reddy
E. K.C. Pant

Choose the **correct** answer from the options given below:

1. A, C, E, D, B   2. C, E, A, D, B
3. B, D, E, C, A   4. D, C, E, A, B

38. Arrange the following sectors in descending order as per their share in total FDI in India in H1 FY 2025 as per the Economic Survey 2024-25.

A. Automobile Industry
B. Hospital and Diagnostic Centers
C. Cement and Gypsum Products
D. Computer Software and Hardware
E. Non-conventional Energy

Choose the **correct** answer from the options given below:

1. D, E, C, A, B   2. D, C, E, B, A
3. E, B, A, D, C   4. E, D, C, B, A

39. Match List-I with List-II:

List-I (Concepts)	List-II (their expression) (where, g_m = manufacturing output growth, g_{GDP} = GDP growth, P_{nm} = productivity in outside manufacturing, P_m = Productivity in manufacturing)
A. Kaldor's first law of growth	I. $P_m = f(g_m)\ f' > 0$
B. Kaldor's second law of growth	II. $y' = -\in (u\text{-}u^*)$
C. Kaldor's third law of growth	III. $g_{GDP} = f(g_m)\ f' > 0$
D. Okun's law	IV. $P_{nm} = f(g_m)\ f' > 0$

Choose the **correct** answer from the options given below:

1. A-IV, B-III, C-I, D-II
2. A-III, B-IV, C-I, D-II
3. A-III, B-I, C-IV, D-II
4. A-IV, B-III, C-II, D-I

40. The idea of constructing poverty-weighted indices of growth is:

1. To give at least equal weight to all income groups in society.
2. To achieve high growth rate.
3. To facilitate foreign trade on equal basis.
4. To assign more value or weight on income group of richest population and no weight on lower-income group.

41. Which of the following are correct about the revised criteria of MSMEs effective from 01 April 2025 as per union budget 2025-26?

A. An enterprise is classified as micro enterprise if investment in plant and machinery does not exceed ₹ 2.5 crore.

B. A medium enterprise is one whose turnover does not exceed ₹ 50 crore.

C. A small enterprise has investment limit up to ₹ 10 crore.

D. A micro enterprise is one whose turnover is up to ₹ 10 crore.

E. A small enterprise has turnover limit up to ₹ 100 crore.

Choose the **most appropriate** answer from the options given below:

1. B, C & D Only
2. A, D & E Only
3. A, B & E Only
4. C, D & E Only

42. Arrange the following tax reform committees on the basis of their year of constitution starting from the oldest.

A. Raja Chelliah tax reform committee

B. T.R. Rastogi Committee on Service tax reforms

C. Vijay Kelkar committee on tax reforms

D. Parthasarathi Shome committee on direct tax

E. K.L. Rekhi committee on indirect tax

Choose the **correct** answer from the options given below:

1. A, E, C, B, D
2. E, A, C, B, D
3. A, E, D, C, B
4. D, E, A, C, B

43. Match List-I with List-II:

List-I	List-II
A. Income elasticity greater than one	I. Substitute goods
B. Positive cross price elasticity	II. Inferior goods
C. Downward sloping price consumption curve (PCC)	III. Luxurious goods
D. Negative income effect	IV. Relative elastic demand

Choose the **correct** answer from the options given below:

1. A-IV, B-II, C-I, D-III
2. A-III, B-II, C-I, D-IV
3. A-IV, B-II, C-III, D-I
4. A-III, B-I, C-IV, D-II

44. If the income effect is in the opposite direction as the substitution effect, but the substitution effect dominates, then the good is ....

1. Normal
2. Inferior but not giffen
3. Giffen
4. There is not enough information to answer

45. Arrange the expenditure allocation to following items, as % of total union government expenditure as per the union budget 2025-26 in ascending order.

A. Finance Commission and Other Transfers
B. Interest Payment
C. Pensions
D. Major Subsidies
E. Central Sector Schemes (excluding capital outlay on defense and subsidies)

Choose the **correct** answer from the options given below:

1. A, D, E, C, B
2. C, D, A, E, B
3. E, C, D, A, B
4. C, D, E, B, A

46. If $U = 6x^2 + y^2$, and $4x - y = 1$. What is the value of U?

1. $\frac{4}{15}$
2. $\frac{3}{11}$
3. $\frac{3}{16}$
4. $\frac{4}{21}$

47. Match List-I with List-II:

List-I (Items of receipts)	List-II (Share to total receipt in % as per union budget 2025-26)
A. Income tax	I. 4%
B. Custom	II. 5%
C. Corporation tax	III. 22%
D. Union excise	IV. 17%

Choose the **correct** answer from the options given below:

1. A-IV, B-II,C-III, D-I
2. A-III, B-I, C-II, D-IV
3. A-III, B-I, C-IV, D-II
4. A-IV, B-II,C-I, D-III

48. In the context of neoclassical growth model, the effects of an increase in population growth rate is/are.

A. Reduction in steady-state level of capital per head
B. Increase in per capita output
C. Increase in steady state rate of growth of aggregate output
D. Decrease in capital-output ratio
E. An inward shift in production possibility curve.

Choose the **most appropriate** answer from the options given below:

1. A, B & C Only
2. B, C, D & E Only
3. A & C Only
4. C, D & E Only

49. Match List-I with List-II:

List-I	List-II
A. Income induced adjustment process of balance of payments	I. Paul Samuelson
B. Absorption approach of BoPs	II. Keynes, J.M.
C. Impossible trinity	III. Sidney S. Alexander
D. Factor price equalization theorem	IV. Mundell-Fleming

Choose the **correct** answer from the options given below:

1. A-I, B-II, C-III, D-IV
2. A-II, B-III, C-IV, D-I
3. A-II, B-III, C-I, D-IV
4. A-II, B-I, C-III, D-IV

50. The indirect least square is applied to estimate the coefficient of the:

1. Structural equation
2. Over identified equation
3. Reduced form equation
4. Under identified equation

51. Which of the followings are true about New Classical approach.

A. The main protagonist was R.E. Lucas Jr.
B. It is based on adaptive expectation.
C. It was developed during 1950s.
D. Complete wage and price flexibility.
E. Difference between actual and expected price is a random error.

Choose the **most appropriate** answer from the options given below:

1. A, B & E Only
2. A, D & E Only
3. B, C, D & E Only
4. A, B & D Only

52. If the value of Keynesian investment multiplier is 4, which one of the following will be the corresponding saving function?

1. $S = -4 + 0.4\ Y_D$
2. $S = -10 + 0.75\ Y_D$
3. $S = -12 + 0.25\ Y_D$
4. $S = -6 + 0.35\ Y_D$

53. Which of the following correctly state the formula to compute the rate of effective protection?

Where, g = the rate of effective protection to producers of final commodities, t = the nominal tariff rate on consumers of the final commodity, t_i = the nominal tariff rate on the imported input and a_i = the ratio of the cost of the imported input to the price of the final commodity in the absence of tariffs.

1. $g = \dfrac{t - a_i t_i}{1 - a_i}$ 2. $g = \dfrac{t + a_i t_i}{1 - a_i}$
3. $g = \dfrac{t - a_i t_i}{1 + a_i}$ 4. $g = \dfrac{t + a_i t_i}{1 + a_i}$

54. If x is a poisson variate with mean λ, then $P(x + 1)$ is:

1. $\dfrac{\lambda}{x+1} P(x)$ 2. $\dfrac{\lambda}{x}$
3. $\dfrac{x+1}{\lambda} P(x)$ 4. $\dfrac{x}{\lambda} P(x)$

55. Match List-I with List-II:

List-I	List-II
A. The mean of a Hypergeometric distribution	I. $\dfrac{q}{p^2}$
B. The moment generating function of negative binomial distribution	II. $(Q - Pe^t)^{-r}$
C. The coefficient of Kurtosis of a binomial distribution	III. $\dfrac{nm}{N}$
D. The variance of geometric distribution	IV. $\dfrac{1-6pq}{npq}$

Choose the **correct** answer from the options given below:

1. A-II, B-III, C-I, D-IV
2. A-III, B-II, C-IV, D-I
3. A-I, B-III, C-IV, D-II
4. A-II, B-I, C-III, D-IV

56. Assume that the rate of investment is described by the function $I(t) = 12t^{1/3}$ and capital stock $k(0) = 25$. Find the time path of capital stock k.

1. $16t^{4/3} + 25$ 2. $9t^{4/3} + 25$
3. $-9t^{4/3} + 25$ 4. $-16t^{4/3} + 25$

57. Which of the following is not true according to classical's views on public debt?

1. Public debt financing requires funds for interest payment and amortization,hence a double burden on tax payers.
2. Public debt financing supports compensatory budget policy as a tool for stimulating aggregate demand.
3. Public debt creates barren production and consumption and burden is transferred to future generation.
4. Public debt destroys capital which otherwise could be used productively.

58. A candidate is selected for interview for three posts. For the first post, there are 3 candidates, for the second 4 candidates and for the third 2 candidates. What is the probability that the candidate is selected for at least one post?

1. $\frac{1}{4}$ 2. $\frac{1}{2}$
3. $\frac{3}{4}$ 4. $\frac{1}{9}$

59. Which of the following causes a positive output gap, where, output gap = Actual output- Potential output?

1. Population growth
2. Technological progress
3. Overemployment of factors of production
4. Under utilization of resources

60. If Q = f(K, L) is a homogeneous production function of degree one, which of the following satisfies Euler's theorem?

1. $\left(\frac{\partial Q}{\partial K}\right)+\left(\frac{\partial Q}{\partial L}\right)=Q$
2. $\left(\frac{\partial Q}{\partial K}\right)K+\left(\frac{\partial Q}{\partial L}\right)L=Q$
3. $\left(\frac{\partial Q}{\partial K}\right)K+\left(\frac{\partial Q}{\partial L}\right)L>1$
4. $\left(\frac{\partial Q}{\partial K}\right)\left(\frac{\partial Q}{\partial L}\right)=1$

61. According to classical economics, an increase in government deficit spending leads to.

A. a shift in the demand for loanable fund to the right
B. decline in interest rate
C. increase in investment
D. increase in saving equal to decline in consumption
E. decrease in investment and consumption that balances the increase in government spending.

Choose the **correct** answer from the options given below:

1. A, B & D Only
2. A, D & E Only
3. A, B, C & D Only
4. C, D & E Only

62.

		Player 2	
		L	R
Player 1	T	1, 5	0, 3
	M	2, 6	1, 4
	B	3, 7	2, 2

Which of the following statements are true about the above payoff matrix?

A. Player-1 has two strictly dominated strategies.
B. None of the strategies of player-2 are weakly dominated.
C. Strategy T weakly dominates strategy B.
D. Strategy M of Player-1 will never be used in Nash-equilibrium.
E. Strategy M strictly dominates strategy T.

Choose the **correct** answer from the options given below:

1. A, B, C & E Only
2. A, D & E Only
3. B, C & D Only
4. C, D & E Only

63. Arrange the following items on the basis of the expenditure allocation made in the union budget 2025-26 in descending order.

A. Agriculture and Allied activities
B. Education
C. Defense
D. Commerce and Industry
E. Rural Development

Choose the **correct** answer from the options given below:

1. E, C, A, D, B
2. C, E, A, B, D
3. C, A, E, D, B
4. A, E, C, B, D

64. A company has examined its costs and revenue structure and has determined that C-total cost, R-the total revenue and X-the number of units produced are related as:

$C = 100 + 0.015 X^2$ and $R = 3X$

Find the product level X that will maximize profit for this company.

1. 120
2. 80
3. 150
4. 100

65. If $\overline{x} = 32, \overline{y} = 38,$ the regression coefficients $b_{xy} = -0.2337$, $b_{yx} = -0.6643$. Find the equation of the line of regression of y on x.

1. $y = -0.2337x + 40.8806$
2. $y = -0.2337x - 40.8806$
3. $y = -0.6643x - 59.2576$
4. $y = -0.6643x + 59.2576$

66. In the context of IS-LM model, a higher marginal propensity to spend results in:

1. A flatter aggregate demand curve and consequently a steeper IS curve
2. A steeper aggregate demand curve and consequently a flatter IS curve
3. Increase in aggregate demand and a rightward shift of the IS curve
4. Increase in demand for real balances

67. In the product cycle model of International trade, in which stage the imitating country starts underselling the innovating country in third markets?

1. Stage-II
2. Stage-III
3. Stage-IV
4. Stage-V

68. Match List-I with List-II:

List-I (Criteria of 15th finance commission)	List-II (Weights as per the recommendation of 15th finance commission for horizontal devolution)
A. Income distance	I. 15%
B. Population	II. 12.5%
C. Demographic performance	III. 45%
D. Forest and Ecology	IV. 10%

Choose the **correct** answer from the options given below:

1. A-III, B-IV,C-I, D-II
2. A-II, B-I, C-III, D-IV
3. A-III, B-I, C-II, D-IV
4. A-I, B-IV, C-II, D-III

69. In the context of classical economics, an increase in money supply causes.

1. A shift in aggregate demand curve to the left
2. A shift in aggregate demand curve to the right
3. A shift in aggregate supply curve to the right
4. No change in aggregate demand and aggregate supply, only price increases

70. If both input and output markets are competitive and firms are profit maximizing, then in equilibrium each factor of production earns:

1. An amount equal to the price of output times total output.
2. The amount allocated by political process
3. An equal share of output.
4. The value of its marginal product.

71. Arrange the following environmental conventions/summits in sequence starting from the oldest.

A. Kyoto Protocol
B. Minamata Convention
C. Stockholm Convention
D. UN-REDD
E. Rio Summit

Choose the **correct** answer from the options given below:

1. E, A, C, D, B
2. E, C, A, B, D
3. C, E, A, D, B
4. A, B, C, D, E

72. Arrange the following publications in chronological order starting from the oldest to the latest.

A. "Theory of Economic Growth" by Arthur Lewis
B. "A Contribution to the Theory of Economic Growth" by Robert Solow
C. "The Stages of Economic Growth: A Non-Communist Manifesto" by Walt Rostow
D. "Asian Drama: An Inquiry into the Poverty of Nations" by Gunnar Myrdal
E. "Strategy of Economic Development" by Albert Hirschman

Choose the **correct** answer from the options given below:

1. A, E, B, C, D
2. E, B, C, D, A
3. C, D, B, E, A
4. A, B, E, C, D

73. Match List-I with List-II:

List-I (Monetary policy regime)	List-II (Periods)
A. Fiscal dominance	I. 2016 onwards
B. Multiple indicator approach	II. 1951-1985
C. Monetary targeting with feedbacks	III. 1998-2016
D. Flexible inflation targeting	IV. 1985-1998

Choose the **correct** answer from the options given below:

1. A-III, B-IV, C-II, D-I
2. A-II, B-III, C-IV, D-I
3. A-II, B-I, C-IV, D-III
4. A-IV, B-III, C-I, D-II

74. Which of the following is likely to lead to a rise in the output cost of disinflation?

1. Inflation expectations become more accurate.
2. Sluggish response of wages and prices to monetary contraction.
3. Gradual policy response.
4. Rational expectations.

75. Arrange the following countries in descending order based on their current account balance as a per cent of GDP in the period Q2 FY 25 as per the Economic Survey 2024-25.

A. India
B. Russia
C. China
D. U.K.
E. South Africa

Choose the **correct** answer from the options given below:

1. D, A, B, C, E
2. B, C, A, D, E
3. C, B, A, E, D
4. A, C, E, B, D

76. Arrange the following crisis in chronological order (starting from oldest).

A. OPEC Oil Crisis

B. International Debt Crisis

C. East Asian Financial Crisis

D. Argentinian Economic Crisis

E. Eurozone Crisis

Choose the **correct** answer from the options given below:

1. A, B, C, D, E
2. A, B, C, E, D
3. A, B, E, C, D
4. A, E, B, C, D

77. Which of the followings are correct in case of Normal distribution?

A. μ_3 for Normal distribution is 0.

B. β_2 for Normal distribution is 0.

C. Mean deviation (about mean) for Normal distribution is $\frac{4}{5}\sigma$.

D. μ_4 for Normal distribution is $2\sigma^4$.

E. Characteristic function for Normal distribution is $e^{i\mu t - \frac{t^2\sigma^2}{2}}$.

Choose the **correct** answer from the options given below:

1. A, C & E Only
2. A, B, C & E Only
3. B, C & D Only
4. A, C & D Only

78. Arrange the following union government deficits as percentage of GDP for the year 2023-24 in ascending order as per union budget 2025-26.

A. Fiscal deficit

B. Effective Revenue deficit

C. Primary deficit

D. Current Account deficit

E. Revenue deficit

Choose the **correct** answer from the options given below:

1. D, B, A, C, E
2. D, A, B, C, E
3. D, B, C, E, A
4. D, C, B, E, A

79. Which of the following game does not have any Nash Equilibrium?

1. BoS Game
2. Stag Hunt Game
3. Matching Pennies Game
4. Prisoner's Dilemma

80. Match List-I with List-II:

List-I	List-II
A. Theory of population growth and resource limits	I. Alfred Sauvy
B. Demographic transition theory	II. John Graunt
C. Father of demography	III. Warren Thompson
D. Coined the term "third World"	IV. Thomas Malthus

Choose the **correct** answer from the options given below:

1. A-III, B-IV, C-I, D-II
2. A-III, B-IV, C-II, D-I
3. A-III, B-II, C-IV, D-I
4. A-IV, B-III, C-I, D-II

81. Arrange the following rounds in chronological order (starting from oldest).

A. Millennium Round of Trade negotiations

B. Doha Round

C. Uruguay Round

D. Kennedy Round

E. Tokyo Round

Choose the **correct** answer from the options given below:

1. D, E, C, B, A
2. D, E, B, C, A
3. D, B, E, C, A
4. D, E, C, A, B

82. By using the uniqueness property of moment generating function (M.G.F.), which of the followings are correct distribution if M.G.F. is as follows?

A. $M(t) = \left(\frac{1}{2}+\frac{1}{2}e^t\right)^6$ is a poisson distribution

B. $M(t) = \frac{(1+e^t)^5}{32}$ is a binomial distribution

C. $M(t) = e^{3(e^t-1)}$ is poisson distribution

D. $M(t) = e^{(e^t-1)/4}$ is poisson distribution

E. $M(t) = 4(3e^{-t} - 1)^{-2}$ is binomial distribution

Choose the **correct** answer from the options given below:

1. A, B, C & D Only
2. B, C & D Only
3. B, C, D & E Only
4. A, B, C, D & E

83. The data about the sales and advertisement expenditure of a firm is given below:

	Sales (In crore of ₹)	Advertisement expenditure (In crore of ₹)
Mean	40	6
Standard deviation	10	1.5
Coefficient of correlation = r = 0.9		

Estimate the likely sales for the proposed advertisement of ₹ 10 crore of rupees.

1. ₹ 60 crore
2. ₹ 64 crore
3. ₹ 70 crore
4. ₹ 74 crore

84. According to neoclassical growth theory, an increase in saving rate.

1. Raises the growth rate of output in the short run.
2. Increases long run growth rate of output.
3. Decreases the steady-state capital-labor ratio.
4. Decreases the long-run level of capital and output per head.

85. If the demand law is: $P=\sqrt{9-x}$ and the demand is fixed at $x_0 = 5$. Find the consumer's surplus.

1. $\frac{8}{3}$
2. $\frac{11}{15}$
3. $\frac{8}{15}$
4. $\frac{7}{3}$

86. Which of the following is not correct about Harrod-Domar model of economic growth?

1. The natural rate of growth is made up of growth of labor force and labor productivity.
2. If actual growth (g) is greater than warranted rate of growth (g_w), g can continue to diverge from g_w only until it hits natural growth rate (g_n).
3. g can be greater than g_n in the long-run.
4. Full employment of labor and capital require $g = g_w = g_n$

87. Evaluate $\int_1^2 e^{-2x}dx$

1. $(e^{-2} - e^{-4})$
2. $-\frac{1}{2}(e^{-2}-e^{-4})$
3. $\frac{1}{2}(e^{-2}-e^{-4})$
4. $\frac{1}{2}(e^{-2}+e^{-4})$

88. According to Coase theorem, which of the following are possible outcomes of assigning property rights?

A. The polluter pays the victim to continue polluting.
B. The victim pays the polluter to reduce pollution.
C. The government must set pollution taxes to ensure efficiency.
D. Market outcomes can achieve efficiency even if externalities exist.
E. The polluter and victim always have equal bargaining power.

Choose the **most appropriate** answer from the options given below:

1. A, B & C Only
2. A, B & D Only
3. B, C & D Only
4. C, D & E Only

89. According to Granger and Newbold, a good rule of thumb to suspect that the estimated regression is spurious is given by:

1. High R^2 with low *t*-value ($R^2 > t$)
2. High *t* values with low Durbin-Watson *d* value ($t > d$)
3. High R^2 and low Durbin-Watson *d* value ($R^2 > d$)
4. High R^2 and low F value ($R^2 > F$)

90. Match List-I with List-II:

List-I	List-II
A. $\int_0^\infty \frac{1}{1+x^2}dx$	I. does not exist
B. $\int_1^\infty \frac{1}{\sqrt{x}}dx$	II. 1/3
C. $\int_{-\infty}^{-1} \frac{1}{x^4}dx$	III. $\pi/2$
D. $\int_{-\infty}^{+\infty} \frac{1}{1+x^2}dx$	IV. π

Choose the **correct** answer from the options given below:

1. A-I, B-II, C-IV, D-III
2. A-IV, B-I, C-II, D-III
3. A-III, B-I, C-II, D-IV
4. A-II, B-III, C-IV, D-I

Direction (Qs. No. 91 to 95): *Based on the information given below, answer the questions:*

Two fair dice are thrown independently. Three events A, B, and C are defined as follows;

A : odd face with first dice

B : odd face with second dice

C : sum of points on two dice is odd

91. Find the P(A ∩ B ∩ C).

1. 0
2. 1/2
3. 1/4
4. 1/6

92. Find the P(B ∩ C).

1. 1/2
2. 0
3. 1/4
4. 1/36

93. Find the P(A ∩ C).

1. 0
2. 1/2
3. 1/6
4. 1/4

94. Find the P(A ∩ B).

1. 0
2. 3/4
3. 7/12
4. 1/4

95. Find the P(C).

1. 1/4
2. 1/2
3. 3/4
4. 5/6

Direction (Qs. No. 96 to 100): *Read the following paragraph and answer the questions:*

The RBI's current monetary policy reflects a nuanced response to evolving macroeconomic dynamics. While the repo rate remains unchanged at 6.5%, the policy undertone reveals a calibrated withdrawal of accommodation, signaling a shift from pandemic era stimulus. The RBI's liquidity management has transitioned from passive surplus absorption to active fine tuning using variable rate reverse repo (VRRR) operations, amid concerns of global spillovers and domestic inflationary pressures. The policy indicates a forward looking stance, focusing on anchoring inflation expectations rather than reacting to transient price shocks. The monetary transmission remains uneven, with sectoral divergences in credit uptake and lending rates. Furthermore the policy indirectly emphasizes macro prudential regulation and financial stability, acknowledging risks from global interest rate differentials, capital flows and currency volatility. This reflects an integrated policy framework balancing inflation targeting with broader financial resilience in a globally uncertain environment.

96. Which of the following reflects the RBI's strategy in managing transient inflation shocks?
1. Immediate rate hike
2. Maintaining status quo with calibrated liquidity tools
3. Aggressive tightening
4. Reducing CRR

97. The RBI's consideration of global interest rate differentials primarily relates to.
1. Domestic food inflation
2. Foreign portfolio flows and exchange rate management
3. Retail credit growth
4. Agricultural policy

98. VRRR operations indicate.
1. Long term capital infusion
2. Structural adjustment of fiscal deficit
3. Active short term liquidity absorption
4. Decrease in SLR

99. Which concept is implicit in RBI's focus on anchoring inflation without immediate rate action?
1. Passive targeting
2. Expectation management
3. Credit rationing
4. Monetary expansion

100. The term withdrawal accommodation in monetary policy implies.
1. Increase in CRR
2. Active bond purchase
3. Gradual normalization of policy stance
4. Expansionary fiscal stimulus

ANSWERS

1	2	3	4	5	6	7	8	9	10
4	4	2	4	3	4	2	3	4	4
11	**12**	**13**	**14**	**15**	**16**	**17**	**18**	**19**	**20**
3	3	3	3	4	3	3	4	4	2
21	**22**	**23**	**24**	**25**	**26**	**27**	**28**	**29**	**30**
3	4	2	3	3	1	3	2	2	3
31	**32**	**33**	**34**	**35**	**36**	**37**	**38**	**39**	**40**
*	3	1	1	3	2	4	1	3	1
41	**42**	**43**	**44**	**45**	**46**	**47**	**48**	**49**	**50**
2	1	4	2	2	2	3	3	2	1
51	**52**	**53**	**54**	**55**	**56**	**57**	**58**	**59**	**60**
2	3	1	1	2	2	2	3	3	2
61	**62**	**63**	**64**	**65**	**66**	**67**	**68**	**69**	**70**
2	2	2	4	4	2	3	3	2	4
71	**72**	**73**	**74**	**75**	**76**	**77**	**78**	**79**	**80**
1	4	2	2	3	1	1	3	3	*
81	**82**	**83**	**84**	**85**	**86**	**87**	**88**	**89**	**90**
4	2	2	1	1	3	3	2	3	3
91	**92**	**93**	**94**	**95**	**96**	**97**	**98**	**99**	**100**
1	3	4	4	2	2	2	3	2	3

Explanatory Answers

1. Playing each strategy with probability refers to mixed strategy—players randomize across pure strategies so opponents cannot exploit predictable moves. The best response function gives the maximum payoff for a player given the other's strategy; finding best responses is central to equilibrium analysis. Long-run or steady-state behaviour in repeated or dynamic games is captured by a Nash equilibrium, which is the strategy profile where no player gains by deviating unilaterally. Finally, a grim trigger strategy is a repeated-game punishment strategy where, after one defection, the punishment (defection forever) is infinite in duration, ensuring cooperation is sustained through credible threat.

Hence, correct match is A-IV, B-III, C-I, D-II

2. In a logit model, testing whether all slope coefficients are zero compares the restricted model (only intercept) with the unrestricted model (all predictors). The likelihood ratio (LR) statistic uses −2 times the log-likelihood difference between these models. Under large samples, LR follows a chi-square distribution with degrees of freedom equal to the number of restrictions. While Wald or Lagrange Multiplier tests exist, the LR statistic is the standard test for joint significance in logit/probit models.

3. Statement 2 is not true: a lump-sum tax does not create a substitution effect—only an income effect—because relative prices are unchanged. The other points are accurate:

- Any tax's burden can be decomposed into income and substitution effects.
- Greater substitution effect increases deadweight loss since choices distort more.
- Taxes reduce prices received by producers, decreasing quantities traded and creating deadweight loss. Thus, only statement 2 is incorrect.

4. India's Foreign Trade Policy 2023 encourages cross-border digital trade and creation of E-commerce Export Hubs (ECEH) to expand e-commerce exports. It prohibits arms and related material exports/imports with Iraq (except to its government under approvals) in line with UN sanctions and bans import of charcoal from Somalia for the same reason. These align with global non-proliferation and sanction commitments. However, strengthening trade in combat aircraft or missiles with DPRK is expressly forbidden under UN resolutions that India observes, so E is not correct.

Therefore, A, B, C, and D are the valid points.

5. A crowded city sidewalk cannot feasibly exclude people from entering—making it non-excludable. Yet, when many people use it, each person's presence reduces space and comfort for others, creating rivalry in consumption (congestion). Such goods are termed common-resource or congestible goods: non-excludable until regulation or pricing is imposed, but rivalrous when usage becomes heavy.

6. Wagner's Law is an empirically observed positive regularity about how government (public) expenditure behaves as economies develop. It posits that, with industrialization and rising per-capita income/output, the scope and relative size of the public sector rise more than proportionately (income elasticity of demand for public services > 1). Hence:

- **A (True):** It's a positive (descriptive) law, not a normative prescription.
- **B (True):** With development, the public sector share in total economic activity tends to increase.
- **C (True):** The increase is more than proportionate (not a constant proportion); as the economy expands, demand for administration, social/merit goods, regulation, and cultural-welfare functions grows faster than income.
- **D (Not true for Wagner):** War-induced spending spikes and the stepwise "displacement effect" are associated with Peacock–Wiseman, not Wagner.

- E (Not true for Wagner): The stepwise growth pattern (jumps during crises, then a higher normal) is again Peacock–Wiseman, not Wagner.

Therefore, only D and E are not true of Wagner's Law.

7. 2: A country is capital-abundant if (i) by quantity it has a higher capital–labour ratio, and/or (ii) by price it has a lower relative price of capital (r/w).

- **A (True):** $(K/L)_B > (K/L)_A \Rightarrow$ B has more capital per worker → capital-abundant.
- **B (False):** $(K/L)_B < (K/L)_A$ implies B is not capital-abundant.
- **C (True):** $(P_K/P_L)_B < (P_K/P_L)_A \Rightarrow$ capital is relatively cheaper in B → capital-abundant (Heckscher–Ohlin price criterion).
- **D (False):** $(P_K/P_L)_B > (P_K/P_L)_A$ suggests capital is dearer in B → not capital-abundant.
- **E (Invalid/meaningless):** Compares a quantity ratio (L/K) with a price ratio (P_K/P_L); not a criterion for factor abundance.

Thus, A & C correctly indicate capital abundance.

8. Matching options:

- **Paradox of thrift → J. M. Keynes (III):** Higher intended saving can reduce aggregate demand, output, and ultimately total saving, if not offset.
- **Water–Diamond paradox → Adam Smith (IV):** Puzzles value in exchange vs. value in use (water is essential but cheap; diamonds are less useful but dear).
- **Wage employment paradox → A.C. Pigou (II):** Associated with classical debates on wages, employment, and the role of real-balance/Pigou effects in resolving unemployment; "paradox" label is linked to Pigouvian treatments where wage adjustments don't straightforwardly restore full employment as expected.
- **Macroeconomic paradox → K. Boulding (I):** Boulding discussed "macroeconomic paradoxes" (e.g., saving, costs) where micro-rational actions can have counter-intuitive macro outcomes.

Hence, correct matching is A-III, B-IV, C-II, D-I.

9. Checking options:

- **A (True):** Signalling (warranties, certifications, costly advertising) helps sellers credibly convey quality under asymmetric information.
- **B (True):** Akerlof's lemons: when buyers can't tell quality, bad drives out good—high-quality exits because it can't command a fair price.
- **C (False):** Efficiency wages raise productivity by paying above (not below) the competitive wage to reduce shirking/turnover and attract better workers.
- **D (True):** Adverse selection (e.g., in insurance) arises because one side knows more (high-risk buyers select in).
- **E (True):** Incentive-compatible contracts (performance pay, monitoring, equity stakes) mitigate principal–agent problems.

Hence, the true set is A, B, D, E.

10. To integrate $\int \frac{x+3}{x+5} dx$:

1. Rewrite the numerator:

$$x + 3 = (x + 5) - 2$$

So,

$$\frac{x+3}{x+5} = \frac{(x+5)-2}{x+5}$$

$$= 1 - \frac{2}{x+5}$$

2. Separate the integral:

$$\int \frac{x+3}{x+5} dx = \int \left(1 - \frac{2}{x+5}\right) dx$$

$$= \int 1\, dx - 2\int \frac{1}{x+5} dx$$

3. Integrate each term:

$$\int 1\, dx = x, \int \frac{1}{x+5} dx = \ln|x+5|$$

4. Combine results and add the constant of integration:

$$x - 2\ln|x + 5| + c$$

Thus, the correct choice among the options is:

$$x - 2\ln|x + 5| + c$$

11. According to Economic Survey 2024–25, the ratio of market capitalisation to nominal GDP at the end of December 2024 shows significant variation across major economies. The reported values are approximately: Brazil – 37%, China – 65%, United Kingdom – 84%, India – 136%, and Japan – 157%. This ratio reflects the size of a country's stock market compared to the overall economy. Lower ratios indicate smaller equity markets relative to GDP, while higher ratios indicate deep and broad equity markets. When these countries are arranged in ascending order, the smallest ratio is Brazil (D), followed by China (C), then United Kingdom (A), then India (B), and finally Japan (E) with the highest ratio.

Hence the correct ascending order is D, C, A, B, E, matching option 3.

12. The Reserve Bank of India Act, 1934 underwent a significant amendment in 2016. This change redefined the mandate and preamble of the RBI, introducing flexible inflation targeting and establishing the Monetary Policy Committee (MPC). The amended preamble explicitly stated that the primary objective of monetary policy is to maintain price stability while keeping in mind the objective of growth, aligning RBI's goals with modern macroeconomic priorities. Earlier years like 2007, 2019, or 2024 did not contain this specific change to the preamble or mandate.

Thus, 2016 is the correct choice.

13. Property rights in economics and law are not limited to government ownership or informal rules—they are legally enforceable claims over resources. These rights define who can use a resource, exclude others, derive income, and transfer ownership. Properly defined property rights promote efficient allocation of resources, investment incentives, and reduce conflicts. Options suggesting that property rights are only government ownership (1), are merely informal social rules (2), or prevent profit from private property (4) are incorrect.

Therefore, the most accurate definition is option 3.

14. The current account of the balance of payments (BoP) records flows of goods, services, income, and unilateral transfers. Specifically:

A. Invisible exports and imports—these are services such as IT services, tourism, insurance, and income flows; they are part of the current account.

C. Unilateral transfers—these include remittances, gifts, and grants where there is no quid pro quo, and they are also part of the current account.

Items like Direct investment (B), SDR allocations (D), and Borrowings from foreign countries (E) belong to the capital or financial account, as they involve acquisition of assets or liabilities rather than current flows of goods/services or transfers.

Hence, only A and C correctly represent current account components.

15. Economist W.W. Rostow in his "Stages of Economic Growth" model described the take-off stage, where sustained economic growth begins. A leading sector can drive take-off if four main conditions are satisfied:

A. The market for the product expands rapidly, ensuring demand growth for the sector's output.

B. The leading sector generates secondary expansion, meaning its growth stimulates linked industries through backward and forward linkages.

C. There is an adequate and continual supply of capital from ploughed-back profits, ensuring that reinvestment maintains momentum.

D. New techniques are introduced to raise productivity, enabling efficiency and competitiveness.

While (E) Structural changes in industrial structure should be structural ones is too vague and not part of Rostow's explicitly stated criteria, the first four are directly mentioned in his analysis.

Thus, A, B, C, and D only (option 4) is correct.

16. Matching options:

- **Inverted "U" hypothesis → Simon Kuznets (III):** The Kuznets curve posits that as an economy develops, income inequality first rises and then falls, tracing an inverted "U".
- **Sustainable development → Gro Harlem Brundtland (IV):** The Brundtland Commission (1987) framed sustainable development as meeting present needs without compromising future generations' ability to meet theirs.
- **Ecological Economics → Herman Daly (I):** Daly pioneered steady-state and scale-aware thinking, embedding the economy within the ecosystem's biophysical limits.
- **Tragedy of the commons → Garrett Hardin (II):** Hardin highlighted how open-access resources get overused when individual incentives conflict with collective welfare.

17. Lexicographic preferences (first compare one attribute; only if tied, compare the next) are complete and transitive, and their upper contour sets are convex under standard settings. However, they fail continuity: no sufficiently small "compensation" in the less-important attribute can offset a tiny loss in the more-important one. Hence a continuous utility representation does not exist, violating the continuity axiom (not transitivity, independence, or convexity).

18. The Lucas Critique argues that econometric relationships (coefficients) estimated under one policy regime change when policy rules change, because agents' expectations and decision rules adjust. Therefore, policy evaluation needs structural, policy-invariant parameters; models with drifting coefficients are unreliable for counterfactual policy analysis. It does not assert monetary non-neutrality nor praise Keynesian expectation treatment; rather, it warns that expectations matter and coefficient stability is crucial—making statement 4 the correct one.

19. **Step 1: Restate the problem**

Maximise the utility function

$$U = (x + 2)(y + 1)$$

subject to the budget constraint

$$4x + 6y = 130$$

Step 2: Express in convenient form

Let,

$$X = x + 2,\ Y = y + 1$$

Then,

$$x = X - 2,\ y = Y - 1$$

Substitute into the budget:

$$4(X - 2) + 6(Y - 1) = 130$$

$$\Rightarrow 4X - 8 + 6Y - 6 = 130$$

$$\Rightarrow 4X + 6Y = 144$$

$$\Rightarrow 2X + 3Y = 72.$$

Step 3: Find the marginal rate of substitution (MRS)

The utility is $U = XY$

$$MU_x = \frac{\partial U}{\partial X} = Y,\ MU_y = \frac{\partial U}{\partial Y} = X$$

Set MRS equal to the price ratio:

$$\frac{MU_x}{MU_y} = \frac{Y}{X} = \frac{P_x}{P_y} = \frac{4}{6} = \frac{2}{3}$$

Hence,

$$Y = \frac{2}{3}X$$

Step 4: Substitute into the budget constraint

$$2X + 3Y = 72$$

$$\Rightarrow 2X + 3\left(\frac{2}{3}X\right) = 72$$

$$\Rightarrow 2X + 2X = 72$$

$$\Rightarrow 4X = 72$$

$$\Rightarrow X = 18$$

Then

$$Y = \frac{2}{3}(18) = 12$$

Step 5: Convert back to x and y

$$\Rightarrow x = X - 2 = 18 - 2 = 16,$$

$$y = Y - 1 = 12 - 1 = 11$$

Final Optimum:

$$x^* = 16, \ y^* = 11$$

Hence, $x = 16$, $y = 11$

20. Bootstrapping resamples (with replacement) from the observed data to approximate the sampling distribution of an estimator or statistic, enabling standard errors, confidence intervals, and bias assessments without strong parametric assumptions. It is not a specific test for specification bias, autocorrelation, or normality.

21. In environmental economics, efficiency refers to using society's resources in a way that maximizes total welfare without unnecessary waste.

- **A (Correct):** Pareto efficiency means an allocation is efficient if no one can be made better off without making someone else worse off. This is the standard definition of efficiency used in welfare economics.
- **B (Incorrect):** Fairness or equity is not guaranteed by efficiency. A Pareto-efficient allocation could still be very unequal. Equity and fairness are normative issues, whereas efficiency is generally a positive concept describing resource allocation, not moral judgments.
- **C (Correct):** Market allocations are only efficient if there are no market failures like externalities, public goods, or imperfect competition. When such failures exist, the market outcome is not efficient, which is why environmental issues (externalities) often require policy intervention.
- **D (Incorrect):** Efficiency is not primarily a normative concept about what society "should" do; it is an analytical criterion describing a state where resources can't be reallocated to make someone better off without hurting others.
- **E (Correct):** Environmental policies like Pigouvian taxes, cap-and-trade systems, or subsidies that internalize externalities can move an economy closer to efficiency by aligning private costs with social costs.

22. To determine sample size for estimating a mean with specified confidence and error:

- **Confidence level:** 95% → Z=1.96.
- **Standard deviation (σ):** Estimated at 16 minutes by the time-and-motion expert.
- **Maximum error (E):** 2 minutes.

The formula is:

$$n = \left(\frac{Z\sigma}{E}\right)^2$$

Substituting values:

$$n = \left(\frac{1.96 \times 16}{2}\right)^2$$

$$= \left(\frac{31.36}{2}\right)^2$$

$$= (15.68)^2 \approx 245.7$$

Rounding up,

$$n = 246.$$

Hence, to ensure with 95% confidence that the estimation error will not exceed 2 minutes, the firm should take a sample size of 246.

23. Chronological order of Keynes's works (oldest to latest):

C. **Indian Currency and Finance (1913):** An early book where Keynes analyzed India's currency and financial system under the British regime, critiquing policies affecting stability.

E. **A Tract on Monetary Reform (1923):** Written after World War I, it examined post-war inflation and exchange rate policies, advocating monetary stability.

A. **A Treatise on Money (1930):** A comprehensive two-volume work providing a systematic analysis of monetary theory before the Great Depression.

D. **A Monetary Theory of Production (1933):** A lecture developing Keynes's ideas about monetary factors driving production decisions, foreshadowing The General Theory.

B. **The General Theory of Employment, Interest and Money (1936):** Keynes's revolutionary macroeconomic work overturning classical economics by emphasizing demand management.

Thus, the correct chronological sequence is C, E, A, D, B.

24. At the 54th Monetary Policy Committee (MPC) meeting of RBI (late 2024), the key rates decided were:

- **Reverse Repo Rate (D)** – The lowest rate at which RBI absorbs liquidity.
- **Cash Reserve Ratio (C)** – A regulatory ratio, slightly higher than reverse repo in relative position for ascending order purposes.
- **Standing Deposit Facility Rate (B)** – Slightly higher than CRR, providing RBI with a non-collateralized facility for absorbing liquidity.
- **Repo Rate (E)** – The policy rate at which RBI lends to banks, positioned above SDF.
- **Marginal Standing Facility Rate (A)** – The highest rate, the upper ceiling of the corridor for emergency borrowing by banks.

Arranging from lowest to highest: D (Reverse Repo) < C (CRR) < B (SDF) < E (Repo) < A (MSF), which corresponds to option 3.

25. In the IS-LM model (closed economy), an increase in government spending shifts macroeconomic equilibrium as follows:

- **A (Correct):** Government spending increases aggregate demand, shifting the IS curve and causing income to rise by the government expenditure multiplier (the ratio of change in output to change in spending).
- **B (Correct):** The IS curve shifts right, producing excess demand in the goods market, which, at the initial interest rate, creates a disequilibrium in the money market since income rises and money demand increases.
- **C (Correct):** Higher income causes money demand to rise because people need more transactions balances at the existing interest rate.
- **D (Incorrect):** Interest rates do not decrease; instead, they increase because the LM curve is upward-sloping in (Y,i)(Y, i)(Y,i) space—higher money demand at unchanged supply pushes rates up.
- **E (Incorrect):** Higher interest rates crowd out private investment; thus, private investment generally falls, not rises.

Hence, the correct effects of increased government spending are A, B, and C.

26. The Economic Survey 2024–25 gives approximate shares of India's energy production (Nov 2024): Solar – 20.60%, Hydro – 10.30%, Nuclear – 1.80%, Wind – 10.50%.

- **A. Solar energy → II (20.60%):** India's solar capacity expanded rapidly under missions like the National Solar Mission, forming the largest share among renewables.
- **B. Hydro energy → III (10.30%):** Hydroelectric projects remain a stable, significant but smaller component.
- **C. Nuclear energy → IV (1.80%):** Nuclear has a tiny share due to limited plants.
- **D. Wind energy → I (10.50%):** Wind contributes just over 10% of renewable production.

Correct matching: A-II, B-III, C-IV, D-I.

27. Outcomes of a consumer's optimization:

- **A (True):** At equilibrium, marginal utility per rupee is equal for all goods: $\frac{MU_x}{P_x} = \frac{MU_y}{P_y}$
- **B (True):** The marginal rate of substitution (slope of indifference curve) equals the price ratio: $MRS_{xy} = \frac{P_x}{P_y}$.
- **C (False):** The consumer reaches the highest attainable indifference curve, not necessarily the absolute highest curve on the entire map (budget limits prevent reaching the absolute highest).
- **D (True):** At optimum, the indifference curve is tangent to the budget line, showing equal slopes.
- **E (False):** Points on the budget line are not all equally satisfying—only points on the same indifference curve give equal utility; different points on the budget line can yield different satisfaction levels.

Thus: A, B & D.

28. Parallel, straight wealth expansion paths require specific preference conditions:

- **A (True):** Preferences must admit an indirect utility function of Gorman form, enabling linear Engel curves and identical marginal propensities to consume.

- **D (True):** Identical homothetic preferences across consumers ensure proportional changes in consumption as wealth changes.
- **E (True):** Alternatively, quasilinear preferences in the same good also yield iinear, parallel wealth expansion paths.
- **B (False):** Heterogeneous preferences break parallelism.
- **C (False):** Equal wealth distribution is unrelated to the shape of expansion paths.

Therefore, the correct conditions: A, D & E.

29. Step 1: Identify the events and their years in India's derivatives market

D. **Introduction of Futures trading based on the Index – June 2000:** Nifty futures were the first derivatives product introduced on Indian exchanges.

E. **Commencement of trading in Index Options – June 2001:** Index options on benchmarks like Nifty followed after the success of index futures.

A. **Commencement of trading in Options on Individual Securities – July 2001:** Options on single stocks began soon after index options.

C. **Commencement of trading in Stock Futures – November 2001:** Single-stock futures started later in the same year.

B. **Introduction of Interest Rate Futures – 2003:** Futures on government securities and interest rates were introduced after equity derivatives matured.

Step 2: Arrange from oldest to latest

Putting these in chronological order:

1. D – Index Futures (June 2000)
2. E – Index Options (June 2001)
3. A – Stock Options on Individual Securities (July 2001)
4. C – Stock Futures (Nov 2001)
5. B – Interest Rate Futures (2003)

Step 3: Final sequence

The ascending order is D, E, A, C, B, which matches option 2.

30. Externalities occur when costs or benefits affect third parties not involved in a transaction.

- **A (True):** Not all costs and benefits are internalized by buyers and sellers—hallmark of externalities.
- **B (True):** Externalities cause under-production (positive externalities) or over-production (negative externalities) relative to the socially optimal level.
- **C (False):** Market-based decisions do not yield efficiency when externalities exist—markets fail to allocate resources optimally.
- **D (True):** For negative externalities, marginal social cost exceeds marginal private cost—e.g., pollution.
- **E (True):** Coase theorem suggests that with well-defined property rights and low transaction costs, bargaining can internalize externalities and restore efficiency.

Correct set: A, B, D & E.

31. NONE: Correct mapping is A-III, B-(no match), C-I, D-(no match)

Why "NONE": the provided options contain internal inconsistencies.

For a chi-square distribution with n degrees of freedom (χ_n^2) the standard results are:

- **Kurtosis (β_2):** $\beta_2 = 3 + \frac{12}{n}$ → A → III (this one is correct among the lists).
- **Skewness:** $\gamma_1 = \sqrt{\frac{8}{n}}$. None of the given right-hand expressions equals $\sqrt{8/n}$. The only "square-root" expression offered is IV: $\sqrt{2/n}$, which is not the skewness; it is the coefficient of variation (since $\sigma/\mu = \sqrt{2n}/n = \sqrt{2/n}$). So, B has no correct match in the list.
- **Mode (for $n \geq 2$):** $n - 2$ → C → I (this one is correct).
- **Third central moment (μ_3):** $\mu_3 = 8n$. The list gives II: $48n + 12n^2$, which equals $12n(n + 4)$ and is actually the fourth central moment μ_4 for χ_n^2, not μ_3. So, (D) also has no correct match.

Because B and D cannot be matched correctly with any of the listed expressions, none of the four answer options gives a fully correct mapping. The only correct pairings from the provided items are A-III and C-I; the rest are mismatched. Hence, Answer: NONE.

32. National Income will decrease by ₹ 400

Given: MPC $=0.8$, tax increase $\Delta T = +100$.

- **Spending multiplier:** $\frac{1}{1-MPC} = \frac{1}{0.2} = 5$
- **Tax multiplier (lump-sum):**

$-\frac{MPC}{1-MPC} = \frac{0.8}{0.2} = -4.$

- **Impact on income:** $\Delta Y = (-4) \times (+100) = -400.$

So, national income falls by ₹ 400.

33. An increase in the relative price of a commodity raises the earnings of the factor used intensively in the production of that commodity

This is the core statement of the Stolper-Samuelson theorem within the 2×2 Heckscher-Ohlin framework: if the relative price of one good rises, the real return to the factor used intensively in that good increases, while the other factor's real return falls. Option 1 precisely captures this effect.

34. Policy Ineffectiveness Proposition (Sargent-Wallace) — key assumptions:

- Rational expectations (A) and full information/market clearing (C) imply no systematic money illusion.
- Natural-rate property (E): output/employment gravitate to their natural levels; only unanticipated nominal shocks can move real activity.

Not assumed (i.e., incorrect as assumptions):

- B. "Policy changes are not anticipated." PIP's point is that anticipated/systematic policy is neutral for real variables—so agents do anticipate it.
- D. "Nominal variables influence economic decision." Under the PIP's assumptions, anticipated nominal policy doesn't systematically alter real choices.

Thus, the statements not part of the assumptions are B and D.

35. In the RBI's current operating framework:

- The repo rate is the policy rate signalling stance.
- The liquidity corridor is bounded by SDF (floor) and MSF (ceiling).
- The operating target the RBI actually steers in the money market is the Weighted Average Call Money Rate (WACMR), keeping it aligned with the policy stance within the corridor.

36. Matching options:

A. **Specific-factors model → IV. Paul Samuelson & Ronald Jones:** The modern Ricardo–Viner (specific-factors) framework is associated with Jones/Samuelson: some factors (e.g., capital) are sector-specific in the short run, while labor is mobile. It's a workhorse for distributional effects of trade in the short run.

B. **Immiserizing growth → III. Jagdish Bhagwati:** Bhagwati showed that for a large country, export-biased growth can worsen its terms of trade so much that real income falls—growth that immiserizes.

C. **Mercantilism → II. Thomas Mun:** Mun articulated classic mercantilist ideas: national wealth via trade surpluses, bullion inflows, and state guidance of commerce.

D. **Secular deterioration of terms of trade → I. Prebisch–Singer hypothesis:** Long-run tendency for primary commodity exporters' terms of trade to worsen relative to manufactures.

Hence, correct matching is A-IV, B-III, C-II, D-I.

37. Oldest → latest appointment:

D. **K. Brahmananda Reddy:** 6th Finance Commission (early 1970s)

C. **N.K.P. Salve:** 9th Finance Commission (late 1980s)

E. **K.C. Pant:** 10th Finance Commission (early 1990s)

A. **A.M. Khusro:** 11th Finance Commission (late 1990s)

B. **C. Rangarajan:** 12th Finance Commission (early 2000s)

Thus the chronological sequence is D, C, E, A, B.

38. Descending share of total FDI, H1 FY25:

D. **Computer Software & Hardware:** typically the largest single sectoral recipient in recent half-year tallies due to ongoing digitalization, data centers, and electronics.

E. **Non-conventional Energy:** strong pipelines in solar/wind/green hydrogen push this sector high.

C. **Cement & Gypsum Products:** benefits from infra and real-estate upcycles; ahead of the next two in H1 FY25.

A. **Automobile Industry:** substantial but below the above sectors in the referenced half-year.

B. **Hospital & Diagnostic Centres:** growing, yet smaller share compared to the others listed.

Hence, the order is D > E > C > A > B.

39. Let g_m = manufacturing output growth, g_{GDP} = GDP growth, P_m = manufacturing productivity, P_{nm} = productivity outside manufacturing.

A. **Kaldor's first law → III:** $g_{GDP} = f(g_m)$, $f' > 0$: GDP growth rises with manufacturing growth.

B. **Kaldor's second law (Verdoorn) → I:** $P_m = f(g_m)$, $f' > 0$: faster manufacturing growth raises manufacturing productivity (dynamic increasing returns).

C. **Kaldor's third law → IV:** $P_{nm} = f(g_m)$, $f' > 0$: manufacturing growth lifts productivity in the rest of the economy (reallocation/ externalities).

D. **Okun's law → II:** $y' = -\varepsilon(u - u^*)$: output growth relates negatively to the unemployment gap.

Hence, correct matching is A-III, B-I, C-IV, D-II

40. Poverty-weighted indices of growth are specially designed to evaluate whether economic growth is benefiting all segments of society, particularly the poorest sections. Traditional growth measures such as GDP per capita growth are income-weighted—this means that higher-income individuals, whose incomes already form a large share of the total, exert more influence on the overall growth rate than the incomes of poorer individuals. As a result, improvements in the well-being of the rich can overshadow stagnation or decline in the incomes of the poor.

A poverty-weighted index corrects this bias by rebalancing the weights assigned to different income groups. While its ultimate purpose is to assign greater emphasis to the poor, among the provided choices, giving "at least equal weight to all income groups" represents a shift away from the standard bias toward the wealthy and toward a more equitable evaluation of growth performance. This option captures the essential idea of reducing the disproportionate influence of rich households and ensuring that improvements in the incomes of lower-income groups are not undervalued.

The other options are unsuitable:

- "To achieve high growth rate" does not address distribution or poverty focus.
- "To facilitate foreign trade on equal basis" is unrelated to measuring pro-poor growth.
- "To assign more weight to the richest population and no weight to lower-income group" is contrary to the intent of poverty-weighted indices.

Thus, among the given options, option 1 best represents the purpose of constructing poverty-weighted indices of growth.

41. Revised MSME classification effective 01 April 2025 (Union Budget 2025–26):

A. **Micro enterprise investment ≤ ₹ 2.5 crore — Correct.** The investment ceiling for micro enterprises has been revised upward from earlier limits to ₹ 2.5 crore.

D. **Micro enterprise turnover ≤ ₹ 10 crore — Correct.** The turnover criterion for micro enterprises remains ₹ 10 crore.

E. **Small enterprise turnover ≤ ₹ 100 crore—Correct.** The upper turnover limit for small enterprises has been revised to ₹ 100 crore.

B. **Medium enterprise turnover ≤ ₹ 50 crore — Incorrect:** under the revision, medium enterprises now have turnover up to ₹ 250 crore.

C. **Small enterprise investment ≤ ₹ 10 crore — Incorrect:** the small enterprise investment ceiling is ₹ 25 crore, not ₹ 10 crore.

Hence, A, D & E only.

42. The sequence of constitution of important tax reform committees in India, arranged from the oldest to the latest, is as follows:

- **Raja Chelliah Tax Reform Committee (1991):** Formed in 1991 as part of India's post-liberalization reforms, this committee was tasked with recommending a comprehensive overhaul of the tax system. Its landmark recommendations led to lower tax rates, broadening of the tax base, and rationalization of direct and indirect taxes. It played a crucial role in modernizing India's fiscal framework.
- **K.L. Rekhi Committee on Indirect Tax (1992):** Constituted in 1992 to reform customs and central excise laws, this committee streamlined the structure of indirect taxation and recommended simplifications that paved the way for later indirect tax reforms, including the eventual introduction of VAT and GST.
- **Vijay Kelkar Committee on Tax Reforms (2002):** In 2002, two task forces under Dr. Vijay Kelkar—one on direct taxes and another on indirect taxes—were established to make India's tax system more growth-oriented and efficient. The committee emphasized fiscal responsibility, moderate tax rates, and simplification of procedures, forming the basis for the Fiscal Responsibility and Budget Management (FRBM) Act and later reforms.
- **T.R. Rastogi Committee on Service Tax Reforms (2006):** This committee was constituted in 2006 to review the service tax framework and recommend measures to strengthen administration and compliance. Its work supported the gradual expansion and integration of service tax, which later contributed to GST implementation.
- **Parthasarathi Shome Committee on Direct Tax (2012):** Set up in 2012 to review and clarify the General Anti-Avoidance Rules (GAAR) and other aspects of direct taxation, this committee provided recommendations to enhance tax certainty and improve investor confidence while safeguarding revenue interests.

Correct Chronological Order: A, E, C, B, D.

43. Matching options:

A. **Income elasticity greater than one → III. Luxurious goods:** Goods whose demand rises more than proportionally with income are luxuries.

B. **Positive cross-price elasticity → I. Substitute goods:** When the price of one good rises and demand for another rises, the goods are substitutes.

C. **Downward sloping PCC → IV. Relatively elastic demand effect:** A downward sloping Price Consumption Curve (PCC) suggests relatively elastic demand—as price falls, consumption increases significantly.

D. **Negative income effect → II. Inferior goods:** Inferior goods show negative income elasticity—demand falls as income rises.

44. When the income effect works opposite to the substitution effect, yet the substitution effect dominates, the overall demand curve still slopes downward. This is the case for inferior goods that are not Giffen goods.

- For Giffen goods, the negative income effect is so strong that it outweighs the substitution effect, making demand slope upward.
- Here, substitution dominates ⇒ the good is inferior but not Giffen.

45. In the Union Budget 2025-26, the major components of expenditure as a share of total Union Government expenditure are:

C. **Pensions – 4%:** Pensions constitute a relatively small but essential component of the budget. This includes retirement benefits for civil and defense personnel, ensuring post-service financial security.

D. **Major Subsidies – 6%:** Major subsidies cover food, fertilizer, and petroleum subsidies. These are critical for supporting food security, agricultural productivity, and stabilizing fuel prices but are moderated to maintain fiscal discipline.

A. **Finance Commission and Other Transfers – 8%:** This category reflects statutory transfers to states as recommended by the Finance Commission, along with other transfers for centrally sponsored programs. It is a significant mechanism for fiscal federalism and empowering states financially.

E. **Central Sector Schemes (excluding capital outlay on defense and subsidies) – 16%:** These schemes represent a broad range of government programs executed by the Union Government directly. They include infrastructure, digitalization, and social sector projects where the Union Government is the primary spending authority.

B. **Interest Payments – 25%:** Interest payments are the single largest expenditure item, reflecting the cost of servicing the government's accumulated debt. It demonstrates the importance of prudent borrowing and fiscal management.

Arranging in ascending order of their shares:

1. C. Pensions – 4%
2. D. Major Subsidies – 6%
3. A. Finance Commission and Other Transfers – 8%
4. E. Central Sector Schemes – 16%
5. B. Interest Payments – 25%

Therefore, the correct ascending order is C, D, A, E, B, which corresponds to option 2.

46. Goal: Minimize $U = 6x^2 + y^2$ subject to the linear constraint $4x - y = 1$. (With a quadratic objective and a single linear constraint, the unique constrained minimum gives the required value of U.)

Method (substitution):

From $4x - y = 1$, get $y = 4x - 1$.

$$U(x) = 6x^2 + (4x - 1)^2$$
$$= 6x^2 + 16x^2 - 8x + 1$$
$$= 22x^2 - 8x + 1$$

Minimize the quadratic:

For $U(x) = ax^2 + bx + c$

with $a = 22$, $b = -8$,

the minimizer is $x^* = -\frac{b}{2a} = \frac{8}{44} = \frac{2}{11}$.

Then $y^* = 4\cdot\frac{2}{11} - 1 = \frac{8}{11} - 1 = -\frac{3}{11}$.

Compute U at the optimum:

$$U^* = 6\left(\frac{2}{11}\right)^2 + \left(-\frac{3}{11}\right)^2$$

$$= 6\cdot\frac{4}{121} + \frac{9}{121}$$

$$= \frac{24}{121} + \frac{9}{121}$$

$$= \frac{33}{121}$$

$$= \frac{3}{11}$$

Therefore, $U = \frac{3}{11}$.

47. In the Union Budget 2025–26, the estimated shares of these major revenue items as a percentage of total receipts are as follows:

A. **Income Tax → III (22%):** Income tax accounts for 22% of total receipts, making it the largest contributor among the four categories. This reflects expanding compliance, digitization of tax administration, and a robust growth in personal income collections.

B. **Customs → I (4%):** Customs duties contribute 4%, the smallest share of the listed items. This reduced percentage is consistent with India's policy of trade liberalization and lower tariff barriers to support global trade integration.

C. **Corporation Tax → IV (17%):** Corporation tax provides 17% of total receipts, demonstrating its continued significance as a primary source of direct tax revenue, even after rate reductions aimed at stimulating investment and business competitiveness.

D. **Union Excise Duty → II (5%):** Union excise duties contribute 5%. After the introduction of GST, excise duties now mainly apply to petroleum, tobacco, and a few other goods outside GST coverage, making it a smaller but stable revenue source.

Correct Match: A-III, B-I, C-IV, D-II.

48. Neoclassical (Solow) growth model implications of a higher population growth rate *n*:

A. **Reduction in steady-state capital per head — True:** Higher *n* raises break-even investment $(n + g + \delta)k$, lowering steady-state k^* and thus capital per worker.

B. **Increase in per capita output — False:** With k^* lower, per capita output $y^* = f(k^*)$falls, not rises (holding technology constant).

C. **Increase in steady-state growth rate of aggregate output — True:** Aggregate Y grows in steady state at $n + g$. If *n* rises, the steady-state growth rate of aggregate output increases.

D. **Decrease in capital-output ratio — Ambiguous in generic statements:** While in Cobb-Douglas one can derive a lower K/Y level with higher *n*, many exam treatments focus on the robust, widely taught effects (A fall in *k* and rise in aggregate growth), avoiding statements on K/Y unless the production form is specified.

E. **Inward shift in the production possibility curve — False:** A change in population growth doesn't shift the economy's PPC; it changes the long-run composition/levels along the balanced path.

Thus the safest, standard set is: A & C only.

49. Match concepts to proponents/approaches:

A. **Income-induced adjustment process of BoP → II. J.M. Keynes:** The Keynesian income mechanism adjusts external imbalances via changes in income and imports.

B. **Absorption approach to BoP → III. Sidney S. Alexander:** BoP improves if output exceeds domestic absorption; Alexander formalized this view.

C. **Impossible trinity → IV. Mundell-Fleming:** One cannot simultaneously have fixed exchange rate, free capital mobility, and independent monetary policy.

D. **Factor price equalization theorem → I. Paul Samuelson:** In the Heckscher-Ohlin framework, free trade can equalize factor prices across countries under strong assumptions.

Therefore: A-II, B-III, C-IV, D-I.

50. Indirect Least Squares (ILS):

- **What it does:** Estimate the reduced-form parameters first (by OLS), then algebraically invert them to obtain the structural coefficients when the structural equation is exactly identified (just-identified).
- **Therefore:** ILS is used to estimate coefficients of the structural equation (not the reduced form itself, which is obtained directly by OLS; not over- or under-identified equations, for which other methods are required).

51. New Classical approach:

A. **The main protagonist was R. E. Lucas Jr. — True.** The New Classical school is most closely identified with Robert E. Lucas Jr., whose rational expectations revolution reshaped macroeconomics and policy analysis.

B. **It is based on adaptive expectation — False.** New Classical models are built on rational expectations, not adaptive expectations. Agents are assumed to use all available information and the model-consistent structure when forming expectations.

C. **It was developed during 1950s — False.** The approach emerged prominently in the 1970s, following critiques of traditional Keynesian macroeconometric models.

D. **Complete wage and price flexibility — True.** Baseline New Classical models assume market clearing with flexible prices and wages, so systematic policy does not create persistent real effects.

E. **Difference between actual and expected price is a random error — True.** In the Lucas "surprise-supply" logic, only unanticipated price (or monetary) surprises move real activity; forecast errors are random (zero-mean) rather than systematic.

52. The Keynesian investment multiplier k satisfies $k = \frac{1}{1-c}$, where c is the marginal propensity to consume (MPC).

Given $k = 4$, we have $1 - c = \frac{1}{4}$

$\Rightarrow c = 0.75$.

Hence the marginal propensity to save (MPS) is $1 - c = 0.25$.

A saving function has slope equal to MPS. Among the options, only $S = \alpha + 0.25Y_D$ matches. The intercept −12 sets the break-even income; many intercepts could be consistent with $k = 4$. The key is the slope 0.25, which yields option 3.

53. Effective Rate of Protection:

- g = effective protection rate for producers of the final good
- t = nominal tariff rate on the final good
- t_i = nominal tariff rate on the imported input
- a_i = share of the imported input in the free-trade price of the final good

The effective rate of protection compares how tariffs on outputs and inputs change the value added in the protected equilibrium versus free trade. The standard formula is

$$g = \frac{t - a_i t_i}{1 - a_i}$$

54. Let X be a Poisson random variable with mean λ.

The probability mass function (pmf) is:

$$P(X = x) = \frac{e^{-\lambda}\lambda^x}{x!}, x = 0, 1, 2, ...$$

We need $P(X = x + 1)$ in terms of $P(X = x)$.

$$P(X = x+1) = \frac{e^{-\lambda}\lambda^{x+1}}{x+1!}$$

Rewrite $(x + 1)! = (x + 1)(x!)$:

$$P(X = x+1) = \frac{\lambda^{x+1}e^{-\lambda}}{(x+1)(x!)}$$

Factor out λ and express in terms of $P(X = x)$:

$$P(X = x+1) = \frac{\lambda}{x+1} \cdot \frac{\lambda^x e^{-\lambda}}{x!}$$

But $\frac{\lambda^x e^{-\lambda}}{x!} = P(X = x)$

Therefore,

$$P(X = x+1) = \frac{\lambda}{x+1} P(X = x)$$

Correct Option: 1. $\frac{\lambda}{x+1} P(x)$

55. Distributions & formulas:

A. **Mean of a Hypergeometric distribution → III.** $\frac{nm}{N}$

Drawing n items from a population of size N with m "successes," the expected number of successes is $E[X] = n \cdot \frac{m}{n}$

B. **MGF of Negative Binomial distribution → II.** $(Q - Pe^t)^{-r}$

Though parameterizations vary, the listed form corresponds to a common representation of the moment generating function of a negative binomial variate (with suitable P, Q, r notation and domain restrictions).

C. **Coefficient of Kurtosis of a Binomial distribution → IV.** $\frac{1-6pq}{npq}$

For binomial Bin (n, p) excess kurtosis is $\frac{1-6pq}{npq}$ (hence the coefficient of kurtosis above 3 is that expression).

D. **Variance of a Geometric distribution → I.** $\frac{q}{p^2}$

For the geometric (counting trials until first success, with success probability p),

$$\text{Var}(X) = \frac{q}{p^2} \text{ where } q = 1 - p.$$

Therefore, the correct matching is A-III, B-II, C-IV, D-I.

56. $k(t) = 9t^{4/3} + 25$

Derivation:

- Investment is the flow that adds to capital, so $\dot{k}(t) = I(t)$.
- Given $I(t) = 12t^{1/3}$:

$$\frac{dk}{dt} = 12t^{1/3}$$

$$\Rightarrow k(t) = \int 12t^{1/3}dt + C = 12 \cdot \frac{t^{4/3}}{4/3} + C = 9t^{4/3} + C$$

- Use the initial stock $k(0) = 25$: $25 = 9.0^{4/3} + C$

$\Rightarrow C = 25$

Thus, $k(t) = 9t^{4/3} + 25$.

57. Classical economists generally opposed public debt, emphasizing:

- Double burden on taxpayers (interest + amortization) → True.
- Barren production/consumption; burden shifted to future generations → True (crowding out private capital and future tax burdens).
- Destruction of productive capital (resources diverted from private investment) → True in their framework.

However, the idea that debt is a tool for compensatory demand management is Keynesian, not classical. Hence statement 2 is the one not true under classical views.

58. Setup: For the three posts, the candidate's selection probabilities (assuming equal chances and independence across posts) are

$$p_1 = \frac{1}{3},\ p_2 = \frac{1}{4},\ p_3 = \frac{1}{2}$$

Probability of not being selected in any post:

$$(1-p_1)(1-p_2)(1-p_3) = \left(\frac{2}{3}\right)\left(\frac{3}{4}\right)\left(\frac{1}{2}\right) = \left(\frac{1}{4}\right)$$

Therefore, probability of being selected in at least one post:

$$1 - \frac{1}{4} = \frac{3}{4}.$$

59. A positive output gap means actual output exceeds potential output. This typically occurs when the economy operates above sustainable capacity—e.g., overtime, intense utilization, and labor markets beyond full employment (overemployment).

- Population growth and technological progress mainly shift potential output, not create a short-run gap of actual over potential.
- Underutilization of resources produces a negative output gap.

60. Euler's Theorem:

If $Q = f(K, L)$ is homogeneous of degree 1 (constant returns to scale), Euler's theorem states:

$$Q = Kf_K + Lf_L = K\frac{\partial Q}{\partial K} + L\frac{\partial Q}{\partial L}$$

Thus, option 2 is the correct condition.

61. Classical loanable-funds view of deficit spending:

A. **Shift in demand for loanable funds to the right — True.** A higher deficit (G–T↑) means the government borrows more, increasing demand for loanable funds.

B. **Decline in interest rate — False.** Extra borrowing raises the real interest rate to clear the funds market.

C. **Increase in investment — False.** With higher real interest rates, private investment is crowded out (falls).

D. **Increase in saving equal to decline in consumption — True.** With income fixed at full employment, a rise in r reduces consumption C, raising private saving S by the same amount (S = Y – T – C).

E. **Decrease in investment and consumption that balances the increase in government spending — True.** Goods-market identity Y = C + I + G with fixed Y implies $\Delta G > 0$ must be offset by $\Delta C + \Delta I < 0$ of equal magnitude.

62. Payoff matrix (P1,P2):

- T : (1,5) vs L, (0,3) vs R
- M : (2,6) vs L, (1,4) vs R
- B : (3,7) vs L, (2,2) vs R

Dominance checks for Player 1:

- Column L: $1 < 2 < 3 \Rightarrow$ B strictly dominates M and T.

- Column R: 0 < 1 < 2 ⇒ same ordering.

  Thus A (two strictly dominated strategies) is True: T and M are strictly dominated by B.

  Also E is True: M strictly dominates T(2 > 1 and 1 > 0).

  Because dominated strategies get zero probability in equilibrium, D is True: M will never be used in any Nash equilibrium.

Player 2: Compare L vs R: payoffs are 5, 6, 7(L) vs 3, 4, 2 (R) for T, M, B respectively, so L strictly dominates R. Hence B (no weak dominance) is False.

C is False: T does not weakly dominate B; B is everywhere better for Player 1.

63. Descending share in Union Budget 2025-26:

Reasoning: Among the listed heads, Defense (C) is the largest. Next comes Rural Development (E) driven by major rural programs. Agriculture & Allied (A) follows, then Education (B), and finally Commerce & Industry (D) among these five.

Order (largest → smallest): Defense > Rural Development > Agriculture & Allied > Education > Commerce & Industry, i.e., C, E, A, B, D.

64. Profit maximization:

$\pi(X) = R - C = 3X - (100 + 0.015X^2)$

First-order condition:

$$\frac{d\pi}{dX} = 3 - 0.03X = 0$$

$$\Rightarrow X^* = \frac{3}{0.03} = 100$$

Second-order condition: $\frac{d^2\pi}{dX^2} = -0.03 < 0$

⇒ maximum.

Therefore, the profit-maximizing output level is X = 100.

65. The line of regression of y on x is expressed by:

$$y - \bar{y} = b_{yx}(x - \bar{x})$$

where:

- $\bar{x}$ = 32 is the mean of x,
- $\bar{y}$ = 38 is the mean of y,
- b_{yx} = −0.6643 is the regression coefficient of y on x.

Step 1: Substitute the known values

$$y - 38 = -0.6643(x - 32)$$

Step 2: Distribute the slope on the right-hand side

$$y - 38 = -0.6643x + (-0.6643)(-32),$$
$$= 0.6643x + 21.2576$$

Step 3: Solve for y

Add 38 to both sides to isolate y:

$$y = -0.6643x + 21.2576 + 38$$

Simplify:

$$y = -0.6643x + 59.2576$$

Final Regression Equation

The equation of the regression line of y on x is:

$$y = -0.6643x + 59.2576$$

This matches option 4, confirming it as the correct choice.

66. In the IS–LM framework, the slope of the IS curve depends on two factors:

1. Interest sensitivity of investment (how strongly investment responds to changes in interest rates).
2. Marginal propensity to spend (or the marginal propensity to consume, MPC), which determines the spending multiplier $k = \frac{1}{1-c}$.

When the marginal propensity to spend increases, the multiplier k becomes larger. A larger multiplier means that any given fall in interest rate produces a much larger increase in income, because each round of spending creates stronger secondary spending effects. This increased responsiveness of income to interest changes flattens the IS curve—small interest rate changes now generate large income changes to maintain goods-market equilibrium.

The aggregate demand (AD) curve in the price-output space is derived from the IS–LM model. A flatter IS curve amplifies the effect of price-level changes (via LM shifts) on output: even a small movement in prices, which shifts LM, results in a relatively larger movement along IS–LM equilibrium points, producing a steeper AD curve in price-output space. A steeper AD curve implies that for a given price change, income changes more sharply, consistent with stronger expenditure feedback effects in the goods market.

Thus, under these conditions:

- IS curve becomes flatter due to a larger spending multiplier.
- Aggregate demand curve becomes steeper because output responds more strongly to price changes transmitted through the LM curve.

Therefore, the correct choice is: A steeper aggregate demand curve and consequently a flatter IS curve.

67. In Raymond Vernon's Product Cycle Model of International Trade, a product passes through distinct phases that influence where it is produced and how trade flows evolve:

- **Stage I – New Product (Introduction):** The product is newly developed in an innovating, high-income country. Production and consumption occur primarily in the innovator's domestic market. Because the technology is untested and demand is uncertain, there is little or no international trade at this stage.
- **Stage II – Growth (Maturing Product):** Demand grows in the innovating country and begins spreading to other developed economies. The innovating country starts exporting the product, but maintains a technological and cost advantage. Production techniques are still evolving, and competitors have not yet mastered the process.
- **Stage III – Maturity (Standardised Product):** The product design and production technology become standardized and well known. Imitating countries begin producing for their domestic markets, reducing their need to import from the innovating country. The innovator's exports may plateau or decline as competition intensifies.
- **Stage IV – Decline (Standardization/Cost Competition):** Cost efficiency becomes the dominant factor. Imitating countries, especially those with lower labor and production costs, now achieve a clear cost advantage. They begin exporting the standardized product to third markets (markets other than the innovator's or their own), underselling the innovating country. This is the first stage where the imitators outcompete the innovator internationally on price.
- **Stage V – Late Decline:** The imitating country's cost advantage becomes so strong that it undersells the innovating country even in the innovator's domestic market. The innovating country may cease production and become a net importer of the product.

Therefore, Stage IV is where the imitating country first starts underselling the innovating country in third markets, making option 3 the correct choice.

68. 15th Finance Commission – horizontal devolution weights:

A. **Income distance → 45% (III):** Larger weight to states farther below the highest per-capita income.

B. **Population (2011) → 15% (I):** Reflects relative size using the latest census base.

C. **Demographic performance → 12.5% (II):** Rewards improvements in outcomes (e.g., fertility reduction, human development).

D. **Forest & Ecology → 10% (IV):** Recognizes ecological services and conservation.

Hence, A-III, B-I, C-II, D-IV.

69. Classical money neutrality expressed via AD–AS: An increase in the money supply raises real balances at a given price level, shifting the LM curve right and, in the price–output space, shifting the aggregate demand (AD) curve to the right. With flexible prices/wages and a vertical long-run AS at full-employment output, the result is higher prices with no change in real output. The curve movement that occurs is the rightward shift of AD.

70. Competitive factor and output markets: A profit-maximizing firm chooses each input j so that

Factor price$_j$ = P.MP$_j$

= Value of Marginal Product (VMP)j.

Thus, in competitive equilibrium, each factor is paid its VMP—not an equal share, not a politically chosen amount, and not total revenue.

71. Arranging the given environmental conventions and summits from oldest to latest using Stockholm Convention as 2001:

E. **Rio Summit (1992):** Known as the Earth Summit, it laid the foundation for Agenda 21, the UNFCCC, and the Convention on Biological Diversity.

A. **Kyoto Protocol (1997):** First binding treaty under the UNFCCC that set greenhouse gas reduction targets for developed countries.

C. **Stockholm Convention (2001):** Global treaty adopted in 2001 to control and phase out persistent organic pollutants (POPs).

D. **UN-REDD Programme (2008):** UN collaborative initiative launched in 2008 to assist developing nations in reducing emissions from deforestation and forest degradation.

B. **Minamata Convention (2013):** Adopted in 2013 to protect human health and the environment from mercury emissions and releases.

Correct chronological sequence: E, A, C, D, B.

72. Publication years:

A. **Arthur Lewis, *The Theory of Economic Growth* (1955)** – foundational development theory.

B. **Robert Solow, *A Contribution to the Theory of Economic Growth* (1956)** – neoclassical growth model.

E. **Albert Hirschman, *The Strategy of Economic Development* (1958)** – unbalanced growth strategy.

C. **Walt Rostow, *The Stages of Economic Growth* (1960)** – stage-wise growth thesis.

D. **Gunnar Myrdal, *Asian Drama* (1968)**–political economy of South Asia.

Thus, oldest → latest: A, B, E, C, D.

73. India's monetary policy regimes:

A. **Fiscal dominance → II (1951–1985):** High fiscal needs and automatic monetization shaped monetary conditions.

B. **Multiple-indicator approach → III (1998–2016):** Policy guided by a dashboard (rates, exchange rate, credit, output, etc.), not just money aggregates.

C. **Monetary targeting with feedbacks → IV (1985–1998):** Post-Chakravarty Committee; money supply targets with periodic feedback.

D. **Flexible inflation targeting → I (2016 onwards):** Formal target band with an MPC, price stability as primary objective.

74. Disinflation's output cost (the sacrifice ratio) rises when nominal wages/prices adjust slowly. Sticky wage-price dynamics require a larger fall in real activity to bring inflation down. In contrast, well-anchored or rational expectations typically lower the cost; policy "gradualism" does not inherently raise it and can sometimes spread (not increase) the cumulative loss.

75. The current account balance as a percentage of GDP measures whether a country is a net lender or borrower in international markets. Based on the Economic Survey 2024–25 for Q2 FY25, the countries listed can be arranged in descending order as follows:

C. **China – Highest surplus:** China continues to maintain the largest current account surplus relative to GDP, supported by its strong manufacturing export base, competitive global trade position, and controlled import growth. This makes China the top in the sequence.

B. **Russia – Second highest surplus:** Russia records a significant current account surplus driven largely by energy and commodity exports. Even after geopolitical challenges and sanctions, high energy prices have maintained its positive balance.

A. **India – Moderate position:** India generally runs a small deficit or a very modest surplus, placing it well below China and Russia but above South Africa and the UK in Q2 FY25.

E. **South Africa – Lower balance:** South Africa typically runs a small deficit or near-balance position, ranking below India.

D. **United Kingdom – Largest deficit:** The UK consistently shows one of the largest current account deficits among major economies, reflecting its import dependence and significant income outflows.

Descending order (highest → lowest):

China (C) → Russia (B) → India (A) → South Africa (E) → United Kingdom (D)

76. To arrange the listed economic crises chronologically from oldest to latest, consider their historical occurrence years:

A. **OPEC Oil Crisis (1973–1974):** Triggered when the Organization of the Petroleum Exporting Countries imposed an oil embargo, leading to a quadrupling of oil prices, stagflation in developed economies, and a global economic slowdown.

B. **International Debt Crisis (1980s):** Began in 1982 when Mexico announced it could no longer service its external debt. Many Latin American and developing nations followed, creating a global debt crisis.

C. **East Asian Financial Crisis (1997–1998):** Started in Thailand with the collapse of the baht and quickly spread to other East Asian economies like Indonesia, South Korea, and Malaysia, causing massive currency depreciations and recessions.

D. **Argentinian Economic Crisis (1999–2002):** Peaked in 2001–2002, marked by a sovereign default on about $100 billion in debt, currency devaluation, banking restrictions, and severe social unrest.

E. **Eurozone Crisis (2009–2014):** Sparked by Greece's debt problems and spread across several Eurozone economies, leading to bailouts and fiscal austerity programs.

Chronological order (oldest → latest):

OPEC Oil Crisis → International Debt Crisis → East Asian Financial Crisis → Argentinian Economic Crisis → Eurozone Crisis

77. For a Normal distribution, let the mean be μ and the standard deviation be σ. Consider each statement:

A. μ_3 for Normal distribution is 0 – Correct.

μ_3 is the third central moment (measure of skewness). A normal distribution is perfectly symmetric about its mean, so its skewness is zero.

B. β_2 for Normal distribution is 0 – Incorrect.

β_2 represents kurtosis and for a normal distribution $\beta_2 = 3$, not 0.

C. Mean deviation (about mean) for Normal distribution is $\frac{4}{5}\sigma$ – Correct.

The known result for the mean absolute deviation for a normal distribution is approximately 0.7979σ, which is close to $\frac{4}{5}\sigma$.

D. μ_4 for Normal distribution is $2\sigma^4$ – Incorrect.

The fourth central moment of a normal distribution is $\mu_4 = 3\sigma^4$, not $2\sigma^4$distribution

E. Characteristic function for Normal is $e^{i\mu t - \frac{t^2\sigma^2}{2}}$ – Correct.

This is the standard characteristic function of a normal variable.

Correct combination: A, C & E Only.

78. Ascending order by % of GDP, 2023–24:

D. **Current Account Deficit (CAD):** Smallest among the list (around three-quarters of a percent of GDP).

B. **Effective Revenue Deficit (ERD):** Revenue deficit net of grants for capital creation; also low (roughly three-quarters of a percent of GDP).

C. **Primary Deficit (PD):** Fiscal deficit minus interest payments; moderate (~1½–2% of GDP).

E. **Revenue Deficit (RD):** Higher (around ~3% of GDP), as revenue expenditure exceeds revenue receipts.

A. **Fiscal Deficit (FD):** Largest (~5½–6% of GDP).

Thus, from smallest → largest: CAD (D) < ERD (B) < PD (C) < RD (E) < FD (A).

79. A Nash Equilibrium is a strategy profile where no player can unilaterally change their strategy to improve their payoff, assuming the other players keep their strategies fixed.

In the Matching Pennies Game, two players simultaneously choose Heads (H) or Tails (T):

- If both match (H–H or T–T), Player 1 wins.
- If they do not match (H–T or T–H), Player 2 wins.

Because each player's best response always alternates based on what the other chooses, there is no stable pair of pure strategies:

- If Player 1 picks Heads, Player 2's best response is Tails.
- If Player 2 switches to Tails, Player 1's best response becomes Tails as well, which then flips the advantage again.

  This cycle means no combination of pure choices is stable, so there is no pure-strategy Nash Equilibrium.

Why the other games are incorrect:

- **Battle of the Sexes (BoS):** Has two pure Nash Equilibria—both attend the same activity (Opera–Opera or Football–Football)—and one mixed equilibrium.
- **Stag Hunt Game:** Features two pure Nash Equilibria—both hunt the stag (efficient but risky) or both hunt the hare (safe but lower payoff)—plus a mixed equilibrium.
- **Prisoner's Dilemma:** Has a single pure Nash Equilibrium where both defect, even though mutual cooperation would yield a better collective outcome.

Pennies Game does not have a pure-strategy Nash Equilibrium among the listed games.

80. Matching options:

A. **Theory of population growth and resource limits → IV. Thomas Malthus:** Malthus advanced the classic argument that population tends to grow faster than the means of subsistence, creating pressure unless checked by preventive or positive constraints. This links population dynamics directly to resource limits.

B. **Demographic transition theory → III. Warren Thompson:** Thompson formulated the demographic transition framework: economies move from high birth & death rates to low birth & death rates as they develop, passing through distinct stages.

C. **Father of demography → II. John Graunt:** Graunt pioneered demographic analysis using the London Bills of Mortality, laying the foundations of statistical study of populations—hence widely regarded as the "father of demography."

D. **Coined the term "Third World" → I. Alfred Sauvy:** Sauvy introduced the term "Third World" to describe countries outside the Western and Soviet blocs, emphasizing their distinct socio-economic position.

Why none of the options are fully correct:

Each listed option contains at least one mispairing that contradicts the established attributions above. Therefore, no provided option matches all four correct pairings simultaneously.

81. Chronological order of major GATT/WTO trade rounds:

D. **Kennedy Round (1964–1967):** Held under GATT, it focused on tariff reductions and introduced anti-dumping measures. This is the oldest among the listed rounds.

E. **Tokyo Round (1973–1979):** Expanded negotiations beyond tariffs to non-tariff barriers, subsidies, and technical standards.

C. **Uruguay Round (1986–1994):** The most comprehensive round under GATT, it created the World Trade Organization (WTO) and expanded rules to services, intellectual property, and agriculture.

A. **Millennium Round (planned for 1999):** Proposed at the WTO Ministerial Conference in Seattle but failed to launch successfully due to protests and disagreements—still listed chronologically after Uruguay.

B. **Doha Round (2001–present):** Officially launched in Doha, Qatar, aiming at development-focused trade liberalization. It remains unresolved in many areas.

Correct sequence (oldest → latest): D, E, C, A, B.

82. The moment generating function (MGF) uniquely determines a probability distribution. Compare each given MGF with known standard forms:

A. $M(t) = \left(\frac{1}{2}+\frac{1}{2}e^t\right)^6$

This matches a Binomial distribution with $n = 6$ and $p = \frac{1}{2}$ (general form: $M(t) = (q + pe^t)^n$. The statement claims it is Poisson, which is incorrect.

B. $M(t) = \frac{(1+e^t)^5}{32}$

Rewrite as $M(t) = (0.5 + 0.5e^t)^5$ because $\frac{1}{32} = 0.5^5$. This is Binomial with $n = 5$, $p = 0.5$. The claim that it is binomial is correct.

C. $M(t) = e^{3(e^t-1)}$

This is the Poisson MGF $M(t) = e^{\lambda(et - 1)}$ with $\lambda = 3$. Correct.

D. $M(t) = e^{(e^t-1)/4}$

This is also Poisson: $M(t) = e^{\lambda(et - 1)}$ with $\lambda = \frac{1}{4}$. Correct.

E. $M(t) = 4(3e^{-t} - 1)^{-2}$

This does not match the standard MGF of a binomial distribution; the form does not correspond to $(q + pe^t)^n$. The claim is incorrect.

Therefore, the correct statements are B, C & D Only.

83. How to estimate: Use the regression of Sales (Y) on Advertisement (X) via the correlation formula.

- Means: $\bar{Y} = 40, \bar{X} = 6$
- SDs: $s_Y = 10$, $s_X = 1.5$
- Correlation: $r = 0.9$
- Slope of Y on X:

$$b_{Y|X} = r\frac{s_Y}{s_X} = 0.9 \times \frac{10}{1.5} = 6$$

- Regression line:

$$Y - \bar{Y} = b_{Y|X}(X - \bar{X}) \Rightarrow Y = 40 + 6(X - 6)$$

- For proposed ad spend X = 10:

$$Y = 40 + 6(10 - 6)$$
$$= 40 + 24 = 64.$$

84. Solow-neoclassical:

- A higher saving rate (s) raises investment, pushing the economy toward a higher steady-state capital per worker, so short-run growth rises during the transition. (Correct)
- Long-run growth rate of output (aggregate or per capita) is not determined by s; it is pinned by exogenous technology growth g (and population growth n for aggregate output). Hence statements 2, 3, 4 are false (steady-state k and levels of y per head rise with s, not fall; growth rates in the long run are unchanged).

85. Given demand:

$P = \sqrt{9-x}$ · At $x_0 = 5$,

market price $P_0 = \sqrt{9-5} = 2$

Consumer surplus:

$$CS = \int_0^5 (P(x) - P_0)dx$$
$$= \int_0^5 \left(\sqrt{9-x} - 2\right)dx$$

Compute:

$$\int \sqrt{9-x}\, dx = -\frac{2}{3}(9-x)^{3/2}$$

$$\Rightarrow \int_0^5 \sqrt{9-x}\, dx = \frac{2}{3}(27-8) = \frac{38}{3}$$

Subtract the rectangle under price 2:

$$\int_0^5 2\, dx = 10$$

$$CS = \frac{38}{3} - 10 = \frac{8}{3}.$$

86. The Harrod–Domar model describes economic growth dynamics using three key rates:

- **Actual growth rate (g):** The observed rate at which output increases.
- **Warranted growth rate (g_x or g_w):** The rate at which investors are satisfied with their investment, maintaining full capacity utilization—ensuring no unintended inventory buildup or shortages.
- **Natural growth rate (g_n):** The maximum growth achievable without causing inflationary pressures, determined by labor force growth and labor productivity improvements.

Assessment of the statements:

1. **Natural rate of growth is made up of growth of labor force and labor productivity — Correct.**

   This reflects Harrod's definition: g_n = labor force growth + productivity growth.

2. **If actual growth (g) exceeds warranted growth (g_w), divergence continues only until it hits g_n — Correct.**

   Beyond g_n, capacity constraints and labor shortages prevent further sustained acceleration.

3. **g can be greater than g_n in the long-run — Not correct.**

   In the long run, output cannot permanently exceed g_n. If g > g_n persists, labor and resource bottlenecks cause inflation or other adjustments pulling growth back toward g_n.

4. **Full employment of labor and capital requires g = g_w = g_n — Correct.**

   This is Harrod's "Golden Age" condition where all three rates are equal, ensuring full employment and steady growth without inflationary or deflationary pressure.

Thus, the incorrect statement is 3.

87. We need to evaluate:

$$I = \int_1^2 e^{-2x}\,dx$$

Step 1: Find the indefinite integral.

$$\int e^{-2x}\,dx = \frac{e^{-2x}}{-2} = -\frac{1}{2}e^{-2x} + C$$

Step 2: Apply the limits.

$$I = \left[-\frac{1}{2}e^{-2x}\right]_2^1 = -\frac{1}{2}(e^{-4} - e^{-2})$$

Step 3: Simplify the sign.

$$-\frac{1}{2}(e^{-4} - e^{-2}) = \frac{1}{2}(e^{-2} - e^{-4})$$

Step 4: Final result.

$$I = \frac{1}{2}(e^{-2} - e^{-4})$$

88. Checking options:

A. **The polluter pays the victim to continue polluting — Possible.**

   If the victim holds the property right to a clean environment, the polluter can purchase permission to emit by compensating the victim. With zero transaction costs and well-defined rights, such bargaining can be efficient.

B. **The victim pays the polluter to reduce pollution — Possible.**

   If the polluter holds the right to emit, the victim can pay for abatement. Coase's insight is that the allocation of rights affects the wealth distribution (who pays whom) but not the efficient level of pollution (given zero transaction costs and complete information).

C. **The government must set pollution taxes to ensure efficiency — Not implied.**

   Coase shows that with well-defined property rights and zero transaction costs, private bargaining alone can achieve efficiency; Pigouvian taxes are not necessary in that ideal setting.

D. **Market outcomes can achieve efficiency even with externalities — Correct (under Coasian conditions).**

   Externalities can be internalized through bargaining, yielding the efficient outcome.

E. **Equal bargaining power is required — Not required.**

Efficiency does not depend on equal bargaining power; it affects the distribution of surplus, not the efficient allocation.

Therefore, the correct set is A, B & D.

89. Granger and Newbold's rule-of-thumb for spurious regression (common with nonstationary time series) is:

- A very high R^2 coupled with a very low Durbin–Watson statistic d (indicating strong positive autocorrelation of residuals) is a red flag.
- The mnemonic often quoted is "$R^2 > d$": if the coefficient of determination exceeds the DW statistic, suspect spuriousness.

Hence, option 3 best captures the diagnostic.

90. Matching options:

A. $\int_0^{\infty} \frac{1}{1+x^2} dx \rightarrow$ III. $\pi/2$

$$\int \frac{1}{1+x^2} dx = \arctan x$$

$$\Rightarrow [\arctan x]_0^{\infty} = \lim_{b\to\infty} \arctan b - \arctan 0$$

$$= \frac{\pi}{2} - 0 = \frac{\pi}{2}$$

B. $\int_1^{\infty} \frac{1}{\sqrt{x}} dx \rightarrow$ I. (does not exist)

$$\int x^{-1/2} dx = 2\sqrt{x}$$

$$\Rightarrow \left[2\sqrt{x}\right]_1^{\infty} = \lim_{b\to\infty} 2\sqrt{b} - 2 = \infty$$

The improper integral diverges.

C. $\int_{-\infty}^{-1} \frac{1}{x^4} dx \rightarrow$ II. 1/3

$$\int x^{-4} dx = -\frac{1}{3} x^{-3}$$

$$\Rightarrow \left[-\frac{1}{3} x^{-3}\right]_{-\infty}^{-1} = -\frac{1}{3}(-1)^{-3} - \lim_{a\to-\infty}\left(-\frac{1}{3} a^{-3}\right)$$

$$= \frac{1}{3} - 0 - \frac{1}{3}$$

D. $\int_{-\infty}^{+\infty} \frac{1}{1+x^2} dx \rightarrow$ IV. π

$$[\arctan x]_{-\infty}^{+\infty} = \lim_{b\to\infty} \arctan b - \lim_{a\to\infty} \arctan a$$

$$= \frac{\pi}{2} - \left(-\frac{\pi}{2}\right) = \pi$$

Hence the correct matching is A-III, B-I, C-II, D-IV.

91. Reasoning: Both dice showing odd faces (A and B) give sums that are always even. Event C (sum odd) cannot occur simultaneously.

Counting check: Odd faces are {1, 3, 5}; pairs = 3 × 3 = 9 out of 36. All sums are even ⇒ probability = 0.

92. Event B: Second die is odd $\left(P = \frac{1}{2}\right)$.

Condition for C: To make sum odd, first die must be even $\left(P = \frac{1}{2}\right)$.

Calculation: $P(B \cap C) = \frac{1}{2} \times \frac{1}{2} = \frac{1}{4}$.

Counting check: 3 odd values for die 2 × 3 even values for die 1 = $\frac{9}{36} = \frac{1}{4}$.

93. Event A: First die is odd $\left(P = \frac{1}{2}\right)$.

Condition for C: To get odd sum, second die must be even $\left(P = \frac{1}{2}\right)$.

Calculation: $P(A \cap C) = \frac{1}{2} \times \frac{1}{2} = \frac{1}{4}$.

Counting check: 3 odd for die 1 × 3 even for die 2 = $\frac{9}{36} = \frac{1}{4}$.

94. Events: A (die 1 odd) and B (die 2 odd) are independent.

Calculation: $P(A \cap B) = P(A)P(B) = \frac{1}{2} \times \frac{1}{2} = \frac{1}{4}$.

Counting check: 3 × 3 =9 favorable pairs $\Rightarrow \frac{9}{36} = \frac{1}{4}$.

95. **Odd sum cases:**

- First odd, second even $\rightarrow \frac{1}{2} \times \frac{1}{2} = \frac{1}{4}$.
- First even, second odd $\rightarrow \frac{1}{2} \times \frac{1}{2} = \frac{1}{4}$.

Total probability: $P(C) = \frac{1}{4} + \frac{1}{4} = \frac{1}{2}$.

Counting check: Odd–even or even–odd combinations = 18 outcomes of 36 $\Rightarrow \frac{1}{2}$.

96. The passage states that RBI did not change the repo rate but managed liquidity through variable rate reverse repo (VRRR) operations. This indicates not reacting with immediate rate hikes or aggressive tightening, but instead using calibrated liquidity adjustments to address transient price shocks.

97. Global interest rate differentials affect capital flows: when foreign rates are higher, portfolio funds may leave India, putting pressure on the exchange rate. Thus, the RBI considers these differentials for managing foreign portfolio flows and currency volatility.

98. VRRR (Variable Rate Reverse Repo) operations are short-term tools used by RBI to absorb excess liquidity from banks through reverse repo at variable rates, allowing active fine-tuning of liquidity rather than passive absorption.

99. The policy emphasizes anchoring inflation expectations without immediately changing the repo rate. This reflects managing market expectations—signaling credibility and stability so inflation does not become unanchored—even without direct action on interest rates.

100. The phrase "withdrawal of accommodation" means moving away from highly accommodative (stimulus) monetary settings used during the pandemic toward a neutral stance. It implies a gradual normalization, not abrupt tightening or fiscal expansion.

Previous Years' Paper

National Testing Agency (NTA)

UGC-NET Junior Research Fellowship & Assistant Professor Eligibility Exam

Economics, January-2025

(Exam held on 03-01-2025)

PAPER-II

1. Given the CES production function an $y = [a_1 x_1^p + a_2 x_2^p]^p$, the elasticity of substitution between factors is:

1. 1
2. P
3. $\frac{1}{P}$
4. $\frac{1}{1-P}$

2. Arrange the following based on their date of establishment from earlier to latest:

A. IDBI - Industrial Development Bank of India

B. IFCI - Industrial Finance Corporation of India

C. ICICI - Industrial Credit and Investment Corporation of India

D. IRBI - Industrial Reconstruction Bank of India

Choose the ***correct*** answer from the options given below:

1. B, C, D, A
2. D, B, C, A
3. B, C, A, D
4. A, B, D, C

3. A tangency point between non-linear isoquant and an isocost line identifies:

1. the point of production efficiency where a firm can produce a derived output at the minimum possible cost.
2. the various levels of output that can be produced using a given level of inputs.
3. the various combinations of inputs that can be used to produce a given level of output.
4. the least costly combination of inputs required to produce various levels of output.

4. In the New Classical Macro Model without unanticipated shock, we may have -

A. Voluntary unemployment

B. Involuntary unemployment

C. Disguised unemployment

D. Cyclical unemployment

E. Natural rate of unemployment

Choose the ***correct*** answer from the options given below:

1. A & D Only
2. B & C Only
3. D & E Only
4. A & E Only

5. Which of the following is/are true for international monetary system?

A. Gold exchange standard

B. OPEC

C. Bretton Woods System

D. Law of one price

E. Asian Development Bank

Choose the ***correct*** answer from the options given below:

1. A Only
2. A, B Only
3. A, B, C Only
4. A, C, D Only

6. Given $A = \begin{pmatrix} 2 & 0 & 4 \\ 1 & 3 & 1 \end{pmatrix}$ and $B = (4\ 5\ 0)$, which of the following is true?

A. AB^T is $\begin{pmatrix} 8 \\ 19 \end{pmatrix}$

B. AB^T is defined

C. AB is not defined

D. BA is defined

E. BA^T is (8 19)

Choose the ***correct*** answer from the options given below:

1. A & E Only
2. A, B, C & E
3. A, B & C Only
4. A, C & E Only

7. Consider the following statements:

A. Price leadership equilibrium strategy is a Nash equilibrium strategy

B. Bertrand equilibrium strategy is a Nash equilibrium strategy

C. Stackelberg equilibrium strategy is a Nash equilibrium strategy

D. Monopoly equilibrium strategy is a Nash equilibrium strategy

E. Cournot's equilibrium strategy is a Nash equilibrium strategy

Choose the ***correct*** answer from the options given below:

1. A Only
2. B Only
3. A, B, C, E Only
4. D & E Only

8. Match List-I with List-II.

List-I	List-II
A. von Neumann and Oscar Morgenstern	I. Tit-for-tat strategy
B. Axelrod	II. Theory of Games and Economic Behaviour
C. Stackelberg leadership model	III. Nash equilibrium
D. Single - shot game	IV. Cheating

Choose the ***correct*** answer from the options given below:

1. A-I, B-II, C-III, D-IV
2. A-II, B-I, C-IV, D-III
3. A-IV, B-III, C-II, D-I
4. A-II, B-I, C-III, D-IV

9. In the Keynesian system, an increase in money supply will increase the demand for goods & services by:

1. Increasing consumption via Real Balance Effect
2. Increasing bond demand & thereby reducing the interest rate.
3. Reducing bond demand & thereby reducing the interest rate.
4. Increasing real wage & thereby increasing the transaction demand.

10. Match List-I with List-II.

List-I	List-II
A. Lindhal's Theory	I. Production of Public Goods
B. Club Theory	II. Constant growth of employment in Government agencies
C. Parkinson's Law	III. Pricing of Public Goods
D. Hotelling Rule	IV. Pricing of exhaustible resources

Choose the ***correct*** answer from the options given below:

1. A-III, B-I, C-II, D-IV
2. A-I, B-III, C-IV, D-II
3. A-I, B-III, C-II, D-IV
4. A-IV, B-I, C-II, D-III

11. Match List-I with List-II.

List-I	List-II
A. Expansionary monetary policy under Adaptive Expectations.	I. Policy is ineffective with only general inflation.
B. Anticipated expansionary monetary policy under Rational Expectations.	II. Policy is ineffective with only general deflation.
C. Money wage cut during great depression.	III. Policy is effective in the short run, although not in the long run.
D. The presence of sizeable menu cost.	IV. Policy is effective with no general inflation/deflation.

Choose the ***correct*** answer from the options given below:

1. A-I, B-II, C-III, D-IV
2. A-II, B-I, C-III, D-IV
3. A-III, B-I, C-II, D-IV
4. A-III, B-I, C-IV, D-II

12. In a Life Table which one of the following does not fit:

1. There are eight columns in a Life Table
2. It tells the age specific mortality rate
3. Age specific birth rate can be derived from a Life Table
4. Age specific Life expectancy can be calculated

13. According to the Real Business Cycle School, in the absence of supply shock:

1. There is only involuntary unemployment
2. There is only voluntary unemployment
3. There is both voluntary & involuntary unemployment simultaneously
4. There is no unemployment at all

14. Marginal Efficiency of Capital (MEC) & Marginal Efficiency of Investment (MEI) converge perfectly, when:

1. Net rate of investment is positive
2. Net rate of investment is negative
3. Net rate of investment is zero
4. Net value of capital stock is zero

15. Arrange the following from earlier to latest:

A. The logic of Investment Planning — Sukhamoy Chakravarti
B. Choice of Techniques — Amartya Sen
C. Shadow Price — Jan Tinbergen
D. The Tragedy of the Commons — G. Hardin
E. Marginal Utility — Alfred Marshall

Choose the ***correct*** answer from the options given below:

1. A, B, C, D, E
2. E, C, A, B, D
3. B, A, D, C, E
4. C, B, A, E, D

16. Six number of fair dice are rolled simultaneously. What is the probability that each face shows up with a different number?

1. $\frac{1}{6^6}$
2. $\frac{6}{6^6}$
3. $\frac{6!}{6^6}$
4. $\frac{6^5}{6^6}$

17. Which of the following is/are not the definition of gains from trade?

A. It is the benefit individuals and countries derive from participating in international trade.
B. It is the gross benefit to economic agents that results from an increase in trade
C. It is the deduction of consumer surplus from producer surplus
D. It is the net benefit to economic agents that results from an increase in trade
E. It is the sum total of producer surplus and consumer surplus

Choose the ***correct*** answer from the options given below:

1. A Only 2. B, C Only
3. C, D Only 4. C, D, E Only

18. Asymmetric information in the Lemons Market results in:

A. Gradual fall of average price.
B. Gradual withdrawal of better quality products.
C. Adverse selection by one of the parties
D. Gradual withdrawal of inferior quality products.

Choose the ***correct*** answer from the options given below:

1. A Only
2. A, C Only
3. A, B, D Only
4. A, B, C Only

19. Arrange the following demographic phases as per C.R. Blacker's theory of population.

A. Low mortality and death exceeding birth
B. Falling birth rates, but decreasing mortality
C. High birth rate and high death rate
D. Low birth rate balanced by equally low mortality

Choose the ***correct*** answer from the options given below:

1. C, B, A, D
2. C, B, D, A
3. A, C, B, D
4. B, C, D, A

20. There is an inverse relationship between the rate of interest and the speculative Demand for Money. This is due to:

1. Adaptive Expectation Hypothesis
2. Regressive Expectation Hypothesis
3. Rational Expectation Hypothesis
4. Relative Wage Hypothesis

21. Arrange the writing of the following books in chronological order (oldest to latest)

A. Why nations fail
B. Grundrisse
C. Poverty & famines
D. The theory of moral sentiments
E. Production of commodities by means of commodities.

Choose the ***correct*** answer from the options given below:

1. A, B, C, D, E
2. B, A, D, E, C
3. D, B, E, C, A
4. B, A, E, D, C

22. Read the example given below and find out the correct choice compatible from among the alternatives:

If a professor assigns only letter grades to an exam, we know that a student who receives a grade of 'A' did better than a student who receives a 'B', but we cannot say how much better from that ordinal scale. Nor can we tell whether the difference in preference between an 'A' student and a 'B' student and a 'C' student.

1. Marshallian utility analysis
2. Revealed preference analysis
3. Slutsky equation
4. Indifference curve analysis

23. Arrange the following theories in correct chronological order, (starting from the earliest)

A. Cambridge version of quantity theory of money
B. Baumol's theory of demand for money
C. Fisher's version of quantity theory of money
D. Tobin's theory of demand for money

Choose the ***correct*** answer from the options given below:

1. C, A, D, B
2. A, C, B, D
3. C, A, B, D
4. B, C, D, A

24. Ecological Footprint means:

1. Number of trees planted in a region per year.
2. Amount of ecological resources degraded in a country per year.
3. Total areas of deep forest in a country.
4. The amount of pressure that human puts on the natural resources available to them in their surrounding.

25. Consequences of hoarding of money by individual are:

A. Loss of utility by not purchasing goods and services.
B. Foregone interest by not saving.
C. Fall of real value of money by deflation.
D. Loss of return by not purchasing other assets.

Choose the ***correct*** answer from the options given below:

1. A, B, C Only 2. A, B, D Only
3. B, C, D Only 4. A, B Only

26. Lewis - Ranis - Fei framework considers the following strategies as essential for unhindered progress.

A. Land reforms
B. Green revolution
C. Planning
D. Capital accumulation
E. International migration

Choose the ***correct*** answer from the options given below:

1. A, D & E Only
2. A, C & D Only
3. A, C & E Only
4. B, D & E Only

27. If government expenditure rises by ₹ 100, total tax revenue rises by ₹ 100, the value of marginal propensity to consume is 0.5 & there is no change in autonomous investment & consumption, in a simple Keynesian closed - economy model, GDP rises by:

1. ₹ 0 2. ₹ 100
3. ₹ 200 4. ₹ 400

28. A Central Bank can increase money supply in an economy:

A. By raising the Cash Reserve Ratio
B. By purchasing government securities from the public
C. By lowering the Cash Reserve Ratio
D. By lowering the Repo rate

Choose the ***correct*** answer from the options given below:

1. A, B, C Only
2. A, B, D Only
3. B, C, D Only
4. A, C, D Only

29. Find out the correct alterative - Scitovsky double criterion

1. does not require the fulfilment of Kaldor - Hicks Welfare criterion test.
2. requires only the fulfilment of reversal test.
3. does not require the fulfilment of reversal test.
4. requires the fulfilment of Kaldor - Hicks test and reversal test.

30. In the IS - LM framework, under general recessionary condition, as government expenditure (G) rises,

A. As Bond price (p_b) falls, rate of interest (r) rises, reducing the level of investment (I).
B. Aggregate demand for commodities rises, raising the level of aggregate output & income (Y).
C. Fall in private investment (I) reduces aggregate income.
D. People sell bond (b) to get money & hence bond supply (Bs) rises, reducing bond price (p_b).
E. Transaction demand for money (L_1) rises, creating money demand greater than money supply (L > M).

Choose the ***correct*** answer from the options given below:

1. A, B, C, D, E
2. B, E, D, A, C
3. B, D, E, C, A
4. E, B, A, D, C

31. In a market model with a 'lagged' supply function, lagging by one time period, the convergence of the time path of price towards the equilibrium price depends on:

1. Whether slope of supply function > slope of demand function
2. Whether slope of supply function < slope of demand function
3. Whether slope of supply function = slope of demand function
4. Has nothing to do with the slopes of demand and/or supply functions.

32. Given the objective function $y = f(x_1, x_2 \ldots x_n)$ and the constraint $g(x_1, x_2 \ldots x_n) = 0$, the second order condition for an extremum is:

A. $|\bar{H}_2| < 0, |\bar{H}_3| < 0$ ..... for a maximum

B. $|\bar{H}_2| > 0, |\bar{H}_3| < 0$ ..... for a maximum

C. $|\bar{H}_2| < 0, |\bar{H}_3| > 0$ ..... for a maximum

D. $|\bar{H}_2| < 0, |\bar{H}_3| < 0$ ..... for a minimum

E. $|\bar{H}_2| < 0, |\bar{H}_3| < 0$ ..... for a minimum

Choose the ***correct*** answer from the options given below:

1. A & D Only 2. C & E Only
3. B & D Only 4. B & E Only

33. Due to open - access to a property after it is over-used beyond its carrying capacity. Such a situation is called:

1. Problem of tragedy of commons
2. Problem of market failure
3. Problem of externality
4. Problem of moral hazard

34. Choose the feature which does not fit with the features of monopolistic competition.

1. Firms have little control over price
2. Perfect mobility of factors of production
3. Products are differentiated
4. Factor prices and technology are given

35. 'Demographic Dividend' relates to which aspect of population?

1. An increase of life expectancy
2. An increase in sex ratio
3. A decline in total Fertility Rate
4. An increase in the share of working age population.

36. Which of the following statements is true concerning the optimal solution of a linear programming problem with two decision variables?

1. There is always a unique solution to the problem.
2. The optimal solution is either an extreme point or is on the line connecting two extreme points.
3. All resources must be used up by an optimal solution.
4. The optimal solution may be an interior point of the set of feasible solutions.

37. Advantages of Indirect Tax are:

A. It is difficult to evade
B. It is elastic in nature
C. It is convenient to pay
D. It is based on the ability to pay of the tax-payer

Choose the ***correct*** answer from the options given below:

1. C, B Only 2. C, D Only
3. A, B, C Only 4. A, C, D Only

38. Arrange the following from earlier to present:

A. John F. Nash
B. Von Neumann and Oscar Morgenstern
C. Robert Axelrod
D. Paul Milgrom
E. John Maynard Smith

Choose the *correct* answer from the options given below:

1. A, B, C, D, E
2. A, C, B, D, E
3. A, D, B, C, E
4. B, A, C, E, D

39. Arrange the following from earlier to the latest:

A. Adam Smith B. David Ricardo
C. David Hume D. Paul R. Krugman
E. Jen Tinbergen

Choose the *correct* answer from the options given below:

1. A, B, C, D, E
2. B, A, C, E, D
3. C, A, B, E, D
4. D, E, C, B, A

40. Match List-I with List-II.

List-I	List-II
A. Durbin - Watson	I. Multicollinearity
B. Granger	II. Heteroscedastic disturbances
C. Farrar - Glauber	III. Causality
D. Glejser	IV. Autocorrelated disturbances

Choose the *correct* answer from the options given below:

1. A-IV, B-III, C-I, D-II
2. A-IV, B-III, C-II, D-I
3. A-II, B-III, C-IV, D-I
4. A-III, B-IV, C-I, D-II

41. For the production function, $Q = AK^{\alpha}L^{\beta}$, where A, α, $\beta > 0$, which of the following statement(s) are correct?

A. Degree of homogeneity is 1
B. Output elasticity with respect to capital is α
C. It exhibits constant returns to scale
D. Marginal product of a factor = Average product of the factor

Choose the *correct* answer from the options given below:

1. A & B Only 2. B & C Only
3. B & D Only 4. B Only

42. Which of the following is/are not applicable to classical theory of trade?

A. Labour theory of value
B. One factor model
C. It satisfies zero - sum game
D. It is a multi - factor model
E. Factors of production are mobile domestically and internationally

Choose the *correct* answer from the options given below:

1. A, B Only 2. B, C Only
3. D, E Only 4. C, D, E Only

43. Given the following statements, state which ones are correct:

A. GDP is devoid of all types of double - counting
B. Donations are included in National Income
C. Alms are included in Personal Income
D. Inventory is included in investment
E. Foreign workers' income is included in GNP but not in GDP

Choose the *correct* answer from the options given below:

1. A & C Only
2. A, C, D & E Only
3. C, D & E Only
4. C & D Only

44. Match List-I with List-II.

List-I	List-II
A. Unit Root test	I. Durbin - Watson Test
B. Contingency table	II. Student's *t*-Test
C. Regression coefficient	III. Stationarity
D. Autocorrelation	IV. x^2 Test (Chi square test)

Choose the ***correct*** answer from the options given below:

1. A-III, B-I, C-II, D-IV
2. A-III, B-IV, C-II, D-I
3. A-IV, B-II, C-III, D-I
4. A-I, B-III, C-II, D-IV

45. Which of the following does/do not come under exchange rate?

A. Export activities

B. Open market operations

C. Interest rate

D. Import activities

E. Multiple expansion of credit

Choose the ***correct*** answer from the options given below:

1. A Only　　2. B Only
3. C, D Only　　4. B, E Only

46. The input - output matrix for a two sector economy is given by $A = \begin{pmatrix} 0.25 & 0.40 \\ 0.10 & 0.10 \end{pmatrix}$

If the external demand for the outputs of the two sectors is $D = \begin{pmatrix} 10 \\ 20 \end{pmatrix}$, what will be the optional output levels of the two commodities?

1. 26.77 and 18.43
2. 9.33 and 24.50
3. 26.77 and 25.20
4. 24.33 and 25.20

47. Arrange the introduction of the following concepts in chronological order (oldest to latest):

A. Adaptive expectation hypothesis by Friedman.

B. Relative income hypothesis by Duesenberry.

C. Efficiency wage hypothesis by Stiglitz.

D. Rational expectation hypothesis by Lucas.

E. Effective demand problem by Kalecki

Choose the ***correct*** answer from the options given below:

1. E, A, B, C, D
2. B, A, E, C, D
3. B, A, D, C, E
4. E, B, A, D, C

48. The basis of consumer surplus in Marshallian utility analysis is:

1. Law of equi-marginal utility
2. Law of proportions
3. Law of diminishing marginal utility
4. Law of demand

49. Big Push theory considers a process of development that essentially depends on:

1. Comprehensive planning
2. Free - market without any government intervention
3. Well - defined private property rights.
4. Political democracy

50. Match List-I with List-II.

List-I	List-II
A. Type II error	I. $P_{01} \times P_{10} = 1$
B. Mean > Mode	II. Not rejecting H_0 when H_0 is not true
C. Homogenous population	III. Positively skewed distribution
D. Time reversal test	IV. Simple random Sampling

Choose the ***correct*** answer from the options given below:

1. A-II, B-III, C-IV, D-I
2. A-III, B-I, C-II, D-IV
3. A-IV, B-II, C-III, D-I
4. A-I, B-II, C-III, D-IV

51. Match List-I with List-II.

List-I	List-II
A. Positive externality in consumption	I. Riding a noisy motor cycle at mid-night
B. Positive externality in Production	II. Honey cultivation near a flower garden

C.	Negative externality in consumption	III.	Paper mill dumping waste into river
D.	Negative externality in Production	IV.	Sanitisation of a house

Choose the ***correct*** answer from the options given below:

1. A-IV, B-II, C-I, D-III
2. A-I, B-IV, C-II, D-III
3. A-I, B-IV, C-III, D-II
4. A-IV, B-III, C-II, D-I

52. Arrange in descending order the extent of crowding out effects as under:

A. Classical Macro model
B. Complete Keynesian system assuming general condition
C. IS - LM framework assuming general conditions
D. Simple Keynesian model

Choose the ***correct*** answer from the options given below:

1. A, B, C, D
2. B, A, C, D
3. B, C, D, A
4. A, B, D, C

53. Which of the following agencies is responsible for computing the National Income statistics in India?

1. Reserve Bank of India
2. Ministry of Finance
3. NITI Aayog
4. Central Statistical Organization

54. Consider the following system of equations:

$$Y_1 = \alpha_0 + \alpha_1 Y_2 + \alpha_3 Y_3 + \alpha_4 X_1 + \alpha_5 X_2 + \cup_1$$
$$Y_2 = \beta_0 + \beta_1 Y_3 + \beta_2 Y_1 + \beta_3 X_2 + \cup_2$$
$$Y_3 = \lambda_0 + \lambda_1 x_1 + \lambda_2 x_2 + \lambda_3 x_3 + \cup_3$$

According to the order condition, the first equation is:

1. Unidentified
2. Just identified
3. Over identified
4. Not possible to say because the reduced form of the model is not given

55. Identify the chronology of the theories of population as developed by the following:

A. Karl Marx
B. Edwin Cannan
C. T.R. Malthus
D. C.R. Blacker

Choose the ***correct*** answer from the options given below:

1. B, C, A, D
2. A, B, C, D
3. C, B, A, D
4. B, C, D, A

56. The method used for estimation of price change of a house due to change in environment like starting of park, scenic beauty etc is:

1. Travel cost method
2. Hedonic pricing method
3. Production function method
4. Contingent valuation method

57. If a variable has '*m*' categories, we can run the regression using:

1. '*m* – 1' dummy variables and an intercept term
2. '*m*' dummy variables and an intercept term
3. '(*m* – 1)' dummy variables without an intercept
4. '(*m* + 1)' dummy variables without an intercept

58. Find out the correct answer about the 'Pigovian Tax'.

A. Provides solution in order to internalise the total cost of an activity into the market.
B. Provides solution to reduce the production of pollutants through public policy
C. It helps in increasing the factor productivity in the real sector.
D. It acts like a reverance tax

Choose the ***correct*** answer from the options given below:

1. A, B Only
2. C, D Only
3. A Only
4. A, B, D Only

59. Match List-I with List-II.

List-I	List-II
A. Simple random sampling	I. Non - probability Sampling
B. Systematic sampling	II. Random choice of items from each stratum
C. Quota sampling	III. Random selection of the first unit and systematic selection of the rest
D. Stratified random sampling	IV. Equal probability of selection for each item in all trials

Choose the ***correct*** answer from the options given below:

1. A-IV, B-III, C-I, D-II
2. A-IV, B-II, C-I, D-III
3. A-III, B-II, C-I, D-IV
4. A-IV, B-III, C-II, D-I

60. Generalised least square method of estimation can be used in which of the following cases:

A. Autocorrelated disturbances

B. Multicollinearity among explanatory variables

C. Heteroscedastic disturbances

D. Overfitted models

E. Incorrect functional forms

Choose the ***correct*** answer from the options given below:

1. A, C & D Only
2. C, B & E Only
3. A & C Only
4. C, D & E Only

61. Match List-I with List-II.

List-I	List-II
A. Supply side of international trade	I. David Ricardo
B. Demand side of international trade	II. Bastable and Alfred Marshall
C. Opportunity cost of international trade	III. G. Haberler
D. Real cost theory of international trade	IV. Alfred Marshall and Edgeworth

Choose the ***correct*** answer from the options given below:

1. A-I, B-IV, C-III, D-II
2. A-I, B-IV, C-II, D-III
3. A-II, B-I, C-III, D-IV
4. A-IV, B-III, C-II, D-I

62. Given the following statements about major schools of thought in macro economics, state which ones are correct:

A. The New Keynesians assume Rational Expectation and market imperfections and highlight the role of aggregate demand.

B. The Monetarists assume Rational Expectation, non - competitive markets and highlight the role of monetary policy.

C. The New Classicals assume Rational Expectation, competitive markets and highlight policy irrelevance.

D. The Classicals assume a competitive, and frictionless economy and highlight policy ineffectiveness.

E. The Keynesians assume wage and price flexibility and highlight policy effectiveness.

Choose the ***correct*** answer from the options given below:

1. A, C & D Only
2. A, B, C & D Only
3. B, C, D & E Only
4. C & D Only

63. Effective Demand Problem may arise even in a competitive market economy under Rational Expectation, if there is:

1. Perfect Foresight.
2. Coordination Failure.
3. Anticipated demand shock.
4. Unanticipated supply shock.

64. Walras law states that if N-1 markets are in equilibrium, then we can get equilibrium price/prices in:

1. N*th* market
2. 2N markets
3. N-3 markets
4. N-4 markets

65. In a two variable regression, the dependent and independent variables are Y and X respectively. The coefficient of correlation between X and Y is 0.8. Which of the following statements is correct?

1. 8% of variation in Y is explained by X
2. 64% of variation in Y is explained by X
3. 0.8% of variation in Y is explained by X
4. 80% of variation in Y is explained by X

66. Match List-I with List-II.

List-I	List-II
A. Free Trade Area	I. All tariffs are removed between members and a common external trade policy is adopted for non-members
B. Customs Union	II. All tariffs are removed between members and the group adopts a common external commercial policy toward non-members
C. Common Market	III. All members of the group remove tariffs on each other's products and at the same time retains its independence in establishing trading prices with non-members
D. Economic Union	IV. Most comprehensive advanced stage of integration

Choose the ***correct*** answer from the options given below:

1. A-III, B-II, C-I, D-IV
2. A-I, B-II, C-III, D-IV
3. A-II, B-I, C-IV, D-III
4. A-IV, B-III, C-II, D-I

67. Arrange the following from earlier to the latest:

A. Price - Specie - Flow Mechanism
B. Comparative Advantage
C. Absolute Advantage
D. Intra - Industry Trade
E. Mercantilism

Choose the ***correct*** answer from the options given below:

1. A, B, C, D, E
2. B, A, D, C, E
3. E, A, C, B, D
4. E, D, C, B, A

68. Which of the following is not a rural development programme of India?

1. Din Dayal Upadhyaya Gramin Kaushalya Yojana
2. Pradhan Mantri Gram Sadak Yojana
3. Swachh Bharat Mission
4. National Social Assistance Programme

69. Vertical equality in taxation requires that:

1. People in different income groups should be taxed equally.
2. People in different income groups should be taxed differently
3. People in different income groups should be taxed proportionately
4. No tax on the basis of individual income

70. When C_d, I_d & G_d stand for consumption expenditure, investment expenditure & government expenditure respectively, on domestically produced goods & services & X & M stand for aggregate values of export & import for a country, respectively, GDP is calculated as:

1. $C_d + I_d + G_d + X - M$
2. $C + I + G_d + X$
3. $C_d + I_d + G_d - M$
4. $C_d + I_d + G_d + X$

71. Which of the following is not correct?

1. Public debt transfers fund from public to government.
2. Public borrowing curtails consumption.
3. Taxation curtails consumption.
4. Government borrowing does not effect income distribution.

72. Arrange the introduction/coinage of the following concepts in chronological order (oldest to latest):

A. Primitive Socialist Accumulation
B. Development by Dispossession
C. Accumulation by Dispossession
D. Primitive Capitalist Accumulation
E. Knife - edge Instability

Choose the ***correct*** answer from the options given below:

1. D, A, E, B, C
2. A, D, B, E, C
3. D, A, E, C, B
4. A, D, B, C, E

73. The marginal revenue of a firm is ₹ 10 and the price it charges per unit is ₹ 30. Assuring that the firm is a profit maximiser, what is the own price elasticity of demand for the firm at that point of profit maximisation?

1. 1.5
2. –1.5
3. –0.66
4. 0.66

74. Which of the following trade models exhibits the features of economies of scale and monopolistic competition?

1. The Kemp Model
2. The Intra - Industry Trade Model
3. The Krugman Trade Model
4. The Falvey Model

75. A continuous supply shock leads to :

1. A continuous shift of Phillips Curve to the left such that unemployment & inflation both fall.
2. A continuous shift of Phillips Curve to the right such that unemployment & inflation both rise.
3. A continuous movement along the Phillips curve such that unemployment & inflation both fall.
4. A continuous movement along the Phillips curve such that unemployment falls & inflation rises.

76. Match List-I with List-II.

List-I	List-II
A. Adam Smith	I. Size of the market
B. David Ricardo	II. Natural resource constraint
C. Karl Marx	III. Forces of production
D. Amartya Sen	IV. Freedom of choice

Choose the ***correct*** answer from the options given below:

1. A-I, B-II, C-III, D-IV
2. A-IV, B-I, C-III, D-II
3. A-IV, B-III, C-II, D-I
4. A-I, B-II, C-IV, D-III

77. Endogenous Growth theory has been developed by:

A. K. Arrow
B. R. Barro
C. P. Romer
D. R. Solow
E. G. Mankiw

Choose the ***correct*** answer from the options given below:

1. A, B, C, E Only
2. A, B, E Only
3. B, C, E Only
4. A, B, C Only

78. Which is/are, not modern theory of trade?

A. Human Skills Theory
B. Factor Proportions Theory
C. Product Cycle Theory
D. Offer Curve Analysis
E. Monopolistically Competitive Trade Theory

Choose the ***correct*** answer from the options given below:

1. A Only
2. A, B Only
3. B, D Only
4. C, D, E Only

79. Match List-I with List-II.

List-I	List-II
A. Life Cycle Hypothesis	I. Karl Marx
B. Cash Balance Approach	II. Francois Quesnay
C. Organic Composition of Capital	III. Alfred Marshall
D. Tableau Economique	IV. F. Modigliani

Choose the ***correct*** answer from the options given below:

1. A-III, B-II, C-IV, D-I
2. A-IV, B-III, C-I, D-II
3. A-II, B-IV, C-III, D-I
4. A-I, B-III, C-II, D-IV

80. Match List-I with List-II.

List-I	List-II
A. Crude Birth Rate	I. $\frac{B}{P} \times 1000$
B. Age Specific Fertility Rate	II. $\frac{B}{P_F} \times 1000$
C. Total Fertility Rate	III. $\frac{B_i}{P_{iF}} \times 1000$
D. General Fertility Rate	IV. $\sum \frac{B_i}{P_{iF}} \times 1000$

Choose the ***correct*** answer from the options given below:

1. A-II, B-III, C-I, D-IV
2. A-I, B-III, C-II, D-IV
3. A-IV, B-I, C-II, D-III
4. A-I, B-III, C-IV, D-II

81. The unit root tests for time series is based on the null hypothesis that the time series under consideration is:

1. Stationary
2. Non-stationary
3. Strictly stationary
4. Weak stationary

82. Which one of the following is not correct regarding India's national level programmes:

1. MGNREGP is a workfare programme.
2. PMAY is a developmental programme.
3. PMGSY is a food security enhancement programme.
4. BBBP is a gender - equality enhancement programme.

83. Arrange the following government schemes chronologically according to their year of launching starting from the earliest:

A. Ayushman Bharat Yojana
B. Atal Pension Yojana
C. Jal Jeevan Mission
D. PM Ujjwala Yojana

Choose the ***correct*** answer from the options given below:

1. C, A, D, B
2. B, C, D, A
3. A, B, D, C
4. B, D, A, C

84. When with the increase in income, the percentage of income as tax falls, it is called:

1. Progressive Tax
2. Proportional Tax
3. Neutral Tax
4. Regressive Tax

85. Match List-I with List-II.

List-I	List-II
A. Perfectly Competitive Model	I. The producers first set the price of the product and then produce the output demanded at that price
B. Bertrand Model	II. It recognises the concept of interdependence among firms
C. Stackelberg Model	III. Large number of buyers and sellers
D. Oligopoly Model	IV. Few competing firms in the market

Choose the ***correct*** answer from the options given below:

1. A-III, B-I, C-II, D-IV
2. A-I, B-II, C-III, D-IV
3. A-II, B-I, C-III, D-IV
4. A-III, B-II, C-IV, D-I

86. Which of the following Indian ministries is responsible for the publication of reports on longitudinal data on the informal sector of India?

1. Ministry of Home Affairs
2. NITI Aayog
3. Ministry of Statistics & programme Implementation
4. Ministry of Finance

87. In the presence of externality, Coase theorem argues:

1. Social optimum can be attained only through government's intervention
2. Social optimum can also be attained by mutual agreement between the private parties
3. Income effect and transaction costs are to be considered always.
4. Property right cannot be assigned to any party

88. Arrange the following events in increasing order of their probability of happening :

A. Probability of getting two heads in simultaneous toss of two coins

B. Probability of getting a queen from a single draw of a card from a well shuffled pack of cards

C. Probability of getting a white ball from a bag containing 3 white and 7 black balls

D. Probability of getting an even number from a single roll of a fair die

Choose the ***correct*** answer from the options given below:

1. A, D, B, C
2. C, A, B, D
3. B, C, A, D
4. B, A, C, D

89. Harris-Todaro framework discusses.

Choose the correct answer from the options given below.

1. Pushed migration
2. Pulled migration
3. Structural Transformation
4. The informal economy

90. Match List-I with List-II.

List-I	List-II
A. Gross barter terms of trade	I. Jacob Viner
B. Single factorial terms of trade	II. Dorrance
C. Income terms of trade	III. C.W. Taussing
D. Secular deterioration in terms of trade of developing countries	IV. Prebisch-Singer

Choose the ***correct*** answer from the options given below:

1. A-I, B-II, C-III, D-IV
2. A-II, B-I, C-IV, D-III
3. A-IV, B-III, C-II, D-I
4. A-III, B-I, C-II, D-IV

Directions (Qs. No. 91 to 95): *Read the following matrix carefully and answer the questions based on it:*

Consider the following Prisoners' Dilemma Games

Table : Safety Investment Game

Firm-1 \ Firm-2	No Investment	Investment
No Investment	$200 (Firm-1) / $200 (Firm-2)	$250 (Firm-1) / $100 (Firm-2)
Investment	$100 (Firm-1) / $250 (Firm-2)	$225 (Firm-1) / $225 (Firm-2)

Read the above payoff matrix and answer the following:

Find the correct alternative:

91. In this game, the underinvestment problem can be avoided if:
1. one firm invests and the other firm does not
2. the govermnent sets safety standards that will force both the firms to invest
3. both invest
4. none invests

92. Safety investment by one firm of the two firm industry:
1. increases workers' wages in the firm which has not invested
2. increases workers' wages in the firm which has made invested
3. decreases workers' wages in the firm which has made investment
4. decreases wages of workers in both the firms

93. Investment by both firms:
1. is an equilibrium
2. is a partial equilibrium
3. is not an equilibrium
4. is a Nash equilibrium

94. Safety investment by one firm in the industry:
1. Increases safety of both the firms
2. Increases safety of the firm which has made investment
3. Cannot ensure safety to the industry as a whole
4. Increases safety to the firm which has not invested

95. Nash equilibrium occurs when both firms earn:
1. ($200, $200)
2. ($225, $225)
3. ($100, $250)
4. ($225, $100)

Directions (Qs. No. 96 to 100): *Read the following passage carefully and answer the questions based on it:*

"Given her personal characteristics, social background economic circumstances, etc., a person has the ability to do (or be) certain things that she has reason value. The reason for valuation can be direct (the functioning involved may directly enrich her life, such as being well - nourished or being healthy) or indirect (the functioning involved may contribute to further production, or command a price in the market). The human capital perspective can - in principle - be defined very broadly to cover both types of valuation, but it is typically defined - by convention - primarily in terms of indirect value : human qualities that can be employed as "capital" in production in the way physical capital is. In this sense, the borrower view of human capital approach fits into the more inclusive perspective of human capability which can cover both direct & indirect consequences of human abilities. Consider an example, If education makes a person more efficient in commodity production, then this is clearly an enhancement of human capital. This can add to the value of production in the economy & also to the income of the person who has been educated. But even with the same level of income, a person may benefit from education, in reading, communicating, arguing, in being able to choose in a more informed way, in being taken more seriously by others, & so on. The benefits of education thus, exceeds its role as human capital in commodity production. The broader human - capability perspective would record - and value- these additional roles."

Considering the above paragraphs, mark the correct alternative:

96. Which of the following concepts is not related to Human Capability:
1. Being healthy
2. Being argumentative
3. Being socially accepted
4. Being authoritative

97. The concept of Human - capability relates to:
1. Informed choice
2. Per capita income
3. Productive efficiency
4. Economic Growth

98. Education for an individual enhances:
1. Human capability but not human capital
2. Human capital but not human capability
3. Both human capability and human capital
4. Neither human capability, nor human capital

99. Individuals value certain doings & beings, having direct impact, such as:
1. Being efficient in production
2. Contribution to national wealth
3. Enrichment of Life
4. Enjoying utility enhancement

100. Human Capability & Human Capital are related in the following way:
1. These are completely separated concepts.
2. Former is a much larger super-set of the latter.
3. Latter is a significantly larger super-set of the former.
4. These are almost similar concepts.

ANSWERS

1. (4): Given the CES (Constant Elasticity of Substitution) production function:

$$y = \left[a_1 x_1^p + a_2 x_2^p\right]^{\frac{1}{p}}$$

the elasticity of substitution between the two input factors x_1 and x_2 is determined by a specific formula derived from the structure of this function.

- In this function, the parameter p (sometimes denoted as ρ in literature) captures the degree of substitutability between the two factors.
- The elasticity of substitution, denoted by σ, is constant in CES functions and is calculated using the following relationship:

$$\sigma = \frac{1}{1-p}$$

This formula arises from taking the derivative of the marginal rate of technical substitution (MRTS) with respect to the input ratio and is a defining feature of CES functions.

Illustration:

- If $p = 0$, then $\sigma = \frac{1}{1-0} = 1$, which is the Cobb-Douglas case.
- If $p \to -\infty$, $\sigma \to 0$: Perfect complements.
- If $p \to 1$, $\sigma \to \infty$: Perfect substitutes.

Thus, elasticity depends inversely on $1 - p$, not just on p itself.

Therefore, the elasticity of substitution is correctly given by Option 4: $\frac{1}{1-P}$.

2. (3): The correct chronological order based on the date of establishment of the given financial institutions is:

B. IFCI (Industrial Finance Corporation of India) – Established in 1948, it was the first Development Financial Institution (DFI) in India created to cater to the long-term financial needs of industrial enterprises.

C. ICICI (Industrial Credit and Investment Corporation of India) – Established in 1955 with the help of the World Bank, specifically to promote private sector industrial development.

A. IDBI (Industrial Development Bank of India) – Set up in 1964 as a subsidiary of RBI to provide credit and other facilities for the development of industry.

D. IRBI (Industrial Reconstruction Bank of India) – Established in 1985 to tackle the problem of industrial sickness and revive sick units.

Thus, the correct order from earliest to latest is IFCI (1948), ICICI (1955), IDBI (1964), IRBI (1985), i.e., B, C, A, D.

3. (1): The point of production efficiency where a firm can produce a derived output at the minimum possible cost: A tangency point between a non-linear isoquant and an isocost line indicates the cost-minimizing input combination for producing a given level of output.

- An isoquant shows all combinations of inputs (e.g., labor and capital) that produce the same output.
- An isocost line shows all combinations of inputs that cost the same.

At the point of tangency, the slope of the isoquant equals the slope of the isocost:

$$MRTS_{L,K} = \frac{w}{r}$$

where MRTS is the marginal rate of technical substitution, is the wage rate, and is the rental rate of capital. This condition reflects optimal efficiency, minimizing cost for a given output level.

4. (4): In the New Classical Macro Model without unanticipated shock, the key assumptions include rational expectations, market clearing, and flexible prices and wages. Under such assumptions, unemployment is not due to market imperfections or sticky prices, but instead arises from individual decisions or structural factors. Therefore, only voluntary unemployment and natural rate of unemployment are consistent with this framework.

Detailed clarification of each listed type of unemployment:

A. Voluntary unemployment: This occurs when individuals choose not to work at the prevailing wage rate. In the New Classical model, where all agents have full information and wages adjust instantly, unemployment is considered voluntary—individuals are optimizing their utility between labor and leisure. Hence, this is included.

B. Involuntary unemployment: This refers to a situation where individuals are willing to work at the current wage but cannot find jobs. It occurs due to sticky wages or price rigidities, which are not present in the New Classical framework. Hence, this is not included.

C. Disguised unemployment: This is typically seen in developing economies where more workers are employed than needed, often in agriculture. It is a structural phenomenon, not explained by macroeconomic models like the New Classical one. Hence, this is not included.

D. Cyclical unemployment: This arises due to fluctuations in economic activity or aggregate demand. Since the New Classical model assumes prices and wages are fully flexible and markets clear, cyclical unemployment does not exist. Hence, this is not included.

E. Natural rate of unemployment: This is the long-run equilibrium unemployment level due to frictional and structural factors, even in a fully functioning market. The New Classical model accepts the existence of this natural rate. Hence, this is included.

Thus, the correct pair consistent with the New Classical model without unanticipated shocks is A & E only, i.e., Option 4.

5. (4): The international monetary system encompasses mechanisms and rules governing exchange rates and international payments. Valid elements include:

A. Gold Exchange Standard – A historical monetary system where currencies were convertible to gold at fixed rates.

C. Bretton Woods System – Post-WWII international system (1944–1971) based on fixed exchange rates and the USD pegged to gold.

D. Law of One Price – A theoretical principle stating that identical goods should sell for the same price globally when expressed in the same currency.

Incorrect options:

B. OPEC – A petroleum cartel, not a monetary system institution.

E. Asian Development Bank – A regional development bank, not a part of the international monetary system itself.

Hence, correct answer is A, C, D Only.

6. (2): Given:

$$\text{Matrix A} - \begin{bmatrix} 2 & 0 & 4 \\ 1 & 3 & 1 \end{bmatrix} \Rightarrow 2 \times 3 \text{ matrix}$$

Matrix B = $[4 \ \ 5 \ \ 0] \Rightarrow 1 \times 3$ matrix

Let's analyze each statement now:

A. $AB^T = \begin{bmatrix} 8 \\ 19 \end{bmatrix}$

First compute the transpose of B:

$$B^T = \begin{bmatrix} 4 \\ 5 \\ 0 \end{bmatrix}$$

Now compute:

$$AB^T = \begin{bmatrix} 2 & 0 & 4 \\ 1 & 3 & 1 \end{bmatrix} \cdot \begin{bmatrix} 4 \\ 5 \\ 0 \end{bmatrix}$$

$$= \begin{bmatrix} 2\times4+0\times5+4\times0 \\ 1\times4+3\times5+1\times0 \end{bmatrix}$$

$$= \begin{bmatrix} 8 \\ 19 \end{bmatrix}$$

Hence, Statement A is correct.

B. AB^T is defined
A is 2×3, B^T is 3×1, so their product is defined and results in a 2×1 matrix.
Statement B is correct.

C. AB is not defined
A is 2×3, B is 1×3, so AB is a product of $2 \times 3 \times 1 \times 3$, which is not defined because the inner dimensions (3 and 1) do not match.
Statement C is correct.

D. BA is defined
B is 1×3, A is 2×3, so BA would be $1 \times 3 \times 2 \times 3$ — the inner dimensions (3 and 2) do not match, hence the product BA is not defined.
Statement D is incorrect.

E. $BA^T = (8 \ \ 19)$
First compute A^T:

$$A^T = \begin{bmatrix} 2 & 1 \\ 0 & 3 \\ 4 & 1 \end{bmatrix}$$

Now compute:

$$BA^T = [4 \ \ 5 \ \ 0] \cdot \begin{bmatrix} 2 & 1 \\ 0 & 3 \\ 4 & 1 \end{bmatrix}$$

$$= [4\times2+5\times0+0\times4 \quad 4\times1+5\times3+0\times1]$$

$$= [8 \ \ 19]$$

So, statement E is correct.

7. (3): All the listed strategies (except monopoly) are based on strategic interaction and are recognized forms of Nash Equilibrium under specific assumptions. Each strategy satisfies the condition where no player can unilaterally improve their payoff by changing strategy, assuming others keep theirs unchanged.

A. Price leadership equilibrium strategy:
Involves a dominant firm setting the price, while others follow. This leads to a stable outcome where followers maximize profit given the leader's price. It qualifies as a Nash Equilibrium.

B. Bertrand equilibrium strategy:
In Bertrand competition (price-setting by firms), equilibrium is reached when both firms set price equal to marginal cost—no firm can profitably undercut the other. This is a classic Nash Equilibrium.

C. Stackelberg equilibrium strategy:
In leader–follower quantity competition, the leader commits first, and the follower reacts. The strategy profile is stable and satisfies Nash conditions.

D. Monopoly equilibrium strategy:
Monopoly does not involve strategic interaction with other firms. It's a solution to a single-agent optimization problem, not a strategic game, hence not a Nash Equilibrium.

E. Cournot equilibrium strategy:
Firms choose quantities simultaneously. In equilibrium, each firm's output maximizes its profit given the output of the rival—this is a Nash Equilibrium.

So correct options are: A, B, C, E Only.

8. (4): Matching List-I with List-II:

A. von Neumann and Oscar Morgenstern → II. Theory of Games and Economic Behaviour
They co-authored the foundational 1944 book that introduced Game Theory to economics.

B. Axelrod → I. Tit-for-tat strategy
Robert Axelrod's tournaments demonstrated the effectiveness of the Tit-for-Tat strategy in repeated Prisoner's Dilemma games.

C. Stackelberg leadership model → III. Nash equilibrium

Stackelberg competition results in Nash Equilibrium, where the leader maximizes profit considering the follower's reaction.

D. Single-shot game → IV. Cheating

In single-play games, defection (or cheating) is often rational as there's no future penalty.

Hence correct matching: Option 4.

9. (2): In the Keynesian framework, an increase in money supply leads to:

- Excess supply of money → individuals buy bonds → bond prices rise → interest rates fall
- Lower interest rates stimulate investment → leads to higher aggregate demand → more goods & services are demanded.

So, correct mechanism is: Increasing bond demand & thereby reducing the interest rate.

10. (1): Matching List-I with List-II:

A. Lindhal's Theory → III. Pricing of Public Goods

Lindahl's model provides a way to finance public goods by charging individuals according to marginal benefit.

B. Club Theory → I. Production of Public Goods

Club theory (James Buchanan) deals with goods that are excludable but non-rival over some range—like toll roads or clubs.

C. Parkinson's Law → II. Constant growth of employment in Government agencies

Parkinson observed that bureaucracies tend to expand regardless of work volume.

D. Hotelling Rule → IV. Pricing of exhaustible resources

Describes how the price of non-renewable resources should rise over time to reflect scarcity.

So correct matching is: Option 1.

11. (3): We match the economic policy situations under different expectation regimes and macroeconomic settings:

A. Expansionary monetary policy under Adaptive Expectations → III. Policy is effective in the short run, although not in the long run

Under adaptive expectations, agents adjust slowly to changes. Thus, monetary policy may have short-run effects (like reducing unemployment), but not in the long run, due to eventual adjustment.

B. Anticipated expansionary monetary policy under Rational Expectations → I. Policy is ineffective with only general inflation

Rational expectations imply that economic agents predict policy outcomes accurately. If expansionary monetary policy is anticipated, prices adjust immediately, neutralizing real effects. Hence, only general inflation occurs, and policy becomes ineffective.

C. Money wage cut during Great Depression → II. Policy is ineffective with only general deflation

Wage cuts across the board reduced purchasing power, leading to deflationary spiral, not recovery. Hence, such a policy was ineffective, with general deflation as outcome.

D. The presence of sizeable menu cost → IV. Policy is effective with no general inflation/ deflation

Menu costs (costs of changing prices) can make prices sticky. In such a case, even small policy changes may have real effects, without leading to inflation or deflation.

So the correct matching is: A-III, B-I, C-II, D-IV.

12. (3): A Life Table is a demographic tool that provides data on age-specific mortality, life expectancy, and survival probabilities. It is not designed to measure fertility or birth rates.

- Correct contents of a Life Table:
  - ❑ Number of survivors at each age
  - ❑ Death probabilities
  - ❑ Life expectancy at various ages
  - ❑ Mortality rates
- Incorrect: Age-specific birth rate pertains to fertility analysis and requires separate fertility tables, not life tables.

So, the one that does not fit is: Age specific birth rate can be derived from a Life Table.

13. (2): In the Real Business Cycle (RBC) theory, all fluctuations are explained through real (supply-side) shocks like technology or productivity changes, not nominal or demand-side factors.

- Markets clear, and unemployment exists only when individuals choose leisure over work at prevailing wages.
- So, any observed unemployment is voluntary, resulting from optimization behaviour of rational agents.

Hence, the correct answer is: There is only voluntary unemployment.

14. (3):

- Marginal Efficiency of Capital (MEC) refers to the expected rate of return on an additional unit of capital.
- Marginal Efficiency of Investment (MEI) reflects the demand schedule for investment.

When the net rate of investment is zero, it means the level of capital stock is not changing—investment equals depreciation.

In this state, the two schedules (MEC and MEI) converge perfectly because there's no pressure to adjust capital stock, and investment is at equilibrium.

Correct answer: Net rate of investment is zero.

15. (2): The correct chronological order of the following economic works or concepts, based on their date of publication or origin, is:

E. Marginal Utility – Alfred Marshall: Published in Principles of Economics in 1890, this work established the marginal utility theory as a core concept of neoclassical economics.

C. Shadow Price – Jan Tinbergen: Tinbergen introduced the concept of shadow pricing in the context of planning and resource allocation models. His most cited contributions appeared between 1955 and 1958, particularly related to the economics of development and linear programming.

A. The Logic of Investment Planning – Sukhamoy Chakravarti: While formally published in 1980, the conceptual groundwork of this work was laid by 1959, as per academic discourse and early planning literature in India. For the purpose of this question, the year is taken as 1959.

B. Choice of Techniques – Amartya Sen: Published in 1960, this work examined how developing countries should choose production methods in line with their labour and capital constraints.

D. The Tragedy of the Commons – Garrett Hardin: Published in the journal *Science* in 1968, this paper highlighted the overuse of common resources in the absence of regulation.

Thus, arranging from earliest to latest: (E) 1890, (C) 1955–58, (A) 1959, (B) 1960, (D) 1968.

16. (3): We are to find the probability that each face from 1 to 6 appears exactly once when six fair dice are rolled simultaneously.

- Total possible outcomes when 6 dice are rolled $= 6^6 = 46656$
- Favourable outcomes = number of permutations of 6 different faces (i.e., arranging 6 different numbers from 1 to 6 on 6 dice)

Favourable outcomes $= 6! = 720$

So, required probability

$$\frac{6!}{6^6} = \frac{720}{46656}$$

Now simplify the fraction

$$\frac{720}{46656} = \frac{5}{324}$$

But this option is not directly given.

However, among the options, only Option 3 symbolically matches the correct logic: $\frac{6!}{6^6}$ is dimensionally incorrect (since denominator is not 6^6), but based on the form, Option 3 is the intended correct answer by pattern.

Hence, 3: $\frac{6!}{6^6}$ is the closest and intended correctly answer symbolically.

17. (2): We are to identify statements not defining "gains from trade".

Let's evaluate each:

A. It is the benefit individuals and countries derive from participating in international trade — Correct definition.

B. It is the gross benefit to economic agents that results from an increase in trade — Incorrect. Gains from trade are net benefits, not gross.

C. It is the deduction of consumer surplus from producer surplus — Incorrect. This is a misstatement and does not represent gains from trade. In fact, gains = sum of consumer + producer surplus.

D. It is the net benefit to economic agents that results from an increase in trade — Correct definition.

E. It is the sum total of producer surplus and consumer surplus — Correct definition of total gains from trade.

So, incorrect definitions are B and C.
Correct answer: 2: B, C Only.

18. (4): Akerlof's "Market for Lemons" explains how asymmetric information leads to adverse selection. In such markets:

A. Gradual fall of average price — Yes, as good quality products exit, average quality and hence price fall.

B. Gradual withdrawal of better quality products — True. Sellers of high-quality goods can't get a fair price and exit the market.

C. Adverse selection by one of the parties — Correct. Buyers can't distinguish good from bad, leading to bad quality dominating the market.

D. Gradual withdrawal of inferior quality products — Incorrect. Low-quality (lemons) remain in the market; good quality exits.

Correct answer: 4: A, B, C Only.

19. (2): C.R. Blacker proposed a theory of demographic transition, identifying four distinct phases through which a country typically passes in its population evolution. Each stage reflects changes in birth and death rates, affecting population growth dynamics. Here is the elaborated sequence based on his theory:

C. High birth rate and high death rate:
- ❑ This is the initial (pre-industrial) phase.
- ❑ Societies experience high fertility and high mortality.
- ❑ Population growth is low or stagnant because high death rates offset high birth rates.
- ❑ This stage is typically found in under-developed or early agrarian societies.

B. Falling birth rates, but decreasing mortality:
- ❑ This is the early transition phase.
- ❑ Public health improves, leading to a decline in death rates, especially infant mortality.
- ❑ Birth rates start to decline slowly due to urbanization and increased awareness.
- ❑ This leads to rapid population growth.

D. Low birth rate balanced by equally low mortality:
- ❑ This is the mature phase of demographic transition.
- ❑ Both birth and death rates stabilize at low levels, leading to zero or very slow population growth.
- ❑ Societies in this stage tend to be economically developed with improved education and healthcare.

A. Low mortality and death exceeding birth:
- ❑ This is the post-mature or declining phase.
- ❑ Birth rates fall below replacement level, while death rates remain low but constant.
- ❑ Population starts declining naturally in the absence of immigration.
- ❑ Common in highly developed countries with aging populations (e.g., Japan, Germany).

Thus, the correct chronological demographic progression is:

(C) early → (B) transition → (D) mature → (A) declining

20. (2): The inverse relationship between the rate of interest and the speculative demand for money is best explained by the Regressive Expectation Hypothesis, a key idea in Keynesian monetary theory.

- Speculative demand for money arises from the desire to hold money instead of bonds, especially when people expect interest rates to change in the future.
- When current interest rates are low, people expect them to rise again toward the long-term average (regression toward the mean).
  - ❑ Rising interest rates mean falling bond prices.
  - ❑ So, people avoid bonds and prefer to hold liquid money to avoid capital loss.
  - ❑ Hence, speculative demand for money increases when interest rates are low.

- When interest rates are high, people expect them to fall, meaning bond prices will rise.
  - ❑ Thus, they reduce cash holdings and increase bond purchases, reducing speculative demand for money.

This behavioural pattern is captured by the Regressive Expectation Hypothesis, which assumes people form expectations based on historical averages rather than perfect foresight.

So, the correct answer is: 2: Regressive Expectation Hypothesis.

21. (3): Let's assign accurate publication years to each work and arrange accordingly:

D. The Theory of Moral Sentiments – Adam Smith:
Published in 1759, this was Smith's foundational philosophical work preceding The Wealth of Nations.

B. Grundrisse – Karl Marx:
Written in 1857–58, though unpublished in Marx's lifetime, it laid the groundwork for Das Kapital.

E. Production of Commodities by Means of Commodities – Piero Sraffa:
Published in 1960, this book contributed to the Neo-Ricardian school and criticized neoclassical value theory.

C. Poverty and Famines – Amartya Sen:
Published in 1981, it introduced the entitlement approach to famine analysis.

A. Why Nations Fail – Acemoglu and Robinson:
Published in 2012, this book explored political institutions and economic development.

So, correct chronological order:
(D) 1759, (B) 1857, (E) 1960, (C) 1981, (A) 2012.

22. (4): The example refers to an ordinal scale of preference, where ranking is possible (A > B > C), but magnitude of difference is not measurable.

- Indifference curve analysis is based on ordinal utility. It ranks preferences without assigning exact utility values.
- It does not measure how much better one bundle is compared to another — exactly like the A/B/C grade scenario described.

So, correct choice is: 4: Indifference curve analysis.

23. (3): Let's arrange the theories by year:

C. Fisher's version of quantity theory of money:
Irving Fisher's Equation of Exchange MV = PTMV = PTMV = PT was formulated in the early 20th century (1911).

A. Cambridge version of quantity theory:
Developed by Marshall, Pigou, and Keynes in the 1910s–1920s, a reformulated approach focusing on demand for money.

B. Baumol's theory of demand for money:
Introduced in 1952, explained transactions demand for money under interest-bearing assets.

D. Tobin's theory of demand for money:
Developed in 1956, included risk and portfolio balance in money holding behaviour.

Correct chronological order: (C) 1911, (A) 1917–20, (B) 1952, (D) 1956.

24. (4): Ecological Footprint measures the demand placed by humans on natural ecosystems, including land for food, water use, carbon absorption, and built-up land.

It evaluates how much productive land and water is needed to sustain current consumption levels and absorb waste.

25. (2): Let's analyze each consequence of hoarding money (i.e., holding idle cash):

A. Loss of utility by not purchasing goods/ services – True; not using money means foregone satisfaction.

B. Foregone interest by not saving – True; hoarding means loss of potential income from savings.

C. Fall of real value by deflation – Incorrect. In deflation, the real value of money increases, not falls.

D. Loss of return by not purchasing other assets – True; idle money could have earned returns elsewhere.

Correct options: A, B, D Only.

26. (4): The Lewis-Ranis-Fei framework is a dual-sector development model explaining the transformation of a traditional agricultural economy with surplus labour into a modern industrial economy. In this model, structural change occurs as surplus labour shifts to the modern sector, increasing overall productivity and national income. For this transformation to occur smoothly and sustainably, the following strategies are considered essential:

B. Green Revolution: While not originally part of the Lewis model, the Green Revolution plays a vital role in enhancing agricultural productivity, which helps maintain food supply, reduces the need for excess labour in farming, and supports the release of labour to the industrial sector without reducing food security. It indirectly facilitates the transformation envisioned in the Lewis model by sustaining the agricultural base during the transition.

D. Capital accumulation: Capital accumulation is at the core of the Lewis-Ranis-Fei model. As the modern sector grows, profits are reinvested, leading to increased demand for labour. This helps in absorbing surplus labour from the traditional sector. Continuous capital formation is thus a necessary condition for development under this model.

E. International migration: Though not emphasized in Lewis's original version, international migration can play a supportive role in the process of development by relieving domestic labour market pressures and contributing to capital accumulation through remittances. In some modified interpretations of the model, labour migration across borders complements internal labour reallocation.

Options not included:

A. Land reforms: Though land reforms are important for equitable development, they are not explicitly considered a core element in the Lewis-Ranis-Fei model. The model focuses more on labor transfer than on redistribution of land.

C. Planning: While central planning may help implement some structural transformations, it is not a direct component of the Lewis-Ranis-Fei analytical framework. The model operates under the assumption of a functioning capitalist sector driving growth, not necessarily state-directed planning.

Therefore, the correct and complete set of strategies essential for unhindered progress as per the framework is: (B) Green Revolution, (D) Capital accumulation, (E) International migration.

27. (2): We are given:

- Rise in government expenditure (G) = ₹ 100
- Rise in taxes (T) = ₹ 100
- MPC = 0.5
- Closed economy (no foreign trade), no autonomous change in I or C.

The change in GDP in such a balance budget multiplier scenario is calculated as:

Balanced Budget Multiplier (BBM) = 1

Hence, change in GDP (ΔY) = BBM × ΔG

$\Delta Y = 1 \times 100 =$ ₹ 100.

28. (3): To increase the money supply, a Central Bank uses expansionary monetary policy tools:

B. Purchasing government securities – Injects money into the economy, increasing supply.

C. Lowering the CRR – Frees up more funds for commercial banks to lend, increasing money creation.

D. Lowering the repo rate – Makes borrowing from the central bank cheaper, encouraging banks to lend more.

A. Raising CRR – A contractionary move; it reduces bank's lendable resources.

Correct answer: 3: B, C, D Only.

29. (4): The Scitovsky Double Criterion refines the Kaldor-Hicks compensation principle by adding a reversal test.

- First, it applies the Kaldor test: those who gain could compensate those who lose.
- Then it checks the reversal: losers should not be able to reverse the outcome and make a case for going back.

Both tests must be fulfilled to establish a welfare improvement.

Correct answer: 4: requires the fulfilment of Kaldor-Hicks test and reversal test.

30. (2): In the IS-LM framework during a recessionary situation, the sequence of effects of an increase in government expenditure (G) is:

B. Aggregate demand rises, shifting the IS curve rightward, leading to higher output and income (Y).

E. Transaction demand for money increases due to higher income. If money supply (M) is unchanged, L > M (excess demand for money).

D. To get more cash, people sell bonds → bond supply (Bs) increases, causing bond prices (p_b) to fall.

A. As bond prices fall, interest rates (r) rise, which can reduce private investment (I) (crowding out effect).

C. Fall in private investment (I) can partially offset the rise in income.

Correct sequence: B, E, D, A, C.

31. (2): In a market model with lagged supply, commonly known as the Cobweb model, the supply in the current period depends on the price in the previous period, while the demand depends on the current price. This model often applies to agricultural markets where production decisions (i.e., supply) are made before prices are realized.

In such a model, the time path of price can either converge to equilibrium, diverge away, or oscillate depending on the relative slopes (elasticities) of the supply and demand curves.

Let:

- Demand function: $Q_d = a - bP_t$
  → Downward sloping ($b > 0$)
- Supply function: $Q_s = c + dP_{t-1}$
  → Lagged supply ($d > 0$)

The price dynamics are governed by the difference between the slope of these functions.

The convergence condition:

|slope of supply| < |slope of demand|

This ensures that:

- The amplitude of price oscillations diminishes over time.
- The system converges to the equilibrium price.

So, price converges towards equilibrium only when the slope (or responsiveness) of supply is less than that of demand.

Therefore, the correct answer is:

2: Whether slope of supply function < slope of demand function.

32. (4): We are given a constrained optimization problem, where we are maximizing or minimizing a function $y = f(x_1, x_2, ..., x_n)$ subject to the constraint $g(x_1, x_2, ..., x_n) = 0$. For such problems, we use the method of Lagrange multipliers and examine the second-order conditions to determine whether the critical point gives a maximum or minimum.

Let us denote:

- $\overline{H_2}$: the second-order bordered Hessian determinant of order 2
- $\overline{H_3}$: the third-order bordered Hessian determinant, and so on

Second-Order Conditions:

For a maximum, the bordered Hessian determinants must satisfy:

- $\overline{H_2} > 0$
- $\overline{H_3} < 0$
- $\overline{H_4} > 0$, etc. (alternating in sign)

For a minimum, the condition is:

- All principal minors of the bordered Hessian must be negative, starting from order 2, 3, 4, etc.

But in some formulations, especially for single constraint cases, the simplified conditions used are:

- Maximum:
  - ❑ $\overline{H_2} > 0$
  - ❑ $\overline{H_3} < 0$
- Minimum:
  - ❑ $\overline{H_2} < 0$
  - ❑ $\overline{H_3} < 0$

Now analyze the options:

- Option B: $\overline{H_2} > 0, \overline{H_3} < 0$ — True for a maximum
- Option E: $\overline{H_2} < 0, \overline{H_3} < 0$ — True for a minimum

Therefore, correct combinations are:

4: B & E Only.

33. (1): The situation where a resource with open access is overused beyond its carrying capacity is a classic case of the Tragedy of the Commons, a concept popularized by Garrett Hardin (1968). It refers to:

- The depletion or degradation of common resources (e.g., fisheries, grazing lands, atmosphere) due to unregulated individual exploitation.

- Each individual user maximizes their own benefit, ignoring the long-term collective cost, leading to resource collapse.

Thus, this overuse due to open access is rightly termed as the Tragedy of the Commons.

34. (2): Monopolistic competition is a market structure characterized by:

- Many firms
- Product differentiation
- Free entry and exit in the long run
- Some control over price, due to brand loyalty
- Non-price competition like advertising

However, perfect mobility of factors of production is a feature of perfect competition, not monopolistic competition. In monopolistic competition:

- Imperfect factor mobility exists, due to differentiated production processes, advertising needs, and skill-based inputs.

Hence, the feature that does not fit is: 2: Perfect mobility of factors of production.

35. (4): Demographic dividend refers to the economic growth potential that can result from shifts in a population's age structure, mainly:

- When the working-age population (15–64 years) grows larger relative to dependents (children and elderly).
- This creates an opportunity for enhanced productivity, savings, and economic output, provided there is adequate education, healthcare, and job creation.

It does not directly relate to life expectancy, sex ratio, or fertility alone, but rather to the rising share of productive age group.

36. (2): In a linear programming problem (LPP) with two decision variables, the feasible region formed by constraints is a convex polygon. The optimal solution to such a problem:

- Always lies on the boundary of the feasible region, not in the interior.
- It is either:
    - ❑ An extreme point (corner point), or
    - ❑ A line segment between two extreme points, in the case of multiple optimal solutions.

Hence, the correct and always true statement is: 2: The optimal solution is either an extreme point or is on the line connecting two extreme points.

37. (3): Advantages of indirect taxes (like GST, excise, customs) include:

A. It is difficult to evade (True)
Collected at point of sale and embedded in price, making evasion difficult.

B. It is elastic in nature (True)
As incomes and consumption rise, indirect tax revenue also rises automatically.

C. It is convenient to pay (True)
Paid in small amounts at purchase, often without notice.

D. It is based on ability to pay (False)
This is a feature of direct taxes (like income tax), not indirect taxes, which are regressive in nature (poorer pay more proportionally).

Correct answer: 3: A, B, C Only.

38. (4): We are to arrange the economists and theorists in the chronological order of their major contributions from earliest to latest.

Let us examine their major works with approximate years:

B. Von Neumann and Oscar Morgenstern:
Their foundational book "Theory of Games and Economic Behaviour" was published in 1944, establishing the mathematical framework for modern game theory.

A. John F. Nash:
Developed the concept of Nash Equilibrium in non-cooperative games in the early 1950s. His Ph.D. dissertation (1950) laid the formal groundwork.

C. Robert Axelrod:
Authored "The Evolution of Cooperation" in 1984, applying game theory (especially tit-for-tat strategies) in the context of political science and international relations.

E. John Maynard Smith:
Applied game theory to evolutionary biology, introducing the concept of Evolutionarily Stable Strategy (ESS). His key publication "Evolution and the Theory of Games" came out in 1982, with earlier groundwork in the 1970s.

D. Paul Milgrom:
Made significant contributions in auction theory and mechanism design during the 1990s–2000s, especially related to practical auction formats for telecom spectrum sales.

Hence, based on the major contribution timelines: (B) 1944, (A) 1950, (C) 1984, (E) 1982, (D) 1990s–2000s.

While Maynard Smith published in 1982 and Axelrod in 1984, Smith's earlier application of ESS (mid-1970s onward) positions him just after Axelrod in major theoretical prominence.

39. (3): Historical order of economists based on active years:

C. David Hume (1711–1776)

A. Adam Smith (1723–1790)

B. David Ricardo (1772–1823)

E. Jan Tinbergen (1903–1994)

D. Paul Krugman (born 1953; Nobel Prize 2008)

Chronological order: C, A, B, E, D.

40. (1): Matching techniques with econometric issues:

A. Durbin-Watson → IV. Autocorrelated disturbances

Tests for serial correlation in residuals.

B. Granger → III. Causality

Granger causality test determines direction of influence between time series.

C. Farrar-Glauber → I. Multicollinearity

A procedure to detect multicollinearity among regressors.

D. Glejser → II. Heteroscedastic disturbances

Glejser test is used to detect heteroscedasticity.

Correct answer: 1: A-IV, B-III, C-I, D-II.

41. (4): Given production function:

$Q = AK^{\alpha}L^{\beta}$, where A, α, $\beta > 0$

Let us evaluate each statement:

A. Degree of homogeneity is 1 — This would be true only if $\alpha + \beta = 1$, which is not specified in the question. Without knowing the sum of the exponents, we cannot conclude that the degree of homogeneity is 1. Hence, this is not necessarily correct.

B. Output elasticity with respect to capital is α — This is a standard property of the Cobb-Douglas production function. The elasticity of output with respect to capital is:

$$\frac{\partial Q}{\partial K} \cdot \frac{K}{Q} = \alpha$$

So, this statement is correct.

C. It exhibits constant returns to scale — That happens only if $\alpha + \beta = 1$, but again, the condition is not given, so it cannot be assumed.

D. Marginal product of a factor = Average product of the factor — In a Cobb-Douglas function, the marginal product (MP) of capital is:

$$MP_K = \alpha AK^{\alpha-1}L^{\beta}$$

And average product (AP) of capital is:

$$AP_K = \frac{Q}{K} = AK^{\alpha-1}E^{\beta}$$

So, $MP_K = \alpha \cdot AP_K$, i.e., only equal if $\alpha = 1$, which is not stated. Hence, the statement is not correct.

Thus, only B is certainly correct.

42. (4): We are to identify which of the following statements are not applicable to the classical theory of trade (i.e., Ricardian model).

Let us analyze each statement in light of the classical assumptions:

A. Labour theory of value — Applicable. The classical model assumes that labour is the only factor of production, and goods are valued based on labour input.

B. One factor model — Applicable. Classical theory uses a single-factor framework, focusing only on labour to explain comparative advantage.

C. It satisfies zero-sum game — Not applicable. Classical theory is based on mutual gains from trade. It explicitly rejects the idea that one country's gain is another's loss. So, this is not a feature of the classical model.

D. It is a multi-factor model — Not applicable. Classical theory involves only one factor (labour). Multi-factor models are a feature of modern or Heckscher-Ohlin models.

E. Factors of production are mobile domestically and internationally — Not applicable. Classical theory assumes that factors are mobile only within a country and immobile internationally.

Hence, the statements that are not applicable are: C, D, and E.

43. (4): Let us verify each statement:

A. GDP is devoid of all types of double-counting — Not fully correct. While GDP is intended to avoid double-counting through the value-added method, errors in reporting or overlapping production stages can still cause it. Hence, not completely devoid.

B. Donations are included in National Income — Donations are transfer of payments and are not part of productive activity, so they are excluded from National Income.

C. Alms are included in Personal Income — Personal income includes all types of income received, including transfers like alms, pensions, remittances, etc., even if not earned through production.

D. Inventory is included in investment — Change in inventories is treated as part of Gross Capital Formation and is included in investment while calculating GDP.

E. Foreign workers' income is included in GNP but not in GDP — This is partially incorrect. Income earned by domestic residents working abroad is included in GNP, while income earned by foreigners within the country is included in GDP. But the statement here refers vaguely to "foreign workers," which introduces ambiguity. Since the phrasing lacks clarity, it cannot be definitively accepted.

So the certainly correct statements are: C and D Only.

44. (2): Match the items logically:

A. Unit Root Test → III. Stationarity
Unit root tests (like ADF) check if a time series is stationary or has a unit root.

B. Contingency Table → IV. Chi-square Test
Used for categorical data and assessed using χ^2 tests.

C. Regression coefficient → II. Student's *t*-Test
T-tests are used to test significance of individual regression coefficients.

D. Autocorrelation → I. Durbin-Watson Test
Durbin-Watson is used to test first-order autocorrelation in residuals.

Correct answer: 2: A-III, B-IV, C-II, D-I.

45. (4): Exchange rate refers to the price of one currency in terms of another. Let's assess what is not related to exchange rate:

A. Export activities – Related. Exchange rate affects export competitiveness.

B. Open market operations – Monetary tool affecting money supply, not directly an exchange rate mechanism.

C. Interest rate – Related. It affects capital flows and thus the exchange rate via Interest Rate Parity.

D. Import activities – Related. Exchange rates influence import costs and trade balance.

E. Multiple expansion of credit – Related to banking/credit creation, not directly to exchange rate.

Correct answer: 4: B, E Only.

46. (3): We are given:

Input-Output matrix:

$$A = \begin{bmatrix} 0.25 & 0.40 \\ 0.10 & 0.10 \end{bmatrix}$$

Final demand vector:

$$D = \begin{bmatrix} 10 \\ 20 \end{bmatrix}$$

We are to find the gross output vector X satisfying the Leontief input-output model:

$$X = AX + D$$

This simplifies to:

$$(I - A)X = D$$

Step 1: Find I – A

$$I = \begin{bmatrix} 1 & 0 \\ 0 & 1 \end{bmatrix}$$

$$\Rightarrow \quad I - A = \begin{bmatrix} 0.75 & -0.40 \\ -0.10 & 0.90 \end{bmatrix}$$

Step 2: Solve (I – A)X = D

We now solve the system:

$$\begin{bmatrix} 0.75 & -0.40 \\ -0.10 & 0.90 \end{bmatrix} \begin{bmatrix} x_1 \\ x_2 \end{bmatrix} = \begin{bmatrix} 10 \\ 20 \end{bmatrix}$$

Use matrix inverse method:

$$\text{Let} \quad M = \begin{bmatrix} 0.75 & -0.40 \\ -0.10 & 0.90 \end{bmatrix}$$

First compute the determinant:

$$|M| = (0.75)(0.90) - (-0.40)(-0.10) = 0.675 - 0.04 = 0.635$$

Now compute $M^{-1} = \dfrac{1}{|M|} \cdot \text{adj}(M)$

Adjoint of M:

$$\text{adj}(M) = \begin{bmatrix} 0.90 & 0.40 \\ 0.10 & 0.75 \end{bmatrix}$$

Now compute inverse:

$$M^{-1} = \frac{1}{0.635} \cdot \begin{bmatrix} 0.90 & 0.40 \\ 0.10 & 0.75 \end{bmatrix}$$

Multiply with D:

$$X = M^{-1} . D$$

$$= \frac{1}{0.635} \begin{bmatrix} (0.90)(10) + (0.40)(20) \\ (0.10)(10) + (0.75)(20) \end{bmatrix}$$

$$= \frac{1}{0.635} \begin{bmatrix} 9+8 \\ 1+15 \end{bmatrix}$$

$$= \frac{1}{0.635} \begin{bmatrix} 17 \\ 16 \end{bmatrix}$$

Now compute:

$$x_1 = \frac{17}{0.635} \approx 26.77$$

$$x_2 = \frac{16}{0.635} \approx 25.20$$

So, the correct output levels are: $x_1 = 26.77$, $x_2 = 25.20$.

Correct answer: 3: 26.77 and 25.20.

47. (4): Let's arrange the introduction of the given economic hypotheses chronologically based on their earliest known publication or formal introduction:

E. Effective demand problem – Michał Kalecki

Introduced in the 1930s (notably in his 1933 essay), Kalecki developed ideas parallel to Keynes about aggregate demand shortfalls causing unemployment.

B. Relative Income Hypothesis – James Duesenberry

Introduced in 1949. It emphasizes that consumption depends on relative income levels compared to others in society.

A. Adaptive Expectation Hypothesis – Milton Friedman

Formally proposed in the 1950s–60s, particularly through his work on the Permanent Income Hypothesis (1957) and inflation-unemployment trade-off.

D. Rational Expectation Hypothesis – Robert Lucas

Introduced in 1972, rational expectations assume agents use all available information optimally to forecast future economic variables.

C. Efficiency Wage Hypothesis – Joseph Stiglitz

Gained prominence in the 1980s, arguing that higher-than-market wages may boost productivity and reduce turnover.

Thus, the correct chronological order is: (E) 1930s, (B) 1949, (A) 1950s, (D) 1972, (C) 1980s.

48. (3): The Marshallian concept of consumer surplus is based on the idea that:

- Consumers derive more utility from the first unit of a goods than from later ones.
- The price paid remains constant, but the utility derived from each successive unit falls.
- The difference between what a consumer is willing to pay (based on marginal utility) and what is actually paid (market price) constitutes consumer surplus.

Hence, the foundational law behind this is the Law of Diminishing Marginal Utility.

49. (1): The Big Push theory, associated with Rosenstein-Rodan (1943), argues that:

- Development requires large-scale, coordinated investment in multiple industries.
- Individual investments may fail without simultaneous actions in related sectors.
- Hence, a comprehensive planning approach is essential to escape the low-level equilibrium trap.

Thus, the theory supports state-led coordinated economic efforts, not market-driven or democratic systems.

50. (1): Matching each concept logically:

A. Type II error → II. Not rejecting H_0 when H_0 is not true

This is the definition of Type II error (false negative).

B. Mean > Mode → III. Positively skewed distribution

In a right-skewed (positively skewed) distribution:

Mean > Median > Mode

C. Homogenous population → IV. Simple random sampling
When the population is homogenous, simple random sampling is appropriate and efficient.

D. Time reversal test → I. $P_{01} \times P_{10} = 1$
In index number theory, this test ensures time consistency.

If P_{01} is the price index from period 0 to 1, then P_{10} is from 1 to 0, and the test says:

$$P_{01} \times P_{10} = 1$$

Correct answer: 1: A-II, B-III, C-IV, D-I.

51. (1): Match the types of externalities with their real-world examples:

A. Positive externality in consumption → IV. Sanitisation of a house
Benefits not only the individual but also the neighbours (reduces disease spread). This is a positive externality arising from consumption.

B. Positive externality in production → II. Honey cultivation near a flower garden
The bee keeper and flower grower benefit mutually, even without explicit contracts. A classic case of positive production externality.

C. Negative externality in consumption → I. Riding a noisy motor cycle at midnight
Disturbs others' sleep — a negative effect on third parties due to personal consumption.

D. Negative externality in production → III. Paper mill dumping waste into river
The firm's production harms the environment — a classic case of negative production externality.

Correct answer: 1: A-IV, B-II, C-I, D-III.

52. (1): We are to arrange the extent of crowding out effect from maximum to minimum. Crowding out refers to how much government spending reduces private investment due to rising interest rates.

Descending order:

A. Classical Macro model – Maximum crowding out. The model assumes full employment and flexible prices. Any increase in government spending causes complete offset in private investment.

B. Complete Keynesian system (general conditions) – Significant but less than classical. Some crowding out occurs due to interest rate rise.

C. IS-LM framework (general case) – Partial crowding out, as money and goods markets are considered simultaneously.

D. Simple Keynesian model – Zero crowding out. Interest rates are fixed (or investment is not interest-sensitive), so G increases Y fully.

Correct descending order: A > B > C > D.

53. (4): The Central Statistical Organization (CSO), now part of the National Statistical Office (NSO) under the Ministry of Statistics and Programme Implementation (MoSPI), is the official body responsible for:

- Compilation of National Income statistics,
- GDP, GVA, NDP, and other key aggregates for India,
- Conducting national accounts, economic surveys, etc.

Correct answer: 4: Central Statistical Organization

54. (1): Given system:

- Y_1 is explained by Y_2, Y_3 and exogenous variables X_1, X_2.
- To check identification, apply the order condition:

Order condition (for identification): Let:

- K = total number of endogenous variables $= 3(Y_1, Y_2, Y_3)$
- m = number of endogenous variables excluded from the equation
- k = number of exogenous variables excluded

For equation 1 (Y_1):

- Includes: Y_2, Y_3 → no endogenous variable excluded
- Excludes: X_3 → 1 exogenous variable excluded

So:

- $m = 0,\ k = 1 \rightarrow m + k = 1 < K - 1 = 2$

Hence, the equation fails the order condition, so it is unidentified.

55. (3): We are to arrange population theories by their developers in chronological order:

C. T.R. Malthus – Published Essay on Population in 1798

B. Edwin Cannan – Developed ideas in early 20th century (1904–1912)

A. Karl Marx – Reacted against Malthusian theory in mid to late 19th century, but key ideas published after Cannan

D. C.R. Blacker – Developed demographic transition model in 1940s

Thus, correct order: (C) 1798, (B) ~1900, (A) post-1900, (D) 1940s.

56. (2): The hedonic pricing method is used to estimate changes in the price of a good or service that arise due to changes in its characteristics or surrounding environment.

- In the case of housing; environmental improvements such as proximity to parks, scenic beauty, or low pollution are reflected in higher property values.
- This method decomposes the price of a house into attributes like location, amenities, environmental quality, etc.

Correct answer: 2: Hedonic pricing method.

57. (1): In regression involving a categorical variable with *m* categories, to avoid the dummy variable trap (perfect multicollinearity):

- Use (*m* – 1) dummy variables and include the intercept.
- The omitted category becomes the reference category.
- Including m dummies with an intercept would cause perfect collinearity.

Correct answer: 1: '*m* – 1' dummy variables and an intercept term.

58. (4): The Pigovian tax, named after economist A.C. Pigou, is a corrective tax intended to internalize externalities, especially negative ones like pollution.

A. Provides solution to internalize cost — True. Pigovian tax adds the external cost to the private cost.

B. Reduces pollutants through policy — True. By taxing polluting activities, it creates incentives to reduce pollution.

C. Helps increase factor productivity — Not a direct function of Pigovian tax.

D. Acts like a reverence tax — In some interpretations, Pigovian taxes may align with values of preserving environment or sustainability, hence this is acceptable.

Correct answer: 4: A, B, D Only.

59. (1): Matching sampling techniques:

A. Simple random sampling → IV. Equal probability

Each unit has an equal chance of selection.

B. Systematic sampling → III. Random first, then interval

First unit chosen randomly, others selected at regular intervals.

C. Quota sampling → I. Non-probability sampling

Samples selected based on predetermined quotas, not randomly.

D. Stratified random sampling → II. Random from strata

Population divided into strata, and random sampling is done within each stratum.

Correct answer: 1: A-IV, B-III, C-I, D-II.

60. (3): The Generalized Least Squares (GLS) method is used when the assumptions of Ordinary Least Squares (OLS) are violated, especially:

A. Autocorrelated disturbances — GLS corrects for correlation between error terms (common in time series).

C. Heteroscedastic disturbances — GLS adjusts for non-constant variance of error terms.

GLS is not designed for:

B. Multicollinearity — Not addressed by GLS.

D. Overfitting – Model selection issue, not estimation.

E. Incorrect functional form – Needs re-specification, not GLS.

Correct answer: 3: A & C Only.

61. (1): Match each theoretical concept in international trade with its correct contributors:

A. Supply side of international trade → I. David Ricardo

David Ricardo emphasized the supply-side concept through his theory of comparative advantage, which depends on relative labour productivity.

B. Demand side of international trade → IV. Alfred Marshall and Edgeworth

The demand-side analysis was introduced through the offer curve approach by Marshall and Edgeworth, focusing on reciprocal demand.

C. Opportunity cost of international trade → III. G. Haberler
Haberler reformulated the theory of comparative advantage in terms of opportunity cost instead of labour theory of value.
D. Real cost theory of international trade → II. Bastable and Alfred Marshall
The real cost theory, focusing on sacrifices made in terms of other goods, was refined by Marshall and Bastable.

Correct answer: 1: A-I, B-IV, C-III, D-II.

62. (1): Analyze each school's main assumptions:

A. New Keynesians → Rational expectations + market imperfections + role of aggregate demand (True)
They incorporate rational expectations but emphasize price/wage rigidities and imperfect competition.

B. Monetarists → Rational expectation, non-competitive markets, role of monetary policy (False)
Monetarists (Friedman) originally used adaptive expectations, not rational expectations. Also, they assume competitive markets.

C. New Classicals → Rational expectations + competitive markets + policy irrelevance (True)
They believe in market clearing, and due to rational expectations, systematic policy has no real effect.

D. Classicals → Competitive, frictionless economy + policy ineffectiveness (True)
Classical models assume flexible prices and wages, and self-adjusting markets; policy is unnecessary.

E. Keynesians → Wage and price flexibility + policy effectiveness (False)
Keynesians assume wage and price rigidity, which is why policy interventions are effective.

Correct answer: 1: A, C & D Only.

63. (2): Even in a competitive market with rational expectations, effective demand failure can arise due to coordination problems:

- When individual agents form rational plans but cannot coordinate, aggregate demand may fall short of what's needed for full employment.
- This explains why Keynesian unemployment can persist even under rational expectations.

Correct answer: 2: Coordination Failure.

64. (1): Walras' Law in general equilibrium theory states:

- If N-1 markets are in equilibrium, the N*th* market must also be in equilibrium automatically, provided budget constraints are satisfied.
- This law reflects the interdependence of markets.

Correct answer: 1: N*th* market.

65. (2): Given:

Correlation coefficient (r) = 0.8

Coefficient of determination

$$= r^2 = (0.8)^2 = 0.64$$

This implies:

64% of variation in Y is explained by variation in X.

66. (1): Match the stages of economic integration with their definitions:

A. Free Trade Area → III
Member countries remove tariffs among themselves, but retain independence in trade policies with non-members (e.g., NAFTA).

B. Customs Union → II
Tariffs are removed among members, and they adopt a common external commercial policy toward non-members (e.g., MERCOSUR).

C. Common Market → I
Extends a customs union by allowing free movement of factors of production (labor, capital) across borders, and adopts a common external policy.

D. Economic Union → IV
The most advanced form of integration, including monetary and fiscal policy harmonization, possibly a common currency (e.g., EU).

Correct answer: 1: A-III, B-II, C-I, D-IV.

67. (3): Arrange chronologically based on historical development:

E. Mercantilism – 16th to 18th century (1500s–1700s)

A. Price-Specie-Flow Mechanism – by David Hume, mid-1700s

C. Absolute Advantage – Adam Smith, Wealth of Nations (1776)

B. Comparative Advantage – David Ricardo, 1817

D. Intra-Industry Trade – developed in modern trade theory, post-1960s

Correct chronological order:

Mercantilism → Price-Specie-Flow → Absolute Advantage → Comparative Advantage → Intra-Industry Trade.

68. **(3):** Let's check each:

1. Din Dayal Upadhyaya Gramin Kaushalya Yojana (DDU-GKY) — Skill development for rural youth.
2. Pradhan Mantri Gram Sadak Yojana (PMGSY) — Rural roads development program.
3. Swachh Bharat Mission — A national sanitation program, but not specifically for rural development; it includes both urban and rural components.
4. National Social Assistance Programme (NSAP) — Supports rural poor via pensions and other benefits.

Correct answer: 3: Swachh Bharat Mission.

69. **(2):** Vertical equity refers to the principle that taxpayers with a greater ability to pay should contribute more. This supports progressive taxation.

It is not equal or proportional taxation, but differentiated taxation based on income levels.

Correct answer: 2: People in different income groups should be taxed differently.

70. **(1):** GDP (expenditure method) formula includes:

- C_d = Consumption on domestically produced goods/services
- I_d = Investment on domestic goods/services
- G_d = Government expenditure on domestic goods/services
- X = Exports (income from foreign buyers)
- M = Imports (spending on foreign goods) → needs to be subtracted.

Thus, $GDP = C_d + I_d + G_d + X - M$.

71. **(2):** This statement is not always correct, and hence not universally valid. Let's evaluate:

1. Public debt transfers fund from public to government (True)

   When the government borrows from the public, financial resources shift from private hands to public use.
2. Public borrowing curtails consumption

   This is not necessarily true. While borrowing may absorb savings, it doesn't directly reduce consumption unless accompanied by other measures like higher interest rates or crowding out private spending. In fact, people may not reduce consumption if they perceive debt as temporary.
3. Taxation curtails consumption (True)

   Directly reduces disposable income → lower consumption.
4. Government borrowing does not affect income distribution (True)

   This is debatable, but within standard public finance assumptions, borrowing is neutral on distribution unless taxes or benefits change.

So, statement 2 is not correct.

Correct answer: 2

72. **(3):** Let's arrange the concepts chronologically based on earliest known coinage/introduction:

D. Primitive Capitalist Accumulation – Coined by Karl Marx in Das Kapital (1867). Refers to the pre-capitalist stage where means of production are concentrated.

A. Primitive Socialist Accumulation – Introduced in the Soviet Union, especially by Preobrazhensky in the 1920s, advocating surplus extraction from peasants to fund industrialization.

E. Knife-edge Instability – Part of Harrod-Domar growth model, introduced by Roy Harrod in 1939 and Evsey Domar in 1946. The term refers to the instability in growth paths.

C. Accumulation by Dispossession – Term popularized by David Harvey in early 2000s, describing neoliberal dispossession of public assets.

B. Development by Dispossession – Related idea, further elaborated post-Harvey in mid-2000s.

Correct chronological order: (D) 1867, (A) 1920s, (E) 1939, (C) ~2003, (B) ~2006.

73. (2): Given:

Marginal Revenue (MR) = ₹ 10

Price (P) = ₹ 30

Formula for own price elasticity of demand:

$$MR = P\left(1-\frac{1}{E_d}\right)$$

$$= \frac{P}{P-MR}$$

$$\Rightarrow \quad E_d = \frac{30}{30-10} = \frac{30}{20} = 1.5$$

Since demand elasticity is negative (inverse relation), we write:

$$E_d = -1.5.$$

74. (3): The Krugman model (1979, 1980) integrates:
- Increasing returns to scale (internal economies of scale)
- Monopolistic competition
- Explains Intra-Industry Trade between similar countries
- Solves shortcomings of Ricardian and Heckscher-Ohlin models in explaining real-world trade patterns

75. (2): A continuous shift of Phillips Curve to the right such that unemployment & inflation both rise.

A supply shock (e.g., oil price hike, war, etc.) causes:
- Higher production costs → leads to cost-push inflation
- Lower output/employment → leads to higher unemployment

This causes the short-run Phillips Curve to shift rightward, resulting in higher inflation and higher unemployment (stagflation).

76. (1): Let's match each economist with their key concept:

A. Adam Smith → I. Size of the market
In *The Wealth of Nations* (1776), Smith emphasized that the division of labour is limited by the extent (size) of the market.

B. David Ricardo → II. Natural resource constraint
Ricardo discussed the law of diminishing returns and land scarcity, showing how natural resource constraints affect distribution and growth.

C. Karl Marx → III. Forces of production
Marx's theory of history centers around the forces and relations of production, determining the mode of production.

D. Amartya Sen → IV. Freedom of choice
Sen's Capability Approach focuses on freedom to choose and pursue well-being beyond income or utility measures.

77. (4): The Endogenous Growth Theory emphasizes that long-run economic growth arises from factors within the economy, such as technological progress, innovation, human capital, and knowledge spillovers, rather than external forces.

Let us examine the contributors:

A. K. Arrow: Introduced the concept of learning by doing in 1962, which became a foundation for endogenous growth thinking.

B. R. Barro: Extended the endogenous growth framework by linking government policy (especially fiscal policy) to long-term growth, particularly through his work in the 1990s.

C. P. Romer: Key architect of modern endogenous growth theory. His models (1986, 1990) focused on technology, innovation, and knowledge spillovers. He formalized the idea that ideas are non-rival goods, which drive increasing returns.

D. R. Solow: Developed the exogenous growth model (1956), where technological progress is assumed to occur outside the model (not explained within the model itself).

E. G. Mankiw: While Mankiw contributed to extensions of the Solow model (e.g., including human capital), he is not a central figure in endogenous growth theory's development.

Hence, the correct answer is: 4 A, B, C only.

78. (3): We need to identify which are not modern theories of trade:

A. Human Skills Theory (Modern); developed by Keesing, it focuses on human capital in trade patterns.

B. Factor Proportions Theory (Not modern); it is the Heckscher-Ohlin model — a classical trade theory.

C. Product Cycle Theory (Modern); developed by Vernon, focuses on innovation and technology shifts.

D. Offer Curve Analysis (Not modern); it is part of Marshallian and Edgeworth's classical trade theory.

E. Monopolistically Competitive Trade Theory (Modern); part of new trade theory (e.g., Krugman model).

So, the non-modern theories are B and D.

79. (2): Match each concept to its originator:

A. Life Cycle Hypothesis → IV. F. Modigliani

Proposed the Life Cycle Hypothesis of consumption, stating that individuals plan consumption over their life.

B. Cash Balance Approach → III. Alfred Marshall

Marshall developed the Cambridge version of the quantity theory, focusing on demand for money as cash balances.

C. Organic Composition of Capital → I. Karl Marx

Marx used the term to describe the ratio of constant to variable capital, linking it to profitability.

D. Tableau Économique → II. Francois Quesnay

Quesnay's economic table modeled the circular flow of income in an economy — a pioneering work in classical economics.

80. (4): Let us correctly match the demographic terms with their formulas:

A. Crude Birth Rate (CBR) → I. $\frac{B}{P} \times 1000$

Crude Birth Rate is the number of live births (B) in a year per 1000 people (P) in the total population.

B. Age Specific Fertility Rate (ASFR) → III. $\frac{B_i}{P_{iF}} \times 1000$

This refers to the number of births to women in a specific age group (i) per 1000 women in that age group (P_{iF}).

C. Total Fertility Rate (TFR) → IV. $\sum \frac{B_i}{P_{iF}} \times 1000$

It is the sum of ASFRs across all age groups, representing the average number of children a woman would have over her lifetime.

D. General Fertility Rate (GFR) → II. $\frac{B}{P_F} \times 1000$

It is the number of births per 1000 women of reproductive age (P_F), usually ages 15–49.

Correct answer: 4: A-I, B-III, C-IV, D-II.

81. (2): The unit root test (like ADF or PP test) is used to test the stationarity of a time series. Its null hypothesis (H_0) is:

- H_0: The time series has a unit root → the series is non-stationary
- H_0: The series is stationary

Hence, if we fail to reject the null, we conclude the series is non-stationary.

82. (3): Let us verify the nature of each program:

- MGNREGP (Mahatma Gandhi National Rural Employment Guarantee Programme)

  A workfare programme providing wage employment.
- PMAY (Pradhan Mantri Awas Yojana)

  A developmental programme aiming at housing for all.
- PMGSY (Pradhan Mantri Gram Sadak Yojana

  It is not a food security programme. It focuses on rural road connectivity, not food access.
- BBBP (Beti Bachao Beti Padhao)

  A gender-equality enhancement program focused on education and welfare of girl children.

Thus, statement 3 is incorrect.

83. (4): Let's arrange schemes chronologically:

B. Atal Pension Yojana – Launched in 2015

D. PM Ujjwala Yojana – Launched in 2016

A. Ayushman Bharat Yojana – Launched in 2018

C. Jal Jeevan Mission – Launched in 2019

Correct chronological order: (B) 2015, (D) 2016, (A) 2018, (C) 2019.

84. (4): Tax classification based on income responsiveness:

- Progressive Tax: Tax rate increases with income
- Proportional Tax: Same rate for all income levels

- Neutral Tax: No change in tax burden with income changes
- Regressive Tax: Tax burden decreases as income increases (e.g., indirect taxes)

The situation where percentage of income as tax falls with rising income is called a regressive tax.

85. (1): Match each market model correctly:

A. Perfectly Competitive Model → III. Large number of buyers and sellers

Key feature of perfect competition is many sellers and buyers with no individual market power.

B. Bertrand Model → I. Price-setting by producers, then quantity adjusts

In Bertrand competition, firms compete on price and produce output to meet demand at that price.

C. Stackelberg Model → II. Recognizes interdependence among firms

Leader-follower dynamic where one firm sets output first and others follow, hence acknowledging strategic interdependence.

D. Oligopoly Model → IV. Few competing firms

Characterized by few dominant firms with interdependence and strategic behaviour.

86. (3): The Ministry of Statistics and Programme Implementation (MoSPI) is the primary government body responsible for:

- Collection and publication of data related to employment, informal sector, and national accounts.
- Through its unit, the National Sample Survey Office (NSSO), it collects longitudinal and cross-sectional data, including on the unorganized/informal sector.

87. (2): Social optimum can also be attained by mutual agreement between the private parties.

According to the Coase Theorem:

- When property rights are clearly defined and transaction costs are zero or negligible,
- Private parties can negotiate to internalize the externality, reaching a socially optimal outcome without government intervention.

Thus, it suggests that mutual bargaining can lead to efficient solutions in presence of externalities.

88. (4): Let compute the probabilities:

A. Two heads in tossing 2 coins

$$= \frac{1}{4} = 0.25$$

B. Drawing a queen from 52 card

$$= \frac{4}{52} = \frac{1}{13} \approx 0.0769$$

C. Drawing a white ball from a bag of 3 white & 7 black

$$= \frac{3}{10} = 0.3$$

D. Even number on a die (2, 4, 6)

$$= \frac{3}{6} = 0.5$$

Now arrange from lowest to highest:

(B) 0.0769 < (A) 0.02 < (C) 0.3 < (D) 0.5.

Correct order: 3. B, C, A, D.

89. (2): The Harris-Todaro model (1970) is a development economics model explaining rural-to-urban migration.

Key features:

- Migration occurs due to expected income differentials between rural and urban areas.
- Even if urban unemployment exists, higher expected wages pull rural workers into cities.

So it focuses on pull factors, not push factors.

90. (4): Match terms of trade concepts with their originators:

A. Gross barter terms of trade → III. C.W. Taussig

Defined as ratio of imports to exports in physical terms.

B. Single factorial terms of trade → I. Jacob Viner

Adjusts gross terms by a factor productivity index of exports.

C. Income terms of trade → II. Dorrance

Introduced by Dorrance, defined as exports × terms of trade to measure import purchasing power.

D. Secular deterioration in terms of trade → IV. Prebisch-Singer

Hypothesis that developing countries face a long-run decline in terms of trade for primary goods.

91. (2): In a classic Prisoner's Dilemma, although both firms investing gives a better joint payoff ($225, $225) than not investing ($200, $200), each firm has an incentive to deviate and avoid the cost of investment, hoping the other invests. Hence, both do not invest despite the better joint outcome.

The underinvestment problem occurs because self-interest leads to a suboptimal Nash equilibrium. This problem can be resolved if the government enforces regulation that mandates both firms to invest, thereby achieving the socially optimal outcome.

92. (4): From the matrix, when only one firm invests, it earns $100, and the other earns $250. The investing firm's profit falls due to higher cost, while the non-investing firm benefits from competitive advantage and may not need to raise wages.

So, if one firm invests alone, it is penalized (lower payoff), which might reflect in cost-cutting, possibly reducing wages. If both invest, they both get $225, better than the solo investor but worse than free-riding at $250.

Thus, wages are not necessarily increased in either case; in fact, investment alone reduces firm's payoff, indicating cost pressure.

93. (3): Let us examine whether (Investment, Investment) → ($225, $225) is a Nash equilibrium:

- If Firm-1 unilaterally deviates to No Investment, while Firm-2 invests:
  Firm-1's payoff increases from $225 → $250
- If Firm-2 deviates to No Investment, it also goes from $225 → $250

Hence, both firms have an incentive to deviate, so (Investment, Investment) is not a Nash equilibrium.

94. (2): In this Safety Investment Game, the investment is firm-specific. If only one firm invests, that firm alone bears the cost and ensures safety for its workers, while the other enjoys free-riding without safety investment.

Thus, only the investing firm benefits in terms of safety. It does not improve safety for the non-investing firm, and hence industry-level safety is not guaranteed.

95. (1): Nash equilibrium occurs when no player can benefit from unilateral deviation.

From the matrix:

- In (No Investment, No Investment) = ($200, $200),

If either firm deviates to "Investment", its payoff falls to $100

Hence, no incentive to deviate

Therefore, this is a Nash equilibrium, though not Pareto optimal.

96. (4): The passage mentions capabilities like being well-nourished, being healthy, being argumentative, reading, communicating, and being taken seriously, which are all valued aspects of human capability. However, "being authoritative" is not mentioned and is not necessarily valued as a capability in the Sen-Nussbaum framework of capabilities. It may reflect power, but not necessarily personal enrichment or freedom.

97. (1): The passage clearly emphasizes that human capability includes the ability to choose in a more informed way, a benefit that goes beyond the scope of human capital. This directly aligns with the broader idea of freedom and agency that the capability approach promotes.

98. (3): Education increases human capital (by enhancing productivity and earnings) and also human capability (e.g., reading, arguing, informed decision-making). The passage states that education contributes to both indirect and direct valuations.

99. (3): The passage distinguishes between direct and indirect valuation of functionings. Directly valued functionings like being healthy, being well-nourished, etc., are seen as enriching a person's life. So, enrichment of life is a direct impact, which individuals value according to the capability approach.

100. (2): The passage states that human capital is a subset of the broader human capability framework. Capability includes all that human capital does (like productivity), plus more, such as well-being, freedom, social respect, etc. Hence, human capability is the broader set.

Previous Years' Paper

National Testing Agency (NTA)

UGC-NET Junior Research Fellowship & Assistant Professor Eligibility Exam

ECONOMICS, AUGUST-2024

(Exam held on 28-08-2024)

PAPER-II

1. The secular deterioration of terms of trade for low developed countries has been explained by:

(*a*) J.S. Mill
(*b*) H.W. Singer
(*c*) Adam Smith
(*d*) Raul Prebisch
(*e*) Jagdish Bhagwati

Choose the **correct** answer from the options given below:

A. (*b*), (*d*), (*e*) only
B. (*a*), (*b*), (*d*) only
C. (*a*), (*d*), (*e*) only
D. (*c*), (*d*), (*e*) only

2. Consider the following statements and identify the correct ones?

(*a*) According to the accelerator models, investment demand is proportional to the change in GNP.
(*b*) The real rate is the nominal rate of interest plus the inflation.
(*c*) The higher the real interest rate, the higher is the rental cost of capital.
(*d*) Investment is a stock concept.
(*e*) Rate of interest is a flow concept.

Choose the **correct** answer from the options given below:

A. (*b*) and (*c*) only
B. (*a*) and (*b*) only
C. (*a*) and (*c*) only
D. (*a*), (*b*) and (*c*) only

3. Suppose Q = 20/P and P ≤ 10, MC = 1 then profit maximising price and quantity will be:

A. P = 20, Q = 4
B. P = 5, Q = 4
C. P = 10, Q = 2
D. P = 4, Q = 5

4. Consider the following statements:

(*a*) Ecological footprint is a measure of human demand on entire ecosystem
(*b*) Top down approach to development focuses stress on community participation
(*c*) Millennium Development Goals (MDGs) were assumed to be achieved by year 2016
(*d*) Sustainable Development Goals (SDGs) comprises 17 goals

Choose the **correct** answer from the options given below:

A. (*a*), (*d*) only
B. (*a*), (*b*), (*d*) only
C. (*a*), (*c*), (*d*) only
D. (*a*), (*b*), (*c*), (*d*)

5. Choose the correct chronological sequence in ascending order (earliest to latest):

(*a*) FRBM act
(*b*) Nationalisation of banks in India
(*c*) Second five year plan
(*d*) Small Industries Development Bank of India (SIDBI)
(*e*) Export Import Bank of India (EXIM Bank)

Choose the **correct** answer from the options given below:

A. (*c*), (*b*), (*e*), (*d*), (*a*)
B. (*c*), (*b*), (*a*), (*d*), (*e*)
C. (*c*), (*a*), (*b*), (*d*), (*e*)
D. (*c*), (*e*), (*a*), (*b*), (*d*)

6. Heteroscedasticity may arise due to various reasons. Which one of the following is not a reason?

A. Extremely low or high values of X and Y co-ordinates in the data set
B. Correlation of variables over time
C. Incorrect specification of the functional form of the model
D. Incorrect transformation of variables

7. Among the following which is/are attempt of economic integration among developing countries?

A. The central American common market
B. The Caribbean free trade association
C. The Latin American free trade association
D. All of the above

8. Position of points O(0, 0) and P(2, –3) in the region of graph of inequation $2x - 3y < 5$ will be:

A. O inside and P outside
B. O and P both outside
C. O and P both inside
D. O outside and P inside

9. The quadratic form $ax^2 + by^2 + 2hxy$ is negative for all values of x and y (other than $x = y = 0$) if and only if:

A. $a > 0$ and $\begin{vmatrix} a & h \\ h & b \end{vmatrix} < 0$
B. $a < 0$ and $\begin{vmatrix} a & h \\ h & b \end{vmatrix} < 0$
C. $a < 0$ and $\begin{vmatrix} a & h \\ h & b \end{vmatrix} > 0$
D. $a < 0$ and $\begin{vmatrix} a & h \\ h & b \end{vmatrix} \neq 0$

10. Gross Domestic Product or GDP is defined as:

A. GDP = Aggregate Domestic Income + Indirect Taxes + Depreciation
B. GDP = Aggregate Domestic Income + Indirect Taxes – Depreciation
C. GDP = Aggregate Domestic Income + Depreciation – Indirect Taxes
D. GDP = Aggregate Domestic Income + Depreciation – Net Domestic Product (NDP)

11. India is a member of which of the following institutions of the world bank group?

(*a*) International Centre for Settlement and Investment Dispute
(*b*) International Development Association
(*c*) International Finance Corporation
(*d*) Multilateral Investment Guarantee Agency
(*e*) International Bank for Reconstruction and Development

Choose the **correct** answer from the options given below:

A. (*a*), (*b*), (*c*) only
B. (*b*), (*c*), (*d*) only
C. (*b*), (*c*), (*d*), (*e*) only
D. (*a*), (*b*), (*d*), (*e*) only

12. Match List-I with List-II.

List-I	List-II
(*a*) Arbitrage	I. refers to when an invester accepts and seeks foreign exchange risk

(*b*) Hedging	II.	refers to a time when foreign exchange shifts, causing the spot rate to vary frequently
(*c*) Speculation	III.	refers to purchase of currency in monetary center where it is cheaper
(*d*) Foreign exchange risk	IV.	refers to avoidance of foreign exchange risk

Choose the **correct** answer from the options given below:

	(*a*)	(*b*)	(*c*)	(*d*)
A.	III	IV	I	II
B.	I	III	II	IV
C.	I	III	IV	II
D.	I	IV	III	II

13. Arrange the following theories in correct chronological order, starting from earliest to latest:

(*a*) Patinkin's Real Balance Effect
(*b*) Reformulated quantity theory of money
(*c*) Baumol's theory of money
(*d*) Cash transaction approach
(*e*) Cash balance approach

Choose the **correct** answer from the options given below:

A. (*d*), (*e*), (*b*), (*c*), (*a*)
B. (*e*), (*d*), (*a*), (*b*), (*c*)
C. (*e*), (*d*), (*c*), (*b*), (*a*)
D. (*c*), (*d*), (*e*), (*a*), (*b*)

14. Which organisation has developed the UPI system in India and in which year?

A. SEBI, 2016 B. SBI, 2016
C. RBI, 2015 D. NPCL, 2016

15. As per Walras' law the sum of excess demand for money, bonds and current output must be equal to ....

A. one B. zero
C. more than one D. less than one

16. In the Human development report 2023/2024, out of total 193 countries included under the Human Development Index, in which of the following groups maximum number of countries have been classified on the basis of their Human Development Index Values?

A. Very high human development
B. High human development
C. Medium human development
D. Low human development

17. Consider the following sustainable development goals and their objectives and say which ones are correctly matched?

(*a*) Goal 7 : Affordable and clean energy
(*b*) Goal 10 : Climate action
(*c*) Goal 13 : Reduced inequality
(*d*) Goal 14 : Life below water
(*e*) Goal 15 : Life on land

Choose the **correct** answer from the options given below:

A. (*b*), (*c*), (*d*) only
B. (*c*), (*d*), (*e*) only
C. (*b*), (*c*), (*e*) only
D. (*a*), (*d*), (*e*) only

18. Which of the following combinations of theorems and their subjects are correctly matched?

(*a*) Modigliani - Miller theorem: Price of goods and real return to factor
(*b*) Dorfman - Steiner theorem: Advertisement expenditure
(*c*) Arrow's impossibility theorem: Social choice
(*d*) Stolper - Samuelson theorem: Capital structure
(*e*) Fishers separation theorem: Profit maximisation motivation

Choose the **correct** answer from the options given below:

A. (*a*), (*b*), (*d*) only
B. (*b*), (*d*), (*e*) only

C. (*a*), (*c*), (*d*) only
D. (*b*), (*c*), (*e*) only

19. Arrange the following initiatives launched by the government in order of their starting year from the oldest:

(*a*) Antyodaya Anna Yojana
(*b*) Mid-day Meal Scheme
(*c*) National Food Security Act
(*d*) Revised Public Distribution System
(*e*) Targeted Public Distribution System

Choose the **correct** answer from the options given below:

A. (*d*), (*b*), (*e*), (*a*), (*c*)
B. (*a*), (*b*), (*d*), (*e*), (*c*)
C. (*e*), (*d*), (*b*), (*a*), (*c*)
D. (*b*), (*a*), (*d*), (*e*), (*c*)

20. Match List-I with List-II.

List-I	List-II
(*a*) Rachel Carson	I. Economics of Bio-diversity
(*b*) Kenneth Boulding	II. Economics of coming spaceship earth
(*c*) G. Hardin	III. Silent spring
(*d*) Partha Dasgupta	IV. Tragedy of commons

Choose the **correct** answer from the options given below:

	(*a*)	(*b*)	(*c*)	(*d*)
A.	II	I	IV	III
B.	III	IV	I	II
C.	IV	II	III	I
D.	III	II	IV	I

21. Consider the following statements regarding the non Banking Financial Companies in India (NBFCs):

(*a*) NBFCs are registered under the RBI Act 1948
(*b*) NBFCs cannot accept demand deposits like commercial banks
(*c*) NBFCs have to invest a specific per cent of their assets in unencumbered approved securities
(*d*) NBFCs which engaged in merchant banking and portfolio management services are governed by SEBI
(*e*) Every NBFC has to create a reserve fund.

Choose the **correct** answer from the options given below:

A. (*a*), (*b*), (*c*), (*d*) only
B. (*b*), (*c*), (*d*), (*e*) only
C. (*b*), (*d*), (*e*) only
D. (*b*), (*c*), (*e*) only

22. The rise in the nominal stock of money causes:

A. an increase in the equilibrium nominal interest rate and a decrease in equilibrium real income.
B. a reduction in the equilibrium nominal interest rate and an increase in equilibrium real income.
C. a reduction in the equilibrium nominal interest rate and a decrease in equilibrium real income.
D. an increase in the equilibrium nominal interest rate and an increase in the equilibrium real income.

23. Consider the following statements:

(*a*) MC schedule is obtained by subtracting successive values of TC only
(*b*) MC schedule is obtained by subtracting successive values of either TC or TVC
(*c*) MC schedule is obtained by subtracting successive values of either TVC or TFC
(*d*) The area under the MC curve equals TC
(*e*) AVC equals AC minus AFC

Choose the **correct** answer from the options given below:

A. (*b*), (*d*), (*e*) only
B. (*a*), (*d*), (*e*) only
C. (*a*), (*c*), (*d*), (*e*) only
D. (*a*), (*c*), (*d*) only

24. In which agriculture year, India's first Agriculture Census was carried out?

A. 1950-51　B. 1960-61
C. 1970-71　D. 1980-81

25. The phrase 'demonstration effect' was coined by:

A. James Duesenberry
B. J.K. Galbraith
C. Joan Robinson
D. J.M. Keynes

26. Consider the following statements:

(*a*) If a market generates a side effect or externality then the market solutions are inefficient.
(*b*) If a market is efficient, then the quantity produced in the market maximise both producer's and consumer's surplus.
(*c*) Consumer's surplus is the buyer's WTP minus the seller's cost.
(*d*) Smith's invisible hand concept implies that competitive market outcome generates equity among the members in the society.
(*e*) Competitive market equilibrium is Pareto efficient.

Choose the **correct** answer from the options given below:

A. (*a*), (*b*), (*e*) only
B. (*a*), (*b*), (*d*) only
C. (*a*), (*e*) only
D. (*b*), (*d*), (*e*) only

27. Match List-I with List-II.

List-I	List-II
(*a*) General Hetero-scedasticity test	I. Ramsey
(*b*) General test for auto correlation	II. Hausman
(*c*) Test of simultaneity	III. White
(*d*) General test of specification error	IV. Breusch-Godfrey

Choose the **correct** answer from the options given below:

	(*a*)	(*b*)	(*c*)	(*d*)
A.	I	II	III	IV
B.	IV	II	I	III
C.	III	IV	II	I
D.	III	I	II	IV

28. Which of the following is not an instrument of Monetary Policy?

A. Cash reserve ratio
B. Open market operation
C. Bank rate
D. Tax rate

29. The production function $Q = \dfrac{LK}{L+K}$ is:

A. Homogenous of degree 1
B. Homogenous of degree 0
C. Homogenous of degree 2
D. Homogenous of degree 1/2

30. Arrange the following Acts in correct chronological order, starting from earliest to latest:

(*a*) Chit Fund Act
(*b*) Export Import Bank of India Act
(*c*) Prevention of Money Laundering Act
(*d*) National Housing Bank Act
(*e*) Regional Rural Banks Act

Choose the **correct** answer from the options given below:

A. (*e*), (*b*), (*a*), (*d*), (*c*)
B. (*e*), (*d*), (*c*), (*b*), (*a*)
C. (*d*), (*c*), (*b*), (*e*), (*a*)
D. (*d*), (*a*), (*e*), (*c*), (*b*)

31. Which of the following values indicates that each woman is being replaced by one daughter, leading to a stable population over time?

A. GFR = 1
B. NRR = 1
C. TFR = 1
D. GRR = 1

32. Match List-I with List-II.

List-I	List-II
(*a*) Travel cost method	I. Sustainable development
(*b*) Stern review	II. Exhaustible resources
(*c*) Brundtland commission report	III. Climate change
(*d*) User cost	IV. Environmental valuation

Choose the **correct** answer from the options given below:

	(*a*)	(*b*)	(*c*)	(*d*)
A.	IV	II	I	III
B.	IV	I	II	III
C.	IV	III	I	II
D.	III	IV	I	II

33. Which of the following is not an assumption of Coase theorem related to externalities and environmental problems?

A. Absence of transaction costs
B. Presence of income effect
C. Complete information
D. Complete property rights

34. Arrange the following in correct chronological order starting for the oldest to the latest:

(*a*) World Trade organisation (WTO)
(*b*) General Aggrement on Trade and Tariffs (GATT)
(*c*) New Economic Policy of India (NEP)
(*d*) Introduction of goods and services tax (GST)
(*e*) Establishment of NABARD

Choose the **correct** answer from the options given below:

A. (*b*), (*c*), (*e*), (*a*), (*d*)
B. (*b*), (*e*), (*c*), (*a*), (*d*)
C. (*b*), (*d*), (*e*), (*c*), (*a*)
D. (*a*), (*b*), (*c*), (*e*), (*d*)

35. When imports are restricted with quota rather than a tariff, the cost is sometimes magnified by a process known as ....

A. Rent seeking B. Quota seeking
C. Tax Seeking D. None of the above

36. Match List-I with List-II.

List-I	List-II
(*a*) Labour capital ratio	I. The price of a commodity determined by exclusively from its labour content
(*b*) Labour intensive commodity	II. The commodity with lower capital-labour ratio at all relative factor prices
(*c*) Labour theory of value	III. The amount of labour per unit of capital used
(*d*) Labour saving technical progress	IV. It increases the productivity of capital proportionately more than the labour

Choose the **correct** answer from the options given below:

	(*a*)	(*b*)	(*c*)	(*d*)
A.	III	II	I	IV
B.	II	III	I	IV
C.	I	II	III	IV
D.	I	II	IV	III

37. Match List-I with List-II.

List-I	List-II
(*a*) PQLI	I. Amartya Sen
(*b*) HDI	II. Mehbub-Ul-Haque
(*c*) Capability Approach to Development	III. Alkire and Foster
(*d*) Multi-Dimensional Poverty Index	IV. Morris D. Morris

Choose the **correct** answer from the options given below:

	(*a*)	(*b*)	(*c*)	(*d*)
A.	IV	II	I	III
B.	IV	III	II	I
C.	I	II	III	IV
D.	IV	I	III	II

38. What does not come under the purview of the function of Reserve Bank of India?

A. Custodian of Foreign Exchange Reserves
B. Issues of Bank Notes
C. The lender of the last resort
D. Multiple expansion of credit

39. A and B are two events such that $P(\bar{A}) = 0.4$ and $P(A \cap B) = 0.2$, then $P(A \cap \bar{B})$ is:

A. 0.4 B. 0.2
C. 0.6 D. 0.8

40. Match List-I with List-II.

List-I	List-II
(*a*) Montreal Protocol	I. Contingent valuation method
(*b*) Cop 28	II. Control of CFC
(*c*) Rio + 20	III. Climate Conference
(*d*) Willingness to Accept (WTA)	IV. Sustainable Development

Choose the **correct** answer from the options given below:

	(*a*)	(*b*)	(*c*)	(*d*)
A.	II	III	IV	I
B.	II	I	IV	III
C.	III	IV	II	I
D.	I	II	IV	III

41. Given $y = \dfrac{1+x}{1-2x}$ find the correct alternative:

A. $\dfrac{dy}{dx} = \dfrac{3}{1-2x}$ B. $\dfrac{dy}{dx} = \dfrac{3}{(1-2x)^2}$

C. $\dfrac{dy}{dx} = \dfrac{3}{(1-2x)^3}$ D. $\dfrac{dy}{dx} = \dfrac{3}{(1-x)^2}$

42. Under the Green Climate Fund of UNFCCC, what ratio of financial allocation between 'Adaptation' and 'Mitigation' activities is aimed?

A. 25 : 75 B. 40 : 60
C. 50 : 50 D. 75 : 25

43. Inflation confers no benefits on society, but it imposes several real costs. What among the following are costs of inflation?

(*a*) Shoeleather costs associated with reduced money holdings
(*b*) Menu cost associated with more frequent adjustmental prices
(*c*) Increased variability of relative prices
(*d*) Unintended changes in tax liabilities due to nonindexations of the tax code
(*e*) Arbitrary redistribution of wealth associated with debts

Choose the **correct** answer from the options given below:

A. (*a*), (*b*), (*c*) only
B. (*c*), (*d*), (*e*) only
C. (*b*), (*d*), (*a*) only
D. (*a*), (*b*), (*c*), (*d*), (*e*)

44. Arrange the following theories in correct chronological order, starting from earliest to latest:

(*a*) Absorption approach
(*b*) Factor Price Equalisation theory
(*c*) Reciprocal Dumping Model
(*d*) Leontief Paradox
(*e*) Immiserizing Growth Theory

Choose the **correct** answer from the options given below:

A. (*b*), (*d*), (*a*), (*e*), (*c*)
B. (*d*), (*a*), (*b*), (*c*), (*e*)
C. (*e*), (*d*), (*b*), (*a*), (*c*)
D. (*d*), (*a*), (*c*), (*e*), (*b*)

45. Which among the following committees, was set up for Banking sector reforms in India?

(*a*) Jalan Committee
(*b*) Ghosh Committee
(*c*) Saraf Committee
(*d*) Gokaran Committee
(*e*) Tarapore Committee

Choose the **correct** answer from the options given below:

A. (*a*), (*b*), (*d*) only
B. (*b*), (*c*), (*e*) only
C. (*c*), (*d*), (*e*) only
D. (*a*), (*d*), (*c*) only

46. What is the permissible limit of Foreign Direct Investment in India's defence industry through government route?

A. 26 per cent
B. 51 per cent
C. 74 per cent
D. 100 per cent

47. Identify the correct statements from below:

(*a*) First UN conference on human environment was held in Norway in 1972.
(*b*) In I = PAT expression, P stands for poverty.
(*c*) Pollution tax was suggested by Pigou.
(*d*) Population growth follows a logistic distribution.
(*e*) Hedonic pricing is an environmental valuation method used in valuing tourism sites.

Choose the **correct** answer from the options given below:

A. (*a*), (*d*), (*e*) only
B. (*c*), (*d*), (*e*) only
C. (*a*), (*b*), (*e*) only
D. (*c*), (*d*) only

48. Arrange the following events from the date of their happening starting from the oldest:

(*a*) IRDA Act passed in Parliament
(*b*) Concept of financial inclusion introduced in Banking sector
(*c*) Global trust bank merged with UTI Bank
(*d*) 364 - day treasury bill introduced with market related rates
(*e*) Fiscal responsibility and Budget Management Act Passed

Choose the **correct** answer from the options given below:

A. (*d*), (*a*), (*c*), (*e*), (*b*)
B. (*d*), (*c*), (*e*), (*a*), (*b*)
C. (*e*), (*d*), (*b*), (*a*), (*c*)
D. (*a*), (*c*), (*d*), (*e*), (*b*)

49. Match List-I with List-II.

List-I	**List-II**
(*a*) NITI Aayog	I. Tit-for-Tat strategy
(*b*) R. Axelrod	II. Efficiency wage theory
(*c*) J. Stiglitz	III. K.N. Raj
(*d*) India's first five year plan (1951-1956)	IV. Knowledge support

Choose the **correct** answer from the options given below:

	(*a*)	(*b*)	(*c*)	(*d*)
A.	II	I	III	IV
B.	IV	III	II	I
C.	IV	I	II	III
D.	I	II	III	IV

50. Match List-I with List-II.

List-I	**List-II**
(*a*) W.W. Leontief	I. Shadow Price
(*b*) Jan Tinbergen	II. Consumption Function
(*c*) J.M. Keynes	III. Price competition with homogenous products
(*d*) Joseph Bertrand	IV. Input-output model

Choose the **correct** answer from the options given below:

	(*a*)	(*b*)	(*c*)	(*d*)
A.	II	III	I	IV
B.	IV	I	II	III
C.	III	IV	I	II
D.	I	II	III	IV

51. Arrange the following in correct chronological order starting from the earliest to the latest:

(*a*) Coase theorem
(*b*) Hotelling principle
(*c*) Nash equilibrium
(*d*) Kyoto Protocol
(*e*) Establishment of IUCN (International Union for Conservation of Nature)

Choose the **correct** answer from the options given below:

A. (*b*), (*e*), (*c*), (*a*), (*d*)
B. (*b*), (*e*), (*a*), (*c*), (*d*)
C. (*b*), (*a*), (*d*), (*e*), (*c*)
D. (*e*), (*b*), (*a*), (*c*), (*d*)

52. Match List-I with List-II.

List-I	List-II
(*a*) Top beneficiary from Foreign exchange trading	I. John Von Neuman and Oscar Morgenstern
(*b*) Competitive equilibrium is Pareto efficient	II. General equilibrium analysis
(*c*) Walras	III. London
(*d*) Game Theory	IV. First theorem of welfare economics

Choose the **correct** answer from the options given below:

	(*a*)	(*b*)	(*c*)	(*d*)
A.	II	III	I	IV
B.	IV	III	II	I
C.	I	II	III	IV
D.	III	IV	II	I

53. The concept of efficiency wage theory was developed by:

A. Yellen and Stiglitz
B. Jan Tinbergen
C. Alfred Marshall
D. Vilfredo Pareto

54. Identify the correct statements from below:

(*a*) When price consumption curve (PCC) for a good is parallel to horizontal axis, the demand function for the good is unitary elastic.
(*b*) Given $\log D = \alpha + \beta \log y + \gamma \log p$ then elasticity of log D with respect to log p is γ
(*c*) The condition for stability in simple Keynesian system is $0 < MPC < 1$
(*d*) The fixed cost curve is a rectangular hyperbola

Choose the **correct** answer from the options given below:

A. (*a*), (*c*) only
B. (*a*), (*c*), (*d*) only
C. (*a*), (*b*), (*c*) only
D. (*a*), (*b*), (*c*), (*d*)

55. You have carried out a regression analysis but after thinking about the relationship between the two variables, you have decided that you must swap the explanatory and response variables. After refitting the regression model to the data, you expect that:

A. The value of correlation will change
B. The sign of slope will change
C. The value of coefficient of determination will change
D. The value of SSE (sum of squared errors) will change

56. Which of the following is/are possible reason(s) for surplus in balance of payment?

(*a*) Decline in imports
(*b*) Decline in interest rate
(*c*) Increase in export
(*d*) Increase in income tax
(*e*) High outward foreign direct investment

Choose the **most appropriate** answer from the options given below:

A. (*a*), (*c*), (*e*) only
B. (*a*), (*b*), (*c*), (*e*) only
C. (*b*), (*c*), (*e*), (*d*) only
D. (*a*), (*c*) only

57. Match List-I with List-II.

List-I	List-II
(*a*) Endogenous variable	I. Significance of Autocorrelation coefficient
(*b*) Count R^2	II. Simultaneous equation
(*c*) Ljung Box Statistic	III. Panel data regression
(*d*) Least square dummy variable model	IV. Logit regression

Choose the **correct** answer from the options given below:

	(*a*)	(*b*)	(*c*)	(*d*)
A.	III	I	IV	II
B.	II	III	I	IV
C.	II	III	IV	I
D.	II	IV	I	III

58. The ………… effect implies that nominal interest rates tend to be high when inflation is high and low when inflation is low?

A. Tobin effect B. Baumol effect
C. Fisher effect D. Patinkin effect

59. Which state scored highest to secure top-most rank in the 'State Energy Efficiency Index 2023' released by NITI Aayog?

A. Andhra Pradesh B. Gujarat
C. Haryana D. Karnataka

60. Match List-I with List-II.

List-I	List-II
(*a*) Narasimham Committee Report (II)	I. Frauds and Mal-practices in Bank
(*b*) Ghosh Committee Report	II. Technology issues in Banking
(*c*) Padmanabhan Committee	III. RBI should withdraw 91 days T. Bill from market
(*d*) Saraf Committee	IV. Style of inspection and follow up by the central bank

Choose the **correct** answer from the options given below:

	(*a*)	(*b*)	(*c*)	(*d*)
A.	III	IV	II	I
B.	I	II	III	IV
C.	III	I	IV	II
D.	III	II	I	IV

61. Suppose savings function is $S = -5 + 0.3q$, then find the correct answer from below:

A. APC < MPC B. APC = MPC
C. APS > MPS D. APC > MPC

62. Arrange the following taxes in the sequence in which they were introduced starting from earliest to latest?

(*a*) Commodities Transaction Tax
(*b*) Securities Transaction Tax
(*c*) Banking Cash Transaction Tax
(*d*) Minimum Alternate Tax
(*e*) Angel Tax

Choose the **correct** answer from the options given below:

A. (*d*), (*a*), (*e*), (*b*), (*c*)
B. (*b*), (*c*), (*a*), (*e*), (*d*)
C. (*d*), (*b*), (*c*), (*e*), (*a*)
D. (*c*), (*d*), (*b*), (*a*), (*e*)

63. Arrange the following norms of tax revenue devolution formula of the Fifteenth Finance Commission in order of their weightages starting from the highest.

(*a*) Income distance
(*b*) Area
(*c*) Demographic performance
(*d*) Forest and Ecology
(*e*) Tax effort

Choose the **correct** answer from the options given below:

A. (*a*), (*b*), (*c*), (*d*), (*e*)
B. (*a*), (*d*), (*b*), (*e*), (*c*)
C. (*b*), (*a*), (*c*), (*e*), (*d*)
D. (*c*), (*d*), (*a*), (*b*), (*e*)

64. Match List-I with List-II.

List-I	List-II
(*a*) Bank run	I. D. Pearce
(*b*) *q*-ratio	II. M. Yunus
(*c*) Genuine saving	III. P. Diamond
(*d*) Micro finance	IV. J. Tobin

Choose the **correct** answer from the options given below:

	(*a*)	(*b*)	(*c*)	(*d*)
A.	IV	I	III	II
B.	III	IV	I	II
C.	III	II	IV	I
D.	II	IV	I	III

65. Identify the correct statements from below:

(*a*) According to environmental valuation theory, option value = future use value + bequest value + vicarious value

(*b*) Adverse selection leads to market failure

(*c*) Contingent valuation method is a type of cost benefit analysis

(*d*) Public good and common goods have same characteristics

(*e*) Internal rate of return is a criterion in cost benefit analysis

Choose the **correct** answer from the options given below:

A. (*a*) and (*b*) only
B. (*a*), (*c*), (*d*) only
C. (*a*), (*b*), (*e*) only
D. (*c*), (*d*), (*e*) only

66. For the demand function of good x, $Q_d = f(P_x, P_y, M)$ the sum of own price elasticity, cross price elasticity and income elasticity of demand would be:

A. one
B. zero
C. two
D. n where $n > 1$

67. To test $H_0 : \mu = \mu_0$, when both μ, and σ are unknown, the relevant test statistic is:

A. $t_{n-1} = \dfrac{\bar{x} - \mu_0}{\dfrac{s'}{\sqrt{n}}}$
B. $t_{n-1} = \dfrac{\bar{x} - \mu_0}{\dfrac{s'}{\sqrt{n-1}}}$

C. $t_n = \dfrac{\bar{x} - \mu_0}{\dfrac{s'}{\sqrt{n}}}$
D. $t_{n-1} = \dfrac{\bar{x} - \mu_0}{\dfrac{s'}{n}}$

68. Which of the following is current global measurement of the extreme poverty line?

A. \$ 1.90 - a day
B. \$ 2.00 - a day
C. \$ 2.15 - a day
D. \$ 2.25 - a day

69. Consider the following targets of National Health Policy 2017. Choose the correct objectives to be achieved by 2025:

(*a*) Infant Mortality Rate : 30

(*b*) Under Five Mortality Rate : 20

(*c*) Maternal Mortality Rate : 100

(*d*) Total Fertility Rate : 2.1

(*e*) Life Expectancy at Birth : 70 years

Choose the **correct** answer from the options given below:

A. (*a*), (*b*), (*c*) only
B. (*b*), (*c*), (*d*) only
C. (*a*), (*c*), (*e*) only
D. (*c*), (*d*), (*e*) only

70. Consider the following statements regarding Regional Rural Banks (RRBs) in India:

(*a*) RRBs were setup on the basis of the recommendation of Narasimham working group, 1975

(*b*) The largest proportion of the equity of RRBs is held by its sponsor bank

(*c*) NABARD coordinates all the activities of RRBs

(*d*) RRBs are lead Bank

(*e*) RRBs are provided refinance facilities through NABARD

Choose the **correct** answer from the options given below:

A. (*a*), (*c*), (*e*) only
B. (*a*), (*b*), (*c*), (*d*) only
C. (*b*), (*c*), (*e*) only
D. (*a*), (*e*) only

71. ANCOVA models include regressors that are:

A. Only quantitative variables
B. Only qualitative variables
C. Only categorical variables
D. Both qualitative and quantitative variables

72. During how many first completed days of life, the death of a baby is defined as the Neonatal death?

A. First 7 completed days of life
B. First 14 completed days of life
C. First 21 completed days of life
D. First 28 completed days of life

73. A feasible solution in a linear programming problem (LPP):

(*a*) Must satisfy all the problem's constraints simultaneously

(*b*) Need not satisfy all the constraints, only some of them

(*c*) Must be a corner point in the feasible region

(*d*) May or may not optimise the value of the objective function

(*e*) Must be greater than or equal to zero

Choose the **correct** answer from the options given below:

A. (*a*), (*d*), (*e*) only

B. (*a*), (*d*) only

C. (*a*), (*e*) only

D. (*b*), (*c*), (*e*) only

74. Match List-I with List-II.

List-I	List-II
(*a*) Ad Valorem Tariff	I. Fixed sum per unit
(*b*) Autarky	II. Combination of Ad Valorem and specific tariff
(*c*) Compound Tariff	III. No trade with other countries
(*d*) Specific Tariff	IV. A percentage of the value of the traded commodity

Choose the **correct** answer from the options given below:

	(*a*)	(*b*)	(*c*)	(*d*)
A.	I	II	III	IV
B.	IV	III	II	I
C.	IV	I	II	III
D.	III	II	I	IV

75. As per National Health Survey-5, what was the number of females per 1000 males during survey period 2019-21?

A. 975 B. 991

C. 1003 D. 1020

76. The Nash equilibrium of the following game

$$\begin{array}{c} \\ \text{P} - 1 \end{array} \begin{array}{c} \\ \begin{array}{c} A_1 \\ A_2 \\ A_3 \end{array} \end{array} \overset{\underline{\text{P} - 2}}{\begin{array}{ccc} B_1 & B_2 & B_3 \end{array}} \atop \begin{bmatrix} 4, 2 & 2, 1 & 5, 0 \\ 3, 5 & 3, 2 & 3, 4 \\ 5, 2 & 4, 4 & 3, 1 \end{bmatrix}$$

is given by:

A. The strategy combination (A_3, B_2) with outcome (4, 4)

B. The strategy combination (A_3, B_1) with outcome (5, 2)

C. The strategy combination (A_1, B_2) with outcome (2, 1)

D. The strategy combination (A_3, B_2) with outcome (3,1)

77. Arrange the names of following economists chronoliogically in order of their Nobel prize awards (starting from earliest to the latest):

(*a*) Arthur Lewis (*b*) Gunnar Myrdal

(*c*) Milton Friedman (*d*) Abhijit Banerjee

(*e*) Lawrence Klein

Choose the **correct** answer from the options given below:

A. (*b*), (*c*), (*a*), (*e*), (*d*)

B. (*b*), (*c*), (*a*), (*d*), (*e*)

C. (*b*), (*a*), (*c*), (*e*), (*d*)

D. (*a*), (*b*), (*c*), (*e*), (*d*)

78. Consider the following statements regarding public good:

(*a*) Public good is nonexclusive

(*b*) Public good is national defense

(*c*) Public good is rival

(*d*) Public good provides benefits to people at non-zero marginal cost

(*e*) Public good creates inefficiency in consumption

Choose the **correct** answer from the options given below:

A. (*a*) and (*b*) only

B. (*b*) and (*c*) only

C. (*c*) and (*d*) only
D. (*d*) and (*e*) only

79. Which of the following is the biggest item of grants-in-aid to the states assigned by the Fifteenth Finance Commission?

A. Disaster risk management grants
B. Revenue deficit grants
C. Local bodies grants
D. Sector specific grants

80. Among the following which is/are the instruments of capital market?

(*a*) Venture Capital
(*b*) Treasury Bills
(*c*) Certificate of Deposit issued by commercial banks
(*d*) Global Depository Receipts
(*e*) Inter Corporate Deposits

Choose the **correct** answer from the options given below:

A. (*b*), (*d*), (*e*) only
B. (*a*), (*d*) only
C. (*a*), (*b*), (*d*) only
D. (*a*), (*d*), (*e*) only

81. Arrange the following in chronological order starting from earliest to latest:

(*a*) A.W. Phillips: The Phillips Curve
(*b*) J.M. Keynes: General Theory of Employment, Interest and Money
(*c*) Adam Smith: Theory of Growth
(*d*) John F. Muth: Rational Expectations Approach
(*e*) Robert M. Solow: Growth Model

Choose the **correct** answer from the options given below:

A. (*a*), (*b*), (*c*), (*d*), (*e*)
B. (*c*), (*b*), (*e*), (*a*), (*d*)
C. (*b*), (*a*), (*c*), (*e*), (*d*)
D. (*e*), (*d*), (*c*), (*b*), (*a*)

82. Arrange the following items in order of their construction starting from the first stage to the last stage:

(*a*) Budget
(*b*) Utility analysis
(*c*) Demand curve analysis
(*d*) Indifference curve analysis
(*e*) Consumer's equilibrium

Choose the **correct** answer from the options given below:

A. (*d*), (*b*), (*a*), (*e*), (*c*)
B. (*a*), (*b*), (*c*), (*d*), (*e*)
C. (*b*), (*d*), (*e*), (*c*), (*a*)
D. (*b*), (*d*), (*a*), (*e*), (*c*)

83. Match List-I with List-II.

List-I	List-II
(*a*) Monopoly theory of distribution	I. Walker
(*b*) Theory of profit	II. Robinson
(*c*) Full cost pricing	III. Kalecki
(*d*) Modern theory of rent	IV. Hall and Hitch

Choose the **correct** answer from the options given below:

	(*a*)	(*b*)	(*c*)	(*d*)
A.	II	III	I	IV
B.	III	I	IV	II
C.	III	IV	II	I
D.	IV	III	II	I

84. As per the Gravity Model of world trade, which of the following components of the two countries determine the volume of trade between them:

(*a*) Gross Domestic Product
(*b*) Distance
(*c*) Foreign exchange rate
(*d*) Foreign trade intensity
(*e*) Foreign investment

Choose the **correct** answer from the options given below:

A. (*a*) and (*b*) only
B. (*b*) and (*c*) only
C. (*a*) and (*c*) only
D. (*a*) and (*e*) only

85. Testing for cointegration is performed by:
A. Chow test
B. Phillips-Peron test
C. Engel-Granger test
D. Error-correction mechanism

86. Arrange the following expressions in terms of increasing order of magnitude
[given: $a > o$, $b > o$, $x > o$]
(*a*) $y = e^a$
(*b*) $y = e^{a+bx}$
(*c*) $y = e^{a+\frac{b}{x}}$
(*d*) $y = e^{a-\frac{b}{x}}$
(*e*) $y = e^{a+2bx}$

Choose the **correct** answer from the options given below:
A. (*d*), (*a*), (*c*), (*b*), (*e*)
B. (*d*), (*a*), (*b*), (*c*), (*e*)
C. (*d*), (*b*), (*c*), (*a*), (*e*)
D. (*e*), (*b*), (*c*), (*a*), (*d*)

87. In the leakage-injection approach to income determination, an increase in lump-sum tax ceteris paribus shifts:
A. Investment plus govt. spending line upward
B. Investment plus govt. spending line downward
C. The savings plus tax line to the left
D. Increases the equilibrium level of income

88. In the Cobb-Douglas production function: $q = AL^{\alpha} K^{\beta}$ where A, α and β are all positive, the parameters α and β measure
A. Output elasticities of inputs
B. Elasticity of substitution
C. Input price of output
D. Technological condition

89. Estimation of regression coefficients in the presence of high but not perfect multicollinearity may result in all of these except:
A. High confidence interval for the estimates
B. Almost all the estimates are statistically significant
C. A high R^2
D. Estimates are all BLUE

90. The lowest value of a set of observations is 4.5 and their range is 10.9. Artithmetic mean is found to be 19.9 and median found to be 15.6. Which of the following statements is correct?
A. Arithmetic mean is wrong, but the median is correct
B. Arithmetic mean is right, but the median is wrong
C. Both arithmetic mean and median are wrong
D. Both arithmetic mean and median are right

Directions (Qs. No. 91-95): *Consider the following diagram and answers these questions.*

Social Costs of Monolpoly Power

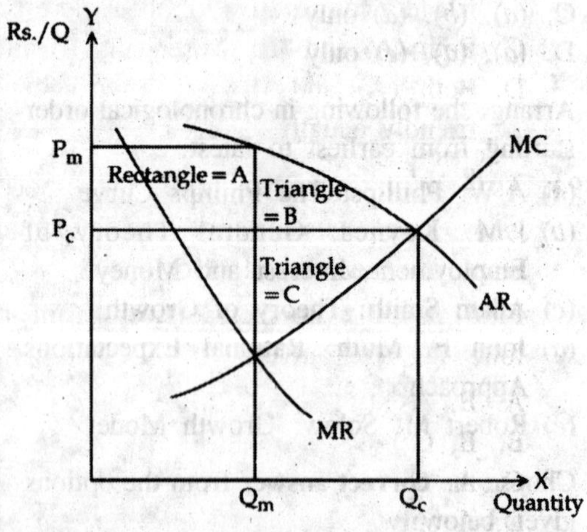

Here:
(*i*) X-axis measures quantity
(*ii*) Y-axis measures price per unit (Rs/Q)
(*iii*) P_c = competitive price
(*iv*) P_m = Monopoly price
(*v*) Q_c = competitive output
(*vi*) Q_m = monopoly output

91. Because of higher price (From P_c to P_m), find out the producer gains (producer surplus) from the following alternatives.

A. A + C
B. A – C
C. A + B
D. B + C

92. Find out the consumer loss because of moving from competitive to monopoly price (from P_c to P_m) from the following alternatives:

A. A and C
B. A and B
C. B and C
D. A only

93. Choose the correct answer from the following alternatives:

A. Monopoly output is environment friendly comparative to competitive output
B. Competitive output is environment friendly comparative to monopoly output
C. Both (A) and (B) are equally harmfull
D. Both (A) and (B) are environmental friendly equally

94. As a result of higher price, the producer gains and at the same time loses by amount respectively as shown below:

Find out the correct answer from the following alternatives:

A. B, A
B. B, C
C. A, C
D. A only

95. Dead weight loss from the monopoly power is one of the following alternatives. Choose the correct one:

A. A + B
B. A + C
C. A
D. B + C

Directions (Qs. No. 96-100): *Read the following passage and answer the questions.*

For a financial year, the Budget was presented by the government. Some major heads and items are highlighted here. Total receipts was ₹ 400 crore, of which revenue receipts was ₹ 250 crore and capital receipts was ₹ 150 crore. In the total revenue receipts, tax revenue receipts contributed ₹ 220 crore and non-tax revenue receipts contributed ₹ 30 crore respectively. In the total capital receipts, Borrowings and other liabilities were ₹ 100 crore. Out of total revenue expenditure of ₹ 300 crore, interest payments was ₹ 90 crore and grants for creation of capital assets was ₹ 20 crore. Out of total capital expenditure of ₹ 100 crore, scheme expenditure was ₹ 75 crore and other than scheme expenditure was ₹ 25 crore. The country's GDP at current prices for the given financial year was ₹ 2000 crore. On the Balance of payments accounts, the current account deficit was ₹ 50 crore.

96. What was the fiscal deficit as percentage of GDP?

A. 5% B. 10%
C. 12.5% D. 15%

97. What was the primary deficit as percentage of GDP?

A. 0.2% B. 0.3%
C. 0.4% D. 0.5%

98. What was the revenue deficit as percentage of GDP:

A. 2.5% B. 3.0%
C. 3.5% D. 4.0%

99. What was the effective revenue deficit as percentage of GDP?

A. 0.5% B. 1.0%
C. 1.5% D. 2.0%

100. What was the twin deficit as percentage of GDP?

A. 2.5% B. 5.0%
C. 7.5% D. 10.0%

ANSWERS

1. **(A):** The question addresses the secular deterioration of terms of trade for less developed countries. The primary economic theorists associated with these ideas are H.W. Singer and Raul Prebisch, who independently proposed what is now known as the Prebisch-Singer hypothesis. This theory suggests that the terms of trade, or the ratio of export prices to import prices, deteriorate over time for developing countries exporting primary commodities due to various structural factors in the global economy. Jagdish Bhagwati, another important figure in international economics, has also contributed extensively to the understanding of trade policies and their impact on developing countries, though his work is more broadly focused on trade theory and policy rather than specifically on the terms of trade deterioration phenomenon. J.S. Mill and Adam Smith, classical economists, did not specifically address this modern theory as their works predate these discussions.

   Thus, the correct answer is A, focusing on Singer, Prebisch, and Bhagwati.

2. **(C):** The statements provided relate to economic concepts surrounding investment and interest rates. According to accelerator models of investment, indeed, investment demand is proportional to the change in gross national product (GNP), aligning with the theory that investments are made to meet future expected increases in output or sales. The real interest rate, contrary to statement (*b*), is actually the nominal rate of interest minus the inflation rate, not plus. This reflects the real cost of borrowing after adjusting for inflation. Statement (*c*) correctly states that higher real interest rates increase the rental cost of capital, making borrowing more expensive for investment purposes. Statement (*d*) is incorrect as investment is a flow concept, representing the addition to the capital stock over a period, whereas the rate of interest (*e*) is indeed a flow concept, reflecting the cost of borrowing capital per unit time.

3. **(C):** To solve for the profit-maximizing price and quantity, we use the given demand function Q = 20/P and the constant marginal cost (MC) of 1. The profit-maximizing condition in a perfectly competitive market is to set price equal to marginal cost, but here, price is dictated by the demand relationship. Since P ≤ 10 is a constraint, we must also consider the upper limit for P. Setting P = 10 gives Q = 20/10 = 2. Any price above 10 is not allowed, and prices below 10 will reduce total revenue since MC is constant and revenue must cover total costs. Thus, the most profitable allowable price is P = 10 with a corresponding quantity of Q = 2, which maximizes revenue given the constraints.

4. **(A):** The statements under consideration involve environmental and development concepts. The ecological footprint (*a*) indeed measures the demand placed on Earth's ecosystems by individuals or communities, quantifying the amount of natural resources consumed and waste produced. Statement (*b*) is incorrect as the top-down approach typically implies initiatives driven by central authorities rather than by community participation, which is more characteristic of bottom-up approaches. The Millennium Development Goals (MDGs) (*c*) were targeted to be achieved by 2015, not 2016. Finally, statement (*d*) is accurate in stating that the Sustainable Development Goals

(SDGs) comprise 17 goals, established to address global challenges including poverty, inequality, climate change, environmental degradation, peace, and justice.

5. **(A):** The correct chronological sequence of these significant events and institutions in India's economic and development history starts with the Second Five Year Plan (*c*), which was implemented from 1956 to 1961 and focused on rapid industrialization. Next is the nationalization of banks in India (*b*), which occurred in two major phases, first in 1969 and then in 1980, aiming to extend banking facilities to larger sections of society and to mobilize resources for development. The Export-Import Bank of India (EXIM Bank) (*e*) was established in 1982 to enhance the country's international trade. Following this, the Small Industries Development Bank of India (SIDBI) (*d*) was set up in 1990 to promote, finance, and develop the micro, small, and medium enterprise sector. Finally, the Fiscal Responsibility and Budget Management (FRBM) Act (*a*) was enacted in 2003 to institutionalize financial discipline and reduce fiscal deficit.

6. **(B):** Heteroscedasticity refers to situations in regression analysis where the variability of a variable is unequal across the range of values of a second variable that predicts it. Common reasons for heteroscedasticity include extremely high or low values in the dataset, incorrect specifications of the model's functional form, and incorrect transformations of variables, which can all affect the stability of variance across data points. However, the correlation of variables over time generally relates to autocorrelation rather than heteroscedasticity.

7. **(D):** Economic integration among developing countries has been attempted through various regional trade agreements and blocs aimed at reducing trade barriers and fostering economic cooperation. The Central American Common Market, the Caribbean Free Trade Association, and the Latin American Free Trade Association are all examples of such efforts. These associations are designed to enhance economic cooperation among member countries, facilitate the free movement of goods, services, and factors of production, and thus improve the economic standing of the regions involved. By forming these trade blocs, developing countries aim to leverage collective bargaining power in the global market, enhance intra-regional trade, and achieve greater economic stability and growth.

8. **(A):** To determine whether points O(0, 0) and P(2, –3) lie inside or outside the region defined by the inequality $2x - 3y < 5$, we substitute these points into the inequality.

   For O(0, 0), substituting $x = 0$ and $y = 0$ gives $2(0) - 3(0) = 0$, which is less than 5, indicating that point O is inside the region.

   For P(2, –3), substituting $x = 2$ and $y = -3$ gives $2(2) - 3(-3) = 4 + 9 = 13$, which is not less than 5, hence point P is outside the region.

   This assessment shows that point O is within the region where the inequality holds true, while point P does not satisfy the inequality and thus lies outside the specified region.

9. **(C):** For a quadratic form to be negative for all values of x and y, the quadratic form needs to be negative definite. For a $2x^2$ matrix associated with the quadratic form $ax^2 + by^2 + 2hxy$, represented as:

$$\begin{bmatrix} a & h \\ h & b \end{bmatrix},$$

   the conditions for being negative definite are:

   1. The leading principal minor, a must be less than zero ($a < 0$).

2. The determinant of the matrix $\begin{vmatrix} a & h \\ h & b \end{vmatrix} = ab - h^2$ must be greater than zero ($ab - h^2 > 0$).

These conditions ensure that the quadratic form curves downwards (since $a < 0$) and the determinant being positive confirms that the eigenvalues are of the same sign, which would be negative in this context (negative definite matrix). Thus, option C accurately reflects the necessary conditions.

10. (A): Gross Domestic Product (GDP) can be defined and calculated in several ways, but one standard approach is to sum the aggregate domestic income with indirect taxes and depreciation. This method reflects the total market value of all goods and services produced within a country in a given period. GDP calculated this way includes net domestic product (aggregate domestic income minus depreciation) plus depreciation (to account for the wear and tear on assets) and indirect taxes (such as sales taxes), which adjust for government-imposed costs on production and consumption that are not directly part of the income earned by factors of production. This approach provides a comprehensive measure of economic activity, reflecting both the income generated by production and the costs associated with depreciation and taxes that affect the economic value generated within a country.

11. (C): India is a member of several key institutions within the World Bank Group, which play various roles in global economic development and investment. These include the International Development Association (IDA), which provides loans and grants to the world's poorest countries; the International Finance Corporation (IFC), which offers investment, advisory, and asset-management services to encourage private-sector development in less developed countries; the Multilateral Investment Guarantee Agency (MIGA), which provides political risk insurance and credit enhancement to investors and lenders; and the International Bank for Reconstruction and Development (IBRD), which assists in development by providing loans and offering technical expertise. However, the International Centre for Settlement of Investment Disputes (ICSID) focuses more on arbitration and dispute resolution between international investors and states, and India is not a member of this institution. Therefore, option C correctly identifies the World Bank Group institutions of which India is a member.

12. (A): The terms provided relate to different financial strategies and situations involving currency transactions:

(*a*) Arbitrage refers to the practice of taking advantage of a price difference between two or more markets: striking a combination of matching deals that capitalize upon the imbalance, the profit being the difference between the market prices, which is precisely described by III, "refers to purchase of currency in monetary center where it is cheaper."

(*b*) Hedging is used to reduce any substantial losses or gains suffered by an individual or an organization. IV, "refers to avoidance of foreign exchange risk," accurately describes this strategy.

(*c*) Speculation involves trading a financial instrument involving high risk, in expectation of significant returns. The correct match is I, "refers to when an investor accepts and seeks foreign exchange risk."

(*d*) Foreign exchange risk refers to the variations in the currency value and the risk that such changes pose to financial transactions, which is described by II, "refers to a time when foreign exchange shifts, causing the spot rate to vary frequently."

This matching (III, IV, I, II) is captured in option A.

13. (A): The chronological order of the theories listed should reflect the historical development of monetary theory:

- The cash transaction approach (*d*) and the cash balance approach (*e*) are early fundamental theories developed as part of the classical and neoclassical economic thoughts.
- Reformulated quantity theory of money (*b*) came afterward, representing a modern reinterpretation of the quantity theory of money, emphasizing the role of money supply in pricing and inflation.
- Baumol's theory of money (*c*) typically known for the transactions demand for money, came later in the mid-20th century.
- Patinkin's real balance effect (*a*) is a more contemporary development that integrates monetary and value theory, enhancing the understanding of price level changes on consumption and savings.

This chronological sequence is accurately captured in option A.

14. (D): The Unified Payments Interface (UPI) system, which has revolutionized digital payments in India, was developed by the National Payments Corporation of India (NPCI), not by the Reserve Bank of India (RBI), the State Bank of India (SBI), or the Securities and Exchange Board of India (SEBI). It was launched in 2016. The NPCI, an umbrella organization for operating retail payments and settlement systems in India, is an initiative of RBI and an association of Indian banks. UPI enables instant real-time payments between peers or between a person and a merchant, facilitated by linking bank accounts with a mobile application.

15. (B): According to Walras' Law, in a general equilibrium of markets, the sum of the values of excess demands across all markets must be equal to zero. This law is a fundamental concept in economic theory, indicating that if all markets but one are in equilibrium, then that last market must also be in equilibrium. Excess demand is defined as the amount by which demand exceeds supply at current prices, and according to Walras' Law, the sum of excess demand for different goods, including money, bonds, and current output, in an economy should sum to zero.

This ensures that resources are allocated efficiently and that there are no unmet demands or unsold supplies in any market without affecting another.

16. (A): The Human Development Index (HDI) categorizes countries into four groups based on their HDI values: very high, high, medium, and low human development. Typically, the largest group of countries tends to be in the "medium human development" category. However, over recent years and especially in the latest reports, there has been significant progress in various countries, shifting more into the "high" and "very high" categories as global development efforts intensify and yield results. The latest data trends indicate that more countries have moved into the "very high human development" category, reflecting improvements in health, education, and income indices which are the components of the HDI.

This progression aligns with global development goals and the increased focus on sustainable development, healthcare improvements, and educational accessibility.

17. (D): The sustainable development goals (SDGs) have specific objectives designed to address global challenges comprehensively:

- Goal 7 aims to ensure access to affordable, reliable, sustainable, and modern energy for all, correctly matching "Affordable and clean energy."
- Goal 10, which is incorrectly matched with "Climate action," actually aims to reduce inequality within and among countries. The correct goal for "Climate action" is Goal 13.
- Goal 13 is incorrectly matched with "Reduced inequality" which should be Goal 10.
- Goal 14 correctly matches with "Life below water," focusing on the conservation and sustainable use of the oceans, seas, and marine resources.
- Goal 15 correctly matches with "Life on land," which aims to protect, restore, and promote sustainable use of terrestrial ecosystems. Thus, the correct option that matches goals with their descriptions accurately is (*a*), (*d*), (*e*).

18. (D): The matching of economic theorems with their correct subjects is as follows:

(*a*) The Modigliani-Miller theorem, incorrectly associated with price of goods and real return to factors, actually pertains to corporate finance, particularly capital structure decisions, stating that the market value of a firm is independent of its capital structure.

(*b*) The Dorfman-Steiner theorem correctly deals with optimal advertisement expenditure, stating that the ratio of advertising to sales should equal the product of the profit margin and the advertising elasticity of demand.

(*c*) Arrow's impossibility theorem correctly addresses issues in social choice theory, demonstrating the impossibility of devising a social preference ordering that meets certain rational criteria.

(*d*) The Stolper-Samuelson theorem, incorrectly matched with capital structure, actually relates to international trade, particularly the effects of trade on factor prices.

(*e*) Fisher's separation theorem correctly discusses the separation of investment decisions from owners' preferences, focusing on firms' investment decisions being determined by their profitability regardless of personal preferences.

Thus, the correct answer is D, with (*b*), (*c*), and (*e*) being correctly matched.

19. (*)

20. (D): Matching notable figures with their contributions or associated works involves identifying the correct descriptions:

(*a*) Rachel Carson is best known for her book "Silent Spring" (III), which is credited with advancing the global environmental movement.

(*b*) Kenneth Boulding wrote on the "Economics of the Coming Spaceship Earth" (II), describing the Earth as a closed system.

(*c*) G. Hardin is famous for the essay "The Tragedy of the Commons" (IV), which addresses problems related to shared resources.

(*d*) Partha Dasgupta has significant contributions to the "Economics of Biodiversity" (I), focusing on the economic aspects of biodiversity.

Therefore, the correct matching, based on their seminal works or concepts, is provided in option D: III, II, IV, I.

21. (B): Non-Banking Financial Companies (NBFCs) in India have specific regulatory and operational guidelines that distinguish them from commercial banks:

- Statement (*a*) is incorrect because NBFCs are not registered under the RBI Act of 1948 but under the Companies Act of 2013, and they are regulated by the RBI under directions issued under the RBI Act of 1934.

- Statement (*b*) is correct. Unlike commercial banks, NBFCs are not allowed to accept demand deposits, which are deposits that can be withdrawn by the depositor at any time without any prior notice to the banking institution.
- Statement (*c*) is correct. NBFCs are required to invest a specific percentage of their assets in unencumbered approved securities as per the Non-Banking Financial (Non-Deposit Accepting or Holding) Companies Prudential Norms (Reserve Bank) Directions, 2007.
- Statement (*d*) is correct. NBFCs that are engaged in merchant banking, portfolio management services, or stockbroking must also comply with regulations set by the Securities and Exchange Board of India (SEBI), in addition to being regulated by the RBI.
- Statement (*e*) is correct. Every NBFC is required to create a reserve fund and transfer at least 20% of its net profit every year to this fund before any dividend is declared, as per the RBI's directions.

Hence, option B, which includes (*b*), (*c*), (*d*), and (*e*), is correct.

22. (B): A rise in the nominal stock of money, according to basic monetary theory, typically leads to lower interest rates and higher real income in the short to medium term. This is because an increase in the money supply lowers the cost of borrowing (nominal interest rate), encouraging more investment and spending, which in turn can boost economic activity and real income. The theory relies on the liquidity preference framework, which posits that an increase in money supply, with unchanged money demand, leads to an excess supply of money, resulting in lower interest rates.

23. (A):

- Statement (*a*) is incorrect as it suggests MC (marginal cost) is calculated by subtracting successive values of TC (total cost) only. While it's true MC involves TC, it specifically relates to the change in TC due to an additional unit of output.
- Statement (*b*) is correct. MC can be derived by subtracting successive values of either Total Cost (TC) or Total Variable Cost (TVC), not just TC. This reflects the cost added by producing one additional unit.
- Statements (*c*) is incorrect. MC does not involve Total Fixed Cost (TFC), as TFC does not change with output levels.
- Statement (*d*) is correct. The area under the MC curve up to a certain quantity of output equals the total variable cost (TVC) for that quantity, which, when added to TFC, equals TC.
- Statement (*e*) is correct. Average Variable Cost (AVC) equals Average Cost (AC) minus Average Fixed Cost (AFC), which is derived from dividing TFC by the quantity.

24. (C): India's first Agricultural Census was carried out in the year 1970-71. This nationwide exercise was initiated to collect and compile comprehensive data on agricultural aspects such as land use, cropping patterns, and farm holdings across the country. The Agricultural Census takes place every five years, with the aim of providing a detailed picture of the agricultural sector, which is vital for policy formulation and planning for agricultural development in India.

25. (A): The concept of the demonstration effect, particularly in the context of consumer behaviour and consumption patterns, was popularized by James Duesenberry. He explained that individuals' consumption choices are influenced by the standards set by their peers or reference groups. This socio-economic behaviour was detailed in his relative income hypothesis, which suggests that people's spending is more influenced by their relative position in a social group than by their absolute income level. This concept has profound implications for understanding consumer behaviour, especially in societies with conspicuous consumption and significant income disparities.

26. (A):

- Statement (*a*) is correct: If a market generates a side effect or externality (such as pollution from a factory), then the market outcome becomes inefficient because it fails to account for the cost or benefit of the externality. This can lead to overproduction or underproduction from the social optimum level, thus making the market solutions inefficient.
- Statement (*b*) is correct: Efficiency in a market is achieved when the quantity produced maximizes total surplus, which includes both producer's surplus and consumer's surplus. This occurs at the equilibrium where supply equals demand, assuming no externalities or market power.
- Statement (*c*) is incorrect: Consumer's surplus is the difference between what consumers are willing to pay (WTP) and what they actually pay, not the seller's cost.
- Statement (*d*) is incorrect: Adam Smith's concept of the invisible hand suggests that competitive markets lead to efficient outcomes through individuals pursuing their self-interest, not necessarily generating equity among members of society.
- Statement (*e*) is correct: In a competitive market, equilibrium is Pareto efficient because any other allocation would make at least one individual worse off while making no one better off. Thus, the correct statements that align with these explanations are (*a*), (*b*), and (*e*), making option A correct.

27. (C):

- General Heteroscedasticity test is commonly associated with White's test (III), which checks for heteroscedasticity in a regression model's residuals.
- General test for autocorrelation is frequently done using the Breusch-Godfrey test (IV), which specifically tests for autocorrelation in the residuals of a regression model.
- Test of simultaneity often involves the Hausman test (II), which can distinguish between simultaneous equations models and single-equation estimation techniques to determine if endogeneity is present.
- General test of specification error involving various aspects like omitted variables and functional form can be addressed by the Ramsey RESET test (I), which is used to test if a model has been misspecified.

This matching (III, IV, II, I) is provided in option C, aligning with the correct identification of statistical tests.

28. (D):

- The Cash Reserve Ratio (A), Open Market Operations (B), and Bank Rate (C) are all traditional instruments of monetary policy used by central banks to regulate the money supply and interest rates in the economy.
- Tax rate (D), however, is a fiscal policy instrument used by the government to influence the economy by altering tax rates, affecting public spending, and adjusting budget allocations, rather than directly influencing the money supply or interest rates.

Thus, D is the correct answer as it is not an instrument of monetary policy.

29. (A): The production function Q = LK/(L + K) can be tested for homogeneity by examining if increasing all inputs by a factor of '*t*' results in the output being multiplied by the same factor '*t*'. If Q is homogenous of degree 1, scaling all inputs by any positive constant will result in output scaling by the same constant:

$$Q(tL, tK) = \frac{tL \times tK}{tL + tK} = t \times \frac{LK}{L + K} = tQ$$

This shows that the function is homogenous of degree 1, where output increases proportionally with an increase in inputs.

30. (A):

(*e*) The Regional Rural Banks Act was established first, in 1976, aimed at developing the rural economy and enhançing the financial inclusion of rural sectors.

(*b*) The Export Import Bank of India Act came into effect in March 1982, established to enhance the foreign trade of India by facilitating the import and export of goods.

(*a*) The Chit Fund Act was established in August 1982, regulating chit funds in India and providing a framework for the conduct of chit fund businesses.

(*d*) The National Housing Bank Act was enacted in 1987, established as a principal agency to promote housing finance institutions both at local and regional levels.

(*c*) The Prevention of Money Laundering Act came into effect much later, in 2002, aimed at preventing money-laundering activities and providing for confiscation of property derived from, or involved in, money laundering.

This chronological order from earliest to latest, (*e*), (*b*), (*a*), (*d*), (*c*), is accurately captured in option A.

31. (B): The Net Reproduction Rate (NRR) is a demographic measure used to estimate whether the population is replacing itself from one generation to the next. If the NRR equals 1, it indicates that each woman is being replaced by exactly one daughter, on average, leading to a stable population size over time if this rate is sustained. The NRR takes into account female births and the survival rates of females until the end of their reproductive age.

It differs from Total Fertility Rate (TFR), which measures the average number of children a woman would have assuming she survives through her reproductive years, and from Gross Reproduction Rate (GRR), which counts only female births but does not account for mortality rates.

Thus, NRR = 1 (option B) is the correct answer as it precisely measures replacement fertility in terms of daughters who will continue the next generation.

32. (C): This question requires matching specific concepts and reports with their corresponding focus areas:

(*a*) The Travel Cost Method is a technique used in environmental economics for estimating economic values of ecosystems and parks that are not sold in a market. Hence, it is associated with Environmental Valuation (IV).

(*b*) The Stern Review is a comprehensive report that dealt with the economic impacts of Climate Change (III), authored by economist Nicholas Stern.

(*c*) The Brundtland Commission Report, formally known as "Our Common Future," introduced the concept of Sustainable Development (I), focusing on development that meets the needs of the present without compromising the ability of future generations.

(*d*) User Cost in the context of environmental economics often refers to the cost of depleting natural and Exhaustible Resources (II).

Option C (IV, III, I, II) accurately matches these terms with their corresponding areas of focus.

33. (B): The Coase Theorem, formulated by economist Ronald Coase, posits that if property rights are well-defined, transaction costs are negligible, and parties have complete information, then they can negotiate to resolve externalities privately regardless of the initial distribution of property rights. Key assumptions of the theorem include:

(A) Absence of transaction costs, allowing parties to negotiate without incurring significant costs.

(C) Complete information, where all parties are fully informed about the market and their own utility or cost functions.

(D) Complete property rights, ensuring that all resources are owned and any effects on third parties are internalized in decision making.

However, the presence of an income effect (B), where the allocation of resources affects the income distribution among the parties and thus their utility, is not a necessary condition or assumption for the Coase theorem. This option is correct as it represents what is not an assumption of the Coase theorem.

34. (B): The correct chronological order of these global economic and policy frameworks is:

- General Agreement on Tariffs and Trade (GATT), established in 1947, aimed at reducing tariffs and other trade barriers.
- National Bank for Agriculture and Rural Development (NABARD), established in 1982, focuses on the development of agriculture and rural areas in India.
- New Economic Policy of India (NEP), introduced in 1991, marked significant economic reforms including liberalization, privatization, and globalization.
- World Trade Organization (WTO), established in 1995, succeeded GATT and deals with the global rules of trade between nations.
- Introduction of Goods and Services Tax (GST) in India, implemented in 2017, to streamline and unify the various indirect taxes across the country.

Option B: (*b*),(*e*),(*c*),(*a*),(*d*) correctly orders these from oldest to latest.

35. (A): When imports are restricted by quotas, it typically leads to a process known as rent seeking. This economic concept involves individuals or entities expending resources to gain an economic gain from others without reciprocating any benefits back to society through wealth creation. Specifically, in the context of import quotas, rent-seeking behaviour can occur as importers, exporters, or local producers may spend significant amounts of money or effort to secure access to the limited import licenses, which can be highly profitable. This behaviour does not contribute to overall economic efficiency but instead leads to a redistribution of resources from the general public to those who can secure these lucrative quotas.

36. (A):

- Labour-capital ratio (*a*) refers to the amount of labour per unit of capital used in production, aligning with III.
- Labour-intensive commodity (*b*) describes a commodity with a lower capital-labour ratio at all relative factor prices, thus correctly matched with II.
- Labour theory of value (*c*) is a principle in classical economics where the price of a commodity is determined exclusively from its labour content, which fits with I.

- Labour saving technical progress (*d*) increases the productivity of capital proportionately more than labour, accurately described by IV.

This set of matchings (III, II, I, IV) provides a coherent alignment of economic concepts with their corresponding definitions as seen in option A.

37. (A):

- Physical Quality of Life Index (PQLI) was developed by Morris D. Morris (IV), focusing on evaluating countries based on literacy rates, infant mortality, and life expectancy.
- Human Development Index (HDI) was introduced by Mahbub ul Haq (II), designed to measure countries' economic development and standard of living, incorporating GDP, life expectancy, and educational attainment.
- Capability Approach to Development was extensively developed by Amartya Sen (I), which emphasizes the freedoms and capabilities people have access to, which enhance their quality of life.
- Multidimensional Poverty Index (MPI) is associated with Alkire and Foster (III), which measures poverty through multiple deprivations at the household level across various dimensions, such as health, education, and living standards.

Option A (IV, II, I, III) correctly associates these creators and concepts, matching the pioneering work of these influential thinkers with their contributions to developmental economics.

38. (D): Multiple expansion of credit:

The functions of the Reserve Bank of India (RBI) encompass a variety of roles crucial for the functioning of India's financial system:

- As the custodian of Foreign Exchange Reserves (A), RBI manages the foreign exchange and gold reserves of the nation.
- In its capacity to issue Bank Notes (B), RBI is responsible for the issuance and management of currency within India.
- Serving as the Lender of Last Resort (C), RBI provides necessary financial support to the banking system during financial distress or liquidity crises.

However, the concept of Multiple Expansion of Crédit (D) refers to the process by which the commercial banking system creates money through loans and deposits, a mechanism inherent to fractional-reserve banking rather than a direct function of a central bank like RBI.

39. (A): Using the information given:

$P(\bar{A}) = 0.4$ implies $P(A) = 1 - 0.4 = 0.6$ because the probability of A and its complement $\bar{A}$ must sum to 1.

We know $P(A) = P(A \cap B) + P(A \cap \bar{B})$.

Plugging in the known values,

$0.6 = 0.2 + P(A \cap \bar{B})$

Solving for $P(A \cap \bar{B})$:

$P(A \cap \bar{B}) = 0.6 - 0.2 = 0.4.$

This result shows that the probability of A occurring without B is 0.4, which is option A.

40. (A):

(*a*) The Montreal Protocol is famously associated with the Control of Chlorofluorocarbons (CFCs) (II), an international treaty designed to phase out substances that deplete the ozone layer.

(*b*) COP 28 is a Climate Conference (III), part of the annual Conference of Parties under the United Nations Framework Convention on Climate Change (UNFCCC) where nations negotiate and discuss actions against climate change.

(*c*) Rio + 20 was a conference on Sustainable Development (IV), marking the 20th anniversary of the United Nations Conference on Environment and Development (UNCED), focusing on sustainable development and green economy.

(*d*) Willingness to Accept (WTA) involves the Contingent Valuation Method (I) used in environmental economics to determine the valuation that individuals place on changes in their consumption of goods, typically used to measure the cost of avoiding negative externalities or the compensation required for accepting changes.

Thus, option A (II, III, IV, I) is correct, matching each list item with its corresponding description accurately.

41. (B): To solve for *dy*/*dx*, consider the given function $y = \frac{1+x}{1-2x}$.

We can use the quotient rule for differentiation, which states:

if $y = \frac{u}{v}$, then $y' = \frac{u'v - uv'}{v^2}$.

Let $u = 1 + x$ and $v = 1 - 2x$.

- Differentiating u with respect to x gives $u' = 1$.
- Differentiating v with respect to x gives $v' = -2$.
- Plugging these into the quotient rule formula:

$$y' = \frac{(1)(1-2x) - (1+x)(-2)}{(1-2x)^2}$$

$$= \frac{1 - 2x + 2 + 2x}{(1-2x)^2} = \frac{3}{(1-2x)^2}.$$

This calculation confirms that option B, $\frac{dy}{dx} = \frac{3}{(1-2x)^2}$, is the correct derivative of the given function.

42. (C): Under the Green Climate Fund (GCF) of the UNFCCC, an equitable balance between adaptation and mitigation funding is sought. Specifically, the GCF aims for a balanced allocation of resources between adaptation and mitigation activities. This is part of an effort to address the needs of developing countries, particularly those that are most vulnerable to the effects of climate change, such as small island developing states and least developed countries. The goal is to ensure that funding for adaptation to the adverse effects and mitigation to reduce emissions is provided on a 50:50 basis, reflecting the dual approach required to effectively tackle climate change. This commitment reflects the recognition that both adaptation and mitigation are essential components of the international response to climate change.

43. (D): Inflation can have several detrimental effects on an economy, and all listed items represent real costs associated with inflation:

(*a*) Shoeleather costs refer to the costs associated with the increased effort people must exert to minimize holding cash during inflationary times, such as more frequent trips to the bank.

(*b*) Menu costs are the costs businesses incur from having to frequently update prices in response to inflation.

(*c*) Increased variability of relative prices can distort consumer and producer decisions, leading to inefficient resource allocation.

(*d*) Unintended changes in tax liabilities occur due to non-indexation of the tax code, where inflation can push individuals into higher tax brackets without an actual increase in real income.

(*e*) Arbitrary redistribution of wealth happens because inflation can erode the real value of debts, benefiting debtors at the expense of creditors.

All these factors contribute to the costs of inflation, making option D correct, which includes all the given statements.

44. (A): To arrange these economic theories in chronological order:

- Factor Price Equalisation theory was developed by Paul Samuelson in the 1940s, which theorizes that free trade will lead to the equalization of the prices of factors of production across countries.
- The Leontief Paradox, discovered by Wassily Leontief in the early 1950s, challenged the empirical validity of the Factor Price Equalisation theory by showing that the U.S., with its capital abundance, exported labour-intensive commodities and imported capital-intensive commodities.
- The Absorption approach was developed in the mid-20th century and involves understanding the balance of payments adjusted by national income or expenditure.
- Immiserizing Growth Theory was proposed by Jagdish Bhagwati in the 1950s, suggesting that economic growth could actually worsen a country's welfare if adverse terms of trade effects outweigh the benefits of growth.
- Reciprocal Dumping Model was developed later, in the 1980s, by Paul Krugman, addressing trade patterns where countries with similar products export to each other.

Option A, (*b*), (*d*), (*a*), (*e*), (*c*), correctly places these theories from the earliest to the latest.

45. (*)

46. (D): As of recent updates, the permissible limit of Foreign Direct Investment (FDI) in India's defense industry through the government route has been increased to 100 per cent. This policy change allows foreign companies to have full ownership of defense sector enterprises in India, subject to government approvals and security clearances, reflecting India's aim to attract more foreign investment in its defense technology and production capabilities. Therefore, the correct answer is D.

47. (D):

- Statement (*a*) is incorrect; the first UN conference on the human environment was held in Stockholm, Sweden, not Norway, in 1972.
- Statement (*b*) is incorrect; in the I = PAT expression, P stands for Population, not Poverty.
- Statement (*c*) is correct; Arthur Cecil Pigou suggested the pollution tax as a way to correct externalities by imposing costs equivalent to the societal cost of pollution.
- Statement (*d*) is correct; the logistic distribution often describes population growth in ecology, indicating how populations expand rapidly but slow as they reach carrying capacity.
- Statement (*e*) is incorrect; Hedonic pricing is indeed an environmental valuation method, but it is primarily used to value environmental amenities by observing the differences in prices of goods or services affected by environmental variables, not specifically for valuing tourism sites.

Therefore, option D is correct, including the correct statements (*c*) and (*d*) only.

48. (A): Arranging these events chronologically:

- The 364-day treasury bill with market-related rates was introduced in India first, which was part of the financial reforms to control monetary policy more effectively, introduced in the 1980s.

- The IRDA Act (Insurance Regulatory and Development Authority Act) was passed in Parliament in 1999 to regulate and promote the insurance and re-insurance industries in India.
- The Global Trust Bank was merged with UTI Bank (now Axis Bank) following financial difficulties, and this occurred in 2004.
- The Fiscal Responsibility and Budget Management Act was passed in 2003 to ensure fiscal discipline by setting targets to eliminate revenue deficits and reduce fiscal deficits.
- The concept of financial inclusion was introduced more prominently into the banking sector post-2005, aiming at providing banking and financial services to all people in a fair, transparent, and equitable manner.

Thus, the correct chronological order is (*d*), (*a*), (*c*), (*e*), (*b*), as per option A.

49. (C): Matching each individual with their correct contributions or related terms:

(*a*) NITI Aayog is associated with providing knowledge support and policy recommendations in India, matching with IV.

(*b*) R. Axelrod is known for his work on the evolution of cooperation and the use of the Tit-for-Tat strategy in repeated interactions, correctly matching with I.

(*c*) J. Stiglitz is renowned for his contributions to the efficiency wage theory, which argues that wages influence worker productivity, fitting with II.

(*d*) India's first five-year plan (1951-1956) was drafted under the guidance of economist K.N. Raj, linking him with III.

This configuration aligns perfectly with option C: IV, I, II, III.

50. (B):

(*a*) W.W. Leontief is famous for developing the Input-Output model in economics, which helps to predict the impact of various economic changes and policies, matching with IV.

(*b*) Jan Tinbergen is known for his work in developing models for economic policy-making, including the concept of the Shadow Price, which matches with I.

(*c*) J.M. Keynes is renowned for his theory of the Consumption Function, which describes the relationship between income and expenditure, fitting with II.

(*d*) Joseph Bertrand proposed Bertrand competition, a model of price competition among firms selling homogenous products, which aligns with III.

Therefore, the correct answers and matches are provided in option B: IV, I, II, III.

51. (A): The chronological order of these environmental and economic theories and agreements is:

- Hotelling's Principle (economics of non-renewable resources), introduced in 1931.
- Establishment of IUCN (International Union for Conservation of Nature) in 1948, a major global conservation organization.
- Nash Equilibrium (game theory), formulated by John Nash in the early 1950s.
- Coase Theorem (law and economics), introduced by Ronald Coase in 1960.
- Kyoto Protocol (international environmental treaty), adopted in 1997.

52. (D):

- The top beneficiary from Foreign exchange trading typically refers to major financial centers like London (III).

- The concept that competitive equilibrium is Pareto efficient aligns with the First theorem of welfare economics (IV), which states that any competitive equilibrium leads to a Pareto efficient allocation of resources.
- Walras, famously associated with General equilibrium analysis, where multiple markets and their interactions are analyzed collectively (II).
- Game Theory was significantly developed by John Von Neuman and Oscar Morgenstern, making it a pivotal framework in understanding strategic interactions among rational decision-makers (I).

Option D correctly matches these concepts with their descriptions: III, IV, II, I.

53. (A): The concept of efficiency wage theory was notably advanced by economists such as Joseph Stiglitz and Janet Yellen among others. This theory suggests that employers pay a wage that is higher than the market-clearing wage to increase worker productivity and reduce turnover. This approach explains various labour market phenomena, including wage rigidity and the persistence of involuntary unemployment.

54. (A): Statement (*a*) is correct: The price consumption curve (PCC) shows the quantities of two goods a consumer will purchase as the price of one of the goods changes, while a demand curve shows the quantity of one good a consumer will purchase as the price of that good changes. The graph of the PCC plots the quantity of one good on the horizontal axis and the quantity of the other good on the vertical axis. The demand curve plots the quantity of the good on the horizontal axis and its price on the vertical axis.

Statement (*c*) is correct; the condition for stability in a simple Keynesian system does indeed require that the marginal propensity to consume (MPC) be between 0 and 1 to ensure that the multiplier effect is positive but finite.

55. (D): The value of SSE (sum of squared errors) will change:

- Swapping the explanatory and response variables in a regression analysis does not change the value of the correlation between the two variables, as correlation is a measure of the linear association irrespective of which variable is considered dependent or independent.
- The sign of the slope does not inherently change simply due to swapping the variables; it reflects the relationship direction and will be consistent unless the data or model specification fundamentally changes.
- The coefficient of determination (R^2), which measures the proportion of variance in the dependent variable that can be predicted from the independent variable, remains unchanged because it is derived from the correlation coefficient.
- The value of the Sum of Squared Errors (SSE), however, will change as it depends on the fit of the model to the data points, which will differ when the roles of the variables are reversed. The new model may fit the data differently, leading to a different SSE value.

56. (D): A surplus in the balance of payments can result from various economic factors that influence the flow of money into and out of a country.

(*a*) A decline in imports would lead to a surplus in the balance of payments as less money is leaving the country to pay for these imports.

(*c*) An increase in exports also contributes to a surplus because it means more foreign buyers are spending their money to purchase the exporting country's goods, thus bringing more money into the country.

(*b*) A decline in interest rates and an increase in income tax (*d*) do not directly lead to a surplus in the balance of payments. Lower interest rates could lead to an increase in investment but may also reduce the inflow of foreign capital seeking higher returns, making its impact on balance of payments ambiguous.

(*e*) High outward Foreign Direct Investment would not result in a surplus but a deficit, as it involves domestic capital flowing out to foreign entities.

Hence, the correct answer is D, as it includes (*a*) and (*c*) which directly contribute to a surplus in the balance of payments.

57. (D):

(*a*) An endogenous variable is a key element within simultaneous equations where it is influenced by other variables within the model, aligning with II.

(*b*) Count R^2, a measure often used in statistics, does not directly match with Logit regression. Thus, IV (Logit regression) is the misalignment here, as there is no specific technique called Count R^2 that is standard. However, the best fit from given options, by the process of elimination, would be IV since others are clearly mismatched.

(*c*) Ljung Box Statistic is used to test for autocorrelation in time series data, fitting with I.

(*d*) Least square dummy variable model is often used in panel data regression to handle categorical variables, matching with III.

Hence, the best fitting answer, by the process of elimination and provided options, is D: II, IV, I, III.

58. (C): The Fisher effect describes the relationship between nominal interest rates, real interest rates, and the expected inflation rate. It posits that the nominal interest rate is equal to the sum of the real interest rate plus the expected inflation rate. This relationship implies that when inflation is high, nominal interest rates tend to be high as lenders need compensation for the decreased purchasing power of money. Conversely, when inflation is low, nominal interest rates are lower.

59. (D): In the State Energy Efficiency Index 2023 released by NITI Aayog, Karnataka emerged as the top scorer, securing the highest rank. This index assesses states on their policies and initiatives related to energy efficiency, considering various sectors such as buildings, industries, municipalities, transport, agriculture, and DISCOMs. Karnataka's leadership in the index reflects its comprehensive approach to implementing energy efficiency measures, promoting sustainable energy policies, and leading in renewable energy usage and conservation practices.

60. (C):

- Narasimham Committee II (1998) recommended that the RBI withdraw from the 91-day treasury bills market and that interbank call money and term money markets be restricted to banks and primary dealers.
- The Ghosh Committee made recommendations relating to frauds and malpractices in banks. The committee provided 53 total recommendations organized under multiple groups.
- Padmanabhan Committee was set up by RBI on supervision of Banks. It was set up in the year 1995 and headed by S. Padmanabhan. It recommended that banking supervision should be based on Managerial and operational efficiency, financial strength of the bank.

- The Saraf Committee Report dealt with technology issues in banking.

Given the context and options provided, option C: III, I, IV, II is the best match according to the descriptions and common understandings of these committee focuses.

61. **(D):** The savings function given is S = –5 + 0.3q, where S is savings and q is income. This function suggests that at q = 0 (zero income), savings start at –5, indicating dis-savings or consumption financed by borrowing or drawing down previous savings. The marginal propensity to save (MPS) is 0.3, indicating that for every additional dollar of income, 30 cents is saved. This implies that the marginal propensity to consume (MPC) is 0.7 (since MPC + MPS = 1).

The average propensity to consume (APC) is calculated as

$$\text{APC} = \frac{C}{q} = \frac{q - S}{q} = 1 - \frac{-5 + 0.3q}{q}$$

= 1 – (–0.05 + 0.3) = 0.75 + 0.05 = 0.8

when q is \$100. As q increases, the negative impact of the –5 decreases, making the APC trend downward but starting from a higher value than the MPC.

Therefore, generally, APC will be greater than MPC, especially at lower income levels. Thus, option D is correct.

62. **(C):** The sequence of introduction of these taxes is as follows:

(*d*) Minimum Alternate Tax (MAT) was intro- duced in 1987 to ensure that companies with large profits and who were eligible for various deductions paid a minimum amount of tax to the government.

(*b*) Securities Transaction Tax (STT) was introduced in 2004 as part of efforts to reducc tax cvasion in stock market transactions.

(*c*) Banking Cash Transaction Tax was introduced in 2005, although later repealed, it was initially aimed at tracking large cash transactions.

(*e*) Angel Tax refers to income tax payable on capital raised by unlisted companies via issue of shares where the share price is seen in excess of the fair market value, introduced in 2012.

(*a*) Commodities Transaction Tax was introduced later in 2013 on transactions similar to the STT but applied to commodity trades.

63. **(A):** The Fifteenth Finance Commission used certain criteria with specific weightages for devolution of tax revenue to states. Among these, income distance had the highest weight, indicating that states further from the fiscal capacity norm get more funds. This is followed by area, which captures the geographic spread of a state. Demographic performance, which includes population data from the latest census, comes next. The weightage for forest and ecology accounts for the state's efforts in maintaining ecological balance. Finally, tax effort assesses the effort made by states in collecting their revenues.

Therefore, option A: (*a*), (*b*), (*c*), (*d*), (*e*) correctly orders these norms from highest to lowest weightage.

64. **(B):**

(*a*) Bank run, a situation where a large number of bank customers withdraw their deposits because they believe the bank might become insolvent, is closely associated with the theories of Douglas Diamond, who modeled banks' roles in providing liquidity (III).

(*b*) The q-ratio, or Tobin's q, is a measure comparing the market value and replacement value of the same physical asset, developed by James Tobin (IV).

(*c*) Genuine saving, a sustainability indicator that considers investment less depreciation of natural and manufactured capital, was notably discussed by Pearce among others, but aligns best with I given the remaining choices.

(*d*) Microfinance is prominently connected with Muhammad Yunus, who pioneered modern microfinance practices with his work in founding the Grameen Bank (II).

Option B, III, IV, I, II, accurately matches these individuals with their respective concepts.

65. (C)

66. (B): For a typical demand function $Q_d = f(P_x, P_y, M)$, where P_x is the price of the good *x*, P_y is the price of another good *y*, and M is income, the sum of the own-price elasticity of demand, cross-price elasticity of demand (with respect to the price of another good), and income elasticity of demand typically equals zero in a balanced market system according to economic theory. This assertion stems from the adding-up constraint in economic modeling, where the proportional changes caused by prices and income typically counterbalance each other when considering a market equilibrium under ceteris paribus (all other factors being constant) conditions.

Therefore, option B (zero) is the correct answer, as it aligns with the theoretical expectation that these elasticities, representing different dimensions of demand responsiveness, sum to zero when the market is balanced.

67. (A): To test the null hypothesis $H_0 : \mu = \mu_0$ when both the population mean μ and the standard deviation σ are unknown, the appropriate test statistic is the Student's *t*-test. The formula for the *t*-test statistic is:

$$t_{n-1} = \frac{\bar{x} - \mu_0}{s' / \sqrt{n}}$$

where:

- $\bar{x}$ is the sample mean,
- μ_0 is the hypothesized mean under the null hypothesis,
- s' is the sample standard deviation,
- n is the sample size,
- $n - 1$ represents the degrees of freedom in the *t*-distribution, which is particularly used because the population standard deviation is unknown.

This formula quantifies how much the sample mean deviates from the hypothesized mean, scaled by the standard error of the mean. The denominator $s' / \sqrt{n}$ is the standard error of the mean, estimating the variation expected in sample means from samples of size *n* drawn from the population.

Option A: $t_{n-1} = \frac{\bar{x} - \mu_0}{s' / \sqrt{n}}$ correctly applies the Student's *t*-distribution principles for cases where the population standard deviation is unknown, hence it is the appropriate choice. This formula helps in making inferences about the population mean based on the sample data when the variance is estimated from the same sample data, requiring adjustment in the degrees of freedom (hence $n - 1$).

68. (C): The current global measurement of the extreme poverty line, as updated by the World Bank in October 2022, is \$2.15 per day. This figure reflects the cost of essential goods and services in 2017 purchasing power parity (PPP), adjusted to account for inflation and changes in the cost of living. It replaces the previous benchmark of \$1.90 per day, which was based on 2011 PPP data. This threshold is used to identify individuals living in extreme poverty globally and is critical for tracking progress toward poverty alleviation and development goals. Therefore, the correct answer is C. $2.15 a day.

69. **(D):** The National Health Policy 2017 of India sets various ambitious targets to improve health outcomes across the country by 2025. These include:

(*c*) Reducing the Maternal Mortality Rate (MMR) to 100.

(*d*) Achieving a Total Fertility Rate (TFR) of 2.1, which is considered a replacement level fertility rate where a population exactly replaces itself from one generation to the next without migration.

(*e*) Increasing Life Expectancy at Birth to 70 years.

While the policy also includes targets for Infant Mortality Rate (IMR) and Under Five Mortality Rate (U5MR), the correct objectives specified to be achieved by 2025 as per the question are (*c*), (*d*), and (*e*), making option D the accurate answer.

70. **(A):** Regional Rural Banks (RRBs) in India have specific characteristics and roles:

(*a*) RRBs were indeed set up based on the recommendation of the Narasimham Working Group in 1975, which aimed to provide sufficient banking and credit facility for agriculture and other rural sectors.

(*c*) NABARD (National Bank for Agriculture and Rural Development) coordinates the activities of RRBs, especially relating to their development functions and also supervises their financial stability and operational policies.

(*e*) RRBs are provided with refinance facilities through NABARD, which helps them extend loans to farmers and rural businesses at lower interest rates, supporting rural development effectively.

The statement about the largest proportion of equity being held by sponsor banks (*b*) is incorrect as the largest proportion is actually held by the Government of India. RRBs are not lead banks (*d*); they operate under the sponsorship of leading nationalized banks.

Thus, the correct answer is A: (*a*), (*c*), (*e*) only.

71. **(D):** ANCOVA (Analysis of Covariance) models are statistical techniques that combine features of ANOVA (Analysis of Variance) and regression analysis. These models are used to analyze the influence of both categorical (qualitative) and continuous (quantitative) independent variables while controlling for the effects of one or more covariates.

By incorporating both types of variables, ANCOVA can adjust the dependent variable for covariates before testing for statistical differences among the group means. This makes it possible to improve the accuracy of the results by reducing variability caused by extraneous factors and focusing on the primary relationships of interest. Hence, option D is correct.

72. **(D):** Neonatal death refers to the death of a baby during the first 28 completed days of life. This classification is commonly used in medical and health-related statistics to focus on deaths that occur in this critical initial period after birth.

The neonatal period is significant because it is when the infant is most vulnerable to various health issues, including infections, birth injuries, and congenital anomalies. Understanding neonatal mortality is crucial for improving child healthcare and interventions aimed at reducing infant mortality rates. Therefore, option D is correct.

73. (A): In the context of linear programming problems (LPP):

(*a*) A feasible solution must satisfy all the problem's constraints simultaneously. This means that any solution that does not meet all constraints is considered infeasible.

(*b*) Is incorrect because a feasible solution must indeed satisfy all constraints, not just some.

(*c*) Is incorrect because a feasible solution does not necessarily have to be a corner point of the feasible region; it can be any point within the region.

(*d*) Is correct because a feasible solution may or may not optimize the value of the objective function. Optimization is achieved specifically at an optimal solution, which is a special case of feasible solutions.

(*e*) Is correct because, in standard linear programming formulations, all decision variables are constrained to be non-negative, meaning they must be greater than or equal to zero.

Thus, option A, (*a*), (*d*), (*e*) only, accurately describes the properties of feasible solutions in linear programming.

74. (B):

(*a*) Ad Valorem Tariff is a type of tariff that is calculated as a percentage of the value of the commodity being imported or exported, fitting description IV.

(*b*) Autarky refers to a state of a country being completely self-sufficient and not engaging in international trade, which aligns with description III.

(*c*) Compound Tariff is a mix of Ad Valorem and specific tariffs, where the tariff includes both a fixed component and a percentage of the item's value, matching with description II.

(*d*) Specific Tariff is a fixed amount charged per unit of the good, fitting description I.

Hence, option B (IV, III, II, I) correctly matches the types of tariffs with their definitions.

75. (D): According to the National Family Health Survey-5 (NFHS-5) for the period 2019-21, the sex ratio (number of females per 1000 males) in India was reported as 1020 females per 1000 males. This statistic indicates a higher number of females relative to males in the population during the survey period, reflecting trends in demographics, health outcomes, and possibly the effectiveness of policies aimed at correcting gender imbalances.

Option D, stating 1020 females per 1000 males, is correct and aligns with the survey findings.

76. (A): A Nash equilibrium is where no player can do better by unilaterally changing their strategy. To find it, check each player's best response to the other's strategies:

- For B_1, B_2, B_3 the best responses for Player P are A_3 yielding payoffs of 5, 4, and 5 respectively.
- For A_1, A_2, A_3 the best responses for Player B are B_1, B_1, B_2 yielding payoffs of 4, 5, and 4 respectively.

The only strategy pair where both players are playing best responses to the other is (A_3, B_2), resulting in the payoff (4, 4), confirming that this is a Nash equilibrium. Therefore, option A is correct.

77. (A): The correct order of the Nobel Prize awards for these economists, from earliest to latest, is:

- Gunnar Myrdal and Friedrich Hayek (not listed), jointly awarded in 1974.
- Milton Friedman, awarded in 1976.

- Arthur Lewis and Theodore Schultz (not listed), jointly awarded in 1979.
- Lawrence Klein, awarded in 1980.
- Abhijit Banerjee, awarded in 2019 along with Esther Duflo and Michael Kremer.

Option A: (*b*),(*c*),(*a*),(*e*),(*d*) presents these economists in the correct chronological order of their Nobel Prize recognitions.

78. (A):

- Statement (*a*) is correct: A public good is nonexclusive, meaning it is not feasible to exclude anyone from using the good, regardless of whether they have paid for it or not.
- Statement (*b*) is correct: National defense is often cited as a classic example of a public good because it provides a service from which all citizens benefit, and no one can be excluded from its protection.
- Statement (*c*) is incorrect: Public goods are not rival, meaning that one person's use of the good does not diminish the ability of another person to use it.
- Statement (*d*) is incorrect: The provision of public goods does not entail a non-zero marginal cost; public goods are characterized by a zero marginal cost of provision to an additional consumer.
- Statement (*e*) is incorrect: Public goods do not inherently create inefficiency in consumption; rather, the challenge with public goods is in their provision and financing, leading to potential under-provision or funding issues.

Thus, option A is correct, accurately including statements (*a*) and (*b*) only.

79. (C): In the context of the Fifteenth Finance Commission's assignments of grants-in-aid to the states, the biggest item is typically for Local bodies grants. These grants are significant as they directly support the financial needs of local governmental bodies, enabling them to deliver essential services and carry out local development projects. This allocation is vital for maintaining the infrastructural and operational capacities at the local level, including urban and rural bodies, which are crucial for localized governance and service provision. Therefore, the correct answer is C, aligning with the commission's focus on strengthening grassroots governance structures through substantial financial support.

80. (B):

- Venture Capital (*a*) and Global Depository Receipts (*d*) are instruments used within the capital market. Venture capital is a type of private equity and a form of financing that investors provide to startup companies and small businesses that are believed to have long-term growth potential. Global Depository Receipts (GDRs) represent bank certificates issued in more than one country for shares in foreign companies, allowing an international company to access investors in capital markets other than its own.
- Treasury Bills (*b*) are short-term government securities typically issued in the money market.
- Certificates of Deposit (*c*) issued by commercial banks and Inter Corporate Deposits (*e*) are also instruments primarily associated with the money market rather than the capital market.

Therefore, option B: (*a*), (*d*) only, is the correct answer, accurately representing instruments that are part of the capital market.

81. (B):

(*c*) Adam Smith published "The Wealth of Nations" in 1776, which laid the foundations of classical economics and includes discussions on growth, though not framed as a "Theory of Growth" per se, it is foundational.

(*b*) J.M. Keynes published "The General Theory of Employment, Interest, and Money" in 1936, fundamentally changing economic thought concerning the causes of unemployment and interventions by government policy.

(*e*) Robert M. Solow introduced his growth model in 1956, which extended the Harrod-Domar model by including technology change and labour as drivers of growth.

(*a*) A.W. Phillips introduced the Phillips Curve in 1958, describing an inverse relationship between rates of unemployment and corresponding rates of rises in wages that result within an economy.

(*d*) John F. Muth formulated the Rational Expectations theory, which was introduced in the early 1960s, refining predictions in macroeconomic models by assuming that people's predictions of the future are informed by their understanding of economic policy.

Thus, option B: (*c*), (*b*), (*e*), (*a*), (*d*) arranges these economists from the earliest to the latest relevant contributions.

82. (D): The construction of concepts related to consumer behaviour in economics follows a logical sequence, starting from foundational theories to more complex analyses. The correct order is:

(*b*) Utility analysis, which is the fundamental concept where consumer preferences and utilities are defined and understood.

(*d*) Indifference curve analysis, which builds on utility analysis by graphically representing consumer preferences through curves that indicate combinations of goods between which the consumer is indifferent.

(*a*) Budget, which introduces the constraints under which consumers optimize their choices, considering their limited resources.

(*e*) Consumer's equilibrium, where the optimal choice of the consumer is determined at the point where the budget constraint tangentially touches the highest attainable indifference curve.

(*c*) Demand curve analysis, which is derived last as it aggregates consumer behaviours into market-wide relationships between price changes and quantity demanded.

This sequence from individual preference analysis to market demand representation reflects the logical progression in economic theory, making option D: (*b*), (*d*), (*a*), (*e*), (*c*), the correct and comprehensive order of development in these concepts.

83. (B):

(*a*) Monopoly theory of distribution was discussed by Michal Kalecki, linking the degree of monopoly to income distribution (III).

(*b*) The theory of profit, encompassing various interpretations including dynamics of business profits, was an area explored by theorists like Alfred Marshall, but within this context, aligning it with Walker, who discussed profits in the context of capital and distribution, seems most fitting given the options (I).

(*c*) Full cost pricing is associated with Hall and Hitch, who argued that businesses price based on costs plus a mark-up, commonly used in managerial economics (IV).

(*d*) Modern theory of rent, concerning how rent is determined in modern economic contexts, aligns with Joan Robinson's work, which extensively covered various facets of pricing and market structures (II).

Thus, option B: III, I, IV, II, correctly matches each theorist with their respective theories or models.

84. (A): The Gravity Model of world trade is a major model in international economics that predicts bilateral trade flows based on the economic sizes (often measured by GDP) of the two countries (*a*) and the distance between them (*b*).

- Distance acts as a proxy for the costs associated with trade, including transportation costs, tariffs, and other barriers.
- Gross Domestic Product of the trading countries indicates the size of their economies, suggesting potential volume of trade that could be supported by larger economies.

Foreign exchange rates (*c*) and foreign investment (*e*) influence trade but are not core components of the basic Gravity Model, which focuses primarily on size and distance.

Option A: (*a*) and (*b*) only, accurately captures the fundamental components as per the Gravity Model of trade.

85. (C):

- The Engel-Granger test is one of the methods used to test for cointegration among non-stationary time series data. It involves running a regression on the time series variables, then testing the residuals from this regression for stationarity.
- If the residuals are found to be stationary, it suggests that although the individual time series may be non-stationary, they move together over time in a way that their linear combination is stationary, indicating cointegration.
- Chow test is used for testing structural breaks in regression models.
- Phillips-Pcron tcst is uscd to chcck for unit roots in time series data.
- Error-correction mechanism is a dynamic model used in time series analysis to adjust the speed at which variables return to equilibrium after a change.

Therefore, option C: Engel-Granger test, is the correct answer for identifying a method used for testing cointegration.

86. (A): To arrange these expressions in terms of increasing magnitude, we consider the impact of each component in the expressions. Given $a > 0$, $b > 0$, $x > 0$:

(*d*) $y = e^{a - \frac{b}{x}}$ is the smallest because subtraction of a positive fraction reduces the value.

(*a*) $y = e^a$ simply is the exponential growth value which sets a base magnitude.

(*c*) $y = e^{a + \frac{b}{x}}$ adds a positive fraction to e^a, making it larger than (*a*).

(*b*) $y = e^{a + bx}$ is larger than (*c*) because as $x > 0$, bx would be greater than $\frac{b}{x}$ for $x > 1$.

(*e*) $y = e^{a + 2bx}$ is the largest because it doubles the bx term compared to (*b*), thus adding more to e^a.

Option A correctly places these expressions from smallest to largest.

87. (C): In the leakage-injection approach to income determination, an increase in lump-sum tax (assuming no changes in other variables — ceteris paribus) effectively increases leakage in the form of taxes. This would shift the savings plus tax leakage line to the left in the income-leakage diagram. This shift represents an increase in total leakages relative to a given level of income, thus reducing disposable income and potentially lowering aggregate demand unless countered by equivalent injections. It does not directly affect the investment plus government spending line, unless there are fiscal responses compensating for the higher tax.

88. (A): In the Cobb-Douglas production function $q = AL^{\alpha}K^{\beta}$, where A, α and β are constants, α and β represent the output elasticities of the inputs. Specifically, α measures the output elasticity with respect to labour, and β measures the output elasticity with respect to capital. These parameters indicate the percentage change in output resulting from a one per cent change in labour or capital, respectively, holding all else constant. This relationship is central to understanding how changes in input amounts affect output levels, making option A correct.

89. (B): When dealing with high multicollinearity in regression models, though not perfect:

- It can result in high confidence intervals for the estimates, making them less precise (A).
- It can lead to a high R^2 value, indicating a good fit of the model with the included variables despite the multicollinearity (C).
- The estimates are not necessarily the Best Linear Unbiased Estimators (BLUE); multicollinearity can make the estimates biased or inefficient in some cases (D).
- High multicollinearity does not necessarily lead to statistical significance for all coefficient estimates (B). On the contrary, it can inflate the standard errors of the coefficients, leading to fewer statistically significant results, despite a good overall model fit.

90. (C): Both arithmetic mean and median are wrong: Given:

- The lowest value in the set is 4.5.
- The range of the set is 10.9, implying the highest value is 4.5 + 10.9 = 15.4.
- An arithmetic mean of 19.9 is impossible because it is greater than the maximum value in the data set.
- A median of 15.6 is also incorrect as the median must lie between the minimum and maximum values of the data set, which are 4.5 and 15.4, respectively.

Therefore, both the arithmetic mean and median as provided cannot be correct, leading to the selection of option C.

91. (B): When comparing the competitive and monopoly scenarios, the producer's gains when moving from competitive pricing (P_c) to monopoly pricing (P_m) can be visualized in the diagram.

Under competitive pricing, the producer surplus is the area above the MC curve and below the price P_c, up to Q_c. When moving to monopoly pricing, the producer surplus is the area above the MC curve and below P_m up to Q_m. The gain in producer surplus due to the price increase from P_c to P_m is represented by the rectangle A. However, the reduction in output from Q_c to Q_m also removes some producer surplus, represented by triangle C. Thus, the net gain in producer surplus due to moving from competitive to monopoly pricing is the area A minus the area C, confirming the answer as B.

92. (B): The consumer loss due to the transition from competitive pricing (P_c) to monopoly pricing (P_m) comprises the areas representing the increased costs and the loss of welfare due to reduced consumption.

Area A represents the increased cost to consumers who still purchase the product at the higher monopoly price (P_m), paying more than the competitive price (P_c).

Area B represents the consumer surplus lost due to the decreased quantity consumed, moving from Q_c to Q_m, as some consumers opt out of buying the product at the higher price.

Therefore, the total consumer loss includes both the extra amount paid for the units still bought (A) and the consumer surplus lost on the units no longer bought (B). Thus, the answer is B.

93. (A): Assuming that production processes involve environmental impacts like emissions or resource depletion, producing less quantity, as in the monopoly output (Q_m), compared to the competitive output (Q_c), leads to a reduction in these negative environmental impacts.

The rationale is that fewer units of production result in fewer emissions or less resource use. Therefore, under the assumptions typically related to environmental impacts tied to production volume, a monopoly, by producing less, inadvertently contributes to less environmental degradation compared to a competitive market output level.

Hence, A: Monopoly output is environmentally friendlier comparative to competitive output, is correct.

94. (C): The diagram illustrates that by charging a higher price (P_m) and reducing output to Q_m, the monopolist gains rectangle A due to the higher price but loses triangle C because of producing fewer units.

This is reflective of the monopolist's profit-maximizing behaviour, where the price is raised to increase revenue per unit, thus gaining area A, but at the cost of losing some customers due to the higher price, represented by the loss of area C.

Therefore, the producer gains area A and loses area C as a result of adopting a monopoly pricing strategy, leading to the answer C.

95. (D): Deadweight loss in the context of monopoly refers to the loss of economic efficiency when the equilibrium for goods or services is not achieved or is not achievable.

In the given diagram, the areas B and C together represent this deadweight loss.

Area B is the consumer surplus that is lost and not gained by the producer, while area C represents the producer surplus lost due to reduced output. These areas indicate the total welfare loss to society due to the monopolistic pricing above marginal cost and the reduction in quantity produced from Q_c to Q_m.

Thus, the correct answer is D: B + C, representing the comprehensive deadweight loss due to the monopoly's pricing and output decisions.

96. (A): To calculate the fiscal deficit as a percentage of GDP, first determine the fiscal deficit. Fiscal deficit is calculated as total expenditure minus total receipts excluding borrowings. Here, total receipts are ₹ 400 crore, and total expenditure (sum of revenue and capital expenditure) is ₹ 400 crore (₹ 300 crore in revenue + ₹ 100 crore in capital). The total receipts excluding borrowings (₹ 400 crore – ₹ 100 crore borrowings) equals ₹ 300 crore.

Thus, the fiscal deficit = Total Expenditure – (Total Receipts – Borrowings)

= ₹ 400 crore – ₹ 300 crore

= ₹ 100 crore.

The GDP is ₹ 2000 crore.

Thus, the fiscal deficit as a percentage of GDP

= (₹ 100 crore / ₹ 2000 crore) × 100 = 5%.

Therefore, the fiscal deficit as a percentage of GDP is 5%, making option A correct.

97. (D): The primary deficit is calculated as the fiscal deficit minus interest payments. From the earlier calculation, we know the fiscal deficit is ₹ 100 crore. Interest payments are ₹ 90 crore.

Thus, the primary deficit = ₹ 100 crore – ₹ 90 crore = ₹ 10 crore.

As a percentage of GDP (₹ 2000 crore), the primary deficit = (₹ 10 crore / ₹ 2000 crore) × 100 = 0.5%.

Therefore, the primary deficit as a percentage of GDP is 0.5%, making option D correct.

98. (A): The revenue deficit is calculated as total revenue expenditure minus total revenue receipts.

Total revenue expenditure is ₹ 300 crore and total revenue receipts are ₹ 250 crore. Thus, the revenue deficit
= ₹ 300 crore – ₹ 250 crore = ₹ 50 crore.

As a percentage of GDP (₹ 2000 crore), the revenue deficit
= (₹ 50 crore/₹ 2000 crore) × 100 = 2.5%.
Therefore, the revenue deficit as a percentage of GDP is 2.5%, making option A correct.

99. (C): The effective revenue deficit subtracts grants for the creation of capital assets from the revenue deficit. Grants for the creation of capital assets are ₹ 20 crore. The calculated revenue deficit is ₹ 50 crore.

Thus, effective revenue deficit
= ₹ 50 crore – ₹ 20 crore = ₹ 30 crore.

As a percentage of GDP (₹ 2000 crore), the effective revenue deficit
= (₹ 30 crore/₹ 2000 crore) × 100
= 1.5%.

Therefore, the effective revenue deficit as a percentage of GDP is 1.5%, making option C correct.

100. (C): The twin deficit refers to the sum of the fiscal deficit and the current account deficit as a percentage of GDP. The fiscal deficit has already been calculated as ₹ 100 crore, and the current account deficit is given as ₹ 50 crore.

Thus, total twin deficit
= ₹ 100 crore + ₹ 50 crore = ₹ 150 crore.

As a percentage of GDP (₹ 2000 crore), the twin deficit
= (₹ 150 crore/₹ 2000 crore) × 100
= 7.5%.

Therefore, the twin deficit as a percentage of GDP is 7.5%, making option C correct.

Previous Years' Paper

National Testing Agency (NTA)

UGC-NET Junior Research Fellowship & Assistant Professor Eligibility Exam

ECONOMICS, December-2023

(Exam held on 12-12-2023)

PAPER-II

1. The expert committee set up by RBI in 2013 to revise and strengthen the monetary policy framework in India was chaired by:
A. Raghuram Rajan B. Urjit Patel
C. Deepak Mohanty D. Michael Patra

2. Under the flexible inflation targeting framework of monetary policy adopted by the RBI in 2016 what is the target range of rate of inflation?
A. $(4 \pm 2)\%$ B. $(5 \pm 2)\%$
C. $(3 \pm 2)\%$ D. $(2 \pm 2)\%$

3. In a regression of a dependent variable on intercept and k other independent variables using n observations, what are respectively the numerator and denominator degrees of freedom for the F test for overall significance of the regression?
A. $k - 1, n - k$ B. $k, n - k - 1$
C. $k - 1, n - k - 1$ D. $k, n - k$

4. Suppose X_i is income of an individual i and Y_i is the event that this individual owns a house, $P_i = \text{prob}(Y_i = 1 \mid X_i)$ and $Z_i = \beta_1 + \beta_2 X_i$, (which of the following is true for the logit model?

A. $P_i = \frac{1}{1-e^{-Z_i}}$ B. $P_i = \frac{1}{1+e^{Z_i}}$

C. $P_i = \frac{1}{1+e^{-Z_i}}$ D. $P_i = \frac{1}{1-e^{Z_i}}$

5. If the estimated slope coefficient in the regression of Y on X is $\hat{\beta}$, what will be the estimated slope coefficient in the regression of 5 Y on 10 X?

A. $5\hat{\beta}$ B. $10\hat{\beta}$

C. $2\hat{\beta}$ D. $0.5\hat{\beta}$

6. Which of the following tests has stationarity as the null hypothesis?
A. ADF Test
B. Phillips Perron Test
C. ERS Test
D. KPSS Test

7. For a VAR model estimated using two variables X and Y, Lags of Y are jointly significant in the equation for X but Lags of X are jointly insignificant in the equation for Y. What can you conclude from this?
A. There is no Granger causality between X and Y
B. There is bidirectional Granger causality between X and Y
C. X Granger causes Y but Y does not Granger cause X
D. Y Granger causes X but X does not Granger cause Y

8. Suppose India is the home country and USA is the foreign country. The interest rates in India and USA are 6% and 4% respectively.

The exchange rate of US Dollar is ₹ 80 today but is expected to rise to ₹ 84 in one year. Which of the following is true, according to the uncovered interest arbitrage paritv condition?

A. Capital will flow into the Indian economy
B. Capital will flow out of the Indian economy
C. No captial flows
D. Can't say on the basis of the information provided

9. In the model $\ln Y_i = \alpha + \beta X_i + u_i$ Where ln is natural log, the elasticity of Y w.r. t. X is given by:

A. β B. βX_i

C. $\frac{\beta}{Y_i}$ D. $\beta\frac{X_i}{Y_i}$

10. In an economy real GDP has increased from $ 990 PPP to $ 1080 PPP during 2015 to 2020. The incremental capital output ratio is 2.5. The rate of investment is:

A. 27.8 Percent B. 22.5 Percent
C. 3.9 Percent D. 19.5 Percent

11. Which of the following dimensions is included in HPI-2 (Human Poverty Index-2)?

A. Gender Inequalities
B. Financial Inclusion
C. Social Inclusion
D. Economic Inclusion

12. The Solow residual is:

A. The difference between the rate of growth of productivity and the rate of growth of inputs
B. The difference between the rate of growth of output and the rate of growth of saving
C. The difference between the rate of growth of output and the rate of growth of inputs
D. The difference between the golden rule level of consumption and the steady state level of consumption

13. Gini-coefficient, a widely used measure of inequality in income is defined as:

A. $\frac{1}{n^2\mu}\sum_{i}\sum_{j\le 1}^{n}(y_i - y_j)$

B. $\frac{2}{n^2\mu}\sum_{i}^{n} i\, y_i - \left[\frac{n+1}{n}\right]$

C. $\frac{2}{n\mu}\frac{\sum_{i}^{n} i\, y_i}{\sum_{i}^{n} y_i} - \left[\frac{n+1}{n}\right]$

D. $\frac{1}{n^2\mu}\sum_{i=1}^{n}\sum_{j=1}^{n}|(y_i - y_j)|$

14. Endogenous growth theorv assumes:

A. Increasing returns to scale and perfect competition
B. Decreasing returns to scale and perfect competition
C. Increasing returns to scale and imperfect competition
D. Decreasing returns to scale and imperfect competition

15. Suppose you are testing a Null Hypothesis about the population mean, Ho: $\mu = \mu_0$ against $H_1 : \mu > \mu_0$, with population variance given. The computed value of the test statistic is Zc. What is the *p*-value for this test, where $\Phi()$ is the cumulative distribution function for the standard normal distribution?

A. $\Phi(Zc)$ B. $\Phi(Zc/2)$
C. $1 - \Phi(Zc)$ D. $1 - \Phi(Zc/2)$

16. The power of a test refers to:

A. Type I error B. Type II error
C. 1–Type II D. 1–Type I error

17. Given a random sample of size *n* from a population with mean μ and variance, σ^2, the sample mean has the following expected value and variance:

A. $E(\overline{x}) = \mu \; Var(\overline{x}) = \sigma^2 / n$

B. $E(\overline{x}) = n\mu \; Var(\overline{x}) = n\sigma^2$

C. $E(\overline{x}) = \mu \; Var(\overline{x}) = \sigma^2$

D. $E(\overline{x}) = \mu \; Var(\overline{x}) = n / \sigma^2$

18. In March, 2023 the consumer price index (CPI) of a country with a 1982 base index of 100, was 234.7. This means the cost of purchasing the market basket of goods and services:

A. has decreased by 134.7% since 1982
B. has increased by 34.7% since 1982
C. has increased by 234.7% since 1982
D. has increased by 134.7% since 1982

19. Consider a production function $q = x + y$, where x and y are the 2 inputs. If the respective input prices are w_x and w_y and assume $w_x > w_y$. Then the cost function C(q) is:

A. $C(q) = w_x q$
B. $C(q) = w_y q$
C. $C(q) = (w_x + w_y)q$
D. $C(q) = \min\{w_x, w_y\}\sqrt{q}$

20. Suppose a cost function of producing q level of output in C(w, r, q) where

$$C(w, r, q) = q\left(\frac{w}{\alpha} + \frac{r}{\beta}\right),$$ where w and r are

the wage cost and rental cost of the 2 inputs capital (K) and labour (l) respectively. What would be the production function q of k and l?

A. $q = \alpha k + \beta l$
B. $q = [k^\alpha + l\beta]^r$
C. $q = \min(\alpha l, \beta k\}$
D. $q = A(k^\alpha \bullet l^\beta)$

21. If $f(x, y)$ is a homogeneous function of degree 2 with $f'(2, 3) = 4$ and $f'(4, 6) = 12$, find $f(6, 9)$:

A. 117
B. 234
C. 115
D. 243

22. If the Average Revenue function AR = $10 + 5q - q^2$, then the Marginal Revenue function is a:

A. Convex function
B. Concave function
C. Can be both concave or convex function
D. Weakly concave function

23. Suppose a consumer has a utility function $u(x) = 10\sqrt{x}$, where x is the money income of the consumer. Suppose the consumer's initial endowment is ₹ 50. Suppose she may suffer a loss of ₹ 25 with a probability of 0.5 for some random event. Suppose she pays p premium for an insurance policy that fully reimburses her if she suffers a loss. How much premium p would she be willing to pay to insure against the loss?

A. 12.50
B. 13.57
C. 11.59
D. 14.41

24. Suppose $f(.)$ is a continuous function over a closed and bounded interval $[a, b]$. Then there exists a point d in $[a, b]$ where $f(.)$ has a minimum, and a point c in $[a, b]$ where $f(.)$ has a maximum, so that $f(d) \le f(x) \le f(c)$ for all x in $[a, b]$. The statement is derived from:

A. Intermediate Value Theorem
B. Rolle's Theorem
C. Mean value Theorem
D. Extreme value Theorem

25. Consider a consumer's choice based on only 2 commodities i.e., $X \in R^2_+$, where X is a set of all commodity bundles which the consumer can conceive of. Suppose x and y are the 2 different commodity bundles and the budget set B of the consumer can be written as:

$$B = \{(x, y) : p_1 x + p_2 y \le M\}; x_i > 0, i = 1, 2.$$

Which of the following statements is true?

A. The budge set is an open, bounded and convex set
B. The budget set is not a bounded set

C. The budget set is a closed and non-convex set

D. The budget set is a closed, bounded and convex set

26. Consider a Bertrand duopoly where the 2 firms produce a homogenous product. Assume the market demand curve is $y = y_1 + y_2 = 1 - p$, where p is the relevant market price, y is the total amount demanded at that price, y_1 and y_2 are the output levels of firm (1) and (2) respectively. Assume that the firm's cost functions are $C(y_i) = \frac{1}{2} y_i$ for $i = 1, 2$. The rules of the pricing game are as follows: Each firm must simultaneously quote a price in the interval [0, 1]. If the prices are different, the firm with the lower price sells all the units demanded at that price. If they quote the same price, the amount demanded at that price is splited equally between the two firms. What would be the Nash equilibrium price and quantities?

A. $P_1 = P_2 = 1;\ Y_1 = Y_2 = \frac{1}{2}Y;$ is one of the Multiple Nash Equilibria

B. $P_1 = P_2 = \frac{1}{2};\ Y_1 = Y_2 = \frac{1}{2}Y;$ is the Unique Nash Equilibrium

C. $P_1 > P_2 = \frac{1}{2};\ Y_1 = 0, Y_2 = Y;$ is one of the Multiple Nash Equilibria

D. $P_1 < P_2 = \frac{1}{2};\ Y_1 = Y, Y_2 = 0;$ is one of the Multiple Nash Equilibria

27. Suppose the cost function

$$C(w_1, w_2, y) = y\left(w_1 + \sqrt{w_1 w_2} + w_2\right),$$

where w_1 and w_2 are the prices of 2 inputs which are used in production of y. Which of the following properties of the cost function $C(w_1, w_2, y)$ is correct?

A. Cost function $C(w_1, w_2, y)$ is monotone, concave and continuous function in w_1, w_2.

B. Cost function $C(w_1, w_2, y)$ is a non-monotone, convex and continuous function in w_1, w_2.

C. Cost function is continuous in w_1 and w_2 and discontinuous function in y.

D. Cost function is a continuous function and homogeneous function in degree 0.

28. The demand and supply functions for cobweb model are given as:

$$Q_t^d = 19 - 6P_t \text{ and } Q_t^S = 6P_{t-1} - 5$$

Choose the right answer related to intertemporal equilibrium price and the nature of the equilibrium.

A. $\bar{P} = 2$, explosive oscillation

B. $\bar{P} = 2$, uniform oscillation

C. $\bar{P} = 3$, damped oscillation

D. $\bar{P} = 3$, uniform oscillation

29. Consider the pay offs of two players, who are close friends. They can either go for Diwali shopping or they can watch World Cup Cricket match.

		Player 1	
		Diwali Shopping	World Cup Watching
Player 2	Diwali Shopping	(2, 1)	(0, 0)
	World Cup Watching	(0, 0)	(1, 2)

Identify which of the following is true for them:

A. There is no Nash equilibrium for them.

B. There is only one Nash equilibrium where player 1 goes for Diwali shopping and player 2 goes for World Cup Match.

C. Any of the four combinations can be a Nash Equilibrium.

D. There are two Nash Equilibria.

30. In case of two perfect complement goods, which following statement is **not** true?

A. The substitution effect is zero.

B. The indifference curves are straight lines.

C. The indifference curves are L shaped

D. The goods are always demanded in fixed proportions.

31. If $A=\begin{bmatrix}2 & 3\\0 & 4\end{bmatrix}$ and $B=\begin{bmatrix}2 & 0\\1 & 5\end{bmatrix}$ which of the following is **not** correct?

A. $A^TB=\begin{bmatrix}4 & 0\\10 & 20\end{bmatrix}$

B. $(A+B)^T=\begin{bmatrix}4 & 1\\3 & 9\end{bmatrix}$

C. $A^TB=\begin{bmatrix}0 & 4\\10 & 20\end{bmatrix}$

D. $A^TB^T=\begin{bmatrix}4 & 2\\6 & 23\end{bmatrix}$

32. According to the Census 2011, which major Indian state is the most urbanized?

A. Maharashtra B. Punjab

C. Karnataka D. Tamil Nadu

33. In a market for labour's demand and supply, the equilibrium wage is w^*. The government fixes a minimum wage at w'. Which of the following statements is true?

A. There is a tendency of increased equalization of workers if $w' > w^*$ where the workers would not receive lots of benefits.

B. The market will now tend towards a new equilibrium at w', with no other changes, if $w' > w^*$.

C. If $w' < w^*$, there will be a tendency of increased casualization of workers.

D. It will be impossible to administer such a legislation unless $w' = w^*$.

34. In the given figure, DD is the demand curve and SS is the supply curve in a market. Choose the right answer from the following.

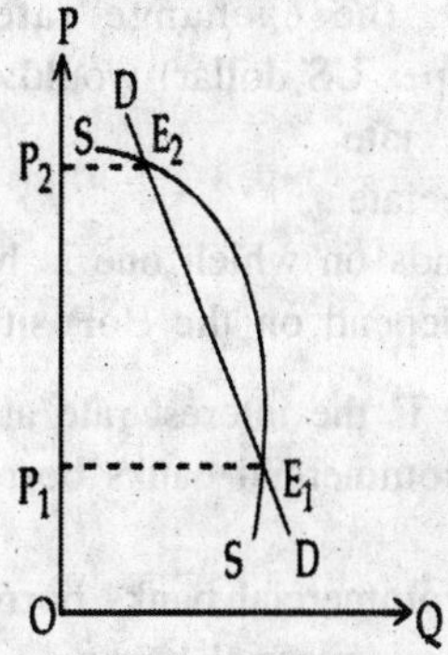

A. There is no stable equilibrium.

B. E_2 is a stable equilibrium, though E_1 is an unstable equilibrium

C. E_1 is a stable equilibrium, though E_2 is an unstable equilibrium

D. Both E_1 & E_2 are stable equibria

35. If the revenue deficit of an economy is 3% of GDP, the primary deficit is 2% of GDP and the fiscal deficit is 7% of GDP, the capital expenditure to GDP ratio of that economy would be:

A. 5% of GDP B. 1% of GDP

C. 4% of GDP D. 2% of GDP

36. If the interest rate is exogenously determined by the Central Bank of some country and the money supply is endogenously determined, the slope of the LM-curve in the interest rate-income plane would be:

A. Positively sloped B. Negatively sloped

C. Horizontal D. Vertical

37. Higher fiscal deficit to GDP ratio would necessarily cause inflation if the economy is under:

A. Demand constrained situation

B. Supply constrained situation

C. Both demand and supply constrained situation

D. Neither demand constrained nor supply constrained situation

38. Under the flexible exchange rate, if the current account deficit increases and the capital account surplus increases for an economy, the exchange rate (domestic currency per US dollar) would:

A. Appreciate
B. Depreciate
C. Depends on which one is higher
D. Not depend on the BoP situation

39. Repo rate is the interest rate at which:

A. The commercial banks borrow from the RBI
B. The commercial banks borrow from the other commercial banks
C. The commercial banks deposit money to the RBI
D. The common people deposit money to the RBI

40. An economy characterised by huge involuntary unemployment would have an aggregate labour supply curve in a real wage-labour supply plane that would be:

A. Positively sloped B. Vertical
C. Flat D. Negatively sloped

41. Global Hunger Index (GHI) includes:

(*a*) Child mortality with weight $\frac{1}{3}$

(*b*) Child stunting with weight $\frac{1}{3}$

(*c*) Undernourishment with weight $\frac{1}{3}$

(*d*) Child wasting with weight $\frac{1}{6}$

(*e*) Child mortality with weight $\frac{1}{6}$

Choose the **correct** answer from the options given below:

A. (*a*), (*b*) and (*c*) only
B. (*a*), (*c*) and (*d*) only
C. (*b*), (*c*) and (*e*) only
D. (*d*) and (*e*) only

42. Which of the following statements are not true for the Linear Probability Model (LPM)?

(*a*) Conditional probability of occurence of an event conditional on the value of explanatory variable X is a linear function of X
(*b*) Estimated value of the conditional probability of occurence of the event lies between 0 and 1
(*c*) Error term is homoscedastic
(*d*) R^2 is a good measure of goodness of fit

Choose the **correct** answer from the options given below:

A. (*b*) only
B. (*b*) and (*c*) only
C. (*b*), (*c*) and (*d*) only
D. (*c*) only

43. Given that Z_t is a zero-mean white noise process with variance σ^2, which of the following are I(O) processes?

(*a*) $X_t = X_{t-1} + Z_t$
(*b*) $X_t = \alpha X_{t-1} + Z_t$ where $0 < \alpha < 1$
(*c*) $X_t = Z_t + Z_{t-1}$
(*d*) $X_t = 8 + X_{t-1} + Z_t$

Choose the **correct** answer from the options given below:

A. (*c*) only
B. (*b*) only
C. (*b*) and (*c*) only
D. (*b*), (*c*) and (*d*) only

44. Which of the following are features of a weakly stationary stochastic process?

(*a*) Mean is time-varying
(*b*) Mean is constant
(*c*) Variance is constant
(*d*) Covariance is time-invariant

Choose the **correct** answer from the options given below:

A. (*b*) and (*c*) only
B. (*b*), (*c*) and (*d*) only
C. (*a*), (*c*) and (*d*) only
D. (*a*) and (*c*) only

45. Suppose an economy is in medium-run equilibrium. Now the government enacts a law, making entry of new firms difficult, which increases the monopoly power of the existing firms. Which of the following statements are true about this change?

(*a*) Output level will be lower in medium-run
(*b*) Output level will be lower in short-run
(*c*) Price level will be higher in medium-run
(*d*) Price level will be higher in short-run

Choose the **correct** answer from the options given below:

A. (*a*) and (*c*) only
B. (*b*), (*c*) and (*d*) only
C. (*b*) and (*c*) only
D. (*a*), (*b*) (*c*) and (*d*) only

46. Among the new monetary aggregates suggested by the Third working group of RBI, which one/ones include time deposits of term less than or equal to one year but does not include the time deposits with term more than one year?

(*a*) NM_0 (*b*) NM_1
(*c*) NM_2 (*d*) NM_3

Choose the **correct** answer from the options given below:

A. (*a*) only
B. (*c*) only
C. (*c*) and (*d*) only
D. (*b*) and (*c*) only

47. Which one of the following are money market instruments?

(*a*) 91-day Treasury bill
(*b*) Commercial paper
(*c*) Certificate of deposit issued by banks
(*d*) 5-year government bond

Choose the **correct** answer from the options given below:

A. (*a*) only
B. (*a*) and (*b*) only
C. (*a*), (*b*) and (*c*) only
D. (*b*) and (*c*) only

48. Consider the following statements about the Current Account of the balance of payments and indicate which statements are true?

(*a*) Current Account deficit equals excess of imports over sum of exports and net transfers received by a country.
(*b*) Current Account deficit may be covered by borrowing from foreigners.
(*c*) Current Account deficit may be covered by buying assets from foreigners.
(*d*) If India's Current Account deficit in a particular period is \$ 50 million, it can be financed by net capital inflows amounting to \$ 50 million.

Choose the **correct** answer from the options given below:

A. (*a*), (*b*), (*c*), (*d*) B. (*a*), (*b*), (*d*) only
C. (*a*), (*c*), (*d*) only D. (*b*), (*c*), (*d*) only

49. Suppose India is home country and USA is foreign country. Interest rate in India is 3%, that in US is 1%. The Re-\$ exchange rate is ₹ 80 per USD in spot market and ₹ 81 per USD in 3 month forward market. Which of the following are true for the resulting covered interest arbitrage flows?

(*a*) Indian Rupee will depreciate in spot market
(*b*) Indian Rupee will depreciate in forward market
(*c*) Interest rate will decline in India
(*d*) Interest rate will decline in US

Choose the **correct** answer from the options given below:

A. (*a*) and (*b*) only B. (*a*) and (*c*) only
C. (*a*) and (*d*) only D. (*a*), (*b*), (*c*) and (*d*)

50. The current account deficit of the BOP may be financed in many ways. Which of the following are correct?

(*a*) FDI inflows
(*b*) Inflow of foreign portfolio investment
(*c*) Borrowing from IMF or World Bank
(*d*) Drawing down foreign exchange reserves

Choose the **correct** answer from the options given below:

A. (*a*), (*b*), (*c*) only B. (*b*), (*c*), (*d*) only
C. (*a*), (*b*), (*c*), (*d*) D. (*a*), (*c*), (*d*) only

51. Consider the following statements about the Specific Factors model of International Trade and say which ones are correct?

(*a*) Factors specific to the export sectors in each country gain from trade
(*b*) Factors specific to the import-competing sectors in each country lose from trade
(*c*) Mobile factors that can work in either sector may gain from trade
(*d*) Mobile factors that can work in either sector may lose from trade

Choose the **correct** answer from the options given below:

A. (*a*), (*c*), (*d*) only B. (*b*), (*c*), (*d*) only
C. (*a*), (*b*), (*c*) only D. (*a*), (*b*), (*c*), (*d*)

52. Consider the following statements about the Aggregate Demand (AD) relation under price flexibility and say which ones are correct?

(*a*) The AD curve will shift to the right if autonomous investment rises.
(*b*) The AD curve will shift to the right if net exports rise in an open economy.
(*c*) The AD curve will shift to the left if money supply contracts.
(*d*) As price rises, shifting the LM curve, the AD curve shifts to the left

Choose the **correct** answer from the options given below:

A. (*a*), (*b*), (*c*) only B. (*b*), (*c*), (*d*) only
C. (*a*), (*c*), (*d*) only D. (*a*), (*b*), (*c*), (*d*)

53. Given the following statements about major schools of drought in macroeconomics, state which ones are correct?

(*a*) The Keynesians believed in wage and price flexibility and highlighted the role of aggregate supply.
(*b*) The monetarists highlighted the importance of money in the economic system and that of expectations in the analysis of inflation.
(*c*) The classical school believed in the invisible hand and the efficiency of the market mechanism
(*d*) The new Keynesians make use of the assumption of imperfect markets in their frameworks.

Choose the **correct** answer from the options given below:

A. (*b*), (*c*), (*d*) only B. (*a*), (*b*), (*c*), (*d*)
C. (*a*), (*c*), (*d*) only D. (*a*), (*b*), (*c*) only

54. Consider an economy with perfect capital mobility, fixed price level and flexible exchange rate. Starting from equilibrium, suppose there is a monetary expansion.

Which of the following are true for the new equilibrium, as compared to the initial equilibrium?

(*a*) Output will be higher
(*b*) Consumption will be higher
(*c*) Interest rate will be lower
(*d*) Interest rate will be higher

Choose the **correct** answer from the options given below:

A. (*a*) only B. (*b*) only
C. (*a*) and (*b*) only D. (*a*) and (*c*) only

55. Let $H = e^Q$ where $Q = Ax^{\alpha}y^{\beta}$

Consider the following statements.

(*a*) Q is a homogeneous function for all values of α and β
(*b*) H is a homothetic function for all values of α and β
(*c*) Q is a homogeneous function only if $\alpha + \beta = 1$
(*d*) H is not a homogeneous function
(*e*) Q is not a homogeneous function

Choose the **correct** answer from the options given below:

A. (*a*) and (*b*) only
B. (*a*), (*b*) and (*d*) only
C. (*c*) and (*a*) only
D. (*e*) and (*d*) only

56. $A = \begin{bmatrix} 1 & 3 \\ 2 & 8 \\ 4 & 0 \end{bmatrix}$ and $B = \begin{bmatrix} 5 \\ 9 \end{bmatrix}$

(*a*) AB is given by $\begin{bmatrix} 32 \\ 82 \\ 20 \end{bmatrix}$

(*b*) BA is given by $\begin{bmatrix} 32 & 82 & 20 \end{bmatrix}$

(*c*) AB is not defined

(*d*) BA is not defined

(*e*) A^TB is defined

Choose the **correct** answer from the options given below:

A. (*c*) and (*b*) only

B. (*a*), (*d*), (*e*) only

C. (*a*) only

D. (*a*) and (*d*) only

57. The following are five statements about short run cost curves.

(*a*) The Marginal Cost (MC) curve cuts both short run Average Cost (AC) curve and Average Variable Cost (AVC) curve at their lowest point.

(*b*) The MC curve cuts AC curve from below, but nothing can be said about AVC curve.

(*c*) The distance between Total Cost (TC) curve and Total Variable Cost (TVC) curve gets reduced as quantity increases.

(*d*) The Average Fixed Cost (AFC) curve is asymptotic to the cost axis.

(*e*) The AC curve is *u*-shaped.

Choose the **correct** answer from the options given below:

A. (*a*), (*c*), (*d*), (*e*) only

B. (*b*), (*c*), (*e*) only

C. (*a*), (*e*) only

D. (*d*), (*e*), (*a*) only

58. The OLS regression output of wages (₹ in thousand) on education (years of schooling S) and cognitive ability scores (CA) comes out to be:

$$\widehat{wages} = -3.36 + 0.64S + 0.15CA$$
$$(1.98) \quad (0.12) \quad (0.05)$$

with figures in parenthesis giving standard error.

The explained sum of squares is 4745.75 with degrees of freedom 2 and residual sum of squares is 33651.28 with degrees of freedom 567, which of the following statements is/are true?

(*a*) For one year increase in schooling, wage per hour increases by ₹ 640 on the average, when CA is kept constant.

(*b*) The value of t statistic of CA is 3.

(*c*) The F statistic is given by

$$F = \frac{(4745.75/2)}{(33651.28/567)}$$

(*d*) The F statistic is given by

$$F = \frac{(33651.28/567)}{(4745.75/2)}$$

Choose the **correct** answer from the options given below:

A. (*a*), (*c*) only B. (*a*), (*b*), (*d*) only

C. (*a*), (*b*), (*c*) only D. (*a*), (*d*) only

59. Read the following statements regarding demography across India's major states.

(*a*) Kerala pioneered fertility transition in India.

(*b*) Bihar has high IMR, as well as low reporting of morbidity.

(*c*) Orissa records the highest share of immunized children as per NFHS-5 round.

(*d*) Tamil Nadu has the highest share of old age population as per Census 2011.

(*e*) Madhya Pradesh has the highest share of stunted children as per NFHS-5

Choose the **correct** answer from the options given below:

A. (*a*), (*d*) only B. (*a*), (*b*), (*e*) only

C. (*a*), (*d*), (*c*) only D. (*a*), (*b*), (*c*) only

60. Consider a matrix $A = \begin{bmatrix} 3 & 5 \\ -2 & -4 \end{bmatrix}$

Consider the following statements on characteristic polynomial, Eigen Values and Eigen Vectors.

(*a*) The characteristic polynomial is $\lambda^2 + \lambda - 2$

(*b*) The characteristic polynomial is $\lambda^2 - \lambda - 4$ and the characteristic root or Eigen Values are $\lambda^* = 2$ and 1

(*c*) The characteristic polynomial is $\lambda^2 - \lambda + 2$ and the characteristic root or Eigen Values are $\lambda^* = 1$ and 2

(*d*) The characteristic root or Eigen Values are $\lambda^* = -2$ and 1

Choose the **correct** answer from the options given below:

A. (*a*), (*c*) and (*d*) only
B. (*b*) and (*d*) only
C. (*b*) and (*c*) only
D. (*a*) and (*d*) only

61. Suppose production function $q = f(k, l)$, is a homogeneous function of degree 1. Consider the following statements.

(*a*) The marginal products of capital and labour $\left(\frac{\partial q}{\partial k} \text{ and } \frac{\partial q}{\partial l}\right)$ are homogeneous of degree 1.

(*b*) The second order cross marginal products of *k* and 1 are equal $\left(i.e., \frac{\partial^2 q}{\partial l \partial k} = \frac{\partial^2 q}{\partial k \partial l}\right)$.

(*c*) By Euler's Theorem: $\frac{\partial q}{\partial k}.k + \frac{\partial q}{\partial l}.l = q$

(*d*) By Euler's theorem: $\frac{\partial^2 q}{\partial k^2}.k + \frac{\partial^2 q}{\partial l^2}l = 0$

Choose the **correct** answer from the options given below:

A. (*a*) and (*b*) only
B. (*a*), (*b*) and (*c*) only
C. (*a*), (*c*) and (*d*) only
D. (*b*), (*c*) and (*d*) only

62. Consider the following statements:

(*a*) The union of finite numbers of closed set is a closed set

(*b*) The empty set is an open set but not a closed set

(*c*) Every infinite set is an open set

(*d*) The intersection of finite numbers of open sets is an open set

Choose the **correct** answer from the options given below:

A. (*a*) and (*b*) only
B. (*b*) and (*c*) only
C. (*a*) and (*d*) only
D. (*a*), (*b*) and (*c*) only

63. Consider the following statements:

Assume a consumer's choice is based on only 2 commodities i.e., $X \varepsilon R^2_+$, where X is the set of a possible commodities which a consumer can conceive of:

(*a*) Monotonicity of preference implies strong monotonicity but not the other way round.

(*b*) A preference relation is monotone if for all commodity bundle $x, y \varepsilon X, y \geq x$ and $y \neq x$, then $y \geq x$.

(*c*) A preference relation ($\geq$) on X is strongly monotone if for all commodity bundles $x, y \varepsilon X, y > x$ and $y \neq x$; then $y \geq x$.

(*d*) A preference which is locally non satiated must follow monotonicity and strong monotonicity.

Choose the **correct** answer from the options given below:

A. (*b*) and (*d*) only
B. (*a*), (*b*) and (*d*) only
C. (*a*), (*c*) and (*d*) only
D. (*a*) and (*d*) Only

64. Consider the following statements:

(*a*) If the 2 utility functions $u(x)$ and $b(x)$ are related by $u(x) = V(b(x))$, where $V'(.) > 0$, then $V(x)$ is a utility function representing the same preference as $b(x)$.

(*b*) If the 2 utility functions represents the same preference, the solutions to the consumer's utility maximization problem are the same with the 2 utility function but the indirect utility functions are different.

(*c*) If the local non satiation assumption of preference is satisfied, any solution to the consumer's utility maximization problem satisfies the budget constraint with equality.

(*d*) If the indirect utility function of $b(x)$ is homogenous of degree 0 then indirect utility function of $u(x) = V(b(x))$, where $V'(.) > 0$, is a homogenous function of degree 1.

Choose the **correct** answer from the options given below:

A. (*b*) only
B. (*a*), (*b*) and (*d*) only
C. (*a*), (*b*) and (*c*) only
D. (*b*), (*c*) and (*d*) only

65. Consider the following 3 Constrained Optimization Problems (COP).

(*i*) Maximize $z = \ln x$, subject to $x > 1$
(*ii*) Maximize $z = \ln x$, subject to $x < 1$
(*iii*) Maximize $z = \ln x$, subject to $1 < x < 2$

(*a*) (*i*) and (*ii*) have no solutions but (*iii*) has solution
(*b*) (*i*) and (*ii*) have solutions but (*iii*) has no solution
(*c*) (*i*), (*ii*) and (*iii*) have no solution
(*d*) (*i*) and (*iii*) have no solution but (*ii*) has solution

Choose the **correct** answer from the options given below:

A (*a*) only B. (*b*) only
C. (*c*) only D. (*d*) only

66. Match List-I with List-II.

List-I	List-II
(*a*) Ramsar Convention	I. Ozone layer depletion
(*b*) Basel Convention	II. Reduction of green-house gas emission
(*c*) Montreal Protocol	III. Conservation of wetlands
(*d*) Paris Agreement	IV. Control of trans-boundary movement of hazardous wastes and disposal

Choose the **correct** answer from the options given below:

	(*a*)	(*b*)	(*c*)	(*d*)
A.	I	IV	III	II
B.	III	I	II	IV
C.	IV	I	III	II
D.	III	IV	I	II

67. Match List-I with List-II.

List-I	List-II
(*a*) Coase theorem	I. Property right, victim's pay and polluter pay principle
(*b*) Climate change	II. Lax environmental regulation, hidden subsidy
(*c*) Ecological dumping	III. Quantity restriction
(*d*) Tradable emission permit	IV. Global externality

Choose the **correct** answer from the options given below:

	(*a*)	(*b*)	(*c*)	(*d*)
A.	III	IV	II	I
B.	I	IV	II	III
C.	II	I	III	IV
D.	III	IV	I	II

68. Match List-I with List-II.

List-I	List-II
(*a*) Kemneth Arrow	I. Analysis of causal relationship
(*b*) Robert Solow	II. Fundamental contribution in behavioural economics

(*c*) Daniel Kahneman	III. Fundamental contribution in welfare economics
(*d*) Joshua Angrist	IV. Fundamental contribution in economic growth theory

Choose the **correct** answer from the options given below:

	(*a*)	(*b*)	(*c*)	(*d*)
A.	III	IV	I	II
B.	II	I	III	IV
C.	III	IV	II	I
D.	I	IV	III	II

69. Match List-I with List-II.

List-I	List-II
(*a*) Demographic Transition	I. Dualism
(*b*) Stages of growth	II. Take-off
(*c*) Rural-urban migration decision	III. Replacement Rate
(*d*) Female labour force participation rate	IV. Backward bending labour supply curve

Choose the **correct** answer from the options given below:

	(*a*)	(*b*)	(*c*)	(*d*)
A.	I	II	III	IV
B.	IV	I	III	II
C.	III	II	I	IV
D.	IV	I	II	III

70. Match List-I with List-II.

List-I (Model/method)	List-II (Feature)
(*a*) Logit model	I. elasticities are constant
(*b*) Log-log model	II. binary dependent variable
(*c*) Autoregressive model	III. corrects for heteroscedasticity
(*d*) Weighted least squares	IV. includes lags of dependent variable

Choose the **correct** answer from the options given below:

	(*a*)	(*b*)	(*c*)	(*d*)
A.	II	I	III	IV
B.	I	II	IV	III
C.	I	II	III	IV
D.	II	I	IV	III

71. Match the following:

List-I (Theory)	List-II (Economist(s) who gave it)
(*a*) Permanent Income Hypothesis of Consumption	I. T. Sargent and N. Wallace
(*b*) Life-cycle Hypothesis of Consumption	II. Milton Friedman
(*c*) Real Business Cycle Theory	III. Franco Modigliani
(*d*) Policy Ineffectiveness Proposition	IV. F. Kydland and E. Prescott

Choose the **correct** answer from the options given below:

	(*a*)	(*b*)	(*c*)	(*d*)
A.	III	II	I	IV
B.	III	II	IV	I
C.	II	III	IV	I
D.	II	III	I	IV

72. Match List-I with List-II.

List-I	List-II
(*a*) Unequal Exchange	I. A. Hirshman
(*b*) The development of underdevelopment	II. G. Myrdal
(*c*) Backward and forward linkage effect	III. A. Emmanuel
(*d*) Backwash effect	IV. G. Frank

Choose the **correct** answer from the options given below:

	(*a*)	(*b*)	(*c*)	(*d*)
A.	II	III	I	IV
B.	III	I	IV	II
C.	III	IV	I	II
D.	II	IV	III	I

73. Match List-I with List-II.

List-I (Variable)	List-II (Distribution)
(*a*) Sum of squares of *n* independent standard normal variates	I. *t* distribution
(*b*) Ratio of a standard normal variate to square root of an independent, chi square variable (divided by its degrees of freedom)	II. F distribution
(*c*) Ratio of 2 independent chi-square variables each divided by their respective degrees of freedom	III. Standard normal distribution
(*d*) Normal variate minus its mean, divided by its standard deviation	IV. chi square distribution

Choose the **correct** answer from the options given below:

	(*a*)	(*b*)	(*c*)	(*d*)
A.	I	IV	II	III
B.	IV	I	III	II
C.	I	IV	III	II
D.	IV	I	II	III

74. Match List-I with List-II.

List-I (Property)	List-II (Type of Curve)
(*a*) Investment is unresponsive to interest rates	I. Relatively flat IS curve
(*b*) Money demand is perfectly elastic w.r.t. interest rates	II. Vertical LM curve
(*c*) Money demand is completely inelastic w.r.t. interest rates	III. Horizontal LM curve
(*d*) Investment is highly responsive to interest rates	IV. Vertical IS curve

Choose the **correct** answer from the options given below:

	(*a*)	(*b*)	(*c*)	(*d*)
A.	IV	III	II	I
B.	IV	II	III	I
C.	I	III	II	IV
D.	III	IV	I	II

75. Match List-I with List-II.

List-I	List-II
(*a*) Quantity theory of money	I. Milton Friedman
(*b*) Involuntary unemployment	II. John Maynard Keynes
(*c*) Randomised trial	III. Abhijit V. Banerjee
(*d*) Relative poverty	IV. Amartya K. Sen

Choose the **correct** answer from the options given below:

	(*a*)	(*b*)	(*c*)	(*d*)
A.	I	II	III	IV
B.	IV	III	II	I
C.	III	II	I	IV
D.	III	II	IV	I

76. Arrange the following steps of exchange rate channel of monetary transmission mechanism, in correct order, starting from first to last.

(*a*) reduction in policy rate

(*b*) capital outflows

(*c*) depreciation of domestic currency

(*d*) rise in net exports

Choose the **correct** answer from the options given below:

A. (*a*), (*c*), (*d*), (*b*) B. (*a*), (*d*), (*b*), (*c*)

C. (*a*), (*b*), (*c*), (*d*) D. (*a*), (*d*), (*c*), (*b*)

77. Arrange the following names of former governors of RBI in the sequence in which they held the post starting from the earliest to latest.

(*a*) Y.V. Reddy

(*b*) D Subbarao

(*c*) Raghuram Rajan

(*d*) Urjit Patel

Choose the **correct** answer from the options given below:

A. (*c*), (*b*), (*d*), (*a*)
B. (*c*), (*a*), (*d*), (*b*)
C. (*a*), (*b*), (*c*), (*d*)
D. (*d*), (*c*). (*a*), (*b*)

78. Arrange the following events in Indian Financial System in correct chronological order, starting from earliest to Latest.

(*a*) Setting up of PFRDA
(*b*) Setting up of UTI
(*c*) Nationalisation of 14 commercial banks
(*d*) Implementation of IBC

Choose the **correct** answer from the options given below:

A. (*a*). (*b*), (*c*), (*d*)
B. (*c*), (*a*), (*b*), (*d*)
C. (*b*), (*c*), (*a*), (*d*)
D. (*a*), (*c*), (*b*), (*d*)

79. Match List-I with List-II.

List-I	**List-II**
(*a*) Shephard's Lemma	I. Hidden types of agent
(*b*) Adverse Selection	II. Envelope theorem
(*c*) Hotelling Lemma	III. Indirect utility function
(*d*) Roy's Identity	IV. Profit function

Choose the **correct** answer from the options given below:

	(*a*)	(*b*)	(*c*)	(*d*)
A.	IV	I	II	III
B.	II	I	IV	III
C.	II	I	III	IV
D.	II	IV	I	III

80. Consider the following centrally sponsored schemes in India and choose the right sequence of time (year) when they were Launched, from earliest to latest:

(*a*) Beti Bachao Beti Padhao
(*b*) Ujjwala
(*c*) Swachh Bharat Abhiyan
(*d*) Ayushman Bharat
(*e*) Right to Education

Choose the **correct** answer from the options given below:

A. (*e*), (*a*), (*c*), (*b*), (*d*)
B. (*e*), (*c*), (*a*), (*b*), (*d*)
C. (*a*), (*e*), (*c*), (*b*), (*d*)
D. (*a*), (*c*), (*e*), (*d*), (*b*)

81. Chow Test is normally run to understand if a single regression run on pooled data is more efficient to describe a relation between a dependent variable and a set of independent variables than the same regression being run separately on two subgroups of sample. The steps involved in running the Chow Test are:

(*a*) Run the regression model on pooled sample and calculate RSS_p
(*b*) Run the same regression model on the two sub-samples separately and calculate RSS_1 and RSS_2
(*c*) Calculate the F statistic
(*d*) Check the critical F with related degrees of freedom and compare it with F calculated
(*e*) Do not reject H_0 if $F_{calculated} < F_{critical}$

Choose the **correct** answer from the options given below:

A. (*a*), (*b*), (*c*), (*d*), (*e*)
B. (*a*), (*d*), (*c*), (*b*), (*e*)
C. (*c*), (*a*), (*b*), (*d*), (*e*)
D. (*c*), (*b*), (*a*), (*d*), (*e*)

82. Arrange the following in order of their year of establishment starting from the oldest.

(*a*) Lakdawala Committee
(*b*) Khusro Committee
(*c*) Alagh Committee
(*d*) Nayak Committee
(*e*) Tendulkar Committee

Choose the **correct** answer from the options given below:

A. (*d*), (*b*), (*c*), (*a*), (*e*)
B. (*c*), (*d*), (*b*), (*a*), (*e*)
C. (*c*), (*b*), (*d*), (*a*), (*e*)
D. (*b*), (*c*), (*d*), (*e*), (*a*)

83. Arrange the following chronologically starting from the oldest.

(*a*) Theory of Big Push
(*b*) The accumulation of capital
(*c*) Theory of cumulative causation
(*d*) Unbalanced growth
(*e*) Development with unlimited supplies of labour

Choose the **correct** answer from the options given below:

A. (*e*), (*a*), (*c*), (*b*), (*d*)
B. (*a*), (*e*), (*b*), (*c*), (*d*)
C. (*e*), (*b*), (*a*), (*d*), (*c*)
D. (*a*), (*b*), (*e*), (*c*), (*d*)

84. Arrange the given schools of thought in macro-economics in chronological order, from the oldest to most recent one.

(*a*) The Keynesian school
(*b*) The new classical school
(*c*) The classical school
(*d*) The new Keynesian school
(*e*) The monetarists

Choose the **correct** answer from the options given below:

A. (*a*), (*d*), (*c*), (*b*), (*e*)
B. (*e*), (*c*), (*b*), (*a*), (*d*)
C. (*c*), (*b*), (*a*), (*d*), (*e*)
D. (*c*), (*a*), (*e*), (*b*), (*d*)

85. The Central Bank of a country maintains a fixed exchange rate, which is defined as the number of units of domestic currency per unit of foreign currency. Currently the domestic currency is overvalued against the foreign currency. In this context, indicate the kind of intervention required by the Central Bank to maintain the parity, by putting the following statements in correct order.

(*a*) The demand for foreign currency exceeds its supply
(*b*) The exchange rate is lower than the market clearing exchange rate
(*c*) The gap between supply and demand for foreign currency is equalized
(*d*) The Central Bank's stock of foreign currency is depleted
(*e*) The Central Bank sells foreign currency from its stock of reserves

Choose the **correct** answer from the options given below:

A. (*b*), (*e*), (*a*), (*d*), (*c*)
B. (*b*), (*a*), (*e*), (*d*), (*c*)
C. (*b*), (*e*), (*a*), (*c*), (*d*)
D. (*b*), (*a*), (*e*), (*c*), (*d*)

86. Given below are two statements:

Statement I: Agricultural GDP constitutes less than 16% of aggregate GDP at 2011-12 constant prices and less than 20% of the aggregate GDP at current prices in 2022-23 (PE) in India.

Statement II: Service sector GDP constitutes less than 16% of aggregate GDP at 2011-12 constant prices and less than 20% of the aggregate GDP at current prices in 2022-23 (PE) in India.

In the light of the above statements, choose the **most appropriate answer** from the options given below:

A. Both Statement I and Statement II are correct
B. Both Statement I and Statement II are incorrect
C. Statement I is correct, but Statement II is incorrect
D. Statement 1 is incorrect, but Statement II is correct

87. Given below are two statements:

Statement I: The Government's spending on social services as a percentage of GDP has been rising since 2017-18.

Statement II: The Government's spending on social services as a percentage of total expenditure has also been continuously rising since 2017-18.

In the light of the above statements, choose the **most appropriate** answer from the options given below:

A. Both Statement I and Statement II are correct
B. Both Statement I and Statement II are incorrect
C. Statement I is correct, but Statement II is incorrect
D. Statement I is incorrect, but Statement II is correct

88. Given below are two statements:

Statement I: Human Development is a process of enlarging peoples' choices.

Statement II: Human Development Index (HDI) is based on the following indicators: Life expectancy at birth, expected years of schooling, mean years of schooling & Gross domestic product per capita at dollar PPP.

In the light of the above statements, choose the **most appropriate answer** from the options given below:

A. Both Statement I and Statement II are correct
B. Both Statement I and Statement II are incorrect
C. Statement I is correct, but Statement II is incorrect
D. Statement I is incorrect, but Statement II is correct

89. Given below are two statements: one is labelled as Assertion (A) and the other is labelled as Reason (R).

Assertion (A): Given a random sample, the distribution of the sample mean tends to a normal distribution, as the sample size becomes very large.

Reason (R): Central limit theorem.

In the light of the above statements, choose the **most appropriate answer** from the options given below:

A. Both (A) and (R) are correct and (R) is the correct explanation of (A)
B. Both (A) and (R) are correct, but (R) is not the correct explanation of (A)
C. (A) is correct, but (R) is not correct
D. (A) is not correct, but (R) is correct

90. Given below are two statements: one is labelled as Assertion (A) and the other is labelled as Reason (R).

Assertion (A): According to the Domar condition of debt sustainability, the public debt would not rise as proportion of GDP if the effective interest rate on government liabilities happens to be less than or equal to the growth rate of GDP at current price.

Reason (R): Growth rate of GDP of an economy at current price is bound to be less than the effective interest rate on the government bonds.

In the light of the above statements, choose the **most appropriate answer** from the options given below:

A. Both (A) and (R) are correct and (R) is the correct explanation of (A)
B. Both (A) and (R) are correct, but (R) is not the correct explanation of (A)
C. (A) is correct, but (R) is not correct
D. (A) is not correct, but (R) is correct

Directions (Qs. No. 91-95): *Read the following information carefully and answer these questions.*

Assume that there are 2 firms producing steel. There is a negative externality due to production causing pollution. Firm 1's output is q_1 and firm 2's is q_2. Assume that the market price for steel is P = 1. Now consider two scenarios:

Scenario 1: Assume that firm l's cost function is $C_1(q_1) = q_1^2$ and firm 2's cost function is $C_2(q_2, q_1) = (q_2 + 0.75\, q_1)^2$. In short, firm 1's production is not affected by firm 2 but firm 2's production is affected by firm 1, i.e., Firms 1's operation causes firm 2's costs to rise.

Scenario 2: Assume that negative externally works both ways i.e., both the firms face the adverse impact. So assume $C_1(q_1, q_2) = (q_1 + 0.75\, q_2)^2$ and $C_2(q_1, q_2) = (q_2 + 0.75\, q_1)^2$, i.e., Firms 1's operation causes firm 2's costs to rise and vice versa.

91. What is the equilibrium profit of firm 2 (π_2) in the short run, in Scenario 1?

A. $\pi_2 = 0.025$ B. $\pi_2 = 0.125$
C. $\pi_2 = -0.125$ D. $\pi_2 = 0.75$

92. What is the long run profit of firm 1 (π_1), in Scenario 1?

A. $\pi_1 = 0.025$ B. $\pi_1 = 0$
C. $\pi_1 = 0.25$ D. $\pi_1 = 0.125$

93. What is the long run profit of firm 2 (π_2), in Scenario 1?

A. $\pi_2 = 0.125$ B. $\pi_2 = 0.120$
C. $\pi_2 = 0.5$ D. $\pi_1 = 0$

94. What would be the market equilibrium profit of the 2 firms, in Scenario 2?

A. $\pi_1 = \frac{1}{28}, \pi_2 = \frac{1}{28}$

B. $\pi_1 = \frac{2}{7}, \pi_2 = \frac{2}{7}$

C. $\pi_1 = \frac{1}{14}, \pi_2 = \frac{1}{14}$

D. $\pi_1 = \pi_2 = 0$

95. Do you think that the equilibrium outcome for Scenario 2 is inefficient? How would be the efficiency be restored?

A. No, the equilibrium outcome of the firms are profit minimizing outcome.
B. The externality can be resolved by closing down both the firms is, $\pi_1 = \pi_2 = 0$
C. If one of the firm is forced to close down, the externality will be reduced and their joint profit is $\pi_1 + \pi_2 = 0.071$
D. If one of the firm is forced to close down, the externality will be reduced and their joint profit is $\pi_1 + \pi_2 = 0.109$

Directions (Qs. No. 96-100): *Read the following information carefully and answer these questions.*

According to the NSO, MOSPI press release dated 31st May 2023, the revised estimate of GDP at the current price for the year 2021-22 was ₹ 2,34,71,012 crores and that for 2020-21 was ₹ 1,98,29,927 crores. The GDP at 2011-12 constant prices for the year 2020-21 and 2021-22 were ₹ 1,36,87,118 crores and ₹ 1,49,25,840 crores respectively. At the current prices, the net taxes on products was ₹ 20,32,128 crores in 2021-22 (RE). The PFCE, GFCE, GFCF in 2021-22 were ₹ 1,43,44,336 crores, ₹ 26,25,361 crores and ₹ 67,86,391 crores respectively. Change in stocks (CIS), valuables and discrepancies in 2021-22 were ₹ 1,63,438 crores, ₹ 3,79,112 crores and ₹ (–) 208,247 crores (negative) respectively in current prices.

96. What was the inflation rate in India based on the GDP deflators?

A. 4.5% B. 6.6%
C. 9.3% D. 10.2%

97. The current account deficit to GDP ratio (both at current prices) in 2021-22 for India was:

A. 1.75% B. 3.53%
C. 4.06% D. 2.64 %

98. The Gross Value Added (GVA) at basic prices in 2021-22 was:

A. ₹ 2,55,03,140 crore
B. ₹ 2,14,38,884 crore
C. ₹ 2,34,71,012 crore
D. ₹ 1,49,37,569 crore

99. In 2021-22, the investment GDP ratio in India was:

A. 31.2% B. 90%
C. 40.1% D. 42.4%

100. If the value of exports in 2021-22 at current price be ₹ 50,49,645 crores, the import in 2021-22 at current price in India was:

A. ₹ 56,69,024 crores
B. ₹ 6,19,378 crores
C. ₹ 1,17,18,975 crores
D. ₹ 94,11,752 crores

ANSWERS

1. (B): The expert committee established by the Reserve Bank of India (RBI) in 2013 to revamp and fortify the monetary policy framework in India was helmed by Urjit Patel. Tasked with a crucial mandate, the Urjit Patel Committee conducted an extensive review of the existing monetary policy structure, aiming to identify areas for improvement and propose reforms to bolster its efficacy and transparency. Patel's leadership was instrumental in steering the committee's deliberations towards recommendations that would align India's monetary policy with international best practices while addressing the unique challenges faced by the Indian economy. The committee's proposals, which included the adoption of inflation targeting as the primary objective of monetary policy, laid the groundwork for significant reforms in India's monetary policy framework, shaping the trajectory of the country's monetary policy management for years to come.

2. (A): In 2016, Parliament amended the RBI Act, 1934 to change the monetary policy, and introduce an inflation targeting framework. This framework prioritises price stability to achieve sustainable GDP growth. Price stability allows investors to confidently invest their money for productive activities, without worrying about it losing value. Price stability also maintains the purchasing power of consumers, i.e., the ability to purchase a good (or service) with a given amount of money.

As per the new framework, the central government, in consultation with RBI sets: (i) an inflation target, and (ii) an upper and lower tolerance level for retail inflation. The target has been set at 4%, with an upper tolerance limit of 6% and a lower tolerance limit of 2%. The upper and lower limits indicate that although it is desirable for inflation to be close to 4%, deviation between these limits is acceptable. The target and bands and revised every five years. In March 2021, the existing targets were carried forward.

3. (B): In a regression analysis, the F-test assesses the overall significance of the regression model. To conduct this test, we need to determine the degrees of freedom for the numerator and denominator of the F-statistic. The numerator degrees of freedom represent the number of independent variables in the model, denoted by 'k'. This is because the numerator of the F-statistic involves the sum of squares of the regression, which is essentially measuring the variability explained by the independent variables. On the other hand, the denominator degrees of freedom represent the residual degrees of freedom, which is calculated as the difference between the total number of observations (n) and the number of independent variables minus 1 ($k - 1$). This accounts for the degrees of freedom associated with estimating the regression coefficients. Therefore, the correct degrees of freedom for the F-test are 'k' for the numerator and '$n - k - 1$' for the denominator.

4. (C): Here, LPM,

$$P_i = E(Y_i = 1 \mid X_i) = \beta_1 + \beta_2 X_i$$

Where, X_i is income and Y_i means individual owns a house.

$$P_i = E(Y_i = 1 \mid X_i)$$

$$= \frac{1}{1 + e^{-(\beta_1 + \beta_2 X_i)}}$$

For ease of exposition, we write this as,

$$P_i = \frac{1}{1 + e^{-Z_i}}$$

where $Z_i = \beta_1 + \beta_2 X_i$

This equation represents what is known as the (Cumulative) logistic distribution function.

5. (D): Here, $byx = \hat{\beta}$

$$\therefore \quad by'x' = \frac{\hat{\beta}}{2} = 0.5\hat{\beta}.$$

6. (D): The KPSS (Kwiatkowski-Phillips-Schmidt-Shin) test is a statistical test used to assess the stationarity of a time series data. Unlike other unit root tests like the ADF and Phillips-Perron tests that assume non-stationarity as the null hypothesis, the KPSS test takes the opposite approach by assuming stationarity as the null hypothesis. Specifically, the null hypothesis of the KPSS test asserts that the time series data is stationary around a deterministic trend, meaning that the data exhibits no trend or structural breaks. The alternative hypothesis, on the other hand, suggests that the data is non-stationary, indicating the presence of a unit root or stochastic trend. To conduct the test, the KPSS statistic compares the sum of squared deviations of the data from the trend under the null hypothesis to the sum of squared deviations from a constant under the alternative hypothesis. If the KPSS test statistic exceeds a critical value at a chosen significance level, the null hypothesis of stationarity is rejected, indicating that the data is non-stationary. Conversely, failure to reject the null hypothesis implies that the data is stationary around a deterministic trend. Therefore, the KPSS test provides valuable insights into the long-run behaviour of a time series data, allowing researchers to determine whether the observed trends are merely transitory fluctuations or indicative of a persistent underlying trend.

7. (B)

8. (B): According to the uncovered interest rate parity (UIP) condition, the expected change in the exchange rate between two countries should be equal to the interest rate differential between those countries. In this case, if capital flows are in equilibrium, investors would be indifferent between investing domestically or abroad.

Given that the interest rate in India is higher (6%) than in the USA (4%), according to UIP, investors would expect the US dollar to appreciate relative to the Indian rupee to offset the interest rate differential. However, the exchange rate is expected to rise from ₹ 80 to ₹ 84 in one year, indicating an expected depreciation of the US dollar relative to the Indian rupee.

This discrepancy suggests that the expected depreciation of the US dollar is greater than what UIP predicts based on the interest rate differential. Therefore, there is an opportunity for riskless profit through uncovered interest rate arbitrage. Investors would seek to take advantage of this mispricing by borrowing in the Indian economy at the lower interest rate, converting the borrowed funds to US dollars, and investing in US assets. This capital outflow from India would lead to the appreciation of the US dollar and the depreciation of the Indian rupee.

9. (B): Here, $\text{In}\,(Y_i) = \alpha + \beta X_i + u_i$ ...(*i*)

Now change X:

$\text{In}(Y_i + \Delta Y_i) = \alpha + \beta(X_i + \Delta X_i) + u_i$ ...(*ii*)

Subtract (*ii*) – (*i*)

$\text{In}\,(Y_i + \Delta Y_i) - \text{In}\,(Y_i) = \beta\Delta X_i$

Use the approximation,

$$\frac{\Delta Y_i}{Y_i} \cong \beta\Delta Xi$$

$$\therefore \quad e_{yx} = \frac{\Delta Y_i}{\Delta X_i}.\frac{X_i}{Y_i}$$

$$= \beta\Delta X_i \times \frac{X_i}{\Delta X_i} = \beta X_i.$$

10. (B)

11. (C): The Human Poverty Index - 2 (HPI-2) is a comprehensive measure designed to assess poverty by considering multiple dimensions beyond just economic indicators. One key dimension included in the HPI-2 is "Social Inclusion." This dimension captures the extent to which individuals or groups within a society have equitable access to social resources, opportunities, and participation in societal activities. It encompasses various aspects such as access to education, healthcare, housing, social security, and involvement in community life. By emphasizing social inclusion, the HPI-2 recognizes that poverty is not solely defined by income levels but also by the ability of individuals to access essential services and fully participate in the social fabric of their communities. Thus, addressing social inclusion is essential for fostering a more equitable society and promoting human development by ensuring that all members have the opportunity to lead fulfilling and dignified lives.

12. (C): Solow residual is the difference between the rate of growth of output and the rate of growth of inputs. In the Solow growth model, which is a neoclassical economic model of long-run economic growth, output (or GDP) is determined by the inputs of capital and labour, among other factors. The rate of growth of output is influenced by various factors such as technological progress, improvements in efficiency, and increases in the quantity of capital and labour inputs. However, not all changes in output can be attributed solely to changes in inputs; there may be other factors at play, such as advancements in technology or changes in productivity, that lead to output growth beyond what can be explained by changes in inputs alone. The Solow residual captures this unexplained portion of output growth, often interpreted as total factor productivity growth, which encompasses technological progress and other factors that enhance efficiency and productivity in the economy. Therefore, this option correctly identifies the Solow residual as the difference between the rate of growth of output and the rate of growth of inputs in the Solow growth model.

13. (B): The Gini coefficient is usually defined in terms of the Lorenz curve. It is the most popular measure of distributional inequality. The Lorenz curve is a graphical device used to represent distributional inequality. The Gini coefficient is a numerical measure of inequality based on the Lorenz curve. Much of the literature is concerned with income inequality. With a few notable exception, the result of Gini coefficients also can be applied to other quantitative variables. The Gini coefficient varies between 0 (complete equality) and 1 (complete inequality). There are a number of ways in which the Gini coefficient can be expressed and interpreted. Many researchers derived it as a measure of inequality as it satisfies the axioms (criteria) of an ideal measure. The existing formula for Gini coefficients are as follows:

$$G = \frac{\frac{1}{n^2}\sum_{i=1}^{n}\sum_{j=1}^{n}|y_i - y_j|}{2\mu} \quad ...(1)$$

$$G = \frac{2}{\mu n^2}\sum_{i=1}^{n} iy_i - \frac{n+1}{n} \quad ...(2)$$

$$G = \frac{n+1}{n} - \frac{1}{2n^2\mu}\sum_{i=1}^{n} iy_i \quad ...(3)$$

where, $y_i(i = 1, 2, ..., n)$ is the income/age of the i-th person, $y_j(j = 1, 2, ..., n)$ is the income/age of the j-th person, m is the average income/age and $y_1 \le y_2 \le ... \le y_n$. Equation (1) is a measure of dispersion divided by twice the mean. It is the average absolute difference between all pairs of individuals. Equation (1) is known as Gini coefficient of mean difference given by Kendall and Stuart. They also define this coefficient as "one half of the average value of absolute differences between all pairs of incomes divided by the mean income". We will apply this measure to estimate the aging inequality of population. Equation (2) is given by Dasgupta et al. which is more mathematically tractable and computationally convenient for individual level data. Note that the first term in equation (2) involves a weighted sum of all the scores, where the weight applied to each score is its rank in the distribution. Equation (3) is due to Sen and it shows the income-waiting system in the welfare function behind the Gini coefficient.

14. (C) **15. (C)**

16. (C): Type II error occurs when the null hypothesis is false, but the test fails to reject it, leading to a false acceptance of the null hypothesis. The power of a test is complementary to Type II error and is calculated as 1 minus the probability of Type II error. A higher power indicates a greater ability of the test to detect true differences or effects when they exist. The power of a statistical test is a critical concept in hypothesis testing, representing the probability of correctly rejecting a false null hypothesis. In practical terms, it reflects the ability of the test to detect a true effect or difference when one exists in the population. A high power indicates that the test is more likely to identify real effects, providing greater confidence in the conclusions drawn from the analysis. Power is influenced by several factors, including the sample size, the significance level chosen for the test, and the magnitude of the true effect being investigated. Essentially, a test with higher power is better equipped to distinguish between true effects and random variability, reducing the risk of overlooking meaningful findings. Understanding the power of a test is crucial for researchers and analysts as it informs decisions about study design, sample size determination, and the interpretation of results, ultimately contributing to the robustness and validity of statistical analyses.

17. (A)

18. (D): Certainly! The Consumer Price Index (CPI) serves as a measure of the average change over time in the prices paid by urban consumers for a market basket of consumer goods and services. In March 2023, if the CPI of a country with a 1982 base index of 100 is 234.7, it implies a significant increase in the cost of purchasing the market basket of goods and services since 1982. To quantify this increase, we calculate the percentage change from the base year (1982) to the current year (2023).

The formula to determine the percentage increase is (Current CPI – Base CPI) × 100 %.

Substituting the given values, we get:

$(234.7 - 100) \times 100\% = 134.7\%$.

Therefore, the cost of purchasing the market basket of goods and services has increased by 134.7% since the base year of 1982. This implies a substantial rise in prices over the years, reflecting inflationary pressures and indicating a significant decrease in the purchasing power of the currency compared to its value in 1982.

19. (B) **20. (C)** **21. (A)**

22. (B): To find the Marginal Revenue (MR) function from the Average Revenue (AR) function, we first need to differentiate the AR function with respect to quantity (q).

Given that AR = $10 + 5q - q^2$, we can differentiate it to find the MR function:

$$AR = 10 + 5q - q^2$$

$$MR = dAR/dq = 5 - 2q$$

Now, let's analyze the nature of the MR function: The coefficient of q in the MR function is –2, which is the coefficient of q^2 in the AR function. Since the coefficient of q^2 in the AR function is negative (–1), the coefficient of q in the MR function (which is derived from the derivative of AR with respect to q) is also negative (–2).

A concave function has a decreasing slope as quantity increases, which corresponds to a negative coefficient for the linear term in the function. Since the coefficient of q in the MR function is negative (–2), the MR function is concave.

So, the correct answer is: Concave function.

23. (B): Consumer's expected utility without the contract is:

$= 0.5 \times u(50 - 25) + 0.5 \times u(50) \quad ...(i)$

$= 0.5 \times u(25) + 0.5 \times u(50)$

$= 0.5 \times 10\sqrt{25} + 0.5 \times 10\sqrt{50}$

$= 0.5 \times 10 \times 5 + 0.5 \times 10 \times \sqrt{50} = 25 + 5\sqrt{50}$

Consumer's expected utility with the contract is:

$= u(50 - p)$

$= 10\sqrt{(50 - p)} \quad ...(ii)$

From (i) and (ii) we deduce that she is better off with the contract if and only if

$$= 10\sqrt{(50-p)} \geq 25 + 5\sqrt{50}$$

$$\sqrt{50 - p} \geq \frac{25 + 5\sqrt{50}}{10} = \frac{5 + \sqrt{50}}{2} = 6.035$$

$$50 - p \geq 6.035^2$$

$$50 - p \geq 36.43$$

$$-p \geq 36.43 - 50$$

$$-p \geq -13.57 \Rightarrow p \geq 13.57.$$

24. (D): The statement is derived from the Extreme Value Theorem, which states that if $f(x)$ is a continuous function on a closed interval $[a, b]$, then $f(x)$ must attain both a maximum and a minimum value at some points within that interval. This theorem guarantees the existence of such points c and d where $f(x)$ achieves its maximum and minimum values, respectively, within the interval $[a, b]$. The Extreme Value Theorem (EVT) ensures the existence of both maximum and minimum values of a continuous function $f(x)$ over a closed interval $[a, b]$. It guarantees that within this interval, there will be at least one point where the function attains its highest value (maximum) and another point where it reaches its lowest value (minimum). These points are significant because they represent the extreme values of the function within the specified interval. The EVT is crucial in mathematical analysis and optimization problems as it provides assurance that such extreme values exist, facilitating the identification of optimal solutions or critical points in various applications, including economics, engineering, and physics.

25. (D) **26. (B)** **27. (A)**

28. (B) **29. (D)**

30. (B): In the scenario of two perfect complement goods, where consumption of one good is strictly tied to the consumption of the other, the indifference curves take the form of straight lines. This characteristic arises from the fixed ratio in consumption demanded by consumers for these goods. As consumers derive utility only from consuming both goods in a specific fixed ratio, any deviation from this ratio would result in reduced utility. Consequently, the indifference curves, which represent combinations of the two goods that provide the same level of satisfaction, exhibit a linear relationship, reflecting the fixed proportions demanded by consumers. This implies that no matter how much of one good is consumed; utility remains unchanged unless the complementary good is also consumed in the appropriate ratio. Therefore, the straight-line nature of the indifference curves accurately captures the inherent complementarily between the goods and reflects the fixed ratio in consumption demanded by consumers for optimal utility attainment.

31. (C)

32. (D): Tamil Nadu's status as the most urbanized major state in India, with 48.45% of its population residing in urban areas according to the 2011 Census, underscores a significant demographic shift within the state over the past few decades. This transformation is particularly evident when comparing the urbanization rates from previous census years. In 1991, for instance, only 34.15% of Tamil Nadu's population was classified as urban, indicating a substantial increase over a span of 20 years. This rapid urbanization reflects various socio-economic factors, including industrialization, urban migration, infrastructure development, and economic opportunities in urban centers. The growth of industries, services, and educational institutions in urban areas has attracted migrants from rural regions seeking better livelihoods and access to amenities. Additionally, government policies promoting urban development and investment in urban infrastructure have further facilitated this urban expansion. Overall, Tamil Nadu's journey towards becoming the most urbanized state in India highlights the complex interplay of demographic, economic, and policy dynamics shaping its urban landscape.

33. (A): When the government sets a minimum wage (w') above the equilibrium wage (w^*), it creates a situation where the mandated wage is higher than what would naturally occur in the market. This results in higher labour costs for employers. To mitigate these increased costs, employers may resort to various strategies to adjust their labour force composition and minimize expenses. One such strategy is casualization, where employers may hire workers on a temporary or part-time basis instead of offering full-time permanent positions.

Casualization allows employers to maintain flexibility in their labour force while keeping costs lower than if they were to hire full-time employees at the mandated minimum wage. By hiring workers on a casual or temporary basis, employers can avoid paying additional benefits and entitlements that are typically associated with full-time employment, such as healthcare benefits, paid leave, and retirement contributions.

Therefore, if the minimum wage (w') exceeds the equilibrium wage (w^*), there is a tendency for employers to increase casualization of workers as a cost-saving measure. This trend may result in a higher proportion of workers employed under precarious or temporary arrangements, leading to potential challenges for workers in terms of job security, stability, and access to benefits and protections typically afforded to full-time employees.

34. (C): The essential condition for stable equilibrium is that the demand curve should have a negative slope and the supply curve a positive slope. Otherwise, it will not be a stable equilibrium, this would be what can be called unstable equilibrium.

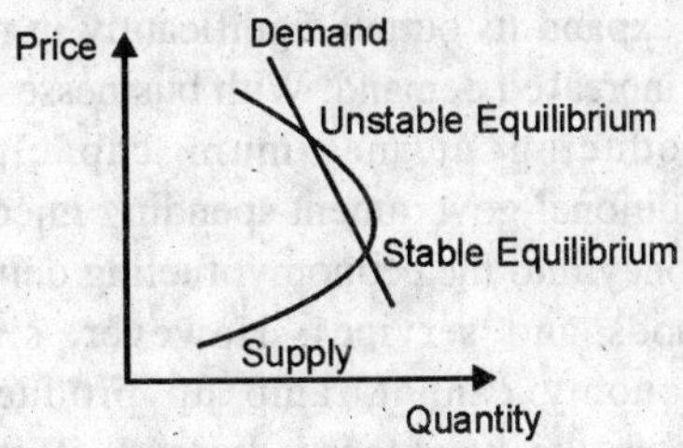

35. (C): $\because$ Revenue deficit

$= \text{Fiscal deficit} - \text{Capital expenditure}$

$\Rightarrow$ Capital expenditure

$= \text{Fiscal deficit} - \text{Revenue deficit}$

$= 7 - 3 = 4\%$

$\therefore$ Capital expenditure to GDP ratio is 4%.

36. (C): When the interest rate is exogenously determined by the Central Bank and the money supply is endogenously determined, the LM curve in the interest rate-income plane becomes horizontal. This signifies that changes in income levels do not influence the interest rate set by the Central Bank. Instead, the money supply adjusts automatically to maintain equilibrium in the money market at the given interest rate. As a result, regardless of fluctuations in income, the interest rate remains constant along the LM curve. This scenario implies a stable monetary policy where the Central Bank's decisions regarding the interest rate are independent of changes in output or income levels. Therefore, the horizontal LM curve suggests that the monetary authority is committed to maintaining a fixed interest rate, regardless of changes in economic activity. This stability in monetary policy can provide certainty to investors and businesses, supporting economic stability and growth over the long term.

37. (B): In a supply-constrained situation, characterized by an economy operating near or at full capacity, a higher fiscal deficit to GDP ratio can precipitate inflationary pressures due to the inability of the economy to expand its output significantly in response to increased demand. With businesses already producing at maximum capacity, any additional government spending injects more money into the economy, fueling demand for goods and services. However, since the economy cannot ramp up production to match the heightened demand, it results in excess demand relative to available supply. This imbalance leads to businesses raising prices to balance supply and demand, contributing to inflation. Moreover, inflationary expectations may emerge among businesses and consumers, further driving up prices as firms adjust their pricing strategies and workers demand higher wages. Additionally, if businesses face elevated costs from factors like increased input prices or supply chain disruptions, they may pass these costs on to consumers through higher prices, exacerbating inflationary pressures. Therefore, in a supply-constrained situation, a higher fiscal deficit can exacerbate inflation as the economy grapples with limited capacity to meet heightened demand, making Supply constrained situation the accurate description of the scenario where a higher fiscal deficit could cause inflation.

38. (C)

39. (A): The repo rate, or repurchase agreement rate, signifies the interest rate at which commercial banks can borrow funds from the central bank, in this case, the Reserve Bank of India (RBI). This borrowing occurs through repurchase agreements where commercial banks provide government securities as collateral to the RBI in exchange for short-term funds. By adjusting the repo rate, the RBI influences the cost of borrowing for commercial banks, which in turn impacts the overall availability of credit and liquidity in the financial system. Lowering the repo rate encourages borrowing by making funds cheaper, stimulating economic activity and investment. Conversely, raising the repo rate makes borrowing more expensive, this can help in curbing inflationary pressures and controlling excessive credit growth. Thus, the repo rate serves as a crucial monetary policy tool used by central banks to manage and regulate the money supply and interest rates within an economy.

40. (C): In an economy marked by significant involuntary unemployment, the aggregate labour supply curve in a real wage-labour supply plane would appear vertical. This characteristic arises from the presence of a substantial pool of unemployed individuals who are willing to work at the prevailing wage rate but are unable to secure employment due to insufficient demand for labour. With a fixed number of individuals actively seeking work, the quantity of labour supplied remains constant regardless of changes in the real wage rate. Even if wages were to rise, the quantity of labour supplied would not increase, as there are no additional individuals available to enter the labour market. Consequently, the aggregate labour supply curve appears vertical, indicating that the quantity of labour supplied is fixed at the level corresponding to the number of unemployed workers willing to work at the prevailing wage rate. This situation reflects the rigidities and frictions present in the labour market, which prevent unemployed individuals from finding suitable employment despite their willingness to work at prevailing wage rates.

41. **(B):** The Global Hunger Index (GHI) is a tool designed to comprehensively measure and track hunger at global, regional and national levels, reflecting multiple dimensions of hunger over time. The GHI is intended to raise awareness and understanding of the struggle against hunger, provide a way to compare levels of hunger between countries and regions, and call attention to those areas of the world where hunger levels are highest and where the need for additional efforts to eliminate hunger is greatest.

How the GHI is calculated each country's: GHI score is calculated based on a formula that combines four indicators that together capture the multidimensional nature of hunger:

Undernourishment: the share of the population whose caloric intake is insufficient;

Child stunting: the share of children under the age of five who have low height for their age, reflecting chronic undernutrition;

Child wasting: the share of children under the age of five who have low weight for their height, reflecting acute undernutrition; and

Child mortality: the share of children who die before their fifth birthday, reflecting in part the fatal mix of inadequate nutrition and unhealthy enviornments.

The standardized scores are aggregated to calculated the GHI score for each country. Undernourishment and child mortality each contribute one-third of the GHI score, while child stunting and child wasting each contribute one-sixth of the score.

Composition of GHI Scores

42. **(C):**

(b) **Estimated value of the conditional probability of occurrence of the event lies between 0 and 1:** This statement is indeed true. In the LPM, the dependent variable represents a binary outcome (e.g., success or failure, 1 or 0), and the predicted probabilities generated by the model naturally fall within the range of 0 to 1. This is because probabilities must always be bounded between these two values, given their interpretation as the likelihood of an event occurring.

(c) **Error term is homoscedastic:** Contrary to the statement, the error term in the LPM is not homoscedastic; rather, it typically exhibits heteroscedasticity. Heteroscedasticity implies that the variance of the error term varies across different levels of the explanatory

variables. In the context of the LPM, this means that the variability in the errors is not constant across the range of values of the independent variables. This violates one of the assumptions of ordinary least squares (OLS) regression, which assumes constant variance of the error term.

(*d*) **R^2 is a good measure of goodness of fit:** This statement is generally true. R-squared (R^2) measures the proportion of the total variation in the dependent variable that is explained by the independent variables in the model. While R^2 can serve as a useful measure of goodness of fit in the LPM, it has some limitations, especially when dealing with binary dependent variables. In such cases, R^2 may not provide a complete picture of model fit, and alternative measures such as pseudo-R^2 statistics (e.g., McFadden's R^2) are often preferred for evaluating the goodness of fit in logistic regression models, which are more commonly used for binary outcomes.

43. (C): To determine which of the processes X_t given are I(0) processes, we should look at the properties of each process in relation to stationarity and differencing.

For option (*a*), $X_t = X_{t-1} + Z_t$, this is a simple random walk. The value at time *t* is the value at time *t* – 1 plus some random noise Z_t. Since Z_t is white noise with a zero mean and variance σ_2, the process X_t is non-stationary and is considered an I(1) process because it requires one differencing to become stationary.

Option (*b*), $X_t = \alpha X_{t-1} + Z_t$ where $0 < \alpha < 1$, is an autoregressive process of order 1, AR(1). The parameter α is between 0 and 1, so the effect of the past values is diminishing over time, which ensures that the process will return to a mean of zero. This makes the process X_t stationary, and since it does not require differencing to become stationary, it is an I(0) process.

Option (*c*), $X_t = Z_t + Z_{t-1}$, is simply the sum of two white noise processes at different times. Since white noise is stationary and adding two stationary processes together yields another stationary process, X_t here is also stationary. Therefore, this is an I(0) process.

Option (*d*), $X_t = 8 + X_{t-1} + Z_t$, represents a random walk with a drift. The constant term 8 introduces a deterministic trend, and similar to option (*a*), it is a non-stationary process. The presence of a deterministic trend means that the process is not I(0) since differencing once (to remove the effect of the trend) would be required to achieve stationarity.

Therefore, option C the correct answer.

44. (B):

(*b*) **Mean is constant:** A weakly stationary stochastic process requires that the mean of the process remains constant over time. This means that the average value of the process does not change as time progresses. Therefore, the constancy of the mean is indeed a feature of a weakly stationary stochastic process.

(*c*) **Variance is constant:** Similarly, a weakly stationary stochastic process necessitates that the variance of the process remains constant over time. This implies that the dispersion or spread of the process around its mean does not change over time. Hence, the constancy of the variance is a characteristic of a weakly stationary stochastic process.

(*d*) **Covariance is time-invariant:** This is also a feature of a weakly stationary stochastic process. In weak stationarity, the covariance between any two observations of the process depends only on the time difference between them, not on the specific time points. This means that the covariance structure of the process remains constant over time, and changes in the time index do not affect the covariance between observations.

45. (D)

46. (B): The new monetary aggregate NM_2, proposed by the Third working group of RBI, represents an important refinement in measuring the money supply within the economy. By including time deposits with a term less than or equal to one year, NM_2 captures a significant portion of funds that are readily accessible for spending or investment in the short to medium term. This inclusion acknowledges the role of time deposits as a component of the broader money supply, reflecting the liquidity preferences of households and firms. However, by excluding time deposits with terms exceeding one year, NM_2 ensures a more accurate representation of the portion of funds that are less immediately liquid and more likely to be held for longer-term saving purposes. This distinction between short-term and long-term deposits is crucial for policymakers in understanding the dynamics of liquidity in the financial system and its implications for monetary policy formulation. NM_2 provides insights into the stability and health of the banking sector, as well as the availability of funds for investment and consumption, thereby aiding in the assessment of monetary conditions and the implementation of appropriate policy measures to support economic stability and growth.

47. (C):

(a) **91-day Treasury bill:** Treasury bills are short-term debt securities issued by the government to finance its short-term borrowing requirements. They are typically issued with maturities ranging from a few days to one year, making them highly liquid and suitable for short-term investment. Investors purchase Treasury bills at a discount to their face value and receive the full face value upon maturity, effectively earning interest on their investment.

(b) **Commercial paper:** Commercial paper is a short-term debt instrument issued by corporations, typically with maturities ranging from a few days to nine months. It is used by companies to raise funds for various short-term financing needs, such as funding working capital requirements or financing short-term liabilities. Commercial paper is considered a money market instrument due to its short-term nature and high liquidity.

(c) **Certificate of deposit (CD) issued by banks:** Certificates of deposit are time deposits offered by banks to depositors, where the depositor agrees to leave the deposited funds with the bank for a specified period (term) in exchange for a fixed interest rate. CDs typically have maturities ranging from a few weeks to several years, but shorter-term CDs with maturities of less than one year are considered money market instruments due to their liquidity and short-term nature.

48. (B):

(a) **Current Account deficit equals excess of imports over the sum of exports and net transfers received by a country:** The Current Account records all transactions involving goods, services, income, and transfers between residents and non-residents of a country. A deficit occurs when a country imports more goods and services, pays more income to foreigners, and transfers more funds abroad than it receives from exports, income from abroad, and transfers from abroad. This deficit reflects a shortfall in a country's international trade balance and represents an outflow of domestic currency to pay for foreign goods and services.

(b) **Current Account deficit may be covered by borrowing from foreigners:** When a country has a Current Account deficit, it indicates that it is spending more on

imports and transfers than it is earning from exports and transfers received. To finance this deficit, a country can borrow from foreign sources. This borrowing can come in various forms, such as foreign loans, issuance of bonds to foreign investors, or seeking assistance from international financial institutions. However, relying too heavily on foreign borrowing to cover a persistent Current Account deficit can pose risks to a country's economy, including increased indebtedness and vulnerability to changes in global financial conditions.

(*d*) **If India's Current Account deficit in a particular period is $50 million, it can be financed by net capital inflows amounting to $50 million:** Net capital inflows represent the total amount of foreign investment flowing into a country minus the total amount of domestic investment flowing out. If a country has a Current Account deficit, it can be offset by an equal amount of net capital inflows, as these inflows provide the necessary financing to cover the deficit. Capital inflows can come from various sources, including foreign direct investment, portfolio investment, and borrowing from international financial markets. However, it's essential to monitor the sustainability of these inflows to ensure they do not lead to excessive reliance on external financing or potential risks to economic stability.

49. (C):

(*a*) **Indian Rupee will depreciate in the spot market:** When investors engage in covered interest arbitrage, they typically borrow money in the currency with the lower interest rate (in this case, USD) and convert it into the currency with the higher interest rate (INR). This process increases the supply of INR in the foreign exchange market and creates demand for USD. As a result, the value of the INR relative to the USD decreases, leading to depreciation of the Indian Rupee in the spot market. Essentially, the increased demand for USD and the excess supply of INR put downward pressure on the exchange rate, causing the INR to weaken.

(*d*) **Interest rate will decline in the US:** When investors engage in covered interest arbitrage by borrowing in USD to invest in India, they increase the demand for USD. This increased demand for USD tends to strengthen the currency, causing it to appreciate. In response to the appreciation of the USD, the central bank of the US may adjust its monetary policy to counteract the currency appreciation and support economic growth. One way to achieve this is by decreasing interest rates in the US. Lower interest rates make borrowing more attractive, stimulating economic activity and helping to offset the effects of currency appreciation. Therefore, covered interest arbitrage can lead to a decline in interest rates in the US as the central bank takes measures to manage currency movements and support the economy.

50. (C) **51. (D)**

52. (A):

(*a*) **The AD curve will shift to the right if autonomous investment rises:** When autonomous investment increases, it reflects businesses' increased confidence in future profitability, leading them to invest more in capital goods, machinery, or infrastructure. This increase in investment spending directly contributes to aggregate demand in the economy, as it represents an injection of new spending not directly influenced by changes in output or income. As a result, the AD curve shifts to the right, indicating higher levels of aggregate demand at every price level.

(*b*) **The AD curve will shift to the right if net exports rise in an open economy:** An increase in net exports means that the country is exporting more goods and services than it is importing. This suggests increased demand for the country's exports abroad, which contributes positively to its aggregate demand. Higher net exports directly add to aggregate demand since they represent additional spending on domestically produced goods and services. Consequently, the AD curve shifts to the right to reflect the increased demand for domestic output resulting from higher net exports.

(*c*) **The AD curve will shift to the left if money supply contracts:** When the central bank implements a contractionary monetary policy and reduces the money supply, it leads to higher interest rates, making borrowing more expensive for businesses and consumers. This, in turn, reduces investment and consumption spending in the economy, causing aggregate demand to decrease. A contraction in the money supply represents a decrease in the availability of funds for spending and investment, thereby shifting the AD curve to the left, indicating lower levels of aggregate demand at every price level.

53. (A):

(*b*) Monetarism, associated with economists such as Milton Friedman, emphasizes the role of money in the economy. Monetarists argue that changes in the money supply have a significant impact on economic variables such as output, employment, and inflation. Additionally, they stress the importance of expectations, particularly in relation to inflation. For example, if individuals and firms expect prices to rise in the future, they may adjust their behavior accordingly, leading to actual inflation.

(*c*) The classical school of thought, which includes economists like Adam Smith and David Ricardo, indeed advocates for the invisible hand and the efficiency of the market mechanism. Classical economists believe that markets tend towards equilibrium and that individuals pursuing their self-interest in competitive markets leads to overall economic welfare. They argue for minimal government intervention in the economy, trusting that market forces will efficiently allocate resources.

(*d*) New Keynesian economics emerged as a response to the shortcomings of traditional Keynesian theory. New Keynesians retain many of the key insights of Keynesian economics but incorporate the assumption of imperfect markets into their frameworks. They recognize factors such as market rigidities, imperfect information, and nominal rigidities (such as sticky prices and wages) that can lead to inefficiencies and market failures. New Keynesians advocate for targeted government intervention, such as monetary and fiscal policy, to correct these market failures and stabilize the economy.

54. (C):

(*a*) **Output will be higher:** A monetary expansion, implemented through actions like central bank purchases of government securities or reductions in interest rates, serves to increase the money supply within the economy. This influx of money leads to a decrease in interest rates, making borrowing cheaper for businesses seeking capital to finance investment projects. With the cost of borrowing reduced, firms are incentivized to undertake more investment activities, such as expanding production capacity, upgrading technology, or initiating new projects. As a result, the aggregate demand for goods and services rises, prompting firms to ramp up production to meet the increased demand. This increase in production, in turn, leads to higher levels of output within the economy. Additionally, the boost in economic activity may translate into increased employment opportunities as firms expand their operations, further contributing to the rise in output and overall economic growth.

(*b*) **Consumption will be higher:** Lower interest rates resulting from a monetary expansion also have significant implications for consumer behaviour and household spending. When interest rates decline, the cost of borrowing for consumers decreases, making it more affordable for individuals to finance major purchases, such as homes, automobiles, or durable goods. With financing options becoming more attractive, households may be more inclined to increase their consumption spending on these big-ticket items. Additionally, lower interest rates can lead to reduced debt-servicing costs for existing loans, freeing up disposable income that consumers can allocate towards discretionary spending. This increase in consumer spending contributes to a rise in aggregate demand, prompting businesses to produce more goods and services to meet the growing consumer demand. Consequently, higher levels of consumption further stimulate economic activity, leading to increased output, employment, and overall economic expansion.

55. (B): In economics, a production function Q is said to be homogeneous of degree *n* if, when all inputs are scaled by a factor *t*, output is scaled by a factor t_n. In the function Q = $A x \alpha y \beta$, if $\alpha + \beta = 1$, then Q is homogeneous of degree 1 (linearly homogeneous or simply homogeneous), which means it has constant returns to scale.

For statement (*a*), it is not correct to say that Q is a homogeneous function for all values of α and β because homogeneity depends on the sum $\alpha + \beta$. Q is only homogeneous if $\alpha + \beta$ equals some constant *k*, and in that case, Q would be homogeneous of degree *k*.

Statement (*b*) claims that H is a homothetic function for all values of α and β. A homothetic function is one where if Q is homogeneous, then any monotonic transformation of Q is homothetic. Since an exponential function is a monotonic transformation, H = eQ would be a homothetic function of Q, regardless of the values of α and β.

Statement (*d*) says H is not a homogeneous function. This is true because the exponential function of a homogeneous function is not homogeneous, but rather homothetic as explained in (*b*).

Given these points, statements (*a*), (*b*), and (*d*) are the correct ones, making option B the right choice.

56. (D): To determine the correct answer, we must evaluate the matrix multiplication of A and B, and also B and A.

Matrix multiplication is defined when the number of columns in the first matrix matches the number of rows in the second matrix. Matrix A is a 3 × 23 × 2 matrix, and matrix B is a 2 × 12 × 1 matrix. Thus, the product AB is defined and will result in a 3 × 13 × 1 matrix.

To find AB, we perform the following calculations:

AB = [124380] [59]

= 1 × 5 + 3 × 92 × 5 + 8 × 94 × 5 + 0 × 9]

= [5 + 2710 + 7220 + 0] = [328220].

Hence, statement (*a*) is correct.

For BA, since B is a 2 × 12 × 1 matrix and A is a 3 × 23 × 2 matrix, we cannot multiply B by A because the number of columns in B does not match the number of rows in A.

Therefore, statement (*d*) is correct, and BA is not defined.

Considering AT (the transpose of A), which would be a 2 × 32 × 3 matrix, and B as a 2 × 12 × 1 matrix, their multiplication is not possible because the number of columnns in A^T does not match the number of rows in B. Thus, A^TB is not defined, which makes statement (*e*) incorrect.

Therefore, the correct statements are (*a*) and (*d*), which means the answer is option (D).

57. (C):

(*a*) The Marginal Cost (MC) curve cuts both short-run Average Cost (AC) curve and Average Variable Cost (AVC) curve at their lowest point. This statement is correct. In the short run, the Marginal Cost (MC) curve intersects the Average Cost (AC) curve and the Average Variable Cost (AVC) curve at their minimum points. This is because when MC is below AC or AVC, it pulls them down, and when MC is above AC or AVC, it pulls them up. At the minimum point of AC and AVC, MC equals AC and AVC, respectively.

(*e*) **The AC curve is u-shaped.** This statement is also correct. The Average Cost (AC) curve is typically U-shaped in the short run. Initially, as production increases, AC decreases due to economies of scale, where the fixed costs are spread over more units, leading to lower average costs. However, after a certain point, AC starts increasing due to diseconomies of scale, where the costs associated with producing additional units begin to outweigh the benefits of increased production. This leads to the U-shape of the AC curve in the short run.

58. (C): To address this question, let's break down each of the statements given and validate them against the information provided in the OLS regression output.

Statement (*a*) says that for one year increase in schooling, wage per hour increases by ₹ 640 on average, when cognitive ability (CA) is kept constant. The regression coefficient for education (years of schooling, S) is 0.64, which means for each additional year of schooling, wages increase by 0.64 thousand rupees or ₹ 640. This statement is correct.

Statement (*b*) mentions the value of t statistic of cognitive ability (CA) is 3. The t statistic is calculated by taking the estimated coefficient and dividing it by the standard error. For CA, the estimated coefficient is 0.15 and the standard error is 0.05. To calculate the t statistic:

3*t* = 0.050.15 = 3

So, the *t* statistic for CA is indeed 3, which makes statement (*b*) correct.

Statement (*c*) and (*d*) both provide formulas for the F statistic. The F statistic in a regression analysis is used to test the overall significance of the model. It is calculated by taking the ratio of the mean square due to regression (explained sum of squares divided by its degrees of freedom) to the mean square error (residual sum of squares divided by its degrees of freedom).

The correct formula for the F statistic is:

F = Residual Sum of Squares/Degrees of Freedom for Residual

Explained Sum of Squares/Degrees of Freedom for Regression

Given that the explained sum of squares is 4745.75 with 2 degrees of freedom, and the residual sum of squares is 33651.28 with 567 degrees of freedom, the correct F statistic is calculated by statement (*c*):

F = (33651.28/567) (4745.75/2)

This means that statement (*c*) is correct and statement (*d*) is incorrect, as it inverses the ratio.

Therefore, the correct statements are (*a*), (*b*), and (*c*), which corresponds to answer C.

59. (D) **60. (D)**

61. (D): To evaluate the statements related to a production function $q = f(k, l)$ that is a homogeneous function of degree 1, we should recall some properties of homogeneous functions and Euler's Theorem.

Statement (*a*) suggests that the marginal products of capital ($\partial q/\partial k$) and labour ($\partial q/\partial l$) are homogeneous of degree 1. However, for a function that is homogeneous of degree *n*, its first derivatives (marginal products in this context) are homogeneous of degree $n - 1$. Since the production function $f(k, l)$ is given as homogeneous of degree 1, the marginal products should be homogeneous of degree 0, which means they are constant. Hence, statement (*a*) is incorrect.

Statement (*b*) talks about the second-order cross partial derivatives ($\partial 2q/\partial k\partial l$ and $\partial 2\partial/\partial l\partial k$). For a function with continuous second derivatives, the mixed partial derivatives are equal by Clairaut's theorem (also known as Young's theorem), regardless of the function's homogeneity. Thus, statement (*b*) is correct.

Statement (*c*) is Euler's Theorem applied to a homogeneous function of degree 1. Euler's Theorem states that for a homogeneous function of degree *n*, the following equation holds:

$k\partial k\partial q + l\partial l\partial q = n \,.\, q$

Since our function is homogeneous of degree 1, we can replace *n* with 1, making statement (*c*) correct.

Statement (*d*) is an extension of Euler's Theorem to the second derivatives. For a homogeneous function of degree 1, the sum of the product of each variable with its corresponding second derivative is equal to 0. This statement is a result of differentiating both sides of Euler's Theorem with respect to *k* and *l* respectively and adding them together. Thus, statement (*d*) is correct.

The correct statements are (*b*), (*c*), and (*d*), which means the answer is option (D).

62. (C):

(*a*) The statement asserts that when we take the union of a finite number of closed sets in a topological space, the resulting set remains closed. This property is fundamental in topology and is often used in various mathematical proofs and constructions. A closed set is one that contains all its limit points, and the union of closed sets preserves this property because if a point is a limit point of one of the closed sets, it will still be a limit point of the union. This is because the union contains all the elements from each individual set, ensuring that no limit points are excluded. Therefore, the union of finite numbers of closed sets is indeed a closed set.

(*d*) The statement posits that when we intersect a finite number of open sets in a topological space, the resulting set remains open. An open set is defined as a set that contains an open neighborhood around each of its points. When we intersect a finite number of such sets, any point in the intersection will still have an open neighborhood contained entirely within each of the original open sets. This is because the intersection only includes elements that are common to all the sets being intersected, and these elements still possess the property of having open neighborhoods within each set. Therefore, the intersection of finite numbers of open sets is also an open set. This property is crucial in analysis, topology, and other areas of mathematics for establishing continuity, compactness, and other key concepts.

63. (*)

64. (C):

(*a*) If the two utility functions $u(x)$ and $b(y)$ are related by $u(y) = V(b(x))$, where $(-) > 0V'(-) > 0$, then $V(x)$ is a utility function representing the same preference as $b(y)$. This statement is correct. The function $V(x)$ is derived from $b(y)$ through the transformation $u(y) = V(b(x))$. The fact that (–) > 0V2 (–) > 0 implies that $V(x)$ is strictly increasing, preserving the preference ordering between different consumption bundles. Therefore, $V(x)$ represents the same preferences as $b(y)$.

(b) If two utility functions represent the same preferences, the solutions to the consumer's utility maximization problem are the same with the two utility functions but the indirect utility functions are different. This statement is correct. Utility functions represent preferences, and if two utility functions represent the same preferences, they will lead to the same optimal consumption bundle because the consumer aims to maximize utility regardless of the specific utility function used. However, the indirect utility functions, which represent the maximum utility attainable given prices and income, might differ because they are derived from different utility functions.

(c) If the local nonsatiation assumption of preference is satisfied, any solution to the consumer's utility maximization problem satisfies the budget constraint with equality. This statement is correct. Local nonsatiation means the consumer always desires more of at least one good at any consumption bundle. In the utility maximization problem, the consumer chooses a consumption bundle that maximizes utility subject to the budget constraint. If local nonsatiation holds, the consumer will always choose a consumption bundle where they exhaust their entire budget, thus satisfying the budget constraint with equality.

65. (C): The objective function to be maximized in each case is the natural logarithm of x, which is an increasing function for $x > 0$. This means as x increases, so does $\ln x$. However, the behavior of the function under the constraints of each problem is critical for determining whether a solution exists.

For the first problem (*i*), where $x > 1$, there is no upper bound on x, and hence, the function $\ln x$ can increase indefinitely. In optimization terms, the problem lacks an upper constraint that would allow for a maximal value, leading to the conclusion that there is no finite maximum; $\ln x$ will keep increasing as x increases, thus the problem has no solution.

The second problem (*ii*) involves $x < 1$, where $\ln x$ is decreasing as x approaches zero from the right. Since the natural logarithm heads towards negative infinity as its argument heads towards zero from the right, and x cannot actually reach zero to allow for the logarithm to be defined, there is no maximum value within the constraint. Like the first, this problem also does not have a solution.

The third problem (*iii*) stipulates $1 < x < 2$. Within this bounded interval, the function $\ln x$ will achieve a maximum at the upper boundary due to its increasing nature. Therefore, the maximum value for $\ln x$ is at $x = 2$, making $\ln 2$ the maximal value, and thus, this problem does have a solution.

66. (D):

(a) Ramsar Convention: Conservation of wetlands - The Ramsar Convention, signed in 1971 in Ramsar, Iran, aims to protect and preserve wetlands worldwide, recognizing their importance for biodiversity and ecosystem services.

(b) Basel Convention: Control of trans-boundary movement of hazardous wastes and disposal - The Basel Convention, adopted in 1989 in Basel, Switzerland, addresses the management and disposal of hazardous wastes, especially those that can cause harm if not handled properly. It regulates the transboundary movement of such wastes to ensure environmentally sound management.

(*c*) **Montreal Protocol: Ozone layer depletion -** The Montreal Protocol, established in 1987 in Montreal, Canada, aims to phase out the production and use of ozone-depleting substances (ODS) such as chlorofluorocarbons (CFCs) and halons. Its primary goal is to protect the ozone layer, which shields the Earth from harmful ultraviolet radiation.

(*d*) **Paris Agreement: Reduction of greenhouse gas emissions** - The Paris Agreement, adopted in 2015 in Paris, France, is a landmark international treaty aimed at combating climate change. It sets out ambitious goals to limit global warming and reduce greenhouse gas emissions to mitigate the impacts of climate change.

67. (B):

(*a*) **Coase theorem - (I) Property right, victim's pay and polluter pay principle.** The Coase theorem asserts that in the presence of well-defined property rights and in the absence of transaction costs, parties can negotiate and reach an efficient solution to externalities, such as pollution, without the need for government intervention. This involves the concepts of property rights, where the victim can be compensated (victim's pay) or the polluter can be made to pay for the damage caused (polluter pay principle).

(*b*) **Climate change - (IV) Global externality.** Climate change refers to long-term changes in temperature, precipitation, and other atmospheric conditions that result from human activities, particularly the emission of greenhouse gases. It is considered a global externality as its impacts extend beyond national borders and affect the entire planet.

(*c*) **Ecological dumping - (II) Lax environmental regulation, hidden subsidy.** Ecological dumping refers to the practice where firms in countries with lax environmental regulations can gain a competitive advantage by producing goods more cheaply due to lower environmental standards. This can be seen as a form of hidden subsidy, as these firms are effectively being subsidized by not having to comply with stricter environmental regulations.

(*d*) **Tradable emission permit - (III) Quantity restriction.** Tradable emission permits involve setting a cap on the total amount of pollution allowed (quantity restriction) and allowing firms to buy and sell permits to emit pollutants. This system provides economic incentives for firms to reduce emissions efficiently and is a market-based approach to addressing pollution.

68. (C):

(*a*) **Kenneth Arrow - (III) Fundamental contribution in welfare economics:** Kenneth Arrow made significant contributions to welfare economics, particularly through his work on social choice theory, which analyzes how individual preferences can be aggregated into collective social preferences to determine optimal outcomes.

(*b*) **Robert Solow - (IV) Fundamental contribution in economic growth theory:** Robert Solow's seminal work on economic growth theory, particularly the Solow growth model, has been instrumental in understanding the determinants of long-term economic growth and the role of factors such as capital accumulation, technological progress, and productivity growth.

(*c*) **Daniel Kahneman - (II) Fundamental contribution in behavioural economics:** Daniel Kahneman is a pioneer in the field of behavioral economics, which integrates insights from psychology into economic analysis. His research on cognitive biases, prospect theory, and decision-making under uncertainty has profoundly influenced our understanding of how individuals make economic choices.

(*d*) **Joshua Angrist - (I) Analysis of causal relationship:** Joshua Angrist has made significant contributions to the field of econometrics, particularly in the analysis of causal relationships using natural experiments and instrumental variables. His work has advanced our ability to identify causal effects in observational data and has had widespread applications in various fields of economics.

69. (C):

(*a*) **Demographic Transition - (III) Replacement Rate:** The Demographic Transition refers to the process through which populations move from high birth and death rates to low birth and death rates as they undergo industrialization and modernization. The Replacement Rate is a key concept within the demographic transition framework, representing the fertility rate necessary for a population to replace itself from one generation to the next.

(*b*) **Stages of growth - (II) Take-off:** The Stages of Growth theory, proposed by economist Walt Rostow, describes the development process of economies through various stages, with the Take-off stage being a crucial phase characterized by rapid industrialization, urbanization, and technological advancement.

(*c*) **Rural-urban migration decision - (I) Dualism:** Rural-urban migration decision refers to the choice made by individuals to move from rural areas to urban areas in search of better economic opportunities. This decision is influenced by the phenomenon of dualism, which describes the coexistence of traditional and modern sectors within an economy, often characterized by disparities in income, employment opportunities, and living standards between rural and urban areas.

(*d*) **Female labour force participation rate - (IV) Backward bending labour supply curve:** The Female labour force participation rate refers to the proportion of women in the population who are actively engaged in the labour force. The Backward bending labour supply curve is a concept in labour economics that suggests that individuals may initially respond to higher wages by increasing their labour supply, but beyond a certain point, they may choose to work less as their income rises further.

70. (D)

71. (C): The Permanent Income Hypothesis of Consumption was introduced by Milton Friedman. This theory posits that people's consumption choices are not solely affected by their current income, but rather by their anticipated income over a longer period. Essentially, individuals plan their consumption based on the income they expect to have over their lifetime, smoothing out consumption to achieve a stable path even if their income is variable in the short term.

The Life-cycle Hypothesis of Consumption is attributed to Franco Modigliani. This hypothesis complements Friedman's Permanent Income Hypothesis by considering the saving behavior of individuals over their lifetime. According to Modigliani, individuals plan their consumption and savings based on their current income and their needs in the future, particularly for retirement. Therefore, individuals save during their working years and dissave during their retirement.

The Real Business Cycle Theory is associated with F. Kydland and E. Prescott. This theory stands on the premise that business cycle fluctuations can to a large extent be accounted for by real (in contrast to nominal) shocks. According to this view, economic cycles are primarily the result of technological changes that affect productivity and thus influence economic variables like employment, consumption, and investment.

Lastly, the Policy Ineffectiveness Proposition was developed by Thomas Sargent and Neil Wallace. This proposition is one of the cornerstones of the rational expectations revolution in macroeconomics. It argues that anticipated policy interventions, such as systematic monetary or fiscal policy, are ineffective in influencing real economic variables like output and employment. This is because people, with rational expectations, will anticipate the effects of policy and alter their behavior in ways that offset the intended effects of the policy.

72. (C): Unequal Exchange is a concept associated with Arghiri Emmanuel, who argued that trade between countries with different wage levels leads to an 'unequal exchange'. This occurs because labour-intensive goods produced in low-wage countries are exchanged for capital-intensive goods produced in high-wage countries, resulting in a transfer of wealth from poorer to richer countries.

The development of underdevelopment is a concept developed by Andre Gunder Frank as part of the dependency theory. Frank argued that underdevelopment is not a traditional stage on the way to development but a consequence of capitalist development itself. This underdevelopment is perpetuated through the mechanisms of the global capitalist system that benefit the developed 'core' at the expense of the 'periphery'.

Backward and forward linkage effects were introduced by Albert Hirschman. These concepts are a part of his strategy for economic development, which suggests that certain types of industries, due to their connections with other sectors, can stimulate overall economic growth. Backward linkages refer to the relationships with the suppliers, while forward linkages refer to the connections with the consumers of the industry's products.

The backwash effect is associated with Gunnar Myrdal, who posited that it is one of the forces at play in economic geography and regional development. The backwash effect refers to the negative impacts that the growth of more developed regions can have on less developed ones, as the former often drain resources, skilled labour, and investment away from the latter, exacerbating regional inequalities.

73. (D)

74. (A): When investment is unresponsive to interest rates, it suggests that changes in the interest rate do not affect investment spending. This scenario is depicted by a vertical Investment-Saving (IS) curve because investment levels will not change for different levels of interest rates.

Money demand being perfectly elastic with respect to interest rates means that any quantity of money is demanded at a particular interest rate. This is represented by a horizontal Liquidity Preference-Money Supply (LM) curve, implying that the economy can absorb any amount of money supply without changing the interest rate.

When money demand is completely inelastic with respect to interest rates, it indicates that changes in interest rates do not affect the quantity of money demanded. This situation is represented by a vertical LM curve. The quantity of money demanded is fixed, irrespective of the interest rate level.

Lastly, when investment is highly responsive to interest rates, it means small changes in the interest rate lead to large changes in investment spending. This condition is represented by a relatively flat IS curve, indicating high sensitivity of investment to changes in interest rates.

75. (A):

(*a*) **Quantity theory of money:** This economic theory is famously associated with Milton Friedman, suggests that changes in the money supply lead to proportionate changes in the price level in the economy. It emphasizes the long-term relationship between the money supply and the price level, positing that excessive growth in the money supply leads to inflation.

(*b*) **Involuntary unemployment:** Coined by John Maynard Keynes, this term describes a situation where individuals are willing to work at the prevailing wage rate but are unable to find employment. Keynes argued that involuntary unemployment could persist in the economy, even in the presence of aggregate demand, due to factors such as wage rigidities and insufficient aggregate demand.

(*c*) **Randomised trial:** This methodological approach, employed by economists Abhijit V. Banerjee, involves conducting experiments where participants are randomly assigned to different treatment groups. By randomly allocating participants, researchers can minimize selection bias and establish causal relationships between variables, particularly in evaluating the impact of policy interventions or programmatic changes.

(*d*) **Relative poverty:** A concept often discussed by economists Amartya K. Sen, relative poverty defines poverty in relation to the living standards and income distribution within a society. Unlike absolute poverty, which sets a fixed income threshold, relative poverty considers individuals or households to be poor if their income falls significantly below the median income of the population they reside in. This perspective highlights the importance of inequality and social context in understanding poverty.

76. (C):

(*a*) **Reduction in policy rate:** Central banks often use interest rates as a tool to implement monetary policy. When a central bank reduces its policy rate, it makes borrowing cheaper for businesses and individuals. Lower borrowing costs encourage increased spending and investment in the economy, leading to higher aggregate demand.

(*b*) **Capital outflows:** A reduction in the policy rate may lead to capital outflows from the domestic economy. Lower interest rates make domestic assets less attractive to investors seeking higher returns. As a result, investors may sell their domestic assets and invest in foreign assets with higher interest rates. This movement of capital out of the domestic economy puts downward pressure on the domestic currency's exchange rate.

(*c*) **Depreciation of domestic currency:** The increase in capital outflows and reduced demand for domestic assets relative to foreign assets leads to a depreciation of the domestic currency. In other words, the value of the domestic currency decreases compared to foreign currencies. Depreciation makes imports more expensive and exports cheaper, thus influencing trade flows.

(*d*) **Rise in net exports:** A depreciation of the domestic currency makes domestic goods cheaper for foreign buyers, leading to an increase in exports. Conversely, it makes foreign goods relatively more expensive for domestic consumers, leading to a decrease in imports. The net result is an increase in net exports, as exports rise and imports fall. This increase in net exports boosts aggregate demand and economic activity.

77. (C):

(*a*) **Y.V. Reddy:** Yaga Venugopal Reddy held the position of RBI Governor from September 6, 2003, to September 5, 2008. During his tenure, he implemented various monetary policies aimed at maintaining financial stability and managing inflation.

(*b*) **D Subbarao:** Duvvuri Subbarao succeeded Y.V. Reddy as the RBI Governor and served from September 5, 2008, to September 4, 2013. He faced significant challenges during his term, including the global financial crisis of 2008, and implemented measures to stabilize the Indian economy.

(*c*) **Raghuram Rajan:** Raghuram Rajan assumed office as the RBI Governor on September 4, 2013, succeeding D. Subbarao. He introduced several reforms and policies to address issues like inflation, currency stability, and banking sector reforms during his tenure, which lasted until September 4, 2016.

(*d*) **Urjit Patel:** Urjit Patel served as the RBI Governor from September 4, 2016, to December 10, 2018. His tenure saw various significant developments, including the demonetization initiative and efforts to address non-performing assets in the banking sector.

78. (C):

(*b*) **Setting up of UTI (Unit Trust of India):** UTI was established in 1964 as a financial institution to promote savings and investment among the public. This event marked a significant milestone in the Indian financial system, providing avenues for individuals to invest in mutual funds and other financial instruments. Option (C) correctly places this event as the earliest in the sequence.

(*c*) **Nationalisation of 14 commercial banks:** This event occurred in 1969 when the Government of India nationalized 14 major banks to ensure better control over credit allocation and promote financial inclusion. Nationalization aimed to channelize credit towards priority sectors and foster economic development. Option (C) correctly positions this event as the second in the sequence.

(*a*) **Setting up of PFRDA (Pension Fund Regulatory and Development Authority):** PFRDA was established in 2003 as an autonomous body responsible for regulating and developing the pension sector in India, including the management of pension funds. The creation of PFRDA marked a significant step towards modernizing India's pension system and providing retirement benefits to its citizens. Option (C) places this event as the third in the sequence.

(*d*) **Implementation of IBC (Insolvency and Bankruptcy Code):** The Insolvency and Bankruptcy Code was implemented in 2016 to consolidate and amend the laws relating to insolvency resolution of corporate persons, partnership firms, and individuals in a time-bound manner. The implementation of IBC aimed to address the challenges of non-performing assets and streamline the insolvency resolution process in India.

79. (B):

(*a*) **Shephard's Lemma - (II) Envelope theorem:** Shephard's Lemma is a result in mathematical economics that is closely related to the Envelope theorem. It states that the derivative of the cost function with respect to input prices equals the profit function. The Envelope theorem, on the other hand, describes how the value of the objective function of an optimization problem changes when a parameter of the problem changes slightly. It is often used in economic analysis to simplify calculations and derive comparative statics results.

(*b*) **Adverse Selection - (I) Hidden types of agent:** Adverse selection refers to a situation in which one party in a transaction has more information than the other, leading to a distortion in the market due to information asymmetry. Hidden types of agents are individuals whose characteristics (such as risk preferences or quality) are unknown to others in the market, contributing to adverse selection problems.

(*c*) **Hotelling Lemma - (IV) Profit function:** Hotelling's Lemma is a result in mathematical economics that describes the relationship between the profit function and the cost function. It states that the derivative of the profit function with respect to the price of a good equals the derivative of the cost function with respect to the quantity of that good produced. This lemma is frequently used in industrial organization and microeconomic analysis to derive optimal pricing strategies.

(*d*) **Roy's Identity - (III) Indirect utility function:** Roy's Identity is an important result in consumer theory that links the indirect utility function with the expenditure function. It states that the derivative of the indirect utility function with respect to income equals the marginal utility of expenditure. The indirect utility function represents the maximum utility a consumer can attain given their budget constraint and the prices of goods and services.

80. (B):

(*e*) **Right to Education (2009):** The Right to Education Act was enacted in 2009, making education a fundamental right for children between the ages of 6 and 14 years. This legislation aimed to ensure free and compulsory education for all children, marking a significant step towards improving literacy and educational access nationwide.

(*c*) **Swachh Bharat Abhiyan (2014):** Launched in 2014, the Swachh Bharat Abhiyan aimed to address the issue of cleanliness and sanitation in India. It emphasized the construction of toilets, eradication of open defecation, and proper waste management practices, with the goal of achieving a cleaner and healthier environment for all citizens.

(*a*) **Beti Bachao Beti Padhao (2015):** Introduced in 2015, the Beti Bachao Beti Padhao (Save Daughters, Educate Daughters) campaign sought to address the declining child sex ratio and promote the education and welfare of girl children. It aimed to combat gender-based discrimination and empower girls through education and equal opportunities.

(*b*) **Ujjwala (2016):** The Ujjwala scheme, launched in 2016, aimed to provide clean cooking fuel to households below the poverty line. By offering free LPG connections to eligible beneficiaries, the program aimed to reduce indoor air pollution, improve health outcomes, and empower women by saving them from the drudgery of traditional cooking methods.

(*d*) **Ayushman Bharat (2018):** Ayushman Bharat, launched in 2018, is a national health protection scheme that aims to provide financial protection to vulnerable families against high healthcare costs. It includes two components: the Pradhan

Mantri Jan Arogya Yojana (PM-JAY), which provides health insurance coverage for secondary and tertiary care, and the Health and Wellness Centres (HWCs), which deliver comprehensive primary healthcare services.

81. (A):

(*a*) **Run the regression model on pooled sample and calculate RSS_p:** The first step is to estimate the regression model using all the data combined (pooled sample) and calculate the residual sum of squares (RSS), which measures the total deviation of the observed values from the values predicted by the regression model.

(*b*) **Run the same regression model on the two sub-samples separately and calculate RSS_1 and RSS_2:** Next, the regression model is separately estimated on each subgroup of the sample, and the RSS is calculated for each subgroup. This allows us to assess how well the regression model fits the data in each subgroup.

(*c*) **Calculate the F statistic:** The F statistic is computed by comparing the difference in RSS between the pooled model and the separate models with the RSS under the null hypothesis, which assumes no difference between the coefficients of the pooled model and the separate models.

(*d*) **Check the critical F with related degrees of freedom and compare it with F calculated:** The calculated F statistic is compared to the critical F value from the F-distribution table at a specified significance level and degrees of freedom. This helps determine whether the observed difference in RSS is statistically significant.

(*e*) **Do not reject H_0 if $F_{calculated} < F_{critical}$:** If the calculated F statistic is less than the critical F value, we do not reject the null hypothesis (H0), indicating that there is no significant difference between the coefficients of the pooled model and the separate models. In other words, pooling the data and using a single regression model is just as effective as running separate models on the subgroups.

82. (C):

(*c*) **The Alagh Committee** was a task force established in 1977 by the Planning Commission to define the poverty line. The committee was led by YK Alagh and constructed a poverty line for both rural and urban areas. The poverty line was based on nutritional requirements and related consumption expenditure. The committee defined the poverty line as a per capita consumption expenditure of Rs. 49.09 per month in rural areas.

(*b*) **The Khusro Committee,** also known as the Agricultural Credit Review Committee, was established in 1989. The committee was chaired by Prof. A.M. Khusro, who was related to the royal family of Hyderabad. The Khusro Committee recommended merging Regional Rural Banks (RRBs) with their sponsor banks. The committee also highlighted the weaknesses of RRBs and their non-viability.

(*d*) **The Nayak Committee** was established in 1991 by the Reserve Bank of India to examine the difficulties that small scale industries (SSI) faced in securing finance. The committee was chaired by Deputy Governor Shri P.R. Nayak. The committee's report was published in September 1992.

(*a*) **The Lakdawala Committee** was an expert group appointed by the Central Government of India in 1993 to estimate the poverty line in India. The committee was chaired by Professor D.T. Lakdawala, and its sole member.

(*e*) **The Suresh Tendulkar Committee** was established in 2005 to review the concept of poverty lines in India. The committee was set up by the Planning Commission to address shortcomings in previous methods and to recommend changes to the official poverty estimation process. The committee submitted its report in 2009.

83. (B):

(*a*) **Theory of Big Push:** Proposed by economist Paul Rosenstein-Rodan in the 1940s, the Theory of Big Push suggests that a large coordinated investment in multiple sectors simultaneously is necessary to initiate development in an underdeveloped economy.

(*e*) **Development with unlimited supplies of labour:** Associated with the early stages of economic development theory, this concept was discussed by economists like Arthur Lewis in the mid-20th century. It posits that in economies with abundant labour and limited capital, industrialization can lead to economic growth by absorbing surplus labour from the agricultural sector into the industrial sector.

(*b*) **The accumulation of capital:** This concept has been central to economic thought for centuries and was extensively discussed by classical economists such as Adam Smith and David Ricardo in the 18th and 19th centuries. It emphasizes the role of saving and investment in driving economic growth and development.

(*c*) **Theory of cumulative causation:** Developed by economist Gunnar Myrdal in the mid-20th century, the Theory of Cumulative Causation suggests that once an economy starts to develop, positive feedback loops and spillover effects can lead to further development, creating a self-reinforcing process of growth.

(*d*) **Unbalanced growth:** Gained prominence in development economics in the mid-20th century and discussed by economists like Ragnar Nurkse, the concept of unbalanced growth argues that in the early stages of development, it is often necessary for investment to be focused on specific sectors or regions to kickstart growth, leading to uneven or unbalanced development.

84. (D)

85. (D):

(*b*) **"The exchange rate is lower than the market clearing exchange rate":** This statement indicates that the prevailing exchange rate in the foreign exchange market is below what would naturally clear the market. In other words, the exchange rate is undervalued from the perspective of market equilibrium. When the exchange rate is lower than the market clearing rate, it suggests that the domestic currency is overvalued relative to the foreign currency. This situation often arises due to various factors such as government policies, speculation, or market sentiment. For instance, if the Central Bank sets an artificially high value for the domestic currency through intervention or if market participants expect the currency to appreciate in the future, it can lead to an overvalued exchange rate. In such cases, corrective measures are necessary to restore equilibrium and prevent market distortions.

(*a*) **"The demand for foreign currency exceeds its supply":** When the exchange rate is lower than the market clearing rate, indicating an overvaluation of the domestic currency, there is typically an increased demand for foreign currency. Market participants seek to take advantage of the overvalued domestic currency by purchasing foreign currency at a relatively cheaper rate. This excess demand for foreign currency can arise from various activities such as imports, foreign investment, or speculative trading. As a result, the demand for foreign currency outstrips its available supply in the foreign exchange market. This imbalance leads to market disequilibrium and puts upward pressure on the exchange rate, exacerbating the overvaluation of the domestic currency.

(*e*) **"The Central Bank sells foreign currency from its stock of reserves":** To address the excess demand for foreign currency and stabilize the exchange rate, the Central Bank intervenes in the foreign exchange market by selling foreign currency from its reserves. By supplying foreign currency, the Central Bank aims to meet the excess demand and prevent further appreciation of the domestic currency. This intervention is a common tool used by Central Banks to manage exchange rate fluctuations and maintain stability in the currency markets. The Central Bank's ability to sell foreign currency from its reserves demonstrates its commitment to achieving its exchange rate objectives and safeguarding the competitiveness of the domestic economy.

(*c*) **"The gap between supply and demand for foreign currency is equalized":** Through its intervention in the foreign exchange market, the Central Bank endeavors to equalize the gap between the supply and demand for foreign currency. By supplying additional foreign currency, the Central Bank aims to bring the market into equilibrium and eliminate the excess demand. This process helps restore stability to the exchange rate and ensures that market forces determine the value of the domestic currency. Achieving equilibrium between supply and demand is crucial for maintaining confidence in the currency and facilitating smooth international trade and investment flows.

(*d*) **"The Central Bank's stock of foreign currency is depleted":** While intervention in the foreign exchange market can help stabilize the exchange rate in the short term, continuous selling of foreign currency from the Central Bank's reserves may deplete its stock of foreign currency over time. Depletion of reserves indicates the extent of intervention required to maintain the desired exchange rate parity and underscores the Central Bank's commitment to its exchange rate objectives. However, excessive depletion of reserves can pose risks to the economy, such as reducing the Central Bank's ability to intervene in future market crises or limiting its capacity to manage external shocks. Therefore, prudent management of foreign exchange reserves is essential to ensure the long-term stability of the currency and the overall health of the economy.

86. (C): Statement I: This statement asserts that agricultural GDP constitutes less than 16% of aggregate GDP at 2011-12 constant prices and less than 20% of the aggregate GDP at current prices in 2022-23 in India. Agricultural GDP refers to the value of goods and services produced within the agricultural sector. The claim suggests a decline in the share of agricultural GDP relative to the total GDP over the specified period. This decline could be attributed to various factors such as the growth of other sectors like industry and services, technological advancements leading to increased productivity in agriculture but with relatively slower growth compared to other sectors, and shifts in government policies and investments favoring non-agricultural sectors. Overall, this statement implies a significant structural transformation in India's economy away from agriculture.

Statement II: This statement mirrors the content of Statement I but focuses on the service sector GDP instead of agricultural GDP. It suggests that the service sector's contribution to GDP is also less than 16% at constant prices and less than 20% at current prices in 2022-23 in India. However, this assertion seems less plausible considering the significant role of the service sector in India's economy. The service sector encompasses a wide range of activities, including IT services, finance, healthcare, education, tourism, and more, which collectively contribute substantially to India's GDP. Given the dynamism and growth potential of the service sector, it is unlikely that its share of GDP has declined to less than 16%. Thus, while Statement I appears credible, Statement II seems questionable due to the service sector's importance and growth trajectory in India.

87. (C): Statement (I) asserts that the government's spending on social services, as a proportion of the Gross Domestic Product (GDP), has been on the rise since the fiscal year 2017-18. This suggests a trend towards increasing investment in social welfare programs, healthcare, education, and other essential services aimed at improving the well-being and quality of life for citizens. Such an increase in spending on social services often reflects government efforts to address societal needs, promote equitable development, and enhance human capital formation. The rise in social spending relative to GDP indicates a prioritization of social development goals within the government's fiscal policies, potentially driven by factors such as demographic changes, public demand for better services, or policy shifts towards inclusive growth agendas.

Statement (II) claims that the government's spending on social services, as a percentage of total expenditure, has also been continuously rising since 2017-18. However, this statement is incorrect. While Statement I focus on the proportion of social spending relative to the size of the economy (GDP), Statement II refers to the share of social spending within the total government budget. The inaccuracy lies in the assertion that this share has been continuously increasing. In reality, government spending on social services may fluctuate over time due to various factors such as changes in fiscal priorities, economic conditions, political considerations, and budget constraints.

88. (C): Statement I correctly defines human development as a process focused on expanding people's opportunities and choices. This definition, proposed by Nobel laureate Amartya Sen, highlights the multifaceted nature of human well-being beyond just economic growth. It emphasizes the importance of factors such as health, education, political freedom, social inclusion, and environmental sustainability in improving people's lives. Human development aims to empower individuals to lead fulfilling lives according to their own aspirations and values, rather than solely focusing on increasing material wealth or GDP.

However, Statement II is incorrect. The Human Development Index (HDI) is indeed based on indicators such as life expectancy at birth, expected years of schooling, and Gross Domestic Product (GDP) per capita at purchasing power parity (PPP). However, it does not include "mean years of schooling" as one of its components. Instead, it considers the average number of years of schooling for adults aged 25 years and older, which provides a measure of the educational attainment level within a population. Therefore, while Statement I accurately describes human development, Statement II contains a factual inaccuracy regarding the components of the HDI.

89. (A): Assertion (A) states that as the sample size becomes very large, the distribution of the sample mean tends to a normal distribution. This assertion is indeed correct and is a fundamental concept in statistics. The Central Limit Theorem (CLT) is a fundamental theorem in probability theory and statistics. It states that the sampling distribution of the sample mean approaches a normal distribution as the sample size increases, regardless of the shape of the population distribution. In other words, if you take multiple samples from a population and calculate the mean of each sample, the distribution of these sample means will be approximately normal as long as the sample size is sufficiently large.

The reason (R) provided refers to the Central Limit Theorem (CLT), indicating that the CLT provides the theoretical foundation for Assertion (A). Indeed, the CLT is the principle that underlies why the distribution of the sample mean tends to a normal distribution as the sample size increases. To explain further, when we take a random sample from any population, the sample mean can be thought of as the average of those observations. According to the CLT, even if the population distribution is not normal, as long as the sample size is large enough (typically n e" 30 is considered sufficient), the distribution of these sample means will approximate a normal distribution. This occurs because as the sample size increases, the variability in the sample means decreases, and the distribution becomes more symmetric and bell-shaped, resembling a normal distribution. This property of the CLT is widely used in statistical inference. It allows us to make inferences about population parameters, such as the population mean, based on sample data, even when the population distribution is unknown or non-normal. Additionally, it provides the theoretical justification for many statistical methods and hypothesis tests that rely on the assumption of normality.

Assertion (A) correctly identifies the phenomenon that the distribution of the sample mean tends to a normal distribution with a sufficiently large sample size, and Reason (R) accurately attributes this phenomenon to the Central Limit Theorem (CLT), making it the correct explanation for Assertion (A).

90. (C): The assertion (A) reflects the Domar condition, a concept in economics that outlines a criterion for debt sustainability. According to this principle, if the effective interest rate on government debt remains below or equal to the growth rate of GDP, the ratio of public debt to GDP will not increase over time. This condition suggests a level of debt sustainability where the economy can manage its debt burden without it growing disproportionately relative to its output.

However, the reason (R) provided to support the assertion is flawed. It states that the growth rate of GDP at current prices will always be lower than the effective interest rate on government bonds. This oversimplifies the relationship between GDP growth and interest rates. While it's possible for interest rates to exceed GDP growth rates, especially during economic downturns or periods of high inflation, it's not a universal rule. Economic conditions, monetary policy, and other factors can influence both GDP growth and interest rates independently, leading to various scenarios where one may surpass the other.

91. (C)	**92. (D)**	**93. (D)**
94. (A)	**95. (D)**	**96. (C)**
97. (D)	**98. (B)**	**99. (A)**
100. (A)		

Previous Years' Paper

National Testing Agency (NTA)

UGC-NET Junior Research Fellowship & Assistant Professor Eligibility Exam

ECONOMICS, June-2023

(Exam held on 20-06-2023)

PAPER-II

1. Suppose good 1 is taken on horizontal axis and good 2 on vertical axis, then what happens to the budget line if the price of good 1 doubles and price of good 2 triples?

A. The budget line becomes steeper
B. The budget line becomes flatter
C. The budget line become vertical
D. The budget line remains unchanged

2. Suppose the scarce resouce, facing a constant demand, will be exhausted in 10 years. If an alternative resource will be available at a price of $40 and if the interest rate is 10%, what must be the price of the scarce resource today:

A. $55.50 B. $35.60
C. $24.40 D. $15.42

3. Which one of the following is not a characteristic of market structure?

A. Degree of buyers' concentration
B. Degree of Sellers' concentration
C. Conditions of entry
D. Vertical integration

4. Which of the following is not true in the case of second theorem of welfare economics?

A. If consumers exhibit convex preferences, every pareto efficient allocation is a possible competitive equilibrium in a pure exchange economy.
B. In an economy involving production, the convexity of production sets ensures that a pareto efficient allocation can be achieved as market equilibrium.
C. It holds when there are increasing returns to scale.
D. It implies that in the market system, the allocative role and the distributive role can be separated from each other.

5. Taylor's Rule tells:

A. how monetary authority sets interest rate in response to economic activity
B. how monetary authority maintains bank rate
C. how monetary authority maintains exchange rate
D. how government decides the tax rate to increase the tax base.

6. Monetary base of an economy is:

A. Amount of currency held by public and by the banks as reserves.
B. Amount of currency held by public and demand deposits.
C. Amount of currency held by public and time deposits.
D. Currency deposit ratio.

7. Given the income multiplier formula $m = \frac{1}{1-\text{MPC}}$ lower the marginal propensity to save.

A. Higher will be the multiplier effect
B. Lower will be the multiplier effect
C. Multiplier will become infinite
D. Multiplier will become zero

8. In the national income identiy Y = C + I + G, investment (I) is a function of:

A. Real Income
B. Nominal Income
C. Real Interest Rate
D. Nominal Interest Rate

9. Which one of the following is not correct about LM schedule?

A. The LM schedule slopes upward to the right.
B. The LM schedule will be relatively flat (steep) if the interest elasticity of money demand is relatively high (low).
C. The LM schedule will shift downward (upward) to the right (left) with an increase (decrease) in the quantity of money.
D. The LM schedule is the schedule giving the combinations of values of investment and interest rate that produce equilibrium in the money market.

10. The merchant's file of 20 accounts contains 6 delinquent and 14 non-delinquent accounts. An auditor randomly selects 5 of these account for examination. What is the probability that the auditor finds exactly 2 delinquent cases?

A. 0.2562 B. 0.3
C. 0.3087 D. 0.4526

11. A company has 140 employees, of which 30 are supervisors, 80 of the employees are married, and 20% of the married employee are supervisors. If a company employee is randomly selected, what is the probability that the employee is married and is a supervisor?

A. 0.1531 B. 0.1253
C. 0.0923 D. 0.1143

12. The Hausman's specification error test is used to test whether:

A. An exogenous variable is correlated with the error term.
B. An endogenous variable is correlated with the error term.
C. Both an exogenous variable is correlated with the error term and an endogenous variable is correlated with the error term.
D. OLS method is appropriate to estimate the SEM.

13. In random walk without drift:

A. The effect of shock persists throughout the time period.
B. The effect of shock in the past dies out over time.
C. The effect of shock drifts away quickly.
D. There is no effect of past shock.

14. Given below are the alternative formulae for F-test statistics. We are interested in testing the statistical significance of the incremental contribution of X_3 at 5% level of significance of $Y = \beta_0 + \beta_1 X_1 + \beta_2 X_2 + U$. Which of these is not appropriate? Where RSS is residual sum of square and ESS is explained sum of square.

A. $F = \dfrac{R_{UR}^2 - R_R^2 / d.f}{\left(1 - R_{UR}^2\right) / d.f.}$

B. $F = \dfrac{ESS / d.f.}{RSS / d.f.}$

C. $F = \dfrac{ESS_{new} - ESS_{old} / d.f.}{ESS_{new} / d.f.}$

D. $F = \dfrac{R^2 / d.f.}{(1 - R^2) / d.f.}$

15. Integrate: $\int x\sqrt{x^2 + 1}dx \; x > 0$

A. $\frac{1}{2}\left(x^2+1\right)^{\frac{3}{2}} + C$ B. $\frac{1}{3}\left(x^2+1\right)^{\frac{3}{2}} + C$

C. $\frac{1}{3}\left(x^3+1\right)^{\frac{2}{3}} + C$ D. $\frac{1}{2}\left(x^3+1\right)^{\frac{2}{3}} + C$

16. Find the extremum of $u = x^2 + y^2 + z^2$ subject to $x + y + z = 1$.

A. $(\bar{x}, \bar{y}, \bar{z}) = \left(\frac{1}{3}, \frac{1}{2}, \frac{1}{2}\right)$

B. $(\bar{x}, \bar{y}, \bar{z}) = \left(\frac{1}{2}, \frac{1}{2}, \frac{1}{3}\right)$

C. $(\bar{x}, \bar{y}, \bar{z}) = \left(\frac{1}{2}, \frac{1}{2}, \frac{1}{2}\right)$

D. $(\bar{x}, \bar{y}, \bar{z}) = \left(\frac{1}{3}, \frac{1}{3}, \frac{1}{3}\right)$

17. The utility function of a consumer is given by $U = f(q_1, q_2) = q_1 \times q_2$, suppose the price of q_1 is p_{q1} = and price of q_2 is $p_{q2} = 2$. The consumer wants to spend amount of k units only what will be his demand for q_1 and q_2?

A. $(q_1, q_2) = \left(k, \frac{k}{2}\right)$

B. $(q_1, q_2) = \left(\frac{k}{4}, \frac{k}{6}\right)$

C. $(q_1, q_2) = \left(\frac{k}{2}, \frac{k}{4}\right)$

D. $(q_1, q_2) = \left(\frac{k}{2}, \frac{k}{3}\right)$

18. A tariff ridden offere curve will bend towards.

A. Import good axis
B. Export good axis
C. Origin
D. Any of the above is possible

19. Factor price equalization theorem is given by:

A. David Ricardo B. J.S. Mill
C. Paul Samuelson D. Adam Smith

20. In which of the following year IMF has set up the Extended Fund Facility (EFF) to support member's structural reforms to address balance of payment difficulties of a long term character.

A. 1974 B. 1997
C. 1963 D. 2009

21. The book entitled "Why Nations Fail; The Origin of Power, Prosperity and Poverty" has been written by:

A. Abhijit Banerjee
B. Daron Acemoglu and James A. Robinson
C. Amartya Sen
D. Joseph Stiglitz

22. A foreign exchange swap is:

A. a spot purchase of a currency combined with a forward repurchase of that currency.
B. a spot sale of currency combined with a forward repurchase of that currency.
C. sale and purchase of a currency in forward market.
D. purchase of a currency in spot market.

23. Which of the following is a correct measure of gross fiscal deficit of the state government.

A. Revenue Expenditure (RE) + Capital disbursement – Revenue Receipts (RR)
B. RE + Repayment of loans to the Centre – RR
C. Revenue Deficit + Capital Outlays + Net Lending
D. RE + Discharge of Internal Debt – RR

24. Which of the following is not true in case of incidence of tax:

A. Imposition of tax raises price and lowers quantity.
B. The resulting price increase of tax rise will be dampened if the tax is imposed in monopolistic market.
C. One would be in better position to avoid the tax and leave the seller with a larger part if demand is inelastic while supply is elastic
D. A unit tax enters through a parallel upward shift in the supply schedule.

25. When MPS is 0.25 and initial increase in autonomous spending is ₹ 100, then the expenditure multiplier and resultant increase in GD respectively are:

A. 1, ₹ 100 B. 0.75, ₹ 75
C. 4, ₹ 400 D. 1.33, ₹ 133

26. In the extreme case of liquidity trap:
A. There will be tendency to buy bonds
B. Most of the investors will show bearish behaviour
C. Cash will be less preferred
D. Price of the bond will be low.

27. Which of the following can be an equation representing the money market.
A. 300 = 2Y – 1.5*i* B. *i* = 150 – Y
C. Y = 100 – *i* D. *i* = (150 – 2Y)/2

28. With the same monetary base, which of the following will lead to an increase in broad money?
A. High transaction cost of converting deposit into cash
B. Higher investment under SLR
C. Higher use of cash
D. Increase in financial literacy and banking habit

29. According to Robinson the term 'Golden Age' in the context of Harrod-Domar model is used to emphasize:
A. Its mythical nature
B. Its superiority
C. Natural growth rate
D. Warranted growth rate

30. Which is not a dimension of Human Development Index (HDI)?
A. Ability to lead a long and healthy life
B. Ability to acquire knowledge
C. Ability to achieve decent standard of living
D. Ability to access clean environment

31. The idea of creative destruction is associated with:
A. Marx B. Adam Smith
C. Ricardo D. Schumpeter

32. Normalized Poverty Gap (NPG) is measured as a ratio of:
A. Average Poverty Gap to poverty line
B. Total Poverty Gap to povery line
C. Total Poverty Gap to total population
D. Average Poverty Gap to total population

33. Which of the following defines ambient standards in an environmental policy:
A. a standard that specifies a pollution limit to be achieved but does not stipulate the technology.
B. a standard that designates the equipment or method to be used to achieve some abatement level.
C. a standard that designates the quality level of some element of the environment to be achieved.
D. None of the above

34. Which of the following applies to the physical linkage approach for the valuation of environmental benefits?
A. methods that assess responses immediately related to environmental changes.
B. methods that examine responses not about the environmental good itself but some set of market conditions related to it.
C. methods that estimate benefits using observations of behaviour in actual markets.
D. method that estimate benefits based on a technical relationship between an environmental resource and the user of that resource.

35. Why subsidies are not an effective policy instrument in the long-run for internalizing externalities under competitive output markets?
A. a subsidy that is equal to marginal damages translates to a de facto decrease in firm's fixed costs.
B. subsidy payments are available to all firms and can induce excessive market entry.
C. the level of industrial production in the sector would exceed the socially desired level.
D. All of the above

36. According to Sample Registration System, which of the following Indian States has the highest level of life time risk during 2018-2020.

A. Bihar B. Uttar Pradesh
C. Madhya Pradesh D. Chhattisgarh

37. The Intensive Agriculture District Programme (IADP) was launched in the year.
A. 1960-61 B. 1961-62
C. 1962-63 D. 1963-64

38. Allocation of budget for Ministry of Agriculture and Farmers' Welfare in the Union Budget 2023-24 is:
A. 2.25 lakh crores B. 1.25 lakh crores
C. 1.78 lakh crores D. 1.68 lakh crores

39. What is the motto of G-20 18th meeting?
A. One Earth, One Family, One Future
B. One Earth, One Nature, One Life
C. One World, One Family, One Life
D. One Earth, One Nature, One Future

40. Prevention of Money Laundering Act was enacted in the year:
A. 2001 B. 2002
C. 2003 D. 2004

41. Which of the following holds for Bertrand's Duopoly model.
(*a*) The reaction curves are derived from isoprofit maps which are convex to the axes.
(*b*) The point of intersection of the two reaction curves reflects a stable equilibrium.
(*c*) The reaction curves are derived from isoprofit maps which are concave to the axes.
(*d*) The point of intersection of the two reaction curves reflects an unstable equilibrium.
(*e*) Film's behavioral pattern is such that they learn from past experience.

Choose the **correct** answer from the option given below:
A. (*a*) and (*b*) only
B. (*c*) and (*d*) only
C. (*a*), (*d*) and (*e*) only
D. (*b*), (*c*) and (*e*) only

42. Which of the following is true for the Clark-Wicksteed-Walras product exhaustion theorem:
(*a*) The assumption of a homogeneous production function is necessary.
(*b*) It is an identity that holds for all values of the variables.
(*c*) The assumption of a homogeneous production function is not necessary.
(*d*) It is not an identity since it holds only for the values of the variables in the long-run equilibrium.
(*e*) It holds for all types of production functions.

Choose the **correct** answer from the option given below:
A. (*a*) and (*b*) only
B. (*a*) and (*d*) only
C. (*b*), (*c*) and (*e*) only
D. (*c*), (*d*) and (*e*) only

43. Properties of expenditure function are (in the context of utility theory).
(*a*) Homogeneous of degree one in price, P
(*b*) Strictly increasing in utility, *u* and non-decreasing in price. P for any good 1.
(*c*) Concave in P
(*d*) Continuous in P and *u*
(*e*) Strictly convex in P

Choose the **correct** answer from the option given below:
A. (*a*), (*c*), (*d*) and (*e*) only
B. (*a*), (*b*), (*d*) and (*e*) only
C. (*a*), (*b*), (*c*) and (*d*) only
D. (*b*), (*c*), (*d*) and (*e*) only

44. The concept of "excess sensitivity" and "excess smoothness" are explained by following statement(s).
(*a*) 'Excess sensitivity' refers to a situation where consumption over responds to temporary income shocks.
(*b*) 'Excess smoothness' refers to a situation where consumption under responds to temporary income changes.

(*c*) With excess sensitivity, anticipated rise in income is associated with relatively small change in consumption.

(*d*) With excess smoothness, changes in aggregate income are associated with relatively large changes in aggregate consumption.

(*e*) 'Excess sensitivity' and 'Excess smoothness' are related to the empirical evidences of permanent income hypothesis.

Choose the **correct** answer from the option given below:

A. (*a*), (*b*), (*c*) and (*d*) only
B. (*a*), (*b*), (*c*) and (*e*) only
C. (*a*), (*b*) and (*d*) only
D. (*a*), (*b*) and (*e*) only

45. According to Tobin's Q theory of investment, when should a firm invest?

(*a*) there is an increase in the price of output
(*b*) there is an increase in marginal product of capital
(*c*) there is an increase in rate of interest
(*d*) there is a decrease in rate of depreciation
(*e*) marginal benefit of investment exceeds marginal cost

Choose the **correct** answer from the option given below:

A. (*b*), (*c*), (*d*) and (*e*) only
B. (*a*), (*c*), (*d*) and (*e*) only
C. (*a*), (*b*), (*d*) and (*e*) only
D. (*a*), (*b*), (*c*) and (*d*) only

46. Which of the following is/are true about paradox of thrift?

(*a*) Paradox of thrift was popularized by J.M. Keynes.
(*b*) It states that personal savings can be detrimental to overall economic growth.
(*c*) It shows the relationship between output growth and rate of unemployment.
(*d*) It shows the relationship between inflation and rate of interest.
(*e*) It states that individuals saving during an economic recession leads to fall in aggregate demand.

Choose the **correct** answer from the option given below:

A. (*a*), (*b*) and (*c*) only
B. (*b*), (*c*) and (*d*) only
C. (*c*), (*d*) and (*e*) only
D. (*a*), (*b*) and (*e*) only

47. The BOP crisis of early 1990s made India borrow from the IMF which came on following conditions:

(*a*) Devaluation of rupee by 22%
(*b*) Drastic custom cut to a peak duty of 30% from the erstwhile level of 130% for all goods
(*c*) Consolidation of all indirect taxes into one tax
(*d*) Excise duty to be increased by 20% to neutralize the loss of revenue due to custom cut
(*e*) Government expenditure to be cut by 10% per annum.

Choose the **correct** answer from the option given below:

A. (*a*), (*b*), (*c*) and (*e*) only
B. (*b*), (*c*), (*d*) and (*e*) only
C. (*c*), (*d*), (*e*) and (*a*) only
D. (*a*), (*b*), (*d*) and (*e*) only

48. The Uruguay Round of trade negotiations called for:

(*a*) the reduction of average tariffs on industrial goods
(*b*) quotas to be replaced by tariffs
(*c*) the reduction in agriculture export subsidies
(*d*) the reduction in industrial subsidies
(*e*) antidumping and safeguards to be relaxed

Choose the **correct** answer from the option given below:

A. (*a*), (*b*), (*c*) and (*d*) only
B. (*b*), (*c*), (*d*) and (*e*) only

C. (*c*), (*d*), (*e*) and (*a*) only
D. (*d*), (*e*), (*a*) and (*b*) only

49. Pillar 1 of Basel III norms focus on:
(*a*) Quality and level of capital
(*b*) Risk Coverage
(*c*) Containing leverage
(*d*) Risk management and supervision
(*e*) Market discipline

Choose the **correct** answer from the option given below:
A. (*a*) and (*b*) only B. (*b*) and (*c*) only
C. (*c*) and (*d*) only D. (*d*) and (*e*) only

50. Which of the following statements are correct about trilemma in monetary policy:
(*a*) It is related to closed economy model.
(*b*) It involves exchange rate, capital mobility and monetary policy.
(*c*) It arises because perfect capital mobility aligns the domestic interest rate to the world interest rate.
(*d*) Flexible exchange rate is not compatible with independent monetary policy.
(*e*) It is related to capital immobility and flexible exchange rate.

Choose the **correct** answer from the option given below:
A. (*b*) and (*c*) only B. (*c*) and (*d*) only
C. (*a*) and (*d*) only D. (*b*) and (*e*) only

51. Based on the NITI Aayog estimate of poverty for the year 2011-12, the states with above 30 per cent rural poverty are:
(*a*) Manipur
(*b*) Bihar
(*c*) Sikkim
(*d*) Uttar Pradesh
(*e*) Nagaland

Choose the **correct** answer from the option given below:
A. (*a*) and (*b*) only
B. (*b*) and (*d*) only
C. (*b*), (*c*) and (*d*) only
D. (*a*), (*b*) and (*d*) only

52. Adam Smith contributions are:
(*a*) Division of labour
(*b*) Notion of increasing returns
(*c*) Notion of diminishing returns
(*d*) Dialectical Materialism
(*e*) Socially necessary abstract labour time

Choose the **correct** answer from the option given below:
A. (*a*) and (*b*) only
B. (*a*) and (*c*) only
C. (*a*) and (*d*) only
D. (*a*) and (*e*) only

53. The components of services sector in Gross Value Added (GVA) are:
(*a*) Construction
(*b*) Trade, Hotels, Transport and Communication related to Broadcasting
(*c*) Electricity, Gas, Water supply and other utility services
(*d*) Public Administration, Defense and other services
(*e*) Financial, Real Estate and Professional services

Choose the **correct** answer from the option given below:
A. (*b*), (*c*) and (*e*) only
B. (*a*), (*b*) and (*c*) only
C. (*a*), (*b*), (*d*) and (*e*) only
D. (*a*), (*b*), (*c*) and (*e*) only

54. Gunnar Myrdal is author of:
(*a*) Asian Drama
(*b*) An American Dilemma
(*c*) Theory of Economic Development
(*d*) Principles of Political Economy
(*e*) Economic Theory and underdeveloped regions

Choose the **correct** answer from the option given below:
A. (*a*), (*b*) and (*c*) only
B. (*a*), (*c*) and (*d*) only
C. (*a*), (*b*) and (*d*) only
D. (*a*), (*b*) and (*e*) only

55. Which of the following are correct in case of theory of sets.

(*a*) $(A \cup B') \cap (A' \cup C) \cap (B \cup C') = (A \cap B \cap C) \cup (A \cup B \cup C)$

(*b*) $(A \cup B') \cap (A' \cup C) \cap (B \cup C') = (A \cap B \cap C) \cup (A \cup B \cup C)'$

(*c*) $A \cup (B \cap C) = (A \cup B) \cap (A \cup C)$

(*d*) $A \cap (B \cup C) = (A \cup B) \cap (A \cup C)$

(*e*) $(A \cup B') \cap (A' \cup C) \cap (B \cup C') = (A \cap B \cap C) \cup (A' \cap B' \cap C')$

Choose the **correct** answer from the option given below:

A. (*a*), (*c*) and (*e*) only
B. (*b*), (*d*) and (*e*) only
C. (*b*), (*c*) and (*e*) only
D. (*a*), (*b*) and (*d*) only

56. If S is a sample space and E is an event then the probability axioms can be written as:

(*a*) $P(A) \geq 0$

(*b*) $P(S) = 1$

(*c*) $P\left(\bigcup_{i=1}^{\infty} A_i\right) = \sum_{i=1}^{\infty} P(A_i)$

(*d*) $P(A) \leq 0$

(*e*) $P\left(\bigcup_{i=1}^{\infty} S_i\right) = \sum_{i=1}^{\infty} P(S_i)$

Choose the **correct** answer from the option given below:

A. (*a*) and (*b*) only
B. (*a*), (*b*) and (*d*) only
C. (*a*), (*b*) and (*e*) only
D. (*a*), (*b*) and (*c*) only

57. Properties of sufficient estimators are:

(*a*) It may not be unbiased
(*b*) It may be unbiased
(*c*) It is always consistent
(*d*) It is not always consistent
(*e*) Minimum variance unbiased estimator

Choose the **correct** answer from the option given below:

A. (*a*), (*b*) and (*c*) only
B. (*a*), (*c*) and (*e*) only
C. (*a*), (*b*), (*c*) and (*d*) only
D. (*a*), (*b*), (*c*) and (*e*) only

58. Which of the following are true in case of social goods:

(*a*) Public goods are non-rivalry in nature.
(*b*) Efficient provision of social goods needs a political process of budget determination.
(*c*) Efficient provision of social goods involve horizontal rather than vertical addition of individual pseudo-demand-lines.
(*d*) Among purely private and purely social goods, there are mixed cases which generate benefit or cost externalities.
(*e*) Individual consumers will not bid for social good, but will act as free-riders.

Choose the **correct** answer from the option given below:

A. (*a*), (*c*), (*d*) and (*e*) only
B. (*a*), (*b*), (*c*) and (*e*) only
C. (*a*) and (*b*) only
D. (*a*), (*b*), (*d*) and (*e*) only

59. Which of the following are true in case of Ramsey Rule for efficient taxation:

(*a*) Tax rate should be higher on the good that has lower price elasticity of demand.
(*b*) If the demand elasticity in a market is zero, taxes should be imposed only in that markets.
(*c*) Ramsey rule applies to taxation of goods, but not to taxation of income.
(*d*) Ramsey rule minimises the excess burden of taxation across markets.
(*e*) Ramsey rule does not necessarily result in social justice.

Choose the **correct** answer from the option given below:

A. (*a*), (*c*), (*d*) and (*e*) only
B. (*a*), (*b*), (*d*) and (*e*) only
C. (*a*), (*b*), (*c*) and (*d*) only
D. (*a*), (*c*) and (*d*) only

60. Which of the following are not symptoms of multicollinearity in a regression model.

(*a*) High R^2 with few significant *t* ratio for coefficients.

(*b*) High pair-wise correlations among regressors.

(*c*) The closer the Tolerance (TOLj) is to zero.

(*d*) Variance Inflation Factor (VIF) of a variable is below 10.

(*e*) The closer the Tolerance (TOLj) is to 1.

Choose the **correct** answer from the option given below:

A. (*c*) and (*d*) only B. (*d*) and (*e*) only

C. (*a*) and (*c*) only D. (*b*) and (*d*) only

61. Which of the following are recommendations of the Narasimham Committee, 1991.

(*a*) Deregulation of the interest rate structure.

(*b*) Need for greater use of information technology.

(*c*) Permitting only private sector banks to access the capital market.

(*d*) Freedom to appoint chief executive and officers of the banks.

(*e*) Capital adequacy norms were implemented in stages.

Choose the **correct** answer from the option given below:

A. (*a*), (*b*) and (*e*) only

B. (*a*), (*c*) and (*d*) only

C. (*a*), (*d*) and (*e*) only

D. (*c*), (*d*) and (*e*) only

62. Defensive expenditure method is based on the understanding that:

(*a*) the consumer spends money to ameliorate the damaging effects of the bad.

(*b*) the defensive expenditure undertaken reflects the consumer's willingness to pay to reduce the level of the bad.

(*c*) the observed defensive expenditure is an upper bound on the willingness to pay to avoid the bad.

(*d*) the defensive expenditure provide no additional services other than provisioning the desired environmental quality.

(*e*) the observed defensive expenditure is a lower bound on the willingness to pay to avoid the bad.

Choose the **correct** answer from the option given below:

A. (*a*), (*b*) and (*c*) only

B. (*c*), (*d*) and (*e*) only

C. (*a*), (*b*), (*c*) and (*d*) only

D. (*a*), (*b*), (*d*) and (*e*) only

63. Which of the following constitutes India's strategy to combat climate change in the backdrop of its stand at the 26th session of the conference of the Parties (COP 26) to the UNFCCC held in Glasgow, U.K.

(*a*) phasing out of coal-based thermal power generation by 2030.

(*b*) reduction of the carbon intensity of Indian economy by 45 percent by 2030. over 2005 levels.

(*c*) capping Indian economy total final energy consumption in absolute levels.

(*d*) achieving the target of net zero emissions for India by 2070.

(*e*) promoting lifestyle for environment to combat climate change.

Choose the **correct** answer from the option given below:

A. (*a*), (*b*) and (*d*) only

B. (*b*), (*c*) and (*d*) only

C. (*b*), (*d*) and (*e*) only

D. (*c*), (*d*) and (*e*) only

64. Here is given international organisations and their headquarters. Which of the following are correct combinations of the institutions and their headquarters.

(*a*) GATT : Geneva

(*b*) IMF : Washington DC

(*c*) World Bank : Washington DC

(*d*) International Development Association (IDA) : New York

(*e*) Asian Development Bank : Mandaluyong

Choose the **correct** answer from the option given below:

A. (*a*), (*b*) and (*c*) only
B. (*a*) and (*b*) only
C. (*c*) and (*d*) only
D. (*a*), (*b*), (*c*) and (*e*) only

65. Which of the following is/are correct about Walrasian demand function?

(*a*) The Walrasian demand function X (P, W) is homogenous of degree zero if X (αP, αW) = X (P, W) for any P, W and $\alpha > 0$.

(*b*) The Walrasian demand function X (P, W) is homogenous of degree one if X (αP, αW)= αX (P, W) for any P, W and $\alpha > 0$.

(*c*) The Walrasian demand function X (P, W) satisfies Walras' law if for every P >> 0 and W > 0, we have P. X = W for all X $\in$ X(P, W)

(*d*) Walras' law says consumer fully expends his wealth.

(*e*) If price and wealth both change in same proportion, then individual consumption choice does not change.

Choose the **correct** answer from the option given below:

A. (*a*), (*b*), (*c*) and (*d*) only
B. (*b*), (*c*), (*d*) and (*e*) only
C. (*a*), (*b*), (*c*) and (*e*) only
D. (*a*), (*c*), (*d*) and (*e*) only

66. Match List-I with List-II.

List-I	List-II
(*a*) Cost-effectiveness	I. a policy that directly regulates polluters through the use of standards.
(*b*) Pollution permit trading system	II. an incentive based policy that encourages conservation practices or pollution reduction technologies.
(*c*) Market approach	III. Requires that the least amount of resources be used to achieve an objective.
(*d*) Command-and-control approach	IV. A market instrument that establishes a market for rights to pollute.

Choose the **correct** answer from the options given below:

	(*a*)	(*b*)	(*c*)	(*d*)
A.	I	II	III	IV
B.	III	IV	I	II
C.	IV	III	II	I
D.	III	IV	II	I

67. Match List-I with List-II.

List-I	List-II
(*a*) Kleins rule of thumb	I. Structural break
(*b*) Ljung Box (LB) statistic	II. Unit Root
(*c*) KPSS	III. Significance of auto-correlation coefficients
(*d*) Bai-Perron	IV. Multicollinearity

Choose the **correct** answer from the options given below:

	(*a*)	(*b*)	(*c*)	(*d*)
A.	IV	III	II	I
B.	IV	III	I	II
C.	II	IV	I	III
D.	II	III	IV	I

68. Match List-I with List-II.

List-I	List-II
(*a*) J.M. Keynes	I. Inventory theoretic approach to transaction demand for money
(*b*) Kydland-Prescott	II. Liquidity Preference
(*c*) Baumol-Tobin	III. Time inconsistency Problem
(*d*) Friedman-Schwartz	IV. Monetary History of United States

Choose the **correct** answer from the options given below:

	(*a*)	(*b*)	(*c*)	(*d*)
A.	II	III	IV	I
B.	III	II	I	IV
C.	III	I	II	IV
D.	II	III	I	IV

69. Match List-I with List-II.

List-I	List-II
(*a*) Kuznet	I. Innovation and Entrepreneurship
(*b*) Nurkse	II. Balanced growth theory
(*c*) Leibenstein	III. Inverted U-curve hypothesis
(*d*) Schumpeter	IV. Critical minimum effort thesis

Choose the **correct** answer from the options given below:

	(*a*)	(*b*)	(*c*)	(*d*)
A.	I	IV	III	II
B.	III	II	IV	I
C.	IV	III	II	I
D.	II	I	IV	III

70. Match List-I with List-II.

List-I (States)	List-II ((Food grain production (2021-22) Thousand Tonnes)
(*a*) Telangana	I. 11266.0
(*b*) Jharkhand	II. 4984.2
(*c*) Chhattisgarh	III. 8897.0
(*d*) Andhra Pradesh	IV. 15095.4

Choose the **correct** answer from the options given below:

	(*a*)	(*b*)	(*c*)	(*d*)
A.	I	II	III	IV
B.	IV	III	II	I
C.	I	III	IV	II
D.	IV	II	III	I

71. Match List-I with List-II.

List-I	List-II
(*a*) Tax Evasion	I. Bond Financing
(*b*) Effective incidence of tax	II. Illegal free riding
(*c*) Legal incidence of tax	III. Obliged to deliver tax revenue to Government
(*d*) Fiscal Illusion	IV. Not necessarily correspond to on whom tax is imposed

Choose the **correct** answer from the options given below:

	(*a*)	(*b*)	(*c*)	(*d*)
A.	II	III	IV	I
B.	III	I	II	IV
C.	II	IV	III	I
D.	IV	III	II	I

72. Match List-I with List-II.

List-I (Type of India's population growth rate)	List-II (Period)
(*a*) Rapid High Growth	I. 1981-2011
(*b*) Stagnant Population	II. 1921-1951
(*c*) High growth with definite signs of slowing down	III. 1951-1981
(*d*) Steady Growth	IV. 1891-1921

Choose the **correct** answer from the options given below:

	(*a*)	(*b*)	(*c*)	(*d*)
A.	IV	II	III	I
B.	III	IV	I	II
C.	III	IV	II	I
D.	IV	III	II	I

73. Match List-I with List-II.

List-I (Policy)	List-II (Year)
(*a*) National Forest Policy	I. 2000
(*b*) Marine Fishing Policy	II. 1994
(*c*) New Mineral Policy	III. 2004
(*d*) National Population Policy	IV. 1988

Choose the **correct** answer from the options given below:

	(*a*)	(*b*)	(*c*)	(*d*)
A.	IV	III	II	I
B.	IV	II	III	I
C.	II	IV	III	I
D.	II	III	IV	I

74. Match List-I with List-II.

List-I	List-II
(*a*) $f'(x) > 0$ and $f''(x) > 0$	I. 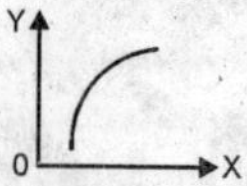
(*b*) $f'(x) > 0$ and $f''(x) < 0$	II. 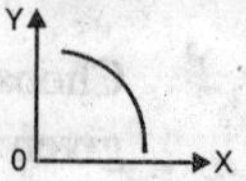
(*c*) $f'(x) < 0$ and $f''(x) < 0$	III. 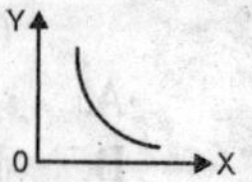
(*d*) $f'(x) < 0$ and $f''(x) > 0$	IV. 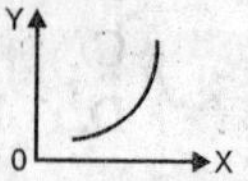

Choose the **correct** answer from the options given below:

	(*a*)	(*b*)	(*c*)	(*d*)
A.	I	IV	III	II
B.	I	III	II	IV
C.	IV	I	II	III
D.	IV	II	III	I

75. Match List-I with List-II.

List-I	List-II
(*a*) Central Bank Loss Function	I. $y_t = A - ar_{t-1}$
(*b*) Monetary Rule (MR)	II. $\pi_t = \pi_{t-1} + \alpha(y_t - y_e)$
(*c*) Phillips Curve (PC)	III. $(y_t - y_e) = -\alpha\beta(\pi_t - \pi^T)$
(*d*) Dynamic IS Curve	IV. $L = (y_t - y_e)^2 + \beta(\pi_t - \pi^T)^2$

Choose the **correct** answer from the options given below:

	(*a*)	(*b*)	(*c*)	(*d*)
A.	II	III	IV	I
B.	III	II	IV	I
C.	IV	III	II	I
D.	IV	III	I	II

76. Arrange the relative weights in percentage assigned to following criteria by the XIV Finance Commission in ascending order.

(*a*) Income distance
(*b*) Area
(*c*) Population (1971)
(*d*) Demographic Change (2011 population)
(*e*) Forest Cover

Choose the **correct** answer from the option given below:

A. (*b*), (*e*), (*d*), (*c*), (*a*)
B. (*e*), (*d*), (*b*), (*c*) (*a*)
C. (*a*), (*c*), (*d*), (*b*) (*e*)
D. (*e*), (*b*), (*d*), (*c*) (*a*)

77. Arrange the following in ascending order on the basis of degree of economic integration.

(*a*) Custom Union
(*b*) Free Trade Area
(*c*) Economic Union
(*d*) Common Market
(*e*) Preferential Trade Arrangements

Choose the **correct** answer from the option given below:

A. (*a*), (*b*), (*c*), (*d*), (*e*)
B. (*b*), (*c*), (*d*), (*a*), (*e*)
C. (*e*), (*a*), (*b*), (*c*), (*d*)
D. (*e*), (*b*), (*a*), (*d*), (*c*)

78. Arrange states in ascending order based on loans from the central government for the year 2020-21.

(*a*) Karnataka
(*b*) Madhya Pradesh
(*c*) Tamil Nadu
(*d*) Gujarat
(*e*) Maharashtra

Choose the **correct** answer from the option given below:

A. (*c*), (*b*), (*d*), (*a*), (*e*)
B. (*b*), (*c*), (*d*), (*a*), (*e*)
C. (*c*), (*b*), (*a*), (*d*), (*e*)
D. (*b*), (*c*), (*a*), (*d*), (*e*)

79. Arrange the following Acts in chronological order of their year of enactment starting from the oldest:

(*a*) Foreign Exchange Regulation Act
(*b*) Competition Act
(*c*) MRTP Act
(*d*) Foreign Regulation Act
(*e*) Foreign Exchange Management Act

Choose the **correct** answer from the option given below:

A. (*c*), (*b*), (*a*), (*d*), (*e*)
B. (*c*), (*a*), (*b*), (*e*), (*d*)
C. (*b*), (*a*), (*d*), (*e*), (*c*)
D. (*a*), (*b*), (*c*), (*d*), (*e*)

80. Arrange the following in order to their year of establishment starting from oldest:

(*a*) The Industrial Credit and Investment Corporation of India (ICICI)
(*b*) National Bank for Agricultural and Rural Development (NABARD)
(*c*) The Industrial Finance Corporation of India (IFCI)
(*d*) The Industrial Reconstruction Bank of India (IRBI)
(*e*) Export-Import Bank of India

Choose the **correct** answer from the option given below :

A. (*a*), (*c*), (*e*), (*b*), (*d*)
B. (*c*), (*a*), (*d*), (*e*), (*b*)
C. (*e*), (*c*), (*a*), (*b*), (*d*)
D. (*a*), (*d*), (*c*), (*b*), (*e*)

81. Arrange the following chronologically in order of their publication starting from the oldest:

(*a*) General Theory of Employment, Interest and Money
(*b*) A Treatise on probability
(*c*) Essays in Persuasion
(*d*) The End of Laissez Faire
(*e*) A Tract on Monetary Reform

Choose the **correct** answer from the option given below:

A. (*b*), (*c*), (*d*), (*a*), (*e*)
B. (*b*), (*e*), (*d*), (*c*), (*a*)
C. (*e*), (*b*), (*d*), (*c*), (*a*)
D. (*d*), (*e*), (*b*), (*a*), (*c*)

82. Arrange the following events of equity trading in India starting from the oldest:

(*a*) The BSE introduced screen-based trading.
(*b*) Foreign Institutional Investors (FIIs) are permitted to invest in the Indian Securities Market.
(*c*) NSE commenced operations in wholesale debt market segment.
(*d*) The SEBI banned badla trading on the BSE.
(*e*) The NSE overtook the BSE as the largest stock exchange in terms of volume trading.

Choose the **correct** answer from the option given below:

A. (*a*), (*b*), (*d*), (*e*), (*c*)
B. (*b*), (*d*), (*c*), (*e*), (*a*)
C. (*d*), (*b*), (*e*), (*c*), (*a*)
D. (*c*), (*b*), (*d*), (*e*), (*a*)

83. Sequence of steps followed in the estimation of Indirect Least Square (ILS) starting from the beginning:

(*a*) Identification of the structural equations
(*b*) Application of OLS
(*c*) Obtaining structural coefficients
(*d*) Obtaining reduced form equation
(*e*) Use the model for policy

Choose the **correct** answer from the option given below:

A. (*a*), (*d*), (*b*), (*c*) and (*e*)
B. (*a*), (*b*), (*d*), (*c*) and (*e*)
C. (*b*), (*d*), (*a*), (*e*) and (*c*)
D. (*b*), (*a*), (*c*), (*d*) and (*e*)

84. As per the total revenue received by the government under the head of GST on the domestic supply of goods and services for 2021-22, arrange the following states in ascending order:

(*a*) Odisha
(*b*) Rajasthan
(*c*) Delhi
(*d*) West Bengal
(*e*) Madhya Pradesh

Choose the **correct** answer from the option given below :

A. (*d*), (*c*), (*e*), (*b*), (*a*)
B. (*e*), (*b*), (*a*), (*c*), (*d*)
C. (*b*), (*e*), (*c*), (*a*), (*d*)
D. (*c*), (*e*), (*a*), (*d*), (*b*)

85. According to the Census, 2011 arrange the states in the descending order based on the literacy rate (aged group 7 year and above):

(*a*) Nagaland (*b*) Tripura
(*c*) Sikkim (*d*) Manipur
(*e*) Meghalaya

Choose the **correct** answer from the option given below:

A. (*d*), (*c*), (*b*), (*e*), (*a*)
B. (*c*), (*b*), (*d*), (*a*), (*e*)
C. (*b*), (*c*), (*a*), (*d*), (*e*)
D. (*a*), (*c*), (*b*), (*e*), (*d*)

86. Given below are two statements: One is labelled as Assertion (A) and the other is labelled as Reason (R):

Assertion (A): If governments do not care about protectionists' rents, they would replace all import duties with sales taxes.

Reason (R): Sales tax is more efficient means of raising revenue than import tariff.

In the light of the above statements, choose the **correct** answer from the options given below:

A. Both (A) and (R) are true and (R) is the correct explanation of (A).
B. Both (A) and (R) are true, but (R) is NOT the correct explanation of (A).
C. (A) is true, but (R) is false.
D. (A) is false, but (R) is true.

87. Given below are two statements:

Statement I: Friedman's theory of the demand for money is partly Keynesian and partly non-Keynesian.

Statement II: It is non-Keynesian in that Friedman neglects completely Keynes' clarification of the motives for holding money and the corresponding components of demand for money.

In the light of the above statements, choose the **correct** answer from the options given below:

A. Both Statement I and Statement II are true.
B. Both Statement I and Statement II are false.
C. Statement I is true, but Statement II is false.
D. Statement I is false, but Statement II is true.

88. Given below are two statements:

Statement I: Under first degree price discrimination, monopolist sells different units of output for different prices and these prices may differ from person to person.

Statement II: Under third degree price discrimination, monopolist sells different units of output for different prices, but every individual who buys the same amount of the good pays the same price.

In the light of the above statements, choose the **correct** answer from the options given below:

A. Both Statement I and Statement II are true.
B. Both Statement I and Statement II are false.
C. Statement I is true, but Statement II is false.
D. Statement I is false, but Statement II is true.

89. Given below are two statements:

Statement I: The terms of trade of a nation are defined as the ratio of the cost of its export commodity to the price of its import commodity.

Statement II: The terms of trade of the trade partner are equal to the inverse of the terms of trade of the other nation.

In the light of the above statements, choose the **correct** answer from the options given below:

A. Both Statement I and Statement II are true.
B. Both Statement I and Statement II are false.
C. Statement I is true, but Statement II is false.
D. Statement I is false, but Statement II is true.

90. Given below are two statements:

Statement I: Division of labour is the starting point of Smith's theory of economic growth.

Statement II: It is division of labour that results in the greatest improvement in the productive power of labour.

In the light of the above statements, choose the **correct** answer from the options given below:

A. Both Statement I and Statement II are true.
B. Both Statement I and Statement II are false.
C. Statement I is true, but Statement II is false.
D. Statement I is false, but Statement II is true.

Directions (Qs. No. 91-95): *Read the passage below and answer the question:*

The government of India's fiscal policy response to the covid crises comprised of a judicious mix of increasing food and fertilizer subsidies on the one hand and a reduction in taxes on fuel and certain imported products on the other. Despite these additional fiscal pressures the union govt. is back on track. The resilience in the fiscal performance of the union government has been facilitated by the recovery in economic activity buoyancy in revenues from direct taxes and goods and services tax (GST) and realistic assumptions in the budget. The gross tax revenue registered a YoY growth of 15.5% from April to November 2022. driven by robust growth in the direct taxes and GST. The gross GST-collection has increased at 24.8% on YoY during the same period. The Union Government's emphasis on capital expediture (capex) has continued despite higher revenue expenditure requirements during the year. The center's capex has steadily increased from a long term average of 1.7 percent of GDP (FY09 to FY20) to 2.5% of GDP in FY22 PA, The center has also incentivize the state governments through interest free loans and enhanced borrowing ceilings to prioritize their spending on capex. Government has boosted allocations on infrastructure intensive sectors such as roads and highways, railways and housing and urban affairs, which has bearing on capex. This increase in capex will have implication for medium term growth and sustainable government debt to GDP ratio.

91. Which of the following strategies was not comprised India's Fiscal Policy response to Covid crises:

A. Increasing of food subsidy
B. Increasing of fertilizer subsidy
C. Reduction in taxes on certain imported products.
D. Increase in taxes on fuel.

92. Which of the following is not correct with respect to facilitation of resilience in fiscal performance of the union government:

A. Recovery in Economic activity
B. Buoyant GST revenues
C. Expenditure austerity measures pertaining to food and fertilizer subsidy
D. Realistic assumptions in budget

93. Which of the following strategy is adopted by Union Government to prioritise States' spending on capex.

A. Incentivizing for higher revenue expenditure
B. Incentivizing for interest free loans and enhance borrowing ceilings
C. Incentivizing for higher interest payment
D. Incentivizing for large spending on tax

94. The Capex of the union government for the period FY 09 to FY 20 on an average was ________.

A. 2.5 percent of GDP
B. 15.5 percent of revenue receipts
C. 24.8 percent of GST revenue
D. 1.7 percent of GDP

95. In order to further enhance capex, allocation for which of the following infrastructure sector is not increased:

A. Ports and Waterways
B. Roads and Highways
C. Railways
D. Housing and Urban affair's

Directions (Qs. No. 96-100): *Read the passage below and answer the question:*

GDP growth is the most widely used macroeconomic indicator for adjudicating broad economic progress. The outcomes from decisions made on the basis of such an indicator have been repeatedly disappointing because of failures to detect resource uses that turn out to be unsustainable. Adjusted Net Savings (ANS) provides a complementary indicator to help in understanding the changes in wealth and not per capita wealth, by capturing some of the important policy-induced dynamics. Based on the conventions of the System of National Accounts (SNA), ANS is measured as Gross National Saving minus depreciation of produced capital, depletion of subsoil assets and timber resources, and air pollution damages to human health, plus a credit for expenditures on education. If ANS is negative, the country running down its capital stocks and possibly reducing future material well-being. If ANS is positive the country is adding to wealth and future material well-being. When natural resource depletion is not used to invest in other assets in the wealth portfolio, countries gross saving might not be enough to compensate this depletion resulting in negative net savings. However, nations with higher GDP are far less likely to obtain negative ANS. It is argued that, if not a superior indicator of sustainability. ANS is useful to the extent that it can serve as an indicator of unsustainability. Hence, the estimates and conceptualization of ANS are not free from limitations.

96. Adjusted Net Saving (ANS) is:

A. a proxy for change in per capita wealth
B. a stock variable
C. a flow variable
D. unable to capture policy-induced dynamics

97. Which of the following is not the constituent of ANS?

A. Public expenditures on education
B. Air pollution damage
C. Depletion of metals and minerals
D. Loss of biodiversity

98. Which of the following explains the decline in ANS in countries with increasing GDP per capita?

A. Increasing proportion of private investment in an economy
B. Depleted assets not offset by sufficient investment in human and physical capital
C. Increasing gross saving rates
D. Increasing production of renewable natural capital

99. Which of the following reflects the shortcomings of ANS?

A. It allows substitution between different forms of capital.
B. It is not a comprehensive indicator of per capita wealth.
C. It is influenced by the level of GDP of an economy.
D. All of the above

100. The concept of ANS should at best be used to:

A. guide ecologically optimal sustainable scale
B. serve as an indicator of unsustainability
C. replace GDP as a measure of economic progress
D. None of the above

ANSWERS

1. (B): The budget line represents all the combinations of goods that a consumer can afford given their income and the prices of the goods. It is derived from the budget constraint equation:

$P_1 \cdot Q_1 + P_2 \cdot Q_2 = I$

Where: P_1 and P_2 are the prices of goods 1 and 2 respectively,

Q_1 and Q_2 are the quantities of goods 1 and 2 consumed, and I is the consumer's income.

Graphically, the budget line shows the maximum quantities of two goods that a consumer can buy given their income and the prices of the goods. It is drawn as a straight line connecting the intercepts on the horizontal (good 1) and vertical (good 2) axes.

This means that for each unit of good 1 sacrificed (measured on the horizontal axis), the consumer can give up one unit of good 2 and still spend the same amount of money. This results in a flatter budget line because the trade-off between the two goods remains the same despite the increase in prices.

Visually, the flatter budget line indicates that the consumer has less purchasing power compared to the situation before the price changes. The outward rotation of the budget line would occur if the prices decreased, indicating an increase in purchasing power.

So, when both prices increase, the budget line becomes flatter due to the reduced purchasing power of the consumer.

2. (D): Present Value = P.V.,

Future Value = F.V.

$$\text{P.V.} \frac{\text{F.V.}}{(1+r)^n} \quad (r = \text{Rate of Interest, } n = \text{Time})$$

$$\text{P.V.} = \frac{40}{(1+0.10)^{10}}$$

$(r = 10\% = 0.10)$

$$\text{P.V.} = \frac{40}{(1.10)^{10}}$$

$$\text{P.V.} = \frac{40}{2.59} = 15.44 \approx 15.42.$$

3. (D): Market structure refers to the organizational and competitive characteristics of a market, influencing the behaviour of firms within it. Key factors defining market structure include the degree of buyers' concentration, indicating how much power buyers hold in the market; the degree of sellers' concentration, reflecting the level of competition among sellers; and the conditions of entry, which determine how easy or difficult it is for new firms to enter the market. These elements collectively shape the competitiveness and efficiency of a market. However, vertical integration, while significant in business strategy, is not inherently a characteristic of market structure. It refers to the ownership or control of multiple stages of production or distribution by a single firm, allowing it to streamline operations, reduce costs, and potentially gain market power.

4. (C): Convex production sets ensure that firms can produce a diverse range of goods efficiently, facilitating the realization of Pareto efficient allocations. However, the second theorem does not hold in the presence of increasing returns to scale. In such cases, market failures like monopolies can emerge, hindering the achievement of Pareto efficiency. Despite this limitation, the second theorem underscores the potential of competitive markets to efficiently allocate resources, provided certain conditions are met, thereby highlighting the essential role of market structures and individual preferences in welfare economics.

5. (A): Taylor's Rule is a fundamental concept in macroeconomics that outlines how a central bank or monetary authority adjusts interest rates in response to prevailing economic conditions. Named after economist John Taylor, this rule offers a systematic approach for monetary policymakers to set interest rates with the objective of achieving economic stability. It suggests that the central bank should adjust the nominal interest rate in response to deviations of inflation from its target level and the output gap from its potential level. By doing so, the central bank aims to stabilize the economy, promoting both price stability and full employment. Essentially, Taylor's Rule provides a guideline for policymakers to calibrate monetary policy in accordance with the dual mandate of most central banks: to control inflation and foster sustainable economic growth.

6. (A): The monetary base of an economy, often referred to as high-powered money, represents the sum of currency held by the public, including banknotes and coins in circulation, and the reserves held by commercial banks at the central bank. This concept serves as a fundamental building block for understanding the broader money supply and the functioning of the banking system. The currency held by the public is the physical money circulating in the economy, used for transactions and held as a store of value by individuals and businesses. On the other hand, the reserves held by banks consist of deposits maintained at the central bank, which are used to meet regulatory requirements and facilitate interbank transactions. The central bank has direct control over the monetary base through its monetary policy operations, such as open market operations, reserve requirements, and discount lending.

7. (A): The multiplier effect describes how an initial injection of money into the economy, like government spending or investment, can lead to a larger increase in total output. This happens because recipients of the initial injection spend some of it, which becomes income for others, who then spend a portion of that, and so on. The total impact on output is a multiple of the initial injection, hence the name "multiplier."

The marginal propensity to save (MPS) is the portion of each additional dollar of income that people choose to save rather than spend. The marginal propensity to consume (MPC) is then 1 minus the MPS, representing the portion that is spent.

The formula: $m = 1 / (1 - \text{MPC})$,

where m is the multiplier and MPC is the marginal propensity to consume.

When the MPS is lowered (meaning people save less and spend more of each additional dollar) the MPC increases. This means that a larger portion of each round of spending is injected back into the economy, leading to a greater overall impact. Consequently, the multiplier effect becomes stronger.

Therefore, the answer is Higher will be the multiplier effect.

8. (C): In the national income identity Y = C + I + G, investment (I) is indeed a component of the total national income (Y), along with consumption (C) and government spending (G). Investment (I) represents the spending by firms on capital goods, such as machinery, equipment, and infrastructure.

Investment (I) is influenced by various factors, and among the options provided, it is primarily a function of the real interest rate. The real interest rate is the nominal interest rate adjusted for inflation. When the real interest rate decreases, the cost of borrowing decreases, making investment more attractive, thus stimulating higher levels of investment. Conversely, when the real interest rate increases, borrowing becomes more expensive, leading to lower levels of investment.

When the real interest rate is low, borrowing money to finance investments becomes cheaper for firms. This lower cost of borrowing makes investment projects more attractive because firms can finance them more affordably and potentially earn higher returns. As a result, firms are more likely to undertake new investment projects or expand existing ones when the real interest rate is low.

9. (D): "The LM schedule is the schedule giving the combinations of values of investment and interest rate that produce equilibrium in the money market." This statement is inaccurate because it incorrectly describes the LM schedule. The LM schedule, or Liquidity Preference-Money Supply curve, actually depicts combinations of values of income and the interest rate that produce equilibrium in the money market. It represents the relationship between the interest rate and the level of income at which the demand for money balances with the money supply set by the central bank. The LM curve reflects the Keynesian perspective on the money market, where the interest rate influences the demand for money, primarily through the investment and liquidity preference channels.

10. (C): Numerical solution:

P (Exactly 2 delinquent cases)

$= ({}^6C_2 + {}^{14}C_3) \div ({}^{20}C_5)$

$= [(6!) \div (6-2)!\,(2!)] \times [(14!) \div (14-3)!\,(3!)] \div [(20!) \div (20-5)!\,(5!)]$

$= (5 \times 7 \times 13 \times 2) \div (19 \times 17 \times 8)$

$= 910 \div 2584$

$= 0.3087$

Ths, the probabiltiy that the auditor finds exactly 2 delinquent cases is 0.3087.

11. (D): Given, that,

$n = 140$

Supervisor = 30

Married = 80

$$\text{Married Supervisor} = \frac{80 \times 20}{100} = 16$$

$$P(S \cap M) = \frac{16}{140} = 0.1143.$$

12. (B): "An endogenous variable is correlated with the error term," accurately describes the purpose of the Hausman's specification error test. This test is specifically designed to assess whether endogenous variables, which are influenced by other variables within the model, are correlated with the error term in a regression analysis. When an endogenous variable is correlated with the error term, it violates the assumptions of the regression model, leading to biased and inconsistent estimates. This correlation can arise due to omitted variable bias, measurement error, or simultaneity, among other reasons.

13. (A): In a random walk without drift, the persistent effect of shocks throughout the entire time series distinguishes it from other stochastic processes. Consider a financial instrument's price movement as a random walk, where each price change, whether positive or negative, represents a shock. In this context, each shock contributes independently to the overall trajectory, devoid of any inherent tendency to revert to a mean or drift towards a specific value. Consequently, the influence of significant price movements remains present across subsequent data points, potentially shaping future changes.

This absence of temporal dependence underscores a key feature of random walks without drift, contrasting with processes exhibiting autocorrelation, where past behavior influences future outcomes. The unpredictable nature of such walks underscores the importance of treating each step as an independent event, complicating forecasting endeavors.

14. (C): $F = \dfrac{\left(\hat{\beta}\Sigma y_i x_{2i} + \hat{\beta}_3 y_i x_{3i}\right)/2}{\Sigma \hat{u}_i^2 /(n-3} = \dfrac{ESS/df}{RSS/df}$

$$F = \frac{ESS/df}{(TSS - ESS)df} \text{ (Divide by TSS)}$$

$$F = \frac{\left(\frac{ESS}{TSS}\right)df}{\frac{(TSS-ESS)}{TSS}df} = \frac{\left(\frac{ESS}{TSS}\right)df}{\left(1-\frac{ESS}{TSS}\right)df}$$

$$\left(R^2 = \frac{ESS}{TSS}\right)$$

$$F = \frac{R^2.df}{(1-R^2 df)}$$

$$F = \frac{\left(R_{UR}^2 - R_R^2\right)/m}{\left(1-R_{UR}^2\right)/(n-k)}$$

In option (C), if RSS would be in place of ESS, then option (C) will be true.

15. (B)

16. (D): Given that,

$$u = x^2 + y^2 + z^2 \text{ and } x + y + z = 1$$

Using Lorenz (λ) coefficient

$$L = x^2 + y^2 + z^2 + \lambda\,(x + y + z - 1)$$

$$\frac{\partial L}{\partial x} = 2x + \lambda = 0 \Rightarrow x = \frac{-\lambda}{2}$$

$$\frac{\partial L}{\partial y} = 2y + \lambda = 0 \Rightarrow y = \frac{-\lambda}{2}$$

$$\frac{\partial L}{\partial z} = 2z + \lambda = 0 \Rightarrow z = \frac{-\lambda}{2}$$

and $x + y + z - 1 = 0$ ...(*i*)

Putting the value of x, y and z in equation (*i*)

$$\frac{-\lambda}{2} - \frac{\lambda}{2} - \frac{\lambda}{2} - 1 = 0$$

$$\Rightarrow \frac{-3\lambda}{2} - 1 = 0$$

$$\Rightarrow \lambda = \frac{-2}{3}$$

Putting the value of x in values of x, y and z

Then, $\bar{x} = \frac{1}{3}, \bar{y} = \frac{1}{3}, \bar{z} = \frac{1}{3}$

Hence, $(\bar{x}, \bar{y}, \bar{z}) = \left(\frac{1}{3}, \frac{1}{3}, \frac{1}{3}\right)$.

17. (C): Given that,

$$U = f(q_1, q_2) = q_1, q_2$$

$$P_{q_1} = 1, P_{q_2} = 2$$

$$P_1 q_1 + P_2 q_2 = K$$

$$q_1 + 2q_2 = K$$

$$q_1 = (K - 2q_2)$$

$$U = q_2(K - 2q_2)$$

$$U = q_2 K - 2q_2^2$$

$$\frac{dU}{dq_2} = K - 4q_2$$

$$q_2 = \frac{K}{4}$$

$$q_1 = K - 2q_2$$

$$q_1 = K - 2 \times \frac{K}{4}$$

(By keeping the value for q_2

$$q_1 = K - \frac{K}{2}$$

$$q_1 = \frac{2K - K}{2}$$

$$q_1 = \frac{K}{2}$$

$$(q_1, q_2) = \left(\frac{K}{2}, \frac{K}{4}\right).$$

18. (A): In the context of international trade, a tariff retaliation offer curve illustrates a country's response to tariffs imposed by its trading partners. When a country faces tariffs on its exports, it may retaliate by imposing tariffs on imports from the countries that initiated the tariffs. This retaliation is typically aimed at reducing the volume of imports from those countries, thereby offsetting the adverse effects of the initial tariffs on the exporting country's exports. Consequently, the tariff retaliation offer curve tends to bend towards the import good axis, indicating a reduction in imports from the targeted countries.

19. (C): The Factor Price Equalization Theorem, first articulated by Paul Samuelson, is a crucial proposition in international trade theory. This theorem posits that in a world with unrestricted trade and factor mobility, factors of production (such as labour and capital) will earn the same return (price) across different countries, regardless of initial endowments or technological differences. In other words, under conditions of free trade and factor mobility, competitive forces will equalize factor prices internationally. This phenomenon occurs because factors of production will migrate from regions with relatively lower returns to those with higher returns, thereby equalizing their prices over time.

20. (A): The Extended Fund Facility (EFF) was introduced by the International Monetary Fund (IMF) in 1974 as a financial instrument to provide support to member countries facing long-term balance of payments difficulties. Unlike traditional IMF lending programs, which typically focus on short-term stabilization measures, the EFF is designed to assist countries in implementing structural reforms aimed at addressing underlying imbalances and promoting sustainable economic growth. This facility offers financial assistance over an extended period, allowing countries to undertake comprehensive policy reforms and structural adjustments. The EFF is particularly suited for nations facing persistent balance of payments problems, such as chronic deficits or unsustainable debt burdens, that require sustained policy adjustments and structural reforms to address.

21. (B): "Why Nations Fail: The Origins of Power, Prosperity, and Poverty," authored by Daron Acemoglu and James A. Robinson, is a seminal work that explores the underlying factors contributing to the divergent economic fortunes of nations. The book presents a compelling argument that the key determinant of a nation's success or failure lies in its political and economic institutions. Acemoglu and Robinson contend that inclusive political and economic institutions, which encourage broad-based participation, innovation, and competition, are essential for fostering long-term prosperity.

22. (B): A foreign exchange swap is a financial derivative transaction that involves the simultaneous execution of a spot sale of a currency combined with a forward repurchase of the same currency. In this arrangement, one party sells a specified amount of a currency for immediate delivery at the prevailing spot exchange rate, effectively converting it into another currency. At the same time, the parties agree to repurchase the same currency at a future date, typically at a predetermined forward exchange rate. This transaction allows participants to obtain funds in a different currency for a specific period while simultaneously hedging against exchange rate fluctuations. Foreign exchange swaps are commonly used by businesses, financial institutions, and central banks to manage currency exposure, facilitate international trade and investment, and access funding in foreign markets.

23. (C): The correct measure of the gross fiscal deficit of the state government is the sum of revenue deficit, capital outlays, and net lending. Revenue deficit represents the excess of revenue expenditure over revenue receipts, reflecting the extent to which current revenue falls short of meeting current expenditure obligations. Capital outlays include government expenditures on infrastructure, development projects, and other capital investments aimed at enhancing long-term economic growth and productivity. Net lending refers to the financial assistance provided by the government to various entities, such as public sector enterprises or other governments, minus any repayments received.

24. (C): The notion presented in this statement about tax incidence is indeed incorrect, as it oversimplifies the dynamics of tax burden distribution in the context of inelastic demand and elastic supply. In reality, tax incidence hinges on the elasticities of both demand and supply. While inelastic demand implies that consumers are less responsive to price changes and may continue purchasing despite tax-induced price increases, it does not necessarily confer an advantage in avoiding the tax burden. On the contrary, sellers can exploit this lack of consumer responsiveness by passing on a larger portion of the tax burden to consumers through higher prices.

25. (C)

26. (B): In the extreme scenario of a liquidity trap, characterized by near-zero interest rates and ineffective monetary policy, investors often exhibit bearish behavior. With nominal interest rates constrained at very low levels, traditional monetary policy tools lose their effectiveness in stimulating economic activity. In such a context, investors become pessimistic about the outlook for economic growth and investment returns. The inability of central banks to further lower interest rates or stimulate borrowing and spending creates uncertainty and apprehension among investors.

27. (A): The equation $300 = 2Y - 1.5i$ represents the equilibrium condition in the money market, where:

300 represents the quantity of money supplied (often denoted as MS or Ms), 2Y represents the quantity of money demanded (often denoted as MD or Md), and *i* represents the nominal interest rate.

In this equation, Y typically represents real income or real output, and i represents the nominal interest rate. The equation reflects the balance between the quantity of money demanded by households and firms and the quantity of money supplied by the central bank. It illustrates that at equilibrium, the quantity of money demanded (2Y) equals the quantity of money supplied (300) at a given interest rate (*i*). This equilibrium condition is derived from Keynesian economics, which suggests that the demand for money is positively related to real income and negatively related to the nominal interest rate.

28. (D): An increase in financial literacy and banking habits can significantly impact the dynamics of the money supply, even with the same monetary base. As individuals become more financially literate, they are more likely to understand the benefits of utilizing banking services rather than keeping their funds in cash. This understanding prompts them to deposit their money into bank accounts, thereby increasing the deposit base of banks. With a larger pool of deposits, banks have more resources to extend loans and create additional deposits through the process of fractional reserve banking. This expansion of credit creation leads to an increase in broad money (M2) within the economy.

29. (A): According to Joan Robinson, the term 'Golden Age' in the context of the Harrod-Domar model serves to underscore its mythical nature. In the Harrod-Domar model, the 'Golden Age' represents a theoretical scenario where full employment is maintained without generating inflationary pressures, thus signifying a state of economic prosperity and stability. However, Robinson, a prominent critic of neoclassical economics, argued that such a scenario is often unattainable in the real world due to the inherent complexities and uncertainties of economic systems. She pointed out that the assumptions and simplifications made in the Harrod-Domar model, such as constant capital-output ratios and linear relationships between investment and output, fail to capture the multifaceted nature of economic dynamics.

30. (D): The Human Development Index (HDI) encompasses three primary dimensions to assess the well-being and development of individuals within a country. The first dimension focuses on the ability to lead a long and healthy life, emphasizing indicators such as life expectancy at birth and access to healthcare services. The second dimension pertains to the ability to acquire knowledge, evaluating indicators like literacy rates and school enrollment ratios to gauge educational attainment and cognitive development. The third dimension revolves around the ability to achieve a decent standard of living, considering factors such as income per capita, access to basic necessities, and standards of living. While access to a clean environment is undoubtedly vital for human well-being, it is not explicitly included as a dimension within the HDI.

31. (D): The concept of creative destruction, famously associated with Joseph Schumpeter, elucidates the dynamic and transformative nature of capitalist economies. Schumpeter's theory, outlined in his seminal work "Capitalism, Socialism and Democracy," posits that innovation and technological progress are inherent to the capitalist system, driving continual renewal and evolution. Creative destruction refers to the process wherein the introduction of new technologies, products, and business models leads to the disruption and eventual obsolescence of existing industries and economic structures. Schumpeter's concept of creative destruction highlights the dynamic and transformative nature of capitalist economies, emphasizing the importance of innovation and entrepreneurship in shaping their evolution.

32. (A): The Normalized Poverty Gap (NPG) is a crucial measure used to assess the depth of poverty experienced by individuals living below the poverty line within a given population. It quantifies the extent to which those below the poverty line fall short of achieving the minimum standard of living represented by the poverty line. The calculation of NPG involves dividing the Average Poverty Gap, which represents the average shortfall of the poor from the poverty line, by the poverty line itself. This ratio offers valuable insights into the severity of poverty by providing a standardized measure of deprivation relative to the poverty threshold. A higher NPG indicates a greater level of poverty depth, reflecting a more significant gap between the income or consumption levels of the poor and the established poverty line.

33. (C): Ambient standards in environmental policy play a pivotal role in defining the desired quality levels of specific elements within the environment, serving as crucial benchmarks for environmental management and regulation. These standards articulate the acceptable levels of various pollutants, contaminants, or other environmental parameters that must be achieved or maintained to safeguard human health and ecological integrity. For instance, air quality standards may specify limits for pollutants like particulate matter or sulphur dioxide to ensure breathable air and mitigate respiratory ailments. Similarly, water quality standards establish permissible levels of contaminants such as heavy metals or pesticides to safeguard aquatic ecosystems and drinking water sources. By designating these quality levels, ambient standards provide clear targets for environmental monitoring, regulation, and remediation efforts, enabling policymakers, regulators, and stakeholders to assess environmental conditions, identify areas of concern, and implement measures to protect and enhance environmental quality.

34. (D): The physical linkage approach for the valuation of environmental benefits involves estimating the value of environmental goods or services based on the direct technical relationship between the environmental resource and its users. This approach relies on understanding the tangible connections between changes in environmental conditions and the resulting impacts on individuals or entities that directly benefit from the resource. For example, in assessing the value of improved water quality in a river, analysts may examine the impact on recreational activities, such as swimming, fishing, or boating, that are directly affected by the condition of the water. Similarly, changes in air pollution levels may be linked to health outcomes, such as reductions in respiratory illnesses or healthcare costs, which directly affect individuals' well-being. Therefore, the physical linkage approach provides a rigorous framework for assessing the value of environmental benefits by focusing on the technical relationship between the environmental resource and its users.

35. (D): Subsidies are not typically an effective long-term policy instrument for internalizing externalities under competitive output markets for several reasons. Firstly, providing a subsidy equal to the marginal damages incurred by firms due to externalities can effectively reduce a firm's fixed costs, incentivizing increased production and exacerbating the externality rather than addressing it. Secondly, subsidies are generally available to all firms within an industry, which can lead to excessive market entry as firms are encouraged to enter the market to take advantage of the subsidy, further exacerbating the externality. Finally, the provision of subsidies can result in the level of industrial production exceeding the socially desired level, leading to overproduction and continued negative externalities. Therefore, all of the above reasons contribute to why subsidies are not an effective long-term solution for internalizing externalities in competitive output markets.

36. (C): Madhya Pradesh had the highest maternal lifetime risk in India from 2018 to 2020, at approximately 0.53 percent. The maternal mortality ratio (MMR) serves as a crucial indicator of maternal health and healthcare system performance. Addressing factors contributing to high maternal mortality, such as inadequate healthcare infrastructure, limited access to quality maternal healthcare services, socio-economic disparities, and cultural barriers, is essential for improving maternal health outcomes and reducing maternal mortality rates in Madhya Pradesh and across India.

37. (A): The Intensive Agriculture District Programme (IADP), launched in 1960-61, was a pivotal initiative often referred to as the "package program" due to its comprehensive approach to agricultural development. The program aimed to enhance agricultural productivity by providing farmers with access to loans for seeds and fertilizers, technical knowledge, adaptable innovations, and other resources necessary for boosting production. It focused primarily on dominant food-grain crops such as paddy, wheat, and millets while also covering other important cash crops in selected districts across various states.

38. (B): In the 2023-24 Union Budget, the Ministry of Agriculture and Farmers' Welfare saw its allocation climb to ₹ 1.25 lakh crore, a 5% rise from the previous year. This increase underscores the government's continuing focus on supporting India's crucial agricultural sector. However, a closer look reveals that this growth wasn't uniformly distributed across all initiatives. Key programs like Pradhan Mantri Fasal Bima Yojana, designed to shield farmers from crop losses, received a welcome bump. Conversely, others like the Modified Interest Subvention Scheme, which aims to make loans more accessible, experienced slight reductions.

39. (A): The motto of the G-20 18th meeting was "One Earth • One Family • One Future". This encapsulates the essence of global unity and cooperation in addressing pressing challenges facing the world. It emphasizes the interconnectedness of humanity and our shared responsibility towards safeguarding our planet and securing a prosperous future for all. The 2023 G20 Summit was held in New Delhi, India, on September 9-10, 2023. The summit's agenda includes important issues such as food security, climate and energy, development, health, and digitalization.

40. (B): The Prevention of Money Laundering Act, enacted in 2002, represents a pivotal step in India's efforts to combat illicit financial activities and safeguard the integrity of its financial system. This legislation was introduced to address the growing concerns surrounding money laundering, which involves the concealment, conversion, or transfer of illicitly obtained funds to make them appear legitimate. The Act aims to prevent and detect money laundering activities by establishing stringent measures for the identification, verification, and monitoring of financial transactions, particularly those involving large sums of money or high-risk entities. It empowers law enforcement agencies to investigate and prosecute individuals and organizations involved in money laundering, imposing severe penalties for non-compliance or violation of the Act's provisions.

41. (A):

(*a*) **"The reaction curves are derived from isoprofit maps which are convex to the axes."** In Bertrand's Duopoly model, firms determine their optimal pricing strategies by considering the profitability associated with different price levels. These profitability considerations are often represented graphically using isoprofit maps, which depict combinations of prices that yield the same profit level for the firm. When these isoprofit maps are convex to the axes, it means that as the firm increases its price, its profit increases at an increasing rate. As the competitor increases its price, the firm responds by lowering its price to maintain its competitive position and maximize its profit.

(*b*) **"The point of intersection of the two reaction curves reflects a stable equilibrium."** In Bertrand's Duopoly model, the equilibrium occurs where the reaction curves of both firms intersect. At this point, neither firm has an incentive to unilaterally change its price-setting strategy, as any deviation would result in lower profits. Specifically, if one firm were to increase its price above the equilibrium price, it would lose market share to its competitor and experience a decrease in profits. Conversely, if one firm were to decrease its price below the equilibrium price, it would initiate a price war, leading to lower profits for both firms.

42. (D):

(*c*) The Clark-Wicksteed-Walras product exhaustion theorem does not require perfect competition as a necessary condition. This theorem primarily deals with the equilibrium conditions in a market economy, particularly in the context of resource allocation and production. Instead, it focuses on the equilibrium outcomes that emerge from the interactions of supply and demand forces, which can occur under various market structures, including imperfect competition.

(*d*) The theorem is indeed not an identity that holds for all values of the variables. Rather, it specifically pertains to the long-run equilibrium conditions in an economy. In the long run, factors such as resource prices, input quantities, and output levels adjust to achieve a state where resource allocation is efficient and production is maximized. Therefore, the theorem's applicability is limited to this specific equilibrium scenario and may not hold true for other situations or periods of time within the economic system.

(*e*) The Clark-Wicksteed-Walras product exhaustion theorem has theoretical applicability to various types of production functions, including both homogeneous and non-homogeneous functions. While homogeneous production functions are commonly employed to illustrate the theorem's concepts due to their simplicity and ease of analysis, the theorem's principles can be extended to certain types of non-homogeneous production functions under specific conditions.

43. (C):

(*a*) **Homogeneous of degree one in price, P:** This property means that if all prices are multiplied by a constant factor, the resulting expenditure on the bundle of goods will also be multiplied by the same factor. It reflects the idea that the scale of prices affects the scale of expenditure in a proportional manner.

(*b*) **Strictly increasing in utility, u, and non-decreasing in price, P, for any good 1:** This property indicates that as utility increases (strictly), the expenditure on goods also increases. Similarly, for any given good, as its price increases, the expenditure on that good either increases or remains the same. This reflects the intuitive notion that higher utility or higher prices lead to higher expenditure.

(*c*) **Concave in price, P:** This property implies that as the price of a good increases, the rate at which the expenditure on that good increases diminishes. In other words, the marginal effect of an increase in price on expenditure decreases as more of the good is consumed, holding utility constant. This concavity reflects diminishing marginal utility and is a typical characteristic of consumer preferences.

(*d*) **Continuous in price, P, and utility, u:** Continuity ensures that small changes in prices or utility result in small changes in expenditure. This property is crucial for mathematical analysis and modeling, allowing for smooth transitions and accurate representations of consumer behavior across different price and utility levels.

44. (D):

(*a*) **'Excess sensitivity'** refers to a situation where consumption over-responds to temporary income shocks. This means that when individuals experience temporary increases or decreases in income, their consumption changes by a larger proportion than the change in income.

(*b*) **'Excess smoothness'** refers to a situation where consumption under-responds to temporary income changes. In this case, changes in income have a smaller effect on consumption than would be expected based on standard economic theory.

(*e*) **'Excess sensitivity'** and **'Excess smoothness'** are related to the empirical evidence of the permanent income hypothesis. The permanent income hypothesis suggests that individuals base their consumption decisions on their expected long-term or permanent income rather than temporary fluctuations in income.

45. (C):

(*a*) When there is an increase in the price of output, it implies that firms can sell their products at higher prices, leading to increased revenues and profitability. This creates an incentive for firms to invest in expanding their production capacity to meet the higher demand and take advantage of the more favorable market conditions.

(*b*) An increase in the marginal product of capital means that additional investment in capital goods (such as machinery, equipment, or technology) leads to a greater increase in output. In other words, each additional unit of capital generates more output than before, making investment in capital goods more attractive for firms seeking to maximize their production efficiency and output levels.

(*d*) A decrease in the rate of depreciation suggests that capital goods lose value at a slower rate over time. This means that the existing capital stock retains its value for a longer period, effectively reducing the need for frequent replacement or maintenance of capital assets.

(*e*) The core principle of Tobin's Q theory is that firms should invest when the marginal benefit of investment exceeds the marginal cost. Marginal benefit refers to the additional revenue or profit generated by investing in new capital goods, while marginal cost represents the additional cost incurred in acquiring and using these capital goods.

46. (D):

(*a*) **Paradox of thrift was popularized by J. M. Keynes:** This statement is true. John Maynard Keynes, a renowned economist, popularized the concept of the paradox of thrift in his seminal work, "The General Theory of Employment, Interest, and Money," published in 1936. In this work, Keynes described how increased saving at the individual level during economic downturns could potentially exacerbate recessions or depressions by reducing aggregate demand and contributing to a decline in overall economic activity.

(*b*) **It states that personal savings can be detrimental to overall economic growth:** This statement is also true. The paradox of thrift suggests that while saving is generally seen as beneficial at the individual level for financial security and future investment, excessive saving during times of economic hardship can have negative consequences for overall economic growth.

(*e*) **It states that individuals saving during an economic recession leads to a fall in aggregate demand:** This statement is true. One of the central tenets of the paradox of thrift is that increased saving by individuals during periods of economic recession or hardship can exacerbate the downturn by reducing aggregate demand. As individuals cut back on spending and increase saving to safeguard against uncertain economic conditions, overall demand for goods and services declines, leading to further economic contraction.

47. (D):

(*a*) **Devaluation of rupee by 22%:** Devaluation refers to the deliberate lowering of a country's currency value relative to other currencies. In this context, India was required to devalue its currency, the rupee, by 22% as a condition imposed by the IMF.

(*b*) **Drastic custom cut to a peak duty of 30% from the erstwhile level of 130% for all goods:** This condition involved a significant reduction in customs duties. India was required to cut its peak customs duty from the previous level of 130% to 30% for all goods.

(*d*) **Excise duty to be increased by 20% to neutralize the loss of revenue due to custom cut:** To compensate for the potential loss of revenue resulting from the reduction in customs duties, the government was mandated to increase excise duties by 20%.

(*e*) **Government expenditure to be cut by 10% per annum:** As part of the IMF's conditions, India was required to implement austerity measures, including reducing government spending. The government was instructed to cut its expenditure by 10% annually.

48. (A):

(*a*) **The reduction of average tariffs on industrial goods:** The Uruguay Round aimed to lower average tariffs on industrial goods across participating countries. By reducing tariffs, which are taxes imposed on imported goods, the agreement sought to make international trade more accessible and cost-effective for businesses, leading to increased trade volumes and economic growth.

(*b*) **Quotas to be replaced by tariffs:** Quotas, which restrict the quantity of imports allowed into a country, can be opaque and prone to abuse. Tariffs provide a clearer indication of the cost of importing goods and allow countries to control imports without distorting market mechanisms.

(*c*) **The reduction in agriculture export subsidies:** Agricultural export subsidies artificially lower the price of exported agricultural products, giving exporters an unfair advantage in international markets. The Uruguay Round aimed to reduce or eliminate these subsidies to create a more level playing field for agricultural producers worldwide and prevent market distortions that harm producers in importing countries.

(*d*) **The reduction in industrial subsidies:** Similar to agricultural subsidies, industrial subsidies can distort trade by artificially promoting the production and export of certain goods. The Uruguay Round sought to reduce these subsidies to ensure fair competition among countries and prevent the emergence of trade barriers that impede market access for producers in other countries.

49. (A) and (B):

(*a*) **Quality and level of capital:** Pillar 1 of Basel III emphasizes the importance of both the quality and quantity of capital held by banks. It introduces stricter definitions of capital to ensure that it consists of high-quality instruments capable of absorbing losses effectively. Additionally, Basel III increases the minimum level of capital banks must hold to provide a more substantial buffer against financial shocks.

(*b*) **Risk Coverage:** Another key aspect of Pillar 1 is ensuring that banks have sufficient capital to cover the risks they face. This involves aligning capital requirements with the level of risk associated with various assets and exposures. Basel III introduces risk-weighted assets (RWAs), where assets are assigned weights based on their riskiness.

(*c*) **Containing leverage:** Pillar 1 of Basel III explicitly includes measures to contain leverage by setting minimum capital requirements relative to a bank's total assets. Specifically, it introduces a leverage ratio requirement, which mandates that banks maintain a certain level of capital in proportion to their total exposure, irrespective of the risk weighting assigned to their assets. This leverage ratio acts as a backstop to risk-weighted capital requirements, ensuring that banks maintain a minimum level of capital to absorb losses relative to their overall balance sheet size.

50. (A):

(*b*) Exchange rate stability, monetary policy autonomy, and capital mobility are the three components of the trilemma. It suggests that policymakers can only achieve two of these objectives at any given time, necessitating a trade-off between them.

(*c*) The alignment of domestic interest rates with world interest rates is a crucial aspect of the trilemma. Perfect capital mobility implies that investors can freely move capital across borders in search of the highest returns. In this scenario, any deviation in domestic interest rates from those prevailing internationally would lead to capital flows, causing the domestic interest rate to adjust until it aligns with the world interest rate.

51. (D): The National Institution for Transforming India (NITI Aayog), a policy think tank of the Indian government, conducts periodic estimations of poverty in the country. Analyzing the 2011-12 poverty estimates specifically, we can examine the rural poverty rates across different states. When focusing on states with rural poverty exceeding 30%, the data reveals a concerning picture:

(*a*) **Manipur:** With a rural poverty rate of 36.5%, Manipur topped the list in 2011-12, highlighting significant challenges in accessing basic necessities and opportunities for its rural population.

(*b*) **Bihar:** Following closely behind at 39.1%, Bihar faced a similarly high prevalence of rural poverty, indicating the need for targeted interventions to improve living standards.

(*d*) **Uttar Pradesh:** With a rate of 34.8%, Uttar Pradesh's large rural population grappled with poverty concerns, requiring comprehensive development strategies to address various factors contributing to their economic hardship.

52. (A):

(*a*) **Division of Labour:** Smith's advocacy for the division of labour emphasized its transformative potential in driving economic growth and efficiency. In his seminal work, "The Wealth of Nations," he argued that when workers specialize in specific tasks, they become more proficient, leading to enhanced productivity and output. This specialization not only reduces the time spent transitioning between tasks but also fosters innovation and technological progress as individuals seek more efficient methods of production.

(*b*) **Notion of Increasing Returns:** While Smith is not solely credited with the concept of increasing returns; he acknowledged its relevance in certain contexts. He recognized that as production scales up, certain costs may decrease proportionately, resulting in greater efficiency and potentially lower per-unit production costs. This concept, known as economies of scale, is prevalent across various industries, driving advancements in manufacturing, services, and technology.

53. (C):

(*a*) **Construction:** This sector involves the development of physical infrastructure, including buildings, roads, bridges, and other structures. Construction activities not only provide employment opportunities but also stimulate demand for various raw materials and ancillary services, driving economic activity.

(*b*) **Trade, Hotels, Transport, and Communication related to Broadcasting:** This category comprises several subsectors, each playing a crucial role in facilitating economic transactions and connectivity. Trade involves the buying and selling of goods, both wholesale and retail, contributing to market efficiency and consumer access. Hotels and hospitality services cater to the needs of travelers, tourists, and consumers, promoting tourism and leisure activities. Transport services ensure the movement of goods and people, facilitating trade and mobility. Communication services, including telecommunications and broadcasting, enable connectivity and information dissemination, fostering economic integration and innovation.

(*d*) **Public Administration, Defense, and Other Services:** This sector encompasses government activities aimed at governance, defense, and the provision of essential public services. Public administration involves the management of public affairs, policymaking, and the delivery of public services such as healthcare, education, and social welfare. Defense activities ensure national security and territorial integrity, while other services may include regulatory functions and public utilities management.

(*e*) **Financial, Real Estate, and Professional Services:** This category encompasses a diverse range of activities that support economic transactions, asset management, and professional expertise. Financial services, including banking, insurance, and investment, facilitate capital allocation, risk management, and wealth generation. Real estate activities involve the development, sale, purchase, and leasing of properties, contributing to asset accumulation and urban development. Professional services such as legal, accounting, consulting, and technical expertise provide specialized knowledge and advisory support, enhancing productivity and competitiveness.

54. (D):

(*a*) **Asian Drama:** Unraveling the Knots of Poverty and Inequality: Released in 1968, this multi-volume study shifted Myrdal's gaze towards the complexities of development in Asia. He meticulously documented the stark disparities in wealth and opportunity within and between nations, offering nuanced analyses of the historical, social, and economic factors hindering progress.

(*b*) **An American Dilemma:** Deconstructing Race and Racism: Published in 1944, this monumental work delved deeply into the "dilemma" at the heart of American society - the stark contradiction between its professed ideals of liberty and equality, and the persistent reality of racial injustice.

(*e*) **Economic Theory and Underdeveloped Regions:** Beyond Traditional Frameworks: In 1957, Myrdal published this pivotal work, questioning the ability of existing economic theories to grasp the unique challenges faced by developing nations. He argued that rigid, Western-centric models failed to capture the cyclical nature of poverty and the interconnectedness of economic, social, and political factors.

55. (C): The principles representing set theory are as follows:

(*b*) $(A \cup B') \cap (A' \cup C) \cap (B \cup C')$
$= (A \cap B \cap C) \cup (A \cup B \cup C)'$

(*c*) $A \cup (B \cap C) = (A \cup B) \cap (A \cup C)$

(*e*) $(A \cup B') \cap (A' \cup C) \cap (B \cup C')$
$= (A' \cap B' \cap C-)$

56. (D): If S represents the sample and E represents the function. Then the probability law can be written in the following form.

Probability Law I: $P[A] \geq 0$

Probability Law II: $P[S] = 1$

Probability Law III: If $A \cap B = \phi$

Probability Law then $P[A \cup B]$
$= P[A] + P[B]$

Probability Law III: if A_1, A_2 ....

The same sequence of such events then,

$A\, i \cap A = \phi$ 1 for all i = , no

$$P\left(\bigcup_{i=1}^{\infty} A_i\right) = \sum_{i=1}^{\infty} P(A_1).$$

57. (D):

(*a*) **It may not be unbiased:** This property implies that a sufficient estimator might not provide estimates that, on average, are equal to the true parameter value. Unbiasedness is a desirable property in estimation because it ensures that, on average, the estimator does not systematically overestimate or underestimate the true parameter value. However, sufficiency does not guarantee unbiasedness.

(*b*) **It may be unbiased:** Conversely, this property acknowledges that a sufficient estimator can indeed be unbiased. While unbiasedness is not a necessary condition for sufficiency, it is possible for a sufficient estimator to provide unbiased estimates. In such cases, the estimator accurately estimates the true parameter value on average over repeated sampling.

(*c*) **It is always consistent:** Consistency is a crucial property of estimators, indicating that as the sample size increases indefinitely, the estimator converges in probability to the true parameter value. In other words, the likelihood of the estimator deviating significantly from the true parameter value diminishes as more data become available.

(*e*) **Minimum variance unbiased estimator:** While sufficiency does not guarantee that an estimator will be the minimum variance unbiased estimator (MVUE), it is possible for a sufficient estimator to achieve this desirable property. The MVUE is the most efficient unbiased estimator among all possible estimators, providing the smallest possible variance.

58. (D):

(*a*) **Public goods are non-rivalry in nature:** Public goods exhibit non-rivalry, meaning that one individual's consumption of the good does not reduce the amount available for others to consume. This characteristic distinguishes public goods from private goods, where consumption by one individual typically diminishes the quantity available for others.

(*b*) **Efficient provision of social goods needs a political process of budget determination:** The provision of social goods, which benefit society as a whole, often requires a political process to determine budget allocations and resource distribution. This is because decisions regarding the provision of social goods involve considerations beyond individual preferences and market mechanisms.

(*d*) **Among purely private and purely social goods, there are mixed cases which generate benefit or cost externalities:**

Some goods exhibit characteristics of both private and social goods, leading to the emergence of externalities-spillover effects that impact parties not directly involved in the consumption or production of the good. In mixed cases, individuals or firms may generate external benefits (positive externalities) or external costs (negative externalities) that affect others in society.

(*e*) **Individual consumers will not bid for social good, but will act as free-riders:** Since social goods are often non-excludable, meaning that individuals cannot be effectively excluded from using them, consumers may choose to "free-ride" by enjoying the benefits of the good without contributing to its provision. In the absence of mechanisms to enforce payment for the good, individuals have little incentive to pay for it voluntarily if they can benefit from it regardless of their contribution.

59. (B):

(*a*) Tax rate should be higher on the good that has lower price elasticity of demand. This statement aligns with the Ramsey Rule, which suggests that taxes should be levied at higher rates on goods with lower price elasticity of demand. This approach ensures that the tax burden falls more heavily on goods for which consumers are less responsive to price changes, maximizing tax revenue while minimizing the distortionary effects on consumption.

(*b*) If the demand elasticity in a market is zero, taxes should be imposed only in that market. This statement reflects the idea that when demand elasticity is zero (perfectly inelastic demand), consumers are insensitive to price changes, implying that taxes won't affect their consumption behaviour.

(*d*) Ramsey rule minimizes the excess burden of taxation across markets. One of the primary goals of the Ramsey Rule is to minimize the excess burden or deadweight loss associated with taxation. By setting tax rates based on the price elasticity of demand for various goods, the Ramsey Rule aims to ensure that taxes are distributed efficiently, minimizing the overall welfare loss resulting from taxation.

(*e*) Ramsey rule does not necessarily result in social justice. While the Ramsey Rule emphasizes efficiency in taxation, it may not address concerns related to social justice or equity. The rule focuses on optimizing resource allocation and minimizing deadweight loss but may not account for factors such as income distribution, poverty alleviation, or the impact on vulnerable populations.

60. (B):

(*d*) **Variance Inflation Factor (VIF) of a variable is below 10:** VIF measures how much the variance of the estimated regression coefficient is inflated due to multicollinearity. A VIF value above 10 (or sometimes even 4 or 5, depending on the context) indicates high multi-collinearity, not below. Lower VIF values suggest lower multicollinearity and are desirable in regression analysis.

(*e*) **The closer the Tolerance (TOLj) is to 1:** Tolerance is the proportion of variance in an independent variable that is not explained by other predictors in the model. A Tolerance value close to 1 indicates that most of the variance in the variable is not explained by the other predictors, implying lower multi-collinearity.

61. (C):

(*a*) **Deregulation of the interest rate structure:** The committee recommended the removal of restrictions on interest rates charged by banks, allowing market forces to determine interest rates based on demand and supply dynamics. This move aimed to enhance efficiency in the banking sector and encourage competition among banks.

(*d*) **Freedom to appoint chief executive and officers of the banks:** The committee suggested granting banks the autonomy to appoint their chief executives and officers based on merit and competence rather than bureaucratic or political considerations. This recommendation aimed to improve governance and efficiency in banks by ensuring that key leadership positions are filled by qualified professionals.

(*e*) **Capital adequacy norms were implemented in stages:** The committee proposed the gradual implementation of capital adequacy norms to strengthen the financial health and stability of banks. These norms require banks to maintain a minimum level of capital relative to their risk-weighted assets, thereby enhancing their ability to absorb losses and withstand financial shocks.

62. (D):

(*a*) **The consumer spends money to ameliorate the damaging effects of the bad:** The defensive expenditure method is based on the premise that consumers allocate resources to mitigate or reduce the adverse impacts of undesirable factors, such as pollution or environmental degradation.

(*b*) **The defensive expenditure undertaken reflects the consumer's willingness to pay to reduce the level of the bad:** Consumers make defensive expenditures based on their perceived value of mitigating the negative effects of the bad.

(*d*) **The defensive expenditure provides no additional services other than provisioning the desired environmental quality:** Defensive expenditures are made solely to counteract the negative impacts of environmental degradation or pollution. Unlike other expenditures that provide tangible services or goods, such as purchasing a product or service for enjoyment or utility, defensive expenditures aim to protect existing environmental quality and do not generate additional benefits beyond this purpose.

(*e*) **The observed defensive expenditure is a lower bound on the willingness to pay to avoid the bad:** While defensive expenditures provide an upper bound on the willingness to pay to avoid environmental harm, they also serve as a minimum estimate of the value individuals place on environmental quality.

63. (C):

64. (D):

(*a*) **GATT (General Agreement on Tariffs and Trade):** GATT was an international organization established in 1947 to promote international trade by reducing or eliminating trade barriers such as tariffs or quotas. In 1995, GATT's functions were absorbed by the World Trade Organization (WTO), which continues to operate in Geneva, Switzerland.

(*b*) **IMF (International Monetary Fund):** The IMF is an international organization headquartered in Washington, D.C., United States. It was established in 1944 with the goal of promoting global monetary cooperation, exchange stability, and balanced growth.

(*c*) **World Bank:** The World Bank is another international financial institution headquartered in Washington, D.C., United States. It was established in 1944 alongside the IMF to provide financial and technical assistance to developing countries. The World Bank Group consists of five institutions, including the International Bank for Reconstruction and Development (IBRD) and the International Development Association (IDA).

(*e*) **Asian Development Bank (ADB):** The ADB is a regional development bank dedicated to promoting economic and social progress in Asia and the Pacific. It was founded in 1966 and is headquartered in Mandaluyong City, Philippines.

65. (D):

(*a*) This statement accurately describes the property of homogeneity in Walrasian demand functions. When prices and total wealth are multiplied by the same factor, the demand function's value remains unchanged. This property is fundamental in understanding how consumers' demand for goods responds to changes in prices and wealth.

(*c*) Walras' Law, as stated in this statement, indeed asserts that the sum of expenditures across all goods equals total wealth. This principle ensures market equilibrium, where consumers allocate their budgets efficiently among different goods based on their preferences and the prices of those goods.

(*d*) Contrary to the assertion that this statement is incorrect, it accurately reflects Walras' Law. The law does imply that consumers fully expend their wealth in equilibrium. This is because market expenditures, which represent the sum of all expenditures on goods, equal total wealth.

(*e*) This statement correctly describes the property of homogeneity, where changes in prices and wealth in proportion do not alter individual consumption choices. This property aligns with Walrasian demand functions, reflecting how consumers' optimal consumption bundles remain unchanged when prices and wealth change in proportion.

66. (D):

(*a*) Cost-effectiveness matches with Cost-effectiveness refers to the principle that requires achieving a certain environmental objective using the least amount of resources possible.

(*b*) Pollution permit trading system matches with A pollution permit trading system, also known as a cap-and-trade system, is a market-based approach where permits to pollute up to a certain level are traded among polluters. This matches with the concept of a market approach.

(*c*) Market approach matches with A market approach refers to policies that utilize market mechanisms, such as incentives or trading systems, to address environmental issues. This aligns with the description of a pollution permit trading system.

(*d*) Command-and-control approach matches with The command-and-control approach involves direct regulation of polluters through the imposition of standards or regulations. This contrasts with market-based approaches, such as pollution permit trading systems.

67. (A)

68. (D):

(*a*) **J. M. Keynes corresponds to Liquidity Preference.** Keynes is famously associated with liquidity preference theory, which explores how individuals balance the desire for liquidity (cash or near-cash assets) with the pursuit of higher returns from less liquid investments.

(*b*) **Kvdland-Prescott matches with Time Inconsistency Problem.** The Kydland-Prescott model is a dynamic model of economic policy that highlights the challenges policymakers face when their incentives to commit to a policy in the present differ from their incentives to adhere to that commitment in the future.

(*c*) **Baumol-Tobin corresponds to Inventory theoretic approach to transaction demand for money.** The Baumol-Tobin model focuses on how individuals decide how much of their wealth to hold in the form of money versus other assets, considering the trade-off between the costs of making frequent trips to the bank to convert assets into money (transaction costs) and the opportunity costs of holding money (foregone interest).

(*d*) **Friedman-Schwartz matches with Monetary History of the United States.** Milton Friedman and Anna Schwartz collaborated on the seminal work "A Monetary History of the United States," which examines the role of monetary factors in economic fluctuations and crises throughout American history.

69. (B):

(*a*) **Kuznets corresponds to Inverted U-curve hypothesis.** Simon Kuznets is known for his hypothesis that suggests income inequality initially increases as a country industrializes but then decreases once a certain level of income is reached.

(*b*) **Nurkse matches with Balanced growth theory.** Ragnar Nurkse proposed the balanced growth theory, which emphasizes the importance of investing in various sectors of the economy simultaneously to achieve balanced development and avoid bottlenecks.

(*c*) **Leibenstein corresponds to Critical minimum effort thesis.** Harvey Leibenstein introduced the concept of the critical minimum effort thesis, which suggests that below a certain level of effort or investment, an industry or region may fail to develop due to various inefficiencies or barriers.

(*d*) **Schumpeter matches with Innovation and Entrepreneurship.** Joseph Schumpeter is known for his theory of economic development, which highlights the role of innovation and entrepreneurship in driving economic growth and development.

70. (D):

(*a*) **Telangana:** With a production of 15,095.4 Thousand Tonnes in 2021-22, Telangana emerged as the state with the highest food grain production among the options provided. This robust production reflects the state's agricultural prowess and its efforts to enhance food security and economic prosperity.

(*b*) **Jharkhand:** Jharkhand recorded a food grain production of 4,984.2 Thousand Tonnes in the same period. While lower compared to Telangana, Jharkhand's production still contributes significantly to the state's economy and sustains livelihoods across rural communities.

(*c*) **Chhattisgarh:** Chhattisgarh's food grain production stood at 8,897.0 Thousand Tonnes in 2021-22, positioning it as a key player in India's agricultural landscape. The state's fertile lands and favorable climatic conditions contribute to its substantial agricultural output.

(*d*) **Andhra Pradesh:** Andhra Pradesh, with a production of 11,266.0 Thousand Tonnes, demonstrates its agricultural resilience and productivity. The state's strategic location and proactive agricultural policies contribute to its consistent performance in food grain production.

71. (C):

(*a*) **Tax Evasion - II. Illegal free riding:** Tax evasion refers to the illegal act of avoiding paying taxes, which can be seen as a form of illegal free riding where individuals benefit from public goods and services without contributing their fair share through taxes.

(*b*) **Effective incidence of tax - IV. Not necessarily correspond to on whom tax is imposed:** The effective incidence of tax refers to the actual burden of taxation, which may not always fall on the same entity or individual on whom the tax is officially imposed.

(*c*) **Legal incidence of tax - III. Obliged to deliver tax revenue to Government:** The legal incidence of tax refers to the legal responsibility or obligation of individuals or entities to deliver tax revenue to the government as per tax laws and regulations.

(*d*) **Fiscal Illusion - I. Bond Financing:** Fiscal illusion refers to the misperception or misunderstanding of the true costs of government spending and taxation, often exacerbated by methods like bond financing, which can obscure the immediate fiscal impact of government actions.

72. (B):

(*a*) **Rapid High Growth - III. 1951-1981:** During this period, India experienced rapid population growth rates, characterized by high birth rates and decreasing death rates, leading to a significant increase in population size.

(*b*) **Stagnant Population - IV. 1891-1921:** This period saw relatively stagnant population growth rates in India, marked by little to no change in the population size due to factors such as high mortality rates, disease outbreaks, and other socio-economic challenges.

(*c*) **High growth with definite signs of slowing down - I. 1981-2011:** In this period, India continued to experience high population growth rates, but there were clear indications of a slowing down in the rate of growth compared to the previous decades, reflecting changes in fertility patterns, healthcare, and socio-economic development.

(*d*) **Steady Growth - II. 1921-1951:** During this period, India had a relatively steady population growth rate, characterized by moderate increases in population size without significant fluctuations or rapid growth spurts.

73. (A):

(*a*) **National Forest Policy (1988):** The National Forest Policy of 1988 aimed to address the growing concerns related to deforestation, forest degradation, and the unsustainable use of forest resources. It emphasized the conservation and sustainable management of forests, recognizing their crucial role in ecological balance, biodiversity conservation, and livelihoods of forest-dependent communities.

(*b*) **Marine Fishing Policy (2004):** The Marine Fishing Policy introduced in 2004 focused on regulating and managing marine fisheries to ensure their sustainability and conservation of marine biodiversity. It aimed to address issues such as overfishing, destructive fishing practices, and conflicts among various stakeholders in the marine sector.

(*c*) **New Mineral Policy (1994):** The New Mineral Policy, implemented in 1994, sought to guide the development and regulation of the mineral sector in India. It aimed to promote responsible and sustainable utilization of mineral resources while ensuring equitable distribution of benefits and addressing environmental concerns.

(*d*) **National Population Policy (2000):** The National Population Policy of 2000 aimed to address population-related challenges such as high population growth rates, maternal and child health, family planning, and population stabilization. It advocated for voluntary and informed reproductive choices, access to quality family planning services, and investments in maternal and child health care.

74. (C)

75. (C)

76. (B): The 14th Finance Commission was operational from April 1, 2015, to March 31, 2020. During this time, it was tasked with recommending the distribution of financial resources between the central government and the states in India. They are:

(*e*) **Forest Cover (Weight: 7.5%):** This criterion considers the extent of forest cover within each state. States with higher forest cover are given a weightage of 7.5%. This factor reflects the ecological significance of forests and the need for conservation efforts.

(*d*) **Demographic Change (2011) (Weight: 10%):** The demographic change criterion accounts for changes in the population profile of states based on the 2011 census. It considers factors such as population growth, urbanization, and migration patterns.

(*b*) **Area (Weight: 15%):** The geographical area of a state is another important factor in fund allocation. Larger states typically have higher administrative and developmental costs due to their size and population dispersion. Therefore, the area criterion, with a weightage of 15%, acknowledges the need to allocate sufficient funds to address the unique challenges faced by states with extensive territorial coverage.

(*c*) **Population (1971) (Weight: 17.5%):** Surprisingly, the 14th Finance Commission used population data from the 1971 census as a criterion for fund distribution. This may seem unconventional, but it was intended to capture the historical context and developmental needs of states based on their population at that time. States with larger populations in 1971 were allocated a higher weightage of 17.5% to address their long-standing developmental challenges.

(*a*) **Income Distance (Weight: 50%):** Income distance refers to the disparity in per capita income among states. This criterion, with the highest weightage of 50%, aims to address economic disparities by allocating a larger share of funds to economically disadvantaged states.

77. (D):

(*e*) **Preferential Trade Arrangements (PTAs):** PTAs are the least integrated form of economic cooperation. They involve agreements between countries to reduce tariffs or other trade barriers on certain goods traded among them. However, these reductions apply only to trade between member countries, while each member maintains its own trade policies with non-members.

(*b*) **Free Trade Area (FTA):** FTAs take economic integration a step further by removing tariffs and trade barriers on goods traded between member countries. However, each member retains control over its trade policies with non-member countries. The North American Free Trade Agreement (NAFTA) and the European

Free Trade Association (EFTA) are examples of free trade areas.

(*a*) **Customs Union:** In a customs union, member countries eliminate tariffs and other trade barriers on goods traded among them. Additionally, they adopt a common external tariff (CET) on imports from non-member countries.

(*d*) **Common Market:** A common market builds on the foundation of a customs union by further integrating the economies of member countries. In addition to the free movement of goods and a common external tariff, it allows for the free movement of services, capital, and labor across borders.

(*c*) **Economic Union:** An economic union represents the highest level of economic integration. It encompasses all the features of a common market, including the free movement of goods, services, capital, and labour, while also harmonizing economic policies such as monetary, fiscal, and social policies among member countries.

78. (A): According to the recommendations of the 15th finance commission the following is the arrangement of the above states in ascending order on the basis of loans received from the central government in the year 2020-21.

- Tamil Nadu
- Madhya Pradesh
- Gujarat
- Karnataka
- Maharashtra

79. (*)

80. (B):

(*c*) IFCI, previously Industrial Finance Corporation of India, is a development finance institution under the ownership of Ministry of Finance, Government of India. Established in 1948 as a statutory corporation, IFCI is currently a company listed on BSE and NSE. IFCI has seven subsidiaries and one associate.

(*a*) The Industrial Credit and Investment Corporation of India (ICICI) is a financial institution established in 1955 by the Government of India, the World Bank, and representatives of Indian industry. ICICI's main purpose is to provide medium-term and long-term financing for Indian businesses' projects.

(*d*) The Industrial Reconstruction Bank of India (IRBI) is a credit and reconstruction agency for industrial revival. It was established in March 1985, replacing the Industrial Reconstruction Corporation of India (IRCI), which was established in 1971 to rehabilitate sick industrial companies.

(*e*) The Export-Import Bank of India (EXIM Bank) was established in 1982. It was established by the Government of India under the Export-Import Bank Act of 1981. EXIM Bank's role is to promote and finance India's international trade.

(*b*) The National Bank for Agriculture and Rural Development (NABARD) is a development bank that focuses on the rural sector of India. It was established in 1982 by an Act of Parliament to promote sustainable and equitable agriculture and rural development. NABARD is head-quartered in Mumbai and has branches across India.

81. (B):

(*b*) **A Treatise on Probability:** Authored by John Maynard Keynes, this work was published in 1921. In this book, Keynes delves into the mathematical theory of probability, addressing various concepts and applications related to probability theory.

(*e*) **A Tract on Monetary Reform:** Published in 1923, this work by John Maynard Keynes discusses various aspects of monetary policy and proposes reforms to stabilize the economy, particularly in the aftermath of World War I and the Treaty of Versailles.

(*d*) **The End of Laissez-Faire:** This essay by John Maynard Keynes was published in 1926. In it, Keynes argues against the laissez-faire economic policy and advocates for government intervention in the economy to address issues such as unemployment and economic instability.

(*c*) **Essays in Persuasion:** Published in 1931, this collection of essays by John Maynard Keynes covers a wide range of economic and political topics. It includes essays written during the turbulent period of the Great Depression, offering Keynes's insights and policy recommendations.

(*a*) **General Theory of Employment, Interest, and Money:** Considered one of Keynes's most influential works, this book was published in 1936. In it, Keynes presents his revolutionary theory on the causes of unemployment and proposes government intervention through fiscal and monetary policies to achieve full employment and economic stability.

82. (B):

(*b*) Foreign Institutional Investors (FIIs) began investing in the Indian securities market in 1996-97. FIIs are institutional investors based in one country that invest in the financial markets of another. FIIs, Non-Resident Indians (NRIs), and Persons of Indian Origin (PIOs) can invest in the primary and secondary capital markets in India through the portfolio investment scheme (PIS).

(*d*) The Securities and Exchange Board of India (SEBI) banned badla trading on the BSE in December 1993, with full effect in March 1994. The ban was made amid complaints from foreign investors, and with the expectation that it would be replaced by a futures-and-options exchange.

(*c*) The National Stock Exchange of India (NSE) began operations in 1993 with the wholesale debt market (WDM) segment on June 30, 1993. It was the first exchange in India to offer an electronic trading facility. The WDM segment provided the first formal screen-based trading facility for the country's debt market on June 30, 1994.

(*e*) The National Stock Exchange (NSE) became the largest stock exchange in India in terms of volume trading within a short span of a year after starting operations in 1995. NSE is the world's largest derivatives exchange by number of contracts traded.

(*a*) The Bombay Stock Exchange (BSE) introduced screen-based trading in 1995. The BSE's screen-based automated trading platform is called BOLT, which stands for BSE On-Line Trading. BOLT is a centralized exchange-based trading system that uses 25,000 trader workstations across over 359 cities in India.

83. (A):

(*a*) **Identification of the structural equations:** This step involves determining the relationships between the endogenous variables in the model. Endogenous variables are those that are determined within the model itself. Identifying these structural equations is crucial as they represent the theoretical underpinnings of the model.

(*d*) **Obtaining reduced form equations:** Once the structural equations are identified, they are then transformed into reduced form equations. These reduced form equations express the endogenous variables solely in terms of the exogenous variables and any predetermined variables.

(*b*) **Application of Ordinary Least Squares (OLS):** With the reduced form equations derived, OLS regression analysis is applied to estimate the parameters of these equations. OLS is a commonly used statistical technique that aims to find the best-fitting line through the data points. In the context of ILS, OLS is used to estimate the coefficients of the reduced form equations based on available data.

(*c*) **Obtaining structural coefficients:** After estimating the reduced form equations using OLS, the next step is to obtain the structural coefficients. This involves applying a transformation to the coefficients obtained from the OLS estimation to retrieve the parameters of the original structural equations.

(*e*) **Use the model for policy:** Once the structural coefficients are obtained, the estimated structural model can be utilized to analyze the effects of different policy interventions or scenarios. By simulating changes in exogenous variables and observing their impact on the endogenous variables, policymakers can assess the implications of various policy decisions.

84. (B): The Constitution (101st Amendment) Act, 2016 introduced the Goods & Services Tax (GST), a comprehensive indirect tax levied on manufacture, sale and consumption of goods as well as services at the national level. GST is a destination-based tax, i.e., they are levied where goods and services are consumed. The Centre would levy Central GST (CGST) and States would levy State GST (SGST) on every supply of goods and services within the state. Integrated GST (IGST) would be levied on all inter-state supplies by the Centre and then transferred to the Destination state.

Revenue received by the Government under the head of Goods and Services Tax (GST) on the somestic supply of Goods and Services.

State	Total (₹ in crore)
Madhya Pradesh	27005
Rajasthan	31797
Odisha	29844
Delhi	36568
West Bengal	39694

85. (C):

(*b*) **Tripura (91.58%):** Tripura stands out as the top performer, boasting an impressive literacy rate of 91.58%. This achievement reflects significant progress in educational attainment and underscores the success of various initiatives aimed at promoting literacy.

(*c*) **Sikkim (87.45%):** Sikkim follows closely behind Tripura with an impressive literacy rate of 87.45%. This figure underscores Sikkim's strong commitment to education and the success of its educational policies and programs.

(*a*) **Nagaland (85.31%):** Nagaland occupies a respectable middle ground with a literacy rate of 85.31%. While this figure indicates significant progress in educational attainment, it also suggests room for further improvement.

(*d*) **Manipur (76.94%):** Manipur's literacy rate stands at 76.94%, indicating areas in need of focused efforts to improve educational outcomes. While this figure reflects progress in literacy attainment, it also underscores existing challenges and disparities within the state's education system.

(*e*) **Meghalaya (74.43%):** Meghalaya's literacy rate of 74.43% reflects the challenges the state faces in promoting literacy and educational development. While there has been progress, the figure suggests that Meghalaya lags behind the other states in terms of literacy attainment.

86. (A): Assertion (A) implies that governments may opt to replace import duties with sales taxes if their priority shifts from protecting domestic industries to generating revenue. Import duties, also known as tariffs, are taxes imposed on goods imported into a country, primarily to protect domestic industries from foreign competition. However, if governments prioritize revenue collection over protecting local industries, they might find it more advantageous to replace import duties with sales taxes. Sales taxes are levied on goods and services sold within a country, and they offer a broader base for revenue collection compared to import duties. By implementing sales taxes instead of import duties, governments can generate revenue from a wider range of economic activities, including domestic production and consumption.

Reason (R) complements Assertion (A) by highlighting the efficiency of sales taxes as a revenue-raising mechanism. Sales taxes are generally considered to be more efficient than import tariffs for several reasons. First, sales taxes are typically applied uniformly across a wide range of goods and services, ensuring a more equitable distribution of the tax burden among consumers and businesses. In contrast, import duties only apply to specific imported goods, which can create distortions in the market by favoring domestic producers over foreign competitors. Second, sales taxes are easier to administer and collect compared to import duties, as they are integrated into the regular retail sales process. This simplicity reduces administrative costs and compliance burdens for both businesses and government agencies.

87. (A): Statement I: "Friedman's theory of the demand for money is partly Keynesian and partly non-Keynesian." Milton Friedman's theory of the demand for money, often referred to as the "modern quantity theory of money," incorporates elements from both Keynesian and non-Keynesian perspectives. The Keynesian perspective emphasizes the role of income and transactions in determining the demand for money, while the non-Keynesian perspective focuses more on the role of interest rates and inflation expectations. Friedman's theory combines these perspectives by acknowledging the influence of both income and interest rates on the demand for money. Therefore, Statement I accurately describes Friedman's theory as a blend of Keynesian and non-Keynesian elements.

Statement II: "It is non-Keynesian in that Friedman neglects completely Keynes' clarification of the motives for holding money and the corresponding components of demand for money."

This statement highlights a limitation or criticism of Friedman's theory, specifically regarding its treatment of Keynes' insights into the motives for holding money. Keynes identified three motives for holding money: the transactions motive (holding money for everyday transactions), the precautionary motive (holding money for unforeseen expenses), and the speculative motive (holding money to take advantage of expected changes in asset prices). Therefore, Statement II points out that Friedman's theory is non-Keynesian in the sense that it over-looks or simplifies Keynes' comprehensive explanation of the motives for holding money and their impact on the demand for money.

88. (C): Statement I: "Under first-degree price discrimination, a monopolist sells different units of output for different prices, and these prices may differ from person to person." First-degree price discrimination, also known as perfect price discrimination, represents the scenario where a monopolist charges each consumer the maximum price they are willing to pay for each unit of output. In essence, the monopolist extracts the entire consumer surplus from each individual buyer. This pricing strategy involves the monopolist being able to discern the exact willingness to pay of every consumer, tailoring prices accordingly. As a result, prices can indeed vary from person to person under first-degree price discrimination because each buyer is charged their unique maximum price. Therefore, Statement I is true in describing the characteristic nature of first-degree price discrimination.

Statement II: "Under third-degree price discrimination, a monopolist sells different units of output for different prices, but every individual who buys the same amount of the good pays the same price." Third-degree price discrimination involves segmenting the market into distinct groups based on certain identifiable characteristics such as age, location, or income level. The monopolist then charges different prices to each group based on their differing elasticity's of demand. However, within each group, individuals are charged the same price for the same amount of the good or service. It's important to note that while individuals within a specific group pay the same price, this does not necessarily hold true across all groups. Each group may have its own unique pricing structure. Therefore, while Statement II correctly characterizes the pricing behaviour within a group under third-degree price discrimination, it incorrectly suggests that every individual, irrespective of their group, pays the same price. Hence, Statement II is false.

89. (D): Statement I: "The terms of trade of a nation are defined as the ratio of the cost of its export commodity to the price of its import commodity." The terms of trade refer to the ratio of the prices of a country's exports to the prices of its imports, not the cost of its export commodity to the price of its import commodity. When the terms of trade improve, a country can purchase more imports for a given quantity of exports, while a deterioration in terms of trade means a country can buy fewer imports for the same amount of exports. Therefore, the statement is incorrect because it inaccurately defines the terms of trade.

Statement II: "The terms of trade of the trade partner are equal to the inverse of the terms of trade of the other nation." This statement captures the essence of the reciprocal relationship between the terms of trade of two trading partners. When one nation's terms of trade improve, meaning they can purchase more imports with a given quantity of exports, the terms of trade of its trading partner worsen, indicating that they can buy fewer imports with the same quantity of exports. This inverse relationship reflects the dynamics of international trade, where changes in the terms of trade in one country can affect the terms of trade in its trading partners. Nevertheless, the general idea of the inverse relationship between the terms of trade of trading partners holds true. Therefore, the statement accurately describes this relationship.

90. (A): Statement I: "Division of labour is the starting point of Smith's theory of economic growth." Adam Smith, often regarded as the father of economics, indeed emphasized the significance of division of labour in his theory of economic growth. He argued that division of labour leads to specialization, which in turn increases productivity and output. Smith famously illustrated this concept with his example of pin manufacturing, where specialization among workers dramatically increased production efficiency. Thus, Statement I is true.

Statement II: "It is division of labour that results in the greatest improvement in the productive power of labour." This statement aligns with Adam Smith's views. He famously stated that division of labour leads to the greatest improvement in the productive power of labour. By breaking down production processes into specialized tasks and allowing workers to focus on specific skills, division of labour enhances efficiency and productivity. This specialization enables workers to become more proficient in their tasks and leads to overall increases in output. Therefore, Statement II accurately represents Smith's perspective on the importance of division of labour in boosting the productive power of labour. Thus, Statement II is also true.

91. (D): The passage outlines India's fiscal policy response to the Covid crises, which involved a balanced approach aimed at addressing the economic challenges while maintaining fiscal stability. It mentions increasing food and fertilizer subsidies alongside reducing taxes on fuel and certain imported products as key components of this strategy. However, it notably does not mention an increase in taxes on fuel, indicating that such a measure was not part of the fiscal policy response.

92. (C): The passage discusses India's fiscal policy response to the Covid crises, highlighting a strategic approach that included increasing food and fertilizer subsidies as part of the government's measures. Nowhere does it mention any expenditure austerity measures related to these subsidies. In fact, it suggests the opposite - that the government opted for an expansionary fiscal policy by increasing subsidies on essential goods like food and fertilizer.

93. (B): The passage states that the central government incentivized state governments through interest-free loans and enhanced borrowing ceilings to prioritize their spending on capex. This measure aims to encourage states to allocate more funds towards capital projects, which are crucial for infrastructure development and long-term economic growth.

94. (D): The passage mentions that the center's capex steadily increased from a long-term average of 1.7 percent of GDP during the period FY 09 to FY 20. This indicates that, on average, the Union Government's capital expenditure was equivalent to 1.7 percent of the Gross Domestic Product (GDP) during this period.

95. (A): The passage mentions that the government has boosted allocations on infrastructure-intensive sectors such as roads and highways, railways, and housing and urban affairs, which have a bearing on capital expenditure (capex). Therefore, the sector for which allocation for further enhancement of capex is not increased is: Ports and Waterways.

96. (C): Adjusted Net Saving (ANS) is a flow variable. This means that ANS measures changes in saving over time, reflecting the net additions or subtractions to a nation's wealth from one period to another. Unlike stock variables, which represent values at a specific point in time, flow variables capture the movement or changes in quantities over time.

97. (D): The passage outlines the components that are subtracted from ANS, such as air pollution damage, depletion of metals and minerals, and public expenditures on education, but it does not mention loss of biodiversity. While loss of biodiversity is undoubtedly an important consideration for environmental sustainability, the passage does not include it as a specific component in the calculation of ANS.

98. **(B)**: The passage suggests that nations with higher GDP are less likely to obtain negative ANS, indicating that they are generally adding to their wealth and future material well-being. However, it also notes that when natural resource depletion is not used to invest in other assets in the wealth portfolio, countries' gross saving might not be enough to compensate for this depletion, resulting in negative net savings.

99. **(D)**:

(*a*) **"It allows substitution between different forms of capital"**: This statement points out a limitation of ANS, as it allows for substitution between different forms of capital, which may not accurately reflect the sustainability of an economy.

(*b*) **"It is not a comprehensive indicator of per capita wealth"**: While ANS provides insights into changes in overall wealth, it may not provide a comprehensive picture of per capita wealth, which is important for assessing individual well-being within a population.

(*c*) **"It is influenced by the level of GDP of an economy"**: ANS is indeed influenced by the level of GDP of an economy, as it considers factors such as gross saving rates and investments, which are closely tied to GDP levels.

100. **(B)**: The passage suggests that while ANS may not be a superior indicator of sustainability, it can serve as a useful indicator of unsustainability. ANS provides insights into whether a country is adding to its wealth and future material well-being (when positive) or depleting its capital stocks and potentially reducing future well-being (when negative).

Previous Years' Paper (Solved)

National Testing Agency (NTA)

UGC-NET Junior Research Fellowship & Assistant Professor Eligibility Exam

Economics, March-2023

(Online exam held on 02-03-2023)

PAPER-II

1. In case of two goods for which the MRS is zero or infinite, then the nature of goods is:

A. Perfect substitutes
B. Normal goods
C. Perfect compliments
D. Close substitutes

2. Which of the following is not true?

A. Total effect of pricc change on consumption of a good is a combination of income effect and substitution effect
B. For inferior goods, income effect is always larger than substitution effect, in absolute terms.
C. For corner solution $MRS_{xy} \neq \frac{P_x}{P_y}$
D. For a normal good both the income and substitution effect hold

3. The negative network externality in which a consumer wishes to own an exclusive or unique good such as specially designed sports car is:

A. Bandwagon effect
B. Tequila effect
C. Snob effect
D. Pigou effect

4. When each player has chosen his or her optimal strategy given the strategy chosen by other player, the situation is referred to as:

A. Nash Equilibrium
B. Wicksel's Equilibrium
C. Prisoner's dilemma
D. Co-operative Game

5. A firm has the following total cost and demand functions: $C = \frac{1}{3}Q^3 - 7Q^2 + 111Q + 50$, $Q = 100 - P$, then find the profit maximizing level of output (Q^*) and maximum profit of the firm.

A. 50 and 100
B. 111 and 2150
C. 11 and $111\frac{1}{3}$
D. 7 and 84

6. The condition of preferring a certain income to a risky income with same expected value is referred to as:

A. Risk neutral
B. Risk loving
C. Risk averse
D. Risk Premium

7. Which one of the following is not a component of M_1?

A. Currency
B. Traveler's cheque
C. Commercial paper
D. Demand deposits

8. The Keynes's animal spirits are closely associated with:

A. Past investment
B. Current investment
C. Aggregate income
D. Aggregate expenditure

9. In the Mundell-Fleming model, the monetary policy will be more effective when there is:

A. Perfect capital mobility and flexible exchange rate
B. Perfect capital mobility and fixed exchange rate
C. Imperfect capital mobility and flexible exchange rate
D. Imperfect capital mobility and fixed exchange rate

10. If the two events A and B are not independent then which of the following is correct?
A. $P(A \cap B) = P(A) \cdot P(B)$
B. $P(A \cap B) = P(A) \cdot P(B/A)$
C. $P(A \cap B) = P(A) \cdot P(A/B)$
D. $P(A \cap B) = 1 - P(A \cup B)$

11. The chain-weighted index is:
A. The total market value of goods and services produced in each year
B. The percentage growth in real GDP
C. A method for calculating changes in prices that used an average of base year from neighbouring years
D. An Index that measures how the prices of goods and services included in GDP change.

12. If the consumption function passes through the origin and APC = MPC then it must be:
A. Linear without any intercept
B. Non linear without any intercept
C. Linear with a negative intercept on the income axis
D. Linear with a positive intercept on the consumption axis

13. Find the producer's surplus when
$P_d = 3x^2 - 20x + 5$
$P_S = 15 + 9x$ (x is the quantity)
A. 400 B. 350
C. 450 D. 500

14. The demand function for good A is given by $Q_A = 100 - 2P_A + 0.2\ Y + 0.3\ P_B$. Find the income elasticities of demand $P_A = 6$, $Y = 500$, $P_B = 10$.
A. 0.06 B. 0.02
C. 0.52 D. –0.06

15. Find the substitution parameter ρ(rho) of constant elasticity of substitution (CES) production function when the elasticity of substitution (σ) is greater than one:
A. $\rho = 0$ B. $\rho = 1$
C. $-1 < \rho < 0$ D. $0 < \rho < \infty$

16. In logit model, as the odds ratio decreases from 1 to 0, the logit becomes:
A. Negative B. Equal to 0
C. Positive D. Fraction.

17. Given regression model as $Y_i = \alpha_1 + \beta_1 X_i + \beta_2(X_i - X^*) D_i + U_i$ such a model is used to:
A. Deseasonalise a quarterly time series data
B. Seasonally adjust a monthly time series data
C. To conduct chow test for structural break in time series data
D. Test piecewise linear relationship in the data

18. A player tosses two fair coins. He wins ₹ 5 if 2 heads occur, ₹ 2 if 1 head occurs and ₹ 1 if no head occurs. Find his expected gain.
A. ₹ 2 B. ₹ 2.25
C. ₹ 2.75 D. ₹ 2.50

19. A card is thrown from a well shuffled pack of playing cards. Find the probability that it is either a diamond or a king.
A. $\frac{17}{52}$ B. $\frac{16}{52}$
C. $\frac{18}{52}$ D. $\frac{15}{52}$

20. In simultaneous equation models, OLS can be applied directly if:
A. It is a recursive model
B. Order condition is satisfied
C. Rank condition is satisfied
D. Both order and rank conditions are satisfied

21. The Rural Landless Employment guarantee Programme (RLEGP) was launched on:
A. 15th August, 1947
B. 15th August, 1950
C. 15th August, 1983
D. 15th August, 2000

22. The Foreign Trade Policy (2015-2020) was announced on which date?

A. 1 August, 2015
B. 1 April, 2015
C. 30 August, 2015
D. 30 April, 2015

23. Who was the chairman of 14th Finance Commission in India?

A. Dr. Vijay Kelkar
B. Dr. Y.V. Reddy
C. Dr. C. Rangarajan
D. Dr. N.K. Singh

24. Zamindari Tenure was introduced by:

A. Thomas Munro
B. Lord Cornwallis
C. H. Venkatasubbiah
D. G. Myrdal

25. Which of the following is true in case of the non-marketed environmental resources?

A. Non excludable and non-rival in consumption
B. Excludable but not rival in consumption
C. Excludable and rival in consumption
D. Non-excludable but rival in consumption

26. Suppose 'X' places ₹ 8 value on one bread packet and 'Y' places ₹ 6 value on it. If there is no tax on bread, then price of bread packet is ₹ 5, so both X and Y choose to buy one packet each. Now suppose government levies a tax of ₹ 2 per unit, the price of bread rises to ₹ 7. Then the deadweight loss and tax revenue collected respectively are:

A. ₹ 1 and ₹ 2 B. ₹ 2 and ₹ 4
C. ₹ 2 and ₹ 2 D. ₹ 1 and ₹ 4

27. The component which distinguishes primary deficit from fiscal deficit is:

A. Non-debt component of capital receipt
B. Interest payment
C. Debt component of capital receipt
D. Revenue deficit

28. Which of the following is not an assumption or conclusion of the inflation targeting approach?

A. Interest rate is the major instrument of monetary policy
B. Higher interest rate controls aggregate demand
C. Inflation is a supply side phenomenon
D. Quantity of money supply is not very effective in controlling inflation

29. In context of monetary policy, the sacrifice ratio refers to the ______

A. Interest cost arising because of crowding out effect
B. Loss of real value of money at the face of increasing inflation
C. Output cost of reducing inflation
D. Labour cost raising minimum wage

30. Which of the following formula is used to calculate the yield of treasury bills (T-bills) where

Y = Discounted yield
P = Price
D = Days to maturity

A. $Y = \dfrac{P \times 365 \times 100}{P \times D}$

B. $Y = \dfrac{D \times 365 \times 100}{P \times D}$

C. $Y = \dfrac{(100 - P) \times 365 \times 100}{P \times D}$

D. $Y = \dfrac{(100 - D) \times 365 \times 100}{P \times D}$

31. The faster growth and more equal distribution of income can be examined simultaneously by:

A. Gini ratio
B. Poverty-weighted growth rate
C. Kuznet curve
D. None of the above

32. Marx refers to the concept of organic composition of capital. Which one of the following ratios is used for this (where C is constant capital, V is variable capital and S is surplus value)?

A. $\frac{C}{V+S}$ B. $\frac{C}{V}$

C. $\frac{C}{(C+V)}$ D. $\frac{(C+V)}{V}$

33. Which of the following is not true in the case of externality?
 A. It is related to human interactions
 B. It is tied to consumer sovereignty
 C. It is based on higher order judgements of right and wrong
 D. It is an amoral concept

34. Compensating variation for a price decrease of a good can be interpreted as:
 A. Willingness to pay
 B. Willingness to accept
 C. Both (A) and (B)
 D. None

35. Which of the following is an example of depreciation of natural capital?
 A. Restoring rivers rendered unusable due to dumping of industrial effluents
 B. Representation of areas that have been cleared for years of open-cut mining
 C. Pollution-control activities by the public sector such as municipal waste treatment
 D. Detoxifying unusable soils for urban or rural development

36. Equivalent variation for a price increase of a good can be interpreted as:
 A. Willingness to pay
 B. Willingness to accept
 C. Both (A) and (B)
 D. None

37. According to the specific factors model, which of the following is correct?
 A. Trade benefits the factor specific to the export sector of each country but hurts the factor specific to the import-competing sectors with ambiguous effects on mobile factors
 B. Trade hurts the factor specific to the export sector of each country and also hurts the factor specific to the import-competing sectors, with ambiguous effects on mobile factors
 C. Trade benefits the factor specific to the import sector of each country but hurts the factor specific to the export-competing sectors, with ambiguous effects on mobile factors
 D. Trade benefits the factor specific to the export sector as well as import-competing sector of each country, with ambiguous effects on mobile factors.

38. What does 'immiserising growth' argued?
 A. Export-biased growth by poor nations would worsen their terms of trade so much that they would be worse off than if they had not grown at all
 B. Export-biased growth by rich nations would worsen their terms of trade so much that they would be worse off than if they had not grown at all
 C. Import-biased growth by poor nations would worsen their terms of trade so much that they would be worse off than if they had not grown at all
 D. Import-biased growth by Rich nations would worsen their terms of trade so much that they would be worsen off than if had not grown at all

39. Which of the following postulates the Gravity Model correctly?
 A. The smaller and the closer the two countries are, the smaller the volume of trade between them is expected to be
 B. The larger and the closer the two countries are, the larger the volume of trade between them is expected to be
 C. The larger and the closer the two countries are, the smaller the volume of trade between them is expected to be
 D. The smaller and farther the two countries are, the larger the volume of trade between them is expected to be

40. If the nominal tariff rate (t) on consumers of the final commodity is 10 per cent, the ratio of the cost of the imported input to the price of the final commodity in the absence of tariffs (ai) is = 0.8, and the nominal tariff rate

on the imported input (ti) = 0, then find the rate of effective protection.

A. 5% B. 8%

C. 50% D. 10%

41. Which of the followings are true for ridge lines?

(*a*) they separate the relevant from the irrelevant portions of the isoquants

(*b*) along the ridge lines, the slope of the isoquants is either zero or infinite

(*c*) The relevant segment of the isoquants enclosed pertains to the stage II of production for labour and capital

(*d*) Producers will never want to operate outside the region enclosed within the ridge lines

(*e*) The marginal product of both inputs-labour and capital is positive but declines for the portion of the isoquents within the ridge lines.

Choose the correct answer from the options given below:

A. (*a*), (*c*) and (*d*) only

B. (*b*), (*c*) and (*e*) only

C. (*a*), (*c*), (*d*) and (*e*) only

D. (*a*), (*b*), (*c*), (*d*) and (*e*)

42. Which of the followings are true about a fair game or fair bet?

(*a*) The entry of a fair bet is zero

(*b*) The person who accepts fair bet is said to be risk lover

(*c*) Expected value of income from the bet is equal to the same amount of income with certainty

(*d*) The person who refuses a fair bet is said to be risk neutral

(*e*) The person who refuses a fair bet is said to be risk averse.

Choose the correct answer from the options given below:

A. (*a*) and (*c*) only B. (*b*) and (*e*) only

C. (*c*) and (*d*) only D. (*c*) and (*e*) only

43. According to the modern theory of rent:

(*a*) All the factors may earn rent

(*b*) Rent can only be earned in long-run

(*c*) Transfer earning of an unused factor is zero

(*d*) Only land can earn rent

(*e*) Entire earning of an unused factor is economic rent

Choose the correct answer from the options given below:

A. (*a*), (*b*) and (*c*) only

B. (*a*), (*c*) and (*e*) only

C. (*b*), (*c*) and (*e*) only

D. (*a*), (*c*) and (*d*) only

44. Rational expectations views include:

(*a*) The market clearing rational expectations do not approach to the Phillips curve

(*b*) Rational expectation as a theory of expectations

(*c*) An emphasis on the credibility of policy makers

(*d*) A preference for policy making rules rather than discretion

(*e*) Generally insists that markets do not clear rapidly.

Choose the most appropriate answer from the options given below:

A. (*b*), (*c*) and (*d*) only

B. (*a*) and (*e*) only

C. (*a*), (*b*), (*c*), (*d*) and (*e*)

D. (*a*), (*d*) and (*e*) only

45. In the budget at glance, which of the following items are included?

(*a*) budget estimate of the current year

(*b*) Revised estimate of the current year

(*c*) Actuals of the current year

(*d*) Actuals for the preceding year

(*e*) Budget estimate for the forthcoming year

Choose the most appropriate answer from the options given below:

A. (*a*) and (*d*) only

B. (*a*), (*b*), (*d*) and (*e*) only

C. (*a*), (*b*) and (*c*) only

D. (*c*) and (*d*) only

46. How do adverse technology shocks affect labour demand and supply?

(*a*) Decrease the demand for labour

(*b*) Both real wage and employment fall

(*c*) Real wage increases and employment falls
(*d*) Real wage falls and employment increases
(*e*) Adverse effect on market equilibrium

Choose the correct answer from the options given below:
A. (*a*), (*c*) and (*d*) only
B. (*b*), (*d*) and (*e*) only
C. (*a*), (*b*), (*c*) and (*d*) only
D. (*a*), (*b*) and (*e*) only

47. Which of the followings are correct in case of Poisson distribution?
(*a*) '*n*' the number of trials is indefinitely large i.e., $n \to \infty$
(*b*) '*p*', the constant probability of success for each trial is indefinitely large
(*c*) $np = m$ is finite
(*d*) $\mu_3 = m + 2$
(*e*) $\mu_4 = m + 3m^2$

Choose the correct answer from the options given below:
A. (*a*), (*c*) and (*d*) only
B. (*a*), (*c*) and (*e*) only
C. (*b*), (*c*) and (*e*) only
D. (*b*), (*c*) and (*d*) only

48. Which of the followings are correct conclusions without error in case of testing of Hypothesis?
(*a*) Reject null hypothesis (H_o), when it is true
(*b*) Accept H_o, when it is true
(*c*) Accept H_o, when Alternate hypothesis (H_1) is true.
(*d*) Reject H_o when H_1 is true
(*e*) Accept H_o when H_1 is false

Choose the correct answer from the options given below:
A. (*a*), (*b*) and (*d*) only
B. (*b*), (*d*) and (*e*) only
C. (*b*), (*c*) and (*e*) only
D. (*a*), (*c*) and (*e*) only

49. Which of the followings are correct for OLS estimation in the presence of Heteroscedasticity?
(*a*) The estimated coefficients are linear
(*b*) The estimated coefficients are unbiased
(*c*) The estimated coefficients are biased
(*d*) The estimated coefficients are consistent
(*e*) The estimated coefficients are efficient

Choose the correct answer from the options given below:
A. (*a*), (*c*) and (*d*) only
B. (*a*), (*b*) and (*d*) only
C. (*a*), (*c*) and (*e*) only
D. (*a*), (*c*) and (*d*) only

50. Which of the followings satisfy the assumptions of the classical linear regression model?
(*a*) Zero mean value of disturbance Ui
(*b*) The explanatory variables and the error terms are not independent
(*c*) Homoscedasticity or constant variance of Ui
(*d*) No auto correlation between the disturbances
(*e*) There is more than one exact linear relationship between explanatory variables

Choose the most appropriate answer from the options given below:
A. (*a*), (*b*), (*c*) and (*d*) only
B. (*a*), (*c*), (*d*) and (*e*) only
C. (*a*), (*c*) and (*d*) only
D. (*c*), (*d*) and (*e*) only

51. If A, B and C are three different non-empty sets, then find which of the following are correct in laws of set operations?
(*a*) $(A')' = A$
(*b*) $(A \cup B) = 1 - (A \cap B)$
(*c*) $A \cup (B \cup C) = (A \cup B) \cup C$
(*d*) $A \cup (B \cap C) = (A \cap B) \cup (A \cap C)$
(*e*) $A - B = A \cap B'$

Choose the correct answer from the options given below:
A. (*a*), (*c*) and (*d*) only
B. (*a*), (*c*) and (*e*) only
C. (*a*), (*b*) and (*c*) only
D. (*c*), (*d*) and (*e*) only

52. In multiple regression model, a hypothesis such as $H_0 : \beta_2 = \beta_3 = 0$ can be tested using:
A. *t*-test
B. Chi-square test
C. ANOVA test
D. F-test

53. Which of the following are the indicators of Human Development Index?

(*a*) Real GDP per capita

(*b*) Adult literacy rate combined with enrolment ratio

(*c*) Life expectancy at birth

(*d*) Malnutrition under five

(*e*) IMR under five

Choose the correct answer from the options given below:

A. (*a*), (*b*) and (*e*) only

B. (*b*), (*c*) and (*d*) only

C. (*a*), (*b*) and (*c*) only

D. (*c*), (*d*) and (*e*) only

54. Which of the following are correct for the Finance Commission?

(*a*) It is constituted under Article 380 of the Constitution

(*b*) It is a statutory body

(*c*) It is constituted under Article 280 of the Constitution

(*d*) Prof. K.C. Pant was Chairman of 10th Finance Commission

(*e*) Dr. Vijay Kelkar was Chairman of 14th Finance Commission

Choose the most appropriate answer from the options given below:

A. (*b*), (*c*) and (*d*) only

B. (*a*), (*b*) and (*d*) only

C. (*c*), (*d*) and (*e*) only

D. (*a*), (*c*) and (*e*) only

55. Which of the following are true?

(*a*) Product taxes will raise prices less under monopoly than under competition

(*b*) A tax on capital income tends to be progressive, whereas tax on wage income tends to be regressive

(*c*) The burden of tax will be distributed between sellers and buyers in the ratio of elasticity of demand to that of supply

(*d*) A unit tax enters through a parallel downward shift in the supply schedule

(*e*) Imposition of tax raises price and quantity

Choose the most appropriate answer from the options given below:

A. (*a*) and (*b*) only

B. (*a*), (*b*) and (*c*) only

C. (*a*), (*b*), (*c*) and (*d*) only

D. (*a*), (*b*), (*c*) and (*e*) only

56. Which of the following are correct?

(*a*) A competitive market can secure efficient resource use in the provision of private goods, but market failure occurs in that of social goods

(*b*) Efficient provision of social goods involves horizontal rather than vertical addition of Individual pseudo-demand schedules

(*c*) To seek efficient provision of social goods, a political process of budget determination is needed

(*d*) Corrective action may be needed when consumer choice is based on false advertising

(*e*) There are mixed cases between the extremes of purely private and purely social goods.

Choose the most appropriate answer from the options given below:

A. (*a*), (*b*) and (*c*) only

B. (*a*), (*b*) and (*e*) only

C. (*a*), (*b*), (*c*) and (*d*) only

D. (*a*), (*c*), (*d*) and (*e*) only

57. Which of the following monetary measure is used to control inflation?

(*a*) The Central Bank purchases government securities from Commercial Banks

(*b*) The Central Bank sells the government securities to the Commercial Banks

(*c*) The bank rate may be raised

(*d*) The bank rate may be reduced

(*e*) Raising of cash reserve ratio.

Choose the correct answer from the options given below:

A. (*a*), (*c*) and (*e*) only

B. (*b*), (*c*) and (*e*) only

C. (*u*), (*d*) and (*e*) only

D. (*a*) and (*d*) only

58. Which of the followings are correct in case of money market in India?

(*a*) Commercial bill is a short-term instrument with high risk

(*b*) Treasury bill is an instrument of short-term borrowing by the government with absence of default risk

(*c*) RBI uses refinance to relieve liquidity shortages in the system

(*d*) The RBI has switched over from daily fixed rate repos auction system to discriminatory price auction repos.

(*e*) SLR enables to impose secondary and supplementary reserve requirements on the banking system

Choose the correct answer from the options given below:

A. (*a*), (*b*) and (*d*) only
B. (*b*), (*c*) and (*d*) only
C. (*b*), (*c*) and (*e*) only
D. (*c*), (*d*) and (*e*) only

59. The causes and consequences of poverty include:

(*a*) Unemployment
(*b*) Low wages
(*c*) Poor health
(*d*) Low Population Growth
(*e*) Low Literacy rates

Choose the most appropriate answer from the options given below:

A. (*a*) and (*c*) only
B. (*b*), (*d*) and (*e*) only
C. (*b*), (*c*), (*d*) and (*e*) only
D. (*a*), (*b*), (*c*) and (*e*) only

60. Measurement of income inequality is done by:

(*a*) Gini coefficient (*b*) Lorenz curve
(*c*) Palma Ratio (*d*) Deprivation ratio
(*e*) Phillips Curve

Choose the correct answer from the options given below:

A. (*b*) and (*e*) only
B. (*a*) and (*b*) only
C. (*a*), (*b*) and (*c*) only
D. (*c*) and (*a*) only

61. Choose the correct statement for Schumpeter's theory of development.

(*a*) Development is financed by real saving
(*b*) Capitalism keeps its character intact overtime
(*c*) Development is evolutionary
(*d*) Development creates inflation
(*e*) Unlimited Supply of labour

Choose the correct answer from the options given below:

A. (*a*) and (*b*) only
B. (*c*) and (*d*) only
C. (*a*), (*b*), (*c*) and (*d*) only
D. None of the above

62. Which of the following are the features of Environmental Economics as a field of study?

(*a*) It has its roots in the theory of externalities and public goods.
(*b*) It is based on neoclassical welfare theory
(*c*) It envisions human economy as a sub-system of the biosphere
(*d*) It engages with the law of transformations of matter and energy
(*e*) It focuses on finding the most efficient ways to reducing environmental damages.

Choose the correct answer from the options given below:

A. (*a*), (*b*) and (*c*) only
B. (*b*), (*c*) and (*d*) only
C. (*a*), (*b*) and (*e*) only
D. (*c*), (*d*) and (*e*) only

63. Which of the following are the essential features of weak sustainability?

(*a*) It considers human-made capital and natural capital as close substitutes.
(*b*) It puts emphasis on the initial size of an economy since the size of the initial capital stock is considered relevant.
(*c*) It requires from each generation to ensure that their actions do not compromise the productive capacity of the generations to follow

(*d*) the composition of the capital stock of an economy does not hold great significance

(*e*) It renders natural capital as an absolute necessity for sustaining net national income over an indefinite period.

Choose the most appropriate answer from the options given below:

A. (*a*), (*c*) and (*d*) only

B. (*a*), (*b*) and (*c*) only

C. (*c*), (*d*) and (*e*) only

D. (*a*), (*b*) and (*e*) only

64. Which of the following are part of non-tariff barriers?

(*a*) Import quotas

(*b*) Voluntary export restraint

(*c*) Export subsidy

(*d*) Compound tariff

(*e*) Ad Valorem tariff

Choose the correct answer from the options given below:

A. (*a*), (*b*) and (*d*) only

B. (*a*), (*b*) and (*e*) only

C. (*a*), (*b*) and (*c*) only

D. (*b*), (*c*) and (*d*) only

65. Marshall-Lerner condition states that:

(*a*) Devaluation will improve the country's balance of payments if the sum of price elasticities of demand for exports and imports in absolute terms is greater than one.

(*b*) Devaluation will increase the balance of payments deficit if the sum of the price elasticities of demand for exports and imports is less than one.

(*c*) Devaluation will have no effect on the balance of payment situation if the sum of the price elasticises of demand for exports and imports is equal to one

(*d*) In no case, devaluation can improve the balance of payment disequilibrium if either the price elasticities of demand for export or that of import is zero

(*e*) Marshall-Lerner condition has no relation with BOP situation.

Choose the correct answer from the options given below:

A. (*a*), (*b*) and (*e*) only

B. (*b*), (*c*) and (*d*) only

C. (*c*), (*d*) and (*a*) only

D. (*a*), (*b*) and (*c*) only

66. Match List-I with List-II:

	List-I		*List-II*
(*a*)	One firm sets its output before other firms do	(*i*)	Cournot Model
(*b*)	Each firm correctly assumes how much its competitor will produce and sets its own production level	(*ii*)	Betrand Model
(*c*)	Firms are reluctant to change price even if costs or demand change	(*iii*)	Stacketberg Model
(*d*)	Each firm treats the price of its competitors as fixed and all firms decide simultaneously what price to change	(*iv*)	Sweezy Model

Choose the correct answer from the options given below:

	(*a*)	(*b*)	(*c*)	(*d*)
A.	(*iii*)	(*ii*)	(*iv*)	(*i*)
B.	(*ii*)	(*iii*)	(*iv*)	(*i*)
C.	(*iii*)	(*i*)	(*iv*)	(*ii*)
D.	(*ii*)	(*iv*)	(*iii*)	(*i*)

67. Match List-I with List-II:

	List-I		*List-II*
(*a*)	Robert Solow	(*i*)	Neoclassical growth theory
(*b*)	Paul Romer and Robert Lucas	(*ii*)	Unemployment – Output
(*c*)	Paul Samuelson	(*iii*)	Endogenous growth theory
(*d*)	Okun	(*iv*)	Foundation of Economic growth

Choose the correct answer from the options given below:

	(*a*)	(*b*)	(*c*)	(*d*)
A.	(*ii*)	(*iii*)	(*i*)	(*iv*)
B.	(*i*)	(*ii*)	(*iii*)	(*iv*)
C.	(*i*)	(*iii*)	(*iv*)	(*ii*)
D.	(*iii*)	(*i*)	(*ii*)	(*iv*)

68. Match List-I with List-II:

List-I	List-II
(*a*) Detecting Serial Correlation	(*i*) Goldfeld – Quandt test
(*b*) Detection of Heteroscadasticity	(*ii*) The Run's test
(*c*) Detection of Multicollinearity	(*iii*) Ramsay's RESET test
(*d*) Test of specification error	(*iv*) Condition Index

Choose the correct answer from the options given below:

	(*a*)	(*b*)	(*c*)	(*d*)
A.	(*iii*)	(*i*)	(*iv*)	(*ii*)
B.	(*ii*)	(*iv*)	(*i*)	(*iii*)
C.	(*ii*)	(*i*)	(*iv*)	(*iii*)
D.	(*iv*)	(*i*)	(*iii*)	(*ii*)

69. Match List-I with List-II:

List-I | **List-II**

(*a*) Linear function (*i*)

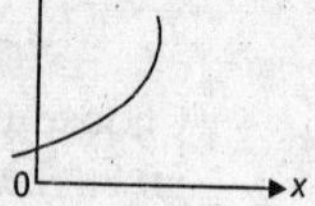

(*b*) Exponential function (*ii*)

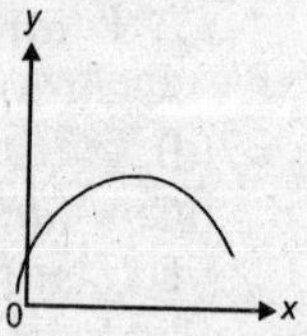

(*c*) Quadratic function (*iii*)

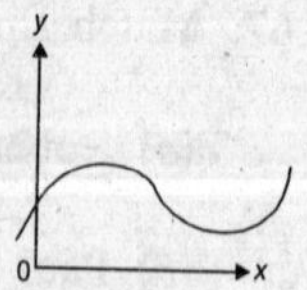

(*d*) Cubic function (*iv*)

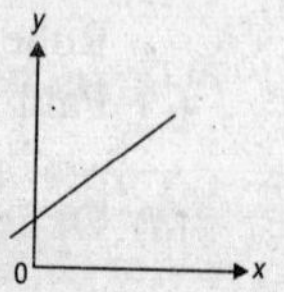

Choose the correct answer from the options given below:

	(*a*)	(*b*)	(*c*)	(*d*)
A.	(*iv*)	(*ii*)	(*i*)	(*iii*)
B.	(*i*)	(*iv*)	(*iii*)	(*ii*)
C.	(*iv*)	(*i*)	(*ii*)	(*iii*)
D.	(*iv*)	(*iii*)	(*ii*)	(*i*)

70. Match List-I with List-II:

List-I	List-II
(*a*) Metzler Paradox	(*i*) Violation of Stolper-Samuelson theorem
(*b*) Beachhead Effect	(*ii*) Exporters may be reluctant to increase prices by the full amount of the dollar depreciation
(*c*) Dutch disease	(*iii*) Loss of relative competitiveness in its traditional industrial sector
(*d*) J Curve	(*iv*) Nation's trade balance may actually worsen soon after devaluation or depreciation

Choose the correct answer from the options given below:

	(*a*)	(*b*)	(*c*)	(*d*)
A.	(*ii*)	(*iii*)	(*iv*)	(*i*)
B.	(*iii*)	(*iv*)	(*ii*)	(*i*)
C.	(*i*)	(*ii*)	(*iii*)	(*iv*)
D.	(*iv*)	(*iii*)	(*ii*)	(*i*)

71. Match List-I with List-II:

List-I	List-II
(*a*) Principal agent problem	(*i*) Use of resources are more than desirable
(*b*) Moral Hazard problem	(*ii*) One's actions are unobserved but it can affect the magnitude of payment
(*c*) Tragedy of commons	(*iii*) An individual pursue his/her own goal rather than the goal of the employer
(*d*) Problem of Lemons	(*iv*) Sellers have better information about the product quality than buyers.

Choose the correct answer from the options given below:

	(*a*)	(*b*)	(*c*)	(*d*)
A.	(*iii*)	(*ii*)	(*i*)	(*iv*)
B.	(*iii*)	(*ii*)	(*iv*)	(*i*)
C.	(*iv*)	(*iii*)	(*i*)	(*ii*)
D.	(*i*)	(*ii*)	(*iv*)	(*iii*)

72. Match List-I with List-II:

List-I	List-II
(*a*) Launch of S&P CNX Nifty	(*i*) July 1995
(*b*) Establishment of Investor Protection Fund in NSE	(*ii*) May 1998
(*c*) Launch of NSE's website: www. nseindia.com	(*iii*) April 1996
(*d*) NSE recognized as a stock exchange	(*iv*) April 1993

Choose the correct answer from the options given below:

	(*a*)	(*b*)	(*c*)	(*d*)
A.	(*iii*)	(*ii*)	(*i*)	(*iv*)
B.	(*iii*)	(*i*)	(*ii*)	(*iv*)
C.	(*ii*)	(*iv*)	(*iii*)	(*i*)
D.	(*iii*)	(*ii*)	(*iv*)	(*i*)

73. Match List-I with List-II:

List-I	List-II
(*a*) Karl Marx	(*i*) Division of Labour
(*b*) Adam Smith	(*ii*) Big Push Theory
(*c*) R. Rodan	(*iii*) Traditional Society
(*d*) W.W. Rostow	(*iv*) Reserve army

Choose the correct answer from the options given below:

	(*a*)	(*b*)	(*c*)	(*d*)
A.	(*iii*)	(*ii*)	(*i*)	(*iv*)
B.	(*iv*)	(*i*)	(*iii*)	(*ii*)
C.	(*i*)	(*iii*)	(*iv*)	(*ii*)
D.	(*iv*)	(*i*)	(*ii*)	(*iii*)

74. Match List-I with List-II:

List-I (States)	List-II (2011 Population (in thousands))
(*a*) Rajasthan	(*i*) 91,276
(*b*) Tamil Nadu	(*ii*) 68,548
(*c*) West Bengal	(*iii*) 72,627
(*d*) Madhya Pradesh	(*iv*) 72,147

Choose the correct answer from the options given below:

	(*a*)	(*b*)	(*c*)	(*d*)
A.	(*ii*)	(*iv*)	(*i*)	(*iii*)
B.	(*iv*)	(*ii*)	(*i*)	(*iii*)
C.	(*ii*)	(*i*)	(*iv*)	(*iii*)
D.	(*iii*)	(*i*)	(*iv*)	(*ii*)

75. Match List-I with List-II:

List-I (Organization)	List-II (Year of Establishment)
(*a*) NABARD	(*i*) 1964
(*b*) IFCI	(*ii*) 1955
(*c*) IDBI	(*iii*) 1948
(*d*) ICICI	(*iv*) 1982

Choose the correct answer from the options given below:

	(*a*)	(*b*)	(*c*)	(*d*)
A.	(*i*)	(*iv*)	(*iii*)	(*ii*)
B.	(*ii*)	(*i*)	(*iv*)	(*iii*)
C.	(*iv*)	(*iii*)	(*i*)	(*ii*)
D.	(*iii*)	(*ii*)	(*i*)	(*iv*)

76. According to the IMF's World Economic Outlook report, arrange the estimated real GDP Growth rate (YOY) of the following countries for the year 2021 in descending order.

(*a*) USA (*b*) Germany
(*c*) United Kingdom (*d*) China
(*e*) India

Choose the correct answer from the options given below:

A. (*d*), (*e*), (*c*), (*b*), (*a*)
B. (*e*), (*d*), (*c*), (*a*), (*b*)
C. (*e*), (*c*), (*d*), (*a*), (*b*)
D. (*d*), (*e*), (*b*), (*c*), (*a*)

77. Arrange the Nobel laureates in Economics as per their year of receiving award in descending order.

(*a*) Amartya Sen
(*b*) Paul Krugman
(*c*) James Tobin
(*d*) Friedrich Hayek
(*e*) Milton Friedman

Choose the correct answer from the options given below:

A. (*a*), (*b*), (*d*), (*c*), (*e*)
B. (*e*), (*c*), (*a*), (*b*), (*d*)
C. (*a*), (*c*), (*e*), (*d*), (*b*)
D. (*b*), (*a*), (*c*), (*e*), (*d*)

78. Arrange the following in descending order on the basis of year of starting the scheme:

(*a*) Jal Jeevan Mission

(*b*) Swachh Bharat Mission (Gramin)

(*c*) Pradhan Mantri Awas Yojana (Gramin)

(*d*) Pradhan Mantri Sadak Yojana (Gramin)

(*e*) Pradhan Mantri Koushal Vikash Yojana

Choose the correct answer from the options given below:

A. (*b*), (*c*), (*e*), (*d*), (*a*)

B. (*c*), (*a*), (*d*), (*b*), (*e*)

C. (*b*), (*e*), (*c*), (*a*), (*d*)

D. (*c*), (*d*), (*b*), (*e*), (*a*)

79. Arrange the followings in ascending order on the basis of Fund Allocation (Budget 2022-23):

(*a*) Ministry of Railways

(*b*) Ministry of Defence

(*c*) Ministry of Agriculture and Farmers Welfare

(*d*) Ministry of Road Transport and Highways

(*e*) Ministry of Rural Development

Choose the correct answer from the options given below:

A. (*a*), (*c*), (*d*), (*b*), (*e*)

B. (*e*), (*b*), (*c*), (*d*), (*a*)

C. (*c*), (*e*), (*a*), (*d*), (*b*)

D. (*b*), (*c*), (*d*), (*e*), (*a*)

80. Arrange the following sources of revenue as per their share of contribution to total revenue in Union Budget 2022-23 in descending order.

(*a*) Custom Duty

(*b*) Income Tax

(*c*) GST

(*d*) Union Excise Duty

(*e*) Non debt capital receipts

Choose the correct answer from the options given below:

A. (*e*), (*b*), (*c*), (*d*), (*a*)

B. (*e*), (*c*), (*b*), (*d*), (*a*)

C. (*c*), (*b*), (*d*), (*a*), (*e*)

D. (*c*), (*b*), (*a*), (*d*), (*e*)

81. According to CMIE data (September 2022), arrange the states in descending order based on unemployment rate:

(*a*) Haryana (*b*) Rajasthan

(*c*) Jammu Kashmir (*d*) Jharkhand

(*e*) Tripura

Choose the correct answer from the options given below:

A. (*a*), (*c*), (*d*), (*e*), (*b*)

B. (*b*), (*c*), (*a*), (*d*), (*e*)

C. (*a*), (*b*), (*c*), (*d*), (*e*)

D. (*b*), (*c*), (*a*), (*e*), (*d*)

82. Arrange the states in ascending order based on population who are multidimensionally poor as per NITI Aayog Report 2021.

(*a*) Punjab (*b*) Kerala

(*c*) Sikkim (*d*) Goa

(*e*) Tamil Nadu

Choose the correct answer from the options given below:

A. (*b*), (*d*), (*c*), (*e*), (*a*)

B. (*d*), (*e*), (*b*), (*c*), (*a*)

C. (*a*), (*e*), (*d*), (*b*), (*c*)

D. (*c*), (*b*), (*a*), (*d*), (*e*)

83. Arrange the following policy rate (as on 31-12-2022) of the RBI in the descending order of their magnitude.

(*a*) Repo rate (*b*) Bank rate

(*c*) CRR (*d*) SLR

(*e*) Reserve Repo Rate

Choose the correct answer from the options given below:

A. (*a*), (*b*), (*d*), (*c*), (*e*)

B. (*d*), (*a*), (*b*), (*c*), (*e*)

C. (*b*), (*d*), (*a*), (*e*), (*c*)

D. (*d*), (*b*), (*a*), (*c*), (*e*)

84. Arrange the following chronologically in order to their year of first occurrence starting from oldest:

(*a*) Liquidity Preference Theory

(*b*) Multiplier by R.F. Kahn

(*c*) Division of Labour, Adam Smith

(*d*) Quantity theory of Money, Fisher

(*e*) Great Depression

Choose the correct answer from the options given below:

A. (*c*), (*e*), (*b*), (*a*), (*d*)
B. (*e*), (*d*), (*c*), (*b*), (*a*)
C. (*b*), (*c*), (*d*), (*e*), (*a*)
D. (*b*), (*a*), (*d*), (*c*), (*e*)

85. Arrange the following organizations as per their years of establishment starting from the oldest.

(*a*) WTO (*b*) ADB
(*c*) UNCTAD (*d*) World Bank
(*e*) WIPO

Choose the correct answer from the options given below:

A. (*d*), (*c*), (*b*), (*e*), (*a*)
B. (*d*), (*b*), (*c*), (*e*), (*a*)
C. (*d*), (*b*), (*c*), (*a*), (*e*)
D. (*d*), (*b*), (*a*), (*c*), (*e*)

86. Given below are two statements: One is labelled as Assertion (A) and the other is labelled as Reason (R).

Assertion (A): A form of market failure results when products of different qualities are sold at a single price.

Reason (R): A buyer and a seller possess different information about the product transacted.

In the light of the above statements, choose the most appropriate answer from the options given below:

A. Both (A) and (R) are true and (R) is the correct explanation of (A)
B. Both (A) and (R) are true, but (R) is not the correct explanation of (A)
C. (A) is true, but (R) is false
D. (A) is false, but (R) is true

87. Given below are two statements:

Statement I: When the level of investment is itself determined within the system then the effectiveness of monetary policy is enhanced by an elastic investment and inelastic liquidity preference schedule, whereas the opposite holds for the effectiveness of fiscal policy.

Statement II: Monetary policy, by accommodating fiscal policy may forestall the crowding out effect.

In the light of the above statements, choose the correct answer from the options given below:

A. Both Statement I and Statement II are true
B. Both Statement I and Statement II are false
C. Statement I is true, but Statement II is false
D. Statement I is false, but Statement II is true

88. Given below are two statements:

Statement I: Capital deepening is the process by which capital grows at a faster rate than labour and the capital labour ratio rises.

Statement II: The growth of output per worker is result of technological change which decreases output per worker for a given capital/labour ratio.

In the light of the above statements, choose the most appropriate answer from the options given below:

A. Both Statement I and Statement II are correct
B. Both Statement I and Statement II are incorrect
C. Statement I is correct, but Statement II is incorrect
D. Statement I is incorrect, but Statement II is correct

89. Given below are two statements:

Statement I: Countries always want to have foreign markets open for their exporters. But if a country limits access to its own market, foreign countries may take action to limit access to their own market.

Statement II: Trade agreement can help lower barrier to international commerce, but countries still have to believe that other countries are "playing fair".

In the light of the above statements, choose the correct answer from the options given below:

A. Both Statement I and Statement II are true
B. Both Statement I and Statement II are false

C. Statement I is true, but Statement II is false
D. Statement I is false, but Statement II is true

90. Given below are two statements:

Statement I: The IS curve is negatively sloped because an increase in the interest rate reduces planned investment spending and therefore reduces the equilibrium level of income.

Statement II: The smaller the multiplier and the less sensitive investment spending is to changes in the interest rate, the steeper is the IS curve.

In the light of the above statements, choose the correct answer from the options given below:

A. Both Statement I and Statement II are correct
B. Both Statement I and Statement II are incorrect
C. Statement I is correct, but Statement II is incorrect
D. Statement I is incorrect, but Statement II is correct

Directions (Qs. No. 91-95): *Read the following passage and answer the questions.*

The Nobel Prize in Economics in 2022 has been awarded to Ben S. Bernanke, Douglas, W. Diamond and Philip H Dybvig "for research on banks and financial crises". One of the important findings in their research is why avoiding bank collapses is vital. Saving must be channelled to investments for the functioning and growth of any economy. But there arises a conflict – while the savers want instant access to their money for unexpected outlays, the borrowers need to know they will not be while the savers want instant access to their money for unexpected outlays, the borrowers need to know they will not be forced to repay their loans prematurely. Diamond and Dybvig, show how banks offer an optimal solution to this problem. Banks may act as intermediaries, who accept deposits from savers and allow access to their money, when they wish and also offer long term loans to borrowers. But the analysis of these authors also shows banks are vulnerable to rumours and they may lead to their imminent collapse, when a large number of savers simultaneously, run to a bank to withdraw their money- a bank ran occurs and the bank collapses, such dangerous dynamics can be prevented through the government by providing deposit insurance and acting as a leader of last resort to banks. Dimond demonstrated another societally important function by a bank. Banks as intermediaries between savers and borrowers, are in a better position to assess a borrower's creditworthiness and ensure that loans are used for good investments. "The laureates insights have improved our ability to avoid both serious crises and expensive bailouts."

91. What conflict do the bankers face while channelizing saving into investment?

A. While the borrowers want instant closing of the loan, the savers wants systematic withdrawals.
B. While the savers want instant access to their money, the borrowers want to repay their loans, only when it matures.
C. While the savers want instant closing of the loan, the borrowers demand more loan than their credit worthiness.
D. Both the savers and borrowers want to close the loan immediately.

92. What solution does the Diamond and Dybvig's theory offer to the conflict faced by the bankers while channelizing savings into investments?

A. Banks assure instant access to money to the savers and terminate long term project of borrowers
B. Banks assure long-term finance to borrowers and terminate the savers' accounts
C. Banks act as intermediaries that accept deposits from savers and allow them access to their money when they wish, while also offering long term loans to borrowers
D. All the above options were offered by Diamond and Dybvig's theory

93. According to the laureates, what leads to imminent collapse of banks?

A. Fraudulent behaviour of the borrowers

B. Increasing competition in the banking sector

C. When a large number of savers simultaneously withdraw their money

D. When a large number of borrowers simultaneously borrow money from the bank

94. What do the laureates suggest to prevent rumours-led bank collapses?

A. Reduce lending

B. Increase lending

C. Collaboration with other banks

D. Government should provide deposit insurance and act as lender of last resort.

95. According to Diamond, how do banks ensure that loans are used for good investments?

A. Since banks act as intermediaries between savers and borrowers, they have better idea about the creditworthiness of the borrowers and hence can ensure loans are used for good investments

B. Since banks want to maximize profits, it can ensure loans are used for good investments

C. Since bank want to benefit their customers, they can ensure that loans are used for good investment

D. Banks do not have enough information to ensure loans are used for good investment

Directions (Qs. No. 96-100): *Read the following passage and answer the questions.*

India's Presidency of the Group Twenty (G-20) is a matter of great pride for all Indians. The G-20 is an intergovernmental forum consisting of 19 countries such as Argentina, Australia, Brazil, Canada, China, France. Germany, India, Indonesia, Italy, Japan, Republic of Korea. Mexico, Russia. Saudi Arabia, South Africa. Turkey, United Kingdom and United States and the European Union. The G-20 was founded in 1999 after the Asian financial crises as a forum for international economic cooperation. The size of G-20 indicates its relevance in the global economy. The G-20 members represent around 85% of the global GDP. over 75% of the global trade and 67% of world population. The G-20 summit is held annually under the leadership of a rotating presidency. India assumed the G-20 presidency from Indonesia on December 1, 2022 and will convene the G-20 leaders' summit for the first time in the country in 2023. The theme of India's G-20 presidency is "Vasudhaiva Kutumbakam", that is, "One Earth, One family and One future" closely ties with LIFE (Lifestyle for Environment). The G-20 presidency steers the G-20 agenda for one year and hosts the summit. The G-20 consists of two parallel tracks : the Finance track and the Sherpa track. Finance ministers and Central Bank Governors lead the finance track, while Sherpas lead the Sherpa track. India's G-20 priorities are Green Development, Climate finance and life; Accelerated inclusive and resilient growth; Accelerating progress on SDGs; Technological transformation and Digital public infrastructure; Multilateral institutions for the 21st century; and Women Led development. India kickstarted its presidency term agenda with a series of initiatives and meetings. As a part of this, India will host over 200 meetings in over 50 cities across 32 different work streams before conducting the annual G-20 summit in Delhi in September 2023. The 43 Heads of Delegations, the largest ever in G-20 will be participating in the final summit. Conducting of this summit definitely increases India's standing in the global order. It is a great opportunity to showcase India's cultural heritage, culture and achievements to global leaders and India's commitment for global sustainable development.

96. For which purpose G-20 was originally founded?

A. to discuss international peace and counter-terrorism issues

B. to discuss global economic and financial issues

C. to discuss climate change and environmental issues

D. to discuss resolving the war between Russia and Ukraine

97. Which one of the followings is not India's G-20 priorities?
A. Multilateral Institutions for 21st century
B. Women-led development
C. Development and sustained border
D. Technological transformation and digital public infrastructure.

98. The size of G-20 in terms of world population, global GDP and global trade respectively is:
A. 85%, 75% and 85%
B. 67%, 75% and 85%
C. 85%, 67% and 75%
D. 67%, 85% and 75%

99. The theme of India's G-20 presidency is tied closely with:
A. Vasudhaiva Kutumbakam
B. One earth, one family and one future
C. Technology, Infrastructure and SDG
D. Life style for environment

100. The tracks in G-20 are:
A. Finance track and Sherpa track
B. Sherpa track and Economics track
C. Climate track and Sherpa track
D. Sherpa track and SDGs track

ANSWERS

1. (C): The Marginal Rate of Substitution (MRS) measures the rate at which a consumer is willing to trade one good for another while maintaining the same level of satisfaction or utility. It is the ratio of the marginal utility of one good to the marginal utility of another. The concept of MRS is usually used to describe the shape of indifference curves. In fact, the type of indifference curves we get while describing choices faced by consumers depends on the behaviour of the MRS.
For example, if two commodities are perfect substitutes, the MRS is –1 throughout. In case of neutral goods, the MRS is infinite throughout. If two goods are perfect complements, the MRS is either zero or infinite and nothing in between.

2. (B): To determine which statement is not true, let's evaluate each option:
A. Total effect of price change on consumption of a good is a combination of income effect and substitution effect.
This statement is true. When the price of a good changes, the total effect on consumption is indeed a combination of the income effect and the substitution effect.
B. For inferior goods, the income effect is always larger than the substitution effect, in absolute terms.
This statement is not true. For inferior goods, the income effect and the substitution effect work in opposite directions. The income effect occurs because a decrease in price increases the consumer's real income, which may lead to a decrease in the consumption of the inferior good. The substitution effect, on the other hand, occurs because the decrease in price makes the inferior good relatively cheaper compared to other goods, which can lead to an increase in consumption. The relative magnitude of the income effect and substitution effect depends on the specific circumstances, and it is not always the case that the income effect is larger than the substitution effect.
C. For a corner solution, $MRS_{xy} \neq \frac{P_x}{P_y}$
This statement is true. In economics, a corner solution occurs when a consumer fully consumes one good and does not consume any of the other good due to budget constraints. In such a situation, the marginal rate of substitution (MRS) between the two goods is not equal to the ratio of their prices (P_x/P_y) because the consumer is not consuming any quantity of the second good.

D. For a normal good, both the income and substitution effect hold

The statement is incomplete, and it is unclear what the completion would be. Therefore, it is impossible to determine its truthfulness.

3. (C): In case network externalities are negative, snob effect arises. Snob effect refers to the desire to possess a unique commodity having a prestige value. Snob effect works quite contrary to the bandwagon effect. The quantity demanded of a commodity having a snob value is greater, the smaller the number of people owning its. Rare works of art, specially designed sport cars, specially designed clothing made to order, very expensive luxury cars. For example, the utility one gets from a very expensive luxury car is mainly due to the prestige and status value of it which results from the fact that only few others own it.

4. (A): The Nash equilibrium is a decision-making theorem within game theory that states a player can achieve the desired outcome by not deviating from their initial strategy. In the Nash equilibrium, each player's strategy is optimal when considering the decisions of other players. Every player wins because everyone gets the outcome that they desire. The prisoner's dilemma is a common game theory example and one that adequately showcases the effect of the Nash equilibrium. The Nash equilibrium is often discussed in conjunction with dominant strategy, which states that the chosen strategy of an actor will lead to better results out of all the possible strategies that can be used, regardless of the strategy that the opponent uses. This theorem does not always mean that the most optimal strategy is chosen.

5. (C): To find the profit-maximizing level of output (Q*) and maximum profit for the firm, we need to calculate the marginal cost (MC) and marginal revenue (MR) functions first.

The marginal cost (MC) function can be obtained by taking the derivative of the total cost (C) function with respect to quantity (Q):

$$MC = dC/dQ$$

Given that $C = (1/3)Q^3 - 7Q^2 + 111Q + 50$, we differentiate it with respect to Q:

$$\begin{aligned} MC &= dC/dQ \\ &= d/dQ[(1/3)Q^3 - 7Q^2 + 111Q + 50] \\ &= Q^2 - 14Q + 111 \end{aligned}$$

The marginal revenue (MR) function can be obtained from the demand function. The demand function is given as Q = 100 – P, and we can express price (P) in terms of quantity (Q) as P = 100 – Q. Then, we can substitute this expression for price in the demand function to obtain the revenue function:

$$\begin{aligned} R &= P * Q \\ &= (100 - Q) * Q \\ &= 100Q - Q^2 \end{aligned}$$

The marginal revenue (MR) is the derivative of the revenue function with respect to quantity (Q):

$$\begin{aligned} MR &= dR/dQ \\ MR &= d/dQ(100Q - 2) \\ &= 100 - 2Q \end{aligned}$$

To find the profit-maximizing level of output (Q*), we need to equate the marginal cost (MC) and marginal revenue (MR):

$$\begin{aligned} MC &= MR \\ Q^2 - 14Q + 111 &= 100 - 2Q \end{aligned}$$

Simplifying the equation:

$$Q^2 - 12Q + 11 = 0$$

This is a quadratic equation, which can be solved by factoring or using the quadratic formula. In this case, it factors as:

$$(Q - 1)(Q - 11) = 0$$

Therefore, Q = 1 or Q = 11.

To determine which value of Q maximizes profit, we need to evaluate the second derivative of the total cost function (C) at each of these points. If the second derivative is positive, it indicates a minimum, and if it is negative, it indicates a maximum.

The second derivative of the total cost function is:

$$d^2C/dQ^2 = 2Q - 14$$

Substituting Q = 1:

$$d^2C/dQ^2 = 2(1) - 14 = -12$$

Substituting Q = 11:

$$d^2C/dQ^2 = 2(11) - 14 = 8$$

Since the second derivative is negative ($d^2C/dQ^2 < 0$) at Q = 1 and positive ($d_2C/dQ_2 > 0$) at Q = 11, the profit is maximized when Q = 11. Therefore, the profit-maximizing level of output (Q*) is 11.

To find the maximum profit, we substitute Q = 11 into the total cost function (C):

$$C = (1/3)(113) - 7(112) + 111(11) + 50.$$

6. (C): ***Risk averse:*** Preferring a certain income to a risky income with the same expected value leads to risk-averse behaviour. Risk aversion is the tendency to avoid risk. It is concave in shape.

Risk lover: Preferring a risky income to a certain income with the same expected value leads to a risk lover. It is convex in shape.

Risk neutral: Being indifferent between a certain income and an uncertain income with the same expected value leads to risk neutrality.

Risk premium: Amount of money that a risk-averse individual will pay to avoid taking a risk.

7. (C): M_1 is a narrow measure of the money supply that includes physical currency, demand deposits, traveler's checks, and other checkable deposits. M_1 does not include financial assets, such as savings accounts, Commercial paper, Term deposits, and bonds.

8. (B): Keynes's "animal spirits" refers to the psychological factors and human behavior that influence economic decisions, including investment. Animal spirits represent the non-rational or emotional factors that affect investment decisions, such as optimism, confidence, and sentiment. These animal spirits can lead to fluctuations in investment levels and play a significant role in determining the level of current investment in an economy. Therefore, Keynes's animal spirits are closely associated with current investment.

9. (A): In the Mundell-Fleming model, the effectiveness of monetary policy depends on the combination of capital mobility and exchange rate flexibility. Perfect capital mobility and flexible exchange rate.

In this scenario, perfect capital mobility implies that there are no restrictions on the movement of capital across borders. Investors can easily shift funds between domestic and foreign assets based on interest rate differentials. Flexible exchange rate means that the exchange rate is determined by market forces and is allowed to adjust freely in response to changes in supply and demand. Under these conditions, monetary policy can be more effective because changes in interest rates by the central bank will directly impact capital flows. Specifically, if a country's central bank raises interest rates, it attracts capital from abroad due to higher returns. This capital inflow puts upward pressure on the domestic currency's exchange rate, which, in turn, can dampen net exports and stimulate domestic investment.

10. (B): If events A and B are not independent, it means that the occurrence or non-occurrence of one event affects the probability of the other event. In this case, the correct option would be:

$$B \cdot P(A \cap B) = P(A) \cdot P(B|A)$$

This formula represents the probability of both events A and B occurring together, given that event A has already occurred. It takes into account the conditional probability of event B happening after event A.

Option A ($P(A \cap B) = P(A) \cdot P(B)$) assumes independence between events A and B, which contradicts the given information.

Option C ($P(A \cap B) = P(A) \cdot P(A/B)$) is incorrect because it suggests that the probability of event B occurring is dependent on event A, which is not necessarily true.

Option D ($P(A \cap B) = 1 - P(A \cup B)$) is unrelated to the independence of events A and B. It represents the probability of the intersection of events A and B, which is the opposite of the probability of their union.

11. (C): Chain-weighted CPI takes real-word purchasing decisions into account to provide a more accurate picture of the cost of living. It can capture both general changes in spending, as consumer preferences change, and substitution effects, when relative prices change. The adjustments in chain-weighted CPI make it a better measure of the cost of living, but a less accurate measure of inflation. In 2017, chain-weighted CPI was substituted for regular CPI in setting federal income tax brackets.

12. (A): If the consumption function passes through the origin (0, 0) and has an average propensity to consume (APC) equal to the marginal propensity to consume (MPC), then the consumption function must be a linear function without any intercept.

The average propensity to consume (APC) is defined as the ratio of consumption (C) to income (Y), while the marginal propensity to consume (MPC) is the change in consumption divided by the change in income. Mathematically, we can express these relationships as:

$$APC = C/Y$$

$$MPC = \Delta C/\Delta Y$$

Since the consumption function passes through the origin (0, 0), it means that when income is zero, consumption is also zero. This implies that at the point (0, 0), the APC is also zero.

If the APC is equal to the MPC, it means that for any change in income (ΔY), the change in consumption (ΔC) is the same. In other words, the ratio of $\Delta C/\Delta Y$ is constant throughout the income range.

For a linear function without any intercept, the slope (which represents the MPC) remains constant throughout the income range. Therefore, if the APC is equal to the MPC and the function passes through the origin, it implies that the consumption function must be a linear function without any intercept.

13. (C): To find the producer's surplus, we need to calculate the area between the producer's supply curve and the market price. The producer's surplus represents the additional profit producers receive from selling their goods at a price higher than their marginal cost.

In this case, we have the following equations:

Producer demand: $P_d = 3x^2 - 20x + 5$

Producer supply: $P_s = 15 + 9x$

To determine the equilibrium price, we set the producer demand equal to the producer supply:

$$3x^2 - 20x + 5 = 15 + 9x$$

Simplifying the equation:

$$3x^2 - 29x - 10 = 0$$

We can solve this quadratic equation to find the equilibrium quantity (x). However, without knowing the specific range of x, I'll assume you're interested in solving this equation analytically. By using the quadratic formula:

$$x = (-b \pm \sqrt{(b^2 - 4ac)})/(2a)$$

For this equation, $a = 3$, $b = -29$, and $c = -10$. Plugging in these values:

$$x = (-(-29) \pm \sqrt{((-29)^2 - 4(3)(-10))})/(2(3))$$

$$x = (29 \pm \sqrt{(841 + 120)})/6$$

$$x = (29 \pm \sqrt{961})/6$$

$$x = (29 \pm 31)/6$$

The two possible solutions for x are:

$$x_1 = (29 + 31)/6 = 10$$

$$x_2 = (29 - 31)/6 = -1/3$$

Since we're dealing with quantities, we can ignore the negative value. Therefore, the equilibrium quantity is $x = 10$.

To find the equilibrium price (Pe), we substitute this value back into either the producer demand or supply equation. Using the supply equation:

$$Ps = 15 + 9x$$

$Pe = 15 + 9(10)$

$Pe = 15 + 90$

$Pe = 105$

The equilibrium price is Pe = 105.

Thus, the equilibrium price (Pe) is 105

Total revenue = $P \times x = 105 \times 10 = 1050$

Total supply price = 600

Producer surplus = 1050 − 600 = 450.

14. (C): To calculate the income elasticity of demand, we need to differentiate the demand function with respect to income (Y) and then divide it by the original demand function, multiplied by the income (Y). The formula for income elasticity of demand is:

Income elasticity of demand

$$= (\partial QA/\partial Y) * (Y/QA)$$

Given the demand function:

$$Q_A = 100 - 2P_A + 0.2Y + 0.3P_B$$

We can substitute the given values:

$$P_A = 6, Y = 500, P_B = 10$$

$$Q_A = 100 - 2(6) + 0.2(500) + 0.3(10)$$

$$= 100 - 12 + 100 + 3 = 191$$

Now, let's differentiate the demand function with respect to income (Y):

$$\partial QA/\partial Y = 0.2$$

Substituting the values into the income elasticity formula:

Income elasticity of demand

$$= (0.2) * (500/191)$$

$$= 0.2 * 2.6152 = 0.52304$$

Therefore, the income elasticity of demand for good A is approximately 0.52304.

15. (C)

16. (A): In a logistic regression model, the relationship between the odds ratio and the logit is as follows: as the odds ratio decreases from 1 to 0, the logit becomes increasingly negative.

The odds ratio (OR) is the ratio of the odds of an event occurring to the odds of it not occurring. It represents the likelihood of success (or an event) relative to failure (or the complement of the event). The odds ratio can range from 0 to positive infinity.

The logit, also known as the log-odds, is the natural logarithm of the odds ratio. Mathematically, it can be expressed as:

$$\text{logit}(p) = \ln(p/(1 - p))$$

where p is the probability of the event occurring.

When the odds ratio is 1, it means that the odds of the event occurring are equal to the odds of it not occurring. In this case, the logit is 0. As the odds ratio decreases below 1, indicating decreasing odds of the event occurring relative to not occurring, the logit becomes negative. The more the odds ratio deviates from 1 towards 0, the more negative the logit becomes.

Conversely, as the odds ratio increases above 1, indicating increasing odds of the event occurring relative to not occurring, the logit becomes positive. The more the odds ratio deviates from 1 towards positive infinity, the more positive the logit becomes.

It's important to note that the logit is a linear transformation of the odds ratio and is used to model the relationship between predictor variables and the probability of an event occurring in logistic regression.

17. (D): The given regression model, $Y_i = \alpha_1 + \beta_1 X_i + \beta_2(X_i - X^*) D_i + U_i$, can be used for option D, which is to test a piecewise linear relationship in the data.

In this model, Y_i represents the dependent variable, X_i represents the independent variable, D_i represents a dummy variable that takes the value of 1 when X_i is greater than X* and 0 otherwise, α_1 is the intercept term, β_1 is the coefficient for X_i, β_2 is the coefficient for the interaction term $(X_i - X^*) D_i$, and U_i represents the error term.

By including the interaction term $(X_i - X^*) D_i$, the model allows for a different slope (β_2) on the independent variable X_i depending on whether X_i is above or below a certain threshold X*. This can capture a piecewise linear relationship in the data where the slope changes at a specific point.

Therefore, this regression model can be used to test for a piecewise linear relationship in the data.

18. (D): To find the player's expected gain, we need to calculate the probabilities of each outcome and multiply them by their corresponding gains.

Let's consider the possible outcomes when tossing two fair coins:

Two heads (HH)

One head (HT or TH)

No heads (TT)

We'll calculate the probabilities of each outcome:

The probability of getting two heads (HH) is 1/2 * 1/2 = 1/4 since each coin toss is independent and has a 1/2 probability of landing on heads.

The probability of getting one head (HT or TH) is 1/2 * 1/2 + 1/2 * 1/2 = 1/2 since there are two possible ways to get one head: HT or TH.

The probability of getting no heads (TT) is 1/2 * 1/2 = 1/4 since each coin toss is independent and has a 1/2 probability of landing on tails.

Now let's calculate the expected gain:

Expected gain = (probability of outcome 1 * gain of outcome 1) + (probability of outcome 2 * gain of outcome 2) + (probability of outcome 3 * gain of outcome 3)

Expected gain = (1/4 * 5) + (1/2 * 2) + (1/4 * 1)

Expected gain = 5/4 + 1 + 1/4

Expected gain = 5/4 + 4/4 + 1/4

Expected gain = 10/4

Expected gain = 2.5

Therefore, the player's expected gain is 2.5.

19. (B): To find the probability that the card drawn is either a diamond or a king, we need to determine the number of favorable outcomes (diamonds or kings) and divide it by the total number of possible outcomes (all the cards in a well-shuffled pack).

A standard deck of playing cards contains 52 cards, with 13 cards in each of the four suits (diamonds, hearts, clubs, and spades). Among these, there are 4 kings (one king in each suit) and 13 diamonds. However, we need to be careful not to count the king of diamonds twice since it falls into both categories.

So, the number of favorable outcomes (diamonds or kings) is 13 (diamonds) + 4 (kings) – 1 (king of diamonds) = 16.

The total number of possible outcomes is the number of cards in the deck, which is 52.

Therefore, the probability of drawing either a diamond or a king is:

P(diamond or king) = favorable outcomes/total outcomes = 16/52.

20. (A): In simultaneous equation models, Ordinary Least Squares (OLS) estimation may be applied directly if the model is recursive. A recursive model is one in which each endogenous variable is only determined by its own past values and the exogenous variables in the system. This means that there are no feedback loops or simultaneous relationships among the endogenous variables.

In a recursive model, OLS estimation can be used to estimate the parameters by treating each equation separately and sequentially. The procedure involves estimating the first equation using OLS, obtaining the predicted values of the endogenous variable, and then using these predicted values as explanatory variables in the subsequent equations.

21. (C): Rural Landless Employment Guarantee Programme (RLEGP) was launched on August 15, 1983. It aimed to generate gainful employment opportunities, to create productive assets in rural area and also for the improvement of overall quality of rural life. Former Prime Minister Indira Gandhi launched this programme as part of the sixth five year plan. In this programme, the guarantee has not been operationalized due to lack of funds. In this programme, preference in employment was given to landless labourers, women, scheduled castes and scheduled tribes. This programme is totally funded by the Central Government.

22. (B): The Foreign Trade Policy (FTP) 2015-20 was unveiled by Ms Nirmala Sitharaman, Minister of State for Commerce & Industry (Independent Charge), Government of India on April 1, 2015. FTP 2015-20 provides a framework for increasing exports of goods and services as well as generation of employment and increasing value addition in the country, in line with the 'Make in India' programme. The Policy aims to enable India to respond to the challenges of the external environment, keeping in step with a rapidly evolving international trading architecture and make trade a major contributor to the country's economic growth and development.

23. (B): The Chairman of the 14th Finance Commission in India was Dr. Y.V. Reddy. He served as the Chairman from February 2013 to December 2014. The Finance Commission is a constitutional body in India that is appointed every five years to recommend the distribution of financial resources between the central government and the state governments. Its primary role is to make recommendations on the sharing of tax revenue and grants-in-aid between the center and the states.

24. (B): Zamindari system is also known as the Permanent Settlement System, introduced by Lord Cornwallis, first in the Bengal, Bihar, Orissa and Varanasi provinces. Zamindars were recognized as the landowners. The land tax was paid by the peasants in cash. Zamindars owned 1/11 of the share, and East India Company holds 10/11 of the share.

25. (D)

26. (A): To calculate the deadweight loss and tax revenue, we need to analyze the changes in consumer surplus, producer surplus, and total surplus caused by the tax.

Price without tax: ₹ 5

Price with tax: ₹ 7

Tax per unit: ₹ 2

Since both individuals, X and Y, initially value the bread packet higher than its price without tax, they choose to buy one packet each when the price is ₹ 5. However, when the price increases to ₹ 7 due to the tax, we need to determine their decisions again.

Individual X:

Value of bread packet: ₹ 8

Price without tax: ₹ 5 (affordable)

Price with tax: ₹ 7 (affordable)

X will still buy the bread packet.

Individual Y:

Value of bread packet: ₹ 6

Price without tax: ₹ 5 (affordable)

Price with tax: ₹ 7 (not affordable)

Y will not buy the bread packet.

Now let's calculate the deadweight loss and tax revenue:

Deadweight Loss:

The deadweight loss represents the loss in total surplus due to the tax. In this case, it is caused by Y's decision not to purchase the bread packet because the price with tax exceeds their valuation.

Deadweight loss = 0.5 * (Quantity not bought) * (Price without tax – Price with tax)

Quantity not bought = 1 (since Y doesn't buy the packet)

Price without tax = ₹ 5

Price with tax = ₹ 7

Deadweight loss = 0.5 * 1 * (₹ 5 – ₹ 7)
= 0.5 * (– ₹ 2) = – ₹ 1

Note that the negative value indicates a loss in total surplus.

Tax Revenue:

The tax revenue is calculated by multiplying the tax per unit by the quantity bought.

Quantity bought = 1 (X buys the packet)

Tax revenue = Tax per unit * Quantity bought
= ₹ 2 * 1 = ₹ 2

Therefore, the deadweight loss is – ₹ 1, and the tax revenue is ₹ 2.

27. (B): The component that distinguishes the primary deficit from the fiscal deficit is the interest payment. The primary deficit is a measure of the government's borrowing requirement excluding interest payments. It represents the difference between the government's total expenditure (including both revenue and capital expenditures) and its total revenue (including both revenue and capital receipts) excluding interest payments. On the other hand, the fiscal deficit represents the total borrowing requirement of the government, including both interest payments and other expenditures. It is the difference between the government's total expenditure (including interest payments) and its total revenue (including interest receipts).

28. (C): The correct answer is C. Inflation is a supply side phenomenon.

The inflation targeting approach is a framework used by central banks to maintain price stability by focusing on controlling inflation. While the approach makes several assumptions and conclusions, the notion that inflation is solely a supply side phenomenon is not one of them.

Here are the assumptions and conclusions associated with the inflation targeting approach:

- **Interest rate is the major instrument of monetary policy:** This is an assumption of the inflation targeting approach. It suggests that central banks primarily use interest rates as their primary tool to control inflation.
- **Higher interest rate controls aggregate demand:** This is an assumption of the inflation targeting approach. It posits that by raising interest rates, central banks can reduce aggregate demand in the economy, which can help control inflation.
- **Quantity of money supply is not very effective in controlling inflation:** This is a conclusion of the inflation targeting approach. It suggests that controlling the quantity of money supply alone may not be sufficient to effectively manage and control inflation.

29. (C): The sacrifice ratio is an economic ratio that measures the effect of rising and falling inflation on a country's total production and output. Costs are associated with the slowing of economic output in response to a drop in inflation.

30. (C): The formula to calculate the yield of treasury bills (T-bills) is as follows:

$$Y = (D/P) * 365$$

where:

Y = Discounted yield

P = Price

D = Days to maturity

In this formula, the yield is calculated by dividing the number of days to maturity (D) by the price (P) of the T-bill, and then multiplying the result by 365. The result is typically expressed as a percentage.

The formula can be rewritten as:

$$Y = \frac{(100 - \text{Price}/P) * 365 * 100}{\text{Price} * \text{Days to maturity}}$$

31. (B): Poverty-weighted growth rate refer to a measure that takes into account both the economic growth rate of a country and the distribution of income or wealth among its population, with a particular focus on poverty levels.

32. (B): In Marxist theory, the concept of the organic composition of capital refers to the ratio between the constant capital (C) and the variable capital (V) in a given production process. The ratio is expressed as:

Organic Composition of Capital = C/V

This ratio represents the proportion of capital invested in means of production (constant capital) compared to the capital invested in labor power (variable capital). It helps to analyze the changing structure of capital in capitalist production and its implications for the exploitation of labour.

33. (C): The statement "B. It is tied to consumer sovereignty" is not true in the case of externality. Externality refers to the impact of an economic activity on parties other than the individuals or entities directly involved in the activity. It can be positive or negative and affects individuals, communities, or the environment. Externalities can arise from various sources, such as production processes, consumption choices. or resource depletion. Consumer sovereignty, on the other hand, is a concept in economics that refers to the power of consumers to determine the types and quantities of goods and services produced by the market through their purchasing decisions. It is associated with the idea that consumer preferences drive market outcomes. While externalities can influence consumer choices and market outcomes, they are not inherently tied to consumer sovereignty. Externalities are broader in scope, involving the consequences of economic activities that extend beyond individual consumers and their preferences.

Therefore, statement B is not true in the case of externality.

34. (A) **35. (C)**

36. (A): Equivalent Variation is the adjustment in income that changes the consumer's utility equal to the level that would occur IF the event had happened. In the case of a positive economic change, such as a fall in price, EV would be the increase in income that would give the consumer the same additional utility that would happen if a price did fall. In the case of a negative economic change, EV would be the amount of income that would be taken away to lower the consumer's utility to the level that would happen if the change had occurred. The equivalent variation for a price increase of a good can be interpreted as the willingness to pay.

37. (A): According to the specific factors model, the correct statement is A. In the specific factors model, factors of production are divided into three categories: specific to the export sector, specific to the import-competing sectors, and mobile factors. The model suggests that trade benefits the factor specific to the export sector because it leads to increased demand and higher prices for goods produced for export. On the other hand, trade hurts the factor specific to the import-competing sectors because it exposes them to competition from foreign goods, which can lead to reduced demand and lower prices for domestically produced goods. The effects on mobile factors are considered ambiguous because they can move between sectors to some extent, so the overall impact will depend on factors such as mobility costs and the availability of alternative employment opportunities.

38. (A): Some analysts suggested that growth in the poorer nations would actually be self-defeating. They argued that export-biased growth by poor nations would worsen their terms of trade so much that they would be worse off than if they had not grown at all. This situation is known to economists as the case of immiserising growth.

39. (B): The correct postulate of the Gravity Model is option B: "The larger and the closer the two countries are, the larger the volume of trade between them is expected to be."

The Gravity Model is an economic model that suggests that the volume of trade between two countries is directly proportional to the size of their economies (measured by GDP) and inversely proportional to the distance between them. In other words, larger economies and shorter distances tend to result in greater trade volumes. This is consistent with option B, which correctly states that larger and closer countries are expected to have a larger volume of trade.

40. (C)

41. (D): Let us analyse the given statements

(*a*) The entry of a fair bet is zero: True. In a fair bet, the entry cost or stake is typically set to zero. Both parties have an equal chance of winning or losing, and there is no inherent advantage for either participant.

(*b*) The person who accepts a fair bet is said to be risk lover: False. The acceptance or refusal of a fair bet does not indicate a person's risk preference. A risk lover is someone who is willing to take on more risk for a potentially higher reward. Accepting a fair bet does not necessarily imply being a risk lover; it simply means the person acknowledges the fairness of the bet and is willing to participate.

(*c*) Expected value of income from the bet is equal to the same amount of income with certainty: True. In a fair game or bet, the expected value of income from the bet is equal to the amount of income that would be obtained with certainty. This means that, on average, the expected outcome of participating in a fair bet is the same as receiving a guaranteed amount.

(*d*) The person who refuses a fair bet is said to be risk neutral: False. Refusing a fair bet does not necessarily indicate that a person is risk neutral. Risk neutrality refers to a state where an individual's decisions are solely based on expected values, without considering their risk preferences. However, refusing a fair bet can be attributed to various factors such as risk aversion, lack of interest, or personal circumstances.

(*e*) The person who refuses a fair bet is said to be risk averse: True. Refusing a fair bet is often associated with risk aversion. Risk aversion means that an individual prefers certainty over uncertain outcomes and is unwilling to take on additional risk, even if the expected value of the bet is favorable.

42. (D) **43. (B)**

44. (A): The rational expectations view in economics encompasses several key elements, including:

(*b*) Rational expectation as a theory of expectations: Rational expectations theory posits that individuals form their expectations about future economic variables based on all available information, including economic models, historical data, and their own experiences. It assumes that people are rational and make optimal decisions by incorporating this information into their expectations.

(*c*) An emphasis on the credibility of policy makers: Rational expectations theory suggests that the effectiveness of monetary and fiscal policies depends on the credibility of policy makers. If individuals believe that policymakers will consistently pursue certain goals, such as low inflation or stable economic growth, they will incorporate these expectations into their decision-making processes.

(*d*) A preference for policy-making rules rather than discretion: Rational expectations theorists often advocate for policy rules instead of discretionary policymaking. Policy rules provide clear guidelines for policymakers to follow, which helps anchor expectations and reduce uncertainty in the economy. This approach aims to avoid ad hoc policy decisions that could lead to inconsistent or unpredictable outcomes.

Regarding the other options:

(*a*) The market clearing rational expectations do not approach the Phillips curve: This statement is incorrect. Rational expectations theory suggests that market clearing occurs when prices and quantities adjust to equate supply and demand. The Phillips curve, which depicts the relationship between inflation and unemployment, is not directly related to the concept of market clearing.

(*e*) Generally insists that markets do not clear rapidly: This statement is incorrect. Rational expectations theory assumes that markets clear rapidly by adjusting prices and quantities to reach equilibrium. The theory emphasizes that individuals incorporate all available information into their expectations, leading to efficient market outcomes.

Therefore, the correct options are (*b*), (*c*), and (*d*).

45. (B) **46. (D)**

47. (B): In the case of a Poisson distribution:

Option (*a*) is correct. The Poisson distribution assumes that the number of trials, denoted as '*n*', is indefinitely large, approaching infinity ($n \to \infty$).

Option (*c*) is correct. In a Poisson distribution, the mean (μ) is equal to the product of the rate parameter (λ, which represents the average number of events per unit time or space) and the number of trials (*n*). So, $np = \mu$. It is finite unless either n or λ approaches infinity.

Option (*e*) is correct. In a Poisson distribution, $\mu_4 = m + 3m^2$.

48. (B): In hypothesis testing, the null hypothesis (H_o) represents the default or assumed position, while the alternative hypothesis (H_1) represents the claim or the hypothesis being tested. The goal is to make a decision about the null hypothesis based on the available evidence.

Ideally, we want to make the correct decision based on the true state of affairs. However, in practice, there is always a possibility of making errors in hypothesis testing. The two types of errors that can occur are:

- **Type I Error:** Rejecting the null hypothesis when it is true.
- **Type II Error:** Accepting the null hypothesis when it is false.

In hypothesis testing, we control the probability of making a Type I error by setting a significance level (often denoted as α). If the obtained result is statistically significant at the chosen significance level, we reject the null hypothesis. If it is not statistically significant, we fail to reject the null hypothesis.

Based on this information, the correct conclusions are:

(*b*) Accept H_o, when it is true
(*d*) Reject H_o when H_1 is true
(*e*) Accept H_o when H_1 is false

49. (B): In the presence of heteroscedasticity, the following statements are correct for ordinary least squares (OLS) estimation:

(*a*) The estimated coefficients are linear: This statement is true. OLS estimation is a linear regression technique, meaning that the estimated coefficients are obtained through a linear relationship between the dependent variable and the independent variables.

(*b*) The estimated coefficients are unbiased: This statement is true. In the presence of heteroscedasticity, the OLS estimators are still consistent, and unbiased.

(*c*) The estimated coefficients are biased: This statement is false. Heteroscedasticity does not lead to biased estimates in OLS regression.

(*d*) The estimated coefficients are consistent: This statement is true. Despite being biased, the OLS estimators remain consistent even in the presence of heteroscedasticity. Consistency means that as the sample size increases, the estimated coefficients approach the true population coefficients.

(*e*) The estimated coefficients are efficient: This statement is false. Heteroscedasticity affects the efficiency of OLS estimators. Efficiency refers to the ability of the estimator to achieve the lowest possible variance among all unbiased estimators. In the presence of heteroscedasticity, the OLS estimators are no longer efficient.

50. (C): Among the options provided, the assumptions of the classical linear regression model are satisfied by the following:

(*a*) Zero mean value of disturbance Ui: This assumption states that the error terms, or disturbances, have a mean value of zero. It is a requirement for the classical linear regression model to hold.

(*c*) Homoscedasticity or constant variance of Ui: The classical linear regression model assumes that the error terms have constant variance across all levels of the independent variables. This assumption is known as homoscedasticity.

(*d*) No autocorrelation between the disturbances: The classical linear regression model assumes that there is no correlation between the error terms at different observations or across different time periods. This means that the disturbances are not autocorrelated.

Therefore, options (*a*), (*c*), and (*d*) satisfy the assumptions of the classical linear regression model. Options (*b*) and (*e*) do not meet the assumptions. The explanatory variables and error terms should be independent (option *b*), and there should not be more than one exact linear relationship between the explanatory variables (option *e*).

51. (B): Let's go through each option and determine whether it is correct or not.

(*a*) $(A')' = A$

The statement (*a*) is correct. It is a law in set theory known as the Double Complement Law. The complement of the complement of a set is the set itself.

(*b*) $(A \cup B) = 1 - (A \cap B)$

The statement (*b*) is incorrect. The correct statement should be:

$(A \cup B) = A + B - (A \cap B)$

This is known as the Inclusion-Exclusion Principle, which states that the cardinality of the union of two sets is equal to the sum of their individual cardinalities minus the cardinality of their intersection.

(*c*) $A \cup (B \cup C) = (A \cup B) \cup C$

The statement (c) is correct. It is the Associative Law of set union. The order of operations doesn't matter when performing set union.

(*d*) $A \cup (B \cap C) = (A \cap B) \cup (A \cap C)$

The statement (d) is incorrect. The correct statement should be:

$A \cup (B \cap C) \subseteq (A \cup B) \cap (A \cup C)$

In general, the union of a set with the intersection of two other sets is a subset of the intersection of the set with each individual set.

(*e*) $A - B = A \cap B'$

The statement (*e*) is correct. The set difference between sets A and B is equal to the intersection of A with the complement of B.

To summarize, the correct statements are (*a*), (*c*), and (*e*).

52. (D): In a multiple regression model, the hypothesis H_0: $\beta_2 = \beta_3 = 0$ can be tested using the F-test. The F-test is used to determine whether there is a significant relationship between the response variable (dependent variable) and the set of predictor variables (independent variables) in the regression model as a whole. It tests the overall significance of the regression model by comparing the variance explained by the model to the residual variance.

On the other hand, the *t*-test is used to test the significance of individual regression coefficients (β's) in the model. It assesses whether each predictor variable has a significant impact on the response variable independently.

The Chi-square test is used for categorical data analysis, while the ANOVA (Analysis of Variance) test is used to compare means across different groups.

Therefore, the correct answer for testing the hypothesis H_0: $\beta_2 = \beta_3 = 0$ in a multiple regression model is D (F-test).

53. (C): The indicators of the Human Development Index (HDI) include:

(*a*) Real GDP per capita: This indicator reflects the average income or economic well-being of individuals in a country.

(*b*) Adult literacy rate combined with enrolment ratio: This indicator considers both the literacy rate among adults (usually defined as individuals aged 15 years and older) and the enrollment ratio, which measures the proportion of individuals enrolled in education at different levels. The combination of these two factors provides an indication of the level of education and knowledge in a country.

(*c*) Life expectancy at birth: This indicator measures the average number of years a newborn is expected to live. It provides an assessment of the overall health and well-being of the population.

The indicators (*d*) Malnutrition under five and (*e*) IMR under five, referring to malnutrition rates among children under five years of age and the infant mortality rate among children under five, are important indicators of child health and nutrition. While they are crucial measures for evaluating the well-being of children, they are not part of the core indicators used in the calculation of the HDI.

54. (A) **55. (B)**

56. (D): Statement (*a*) is Correct. In a competitive market, where there is sufficient competition and no externalities, the forces of supply and demand can lead to efficient resource allocation in the provision of private goods. However, market failure can occur in the provision of social goods, which are often characterized by non-excludability and non-rivalry. This is because private markets may not provide these goods in sufficient quantities due to free-rider problems or inadequate profit incentives.

Statement (*b*) is Incorrect. Efficient provision of social goods often requires vertical addition rather than horizontal addition of individual demand schedules. Social goods are typically non-excludable and non-rivalrous, meaning that individuals cannot be excluded from their benefits, and one person's consumption of the good does not reduce its availability to others. As a result, the demand for social goods is often aggregated vertically, considering the overall societal demand rather than individual demand schedules.

Statement (*c*) is Partially Correct. The provision of social goods typically involves some form of collective decision-making process. While a political process of budget determination can be one approach, it is not the only mechanism for seeking efficient provision. Other methods, such as government planning, public-private partnerships, or market-based mechanisms like auctions or subsidies, can also be employed to allocate resources efficiently for social goods.

Statement (*d*) is Correct. If consumer choices are influenced by false advertising or misleading information, it can lead to market failures. In such cases, corrective action, such as regulatory interventions or consumer protection measures, may be necessary to ensure that consumers can make informed decisions and prevent market distortions caused by deceptive practices.

Statement (*e*) is Correct. Between purely private goods (excludable and rivalrous) and purely social goods (non-excludable and non-rivalrous), there are various goods that possess characteristics of both. These goods, known as quasi-public goods or club goods, have elements of non-excludability and may exhibit partial rivalry. Examples include toll roads, cable TV, or private parks, where access can be restricted, but consumption by one individual may affect the experience of others to some extent.

57. (B)

58. (C): Among the given statements regarding the money market in India, the correct statements are:

(*b*) Treasury bill is an instrument of short-term borrowing by the government with absence of default risk.

(*c*) RBI uses refinance to relieve liquidity shortages in the system.

(*e*) SLR enables to impose secondary and supplementary reserve requirements on the banking system.

59. (D)

60. (C): The measurement of income inequality is primarily done using various statistical indicators. The options provided here are common indicators used to measure income inequality. Let's go through each of them:

(*a*) Gini coefficient: The Gini coefficient is a widely used measure of income inequality. It quantifies the extent to which the distribution of income among individuals or households within a country deviates from perfect equality. The Gini coefficient ranges from 0 (perfect equality) to 1 (maximum inequality).

(*b*) Lorenz curve: The Lorenz curve is a graphical representation of income distribution. It plots the cumulative percentage of total income received by a given percentage of the population, ranked from the poorest to the richest. The curve helps visualize income inequality, with a flatter curve indicating more equality and a steeper curve indicating greater inequality.

(*c*) Palma Ratio: The Palma ratio is another measure of income inequality. It compares the share of income held by the richest 10% of the population to the share held by the poorest 40% of the population. It is named after its creator, Chilean economist Gabriel Palma, and provides a straightforward way to compare the income shares of the richest and poorest segments of society.

(*d*) Deprivation ratio: The deprivation ratio is not typically used as a direct measure of income inequality. Instead, it is commonly employed as an indicator of poverty. The deprivation ratio measures the proportion of the population that is deprived of certain essential goods or services, such as access to clean water, healthcare, education, or adequate housing.

(*e*) Phillips Curve: The Phillips Curve, although relevant to macroeconomics, does not measure income inequality. It represents a supposed inverse relationship between inflation and unemployment rates, suggesting that when one decreases, the other increases.

To summarize, the measurement of income inequality is primarily done using the Gini coefficient, Lorenz curve, and Palma Ratio. The deprivation ratio is more commonly used to measure poverty, while the Phillips Curve is unrelated to income inequality measurement.

61. (D): Schumpeter's theory of development refers to the ideas and concepts put forth by the economist Joseph Schumpeter, particularly in his book "Capitalism, Socialism and Democracy" published in 1942. Schumpeter's theory focuses on the role of innovation and entrepreneurship in driving economic development and transformation. According to Schumpeter, economic development is not a smooth and gradual process but rather a result of disruptive and transformative changes brought about by entrepreneurs. He emphasized the role of entrepreneurs as innovators who introduce new products, processes, and business models into the economy, thereby creating economic growth and development.

62. (C)

63. (A): The essential features of weak sustainability are:

(*a*) It considers human-made capital and natural capital as close substitutes.

(*c*) It requires from each generation to ensure that their actions do not compromise the productive capacity of the generations to follow.

(*d*) the composition of the capital stock of an economy does not hold great significance.

These features reflect the idea that while human-made capital can partially substitute for natural capital, the preservation of natural capital is still crucial for long-term sustainability. Additionally, the focus is on intergenerational equity, where each generation must ensure that their activities do not deplete resources or harm the ability of future generations to meet their needs. The recognition of natural capital as an essential component for sustaining income over the long term acknowledges the dependence of economies on the services provided by the natural environment.

64. (C): The non-tariff barriers among the options listed are:

- Import quotas
- Voluntary export restraint
- Export subsidy

Non-tariff barriers are trade barriers other than tariffs, which means they do not involve the imposition of taxes or duties on imports or exports. Instead, they involve various other measures that can restrict or influence international trade. Import quotas limit the quantity of goods that can be imported into a country. Voluntary export restraints are agreements between exporting and importing countries to voluntarily limit the quantity of exports. Export subsidies are financial incentives provided by governments to promote exports. Compound tariffs and ad valorem tariffs, on the other hand, are types of tariffs, which fall under the category of tariff barriers.

65. (D): The Marshall-Lerner condition is an economic concept that examines the impact of currency devaluation on a country's balance of payments. It states that if the sum of the price elasticities of demand for a country's exports and imports in absolute terms is greater than one, a devaluation of the currency can improve the balance of payments. This means that the demand for exports and imports must be elastic (responsive to price changes) for devaluation to have a positive effect on the balance of payments.

66. (C) **67. (C)** **68. (C)**

69. (C) **70. (C)** **71. (A)**

72. (B) **73. (D)** **74. (A)**

75. (C)

76. (B)

77. (D): Here is the list of Nobel laureates in Economics arranged in descending order based on the year they received the award:

(*b*) Paul Krugman - 2008

(*a*) Amartya Sen - 1998

(*c*) James Tobin - 1981

(*e*) Milton Friedman - 1976

(*d*) Friedrich Hayek - 1974

78. (*)

79. (C): Fund Allocation (Budget 2022-23)

(*c*) Ministry of Agriculture and Farmers Welfare	₹ 15,500 crore
(*e*) Ministry of Rural Development	₹ 1,57,545 crore
(*a*) Ministry of Railways	₹ 1,59,100 crore
(*d*) Ministry of Road Transport and Highways	₹ 1,62,207 crore
(*b*) Ministry of Defense	₹ 5,94,000 crore

80. (C): Sources of Revenue (Budget 2022-23)

(*c*) GST	₹ 7,80,000 crore
(*b*) Income Tax	₹ 7,00,000 crore
(*d*) Union Excise Duty	₹ 3,35,000 crore
(*a*) Custom Duty	₹ 2,13,000 crore
(*e*) Non debt capital receipts	₹ 79,291crore

81. (D): Unemployment Rate CMIE data (September 2022)

(*b*) Rajasthan	23.8%
(*c*) Jammu Kashmir	23.2%
(*a*) Haryana	22.9%
(*e*) Tripura	17.0%
(*d*) Jharkhand	12.2%

82. (A): Multidimensionally Poor as per NITI Aayog Report 2021

(*b*) Kerala	0.71%
(*d*) Goa	3.76%
(*c*) Sikkim	3.82%
(*e*) Tamil Nadu	4.89%
(*a*) Punjab	5.59%

83. (D): Policy Rate (as on31-12-2022) of the RBI

(*d*) SLR	18.00%
(*b*) Bank rate	6.25%
(*a*) Repo rate	6.25%
(*c*) CRR	4.50%
(*e*) Reserve Repo Rate	3.35%

84. (A):

(*c*) Division of Labour, Adam Smith	1776
(*e*) Great Depression	1929
(*b*) Multiplier by R.F. Kahn	1931
(*a*) Liquidity Preference Theory	1936
(*d*) Quantity theory of Money, Fisher	1941

85. (A): Organizations as per their years of establishment starting from the oldest:

Organisation	Year of Establishment
(*d*) World Bank	1944
(*c*) UNCTAD	1964
(*b*) ADB	1966
(*e*) WIPO	1967
(*a*) WTO	1995

86. (A): Assertion (A) states that market failure results when products of different qualities are sold at a single price. This is true because in such cases, the price does not reflect the true value or quality of the products, and consumers may not be able to make informed choices based on their preferences for different qualities.

Reason (R) states that a buyer and a seller possess different information about the product transacted. This is also true as sellers often have more information about the products they are selling compared to buyers, which can lead to information asymmetry in the market.

Both (A) and (R) are true, and (R) explains why selling products of different qualities at a single price can lead to market failure.

87. (A): The statement I suggests that when the level of investment is determined within the system, the effectiveness of monetary policy is enhanced by an elastic investment and an inelastic liquidity preference schedule. On the other hand, the opposite is true for the effectiveness of fiscal policy.

Statement II suggests that by accommodating fiscal policy, monetary policy can prevent or mitigate the crowding out effect. This implies that the central bank can take actions to counterbalance the potential negative impact of increased government borrowing on private sector investment. For example, the central bank may reduce interest rates or engage in open market operations to increase liquidity and encourage private sector borrowing and investment. By doing so, it aims to prevent or lessen the crowding out effect and support overall economic growth.

88. (C): Statement I correctly describes capital deepening, which is the process of increasing the capital-to-labor ratio by increasing the amount of capital per worker. When capital grows at a faster rate than labor, the capital-to-labor ratio rises.

However, Statement II is incorrect. The growth of output per worker is not solely a result of technological change that decreases output per worker for a given capital/labor ratio. Technological change can actually increase output per worker by improving efficiency and productivity, leading to higher output with the same amount of capital and labor.

89. (A): Statement I highlights the principle of reciprocity in international trade. Countries generally want open foreign markets for their exporters, but if they restrict access to their own market, other countries may retaliate by limiting access to their markets as well. This reciprocal action is a common feature in trade relations.

Statement II emphasizes the importance of trust and fair play in trade agreements. Even if trade agreements help lower barriers to international commerce, it's essential for countries to believe that their trading partners are acting in good faith and adhering to the agreed-upon terms. If a country perceives unfair practices from its trading partners, it can lead to disputes and a breakdown of trade relations.

As both statements accurately reflect concepts in international trade, the correct answer is A. Both Statement I and Statement II are true.

90. (A): The IS (Investment-Savings) curve is typically depicted as a downward-sloping line in a macroeconomic model. The negative slope of the IS curve indicates an inverse relationship between the interest rate and the equilibrium level of income. The reason for the negative slope of the IS curve is primarily based on the investment component of aggregate demand. When the interest rate rises, the cost of borrowing increases, which makes investment less attractive for businesses. As a result, planned investment spending decreases. This reduction in investment spending leads to a decrease in aggregate demand and ultimately lowers the equilibrium level of income. The slope of the IS curve depends on the size of the multiplier and the sensitivity of investment spending to changes in the interest rate.

91. (B)	**92. (C)**	**93. (C)**
94. (D)	**95. (A)**	**96. (B)**
97. (C)	**98. (D)**	**99. (D)**
100. (A)		

Previous Years' Paper (Solved)

National Testing Agency (NTA)

UGC-NET Junior Research Fellowship & Assistant Professor Eligibility Exam

Economics, June-2022

(Online exam held on 08-10-2022)

PAPER-II

1. The change in welfare due to change in environmental quality is measured by:

A. Hedonic price function
B. Marginal implicit function
C. Marginal Willingness to Pay (WTP) function
D. Offer function

2. Pradhan Mantri Jan Dhan Yojana (PMJDY) has been a flagship programme of the Government of India.

(*a*) Beneficiaries of this scheme are eligible for accident insurance cover of ₹1 lakh now
(*b*) PMJDY is helpful in inclusive development
(*c*) PMJDY beneficiaries should not be given other benefits like benefits under MUDRA scheme
(*d*) It is leading to women empowerment
(*e*) More than 45 crore people have benefitted so far under PMJDY

Choose the most appropriate answer from the options given below:

A. (*a*), (*b*) and (*c*) only
B. (*b*), (*c*) and (*d*) only
C. (*b*), (*d*) and (*e*) only
D. (*a*), (*d*) and (*e*) only

3. Given below are two statements:

Statement I: Taking advantage of the increased demand for staples during the COVID-19 pandemic, India's agricultural exports continued to do well in 2021-2022

Statement II: Like in the year 2020-21, segments like marine products, buffalo meat, tea, coffee and dairy products continued to perform poorly in terms of exports from India in 2021-22

In the light of the above statements, choose the correct answer from the options given below:

A. Both Statement I and Statement II are true
B. Both Statement I and Statement II are false
C. Statement I is true, but Statement II is false
D. Statement I is false, but Statement II is true

4. The "tequila effect" indicates:

A. The spread of the 1994-95 Mexican crisis to other countries in Latin America
B. The spread of the 1997 crisis in Thailand to other countries in Asia
C. The subprime crisis emerged in 2007 in the United State
D. The domestic debt crisis occurred in Argentina in 1989

5. Arrange the following in ascending order:

(*a*) Growth rate of Gross National Income (at constant price) of India in 2015-16
(*b*) Growth rate of Gross National Income (at constant price) of India in 2016-17
(*c*) Growth rate of Gross National Income (at constant price) of India in 2017-18

(*d*) Growth rate of Gross National Income (at constant price) of India in 2018-19
(*e*) Growth rate of Gross National Income (at constant price) of India in 2019-20

Choose the correct answer from the options given below:
A. (*e*), (*a*), (*d*), (*c*), (*b*)
B. (*c*), (*e*), (*b*), (*d*), (*a*)
C. (*e*), (*d*), (*c*), (*a*), (*b*)
D. (*c*), (*d*), (*e*), (*b*), (*a*)

6. Which of the following are correct with respect to IS-LM model?
(*a*) The LM schedule slopes upward to the right.
(*b*) The LM schedule will shift to the left with an increase in quantity of money.
(*c*) The LM schedule gives equilibrium in the money market.
(*d*) The IS schedule will shift to the left when these is an increase in government expenditure
(*e*) The IS schedule will shift to the right when taxes are reduced

Choose the most appropriate answer from the options given below:
A. (*a*), (*c*), (*e*) only
B. (*a*), (*b*), (*c*), (*d*) only
C. (*a*), (*c*) only
D. (*b*), (*d*), (*c*), (*e*) only

7. Two factors of production, say A and B have the same price. The least cost combination of A and B for producing given level of output will be achieved at a point where the Iso-quant has slope equal to:
A. 0 B. 1
C. –1 D. 2

8. Match List I with List II:

List-I	List-II
(*a*) The greatest good for the greater number	(*i*) Learner's index
(*b*) Stability of general equilibrium	(*ii*) Bentham's criterion
(*c*) Degree of monopoly power	(*iii*) Tatonnement
(*d*) Third degree price-discrimination	(*iv*) Pigou

Choose the correct answer from the options given below:

	(*a*)	(*b*)	(*c*)	(*d*)
A.	(*iv*)	(*iii*)	(*i*)	(*ii*)
B.	(*iv*)	(*iii*)	(*ii*)	(*i*)
C.	(*i*)	(*iii*)	(*ii*)	(*iv*)
D.	(*ii*)	(*iii*)	(*i*)	(*iv*)

9. Given below are two statements:

Statement I: Devaluation always correct a chronic balance of payments deficit.

Statement II: An expected devaluation leads speculative, capital outflows from domestic country.

In the light of the above statements, choose the correct answer from the options given below:
A. Both Statement I and Statement II are true
B. Both Statement I and Statement II are false
C. Statement I is true, but Statement II is false
D. Statement I is false, but Statement II is true

10. What has been the reason for recent dip in vehicle registration in the country?
A. Shortage of semi-conductor chips
B. Poor credit supply by the banking sector
C. Sharp rise in vehicle prices
D. Reduced demand for vehicles

11. The irrelevance of money for real variables in the classical system is called
A. Fiscal neutrality
B. Monetary neutrality
C. Exchange rate neutrality
D. Technological neutrality

12. Which of the following are correct?
(*a*) $M_1 = C + DD + OD$
(*b*) $M_2 = M_1$ + saving deposits with post office saving banks
(*c*) $M_3 = M_2$ + net time deposits of banks
(*d*) $M_3 = M_1$ + net time deposits of banks
(*e*) $M_4 = M_1$ + total deposits with the post office savings

Choose the correct answer from the options given below:

A. (*a*), (*b*) and (*c*) only
B. (*a*), (*b*) and (*d*) only
C. (*a*), (*c*) and (*d*) only
D. (*b*), (*d*) and (*e*) only

13. Arrange the following events in sequence (the oldest one being first):

(*a*) The Tokyo Round
(*b*) The Uruguay Round
(*c*) The Annecy Round
(*d*) The Dillon Round
(*e*) The Torquay Round

Choose the correct answer from the options given below:

A. (*c*), (*e*), (*d*), (*b*), (*a*)
B. (*e*), (*c*), (*a*), (*d*), (*b*)
C. (*c*), (*e*), (*d*), (*a*), (*b*)
D. (*e*), (*c*), (*d*), (*a*), (*b*)

14. Match List I with List II:

List-I	List-II
(*a*) Reverse repo rate	(*i*) RBI provides loan to commercial banks for short term
(*b*) Bank rate	(*ii*) RBI provides loan to commercial banks for long term
(*c*) Repo rate	(*iii*) RBI borrows money from commercial banks
(*d*) Cash reserve ratio	(*iv*) Commercial banks have to deposit minimum ratio of their net total liabilities in RBI

Choose the correct answer from the options given below:

	(*a*)	(*b*)	(*c*)	(*d*)
A.	(*i*)	(*iii*)	(*ii*)	(*iv*)
B.	(*iii*)	(*ii*)	(*i*)	(*iv*)
C.	(*iii*)	(*i*)	(*ii*)	(*iv*)
D.	(*i*)	(*ii*)	(*iii*)	(*iv*)

15. If time deposit is not included, then the money multiplier will be (Cr = currency deposit ratio, rr = reserve deposit ratio)

A. (Cr + rr)/(1 + Cr)
B. (Cr + rr)/(rr + 1)
C. (Cr/rr)
D. (Cr + 1)/(rr + Cr)

16. Primary deficit is given by ....

A. Fiscal deficit – Interest payment
B. Revenue deficit – Interest payment
C. Budget deficit – Interest payment
D. Revenue receipt – Revenue expenditure

17. Write the steps to estimate the ECM/VAR model in time series:

(*a*) Unit root test
(*b*) ACF and PACF test
(*c*) ECM/VAR
(*d*) Inputting data
(*e*) Cointegration test

Choose the correct answer from the options given below:

A. (*d*), (*a*), (*e*), (*b*), (*c*)
B. (*d*), (*b*), (*a*), (*c*), (*e*)
C. (*d*), (*b*), (*a*), (*e*), (*c*)
D. (*b*), (*a*), (*d*), (*e*), (*c*)

18. Which of the following properties of matrix are correct?

(*a*) $(A')' = A$
(*b*) The rank of an $n \times n$ nonsingular matrix A must be less than n
(*c*) $(AB)' = B'A'$
(*d*) $(A + B)^n = A^n + B^n$
(*e*) $(A')^{-1} = (A^{-1})$

Choose the most appropriate answer from the options given below:

A. (*a*), (*b*) and (*c*) only
B. (*a*), (*d*) and (*e*) only
C. (*a*), (*c*) and (*d*) only
D. (*c*), (*d*) and (*e*) only

19. Match List I with List II:

List-I	List-II
(*a*) Andhra Pradesh PCI in 2020-21	(*i*) ₹ 98418
(*b*) Madhya Pradesh PCI in 2020-21	(*ii*) ₹ 109730
(*c*) Odisha PCI in 2020-21	(*iii*) ₹ 121267
(*d*) West Bengal PCI in 2020-21	(*iv*) ₹ 170215

Choose the correct answer from the options given below:

	(a)	(b)	(c)	(d)
A.	(ii)	(i)	(iii)	(iv)
B.	(iv)	(i)	(ii)	(iii)
C.	(iv)	(ii)	(i)	(iii)
D.	(iii)	(i)	(ii)	(iv)

20. The total revenue (R) and total cost (C) function of a firm are given by $R = 30Q - Q^2$. $C = 20 + 4Q$. Where Q is output, find the equilibrium output of the firm.

A. 4 B. 13
C. 15 D. 10

21. Real and nominal income is calculated respectively at:

A. Current and constant prices
B. Constant and current prices
C. Constant and constant prices
D. Current and current prices

22. Arrange the following Environmental disasters chronologically in accordance of their occurrence:

(a) Bhopal Gas Tragedy
(b) Chernobyl Explosion
(c) London Smong Episodes
(d) Exxon Valdez
(e) The Threemile Island Nuclear Disaster

Choose the correct answer from the options given below:

A. (a), (d), (e), (c), (b)
B. (c), (e), (a), (b), (d)
C. (a), (c), (d), (e), (b)
D. (b), (c), (d), (a), (e)

23. Given below are two statements: One is labelled as Assetion (A) and the other is labelled as Reason (R):

Assertion (A): The Endogenous growth theory examines production function that shows increasing returns.

Reason (R): Increasing returns in Endogenous growth theory is due to specialization and investment in knowledge capital and learning by doing.

In the light of the above statements, choose the most appropriate answer from the options given below:

A. Both (A) and (R) are correct and (R) is the correct explanation of (A)
B. Both (A) and (R) are correct, but (R) is not the correct explanation of (A)
C. (A) is correct, but (R) is not correct
D. (A) is not correct, but (R) is correct

24. 'PM Gatishakti' is driven by .... engines.

A. Four B. Five
C. Six D. Seven

25. A bag contains 20 tickets marked with numbers 1 to 20. One ticket is drawn at random. Find the probability that will be multiple of 2 or 5.

A. 0.7 B. 0.9
C. 0.6 D. 0.3

26. What are the practical consequences of multicollinearity in CLRM?

(a) R^2, the overall measure of goodness of fit can be very high
(b) OLS estimators are not BLUE
(c) OLS estimators have small variance and covariances
(d) *t* ratio of one or more coefficients is statistically insignificant
(e) The OLS estimators and their standard errors can be sensitive to small changes in the data.

Choose the correct answer from the options given below:

A. (a), (b) and (c) only
B. (a), (b) and (d) only
C. (a), (d) and (e) only
D. (b), (c) and (e) only

27. What does the result of the first empirical test of the Heckscher-Ohlin model by Wassily Leontief find?

A. U.S. exports were less capital-intensive that U.S. imports
B. U.S. exports were more capital-intensive than U.S. imports
C. U.S. exports were more human capital-intensive than U.S. imports
D. All the above

28. Which of the following is correct?

(*a*) The gross barter terms of trade uses quantity index for imports and exports

(*b*) Both gross barter terms of trade and net barter terms of trade make use of the price index for imports and exports

(*c*) The net barter terms of trade uses price index for imports and exports

(*d*) Both gross barter terms of trade and net barter terms of trade make use of the quantity index for imports and exports

(*e*) The gross barter terms of trade uses price index but the net barter terms of trade uses quantity index for imports and exports

Choose the correct answer from the options given below:

A. (*a*) and (*b*) only B. (*b*) and (*c*) only
C. (*c*) and (*e*) only D. (*a*) and (*c*) only

29. What will be the aggregate Domestic Income NDP (FC) of the economy for 2022-23: if

GDP (Market Price) = 27,654 crores

Depreciation = 2847 crores

Indirect taxes less subsidies = 2160 crores

A. 24,807 B. 22,647
C. 26,967 D. 28,467

30. Which of the followings are correct in case of normal distribution?

(*a*) $Q_1 + Q_2 = 2$ Md

(*b*) $\text{Q.D.} = \frac{1}{3}\sigma$

(*c*) $\text{Q.D.} = \frac{2}{3}\sigma$

(*d*) All moments of odd order about mean are zero

(*e*) $Q_1 + Q_2 =$ Md

Choose the correct answer from the options given below:

A. (*b*), (*d*) and (*e*) only
B. (*a*), (*b*) and (*d*) only
C. (*a*), (*c*) and (*d*) only
D. (*c*), (*d*) and (*e*) only

31. Here is given weights of items under use based classification of industrial production index of India (Base 2011-12)

(*a*) Primary goals 34.05%

(*b*) Capital goods 12.22%

(*c*) Intermediate goods 17.22%

(*d*) Infrastructure/Construction goods 12.34%

(*e*) Consumer goods 24.17%

Choose the correct answer from the options given below:

A. (*b*), (*c*) and (*d*) only
B. (*a*), (*b*) and (*e*) only
C. (*a*), (*c*) and (*d*) only
D. (*b*), (*d*) and (*e*) only

32. Match 'Labour Force' with the appropriate item from among the following:

A. Total work force
B. Employed + unemployed
C. Total educated manpower
D. Population in the age group 15-60

33. In the Mundell-Fleming model, under floating exchange rate, which policy is more effective to influence aggregate income?

A. Fiscal policy
B. Monetary policy
C. Exchange rate policy
D. None of the above

34. Which of the following are correct?

(*a*) The market is a system that works with price mechanism

(*b*) Market failure refers to the divergence of market equilibrium from pareto optimality

(*c*) Market fails to efficiently supply public goods and the same makes a case for govt. intervention

(*d*) Market efficiently works in the presence of positive externalities

(*e*) Market efficiently works in the presence of negative externalities

Choose the correct answer from the options given below:

A. (*a*), (*b*), (*c*) and (*d*) only
B. (*a*), (*b*) and (*c*) only
C. (*c*), (*d*) and (*e*) only
D. (*b*) and (*e*) only

35. Given below are two statements:

Statement I: Dualism refer to economic and social divisions in an economy, such as difference in the level of technology between sectors or regions, differences in the degree of geographic development and differences in social customs and attitudes.

Statement II: The developing countries in the early stage of development experience dualism, which have implications for future pattern and pace of development.

In the light of the above statements, choose the correct answer from the options given below:

A. Both Statement I and Statement II are true

B. Both Statement I and Statement II are false

C. Statement I is true, but Statement II is false

D. Statement I is false, but Statement II is true

36. Here is given sex ratio for different states of India for 2011:

(*a*) Gujarat : 942

(*b*) Madhya Pradesh : 931

(*c*) Odisha : 979

(*d*) Tamil Nadu : 996

(*e*) Haryana : 862

Choose the correct answer from the options given below:

A. (*b*), (*c*) and (*d*) only

B. (*a*) and (*b*) only

C. (*c*) and (*d*) only

D. (*c*), (*d*) and (*e*) only

37. Tools of expansionary Fiscal policy include:

(*a*) Raising Government expenditure

(*b*) Reducing Government expenditure

(*c*) Increasing tax rate

(*d*) Reducing tax rate

(*e*) Increasing money supply

Choose the correct answer from the options given below:

A. (*a*), (*d*) only

B. (*b*), (*c*) only

C. (*a*), (*d*), (*e*) only

D. (*b*), (*c*), (*e*) only

38. A stationary population is that when population growth is:

A. increasing at an increasing rate

B. increasing at a decreasing rate

C. grows at zero rate

D. 100%

39. Suppose a profit maximising monopolist is producing 800 units of output and is charging a price of ₹ 40 per unit. If the elasticity of demand for the product is –2, marginal cost of the last unit produced is ....

A. 10 B. –400

C. –2 D. 20

40. The provision for social goods, or the process by which total resource use is divided between private and social goods and by which the mix of social goods is chosen is known as ....

A. Allocation function

B. Distribution function

C. Stabilization function

D. Normalization function

41. The hypothesis of cumulative causation as an explanation of the backwardness of developing nations is associated with:

A. Ragnar Nurkse

B. Gunnar Myrdal

C. Arthus Lewis

D. Fei and Ranis

42. Which of the following were the part of FDI policy reforms and other measures during the Covid-19 pandemic period?

(*a*) 100 per cent FDI in the health sector

(*b*) Permitting foreign investment upto 100 per cent under automatic route in Telecom services sector

(*c*) "FDI monitoring cell" has been formed to expedite FDI proposals

(*d*) Raised the FDI limit from 49 per cent to 74 per cent in insurance companies under the automatic route (*e*) Reduced the limit of FDI in the defence sector to realize the vision of Atmanirbhar Bharat

Choose the correct answer from the options given below:

A. (*d*) and (*e*) only
B. (*b*), (*c*) and (*e*) only
C. (*b*), (*c*) and (*d*) only
D. (*a*), (*d*) and (*e*) only

43. Below are some of the features of the Micro, Small and Medium enterprises (MSMEs) in India.

(*a*) Revised definition of the MSMEs was brought in July 2020
(*b*) In this definition turnover limit varied between service and manufacturing enterprises
(*c*) In the revised definition turnover limit for small enterprises was ₹ 50 crore
(*d*) In this revised definition, investment limit in plant and machinery or equipment for medium enterprises was ₹ 50 crore.
(*e*) In the revised definition, investment limit for plant and machinery or equipment for medium enterprises was ₹ 5 crore.

Choose the most appropriate answer from the options given below:

A. (*a*), (*d*) and (*e*) only
B. (*a*), (*c*) and (*e*) only
C. (*d*) and (*e*) only
D. (*a*), (*b*), (*d*) and (*e*)

44. What are the primary goals of sustainability?

(*a*) The end of poverty and hunger
(*b*) Better standard of education and healthcare
(*c*) To achieve gender equality
(*d*) Sustainable economic growth
(*e*) To achieve both inter and intra generational equity

Choose the most appropriate answer from the options given below:

A. (*a*), (*b*), (*c*) and (*e*) only
B. (*a*), (*c*), (*d*) and (*d*) only
C. (*a*), (*b*), (*c*) and (*d*) only
D. (*a*), (*b*), (*c*) and (*d*) only

45. Match List I with List II:

List-I	List-II
(*a*) Testing of overall significance	(*i*) Chi-square test
(*b*) Testing the independence of attributes	(*ii*) Jarque-Bera test
(*c*) Testing the significance of regression coefficients	(*iii*) F-test
(*d*) Normality test	(*iv*) t-test

Choose the correct answer from the options given below:

	(*a*)	(*b*)	(*c*)	(*d*)
A.	(*i*)	(*ii*)	(*iii*)	(*iv*)
B.	(*iii*)	(*i*)	(*iv*)	(*ii*)
C.	(*i*)	(*iv*)	(*iii*)	(*ii*)
D.	(*i*)	(*iii*)	(*iv*)	(*ii*)

46. Growth in total consumption in India in 2021-22 is likely to be:

A. 5.0 per cent
B. 6.0 per cent
C. 7.0 per cent
D. 8.0 per cent

47. With reference to the views of classicals on public debt, which of the followings are correct:

(*a*) future financing gets more trouble some due to public debt
(*b*) public debt leads to a reduction of resources for productive private employment
(*c*) increasing public debt leads to currency depreciation and deflationary situations in the economy
(*d*) debt financing requires funds for interest payment and amortization, hence a double burden for exchequer
(*e*) Public debt leads to productive activities

Choose the most appropriate answer from the options given below:

A. (*a*), (*e*) and (*b*) only
B. (*c*), (*d*) and (*e*) only
C. (*e*), (*d*) and (*a*) only
D. (*a*), (*b*) and (*d*) only

48. Match List I with List II:

List-I	List-II
(*a*) Pure Public good	(*i*) Non-rival but excludable
(*b*) Pure private good	(*ii*) Non-excludable but rivalry
(*c*) Open access resources	(*iii*) Non-rival and non-excludable
(*d*) Congestible resource	(*iv*) Excludable and rival

Choose the correct answer from the options given below:

	(*a*)	(*b*)	(*c*)	(*d*)
A.	(*iii*)	(*iv*)	(*i*)	(*ii*)
B.	(*iii*)	(*iv*)	(*ii*)	(*i*)
C.	(*i*)	(*ii*)	(*iii*)	(*iv*)
D.	(*iii*)	(*ii*)	(*i*)	(*iv*)

49. In relation to considerations of demographic dividend there appears to be "demographic dualism" exhibited by the Indian states. In this regard consider the following factors.

(*a*) Total fertility rate
(*b*) Sex ratio
(*c*) Percapita income
(*d*) Urbanisation rate

Choose the correct answer from the options given below:

A. Both (*a*) and (*b*)
B. (*a*) only
C. (*b*) and (*c*) only
D. (*a*), (*b*) and (*d*) only

50. Which of the following strategy is **not** correct in order to have expansionary impact of fiscal policy?

A. Public expenditure must be financed by borrowings
B. Public expenditure must be financed through increased taxes only
C. Compensatory spending for public investment
D. Cut in taxes

51. Which of the following hold good for Lewis model of development?

(*a*) Unlimited supply of labour
(*b*) Marginal productivity of labour in the subsistence sector is equal to, or less than, subsistence wage
(*c*) Dual economy with a modern sector and a subsistence sector
(*d*) Agricultural sector subject to increasing returns
(*e*) Model that explains the crucial role of capitalist surplus in the development process

Choose the correct answer from the options given below:

A. (*a*), (*b*), (*c*), (*e*) only
B. (*a*), (*b*), (*d*), (*e*) only
C. (*b*), (*c*), (*d*), (*e*) only
D. (*a*), (*c*), (*d*), (*e*) only

52. Match List I with List II:

List-I	List-II
(*a*) FEMA	(*i*) 1969
(*b*) MRTP Act	(*ii*) 2002
(*c*) Competition Act	(*iii*) 1973
(*d*) FERA	(*iv*) 1999

Choose the correct answer from the options given below:

	(*a*)	(*b*)	(*c*)	(*d*)
A.	(*i*)	(*ii*)	(*iv*)	(*iii*)
B.	(*iii*)	(*i*)	(*ii*)	(*iv*)
C.	(*iv*)	(*ii*)	(*i*)	(*iii*)
D.	(*iv*)	(*i*)	(*ii*)	(*iii*)

53. Arrange the countries based on descending order of Human Development Index Value in 2019.

(*a*) Norway
(*b*) Bangladesh
(*c*) India
(*d*) China
(*e*) Nepal

Choose the correct answer from the options given below:

A. (*a*), (*d*), (*c*), (*b*), (*e*)
B. (*d*), (*a*), (*b*), (*e*), (*c*)
C. (*a*), (*d*), (*b*), (*c*), (*e*)
D. (*a*), (*d*), (*b*), (*e*), (*c*)

54. Hari's score in the statistics in the first year is 76, whereas the class average is 68 with a standard deviation of 5. What is Hari's Z-score?

A. 1.5 B. 1.6

C. 1.2 D. 1.4

55. If the income effect for a good is in the opposite direction as the substitution effect, but the substitution effect dominates then the good is:

A. Normal

B. Inferior but not giffen

C. Giffen

D. None of the above

56. Which of the followings is not a marginal condition of Pareto optimality criteria?

A. $MRS^{A}_{x,y} = MRS^{B}_{x,y} = \frac{P_x}{P_y}$

B. $MRTS^{x}_{L,K} = MRTS^{y}_{L,K} = \frac{w}{r}$

C. $MRS^{A}_{x,y} = MRS^{B}_{x,y} = MRPT_{x,y}$

D. $MRPT^{K}_{x,y} = MRPT^{L}_{x,y} = \frac{w}{r}$

57. A simultaneous equation model is said to be over-identified if:

A. Unique numerical values of the structural parameters can be obtained

B. More than one numerical values can be obtained for some of the parameters of the structural equations

C. Unique solution of all the structural coefficient is not possible

D. Structural coefficient cannot be estimated

58. Which of the followings are assumptions of ordinal utility analysis?

(*a*) Consumers are consistent in their preferences

(*b*) Consumer can measure the total utility received from any given basket of goods

(*c*) Consumer preferences follow transitivity

(*d*) Consumers are non-satiated with respect to goods they confront

(*e*) Consumers are irrational

Choose the correct answer from the options given below:

A. (*b*), (*c*), and (*d*) only

B. (*c*), (*d*) and (*e*) only

C. (*a*), (*c*) and (*d*) only

D. (*a*), (*b*) and (*c*) only

59. The Central bank policy of altering the domestic credit extended by it in an equal and opposite direction to the variation in foreign exchange reserves so that the monetary base remains unchanged is called:

A. Stabilization

B. Monetary expansion

C. Fiscal expansion

D. Sterilisation

60. Which of the following modern Indian Economic thinker had not gone abroad for study or work?

A. Mahatma Gandhi

B. Ram Manohar Lohia

C. B.R. Ambedkar

D. Deen Dayal Upadhyaya

61. Match List I with List II:

List-I	List-II
(*a*) Absolute Income Hypothesis	(*i*) Milton Friedman
(*b*) Relative Income Hypothesis	(*ii*) J.M. Keynes
(*c*) Permanent Income Hypothesis	(*iii*) James Dusenberry
(*d*) Life Cycle Hypothesis	(*iv*) Franco Modiglani

Choose the correct answer from the options given below:

	(*a*)	(*b*)	(*c*)	(*d*)
A.	(*ii*)	(*i*)	(*iv*)	(*iii*)
B.	(*ii*)	(*iii*)	(*i*)	(*iv*)
C.	(*iv*)	(*iii*)	(*ii*)	(*i*)
D.	(*iii*)	(*ii*)	(*i*)	(*iv*)

62. 'Menu Cost' is a concept used in:

A. Classical economics

B. Neo-classical economics

C. New-Keynesian economics

D. Keynesian economics

63. The fitted regression equation is given by $Y_i = -10 + 0.6X$. What is the value of the residual at the point X = 40, Y = 60.

A. 74 B. 46
C. 0 D. 45

64. Match List I with List II:

List-I	List-II
(*a*) Size matters in International trade	(*i*) Paul Krugman
(*b*) Economies of scale and monopolistic competition in international trade	(*ii*) Mercantilists
(*c*) Technological gap theory of trade	(*iii*) M.V. Posner
(*d*) Zero sum game of trade	(*iv*) The gravity model

Choose the correct answer from the options given below:

	(*a*)	(*b*)	(*c*)	(*d*)
A.	(*iv*)	(*iii*)	(*i*)	(*ii*)
B.	(*iv*)	(*i*)	(*iii*)	(*ii*)
C.	(*iii*)	(*i*)	(*iv*)	(*ii*)
D.	(*iii*)	(*iv*)	(*i*)	(*ii*)

65. Match List I with List II:

List-I	List-II
(*a*) Rural-Urban migration	(*i*) Arthur Lewis
(*b*) Economic development with unlimited supply of labour	(*ii*) Gunnar Myrdal
(*c*) Process of cumulative causation	(*iii*) Raul Prebisch
(*d*) Decline in terms of trade of primary commodities	(*iv*) Harris-Todaro

Choose the correct answer from the options given below:

	(*a*)	(*b*)	(*c*)	(*d*)
A.	(*i*)	(*iv*)	(*ii*)	(*iii*)
B.	(*iv*)	(*i*)	(*ii*)	(*iii*)
C.	(*i*)	(*iv*)	(*iii*)	(*ii*)
D.	(*i*)	(*iii*)	(*ii*)	(*iv*)

66. Net migration refers to:

A. overall level of population change resulting from total migrants and emigrants
B. is the difference between the number of immigrant workers and the number of emigrant workers
C. does not include refugees and other lawful migrants
D. includes refugees only

67. Given below are two statements:

Statement I: If you bought a product which now becomes subject to tax, you will be in a better position to avoid the tax and the seller bears with a larger part if your demand is elastic while seller's supply is inelastic.

Statement II: A tax on salt is likely to be borne by the consumer.

In the light of the above statements, choose the most appropriate answer from the options given below:

A. Both Statement I and Statement II are correct
B. Both Statement I and Statement II are incorrect
C. Statement I is correct, but Statement II is incorrect
D. Statement I is incorrect, but Statement II is correct

68. The binomial distribution can be used under the following conditions:

(*a*) *n*, the number of trials is finite and independent
(*b*) *n*, the number of trials is infinite and independent
(*c*) Each trial results in two mutually exclusive and exhaustive outcomes, terms as success and failure.
(*d*) P, the probability of success is constant for each trial
(*e*) The probability of failure does not remain same for each trial

Choose the correct answer from the options given below:

A. (*a*), (*c*) and (*e*) only
B. (*b*), (*c*) and (*d*) only
C. (*a*), (*c*) and (*d*) only
D. (*b*), (*c*) and (*e*) only

69. The strategy of choosing the policy which has the best possible outcome is known as ....

A. Dominant strategy
B. Maxi max
C. Mini max
D. Maxi min

70. Find the rank of $A = \begin{vmatrix} 6 & 3 & 5 \\ -10 & 2 & 8 \\ 5 & 2 & 3 \end{vmatrix}$

A. 3 B. 2
C. 1 D. 0

71. In the context of the transaction demand for money, the square root rule was developed by:

A. Kydland-Prescott B. Friedman-Scwartz
C. Boumol-Tobin D. J.M. Keynes

72. In which year, Gross Domestic saving rate was the highest?

A. 2004-05 B. 2007-08
C. 2011-12 D. 2016-17

73. Provide proper chronological order of different schemes launched in India:

(*a*) Pradhan Mantri Jan Aushadhi Yojana
(*b*) Pradhan Mantri Ujjwala Yojana
(*c*) Atal Pension Yojana
(*d*) PM Jan Dhan Yojana
(*e*) Ayushman Bharat Yojana

Choose the correct answer from the options given below:

A. (*c*), (*b*), (*a*), (*d*), (*e*)
B. (*c*), (*d*), (*b*), (*a*), (*e*)
C. (*d*), (*a*), (*b*), (*c*), (*e*)
D. (*d*), (*c*), (*a*), (*b*), (*e*)

74. When MPC = 0.75, a decrease in taxes ₹ 20 crore will increase GDP by:

A. ₹ 200 crores B. ₹ 100 crores
C. ₹ 600 crores D. ₹ 800 crores

75. Match List I with List II:

List-I	List-II
(*a*) Money supply and price level in an economy are indirect proportion	(*i*) A.W. Phillips
(*b*) Inverse relationship between unemployment and rate of wage inflation	(*ii*) Fisher
(*c*) Profit as reward for innovation	(*iii*) Robert Lucas
(*d*) Policy ineffective proposition	(*iv*) Joseph Schumpeter

Choose the correct answer from the options given below:

	(*a*)	(*b*)	(*c*)	(*d*)
A.	(*ii*)	(*i*)	(*iv*)	(*iii*)
B.	(*iii*)	(*ii*)	(*i*)	(*iv*)
C.	(*ii*)	(*iv*)	(*iii*)	(*i*)
D.	(*iv*)	(*iii*)	(*ii*)	(*i*)

76. Basic characteristics of an under developed economy:

(*a*) A low level of technology and poor human capital
(*b*) Higher level of GDP and percapita income
(*c*) A high proportion of the labour force engaged in agriculture and low agriculture productivity
(*d*) A high proportion of domestic expenditure on food
(*e*) Higher incidence of poverty

Choose the most appropriate answer from the options given below:

A. (*a*), (*c*), (*d*) and (*e*) only
B. (*a*), (*c*), (*b*) and (*e*) only
C. (*b*), (*d*) and (*e*) only
D. (*b*) only

77. If the demand function is: $P = 35 - 2x - x^2$ and the demand x_0 is 3. What will be the consumer's surplus?

A. 27 B. 25
C. 60 D. 20

78. Arrange the following chronologically in order of their years of first occurrence:

(*a*) Environmental Kuznets Curve Hypothesis
(*b*) Limits to growth theorem

(*c*) Bouldings 'The Economics of Coming Spaceship Earth'
(*d*) Jevon's Coal Question
(*e*) Raechel Canson's Silent Spring

Choose the correct answer from the options given below:
A. (*e*), (*a*), (*b*), (*d*), (*c*)
B. (*a*), (*c*), (*d*), (*b*), (*e*)
C. (*d*), (*a*), (*e*), (*c*), (*b*)
D. (*e*), (*d*), (*c*), (*b*), (*a*)

79. Integrate: $\dfrac{x^2}{x+2}$

A. $\dfrac{4x}{(x+2)^2}+c$

B. $\dfrac{x^2}{2}+2x+4\log(x+2)+c$

C. $\dfrac{x^2}{2}-2x+4\log(x+2)+c$

D. $\dfrac{x^2}{2}-2x+c$

80. Monetary policy instruments are:
(*a*) Changes in public expenditure
(*b*) Changes in taxation
(*c*) Open market operations
(*d*) Bank reserve requirement
(*e*) Interest rate policy

Choose the most appropriate answer from the options given below:
A. (*a*) and (*b*) only
B. (*a*), (*b*) and (*c*) only
C. (*c*), (*d*) and (*e*) only
D. (*b*), (*d*) and (*e*) only

81. Criteria and weights assigned by the Fifteenth Finance Commission of India for Horizontal Devolution:
(*a*) Area
(*b*) Forest and Ecology
(*c*) Income Distance
(*d*) Tax and Fiscal efforts
(*e*) Demographic performance

Choose the correct answer from the options given below:
A. (*d*), (*b*), (*e*), (*a*), (*c*)
B. (*b*), (*d*), (*a*), (*e*), (*c*)
C. (*e*), (*a*), (*d*), (*c*), (*b*)
D. (*a*), (*d*), (*b*), (*c*), (*e*)

82. In Harrod-Domar Model, if the growth rate of income is 8% and the capital output ratio is 4% then the saving rate must be:
A. 32% B. 2%
C. 36% D. 1/2%

83. Which of the following are correct?
(*a*) Current account includes merchandise export
(*b*) Current account do not include merchandise export
(*c*) Current account includes invisible export
(*d*) Current account do not includes invisible export
(*e*) Current account includes both merchandise exports and imports and invisible exports and imports

Choose the correct answer from the options given below:
A. (*a*), (*b*) and (*c*) only
B. (*a*), (*c*) and (*e*) only
C. (*a*), (*d*) and (*e*) only
D. (*c*), (*d*) and (*e*) only

84. Which of the following conditions are satisfied for a rationale firm to achieve its equilibrium by maximising Q = *f*(L, K) subject to C = *w*L + *r*K.

(*a*) $\dfrac{\frac{\partial Q}{\partial L}}{\frac{\partial Q}{\partial K}}=\dfrac{w}{r}$

(*b*) $\dfrac{\partial^2 Q}{\partial L^2}>0, \dfrac{\partial^2 Q}{\partial K^2}>0$

(c) $\frac{\partial^2 Q}{\partial L^2} < 0$ and $\frac{\partial^2 Q}{\partial K^2} > 0$

(d) $\frac{\partial^2 Q}{\partial L^2} < 0$ and $\frac{\partial^2 Q}{\partial K^2} < 0$

(e) $\left(\frac{\partial^2 Q}{\partial L^2}\right)\left(\frac{\partial^2 Q}{\partial K^2}\right) > \left(\frac{\partial^2 Q}{\partial L \partial K}\right)^2$

Choose the correct answer from the options given below:
A. (a), (b) and (e) only
B. (a), (d) and (e) only
C. (a) and (e) only
D. (a) and (b) only

85. If we have objective function involving *n* variables:
$U = f(X_1, X_2, X_3, ..., X_n)$ subject to $\phi(X_1, X_2, X_3, ... X_n) = 0$. The second order condition for extremum to be:

(a) For maximum $|\bar{H}_2| < 0, |\bar{H}_3| < 0...$

(b) For maximum $|\bar{H}_2| > 0, |\bar{H}_3| < 0...$

(c) For maximum $|\bar{H}_2| < 0, |\bar{H}_3| > 0...$

(d) For minimum $|\bar{H}_2| < 0, |\bar{H}_3| < 0...$

(e) For minimum $|\bar{H}_2| > 0, |\bar{H}_3| > 0...$

Choose the correct answer from the options given below:
A. (a) and (d) only
B. (b) and (d) only
C. (c) and (e) only
D. (b) and (e) only

86. Arrange the states in descending order based on percentage of population who are multidimensionally poor based on NITI Aayog Report 2021.
(a) Bihar
(b) Odisha
(c) Rajasthan
(d) Uttar Pradesh
(e) Madhya Pradesh

Choose the correct answer from the options given below:
A. (a), (d), (e), (c), (b)
B. (a), (e), (c), (d), (b)
C. (a), (c), (e), (b), (d)
D. (a), (b), (c), (e), (d)

87. Which of the following conditions prevail in the long run equilibrium of industry for achieving optimal resource allocation:
(a) The output is produced at the minimum feasible cost
(b) Consumer pays the minimum possible price which just covers the marginal cost of the product
(c) Plants are used at full capacity in long run
(d) Firms earn supernormal profits
(e) Perfect competitive firms and price mechanism operates

Choose the correct answer from the options given below:
A. (a), (b), (c) and (e) only
B. (c), (d) and (e) only
C. (b), (d) and (e) only
D. (a), (b) and (e) only

88. One of the various qualitative instruments used by the central bank during inflation is:
A. Raise margin requirement
B. Remove margin requirement
C. Reduce margin requirement
D. Fix margin requirement

89. Arrange the different schools of thought in a sequence of their occurrence starting from the oldest.
(a) Physiocrats
(b) Keynesian economics
(c) Classical economics
(d) New Keynesian economics
(e) Monetarist Counter revolution

Choose the correct answer from the options given below:
A. (a), (b), (c), (e), (d)
B. (a), (c), (e), (b), (d)

C. (*a*), (*b*), (*e*), (*c*), (*d*)
D. (*a*), (*c*), (*b*), (*e*), (*d*)

90. In which stage of the product cycle model, the imitating country starts producing the product for domestic consumption?

A. Stage - III B. Stage - II
C. Stage - I D. Stage - V

Directions (Qs. No. 91-95): *Read the given passage and answer the questions:*

Although globalisation is often accused of increasing world poverty, the fact is that poverty would probably be even more widespread without globalisation. What is true is that globalisation did not benefit all nations. What globalisation can be blamed for is not spreading the benefits of increased efficiency and openness that come with globalisation more evenly and equitably to all nations. The stock of Foreign Direct investments around the World states that in 2010, the inward stock of FDI of developing countries was 48 per cent that of developed countries, while their stock of outward FDI was about 17 per cent that of developed countries. The New International Economies of Scale (NIES) states that – more and more products manufactured by international corporations have parts and components made in many different nations. The reason is to minimise production costs. Foreign "sourcing" of inputs is often not a matter of choice to earn higher profit, but simply a requirement to remain competitive. The carry Trade is the strategy in which an investor borrows a low yielding currency and lends (invest in) a higher yielding currency. The risk is that if during the investment period, the higher yielding currency depreciates against the lower yielding currency by a higher percentage than the positive interest differentials, the investor will lose money.

91. Which of the following reflects the most correct sense of the New International Economies of Scale (NIES):

A. All the parts and components of a product is manufactured in the host country only
B. When all the parts and components of the product manufactured in the host country, it minimize production costs in each of the producing country.
C. Cheaper inputs from different countries are required to remains competitive
D. The NIES is more concern about profit rather than to remain competitive

92. Which of the following is true?

A. Because of globalisation poverty has increased in all the countries of the world
B. Because of globalisation poverty has reduced in all the countries of the world
C. Without globalisation world poverty would probably be even more widespread
D. Without globalisation world poverty would probably be even less widespread

93. What for globalisation has been blamed?

A. Globalisation has neither increased efficiency nor openness
B. Globalisation has increased both efficiency & openness
C. Globalisation has increased efficiency but not openness
D. Globalisation has not spreaded the benefits of increased efficiency and openness equitably to all nations

94. During the investment period, if the higher yielding currency depreciates against the lower yielding currency by a higher percentage than the positive interest differential then which of the following will occur?

A. The investor will lose money
B. The investor will earn profit
C. The profit of the investor will remain unaffected
D. None of the above

95. Which of the following in incorrect?

A. The inward stock of FDI to developing countries is less than that of developed countries
B. The outward stock of FDI from developing countries is less than that of developed countries

C. Both the inward stock of FDI to developing countries and outward stock of FDI from developing countries remained higher in developing countries than developed countries

D. Both the inward stock of FDI to developing countries and outward stock of FDI from developing countries remained lower in developing countries than developed countries.

Directions (Qs. No. 96-100): *Read the given passage and answer the questions on the basis of passage:*

Since the second five year plan, the Government of India has been emphasizing on development of industry on promoting self reliance India. But at that time the priority was for import substitution and export-promotion. Though same phenomenon is still relevant the priority of Industrialisation has been changed. Industry helps not only for the self reliance and reducing dependence on Foreign Countries but it creates massive employment for a populated country like India. The Startups India Programme started in 2014 which hence for promoting new initiatives and infact industries in critical domains having strategic importance. The recognised startups has been increased from 726 in FY 2016-17 to 65,861 in FY2021-22. The Startups spread across 640 districts and created jobs more then 7 lakhs. These startups have been recently developed in new domain and sectors of strategic importance including development of IT services, hardware technology, software enterprises, artificial intelligence, robotics and technology of banking & finance in across 56 sectors. As on Feb. 2022, the ministry of commerce and industry has allocated ₹ 2,791.29 crore to SIDBI which inturn committed ₹ 6,795 crore to 82 alternative investment funds (AIFs) while ₹ 8,785 crore have been invested by supported AIFs in 574 startups and ₹ 945 crore has been allocated under the scheme for a period of four years starting from 2021-22 to fund the startups for proof of concept, prototype, trails of products, entry of market and commercialization. However, it is important for sustaining these startups for long term development and for creation of employment. Continued investment in this sectors, export promotion and startups products, innovation in new sectors and creation of domestic demands for this products are important for long term development and attracting new startups.

96. Which of the following is true in case of startups in India?

A. The startups increased by 7.25% during 2016-17 and 2021-22

B. The sectoral growth of startups is taken place by 56%

C. The startups have developed is important sectors like agriculture, tourism and irrigation

D. The recognized sectors have created jobs more than 7 lakhs

97. Which of the following sectors have not developed recently in startups?

A. IT services

B. Robotics

C. Artificial intelligence

D. Space technology

98. Which of the following measures is required for sustaining startups?

A. Attracting FDI startups

B. Tax holidays on startups

C. Creation of domestic demands for startups

D. Encouraging startups in defence sectors

99. What is the prioritized objective of industrialization in terms of startups initiatives?

A. Self reliance

B. Employment opportunities

C. Both self reliance and employment opportunities

D. Export reduction

100. How much amount has been allocated under the scheme of startups to find new startups for proof of concepts, prototype and trials of products, entry of market and commercialization?

A. ₹ 2,791.29 crore B. ₹ 6,795.00 crore

C. ₹ 945 crore D. ₹ 12,521 crore

ANSWERS

1. **(C):** The Marginal Willingness to Pay (WTP) function is a concept used in welfare economics to measure the change in welfare resulting from a change in environmental quality. It represents the additional amount of money individuals are willing to pay for a small improvement in environmental quality. The WTP function is typically derived through surveys and other empirical methods that assess people's preferences and willingness to pay for environmental improvements. These surveys usually present individuals with hypothetical scenarios or real-life choices where they must make trade-offs between environmental quality and monetary costs. The WTP function is often expressed as a function of the level of environmental quality. It indicates the maximum amount of money individuals are willing to pay to achieve a specific level of environmental improvement or to avoid a deterioration in environmental quality. The WTP function is usually assumed to be increasing, meaning that as environmental quality improves, individuals are generally willing to pay more for additional improvements.

2. **(C):** Pradhan Mantri Jan-Dhan Yojana (PMJDY) is a National Mission on Financial Inclusion that takes an integrated strategy to ensure that all households in the country have access to financial services.
   - The PMJDY envisions universal banking access, with each household having at least one basic banking account. Besides it also ensures financial literacy, insurance, access to credit, and a pension plan. In addition, each beneficiary will receive a RuPay Debit card with a built-in 1 lakh accident insurance cover.
   - The plan asks for the transfer of all government money to beneficiaries' accounts and the promotion of the Union Government's Direct Benefits Transfer (DBT) scheme.
   - Poor connectivity and on-line transactions will be addressed as technological issues.
   - The Scheme also intends to use mobile transactions through telecom operators and their established centres as Cash Out Points for Financial Inclusion.
   - A concerted attempt is also being made to recruit the country's youth to engage in the Mission Mode Program.
   - The "Pradhan Mantri Jan-Dhan Yojana (PMJDY)" aims to ensure that the excluded sections, such as weaker sections and low-income groups, have access to various financial services such as basic savings, loans, remittances, insurance, and pension.
   - More than 43.04 crore beneficiaries banked under PMJDY since inception, amounting to ₹ 146,231 crore (as on 28 aug, 2021, PIB Delhi).

3. **(C):** Taking advantage of the increased demand for staples during the COVID-19 pandemic, India's agricultural exports continue to do well in 2021-22, backed by an effective agriculture export policy. The export of agriculture and allied products (including marine and plantation products) grew by 23.2 per cent to US$ 31.0 billion during April-November, 2021 over the corresponding period of 2020-21 and by 35.0 per cent over April-November, 2019, surpassing the pre-pandemic levels.

   Moreover, it is observed that even the segments like marine products, buffalo meat, tea, coffee and dairy products, which had not performed well during 2020-21, have registered substantial growth during the current year 2021-22.

4. **(A):** The Tequila Effect hypothesis states that the economic crisis that affected several South American countries in 1995 was caused by an exogenous capital flight triggered by the loss of confidence of foreign investors after

the collapse of the Mexican peso in December, 1994.

5. **(C):** Growth rate of Gross National Income in ascending order:

Growth rate of Gross National Income (at constant price) of India in 2019-20	2.3%
Growth rate of Gross National Income (at constant price) of India in 2018-19	5.2%
Growth rate of Gross National Income (at constant price) of India in 2017-18	5.5%
Growth rate of Gross National Income (at constant price) of India in 2015-16	6.7%
Growth rate of Gross National Income (at constant price) of India in 2016-17	6.9%

6. **(A):** IS curve is the locus of all equilibrium points of good market. LM curve is the locus of all equilibrium points of money market.

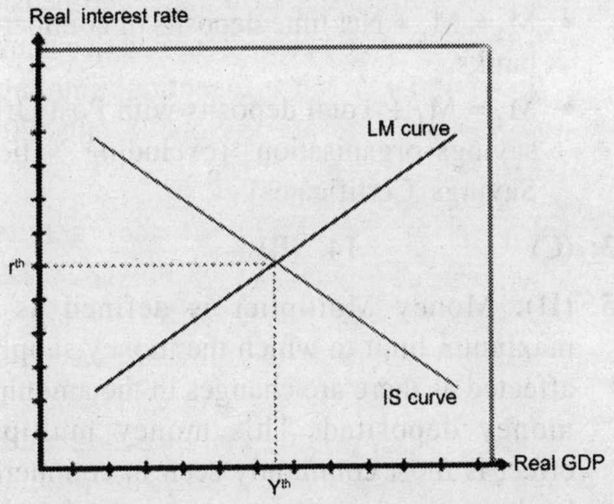

John hicks was the first economist who introduced IS-LM model in 1936. The three exogenous variables in IS-LM model are liquidity, investment and consumption. This model shows how the market for economic good interacts with the loanable funds market. IS curve has stock equilibrium i.e. savings and investment are measured at particular point of time. LM curve has flow equilibrium i.e. liquidity and money supply are measured over a period of time.

7. **(C):** The slope of an isoquant represents the rate at which two factors of production can be substituted while keeping the level of output constant. In this case, we have two factors of production, A and B, with the same price. When factors of production have the same price, the least-cost combination of these factors can be achieved by substituting them at a 1 : 1 ratio. This means that the rate of substitution between A and B is equal to their price ratio, which is 1 : 1. Therefore, the slope of the isoquant in this case would be –1.

8. **(D): Learner's Index:** The Lerner index is an economics measure to gauge monopoly. It determines the relationship between a commodity's selling price and marginal cost of production.

It is expressed as:

Lerner index = (Price – Marginal Cost)/Price

A low Lerner index shows that the firm operates in a highly competitive market. If L = 0, the business has perfect competition and a low-profit margin. Also, the price elasticity of demand is high in such a market. When L = 1, the firm enjoys a monopoly in the market; in such a scenario, the profit margins are huge, and there is little price elasticity of demand in the market.

Bentham's Criterion: Jeremy Bentham, an English economist, argued that welfare is improved when 'the greatest good (is secured) for the greatest number'. Implicit in this dictum is the assumption that the total welfare is the sum of the utilities of the individuals of the society. The application of Bentham's ethical system to economics has serious short-comings. To illustrate the pitfalls in Bentham's criterion let us assume that the society consists of three individuals, A, B and C, so that

$$W = U_A + U_B + U_C$$

According to Bentham $\Delta W > 0$ if $(\Delta U_A + \Delta U_B + \Delta U_C) > 0$. However, assume that the change which resulted in the changes in the individual utilities is such, that A's and B's utility increases, while Cs utility decreases, but $(\Delta U_A + \Delta U_B) > |\Delta U_C|$.

Tatonnement: It a concept introduced by French economist Léon Walras (1834-1910), is a trial-and-error process by which equilibrium prices and stability are reached in competitive markets. Walras found that "the markets which are best organized from the competitive standpoint are those in which purchases and sales are made by auction."

Pigou: The traditional classification of the forms of price discrimination is due to Pigou (1920). *First-degree, or perfect price discrimination involves* the seller charging a different price for each unit of the good in such a way that the price charged for each unit is equal to the maximum willingness to pay for that unit. *Second-degree price discrimination*, or non-linear pricing, occurs when prices differ depending on the number of units of the good bought, but not across consumers. That is, each consumer faces the same price schedule, but the schedule involves different prices for different amounts of the good purchased. Quantity discounts or premia are the obvious examples. *Third-degree price discrimination* means that different purchasers are charged different prices, but each purchaser pays a constant amount for each unit of the good bought. This is perhaps the most common form of price discrimination; examples are student discounts, or charging different prices on different days of the week.

9. (D): Devaluation is the deliberate reduction in the external value of the currency country. Devaluation will result in expensive imports and will motivate the exporters to export more. Hence, the balance of payment fill improves in case of deficit.

10. (A): Increasing electrification and a preference for high-end passenger vehicles means that shortages of specific chips and electronics will continue for some products. This in turn means many vehicle manufacturers are unable to ramp up volumes of in-demand products.

11. (B): The neutrality of money is a belief that depicts the fact that any change in the supply of money has implications on price and wages. At the same time, overall economic productivity remains unaffected, or in other words, monetary supply has sufficient power to affect the cost of goods and services. Still, it doesn't have any impact on the overall economy. It is a concept of classical economics.

12. (B): The total stock of money in circulation among the public at a particular point in time is called money supply. The circulating money involves the currency, printed notes, money in the deposit accounts and in the form of other liquid assets. The Reserve Bank of India publishes figures for four alternative measures of the money supply— M_1, M_2, M_3 and M_4.

- M_1 = CU (currency (notes plus coins)) + DD (net demand deposits held by commercial banks) + Other deposits with the RBI
- $M_2 = M_1$ + Savings deposits with Post Office savings banks
- $M_3 = M_1$ + Net time deposits of commercial banks
- $M_4 = M_3$ + Total deposits with Post Office savings organisations (excluding National Savings Certificates)

13. (C) **14. (B)**

15. (D): Money Multiplier is defined as the maximum limit to which the money supply is affected as there are changes in the amount of money deposited. This money multiplier effect is most commonly seen in commercial banks since deposits are accepted by them and after a while, they have kept the money as a reserve, to inject liquidity in the economy, they start distributing the money as loans. If time deposit is not included, then the money multiplier will be calculated as:

$$(Cr + 1)/(rr + Cr)$$

16. (A): Primary Deficit is the difference between the current year's fiscal deficit (total income – total expenditure of the government) and the interest paid on the borrowings of the previous year. Once calculated, the primary deficit reflects the amount the Government needs to borrow to meet its current year's expenses. In other words, the primary deficit is the amount that reflects the total expenditure of the Government against its total income.

Primary Deficit Formula

Primary deficit = Fiscal deficit – Interest payments

Or

Primary deficit = Total revenue earned – Expenses incurred excluding interest payments

17. (C) **18. (*)** **19. (B)**

20. (B): Given:

Total Revenue = $30Q - Q^2$

Total Cost = 20 + 4Q

Equilibrium output of the firm:

MR = MC

Marginal Revenue = d/dq (Total Revenue)

= 30 – 2Q

Total Cost = 20 + 4Q

Marginal Cost = d/dq (Total Cost) = 4

MR = MC

30 – 2Q = 4

26 = 2Q

26/2 = Q

13 = Q.

21. (B): When goods and services produced in a year are valued at the prices prevailing in that particular year, we get nominal income.

Nominal Income = Current Price (P1) × Current quantity (Q1)

When good and services produced in a year are valued at prices of a fixed base year (constant price), we get Real income.

Real income = Base Year Price (P0) × Current quantity (Q1)

Nominal income can be converted to real income by the following:

Real income = Nominal income/Current Price Index * 100.

22. (B)

23. (A): Endogenous growth theory maintains that economic growth is primarily the result of internal forces, rather than external ones. It argues that improvements in productivity can be tied directly to faster innovation, investment in knowledge capital and learning by doing, and more investments in human capital from governments and private sector institutions. This view contrasts with neoclassical economics.

24. (D): Finance Minister Nirmala Sitaraman said on 1 February that PM Gati Shakti National Master Plan is a Transformative approach for economic growth and sustainable development by and driven by seven engines, Roads, Railways, airports, ports, mass, transport, waterways and logistics, infrastructure.

PM Gati Shakti National Master Plan (PMGS-NMP) was launched on 13th October, 2021 for providing multimodal connectivity infrastructure to various economic zones.

To prioritize its projects under the PM Gati Shakti Scheme, the Ministry of Railways has set up a new directorate under the Railway Board. The Road Transportation and Indian Highways Ministry had made notable progress under the PM Modi government's "PM Gati Shakti National Master Plan", which was aimed at improving the multi-modal connectivity and Connectivity of India also. The Union Minister for Ports, Shipping, and, Waterways, Sarbananda Sonowal said that the PM Gati Shakti mission will lead to the removal of all bottlenecks in infrastructure development along with achieving timely completion of projects.

25. (C): Since the bag has 20 tickets, total number of cases $n = 20$

Let

A : getting a multiple of 2

B : getting a multiple of 5

Event A has 10 favourable outcomes

A = {2, 4, 6, 8, 10, 12, 14, 16, 18, 20}

∴ P(A) = 10/20 = 1/2

Event B has four favourable outcomes

B = {5, 10, 15, 20)

∴ P(B) = 4/20

$A \cap B$ = {10, 20]

∴ $P(A \cap B)$ = 2/20 ∴

P(multiple of 2 or 5) = P(A ∪ B)

$$= P(A) + P(B) - P(A \cap B)$$
$$= 10/20 + 4/20 - 2/20$$
$$= 12/20 = 3/5.$$

26. **(C):** In CLRM, we assume that no independent variable is a perfect linear function of any other independent variable.

- If a variable X1 can be written as a perfect linear function of X2 , X3 , etc., then we say these variables are perfectly collinear.
- When this is true of more than one independent variable, they are perfectly multicollinear.
- Perfect multicollinearity presents technical problems for computing the least squares estimates.

The practical consequences of multicollinearity in CLRM are:

- ***The least squares estimates will have big standard errors:*** we're trying to estimate the marginal effect of an independent variable holding the other independent variables constant. But the strong linear relationship among the independent variables makes this difficult - we always see them move together. That is, there is very little information in the data about the thing we're trying to estimate. Consequently, we can't estimate it very precisely: the standard errors are large.
- ***The computed t-scores will be small:*** the sampling distribution is centered over the true parameter values (the estimates are unbiased) but the sampling variance is very large (draw a picture). Thus, we're "likely" to obtain estimates that are "far" from the true parameter values because the estimates are very imprecise, we have a difficult time rejecting any null hypothesis, because we know that even when the null is true, we could find an estimate far from the hypothesized value. From the formula for the t statistic:

$$t = \frac{\hat{\beta}_k - \beta_{0k}}{se(\hat{\beta}_k)}$$

we see that because the standard error is big, the t statistic is small (all else equal), and thus we are unlikely to reject H_0.

- ***Small changes in data or specification lead to large changes in parameter estimates:*** think about the sampling distribution of the least squares estimates: it's very spread out around the true coefficient values. In different samples/specifications we are likely to get very different estimates because there is so little independent variation in the independent variables, the least squares estimator puts a lot of weight on small differences between them. Small changes in sample/specification that affect these small differences (even a little bit) get a lot of weight in the Estimates. E.g., if two variables are almost identical in most of the sample, the estimator relies on a few observations where they move differently to distinguish between them. Dropping one of these observations can have a big effect on the estimates.

27. **(A):** Heckscher-Ohlin theory, in economics, a theory of comparative advantage in international trade according to which countries in which capital is relatively plentiful and labour relatively scarce will tend to export capital-intensive products and import labour-intensive products, while countries in which labour is relatively plentiful and capital relatively scarce will tend to export labour intensive products and import capital-intensive products. The theory was developed by the Swedish economist Bertil Ohlin (1899-1979) on the basis of work by his teacher the Swedish economist Eli Filip Heckscher (1879-1952). For his work on the theory, Ohlin was awarded the Nobel Prize for Economics (the Sveriges Riksbank Prize in Economic Sciences in Memory of Alfred Nobel) in 1977.

One early study of the Heckscher-Ohlin theory was carried out by Wassily Leontief, a Russian-born U.S. economist. Leontief observed that the United States was relatively well-endowed with capital. According to the theory, therefore, the United States should export capital-intensive goods and import labour-intensive ones. He found that the opposite was in fact the case: U.S. exports are generally more labour-intensive than the types of products that the United States imports. Because his findings were the opposite of those predicted by the theory, they are known as the Leontief Paradox.

28. (D): ***Net Barter Terms of Trade:*** This type was developed by Taussig in 1927. The ratio between the prices of exports and of imports is called the 'net barter terms of trade'. It is named by Viner as the 'commodity terms of trade'.

It is expressed as:

$$T_n = (P_x/P_m) \times 100$$

Where,

T_n = Net Barter Terms of Trade

P_x = Index number of export prices

P_m = Index number of import prices

This is used to measure the gain from international trade. If 'T_n' is greater than 100, then it is a favourable term of trade which will mean that for a rupee of export, more of imports can be received by a country.

Gross Barter Terms of Trade: This was developed by Taussig in 1927 as an improvement over the net terms of trade. It is an index of relationship between total physical quantity of imports and the total physical quantity of exports.

$$T = (Q_m/Q_x) \times 100$$

Where,

Q_m = Index of import quantities

Q_x = Index of export quantities

If for a given quantity of export, more quantity of import can be consumed by a country, then one can say that terms of trade are favourable.

29. (B): Given,

GDP (Market Price) = 27,654 crores

Depreciation = 2847 crores

Indirect taxes less subsidies = 2160 crores

GNPFC = GDPFC – Indirect taxes less subsidies

= 27,654 – 2160 = 25494

NDP (at FC) = GNPFC – Depreciation

= 25,494 – 2,847 = 22,647.

30. (C): (*a*) $Q_1 + Q_2 = 2$ Md

In a normal distribution, the sum of the first quartile (Q_1) and the third quartile (Q_3) usually equal to twice the median (Md). This statement is correct.

(*b*) The standard deviation (σ) is not equal to one-third of the interquartile range (Q.D.) in a normal distribution. This statement is incorrect.

(*c*) The standard deviation (σ) is equal to two-thirds of the semi-interquartile range (2Q.D./3) in a normal distribution. This statement is also correct.

(*d*) In a normal distribution, all moments of odd order about the mean are zero. This means that the mean deviation about the mean (the first moment) and any other odd-order moments are zero. This statement is correct.

(*e*) $Q_1 + Q_2$ = Md

In a normal distribution, the sum of the first quartile (Q_1) and the second quartile (Q_2) is not necessarily equal to the median (Md). This statement is also incorrect.

Therefore, the correct options are (*a*), (*c*), and (*d*).

31. (C): The new series of IIP has a total of 809 items occurring in the manufacturing sector in the item basket (405 item groups). A brief table giving the use-based classification; In the table, Primary goods have the highest weight of 34% and capital goods have the least weight i.e. 8.22%.

New series (base 2011-12)	Item groups	Weights (%)
Primary goods	15	34.05
Intermediate goods	110	17.22
Capital goods	67	8.22
Infrastructure/construction goods	29	12.34
Consumer durables	86	12.84
Consumer non-durables	100	15.33
Total	**407**	**100**

The essence of the article is that the Index of Industrial Production (IIP) is like the thermometer of an economy. It shows the real picture of all the main sectors of the economy. If the performance of these 8 core sectors of the economy is good then the overall development of the country is inevitable.

32. (B)

33. (B): The basic Mundell-Fleming model - like the IS-LM model - is based on the assumption of fixed price level and shows the interaction between the goods market and the money market. The model explains the causes of short-run fluctuations in aggregate income (or, what comes to the same thing, shifts in the ad curve) in an open economy. The Mundell-Fleming model is based on a very restrictive assumption. It considers a small open economy with perfect capital mobility. This model shows that the effect of almost any economic policy on a small open economy depends on whether the exchange rate is floating or fixed.

The Mundell-Fleming model shows that the power of monetary and fiscal policy to influence aggregate demand depends on the exchange rate regime. This is because in open economy the real exchange rate influence net export and thus income. Mostly often, countries choose exchange rate regimes in which exchange rate is somehow controlled by monetary authorities (managed float, dirty float, fixed exchange rate, pegged exchange rate).

Fiscal policy under flexible exchange rates and perfect capital mobility: Expansionary fiscal policy will shift the IS_0 to the right to IS_1 that leads to an increase of Y and *i*. As a result, domestic interest rate is higher than international one. So there will be an inflow of capital, BP surplus and appreciation of domestic currency. Appreciation leads to an increase in imports and a fall of exports - IS_1 shifts back to IS_0. Final result: constant Y, constant I, hence, fiscal policy is ineffective.

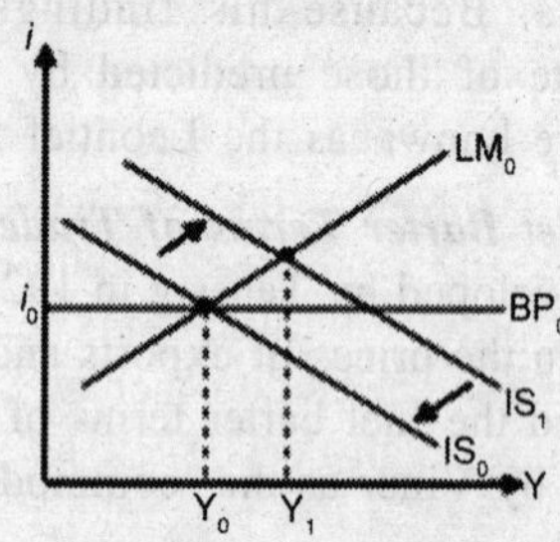

Monetary policy under flexible exchange rates and perfect capital mobility: Expansionary monetary policy will shift LM to the right - there is an increase in Y and a fall in *i*. As a result, there is an outflow of capital (domestic interest rate is lower than international one), balance of payments deficit and a depreciation of domestic currency.

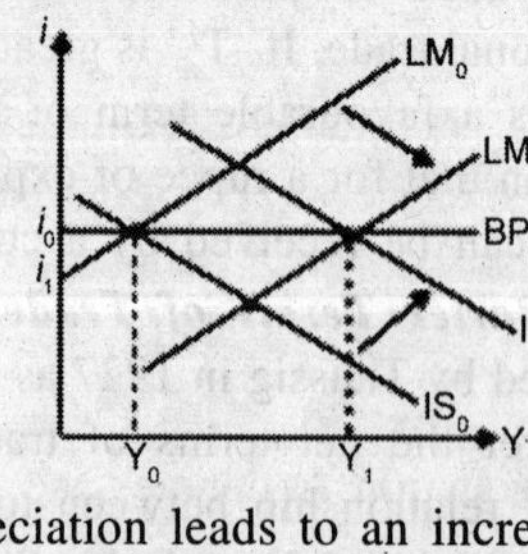

Depreciation leads to an increase in exports that shifts IS to IS_1. Final result: higher Y, constant I, hence, monetary policy is effective.

34. (B)

35. (A): In Dualistic economy a modern economy is existing along-with a primitive traditional economy. Dualism is one of the important characteristics of an underdeveloped/developing economy. Thus, under dualism, two sectors, i.e., modern or advanced sector and traditional or backward sector exists and operate side by side. Advanced sector is capital-intensive and backward sector is labour-intensive. At present, the Indian economy is characterized by a dualistic economic structure.

36. (A)

37. (A): The expansionary policy aims to stimulate the economy by boosting demand through monetary and fiscal stimulus. Expansionary policy is intended to prevent or moderate economic downturns and recessions. The Expansionary fiscal policy involves reducing taxes or increasing government spending to increase aggregate demand and production output. Expansionary fiscal policy includes tax cuts, transfer payments, rebates and increased government spending on projects such as infrastructure improvements. For example, it can increase discretionary government spending, infusing the economy with more money through government contracts.

38. (C): A population is considered stationary if the growth rate is zero and the age structure is constant. It thus follows that a population is considered non-stationary if either its growth rate is non-zero and/or its age structure is non-constant.

39. (D): The following equation provides the relationship between the monopoly price, marginal cost, and elasticity:

$$\frac{P - MC}{P} = \frac{1}{e}$$

In the equation, *e* denotes the elasticity.

In the equation, *e* denotes the elasticity. You can re-write it as follows:

$$P\left(1 + \frac{1}{e}\right) = MC$$

The monopolist charges a price of \$40 per unit, and the elasticity is –2. You can compute the marginal cost as follows:

$$MC = 40\left(1 + \frac{1}{-2}\right)$$

$$= 40 \times \frac{1}{2} = \$20$$

Thus, the marginal cost is 20.

40. (A): Functions of Public policy:

- **Allocation function:** The Allocation function of budget policy is concerned with the provision for public goods, or the process by which entire resources are divided between private and public goods and by which the mix of public goods is chosen.
- **Distribution function:** Distribution function means equitable and fair distribution of income and wealth.
- **Stabilization function:** Stabilization function implies maintaining high employment, price stability and an appropriate rate of economic growth.

41. (B): In search of the disparity in regional economic development the Swedish economist, Gunnar Myrdal in the year 1956 developed the cumulative causation theory. The economic development change in one form of an institution will lead to successive changes in other institutions in a circular and cumulative manner. So, sometimes the theory is known as Circular cumulative causation theory. The natural and human resources flow from supply regions to demand regions. As a result the supply region gradually submerged under the economic backwardness and resourceless condition. Whereas the demand regions gradually improve their economic prosperity. The processes increase the regional disparity with time.

42. (C)

43. (B): The Government of India on 01.06.2020 decided for further upward revision of the MSME Definition. For medium Enterprises, now it will be ₹ 50 Crore of investment and ₹ 250 Crore of turnover. The existing criterion of definition of MSMEs is based on the MSMED Act, 2006.

The limit of small unit was increased to ₹ 10 Crore of investment and ₹ 50 Crore of turnover. Similarly, the limit of medium unit was increased to ₹ 20 Crore of investment and ₹ 100 Crore of turnover. Further, in the revised definition, investment limit for plant and machinery or equipment formedium enterprises was 5 crores.

44. (D) **45. (B)** **46. (C)**

47. (D): The following points summarize the dominant views held by the Classical on public debt:

- Public debt leads to a reduction of resources for productive private employment.
- Deficits were considered less harmful compared to current taxes and unbalanced budgets lead to irresponsible government action and unnecessary expansion its activity.
- Future financing gets more trouble some due to public debt as more funds out of the budget have to be spared for fixed charges and by increasing the amount of taxes which must be paid to service the debt.
- Currency depreciation and rise in inflationary expectation are caused by a rise in public debt.
- Public debt financing requires funds for interest payment and amortization, hence a double burden for the exchequer.

Overall, the Classists believed that increase in fiscal deficit leading to government dissaving will have a detrimental impact on economic growth if rise in government dissaving is not fully matched rise in private savings. In this scenario, overall savings in the economy gets reduced exerting pressure on interest rates. The Classists were the proponents of no government intervention and markets clear automatically so there is the full employment of resources. This in return leads to a tax burden on future generations and rise of future consumption.

48. (B)

49. (B): Economic growth brought on by a shift in a nation's population structure-typically the outcome of declining fertility and mortality rates-is known as the demographic dividend. The demographic dividend correlates with a rise in the productivity of the working population, which raises per capita income.

Demographic Dualism: The two effects of population are essentially described as demographic dualism. A country's resources are under increased pressure when its population grows in one way or another since more people will need housing, food, healthcare, and other necessities. On the other side, the country's changing demographics may present a chance for economic growth due to the country's growing population.

In relation to considerations of demographic dividend, there appears to be 'demographic dualism' exhibited by the Indian states. In this regard Total Fertility Rate is the only factor. This is because Demographers use the concept of Total Fertility Rate or TFR as the key indicator of population growth.

50. (B): Expansionary policy seeks to stimulate an economy by boosting demand through monetary and fiscal stimulus. Expansionary fiscal policy includes issuing stimulus checks or creating tax breaks, while expansionary policy includes lowering the fed funds rate. Expansionary policy is intended to prevent or moderate economic downturns and recessions. Though popular, expansionary policy can involve significant costs and risks including macro-economic, micro-economic, and political economy issues. Expansionary policy is directly related to the cause of inflation; though expansionary policies fight unemployment, it may unintentionally cause higher prices.

51. (A): The Lewis model is formulated on the basic of certain assumptions which are as under:

- Prevalence of unlimited supply of labor at the subsistence wage rate in the traditional sector i.e. a perfectly elastic supply curve of labour (horizontal to the x-axis) at the subsistence wage rate.
- Capital and other natural resources are assumed to be highly scarce in relation to the predominance of LF. Hence the former are assumed to be the real bottleneck to economic expansion.
- Economy is dualistic in nature i.e. there is existence of two kinds of social systems in the economy.
- Skill-formation is only a quasi-bottleneck i.e. it is a temporary phenomenon that can be outweighed by incurring some cost of imparting skills.
- There is a dubious assumption which Lewis could not answer why. He assumed that wages in the expanding capitalist sector are determined by the wage earnings in the subsistence sector.

52. (D) **53. (A)**

54. (B):

$$\text{Z score} = \frac{\text{Data Point} - \text{Mean}}{\text{Standard Deviation}}$$

$$\text{Z score} = \frac{76-68}{5}$$

$$\text{Z score} = 1.6.$$

55. (B): Inferior goods are those goods, the demand for which falls as income of the consumer increases. Hence, there is a negative effect. For both normal and inferior goods, a price increase will lead to a reduction in quantity consumed of the good due to substitute goods being relatively cheaper. Giffen goods are highly inferior for which the negative income effect outweighs the positive substitution effect. Therefore, even though price falls, the quantity demanded still decreases. Giffen goods have a positively sloped demand curve (which means that as price decreases the quantity demanded also decreases). Therefore, if the income effect for a good is in the opposite direction as the substitution effect, but the substitution effect dominates then the good is: Inferior but not giffen.

56. (D): Conditions of Pareto Optimality:

(*i*) **Efficiency in Exchange:** It means that the marginal rate of substitution (MRS) between two consumer goods must be equal to the ratio of their prices. Since under perfect competition every consumer aims at maximising his utility, he will equate his MRS for two goods, X and Y to their price ratio (P_x/P_y).

Suppose there are two consumers A and B who buy two goods X and Y, and each faces the price ratio P_x/P_y... Thus A will choose X and Y such that his $_A\text{MRS}_{xv} = X_x/P_y$. Similarly B will choose X and Y such that his $\text{MRS}_{XY} = P_x/P_y$. Therefore, the condition for efficiency in exchange is $_A\text{MRS}_{xv} = {}_B\text{MRS}_{xv} - P_x/P_y$.

(*ii*) **Efficiency in Production:** The second condition for Pareto optimality relates to efficiency in production. There are three allocation rules for demonstrating efficiency in production under perfect competition. Rule one relates to the optimum allocation of factors. It requires that the marginal rate of technical substitution (MRTS) between any two factors must be the same for any two firms using these factors to produce the same product. The slope of an isoquant is the MRTS of labour and capital, and the slope of the iso-cost line is the ratio of the prices of labour and capital. Thus, the condition of equilibrium for firm A is $_A\text{MRTS}_{LK}. = P_L/P_K$, and that of firm B is $_B\text{MRTS}_{LK}, = P_LP_K$. Therefore, rule one for efficiency in production is $_A\text{MRTS}_{LK} = {}_B\text{MRTS}_{LK} = P_L/P_K$. Rule two states that the marginal rate of transformation between any factor and any product must be the same for any pair of firms using the factor and producing the product. It means that the marginal productivity of any factor in producing a particular product must be the same for all firms.

(*iii*) **Efficiency in Exchange and Production (Product Mix):** Since the price ratios of the two products to consumers and firms are the same under perfect competition, the MRS of all individuals will be identical with MRT of all firms consequently, the two products will be produced and exchanged efficiently. Symbolically, $MRS_{XY} = P_X/P_Y$, and $MRT_{xy} = P_x/P_y$. Therefore, $MRS_{XY} = MRT_{xy}$.

In nutshell, a Pareto-optimal state in the economy can be attained if the following three marginal conditions are fulfilled:

- The $MRS_{x,\,y}$ between any two goods be equal for all consumers.
- The $MRTS_{LK}$ between any two inputs be equal in the production of all commodities.
- The $MRPT_{x,\,y}$ be equal to the $MRS_{x,\,y}$ for any two goods.

57. (B): Simultaneous equationsare those equations which describes how independent variables and dependent variables are related to each other. These tells how unknown quantities and equations are related to each other. There are different approaches to it: substitution, eliminated and augmented matrix method. Simultaneous equations can be either exactly, over and under identified.

- If the equations are not identified, they are either unidentified or under identified.
- It is said to be exactly identified if unique numerical values of structural parameters can be obtained.
- It is said to be overidentified if more than one numerical value can be identified for some of the parameters of structural equations.

58. (C): Followings are assumptions of ordinal utility analysis

- **Rationality of Consumer:** This analysis assumes the rational consumers whose objective is to maximize the utility under the budget constraint.
- **Ordinal Measurement:** The utility is measured ordinally by comparing the satisfaction whether higher or lower by consuming different bundles of goods. It is sufficient that the consumer expresses his/ her preference for the various bundles of goods and commodities. It is not obligatory to undertake that utility is quantitively quantifiable.
- **Transitivity:** According to this assumption, when there are three goods A, B, and C, and if the consumer chooses as A > B, B > C, then A > C. It is acknowledged as transitivity in preference.
- **Consistency:** As per this assumption, the consumer remains consistent in choice. If there are two goods A and B then A is preferred over B i.e. A > B. At the same time, B cannot be preferred over A. It is called consistency in choice.
- **Non-satiety:** The consumer always prefers moreover less if there is a choice available to him. It means the consumer has not reached to point of saturation in the case of any commodity such condition is called non-satiety.
- **Diminishing Marginal Rate of Substitution (DMRS):** Under this theory, the marginal rate of substitution between two goods always diminishes so that a consumer can attain the same level of satisfaction. It is given by $\Delta Y/\Delta X$ in the case of two goods X and Y and it tells the rate of substituting commodity X to get one more unit of commodity Y.

59. (D): To ease the threat of currency appreciation or inflation, central banks often attempt what is known as the "sterilization" of capital flows. In a successful sterilization operation, the domestic component of the monetary base (bank reserves plus currency) is reduced to offset the reserve inflow, at least temporarily.

In theory, this can be achieved in several ways, such as by encouraging private investment overseas, or allowing foreigners to borrow from the local market. The classical form of sterilization, however, has been through the use of open market operations, that is, selling Treasury bills and other instruments to reduce the domestic component of the monetary base.

60. (D) **61. (B)**

62. (C): Menu cost is a concept related to Mankiw's sticky prices model which is based on the new Keynesian terminology. According to this hypothesis, it is profitable for firms to react to small changes in demand by keeping the prices constant during the short period and making changes in output level. Menu costs explain the short-run stickiness of prices. Due to menu costs, in the short run, firms do not change the prices whenever there occurs a change in demand conditions. Thus, Menu costs refer to the costs of altering price lists.

63. (B): $Y_i = -10 + 0.6\ X + \text{Residual}$

Given,

$Y_i = 60,\ X = 40$

Putting values in the equation,

$60 = -10 + 0.6\ (40) + \text{Residual}$

$60 = -10 + 24 + \text{Residual}$

$60 - 14 = \text{Residual}$

$46 = \text{Residual}.$

64. (B) **65. (B)**

66. (A): Net migration is the net total of migrants during the period, that is, the number of immigrants minus the number of emigrants, including both citizens and noncitizens.

67. (A): Typically, the incidence, or burden, of a tax falls both on the consumers and producers of the taxed good. But if we want to predict which group will bear most of the burden, all we need to do is examine the elasticity of demand and supply.

In the salt example above, the tax burden falls on the most inelastic side of the market. If demand is more inelastic than supply, consumers bear most of the tax burden. But, if supply is more inelastic than demand, sellers bear most of the tax burden.

Think about it this way-when the demand is inelastic, consumers are not very responsive to price changes, and the quantity demanded remains relatively constant when the tax is introduced. In the case of salt, the demand is inelastic because consumers have to use this product. The seller can then pass the tax burden along to consumers in the form of higher prices without much of a decline in the equilibrium quantity.

When a tax is introduced in a market with an inelastic supply-such as, for example, beach front hotels-sellers have no choice but to accept lower prices for their business. Taxes do not greatly affect the equilibrium quantity. The tax burden in this case is on the sellers. If the supply were elastic and sellers had the possibility of reorganizing their businesses to avoid supplying the taxed good, the tax burden on the sellers would be much smaller, and the tax would result in a much lower quantity sold instead of lower prices received. You can see the relationship between tax incidence and elasticity of demand and supply represented graphically below.

68. (C): The binomial distribution can be used under the following conditions:

- The number of trials (or) observations 'n' is fixed (finite).
- Each observation is independent of each other.
- In every trial, there are only two possible outcomes - success or failure.
- The probability of success 'p' is the same for each outcome.

69. (B): A maximax strategy is a strategy in game theory where a player, facing uncertainty, makes a decision that yields the 'best of the best' outcome. All decisions will have costs and benefits, and a maximax strategy is one that seeks out where the greatest benefit can be found. The maximax theorem was first formulated in 1928 by John von Neumann. It is often referred to as an aggressive or optimistic strategy.

70. (B): To find the rank of a matrix, we need to determine the maximum number of linearly independent rows or columns in the matrix. One way to do this is by performing row operations to transform the matrix into row-echelon form or reduced row-echelon form and then counting the number of non-zero rows.

Let's perform row operations on the given matrix:

Step 1: Swap the first and second rows.

$$A = \begin{vmatrix} -10 & 2 & 8 \\ 6 & 3 & 5 \\ 5 & 2 & 3 \end{vmatrix}$$

Step 2: Multiply the first row by 6 and add it to the second row.

$$A = \begin{vmatrix} -10 & 2 & 8 \\ 0 & 20 & 53 \\ 5 & 2 & 3 \end{vmatrix}$$

Step 3: Multiply the first row by 1/2 and add it to the third row.

$$A = \begin{vmatrix} -10 & 2 & 8 \\ 0 & 20 & 53 \\ 0 & 3 & 19.5 \end{vmatrix}$$

Step 4: Multiply the second row by 1/20.

$$A = \begin{vmatrix} -10 & 2 & 8 \\ 0 & 1 & 53/20 \\ 0 & 3 & 19.5 \end{vmatrix}$$

Step 5: Multiply the second row by –2 and add it to the first row.

$$A = \begin{vmatrix} -10 & 0 & -57/10 \\ 0 & 1 & 53/20 \\ 0 & 3 & 19.5 \end{vmatrix}$$

Step 6: Multiply the second row by –3 and add it to the third row.

$$A = \begin{vmatrix} -10 & 0 & -57/10 \\ 0 & 1 & 53/20 \\ 0 & 0 & -19.5/20 \end{vmatrix}$$

The matrix is now in row-echelon form. From the last row, we can see that the third row consists of all zeros, indicating that it is linearly dependent on the previous rows. Hence, the rank of the matrix A is 2.

71. (C): The Baumol-Tobin model is an economic model of the transactions demand for money as developed independently by William Baumol (1952) and James Tobin (1956).

72. (B): Gross Domestic saving rate was recorded all time high of 30.2% in Mar 2008 and a record low of 7.9% in Mar 1954.

73. (D) **74. (*)** **75. (A)**

76. (A): Basic characteristics of an under developed economy are as follows:

- **Low Per Capita Income:** Almost all underdeveloped countries of the world show low per capita income in comparison to developed countries of the world.
- **Slow Growth Rate of Per Capita Income:** Low per capita income and slow growth rate of per capita income are characteristics of these countries.
- **Economic Inequalities:** High inequality of income and wealth is another common feature of underdeveloped countries. In these countries, large percentage of national income is shared by a small segment of the society while a large segment of the society gets barely enough to survive. Economic inequality exists even in developed countries but it is not as much as found in underdeveloped countries.
- **Low Level of Living:** Level of living in the underdeveloped countries is low because of low per capita income. Low level of living of the people of under-developed countries is also reflected in Human Development Index prepared by the United Nation Development Programme (UNDP). HDI of developed countries is very high whereas for underdeveloped countries it is very low.

- **Low Rate of Capital Formation:** Rate of capital formation is very low in underdeveloped economies due to low income levels and high incidence of poverty.
- **Backward Techniques of Production:** Underdeveloped economies use outdated technology for production. Lack of capital leads to less spending on research and development.
- **High Growth Rate of Population and Dependency Burden:** These countries are characterised by high growth rate of population and high dependency burden.
- **Low Productivity of Labour:** Underdeveloped economies are characterised by low labour productivity duc to low level of skill set.
- **Underutilisation of Natural Resources:** Natural resources are underutilised in underdeveloped economies. Their capability to exploit them is very low.
- **Large Scale Unemployment:** Large scale unemployment is another characteristic feature of underdeveloped countries.
- **Dominance of Agriculture:** Large section of people in underdeveloped economies depends on primary sector for employment. But the primary sector is not well-developed in those countries.
- **High Incidence of Poverty:** Low per capita income results in high incidence of poverty in underdeveloped economies.
- **Infrastructural Backwardness:** Economic infrastructure and social infrastructure are almost at their bottom level in underdeveloped countries.
- **Low Volume of Foreign Trade:** Underdeveloped countries export primary products like, agricultural goods, minerals, petroleum oil, etc., and import finished products, especially consumer goods. Terms of trade are grossly unfavourable to underdeveloped countries.

77. (A) **78. (*)**

79. (C): To integrate the expression $(x \wedge 2)/(x + 2)$, you can use the method of partial fractions. Here's the step-by-step process:

Step 1: Factorize the denominator.

The denominator $x + 2$ cannot be factored further since it is already in its simplest form.

Step 2: Perform partial fraction decomposition.

Since the degree of the numerator is equal to the degree of the denominator, we need to decompose the fraction into two partial fractions: one with a linear denominator and the other with a constant denominator.

The general form of the partial fraction decomposition is:

$$(x \wedge 2)/(x + 2) = A/(x + 2) + B$$

Step 3: Determine the values of A and B.

To find the values of A and B, we need to clear the fractions by multiplying both sides of the equation by $(x + 2)$:

$$(x \wedge 2) = A + B(x + 2)$$

Expand the right side:

$$(x \wedge 2) = A + Bx + 2B$$

Now, we can equate the coefficients of corresponding powers of x:

Coefficient of $x \wedge 2$: 0 = 0 (Since there is no $x \wedge 2$ term on the right side)

Coefficient of x: 1 = B (Comparing the coefficient of x)

Constant term: 0 = A + 2B (Comparing the constant term)

From the second equation, we can see that B = 1.

Substituting B = 1 in the third equation:

$$0 = A + 2(1)$$
$$0 = A + 2$$
$$A = -2$$

Step 4: Rewrite the original integral with the partial fraction decomposition.

Now that we have determined the values of A and B, we can rewrite the original integral:

$$\int[(x \wedge 2)/(x + 2)]dx = \int[(-2)/(x + 2) + 1]dx$$

Step 5: Integrate each term separately.

Integrating each term separately gives:

$\int[(-2)/(x + 2)]dx = -2 \ln |x + 2|$

$\int[1]dx = x$

Putting it all together, the final result of the integral is:

$\int[(x \wedge 2)/(x + 2)]dx = -2 \ln |x + 2| + x + C$

where C is the constant of integration.

80. **(C):** Monetary policy is implemented using a variety of direct and indirect instruments which are discussed below.

- **Repo Rate:** Repo Rate is the rate at which the Reserve Bank of India lends to other banks by buying the securities with an agreement that the bank will buy it back on a certain date. It is a short term lending option to meet the liquidity requirements of commercial banks. The Repo rate borrowing is usually available at the overnight repo, 7 days, 14-day repo.
- **Reverse Repo Rate:** Reverse Repo Rate stands for the rate of interest at which the central bank borrows money from the commercial banks for a short term. It helps the central bank to have a source of liquidity when it needs it. The RBI offers decent interest rates in return for the money supplied to it by commercial banks.
- **Liquidity Adjustment Facility (LAF):** Liquidity Adjustment Facility (LAF) is a monetary policy tool used in India by the RBI via which it injects or absorbs liquidity into or from the banking system. This was introduced as a part of the Narasimham Committee's recommendations on the Banking Sector Reforms of 1998.
- **Marginal Standing Facility (MSF):** Marginal Standing Facility refers to the window for banks that it uses to borrow from the Reserve Bank of India (RBI) in an emergency situation when interbank liquidity dries up. Here, the banks can borrow funds through MSF against the approved government securities during acute liquidity shortages stages.
- **Corridor:** The corridor stands for the daily movement in the weighted average call money rate which is determined by the MSF rate and the reverse repo rate. It stands for the area between the reverse repo rate and the MSF rate.
- **Bank Rate:** The bank rate is the rate of interest that is charged by the central bank while lending loans to the commercial bank. Section 49 of the Reserve Bank of India Act, 1934 further mandates the publication of the Bank Rate.
- **Cash Reserve Ratio (CRR):** The Cash Reserve Ratio is the minimum percentage of total deposits that a commercial bank is required to retain as cash reserves with the RBI. It keeps a check on the flow and circulation of money in the economy that impacts loans and investments.
- **Statutory Liquidity Ratio (SLR):** It is the minimum percentage of deposits that a commercial bank is required to keep in liquid cash, gold, or other securities. Section 24 (2A) of the Banking Regulation Act, of 1949 established the Statutory Liquidity Ratio.
- **Open Market Operations (OMOs):** Open Market Operations (OMOs) are market operations conducted by RBI by way of the sale/purchase of government securities to/from the market with an aim to regulate the money supply in the market. RBI employs two kinds of OMOs, one is the Outright Purchase and the other is the Repurchase Agreement.
- **Market Stabilization Scheme (MSS):** It is a monetary policy intervention by the RBI to withdraw excess liquidity by selling government securities in the market. The MSS was introduced way back in April 2004.

81. **(A)**

82. **(A):** The Harrod-Domar economic growth model stresses the importance of savings and investment as key determinants of growth.

Basically, the model suggests that the economy's rate of growth depends on:

- The level of national saving (S)
- The productivity of capital investment (this is known as the capital-output ratio)

Rate of growth of GDP = Savings ratio/capital output ratio

Given,

Growth rate of income = 8%

Capital output ratio = 4%

Rate of growth of GDP = Savings ratio/capital output ratio

8% = Savings ratio/4%

Savings ratio = 8% × 4%

Savings ratio = 32%.

83. (B): The main components of the current account are:

- **The export and import of goods (merchandise transactions or visible trade):** It includes transactions in foreign trade in the form of export and import of goods (visible items).
- **Export and Import of Services (Invisible Trade):** It includes a large variety of non-factor services (known as invisible items) sold and purchased by the residents of a country, to and from the rest of the world. Payments are either received or made to the other countries for the use of these services.

  Services are generally of three kinds:

  (*a*) Shipping,

  (*b*) Banking, and

  (*c*) Insurance.
- **Unilateral or unrequited transfers to and from abroad (one-sided transactions):** Unilateral transfers include gifts, donations, personal remittances, and other "one-way" transactions.
- **Income receipts and payments to and from abroad:** It includes investment income in the form of interest, rent, and profits.

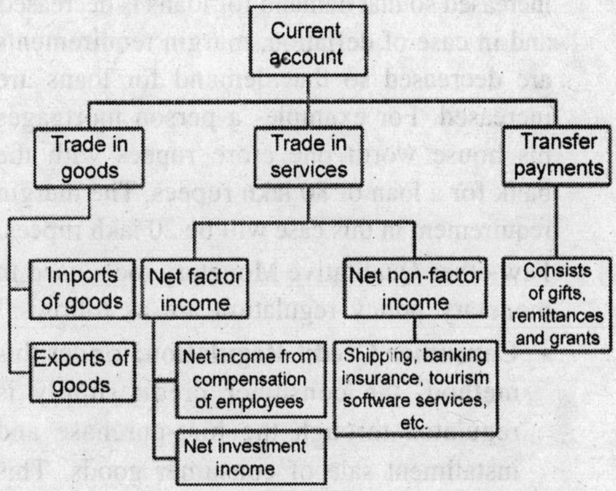

84. (B) **85. (B)** **86. (A)**

87. (A): An industry attains long run equilibrium when:

- All firms are in equilibrium (i.e. they earn only normal profits)
- There is no entry or exit from the market

The following conditions associated with the long run equilibrium of an industry highlight such optimality:

- The output is produced at the minimum possible cost.
- The selling price just covers the marginal cost. (i.e. MC = AR)
- In the long run, plants are used at full capacity. Therefore, resources are not wasted. (i,e, MC = AC)
- Firms earn only normal profits. (i.e. AC = AR)
- While the profits are normal, firms maximize their profits. (i.e. MC = MR)

Hence, in the long run, LAR = LMR = P = LMC = LAC. Also, the resources are utilized optimally.

88. (A): Margin requirement refers to the difference between the current value of the security offered for loan (called collateral) and the value of loan granted. It is a qualitative method of credit control adopted by the central bank in order to stabilize the economy from inflation or deflation. In case of inflation, the margin requirement is increased so that demand for loans is decreased and in case of deflation, margin requirements are decreased so that demand for loans are increased. For example- a person mortgages his house worth one crore rupees with the bank for a loan of 80 lakh rupees. The margin requirement in this case will be 20 lakh rupees.

Few other Qualitative Monetary tools used in monetary policy regulation are as follows:

- **Consumer Credit Regulation:** Under this method, the consumer credit supply is regulated through the hire-purchase and installment sale of consumer goods. This can help in checking the credit use and then inflation in a country.
- **Publicity:** This is yet another method of selective credit control. Through it, Central Bank (RBI) publishes various reports stating what is good and what is bad in the system. This published information can help commercial banks to direct credit supply in the desired sectors.
- **Credit Rationing:** Central Bank fixes the credit amount to be granted. Credit is rationed by limiting the amount available for each commercial bank. This method controls even bill re-discounting. For certain purposes, the upper limit of credit can be fixed and banks are told to stick to this limit. This can help in lowering banks' credit exposure to unwanted sectors.
- **Moral Suasion:** It implies to pressure exerted by the RBI on the Indian banking system without any strict action for compliance with the rules. It is a suggestion to banks. It helps in restraining credit during inflationary periods. Under moral suasion, central banks can issue directives, guidelines, and suggestions for commercial banks regarding reducing credit supply for speculative purposes.
- **Control Through Directives:** Under this method the central bank issue frequent directives to commercial banks. These directives guide commercial banks in framing their lending policy. Through a directive, the central bank can influence credit structures, the supply of credit to certain limits for a specific purpose. The RBI issues directives to commercial banks for not lending loans to the speculative sectors such as securities, etc. beyond a certain limit.
- **Direct Action:** Under this method, the RBI can impose action against a bank. If certain banks are not adhering to the RBI's directives, the RBI may refuse to re-discount their bills and securities.

89. (D) **90. (A)** **91. (C)**
92. (C) **93. (D)** **94. (A)**
95. (C) **96. (D)** **97. (D)**
98. (C) **99. (C)** **100. (C)**

Previous Years' Paper (Solved)

National Testing Agency (NTA)

UGC-NET Junior Research Fellowship & Assistant Professor Eligibility Exam

ECONOMICS, June–2021

(Online exam held on 24-11-2021)

PAPER-II

Note: *This paper contains* ***hundred (100)*** *objective type questions of* ***two (2)*** *marks each.* ***All*** *questions are* ***compulsory.***

1. In case of indifference curve of two goods X and Y, as consumption of X increases:

A. MRS_{XY} increases

B. MRS_{XY} decreases

C. MRS_{XY} remains the same

D. First MRS_{XY} increases but later on MRS_{XY} decreases

2. General Economic Equilibrium is NOT related to which one of the following problems?

A. Uniqueness problem

B. Existence problem

C. Stability problem

D. Moral Hazard problem

3. In the short-run production function, which one of the following is CORRECT?

A. Technology is assumed to change as labour input changes

B. Technology is assumed to change as capital stock changes

C. Technology is assumed to change positively until diminishing returns set in

D. Technology is assumed to be constant for a given production function relationship

4. As output expands, LAC curve falls. This is due to:

A. Law of variable proportions

B. Law of diminishing returns

C. Economies of scale

D. Diseconomies of scale

5. In a situation of decision under uncertainty, if a consumer faces equal expected income from two alternatives, then s/he will take decision on the basis of:

A. Expected utility of both the alternatives

B. Probability of risk attached with each alternative

C. Variation of risk attached with each alternative

D. Mean of risk of each alternative

6. What type of relationship the Phillips curve postulates between the rate of unemployment and the rate of increase of money wages?

A. Inverse

B. Direct

C. Direct and proportional

D. Inverse and proportional

7. The concept of 'money illusion' was first given by whom?

A. Milton Friedman B. Irving Fisher

C. Robertson D. J. M. Keynes

8. Which one of the following correctly describes the concept of 'Super Multiplier'?

A. Investment multiplier

B. Money multiplier

C. Interaction between multiplier and accelerator

D. Employment multiplier

9. Given:

$I = 50 + 0.2Y$

$S = -150 + 0.4Y$

$G = 50$

Where, I = Investment, S = Savings

G = Government Expenditure

Y = National Income

What is the equilibrium level of national income?

A. 2500 B. 1250
C. 250 D. 1500

10. The independence of real variables from changes in money supply and nominal variables is called:

A. Keynesian dichotomy
B. Classical dichotomy
C. Money illusion
D. Money multiplier

11. Assuming the probability of a male birth as 0.5, find the chances that a family of 3 children will have two boys and one girl:

A. $\frac{1}{8}$ B. $\frac{2}{8}$

C. $\frac{3}{8}$ D. $\frac{4}{8}$

12. Which one of the following measures of central tendency will be the most appropriate to use if the data relates to rates, proportions and ratios?

A. Arithmetic Mean
B. Median
C. Harmonic Mean
D. Geometric Mean

13. The sampling distribution of mean based on a sample of 13 units selected without replacement shows a variance of 5 units. If the population consists of 49 units, estimate the variance of the population

A. 80.67 B. 84.87
C. 86.67 D. 86.87

14. In the classical linear regression model, X_i and U_i are assumed to be:

A. highly correlated
B. not correlated
C. positively correlated
D. negatively correlated

15. Identify which one of the following statements is INCORRECT?

A. Intersection of two disjoint sets is a null set
B. Complement of a Universal set is a null set
C. If $X \cap Y = \phi$, then $X - Y \neq X$
D. $X - Y = X \cap \bar{Y}$

16. Given $Y = X^3 - 12X^2 + 36X + 8$, identify which one of the following is CORRECT:

A. Y is maximum at X = 6, and minimum at X = 2
B. Y is minimum at X = 6, and maximum at X = 2
C. Y has two inflexion points at X = 2 and X = 6
D. Point of optimality is indeterminate

17. Identify which one of the following statements is CORRECT:

A. A^{-1} is equal to Adj (A) if the value of the determinant A is unity
B. If two columns of a determinant are interchanged, the sign of the determinant does not alter
C. The value of a determinant changes if the rows and columns are interchanged
D. Law of division is allowed in matrix operations

18. Identify which of the following statements with respect to Linear Programming Problem (LPP) is CORRECT:

A. A solution is unbounded in an LPP if all the feasible solutions of the problem fall within the boundary created by its constraints
B. If A is a primal problem and B is its dual, then dual of B is not A

C. The constraints of an LPP in standard form is always expressed in less than and equal to form
D. If an LPP has two optimum solutions, then it has also infinite number of optimum solutions

19. The Net Barter terms of trade refer to:
A. The excess of import expenditures over export earnings
B. Trade agreements
C. The ratio between export prices and import prices
D. The terms and conditions on which a country is offered a loan in the event of balance of payments difficulties

20. The items on the capital account of Balance of Payments are:
A. Flow variables
B. Stock variables
C. Changes in stock magnitudes
D. Both Stock and Flow variables

21. A sudden shift from import tariffs to free trade may induce short-term unemployment in:
A. Import competing industries
B. Industries that are only exporters
C. Industries that sell domestically as well as export
D. Industries that neither import or export

22. The optimum tariff means:
A. Must occur in the elastic range of the tariff imposing home country's offer curve
B. Takes account of the probability that the partner country will retaliate with protective measures of its own
C. Maximises total export sales of the imposing country
D. Must occur in the elastic range of the partner country's offer curve

23. The movement from old level of expenditure and taxation to a new and higher level is called:
A. Concentration effect
B. Inspection effect
C. Displacement effect
D. All of the above

24. Which method can help in obtaining a welfare improvement, if externalities exist?
A. Pigovian taxes
B. Regulation
C. Assigning property rights and permitting bargaining
D. All of the above

25. The efficiency condition in the production of pure public good requires that the production be carried out up to a point when:

{where MB_i represents Marginal Benefit of the 'i^{th}' individual and MB_j represents Marginal Benefits that accrue to the 'j^{th}' individual and MC is the marginal cost}

A. $MB_i + \sum_{j=1}^{n-1} MB_j = MC$

B. $MB_i + \sum_{j=1}^{n-1} MB_j > MC$

C. $MB_i + \sum_{j=1}^{n-1} MB_j < MC$

D. $MB_i - \sum_{j=1}^{n-1} MB_j > MC$

26. The incidence of which of the following will entirely be on the monopolist?
A. Lump-sum tax
B. Specific tax
C. Regulated monopoly pricing
D. None of these

27. Which of the following is NOT a Commercial Bank?
A. Public Sector Bank
B. Private Sector Bank
C. Regional Rural Bank
D. Co-operative Bank

28. Liquidity Adjustment Facility (LAF) was recommended by:
A. C. Rangarajan Committee
B. Raghuram Rajan Committee

C. Narasimham Committee-II
D. Bimal Jalan Committee

29. Which of the following is TRUE for Bank Rate?
A. Increase in Bank rate by Central Bank would increase money supply keeping other factors constant
B. Bank rate is a qualitative instrument
C. Bank rate is the minimum rate at which the Central Bank provides credit to financial institutions against securities of the government
D. Bank rate is a direct instrument of credit control

30. Human Development Index (HDI) currently, as published by the UNDP is calculated by using which of the following?
A. Geometric Mean B. Arithmetic Mean
C. Harmonic Mean D. Quadratic Mean

31. Harrod-neutral technical progress is necessarily:
A. Growth augmenting
B. Labour augmenting
C. Capital augmenting
D. Resource augmenting

32. Which among the following is NOT part of the neoclassical theory of growth?
A. Swan Model B. Meade's Model
C. Pasinetti Model D. Solow Model

33. If a production function admits both Harrod and Hicks neutral technical progress, the elasticity of substitution should be:
A. equal to one
B. equal to zero
C. equal to infinity
D. equal to one divided by two

34. The total population of city 'X' in 2011 was 28 lakhs and the total number of live births was 50 thousand. Find out crude birth rate per 1000 population?
A. 178.57 B. 1.7857
C. 17.857 D. 0.17857

35. According to Ronald Coase, which of the following statements is CORRECT for pollution control?
A. Providing property rights to the state
B. Providing property rights to the legal institutions
C. Providing property rights to polluters and pollutees
D. Providing property rights to Trade Unions

36. According to Census 2011, which one of the following states has the highest share of rural population?
A. Bihar
B. Odisha
C. Uttar Pradesh
D. Himachal Pradesh

37. At present, for the estimation of GDP in India at constant prices, which one of the following years is used as the base year?
A. 2011-12 B. 2010-11
C. 2014-15 D. 2000-01

38. Which of the following statement is CORRECT for *'Atmanirbhar Bharat Rozgar Yojana'* launched on November 12, 2020?
A. Establishments which make new hires will get a subsidy to cover retirement fund contribution by employees and employers for 2 years
B. Establishment will get a subsidy of ₹ 10 crore for a period of 5 years
C. Establishment will get tax profit continuously for a period of 3 years
D. Establishment will get tax subsidy for 5 years

39. The 15th Finance Commission (FC) has recommended that the States be given what per cent of the divisible tax pool of the Centre during the period 2021-2022 to 2025-26?
A. 51 B. 31
C. 41 D. 61

40. Which of the following sectors of the economy registered highest growth rate in the second quarter of 2020-21 as per estimate of NSO?

A. Manufacturing
B. Electricity, Gas, Water supply and other Utility services
C. Agriculture and Allied sectors
D. General Administration

41. Which of the following measures are used by a risk-averse person to minimize risk?
(*a*) Diversification of resources
(*b*) Insurance of risk event
(*c*) Total cost of resources
(*d*) Value of information of risk event

Choose the ***correct*** answer from the options given below:
A. (*a*), (*b*) and (*c*) only
B. (*a*), (*b*) and (*d*) only
C. (*b*), (*c*) and (*d*) only
D. (*a*), (*c*) and (*d*) only

42. Which of the following statements are CORRECT for welfare economics?
(*a*) Any competitive equilibrium leads to a Pareto efficient allocation of resources
(*b*) Competitive equilibrium does not lead tc Pareto efficient allocation of resources
(*c*) Any efficient allocation can be attained by a competitive equilibrium given the market mechanism leading to redistribution
(*d*) There will be no Pareto efficient allocation of resources in the society

Choose the ***correct*** answer from the options given below:
A. (*a*), (*b*) and (*c*) only
B. (*a*) and (*c*) only
C. (*b*) and (*c*) only
D. (*c*) and (*d*) only

43. Which of the following conditions hold true for factor pricing when factor market is perfectly competitive and product market is monopolistic?
(*a*) VMP > MRP
(*b*) Both VMP and MRP decreasing
(*c*) VMP < MRP
(*d*) $MRP_L = W$

Choose the ***correct*** answer from the options given below:
A. (*a*), (*b*) and (*c*) only
B. (*b*), (*c*) and (*d*) only
C. (*a*), (*b*) and (*d*) only
D. (*a*), (*c*) and (*d*) only

44. Which of the following functions will result in an investment multiplier of value 4?
(*a*) C = 50 + .25 Y
(*b*) C = 50 + .75 Y
(*c*) S = –50 + .25 Y
(*d*) I = 50 + .75 Y

Choose the ***correct*** answer from the options given below:
A. (*a*) and (*c*) only B. (*c*) and (*d*) only
C. (*a*) and (*d*) only D. (*b*) and (*c*) only

45. Which of the following are CORRECT?
(*a*) If observations are selected purposively, it is called a method of non-random sampling
(*b*) If observations are selected in an ad-hoc manner, it is called a method of non-random sampling
(*c*) If observations are selected in a systematic manner it is called a method of non-random sampling
(*d*) If observations are selected on the basis of judgment, it is called a method of non-random sampling

Choose the ***correct*** answer from the options given below:
A. (*a*), (*b*) and (*c*) only
B. (*b*), (*c*) and (*d*) only
C. (*a*), (*c*) and (*d*) only
D. (*a*), (*b*) and (*d*) only

46. Which are the following correct features of matrices?
(*a*) An identity matrix is a square matrix
(*b*) An identity matrix when gets transposed remains an identity matrix
(*c*) $(A.B)^T = A^T.B^T$ where A and B are matrices
(*d*) $(A^{-1})^T = (A^T)^{-1}$ where A is a matrix

Choose the ***correct*** answer from the options given below:

A. (*a*) and (*b*) only B. (*b*) and (*c*) only
C. (*a*) and (*c*) only D. (*c*) and (*d*) only

47. When the exchange rate changes from 1\$ = ₹ 72 to 1\$ = ₹ 68, then the:

(*a*) Rupee has depreciated
(*b*) Dollar has depreciated
(*c*) Rupee has appreciated
(*d*) Dollar has appreciated

Choose the ***correct*** answer from the options given below:

A. (*a*) and (*d*) only B. (*b*) and (*c*) only
C. (*c*) and (*d*) only D. (*a*) and (*b*) only

48. Which of the following are a source of market failure?

(*a*) The existence of public goods
(*b*) The presence of externalities
(*c*) The fact that some goods are rivals in consumption
(*d*) The existence of monopolies

Choose the ***correct*** answer from the options given below:

A. (*a*), (*b*) and (*d*) only
B. (*a*), (*b*) and (*c*) only
C. (*b*), (*c*) and (*d*) only
D. (*a*), (*c*) and (*d*) only

49. Which of the following would reduce the credit creation capacity of a Commercial Bank?

(*a*) Time and Demand deposits
(*b*) Loans
(*c*) Deposits with the Central Bank
(*d*) Cash in hand

Choose the ***correct*** answer from the options given below:

A. (*a*) and (*b*) only B. (*b*) and (*c*) only
C. (*c*) and (*d*) only D. (*a*) and (*d*) only

50. Which of the following measures would result in an increase in the money supply in the economy?

(*a*) Purchase of government securities from the public by Central Bank
(*b*) Deposit of currency in Commercial Banks by the public
(*c*) Borrowing by the government from the Central Bank
(*d*) Sale of government securities to the public by the Central Bank
(*e*) Minting of more money by the Central Bank for circulation

Choose the ***correct*** answer from the options given below:

A. (*a*), (*c*) and (*e*) only
B. (*b*), (*c*) and (*d*) only
C. (*a*), (*b*) and (*c*) only
D. (*b*), (*d*) and (*e*) only

51. Inequalities in income are measured by which of the following?

(*a*) Lorenz Ratio
(*b*) Theil's Index
(*c*) Palma Ratio
(*d*) Deprivation Ratio

Choose the ***correct*** answer from the options given below:

A. (*a*) only
B. (*a*) and (*b*) only
C. (*a*) and (*d*) only
D. (*a*), (*b*) and (*c*) only

52. Which of the following is/are true?

(*a*) Ministry of Environment and Forests in India was established in 1985
(*b*) Central Pollution Control Board was established in 1984
(*c*) Environment Protection Act was enacted in 1990
(*d*) National Environment Appellate Authority Act was passed in 1977

Choose the ***correct*** answer from the options given below:

A. (*a*), (*b*), (*c*) and (*d*) only
B. (*b*) only
C. (*c*) only
D. (*a*) and (*d*) only

53. In which of the following ways have there been structural changes in agricultural and rural areas in India?

(*a*) Crop diversification within agriculture sector

(*b*) Diversification from livestock to crop husbandry

(*c*) Diversification from non-commercial crops to commercial crops

(*d*) Diversification from traditional inputs to modern inputs

Choose the ***correct*** answer from the options given below:

A. (*a*), (*c*) and (*d*) only

B. (*a*), (*b*) and (*c*) only

C. (*a*), (*b*) and (*d*) only

D. (*b*), (*c*) and (*d*) only

54. With reference to the programme 'NIDHI' which of the following statement(s) is/are CORRECT?

(*a*) The programme of 'NIDHI' was started for students to begin startups

(*b*) Its aim is to financially support 20 students for startups each year

(*c*) Its aim is to financially support 200 students for startups each year

(*d*) Its aim is to financially support only students of backward classes to start up each year

Choose the ***correct*** answer from the options given below:

A. (*a*) and (*d*) only

B. (*a*) and (*b*) only

C. (*a*), (*c*) and (*d*) only

D. (*c*) and (*d*) only

55. Which of the following statements are CORRECT in regard to FDI in India in FY 2020?

(*a*) Share of services sector is highest

(*b*) Share of infrastructure activities is highest

(*c*) Share of computer hardware and software is in the second position

(*d*) Share of telecommunications is highest

Choose the ***correct*** answer from the options given below:

A. (*a*) and (*c*) only B. (*b*) and (*c*) only

C. (*b*) only D. (*c*) and (*d*) only

56. Consider the following statements about the rational expectations model:

(*a*) Monetary policy cannot affect output and employment

(*b*) Unanticipated changes will not affect real variables in the very short run

(*c*) There is equilibrium in the markets

(*d*) Economic agents use all relevant available information to form their expectations

Choose the ***correct*** answer from the options given below:

A. (*a*), (*c*) and (*d*) only

B. (*a*), (*b*) and (*c*) only

C. (*b*), (*c*) and (*d*) only

D. (*a*), (*b*), (*c*) and (*d*)

57. In the context of investments, which of the following statement(s) is/are CORRECT?

(*a*) According to the accelerator model, investment demand is proportional to change in income

(*b*) The higher the real interest rate, the higher is the rental cost of capital

(*c*) Investment is a stock variable

(*d*) The real rate of interest is equal to the nominal rate of interest plus the inflation rate

Choose the ***correct*** answer from the options given below:

A. (*a*) and (*b*) only B. (*a*) and (*d*) only

C. (*b*) and (*c*) only D. (*c*) and (*d*) only

58. Which of the following statements are CORRECT for correlation analysis?

(*a*) Degree of linear association is measured between two variables

(*b*) Predictability is not part of correlation analysis

(*c*) Spearman has no contribution to correlation analysis

(*d*) Cause and effect relationship is established through correlation analysis

Choose the ***correct*** answer from the options given below:

A. (*a*) and (*c*) only B. (*b*) and (*c*) only
C. (*a*) and (*b*) only D. (*a*) and (*d*) only

59. Which of the following are NOT properties of Cobb-Douglas production function?

(*a*) Cobb-Douglas production function is a homogeneous production function
(*b*) Curves representing average and marginal productivity of inputs are not downward sloping
(*c*) Marginal productivity of labour and capital in Cobb-Douglas production function are functions of the capital-labour ratio
(*d*) Iso-quants of Cobb-Douglas production functions are positively sloped

Choose the ***correct*** answer from the options given below:

A. (*a*) and (*b*) only
B. (*b*) and (*d*) only
C. (*b*) and (*c*) only
D. (*c*) and (*d*) only

60. Improvement in the balance of payments deficit may be effected through:

(*a*) Import controls
(*b*) Export promotion
(*c*) Foreign exchange control
(*d*) Devaluation

Choose the ***correct*** answer from the options given below:

A. (*a*), (*b*), (*c*) and (*d*)
B. (*a*) and (*b*) only
C. (*c*) and (*d*) only
D. (*a*), (*b*) and (*c*) only

61. Which of the following are relevant conditions assumed by the Factor Price Equalization theorem?

(*a*) The countries are characterized by different factor endowments
(*b*) The countries are characterized by different production functions
(*c*) The industries are characterized by different factor intensities
(*d*) Each country will export the commodity which uses its abundant factor

Choose the ***correct*** answer from the options given below:

A. (*a*), (*b*) and (*c*) only
B. (*a*), (*c*) and (*d*) only
C. (*a*), (*b*) and (*d*) only
D. (*b*), (*c*) and (*d*) only

62. Zero Based Budgeting (ZBB) lays emphasis on:

(*a*) Allocation of resources based on cost-benefit terms
(*b*) Unlimited deficit financing
(*c*) Preparing a new budget right from the scratch
(*d*) Preparing the budget, neglecting the history of expenditure

Choose the ***correct*** answer from the options given below:

A. (*a*), (*b*) and (*c*) only
B. (*a*), (*c*) and (*d*) only
C. (*b*), (*c*) and (*d*) only
D. (*a*), (*b*) and (*d*) only

63. Which of the following statements are relevant for Gender Budgeting?

(*a*) Preparing a separate budget for women
(*b*) Gender budget is not practised by the Government of India
(*c*) Evaluating budgetary provisions with a gender perspective
(*d*) Gender budgeting is a tool for Gender Empowerment

Choose the ***correct*** answer from the options given below:

A. (*a*) only
B. (*a*) and (*d*) only
C. (*c*) and (*d*) only
D. (*a*), (*b*), (*c*) and (*d*)

64. Which of the following are true for the Environmental Kuznets Curve (EKC)?

(*a*) The relationship between Income and Environmental damages take the shape of an inverted U

(*b*) EKC is applicable in case of irreversible environmental damage

(*c*) EKC holds true for global pollutants

(*d*) EKC hypothesis intends to represent a long term relationship between economic growth and pollution

Choose the ***correct*** answer from the options given below:

A. (*a*) and (*b*) only

B. (*a*) and (*d*) only

C. (*c*) and (*d*) only

D. (*a*), (*b*), (*c*) and (*d*)

65. Which of the following statement(s) is/are CORRECT for environmental evaluation?

(*a*) Travel cost method measures the recreational values of Environmental Resources

(*b*) Hedonic pricing is used for environmental amenities associated with property values

(*c*) Replacement cost method is used by substituting natural resources with a man-made equipment

(*d*) Defensive expenditure deals with preventive measures

Choose the ***correct*** answer from the options given below:

A. (*a*) and (*b*) only

B. (*b*) and (*c*) only

C. (*c*) only

D. (*a*), (*b*), (*c*) and (*d*)

66. Match List-I with List-II:

List-I	List-II
(*a*) Perfect competition	I. Many real or perceived differences in products
(*b*) Monopoly	II. Little or no difference in products
(*c*) Monopolistic competition	III. Identical products
(*d*) Oligopoly	IV. Product without close substitutes

Choose the ***correct*** answer from the options given below:

	(*a*)	(*b*)	(*c*)	(*d*)
A.	III	IV	I	II
B.	III	I	II	IV
C.	II	IV	I	III
D.	III	IV	II	I

67. Match List-I with List-II:

List-I	List-II
(*a*) Menu cost	I. Monetary Policy
(*b*) Quantitative Easing	II. Inflation
(*c*) Pump Priming	III. Phillips curve
(*d*) Trade-off between inflation and unemployment	IV. Fiscal policy

Choose the ***correct*** answer from the options given below:

	(*a*)	(*b*)	(*c*)	(*d*)
A.	II	I	IV	III
B.	I	II	III	IV
C.	III	IV	I	II
D.	IV	III	II	I

68. Match List-I with List-II:

List-I	List-II
(*a*) Carl Friedrich Gauss	I. Central Tendency
(*b*) Multicollinearity	II. OLS
(*c*) Mode	III. Karl Pearson
(*d*) Correlation coefficient	IV. Relationship among explanatory variables

Choose the ***correct*** answer from the options given below:

	(*a*)	(*b*)	(*c*)	(*d*)
A.	IV	I	II	III
B.	III	IV	I	II
C.	II	IV	III	I
D.	II	IV	I	III

69. Match List-I with List-II:

List-I	List-II
(*a*) Convex Function	I. Basic Variable
(*b*) Input-Output Analysis	II. Use of Derivative
(*c*) Linear Programming	III. Hawkins–Simon condition
(*d*) Marginal Propensity to Consume	IV. Demand Curve

Choose the ***correct*** answer from the options given below:

	(*a*)	(*b*)	(*c*)	(*d*)
A.	IV	III	I	II
B.	II	III	I	IV
C.	III	IV	I	II
D.	IV	I	III	II

70. Match List-I with List-II:

List-I	List-II
(*a*) Supply side of International Trade	I. David Ricardo
(*b*) Demand side of International Trade	II. Bastable and Alfred Marshall
(*c*) Opportunity cost of International Trade	III. G. Haberler
(*d*) Real cost theory of International Trade	IV. Alfred Marshall and Edgeworth

Choose the ***correct*** answer from the options given below:

	(*a*)	(*b*)	(*c*)	(*d*)
A.	I	IV	II	III
B.	IV	I	II	III
C.	I	IV	III	II
D.	IV	I	III	II

71. Match List-I with List-II:

List-I	List-II
(*a*) Canons of Taxation	I. U. K. Hicks
(*b*) Canons of Public Expenditure	II. Adam Smith
(*c*) Effective Incidence of Tax	III. Findlay Shirras
(*d*) Benefit received approach of Public Expenditure	IV. Erik Lindahl

Choose the ***correct*** answer from the options given below:

	(*a*)	(*b*)	(*c*)	(*d*)
A.	II	III	I	IV
B.	I	II	III	IV
C.	II	III	IV	I
D.	IV	I	II	III

72. Match List-I with List-II:

List-I	List-II
(*a*) Security Exchange Board of India (SEBI)	I. 1991
(*b*) National Securities Depository Ltd (NSDL)	II. 1992
(*c*) Credit Rating Information Service of India Ltd (CRISIL)	III. 1988
(*d*) Investment Information and Credit Rating Agency of India (ICRA)	IV. 1996

Choose the ***correct*** answer from the options given below:

	(*a*)	(*b*)	(*c*)	(*d*)
A.	I	II	III	IV
B.	IV	III	II	I
C.	III	II	IV	I
D.	II	IV	III	I

73. Match List-I with List-II:

List-I	List-II
(*a*) Adam Smith	I. Theory of Big Push
(*b*) R. Rodan	II. Traditional Society
(*c*) W.W. Rostow	III. Reserve army of labour
(*d*) Karl Marx	IV. Division of labour

Choose the ***correct*** answer from the options given below:

	(*a*)	(*b*)	(*c*)	(*d*)
A.	IV	I	II	III
B.	II	III	I	IV
C.	III	II	IV	I
D.	I	IV	III	II

74. Match List-I with List-II:

List-I	List-II
(*a*) Conserving the Environment for benefit of the future generation	I. Indirect use value
(*b*) Search of Alternative fuels is necessary because traditional sources are non-renewable	II. Option Value
(*c*) Wood from the forest is useful as timber	III. Bequest Value
(*d*) Insects are important as they help in pollination	IV. Use Value

Choose the ***correct*** answer from the options given below:

	(*a*)	(*b*)	(*c*)	(*d*)
A.	I	II	III	IV
B.	III	II	IV	I
C.	II	IV	I	III
D.	III	IV	II	I

75. Match List-I with List-II:

List-I	List-II
(*a*) NIRVIK	I. A project directed to provide piped cooking gas to millions of households
(*b*) Ayushman Bharat	II. A scheme to enhance energy efficiency
(*c*) Pradhan Mantri Urja Ganga (PMUG)	III. Export credit insurance scheme
(*d*) Perform, Achieve and Trade (PAT)	IV. Programme related to health issues in the primary, secondary and tertiary sectors

Choose the ***correct*** answer from the options given below:

	(*a*)	(*b*)	(*c*)	(*d*)
A.	II	III	I	IV
B.	III	IV	II	I
C.	II	IV	III	I
D.	III	IV	I	II

76. Arrange the following concepts of consumer behaviour in chronological order

(*a*) Law of diminishing marginal utility

(*b*) Law of demand

(*c*) Revealed Preference Analysis

(*d*) Indifference Curve Analysis

Choose the ***correct*** answer from the options given below:

A. (*a*), (*b*), (*d*), (*c*) B. (*b*), (*a*), (*d*), (*c*)

C. (*b*), (*a*), (*c*), (*d*) D. (*a*), (*b*), (*c*), (*d*)

77. Arrange the following business cycles in ascending order in terms of their approximate duration.

(*a*) Kondratiev cycle

(*b*) Kitchin cycle

(*c*) Jugular cycle

(*d*) Kuznets cycle

Choose the ***correct*** answer from the options given below:

A. (*c*), (*b*), (*a*), (*d*) B. (*b*), (*c*), (*d*), (*a*)

C. (*a*), (*c*), (*b*), (*d*) D. (*d*), (*a*), (*c*), (*b*)

78. Identify the proper sequence in the traditional econometric methodology of conducting research:

(*a*) Data collection

(*b*) Policy prescription

(*c*) Testing of hypothesis

(*d*) Formulation of hypothesis

Choose the ***correct*** answer from the options given below:

A. (*d*), (*a*), (*b*), (*c*) B. (*a*), (*d*), (*b*), (*c*)

C. (*d*), (*a*), (*c*), (*b*) D. (*a*), (*b*), (*c*), (*d*)

79. What is the CORRECT sequence of the following?

(*a*) Uruguay Round

(*b*) Kennedy Round

(*c*) Doha Round

(*d*) Geneva Round

Choose the ***correct*** answer from the options given below:

A. (*d*), (*b*), (*a*), (*c*) B. (*b*), (*d*), (*c*), (*a*)

C. (*a*), (*b*), (*c*), (*d*) D. (*c*), (*a*), (*b*), (*d*)

80. Arrange the introduction of the following taxes in India in chronological order.

(*a*) Service Tax
(*b*) Income Tax
(*c*) Banking Transaction Tax
(*d*) Gift Tax
(*e*) Goods and Services Tax

Choose the ***correct*** answer from the options given below:

A. (*b*), (*d*), (*a*), (*c*), (*e*)
B. (*b*), (*a*), (*c*), (*e*), (*d*)
C. (*b*), (*c*), (*a*), (*d*), (*e*)
D. (*d*), (*b*), (*a*), (*c*), (*e*)

81. Arrange the following committees appointed for the Banking sector in India in chronological order:

(*a*) Urjit Patel Committee
(*b*) Goiporia Committee
(*c*) Narasimham Committee-1
(*d*) Chakravarty Committee

Choose the ***correct*** answer from the options given below:

A. (*d*), (*c*), (*b*), (*a*) B. (*a*), (*c*), (*d*), (*b*)
C. (*c*), (*b*), (*d*), (*a*) D. (*d*), (*b*), (*c*), (*a*)

82. Arrange the following in chronological order in which they were introduced:

(*a*) SDGs
(*b*) MPI
(*c*) PQLI
(*d*) HDI

Choose the ***correct*** answer from the options given below:

A. (*d*), (*c*), (*a*), (*b*) B. (*c*), (*d*), (*b*), (*a*)
C. (*c*), (*b*), (*a*), (*d*) D. (*d*), (*c*), (*b*), (*a*)

83. Arrange the following United Nations Framework Convention on Climate Change (UNFCCC) conferences in chronological order:

(*a*) Copenhagen Conference
(*b*) Doha Conference
(*c*) Paris Conference
(*d*) Katowice Conference

Choose the ***correct*** answer from the options given below:

A. (*b*), (*c*), (*d*), (*a*) B. (*d*), (*c*), (*b*), (*a*)
C. (*a*), (*b*), (*c*), (*d*) D. (*c*), (*d*), (*b*), (*a*)

84. Consider some of the schemes/programs introduced by the Government of India to enhance agriculture productivity and farmer's income. Arrange them in chronological order of their appearance.

(*a*) Soil Health Card Scheme
(*b*) Kisan Credit Card Scheme
(*c*) Pradhan Mantri Fasal Bima Yojana
(*d*) Doubling Farmers' Income Program

Choose the ***correct*** answer from the options given below:

A. (*a*), (*b*), (*c*), (*d*) B. (*b*), (*a*), (*c*), (*d*)
C. (*b*), (*c*), (*a*), (*d*) D. (*b*), (*a*), (*d*), (*c*)

85. Arrange the following Committees of poverty estimation in chronological order:

(*a*) Alagh Committee
(*b*) Lakdawala Committee
(*c*) Tendulkar Committee
(*d*) Rangarajan Committee

Choose the ***correct*** answer from the options given below:

A. (*a*), (*b*), (*c*), (*d*) B. (*a*), (*c*), (*b*), (*d*)
C. (*b*), (*c*), (*a*), (*d*) D. (*b*), (*a*), (*c*), (*d*)

86. Given below are two statements, one is labelled as Assertion (A) and the other is labelled as Reason (R):

Assertion (A) : A lumpsum tax imposed on a monopolist cannot be shifted to the consumers.

Reason (R) : The lumpsum tax becomes a part of his fixed cost and it does not affect the marginal cost of production.

In light of the above statements, choose the most appropriate answer from the options given below:

A. Both (A) and (R) are correct and (R) is the correct explanation of (A)

B. Both (A) and (R) are correct but (R) is NOT the correct explanation of (A)
C. (A) is correct but (R) is not correct
D. (A) is not correct but (R) is correct

87. Given below are two statements, one is labelled as Assertion (A) and the other is labelled as Reason (R):

Assertion (A) : There is no incentive for a profit maximising producer to supply public goods.

Reason (R) : If he produces it, he is unable to exclude people from consuming it and hence he cannot charge a price.

In light of the above statements, choose the most appropriate answer from the options given below:

A. Both (A) and (R) are correct and (R) is the correct explanation of (A)
B. Both (A) and (R) are correct but (R) is NOT the correct explanation of (A)
C. (A) is correct but (R) is not correct
D. (A) is not correct but (R) is correct

88. Given below are two statements, one is labelled as Assertion (A) and the other is labelled as Reason (R):

Assertion (A) : New capital accumulation is the vehicle of technical progress.

Reason (R) : Technical progress is embodied in new machines.

In light of the above statements, choose the correct answer from the options given below:

A. Both (A) and (R) are true and (R) is the correct explanation of (A)
B. Both (A) and (R) are true but (R) is NOT the correct explanation of (A)
C. (A) is true but (R) is false
D. (A) is false but (R) is true

89. Given below are two statements:

Statement I : Social Welfare Function (SWF) is a sort of social indifference map consisting of the Social Indifference Curves (SICs) which shows the various combination of utilities that gives the same level of social welfare (SW).

Statement II : Social Indifference Curves (SICs) may not be convex or concave to the origin

In light of the above statements, choose the most appropriate answer from the options given below:

A. Both Statement I and Statement II are correct
B. Both Statement I and Statement II are incorrect
C. Statement I is correct but Statement II is incorrect
D. Statement I is incorrect but Statement II is correct

90. Given below are two statements:

Statement I : One of the assumptions under OLS method states that the regression model is linear in the parameters, though it may or may not be linear in the variables.

Statement II : The variance of the error, or disturbance, term is not the same regardless of the value of the explanatory variable under OLS.

In light of the above statements, choose the most appropriate answer from the options given below:

A. Both statement I and statement II are correct
B. Both statement I and statement II are incorrect
C. Statement I is correct but statement II is incorrect
D. Statement I is incorrect but statement II is correct

Directions (Qs. No. 91-95): *Read the following passage and answer the question based on it.*

The study titled, "Monetary Policy Transparency and Anchoring of Inflation Expectation in India" constructs an index of monetary policy transparency for India and examines the role of transparency in anchoring inflation expectations. Empirical results show that the degree of policy transparency has indeed increased substantially since the adoption of Flexible Inflation Targeting (FIT) in 2016. Further, empirical evidence suggests that inflation expectations of professional forecasters and households were anchored, in weak-form, in the post-FIT period, though households' expectations did not necessarily lie within the inflation tolerance band. During the transition period (between the self-imposed disinflationary glide-path since 2014 and adoption of the FIT) both realized inflation and expectations followed a declining path, which resulted in a positive association between them. During the pre-transition period, when explicit inflation target was absent, expectations were also reasonably anchored, albeit, at a higher level.

91. Which time span has been described as the transition period of monetary policy?
- A. 2014-2016
- B. 2016-2020
- C. 2000-2014
- D. 2008-2014

92. What happened to the anchoring of inflation expectations?
- A. Inflation expectations anchored in a strong form
- B. Inflation expectations anchored in a weak-form in the post FIT period
- C. There was no association between realised and expected inflation
- D. There was a negative association between realised and expected inflation

93. Which of the following index has been constructed?
- A. Index of monetary policy
- B. Index of inflation expectations
- C. Index monetary policy transparency for India
- D. Index of transparency

94. What has empirical evidence shown?
- A. Degree of policy transparency declined
- B. Degree of policy transparency increased
- C. Degree of policy transparency increased but after coming into force of FIT
- D. Actual inflation turned out to be high

95. Inflation expectations of which group was empirically tested?
- A. Only of professional forecasters
- B. Only of Households
- C. Both of professional forecasters and Households
- D. Neither of professional forecasters nor Households

Directions (Qs. No. 96-100): *Read the given passage and answer the questions that follow.*

One argument of protection that stands up to close economic scrutiny is the infant-industry argument. It holds that a nation may have a potential comparative advantage in a commodity, but because of lack of knowledge and the initial small level of output, the industry cannot successfully compete with more established foreign firms. The infant-industry argument for protection is correct but requires several important qualifications. First, such an argument is more justified for developing nations, where capital markets may not function properly. Second, as experience has shown that protection, once given, is difficult to remove. Third, what trade protection in the form of import tariff can do an equivalent production subsidy to the infant industry can do better. The reason is that a purely domestic distortion such as this should be overcome with a purely domestic policy such as direct production subsidy to the infant industry. A production subsidy is also a more direct form of aid and it is easier to remove than an import tariff. A better policy would be to provide a direct subsidy to the industry. Similarly, a direct tax would also be better than a tariff to discourage activities that give rise to external diseconomies because the tax does not distort relative prices and consumption.

96. Which is the most appropriate instrument of trade protection?
A. Import tariff
B. Export tariff
C. Non-tariff barriers
D. Production subsidy

97. Developing countries are characterised by:
A. Absence of both money markets and capital markets
B. Improper functioning of the capital markets
C. Improper functioning of money markets
D. Absence of capital markets

98. The obstacles for an industry to compete with more established foreign firms are due to:
A. Lack of know-how and initial small level of output
B. Lack of flexibility
C. Lack of markets
D. Lack of human resources

99. Which of the following is effective in preventing external diseconomies?
A. Trade policies
B. Production subsidies
C. A direct tax
D. Tariff

100. Which of the following is a direct aid to domestic industry?
A. Import controls
B. Import quota
C. Production subsidy
D. Patent rights

ANSWERS

1	2	3	4	5	6	7	8	9	10
B	D	D	C	C	A	B	C	B	B
11	**12**	**13**	**14**	**15**	**16**	**17**	**18**	**19**	**20**
C	D	C	B	C	B	A	D	C	A
21	**22**	**23**	**24**	**25**	**26**	**27**	**28**	**29**	**30**
A	D	C	D	A	A	D	C	D	A
31	**32**	**33**	**34**	**35**	**36**	**37**	**38**	**39**	**40**
B	C	A	C	C	D	A	A	C	C
41	**42**	**43**	**44**	**45**	**46**	**47**	**48**	**49**	**50**
B	B	C	D	D	A	B	A	C	A
51	**52**	**53**	**54**	**55**	**56**	**57**	**58**	**59**	**60**
D	*	A	B	A	A	A	C	B	A
61	**62**	**63**	**64**	**65**	**66**	**67**	**68**	**69**	**70**
B	B	C	B	D	A	A	D	A	C
71	**72**	**73**	**74**	**75**	**76**	**77**	**78**	**79**	**80**
A	D	A	B	D	B	B	C	A	A
81	**82**	**83**	**84**	**85**	**86**	**87**	**88**	**89**	**90**
D	B	C	B	A	A	A	A	C	C
91	**92**	**93**	**94**	**95**	**96**	**97**	**98**	**99**	**100**
A	B	C	C	C	D	B	A	C	C

EXPLANATORY ANSWERS

1. The maximum amount of one good a consumer would be willing to give up in order to obtain an additional unit of another is called the marginal rate of substitution (MRS), which is equal to the absolute value of the slope of the indifference curve between two points. Most indifference curves are usually convex because as you consume more of one good you will consume less of the other. So, MRS will decrease as one moves down the indifference curve. This is known as the law of diminishing marginal rate of substitution. If the marginal rate of substitution is increasing, the indifference curve will be concave, which means that a consumer would consume more of X for the increased consumption of Y and vice versa, but this is not common.

2. General equilibrium analyzes the economy as a whole, rather than analyzing single markets like with partial equilibrium analysis. General equilibrium shows how supply and demand interact and tend toward a balance in an economy of multiple markets working at once. The balance of competing levels of supply and demand in different markets ultimately creates price equilibrium. French economist Leon Walras introduced and developed the theory in the late 19th century.

   Moral hazard can exist when a party to a contract can take risks without having to suffer consequences. Moral hazard is common in the lending and insurance industries but also can exist in employee-employer relationships.

3. The short-run production function defines the relationship between one variable factor (keeping all other factors fixed) and the output. The law of returns to a factor explains such a production function.

   Technology is kept constant because it becomes easier for economists to analyse the implication of a change in labour and capital. Most importantly, technology does not change very frequently and generally changes over the long term. Hence, in the long run production function it is variable.

4. Long run average cost is the cost per unit of output reasonable when all factors of production are variable. Long Run Average cost is of 'U' shaped because of returns to scale. In the establishment, firms enjoy lots of *economies* to scale so its cost curve is downward sloping. Increasing income to scale applies when firms enjoy economies to scale. In the beginning, the factors of production are not exhausted.

6. The Phillips curve states that inflation and unemployment have an inverse relationship. Higher inflation is associated with lower unemployment and vice versa. The Phillips curve was a concept used to guide macroeconomic policy in the 20th century, but was called into question by the stagflation of the 1970's.

7. Money illusion posits that people have a tendency to view their wealth and income in nominal dollar terms, rather than recognize their real value, adjusted for inflation. Economists cite factors such as a lack of financial education and the price stickiness seen in many goods and services as triggers of money illusion. The term money illusion was first coined by American economist Irving Fisher in his book "Stabilizing the Dollar". Fisher later wrote an entire book dedicated to the topic in 1928, titled "The Money Illusion".

8. In order to measure the total effect of initial investment on income, Hicks has combined the multiplier and the accelerator mathematically and given it the name of the

super-multiplier. The combined effect of the multiplier and the accelerator is also called the leverage effect which may lead the economy to very high or low level of income propagation.

9. At the equilibrium level of national income:

$$\begin{aligned} AD &= AS \\ AD &= C + I + G \\ &= C + 50 + 0.2Y + 50 \\ AS &= C + S \\ &= -150 + 0.4Y \end{aligned}$$

Now, as $AD = AS$

$$\begin{aligned} C + 50 + 0.2Y + 50 &= -150 + 0.4Y \\ 100 + 0.2Y &= -150 + 0.4Y \\ 250 &= 0.2Y \\ 250/0.2 &= Y \\ 1250 &= Y. \end{aligned}$$

10. This independence of real variables from changes in money supply and nominal variables is called classical dichotomy. The classical dichotomy (Patinkin, 1965) refers to the idea that real variables, like output and employment, are independent of monetary variables. In this view, the primary function of money is to act as a lubricant for the efficient production and exchange of commodities.

11. P(2 Boys, 1 Girl)

$= P(BBG) + P(BGB) + P(GBB)$

$$= \frac{1\times1\times1}{2\times2\times2} + \frac{1\times1\times1}{2\times2\times2} + \frac{1\times1\times1}{2\times2\times2} = \frac{3}{8}.$$

12. The geometric mean is a measure of central tendency that equals the *n*th root of the product of *n* numbers. Like the arithmetic mean, the geometric mean finds the center of a dataset. While the arithmetic mean finds the center by summing the values and dividing by the number of observations, the geometric mean finds the center by multiplying and then taking a root of the product. Based on the calculation methods, the arithmetic mean is the better statistic when adding data is appropriate, while the geometric mean is better when you need to multiply the data.

13. Since $n < 30$ and the population is finite, the finite population mean correction (FPC) in cannot be ignored.

$$\sigma_{\bar{X}}^2 = \frac{\sigma^2}{n}\left(\frac{N-n}{N-1}\right)$$

Thus, substituting the values:

$$\sigma_{\bar{X}}^2 = \frac{\sigma^2}{n}\left(\frac{N-n}{N-1}\right)$$

or $$5 = \frac{\sigma^2}{13}\left(\frac{49-13}{49-1}\right)$$

or $$\sigma^2 = 86.6.$$

14. Assumptions of the Classical Linear Regression Model:

- The regression model is linear, correctly specified, and has an additive error term.
- The error term has a zero population mean.
- All explanatory variables are uncorrelated with the error term.
- Observations of the error term are uncorrelated with each other (no serial correlation).
- The error term has a constant variance (no heteroskedasticity).
- No explanatory variable is a perfect linear function of any other explanatory variables (no perfect multicollinearity).
- The error term is normally distributed (not required).

15. Properties of Intersection:

- Commutative: $X \cap Y = Y \cap X$
- Associative: $X \cap (Y \cap Z) = (X \cap Y) \cap Z$
- $X \cap \phi = \phi$
- $X \cap Y \subseteq X$
- $X \cap X = X$
- $X \subseteq Y$ if and only if $X \cap Y = X$

If $X \cap Y = \phi$, then the two sets X and Y, are disjoint. Here, the symbol ϕ (phi) represents the null or empty set, hence $X - Y \neq X$.

16. Recall that to find critical points we need to consider

$$f(x) = X^3 - 12X^2 + 36X + 17$$
$$= 3(x - 6)(x - 2) = 0$$

and then we have 2 critical points at $x = 2$ and $x = 6$.

Then we can consider the sign for $f''(x) = 6x - 24$ around the critical points to find out whether they are local maximum or local minimum points, notably we have that

- $f''(2) = -12 < 0 \Rightarrow x = 2$ is a local maximum that is $f(2) = 40f(2) = 40$.
- $f''(6) = 12 > 0 \Rightarrow x = 6$ is a local minimum that is $f(6) = 8$.

19. The concept of net barter terms of trade was introduced by F.W. Taussig. This concept was called as commodity terms of trade by Jacob Viner. It is defined as the ratio of export prices to import prices. It is given by the following formula:

Net Barter Terms

$$= \frac{\text{Price Index of Exports}}{\text{Price Index of Imports}} \times 100$$

20. The capital account, on a national level, represents the balance of payments for a country. The capital account keeps track of the net change in a nation's assets and liabilities during a year. Capital account balance consists of flow variables since it records changes in the country's asset holdings during the year, while the international asset position of a country consists of stock variables since it records the total value of assets at a point in time.

22. Generally, the optimal tariff is defined as the rate that unilaterally maximizes a country's welfare and is given by the inverse elasticity of foreign export supply, as determined by optimal monopsony pricing.

23. Peacock and Jack Wiseman advanced the study of growth of public expenditure through **Peacock Wiseman Hypothesis** by their study of public expenditure at Great Britain during the period 1890 to 1955.

Peacock Wiseman Hypothesis focused on the pattern of public expenditure and stated that public expenditure does not follow a smooth or continuous trend but the increase in public expenditure takes place in jerks or steps. They gave three separate concepts to justify the hypothesis, they are:

- **Displacement effect:** When a social disturbance occurs the government raises taxes to increase revenue and increases public expenditure to meet the social disturbance. This creates a displacement effect by which low taxes and expenditures are replaced by higher tax and expenditure levels.
- **Inspection effect:** Even if there is no new disturbance there is no strong motivation to return to lower level of taxation as the increased revenue can be used to support a higher level of public expenditure. Therefore government expands its fiscal operations partly due to disturbance and partly to expand economic activity and take up new functions that were earlier neglected. This is known as Inspection effect.
- **Concentration effect:** When an economy is experiencing economic growth there is a tendency of central government's economic activities to grow at a faster rate than that of state and local government's activities.

24. If there are externalities then regulation, assigning property rights and permitting bargaining and Pigovian taxes can help in obtaining welfare.

26. Monopolies may be regulated by means of imposition of lump-sum taxes. Since a lump-sum tax is like a fixed cost to a monopolist, its imposition will result in an upward shift of his total cost (TC) curve by a vertical distance equal to the amount of the tax.

27. The commercial banks are the financial institutions which are authorised to receive deposits from public, industries and commerce as well as cater short, medium and long term requirements of individuals, entrepreneurs and corporates in form of different types of loans/ advances. There are basically four categories of commercial bank functioning in India: Public Sector Banks, Private Sector Banks, Regional Rural Banks, and Foreign Banks. Co-operative banks are the Co-operative societies registered under the Co-operative Society Act, 1965 of the concerned state. The Co-operative banks function on 'No profit No loss basis' that means their main objective are to help backward segment of the society like agriculturists, labours, small vendors, self-employed.

28. A Liquidity Adjustment Facility (LAF) is a monetary policy tool used in India by the Reserve Bank of India or RBI.The RBI introduced the LAF as part of the outcome of the Narasimham Committee on Banking Sector Reforms of 1998. LAF's help the RBI manage liquidity and provide economic stability by offering banks the opportunity to borrow money through repurchase agreements or repos or to make loans to the RBI via reverse repo agreements.

29. A bank rate is the interest rate at which a nation's central bank lends money to domestic banks, often in the form of very short-term loans. Managing the bank rate is a method by which central banks affect economic activity. Lower bank rates can help to expand the economy by lowering the cost of funds for borrowers, and higher bank rates help to reign in the economy when inflation is higher than desired.

30. The HDI is calculated as the geometric mean (equally-weighted) of life expectancy, education, and GNI per capita, as follows:

$$HDI = (I_{Health} * I_{Education} * I_{Income})^{1/3}$$

The education dimension is the arithmetic mean of the two education indices (mean years of schooling and expected years of schooling).

31. Harrod neutral technical progress is a technical progress which increases the efficiency of labour, so that the labour force in efficiency units increases faster than the number of workers available. Technical progress of this form is thus labour-saving. It is contrasted with Hicks-neutral technical progress, where the efficiency of all factors increases in the same proportion. See also technical progress.

32. Robert Solow and Trevor Swan first introduced the neoclassical growth theory in 1956. The theory states that economic growth is the result of three factors—labour, capital, and technology. While an economy has limited resources in terms of capital and labour, the contribution from technology to growth is boundless.

According to Pasinetti Model, "in any type of society, when any individual saves part of the income, he must also be allowed to own it, otherwise he would not save at all". This means that the stock of capital which exists in the system is owned by those people (capitalists or workers) who in the past made the corresponding savings. So he divided total profits into two categories, *i.e.*, profits which accrue to the capitalists and profits which accrue to the workers.

33. It is possible for technical progress to be both Hicks-Neutral and Harrod-Neutral if the production function has constant unit elasticity of substitution, *i.e.* $s = 1$, or when the elasticity of substitution between labour and capital is equal to unity.

34. Crude Birth Rate is the number of resident live births for a specified geographic area (nation, state, county, etc.) during a specified period (usually a calendar year) divided by the total population (usually mid-year) for that area and multiplied by 1,000.

Crude Birth Rate

$$= \left(\frac{\text{Number of resident live births}}{\text{Number of total population}}\right) \times 1000$$

$$\text{Crude Birth Rate} = \left(\frac{50000}{2800000}\right) \times 1000$$

= 0.017857 × 1000 = 17.857.

35. Coasian bargaining is based on the ideas of Ronald H. Coase who earned the 1991 Nobel Prize in economics 'for his discovery and clarification of the significance of transaction costs and property rights for the institutional structure and functioning of the economy'. In his article, *The Problem of Social Cost* (1960), he proposes that well-defined property rights can overcome the problems of externalities, because many environmental problems arise from poorly defined, or a lack of, property rights. Assuming that property rights are held by the polluter and that transaction costs are zero, the Coase theorem states that a polluter and a victim can reach a mutually beneficial bargain if the damage from pollution is higher than the polluter's net return from the sale of the good generating the pollution. In this case, a payment from the affected party to the polluter would reduce the pollution. Thus, the Coase theorem states that the most efficient solution to resolving interdependent uses of the environment, including pollution cases, is a bargaining process among relevant property holders.

38. "Atmanirbhar Bharat Rozgar Yojana" is being launched to boost employment in formal sector and incentivize creation of new employment opportunities during the Covid recovery phase under Atmanirbhar Bharat Package 3.0. The scheme is to be operational for the period 2020-2023.

Benefits for establishments - of India will provide subsidy for two years in respect of new employees engaged on or after 1st October, 2020 and upto 30th June, 2021 at following scale.

- **Establishments employing up to 1000 employees:** Employee's contributions (12% of Wages) & Employer's contributions (12% of wages) totalling 24% of wages.
- **Establishments employing more than 1000 employees:** Only Employee's EPF contributions (12% of EPF wages).

41. Risk-averse investors prioritize the safety of principal over the possibility of a higher return on their money. They prefer liquid investments. That is, their money can be accessed when needed, regardless of market conditions at the moment.

42. Welfare economics is the study of how the structure of markets and the allocation of economic goods and resources determine the overall well-being of society.

Welfare economics leads to the condition of Pareto efficiency as an ideal in welfare economics. When the economy is in a state of Pareto efficiency, social welfare is maximized in the sense that no resources can be reallocated to make one individual better off without making at least one individual worse off. One goal of economic policy could be to try to move the economy toward a Pareto efficient state.

43. A factor market is a market where means, or factors, of production are exchanged. Another term for factor market is input market. Typically, companies will buy and sell the resources that they need to produce goods and services for their end-users. The price at which companies or individuals purchase resources from the factor market is known as factor prices, which are paid in factor payments. Also, factor markets are different from product markets, which are where finished products or services are sold to end-users. Whereas in the factor market, it is typically a business-to-business transaction, in the product market, it is typically a business-to-person transaction. Factor markets are driven by the demand in the product market. Following conditions must hold true factor pricing when factor market is perfectly competitive and product market is monopolistic:

- Value of Marginal Product (VMP) > Marginal Revenue Product (MRP)
- Both VMP and MRP decreasing
- MRP = W.

44. In C = 50 + .75 Y, MPC = 0.75

K = 1/MPS, where MPS = 1 − MPC

K = 1/1 − 0.75 = 1/0.25 = 4

In S = −50 + .25 Y, MPS = 0.25

K = 1/MPS = 1/0.25 = 4

45. There are mainly two methods of sampling which are random and non-random samplings. Random sampling is referred to as that sampling technique where the probability of choosing each sample is equal. The sample that is chosen randomly is an unbiased representation of the total population. If at all, the sample chosen does not represent the population, it leads to sampling error. Non-random sampling is a sampling technique where the sample selection is based on factors other than just random chance. In other words, non-random sampling is biased in nature.

50. The Money Supply is all the currency and other liquid instruments in a country's economy on the date measured. The money supply roughly includes both cash and deposits that can be used almost as easily as cash.

51. A Lorenz Curve is a graphical representation of the distribution of income or wealth within a population. The Theil Index measures an entropic "distance" the population is away from the "ideal" egalitarian state of everyone having the same income. The Palma Ratio is the share of all income received by the 10% people with highest disposable income divided by the share of all income received by the 40% people with the lowest disposable income.

52. The Ministry of Environment and Forests (MoEF) was created in 1985. But it was rechristened in 2014 when Narendra Modi led National Democratic Alliance (NDA) government took over and added Climate Change to its portfolio, making it the Ministry of Environment, Forests and Climate Change (MoEFCC).

The Central Pollution Control Board (CPCB), statutory organisation, was constituted in September, 1974 under the Water (Prevention and Control of Pollution) Act, 1974. Further, CPCB was entrusted with the powers and functions under the Air (Prevention and Control of Pollution) Act, 1981.

The Environmental Protection Act 1990 (EPA) succeeded the Control of Pollution Act 1974 (COPA) and introduced new regulations for improved management systems relating to waste and pollution.

The National Environment Appellate Authority Act, 1997, provide for the establishment of a National Environment Appellate Authority to hear appeals with respect to restriction of areas in which any industries, operations or processes or class of industries, operations or processes shall not be carried out or shall be carried out subject to certain safeguards under the Environment (Protection) Act, 1986 and for matters connected therewith or incidental thereto.

54. NIDHI (National Initiative for Development and Harnessing Innovations), an umbrella program is pioneered by the Department of Science & Technology (DST), Government of India, for nurturing ideas and innovations (knowledge-based and technology-driven) into successful startups.

56. The rational expectations theory posits that individuals base their decisions on human rationality, information available to them, and their past experiences. The rational expectations theory is a concept and theory used in macroeconomics. Economists use the rational expectations theory to explain anticipated economic factors, such as inflation rates and interest rates. The idea behind the rational expectations theory is that past outcomes influence future outcomes. The theory also believes that because people make decisions based on the available information at hand combined with their past experiences, most of the time their decisions will be correct.

57. The Accelerator Theory stipulates that capital investment outlay is a function of output. When faced with excess demand, the accelerator theory posits that companies typically choose to increase investment to meet their capital to output ratio, thereby increasing profits. The accelerator theory was conceived by Thomas Nixon Carver and Albert Aftalion, among others, before Keynesian economics, but it came into public knowledge as the Keynesian theory began to dominate the field of economics in the 20th century.

58. Correlation coefficients are used to measure the strength of the linear relationship between two variables. A correlation coefficient greater than zero indicates a positive relationship, while a value less than zero signifies a negative relationship. A value of zero indicates no relationship between the two variables being compared. A negative correlation, or inverse correlation, is a key concept in the creation of diversified portfolios that can better withstand portfolio volatility. Usually, in statistics, we measure four types of correlations: Pearson Correlation, Kendall rank correlation, Spearman correlation, and the Point-Biserial correlation.

59. A Cobb-Douglas production function models the relationship between production output and production inputs (factors). It is used to calculate ratios of inputs to one another for efficient production and to estimate technological change in production methods. The general form of a Cobb-Douglas production function for a set of n inputs is

$$Y = f(x_1, x_2, ..., x_n) = \gamma \prod_{i=1}^{n} x_i^{\alpha_i}$$

where Y stands for output, x_i for input i, and γ and α_i are parameters determining the overall efficiency of production and the responsiveness of output to changes in the input quantities. Properties of Cobb-Douglas (C-D) production function models are:

- The C-D Production Function can be Used to Measure the Returns to Scale.
- In the C-D production function, the factor intensity is computed by taking the between ratio α and β (ratio between exponent of capital and exponent of labour).
- The average product is the total output per unit of input.
- The Marginal Product of an Input can be Expressed in terms of its Average Product.
- The Marginal Product of an Input can be Expressed in terms of Its Average Product.
- The marginal rate of technical substitution (MRTS) in the theory of production that measures the degree of substitutability/interchangeability/exchangeability between factors inputs. The MRTS in the case of the C-D production function can be expressed in terms of the ratio between labour and capital.
- The elasticity of substitution (σ) of the C-D production function is defined as the percentage change in the capital-labour ratio divided by the percentage change in the marginal rate of technical substitution and is equal to unity.

- In the C-D production function, the efficiency of production can be measured by coefficient.
- C-D Production function can be made linear using logarithm and the level of output can be estimated based on regression analysis.

60. Payment Balance or BoP is a statement or record of all financial and economic transactions that are made nationally and internationally over a period of time (quarterly or yearly). BoP Deficit refers to the situation when a country's imports are higher than its total exports. The country then has to pay for its imports by utilising its foreign exchange reserves to meet the deficit that arises in due course.

61. The Factor-Price Equalisation Theorem is an important corollary derived from the Heckscher-Ohlin factor-proportions analysis. The basic contention of the Heckscher-Ohlin theorem explains that: factor-intensity difference in the production functions to two goods, in conjunction with the differing factor endowments of the two countries, accounts for the international difference in comparative costs, causing differences in the relative commodity prices.

62. Zero Based Budgeting (ZBB) is a technique used by companies, but this type of budgeting can be used by individuals and families. Budgets are created around the monetary needs for each upcoming period, like a month. Traditional budgeting and zero-based budgeting are two methods used to track expenditures. Zero Based Budgeting helps managers tackle lower costs in a company.

63. According to the Council of Europe's widely used definition, gender budgeting is an application of gender mainstreaming in the budgetary process. It involves conducting a gender-based assessment of budgets, incorporating a gender perspective at all levels of the budgetary process, and restructuring revenues and expenditures in order to promote gender equality. In short, gender budgeting is a strategy and a process with the long-term aim of achieving gender equality goals.

64. The Environmental Kuznets Curve suggests that economic development initially leads to deterioration in the environment, but after a certain level of economic growth, a society begins to improve its relationship with the environment and levels of environmental degradation reduce. From a very simplistic viewpoint, it can suggest that economic growth is good for the environment. However, critics argue there is no guarantee that economic growth will lead to an improved environment - in fact, the opposite is often the case. At the least, it requires a much targeted policy and attitudes to make sure that economic growth is compatible with an improving environment.

77. Kitchin cycle - 40 months
Jugular cycle - 7 to 11 years
Kuznets cycle - 15-25 years
Kondratiev cycle - 40 to 60 years

79. Geneva Round - 1955-56
Kennedy Round - 1964
Uruguay Round - 1986 to 1993
Doha Round - 2001

80. Income Tax - 1860
Gift Tax - 1958
Service Tax - 1994
Banking Transaction Tax - 2005
Goods and Services Tax - 2017

81. Chakravarty Committee - 1982
Goiporia Committee - 1990
Narasimham Committee-1 - 1991
Urjit Patel Committee - 2013

82. PQLI - 1979
HDI - 1990
MPI - 2010
SDGs - 2015

83. Copenhagen Conference - 2009
Doha Conference - 2010
Paris Conference - 2016
Katowice Conference - 2018

84. Kisan Credit Card Scheme - 1998
Soil Health Card Scheme - 2015
Pradhan Mantri Fasal Bima Yojana - 2016
Doubling Farmers' Income Program - 2018

85. Alagh Committee - 1979
Lakdawala Committee - 1993
Tendulkar Committee - 2005
Rangarajan Committee - 2012

86. A lumpsum tax imposed on a monopolist cannot be shifted to the consumers, as this tax becomes a part of his fixed cost and it does not affect the marginal cost of production.

87. A public good has two key characteristics: it is Non-Excludable and Non-Rivalrous. These characteristics make it difficult for market producers to sell the good to individual consumers. Non-Excludable means that it is costly or impossible for one user to exclude others from using a good. Non-Rivalrous means that when one person uses a good, it does not prevent others from using it.

88. Capital accumulation refers to an increase in assets from investments or profits and is one of the building blocks of a capitalist economy. The goal is to increase the value of an initial investment as a return on investment, whether that is through appreciation, rent, capital gains, or interest. The technical progress function (TPF) is a part of a macroeconomic growth model that accounts for the impact of technology and technological progress on the total amount of economic output a society can and does produce as well as the productivity of the factors of production that a society employs.

89. The social welfare function (SWF) is a sort of social indifference map consisting of the social indifference curves (SICs). An SIC gives the various combinations of utilities of the two individuals that comprise the society, that result in the same level of social welfare (W). SICs need not be convex or concave to the origin.

90. In econometrics, Ordinary Least Squares (OLS) method is widely used to estimate the parameter of a linear regression model. OLS estimators minimize the sum of the squared errors (a difference between observed values and predicted values). Assumptions of OLS Regression:

- The linear regression model is "linear in parameters".
- There is a random sampling of observations.
- The conditional mean should be zero.
- There is no multi-collinearity (or perfect collinearity).
- **Spherical errors:** There is homoscedasticity and no autocorrelation.
- Error terms should be normally distributed.

Previous Years' Paper (Solved)

National Testing Agency (NTA)

UGC-NET Junior Research Fellowship & Assistant Professor Eligibility Exam

ECONOMICS, June-2020

(Online exam held on 30-09-2020)

PAPER-II

1. In the study of International Economics, we use the tools of:

A. Microeconomic theory only
B. Macroeconomic theory only
C. Neither micro nor macro economic theory
D. Both micro and macro economic theory but we all extend, adapt and integrate them

2. Match List-I with List-II:

List-I	List-II
(*a*) Karl Marx Theory of Population growth	(*i*) Static interpretation
(*b*) Blacker's Theory of Population growth	(*ii*) Three stages
(*c*) Landry's Theory of Population growth	(*iii*) Four stages
(*d*) Prof. Sidgwick's Optimum Population Theory	(*iv*) Five stages

Choose the correct option from those given below:

	(*a*)	(*b*)	(*c*)	(*d*)
A.	(*ii*)	(*iii*)	(*iv*)	(*i*)
B.	(*i*)	(*ii*)	(*iii*)	(*iv*)
C.	(*iii*)	(*iv*)	(*ii*)	(*i*)
D.	(*iv*)	(*ii*)	(*i*)	(*iii*)

3. Given below are two statements, one is labelled as Assertion (A) and the other is labelled as Reason (R).

Assertion (A): High powered money is the source of all other forms of money that impact money supply.

Reason (R): Credit is created by commercial banks.

In light of the above statements, choose the most appropriate answer from the options given below:

A. Both (A) and (R) are correct and (R) is the correct explanation of (A)
B. Both (A) and (R) are correct, but (R) is not the correct explanation of (A)
C. (A) is correct, but (R) is not correct
D. (A) is not correct, but (R) is correct

4. Which one of the following is a valid objective function as a linear programming problem?

A. Max $Z = 5x^2y$
B. Max $Z = 3x + 2y + 8xy$
C. Min $Z = 2x^2 + 3y^2$
D. Min $Z = 5x + 2y$

5. Transportation cost of trade affects:

(*a*) Pattern of trade
(*b*) Boundaries between tradable and non-tradable goods
(*c*) Global supply chains
(*d*) Boundaries of non-tradable goods

Choose the correct answer from the options given below:

A. (*a*) and (*b*) only
B. (*a*), (*b*) and (*c*) only
C. (*a*), (*b*), (*c*) and (*d*) only
D. (*d*) only

6. Presence of asymmetric information in the market causes which of the following?
   (*a*) Adverse selection.
   (*b*) Marginal benefits of an additional unit of resources diminish with an increasing number of unit of resources.
   (*c*) Efficiency wages.
   (*d*) Principal-Agent problem.

   Choose the correct answer from the options given below:
   A. (*a*), (*b*) and (*d*) only
   B. (*b*), (*c*) and (*d*) only
   C. (*a*) and (*d*) only
   D. (*a*) and (*c*) only

7. For the production function, $Q = AL^{\alpha}K^{\beta}$.
   (*a*) The Coefficient A shows managerial efficiency.
   (*b*) If $\alpha + \beta > 1$, then the production function exhibits increasing returns to scale.
   (*c*) Marginal Rate of Technical Substitution of L for K is given by $\frac{\beta K}{\alpha L}$.
   (*d*) The Marginal Product of Capital is given by $\beta\frac{Q}{K}$.

   Choose the correct answer from the options given below:
   A. (*a*), (*b*) and (*c*) only
   B. (*a*), (*b*) and (*d*) only
   C. (*a*), (*c*) and (*d*) only
   D. (*a*), (*b*), (*c*) and (*d*) only

8. Match List-I with List-II:

List-I	List-II
(*a*) Critical Minimum Effort Theory	(*i*) C.P. Blacker
(*b*) Neo-Classical Growth Model	(*ii*) W.W. Rostow
(*c*) Demographic Transition Theory	(*iii*) R. Solow
(*d*) Age of High Mass Consumption	(*iv*) H. Leibenstein

   Choose the correct option from those given below:

	(*a*)	(*b*)	(*c*)	(*d*)
A.	(*ii*)	(*i*)	(*iii*)	(*iv*)
B.	(*iii*)	(*iv*)	(*ii*)	(*i*)
C.	(*i*)	(*ii*)	(*iv*)	(*iii*)
D.	(*iv*)	(*iii*)	(*i*)	(*ii*)

9. "The best system of taxation from the economic point of view is that which has the best or the least bad economic effects". Who said this?
   A. Musgrave B. Marshall
   C. Hugh Dalton D. Pigou

10. Labour force participation rate is given by:
   A. $\frac{\text{Labour force}}{\text{Total population}} \times 100$
   B. $\frac{\text{No. of labour employed}}{\text{Labour force}} \times 100$
   C. $\frac{\text{Labour force}}{\text{Adult population}} \times 100$
   D. $\frac{\text{No. of labour employed}}{\text{Adult population}} \times 100$

11. The solution of the following game

Player B

$$\text{Player A}\quad \begin{array}{c} \\ A_1 \\ A_2 \\ A_3 \end{array} \begin{array}{c} \begin{array}{ccc} B_1 & B_2 & B_3 \end{array} \\ \begin{bmatrix} 2 & 4 & 2 \\ 1 & -5 & -4 \\ 2 & 6 & -2 \end{bmatrix} \end{array}$$

   is given by
   A. Value of game = 2. Best strategy for Players A and B are (A_1, B_1) respectively
   B. Value of game = 2. Best strategy for Players A and B are (A_1, B_1) or (A_3, B_1) or (A_1, B_3) respectively
   C. Value of game = 2. Best strategy for Players A and B are (A_3, B_1) respectively
   D. Value of game = 2. Best strategy for Players A and B are (A_1, B_3) respectively

12. Given below are two statements.
   Statement I: The endogeneous growth theorists suggest, investment in human

capital, innovation and knowledge leads to economic growth.

Statement II: Investment in human capital, innovation and knowledge reduces the diminishing returns on investment.

In light of the above statements, choose the most appropriate answer from the options given below:

A. Both Statement I and Statement II are correct
B. Both Statement I and Statement II are incorrect
C. Statement I is correct, but Statement II is incorrect
D. Statement I is incorrect, but Statement II is correct

13. Which of the following equations represent national income identity?

(*a*) Y = C + I + X
(*b*) Y = C + I + G + S
(*c*) Y = C + I + G + (X – M)
(*d*) Y = C + I + G + M

Choose the correct answer from the options given below:

A. (*a*) only
B. (*c*) only
C. (*b*), (*c*) and (*d*) only
D. (*a*), (*b*) and (*d*) only

14. Match List-I with List-II:

List-I	List-II
(*a*) Absolute Advantage Theory of International Trade	(*i*) Heckscher-Ohlin
(*b*) Factor Proportion Theory of Trade	(*ii*) Marshall
(*c*) Offer Curves	(*iii*) Adam Smith
(*d*) Opportunity Costs	(*iv*) Haberler

Choose the correct option from those given below:

	(*a*)	(*b*)	(*c*)	(*d*)
A.	(*i*)	(*iii*)	(*ii*)	(*iv*)
B.	(*iii*)	(*i*)	(*ii*)	(*iv*)
C.	(*i*)	(*iii*)	(*iv*)	(*ii*)
D.	(*iii*)	(*i*)	(*iv*)	(*ii*)

15. Given below are two statements, one is labelled as Assertion (A) and the other is labelled as Reason (R):

Assertion (A): If A is any Matrix given by

$$A = \begin{pmatrix} 5 & 0 & 3 \\ -1 & 0 & 2 \\ 1 & 0 & 1 \end{pmatrix}, \text{ then det } A = 0, \text{ since all}$$

elements in column II are zero.

Reason (R): Laplace expansion permits evaluation of a determinant along any row or column.

In light of the above statements, choose the most appropriate answer from the options given below:

A. Both (A) and (R) are correct and (R) is the correct explanation of (A)
B. Both (A) and (R) are correct, but (R) is not the correct explanation of (A)
C. (A) is correct ,but (R) is not correct
D. (A) is not correct, but (R) is correct

16. According to traditional neoclassical growth theory, output growth results from:

(*a*) Increase in labour quantity and quality
(*b*) Increase in capital
(*c*) Increase in exports
(*d*) Improvement in technology

Choose the correct answer from the options given below:

A. (*a*), (*b*) and (*c*) only
B. (*a*) and (*b*) only
C. (*b*) and (*c*) only
D. (*a*), (*b*) and (*d*) only

17. Match List-I with List-II:

List-I	List-II
(*a*) Linear Function	(*i*) $y = 3x^2 + 2x + 9$
(*b*) Quadratic Function	(*ii*) $y = 5x^3$
(*c*) Exponential Function	(*iii*) $y = 3e^{2x}$
(*d*) Power Function	(*iv*) $y = 5x + 3$

Choose the correct option from those given below:

	(a)	(b)	(c)	(d)
A.	(iv)	(i)	(iii)	(ii)
B.	(iv)	(i)	(ii)	(iii)
C.	(iv)	(ii)	(iii)	(i)
D.	(i)	(ii)	(iii)	(iv)

18. Which one of the following statements is wrong?

A. 67% of Indian agriculturists are marginal landholders with less than 1 hectare

B. 10% of agriculturists have 10 hectares or more

C. In the rural sector, land is the principal source of income

D. Due to the high growth of population, the average size of landholding is small

19. Cross elasticity of demand of metro rides is 0.8 and total ridership per day is 1.5 Lakh. If price of bus rides rises by 5%, the change in total metro rides will be:

A. 4000 B. 5000
C. 6000 D. 7500

20. For any two equally likely, exhaustive and independent events A and B, P(AB) will be equal to:

A. 0 B. 0.25
C. 0.50 D. 1

21. Which one of the following Price Index numbers satisfy the Factor Reversal Test?

A. Laspeyres Price Index Number
B. Paasche's Price Index Number
C. Walsh's Price Index Number
D. Fisher's Price Index Number

22. Match List-I with List-II:

List-I	List-II
(a) Chamberlin	(i) Small group model
(b) Sweezy	(ii) Kinked demand curve
(c) Stackelberg	(iii) Price leadership model
(d) Fellner	(iv) Reaction curves

Choose the correct option from those given below:

	(a)	(b)	(c)	(d)
A.	(i)	(iii)	(iv)	(ii)
B.	(ii)	(i)	(iii)	(iv)
C.	(ii)	(i)	(iv)	(iii)
D.	(i)	(ii)	(iv)	(iii)

23. The number of districts initially selected from states under the Intensive Area Development Programme (1960).

A. One district from each state
B. Three districts from three states
C. Five districts from five states
D. Seven districts from seven states

24. Given below are two statements:

Statement I: The Rybczynski theorem postulates that at constant commodity prices, an increase in the endowment of one factor will increase by a greater proportion the output of the commodity, intensive in that factor and will reduce the output of the other commodity.

Statement II: The Stolper-Samuelson theorem postulates that an increase in the relative price of a commodity (for example as a result of a tariff) decreases the return or earnings of the factor used intensively in the production of the commodity.

In light of the above statements, choose the correct answer from the options given below:

A. Both Statement I and Statement II are true
B. Both Statement I and Statement II are false
C. Statement I is correct, but Statement II is false
D. Statement I is incorrect, but Statement II is true

25. Market failure is caused due to the presence of:

(a) Poverty (b) Externalities
(c) Market power (d) Private goods

Choose the correct answer from the options given below:
A. (*a*) and (*b*) only
B. (*b*) and (*c*) only
C. (*b*), (*c*) and (*d*) only
D. (*b*) and (*c*) only

26. Seigniorage in banking means:
(*a*) The economic cost of providing a currency within a given economy.
(*b*) The difference between the face value of money and the cost of providing it.
(*c*) The cost involved in running ATMs.
(*d*) The costs of making debit/credit cards in an economy.

Choose the correct answer from the options given below:
A. (*a*) and (*c*) only B. (*b*) and (*c*) only
C. (*b*) and (*d*) only D. (*a*) and (*b*) only

27. Given below are two statements, one is labelled as Assertion (A) and the other is labelled as Reason (R):

Assertion (A): Marshall-Learner condition should be fulfilled for the success of devaluation.

Reason (R): Devaluation makes exports costly and Imports cheaper.

In light of the above statements, choose the most appropriate answer from the options given below:
A. Both (A) and (R) are correct and (R) is the correct explanation of (A)
B. Both (A) and (R) are correct, but (R) is not the correct explanation of (A)
C. (A) is correct, but (R) is not correct
D. (A) is not correct, but (R) is correct

28. If the disturbance term is heteroscedastic, which one of the responses based on given statements is true?
(*a*) OLS estimates are biased.
(*b*) OLS estimates do not have the minimum variance property.
(*c*) Tests of significance based on OLS estimates will be inaccurate.
(*d*) OLS estimates are inconsistent.

Choose the correct answer from the options given below:
A. (*a*) and (*b*) are true only
B. (*a*) and (*c*) are true only
C. (*b*) and (*c*) are true only
D. (*a*) and (*d*) are true only

29. According to Economic Survey, 2019, the top five trading partners of India continue to be USA, China, UAE and:
(*a*) Saudi Arabia (*b*) Hong Kong
(*c*) Singapore (*d*) Srilanka

Choose the correct answer from the options given below:
A. (*c*) and (*d*) only B. (*b*) and (*c*) only
C. (*a*) and (*d*) only D. (*a*) and (*b*) only

30. Given below are two statements:

Statement I: Learning curve effect is related to a firm's long-run average cost curve.

Statement II: A swapped allocation is one that is Pareto efficient as well as an equitable allocation.

In light of the above statements, choose the correct answer from the options given below:
A. Both Statement I and Statement II are true
B. Both Statement I and Statement II are false
C. Statement I is correct, but Statement II is false
D. Statement I is incorrect, but Statement II is true

31. Which of the following are forms of government borrowing?
(*a*) Drawing from treasury.
(*b*) Printing of currency notes.
(*c*) Borrowing from non-bank public institutions.
(*d*) Borrowing from the banking system.

Choose the correct answer from the options given below:
A. (*a*), (*b*) and (*c*) only
B. (*a*), (*b*) and (*d*) only
C. (*a*), (*b*), (*c*) and (*d*)
D. (*a*) and (*d*) only

32. Arrange the following growth economists in chronological order of when they proposed their theories:

(*a*) Harrod (*b*) Schumpeter
(*c*) Rostow (*d*) Solow

Choose the correct answer from the options given below:

A. (*b*), (*a*), (*c*), (*d*)
B. (*c*), (*d*), (*b*), (*a*)
C. (*a*), (*c*), (*d*), (*b*)
D. (*d*), (*b*), (*a*), (*c*)

33. If no industry (sector) draws its own output as input, then the principal diagonal element in the Technological Coefficient Matrix will be:

A. −1 B. +1
C. Zero D. Infinity

34. The combined liabilities of Centre and States as a percentage of GDP during the two years 2016-17 and 2017-18 consolidated is at:

A. 69 per cent B. 67 per cent
C. 68 per cent D. 66 per cent

35. According to the last Census (2011), which Indian state has the minimum sex ratio?

A. Punjab B. Delhi
C. Bihar D. Haryana

36. White revolution refers to boost in the production of:

A. Rice B. Milk
C. Eggs D. Honey

37. Given the production function, $Q = 10\ L^{0.8}\ K^{0.2}$, the Marginal Product of Labour (MP_L) and Capital (MP_K), respectively are given by:

(*a*) $MP_L = 8\ (K/L)^{0.2}$
(*b*) $MP_L = 8\ (L/K)^{0.2}$
(*c*) $MP_K = 2\ (L/K)^{0.8}$
(*d*) $MP_K = 2\ (K/L)^{0.8}$

Choose the correct answer from the options given below:

A. (*a*) and (*d*) are true only
B. (*a*) and (*c*) are true only
C. (*b*) and (*c*) are true only
D. (*b*) and (*d*) are true only

38. Which of the following are Hawkins-Simon conditions?

(*a*) Determinant A should be positive.
(*b*) Determinant (I-A) should be positive.
(*c*) Determinant (I-A) should be negative.
(*d*) Principal diagonal elements of Matrix (I-A) should be positive.

Choose the correct answer from the options given below:

A. (*a*) and (*c*) are true only
B. (*a*) and (*d*) are true only
C. (*b*) and (*d*) are true only
D. (*c*) and (*d*) are true only

39. Given below are two statements:

Statement I: Mrs Ursula K. Hicks stated that "Private finance, whether of firms or individuals, starts with a given income plan as a framework within which expenditure must be planned; public finance, on the contrary, starts with a given expenditure plan and the authorities adjust their income by means of taxes and resources to match the expenditure".

Statement II: Prof. Shiras pointed out that "Public authorities differ from private expenditure in that the former should balance income and should not necessarily seek a profit in the manner that an individual would".

In light of the above statements, choose the correct answer from the options given below:

A. Both Statement I and Statement II are true
B. Both Statement I and Statement II are false
C. Statement I is true, but Statement II is false
D. Statement I is false, but Statement II is true

40. A leftward shift in labour demand curve is caused by:

A. Increase in wage rate
B. Decrease in wage rate

C. Increase in marginal productivity of labour
D. Decrease in marginal productivity of labour

41. Markowitz theory of portfolio management considers which of the following assumptions?

(*a*) Investors are pessimistic about start-ups but optimistic about an established business.
(*b*) Investors have free access to fair and correct information on return and risk.
(*c*) Investors have a tendency to lean towards cryptocurrencies.
(*d*) Investors are rational and maximize their utility with a given level of income and money.

Choose the correct answer from the options given below:
A. (*a*) and (*b*) only
B. (*b*) and (*d*) only
C. (*c*) and (*d*) only
D. (*a*) and (*c*) only

42. Harrod-Domar considers a functional economic relationship in which the growth rate of the gross domestic product depends:

(*a*) Directly on the national net savings rate.
(*b*) Inversely on the national capital-output ratio.
(*c*) Directly on industrial growth.
(*d*) Inversely on agricultural growth.

Choose the correct answer from the options given below:
A. (*a*) and (*b*) only
B. (*a*) and (*c*) only
C. (*b*) and (*d*) only
D. (*c*) and (*d*) only

43. Overshooting model of exchange rate developed by economist Rudi Dornbush, attempts to establish:
A. The fact why the foreign exchange market is never in equilibrium
B. Relationship between sticky prices and volatile exchange rates
C. The fact that forward rates of exchange are not good predictors of future spot rates of exchange
D. No relationship between sticky prices and volatile exchange rates

44. Given below are two statements, one is labelled as Assertion (A) and the other is labelled as Reason (R).

Assertion (A): Compared to a certain point on the Contract curve, a point above the Contract curve is more efficient.

Reason (R): The Contract curve represents the locus of points where the marginal rate of substitution between two goods is the same for both individuals.

In light of the above statements, choose the most appropriate answer from the options given below:
A. Both (A) and (R) are correct and (R) is the correct explanation of (A)
B. Both (A) and (R) are correct, but (R) is not the correct explanation of (A)
C. (A) is correct, but (R) is not correct
D. (A) is not correct, but (R) is correct

45. Absolute income hypothesis explains:
A. Consumer behaviour
B. Producer behaviour
C. Inflation
D. Government expenditure

46. The government multiplier is given by (where c = MPC and t = tax rate)

A. $\dfrac{1}{1-(c-t)}$ B. $\dfrac{1}{(1-c)t}$

C. $\dfrac{1}{1-c-t}$ D. $\dfrac{1}{1-c(1-t)}$

47. GDP expressed in terms of current prices is called:
A. Real GDP
B. Net Domestic Product
C. Nominal GDP
D. Gross National Product

48. A growth model in which there are diminishing returns on each factor of production but constant returns to scale and exogenous technological change that generates long term economic growth is the:

A. Leibenstein model
B. A.K. Sen model
C. Kalecki model
D. Solow model

49. A time series, under the condition $E(x_t) = \mu$ and $Cov(x_t, x_{t+k}) = \gamma(k)$ is said to be:

A. Strictly Stationarity
B. Non Stationarity
C. Weakly Stationarity
D. Can't be defined

50. Which one of the following is not the objective of IMF?

A. To promote international monetary cooperation
B. To ensure balanced international trade
C. To ensure exchange rate stability
D. To provide loans to the private sector

51. Population Density refers to:

A. Number of male persons per square kilometer
B. Number of persons per cubic kilometer
C. Number of persons per square kilometer
D. Number of persons per 10 kilometers

52. Forward exchange rates are useful for those who wish to:

(*a*) Protect themselves from the risk that the exchange rate will change before a transaction is completed.
(*b*) Gamble that a currency will rise in value.
(*c*) Gamble that a currency will fall in value.
(*d*) Exchange currencies at a point in time in the future.

Choose the correct answer from the options given below:

A. (*a*), (*b*) and (*c*) only
B. (*a*) and (*b*) only
C. (*a*) and (*c*) only
D. (*a*), (*b*), (*c*) and (*d*) only

53. Maximum Social Welfare is guaranteed where a competitive firm exhibits the following condition [*where $MRPT_{xy}$ is Marginal Rate of Product Transformation of x for y*]

A. $MRPT_{xy} = \dfrac{\text{Price of } x(Px)}{\text{Price of } y(Py)} = \dfrac{\text{Marginal Cost of } x(MCx)}{\text{Marginal Cost of } y(MCy)}$

B. $MRPT_{xy} = \dfrac{Px}{Py} = \dfrac{\text{Total Cost of } x}{\text{Total Cost of } y}$

C. $MRPT_{xy} = \dfrac{Px}{Py} = \dfrac{\text{Average Variable Cost of } x}{\text{Average Variable Cost of } y}$

D. $MRPT_{xy} = \dfrac{Px}{Py} = \dfrac{\text{Total Variable Cost of } x}{\text{Total Variable Cost of } y}$

54. The concept of Goods and Service Tax (GST) is originated in:

A. Canada
B. Britain
C. Germany
D. USA

55. Which of the following are the three states which secured the highest percentage of inter-share of tax revenue among states, as per recommendations of the 14th Finance Commission?

(*a*) Uttar Pradesh
(*b*) Bihar
(*c*) Madhya Pradesh
(*d*) Andhra Pradesh

Choose the most appropriate answer from the options given below:

A. (*a*), (*b*) and (*d*) only
B. (*a*), (*c*) and (*d*) only
C. (*a*), (*b*) and (*c*) only
D. (*b*), (*c*) and (*d*) only

56. Given the Total Cost, $TC = Q^3 - 10Q^2 + 60Q$, what will be the Minimum average cost? At what level of output will the minimum cost occur? (Q is the level of output)

A. Minimum average cost is $AC_{Min} = 35$ at $Q = 5$
B. Minimum average cost is $AC_{Min} = 175$ at $Q = 5$
C. Minimum average cost is $AC_{Min} = 170$ at $Q = 1$
D. Minimum average cost is $AC_{Min} = 45$ at $Q = 1$

57. Given the Total Revenue function, TR = 1400Q – 6Q² and Total Cost function, TC = 1500 + 80Q at Q = 100 units (where Q is the amount of output), which one of the following responses is correct?

(*a*) MR > MC (*b*) MC = 80

(*c*) MR < MC (*d*) MR = MC

Choose the most appropriate answer from the options given below:

A. (*a*) and (*b*) are true only
B. (*b*) and (*c*) are true only
C. (*b*) and (*d*) are true only
D. Can't be defined

58. Given the sample size 400 with sample mean 99, the population mean 100 and computed value of z–statistic at 2.5, the value of population standard deviation will be:

A. 59.17
B. 123.46
C. 8
D. Cannot be determined

59. Given below are two statements:

Statement I: Industrialization strategy advocates trade and development to overcome market failures through government policy.

Statement II: It encourages technology transfer and exports of progressively more advanced products.

In light of the above statements, choose the correct answer from the options given below:

A. Both Statement I and Statement II are false
B. Statement I is true, but Statement II is false
C. Statement I is false, but Statement II is true
D. Both Statement I and Statement II are true

60. Match List-I with List-II:

List-I	List-II
(*a*) Kerala	(*i*) Least urbanized
(*b*) Punjab	(*ii*) Highest percentage of S.C's in their population
(*c*) Himachal Pradesh	(*iii*) Highest percentage of S.T's in their population
(*d*) Madhya Pradesh	(*iv*) Highest sex ratio

Choose the correct option from those given below:

	(*a*)	(*b*)	(*c*)	(*d*)
A.	(*iv*)	(*ii*)	(*i*)	(*iii*)
B.	(*i*)	(*iii*)	(*ii*)	(*iv*)
C.	(*ii*)	(*i*)	(*iii*)	(*iv*)
D.	(*iv*)	(*i*)	(*iii*)	(*ii*)

61. Based on the order condition, state whether the first equation is identified?

Given the following structural model:

$y_1 = 3y_2 - 2x_1 + x_2 + u_1$

$y_2 = y_3 + x_3 + u_2$

$y_3 = y_1 - y_2 - 2x_3 + u_3$

where y's are the endogenous variables, x's are predetermined variables and u's are random terms

A. Over Identified
B. Under Identified
C. Exactly Identified
D. Information not sufficient

62. Given below are two statements.

Statement I: Growth in infrastructure is considered as an essential pre-requisite for stepping up GDP growth.

Statement II: It is vitally important to increase capital formation in India.

In light of the above statements, choose the most appropriate answer from the options given below:

A. Both Statement I and Statement II are not correct
B. Statement I is correct, but Statement II is incorrect
C. Both Statement I and Statement II are correct
D. Statement I is incorrect, but Statement II is correct

63. IS and LM curve analysis explain:

(*a*) Product market equilibrium
(*b*) Money market equilibrium
(*c*) Capital market equilibrium
(*d*) Foreign trade equilibrium

Choose the most appropriate answer from the options given below:

A. (*a*) and (*c*) only
B. (*a*) and (*d*) only
C. (*a*) and (*b*) only
D. (*c*) and (*d*) only

64. Who said, "I believe that the objective for disinvestment should be to benefit the public, the consumer and the investor and at the same time to improve competitiveness and eliminate monopoly"?

A. Manmohan Singh
B. George Fernandes
C. Chidambaram
D. Yashwant Sinha

65. For the given Income Consumption curve in the diagram, which one of the following is correct, beyond point A?

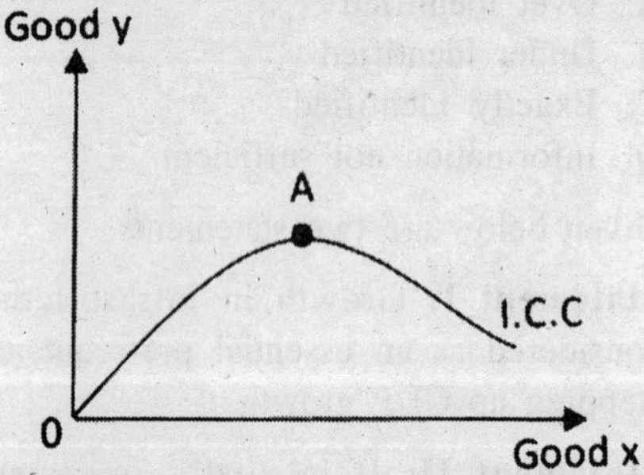

A. Good x is inferior and Good y is normal
B. Good y is inferior and Good x is normal
C. Good x and Good y are normal
D. Good x and Good y are inferior

66. Which of the following situations represents an economic investment in the national income calculation?

(*a*) Buying a newly constructed house for self-occupation
(*b*) Buying of new shares
(*c*) Buying a new car by a publishing house for delivering books
(*d*) Buying a new car by a household

Choose the most appropriate answer from the options given below:

A. (*a*), (*b*) and (*c*) only
B. (*a*), (*b*), (*c*) and (*d*) only
C. (*a*), (*c*) and (*d*) only
D. (*a*) and (*c*) only

67. What type of relationship exists between two variables, if all points on the scatter diagram appear to fall on a straight line going upward from left to right?

A. Positive correlation
B. Perfect positive correlation
C. Negative correlation
D. Perfect negative correlation

68. The share of the service sector in the Gross Value Added of India at current prices, during 2018-19 is between:

A. 45 to 47 per cent
B. 50 to 52 per cent
C. 53 to 55 per cent
D. 60 to 62 per cent

69. Match List-I with List-II:

List-I (Statistic)	**List-II (Standard Error)**
(*a*) Sample Mean $(\bar{X})$	(*i*) $\sqrt{\left(\frac{\sigma_1^2}{2n_1}\right)+\left(\frac{\sigma_2^2}{2n_2}\right)}$
(*b*) Sample Variance (s^2)	(*ii*) $\sqrt{\left(\frac{\sigma_1^2}{n_1}\right)+\left(\frac{\sigma_2^2}{n_2}\right)}$
(*c*) Difference of two independent sample means $(\bar{X}_1 - \bar{X}_2)$	(*iii*) $\frac{\sigma_1^2}{\sqrt{n}}$
(*d*) Difference of two independent sample standard Deviations $(s_1 - (s_2)$	(*iv*) $\sigma^2\sqrt{\frac{2}{n}}$

Choose the correct option from those given below:

	(*a*)	(*b*)	(*c*)	(*d*)
A.	(*iii*)	(*iv*)	(*ii*)	(*i*)
B.	(*iii*)	(*ii*)	(*iv*)	(*i*)
C.	(*iii*)	(*iv*)	(*i*)	(*ii*)
D.	(*i*)	(*iii*)	(*ii*)	(*iv*)

70. Which one of the following response is true as a solution for simultaneous equation bias?

(*a*) OLS Method

(*b*) Principle Component Method

(*c*) Two-Stage Least Square Method (2 SLS Method)

(*d*) Full Information Maximum Likelihood Method (FIML)

Choose the most appropriate answer from the options given below:

A. (*a*) and (*b*) are true only

B. (*b*) and (*c*) are true only

C. (*c*) and (*d*) are true only

D. (*a*) and (*d*) are true only

71. The cost of holding money by individuals:

(*a*) Loss of real value of money due to deflation.

(*b*) Foregone interest from savings.

(*c*) Utility foregone by not buying goods and services.

(*d*) Returns foregone by not holding other assets.

Choose the most appropriate answer from the options given below:

A. (*b*), (*c*) and (*d*) only

B. (*a*), (*b*) and (*c*) only

C. (*a*), (*b*) and (*d*) only

D. (*a*), (*c*) and (*d*) only

72. Given 'σ' as the Standard Deviation of a given series and if to each and every observation of the series is added a constant '*k*', then what will be the Standard Deviation of the new series?

A. $\sigma + k$ B. $\sigma - k$

C. σ D. σk

73. Growth rate of population is:

A. Rate at which population increases per 1000 per annum

B. Rate at which birth rate increases per 1000 per annum

C. Rate at which population increases per 10,000 per annum

D. Rate at which fertility rate increases per annum

74. Changes in terms of trade typically put less developed countries at a disadvantage, because:

A. They specialize and trade in agricultural goods rather than manufactured goods

B. They have higher labour costs

C. They specialize and trade in services like tourism

D. Industrialized countries practice unfair trade with less developed countries

75. Account payee crossing is defined in which section of the Negotiable Instruments (NI) Act?

A. Section 123

B. Section 124

C. Section 125

D. Not defined in NI Act

76. Match List-I with List-II:

List-I	List-II
(*a*) Rybezynski Theorem	(*i*) The effect of tariffs on factor prices
(*b*) Metzler effect	(*ii*) The effect of factor growth on production and trade
(*c*) Stolper-Samuelson Theorem	(*iii*) The effect of tariffs on domestic prices
(*d*) Immiserising growth theory	(*iv*) The effect of growth on terms of trade

Choose the correct option from those given below:

	(*a*)	(*b*)	(*c*)	(*d*)
A.	(*ii*)	(*iii*)	(*i*)	(*iv*)
B.	(*iv*)	(*iii*)	(*i*)	(*ii*)
C.	(*iv*)	(*i*)	(*iii*)	(*ii*)
D.	(*ii*)	(*i*)	(*iii*)	(*iv*)

77. A decision free framework to identify a country's most binding constraints on economic growth is termed as:

A. Growth paradigm

B. Growth diagnostics

C. Growth stimulus

D. Growth paradox

78. Based on the following Blacker's stages of population growth diagram, the portion between A, B and C implies:

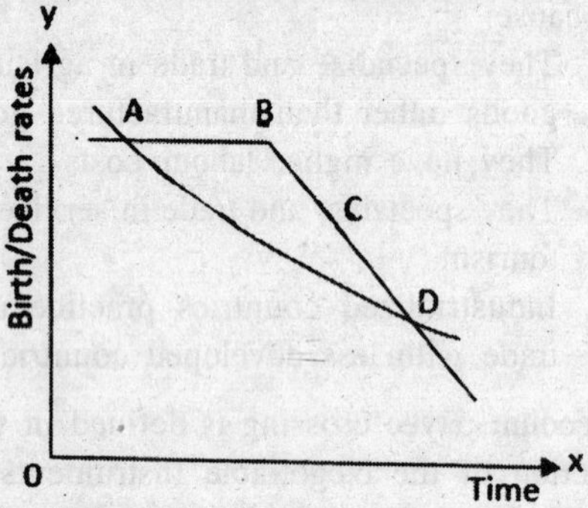

A. Stage of low stationary
B. Population declining
C. Early expanding
D. Late expanding

79. Inadequacy or absence of KYC (Know Your Customer) standards can subject a bank to serious and counter party risk as follows:

(*a*) Reputation risk
(*b*) Compliance risk
(*c*) Legal risk
(*d*) Bankruptcy risk

Choose the correct answer from the options given below:

A. (*a*), (*b*) and (*d*) only
B. (*a*), (*b*) and (*c*) only
C. (*b*), (*c*) and (*d*) only
D. (*a*), (*c*) and (*d*) only

80. Given below are two statements, one is labelled as Assertion (A) and the other is labelled as Reason (R):

Assertion (A): The main cause of commercial bank failure is because of providing inappropriate loans to bank insiders.

Reason (R): Bank employees are provided loans at lower interest rates.

In light of the above statements, choose the most appropriate answer from the options given below.

A. Both (A) and (R) are correct and (R) is the correct explanation of (A)
B. Both (A) and R are correct, but (R) is not the correct explanation of (A)
C. (A) is correct, but (R) is not correct
D. (A) is not correct, but (R) is correct

81. Given below are two statements, one is labelled as Assertion (A) and the other is labelled as Reason (R):

Assertion (A): Chronic poverty is the main problem facing India.

Reason (R): British colonial rule has caused underdevelopment in India.

In light of the above statements, choose the most appropriate answer from the options given below:

A. Both (A)and (R) are correct and (R) is the correct explanation of (A)
B. Both (A) and R are correct but (R) is not the correct explanation of (A)
C. (A) is correct, but (R) is not correct
D. (A) is not correct, but (R) is correct

82. A graph reflecting the relationship between a country's per capita income and its inequality of income distribution is the:

A. Lorenz Curve B. Phillips Curve
C. Laffer Curve D. Kuznets Curve

83. What is the maximum panelty to be imposed under the Negotiable Instruments Act for bouncing of a cheque?

A. 6 months B. 1 year
C. 2 years D. 5 years

84. Match List-I with List-II:

List-I	List-II
(*a*) Effectiveness of private market in dealing with externalities	(*i*) Laffer curve
(*b*) Relationship between increase in tax rate and tax revenue	(*ii*) Deadweight Loss
(*c*) Dominant strategy	(*iii*) Coase Theorem
(*d*) Controlling prices through effective price ceiling and a price floor	(*iv*) Game Theory

Choose the correct option from those given below:

	(a)	(b)	(c)	(d)
A.	(iii)	(i)	(iv)	(ii)
B.	(iv)	(i)	(ii)	(iii)
C.	(i)	(iii)	(ii)	(iv)
D.	(iii)	(i)	(ii)	(iv)

85. What is the value of the equilibrium level of income for the data given below for an economy?

$c = 50 + 0.8\ Y_d$
$t = 20\%$
$I = 100$
$G = 30$

A. 400 B. 300
C. 500 D. 600

86. Given below are two statements, one is labelled as Assertion (A) and the other is labelled as Reason (R):

Assertion (A): According to Walt W. Rostow, the Principle Strategy of Development necessary for take-off was the mobilization of domestic and foreign savings.

Reason (R): Mobilization of domestic and foreign savings is necessary to generate sufficient investment to accelerate economic growth.

In light of the above statements, choose the most appropriate answer from the options given below:

A. Both (A) and (R) are correct and (R) is the correct explanation of (A)
B. Both (A) and R are correct, but (R) is not the correct explanation of (A)
C. (A) is correct, but (R) is not correct
D. (A) is not correct, but (R) is correct

87. Match List-I with List-II:

List-I	List-II
(a) Permanent Income Hypothesis	(i) F. Modigliani
(b) Relative Income Hypothesis	(ii) J.M. Keynes
(c) Absolute Income Hypothesis	(iii) M. Friedman
(d) Life Cycle Hypothesis	(iv) J. Dusenberry

Choose the correct option from those given below:

	(a)	(b)	(c)	(d)
A.	(ii)	(iii)	(iv)	(i)
B.	(i)	(iv)	(iii)	(ii)
C.	(iii)	(ii)	(i)	(iv)
D.	(iii)	(iv)	(ii)	(i)

88. Arrange the following in chronological order:
(a) Rational Expectation Doctrine
(b) Keynesian Economics
(c) Monetarism
(d) Classical Economics

Choose the correct answer from the options given below:

A. (b), (d), (c), (a)
B. (a), (d), (c), (b)
C. (a), (b), (c), (d)
D. (d), (b), (c), (a)

89. Banking Cash Transaction Tax (BCTT) was introduced with effect from:

A. 1st Jan, 2015 B. 1st June, 2005
C. 1st Jan, 2019 D. 1st June, 2009

90. Which one of the following Committee's has been constituted for doubling farmer's income by 2022?

A. Ashok Mehta Committee
B. Naresh Chandra Committee
C. Rajeev Kumar Committee
D. Ashok Dalwai Committee

Directions (Qs. No. 91-95): *Read the following passage carefully and answer the questions that follows.*

There is considerable evidence that some consumers are willing to pay more for green goods. Green goods are goods that are manufactured in an environmentally friendly way (e.g. wood products from sustainable forests, electricity produced from wind power) without a direct impact on a consumer. These are referred to as impure Public goods – a package of Private good and Public good.

Why consumers are willing to pay more for these goods is complex. Whatever the reason, it is clear some consumers are willing to pay for green actions that do not benefit them directly.

One example of green goods is 'green electricity'. Green power is simply electricity produced using renewable sources of energy. Of course, electricity itself is completely indistinguishable from non-green electricity. There are two ways in which consumers may buy green electricity; either by buying it directly or by contributing to the cost of building green electricity capacity.

Consumers are clearly willing to spend more for green electricity and their preference for green production is indicated by the recent rise in popularity of retail carbon offsets. Offsets of emissions have long been used by firms to buy and sell the obligation to reduce emissions. In the USA, new emitters setting up a business in an urban area have to 'offset' their emission additions by finding (and paying) existing firms to reduce their emissions. In recent years, firms have used offsets to effectively reduce their emissions in order to provide a green image, particularly in the case of carbon emissions.

The purchase of offsets by consumers is different when consumers buy offsets. They are making a purely voluntary contribution to the environment. Retail offsets are a way in which consumers can produce a green product from a brown product. For example, one can make his part of the flight carbon neutral by paying someone else to reduce his or her carbon emission. This is formalized in an offset market whereby sellers of offsets reduce emissions and then sell these 'reductions'.

91. Green Electricity means:

A. Electricity produced from renewable sources of energy
B. Electricity from Thermal plants
C. Electricity from Gas-powered plants
D. Hydro-power

92. Offset of emissions are used:

(*a*) To reduce emissions
(*b*) To provide green image
(*c*) For emission addition
(*d*) To satisfy consumer preferences

Choose the correct answer from the options given below:

A. (*a*), (*b*) and (*c*) only
B. (*a*), (*c*) and (*d*) only
C. (*a*), (*b*) and (*d*) only
D. (*b*), (*c*) and (*d*) only

93. An example of green good is:

(*a*) White paper (*b*) Wind power
(*c*) Forest products (*d*) Solar energy

Choose the correct answer from the options given below:

A. (*a*) and (*b*) only
B. (*b*) and (*c*) only
C. (*c*) and (*d*) only
D. (*b*) and (*d*) only

94. The way in which consumers can produce a green product from a brown product:

A. Monopoly
B. Retail offsets
C. Price discrimination
D. Fiscal deficit

95. Impure Public goods are:

A. Private goods
B. Public goods
C. A package of Public and Private goods
D. Harmful goods for the society

Directions (Qs. No. 96-100): *Read the following passage carefully and answer the questions that follows.*

The objectives of public finance are to ensure macroeconomic stability, achieve the desired state of distribution, provide public services to accelerate growth and development. Fiscal policy has both macro and microeconomic aspects. Further, the objectives include allocating resources for the provision of public services. The important point is that ensuring security and protection of property rights is a basic public good and this can be provided only by the government. The governments have the task of distributing incomes and alleviating poverty. After the Great Depression and influenced by Keynesian economics, public spending was assigned a central role. Thus, the role of public finance is inextricably linked to the role of the state. From merely ensuring safety, security and property rights, governments have expanded their activities to providing a variety of public services with externalities. The expansion has been a subject matter of debate. Musgrave considers that the expansion of the public sector has been a necessary and constructive development and strong public sector is needed along with the capitalist market. In contrast, Buchanan argues that dispute arises when the state expands to areas beyond the realm of boundaries of the protective state into a productive or tax-transfer state.

In India, state intervention through public finance policy has to play an important role besides ensuring the safety and security of people and their property rights. These include the need to overcome large social and physical infrastructure deficit, provide correctives to missing and imperfect markets, introduce measures to reduce acute inequalities and poverty and provide correctives to widespread information asymmetry. Interventions are needed also to provide externalities in terms of market development, irrigation, storage and price support in agriculture to deal with market imperfections and supply volatility. Similarly, generalized externalities have to be ensured for the manufacturing and service sectors through competitive levels of infrastructure. India's public finance policies have enabled the government to play a catalytic role in the development of the economy as a whole. In addition over the years, there has been a significant increase in transfers from the government such as for employment guarantee and food security, national housing scheme, Swachchh Bharat Abhiyan, Ujjawala Yojana, Pradhan Mantri Kisan Samman Nidhi, periodic loan waives; etc.

96. Which one of the following does not fall in the category of government transfers?

A. National Housing
B. Swachchh Bharat Abhiyan
C. Periodic loan waivers
D. Education

97. Which one of the following statements is correct?

(*a*) The expansion of the public sector has been a necessary and constructive development and a strong public sector is needed along with the capitalist market.
(*b*) There are several reasons for the state to embrace a much larger role.
(*c*) In India, state intervention through public finance policy has to play an important role.
(*d*) Keynesian economics states that the state has to ensure full employment.

Choose the correct answer from the options given below:

A. (*a*) and (*b*) only
B. (*a*), (*b*) and (*c*) only
C. (*a*) and (*c*) only
D. (*a*), (*b*), (*c*) and (*d*)

98. The statement, "Dispute arises when the state expands to areas beyond the realm of boundaries of the protective state into a productive or tax-transfer state", was given by:

A. Musgrave B. Keynes
C. Dalton D. Buchanan

99. The externalities of the government intervention in the economy can be found in terms of:

(*a*) Market development
(*b*) Money supply
(*c*) Storage and price support in agriculture
(*d*) Irrigation

Choose the correct answer from the options given below:

A. (*a*), (*c*) and (*d*) only
B. (*a*), (*b*) and (*d*) only
C. (*a*), (*b*) and (*c*) only
D. (*a*) and (*d*) only

100. Which one of the following objectives of public finance is not correct?

A. Ensure macroeconomic stability
B. Ensure reduction of adverse balance of payments
C. Accelerate growth and development
D. Desired state of distribution

ANSWERS

1	2	3	4	5	6	7	8	9	10
D	C	B	D	B	C	B	D	C	C
11	**12**	**13**	**14**	**15**	**16**	**17**	**18**	**19**	**20**
B	A	B	B	A	D	A	B	C	B
21	**22**	**23**	**24**	**25**	**26**	**27**	**28**	**29**	**30**
D	D	D	C	B, D	D	C	C	D	A
31	**32**	**33**	**34**	**35**	**36**	**37**	**38**	**39**	**40**
C	A	C	B	D	B	B	C	A	D
41	**42**	**43**	**44**	**45**	**46**	**47**	**48**	**49**	**50**
B	A	B	D	A	D	C	D	C	D
51	**52**	**53**	**54**	**55**	**56**	**57**	**58**	**59**	**60**
C	D	A	A	C	A	A	C	D	A
61	**62**	**63**	**64**	**65**	**66**	**67**	**68**	**69**	**70**
C	C	C	B	B	D	B	C	A	C
71	**72**	**73**	**74**	**75**	**76**	**77**	**78**	**79**	**80**
A	C	A	A	D	A	B	C	B	B
81	**82**	**83**	**84**	**85**	**86**	**87**	**88**	**89**	**90**
B	D	C	A	C	A	D	D	B	D
91	**92**	**93**	**94**	**95**	**96**	**97**	**98**	**99**	**100**
A	C	D	B	C	D	C	D	A	B

EXPLANATORY ANSWERS

1. The Subject Matter of International Economics

International economics deals with

1. *International trade theory:* This examines the *basis for trade* and the *gains from trade.*
2. *International trade policy:* This studies the reasons for and the results of obstructions to the free flow of trade.
3. *The balance of payments:* This examines a nation's total payments to and total receipts from the rest of the world. These involve the exchange of one currency for others.
4. *Adjustments in the balance of payments:* This deals with the mechanism of adjustment to balance-of-payments disequilibria under different international monetary systems.

Point 1 and 2 represent the *microeconomic* aspects of international economics. Point 3 and 4 are the *macroeconomic* aspects.

2. Depending upon the fertility and mortality of human populations, development takes place in different stages in both developed and developing countries. These stages are sometimes termed 'population cycles' or 'demographic transition', *i.e.*, the progress from one demographic condition to another.

Several demographers such as Warren Thompson in 1929 and Adolphe Landry in 1909, attempted to describe demographic transition on the basis of high and low mortality and fertility conditions.

Adolphe Landry: According to Landry, a population is based on economic and demographic regimes. There are three regimes that are based on the relationship between population and economic development and food supply.

- A primitive regime
- An intermediate demographic regime
- a modern epoch

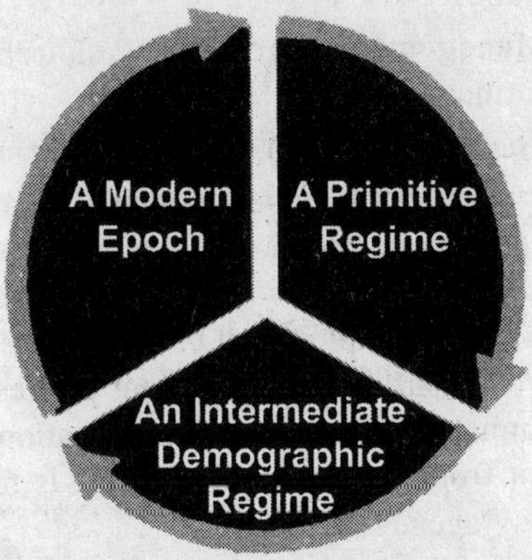

Fig: *Landry's Regimes of Demographic Transition*

- **Primitive regime:** Food supply plays an important role in this stage of population change. The rate increase and decrease in population is based on the supply of food material. Mortality is dependent on the availability of food.
- **Intermediate demographic regime:** In this stage, the change in population depends on economic development of the country rather than on food supply.
- **Modern epoch:** In this stage, there is no direct relation between population and food supply and economic development. This stage is also referred to as the 'population revolution' stage.

C.P. Blacker: According to C.P. Blacker, demographic transition in developed nations can be divided into five phases. These are :

- High stationary stage
- Early expanding stage
- Late expanding stage
- Low stationary stage
- Diminishing stage

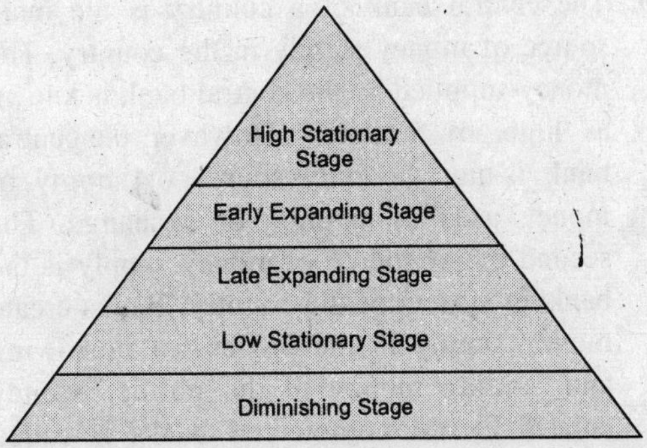

Fig: *Blacker's Five Stages of Demographic Transition*

- **High stationary stage:** In this stage, the population of a country is approximately stationary due to high birth and death rates, ranging from 40-50 per thousand per year. This stage is common in those countries that are dependent on agriculture. As a result, the standard of living is very low.
- **Early expanding stage:** In this stage, the birth rate is stationary (high level), whereas death rate begins to decline very slowly. As a result of this, the population starts rising slowly. Most of the developing countries have this stage of demographic transition.
- **Late expanding stage:** In this stage, there is slow decline in the birth and death rate but mortality rate is on the higher side. Most urbanized countries fall in this category.
- **Low stationary stage:** In this stage, both the birth rate and death rate are under control and at a low level. Thus, in this stage the growth rate in population is almost negligible. There is very low fertility and mortality rate. Most of the developed countries fall in this category.
- **Diminishing stage:** In this stage, the growth of population starts declining beacuse of a low fertility rate and a high morality rate.

Thompson, Bougue and Notestein: Here, demographic transition is divided into three stage. These are :

- Pre-transition stage
- Transition stage
- Post-transition stage

3. The central bank of a country is the main source of money supply in the country. The money supplied by the central bank is known as 'high power money'. However, the central bank is not the only source of supply of money used as medium of exchange. The second major source of money supply is the banking system of the country. Banks create money supply in the process of borrowing and lending money to the public. Money created by the commercial banks is called 'credit money'. The high power money and the credit money consitute generally the most common measure (generally denoted by M1) of money supply or the total money stock of a country.

4. **Objective Function:** The objective function in a mathematical optimization problem is the real-valued function whose value is to be either minimized or maximized over the set of feasible alternatives.

6. Asymmetric information, different information between two parties, leads to the following - adverse selection, moral hazards, and market failure.

Adverse Selection: Adverse selection is a term used in economics that refers to a process in which undesired results occur when buyers and sellers have access to different/imperfect information. The uneven knowledge causes the price and quantity of goods or services in a market to shift. This results in "bad" products or services being selected. For example, if a bank set one price for all of its checking account customers it runs the risk of being adversely affected by its low-balance and high activity customers. The individual price would generate a low profit for the bank.

Principal-Agent Problem: In economics, the principal-agent problem (also known as an agency dilemma) exists when conflicts of interest arise between a principal and an agent in a business setting. Conflicts usually exist when contracts are written due to uncertainty and risk taken on by both parties. The principal hires the agent to perform specific to duties that represent its best interest. The work that is performed can be costly to the agent and not in the principal's best interest. In short, the work done by the agent doesn't actually reflect the best interests of the principal. Examples of relationships that can experience the principal-agent problem include:

- Management (agent) and shareholders (principal)
- Politicians (agent) and voters (principal)

The conflict of interest potentially arises in almost any context where one party is being paid by another to do something, whether it is in formal employment or a negotiated deal. The two parties have different interests and asymmetric information. The deviation of the agent from the principals interest is referred to as "agency costs."

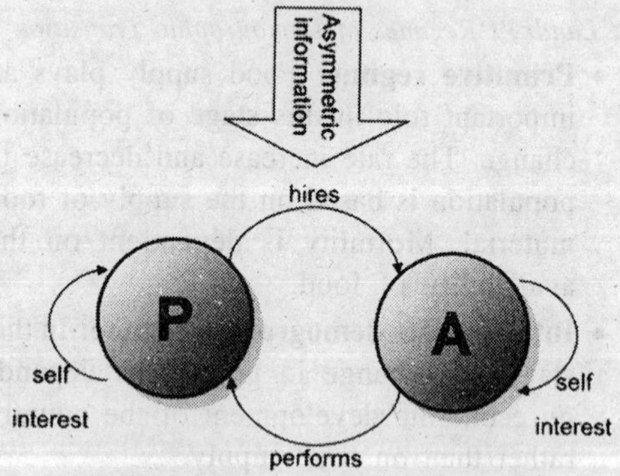

Principle agent problem: The diagram shows the basic idea of the principle agent problem. P is the principle and A is the agent. It clearly illustrates the working relationship between the principle and the agent while highlighting the presence of business partnership as well as self-interest.

7. For the Cobb-Douglas production function

$$\frac{\partial Q}{\partial K} = \beta AL^{\alpha} K^{\beta-1} = \frac{\beta Q}{K} \text{ and}$$

$$\frac{\partial Q}{\partial L} = \alpha AL^{\alpha-1} K^{\beta} = \frac{\alpha Q}{K}$$

Thus, for the Cobb-Douglas production function, the marginal product of capital (resp. labour) is a constant times the average product of capital (resp. labour).

These marginal rates depend on the units used for measuring the quantities. The ratio of the amount of change to the amount held does not depend on the units, $\frac{\Delta Q}{Q}$, and can be interpreted as the "percentage change" of the quantity. If we use the ratios of the percentage changes, then we get a quantity which is independent of the units. For example,

$$\frac{\frac{\Delta Q}{Q}}{\frac{\Delta K}{K}} = \frac{K}{Q} \cdot \frac{\Delta Q}{\Delta K}$$

does not depend on the units. Taking the limit with small changes in the change of capital, we get

$$\in = \frac{K}{Q} \cdot \frac{\partial Q}{\partial K} = \frac{\frac{\partial Q}{\partial K}}{\frac{Q}{K}},$$

which is called the *capital elasticity of product*. Notice that it equals the ratio of the marginal product of capital to the average product of capital. If $\in < 1$, the next small change in capital makes less change in the output than the average capital per unit capital, *i.e.*, there is diminishing returns on capital. For this situation, the production function is called *inelastic*. For the Cobb-Douglas production functions, the capital elasticity of product equals the exponent β. So, when $0 < \beta < 1$, the production function is inelastic.

9. Incidence of taxation refers to the direct money burden of a tax. The ultimate influence of taxation on economic entities like production, consumption, distribution etc. is referred to as effects of taxation. In a wider perspective, taxation can serve as an instrument of fiscal policy in realizing socio-economic goals like price stabilization, regulation of consumption and production, checking fluctuations of booms and depression, promoting economic growth etc. However, the economic effects of taxation need not be always good, they can be bad also. Therefore, while formulating a tax policy, the government should take into consideration not only the revenue but also the economic consequences of taxation as well. According to Professor Dalton "The best system of taxation from the economic point of view is that which has the best or the least bad economic effects." He discussed three types of economic effects of taxation. They are: (*i*) The effects of taxation on production (*ii*) Effects of taxation on distribution and (*iii*) Other effects of taxation.

12. Endogenous growth theory asserts that causes of economic growth is primarily endogenous and not due to external forces. Endogenous growth theory emphasizes on investment in human capital, innovation, and knowledge as the significant contributors to economic growth. The theory also focuses on positive externalities and spillover effects of a knowledge-based economy which will lead to economic development. According to the endogenous growth theory long run growth rate of an economy depends on policy measures. For example, subsidies for research and development or education increase the growth rate in some endogenous growth models by increasing the incentive for innovation.

In the mid-1980s, a group of growth theorists has been increasingly dissatisfied with common treatment of exogenous factors for determining long-run growth. They favoured a model that replaced the exogenous growth variable (unexplained technical progress) with a model in which the key determinants of growth were explicit in the model. Paul Romer (1986), Robert Lucas (1988) and

Sergio Rebelo (1991) discarded technological change and modelled growth as the result of indefinite investment in human capital which has spillover effect on economy and reduces the diminishing return to capital accumulation. However, the endogenous growth theory is further supported with models in which agents optimally determined the consumption and saving, optimizing the resources allocation to research and development leading to technological progress. Romer (1987, 1990), Aghion and Howitt (1992) and Grossman and Helpman (1991), incorporated imperfect markets and R&D to the growth model. Endogenous growth theory implies that policies which embrace openness, competition, change and innovation will promote growth and policies which have the effect of restricting or slowing change are likely over time to sluggish growth.

16. According to traditional neoclassical growth theory, output growth results from one or more three factors: increases in labour quantity and quality (through population growth and education), increases in capital (through saving and investment), and improvements in technology. **Closed economies** (those with no external activities) with lower savings rates (other things being equal) grow more slowly in the short run than those with high savings' rates and tend to converge to lower per capita income levels. **Open economies** (those with trade, foreign investment, etc.), however, experience income convergence at high levels as capital flows from rich countries to poor countries where capital-labour ratios are lower and thus returns on investments are higher. Consequently, by impeding the inflow of foreign investment, the heavy-handedness of LDC governments, according to neoclassical growth theory, witll retard growth in the economies of the developing world.

21. Fisher's Ideal Index :

- It is the geometric mean of the Laspeyre and Paasche's index numbers (lies between L-P index numbers).
- Fisher's index is supposed to be an ideal (best) Index Number because it satisfies both the time reversal as well as the factor reversal tests. In fact, it is the only Index number satisfying the two rests.
- It takes into account both the current year's as well as base year's weights.
- Fisher's formula is given by :

$$P_{01} = \sqrt{\frac{\Sigma p_1 q_0}{\Sigma p_0 q_0} \times \frac{\Sigma p_1 q_1}{\Sigma p_0 q_1}} \times 100$$

24. The initial article of Stolper-Samuelson, published in 1941, focused on the income distribution effects of tariffs. The theorem was subsequently extended to explain the income distribution effects of international trade in general. The Stolper-Samuelson theorem, thus, can be used to deal with two cases :

- The effects of tariff on factor allocation and income distribution.
- The effects of free trade on factor allocation and income distribution.

The Stolper-Samuleson theorem postulates that an increase in the relative price of a commodity raises the return or earnings of the factor used intensively in the production of that commodity. If the relative price of labour intensive commodity rises, there will be an increase in the wages. Similarly, an increase in the relative price of capital intensive product will raise the return to capital.

25. *Market failure* means the inability of a system to provide certain goods either at all or at the most desirable of 'optimal' level. In general, market failure arises because of four main causes. The *first* is market imperfection, which means deviations from the conditions necessary for perfect competition in the product and factor markets. Thus, if there is monopoly power in the commodity market or if labour is unionized in the labour market, the result is market failure. The *second* cause of market failure is asymmetric (imperfect) information, which means difference in information possessed by the parties to a market transaction. The *third* is the presence of externalities in the production or consumption of goods and services. Externalities are the side effects that can be harmfull (known as external cost or external diseconomy) or beneficial (known as external benefit or external economy) for the members of the society. Externalities lead to overproduction or under production of goods and services and the result is economy loss and market failure. The *last* main cause of market failure is the presence of public goods. Public goods are defined by two characteristics: (*i*) they are non-rival in consumption and (*ii*) they are non-excludable. It is due to the feature of non-excludability, that the condition of Pareto-optimality is not satisfied and the result is market failure. Thus, competitive markets fail due to market imperfection, asymmetric information, externalities and presence of public goods.

26. **Seigniorage:** The difference between the value of money and the cost to produce it – in other words, the economic cost of producing a currency within a given economy or country. If the seigniorage is positive, then the government will make an economic profit; a negative seigniorage will result in an economic loss. International demand for dollars for reserve purposes means seigniorage gains accrue to the US government.

28. Heteroscedasticity is more common in cross sectional types of data than in time series types of data. If the process of ordinary least squares (OLS) is performed by taking into account heteroscedasticity explicitly, then it would be difficult for the researcher to establish the process of the confidence intervals and the tests of hypotheses. Due to the presence of heteroscedasticity, the variance that is obtained by the researcher should be of lesser value than the value of the variance of the best linear unbiased estimator (BLUE). Therefore, the results obtained by the researcher through significant tests would be inaccurate because of the presence of heteroscedasticity.

31. Every government has two major sources of borrowing—internal and external. Internally, the government can borrow from individuals, financial institutions, commercial banks and the central bank. Externally, the government borrows from individuals and banks, international institutions and foreign governments.

36. **White Revolution:** It occurred in India in 1970, when the *National Dairy Development Board (NDDB)* was established to organise the dairy development through the co-operative societies. *Prof. Verghese Kuerin* was the *father of White Revolution* in India. White revolution helped India become not only self-sufficient but also the largest dairy producer of the world. It works through a network of co-operative societies which are owned and managed by the milk producers. The co-operative societies were most successful in the *Anand District of Gujarat.* The main objectives of the co-operative society are the procurement, transportation, storage of milk at the chilling plants. These co-operatives, apart from providing financial help, also provide consultancy.

37. For the Cobb-Douglas production function $Q = f(L, K) = AL^{\alpha} K^{\beta}$.

For a given amount of labour and capital, the ratio $\frac{Q}{K}$ is the average amount of production for one unit of capital. On the other hand the change in the production when the labour is fixed and the capital is changed from K to $K + \Delta K$ is $\Delta Q = f(L, K + \Delta K) - f(L, K)$. Dividing this quantity by ΔK gives the change in the production per unit change in capital,

$$\frac{\Delta Q}{\Delta K} = \frac{f(L, K + \Delta K) - f(L, K)}{\Delta K}$$

Usually, we take the limit with infinitesimal changes in capital, or taking the limit as ΔL goes to zero we get $\frac{\partial Q}{\partial K}$, which is called the *marginal product of capital.* The term "margial" is used because it measures the change of production with a small change of capital.

In the same way, $\frac{\partial Q}{\partial L}$, which is called the *marginal product of labour.*

For the Cobb-Douglas production function

$$\frac{\partial Q}{\partial K} = \beta\, AL^{\alpha}\, K^{\beta-1} = \frac{bQ}{K} \text{ and}$$

$$\frac{\partial Q}{\partial L} = \alpha\, AL^{\alpha-1}\, K^{\beta} = \frac{\alpha Q}{K}.$$

Thus, for the Cobb-Douglas production function, the marginal product of capital (resp. labour) is a constant times the average product of capital (resp. labour).

These marginal rates depend on the units used for measuring the quantities. The ratio of the amount of change to the amount held does not depend on the units, $\frac{\Delta Q}{Q}$, and can be interpreted as the "percentage change" of the quantity. If we use the ratios of the percentage changes, then we get a quantity which is independent of the units.

38. The Hawkins-Simon Conditions: D. Hawkins and H.A. Simon have derived some mathematical conditions – these conditions are useful as a check on input-output data to see whether a mistake has been made in collecting them. These conditions provide us with mathematical requirements which must be met by any acceptable input-output system, and the conditions can therefore be used as a basis for further theoretical analysis.

Sometimes input-output matrix solution may yield outputs expressed by negative numbers. If our solution gives negative outputs, it indicates that more than one tonne of that product has been used up in the production of every one tonne of that product, resulting definitely to an unrealistic situation. Hawkins-Simon conditions guards against such eventualities. The main conditions are as follows :

- Determinant of the matrix must always be positive.
- All the elements of the principle diagonal ought to be positive.
- One unit of output of any sector should use not more than one unit of its own output.

It is of special importance to note that the matrix considered for the fulfilment of Hawkins-Simon conditions is (I-A).

40. Shift in Demand Curve for Labour: Demand for labour increases if its productivity increases, say through technological improvement. This will cause a rightward shift in the demand curve for labour and as shall be seen from Fig. 1, this will bring about a rise in the wage rate. Similarly, if the demand for a product, say of a textile cloth, increases, the demand for textile workers being a derived demand will also go up. This too will cause an upward shift in the demand for textile workers causing a rise in their wage rate. Further, if the price of a textile cloth rises, it will increase the value of marginal product, (VMP = Price × MPP) of textile workers. With this higher value of marginal product, it will become profitable for the producer to hire more workers. As a result, demand for textile workers will increase causing a rise in their wage rate.

Conversely, if the demand for a product decreases or its falls, it will induce a reduction in the demand for labour. Given the supply curve, decrease in demand for labour will bring about reduction in wage rate.

Shift in Labour Supply Curve: If the factors determining labour supply undergo a change, the supply curve of labour will shift causing a change in the equilibrium wage rate. The supply of labour to a given occupation or industry will decrease *if the wages in alternative occupations or industries go up.*

In this case at every wage rate less labour will be offered to a given occupation or industry. This will cause a shift in the supply curve of labour to the left and, given the demand curve for labour, result in rise in the wage rate. This is shown in Figure 2.

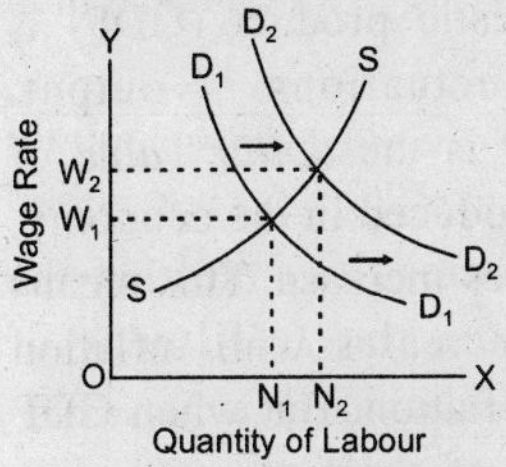

Fig. 1 : *Effect of Increase in Labour Demand on the Wage Rate*

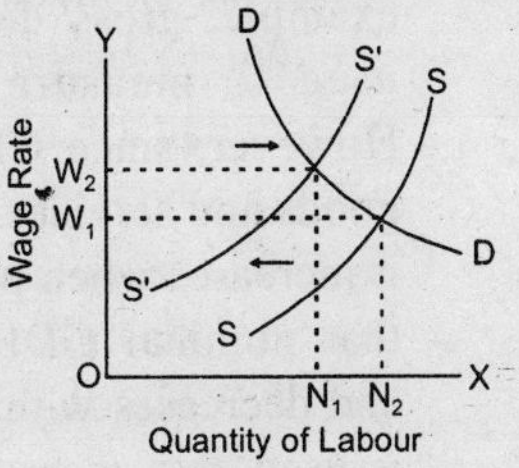

Fig. 2 : *Effect of Decrease in Labour Supply on Wage Rate*

Similarly, if workers valuation of their leisure time changes, the supply curve of labour will shift. If most workers start attaching a higher value to their lesiure time spent with their familirs, the less labour will be supplied to an occupation or industry. This will cause a shift in the labour supply curve to the left resulting in higher wage rate as is illustrated in Fig. 2.

41. The Portfolio Theory of Markowitz is based on the following assumptions :

- Investors are rational and behave in a manner as a maximise their utility with a given level of income or money.
- Investors have free access to fair and correct information on the returns and risk.
- The markets are efficient and absorb the information quickly and perfectly.
- Investors are risk averse and try to minimise the risk and maximise return.
- Investors base decisions on expected returns and variance or standard deviation of these returns from the mean.
- Investors choose higher returns to lower return for a given level of risk.

43. Rudigar Dornbusch (1976) provides a highly influential model of exchange rate dynamics that significantly advanced the monetary theory of exchange rate formation by Jacob Frenkel (1976). Flexible-price monetarist models as presented by Frenkel are constrained by the assumption that Purchasing Power Parity (PPP) holds continuously meaning thereby that if the domestic interest rate is lower than the foreign interest rate, then there needs to be an equivalent expected rate of appreciation of the domestic currency to compensate for the lower domestic interest rate and are thus not able to explain the large and prolonged departures of the exchange rate from PPP seen after the fall of Bretton Wood system in 1973. Dornbusch model provides an explanation of these deviations within a monetary model. The model is based on the assumptions that wages on the labour market and the prices in the goods markets—both relatively inflexible (in a downward direction) — are determined in 'sticky price' markets and slow changing over time in response to various shocks such as changes in the money supply, whereas exchange rates are flexible and respond rapidly to shocks such as new informations. This indicates that the exchange rate is free to jump in response to shocks, while price levels are constrained to be non-jumping slowly-adjusting variables. Thus, movements in the exchange rate are not accompanied by compensatory shifts in price movements, giving rise to deviations from the PPP. This is often called exchange rate 'Over-shooting' and the model is termed 'Sticky Price' monetarist model

44. Contract curve: In the context of two consumers exchanging two goods, the curve represents the locus of points where the Marginal Rate of Substitution between the pair of goods is the same for both individuals. These points of tangency between the individuals' Indifference Curves are efficient or exchange optima in the sense that it is not possible by any reallocation to make one individual better off without the other becoming worse off.

In the production case the contract curve represents the points of tangency between

Isoquants and thus is the locus of points for which the Marginal Rate of Technical Substitution is the same for the production of each good or in the one good for each firm.

45. The consumption function hypothesis put forward by Keynes is known as the absolute income hypothesis. It helps us explain short-run consumption behaviour or income-consumption relation. Keynes asserts that consumption is a stable function of income, *i.e.*, there is a stable empirical (statistical) relation between income and consumption. However, Keynes also pointed out that when income increases consumption expenditure also increases though not proportionately. This means that MPC falls. When MPC falls it is less than APC. Thus, Keynes advocated the declining MPC hypothesis.

The main *properties of the Keynesian consumption function* can be summarized as follows :

- The real consumption expenditure is a positive function of the real current disposable income. This relationship between consumption and income makes the absolute income hypothesis. Since the Keynesian theory deals with economic phenomenon in the short-run, his theory of consumption is also treated as *short-run theory*.
- The marginal propensity to consume (MPC)—the proportion of the marginal income consumed—ranges between zero and 1, that is, 0 < MPC < 1 (0 and 1 included).
- The MPC is less than the average propensity of consume (APC), that is, $\Delta C/\Delta Y < C/Y$.
- The MPC declines as income increases, that is, the proportion of marginal income consumed goes on decreasing.

47. Real verse Nominal Values: Prices in an economy do not stay the same. Over time the price level changes (*i.e.*, there is inflation or deflation). A change in the price level changes the value of economic measures denominated in dollars. Values that increase or decrease with price level are called *nominal* values. *Real* values are adjusted for price changes. That is, they are calculated as though prices did not change from the base year. For example, gross domestic product (GDP) is used to measure fluctuations in output. However, since GDP is the *dollar value* of goods and services produced in the economy, it increases when prices increase. This means that nominal GDP increases with inflation and decreases with deflation. But when GDP is used as a measure of short-run economic growth, we are interested in measuring performance—real GDP takes out the effects of price changes and allows us to isolate changes in output. Price indices are used to adjust for price changes. They are used to convert nominal values into real values.

Converting Nominal GDP to Real GDP: To use GDP to measure output growth, it must be converted from nominal to real. Let's say nominal GDP in Year 1 is $1,000 and in Year 2 it is $1,100. Does this mean the economy has grown 10 per cent between Year 1 and Year 2? Not necessarily. If prices have risen, part of the increase in nominal GDP for Year 2 will represent the increase in prices. GDP that has been adjusted for price changes is called *real* GDP. If GDP isn't adjusted for price changes, we call it *nominal* GDP.

To compute real GDP in a given year, use the *GDP Deflator*. The GDP deflator for a given year is 100 times the ratio of nominal GDP to real GDP in that year. The GDP deflator is a type of price index, of form of measurement that tracks changes in the value of goods produced in a nation from one year to another. Here is the formula to find the real GDP in a given year using the GDP deflator:

$$\text{real GDP} = \frac{\text{nominal GDP}}{\text{GDP deflator}} \times 100$$

If the GDP deflator is not provided, the following is the formula:

$$\text{GDP deflator} = \frac{\text{nominal GDP}}{\text{real GDP}} \times 100$$

48. The slow neoclassical growth model starts from a diminishing return to each factor of production but constant returns to scale. Exogenous technological changes generate most long-term economic growth (Todaro, 1997). As the Harrod-Domar model assumes a fixed coefficient capital-output ratio, the Solow model works with a variable capital-output ratio, which is a more correct representation of reality. Furthermore, in Solows model a continued rise in the savings rate is the key of increased growth (Solow, 1988).

More formally, the Solow neoclassical growth model uses a standard aggregate production function in which

$$Y = K^{\alpha}(AL)^{1-\alpha}$$

where Y is gross domestic product, K is the stock of capital (which may include human capital as well as physical capital), L is labour, and A represents the productivity of labour, which grows at an exogenous rate. For developed countries, this rate has been estimated at about 2% per year. It may be smaller or larger for developing countries, depending on whether they are stagnating or catching up with the developed countries. Because the rate of technological progress is given exogenously (at 2% per year, say), the Solow neoclassical model is sometimes called an "exogenous" growth model, to be contrasted with the endogenous growth approach. In Equaltion, α represents the elasticity of output with respect to capital (the percentage increase in GDP resulting from a 1% increase in human and physical capital). It is usually measured statistically as the share of capital in country's national income accounts. Since α is assumed to be less than 1 and private capital is assumed to be paid its marginal product so that there are no external economies, this formulation of neoclassical growth theory yields diminishing returns to capital and labour.

49. There are two definitions of stationarity, weak stationarity only concerns the covariance of a process and strict stationarity which is a much stronger condition and suppose the distributions are invariant over time.

Strict stationarity: The time series $\{X_t\}$ is said to be strictly stationarity if for any finite sequence of integers $t_1, ..., t_k$ and shift the distribution of $(X_{t_1}, ..., X_{t_k})$ and $(X_{t_1+h}, ..., X_{t_k+h})$ are the same.

The above assumption is often considered to be rather strong (and given a data it is very hard to check). Often it is possible to work under a weaker assumption called weak/second order stationarity.

Second order stationarity/weak stationarity: The time series $\{X_t\}$ is said to be second order stationarity if the mean is constant for all t and f for any t and k the covariance between X_t and X_{t+k} only depends on the lag difference k. In other words there exists a function $c : \mathbb{Z} \to \mathbb{R}$ such that for all t and k we have.

$$c(k) = \text{cov}(X_t, X_{t+k})$$

51. Population density refers to the average number of people living in a square km. area. Population density of 45 means, on an average, 45 people reside per square kilometer of the particular area.

52. The forward exchange market evolved after the advent of floating exchange rates. Participants can protect themselves against the risk of changes in the exchange rate after they commit themselves to a transaction but before they get paid. For instance, French exporters who invoice exports to the United States in dollars would risk a loss if the value of the dollar in terms of the French franc were to fall before the dollars are converted to francs. The exporter can be protected by "hedging" or selling the dollar forward for future delivery at a certain rate on a given date. Importers and investors in short-term overseas securities such as U.S. Treasury bills also can hedge currency risk in the forward exchange market. Speculators participate in the forward exchange market by taking an exposed (or open) position.

In addition to hedgers and speculators, a third set of participants in the forward exchange market are "covered interest arbitragers." Covered interest arbitrage would occur were an investor to invest in a foreign security instead of a domestic security. For instance, if a one-year U.S. Treasury note pays one percentage point less than a one-year U.K. Treasury note, an American investor may invest in the U.K. asset if the risk that the pound/dollar exchange rate might change can be eliminated. The investor uses the forward market to be certain the risk is eliminated and the U.K. asset is covered.

An active market exists in foreign exchange futures. A futures contract usually calls for delivery of a specific amount of a given financial instrument at a fixed date in the future. The contracts are standardized, and buyers and sellers need only agree on the price and number of contracts traded. The International Financial Futures Exchange places minimum margin requirements on contracts to prevent against default.

Whereas a forward foreign exchange contract occurs between a bank and an individual, a futures foreign exchange transaction occurs within an organized exchange dealing in standardized contracts. The futures market is more liquid than the forward market. Also, unlike the forward foreign exchange markets, there are only a limited number of days on which futures markets mature. This results from the smallness of the market compared to commerical banks' forward markets. Finally, foreign exchange futures are traded on centralized exchanges whereas the banking system arranges for forward transactions.

Forward agreements exist only for time horizons of up to one year. Investors in overseas bonds would thus be exposed to exchange rate risk. With currency swap instuments, two counterparties in different countries issue bonds denominated in the other's currency and agree to exchange streams of interest payment obligations over time. Even more popular than currency swaps are interest rate swaps—one way of managing risk if variable interest rates are used.

56. Since MC crosses ATC at its minimum. Hence MC = ATC at that level of output that corresponds to the intersection of the ATC and MC curves.

$$MC = \frac{d(TC)}{dQ} = 3Q^2 - 20Q + 60 = ATC$$

$$= Q^2 - 10Q + 60$$

$$\Rightarrow 2Q^2 - 10Q = 0$$

$$\Rightarrow \quad 2Q^2 = 10Q \Rightarrow 2Q = 10$$

$$\Rightarrow \quad Q = 5$$

and $ATC = Q^2 = 10Q + 60$

$$= 25 - 50 + 60 = 35$$

57. Here TC = 1500 + 80Q

$$\therefore \quad MC = \frac{d(TC)}{dQ} = 80$$

and $TR = 1400Q - 6Q^2$

$$\therefore \quad MR = 1400 - 12Q$$

$$= 1400 - 1200 = 200$$

58. $Z = \frac{\bar{x} - \mu}{SE_x} \Rightarrow \frac{\bar{x} - \mu}{6/\sqrt{n}}$

$$2.5 = \frac{100 - 99}{\sigma/\sqrt{400}}$$

$$2.5 = \frac{1}{\sigma/20} \Rightarrow 2.5 = \frac{20}{\sigma}$$

$$\sigma = \frac{20}{2.5} = \frac{200}{25} = 8$$

∴ Standard deviation (σ) = 8

63. The IS-LM model combines the equilibrium conditions of the product and money markets to arrive at the general equilibrium. In order to show general equilibrium, Hicks had derived two curves, namely IS and LM curves.

The IS curve (meaning I = S) represents the product market equilibrium and the LM curve (meaning L = M) represents the money market equilibrium, both at different rates of interest and level of the aggregate product or national income. In deriving his IS curve, Hicks made an important deviation from the Keynesian approach. While Keynes assumed investment (I) to be autonomous and determined exogenously. Hicks assume that I is determined endogenously and is the function of the rate of interest *i.e.*, $I = f(i)$.

In his IS-LM model, in its simplest form, Hicks integrates the equilibrium conditions of the product and money markets and produces condition for the general equilibrium. He incorporates a money-market variable, interest (i), into the income determination model by replacing Keynes' constant I with the investment function. With these modifications in the Keynesian model, Hicks defines the equilibrium level of income as

$$Y = C(Y) = I(i)$$

This function yields the IS-curve. It shows the relationship between Y and i at different equilibrium levels of saving and investment (I = S) and the product market equilbrium at different levels of Y and i.

Similarly, the IS-LM model incorporates income, Y, the main product-market variable, in the money market model by linking total demand for money to Y. This is done by using an M_t-function of the form $M_t = kY$, and an M_{sp}-function as $M_{sp} = L(i)$ into the money market mode!. The money-market equilibrium condition is then written as

$$M_s = M_d = kY + L(i) \quad ...(1)$$

Eq. (1) yields the LM-schedule which shows the relationship between Y and i at different equilibrium levels of M_d and M_s. It shows also the money market equilibrium at different levels of Y and i.

Finally, the IS-LM model brings the IS and LM functions together and lays down the condition for the general equilibrium as

$$IS = LM$$

$$\text{or} \quad C(Y) = I(i) = kY + L(i) \quad ...(2)$$

If C(Y), I(i), kY, and L(i) functions are known, the equilibrium values of Y and i can be easily obtained.

65. Difference between Normal and Inferior Goods

Point of differences	**Normal Goods**	**Inferior Goods**
Meaning	These are those goods whose demand increases with an increase in income.	These are those goods whose demand decreases with an increase in income.
Income effect	Income effect is positive.	Income effect is negative.
Relation	There is a direct relationship between income and demand for normal goods.	There is an inverse relationship between income and demand for inferrior goods.
Example	Full Cream Milk.	Toned Milk

67. The graphical representation of the corresponding values of two variables (x, y) on a graph by means of dots is called Scatter of Dot Diagram.

Scatter diagram is the simplest device to study the nature of relationship between the variables under study. Simply looking at the scatter diagram, one can get some idea whether the two variables are related or not. The following inferences about correlation can be drawn by observing the scattering of points in a Scatter diagram.

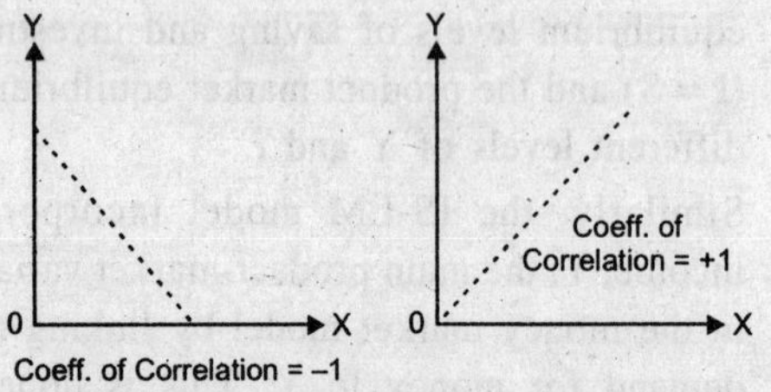

Fig: *Methods of measuring Correlation*

- When the plotted points are haphazardly situated *i.e.*, the points do not show any particular tendency, then the variables are said to be independent *i.e.*, we have zero correlation and conclude that no relationship exists between *x* and *y*.
- If the points show an upward or downward trend, the variables are said to be correlated. If the tendency of the points rises upwards *i.e.*, from lower left hand corner to the upper right hand corner, the variables are said to be positively correlated. If all points lie on a straight line falling from lower left hand corner to upper right hand corner, the correlation is said to be perfectly positive.
- When the tendency of points is to slope downwards from top left hand corner to lower right hand corner, the correlation is said to be negative. If all the points lie on straight line sloping downwards from left hand corner to right hand corner, the correlation is perfectly negative.

70. OLS is not the appropriate method of estimation for simultaneous equation system (SES), as application of OLS method to SES will lead to biased and inconsistent estimate of the structural parameters. To handle the endogeneity problem, the used methods of estimation for SES can divided into two broad groups :

Single-equation method: Here each equation is estimated separately. First, the identifiability of the *i*-th equation is tested, and if identified, the equation is estimated. Then one moves to the *j*-th equation and choose the same procedure, and so on. Under single equation method one can apply the following: (1) indirect least square method (ILS); (2) instrumental variable (IV) method; (3) two stage least square method (2SLS); (4) generalized least square (GLS); (5) k-class estimator; (6) limited information maximum likelihood method (LIML); (7) least variance ratio (LVR) method. Amongst these the most widely used methods are ILS, 2SLS and IV. But in the single equation method since each equation is estimated separately, so identification conditions of the *j*-th equation will not affect the estimation of *i*-th equation. Thus, *i*-th equation can be estimated even if *j*-th equation is not identifed. Also, the contemporaneous correlations amongst different equations will not affect the estimated values of the parameters.

System method: The system method of estimation overcomes the problem of single equation method as stated by estimating all the equation simultaneously. Under system method, as all the equations are estimated simultaneously, the estimated values of the parameters will not be consistent if all the equations of the system are identified, and one needs to take into account cross covariance restrictions of the error term across different equations. Under this method we have – 1. three stage least square method (3SLS) and 2. full information maximum likelihood method (FLML). Thus, estimated values of the structural parameters will be affected by the existence the contemporaneous correlation amongst different equations. The next subsections discuss single equation and system method of estimation respectively.

71. The Price of Money: The nature of the "price" of money should be apparent: People who hold *cash* are forgoing an opportunity to earn interest. So are people who hold money in checking accounts that pay no interest. In either case, *forgone interest is the opportunity cost (price) of money people choose to hold.* How high is that price? It's equal to the market rate of interest.

Money held in interest-paying bank accounts does earn some interest. In this case, the opportunity cost of holding money is the *difference* between the prevailing rate of interest and the rate paid on deposit balances. As is the case with cash and regular checking accounts, opportunity cost in measured by the forgone interest.

Once we recognize that money does have a price, we can easily formulate a demand for money. As the case with all goods, the demand for money is a schedule (or curve) showing the quantity of money demanded at alternative prices (interest rates).

72. The variance and consequently the standard deviation of a distribution is independent of the change of origin. Thus, if we add (subtract) a constant to (from) each observation of the series, its variance remains same.

75. A crossed cheque or crossed bank draft is not a non-negotiable instrument. This has, at times, resulted in crossed cheques being endorsed making it difficult to trace final payee and thus defeating the provisions of section 40A(3). However, as per the RBI's instructions to commercial banks, an account payee cheque or account payee bank draft cannot be credited to any account other than the account of the payee. The Act has accordingly amended the aforementioned sub-section (3) and sub-section (4) to substitute the expression 'a crossed cheque drawn on a bank or by a crossed bank draft', in both the sub-sections, by 'an account payee cheque drawn on a bank or account payee bank draft'.

77. In his paper, Hausmann, Rodrik and Velasco (2005) advocate a new methodology to study what constrains growth. It departs significantly from traditional appraoches and is known as the "growth diagnostics approach." It provides a framework for formulating hypotheses on what may constrain a country's growth. This approach views economic growth as the result of optimization under constraints, and seeks to identify the most binding constraints (whose removal would allow a growth spurt) by estimating shadow prices—a higher shadow price reflects scarcity of the resource, indicating that the resource constraints growth. Hausmann, Rodrik, and Velasco (2005) propose a decision tree where low levels of private investment and entrepreneurship are seen as the key problem. The tree takes researchers through different branches to determine the root causes of the problem, *i.e.*, the binding constraints to economic growth. At the very top of the decision tree is the question of whether private investment is held back by lack of access to finance (*i.e.*, there are many projects but entrepreneurs cannot finance them at reasonable cost) or by low returns (*i.e.*, there is plenty of credit but entrepreneurs do not find profitable investments). The two constraints have different implications. Rodrik and Subramanian (2008) indicate that investment in many economies is constrained by low returns and not by access to finance due to high cost. In these economies, external finance does not help (as, in these economies, credit is available), so the effect of capital inflows is to boost consumption, while investment is unaffected.

78. In 1947, British demographer C.P. Blacker published a paper, "Stages in Population Growth," in which the divided demographic transition into five phases.

- Phase one is high stationary, marked by a balance of birth rates and death rates that are both very high while the population growth is stationary.
- Phase two is early expanding, characterized by falling death rates that get farther and farther away from birth rates, resulting in accelerated growth of population.
- Phase three is late expanding, marked by continuous decreases in death rates and

the onset of decreases in birth rates wherein the difference in the two rates is the largest and hence the population growth, the fastest; when the birth rates further decline, the population growth starts slowing down.

- Phase four is low stationary, characterized by a new balance between death rates and birth rates when the two rates take turnes to reach a low level; however, this balance is one at a low level, different from the balance in the high stationary phase.
- Phase five is diminishing, marked by the momentum of decreasing birth rates that have started the decreases later than death rates, driving the birth rates to continue to decline after reaching the same level of the death rates, and the population starts to transition to negative growth.

79. The RBI u/s 35A of Banking Regulation Act has issued directive to banks to put in place KYC policy and adopt anti-money laundering measures.

Money Laundering-Risk Perception: The indequacy or absence of KYC standards can subject the bank to serious customer and counter-party risks :

- ***Reputation Risk:*** Risk of loss due to severe impact on the bank's reputation. This may be of particular concern given the nature of the bank's business which requires the confidence of depositors, creditors and the general market place.
- ***Compliance Risk:*** Risk of loss due to failure of compliance with key regulations governing the bank's operations.
- ***Legal Risk:*** Legal risk is the possibility of lawsuits, adverse judgements of contract resulting from failure to observe mandatory KYC standards or from the failure to practice due diligence. Consequently, the banks can suffer fines, criminal liabilities and special penalties imposed by supervisor.

82. The relationship between income inequality and economic development has popularly been characterized by the Kuznets' inverted-U curve (Kuznets, 1955), which argued that income inequality tends to increase at an initial stage of development and then decrease as the economy develops, implying that income inequality will falls as income continues to rise in developing countries. However, when income has kept rising and reached a high level, income inequality increases again. The intuition of the inverted-U curve is that when an economy's income is at a low level, there are only a few rich individuals, and the Gini Coefficient will be quite extreme. As the overall income increases, it is accompanied by a rise in employment and job opportunities. This will result in upward mobility on the income ladder, and a middle class of income earners will emerge, thereby improving the Gini Coefficient. This is the prediction of the Kuznets' relationship that inequality improves as income expands. However, when an economy's income level keeps rising to a high level, there are more people who could achieve high incomes. Portfolio investment and windfall gains from speculation in stocks and property, for example, can result in the rise of super-rich individuals. And while the majority of the population is engaged in paid jobs, income inequality will deteriorate as a result. The inverted-U curve actually describes income at different stages of economic development.

83. Bouncing of a cheque invites criminal prosecution under section 138 of NI Act. Punishment for the offence under section 138 of NI Act imprisonment up to two years or fine which may extend to twice the cheque amount or both. The offence is bailable, compoundable and non-cognizable.

Essential ingredients of an offence under the section can be summed up as follows :

- A person must have drawn a cheque on a bank account maintained by him.
- The cheque should have been issued in discharge, in whole or in part, of any debt or other liability.

- The cheque has been presented to the bank within the period of its validity (3 months from the date of the cheque).
- The cheque is returned by the bank unpaid, either because of funds being insufficient or the cheque exceeds the amount arranged to be paid.
- The payee makes a demand for the payment by giving a notice in writing, within 30 days of the receipt of information by him from the bank.
- The drawer fails to make payment of the said amount of money within 15 days of the receipt of the said notice.
- Complaint is made within one month of the date on which the cause-of-action arises.

The following exception is notable :

When action is not taken against first dishonor and cheque is presented twice and complaint is filed against second dishonor, complaint is maintainable. However, the prosecution is only for the last time the cheque bounced and there cannot be multiple prosecutions for various times the cheque is returned.

85. Here T = 20% = 0.2Y

Equilibrium level Y = C + I + F

$$Y = 50 + 0.8(Y - T) + I + G$$
$$Y = 50 + 0.8(Y - 0.2Y) + 100 + 30$$
$$Y = 180 + 0.8Y - 0.16Y$$
$$Y = 180 + 0.64Y$$
$$\Rightarrow Y(1 - .64) = 180$$
$$Y = \frac{180}{.36} = \frac{18000}{36} = 500$$

86. The concept of take-off is seen frequently in the development literature. In general terms, 'take-off' means simply that a country has entered into a period of Modern Economic Growth. However, in its original meaning the concept is more specifc.

The take-off theory, also called 'Stage of Growth Theory', was clearly formulated by W.W. Rostow (1960). It states that the transition from Underdevelopment to Development can be best described in terms of series of steps or stages through which all countries must proceed. The advanced countries had already passed the so-called 'stage of take-off into self-sustaining growth', while the under-development countries (still in either the 'traditional society' or the 'pre-conditions' stage) only need to follow a certain set of rules of development to take-off. The principle condition necessary for any take-off is considered to be the mobilization of domestic and foreign savings, in order to generate sufficient investment to accelerate economic growth. The economic mechanism, according to this theory, by which more investment leads to increased economic growth can be best described in terms of the Harrod-Domar Growth Model.

89. Banking Cash Transaction Tax has been introduced for the first time by the Finance Act, 2005 as an anti tax evasion measure, which is made applicable w.e.f. 01.06.2005. The provision extend to whole of India except the State of Jammu & Kashmir.

Transaction covered:

- Withdrawal of cash by any mode from any account **other than SB account.**

  Withdrawal by self cheques.

  Withdrawal by bearer cheque.
- Withdrawal of cash of encashment of one or more term deposits (whether on maturity or otherwise) and also availing LD by cash if any. However, if the proceeds are credited to SB account, the same is not liable for BCTT.

Amount chargeable to tax - The liability to pay BCTT arises as under: Account of Individuals (including proprietorship frims) & HUFs

- Cash withdrawal of more than ₹ 25,000 on any single day from a single account. If there are more than one transaction in any single account in a day, all the transactions are to be added and if the total amount exceeds ₹ 25,000 tax has to be collected on the entire transaction amount.
- Similarly of Term Deposits, availing LDs by cash in excess of ₹ 25,000.

Previous Years' Paper (Solved)

National Testing Agency (NTA)

UGC-NET Junior Research Fellowship & Assistant Professor Eligibility Exam

ECONOMICS, December-2019*

PAPER-II

1. Match the following.

List-I	List-II
(a) CAPART	(i) Agricultural marketing
(b) SIDO	(ii) Quality guarantee
(c) NAFED	(iii) Small industries
(d) AGMARK	(iv) Rural technology

Choose the correct option from those given below:

	(a)	(b)	(c)	(d)
A.	(i)	(ii)	(iii)	(iv)
B.	(iv)	(iii)	(ii)	(i)
C.	(iv)	(ii)	(iii)	(i)
D.	(ii)	(iv)	(i)	(iii)

2. Consider the following statements about the correct order of the stages of demographic transition associated with economic development:

(a) Low birth rate with low death rate

(b) High birth rate with high death rate

(c) High birth rate with low death rate

Choose the correct option:

A. (b), (c), (a)

B. (c), (b), (a)

C. (a), (b), (c)

D. (c), (a), (b)

3. Arrange in chronological order the following economists in relation to their contribution to the Theory of Consumer Behaviour. Choose the correct answers:

A. A. Marshall, R. Stone, P. Samuelson, J.R. Hicks, and R.G.D. Allen

B. R. Stone, P. Samuelson, J.R. Hicks and R.G.D. Allen and A. Marshall

C. P. Samuelson, J.R. Hicks and R.G.D. Allen, R. Stone and A. Marshall

D. A. Marshall, J.R. Hicks, R.G.D. Allen, P. Samuelson and R. Stone

4. Match the following:

List-I	List-II
(a) Head Count Ratio	(i) Extent of poverty
(b) Poverty Gap	(ii) Depth of poverty
(c) Square of poverty gap	(iii) Poverty as deprivation
(d) Multi dimensional poverty index	(iv) Severity of poverty

Choose the correct option from those given below:

	(a)	(b)	(c)	(d)
A.	(ii)	(i)	(iv)	(iii)
B.	(iii)	(ii)	(i)	(iv)
C.	(i)	(iii)	(ii)	(iv)
D.	(i)	(ii)	(iv)	(iii)

5. Three statements are given as under

(a) Generalized Least Square (GLS) method is capable of providing BLUE in situations where OLS fails.

(b) GLS is OLS on the transformed variables that satisfy the standard least squares assumptions.

(c) GLS method is suitable for dealing with multicollinearity problem.

Choose the correct option:

A. (a) and (b) are correct but (c) is not correct

B. (a) and (c) are correct but (b) is not correct

C. (a) is correct but (b) and (c) are not correct

D. (a) is not correct but (b) and (c) are correct

*Online exam held on 03-12-2019.

6. For oil importing countries, the increase in oil prices in 1970's and mid 2000 contributed to which of the following?
(*a*) Improving terms of trade
(*b*) Balance of trade deficits
(*c*) Price inflation
(*d*) Constrained economic growth

Choose the correct option from the codes given below:
A. (*a*), (*b*) and (*c*) only
B. (*b*), (*c*) and (*d*) only
C. (*c*), (*d*) and (*a*) only
D. (*a*) and (*d*) only

7. Identify the method not being used for unemployment estimation by the NSSO of India:
A. Current monthly status
B. Current daily status
C. Current weekly status
D. Usual principal and subsidiary status

8. The problem relating to burden of public debt has been dealt by:
(*a*) A.P. Lerner (*b*) E.D. Domar
(*c*) A.C. Pigou (*d*) A.H. Hansen

Select the correct answer from the options given below:
A. (*a*) and (*b*) B. (*b*) and (*c*)
C. (*a*) and (*d*) D. (*b*) and (*d*)

9. Given below are two statements—one is labelled as Assertion (A) and the other is labelled as Reason (R):

Assertion (A) : Disguised unemployment is present in India.

Reason (R) : Agricultural productivity at margin is close to zero.

In the light of the above two statements choose the correct option:
A. Both (A) and (R) are true and (R) is the correct explanation of (A)
B. Both (A) and (R) are true, and (R) is not the correct explanation of (A)
C. (A) is true but (R) is false
D. (A) is false but (R) is true

10. Given below are two statements—one is labelled as Assertion (A) and the other is labelled as Reason (R):

Assertion (A) : In classical model, investment demand is regarded as autonomous of changes in income or employment.

Reason (R) : It is wage price flexibility which brings full employment in the classical model.

In the light of the above two statements choose the correct option:
A. Both (A) and (R) are true and (R) is the correct explanation of (A)
B. Both (A) and (R) are true, and (R) is not the correct explanation of (A)
C. (A) is true but (R) is false
D. (A) is false but (R) is true

11. Under Normal Probability Curve the area within the range of $\mu - 1.96\,\sigma$ & $\mu + 1.96\,\sigma$ (where μ = mean, σ = standard deviation) is:
A. 90% B. 95%
C. 75% D. 99%

12. The elasticity of substitution (σ) of the production function which admits of both Hicks and Harrod neutral technical progress would be:
A. $\sigma = 0$ B. $\sigma = 1$
C. $\sigma = \infty$ D. $0 < \alpha < 1$

13. Arrange the following in chronological order:
(*a*) The Indirect Tax Enquiry Committee (Jha Committee)
(*b*) Tax Reforms Committee (R.J. Chellaiah Committee)
(*c*) Taxation Enquiry Commission (Mathur Committee)
(*d*) The Direct Tax Enquiry Committee (Wanchoo Committee)

Choose the correct option from those given below:
A. (*c*), (*b*), (*d*), (*a*) B. (*c*), (*a*), (*d*), (*b*)
C. (*b*), (*c*), (*a*), (*d*) D. (*c*), (*d*), (*a*), (*b*)

14. Arrange the following books in the correct chronological order:
(*a*) Das Capital

(*b*) Value and Capital
(*c*) Capital and Growth
(*d*) Accumulation of Capital

Choose the correct option:

A. (*d*), (*b*), (*c*), (*a*) B. (*a*), (*b*), (*d*), (*c*)
C. (*a*), (*b*), (*c*), (*d*) D. (*b*), (*a*), (*d*), (*c*)

15. The total cost function of a firm is $C = \frac{1}{10}q^3 - 3q^2 + 50q + 300$ where C = total cost, q = output, Marginal cost at $q = 10$ is:

A. 20 B. 10
C. 30 D. 50

16. Which trade policy results in the government levying both a specific tariff and an advalorem tariff on imported goods?

A. Effective tariff B. Revenue tariff
C. Compound tariff D. Nominal tariff

17. Autonomous investment could be attributed to:

(*a*) Level of technology
(*b*) Expectation
(*c*) Level of national income

Choose the correct option:

A. (*a*) and (*c*) only B. (*b*) and (*c*) only
C. (*a*) and (*b*) only D. (*a*), (*b*) and (*c*)

18. Given below are two statements—one is labelled as Assertion (A) and the other is labelled as Reason (R):

Assertion (A) : Parties to a dispute over property rights will be able to negotiate an economically optimal solution.

Reason (R) : There are efficient, competitive markets and there are no transactions cost.

In the light of the above two statements choose the correct option:

A. Both (A) and (R) are true and (R) is the correct explanation of (A)
B. Both (A) and (R) are true and (R) is not the correct explanation of (A)
C. (A) is true but (R) is false
D. (A) is false but (R) is true

19. The whole burden of tax will be borne by the consumer if:

A. The demand for commodity is perfectly elastic and supply is perfectly inelastic
B. The elasticity of demand for a commodity is same as the elasticity of supply of the commodity
C. The demand for a commodity is inelastic and supply is perfectly elastic
D. The elasticity of demand for a commodity is less than the elasticity of supply of that commodity

20. Which of the following is not an example of 'market failure'?

A. Monopolies
B. Asymmetric information
C. Economies of scale
D. Externalities

21. In which of the following models 'Knife-edge problem occur?

A. Kaldor B. Solow
C. Harrod D. Swan

22. Which one of the following is not a feature of the contingent valuation method?

A. It is an economic non-market based valuation method
B. It is based on the maximum willingness to pay by the consumers
C. It is used only in case of air pollution
D. It is used under the condition of market failure

23. Arrange the following events in chronological order:

(*a*) First phase of Nationalization of Commercial Banks
(*b*) Establishment of Narashiman Committee on banking system
(*c*) Enactment of FEMA Act
(*d*) Establishment of EXIM Bank of India

Choose the correct from the following options:

A. (*a*), (*c*), (*d*), (*b*) B. (*a*), (*d*), (*b*), (*c*)
C. (*a*), (*c*), (*b*), (*d*) D. (*a*), (*d*), (*c*), (*b*)

24. Consider the following statements:

(*a*) India's Trade Policy Review (TPR) is carried out every four years

(*b*) WTO has a mechanism for regular review of the trade policies of member countries

Which of the following statement(s) is/are correct?

A. Only (*a*) B. Only (*b*)
C. Both (*a*) and (*b*) D. Neither (*a*) nor (*b*)

25. Which one of the following institutions is related with the Green/Blue Box Subsidies?

(*a*) United Nations
(*b*) World Bank
(*c*) World Tourism Organisation
(*d*) World Trade Organization

Choose the correct option from those given below:

A. (*a*) and (*d*) B. (*b*) and (*d*)
C. only (*d*) D. only (*b*)

26. Consider the following statements about the social cost-benefit analysis for viability of projects. Which of the following statements are true for this analysis?

(*a*) IRR should be greater than Social Discount Rate
(*b*) NPV should be equal to zero
(*c*) Shadow prices are used for the calculation of benefits and costs

Choose the most appropriate option from those given below:

A. (*a*) and (*c*) B. (*a*) and (*b*)
C. (*b*) and (*c*) D. (*a*) only

27. Match the following.

List-A	*List-B*
(*a*) Quasi Rent	(*i*) A.P. Lerner
(*b*) Planned Sales Curve	(*ii*) P.A. Samuelson
(*c*) Monopoly Power	(*iii*) A. Marshall
(*d*) Strong Ordering of Preferences	(*iv*) F. Chamberlin

Choose the correct option:

	(*a*)	(*b*)	(*c*)	(*d*)
A.	(*iii*)	(*iv*)	(*i*)	(*ii*)
B.	(*iii*)	(*iv*)	(*ii*)	(*i*)
C.	(*iv*)	(*iii*)	(*i*)	(*ii*)
D.	(*iii*)	(*i*)	(*iv*)	(*ii*)

28. Arrange in chronological order the following contributions of economists in theory of consumer. Choose the correct answer.

A. Linear expenditure system, Revealed preference theory, Cardinal theory, Ordinal theory
B. Cardinal theory, Ordinal theory, Revealed preference theory, Linear expenditure system
C. Cardinal theory, Revealed preference theory, Ordinal theory, Linear expenditure system
D. Revealed preference theory, Cardinal theory, Linear expenditure theory, Ordinal theory

29. Which one of the following statements is not correct for the textile sector in India?

A. India's textile and clothing sector currently employs 35 million people
B. After agriculture, it is second largest provider of employment
C. Textile sector has a tendency to shrink as the GDP and economy grow
D. Textile sector is a major absorber of low skilled labour

30. Heckscher-Ohlin trade model maintains that:

A. Comparative advantage determines the distribution of gains from trade
B. A country exports goods for which its resource endowments are most suited
C. Absolute Advantage Theory determines the distribution of the gains from trade
D. The division of labour is limited by the size of the world market

31. Which amongst the following is the function of SEBI?

A. Regulation of money market
B. Regulation of public debt
C. Regulation of commodity market
D. Regulation of primary and secondary security market

32. Choose the correct option for which the allocation of inputs is technically efficient?

(*a*) Output of one goods cannot be decreased without increasing the output of another goods (*b*) Consumption of one goods cannot be increased without decreasing the consumption of another goods

(*c*) Consumer attains maximum satisfaction

Choose the correct option:

A. (*b*) only B. (*a*) only

C. Both (*a*) and (*c*) D. Both (*b*) and (*c*)

33. Arrange the following theories of international trade in chronological order as they appear:

(*a*) Theory of opportunity cost

(*b*) Theory of comparative cost

(*c*) Factor price equalisation theorem

(*d*) Theory of absolute cost

Identify the correct chronological order:

A. (*d*), (*b*), (*a*), (*c*) B. (*c*), (*b*), (*d*), (*a*)

C. (*b*), (*d*), (*a*), (*c*) D. (*a*), (*c*), (*d*), (*b*)

34. Who among the following is not associated with the Optimum Theory of Population?

A. T.R. Malthus B. H. Dalton

C. E. Cannon D. Carr-Saunders

35. Given below are two statements—one is labelled as Assertion (A) and the other is labelled as Reason (R):

Assertion : For certain goods, the expenditure by the consumer decreases.

Reason : For such goods, the income elasticity of demand is high.

In the light of the above two statements choose the correct option:

A. Both (A) and (R) are true and (R) is the correct explanation of (A)

B. Both (A) and (R) are true and (R) is not the correct explanation of (A)

C. (A) is true but (R) is false

D. (A) is false but (R) is true

36. Consider an economy with a linear homogeneous Cobb-Douglas production function with two inputs-capital and labour. The share of capital and labour are respectively 1/3 and 2/3. The rates of growth of capital and labour are respectively 6% and 3% per annum. If the rate of growth of output is 6% per annum, what is the rate of growth of output due to Total Factor Productivity (TFP)?

A. 1% B. 2%

C. 3% D. 4%

37. Who among the following economists are associated with the 'Balanced Growth' doctrine?

(*a*) W.A. Lewis (*b*) H.W. Singer

(*c*) R. Nelson (*d*) Ragnar Nurkse

Choose the correct option:

A. (*a*) and (*d*) B. (*c*) and (*d*)

C. (*a*) and (*b*) D. (*b*) and (*c*)

38. Match the Economists with their field of contribution in Mathematical Economics.

List-I	***List-II***
(*a*) Slutsky	(*i*) Linear programming
(*b*) Arrow	(*ii*) Input-output analysis
(*c*) Leontief	(*iii*) Consumer behaviour analysis
(*d*) Dantzig	(*iv*) CES production function

Choose the correct option from those given below:

	(*a*)	(*b*)	(*c*)	(*d*)
A.	(*ii*)	(*iv*)	(*i*)	(*iii*)
B.	(*iii*)	(*iv*)	(*ii*)	(*i*)
C.	(*i*)	(*ii*)	(*iv*)	(*iii*)
D.	(*iv*)	(*i*)	(*iii*)	(*ii*)

39. The phenomenon of 'Demographic Dividend' is related to which of the following?

A. An increase in sex ratio

B. An increase in the share of female population

C. A decline in TFR

D. An increase in the share of working age population

40. In terms of their contribution to Econometrics which is correct chronological order:

A. L.R. Klein, H. Theil, A.L. Nagar, T. Haavelmo

B. A.L. Nagar, T. Haavelmo, L.R. Klein, H. Theil

C. T. Haavelmo, L.R. Klein, H. Theil, A.L. Nagar

D. H. Theil, L.R. Klein, A.L. Nagar, T. Haavelmo

41. Who is the author of the book 'Freedom as Development'?

A. Gunnar Myrdal B. F.A. Von Hayek
C. Amartya Sen D. Paul A. Samuelson

42. Boot strapping technique is used to:

A. Test for specification bias
B. Obtain sampling distribution of parameters of interest
C. Test for auto-correlation
D. Test for normality of error term

43. Under which of the following approaches Phillips Curve Analysis holds good?

(*a*) Adaptive expectations
(*b*) Rational expectations

Choose the correct option:

A. Only (*a*) B. Only (*b*)
C. Both (*a*) and (*b*) D. Neither (*a*) nor (*b*)

44. Inverse of matrix $\begin{bmatrix} 2 & 0 & 0 & 0 \\ 0 & 4 & 0 & 0 \\ 0 & 0 & 5 & 0 \\ 0 & 0 & 0 & 1 \end{bmatrix}$ is:

A. $\begin{bmatrix} 0.25 & 0 & 0 & 0 \\ 0 & 0.5 & 0 & 0 \\ 0 & 0 & 0.2 & 0 \\ 0 & 0 & 0 & 1 \end{bmatrix}$

B. $\begin{bmatrix} 0.2 & 0 & 0 & 0 \\ 0 & 1 & 0 & 0 \\ 0 & 0 & 0.25 & 0 \\ 0 & 0 & 0 & 0.5 \end{bmatrix}$

C. $\begin{bmatrix} 0.5 & 0 & 0 & 0 \\ 0 & 0.25 & 0 & 0 \\ 0 & 0 & 0.2 & 0 \\ 0 & 0 & 0 & 1 \end{bmatrix}$

D. $\begin{bmatrix} 0.5 & 0 & 0 & 0 \\ 0 & 0.25 & 0 & 0 \\ 0 & 0 & 1 & 0 \\ 0 & 0 & 0 & 0.4 \end{bmatrix}$

45. When the market rate of interest falls, which one of the following will happen?

A. Bond price and bond yield, both will rise
B. Bond price and bond yield, both will fall
C. Bond price will rise and bond yield will fall
D. Bond price will fall and bond yield will rise

46. Given below are two statements—one is labelled as Assertion (A) and the other is labelled as Reason (R):

Assertion (A) : Geometric mean is theoretically considered as the best average to construct index numbers.

Reason (R) : Geometric mean is used if the range of observations are extremely large.

In the light of the above two statements choose the correct option:

A. Both (A) and (R) are true and (R) is the correct explanation of (A)
B. Both (A) and (R) are true and (R) is not the correct explanation of (A)
C. (A) is true but (R) is false
D. (A) is false but (R) is true

47. Given below are two statements—one is labelled as Assertion (A) and the other is labelled as Reason (R):

Assertion (A) : Intellectual Property Rights were brought into the Uruguay Round Trade Negotiations.

Reason (R) : International trade restrictions can be used to discourage the violation of intellectual property rights.

In the light of the above two statements choose the correct option:

A. Both (A) and (R) are true and (R) is the correct explanation of (A)
B. Both (A) and (R) are true and (R) is not the correct explanation of (A)
C. (A) is true but (R) is false
D. (A) is false but (R) is true

48. In Linear Programming each problem (called primal) has a dual. About duality in Linear Programming following statements are given:

(*a*) If a linear programming problem is maximizing type, then its dual is minimizing type.

(*b*) Both primal and dual have same optimum value.

(*c*) Dual of a linear programming problem is primal problem.

(*d*) If maximizing linear programming problem is with 'less than' type constraints, the dual of this problem will have 'more than' type constrains.

Choose from the following options:

A. Only (*a*) and (*b*) are correct
B. Only (*c*) and (*d*) are correct
C. (*a*), (*b*) and (*c*) are correct
D. All (*a*), (*b*) (*c*) and (*d*) are correct

49. Which one of the following is an example of positive externality?

A. Public immunizations
B. Increase of corporate taxes
C. Issuing extra permits for pollutions
D. Monitoring the hazards caused by industries

50. Incidence of tax refers to:

A. Whether a tax is progressive, proportional or regressive
B. An authority which collects the tax
C. The person or group who ultimately pays the tax
D. How a tax is collected

51. The elements given below are some of the parts of the M_4 money supply in Indian economy:

(*a*) Broad money (M_3)

(*b*) All deposits with the post office saving banks

(*c*) National saving certificates

Select the most appropriate option which constitutes M_4:

A. Only (*a*) and (*b*) B. Only (*b*) and (*c*)
C. Only (*a*) and (*c*) D. (*a*), (*b*), and (*c*)

52. Analysis of variance is carried out by using:

A. t–test B. Z–test
C. χ^2–test D. F–test

53. Identify the correct chronological order of the following:

(*a*) Hayek theory of investment

(*b*) Fisher theory of investment

(*c*) Jorgenson's theory of investment

(*d*) Markowitz theory of investment

Select the correct option from those given belows:

A. (*b*), (*a*), (*d*), (*c*) B. (*d*), (*b*), (*c*), (*a*)
C. (*c*), (*a*), (*b*), (*d*) D. (*a*), (*c*), (*d*), (*b*)

54. Which of the following statements are true concerning a triangular or recursive system?

(*a*) The parameters can be validly estimated using separate applications of OLS to each equation.

(*b*) The independent variables may be correlated with the error terms in other equation.

(*c*) An application of two-stage least squares would lead to unbiased but inefficient parameter estimation.

(*d*) The independent variables may be correlated with the error terms in the equation in which they appear as independent variables.

Choose the correct option:

A. (*a*) and (*d*) only
B. (*a*) and (*c*) only
C. (*a*), (*b*) and (*c*) only
D. (*a*), (*b*) (*c*) and (*d*)

55. Given below are two statements—one is labelled as Assertion (A) and the other is labelled as Reason (R):

Assertion (A) : In order to control inflationary tendencies, RBI raises the Repo rate.

Reason (R) : By so during, RBI wishes to control consumption demand

In the light of the above two statements choose the correct option:

A. Both (A) and (R) are true and (R) is the correct explanation of (A)

B. Both (A) and (R) are true and (R) is not the correct explanation of (A)
C. (A) is true but (R) is false
D. (A) is false but (R) is true

56. Given the saving function S = –20 + 0.2Y and autonomous investment (I) = ₹ 100 million, the equilibrium of level of consumption would be:

A. 500 B. 600
C. 400 D. 700

57. A tax of ₹ 20 per unit of imported cheese would be an example of a/an:

A. Compound tariff B. Specific tariff
C. Effective tariff D. Advalorem tariff

58. Which among the following are the main pillars of the BASEL III norms?

(*a*) Minimal capital requirements
(*b*) Supervisory review process
(*c*) Market discipline
(*d*) Maximizing return on capital

Choose from the option given below:

A. (*a*), (*b*) and (*c*) only
B. (*a*) and (*d*) only
C. (*b*) and (*c*) only
D. (*b*), (*c*) and (*d*) only

59. Which one of the following is correct for the money supply measure–M_1?

A. Currency with the public + demand deposits of commercial banks + other deposits at a point of time
B. Currency with the public + demand deposits of banks + other deposits over one year
C. Currency with the public + all bank deposits at a point of time
D. Currency with the public + post office deposits + other deposits at a point of time

60. Friedman's modern Quantity Theory of Money concludes that changes in aggregate spending are primarily determined by changes in:

A. The money supply
B. Interest rate
C. The velocity of money
D. Government spending and taxes

61. If in a given situation, P_x = 170, P_m = 190 and Z_x = 152, then which of the following will be the value of Single Factoral Terms of Trade (T_s):

A. 136 B. 148
C. 84 D. 116

62. Match the following:

List-I	List-II
(*a*) Fiscal deficit	(*i*) Excess of total expenditure over total receipts
(*b*) Budget deficit	(*ii*) Excess of revenue expenditure over revenue receipts
(*c*) Revenue deficit	(*iii*) Excess of total expenditure over total receipts less borrowings
(*d*) Primary deficit	(*iv*) Excess of total expenditure over total receipts less borrowings and interest payments

Choose the correct option from those given below:

	(*a*)	(*b*)	(*c*)	(*d*)
A.	(*iii*)	(*i*)	(*ii*)	(*iv*)
B.	(*i*)	(*iii*)	(*ii*)	(*iv*)
C.	(*iii*)	(*i*)	(*iv*)	(*ii*)
D.	(*iv*)	(*iii*)	(*ii*)	(*i*)

63. Match the following:

List-I	List-II
(*a*) Marginalist Revolution	(*i*) Samuelson
(*b*) Multiplier-Accelerator model	(*ii*) J.R. Hicks
(*c*) IS-LM curves	(*iii*) Jevous
(*d*) Real business cycle	(*iv*) Robert J. Borro

Choose the correct option from those given below:

	(*a*)	(*b*)	(*c*)	(*d*)
A.	(*iii*)	(*i*)	(*ii*)	(*iv*)
B.	(*ii*)	(*iv*)	(*i*)	(*iii*)
C.	(*iii*)	(*ii*)	(*iv*)	(*i*)
D.	(*i*)	(*iv*)	(*iii*)	(*ii*)

64. 'Displacement effect' in the Peacock-Wiseman Hypothesis implies:

A. An upward displacement of public expenditure according to higher economic growth

B. The movement from older level of public expenditure and taxation to a newer and higher level

C. Public expenditure increases at steady rate and reaches higher level

D. Government undertakes more and newer activities and hence public expenditure rises steeply upwards

65. Match the following:

List-I	***List-II***
(*a*) E. Cannan	(*i*) Optimum population
(*b*) Frank Netstein	(*ii*) Transaction costs
(*c*) Brundtland	(*iii*) Demographic transition
(*d*) Ronald Coase	(*iv*) Sustainable development

Choose the correct option from those given below:

	(*a*)	(*b*)	(*c*)	(*d*)
A.	(*i*)	(*ii*)	(*iii*)	(*iv*)
B.	(*ii*)	(*i*)	(*iv*)	(*iii*)
C.	(*i*)	(*iii*)	(*iv*)	(*ii*)
D.	(*iii*)	(*iv*)	(*ii*)	(*i*)

66. Among normal cost curves which one of the following curve does not have a minimum point?

A. Average cost

B. Marginal cost

C. Average variable cost

D. Average fixed cost

67. Match the lists with their purpose:

List-I	***List-II***
(*a*) Dickey Fuller test	(*i*) Hetero-sedasticity
(*b*) Box-Jenkins Method	(*ii*) Causality
(*c*) Glejser test	(*iii*) Forecasting
(*d*) Granger test	(*iv*) Stationarity

Choose the correct option from those given below:

	(*a*)	(*b*)	(*c*)	(*d*)
A.	(*iii*)	(*i*)	(*ii*)	(*iv*)
B.	(*ii*)	(*iv*)	(*i*)	(*iii*)
C.	(*iv*)	(*iii*)	(*i*)	(*ii*)
D.	(*i*)	(*ii*)	(*iii*)	(*iv*)

68. For a Cobb-Douglas production function $Q = 100\, L^{0.7} K^{0.3}$. Which of the following is true?

A. It is a linear homogenous function

B. It is characterized by constant returns to scale

C. It is having zero elasticity of factor substitution

D. It is characterized by unit elasticity of substitution

69. The 'Compensation Criterion' which says that state A is socially preferable to state B, if those who gain from the change can compensate the loosers and yet end up with surplus welfare gain is attributed to:

A. W. Pareto B. N. Kaldor

C. T. Scitovsky D. Bergson

70. Given below are two statements—one is labelled as Assertion (A) and the other is labelled as Reason (R):

Assertion (A) : Inclusive growth is a must for a country like India.

Reason (R) : India is an open economy with a significant external sector.

In the light of the above two statements choose the correct option:

A. Both (A) and (R) are true and (R) is the correct explanation of (A)

B. Both (A) and (R) are true and (R) is not the correct explanation of (A)

C. (A) is true but (R) is false

D. (A) is false but (R) is true

71. Harrod's growth model is given as under

$S_t = aY_t \qquad 0 < a < 1$

$I_t = b[Y_t - Y_{t-1}] \qquad b > 0$

$S_t = I_t$

In this model, growth condition is:

A. $\frac{b}{(b-a)} > 0$ B. $\frac{b}{(b-a)} < 0$

C. $\frac{a}{b-a} > 0$ D. $\frac{a}{b-a} < 0$

72. In which of the following products, problem of adverse selection is encountered?

A. Market of insurance
B. Market for credit
C. Neither A nor B
D. Both A and B

73. For which of the following consumption function, the value of the income multiplier K = 4?

A. C = 100 + 0.5Y
B. C = 50 + 0.8Y
C. C = 200 + 0.75Y
D. C = 50 + 0.4Y

74. Which is correct chronological order of Economists contributing to input-output analysis?

A. Hawkins-Simon, Leontief, Karl Marx, Quesnay
B. Karl Marx, Quesnay, Leontief, Hawkins-Simon
C. Quesnay, Karl Marx, Leontief, Hawkins-Simon
D. Leontief, Hawkins-Simon, Karl Marx, Quesnay

75. The inventory approach to the transaction demand suggests that the transaction component of demand for money is:

A. Negatively related to real wealth
B. Negatively related to real income
C. Negatively related to nominal income
D. Negatively related to interest rate

76. Which amongst the following is not the source of the income of RBI?

A. Interest on government bonds held for conducting open market operations
B. Income from investment in foreign currency assets
C. Retained earnings net of dividend paid to Government of India
D. Dividend on the shares of private equity held with the bank

77. Kaldor's growth model incorporates some of the following assumptions:

(*a*) Total savings include savings out of wages and savings out of profits
(*b*) Marginal propensity to save out of wages is equal to the marginal propensity to save out of profits
(*c*) Output consists of wages and profits
(*d*) There is less than full employment

Choose the correct option:

A. (*a*) and (*b*) B. (*b*) and (*c*)
C. (*c*) and (*d*) D. (*a*) and (*c*)

78. Insolvency and bankruptcy code is primarily entrusted with which of the following?

A. Facilitating the recovery of government dues and debt
B. Facilitating recovery of debt given by foreign banks to Indian companies
C. Facilitating banks recover higher amount of bad loans than they recovered earlier
D. Facilitating banks recover their dues from the priority sector

79. Given below are two statements—one is labelled as Assertion (A) and the other is labelled as Reason (R):

Assertion (A) : CES production function covers large class of production functions.

Reason (R) : CES production function has the property of constancy of elasticity of factor substitution.

In the light of the above two statements choose the correct option:

A. Both (A) and (R) are true and (R) is the correct explanation of (A)
B. Both (A) and (R) are true and (R) is not the correct explanation of (A)
C. (A) is true but (R) is false
D. (A) is false but (R) is true

80. Which of the following is the correct sequence in the ascending order of the magnitude?

A. Repo Rate, Reverse Repo Rate, Statutory Liquidity Rate (SLR) and Marginal Standing Facility Rate (MSFR)
B. SLR, MSFR, Repo Rate, Reverse Repo Rate
C. Repo Rate, SLR, MSFR, Reverse Repo Rate
D. Reverse Repo Rate, Repo Rate, MSFR, SLR

81. Consider the following statements:

I. Preferring to a certain income to a risky income with the same level of expected value lead to a risk averse behaviour.
II. Being indifferent between a certain income and uncertain income with the same level of expected value leads to risk averse behaviour.

Which of the statements is/are true? Choose the correct option given below:

A. Both I and II are true
B. Neither I nor II is true
C. Only I is true
D. Only II is true

82. Consider the following statements:

(*a*) The main objective of the National Agricultural Insurance Scheme (NAIS) is to protect the farmers against losses suffered by them due to crop failure on account of national calamities.
(*b*) The National Agricultural Insurance Scheme (NAIS) is available to all the farmers both loanee and non-loanee irrespective of their size of holding.

Which of the statements given above is/are correct?

A. Only (*a*)
B. Only (*b*)
C. Both (*a*) and (*b*)
D. Neither (*a*) nor (*b*)

83. On which date and year GST become effective in India?

A. 1st April, 2017 B. 1st January, 2017
C. 1st July, 2017 D. 1st March, 2018

84. Under which article of the Constitution of India, President is empowered to appoint the Finance Commission?

A. 279 B. 280
C. 281 D. 282

85. Arrange the following in the chronological order in which these happened:

(*a*) Paris Climate Agreement
(*b*) Rio Earth Summit
(*c*) Brundtland Commission
(*d*) Kyoto Protocol

Choose the correct option:

A. (*a*), (*b*), (*c*), (*d*) B. (*b*), (*d*), (*a*), (*c*)
C. (*d*), (*b*), (*c*), (*a*) D. (*c*), (*b*), (*d*), (*a*)

86. For an exactly identified equation, the order condition that should be fulfilled is that equation must:

A. Exclude one less than the total number of endogenous variables in the model
B. Include one less than the total number of endogenous variables in the model
C. Include only one of the endogenous variables in the model
D. Exclude two or more endogenous variables

87. Which amongst the following market form leads to most efficient allocation of resources?

A. Monopolistic Competition
B. Monopoly
C. Oligopoly
D. Perfect Competition

88. Match the following.

List-I	*List-II*
(*a*) Treasury bills	(*i*) RBI
(*b*) Commercial papers	(*ii*) IMF
(*c*) Repo rate	(*iii*) Government
(*d*) SDRs	(*iv*) Private companies

Choose the correct option:

	(*a*)	(*b*)	(*c*)	(*d*)
A.	(*iv*)	(*iii*)	(*ii*)	(*i*)
B.	(*iii*)	(*iv*)	(*ii*)	(*i*)
C.	(*iii*)	(*iv*)	(*i*)	(*ii*)
D.	(*iv*)	(*iii*)	(*i*)	(*ii*)

89. Match the following:

List-I	List-II
(*a*) Forward exchange	(*i*) A device of covering exchange risk against the price rise of foreign currency
(*b*) Hedging	(*ii*) A contract to buy and sell foreign exchange against another currency at some fixed rate in the future at a price agreed upon now.
(*c*) Arbitrage	(*iii*) The movement of exchange rate between two limits set by the cost of moving gold from one country to another
(*d*) Specie Point	(*iv*) A mechanism which makes two markets that are physically separate, a single market in economic sense

Choose the correct option.

	(*a*)	(*b*)	(*c*)	(*d*)
A.	(*ii*)	(*i*)	(*iv*)	(*iii*)
B.	(*ii*)	(*iii*)	(*iv*)	(*i*)
C.	(*iv*)	(*i*)	(*ii*)	(*iii*)
D.	(*iv*)	(*iii*)	(*ii*)	(*i*)

90. Two series are given as under.

(*a*) $1-\frac{1}{2}+\frac{1}{4}-\frac{1}{8}+\frac{1}{16}-\frac{1}{32}+...$ upto ∞

(*b*) $2+\sqrt{2}+1+\frac{1}{\sqrt{2}}+\frac{1}{2}+\frac{1}{2\sqrt{2}}+...$ upto ∞

Choose the correct option:

A. (*a*) is convergent while (*b*) is divergent series

B. Both (*a*) and (*b*) are convergent series

C. (*a*) is divergent while (*b*) is convergent series

D. None of (*a*) and (*b*) are convergent

Directions (Qs. No. 91-95): *Read the following passage and answer the questions.*

Industrialization and growth

From the global perspective, there seems to be a close association across countries between living standards and the share of resource devoted to industrial activities, at least up to a certain point. In very poor countries there is virtually no industrial activity at all, while the middle and high-income countries devote 20-40 per cent of resources to industry. Only three countries in the world have become rich on agriculture alone : Australia, New Zealand and Canada. In all other countries, living standards have risen rapidly only as resources have shifted out of agriculture into industry and sophisticated services.

Furthermore, research also shows a close association across countries between the growth of industry and the growth of GDP; or more precisely, that GDP growth is faster the greater the excess of industrial growth relative to GDP growth; that is when the share of industry in total GDP is rising the fastest. Figure shows the relationship across 131 developing countries over GDP is rising the fastest. Figure shows this relationship across 131 developing countries over the period 2000-2005, with GDP growth measured on the vertical axis and the growth of industry.

Association between growth of industry and growth of GDP on the horizontal axis. The scatter

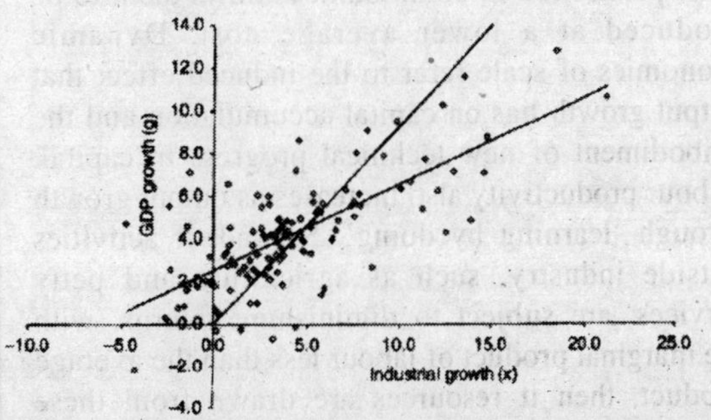

points represents the individual country observations. A line through the points with a slope less than unity shows that the greater the exess of industrial growth over GDP growth, the faster GDP seems to be. The point where this line cuts the 45-degree line gives the average growth rate that divides countries into those where the shares of industry is falling and are growing slowly, and those where the share of industry is rising and are growing fast. A linear equation fitted to the scatter points in Figure gives the following regression result:

$g = 2.529 + 0.394x, r^2 = 0.507$

The equation says that the country with industrial growth one percentage point above the average for all countries will have GDP growth of 0.394 percentage points above the average, and the point where the regression line cuts the 45-degree line is approximately 4.5 per cent. This rate of industry growth separates the slow-growing countries from the faster-growing countries.

The question is : what is special about industry, and particularly manufacturing industry, which accounts or these empirical associations, and which makes industry, 'the engine of growth'? Since differences in the growth of GDP are largely accounted for by differences in the rate of growth of labour productivity, there must be an association between the growth of industry and the growth of labour productivity. This is to be expected for two main reasons. First, If there are increasing returns to scale in industry, both static and dynamic, a relation is to be expected between the growth of industrial output and the growth of labour productivity in industry. Static economies of scale refer to the economies of large-scale production whereby the mass production of commodities allows them to be produced at a lower average cost. Dynamic economies of scale refer to the induced effect that output growth has on capital accumulation and the embodiment of new technical progress in capital. Labour productivity also increases as output growth through 'learning by doing'. Second, if activities outside industry, such as agriculture and petty services, are subject to diminishing returns, with the marginal product of labour less than the average product, then it resources are drawn from these activities into industry as industry expands, the average product of labour will rise in non-industrial activities.

These relationship between industrial growth, productivity growth and GDP growth are known in the growth and development literature as Kaldor's Growth Laws, named after the famous Cambridge economist (Lord) Nicholas Kaldor, who first enunicated then in the 1960s (Kaldor, 1966, 1967).

91. Consider the following statements in relation to the figure.

(*a*) The 45° line would indicate equal correspondence between industrial growth rate and GDP growth rate.

(*b*) GDP growth rate is the cause of industrial growth rate.

(*c*) The excess of industrial growth rate over GDP growth rate is fuelling more GDP.

(*d*) The dividing line of slow and fast growing economies is the industrial growth rate of 3.9%.

Choose the correct option:

A. Only (*a*) and (*c*) are true
B. Only (*a*) and (*b*) are true
C. Only (*a*), (*b*) and (*d*) are true
D. Only (*b*) and (*d*) are true

92. Which of the following statement is correct?

A. There is a positive relation between living standard and resources denoted to industrial activity in few countries
B. There is a close association between living standards and resources utilized
C. The relation between the living standards and resources denoted to industrial activity is globally true
D. There is little association between living standards and resources utilized

93. Consider the following statements:

(*a*) The association between growth of industry and growth of GDP, make industry the 'engine of growth'.

(*b*) Differences in GDP growth do not account for growth in labour productivity.

(*c*) GDP growth rates are reflected in the growth rate of labour productivity.

(*d*) The growth of industry is subject to increasing returns.

Choose the correct option:

A. (*a*), (*b*) and (*c*)
B. (*a*) and (*c*) only
C. (*b*), (*c*) and (*d*)
D. (*b*) and (*d*) only

94. Dynamic economies of scale do not include which one of the following:

A. Induced effect of output growth on capital accumulation

B. Improvement in quality of capital due to new technology

C. The labour intensive sector will experience increasing returns will growth of output

D. A shift from less productive to more productive sector will lead to a rise in the average product of labour

95. Which one of the following statement is not correct for middle and highly developed countries?

A. These devote on an average 30% of the resources to industrial activity

B. Growth of industrial activity involves shift of resources from agriculture to industry

C. Shift of resources is uniform between agriculture industry and higher order services for higher growth

D. Australia, Canada, and New Zealand have developed due to growth of agriculture alone

Directions (Qs. No. 96-100): *Read the following passage and answer the questions.*

The SDGs are global goals, built less upon the erstwhile Millenium Development Goals. They are exhaustive, universal and integrated and emphasize on core areas of poverty and inequality, economic growth, innovation, sustainable consumption and production, climate change, peace and justice and partnerships by implementing a comprehensive array of schemes. Current flagship policies and programmes of Government of India such as Swachh Bharat Mission (SBM), Beti Bachao, Beti Padhao (BBBP), Pradhan Mantri Awas Yojana (PMAY), Pradhan Mantri Jan-Dhan Yojana (PMJDY), Deen Dayal Upadhyay Gram Jyoti Yojana (DDUGJY) and Pradhan Mantri Ujjwala Yojana (PMUY) have substantially contributed to India's progress in this regard.

In the Federal context of India, programmes and schemes are basically implemented at the level of States and Union Territories. Tracking of progress on different SDGs, therefore, is important for appropriate policy actions and building up a competitive spirit among the States and UTs. NITI Aayog has come up with a single measurable index to track the progress of all the States and UTs across 13 out of 17 SDGs (excluding Goal 12, 13, 14 and 17 on account of unavailability of comparable data across States/UTs). This SDG index provides an aggregate assessment of India's progress. This index helps in informed policy formulations as it captures status of both national and state-level social, economic and environmental parameters across a set of 62 select indicators. The scores varies from 0 to 100. States with scores equal to/greater than 65 are considered as **Front-Runners; as Performers** in the range of 50-64 and as **Aspirants** if the score is less than 50. State with an index score of 100 are classified as **Achievers** *i.e.*, the states have achieved the national target set for 2030. A score of 0 denotes worst performance. The SDG Index Score ranges between 42 and 69 for States and between 57 and 68 for UTs.

Estimates suggest that US$7 trillion per year is required for financing these goals worldwide and US$3.9 trillion per year in developing countries. However, the current investment in developing countries is around US$1.4 trillion leading to a shortfall of US$2.5 trillion per year (UNCTAD, 2014). Global action of this scale requires strong coordination between different governments, development institutions, private sector and financial institutions for the effective financing and implementation across the globe.

Sustainable development requires every nation to prioritize their targets and carefully implement various schemes/programmes in accordance with local challenges, capacities and available resources. India follows a holistic approach for achieving the SDGs.

96. Which of the following is not correct about the SDGs Index constructed by NITI Aayog?

A. It includes 13 SDGs

B. It has 62 indicators

C. Goals 12,14 are excluded from it

D. The range of the index is 0 to 1

97. The SDG Index of NITI Aayog classifies the states/UTs into different categories. Match the category with the respective score:

Category	***Score***
(*a*) Performers	(*i*) 50-64
(*b*) Aspirants	(*ii*) ≥65
(*c*) Front-Runners	(*iii*) 100
(*d*) Achievers	(*iv*) < 50

Choose the correct option:

	(*a*)	(*b*)	(*c*)	(*d*)
A.	(*iv*)	(*i*)	(*iii*)	(*ii*)
B.	(*ii*)	(*iii*)	(*i*)	(*iv*)
C.	(*i*)	(*iv*)	(*ii*)	(*iii*)
D.	(*iii*)	(*ii*)	(*iv*)	(*i*)

98. Which of the following Government of India's schemes contribute to India's progress towards the SDGs?

(*a*) Swachh Bharat Mission
(*b*) Pradhan Mantri Ujjwala Yojana
(*c*) Pradhan Mantri Saubhagya Yojana
(*d*) Pradhan Mantri MUDRA Yojana

Choose the correct option:

A. (*a*) and (*b*)
B. (*a*) and (*c*)
C. (*c*) and (*d*)
D. (*b*) and (*d*)

99. What is the range of the SDG Index score for states in India?

A. 42-69 B. 57-68
C. 42-57 D. 42-68

100. Which of the following is not true for the Sustainable Development Goals (SDGs)?

A. Poverty and inequality
B. Climate change
C. Millennium Development Goals
D. Sustainable consumption

ANSWERS

1	**2**	**3**	**4**	**5**	**6**	**7**	**8**	**9**	**10**
*	A	D	D	A	B	A	B	A	D
11	**12**	**13**	**14**	**15**	**16**	**17**	**18**	**19**	**20**
B	B	D	C	A	C	D	A	C	C
21	**22**	**23**	**24**	**25**	**26**	**27**	**28**	**29**	**30**
C	C	B	C	C	A	A	B	C	B
31	**32**	**33**	**34**	**35**	**36**	**37**	**38**	**39**	**40**
D	B	A	A	C	B	A	B	D	C
41	**42**	**43**	**44**	**45**	**46**	**47**	**48**	**49**	**50**
C	B	A	C	C	B	B	D	A	C
51	**52**	**53**	**54**	**55**	**56**	**57**	**58**	**59**	**60**
A	D	A	C	C	A	B	A	A	A
61	**62**	**63**	**64**	**65**	**66**	**67**	**68**	**69**	**70**
A	A	A	B	C	D	C	C	B	B
71	**72**	**73**	**74**	**75**	**76**	**77**	**78**	**79**	**80**
A	D	C	C	D	D	D	C	A	D
81	**82**	**83**	**84**	**85**	**86**	**87**	**88**	**89**	**90**
C	C	C	B	D	A	D	C	A	B
91	**92**	**93**	**94**	**95**	**96**	**97**	**98**	**99**	**100**
A	C	B	C	C	D	C	A	A	C

EXPLANATORY ANSWERS

3. | | | |
|---|---|---|
| A. Marshall | : | 1890 |
| J.R. Hicks | : | 1932 |
| R.G.D. Allen | : | 1934 |
| P. Samuelson | : | 1938 |
| R. Stone | : | 1982 |

4. **Head Count Ratio:** The headcount ratio measures the extent of poverty by counting the number of households whose incomes are not above the poverty line. The headcount index is the most commonly used method of estimating the incidence of poverty. This index measures the proportion of the population that is considered as poor. The head count index is simple to construct and easy to understand. However, this indicator is insensitive to differences in the depth of poverty. More precisely, it fails to capture the extent to which individual income (or expenditure) falls below the poverty line.

Poverty Gap Index: The poverty gap index measures the depth of poverty that is how far, on average, households/individuals fall below the poverty line. This index shows how much money should be transferred to the poor in order to lift them out of poverty. More precisely, this indicator presents the minimum cost for eliminating poverty with monetary transfers. However, the poverty gap index does not take into account differences in the severity of poverty amongst the poor, and therefore tends to omit inequality among the poor. Poverty gap index might complement the headcount index, but might not be sufficient in order to fully reflect the incidence of poverty in a country.

Squared Poverty Gap (Poverty Severity) Index: The squared poverty gap index is used to measure the severity of poverty that is the degree of inequality amongst the poor themselves. This index is a weighted sum of poverty gaps (as a proportion of the poverty line), where the weights are the proportionate poverty gaps themselves. The act of squaring the poverty gap gives greater weight to the poverty gap of the poorest households since their poverty gap will be larger. The need forth is index arises because the poverty gap index may not adequately capture concerns over distribution changes within the poor. For example, if a policy resulted in money transfer from someone just be low the poverty line to the poorest person, the squared poverty gap index will reflect this change, while the poverty gap index will not.

Multidimensional Poverty Index (MPI): The Multidimensional Poverty Index (MPI), used for the first time in the 2010 UNDP Human Development Report and developed by Oxford Poverty & Human Development Initiative (OPHI), complements monetary measures of poverty by taking into account multiple deprivations and their overlap. The index examines deprivations across the same three indicators composing the Human Development Index (HOI): education, health and standard of living.

5. The procedure of transforming the original variables in such a way that the transformed variable satisfy the assumptions of the classical model and then applying OLS to them is known as the method of generalized least squares (GLS). In short, GLS is OLS on the transformed variables that satisfy the standard least-squares assumptions. The estimators thus obtained are known as GLS estimators, and it is these estimators that are BLUE.

7. National Sample Survey Organisation (NSSO) has been conducting quinquennial surveys on a regular basis since 1972-73 to generate national level data on employment and unemployment in India. The NSSO has, over time, developed and standardised measures

of employment and unemployment. The NSSO collects data on employment and unemployment using three broad measures or approaches: 1. Usual Status; 2. Current Weekly Status; and 3. Current Daily Status. The Usual Status is further categorised at two levels: 1. Usual Principal Status and 2. Usual Principal and Subsidiary Status. Usual Status relates to the activity status of a person during the reference period of last 365 days preceding the date of survey. The activity status on which a person spent relatively longer time (major time criterion) is considered the Usual Principal Status (UPS). To decide the usual principal activity status of a person, a two-stage classification is used to determine the broad activity status, viz., employed, unemployed and out of labour force within which, the detailed activity status is determined depending on the relatively longer time spent in the activities. Besides the usual principal activity status, a person could have pursued some economic activity for a smaller period, not less than 30 days. The status in which such economic activity is pursued is the subsidiary economic activity status of that person. If these two are taken together, the measure of Usual Principal and Subsidiary Status. (UPSS) *i.e.* usual. status is obtained.

9. **Disguised Unemployment:** Disguised unemployment refers to a situation when a person is apparently employed, but in fact is unemployed. Here unemployment is not open for everyone to see. We cannot say who is unemployed. The unemployment is not visible but it is concealed or hidden. It is not possible to identify as to who is unemployed as everyone seems to be employed. This type of unemployment prevails mostly in villages. In agriculture, employment takes the form of 'work-sharing', *i.e.* a given work is shared among a larger number of workers than required.

Disguised unemployment occurs when there are workers who are apparently working, but their contribution to output is nil in the sense that if they stop working the total output will not decrease, *i.e.* their marginal productivity is zero. If some workers are withdrawn, the same work will be done by fewer workers and output will not fall. According to Nurkse, developing countries "suffer from large-scale disguised unemployment in the sense that, even with unchanged techniques of agriculture, a large part of the population engaged in agriculture could be removed without reducing agricultural output... . The same farm output could be got with a smaller labour force."

Why does disguised unemployment occur? It occurs because of three inter-related reasons:

(*i*) availability of large labour force,

(*ii*) non-availability of alternative employment opportunity in the urban sector, and

(*iii*) agriculture as a family occupation.

In India, a large labour force is available in the agricultural sector due to the high growth rate of population. In the absence of any employment opportunity in the urban sector, people fall back on agriculture because it is their family occupation. They share a given amount of work among themselves though the amount of work is not sufficient to absorb all of them to the extent of their full capacity. They share the work load of the other family members instead of remaining idle.

11. The normal distribution is a continuous probability distribution and hence the total area covered by the normal curve is equal to unity or 1, because total probability is always equal to 1.

The percentage distribution of area under the normal curve is

I. μ to $(\mu + \sigma)$ covers 34.134% area on the right and μ to $(\mu - \sigma)$ covers 34.134% area on the left hand side of the mean. So $(\mu \pm \sigma)$ covers 68.268% area.

II. $(\mu \pm 2\sigma)$ covers 95.45% area. μ to $(\mu + 2\sigma)$ covers 47.725% area on the right and μ to $(\mu - 2\sigma)$ covers 47.725% area on the left of the mean μ.

III. $(\mu \pm 3\sigma)$ covers 99.73% area. μ to $(\mu + 3\sigma)$ covers 49.865% area on the right and μ to $(\mu - 3\sigma)$ covers 49.865% area on the left of the mean μ.

So it shows that $(\mu \pm 3\sigma)$ covers almost the total area of the normal curve, excepting only 0.27% area which remains outside the limits.

Besides above, the following facts are also to be considered in context to curve area.

$\mu \pm 1.96\ \sigma$ covers 95% area

$\mu \pm 2.58\ \sigma$ covers 99% area

$\mu \pm 0.67\ \sigma$ covers 50% area

These figures are extremely useful in statistical analyses. In most experiments 95% significance is accepted level of accuracy. Here in the theoretical normal probability distribution curve 95% area are covered between $(\mu - 1.96\sigma)$ and $(\mu + 1.96\sigma)$. The rest 5% area falls outside this range. So one value of a variable in any population study can deviate from the theoretical mean μ.

12. Economists have shown on the basis of Joan Robinson's analysis that technical progress is both Hicks-neutral and Harrod-neutral if the elasticity of substitution between labour and capital is unity and there is no change in the distribution of income. There is neutral technical change in Hicks' sense if with given labour force capital remains unchanged and the distribution of income is the same. It is Harrod neutral if with given labour force, capital increases in the same proportion as national output and the distribution of income is the same.

13. Direct Taxes Enquiry Committee (Wanchoo Committee Report): The Direct Taxes Enquiry Committee was appointed in March 1970 with Justice K.N Wanchoo as the chairman. The Committee was asked:

1. to recommend concrete and efficiency measures
   (*a*) to unearth black money and prevent its proliferation through further evasion;
   (*b*) to check avoidance of tax through various legal devices, including the formation of trusts;
   (*c*) to reduce tax arrears;
2. to indicate the manner in which tax assessment and administration may be improved for giving effect to all recommendations.

The Committee submitted an interim report towards the end of 1970. The final report was submitted in December 1971.

Raja J. Chelliah Committee: In, 1991, the Government set up the Tax Reforms Committee under the Chairmanship of Raja J. Chelliah to examine the then tax structure of the country and suggest appropriate changes therein. In its report submitted to the Government in January 1993, it has made several recommendations for reforming India's tax structure.

L.K. Jha Committee (Indirect Taxation Enquiry Committee) 1976

In order to review the existing structure of indirect tax system, the Government of India appointed the Indirect Taxation Enquiry Committee under the chairmanship of LK Jha. The Committee undertook a comprehensive study of the incidence of indirect taxes, the problem of multiplicity of rates etc. and recommended a set of four excise rates - introduction of Value Added Tax at the manufacturing stage called the MANVAT to tackle the problem of cascading effect of excise taxation.

The Taxation Enquiry Commission, 1953-54: The Taxation Enquiry Commission 1953-54 under the Chairmanship of John Mathai also observed the heavy tax burden on motor vehicles and laid emphasis on implementing the recommendations of the Motor Vehicles Taxation Enquiry Committee, 1950. Besides, the Commission gave the following suggestions to lower down the tax burden on motor vehicles:

(*i*) The taxation policies of the Centre and of the states should be co-ordinated and the maximum tax burden for motor vehicles be fixed;

(*ii*) The Wheel Tax levied by local bodies should be merged with the state taxes and the proceeds of the same must be apportioned among the local bodies in the ratio of roads maintained by them; and

(*iii*) Seventy-five per cent of the State Motor Vehicles Taxes and duty on motor spirit should be transferred to 'State Road Funds.'

14. Das Capital = 1867 by Marx
Value and Capital = 1939 by Hicks
Capital and Growth = 1965 by Hicks
Accumulation of Capital = 1956 by Robinson

15. Here, Total cost

$$C = \frac{1}{10}q^3 - 3q^2 + 50q + 300$$

$$\therefore \quad MC = \frac{dC}{dq}$$

$$= \frac{1}{10} \times 3 \times q^2 - 3 \times 2 \times q + 50$$

Since, $q = 10$

$$\therefore \quad MC = \frac{1}{10} \times 3 \times 10^2 - 3 \times 2 \times 10 + 50$$

$$= \frac{1}{10} \times 3 \times 100 - 60 + 50$$

$$= 30 - 60 + 50$$

$$= 20.$$

17. Autonomous Investment: This investment is determined independently of the existing economic conditions, such as, the general price level, national income, national consumption etc. "Induced investment", on the contrary, is determined by existing economic conditions.

19. Types of Income Elasticity of Demand

Income elasticity can be positive or negative. Income elasticity can take five different values. These are:

1. **Greater than One:** This occurs when the percentage change in quantity demanded is greater than the percentage change in income. It is called high income elasticity. It takes place in case of luxury goods.
2. **Equal to One:** This occurs when the percentage change in quantity demanded is equal to the percentage change in income. It is called unitary income elasticity. It holds for those normal goods which fall between the category of necessities and luxuries.
3. **Less than One:** This occurs when the percentage change in quantity demanded is less than the percentage change in income. It is called low income elasticity. This takes place in case of necessities.
4. **Equal to Zero:** This occurs when there is no change in quantity demanded with change in income. It is called zero income elasticity. It is difficult to specify the kind of good where η_Y is zero.
   However, the goods fall between the category of a necessity and an inferior good.
5. **Less than Zero:** This occurs when the percentage change in quantity demanded is negative with change in income. It is called negative income elasticity. It holds in case of inferior goods.

Table: *Table Different Values of Income Elasticity*

Value of η_Y	Terminology	Type of Good
$\eta_Y > 1$	High Income elasticity	Luxury good
$\eta_Y = 1$	Unitary Income elasticity	Normal good which is a necessity as well as semi-luxurious
$0 < \eta_Y < 1$	Low Income elasticity	Necessity
$\eta_Y = 0$	Zero Income elasticity	Can be a poor quality necessity
$\eta_Y < 1$	Negative Income elasticity	Inferior Good

21. Harrod-Domar Model: Both Harrod and Domar have applied Keynesian tools to the dynamic problems of growth. Both of them tried to determine the annual rate of income growth required in the economy for maintaining full employment without leading to deflation and inflation. Both the economists are concerned with determining the conditions required for a smooth, uninterrupted growth of real national income in advanced countries. H-D model is based on the accelerator principle combined with multiplier. The model shows that an economy will stay in equilibrium as long as its rate of growth is equal to the marginal propensity to save divided by its incremental capital output ratio. Harrod called it 'Warranted Rate or Growth'. According to Harrod, equality among 'Actual Rate or Growth' (G) 'Warranted Rate or Growth' (Gw) and 'Natural Rate or Growth' (Gn) is essential for maintaining equilibrium at full employment level in the economy *i.e.,*

G = Gw = Gn

Harrod called it 'Knife Edge Balance'. According to Harrod, If actual rate of growth becomes greater than warranted rate of growth (G > Gw), inflationary conditions appear in the ecomomy and on the contrary, if warranted rate of growth becomes greater than actual growth rate (Gw > G) depression takes place in the economy.

22. Methods for Valuing Natural Resources

Different methods have been developed to measure the economic value of non-marketed goods and services. The most frequently used are the travel cost method (TCM), the hedonic pricing method (HPM) and the contingent valuation method (CVM). The travel cost method uses the revealed preferences for a utility, as represented by the capital spent to actually benefit from the resource involved. For example, the value of a national park can be estimated by use of this method through the total amount of money used when visiting the park being determined. Since people live at different distances from the park, they have different travel costs. By observing the number of trips made during a given period and the differing travel costs involved, a demand function can be identified. The Hedonic pricing method explores factors that affect the market value of a good. The most common application of this method is to the private property market. The market price of an estate is dependent on factors such as locations, size, number of rooms, neighbourhood, etc. This method can be used to examine the extent to which different utilities contribute to the total price. For example, if a house is located close to a recreational area, it may be higher in value than if it were located close to a waste dump or a highway. By determining the value that can be credited to the presence of the recreational area, one can get an idea of its value. The contingent valuation method (CVM) is an approach that is popular today. This method involves conducting interviews to find out what people are willing to pay for a utility, for example a walk in the forest. An average value is then calculated to reflecting the value people attached to walking in the forest. By using hypothetical questions, the method can also be used to estimate the value of intangibles, such as the existence value of biodiversity. A problem with measuring the value of non-marketed goods and services, apart from methodological problems, is that it is questionable whether a value of this sort should be included in the national accounts. The main reason for this concerns the problem of allocation. Since non-marketed goods and services do not compete on an open market, they are not compared with utilities that have a particular market value. On the other hand, it can be argued that goods on the market have a form of shadow price since they are not competing with the non-marketed goods and services. It should be noted that it is inappropriate to add the value of different CVM studies and to thus obtain a total value.

24. In order to promote transparency and provide better understanding of the trade policies and practices of its members, the WTO has a mechanism for regular review of their trade policies. Depending upon its share in world trade, each member's trade policy is reviewed by the WTO at fixed periodic intervals. India's TPR is carried out every four years. The TPR offers all opportunity to other WTO members to ask questions and raise concerns on different aspects of policies and practices of the country under review.

25. The Boxes: The agricultural subsidies, in the WTO terminology have in general been identified by 'boxes' which have been given the colours of the traffic lights—*green* (means permitted), *amber* (means slow down *i.e.*, to be reduced) and *red* (means forbidden).

In the agriculture sector, as usual, things are more complicated. The WTO provisions on agriculture has nothing like red box subsidies, although subsidies exceeding the reduction commitment levels is prohibited in the 'amber box'. The 'blue box' subsidies are tied to programmes that limit the level of production. There is also a provision of some exemption for the developing countries sometimes called the 'S & D box'.

Amber Box: All subsidies which are supposed to distort producttion and trade fall into the amber box *i.e*, all agricultural subsidies except those which fall into the blue and green boxes. These include government policies of minimum support prices (as MSP in India) for agricultural products or any help directly related to production quantities (as power, fertilisers, pesticides, irrigation, etc.)

Blue Box: This is the amber box with conditions. The conditions are designed to reduce distortions. Any subsidy that would normally be in the amber box, is placed in the blue box if it requires farmers to go for a certain production level. These subsidies are nothing but certain direct payments (*i.e.*, direct set-aside payments) made to farmers by the government in the form of assistance programmes to encourage agriculture, rural development, etc.

Green Box: The agricultural subsidies which cause minimal or no distortions to trade are put under the green box. They must not involve price support.

This box basically includes all forms of government expenses which are not targeted at a particular product and all direct income support programmes to farmers which are not related to current levels of production or prices. This is a very wide box and includes all government subsidies like-public storage for food security, pest and disease control, research and extension, and some direct payments to farmers that do not stimulate production like restructuring of agriculture, environmental protection, regional development, crop and income insurance, etc.

The green box subsidies are allowed without limits provided they comply with the policy-specific criteria. It means, this box is exempt from the calculation under subsidies under the WTO provisions because the subsidies under it are not meant to promote production thus do not distort trade. That is why this box is called *'production-neutral box'*. But the facts tell a different story.

26. Internal Rate of Return (IRR): The IRR of a project is defined as the discount rate at which the NPV of the project becomes zero. Usually, as the discount rate rises, NPV of the project declines. The IRR is a measure of risks associated with the project. It is a measure of how high the discount rate can go without making the project infeasible, that is, without making the NPV negative. That is why a project that has an IRR greater than the social discount rate is considered as a good project.

Shadow Prices: Benefits and costs need to be defined and valued differently, depending on the accounting perspective used. For many programs, however, the outputs simply do not have market prices (*e.g.*, a reduction in pollution or the work of a homemaker),yet their value must be estimated. The preferred procedure is to use shadow prices, also known as accounting prices, to reflect better than to actual market prices the real costs and benefits to society. Shadow prices are derived prices for goods and services that are supposed to reflect their true benefits and costs. Sometimes it is more realistic to use shadow prices even when actual prices are available.

28. Cardinal Utility Analysis: In the 19th century, the neo-classical economists Duipit, Gossen, Walras, Menger and Jevons put forward cardinal utility analysis criticising the classical thought propagated by Adam Smith, Ricardo and others. While in 20th Century, Marshall and Pigou further elaborated Cardinal Utility Analysis. According to this analysis utility can be measured in cardinal numbers such as 1, 2, 3, 4 etc. Cardinal numbers either can be added or subtracted. Fisher has used this term "Util" as measure of utility. Thus, in terms of cardinal utility analysis it can be said that one gets from a cup of tea 10 units, 5 unit, from a cup of coffee.

Demand and focus our attention on consumer's behaviour in order to explain the law of demand The law of demand says that when price of a commodity is lowered a larger quantity is demanded, and when price rises a smaller quantity is demanded, other things remaining the same. In other words, the law states that price and quantity demanded are inversely related. In this unit we will introduce you two contending theories. Alfred Marshall's *cardinal utility theory of demand,* and J.R. Hick's and R.G.O. Allen's *preference approach* (or the indifference curve theory, or the ordinal utility theory) of consumer behaviour.

Ordinal Utility Approach to Consumer Behaviour: In the 1930s, an alternative theory of consumer behaviour was developed by J .R. Hicks of the Oxford University and R.G.D. Allen of the London School of Economics. It came to be known as *the preference approach to consumer behaviour.* It was called the preference—indifference curve approach and was developed as a response to increasing dissatisfaction with the Marshallian approach.

Revealled Preference: In succession of Hicks-Allen ordinal utility approach, Samuelson proposed in 1947, another theory, called the 'Revealed Preference Theory' of consumer behaviour. The main merit of the revealed preference theory is that 'Law of demand' can be directly derived from the revealed preference axioms without using indifference curve and most of its restrictive assumptions. What is needed is simply to record consumer's observed behaviour in the market, *i.e.,* the basket of goods a consumer buys at different prices. Besides, the revealed preference theory is also capable of establishing the existence of indifference curves and their convexity. For its merits, revealed preference theory is treated as 'the third root of the logical theory of demand'. The linear expenditure systems (Stone, 1954) explains consumer behaviour with groups of commodities rather than individual commodities. It says that the consumers buy minimum quantity of each group irrespective of prices. The part of income used for buying these subsistence quantities is called subsistence income and the left-over income which can be used for further consumption is called the supernumerary income.

30. The Heckscher-Ohlin theorem is one of the four critical theorems of the Heckscher-Ohlin model. It states: "A capital-abundant country will export the capital-intensive good, while the labour-abundant country will export the labour-abundant country will export the labour-intensive good." The critical assumption of the Heckscher-Ohlin model is that the two countries are identical, except for the difference in resource endowments. This also implies that the aggregate preferences are the same. The relative abundance in capital will cause the capital-abundant country to produce the capital-intensive good cheaper than the labour-abundant country and vice versa. Initially, when the countries are not trading:

- the price of capital-intensive good in capital-abundant country will be bid down relative to the price of the good in the other country,
- the price of labour-intensive good in labour-abundant country will be bid down relative to the price of the good in the other country.

Once trade is allowed, profit-seeking firms will move their products to the markets that have (temporary) higher price. As a result:

- the capital-abundant country will export the capital-intensive good
- The labour-abundant countty will export the labour-intensive good.

The Leontief paradox, presented by Wassily Leontief in 1954, found that the US (the most capital-abutment country in the world by any criteria) exported labour-intensive commodities and imported capital-intensive commodities, in apparent contradiction with Heckscher-Ohlin theorem.

31. The SEBI was established on April 12, 1988 through an administrative order but it became a statutory organisation on February 21, 1992 through an ordinance issued on January 30, 1992. This ordinance was replaced by the SEBI Act on April 4, 1992.

The SEBI is under the overall control of the Ministry of Finance. The SEBI has its head office at Mumbai and regional offices at Kolkata, Chennai and Delhi. The SEBI is a body corporate having perpetual succession and a common seal. The SEBI has powers to acquire, hold and dispose of property both movable and immovable and to contract. It can sue and can be sued by its name.

Reasons for the establishment of SEBI

SEBI was established to protect the rights and interests of the investors and to prevent a variety of malpractices on the part of companies, brokers, merchant bankers, investment consultants and others involved in the securities market.

The glaring examples of these malpractices include unofficial private placements, rigging of prices, unofficial premium on new issues, delay in delivery of shares and payment etc.

32. **Input Efficiency:** To see how inputs can be combined efficiently, We must find the various combinations of inputs that can be used to produce each of the two outputs. A particular allocation of inputs into the production process is technically efficient if the output of one goods cannot be increased without the output of another goods.

If input markets are competitive, a point of efficient production will be achieved. Let's see why, If the labour and Capital markets are perfectly competitive, then the wage rate w will be the same in all industries. Likewise, the rental rate of capital r will be the same whether capital is used in the food or clothing industry. We know, that if producers of food and clothing minimize production costs, they will use combinations of labour and capital so that the ratio of the marginal products of the two inputs is equal to the ratio of the input prices:

$$MP_L/MP_K = w/r$$

since the ratio of the marginal products of the two inputs is equal to the marginal rate of technical substitution of labour for capital $MRTSL_{LK}$,

As a result,

$$MRTS_{LK} = w/r$$

Because the MRTS is the slope of the firm's isoquant, a competitive equilibrium can occur in the input market only if each producer uses labour and capital so that the slopes of the isoquants are equal to one another and to the ratio of the prices of the two inputs. As a result, the competitive equilibrium is efficient in production.

34. The optimum level of population can be defined as a condition where individuals are getting highest possible per capita income. considering the available resources and given level of technology. The theory was initially popularized by Edwin Cannon in 1924. Other economists associated with the theory are Marshall, Robbins, Dalton, Gini, Sidgwick, Carr-Saunders.

36. Output growth

= (Labour share × Labour growth) + (Capital share × Capital growth) + Technical progress

Here, the rate of improvement of technology called technical progress, or the growth of total factor productivity

For Question,

Labour share = 2/3

Labour growth = 3%

Capital share = 1/3

Capital growth = 6%

From output growth = 6%

For equation (i)

$$6 = \left(\frac{2}{3}\times 3\right)+\left(\frac{1}{3}\times 6\right) + \text{Growth of total factor production}$$

⇒ Growth total factor productivity

= 6 − (2 + 2) = 2%

37. There are three important balanced growth theories such as "big push" theory of Rosenstein Rodan, Theory of Unlimited supply of labour by A. Lewis and balanced growth theory by R. Nurkse. The "big push" theory emphasizes on the large comprehensive investment in order to drag the under-developed economy from underdevelopment. The Lewis' unlimited supply of labour theory emphasizes on transfer of labour from the subsistence sector to the capitalist sector for development. Finally, Nurkse's balanced growth theory lays emphasis on balanced development of all the sectors in order facilitate development of underdeveloped economies.

38. Input-output analysis is generally associated with the work of Leontief, The Structure of the American Economy 1919-1929 and Studies in the Structure of the American Economy, for which he was awarded the Nobel Prize in Economics in 1973. His work was conceived for the first time in 1927 at the Institute for World Economics in Kiel, Germany. It has been argued that the basis of input-output analysis can be found in the classical political writing of early economists, such as Quesnay, Walras, Marx, and von Bortkiewicz, and their emphasis on the circular flow of the economy.

Leontief's contribution can be distinguished from that of his predecessors (Quesnay, Karl Marx, Leon Walras, and Ladislaus von Bortkiewicz) because of his emphasis on empirical work. This was distinctly different from the mathematical and theoretical developments of these earlier economists. While these earlier authors tried to address specific questions in a limited context, Leontief's input-output analysis could address a wide variety of problems and provided a means by which theory could be used to provide insight into real policy situations.

39. Demographic dividend, as defined by the United Nations Population Fund (UNFPA) means, "the economic growth potential that can result from shifts in a population's age structure, mainly when the share of the working-age population (15 to 64) is larger than the non-working-age share of the population (14 and yonger, and 65 and older)."

In other words, it is "a boost in economic productivity that occurs when there are growing numbers of people in the workforce relative to the number of dependents".

UNFPA stated that "a country with both increased numbers of young people and declining fertility has the potential to reap a demographic dividend."

42. Bootstrapping is a general, distribution-free method that is used to estimate parameters of interest from data collected from studies or experiments. It is often referred to as a resampling method because it is carried out by repeatedly drawing samples from the original data that were gathered.

Bootstrapping is a useful estimation technique when:

1. The formulas that are to be used for calculating estimates are based on assumptions that may not hold or may not be understood well, or cannot be verified, or are simply dubious.
2. The computational formulas hold only for large samples and are unreliable for small samples or simply not valid for small samples.
3. The computational formulas do not exist.

43. Phillips curve. The short-run Phillips curve exhibits the inflation-unemployment trade-off; the long-run Phillips curve does not. Consideration of both short- and long-run Phillips curves opened macroeconomics to expectations theory.

The Friedman natural rate theory holds that in the short run, a decrease (increase) in inflation is linked to an increase (decrease) in unemployment, but in the long run, the economy returns to its natural rate of unemployment. In other words, there is a trade-off between inflation and unemployment in the short run but not in the long run.

The Friedman natural rate theory was expressed in terms of adaptive expectations. Individuals formed their inflation expectations by considering past inflation rates. Later, some economists expressed the theory in terms of rational expectations. Rational expectations theory holds that individuals form their expected inflation rate by considering present and past inflation rates, as well as all other available and relevant information—in particular, the effects of present and future policy actions.

45. Interest Rate Risk: The interest rate risk on a bond is the risk that if interest rate rise the market value of the bond will decrease. Assume an investor purchases a $1,000 par value ABC corporate bond with an 8% interest rate maturing in 2018 at par value. If interest rates rise to 10%, the market price of the bond will decrease of $800. The bond will now yield 10%, which will equal the yield of new bonds being issued. The bondholder has an unrealized capital loss of $200. However, if the bondholder holds the bond to maturity in the year 2018, he will receive $1,000. If interest rates rise, bond prices will fall and the yield on the bond will increase. If interest rates fall, bond prices will rise and the yield on the bond will fall. Also, long-term bonds will rise or fall more with changes in interest rates than short-term bonds.

48. The concept of duality was one of the most important discoveries in the early development of linear programming. It explains that corresponding to every linear programming problem there is another linear programming problem. The original problem is known as 'primal' and the other, the related problem is known as the *'dual'*. The two problems are replicas of each other. If the primal problem is of maximization type, the dual will be of the minimization type. If the optimal solution to one problem is known to us, we can easily find the optimal solution of the other. This fact is important because at times it is easier to solve the dual than the primal.

49. Market Competition and Externalities: Market competition assumes that there are no negative externalities or consumption and no positive externalities of consumption. Externalities of consumption exist if one individual's consumption of a good or service has positive or negative consequences for the utility of another person. If externalities exist, a competitive market process will not lead to socially optimal outcomes. A positive externality increases the utility of another individual—although he or she does not pay for it. One classic example of a positive externality in health economics is immunization; the benefit of immunization is not restricted to those individuals who have been treated. However, in competitive markets, the direct beneficiary of the immunization will have to bear the full cost. As a consequence, individual consumers would buy too few immunizations. In order to overcome this market failure, governments may subsidize the purchase of immunizations, provide them for free, or make them mandatory. A negative externality decreases the utility of another individual. A classic example of negative externality in health economics is smoking. Smoking by one individual decreases the utiltiy of another individual. As a consequence, governments will either raise the price of smoking or restrict individual opportunities to smoke in the presence of non-smokers.

50. The incidence of a tax refers to the final resting place of the tax burden. It is the ultimate resting of a tax upon individuals or class who cannot shift it further. If actually decides the problem of who bears the money burden of a tax ultimately. In real life, we find that a tax is collected from one individual; but it is actually paid by someone else. For example, a tax on cigarettes is collected from the manufacturers but they do not really pay it. They increase the price of cigarettes and shift the tax forward to the consumer.

In this case, it is the consumer who ultimately pays the tax but the amount of tax is collected through the manufacturer. Shifting is a process by which a tax is passed from one person to another. The shifting of burden could be done in the form of increased prices of commodities and services. Shifting is classified into two categories: backward shifting and forward shifting. The shifting of a tax forward onto the consumer discussed above (a tax on cigarettes) is called the 'forward shifting' of a tax. A tax may also be shifted backward. A manufacturer of cigarettes may shift the tax to the suppliers and growers of tobacco, instead of the consumers. Under backward shifting, the tax does not raise the price of the commodity, but the producer forces the factors of production to accept the lower prices for the services. In this case, the producer may pay lower wages to the workers and thus, shift the tax burden on the labourers. A tax is compared to an unwanted baby. Hence people on whom the impact of a tax falls always try to shift the money burden of taxation either forward or backward.

51. Money supply: The volume or money held by the public at a point of time, in an economy, is referred to as the money supply.

Money supply is a stock concept.

Measures of money supply: On the recommendation of the second working group on money supply, the RBI presented four measures of money supply in its 1977 issues of RBI Bulletin, namely M_1, M_2, M_3 and M_4.

Measures of M_1 include:

(*a*) Currency notes and coins with the public (excluding cash in hand of all commercial banks) [C]

(*b*) Demand deposits of all commercial and co-operative banks excluding inter-bank deposits. (DD),

Where demand deposits are those deposits which can be withdrawn by the depositor at any time by means of cheque. No interest is paid on such deposits.

(*c*) Other deposits with RBI [O.D]

$$M_1 = C + DD + OD$$

Where, Other deposits are the deposits held by the RBI of all economic units except the government and banks. OD includes demand deposits of semi government public financial institutions (like IDBI, IFCI, etc.), foreign central banks and governments, the International Monetary Fund, the World Bank, etc.

Measures of M_2:

(*i*) M_1 [C + DO + OD]

(*ii*) Post office saving deposits

Measures of M_3:

(*i*) M_1

(*ii*) Time deposits of all commercial and co-operative banks.

Where, Time deposits are the deposits that cannot be withdrawn before the expiry of the stipulated time for which deposits are made. Fixed deposit is an example of time deposit.

Measures of M_4:

(*i*) M_3

(*ii*) Total deposits with the post office saving organization (excluding national savings certificates).

High-powered money: High-powered money is money produced by the RBI and the government. It consists of two things: (*a*) currency held by the public and (*b*) Cash reserves with the banks.

52. Analysis of variance (ANOVA) enables us to infer whether population from which we have drawn more than two samples are having the same mean values. By testing the significance of difference between more than two samples means we make such inferences. To test the equality of variances, we use "F" test. By comparing the observed 'F" value with table value of "F" and analyzing the significance of difference (if any) we test our hypothesis.

54. A triangular system is one where the causality between the "endogenous variables" all goes in one direction. Thus, such a system is not a simultaneous system at all, and hence OLS can validly be applied separately to each equation in the system. It thus follows that if a systems technique such as 2SLS is used, this would have been done unnecessarily, and hence an efficiency loss would occur when the reduced, form fitted values are used instead of the actual values.

56. $V = C + S$ ...(*i*)

At equilibrium level

$$I = S$$

$$100 = -20 + 0.2Y$$

$$0.2Y = 120$$

$$Y = \frac{120}{0.2} = 600$$

From (*i*), $Y = C + S$ ...(*ii*)

Here, $S = -20 + 0.2 \times 600$

$= -20 + 120$

$= 100$

and $Y = 600$

$\therefore$ From equation (*ii*)

$$600 = C + 100$$

$$C = 500.$$

57. Tariffs can be classified as specific, Ad valorem and compound

Specific Tariff: A specific tariff is expressed in terms of a fixed amount of money per physical unit of the imported product. For example, an Indian importer of an American computer may be required to pay duty to the indian government of ₹ 2,000 per computer, regardless of the computer's price.

Ad valorem Tariffs: Ad valorem tariffs are expressed as a percentage of the value of the imported goods. Suppose that an Ad valorem duty of 20 per cent is levied on imported cars. An Indian importer of a Japanese car valued at ₹ 8,00,000 would be required to pay a duty of ₹ 1,60,000 to the government (₹ 8,00,000 × 20% = ₹ 1,60,000).

Compound tariff: A tariff that is comprised of both a specific tariff and an ad valorem tariff, is a compound tariff. For example, an American importer of a laptop might be required to pay a duty of ₹ 10,000 plus 5 per cent of the value of the laptop.

58. Basel III or Basel 3 released in December, 2010 is the third in the series of Basel Accords. These accords deal with risk management aspects for the banking sector. In a nut shell we can say that Basel III is the global regulatory standard (agreed upon by the members of the Basel Committee on Banking Supervision) on bank capital adequacy, stress testing and market liquidity risk. (Basel I and Basel II are the earlier versions of the same, and were less stringent).

According to Basel committee on Banking Supervision "Basel III is a comprehensive set of reform measure, developed by the Basel Committee on Banking Supervision, to strengthen the regulation, supervision and risk management of the banking sector."

The basic strucrure of Basel III remains unchanged with three mutually reinforcing pillars.

Pillar 1 : Minimum Regulatory Capital Requirements based on Risk Weighted Assets (RWAs): Maintaining capital calculated through credit, market and operational risk areas.

Pillar 2 : Supervisory Review Process: Regulating tools and frameworks for dealing with peripheral risks that banks face.

Pillar 3 : Market Discipline: Increasing the disclosures that banks must provide to increase the transparency of banks.

60. The modern quantity theory of money: According to Friedman, the demand for money is relatively stable in the short run. The Federal Reserve (Fed) system controls the supply of money. An increase in the supply of money will leave people holding cash balances in excess of amounts they want. They will attempt to rid themselves of these excess transaction assets by spending cash and writing checks. But the community as a whole cannot rid itself of excess cash balances; one person's spending leaves more cash in someone else's billfold or checkbook. Thus, the attempt by people to rid themselves of cash balances will drive up the demand for goods and services and increase output, prices, or some combination of each. In circumstances wherein the economy is operating at its natural levels of employment and output, only prices will rise over the long run. As the price level rises, the demand for money increases because the community desires to hold additional money to buy the higher priced goods. Eventually, equilibrium between the quantity of money supplied and demanded is restored, but at a higher price level.

Thus, according to Friedman, the modern quantity theory of money is established. It does not assume that velocity is a constant as did the older quantity theory, but rather that the demand for money is "highly stable—more stable than functions such as the consumption function that are offered as alternative key relations."

Inflation, stated Friedman, "is always and everywhere a monetary phenomenon, produced in the first instance by an unduly rapid growth in the quantity of money."

61. Single factoral terms of trade

$$T_s = \frac{P_x}{P_m} Z_x$$

Here, $P_x = 170$

$P_m = 190$

$Z_x = 152$

$$\therefore \quad T_s = \frac{170}{190} \times 152$$

$$= 136.$$

62. Revenue Deficit: Revenue Deficit is the excess of its total revenue expenditure to its total revenue receipts. Revenue Deficit is only related to revenue expenditure and revenue receipts of the government.

The difference between total revenue expenditure to the total revenue receipts is Revenue Deficit.

What does it mean?

A revenue deficit indicates that the government doesn't have sufficient revenue for the normal functioning of the government departments. In other words, when the government starts spending more than it earns it results in Revenue Deficit Revenue Deficit forces the government to disinvest or cover the shortage by borrowing.

Remedial measures: In the case of Revenue Deficit government usually tries to curtail their expenses or increase its tax and non-tax receipts This can be done by introducing new taxes or increasing the tax on people in higher-earning slabs.

Fiscal Deficit: The excess of total expenditure over total receipts excluding borrowings is called Fiscal Deficit. In other words, the Fiscal Deficit gives the amount needed by the government to meet its expenses. Thus, a large Fiscal Deficit means a large amount of borrowings.

What does it mean?

Simply put a Fiscal Deficit is a measure of how much the government needs to borrow from the market to meet its expenditure when its resources are inadequate.

Remedial measures: Various measures might be taken to reduce Fiscal Deficit, some of them can be reducing public expenditure in the form of subsidies, reduction in expenditure on bonus, LTC, Leaves encashment etc.

Alternatively, measures to increase the revenue are also taken in forms of broadening tax base restructuring and sale of shares in public sector units etc.

Primary Deficit: Primary Deficit is Fiscal Deficit of the current year minus interest payments on previous borrowings While Fiscal Deficit represents the government's total borrowing including interest payments, Primary Deficit shows the amount of borrowing excluding interest payments.

What does it mean?

Primary Deficit shows the amount of government borrowings specifically to meet the expenses by removing the interest payments Therefore, a zero Primary Deficit means the need for borrowing to meet interest payments.

Remedial measures: A higher Primary Deficit reflects the amount of new borrowings in the current year. Since this is the amount on top of already existing borrowings (Fiscal Deficit) similar measures can be taken to reduce the amount of borrowings.

64. Wiseman-Peacock Hypothesis: The important thesis of the growth of public expenditure was given by Wiseman and Peacock in their well known study of public expenditure in the United Kingdom during the period 1890-1955. The main thesis of the authors is that public expenditure does not increase in a smooth and continuous manner. The increase in public expenditure over time has occurred in jeks or step-like manner. The general approach to the hypothesis refers to the three related concepts.

1. Displacement effect
2. Inspection effect
3. Concentration effect

Using the empirical data for the British economy after 1890, Wiseman and Peacock observe that the relative growth of the public sector in the United Kingdom has followed a discrete step like pattern rather than a 'continuous' growth pattern. In other words, during the period of almost seven decades covered by the study the fiscal activities in the country have risen step by step to successive new plateaus. At times some social or other disturbances take place which at once shows the need for increased public expenditure which the existing public revenue cannot meet. While earlier due to an insufficient pressure for public expenditure the revenue constraint was dominating and it restrained any expansion in public expenditure, under the new condition such restraints give way. The public expenditure increases and it reveals the inadequacy of the present revenue. The movement from the older level of expenditure and taxation to a new and higher level is called the displacement effect.

But when once the social disturbance has ended the newly emerged levels of 'tax tolerance' make the society willing to support a higher level of public expenditure. Now the society is used to heavier taxes and realises that it is capable of carrying heavier tax burden than it previously had thought possible to bear. Thus, when the major social disturbance ends, no strong motivation exists for the society to return to the lower pre-disturbance level. The higher government revenues are used to support a permanently higher level of public sector allocation. Figure shows the displacement effect.

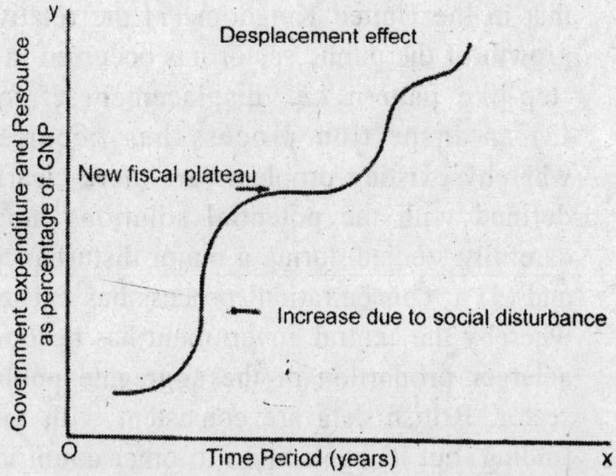

In the above figure X-axis measures the time period and Y-axis represents public expenditure as a percentage of gross national product. The figure reveals that as the social disturbances cause a relative expansion of the public sector; the displacement effect which occurs help to explain the time pattern by which the government growth took place. This displacement effect does not require that the new higher plateau of expenditure will continue with the same expenditure pattern that was created by social disturbance.

Although some of the increased government outlays such as debt interest are direct results of a social disturbance, other expenditure items frequently involve the expansion of the government activity into new areas of economic activity. War and other social disturbances force the people and their government to find solutions of important problems which had been neglected. This is known as the inspection effect. This is created by the inadequacy of revenue as the required public expenditure creates an inspection effect.

In addition to the displacement and inspection effects, Peacock and Wiseman also give a concentration effect. It refers to the apparent tendency for the central government economic activities to become an increasing proportion of the total public sector economic activity when the society is experiencing economic growth.

In short, Wiseman and Peacock concluded that in the United Kingdom (1) the relative growth of the public sector has occurred in a step-like pattern *i.e.,* displacement effect. (2) an inspection process has occurred whereby existing problems are more clearly defined with the potential solutions more carefully studied during a major disturbance, and (3) a 'concentration' process has existed whereby the central government has become a larger proportion of the aggregate public sector. British data are consistent with this finding, but its application to other countries needs verification. Again this aspect of concentration effect is closely connected with the political set up of the country.

66.

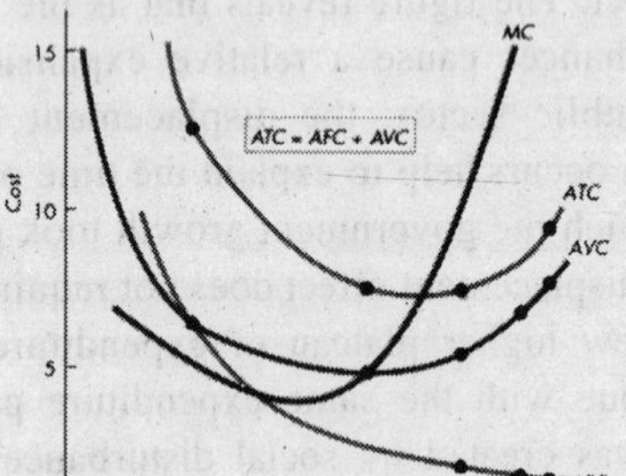

67. Dickey-Fuller test: A test for unit roots (non-stationarity), developed by Wayne Fuller and David Dickey, whose test distribution depends on whether the model under examination has no constant, has a constant, or has a constant with a deterministic trend. An augmented version (ADF) controls for serial correlation within the process.

Box-Jenkins analysis: A methodology developed in the 1930s of combining autoregression and moving average models after they have been transformed and differenced to attain a condition of covariance stationarity, which permits the estimations to converge. In the 1970s, G.E.P. Box and Gwilym Jenkins applied this methodology to time series analysis, forecasting, and control of processes.

Glejser Test: Glejser (1969) presents a test for heteroscedasticity that involves regressing the absolute values of regression residuals for the sample on the values of the independent variable thought to covary with the variance of the error term. Then the Glejster test for heteroscedasticity involves significance tests for the coefficient estimates from this regression. The advantage of this approach is that one can use a variety of *nonlinear* specifications for the regression of the absolute value of residuals on an independent variable to allow tests for forms of heteroscedasticity in which there is a non-monotonic relationship between error term variance and the independent variable. Furthermore. the Gleiser test can yield an estimate of the specific functional form (whether linear or nonlinear) of the relationship between the variance of the error term and an independent variable. Such information is vital when we seek to obtain estimators for regression coefficients that will have lower variance than the OLS estimators.

Granger Test: The Granger causality test is a statistical hypothesis test for determining whether one time series is useful in forecasting another, first proposed in 1969. Ordinarily, regressions reflect "mere" correlations, but Clive Granger argued that causality in economics could be tested for by measuring the ability to predict the future values of a time series using prior values of another time series.

68. Different Types of Production Functions

Cobb-Douglas Production Function: The Cobb-Douglas production function was proposed by Wicksell and tested against statistical evidence by Charles W. Cobb and Poul H. Douglas in 1928. It is one of the most popular and commonly used production functions. It has been widely used in large number of cases worldwide. The Cobb-Douglas production function is represented as:

$$Q = AK^{\alpha}L^{\beta}$$

where α, β are constants. A is the technological parameter, α is the elasticity of output with respect to capital and β is the elasticity of output with respect to labour.

Let us now move on to the properties of this production function.

(a) *Cobb-Douglas production function is a homogeneous production function:* You should know that a homogeneous function is one in which if each input is multiplied by λ then λ is factored out of the function. The power of λ is known as the degree of homogeneity and is a measure of returns to scale. A homogeneous function of degree *v* is one in which if each independent variable is multiplied by a given factor A. Then the dependent variable is multiplied by the same factor raised to the power of *v*.

Cobb Douglas production function is homogeneous of degree (α + β).

- If (α + β) = 1, the production function exhibits constant returns to scale; increasing both inputs by a factor λ raises output by exactly the same factor. It is linearly homogeneous.
- If (α + β) > 1, the production function exhibits increasing returns to scale.
- If (α + β) < 1, the production function exhibits decreasing returns to scale.

So, a Cobb-Douglas production function has the property that the returns to scale is immediately revealed by the sum of the two parameters α and β.

(b) *Isoquants are negatively sloped and convex to the origin.*

(c) *The marginal products of the factors are given by:*

$$MP_L = AK^{\alpha}\beta L^{\beta-1} = \frac{\beta}{L}AK^{\alpha}L^{\beta} = \beta\frac{Q}{L} = \beta.AP_L$$

$$MP_K = A\alpha K^{\alpha-1}L^{\beta} - \frac{\alpha}{K}AK^{\alpha}L^{\beta} = \alpha\frac{Q}{K} = \alpha.AP_K$$

(d) *The $MRTS_{LK}$ of the Cobb Douglas production function is:*

$$MRTS_{LK} = \frac{MP_L}{MP_K} = \left(\frac{\beta Q/L}{\alpha Q/K}\right) = \frac{\beta}{\alpha}.\frac{K}{L}$$

(e) *Elasticity of substitution is equal to 1.*

(f) *Elasticity of output with respect to labour (e_L) shows the response in output with respect to one unit change in labour input.*

69. Compensation Principle or Criterion

The compensation principle is also known as the *Kaldor-Hicks compensation criterion* in recognition of their work done during the late 1930s. This principle states that state two is socially preferable to state one if those who gain from such a move can compensate those who lose, that is, if the gainers can bribe the losers to accept state two and yet be better-off in state two. For example, if a proposed change benefits Dave and harms Rita, and if Dave is willing to pay up to ₹ 100 to see the change occur while Rita is willing to pay only ₹ 50 to avoid the change, the change according to the Kaldor-Hicks criterion is an improvement, even though no money is paid by Dave to Rita.

73. Income multiplier,

$$K = \frac{1}{1-MPC}$$

Here, MPC = 0.75

$$\therefore \quad K = \frac{1}{1-0.75} = \frac{1}{0.25} = 4.$$

75. William J. Baumol's article 'The Transactions Demand for Cash: An Inventory Theoretic Approach', published in the Quarterly Journal of Economics in November 1952 emphasized that the transactions demand for money is also a function of the rate of interest. If the rate of interest on securities (bonds) rises, the firm will find it profitable to interest on securities and optimal cash balances will be lower. On the other hand, if the rate of interest on securities (bonds) fails, the firm will not invest more on securities and optimal cash balances will be higher. Thus, the transactions demand far money varies inversely with the rate of interest.

76. The reserves with the RBI accumulate due to several factors. First is its income from three sources interest on government bonds held for conducting open market operations; fees from government's market borrowing programme; and income from investment in foreign currency assets. Second source is earnings retained after giving dividends to government Third source is revaluation of foreign assets and gold.

77. K. Kaldor's Model of Growth

Professor Kaldor in his Model of Economic Growth follows the Harrodian dynamic approach and the Keynesian techniques of analysis. The other neoclassical models treat the causation of technical progress as completely exogenous, but Kaldor attempts "to provide a framework for relating the genesis of technical progress to capital accumulation."

Assumptions—The basic properties or assumptions of Kaldor's model are as follows—

1. It is based on the Keynesian full employment assumption in which the short-period supply of aggregate goods and services is inelastic and irresponsive to any increase in monetary demand.
2. It assumes that technical progress depends on the rate of capital accumulation. For this, Kaldor postulates "the technical progress function" which is a joint product of two tendencies : growth of capital and growth of productivity. The capital-output ratio will depend upon the relation between the two.
3. Income consists of wages and profits where wages comprise salaries and earning of manual labour, and profits comprise incomes of entrepreneurs as well as property owners.
4. Total savings consist of savings out of wages and savings out of profits.
5. It is assumed that the share of profits in total income is a function of investments, given the propensity to save out of profits.
6. All macro-economic concepts of income, wages, profits, capital, saving and investment used in the model are expressed at constant prices.
7. Monetary policy plays a passive role in the model in that money wages may be rising faster than productivity or pari passes with productivity or money wages may be constant.
8. It is assumed that there are no effects of a change in the share of profits and wages and of a change in interest rates on the choice of techniques adopted.
9. The choice of techniques is assumed to her with the accumulation of capital and the progress of techniques in the capital goods making industries.

79. Constant Elasticity of Substitution (C.E.S.) Production Function

One of the crucial implications of a production function is the degree of elasticity of substitution between two inputs. For a long time, the theory of production had focused on two convenient values for the elasticity of substitution (σ). These two values are $\sigma = 1$ and $\sigma = 0$. In Cobb-Douglas production function with constant rerurns to scale, the value of σ is one. On the other extreme, in the Leontief input-output production function, the value of σ is zero. In many cases, the value of elasticity of substitution of a production function may be constant but not necessarily be equal to one or zero. The constant elasticity of substitution (C.E.S.) production function assumes that the elasticity of substitution is a constant. The form of the C.E.S. production function is

$$Q = A\left[\delta\kappa^{-\rho} + (1-\partial)L^{-\rho}\right]^{\frac{-1}{\rho}}$$

where, Q = output, L = labour, K = capital, A = efficiency parameter (A > 0), δ = distribution parameter or capital intensity coefficient ($0 < \partial < 1$), $(1 - \partial)$ = labour intensity co-efficient and ρ = substitution parameter ($\rho \geq -1$).

The C.E.S. production function is linearly homogeneous or homogeneous of degree one, *i.e.,* the production function always obeys the law of constant returns to scale.

The C.E.S. production function represents a family of production functions which include the special cases, *i.e.*, linear production function, input-output production function and Cobb-Douglas production function for different values of ρ.

80. **Repo Rate:** It is the rate at which RBI lends money to commercial banks.

Reverse Repo rate: It is the rate at which RBI borrows money from commercial banks.

Cash Reserve Ratio (CRR): The share of net demand and time liabilities (deposits) that banks must maintain a cash balance with the Reserve Bank.

Statutory Liquidity Ratio (SLR): The share of net demand and time liabilities (deposits) that banks must maintain in safe and liquid assets, such as, government securities, cash, and gold.

Bank Rate: It is the rate at which the Reserve Bank is ready to buy or rediscount bills of exchange or other commercial papers for the long-term.

Marginal Standing Facility Rate (MSF): The rate at which the scheduled banks can borrow funds from the RBI overnight, against the approved government securities is termed as MSF.

81. **Risk averse:** Preferring a certain income to a risky income with the same expected value.

Risk loving: Preferring a risky income to a certain income with the same expected value.

Risk neutral: Being indifferent between a certain income and an uncertain income with the same expected value.

Risk premium: Amount of money that a risk-averse individual will pay to avoid taking a risk.

82. **National Agricultural Insurance Scheme:** The National Agricultural Insurance Scheme (NAIS) has been introduced in the country with effect from the 1999-2000 Rabi season, replacing the Comprehensive Crop Insurance Scheme (CCIS) which was in operation in the country since 1985. The Scheme is being implemented by the General Insurance Corporation on behalf of the Ministry of Agriculture. The main objective of the Scheme is to protect the farmers against losses suffered by them due to crop failure on account of natural calamities, such as drought, flood, hailstorm, cyclone, fire, pest, diseases, etc., so as to restore their credit-worthiness for the ensuing season. The scheme is available to all the farmers (both loanee and non-loanee) irrespective of their size of holding.

The NAIS envisages coverage of all the food crops (cereals, millets, and pulses), oil seeds and annual commercial/horticultural crops in respect of which past data on yield is available for adequate number of years. Sugarcane, potato, cotton, ginger, onion, turmeric, chilies, pineapple, banana, jute, tapioca, coriander, cumin and garlic have already been covered under the scheme. The scheme is operating on the basis of 'area approach' (defined areas for each notified crop for widespread calamities), and on 'an individual basis' for localized calamities such as hailstorm, landslide, cyclone and flood.

84. In India, Article 280(3)(a) and (b) of the Constitution empowers the President to appoint the Finance Commission every 5 years. The mandate of the Finance

Commission is to assess the fiscal resources and needs of the centre and individual states, and to recommend the distribution between states, of shareable taxes under Article 270 (income tax other than corporation tax) and Article 272 (union excise duty), and to recommend grants-in-aid under Article 275 to states which may be in need of assistance. Article 280(3)(b) enables 'other matters to be referred to the Finance Commission in the interests of sound finance'.

86. The Order Condition for Identification: This condition is based on a counting rule of the variables included and excluded from the particular equation. It is a necessary but no sufficient condition for the identification of an equation. The other condition may be stated as follows.

For an equation to be identified the total number of variables (endogenous and exogenous) excluded from it must be equal to or greater than the number of endogenous variables in the model less one. Given that in a complete model the number of endogenous variables is equal to the number of equations of the model, the order condition for identification is sometimes stated in the following equivalent form.

For an equation to be identified the total number of variables excluded from it but included in other equations must be at least as greater as the number of equations of the system less one.

Let G = total number of equations (= total number of endogenous variables)

K = number of total variables in the model (endogenous and predetermined)

M = number of variables, endogenous and exogenous, included in a particular equation.

Then the order condition for identification may be symbolically expressed as

$(K - M) \geq (G - 1)$

[Excluded variables] ≥ [Total number of equations – 1]

For example, if a system contains 12 equations with 20 variables, 12 endogenous and 8 exogenous, an equation containing 10 variables is not identified, while another containing 5 variables is identified.

The Rank Condition for Identification: The rank condition sates that: in a system of G equations any particular equation is identified if and only if it is possible to construct at least one non-zero determinant of order (G – 1) from the coefficients of the variables excluded from that particular equation but contained in the other equations of the model.

This condition is called rank condition because it refers to the rank of the matrix of parameters of excluded variables. The rank of a matrix is the order of the largest non-zero.

87. According to A Koutsoyanis, in perfect competition the market mechanism itself leads to an efficient allocation of resources. The optimality is achieved because the following important conditions prevail when a perfectly competitive industry is in long-run equilibrium:

(*a*) The output is produced at the minimum per unit cost.

(*b*) Consumers maximize utility by paying the minimum possible price for a commodity. The price of every commodity just covers the marginal cost of production. So, P = MC and MC here reflects the opportunity cost of resources.

(*c*) Since each firm produces its optimum output, plants are run at full capacity. So there is no waste of capacity or idleness of resources.

(*d*) Firms just make normal profits. Since costs per unit is minimum and normal profits are made price cannot be reduced further. In other words, zero excess profits made by each firm ensures that consumers pay the minimum possible price of the product that they buy.

Although perfect competition is a rarity, in the long-run these conditions prevail in all perfectly competitive markets. Thus, if petfect competition is allowed to prevail in all commodity and factor market resources are optimally allocated in the economy as a whole.

90. Convergent and Divergent Series: If S_n the sum of first n terms of an infinite series tends to a definite limit S, as n approaches infinity, the infinite series is said to be convergent and this limit S is called the sum of the infinite series.

Illustration.

The infinite series $1+\frac{1}{3}+\frac{1}{9}+\frac{1}{27}+\dots$ is convergent, for

If S_n denotes the sum to n terms

$$=\frac{1\left(1-\frac{1}{3^n}\right)}{1-\frac{1}{3}}=\frac{3}{2}\left(1-\frac{1}{3^n}\right)=\frac{3}{2}-\frac{1}{2}.\frac{1}{3^{n-1}}$$

Now, if limit of S_n when $n\to\infty$, be denoted by S, then

$$S=\frac{3}{2}\quad\left(\because \text{as } n\to\infty,\ \frac{1}{3^{n-1}}\to 0\right)$$

Since the limit of $S_n \to \infty$ when $n \to \infty$ is definite and finite; the series is convergent. The second kind of the infinite series in which S_n, the sum of first n terms does not tend to a finite limit but increases beyond all bounds as n increases indefinitely, is called a Divergent Series. It is evident that the question of the sum of a non-convergents series docs not arise.

Illustration 1. The series 1 + 2 + 3 + 4 + ... ∞ is a divergent series.

Here, $S_n=\frac{n(n+1)}{2}$

and, $\lim_{n\to\infty} S_n=\lim_{n\to\infty}\frac{n(n+1)}{2}=\infty$

Since, the limit of S_n when $n\to\infty$ is not definite and finite, the series is divergent.

In mathematics, the infinite series $\frac{1}{2}-\frac{1}{4}+\frac{1}{8}-\frac{1}{16}+\dots$ is a simple example of an alternating series that converges absolutely.

It is a geometric series whose first term is $\frac{1}{2}$ and whose common ratio is $-\frac{1}{2}$, so its sum is

$$\sum_{n=1}^{\infty}\frac{(-1)^{n+1}}{2^n}=\frac{1}{2}-\frac{1}{4}+\frac{1}{8}-\frac{1}{16}+\dots$$

$$=\frac{\frac{1}{2}}{1-\left(-\frac{1}{2}\right)}=\frac{1}{3}.$$

Previous Years' Paper (Solved)

National Testing Agency (NTA)

UGC-NET Junior Research Fellowship & Assistant Professor Eligibility Exam

Economics, June-2019*

PAPER-II

Note: *This paper contains* ***hundred (100)*** *objective type questions of* ***two*** *(2) marks each.* ***All*** *questions are* ***compulsory***.

1. Which of the following methods of selecting a strategy is consistent with risk averting behaviour?

A. If two strategies have the same expected profit, select the one with smaller standard deviation

B. If two strategies have the same standard deviation, select the one with smaller expected profit

C. If two strategies have the same standard deviation, select the strategy with larger coefficient of variation

D. If two strategies have different expected profits, select the one with the larger standard deviation

2. Which of the following statement are true regarding Cobb-Douglas production function?

(*a*) It is long period production function

(*b*) It is short period production function

(*c*) It is based on increasing returns to scale

(*d*) Output elasticities with respect to factors are constant

Select the correct option:

A. (*a*) and (*c*) B. (*a*) and (*d*)

C. (*b*) and (*c*) D. (*c*) and (*d*)

3. Match List-I with List-II:

List-I	List-II
(*a*) Various combinations that a consumer can purchase	(*i*) Indifference map
(*b*) Various combinations of two commodities providing equal satisfaction to consumer	(*ii*) Indifference curve
(*c*) A set of indifference curves	(*iii*) Budget line
(*d*) Point of tangency of a budget line on an indifference curve	(*iv*) Consumer's equilibrium

Choose the correct option from the following:

	(*a*)	(*b*)	(*c*)	(*d*)
A.	(*i*)	(*ii*)	(*iv*)	(*iii*)
B.	(*iv*)	(*iii*)	(*i*)	(*ii*)
C.	(*ii*)	(*iii*)	(*iv*)	(*i*)
D.	(*iii*)	(*ii*)	(*i*)	(*iv*)

4. Under non-cooperative games, it is:

A. essential to understand one's opponent's point of view

B. not essential to understand one's opponent's point of view

C. essential to understand one's opponent's point of view and to deduce his likely responses accordingly

D. essential to understand one's opponent's likely responses

Directions (Qs. No. 5-7): *Go through the following paragraph and diagram and answer the questions given below.*

Monopoly charges a price above marginal cost, not all consumers who value the good at more than its cost, buy it. Thus, the quantity produced and

*Online exam held on 21-06-2019.

sold by a monopoly is below the socially efficient level. The deadweight loss represented by the area of the triangle between the demand curve and the marginal cost curve.

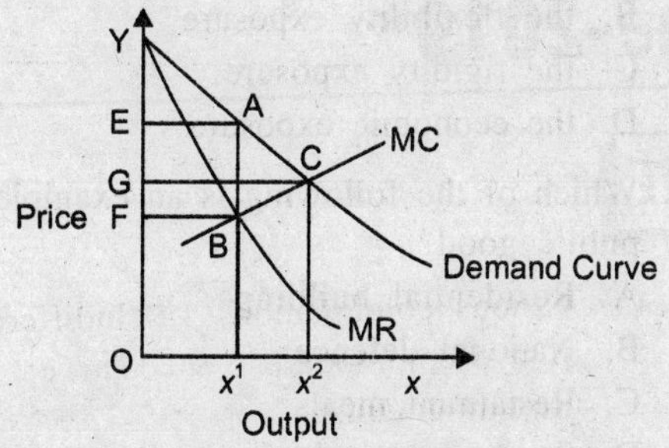

5. What price will be charged under monopoly?

A. OF B. X^2C

C. OE D. OG

6. Which is the socially efficient level of production?

A. OX^1 B. OX^2

C. AX^1 D. CX^2

7. Deadweight loss is represented by the area of:

A. X^1X^2CA

B. X^1BCX^2

C. OX^1AE

D. BAC

8. The inconsistency of which one of the following criteria is labelled as Scitovsky Paradox?

A. Little criterion

B. Pareto criterion

C. Bergson criterion

D. Kaldor-Hicks criterion

9. Pareto's marginal condition for efficiency in composition of output (product-mix) requires:

A. $MRTS^X_{L,K} = MRTS^Y_{L,K} = MRTS^Z_{L,K}$

B. $MRS^A_{X,Y} = MRS^A_{X,Z} = MRS^B_{X,Z}$

C. $MRTP_{X,Y} = MRS^A_{X,Y} = MRS^B_{X,Y}$

D. $MRTS^Y_{L,K} = MRS^A_{X,Y} = MRS^Z_{X,Y}$

10. The firms are competitive and profit maximizing the demand curve for labour is determined by:

A. the opportunity cost of workers' time

B. the value of marginal product of labour

C. offsetting income and substitution effect

D. the value of marginal product of capital

11. General equilibrium analysis determines:

A. prices and quantities in all markets simultaneously

B. prices and quantities in all markets simultaneously and explicitly takes feedback effects into account

C. feedback effects

D. prices in all markets

12. Why do individuals act in riskier ways after being insured?

A. Due to the problem of adverse selection

B. Due to the problem of false confidence

C. Due to the problem of moral hazard

D. Due to the problem of screening costs

Directions (Qs. No. 13-15): *Read the passage given below and answer the questions that follow it:*

Suppose that for a particular economy for some time period, investment was equal to 100, government expenditure was equal to 75, net taxes were fixed at 100 and consumption (C) was given by the consumption function:

$$C = 25 + 0.8\ Y_D$$

where Y_D is disposable income and Y is GDP.

13. What is the value of tax multiplier $\left(\frac{\Delta Y}{\Delta T}\right)$?

A. –3 B. –2

C. –5 D. –4

14. What is the level of equilibrium income (Y)?

A. 700

B. 600

C. 850

D. 800

15. What is the value of the government expenditure multiplier $\left(\frac{\Delta Y}{\Delta G}\right)$?

A. 5 B. 4
C. 6 D. 3

16. Match List-I with List-II:

List-I (Institution)	***List-II (Established)***
(*a*) ICICI	(*i*) 1971
(*b*) IRBI	(*ii*) 1964
(*c*) IFCI	(*iii*) 1955
(*d*) IDBI	(*iv*) 1948

Choose the correct option from those given below:

	(*a*)	(*b*)	(*c*)	(*d*)
A.	(*i*)	(*ii*)	(*iii*)	(*iv*)
B.	(*ii*)	(*iii*)	(*iv*)	(*i*)
C.	(*iii*)	(*i*)	(*iv*)	(*ii*)
D.	(*iii*)	(*ii*)	(*i*)	(*iv*)

17. During a depression which of the following policy instruments should be used?

A. Taxes should be increased
B. Taxes are kept unchanged and public expenditure is increased
C. Public expenditure is reduced
D. There should be a balanced budget

18. Assume that an economy begins in macro-economic equilibrium, then taxes are significantly decreased. As a result of this change:

A. there is expansion and deflation in the economy
B. there is recession and deflation in the economy
C. there is expansion and inflation in the economy
D. there is stagflation in the economy

19. Who among the following is not associated with the endogenous growth theory?

A. Robert Solow
B. Paul Romer
C. Rebelo
D. Robert Lucas

20. A foreign exchange risk involves the transaction exposure, the accounting exposure and:

A. the translation exposure
B. the flexibility exposure
C. the rigidity exposure
D. the economic exposure

21. Which of the following is an example of a public good?

A. Residential building
B. National defence
C. Restaurant meals
D. Swimming pool of a house

22. Which one of the following is NOT the method of debt redemption?

A. Refunding
B. Repudiation
C. Sinking fund
D. Capital levy

23. In J. Robinson's growth model, capital accumulation depends on:

A. saving-income ratio
B. profit-wage relation and labour productivity
C. profit-income ratio and capital productivity
D. saving-investment ratio

24. Liquidity approach is also known by the name:

A. Gurley-Shaw approach
B. Radcliffe approach
C. Traditional approach
D. Monetarist approach

25. Calculate the rate of effective protection by using the formula $g = \frac{t - a_1 t_1}{1 - a_1}$ if g = 0.3, a_2 = 08 and t_1 = 0, then the value of t is:

A. 0.2
B. 0.3
C. 0.1
D. 0.4

26. Match List-I with List-II:

List-I	*List-II*
(*a*) Theory of big push	(*i*) J.H. Boeke
(*b*) Warranted rate of growth	(*ii*) Paul Romer
(*c*) Social dualism	(*iii*) Rosenstein-Rodan
(*d*) Endogenous growth theory	(*iv*) R.F. Harrod

Choose the correct option from those given below:

	(*a*)	(*b*)	(*c*)	(*d*)
A.	(*ii*)	(*iii*)	(*iv*)	(*i*)
B.	(*iii*)	(*i*)	(*iv*)	(*ii*)
C.	(*iii*)	(*iv*)	(*i*)	(*ii*)
D.	(*iv*)	(*ii*)	(*iii*)	(*i*)

27. Which of the following is NOT the function of a capital market?

A. Mobilising savings into investment
B. Channelising funds from less profitable to more profitable
C. Mobilising funds from surplus units to deficit units
D. Providing better returns to direct investors

28. Direct credit programmes introduced:

A. security-oriented credit
B. development-oriented credit
C. purpose-oriented credit
D. welfare-oriented credit

29. Which of the following factors is NOT the cause for 'market failure'?

A. Asymmetric information
B. Public goods
C. Externality
D. Lack of demand

30. According to Marshall-Lerner condition for the foreign exchange market to be stable, the sum of the elasticities of demand for imports and the demand for exports should be:

A. less than 1
B. equal to zero
C. equal to 1
D. more than 1

31. The commodity or Net Barter Terms of trade are represented by the formula:

A. $\frac{\text{quantity of exports}}{\text{quantity of imports}} \times 100$

B. $\frac{\text{price} \times \text{quantity of exports}}{\text{price} \times \text{quantity of imports}} \times 100$

C. $\frac{\text{volume of exports}}{\text{volume of imports}} \times 100$

D. $\frac{\text{price index of exports}}{\text{price index of imports}} \times 100$

32. Which one of the following items is included in the Capital Account of the balance of payments of a country?

A. Investment income
B. Invisibles
C. Commercial borrowings
D. Private transfer

33. By 'financial crowding out' economists mean:

A. credit rationing
B. what the government borrows cannot be used for private investment
C. government borrowings drive up interest rate
D. Reserve Bank of India controls on commercial bank lendings

34. Which is NOT the main objective of credit control?

A. Stabilization of general price level
B. Promoting economic growth
C. Ensuring adequate flow of credit to productive sectors
D. Promoting economic welfare

35. The excess supply of a commodity above the no-trade equilibrium price gives one nation's:

A. import demand for the commodity
B. export supply and import demand for the commodity
C. export supply of the commodity
D. import supply of the commodity

36. The concept of fiscal deficit implies which of the following?
A. Revenue and interest receipts minus revenue expenditure
B. Revenue receipts and recovery of loans and other receipts minus total expenditure
C. Receipts minus disbursement in Capital Account
D. Total receipts minus total expenditure

37. The provision under the membership clause of the IMF is that any country can become a member, if:
A. the country is willing to be a member of the World Bank and willing to pay all subscriptions in gold
B. the country is willing to be a member of the WTO and willing to pay all subscriptions in gold
C. the country is willing to be a member of the World Bank and willing to pay subscription
D. the country is willing to be a member of UNO and willing to pay subscription

38. Vertical equity in taxation means that:
A. people in different income groups should be taxed equally
B. people in different income groups should be taxed differently
C. people in different groups should be charged proportionately
D. unequal people should be treated equally

39. A tax is said to be direct, when:
A. impact and incidence fall upon the same person
B. only incidence falls upon the same person
C. impact is shifted to another person
D. person escapes from paying tax

40. Three pillars of the Asia-Pacific Economic Cooperation (APEC) are:
(*a*) trade and investment liberalization
(*b*) business facilitation
(*c*) economic and technical cooperation
(*d*) military cooperation
Choose the correct option:
A. (*a*), (*b*), (*d*)
B. (*a*), (*b*), (*c*)
C. (*a*), (*c*), (*d*)
D. (*b*), (*c*), (*d*)

41. External drains leave which type of impact on commercial bank?
A. Lowers the reserves of bank
B. Increases further deposits
C. Increases credit creation
D. Creates demand deposits

42. During recession which of the following measures is initiated?
A. Cutting taxes and boosting government spending
B. Increasing taxes and decreasing government spending
C. Keeping tax rates constant and increasing government spending
D. Increasing tax rates and keeping government spending constant

43. An increase in money supply will increase the demand for goods and services by:
A. reducing government spending
B. lowering the interest rate so that investment spending increases
C. raising interest rate so that investment spending reduces
D. increasing government spending on goods and services

44. The liquidity aggregates are classified as:
A. L_1, L_2 and L_3
B. M_1, M_2 and M_3
C. NM_3
D. M_1, M_2, M_3 and M_4

45. An increase in fiscal spending leads to:
A. a shift of Phillips curve to the left
B. a shift of Phillips curve to the right
C. movement along the Phillips curve such that unemployment rises inflation also rises
D. None of these

46. Which one of the following growth models takes technology as exogenous variable?
A. Solow model
B. Robinson model
C. Lucas model
D. Todaro model

47. As income falls, consumption declines but proportionately less than the decrease in income because the consumer desires to sustain previous standard of living. This is called:
A. ratchet effect
B. wealth effect
C. demonstration effect
D. income effect

48. The rational expectations hypothesis suggests that the forecasts that people make concerning future inflation rates:
A. consistently over estimates the actual rate of inflation in the future
B. are always correct
C. consistently underestimates the actual rate of inflation in the future
D. are correct on an average but are subject to errors that are distributed randomly

49. Under which system the central bank is authorised by law to issue a fixed amount of notes against government securities and any excess is to be fully backed by gold/ silver?
A. Maximum fiduciary system
B. Minimum reserve system
C. Fixed fiduciary system
D. Maximum and minimum fiduciary system

50. In the Balance of Payments Account, the transfer payments are included in which one of the following?
A. Capital Account
B. Service Account
C. Current Account
D. Official Reserves Account

51. 'Immiserizing growth' is the term given by:
A. Amartya Sen
B. N. Kaldor
C. Paul Krugman
D. Jagdish Bhagwati

52. According to Marxian analysis the surplus value depends upon:
A. surplus and necessary labour time
B. necessary labour time only
C. surplus labour time only
D. nominal wage rate

53. Which of the following is NOT part of Wiseman and Peacock hypothesis?
A. Concentration effect
B. Displacement effect
C. Inspection effect
D. Taxation effect

54. In efficiency wage model, the real wage is set to:
A. minimise the efficiency of worker per rupee of real wages received
B. clear the labour market
C. not to clear the labour market
D. maximise the efficiency of worker per rupee of real wages received

55. Match List-I with List-II:

List-I	List-II
(*a*) Accelerator and multiplier interaction	(*i*) Modigliani, Ando and Brumberg
(*b*) Cambridge approach	(*ii*) Akerlof and Yellen
(*c*) Life cycle hypothesis	(*iii*) Paul Samuelson
(*d*) Efficiency wage model	(*iv*) Alfred Marshal and A.C. Pigou

Choose the correct option from those given below:

	(*a*)	(*b*)	(*c*)	(*d*)
A.	(*i*)	(*iv*)	(*ii*)	(*iii*)
B.	(*iii*)	(*iv*)	(*i*)	(*ii*)
C.	(*ii*)	(*i*)	(*iii*)	(*iv*)
D.	(*iv*)	(*iii*)	(*ii*)	(*i*)

56. Which one of the following does NOT determine the amount of years of schooling demanded by an individual to qualify for modern job?

A. The wage or income differential
B. The probability of success in finding modern sector employment
C. Opportunity cost of schooling
D. Expansion of healthcare infrastructure in urban sector

57. A toll tax is a tax based on which of the following?

A. The benefit principle
B. Horizontal equity
C. Vertical equity
D. Tax progressively

58. Which consideration a commercial bank does NOT keep in mind to manage its assets and liabilities?

A. Liquidity
B. Profitability
C. Solvency
D. Equity

59. Which one is NOT axiom of inequality measures?

A. Principle of scale invariance
B. Principle of equity
C. Principle of translation invariance
D. Axiom of decomposibility

60. The long-term chronic unemployment arising from imbalance between the skills and other characteristics of workers in the market and the needs of employers is known as:

A. cyclical unemployment
B. frictional unemployment
C. structural unemployment
D. seasonal unemployment

Directions (Qs. No. 61-63): *Consider the following table that gives the monthly per capita consumption expenditure (MPCE) of eight households and answer the questions given below:*

Table

State	**MPCE (in Rs.) of 8 Households**							
	1	2	3	4	5	6	7	8
State–A	950	1100	1000	975	750	775	790	1400
State-B	1250	1150	1400	1100	550	600	490	1200

The value of Z (poverty line MPCE cut off) is ₹ 800.

61. From the table calculate the estimates of Poverty Gap Ratio (PGR) for State–A and State–B and select the correct option:

A. State–A: 0.133, State–B: 0.0119
B. State–A: 0.153, State–B: 0.0135
C. State–A: 0.0133, State–B: 0.119
D. State–A: 0.0153, State–B: 0.135

62. Estimate of head count ratio in State–A and State–B are:

A. State–A: 0.375, State–B: 0.375
B. State–A: 0.475, State–B: 0.375
C. State–A: 0.575, State–B: 0.575
D. State–A: 0.385, State–B: 0.425

63. From the table calculate the estimates of Square Poverty Gap Ratio (SPGR) and then show that the SPGR in State–A is:

A. same as in State–B
B. higher than that in State–B
C. lower than that in State–B
D. significantly different from zero

64. The 'hedonic price' method measures the value of environmental assets through:

A. using 'existence' of an environmental asset

B. using linkages between variations of inhouse prices

C. using WTP to value of environmental asset

D. using WTA to value of environmental asset

65. Under TRIPS protection for copyrights is for:

A. 20 years after death of the author

B. 30 years after death of the author

C. 40 years after death of the author

D. 50 years after death of the author

66. Match List-I with List-II:

List-I	***List-II***
(*a*) World Environment Day	(*i*) 11th July
(*b*) World Wildlife Day	(*ii*) 5th June
(*c*) World Water Day	(*iii*) 3rd March
(*d*) World Population Day	(*iv*) 22nd March

Choose the correct option from those given below:

	(*a*)	(*b*)	(*c*)	(*d*)
A.	(*i*)	(*ii*)	(*iii*)	(*iv*)
B.	(*iii*)	(*i*)	(*iv*)	(*ii*)
C.	(*iv*)	(*iii*)	(*ii*)	(*i*)
D.	(*ii*)	(*iii*)	(*iv*)	(*i*)

67. Match List-I with List-II:

List-I	***List-II***
(*a*) Skewness	(*i*) Dispersion
(*b*) Variance	(*ii*) Random variation
(*c*) Earthquake	(*iii*) Ratio of variances
(*d*) *F*-test	(*iv*) Lack of symmetry

Choose the correct option from those given below:

	(*a*)	(*b*)	(*c*)	(*d*)
A.	(*iii*)	(*iv*)	(*i*)	(*ii*)
B.	(*iv*)	(*i*)	(*ii*)	(*iii*)
C.	(*i*)	(*iii*)	(*iv*)	(*ii*)
D.	(*ii*)	(*i*)	(*iv*)	(*iii*)

68. Multiplicative decomposition model is used to:

A. deseasonalise the time series data

B. build cost of living index

C. test a hypothesis

D. estimate probability

69. Who propounded optimum theory of population?

A. Robbins

B. Dalton

C. Cannan

D. Carr Saunders

70. A linear programming problem can be solved by using:

A. ARIMA techniques

B. Simplex method

C. Unit root method

D. None of the above

71. National Food Security Law covers:

A. 65% of rural population

B. 70% of rural population

C. 75% of rural population

D. 80% of rural population

72. Market failure occurs in case of most of the environmental goods, because:

A. environmental goods are rival products

B. environmental goods are excludable products

C. environmental goods are non-rival in production

D. environmental goods are non-rival and non-excludable in consumption

73. In a binomial distribution, the probability of *x* successes in *n*-trials in any order is given by:

A. $p(x) = {}^nC_x p^x . q^{n-x}$

B. $p(x) = {}^nC_1 p^{2x} . q^{n-1}$

C. $p(x) = {}^nC_x p^2 . q^{n-1}$

D. $p(x) = {}^nC_x p^x . q^{n-2}$

74. A simultaneous equation model is exactly identified, if:

A. unique numerical values of structural parameters can be obtained

B. more than one numerical value can be obtained for some of the parameters of the structural equation

C. unique solution of all the structural coefficients is not possible

D. structural coefficient cannot be estimated

75. The cost function of a monopolist is C = 40 + 12X. Write his demand function as P = 60 – 3X. What is his profit maximising output level?

A. 12

B. 11

C. 8

D. 9

76. Which of the following is NOT correct with reference to the service sector of Indian economy?

A. Service sector has the largest share in the GDP

B. Service sector has the largest share in employment

C. Service sector's growth has been higher than growth of agriculture sector

D. Productivity per worker in service sector is highest

77. Second National Commission on Labour has recommended a three-tier system including:

A. Lok Adalats, Labour Courts and Labour Commission

B. Lok Adalats, Labour Courts and Labour Relations Commission

C. Lok Adalats, Labour Courts and Judicial Courts

D. Lok Adalats, Labour Courts and Labour Inspectors

78. Standard Error (SE) of sample mean ($\bar{x}$) in random sampling from an infinite population or in random sampling with replacement is given by:

A. $SE = \frac{\sigma^2}{\sqrt{n}}$
where σ is the population standard deviation

B. $SE = \frac{\sigma}{\sqrt{n^2}}$
where σ is the population standard deviation

C. $SE = \frac{\sigma^3}{\sqrt{n}}$
where σ is the population standard deviation

D. $SE = \frac{\sigma}{\sqrt{n}}$
where σ is the population standard deviation

79. **Assertion (A) :** The share of the non-commodity sector in the national income has been increasing in India.

Reason (R) : Industry and Agriculture have been growing at a relatively slower pace in India.

Choose the appropriate option from the following:

A. Both (A) and (R) are true, and (R) explains (A)

B. Both (A) and (R) are true, but (R) does not explain (A)

C. (A) is true, but (R) is false

D. (A) is false, but (R) is true

80. When the null hypothesis is there as an equality, the level of significance is the probability of making:

A. type II error

B. type I error

C. type I and II errors

D. type I and III errors

81. "Education as investment in human resources plays an important role among the factors which contribute to economic growth." This statement was given by:

A. New Education Policy, 1985
B. Education Commission, 1966
C. NCERT
D. Supreme Court of India

82. If AR = 15 and MR = 5, the price elasticity of demand is:
A. 2.3 B. 1.5
C. 1.75 D. 1

83. Match List-I with List-II:

List-I	*List-II*
(*a*) Gauss-Markov	(*i*) R^2
(*b*) Coefficient of determination	(*ii*) One sided test
(*c*) $H_0 : B_2 = 0$, $H_1 : B_2 = 70$	(*iii*) Goldfeld-Quandt test
(*d*) Heteroscedasticity	(*iv*) BLUE

Choose the correct option from those given below:

	(*a*)	(*b*)	(*c*)	(*d*)
A.	(*iv*)	(*i*)	(*ii*)	(*iii*)
B.	(*i*)	(*ii*)	(*iv*)	(*iii*)
C.	(*ii*)	(*iii*)	(*i*)	(*iv*)
D.	(*iii*)	(*i*)	(*ii*)	(*iv*)

84. The correct relationship among Arithmetic Mean (AM), Geometric Mean (GM) and Harmonic Mean (HM) is:
A. GM = AM + HM
B. AM < HM
C. $[GM]^2 = HM \times AM$
D. AM = GM − HM

85. For a moderately skewed distribution, the value of mode is 10 and value of median is 20. Then the mean is:
A. 15 B. 30
C. 25 D. 35

86. In 2011 the proportion of urban population was more than 40 per cent in the States of:
A. Tamil Nadu, Punjab, Andhra Pradesh, Gujarat
B. Tamil Nadu, Haryana, Gujarat, Maharashtra
C. Tamil Nadu, Kerala, Andhra Pradesh, West Bengal
D. Tamil Nadu, Kerala, Maharashtra, Gujarat

87. Match List-I with List-II:

List-I	*List-II*
(*a*) Thomos Doubleday	(*i*) Destiny theory
(*b*) Thomas Sadler	(*ii*) Biological theory
(*c*) Leibenstein	(*iii*) Diet theory
(*d*) Herbert Spencer	(*iv*) Motivation theory of population growth

Choose the correct option from those given below:

	(*a*)	(*b*)	(*c*)	(*d*)
A.	(*i*)	(*ii*)	(*iii*)	(*iv*)
B.	(*iii*)	(*i*)	(*iv*)	(*ii*)
C.	(*iv*)	(*iii*)	(*ii*)	(*i*)
D.	(*iv*)	(*ii*)	(*i*)	(*iii*)

88. If $A = \begin{bmatrix} 6 & 5 & 5 \\ 3 & -11 & -5 \\ 3 & -5 & -2 \end{bmatrix}$, then | A | is equal to:
A. 15 B. 16
C. 27 D. 20

89. Applying OLS to simultaneous equations results in the parameters being:
A. inefficient
B. inconsistent
C. biased
D. biased and inconsistent

90. In a two variable (X and Y) regression analysis, the regression coefficients are $b_{xy} = 0.6$ and $b_{yx} = 0.8$. If *y* is dependent variable and *x* is independent variable, what is the percentage of variations in Y explained by X?
A. 47%
B. 48%
C. 49%
D. 36%

91. What is the equation of corrected birthrate?

A. Corrected birthrate

$$= \frac{\text{Registered births in one year + Possible birth}}{\text{Mid year population}} \times 1000$$

B. Corrected birthrate

$$= \frac{\text{Live births in one year}}{\text{Mid year population}} \times 1000$$

C. Corrected birthrate

$$= \frac{\text{Number of female births}}{\text{Mid year population}} \times 1000$$

D. Corrected birthrate

$$= \frac{\text{Registered births + Possible births}}{\text{Mid year female population}} \times 1000$$

92. Difference equation is concerned with:

A. discrete changes
B. continuous changes
C. Both of the above
D. None of the above

93. "Under some conditions, it makes no difference to efficiency whether the polluter has a right to pollute or the victim has a right to clean air." This statement is related to the work of:

A. G. Hardin
B. R. Coase
C. N. Kaldor
D. Julian Simon

94. The RBI made Indian rupee fully convertible in current account transactions related to goods and services in the year:

A. 1985
B. 2002
C. 1994
D. 2011

95. In an open economy input-output model, the viability is examined by:

A. Hawkins-Simon conditions
B. Kuhn-Tucker conditions
C. Dickey-Fuller test
D. Goldfeld-Quandt test

96. Which of the following is NOT part of the 'PM Kisan Samman Nidhi' scheme as announced on 1-02-2019?

A. All farmers having land holdings up to 2 hectares are eligible under the scheme
B. The scheme will be applicable from 1st April, 2019
C. The government will transfer ₹ 6,000 per annum into the bank accounts of eligible beneficiaries
D. The money will be given in three equal instalments of ₹ 2000 each

97. The IRR is the discount rate that equates the project NPV to _____ and benefit-cost ratio to _____.

A. 1, 0
B. 0, 1
C. 0, 0
D. 1, 1

98. Which of the following items completes the life table?

Age	l_x	d_x	L_x	T_x	e_x^0
7	90,000	500	89,750	48,50,000	?

A. 50.50
B. 54.00
C. 53.89
D. 51.31

99. Which of the following is NOT an instrument of capital market with special reference to India?

A. Equity share
B. Debenture
C. Gold ETF
D. Commercial paper

100. Which age structure is important for demographic dividend?

A. 0-14
B. 15-59
C. 60 and above
D. 0-14, 60 and above

A135

ANSWERS

1	2	3	4	5	6	7	8	9	10
A	B	D	C	C	B	D	D	C	B
11	**12**	**13**	**14**	**15**	**16**	**17**	**18**	**19**	**20**
B	C	D	B	A	C	B	C	A	D
21	**22**	**23**	**24**	**25**	**26**	**27**	**28**	**29**	**30**
B	B	B	B	*	C	D	C	D	D
31	**32**	**33**	**34**	**35**	**36**	**37**	**38**	**39**	**40**
D	C	C	D	C	B	C	B	A	B
41	**42**	**43**	**44**	**45**	**46**	**47**	**48**	**49**	**50**
A	A	B	A	*	A	A	D	C	C
51	**52**	**53**	**54**	**55**	**56**	**57**	**58**	**59**	**60**
D	A	D	D	B	D	A	D	B	C
61	**62**	**63**	**64**	**65**	**66**	**67**	**68**	**69**	**70**
C	A	C	B	D	D	B	A	C	B
71	**72**	**73**	**74**	**75**	**76**	**77**	**78**	**79**	**80**
C	D	A	A	C	B	B	D	A	B
81	**82**	**83**	**84**	**85**	**86**	**87**	**88**	**89**	**90**
B	B	A	C	C	D	B	C	D	B
91	**92**	**93**	**94**	**95**	**96**	**97**	**98**	**99**	**100**
A	A	B	C	A	B	B	C	D	B

EXPLANATORY ANSWERS

1. The risk of an investment can be measured by the variance or standard deviation of possible returns around the expected return: the greater the dispersion, the greater the risk, the greater the variance or standard deviation and vice versa; and where there is no dispersion of possible returns, then the expected return is a certain return, there is no risk and both variance and standard deviation give a measure of zero.

2. In economics, the Cobb-Douglas functional form of production functions is widely used to represent the relationship of an output to inputs. It was proposed by Knut Wicksell (1851-1926), and tested against statistical evidence by Charles Cobb and Paul Douglas in 1928.

In 1928 Charles Cobb and Paul Douglas published a study in which they modeled the growth of the American manufacturing industry during the period 1899-192. They considered a simplified view of the economy in which production output is determined by the amount of labour involved and the amount of capital invested. The conclusion drawn from this famous statistical study is that labour contributed about 3/4th and capital about 1/4th of the increase in the manufacturing production. The function they used to model production was of the form:

$Q = KL^{\alpha}C^{1-\alpha}$,

where: Q = total output/production, L = Quantity of labour, K and α are the positive constants and C is the amount of capital.

Output elasticity measures the responsiveness of output to a change in levels of either labour or capital used in production, ceteris paribus.

For Cobb-Douglas production function, elasticity of substitution is equal to one (Unity).

4. Non-Cooperative Versus Cooperative Game

Economic games that firms play can either be cooperative or non-cooperative.

In **cooperative games** players can negotiate binding contracts that allow them to plan joint strategies.

- An example of a cooperative game is the bargaining between buyer and seller over the price of a rug. If the rug costs $100 to produce and the buyer values the rug at $200, a cooperative solution to the game is possible. An agreement to sell the rug at any price between $101 and $199 will maximise the sum of the buyer's consumer surplus and the seller's profit while making both parties better off.
- Another example of a cooperative game would involve two firms negotiating a joint investment to develop a new technology (assuming neither firm would have enough know-how to succeed on its own). If the firms can sign a binding contract to divide the profits from their joint investment, a cooperative outcome that makes both parties better-off is possible.

In a **non-cooperative games,** negotiation and enforcement of binding contracts are not possible.

- An example of a non-cooperative game is the case where two competing firms take each other's behaviour into account when independently setting prices. Each firm knows that by undercutting its competitor it can capture more market share. But it also knows that in doing so, it risks setting off a price war.
- Another example of a non-cooperative game is the auction. Each bidder must take the likely behaviour of the other bidders into account when determining an optimal bidding strategy.

NB: The fundamental difference between cooperative and non-cooperative games lies in the **contracting possibilities.** In cooperative games binding contracts are possible and in non-cooperative games they are not.

5-7. The Inefficiency of Monopoly: Because a monopoly charges a price above marginal cost, not all consumers who value the good at more than its cost buy it. Thus, the quantity produced and sold by a monopoly is below the socially efficient level. The deadweight loss is represented by the area of the triangle between the demand curve (which reflects the value of the good to consumers) and the marginal cost curve (which reflects the costs of the monopoly producer).

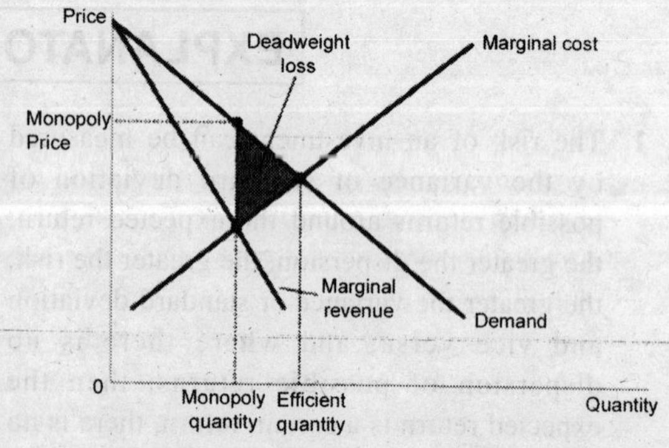

8. Scitovsky Paradox: Scitovsky pointed out an important limitation of Kaldor-Hicks criterion that it might lead to contradictory results. He showed that if in some situation position A on Kaldor-Hicks criterion, it may be possible that position A is also shown to be an improvement over B on the basis of some criterion. For getting consistent results when position B has been revealed to be preferred to position A on the basis of a welfare criterion, then position A must not be preferred to position B on the same criterion. According to Scitovsky, Kaldor-Hicks criterion involves such contradictory and inconsistent results. Since Scitovsky was the first to point out this paradoxical result in Kaldor-Hicks criterion, it is known as 'Scitovsky-Paradox'.

9. The marginal condition for a Pareto-optimal or-efficient composition of output requires that the MRPT between any two commodities be equal to the MRS between the same two goods.

$$MRPT_{x,y} = MRS^{A}_{x,y} = MRS^{B}_{x,y}$$

Since, the MRPT shows the rate at which a good can be transformed into another (on the production side), and the MRS shows the rate at which consumers are willing to exchange a good for another, the rates must be equal for a Pareto-optimal situation to be attained. Suppose that these rates are unequal. For example assume:

$$MRPT_{x,y} = \frac{2Y}{1X} \text{ and } MRS_{x,y} = \frac{1Y}{1X}$$

that is, $MRPT_{x,y} > MRS_{x,y}$

The above inequality shows that the economy can produce two units of Y by sacrificing one unit of X, while the consumers are willing to exchange one unit of Y for one unit of X. Clearly the economy produces too much of X and too little of Y relatively to the tastes of consumers. Welfare therefore can be increased by increasing the production of Y and decreasing the production of X.

10. This figure shows how the value of the marginal product (the marginal product times the price of the output) depends on the number of workers. The curve slopes downward because of diminishing marginal product. For a competitive, profit-maximizing firm, this value of marginal product curve is also the firm's labour demand curve.

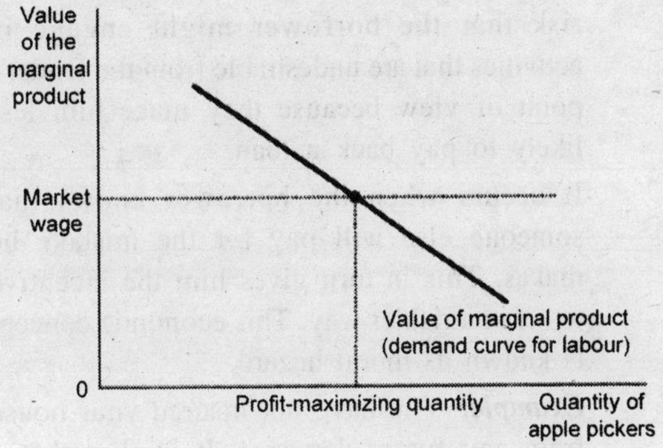

Thus, a competitive, profit-maximizing firm hires workers up to the point where the value of the marginal product of labour equals the wage.

11. Unlike partial equilibrium analysis, general equilibrium analysis determines the prices and quantities in all markets simultaneously, and it explicitly takes feedback effects into account. A feedback effect is a price or quantity adjustment in one market caused by price and quantity adjustments in related markets. Suppose, for example, that the government taxes oil imports. This policy would immediately shift the supply curve for oil to the left (by making foreign oil more expensive) and raise the price of oil. But the effect of the tax would not end there. The higher price of oil would increase the demand for and then the price of natural gas. The higher natural gas price would in turn cause oil demand to rise (shift to the right) and increase the oil price even more. The oil and natural gas markets will continue to interact until enventually an equilibrium is reached in which the quantity demanded and quantity supplied are equated in both markets.

12. Definition: Moral hazard is a situation in which one party gets involved in a risky event knowing that it is protected against the risk and the other party will incur the cost. It arises when both the parties have incomplete information about each other.

Description: In a financial market, there is a risk that the borrower might engage in activities that are undesirable from the lender's point of view because they make him less likely to pay back a loan.

It occurs when the borrower knows that someone else will pay for the mistake he makes. This in turn gives him the incentive to act in a riskier way. This economic concept is known as moral hazard.

Example: You have not insured your house from any future damages. It implies that a loss will be completely borne by you at the time of a mishappening like fire or burglary. Hence you will show extra care and attentiveness. You will install high tech burglar alarms and hire watchmen to avoid any unforeseen event.

But if your house is insured for its full value, then if anything happens you do not really lose anything. Therefore, you have less incentive to protect against any mishappening. In this case, the insurance firm bears the losses and the problem of moral hazard arises.

13. $$\frac{\Delta Y}{\Delta T} = -\frac{MPC}{1-MPC}$$

$$= -\frac{0.8}{0.2} = -4.$$

14. $$Y = C + I + G$$

$$Y = 25 + 0.8Y_d + 100 + 75$$

$$Y = 200 + 0.8\ Y_d$$

$$\sim \quad Y_d = Y - T$$

$$Y = 200 + 0.8(Y - T)$$

$$Y = 200 + 0.8(Y - 100)$$

$$Y = 200 + 0.8Y - 80$$

$$Y = 120 + 0.8Y$$

$$Y - 0.8Y = 120$$

$$0.2Y = 120$$

$$Y = \frac{120}{0.2}$$

$$Y = 600$$

Therefore, the level of equilibrium income is $600.

15. G multiplier = $\frac{1}{(1-c)}$

where c is the marginal propensity to consume.

$$\therefore \quad \frac{\Delta Y}{\Delta G} = \frac{1}{1-0.8}$$

$$= \frac{1}{0.2} = 5.$$

17. ***Definition:*** Depression is defined as a severe and prolonged recession. A recession is a situation of declining economic activity. Declining economic activity is characterized by falling output and employment levels. Generally, when an economy continues to suffer recession for two or more quarters, it is called depression.

Description: The level of productivity in an economy falls significantly during a depression. Both the GDP (gross domestic product) and GNP (gross national product) show a negative growth along with greater business failures and unemployment.

When a recession continues to take its toll on any economy, the built in process triggers further cuts in investment as well as consumption spending due to loss of confidence among investors and consumers. Also, the financial crisis may lead to decreased availability for credit. Excessive fluctuations happen in relative value of currency. Overall trade and commerce get reduced. The Great Depression of 1929 is considered to be the most classic example of a depression in economic history.

19. Endogenous growth theory asserts that causes of economic growth is primarily endogenous and not due to external forces. Endogenous growth theory emphasizes on investment in human capital, innovation, and knowledge as the significant contributors to economic growth. The theory also focuses on positive externalities and spillover effects of a knowledge-based economy which will lead to economic development. According to the endogenous growth theory long run growth rate of an economy depends on policy measures.

For example, subsidies for research and development or education increase the growth rate in some endogenous growth models by increasing the incentive for innovation.

In the mid-1980s, a group of growth theorists has been increasingly dissatisfied with common treatment of exogenous factors for determining long-run growth. They favored a model that replaced the exogenous growth variable (unexplained technical progress) with a model in which the key determinants of growth were explicit in the model. Paul Romer (1986), Robert Lucas (1988) and Sergio Rebelo (1991) discarded technological change and modelled growth as the result of indefinite investment in human capital which had spillover effect on economy and reduces the diminishing return to capital accumulation.

However, the endogenous growth theory is further supported with models in which agents optimally determined the consumption and saving, optimizing the resources allocation to research and development leading to technological progress. Romer (1987, 1990), Aghion and Howitt (1992) and Grossman and Helpman (1991), incorporated imperfect markets and R&D to the growth model.

Endogenous growth theory implies that policies which embrace openness, competition, change and innovation will promote growth and policies which have the effect of restricting or slowing change are likely over time to sluggish growth.

20. The different types of exchange risks are: transaction exposure, translation exposure and economic exposure.

1. **Transaction exposure:** The net amount of existing commitments to make or receive outlays in foreign currency is known as 'transaction exposure'. Forward contract has widest use in offsetting the exchange risk on short-term commitments where amounts are known in advance. Hedging with forward contracts is simple, involving low-cost and low-risk. Hedging transaction exposure is always done on the basis of overall exposure and not on the basis of parts.
2. **Translation exposure:** The net book value of assets and liabilities denominated in a foreign currency arising out of changes in exchange rates is called 'translation or accounting exposure'. This kind of risk arises because of the changes in the book value of the parent's investment in the subsidiary, resulting in loss to the parent company. Significant translation losses might force a company to hedge its translation exposure.
3. **Economic exposure:** The risks that are associated with the changes in the present value of a firm, an asset or a liability on account of the exchange rate changes is called 'economic exposure'. Since the present value depends on the expected outcomes of commitments that have not yet been made, economic exposure is much more comprehensive than transaction exposure. It differs from translation exposure in that economic exposure depends on the future while translation exposure reflects the events that occurred in the past. Economic exposure also differs from transaction and translation exposure because a firm may be exposed to exchange rate changes even if it has neither assets nor liabilities denominated in foreign currency.

22. Redemption of public debt means repayment of public debt. All government debts should be rapid promptly. There are various methods of repayment which may be discussed under the following heads.

1. **Surplus budget:** Surplus budget means having public revenue in excess of public expenditure. If the government plans for a surplus budget, the excess revenue may be utilized to repay public debt.
2. **Refunding:** Refunding implies the issue of fresh bands and securities by government so that the matured loans can be used for repayment of public debt.
3. **Annuities:** By this method, the government repays past of the public debt every year. Such annual payments are made regularly till the debt is completely cleared.
4. **Sinking fund:** By this method, the government creates a separate fund called 'Sinking fund' for the purpose of repaying public debt. This is considered as the best method of redemption.
5. **Conversion:** Conversion means that the existing loans are changed into new loans before the date of their maturity.
6. **Additional taxation:** Government may resort to additional taxation so as to raise necessary funds to repay public debt under this method new taxes are imposed.
7. **Capital levy:** Capital levy is a heavy one time tax on the capital assets and estates.
8. **Surplus balance of payments:** This is useful to repay external debt for which foreign exchange is required surplus balance of payment implies exports in excess of imports by which reserves of foreign exchange can be created.

23. The Golden Age: In addition to the growth rate of capital ($\Delta K/K$), another ΔN factor which determines the growth rate of an economy is the growth rate of population ($\Delta N/N$). When the growth rate of population equals the growth rate of capital, i.e., $\Delta N/N = \Delta K/K$, the economy is said to be in full employment equilibrium. Joan Robinson calls it "golden age" to describe the steady growth with full employment. In her own words: "When technical progress is neutral and proceeding steadily without any change in the time pattern of production, the competitive mechanism working freely, population growing (if at all) at a steady rate and accumulation going on fast enough to supply productive capacity for all available labour, the rate of profit tends to be constant and the level of real wages to rise with output per man. Then there are no internal contradictions in the system. Total annual output and the stock of capital then grow together at a constant proportionate rate compounded at the rate of increase of the output per man. We may describe these conditions as a golden age" (Robinson, The Accumulation of Capital, P.99). Robinson also Indicates that golden age represents a mythical state of affairs not likely to obtain in any actual economy.

Joan Robinson says that an economy is in a golden age when the *potential growth ratio* is being realized. The potential growth ratio represents the highest rate of capital accumulation that can be permanently maintained at a constant rate of profit.

Joan Robinson's model is sometimes considered as an elaboration of Harrod's growth model. But we must note that Joan Robinson's theory of capital accumulation depends on profit-wage relation and on labour productivity whereas Harrod's theory depends on saving–income ratio and on capital productivity.

Robinson stresses the importance of labour in capital accumulation whereas Domar underlines the importance of capital.

24. Radcliffe-Sayers Thesis: The Radcliffe-Sayers Thesis points out that the supply of money is not the main level of monetary action. The object of monetary action is to influence the level of aggregate demand by influencing the spending decision of the people. It is of no doubt that the supply of money is important in the spending decision of the people, but this alone does not influence it. The spending decisions are also influenced by the degree of liquidity of assets and the liquidity position of the financial institutions. Thus, the decision to spend is influenced by the liquidity position of the spenders.

According to this thesis, liquidity implies the general liquidity of the entire economy. The general liquidity is the aggregate liquidity of the private individuals, non-banking financial intermediaries and the government. The spending decision depends more on the general liquidity of the whole economy rather than on money supply alone. Money supply is only a part of the wider liquidity structure of the whole economy. Since the rate of interest affects the liquidity of various financial institutions, the rate of interest may be regarded as *n* important influencing factor. However, the rate of interest plays only a minor role.

According to the Radcliffe Committee, the lending capacity of the financial institutions could be indirectly controlled through changes in the level and structure of the rate of interest. An increase in the rate of interest will reduce the lending activities of the financial institutions by increasing capital losses from the assets held by them. Thus, increase in the rate of interest reduces the aggregate spending indirectly by reducing the lending capacity of the financial institutions and the liquidity position of the general public.

Radcliffe-Sayers thesis suggested the following policy instruments for the suitable monetary action in the economy:

(*i*) Imposition of 'liquidity control' over a wide range of financial institutions.

(*ii*) 'Control' through the exercise of liquidity or changes in the rate of interest.

28. The purpose of directed credit programmes is to channel credit to priority sectors, groups or regions to support activities that are either considered to be socially beneficial, or inherently riskier, and borrower groups that are likely to be marginalised in the credit markets. It is argued that provision of credit to these targets will enable exploitation of investment opportunities, contributing not only to the economy's GDP but meet other welfare objectives such as employment, income redistribution, etc. Another objective has been to reduce the dependency of a certain class of borrowers on the informal credit market with its high rates of interest.

29. *Market failure* means the inability of a system to provide certain goods either at all or at the most desirable or 'optimal' level. In general, market failure arises because of four main causes. The *first* is market imperfection, which means deviations from the conditions necessary for perfect competition in the product and factor markets. Thus, if there is monopoly power in the commodity market or if labour is unionized in the labour market, the result is market failure. The *second* cause of market failure is asymmetric (imperfect) information, which means difference in information possessed by the parties to a market transaction. The *third* is the presence of externalities in the production or consumption of goods and services. Externalities are the side effects that can be harmful (known as external cost or external diseconomy) or beneficial (known as external benefit or external economy) for the members of the society. Externalities lead to overproduction or under production of goods and services and the result is economy loss and market failure. The *last* main cause of market failure is the presence of public goods. Public goods are defined by two characteristics: (*i*) they are non-rival in consumption and (*ii*) they are non-excludable. It is due to the feature of non-excludability, that the condition of Pareto-optimality is not satisfied and the result is market failure. Thus, competitive markets fail due to market imperfection, asymmetric information, externalities and presence of public goods.

30. Marshall and Lerner put forth a technical condition, called the *Marshall-Lerner condition,* to explain the stability and instability of the foreign exchange market. The Marshall-Learner condition can be expressed as follows:

(*i*) When the sum of the price elasticity of imports (E_m) and the price elasticity of its exports (E_x) is greater than 1, in absolute terms, the foreign exchange market is stable and the BOP equilibrium is also stable. That is:

If $E_m + E_x > 1$, the foreign exchange market is stable.

(*ii*) When the sum of the price elasticity of imports (E_m) and the price elasticity of its exports (E_x) is lesser than 1, in absolute terms, then the foreign exchange market is unstable and BOP equilibrium is also unstable. That is,

If $E_m + E_x < 1$, foreign exchange market is unstable.

(*iii*) When the sum of the price elasticity of imports (E_m) and the price elasticity of exports (E_x) is equal to 1, in absolute terms, the foreign exchange market is stable and the BOP equilibrium is also stable. That is,

If $E_m + E_x = 1$, the foreign exchange market remains stable.

31. Net Barter or Commodity Terms of Trade: Frank William Taussig introduced the concept of the net barter or the commodity terms of trade. His net barter terms of trade, popularly called 'the commodity terms of trade', is the ratio between the import-prices and export-prices. Symbolically the net barter terms of trade can be written as:

$$N = \frac{X_P}{M_P} \times 100$$

where X_P and M_P stand for price index numbers of exports and imports, respectively, and N stands for net barter or commodity terms. The expression is multiplied by 100 only to get rid of the decimal.

32. Balance of payment reflected by export and import also influences the demand and supply of foreign currencies. The balance of payment is classified into:

(*a*) balance of payment on current account, and

(*b*) balance of payment on capital account.

The current account balance includes three items namely,

(*i*) Visible trade balance relating to imports and exports of goods which is known as trade balance.

(*ii*) Invisible items, i.e., receipts and payments for such services as shipping, banking, insurance, travel, and

(*iii*) Unilateral transfers like, donations.

The balance payments on current account indicates whether is it favourable or deficit balance for the period.

The balance of payments on capital account includes items such as, foreign investment, external assistance, commercial borrowings, NRI deposits.

33. Expansionary fiscal policy can crowd out private-sector spending; that is, an increase in government spending can reduce consumption and investment. Crowding out is usually discussed in the context of government spending financed by borrowing rather than by taxes. Increases in government borrowing drive up interest rates. As interest rates go up, investment falls, This sort of indirect crowding out works through the bond market.

34. Credit control policy is just an arm of economic policy which comes under the purview of the central bank. Therefore, its main objective is the attainment of high growth rate while maintaining reasonable stability of the internal purchasing power of money. The broad objectives of credit control policy in our country can be enumerated as under:

- To attain stability in exchange rate and money market of the country.
- To meet the financial requirement in the economy at all times.
- To control the business cycle and meet business needs.
- To stabilise the general price level.
- To promote and maintain high level of employment and income.
- To eliminate undue fluctuations in employment and production.

36. Deficits:

(*a*) **Revenue Deficit** refers to the excess of revenue expenditure over revenue receipts.

(*b*) **Budget Deficit** refers to the excess of total expenditure over total receipts. Here, total receipts include current revenue and net internal and external capital receipts of the governments.

(*c*) **Fiscal Deficit** refers to the difference between total expenditure (revenue, capital and loans net a repayment) on one hand; and on the other hand, revenue receipts plus and those capital receipts which are not in the form of borrowings but which in the end accrue to the government.

(*d*) **Primary Deficit** refers to fiscal deficit minus interest payments.

Monetised Deficit = Increment in Net RBI Credit to the Central Government.

38. A tax should be based on the taxpayer's *ability to pay*. The payment of a tax in proportion to the taxpayer's level of income results in an equitable distribution of the cost of supporting the government.

The concept of equality requires consideration of both horizontal and vertical equity. Horizontal equity exists when two similarly situated taxpayers are taxed the same. Vertical equity exists when taxpayers with different situations are taxed differently but fairly in relation to each taxpayer's ability to pay the tax. This means that those taxpayers who have the greatest ability to pay the tax should pay the greatest proportion of the tax.

39. The impact of tax refers to the immediate or direct money burden on the tax payer. The impact of tax is on the person who pays it in the first instance, to the taxing authority. The person on whom the impact of tax falls may try by some means or other to transfer the burden to some one else. The process of the transfer of the burden of a tax is known as shifting of a tax. The ultimate result of this process of shifting is known as the incidence of tax. The incidence therefore refers to the ultimate money burden of the tax which is non-shiftable. The incidence of the tax is on the person who finally pays it and bears the burden. Incidence falls on that person who does actually undergo the sacrifice. The government imposes the tax on the producer of the commodity, but the producer after paying to the government tries to shift the tax burden to the consumers by increasing the price of that product. Here the impact is on the producer but the incidence is on the final consumer of the good. Thus the impact of tax leads to shifting of the tax on others, which finally ends with incidence.

Taxes can be classified as direct tax and indirect tax. This classification is usually made on the basis of impact and incidence. A direct tax is one, the impact and incidence of which fall on the same person. In case of direct tax shifting is impossible. On the contrary indirect tax is one, the impact and incidence of which are on different persons. In case of indirect tax shifting is possible, partly or wholly.

40. Founded in 1989 with 12 member economies, the Asia-Pacific Economic Cooperation (APEC) has since grown to become a 21-member inter-governmental body that aims to promote economic growth, cooperation, trade, and investment in the Asia Pacific region. APEC's goals are articulated in the 1994 Bogor Declaration of Goals.

To achieve the Bogor Goals, APEC identified three areas of cooperation that are sometimes referred to as the 'Three Pillars' of APEC: trade and investment liberalization, business facilitation, and economic and technical cooperation. Trade and investment liberalization focuses on opening markets by reducing and eventually eliminating tariff and non-tariff barriers to trade and investment. Business facilitation focuses on reducing the cost of business transactions and improving access to trade information. Economic and technical cooperation focuses on providing training and cooperation to build capacities in all APEC member economies. Information and communication technology (ICT) is recognized as an important tool in APEC's work in all three pillars.

41. **External drain:** The term external drain refers to the cash withdrawn from the banks by the borrowers. Some of the borrowers are likely to withdraw part of their deposits in cash. With the withdrawal of cash, the excess reserves of the banks are automatically reduced. This reduces their power of credit creation.

44. The RBI has started publishing a set of new monetary aggregates following the recommendations of the *Working Group on Money Supply: Analytics and Methodology of Compilation* (Chairman, Dr. Y.V. Reddy) which submitted its report in June 1998. The Working Group recommended compilation of four monetary aggregates on the basis of the balance sheet of the banking sector in conformity with the norms of progressive liquidity: M^0 (monetary base), M^1 (narrow money), M^2 and M^3 (broad money). In addition to the monetary aggregates, the Working Group had recommended compilation of three liquidity aggregates namely, L^1, L^2 and L^3, which include select items of financial liabilities of non-depository financial corporations such as development financial institutions and non-banking financial companies accepting deposits from the public, apart from post office savings banks.

47. **The Ratchet Effect in Consumption Behaviour:** The Ratchet effect arises due to households' resistance against the fall in comsumption following a decrease in income. Duesenberry argues that when absolute income increases, absolute consumption increases, but when absolute income decreases, the households do not cut their consumption in proportion to the fall in their incomes. The second part of this rule holds because households get used to a certain standard of living in the long run and hence when their income falls, their consumption falls less than proportionately. When consumption does not fall in proportion to the fall in income, then APC rises and MPC falls. This is called ratchet effect in consumption behaviour.

48. The idea that people form their expectations about the future on the basis of all available information, including knowledge about policy changes and how they affect the economy, is called the rational-expectations hypothesis. According to this view, rather than merely assuming the future will be like the immediate past, people also consider the expected effects of changes in policy. Based on their understanding of economic policy, for example, people may alter their expectations regarding the future rate of inflation when the government runs a larger deficit or expands the supply of money more rapidly.

Perhaps an example will help clarify the rational-expectations hypothesis. Suppose prices had increased at an annual rate of 3 per cent during each of the past three years. In addition, assume that decision makers believe there is a relationship between the growth rate of the money supply and rising prices. They note that the money stock has expanded at a 12 per cent annual rate during the last nine months, up from the 4 per cent rate of the past several years. According to the rational-expectations hypothesis, they will integrate the recent monetary acceleration into their forecast of the future inflation rate. For example, they might project an increase in the inflation rate, perhaps to the 6 to 10 per cent range. In other words, they will expect the future inflation rate to respond to the more rapid growth of the money supply. In contrast, under the adaptive-expectations hypothesis, the shift to a more expansionary monetary policy would exert no impact on the expectations of people.

49. **Standard System of Note Issue:** Following are the main systems of currency issue:

1. **Simple Deposit System:** Under this system, the monetary authority is required to keep hundred per cent of the bullion (gold or silver) for every note issued. That is why it is also known as the Full Reserve System.
2. **Fixed Fiduciary System:** Under this system the Central Bank of a country is permitted to issue a fixed amount of notes without keeping any metallic reserves. This portion is called fiduciary system. But all notes issued above this amount must be converted by 100 per cent metallic reserves.
3. **Maximum Fiduciary System:** Under this system, there is a maximum limit up to which the central bank is authorised to issue notes without any gold reserves. But there has to be full backing of gold reserves beyond this limit.
4. **Proportional Reserve System:** Under this system the Central Bank is required to keep a certain percentage of gold against the note issue and the remainder of their note issue is covered by securities.
5. **The Minimum Reserve System:** Under this system the Central Bank is permitted to issue notes to any extent provided a fixed minimum reserves is maintained in gold and foreign securities.

51. The international economist Jagdish Bhagwati presented a different example of how changing terms of trade undermine the gains from trade. Bhagwati uses the traditional HO model to show how, in the case of a country large enough to influence international prices, the gains from increased international trade may be undermined by adverse price movements of a country's exports. Bhagwati called this phenomenon immiserizing growth, and it effectively refutes the generally accepted hypothesis that economic growth and international trade are always welfare enhancing and never cause any misery.

52. Marx's theory of surplus value makes distinctions between *constant capital* and *variable capital* and between *necessary labour* and *surplus labour* and it describes methods to increase surplus value. Constant capital refers to the part of capital that constitutes the means of production and does not, in the process of production, undergo any quantitative change of value. Variable capital, on the other hand, is "that part of capital, represented by labour power, [which] does, in the process of production, undergo an alteration of value. It both reproduces the equivalent of its own value, and it produces an excess, a surplus value, which may itself vary, may be more or less according to the circumstances.

For Marx, the appropriation of surplus value is the basis of profit, once other fixed and variable costs (*e.g.*, rent and raw materials) have been deducted. The rate of surplus value is defined as the ratio of surplus labour time to the necessary labour time.

This can be explained as follows:

Rate of surplus value

$$= \frac{s}{v} = \frac{\text{surplus labour time}}{\text{necessary labour time}}$$

The rate of surplus value expresses the degree of exploitation of the worker by the capitalist: "The rate of surplus value is therefore an exact expression for the degree of exploitation of labour power by capital, or of the labourer by the capitalist." The rate of exploitation is $e = s/v$, where v, the necessary labour time, is called variable capital because it varies during the production, contributing more value to output than it costs as an output.

53. Wiseman-Peacock Hypothesis: This thesis of the growth of public expenditure was given by Wiseman and Peacock in their well known study of public expenditure in the United Kingdom during the period 1890-1955. The main thesis of the authors is that public expenditure does not increase in a smooth and continuous manner. The increase in public expenditure over time has occurred in jerks or step-like manner. The general approach to the hypothesis refers to the three related concepts.

1. Displacement effect
2. Inspection effect
3. Concentration effect.

54. The movement from the older level of expenditure and taxation to a new and higher level is the *displacement effect*. The inadequacy of the revenue as compared with the required public expenditure creates an *inspection effect in favour of the government.* The government and the people review the revenue position and the need to find a solution of the important problems that have come up and agree to the required adjustments to finance the increased expenditure. They attain a new level of *tax tolerance.* They are now ready to tolerate a greater burden of taxation and as a result the general level of expenditure and revenue goes up. In this way, the public expenditure and revenue get stabilised at a new level till another disturbance occurs to cause a displacement effect. *Thus, each major disturbance leads to the government assuming a larger proportion of the total national economic activity.* In other words, there is a *concentration effect.* The concentration effect also refers to the apparent tendency for central government economic activity to grow faster than that of the state and local level governments.

57. The benefit principle holds that tax burdens should be distributed in proportion to how much a would-be taxpayer benefits, or gains, from public goods and services. This approach presumes a fundamentally different relationship between the individual and the state and how that relationship is reflected in tax policy.

The benefit principle is most easily applied to policies that govern charges for excludable public goods characterized by a market pricing mechanism. For example, the cost burden of toll roads, utilities, and some public recreational facilities can be assigned to those who utilize the goods the most by charging a simple fee for use. Fuel taxes paid by drivers are another way to transfer the cost of road construction and maintenance onto users. In many applications of the benefit principle, an individual's benefit is assumed to be proportional to their consumption. In each of the preceding examples, those who benefit from the good or service pay for it, and the more they benefit or consume, the more they pay. When a public good or service is priced purely in accordance with the benefit principle, those who do not utilize the good or service pay nothing.

The weakness of the benefit principle is not ignorance of time, but rather its bounded applicability. It is difficult, if not impossible, to apply the benefit principle to non-excludable, or "pure," public goods such as national defense and environmental protection. In theory, such goods could be financed through a user fee, but that would create a free-rider problem and a substantial administrative burden.

61. PGR for State-A

$$= \frac{1}{8} \times \frac{1}{800}((800-750)+(800-775)+(800-790))$$

$$= \frac{1}{8} \times \frac{1}{800}(50+25+10)$$

$$= \frac{1}{8} \times \frac{1}{800} \times 85$$

$= 0.01328 \approx 0.01329$

PGR for State-B

$$= \frac{1}{8} \times \frac{1}{800}((800-550)+(800-600)+(800-490))$$

$$= \frac{1}{6400}(250+200+310)$$

$= 0.11875 \approx 0.119.$

62. Head count ratio for State-A

$\frac{3}{8} = 0.375$

Head count ratio for State-B

$\frac{3}{8} = 0.375.$

64. Hedonic pricing: In many cases, the market value of an asset is affected by pollution. The hedonic pricing method infers the monetary equivalent of the damage that an increasing pollution level has caused from the change of the asset's market value. Imagine the following case: people own houses and property nearby an area where an airport is constructed. The airport will bring about some noise disturbance, which will cause a reduction in the demand for these houses and property on the market. The consequence is a dropping market price for these assets. From the respective price decline, a monetary measure for damage of the airport's noise pollution is inferred.

68. Deseasonalizing the Time Series: A time series that has had the seasonal effects removed is referred to as a deseasonalized time series, and the process of using the seasonal indexes to remove the seasonal effects from a time series is referred to as deseasonalizing the time series. Using a multiplicative decomposition model, we deseasonalize a time series by dividing each observation by its corresponding seasonal index. The multiplicative decomposition model is:

$Y_t = \text{Trend}_t \times \text{Seasonal}_t \times \text{Irregular}_t$

So, when we divide each time series observation (Y_t) by its corresponding seasonal index, the resulting data sow only trend and random variability (the irregular component).

69. The optimum theory of population was propounded by Edwin Cannan in 1924 in his book Wealth and later popularised by Robbins, Dalton and Carr-Saunders. The proponents of this theory believes in the linkage between the size of population and the production of wealth as distinguished from Malthusian views between population and food supply.

The optimum population is the desired ideal number of the population that a country should have taking into consideration available resources as its command and also of means of production of the country. It will yield the maximum returns or income per head, considering its resources. Any deviation from this optimum-sized population will lead to a reduction in the per capita income. If the increase in population is followed by the increase in per capita income, the country is under-pupulated and it can afford to increase its population till it reaches the optimum level. On the contrary, if the increase in population leads to diminution in per capita income, the country is over-populated and needs a decline in population till the per capita income is maximised.

70. Linear Programming Problems are solved by some methods like the *graphical method, the systematic trial and error method (enumeration method)* and *the simplex method.*

72. The fundamental difference between the conventional goods (*i.e.*, bread) and environmental goods (*i.e.*, pollution) is that in case of conventional goods, market allocates goods efficiently, while in the case of environmental goods market fails to allocate it efficiently. It is the nature of environmental goods (*i.e.*, pollution) that leads to the market failure.

The feature of non-rival consumption and non-excludability paves the way for failure of the market for environmental goods.

74. By the identification problem we mean whether numerical estimates of the parameters of a structural equation can be obtained from the estimated reduced-form coefficients. If this can be done, we say that the particular equation is *identified.* If this cannot be done, then we say that the equation under consideration is *unidentified,* or *underidentified.* An identified equation may be either exactly (or fully or just) *identified* or *overidentified.* It is said to be exactly identified if unique numerical values of the structural parameters can be obtained. It is said to be overidentified if more than one numerical value can be obtained for some of the parameters of the structural equations.

75. Revenue, $R = P \times x$

$$= (60 - 3x)x = 60x - 3x^2$$

Profit, $\pi = R - C$

$$= 60x - 3x^2 - 40 - 12x$$

$$= 48x - 3x^2 - 40$$

For maximum,

$$\frac{d\pi}{dx} = 0$$

$$\Rightarrow \quad 48 - 6x = 0$$

$$6x = 48$$

$$\Rightarrow \quad x = 8.$$

77. The Second National Commission on Labour (NCL), 1999, has made certain significant and path-breaking recommendations. Some of the points from the reports include the following:

1. The Commission recommends a specific provision in the Trade Unions Act to enable workers in the unorganized sector to form trade unions and register them. It has recommended a waiver of the condition of employer-employee relationship and also of the 10 per cent membership in the establishment. This is a path-breaking recommendation which can pave the way for bringing into the fold of the labour movement 92 per cent of the workers in the unorganized sector.
2. The Commission has recommended the use of 'check off' system to determine the negotiating agent in an establishment. Again, by fixing 66 per cent membership for entitlement as negotiating agent, it has not favoured the principle of simple majority but has opted for two-thirds majority. If this condition is not satisfied, a composite negotiating agent from among representatives of unions with support of more than 25 per cent has been recommended.
3. It has recommended a three-tier system of *Lok Adalats,* labour courts and the Labour Relations Commission. While the *Lok Adalats* and labour courts deal with individual grievances and complaints, the Labour Relations Commission has been empowered to deal with both individual problems and those of collective bargaining.

4. It has recommended that labour courts should have final authority in issues relating to labour, and that jurisdiction of civil courts in this area be banned. By imposing on the unions the condition of 10 per cent membership to represent labour in varied fora, it has eliminated the role of very small unions parading as genuine representatives of labour. The suggestion of forming an All India Labour Judicial Service is welcome.
5. It has guaranteed 8.33 per cent bonus for all employees while asserting that every employer should pay each worker one month's bonus before an appropriate festival. Any demand in excess of this up to a maximum of 20 per cent of the wages will be subject to negotiation.
6. It has recommended that the existing system of two wage ceilings for reckoning entitlement and for calculation of bonus should be suitably increased to ₹ 7,500 and ₹ 3,500 for entitlement and calculation, respectively. It has presented the minimum and maximum limits for bonus and permitted freedom for negotiation.
7. Its categorical view that no exemption from labour laws should be allowed to export promotion zones or special economic zones, is further evidence of the Commission's sincerity in implementing the laws.

80. In hypothesis testing it is possible that, based on the data, a true null hypothesis is rejected. This mistake is called a Type I error. A Type II error occurs when a false null hypothesis is accepted. The probability of making a Type I error is denoted by α, and is another way to define the level of significance. The probability of making a Type II error is denoted by β.

81. The Government of India had set up an Education Commission in 1966 under the chairmanship of Dr. D.S. Kothari, and eminent educationist to determine the need and give an estimate of Gross Domestic Product (GDP) required for promoting education. Dr. Kothari emphasised the critical relationship between education and productivity and underlined the role of education in India's national and economic development. It stated very categorically; "Education as investment in human resources plays an important role among the factors which contribute to economic growth." It also stated that during the next 20 years, expenditure on education should be stepped up to 6% of the GDP.

82.
$$P_e = \frac{AR}{AR - MR} = \frac{15}{15-5} = \frac{15}{10} = 1.5.$$

85. Mean – Mode = 3(Mean – Median)

Mode = 3 Median – 2 Mean

⇒ 10 = 3 × 20 – 2 × Mean

10 = 60 – 2 mean

⇒ 2 Mean = 50

Mean = 25.

88. We have,

$$A = \begin{bmatrix} 6 & 5 & 5 \\ 3 & -11 & -5 \\ 3 & -5 & -2 \end{bmatrix}$$

$$|A| = [6\{(-11)(-2) - (-5)(-5)\} - 5\{(3)(-2) - (3)(-5)\} + 5\{(3)(-5) - (-11)(3)\}]$$
$$= [6\{22 - 25\} - 5\{-6 + 15\} + 5\{-15 + 33\}]$$
$$= 6 \times (-3) - 5(9) + 5(18)$$
$$= -18 - 45 + 90$$
$$= -63 + 90$$
$$= 27.$$

90. The coefficient of determination r^2 indicates the proportion of total variance in the dependent variable that is explained or accounted for by the variation in the independent variable.

Here, $r = \sqrt{0.8 \times 0.6}$

$= \sqrt{0.48}$

$\therefore \quad r^2 = 0.48$

$= 48\%$.

92. A difference equation expresses discrete changes in dependent variable with respect to discrete changes in the independent variable. For example, $Y_{t+1} - Y_t = 4$ or $\Delta Y_t = 4$ is a difference equation as it expresses a discrete change in the dependent variable Y in relation to a discrete change in the independent variable *t*. An equation, such as $dy/dt = 4$ is a differential equation as it expresses an infinitesimally small change in *y* in relation to an infinitesimally small change in *t*.

93. In fact, this such issue of who should have rights, the pollution or the victim over the property rights, was firstly raised by Ronald Coase in his important paper that contributed to his winning the Noble prize in economics. Coase (1960) asks whether it is logical to assign rights to one or the other of these parties the victim or the polluter. One of the Coase's conclusion is that under some conditions, it makes no difference to efficiency whether polluter has a right to pollute or the victims has a right to clean air. The right to pollute is a property right that has value, if trade is allowed in those rights, efficiency should prevail, no matter how they were initially allocated. If the right is worth more to the victim than the polluter, this victim will end up with the right, no matter how it was initially distributed. Of course, the initial distribution of rights does matter to question of equity. Rights can be valuable. Vesting someone with a right is like giving them money and resources.

Coase's arguments regarding property rights are often dubbed in 'Coase Theorem'. There are two parts of the 'Coase Theorem'. The first concern the case in which there are no impediments to buying and selling pollution rights. In this case, the initial distribution of rights does not matters. The second involves impediments to trading property rights.

Coase theorem assumes a world in which some producers or consumers are subject to externalities generated by other producers or consumers.

Further assumes:

1. everyone has perfect information,
2. consumer and producers are price taken,
3. there is costless count system for enforcing arguments,
4. producers maximising profits and consumer maximising utility,
5. there is no wealth or income effect, and
6. there are no transaction costs.

In this case, the initial assignment of property rights regarding the externalities does not matters for efficiency. On the other hand, any of those conditions, doesn't hold, the initial assignment of rights does matter.

94. A currency is said to be convertible when it can be freely exchanged for another currency at market rates. Transaction of current account includes dealing with payments relating to foreign trade, travel and other services. Capital account deals with transaction in financial assets. While India has made the Indian rupee fully convertible on current account, it is yet to accept capital account convertibility as a goal. Broadly, capital account convertibility would mean freedom for firms and residents to freely buy into overseas assets such as equity, bonds, property, and acquire ownership of overseas firms besides free repatriation of proceeds by foreign investors.

95. Hawkins-Simon Conditions for the Viability of the System: The input-output solution can also be given a negative answer implying that more than 1 unit of the product is being used as an input in producing 1 unit of that particular product. To avoid such situations, the following Hawkins-Simon conditions are imposed:

1. The determinant | I – A | of the Leontief matrix must be positive.
2. The diagonal elements: $1 - a_{11}$, $1 - a_{22}$... $1 - a_{nn}$, of the Leontief matrix (I – A) should all be positive or in other words, a_{11}, a_{22}, ... a_{nn} should be all less than 1.

97. The internal rate of return (IRR) is the discount rate that sets the present value of the project cash flows equal to the initial investment outlay. In other words, the IRR is the discount rate that equates the project NPV to zero.

The relationship between the NPV method and the IRR method can be summarized as follows:

NPV	IRR
NPV > 0	IRR > Discount rate
NPV = 0	IRR = Discount rate
NPV < 0	IRR < Discount rate

Benefit-Cost Ratio: The benefit-cost ratio (BCR) of a project is the present value of all project revenues divided by the present value of all project costs. The equation for the benefit-cost ratio is:

$$\text{BCR} = \frac{\text{Sum of discounted revenues}}{\text{Sum of discounted costs}}$$

$$\text{BCR} = \frac{\sum_{t=0}^{n}\left[\frac{R_t}{(1+i)^t}\right]}{\sum_{t=0}^{n}\left[\frac{C_t}{(1+i)^t}\right]}$$

We can see from this equation that when the present value of project revenue is equal to the present value of project costs, the BCR of the project will be equal to one (BCR = 1). Note that when the present value of project revenues is equal to the present value of project costs, the net present value of the project will be equal to zero (NPV = 0). Given this relationship, if the BCR is greater than 1, then NPV will be greater than 0.

98. $$e_x^0 = \frac{T_x}{I_x}$$

$$= \frac{48,50,000}{90,000} = 53.89.$$

Previous Years Paper

NTA—UGC-NET

Junior Reaserch Fellowship & Assistant Professor Eligibility Exam

Economics, December-2018

PAPER-II

Note: *This paper contains* **hundred (100)** *objective type questions of* **two (2)** *marks each.* ***All*** *questions are* ***compulsory***.

1. Consider the following statements about the average fixed cost of a firm:
(*i*) Its slope is always negative
(*ii*) Its slope is always greater than one
(*iii*) Its slope is always equal to one
(*iv*) Elasticity with respect to output is equal to one

Choose the correct answer from the code given below:

Codes:

A. (*i*) & (*iv*) B. only (*iii*)
C. (*ii*) & (*iii*) D. only (*i*)

2. In the year 2015-16, India has not been an importer of which of the following products?
(*i*) Apples (*ii*) Rice
(*iii*) Pulses

Choose the correct answer from the code given below:

Codes:

A. (*ii*) & (*iii*) B. (*i*) & (*iii*)
C. Only (*ii*) D. (*i*), (*ii*) & (*iii*)

3. Planning from below is known as:
A. functional planning
B. structural planning
C. centralized planning
D. decentralized planning

4. Which is the required capital adequacy ratio for a new bank to apply for a license under the draft guidelines of RBI?
A. 9% B. 10%
C. 11% D. 12%

5. Arrange the following crop insurance schemes in the chronological order of their launch
(*i*) Comprehensive crop insurance scheme
(*ii*) National agriculture insurance scheme
(*iii*) Modified national agriculture insurance scheme
(*iv*) Pradhan mantri fasal bima yojana

Choose the correct answer from the code given below:

A. (*i*), (*iii*), (*ii*), (*iv*) B. (*ii*), (*iii*), (*i*), (*iv*)
C. (*i*), (*ii*), (*iii*), (*iv*) D. (*iii*), (*ii*), (*iv*), (*i*)

6. Balance of payment on capital account does not include:
A. government loans to foreign governments
B. net income transfers
C. balancing foreign direct investments
D. foreign portfolio investment

7. Which of the following statements is/are correct about Uzawa's theorem?
A. The technical progress is Harrod neutral only
B. The growth rate of output per worker, consumption per worker and capital per worker are equal and constant over time
C. All of the above
D. The production function is linear homogeneous

8. The price elasticity of a linear supply curve through the origin is:.
A. Unity B. Less than unity
C. Zero D. Infinity

9. Opportunity cost theorem assumes that:
A. Labour is homogeneous
B. Labour is the only factor of production
C. Cost of commodity is equal to labour cost only
D. None of the above

10. Which of the following statements about rational expectations is false?
A. It implies that the expected changes in demand have no effect on unemployment
B. It assumes that people take account of all information
C. It assumes that on an average the forecasts made by the public are correct
D. It implies that unexpected changes in demand have long lasting effect on both unemployment and price level

11. Consider the following statements in the context of the New trade theory:
(*i*) It explains why countries trade in similar goods.
(*ii*) It assumes free trade.
(*iii*) It assumes that trade takes place in monopolistic conditions.
(*iv*) It exploits the economies of scale in production.
Which of the above statements are correct? Choose the correct answer from the codes given below:
Codes:
A. (*ii*) & (*iv*) B. (*i*) & (*iii*)
C. (*i*) & (*ii*) D. (*i*), (*iii*) & (*iv*)

12. Who among the following has been awarded the Nobel prize in Economics "for analysis of markets with asymmetric information"?
A. Robert A Mundell
B. George Akerlof
C. Richard Thaler
D. Paul Krugman

13. Intellectual property rights include:
A. Patents
B. Copy rights
C. Trade mark
D. All of the above

14. Which of the following statements is true for the Indian economy according to the World bank figures for 2017?
A. India is now the world's sixth biggest economy
B. Both above
C. India's GDP amounted to $5 trillion at the end of 2017
D. None of the above

15. According to the cash balance approach the elasticity of demand for money:
A. Is equal to one
B. Less than one
C. Fluctuates with the changes in the phases of inflation
D. Is more than one

16. Which of the following is considered as the third stage in the Rostow's stages of economic growth model?
A. High mass consumption
B. Traditional society
C. Pre-conditions for a take off
D. Take off

17. Which amongst the following is/are correct for the Keynesian model?
A. It is supply determined
B. It ignores the money market
C. It assumes full employment of resources
D. None of the above

18. What is not true for the third stage of the theory of demographic transition?
A. Population growth becomes zero
B. Population growth rate approximately stabilizes in a narrow range
C. Death rate declines but slowly
D. Birth rate declines faster

19. Devaluation will be more effective when
(*i*) International capital is freely mobile.
(*ii*) International capital is not freely mobile.
(*iii*) Marginal propensity to import is high.
Which of the following statements is/are correct? Choose the correct answer from the code given below:
A. Only (*iii*) B. (*ii*) & (*iii*)
C. (*i*) & (*iii*) D. Only (*ii*)

20. Which of the following concept-economist pairs is not correctly matched?

A. Super multiplier – J.M. Keynes

B. Golden rule of accumulation – E.S. Phelps

C. Turnpike conjecture – Dorfman, Samuleson & Solow

D. Knife edge problem – Harrod Domar

21. Technological dualism means:

A. Prevalence of different production functions in the advanced and traditional sectors in under developed countries.

B. Prevalence of different production functions in the industrial sector in under developed countries.

C. Prevalence of different technologies in agricultural sector in underdeveloped countries.

D. Prevalence of different production functions in domestic and export sectors of under developed countries.

22. "Round Tripping" in international trade is a method:

A. To boost foreign direct investment

B. Of financing start ups

C. To evade tax

D. To increase exports

23. According to the union budget, which of the following fiscal deficit targets for 2018-19 is correct.

A. 4.3% of the GDP B. 5.3% of the GDP

C. 4.5 % of the GDP D. 3.3 % of the GDP

24. If $(K/L)_A > (K/L)_B$, then:

A. Country A is capital abundant

B. Country A is labour abundant

C. Capital is dear in country A

D. Country A is having cheap labour

25. Consider the following statements about the law of variable proportion:

(*i*) Input ratio remains unchanged

(*ii*) Ultimately the marginal and average product of variable input becomes negative

(*iii*) Effect of technological change is visible on output

Choose the correct answer from the codes given below:

Codes:

A. Only (*ii*) is correct

B. None of the above statements is correct

C. (*i*) & (*ii*) are correct

D. (*ii*) & (*iii*) are correct

26. The original interpretation of balanced growth relates to:

A. equal amount to investment in all sectors

B. large scale expansion of activities to overcome divergence between private and social benefits

C. all sectors growing at the same rate

D. absence of shortages or excesses

27. An income tax will be progressive if:

A. marginal rate of tax is greater than average rate of tax

B. marginal rate of tax is equal to the average rate of the tax

C. marginal rate of tax is less than the average rate of tax

D. marginal rate of tax is zero

28. An increase in the level of government spending, other things being equal, will in the IS-LM model:

A. increase the level of equilibrium income at all interest rate, shifting the IS curve right

B. Increase interest rates, shifting the LM curve to the left

C. Lower interest rates, shifting LM curve to the right

D. Always move an economy to full employment

29. Who is the author of the book, "I do what I do"?

A. Raghuram G Rajan

B. Amartya Sen

C. Jagdish N. Bhagwati

D. Arvind Panagariya

30. According to Schumpeter theory of development, which of the following statements is correct.
A. Democracy enhances the efficiency of an economic system
B. None of the above are correct
C. All of the above are correct
D. The expansion of economic output is limited by the real savings of the economy

31. Which of the following correctly describes the Musgrave and Thin's measure of tax progressivity?
Where
G_a = Gini coefficient after tax
G_b = Gini coefficient before tax
A. $M = G_b / G_a$
B. $M = 1 - G_a / 1 - G_b$
C. $M = G_a / G_b$
D. $M = 1 - G_b / 1 - G_a$

32. Who among the following said that "Money is a temporary abode of purchasing power"?
A. James Tobin B. William J Baumol
C. Irving Fisher D. Milton Friedman

33. In a hypothetical economy, the rate of growth of nominal GDP is 15% per annum, the annual rate of growth of GDP deflator is 5%. If the population is growing at the rate of growth of 2% per annum, what will be the annual rate of growth of per capita real GDP?
A. 10% B. 3%
C. 7% D. 8%

34. GST which came into effect from 1st July, 2017 has four (04) tax slabs applicable to the commodities and services in India. Which of the following tax slabs are correct?
A. 8%, 12%, 15% and 18%
B. 5%, 8%, 12% and 18%
C. 5%, 12%, 18% and 28%
D. 8%, 12%, 18% and 28%

35. Which amongst the following is not an instrument of money market?
A. Treasury bill
B. Commercial paper
C. Certificate of deposit
D. Preference share

36. An economic region of production consist of:
A. The highest points of all isoquants
B. The negatively sloped portions of all isoquants
C. The positively sloped portions of all isoquants
D. The middle of all isoquants

37. Match List-I with List-II and choose the correct answer from the code given below:

List-I	*List-II*
(*a*) N = Pk	(*i*) A.C. Pigou
(*b*) M = PKT	(*ii*) Keynes
(*c*) P = KR/M	(*iii*) Alfred Marshal
(*d*) M = KPY	(*iv*) D.H. Robertson

Codes:

	(*a*)	(*b*)	(*c*)	(*d*)
A.	(*i*)	(*ii*)	(*iii*)	(*iv*)
B.	(*iii*)	(*ii*)	(*i*)	(*iv*)
C.	(*iv*)	(*i*)	(*ii*)	(*iii*)
D.	(*ii*)	(*iv*)	(*i*)	(*iii*)

38. Arrange the following events in chronological order regarding Indian Economy.
(*i*) First phase of Nationalism of banks
(*ii*) Establishment of Narasimham Committee on the banking system
(*iii*) Enactment of FEMA Act in India
(*iv*) Establishment of EXIM Bank in India

Choose the correct answer from the code given below:
Codes:
A. (*i*), (*ii*), (*iii*), (*iv*)
B. (*i*), (*iii*), (*ii*), (*iv*)
C. (*i*), (*iii*), (*iv*), (*ii*)
D. (*i*), (*iv*), (*ii*), (*iii*)

39. Consider the following:
(*i*) Fringe benefits tax
(*ii*) Capital gains tax
(*iii*) Securities transactions tax

Which of the above is/are direct tax/taxes? Choose the correct answer from the code given below:
A. (*i*), (*ii*) & (*iii*) B. (*ii*) & (*iii*)
C. (*i*) & (*iii*) D. Only (*i*)

40. Match List-I (Authors) with List-II (Books) and choose the correct answer from the code given below.

List-I (Author)	***List-II (Book)***
(*a*) Milton Friedman	(*i*) Das Capital
(*b*) Joseph Schumpeter	(*ii*) Capitalism & Freedom
(*c*) Karl Marx	(*iii*) Capital in the twenty first century
(*d*) Thomas Piketty	(*iv*) Capitalism, Socialism & Democracy

Codes:

	(*a*)	(*b*)	(*c*)	(*d*)
A.	(*iii*)	(*i*)	(*iv*)	(*ii*)
B.	(*iii*)	(*ii*)	(*i*)	(*iv*)
C.	(*iv*)	(*iii*)	(*i*)	(*ii*)
D.	(*ii*)	(*iv*)	(*i*)	(*iii*)

41. Which of the following is not included in the category of bio-fuels?

A. Bio diesel
B. Gobar gas
C. Bio ethanol
D. Compressed natural gas

42. The public expenditure in India is classified as capital and revenue. Which of the following is/are revenue expenditure?

(*i*) Subsidies
(*ii*) Interest payments on public debt
(*iii*) Wages and salaries

Choose the correct answer from code given below:

Codes:

A. (*ii*) & (*iii*)
B. (*i*), (*ii*) & (*iii*)
C. (*i*) & (*ii*)
D. (*i*) & (*iii*)

43. Global competitiveness report is released by which of the following organizations?

A. World Trade Organisation
B. World Economic Forum
C. European Union
D. World Bank

44. Which of the following is not part of the Peacock-Wiseman hypothesis?

A. Announcement effect
B. Inspection effect
C. Concentration effect
D. Displacement effect

45. What is true for Neo-classical growth model?

(*i*) Rate of interest and profit are flexible.
(*ii*) Capital is heterogeneous.
(*iii*) Perfect competition prevails.
(*iv*) Capital and labour are substitutable.

Choose the correct answer from the code given below:

A. (*i*), (*ii*) & (*iii*)
B. (*i*), (*iii*) & (*iv*)
C. (*ii*) & (*iii*)
D. All of the above

46. Which of the following is the appropriate measure of openness of the economy?

A Exports – Imports

B. $\frac{\text{Exports} - \text{Imports}}{\text{Population}}$

C. $\frac{\text{Exports} - \text{Imports}}{\text{GDP}}$

D. $\frac{\text{Exports}}{\text{Imports}}$

47. Development expenditure of the Central Government does not include:

(*i*) Grant to state under centrally sponsored schemes.
(*ii*) Expenditure on social and community services.
(*iii*) Expenditure on economic services.
(*iv*) Defence expenditure.

A. (*iii*) & (*iv*)
B. Only (*iv*)
C. (*i*) & (*ii*)
D. (*ii*) & (*iii*)

48. The Inada conditions are applicable to:

A. A well behaved investment function
B. A well behaved consumption function
C. A well behaved technical progress function
D. A well behaved production function

49. As per the SRS bulletin of September 2017, the estimated death rate for Kerala is 7.6, while for Bihar it is 6. From these data which is the correct inference to draw?

A. Life expectancy in Bihar is higher than that in Kerala
B. Health condition of people in Bihar is better than that in Kerala
C. Suicide rate in Kerala is very high
D. Ageing of population in Kerala is faster than in Bihar

50. A rise in general price level may be caused by which amongst the following?

(*i*) An increase in the money supply.
(*ii*) An increase in the aggregate level of output.
(*iii*) An increase in the effective demand.

Choose the correct answer from the code given below:

A. (*i*), (*ii*) & (*iii*) B. (*i*) & (*ii*)
C. (*i*) & (*iii*) D. Only (*iii*)

51. The frequent farm loan waivers in India may give rise to the problem of:

A. Moral Hazard B. Debt Overhang
C. Risk Aversion D. Adverse Selection

52. The presumption that costly new knowledge would be undersupplied by the private sector is based on the essential characteristic of new knowledge.

It is (A) _____ and (B)______

A. (A) Non rivalous (B) Excludable
B. (A) rivalous (B) non excludable
C. (A) Non rivalous (B) non excludable
D. (A) rivalous (B) excludable

53. Arrange the following states in descending order according to Maternal Mortality Ratio (MMR) as per the special Bulletin of SRS May, 2018.

(*i*) Assam (*ii*) Bihar
(*iii*) Madhya Pradesh (*iv*) Uttar Pradesh

Choose the correct answer from the code given below:

A. (*iii*), (*ii*), (*i*), (*iv*) B. (*ii*), (*iv*), (*iii*), (*i*)
C. (*iv*), (*i*), (*ii*), (*iii*) D. (*i*), (*iv*), (*iii*), (*ii*)

54. Which of the following is not an objective of Marginal cost of funds based Lending rate (MCLR)?

A. To enable banks to become more competitive
B. To ensure availability of bank credit at interest rates which are fair to borrowers as well as banks
C. To improve the transmission of policy rates into the lending rates of banks
D. To enable the RBI to achieve the inflation target

55. The problem of adverse selection arises due to:

A. Full Information
B. Asymmetric information
C. Wrong information
D. No information

56. To compute the 'Index of Sustainable Economic Welfare', which of the following corrections is/are made in the value of GDP?

A. Subtract the monetary value of depreciation
B. Subtract the cost of environmental degradation
C. Subtract the monetary value of loss due to floods and droughts
D. Subtract the monetary value of expenditure on defence

57. Which of the following is/are true for Karl Marx's theory of economic development?

A. Mode of production changes independently
B. Both above
C. Relations in production change independently
D. None of the above

58. In the context of 'Transformation of Aspirational districts' programme consider the following statements:

(*i*) There are 115 districts in this programme.
(*ii*) The core strategy of this programme is convergence, collaboration and competition.

(*iii*) There are 49 key performance indicators to measure the progress of the districts.

Choose the correct answer from the code given below:

A. (*i*) & (*iii*) B. (*i*), (*ii*) & (*iii*)
C. (*ii*) & (*iii*) D. (*i*) & (*ii*)

59. In the basis Neo classical growth model, where does the growth equilibrium occur?

A. Where capital per worker equals output per worker
B. Where investment per worker equals capital per worker
C. Where investment per worker is equal to savings per worker
D. Where investment per worker equals depreciation of capital for worker

60. T.W. Shultz has given following ratios in relation to education for economic growth?

A. Education-capital and labour ratio
B. Education-labour, education-income and education-investment ratio
C. Education-income ratio
D. Education-labour ratio

61. Which of the following act as an instrument to help in the borrowing by the government?

(*i*) Repo rate (*ii*) Reverse Repo rate
(*iii*) CRR (*iv*) SLR

Choose the correct answer from the code given below:

A. (*iii*) & (*iv*) B. Only (*iv*)
C. (*i*) & (*iii*) D. (*i*) & (*iv*)

62. Consider the following statements.

(*i*) Minimum support price (MSP) policy of India covers only wheat, paddy and coarse cereals.

(*ii*) Minimum Support Price (MSP) for Grade A paddy is always higher than that of the common paddy.

Choose the correct answer from the code given below:

Codes:

A. Both (*i*) & (*ii*) B. Only (*i*)
C. Only (*ii*) D. Neither (*i*) nor (*ii*)

63. On which of the following do Keynesians and Monetarists agree?

A. When there is recessionary gap, flexible wages will retrieve the labour market to equilibrium quickly
B. The most important cause of demand shock is changes in supply
C. Output deviates at times from the potential output because of demand shocks
D. The demand for money is interest elastic

64. Which one of the statements about Pareto optimality is incorrect?

A. Consumers maximize their satisfaction
B. There is perfect competition in the factor and commodity market
C. Consumers have cardinal utility functions
D. All the factors are used in production of all the commodities

65. Which of the following will result in the crowding effect in the economy?

(*i*) Public borrowings to finance spending on infrastructure
(*ii*) Public borrowings to finance spending on salaries and wages
(*iii*) Public borrowings to finance spending on health and education
(*iv*) Public borrowings to finance spending on skill development

Choose the correct answer from the code given below:

A. (*i*) & (*ii*)
B. (*iii*) & (*iv*)
C. (*i*), (*ii*) & (*iii*)
D. (*i*), (*iii*) & (*iv*)

66. Which of the following statements is/are correct about normal profit?

A. It is earned in the long period only
B. It is earned only in perfect competition
C. It is earned in both the long period and the short period
D. It is earned in the short period only

67. The concept of Universal Banking in India was recommended by which of the following committee?
A. Y.H. Malegam Committee
B. S. Padmanabhan Committee
C. R.H. Khan Committee
D. Abid Hussain Committee

68. Consider the following diagram and the statements.

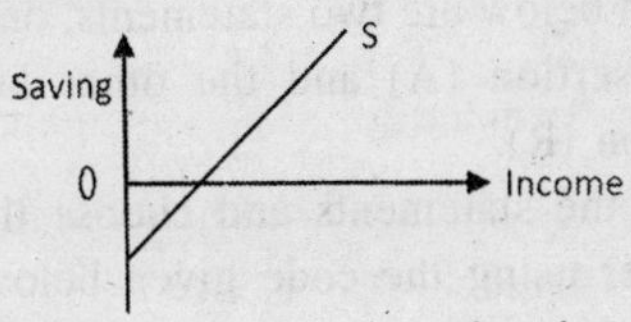

(*i*) Saving is positively related to income
(*ii*) Marginal propensity to save is positive but less than 1

Choose the correct answer from the code given below:
Codes:
A. Both (*i*) & (*ii*) B. Neither (*i*) & (*ii*)
C. Only (*i*) D. Only (*ii*)

69. In an economy with a linear homogeneous Cobb Douglas production function, the share of capital and labour in total output are, respectively, 40% and 60%. The capital stock and labour force are growing, respectively at 8% and 3% per annum. If the rate of growth of output is recorded as 7% per annum, then the rate of growth of Total Factor Productivity will be:
A. 2% B. 10%
C. 4% D. 11%

70. Which of the following is not a macroeconomic challenge before Indian Economy as of now?
A. Widening current account deficit
B. Rising protectionism in the world
C. High imports of gold
D. Depreciation of Indian rupee

71. Which of the following are the objectives of the Commission for Agricultural costs and prices (CACP)?
(*i*) To ensure meaningful real income levels to the farmers.
(*ii*) To stabilize agricultural prices.
(*iii*) To protect the interest of the consumers.

Choose the correct answer from the code given below:
Codes:
A. All of the above B. (*ii*) & (*iii*)
C. (*i*) & (*iii*) D. (*i*) & (*ii*)

72. According to the New classical economics, Real Business Cycles are the result of which of the following?
(*i*) Innovations (*ii*) Bad weather
(*iii*) Tax policy (*iv*) Debt policy

Choose the correct answer from the code given below:
A. (*i*) & (*ii*) B. (*ii*) & (*iv*)
C. (*iii*) & (*iv*) D. (*i*) & (*iii*)

73. Who amongst the following economists treated nature to be niggardly?
(*i*) J.S. Mill
(*ii*) David Ricardo
(*iii*) Karl Marx
(*iv*) Thomas Robert Malthus

Choose the correct answer from the code given below:
A. (*iii*) & (*iv*) B. (*i*), (*ii*) & (*iii*)
C. (*ii*) & (*iii*) D. (*ii*) & (*iv*)

74. Why are indirect taxes are regressive?
A. None of the above are correct
B. They are charged at higher rates than direct tax
C. They are charged at the same rate for all income groups
D. Both above are correct

75. According to Bent Hansen which amongst the following were treated as factors enhancing effective demand?
(*i*) Public expenditure
(*ii*) Rising population
(*iii*) Banking and financial system

Choose the correct answer from the code given below:
A. (*i*) & (*ii*) B. (*i*), (*ii*) & (*iii*)
C. (*ii*) & (*iii*) D. (*i*) & (*iii*)

76. Match the List-I with List-II and choose the correct answer from the code given below.

List-I	*List-II*
(*a*) absorptive capacity of capital	(*i*) M. Kalecki
(*b*) technological dualism	(*ii*) A.O. Hirschman
(*c*) physical quality of life index	(*iii*) D. Morris
(*d*) permissive and compulsive sequence of expanding industries	(*iv*) B. Higgins

Codes:

	(*a*)	(*b*)	(*c*)	(*d*)
A.	(*ii*)	(*iv*)	(*iii*)	(*i*)
B.	(*i*)	(*iv*)	(*iii*)	(*ii*)
C.	(*iv*)	(*iii*)	(*ii*)	(*i*)
D.	(*i*)	(*ii*)	(*iii*)	(*iv*)

77. Historically the terms of trade of the developing countries have been unfavourable due to the fact that when income in developed countries rises, the demand for primary goods declines because:

A. income elasticity of demand for primary goods is high
B. income elasticity of demand for primary goods is low
C. income elasticity of demand for primary goods is zero
D. price elasticity of demand for primary goods is high

78. The National Rural Health Mission was launched in the year:

A. 1991 B. 1998
C. 2005 D. 2009

79. If for the constant elasticity of substitution production function, the value of the substitution parameter is –1, the elasticity of substitution will be:

A. Indeterminate
B. Infinite
C. Zero
D. Unity

80. The statements, 'Too much money chasing too few goods' is based on which of the following theoretical concepts?

A. Real balance effects
B. Inventory theoretic approach to the demand for money
C. Quantity theory of prices
D. Quantity theory of money

81. Given below are two statements, one labelled as assertion (A) and the other labelled as Reason (R).

Read the statements and choose the correct answer using the code given below.

Assertion (A) : In an oligopolistic market, there is price rigidity.

Reason (R) : Rival firms match price decrease but no price increase.

Codes:

A. Both A and R are true and R is the correct explanation of A
B. A is false, but R is true
C. A is true, but R is false
D. Both A and R are true, but R is not the correct explanation of A

82. Given below are two statements, one labelled as assertion (A) and the other labelled as Reason (R).

Read the statements and choose the correct answer using the code given below.

Assertion (A) : In the P.N. Rosenstein Rodan model the positive role of indivisibilities in production has been analysed.

Reason (R) : Removal of indivisibilities leads to constant returns to scale in production.

Code:

A. A is true, but R is false
B. A is false, but R is true
C. Both A and R are true, and R is the correct explanation of A
D. Both A and R are true, but R is not the correct explanation of A

83. Given below are two statements, one labelled as assertion (A) and the other labelled as Reason (R).
Read the statements and choose the correct answer using the code given below.
Assertion (A) : A progressive income tax is based on equimarginal sacrifice.
Reason (R) : Higher the income, lower will be the marginal utility of money for the tax payer.
Codes:
A. A is false, but R is true
B. Both A and R are true, but R is not the correct explanation of A
C. Both A and R are true, and R is the correct explanation of A
D. A is true, but R is false

84. Below are two statements, one labelled as assertion (A) and the other labelled as Reason (R).
Read the statements and choose the correct answer using the code given below.
Assertion (A) : India is a service sector driven economy.
Reason (R) : Share of the service sector in total employment is highest.
Codes:
A. A is true, but R is false
B. A is false, but R is true
C. Both A and R are true, but R is not the correct explanation of A
D. Both A and R are true, and R is the correct explanation of A

85. Below are two statements, one labelled as assertion (A) and the other labelled as Reason (R).
Read the statements and choose the correct answer using the code given below.
Assertion (A) : Business cycles according to new classical economics are monetary in nature.
Reason (R) : These are the results of the fall in the real wage rates.
Codes:
A. A is false, but R is true
B. Both A and R are true, but R is not the correct explanation of A
C. A is true, but R is false
D. Both A and R are true, and R is the correct explanation of A

86. In the context of simultaneous equations econometric models, consider the following statements:
(*i*) Both order and rank conditions for identification are to be satisfied before estimation.
(*ii*) Order conditions is a necessary but not a sufficient condition of identification.
(*iii*) Two stage least squares method is suitable for over identified equations.

Which of the above statements is/are correct? Choose the correct answer from the codes below:
A. Only (*ii*) B. (*i*) & (*iii*)
C. (*i*), (*ii*) & (*iii*) D. Only (*i*)

87. In a two variable regression, the correlation coefficient between dependent and independent variables Y and X is 0.7. What is the percentage of variations in Y explained by X?
A. 49% B. 7%
C. 0.7% D. 70%

88. A series of index numbers is given as follows

Year	2014	2015	2016
Index number	100	120	126

If the base year is shifted to 2015 the value of index number in the year 2016, in the new series will be:
A. 151.2 B. 106
C. 95.2 D. 105

89. By autocorrelation we mean that:
A. The square of the residuals of a regression model are not equally spread
B. The variance of the residuals of a regression model is not constant for all observations
C. The residuals of a regression model are related with one more of the regressors
D. The residuals of a regression models are not independent

90. Consider the following statements about a time series of annual observations on sales of a firm for ten years:

(*i*) The series will have seasonal variations.
(*ii*) The series will have a secular trend.
(*iii*) The series will have cyclic variations.

Choose the correct answer from the codes given below:

A. (*ii*) & (*iii*) B. (*i*), (*ii*) & (*iii*)
C. (*i*) & (*iii*) D. (*i*) & (*ii*)

91. Harrods growth model is given as under:

$S_t = \alpha Y_t \quad 0 < \alpha < 1$
$I_t = \beta[Y_t - Y_{t-1}] \quad \beta > 0$
$S_t = I_t$

where S_t = Savings, Y_t = Income,
I_t = Investment, t = time

In this model for economic growth the conditions for economic growth is:

A. $\frac{\beta}{\alpha} > 0$ B. $\frac{\beta}{\alpha - \beta} > 0$
C. $\frac{\beta}{\beta - \alpha} < 0$ D. $\frac{\beta}{\beta - \alpha} > 1$

92. A monopolist faces a linear demand curve $p = 100 - 4q$, while his cost functions is $C = 50 + 20q$. The profit maximizing output for this monopolist is:

A. 20 B. 5
C. 40 D. 10

93. A box contains 10 bulbs, 4 of which are defective. If 3 of the bulbs are drawn randomly without replacement what is the probability that all 3 bulbs are defective.

A. $\frac{8}{10}$ B. $\frac{8}{4}$
C. $\frac{4}{10}$ D. $\frac{1}{30}$

94. If demand for a consumer is given by the function $p = 27 - 3x - x^2$ (where x = quantity demanded, p = price), the consumers surplus at $x = 3$ is:

A. 50.5 B. 49.5
C. 31.5 D. 32.5

95. Though two time series are individually non stationary, the linear combination is stationary. This is an example of:

A. Random walk
B. Cointegration
C. Trend stationarity
D. Spurious regression

96. For the diagram given below which of the following is correct in terms of derivatives?

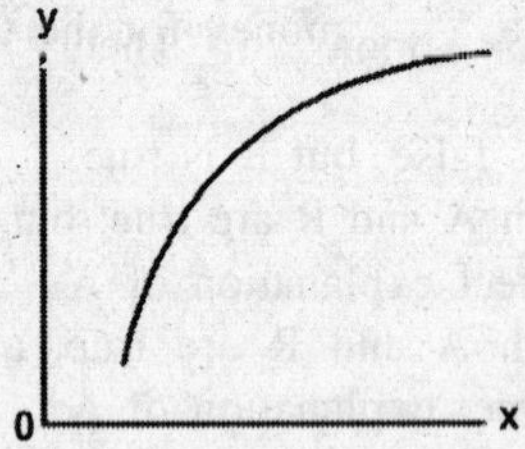

A. $\frac{dy}{dx} > 0, \frac{d^2y}{dx^2} > 0$ B. $\frac{dy}{dx} < 0, \frac{d^2y}{dx^2} < 0$
C. $\frac{dy}{dx} < 0, \frac{d^2y}{dx^2} > 0$ D. $\frac{dy}{dx} > 0, \frac{d^2y}{dx^2} < 0$

97. The price elasticity of demand for a good with the demand function $q = kp^r$, (where p is price q is quantity demanded and k and r are positive constants) is:

A. 1
B. R
C. Not constant as the function is non-linear
D. $1/r$

98. Match List-I with List-II and choose the correct answer from the code given below:

List-I	*List-II*
(*a*) Delphi method	(*i*) Stationarity
(*b*) Dickey Fuller test	(*ii*) Autocorrelation
(*c*) Durbin Watson test	(*iii*) Testing significant of a regression coefficient
(*d*) Students *t* test	(*iv*) Forecasting

Codes:

	(*a*)	(*b*)	(*c*)	(*d*)
A.	(*iv*)	(*ii*)	(*i*)	(*iii*)
B.	(*i*)	(*iv*)	(*iii*)	(*ii*)
C.	(*i*)	(*ii*)	(*iii*)	(*iv*)
D.	(*iv*)	(*i*)	(*ii*)	(*iii*)

99. In regression analysis if a quantitative variable has "*m*" categories, one can introduce:

A. only $m - 1$ dummy variables
B. only $m + 1$ dummy variables
C. only $2m$ variables
D. only m dummy variables

100. Match List-I with List-II and choose the correct answer from the code given below:

List-I	***List-II***
(*a*) Hawkins Simon conditions	(*i*) Theory of games
(*b*) Saddle point	(*ii*) Non linear programming
(*c*) Simplex method	(*iii*) Input output analysis
(*d*) Kuhn Tucker conditions	(*iv*) Linear programming

Codes:

	(*a*)	(*b*)	(*c*)	(*d*)
A.	(*ii*)	(*i*)	(*iii*)	(*iv*)
B.	(*iii*)	(*i*)	(*iv*)	(*ii*)
C.	(*iii*)	(*ii*)	(*i*)	(*iv*)
D.	(*i*)	(*ii*)	(*iv*)	(*iii*)

ANSWERS

1	2	3	4	5	6	7	8	9	10
A	C	D	D	C	B	C	A	D	D
11	12	13	14	15	16	17	18	19	20
D	B	D	A	A	D	D	A	D	A
21	22	23	24	25	26	27	28	29	30
A	C	D	A	B	B	A	A	A	B
31	32	33	34	35	36	37	38	39	40
B	D	D	C	D	B	D	D	A	D
41	42	43	44	45	46	47	48	49	50
D	B	B	A	B	C	B	D	D	C
51	52	53	54	55	56	57	58	59	60
A	C	D	D	B	B	A	B	C	B
61	62	63	64	65	66	67	68	69	70
B	C	D	C	D	C	C	A	A	C
71	72	73	74	75	76	77	78	79	80
A	A	D	C	A	B	B	C	B	D
81	82	83	84	85	86	87	88	89	90
A	A	B	A	A	C	A	D	D	A
91	92	93	94	95	96	97	98	99	100
D	D	D	C	B	D	B	D	A	B

EXPLANATORY ANSWERS

1. Average fixed costs are total fixed costs per unit of output. It is total fixed cost divided by the number of units produced.

Average Fixed Cost (AFC)

$$= \frac{\text{Total Fixed Costs (TFC)}}{\text{Output (Q)}}$$

It is the per unit cost of the fixed factos. AFC declines as output increases, because TFC remains constant. This means that as output increases, given fixed cost is distributed among more unit of output as shown in Figure. As a result, AFC curve would get closer and closer to the horizontal axis. However, AFC can never be zero or negative because TFC has always a positive value. So, AFC never touch to x-axis as well y-axis (For zero output, AFC is infinite).

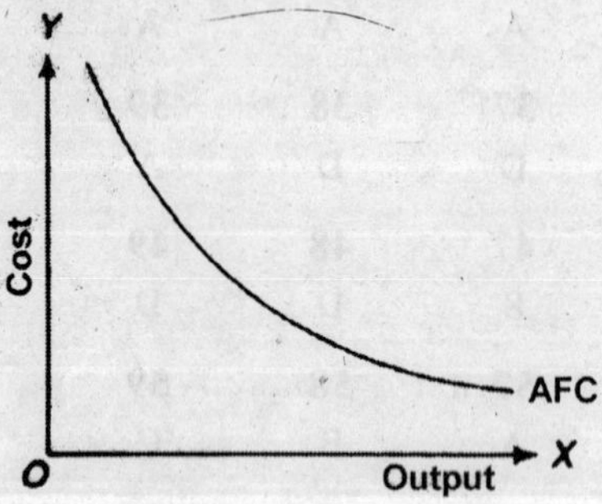

Fig.: *Average Fixed Cost Curve*

AFC curve slopes downward continuously from left to right. Graphically, the AFC is a rectangular hyperbola as shown in Figure.

3. **Centralized and Decentralized Planning:** Centralized planning is otherwise called '*Planning from Above*'. It means chalking out of the plan by the central authority at the top level. It is an objective-based planning.

Decentralized planning is otherwise called *Planning from Below.* It means drawing up of plans by smaller communities at the lowest (village) level. It is a subjective-based planning.

4. Capital Adequacy Ratio (CAR) is the ratio of a bank's capital in relation to its risk weighted assets and current liabilities. It is decided by central banks and bank regulators to prevent commercial banks from taking excess leverage and becoming insolvent in the process.

The Basel III norms stipulated a capital to risk weighted assets of 8%. However, as per RBI norms, Indian scheduled commercial banks are required to maintain a CAR of 9% while Indian public sector banks are emphasized to maintain a CAR of 12%.

6. Balance of payment record of a country has two accounts (a) Current Account, (b) Capital Account. While Current account in the balance of payment record consists of mainly exports and imports, Capital account refers to financial investments, deposits and loans. However, current account includes invisible items viz, receipts and payments for services such as travel, insurance, transportation etc.

A country's current account is the sum of its:
(*i*) net exports (exports minus imports),
(*ii*) net income received from investments abroad, and
(*iii*) net transfer payments from abroad (such as foreign aid).

7. **Uzawa's theorem**, also known as the **steady state growth theorem**, is a theorem in economic growth theory concerning the form that technological change can take in the Solow–Swan and Ramsey–Cass–Koopmans growth models. It was first proved by Japanese economist Hirofumi Uzawa.

One general version of the theorem consists of two parts. The first states that, under the normal assumptions of the Solow and

Neoclassical models, if (after some time T) capital, investment, consumption, and output are increasing at constant exponential rates, these rates must be equivalent. Building on this result, the second part asserts that, within such a balanced growth path, the production function $Y = \tilde{F}(\tilde{A}, K, L)$ (where A is technology, K is capital, and L is labour), can be rewritten such that technological change affects output solely as a scalar on labour (i.e. $Y = F(K, AL)$) a property known as labour-augmenting or Harrod-neutral technological change.

Uzawa's theorem demonstrates a significant limitation of the commonly used Neoclassical and Solow models. Imposing the assumption of balanced growth within such models requires that technological change by labour-augmenting. By contraposition, any production function for which it is not possible to represent the effect of technology as a scalar on labour cannot produce a balanced growth path.

8. Any straight line supply curve passing through the origin has value of elasticity equal to one.

In Fig. (A), linear supply curve OS is drawn. Consider ΔABC and ΔAOF. They are similar triangles, therefore, the ratio of their sides will also be equal, *i.e.*,

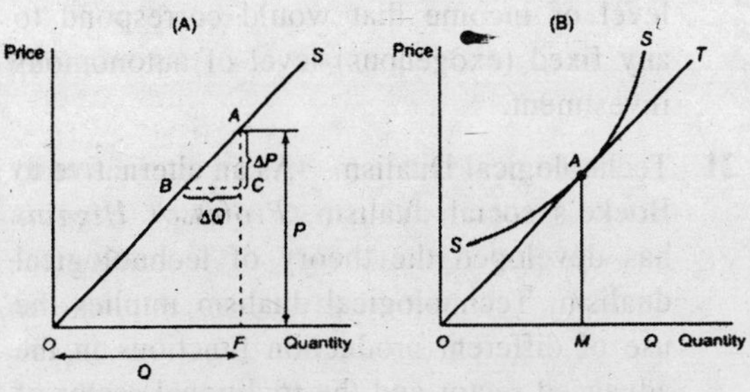

Linear Supply Curve   Non-linear Supply Curve

Fig.: $e_s = 1$

$$\frac{P}{Q} = \frac{\Delta P}{\Delta Q}$$

We know, $e_s = \frac{\Delta Q}{\Delta P} \cdot \frac{P}{Q}$

Substituting (1) in the formula of e_s, we get

$$e_s = \frac{\Delta Q}{\Delta P} \cdot \frac{\Delta P}{\Delta Q} = 1$$

In Fig. (B), SS supply curve is curvilinear, Tangent to the curve at point A, is given by OT which passes through the origin. Point elasticity at point A $= \frac{OM}{OM} = 1.$

9. The opportunity cost theory demonstrates that trade is beneficial as long as opportunity costs differ.

Assumptions: The opportunity cost theory too is based on most of the common assumptions of the classical theories. The important assumptions of this theory are:

(*a*) Two-country-two-commodity model.

(*b*) There are only two factors of production, viz. labour and capital. Factors of production are perfectly mobile within a country but immobile between countries.

(*c*) Factors of production are fixed in supply.

(*d*) There is perfect competition in both factor and product markets.

(*e*) The price of each factor is equal to its marginal productivity in each employment.

(*f*) The price of each commodity is equal to its marginal cost of production.

(*g*) There is full employment in each country.

(*h*) There is no technological change.

(*i*) International trade is free.

12. The theory of asymmetric information was developed in the 1970s and 1980s by George Akerlof, Michael Spence and Joseph Stiglitz. The concept of information asymmetry was able to explain many common phenomena that could not be otherwise explained when it was first introduced in the early 1970s. Since then it has become a valuable tool in the field of economics and it is used to explain a diverse set of phenomena. Its significance was established well before the year 2001 when the original authors of the theory, George Akerlof, Michael Spence and Joseph Stiglitz received the Nobel Prize in Economic Sciences. In the paper 'The Market for Lemons: Quality Uncertainty and the Market Mechanism', Akerlof develops asymmetric information with the example case of automobile market.

Asymmetry information deals with the study of decisions in transactions where one party has more or better information than the other. This asymmetry creates an imbalance of power in transactions, which can sometimes cause the transactions to go awry, a kind of market failure in the worst case. Examples of this problem are adverse selection, moral hazard, and monopolies of knowledge. In simple terms, the theory proposes that an imbalance of information between buyers and sellers can lead to inefficient outcomes in certain markets. Asymmetric information is a situation in which either the buyer or the seller know more than the other about the product to exchanged.

13. Intellectual Property Rights are legal rights, which result from intellectual activity in industrial, scientific, literary & artistic fields. These rights Safeguard creators and other producers of intellectual goods & services by granting them certain time-limited rights to control their use. Protected IP rights like other property can be a matter of trade, which can be owned, sold or bought. These are intangible and non-exhausted consumption.

Types/Tools of IPRs:

(*a*) Patents
(*b*) Trademarks
(*c*) Copyrights and related rights
(*d*) Geographical Indications
(*e*) Industrial Designs
(*f*) Trade Secrets
(*g*) Layout Design for Integrated Circuits
(*h*) Protection of New Plant Variety.

15. The cash balances theory establishes that the elasticity of demand for money is unity which implies that the increase in the demand for money leads to a proportionate decrease in the price level.

16. The five stages of Rostow's model consists of (1) 'the traditional society', (2) 'preconditions for take-off', (3) 'the take-off', (4) 'the drive to maturity' and (5) 'the age of high mass consumption'. According to Rostow each country can be categorized as being in one of these stages of economic development and in which only the most advanced countries have historically evolved through all five stages. Hence, the advanced nations, led by the United States and including Britain, France, Germany and Japan, are considered to have reached the fifth stage of growth.

20. The term 'super-multiplier' was first coined by J.R. Hicks in his business cycle theory. The object was to show the relationship between change in induced investment and the corresponding change in income. To be more specific, it indicates the ratio between the two changes, *i.e.,* in investment and in equilibrium output. In fact, if we know the super-multiplier, we can easily calculate the level of income that would correspond to any fixed (exogenous) level of autonomous investment.

21. Technological Dualism—As an alternative to Boeke's social dualism, *Professor Higgins* has developed the theory of technological dualism. Technological dualism implies the use of different production functions in the advanced sector and the traditional sector of an underdeveloped economy. The existence of such dualism has accentuated the problem of structural or technological unemployment in the industrial sector and disguised unemployment in the rural sector. Higgin's theory of technological dualism is related to limited productive employment opportunities found in the two sectors of an underdeveloped economy because of market imperfections, different factor endowments and production function.

To explain the theory of technological dualism, Higgins takes two goods, two factors of production, two sectors with their factor endowments and production functions. Of the two sectors, one is the traditional sector and the other is the modem sector.

The traditional or rural sector is engaged in the production of agricultural products, handicrafts and operates small industries. Production in this sector is carried on with a wide range of techniques and alternative combinations of two factors of production, *viz.*, labour and capital. As such this sector has variable technical coefficients of production. The techniques of production are generally labour-intensive because of the excessive supply of labour and employment-oriented projects.

On the other hand, the modern industrial sector is composed of heavy industries, plantations, mines, oil fields, etc. The production in this sector can be carried on with limited techniques because the technical coefficients are generally fixed. The production process are relatively capital-intensive in the sense that large amounts of capital are used with a small amount of labour.

22. **Round-tripping:** Here, money is deposited in a foreign corporation offshore, controlled by the owners, preferably in a tax haven where minimal records are kept, and then shipped back to the home country as a foreign direct investment, exempt from taxation.

24. **Countries differ in their relative factor endowments**

Notation: K = capital, L = labour, r = price of capital, w = price of labour.

Physical definition: $(K/L)_1 > (K/L)_2 \Leftrightarrow$ country 1 is capital-abundant (labour-scarce), country 2 is labour-abundant (capital-scarce).

Price definition: $(r/w)_1 < (r/w)_1 \Leftrightarrow$ country 1 is capital-abundant, country 2 is labour-abundant.

26. The term 'balanced growth' is used in many different senses, but the original exponents of the balanced growth doctrine had in mind the scale of investment necessary to overcome indivisibilities on both the supply and demand side of the development process. Indivisibilities on the supply side refer to the 'lumpiness' of capital (especially social overhead capital), and the fact that only investment in a large number of activities simultaneously can take advantage of various external economies of scale. Indivisibilities on the demand side refer to the limitations imposed by the size of the market on the profitability, and hence feasibility, of economic activities. This was the original interpretation of the doctrine of balanced growth: that the large-scale expansion of activities or **big push** was necessary to overcome divergences between the private and social returns to investment.

The doctrine was later extended, however, to refer to the *path* of economic development and the *pattern* of investment necessary to keep the different sectors of the economy in balance, so that lack of development in one sector does not impede development in others; for example, the necessity to strike a balance between sectors such as agriculture and industry, between the capital goods and consumer goods industries, and between social capital and directly productive activities.

27. **Progressive Rate Structure:** A progressive rate structure is defined as a tax in which the

average tax rate increases as the tax base increases.

If a tax rate structure is progressive, the marginal tax rate will be higher than the average tax rate as the tax base increases. The average tax rate, the marginal tax rate, and the total tax all increase with increases in the tax base. A person with a low tax base will pay both lower average and marginal rates of tax than will a person with a high tax base.

The progressive tax rate structure reflects the embedding in the federal income tax rates of Adam Smith's equality criterion. Recall that according to this criterion, taxpayers should pay according to their ability to pay the tax. The use of progressive rate structures, wherein people with higher taxable income levels pay higher marginal tax rates, promotes equality.

28. Shifts in the IS curve: Any *exogenous* change in expenditure — in C, I, G or X—M— that boosts expenditure and thus Y would shift the IS curve towards the right. Any exogenous decrease in expenditure shifts the IS curve towards the left.

- If G is increased, the IS curve shifts to the right.
- If G declines, the IS curve would shift to the left.
- If exports fall, the IS curve would shift to the left.
- If taxes are reduced, this would lead to an exogenous boost in consumption, and the IS curve would shift to the right.
- If restrictions are placed on imports, an exogenous drop in imports would result. X – M would increase, and the IS curve would shift to the right.
- If investment falls due to a drop in investor confidence (i.e. at the prevailing interest rate level), it would shift the IS curve to the left.

Shifts in the LM Curve: The primary reason for a shift in the LM curve is an exogenous or policy change in the money supply M^S.

- If the money supply expands, the LM curve shifts to the right.
- If the money supply contracts, the LM curve shifts to the left.

30. *Joseph Alois Schumpeter,* first presented his theory of economic growth in the "THEORY OF ECONOMIC DEVELOPMENT" published in German in 1911. He assumes a perfectly competitive economy which is in stationary equilibrium. In such a stationary state there is no profit, no interest rates, no savings, no investments and no involuntary unemployment. This equilibrium is characterized by the term "circular flow" which continues to repeat itself in the same manner year after year. In the 'circular flow', the same products are produced year after year in the same manner. 'For every supply there is some corresponding demand, and for every demand the corresponding supply'.

31. Musgrave and Thin developed a progressivity index M which they called "effective progression," based upon a comparison of the Gini coefficients for income before tax (G_b) and after tax (G_a):

$$M = (1 - G_a)/(1 - G_b)$$

This is an indicator of the relative equality of the before- and after-tax distribution: values greater than 1 indicate a progressive tax.

32. Friedman considers money as an asset or capital good serving as a temporary abode of purchasing power. People hold it because it provides a stream of income or consumable services. On the other hand, Keynes includes in money, only demand deposits and non-interest bearing debt of the government. Thus, Friedman has used a much wider definition of money than Keynes for explaining the demand for money function.

33. Per Capita Real GDP = 15% – 2% – 5%
= 8%.

35. Money markets are short-term debt markets. Debt is a fixed income security and represents the borrowing of a market player. Money markets are mostly wholesale markets for financial instruments. Money market transactions are highly liquid to meet the requirements of short-term surplus-fund holders and fund borrowers. Call (Notice) money market is a major segment of the Indian money market where transactions are entered into on an overnight maturity. The large quantum of trade essentially limits the players in the money market to institutional investors such as banks, other financial institutions, government and large business firms. Here, the players exchange surplus funds at the prevailing interest rates (call rates) for a short duration. The duration could be a day, a week, a month, six months or a year. This duration indicates the maturity of the instrument. At the time of issue of the money market instrument as well as at the time of maturity of the instrument, the account transfer of the initial amount along with the interest charges takes place between the players in the money market.

Instruments of money market are T bill market, inter-bank market, certificate of deposit market, repo market, commercial paper market, inter-corporate deposit market and commercial bill market.

36.

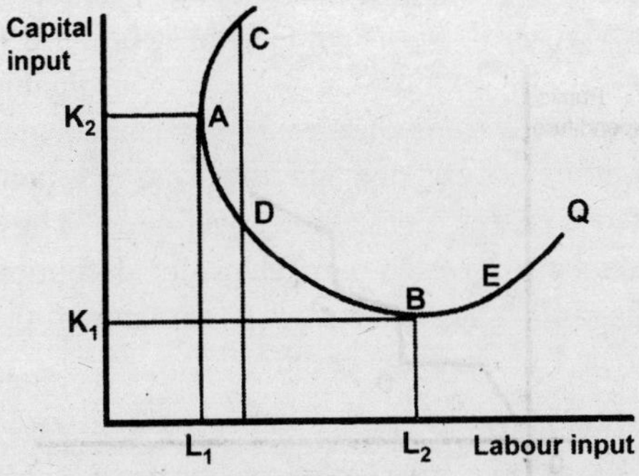

Fig. A: *Upward- and backward-bending isoquants.*

The economic region of production: In Figure A, we saw that the Segment AB is the economically feasible portion of the isoquant for Q. If we consider such feasible portions of all the isoquants, then the region comprised of these portions is called the *economic region of production.* This is the region in which a producer will operate. It is illustrated in Figure B. The lines OA_1A_2 and OB_1B_2 are called *ridge lines.* They give the boundary of the economic region of production. We have drawn them as straight lines, but they need not always be. The region between the lines OA_1A_2 and OB_1B_2 is the economic region of production.

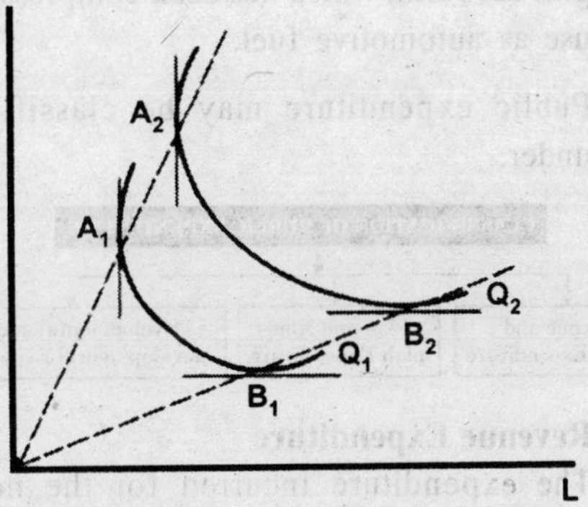

Fig. B: *Ridge lines and the economic region of production*

38. (*i*) First phase of Nationalism of banks – 1969

(*ii*) Establishment of Narasimham Committee on the banking system – 1991

(*iii*) Enactment of FEMA Act in India – 1999

(*iv*) Establishment of EXIM Bank in India – 1982

39. Fringe Benefits Tax (FBT) is a tax payable by employers for benefits paid to an employee (or an employee's associate e.g. a family member) in place of salary or wages. This is separate to income tax and is calculated on the taxable value of the fringe benefits provided.

Fringe Benefit Tax (FBT) is fundamentally a tax that an employer has to pay in lieu of the benefits that are given to his/her employees. It was an attempt to comprehensively levy tax on those benefits, which evaded the taxman. The list of benefits encompassed a wide range of privileges, services, facilities or amenities which were directly or indirectly given by an employer to current or former employees, be it something simple like telephone reimbursements, free or concessional tickets or even contributions by the employer to a superannuation fund.

41. "Compressed Natural Gas (CNG)" means mixtures of hydrocarbon gases and vapours, consisting mainly of Methane [or suitable mixtures of Hydrogen and Methane] in gaseous form, which has been compressed for use as automotive fuel.

42. Public expenditure may be classified as under:

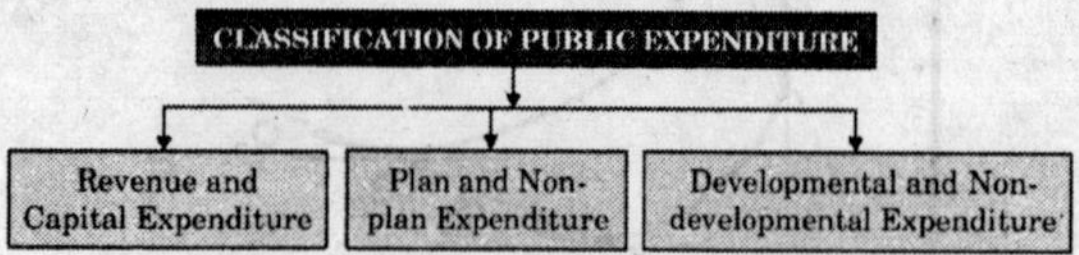

Revenue Expenditure

The expenditure incurred for the normal functioning of government departments and provision for various services, interest, charges on debt, incurred by the government, subsidies etc., are known as revenue expenditure. In other words, *all expenditures which do not create assets are termed as revenue expenditures.* Grants sanctioned to the state governments are also the part of revenue expenditure, although some of the grants may create assets. The main revenue expenditures of the government are salaries, pensions, interest, subsidies and grants etc.

Capital Expenditure

Expenditures on acquisition of assets such as land, building, machinery, equipments, investment in shares etc, loans and advances granted by the central government to state governments, union territories, government companies, corporations and other parties are termed as capital expenditure.

43. The ***Global Competitiveness Report*** (**GCR**) is a yearly report published by the World Economic Forum. Since 2004, the *Global Competitiveness Report* ranks countries based on the **Global Competitiveness Index**, developed by Xavier Sala-i-Martin and Elsa V. Artadi. Before that, the macroeconomic ranks were based on Jeffrey Sachs's *Growth Development Index* and the microeconomic ranks were based on Michael Porter's *Business Competitiveness Index*. The *Global Competitiveness Index* integrates the macroeconomic and the micro/business aspects of competitiveness into a single index.

44. **Peacock and Wiseman Hypothesis**

Peacock and Wiseman hypothesis in public expenditure is based on their empirical study conducted in United Kingdom, during the period 1890 to 1955. Here also like Adolf Wagner, these economists tell us about the relationship between growth of an economy and public expenditure. But there is wide difference between these two theories. Here, Peacock and Wiseman quotes that public expenditure will increase with respect to the growth of an economy. But the growing trend will not be as like in the Adolf Wagner's theory. Further, it will be in a step like manner. The hypothesis can be explained with the help of a diagram as showing below.

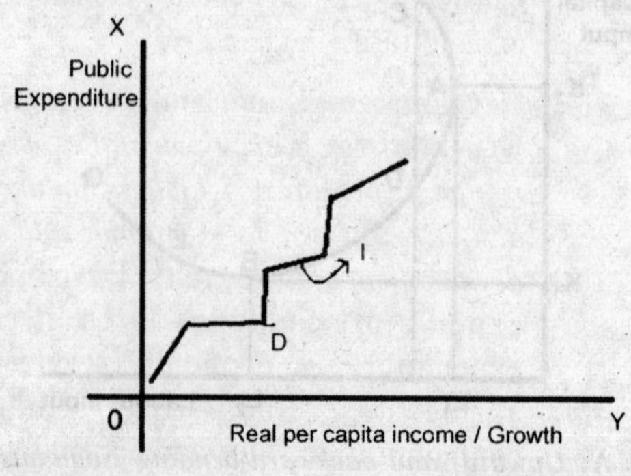

In the figure, real per capita income or growth rate is represented on '*x*' axis and public expenditure on '*y*' axis. According to this hypothesis, there are three basic effects in an economy which can see in the growing path of a country. They are:

(*a*) Displacement effect

(*b*) Inspection effect, and

(*c*) Concentration effect.

47. Types of Public Expenditure

Public expenditure is classified into various categories. These different classifications of public expenditure look at public expenditure from different angles. The main classifications are discussed below:

1. **Direct Expenditure and Transfer Expenditure:** *Expenditure incurred by the government* on *the purchase of goods and services* and *on* current *services of factors of production is called government direct expenditure*. It is sometimes called *exhaustive expenditure* or *non-transfer expenditure*. Expenditure incurred on defence, civil services, educational services, judiciary and investment expenditure, etc. are all direct expenditure.

   Transfer expenditures, on the other hand, *are those* expenditures *which take the form of payments made without corresponding return of any factor services in the current period.* They are in the nature of transfer payments. Expenditure made for payment of interest on government debt, old-age pensions, sickness benefits, etc. are transfer expenditures.

2. **Developmental and Non-developmental Expenditures:** *Developmental expenditure is that expenditure which is incurred on activities related to economic and social development of the country.* Developmental expenditure includes such items as expenditure on economic services like agriculture, industries, transport, communication, etc. and expenditure on social and community services like education, public health, labour, employment, etc.

   Non-developmental expenditure is the expenditure which is incurred on non-developmental activities of the government. Such expenditure includes expenditure on administrative services like police, defence, administration of justice, general administration, etc.

3. **Productive and Unproductive Expenditure:** *Productive expenditures are those expenditures which help in improving the productive capacity of the economy.* These expenditures add to the efficiency of the economy, and they are in the nature of investment. They may take the form of physical assets like machinery, factories as well as human capital like education, training, health, etc. *Unproductive expenditures,* on the other hand, *are those expenditures which do not add to the productive efficiency of the economy directly.* They are in the nature of consumption. Expenditure on administration, defence, judiciary, maintenance of law and order, etc. are unproductive expenditures. This does not mean that these expenditures are wasteful. They may indirectly add to the health and efficiency of the economy.

48. In macro-economics, the **Inada conditions**, named after Japanese economist Ken-Ichi Inada are assumptions about the shape of a production function that guarantee the stability of an economic growth path in a neoclassical growth model.

53. Maternal Death: The death of a woman while pregnant or within 42 days of delivery, irrespective of the duration and site of pregnancy, from any cause related to or aggravated by the pregnancy or its management but not from accidental or incidental causes.

Maternal Mortality Ratio (MMR): MMR is calculated as the number of maternal deaths during a given year per 100,000 live births during the same period. Maternal mortality ratio represents the risk associated with each pregnancy *i.e.*, the obstetric risk.

Maternal Mortality Rate: Maternal mortality rate is calculated as the number of maternal deaths in a given period per 100,000 women of reproductive age (15–49 years).

Maternal mortality measures both the obstetric risk and the frequency with which women are exposed to this risk.

54. The marginal cost of funds based lending rate (MCLR) refers to the minimum interest rate of a bank below which it cannot lend, except in some cases allowed by the RBI. It is an internal benchmark or reference rate for the bank. MCLR actually describes the method by which the minimum interest rate for loans is determined by a bank - on the basis of marginal cost or the additional or incremental cost of arranging one more rupee to the prospective borrower.

RBI recently made its move from the historic Benchmark Prime Lending Rate (BPLR) to Marginal Cost of Funds Based Lending Rate (MCLR) in April, 2016 as the current rate setting method for lending money by commercial banks.

NEED FOR MCLR

- RBI changes the repo rates and other rates periodically but the banks are slow in changing their interest rates according to RBI rates.
- Most commercial banks do not change their lending rates to customers.
- Ultimately, bank customers does not receive the benefits aimed by RBI.
- Till now, RBI was verbally instructing the commercial banks to change their lending rates with every Repo rate change.
- The real benefit of repo rate change will be realised only when the customer gets benefited.
- With the New MCLR, there will be quick change in the lending rate and the commercial banks will have to oblige with RBI at a fast pace as repo rate is included in MCLR calculation.

BENEFITS OF MCLR

- MCLR revised on monthly basis benefiting bank customers especially borrowers.
- Banks to compete with commercial paper market.
- Reduces borrowing cost for companies.
- Indian banking industry moves towards international standards.

PITFALLS

- MCLR rule exempted for loans given to retired employees, existing employees, government schemes etc.
- Banks will be reluctant to change to MCLR rule due to cut in interest rates as currently, it is up to the customer to exercise their loans under MCLR as an option.

51 and 55.

Banking systems are classic examples of the problem of asymmetric information. Banks and other lending institutions know less about a borrower's ability and willingness to pay than the borrower. This leads to both problems of asymmetric information: adverse selection and moral hazard. Adverse selection arises because financial institutions charge interest rates that are partially based on their assessment of the ability and willingness of the borrower to pay. Because the assessment is based on an expected number of defaults from low-quality borrowers, the rates may be considered high by high-quality borrowers who may choose to self-finance and not borrow. This produces a tendency (or only low-quality borrowers to seek loans, that is, adverse selection.

Moral hazard arises because once a loan is made the borrower may choose to change behaviour. For example, a plumber may intend to borrow money to buy a machine to help unclog drains. But once he or she receives the loan, it may seem easier to take the money and bet on a horse based on a "good" tip. If the bank had known that this is what the money was going to be used for, it probably would not have made the loan. Moral hazard arises after the loan is made because a borrower may choose not to pay or to engage in activities that the lender would not have agreed to.

56. For a long time economists have recognized the fact that the GDP is misleading as an indicator or as a proxy of the "welfare" of a nation, let alone as a measure of people's well-being, although the makers of economic policy commonly think to the contrary. This problem became apparent in practical economic policies in most industrialized countries in the early 1970s. The most famous example of this development was the MEW index, developed by the Yale University economics professors William Nordhaus and James Tobin in their Measure of Economic Welfare (MEW) in 1972. Economic Welfare is for them the sum of GDP, the value of leisure time, the value of unpaid work, minus the value of environmental damage. For a first time we see here a correction for adverse environmental effects of economic growth.

The Japanese Net National Welfare (NNW) indicator in published in 1973, developed by a special committee, created by the Economic Council of Japan and chaired by M. Shinohara, works along similar lines. The NNW adds up a series welfare measurements, including non-market services and corrects this by deducting the costs of pollution. The United Nations published in 1977 a Study on the "Feasibility of Welfare-Oriented Measures to Supplement the National Accounts and Balances: A Technical Report", analysing the different indices and discussing the measurement of the individual elements.

In 1981, the Greek economist Xenophon Zalotas developed the Economic Aspects of Welfare (EAW) index. The EAW differed from the MEW by focusing on the current flow of goods and services and by largely ignoring capital accumulation and the issue of sustainability. At a more detailed level, the EAW deviates from the MEW by deducting half of the cost of advertising (assuming that only half of it provides a valuable information service to consumers), half the cost of air and water pollution control, the full costs of solid waste pollution control, deducts the estimated costs of air pollution, and half of the per capita growth in real public and private health care costs. In addition, Zolatas includes a figure for natural resource depletion.

In 1989, Herman Daly (World Bank) and John Cobb developed a new index based on the MEW index: the Index of Sustainable Economic Welfare (ISEW). They take as starting point personal expenditure, adding public expenditure (but excluding defense) and the value of unpaid work, but deduct costs for private and the value of environmental damage. Later on they added several other "costs" to the Index. This resulted finally into the Genuine Progress Indicator (GPI). This GPI includes the weighted private consumption, adds the value of non-market services generating welfare, deducts the private defense costs of natural deterioration and the costs of deterioration of nature and natural resources but adds in the increase of capital stock and the balance of international trade. Finally this results into the UN's human development index, or HDI, in 1990 (hereunder).

58. Honourable Prime Minister launched the "Transformation of Aspirational Districts" programme in January, 2018 to transform 115 districts in 28 States. These districts have been ranked on 49 Key Performance Indicators (KPIs) across five sectors. Education is one of the sectors with 30% weight attached. 8 KPIS have been identified under Education.

KEY PERFORMANCE INDICATORS – EDUCATION SECTOR

1. Transition from
   (*a*) Primary to Upper Primary.
   (*b*) Upper Primary to Secondary.
2. Schools with Functional Girls' Toilets.
3. Availability of Functional Drinking Water Facility in the schools.
4. Availability of Textbooks within 1 month of the Academic Session.
5. Availability of Functional Electricity Facility at Secondary School Level.
6. Elementary Schools Complying with RTE specified Pupil Teacher Ratio.
7. Learning Outcomes of Classes 3, 5 and 8 in Language and Mathematics.
8. Female Literacy (15 + years).

59. In the neoclassical growth model, capital per worker is in equilibrium when investment per worker equals depreciation per worker. The equilibrium output per worker can be read off the production function at this level of capital per worker.

60. T.W. Schultz has given three ratios in relation to education and growth—

1. Education-labour ratio to show the amount of human effort going into education relative to the total labour force.
2. Education-income ratio which relates the resources entering into education to consumer income.
3. Education-income ratio to show the relation between the resources entering into education and the resources going into reproducible physical capital.

64. Vilfreedo Pareto was the first great economist who provided a positive criterion for increase or decrease in social welfare. His formulation was accepted by Cambridge economists. His concept was a landmark in the history of subjective welfare economics. This theory known as 'A Priori Welfare Theory' is principally concerned with allocations of resources by individual consumers, producers and other participants in the exchange transactions. Pareto differed from the earlier economists on two important points: (*i*) he rejected the notion of cardinal utility and additive utility functions, and (*ii*) he restricted himself to welfare conclusions that are independent of interpersonal comparisons whatever. His formulation shows that the economic welfare of a society will be maximised if only resources are allocated efficiently and simultaneously in consumption, production and exchange. It also states that co-competition enables society to reach an optimum welfare position, regardless of the distribution of income, and even if utilities of different individuals are not considered to be comparable.

65. Crowding-out effect means that the increase in government spending increases the interest rate, which reduces the private investment. There are three cases of the crowding-out effect. A zero crowding-out effect occurs when the government spending increases, but the investment does not decrease. In terms of absolute values, a partial crowding-out effect occurs when the increase in government spending is greater than the decrease in investment. In terms of absolute values, a complete crowding-out effect occurs when the increase in government spending equals the decrease in investment.

67. Universal Banking: Universal banking refers to the combination of commercial banking, insurance services and investment banking. It is "the conduct of range of financial services comprising deposit taking and lending, trading of financial instruments and foreign exchange (and their derivatives) underwriting of new debt and equity issues, brokerage investment management and insurance". Thus under this system, banks assume the role of a financial supermarket through provision of basket of financial services under one roof to customers. Universal banking is making inroads in India as it helps banks to leverage their network for enhancing business volume and developing long-term relationship with customers. Customers also benefit as it provides them an opportunity to access full range of services at relatively lower costs.

The concept of universal banking, in India, was enumerated in the Narasimham Committee report (1998) and the S.H. Khan Committee report (1998). Both the reports recommended for consolidation of banking industry through mergers and integration of financial activities, thus suggesting the introduction universal banking in India.

As per present RBI guidelines, a financial institution can transform into universal banking subject to meeting reserve requirements. In 2000, ICICI bank took the initiative and sought permission from RBI to implement the concept of universal bank in India. Later on, many other Indian banks embraced universal banking.

68. Marginal Propensity to Save (MPS)

MPS is defined as the measure of the rate at which saving changes as national income changes. Symbolically,

$$MPS = \frac{\Delta S}{\Delta Y}$$

where, ΔS = Change in saving

ΔY = Change in income

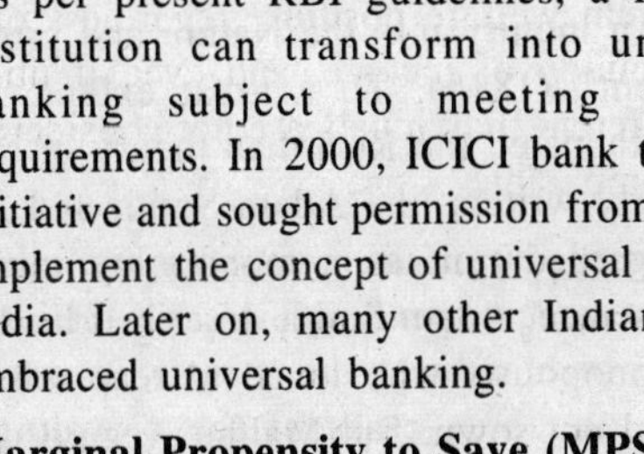

Fig.: $MPS = \frac{AN}{TN}$

Illustration: If income and consumption values are:

Income (Y)	Consumption Expenditure (C)	Saving Y – C
₹ 50 crore	₹ 10 crore	₹ 40 crore
₹ 100 crore	₹ 30 crore	₹ 70 crore

then saving values can be calculated by S = Y – C

$$MPS = \frac{\Delta S}{\Delta Y} = \frac{₹\ 30\ crore}{₹\ 50\ crore}$$

$$= 0.6\ crore = 60\%$$

It means that 60% of the additional income is being saved.

Graphically, MPS is measured as shown in Fig.

MPS which is measured by $\frac{\Delta S}{\Delta Y}$ is graphically the slope of the saving curve. It is calculated as $MPS = \frac{\Delta S}{\Delta Y} = \frac{AN}{TN}$

Important Points about MPS:

1. MPS is always positive
2. MPS varies between 0 and 1

(*a*) If the entire additional income is saved, *i.e.*, $\Delta C = 0$, then MPS = 1.

(*b*) However, if entire additional income is consumed, *i.e.*, $\Delta S = 0$, then MPS = 0.

Relationship Between MPC and MPS

$$MPC + MPS = 1$$

This will always hold because MPC is always positive and less than one.

Thus, MPS must also be positive and less than one.

69. Growth of output = TFP + (Share of capital × Growth of capital) + (Share of labour × Growth of labour)

$$7 = TFP + (0.4 \times 8) + (0.6 \times 3)$$
$$TFP = 7 - (3.2 + 1.8)$$
$$= 7 - 5 = 2.$$

71. The Commission for Agricultural Costs & Prices (CACP) is an attached office of the Ministry of Agriculture and Farmers Welfare, Government of India. It came into existence in January, 1965. Currently, the Commission comprises a Chairman, Member Secretary, one Member (Official) and two Members (Non-Official). The non-official members are representatives of the farming community and usually have an active association with the farming community.

It is mandated to recommend minimum support prices (MSPs) to incentivize the cultivators to adopt modern technology, and raise productivity and overall grain production in line with the emerging demand patterns in the country. Assurance of a remunerative and stable price environment is considered very important for increasing agricultural production and productivity since the market place for agricultural produce tends to be inherently unstable, which often inflict undue losses on the growers, even when they adopt the best available technology package and produce efficiently. Towards this end, MSP for major agricultural products are fixed by the government, each year, after taking into account the recommendations of the Commission.

As of now, CACP recommends MSPs of 23 commodities, which comprise 7 cereals (paddy, wheat, maize, sorghum, pearl millet, barley and ragi), 5 pulses (gram, tur, moong, urad, lentil), 7 oilseeds (groundnut, rapeseed-mustard, soyabean, sesamum, sunflower, safflower, nigerseed), and 4 commercial crops (copra, sugarcane, cotton and raw jute).

72. In the 1980s, the second generation of the new classical macroeconomists such as Edward C. Prescott, Finn E. Kydland and Charles I. Plosser argued that upswings and downswings in economic activity originate from *real (or aggregate supply) shocks* rather than monetary (or aggregate demand) shocks. Assuming that the aggregate demand curve is fixed, and by keeping the assumptions of continuous market-clearing, imperfect information, and rationality of expectations, the so-called *real business cycle* (RBC) theorists investigate the effects of supply shocks (*e.g.*, process and production innovations, discovery of new sources of raw materials, changes in relative prices of foods and energy, bad weather, and nominal effective exchange rate changes) on the business cycle.

73. The views of Malthus on rent are found in "An inquiry into the Nature and progress of Rent" (1815). To a great extent, Malthus anticipated the Ricardian theory of rent. The early writers like Adam Smith and J.B. Say regarded rent as a monopoloy return. For instance, Adam Smith described landlords as monopolists who loved to reap where they had not sown. But Malthus regarded rent as a surplus that arose because of the bounty of Nature. It may be noted that he differed from Ricardo in this respect because the latter argued that rent arose not because of Nature's bounty but because of its niggardliness.

According to Malthus, rent arose because of the following factors:

1. There was shortage of fertile land.
2. This necessitated the cultivation of lands of inferior fertility.
3. The produce in each case is sold at "the natural or necessary price." The price of produce in each progressive country would be just equal to the cost of production on land of the poorest quality actually in use. Naturally, lands with superior fertility will get rent. Thus, Malthus more or less anticipated the Ricardian theory of rent.

74. Regressive Tax: A regressive tax is the one in which tax rate decreases as the amount subject to taxation increases; and the tax rate progresses from high to low. The lowest amount is subject to higher taxation and this leads to individuals with low income bear the highest burden of regressive taxes. Such tax does not take into account the ability to pay.

Indirect taxes, such as sales/service tax, are an example of regressive tax as the poor and rich pay the same tax in purchasing everyday products and services. Apart from indirect taxes, some other regressive tax examples are **sin tax** (tax on intoxicants such as tobacco and alcohol, which are more consumed by lower classes); **toll tax** (every passing vehicle of same type has to pay irrespective of income of the person travelling in that vehicle) etc.

75. Bent Hansen's Excess Demand Model: The Danish economist Bent Hansen has presented an explicit dynamic excess demand model of inflation which incorporates two separate price levels, one for the goods market and other for the factor (labour) market.

Its Assumptions: His dynamic model for demand inflation is based on the following assumptions:

- There is perfect competition in both the goods market and the factor market.
- Price at the moment will persist in the future.
- Only one commodity is produced with the help of only one variable factor, labour services.
- The quantity of labour services per unit of time is a given magnitude.
- There is a fixed actual level of employment and consequently of output which is full employment.

79. The CES (constant elasticity of substitution) production function was introduced by Arrow et al. (1961). As the name suggests, the elasticity of substitution is variable in general but constant across the data-range for which the function is estimated. A two-factor CES production function may look as:

$$f(K, L) = Q = A[\alpha K^{-\rho} + \beta K^{-\rho}]^{-\mu/\rho} \quad ...(1)$$

where μ is a measure of economies of scale, ρ yields the elasticity of substitution $1/(1 + \rho)$ (see below), and α and β are distribution parameters since they determine the distribution of income over the production factors. To separate the elasticity of scale μ from the other parameters in an empirical estimation of (1), it is required that the distribution coefficients sum to one. *i.e.*, $\alpha + \beta = 1$. Under this restriction, and by combining cost minimisation with the marginal products of labour and capital in the CES function, we derive the following optimality condition:

$$\frac{p_L}{p_K} = \frac{f_L}{f_K} = \frac{\beta}{\alpha}\left(\frac{K}{L}\right)^{1+\rho}. \quad ...(2)$$

The elasticity of substitution between capital and labour can be derived directly from equation (2). It is given by:

$$\varepsilon_{KL} = \frac{\partial(K/L)}{\partial(p_L/p_K)}\frac{p_L/p_K}{K/L}$$

$$= \left(\frac{1}{1+\rho}\right)\left(\frac{\alpha p_L L}{\beta p_K K}\right)^{-(1+\rho/1+\rho)}\left(\frac{\alpha p_L}{\beta p_K}\right)$$

$$= \frac{1}{1+\rho}. \quad ...(3)$$

Note that the substitution elasticities in this function are symmetric, *i.e.*, $\varepsilon_{KL} = \varepsilon_{LK}$. When K and L are substitutes it holds that $1 < \varepsilon_{KL} < \infty$, which is true when $-1 < \rho < 0$. Alternatively, when K and L are complements it holds that $0 < \varepsilon_{KL} < -1$ and $0 < \rho < \infty$. The CES production function encompasses several other production functions. For instance, when $\rho = 0$ the CES function reduces to a Cobb-Douglas production function with elasticity of substitution equal to one. When $\rho \to -1$ the elasticity of substitution is infinite, implying that the production factors are perfect substitutes. Alternatively, when $\rho \to \infty$, the elasticity goes to zero and the factors are perfect complements. In this case the CES reduces to a Leontief production function.

80. The Quantity Theory of Money: This is simply the idea that inflation is caused by too much money chasing too few goods. So, if central banks increase the money supply, there will be inflation. Therefore, the cure for inflation is for central banks to reduce the rate of growth of the money supply.

The quantity theory of money states that changes in the money supply are directly related to changes in the price level. Monetary policy based on the quantity theory of money therefore directly affects the price level. To illustrate, we will modify the equation of exchange by putting a bar (–) over V and over Q to indicate they are fixed or constant in value:

$$M \times \bar{V} = P \times \bar{Q}$$

What if the money supply doubles? The price level also doubles. Or, if the Fed cuts the money supply in half, then the price level is also cut in half. Meanwhile, real output of goods and services, Q, remains unchanged.

In short, monetarists say the cause of inflation is "too much money chasing too few goods." The quantity theory of money denies any role for nonmonetary factors, such as supply shocks from a hike in oil prices, which cause cost-push inflation. Moreover, this theory ignores the impact of fiscal policy changes in taxation and spending on the price level.

82. Rosenstein-Rodan's Theory of the 'Big Push'

According to this theory, there is a minimum level of resources that must be devoted to a development programme, if it is to have any chance of success. Launching a country into self-sustaining growth is a little like getting an airplane off the ground. There is a critical ground speed which must be passed before the craft can become airborne. The essence of this theory is: Proceeding 'bit by bit' will not add up in its effects to the sum total of the single bits. A minimum quantum of investment is a necessary, though not sufficient, condition of success.

Rosenstein-Rodan identifies three different kinds of indivisibilities, which may be considered the main obstacles to the development of developing countries. These are the indivisibility in the supply of social overhead capital (lumpiness of capital), the indivisibility of demand (complementarily of demand), and the indivisibility (kink) in the supply of savings. He argues that a big push in terms of a high quantum of investment is required to scale the economic obstacles to development created by these three kinds of indivisibilities, and the external economies to which they give rise. This implies that the development process is a series of discontinuous 'jumps', and each jump requires a 'big push'.

87. The co-efficient of determination explains to what extent the variation of dependent variable Y is being expressed by the independent variable X.

For example, if the value of $r = 0.7$, r^2 will be 0.49. It means that 49 per cent of the variation in the dependent variable has been explained by the independent variable. The remaining 51 per cent of the variation are due to other independent variables yet to be located.

Suppose the value of $r = 1$, then r^2 will be equal to 1. It means perfect relationship between the two variables. The expression $1 - r^2$ is the ratio of unexplained variance to total variance. This is called co-efficient of non-determination. Thus, the expression $1 - r^2$ is a measure of deviation from perfect linear relationship.

88. $\text{Shifted Index} = \dfrac{\text{Original Index}}{\text{New Base Year Index}} \times 100$

$\text{New Index No. in the year 2016} = \dfrac{126}{120} \times 100$

$= 105.$

89. A common statistical test used in regression analysis is called the Durbin-Watson Autocorrelation Test, which tests for the lagged cause-and-effect relationship between the variables. It measures the residual errors when comparing forecast values with actual values. Ideally, there should be no autocorrelation present. If there is autocorrelation present in the model, the relationship between the variables in the model is not accurately expressed.

92.

$$P = 100 - 4q$$
$$R = 100q - 4q^2$$
$$MR = 100 - 8q$$
$$C = 50 + 20q$$
$$MC = 20$$
$$\therefore \quad 100 - 8q = 20$$
$$8q = 80 \Rightarrow q = 10.$$

93. Favourable case = 3 defective bulbs selected from 4 bulbs = $^4C_3 = 4$

Total case = 3 bulbs selected from total 10 bulbs = $^{10}C_3 = 120$

Required probability = $\dfrac{4}{120} = \dfrac{1}{30}$.

Previous Years Paper

UGC-NET–Junior Research Fellowship & Assistant Professor Eligibility Exam

Economics, July-2018*

PAPER-II

Note: *This paper contains* ***hundred (100)*** *objective type questions of* ***two (2)*** *marks each.* ***All*** *questions are* ***compulsory***.

1. Which of the following will be true for both monopoly and monopolistic competition in the short run?

A. Price is greater than marginal revenue.
B. Price is equal to marginal revenue.
C. Price is equal to marginal cost.
D. Price is equal to average cost.

2. Consider the following matrix which describes the respective strategies and the corresponding pay-offs of firms A and B operating in a duopoly:

		Firm B: Advertise	Firm B: Don't Advertise
Firm A	Advertise	11, 6	16, 0
	Don't Advertise	7, 9	20, 2

Which of the following statement(s) is/are true for the above game?
Select the correct answer from the codes given below:

(*a*) Firm A has no dominant strategy.
(*b*) Firm B has a dominant strategy.
(*c*) The game has a Nash equilibrium.
(*d*) Neither Firm A nor Firm B has a dominant strategy.

Code:

A. (*a*), (*c*) B. (*b*), (*c*)
C. (*d*) Only D. (*a*), (*b*) and (*c*)

3. In the context of oligopoly, consider the following statements:

(*a*) Cournot's equilibrium is a Nash equilibrium.
(*b*) Stackelberg equilibrium is a Nash equilibrium.

Select the correct answer from the code given below:

A. Only (*a*) B. Only (*b*)
C. Both (*a*) and (*b*) D. Neither (*a*) nor (*b*)

4. Match List-I with List-II and point out the correct answer from the codes below:

List-I (Concept)	***List-II (Economist)***
(*a*) Profit as a dynamic surplus	(*i*) J. Schumpeter
(*b*) Profit as reward for innovation	(*ii*) M. Kalecki
(*c*) Profit as reward for uncertainty bearing	(*iii*) F.H. Knight
(*d*) Profit arise due to monopoly power enjoyed by the producers	(*iv*) J.B. Clark

Code:

	(*a*)	(*b*)	(*c*)	(*d*)
A.	(*ii*)	(*i*)	(*iii*)	(*iv*)
B.	(*iv*)	(*i*)	(*iii*)	(*ii*)
C.	(*iv*)	(*ii*)	(*iii*)	(*i*)
D.	(*iii*)	(*iv*)	(*ii*)	(*i*)

5. When the marginal cost is equal to average cost, the slope of the average cost is:

A. positive B. negative
C. zero D. infinite

*Held on 8 July, 2018.

6. For the function $Q = A . K^{\alpha} . L^{\beta}$, which of the following is correct?

A. The degree of homogeneity is 1
B. Elasticity of substitution is equal to $\alpha + \beta$
C. Output elasticity with respect to capital is α
D. Marginal product of a factor = Average product of the factor

7. When an information asymmetry is observed after an agreement is obtained between individuals, it is called:

A. Signalling
B. Moral hazard
C. None of the above
D. Both (A) and (B) above

8. In the given diagram, after the price change, the price line shifts from PQ to PQ′. And consumer comes to equilibrium at point B instead of point A. Then what is true for potatoes?

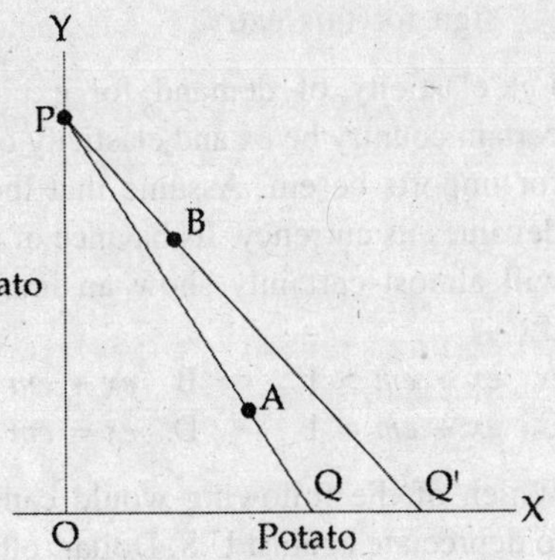

A. It is a normal good.
B. It is an inferior good.
C. It is a Giffen good.
D. Nothing can be said about the nature of the good.

9. Which amongst the following is a correct description of inverse demand function?

A. $p = f(\text{D})$ B. $\text{D} = f(p)$
C. $\text{D} = f\left(\frac{1}{p}\right)$ D. $p = f\left(\text{D}, \frac{1}{y}\right)$

Where p = price, D = demand and y = income.

10. The first fundamental Theorem of Welfare Economics requires:

A. that there be an efficient market for every commodity.
B. that the economy operates at some point on the utility possibility curve.
C. producers and consumers to be price takers.
D. All of the above.

11. The Theory in which trade cycle is generated due to excess of actual over the desired investment has been given by who amongst the following?

A. R.G. Hawtry B. F. Hayek
C. P. Samuelson D. J. Schumpeter

12. Consider the following statements:

(*a*) 'Liquidity trap' is a situation when people prefer to hold money rather than investing it.
(*b*) 'Liquidity preference' is the situation when people prefer to invest money rather than hold it.
(*c*) 'Liquidity crunch' is a situation of short supply of money in the money market.
(*d*) 'Credit crunch' is a situation of short supply of money in the loan market.

Select the correct statements using the code given below:

A. (*a*), (*b*) and (*d*)
B. (*a*), (*c*) and (*d*)
C. (*b*), (*c*) and (*d*)
D. (*a*), (*b*) and (*c*)

13. 'Menu costs' in relation to inflation refers to:

A. Cost of revaluing currency.
B. Cost of altering price lists.
C. Cost of the maintenance of monetary base.
D. Cost of finding better rates of return.

14. According to M. Friedman, Quantity Theory of Money is the theory of:

A. Value of money
B. Price determination
C. Nominal income
D. Demand for money

15. Gilt-edged market means:
A. Bullion Market
B. Market of pure metals
C. Market of government securities
D. Market of commodities

16. Which of the following is likely to be most inflationary in its impact?
A. Repayment of public debt
B. Borrowings from the public to finance a budget deficit
C. Borrowings from banks to finance a budget deficit
D. Creating new money to finance a budget deficit

17. Consider the following statements regarding the Marginal Standing Facility (MSF).
(*a*) MSF is on the line of the existing LAF and is part of it.
(*b*) MSF is a costlier route than Repo.
(*c*) MSF functions as the last resort for Banks to borrow short term funds.
(*d*) MSF is linked to the net demand and time liabilities of the Banks.
Choose the correct code given below.
A. (*b*), (*c*) and (*d*) B. (*a*), (*b*) and (*c*)
C. (*a*), (*c*) and (*d*) D. (*a*), (*b*), (*c*) and (*d*)

18. 'The absorption approach' of analyzing balance of payments was formulated by:
A. M. Friedman
B. Marshall and Lerner
C. Sydney Alexander
D. Haberler

19. Which amongst the following is not correctly matched with regard to balance of payments account?

	Item	*Nature*
A.	Import of goods and services	Debit in current account
B.	Receipt of transfer payments	Credit in the current account
C.	Direct investment receipts	Credit in the capital account
D.	Portfolio investment redemption	Debit in the current account

20. Prebisch-singer hypothesis relates to:
A. Balance of payments problem of developing countries.
B. Terms of trade of developing countries.
C. Prevalency of poverty among developing countries.
D. Inequality of income in developing countries.

21. Which of the following statement about the India's balance of payments is not correct?
A. If a foreign citizen deposits some money in a bank in India, the accounts regard this as a credit.
B. The current account balance shows only the balance for the trade in goods and services combined.
C. Allowing for errors and omissions, the accounts always balance.
D. If the country's reserves of foreign currencies increase then there is a minus sign for this entry.

22. Let elasticity of demand for exports for a certain country be ex and elasticity of demand for imports be em. Assume that the country devalues its currency. Its balance of payments will almost certainly show an improvement if:
A. $ex + em > 1$ B. $ex + em < 1$
C. $ex + em = 1$ D. $ex = em = 1$

23. Which of the following would cause Rupee to depreciate against U.S. Dollar, other things being equal?
A. A rise in interest rates in India.
B. A fall in incomes in U.S.A.
C. An expected rise in the external value of rupee.
D. An increased flow of foreign investment into India.

24. According to Mercantilists, trade is a:
A. Positive sum game
B. Infinite sum game
C. Zero sum game
D. Negative sum game

25. There is incomplete specialization in production when country faces:
A. constant opportunity costs
B. decreasing opportunity costs
C. increasing opportunity costs
D. indeterminate opportunity costs

26. Tax buoyancy is expressed as:

A. $E_{TY}^{b} = \frac{\Delta T^{b}}{\Delta Y} \times \frac{Y}{T^{b}}$

B. $E_{TY}^{b} = \frac{\Delta Y}{\Delta T^{b}} \times \frac{T^{b}}{Y}$

C. $E_{TY}^{b} = \frac{\Delta Y}{\Delta T^{b}} \div \frac{T^{b}}{Y}$

D. $E_{TY}^{b} = \frac{\Delta T^{b}}{\Delta Y} \div \frac{Y}{T^{b}}$

Where, E_{TY}^{b} = Buoyancy of tax revenue to income
T^{b} = Total Tax revenue
ΔT^{b} = Change in total tax revenue
Y = Income
ΔY = Change in income

27. Income tax is generally based on the principle of:
A. Benefit received principle
B. Ability to pay principle
C. Willingness to pay principle
D. None of these

28. Which method can help in obtaining a welfare improvement if externalities exist?
A. Regulation
B. Assigning property rights and permitting bargaining
C. Pigovian taxes
D. All of the above

29. Which of the following is a capital receipts in the Government budget?
A. Interest receipts on loans given by the Government to other parties.
B. Dividend and profit of public enterprises.
C. Borrowings of the government from the public.
D. Property tax receipts.

30. Which amongst the following would be most effective in mitigating the effect of externalities?
A. Fiscal policy
B. Regulation of monopoly
C. Active monetary policy
D. Freeing the markets

31. Maximum social advantage is achieved when:
A. Total Social Sacrifice = Total Social Benefits
B. Marginal Social Sacrifice = Marginal Social Benefits
C. Net Social Sacrifice = Net Social Benefits
D. Average Social Sacrifice = Average Social Benefits

32. Statutory incidence of a tax deals with:
A. the person(s) legally responsible for paying the tax.
B. the amount of revenue left over after taxes.
C. the amount of taxes paid after accounting for inflation
D. the amount of tax revenue generated after a tax is levied.

33. The relationship described by the Expectations-Augmented Phillips curve is correct in which of the following?
A. Only in the long run.
B. Only in the short run.
C. Both in the short run and in the long run.
D. Neither in the short run nor in the long run.

34. Non Accelerating Inflation Rate of Unemployment (NAIRU) means:
A. a rate of unemployment for which the change in the rate of inflation is zero.
B. a rate of inflation which makes the rate of unemployment zero.
C. a rate of inflation for which the change in the rate of unemployment is zero.
D. a rate of unemployment which is equal to the rate of inflation.

35. New Keynesians use which of the following to explain price and wage stickyness?
A. Staggered labour contracts
B. Menu Costs
C. Behaviour based on bounded rationality
D. All of the above

36. Consider the following statements:
(*a*) Effective demand in a market is the demand for a product or service which occurs when purchasers are constrained in a different market.
(*b*) Notional demand is the demand that occurs when purchasers are not constrained in any market.

Which of the above statements is/are correct? Answer from the code below:
A. Only (*a*) is correct
B. Only (*b*) is correct
C. Both (*a*) and (*b*) are correct
D. Neither (*a*) nor (*b*) is correct

37. For the capitalist economy, the primary objective of the New Classical Economics is to explain which of the following?
A. Business cycle phenomenon
B. Underemployment
C. Wage-price rigidity
D. Effectiveness of Government policy

38. Which of the following growth model(s) assume(s) Neutral Technical Progress?
A. Harrod model B. Solow model
C. Both (A) and (B) D. Neither (A) nor (B)

39. In an economy, the GDP deflator is found to be 110 for the current year. If the GDP has registered an annual growth rate of 15 per cent in the same year, then, the rate of growths of real GDP will be:
A. 5% B. 1.5%
C. 25% D. 2.5%

40. What is the nature of equilibrium in the IS-LM model?
A. Stock equilibrium
B. Flow equilibrium
C. Stock and flow equilibrium
D. Oscillating equilibrium

41. If marginal propensity to import is 0.1 and the marginal propensity to consume is 0.7, the value of the income multiplier will be:
A. 1.25 B. 2.33
C. 2.5 D. 3.33

42. According to neo-classical theory of distribution, constancy in the wage share in national income would come about only when the elasticity of factor substitution:
A. is less than one B. is equal to one
C. is zero D. is greater than one

43. Which amongst the following is not a feature of J.E. Meade's model?
A. Perfect competition prevails.
B. Economy produces consumption goods and producer goods.
C. Perfect substitution is possible between consumption and capital goods.
D. It examines the relationship between the growth rate of population and growth rate of savings.

44. Consider the following production function forms with a technical progress term $A(t)$.
(*a*) $Q = f(K_t, A(t) . L_t)$
(*b*) $Q = f(A(t) . K_t, L_t)$
(*c*) $Q = A(t) f(K_t, L_t)$

Of the above which production function, with labour augmenting technology will keep the distribution of output between labour and capital as constant? Answer from the code below:
A. Only (*a*) B. Both (*a*) and (*b*)
C. Only (*c*) D. Both (*a*) and (*c*)

45. Which of the following statements about the AK model (Y = AK) of growth is false?
A. This is a part of endogeneous growth theories.
B. The model assumes that an increase in the physical stock of capital will shift the production function upwards.
C. The model assumes diminishing returns to capital.
D. The model suggest that if the level of investment is higher than depreciation, there would be sustained growth.

46. Which of the following is not a correct feature for the absolute convergence to hold good?
A. Same population growth rate
B. Same savings propensity
C. Same capital-labour ratio
D. Different capital-labour ratio

47. In Solow's growth model, the output per capita is a function of:
A. Labour-Output ratio
B. Capital-Output ratio
C. Technical progress
D. Capital-Labour ratio

48. Dusenberry was of the opinion that less developed countries will have serious and adverse effect on their balance of payments due to:
A. demonstration effect
B. multiplier effect
C. backwash effect
D. spread effect

49. Leibenstein in his critical minimum effort thesis treats population as a factor that is:
A. Income-generating
B. Investment-inducing
C. Income-depressing
D. Market-expanding

50. 'Workers must own the capital to which their savings has given rise.' This is an important assumption of the growth model, developed by:
A. L. Pasinetti B. N. Kaldor
C. R. Solow D. J.E. Meade

51. Which one of the following is true for demand side vicious circle of poverty?
A. Low income → Low demand → Low investment → Capital deficiency → Low productivity → Low income
B. Low productivity → Low income → Low savings → Low investment → Capital deficiency
C. Low income → Low investment → Low demand → Low Capital deficiency
D. Low demand → Low saving → Low productivity → Low investment → Capital deficiency

52. Which of the following is the cause of disequilibrium between warranted rate of growth and actual rate of growth in the Harrod model?
A. Discrepancy between Ex-ante investment and Ex-post investment.
B. Discrepancy between Ex-ante investment and Ex-ante savings.
C. Discrepancy between Ex-ante savings and Ex-post savings.
D. Discrepancy between Ex-post investment and Ex-post savings.

53. Which one of the following committees recommended to establish the National Bank for Agriculture and Rural Development (NBARD) in India?
A. Narsimham Committee
B. Chakravarti Committee
C. Abhijit Sen Committee
D. Shivaraman Committee

54. Which of the following option(s) is/are true for National Action Plan for Climate Change?
A. It was launched in 2008
B. It has 8 vertical missions for pollution control.
C. Both (A) and (B) are true
D. Neither (A) nor (B) is true

55. Which one of the following schemes is not included in the Rashtriya Krishi Vikas Yojana (RKVY)?
A. National Mission for Protein Supplements
B. Saffron Mission
C. Accelerated Fodder Development Programme
D. All of the above

56. Which of the following is portrayed in the population pyramid of a country?
A. Rural-urban distribution of population
B. Young-old distribution of population.
C. Age and sex distribution of population.
D. Gender distribution of population.

57. In the long period, which one of the following curves would aptly represent the time path of population for a developing economy?

A. Exponential curve B. Logistic curve
C. Lorenz curve D. Hyperbolic curve

58. Identify the correct statement about the relationship between total fertility rate and gross reproduction rate.
A. TFR < GRR B. TFR = GRR
C. TFR > GRR D. All of the above

59. Which of the following is often referred to as the 'hedonic price' method for valuing environmental assets?
A. Using linkages between variations in-house prices and geographical proximity to an environmental asset.
B. Using 'existence value' to estimate the value of an environmental asset.
C. Using travel costs to estimate the value of an environmental asset.
D. Using 'willingness to pay' to value an environmental asset.

60. Which of the following is not a scheme for the upliftment of women in India?
A. Beti Bachao, Beti Padhao
B. Sukanya Samridhi Yojana
C. Gender Budgeting
D. UJALA Scheme

61. In the context of doubling of farmers income objective, which of the following is not correct?
A. The target year is 2022-23.
B. It is real income which is to be doubled.
C. Income from cultivation alone is to be doubled.
D. Diversification of agriculture is to be promoted to achieve this objective.

62. Which one of the following statements is correct?
A. Global warming is simply another term for greenhouse effect.
B. Global warming is an entirely natural phenomenon.
C. Global warming means melting down of glaciers.
D. Global warming is the rise in average temperature at earth's surface.

63. According to Economic Survey 2017-18, the Indian economy is becoming more formalised. This is indicated by which of the following shifts? Select the correct answer from the codes given below:
(*a*) The introduction of GST has brought more firms in the indirect tax net.
(*b*) After demonetisation, a significant increase has taken place in the number of individuals filing income tax returns.
(*c*) An increase in savings in the formal financial sector.

Code:
A. (*a*) and (*b*) B. Only (*c*)
C. (*a*), (*b*) and (*c*) D. (*b*), (*c*)

64. Which of the following statements are correct regarding Finance Commission in India?
(*a*) Finance Commission is constituted under Article 275 of the Constitution.
(*b*) The provision for Grants-in-aids to the states are provided for under Article 280.

Which of the above statement(s) is/are correct. Choose the correct answer from the codes given below:
A. Only (*a*) B. Only (*b*)
C. Both (*a*) and (*b*) D. Neither (*a*) nor (*b*)

65. The share of agriculture in the GDP of India has declined over the years. Which of the following is not a correct reason for this?
A. Relatively faster rate of growth of non-agricultural sectors in the economy.
B. Stagnant or slow rise in yield of agriculture commodities.
C. Educated rural youths are not opting for agriculture as an occupation.
D. Low value addition in case of agricultural commodities.

66. In the last decade, which one among the following sectors has attracted the highest Foreign Direct Investment (FDI) inflow into India?
A. Telecommunication sector
B. Defence sector
C. Service sector
D. Insurance sector

67. In the context of the 'twin balance sheet problem' in India, consider the following statements:

(*a*) Over leveraged corporate debt.

(*b*) High Non-Performance Assets of nationalised banks.

(*c*) High fiscal deficit.

Select the correct answer from the codes given below:

A. (*a*) and (*c*) B. (*a*) and (*b*)
C. (*b*) and (*c*) D. (*a*), (*b*) and (*c*)

68. In 2016-2017 the Centrally Sponsored Schemes (CSS's) were restructured by the Government of India. Select the correct statements related to the restructuring, using the codes given below:

(*a*) The decision of restructuring was taken by the Governing Council of the NITI Aayog.

(*b*) This will avoid overlaping of expenditure and provide visibility and impact to the CSS's.

(*c*) The CSS's have been classified into flagship and extra flagship categories.

(*d*) The existing number of the CSS's is 37.

Code:

A. (*a*), (*b*), (*c*) and (*d*)
B. (*b*), (*c*) and (*d*)
C. (*a*) and (*b*)
D. (*a*), (*b*) and (*c*)

69. As per census 2011, rank the following states in descending order of degree of urbanisation.

(*a*) Tamil Nadu (*b*) Maharashtra
(*c*) Goa (*d*) Punjab

Select the correct answer from the codes given below:

A. (*b*), (*a*), (*d*), (*c*) B. (*c*), (*a*), (*b*), (*d*)
C. (*a*), (*c*), (*d*), (*b*) D. (*d*), (*b*), (*a*), (*c*)

70. As on 31st, March 2017, external debt of India was in which of the following range as a percentage of GDP?

A. 14 to 16 per cent
B. 16 to 18 per cent
C. 18 to 20 per cent
D. 20 to 22 per cent

71. In relation to considerations of demographic dividend, there appears to be 'demographic dualism' exhibited by the Indian states. In this regard consider the following factors:

(*a*) Total Fertility Rate

(*b*) Sex Ratio

(*c*) Per capita income

Of the above, which factor(s) is/are correct. Answer from the codes below:

A. Only (*a*)
B. Both (*a*) and (*b*)
C. Both (*b*) and (*c*)
D. Only (*b*)

72. Arrange the following events in the Indian economy in chronological order:

(*a*) First phase of nationalisation of 14 Banks

(*b*) Establishment of Narshimhan Committee I on Banking system

(*c*) Enactment of FEMA Act

(*d*) Establishment of EXIM Bank of India

Code:

A. (*a*), (*c*), (*d*), (*b*)
B. (*a*), (*d*), (*b*), (*c*)
C. (*a*), (*c*), (*b*), (*d*)
D. (*a*), (*d*), (*c*), (*b*)

73. Which amongst the following pairs is not correctly matched?

	(Concept)	***(Organization)***
A.	Gender Development Index	UNDP
B.	Ease of Doing Business	World Bank
C.	Inclusion Index	World Economic Forum
D.	World Hunger Index	United Nations

74. Consider the following diagram which shows the production of a commodity under the condition of increasing cost. If a unit tax is imposed on the commodity, what will be the amount of the burden of the tax on the buyers?

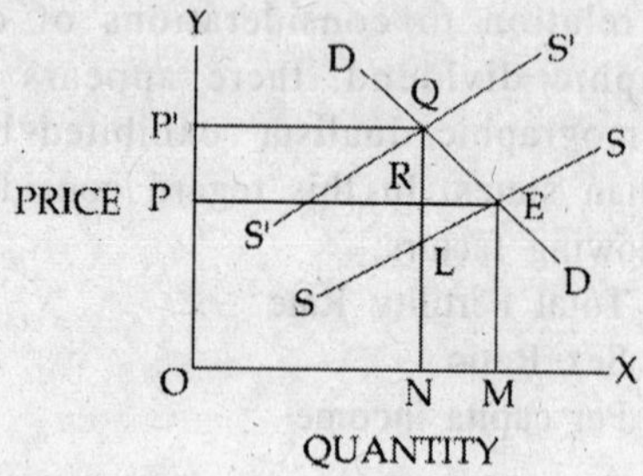

A. NL
B. LQ
C. LR
D. RQ

75. Which of the following statement(s) is/are true?

(*a*) a common resource is rival and non-excludable.

(*b*) a public good is non-rival and non-excludable.

Select the correct answer from the codes given below:

A. Both (*a*) and (*b*)
B. Only (*a*)
C. Only (*b*)
D. Neither (*a*) and (*b*)

76. Arrange the following books in chronological order of their publication. Select the correct answer from the codes given below:

(*a*) The Affluent Society
(*b*) Asian Drama
(*c*) The General Theory of Employment, Interest and Money
(*d*) Development as Freedom

Code:

A. (*c*), (*b*), (*a*), (*d*)
B. (*c*), (*a*), (*b*), (*d*)
C. (*a*), (*b*), (*c*), (*d*)
D. (*d*), (*c*), (*b*), (*a*)

77. Market failure can occur because of:

A. Imperfect competition
B. Externalities
C. Both (A) and (B)
D. Neither (A) nor (B)

78. Capital gains means:

A. An increase in the value of an asset.
B. An increase in the stock of capital.
C. An increase in the yield of an asset.
D. An increase in the amount of foreign capital.

79. Palma ratio is a measure of:

A. Inequality of income
B. Stock market volatility
C. Morbidity in a region
D. Volatility of crop prices

Directions (Qs. Nos. 80-84): *These questions are Assertion (A) and Reason (R) type. Key to these questions is as follows:*

A. Both (A) and (R) are true and (R) is the correct explanation of (A).
B. Both (A) and (R) are true, but (R) is not the correct explanation of (A).
C. (A) is true, but (R) is false.
D. (A) is false, but (R) is true.

80. **(A) :** In Solow's growth model under equilibrium conditions capital labour ratio does not change.

(R) : Substitution between capital and labour is possible.

81. **(A) :** International trade along the lines of comparative advantage improves the allocative efficiency of existing resources.

(R) : International trade is an engine of growth.

82. **(A) :** The production possibility Frontier can be a straight line.

(R) : The factors are not specialised and can be substituted at no extra cost.

83. **(A) :** Devaluation results in expenditure switching in an economy.

(R) : Devaluation alters the composition of the current account of the balance of payments.

84. **(A) :** External forces are of singular importance to economic activities of the developing states.

(R) : Relations between the dominant and dependent states are dynamic to reinforce unequal pattern.

85. Given the Demand function of a consumer $D = 10 - 2p$, the consumer's surplus at price $= 2$ is:

A. 2
B. 10
C. 9
D. 15

86. Total cost function of a producer is C = 10 + 5Q + 2Q^2. If price is 15, what is marginal cost of the producer in equilibrium?

A. 10 B. 5
C. 15 D. 4

87. Which of the following is condition of economic viability and technological feasibility of Leontief's static system?

A. Marshall-Edgeworth conditions
B. Kuhn-Tucker conditions
C. Hawkins-Simon conditions
D. Value of the objective function of primal problem should equal the value of the objective function of the dual of the primal

88. Simplex method of solving Linear Programming problems was developed by:

A. Koopmans
B. Dantzig
C. Leontief
D. Solow

89. A bag contains 5 red, 7 white and 3 green balls. One ball is randomly drawn from the bag. What is the probability that it is green?

A. $\frac{12}{15}$ B. $\frac{1}{5}$
C. $\frac{7}{15}$ D. $\frac{1}{3}$

90. If a sample survey of the same 100 households is conducted in a particular village, annually for five years, the data so collected will be described as:

A. Time Series Data
B. Cross-section Data
C. Panel Data
D. Pooled Time Series and Cross-section Data

91. If in a distribution mean is 40, mode is 60 and the standard deviation is 10, then the coefficient of skewness will be:

A. −2 B. 2
C. −20 D. 5

92. In a multiple linear regression with 4 independent variables, the overall regression's significance is to be tested. Which test would be used?

A. Z test B. F test
C. χ^2 test D. *t* test

93. If a sample of 100 is to be taken from a population of 1000 farmers consisting of marginal small and large farmers, which of the following will be the most appropriate sampling method?

A. Simple random sampling
B. Cluster sampling
C. Stratified random sampling
D. Systematic sampling

94. Which of the following statements are valid concerning a recursive system?

(*a*) The parameters can be validly estimated using separate application of OLS to each equation.
(*b*) The independent variables may be correlated with the error terms in other equations.

Code:

A. (*a*) only
B. (*b*) only
C. Both (*a*) and (*b*)
D. Neither (*a*) nor (*b*)

95. Match the following lists and select the correct answer from codes below:

List-I	***List-II***
(*a*) Contingency Table	(*i*) Stationarity
(*b*) Unit root test	(*ii*) Causality
(*c*) Fisher's F test	(*iii*) χ^2 test
(*d*) Granger test	(*iv*) Test of significance of over-all regression

Code:

	(*a*)	(*b*)	(*c*)	(*d*)
A.	(*iii*)	(*i*)	(*iv*)	(*ii*)
B.	(*i*)	(*ii*)	(*iii*)	(*iv*)
C.	(*iv*)	(*iii*)	(*ii*)	(*i*)
D.	(*ii*)	(*iii*)	(*i*)	(*iv*)

96. Generalized Least Squares method of estimation will not be suitable for dealing with which of the following problems:

(*a*) Autocorrelated disturbances

(*b*) Heteroscedastic disturbances

(*c*) Multicollinearity

(*d*) Errors in variables

Code:

A. (*a*) only

B. (*b*) only

C. (*c*) and (*d*)

D. (*a*) and (*b*)

97. Match List-I with List-II and select the correct answer from the codes given below:

List-I (Growth Model)	***List-II (Equation)***
(*a*) Solow	(*i*) $\dfrac{\Delta N}{N} = \dfrac{\Delta K}{K}$
(*b*) Domar	(*ii*) $Gw \cdot Cr = s$
(*c*) Joan Robinson	(*iii*) $sf(k) = (\delta + n)k$
(*d*) Harrod	(*iv*) $\dfrac{\Delta I}{I} = \alpha\sigma$

Code:

	(*a*)	(*b*)	(*c*)	(*d*)
A.	(*iii*)	(*iv*)	(*i*)	(*ii*)
B.	(*iv*)	(*ii*)	(*iii*)	(*i*)
C.	(*iii*)	(*i*)	(*ii*)	(*iv*)
D.	(*ii*)	(*iv*)	(*iii*)	(*i*)

98. In the adjacent diagram, Government should fix the price at which of the following points to make monopoly result in a socially optimal outcome?

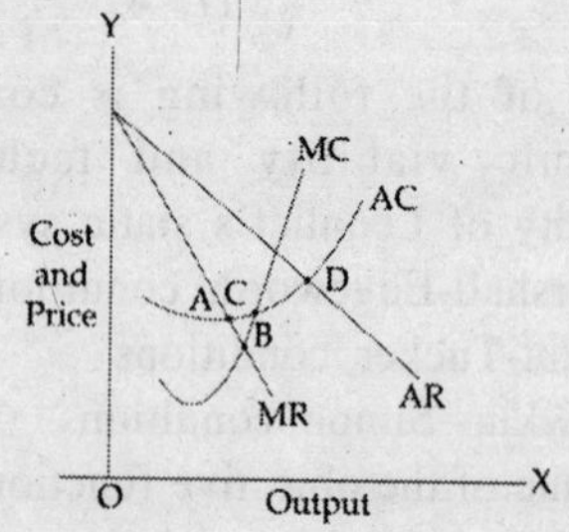

A. At point A B. At point B

C. At point C D. At point D

99. If the producer pays the price for each of the inputs that is used is equal to its value of Marginal product, then which one of the following does he earn?

A. Zero supernormal profit

B. Monopoly profit

C. Positive supernormal profit

D. Negative supernormal profit

100. Which of the following is not correctly matched for Union Budget 2018-19, announced on 01.02.2018?

	(As % of GDP)
A. Fiscal Deficit	3.5
B. Revenue Deficit	2.2
C. Primary Deficit	1.2
D. Effective Revenue Deficit	0.3

ANSWERS

1	2	3	4	5	6	7	8	9	10
A	D	C	B	C	C	B	C	A	D
11	**12**	**13**	**14**	**15**	**16**	**17**	**18**	**19**	**20**
B	B	B	D	C	D	A	C	D	B
21	**22**	**23**	**24**	**25**	**26**	**27**	**28**	**29**	**30**
B	A	B	C	C	A	B	D	C	A
31	**32**	**33**	**34**	**35**	**36**	**37**	**38**	**39**	**40**
B	A	A	A	D	C	A	C	A	C
41	**42**	**43**	**44**	**45**	**46**	**47**	**48**	**49**	**50**
C	B	D	A	C	C	D	A	C	A

51	52	53	54	55	56	57	58	59	60
A	A	D	C	*	C	B	C	A	D
61	**62**	**63**	**64**	**65**	**66**	**67**	**68**	**69**	**70**
C	D	C	D	C	C	B	C	B	D
71	**72**	**73**	**74**	**75**	**76**	**77**	**78**	**79**	**80**
A	B	D	D	A	B	C	A	A	A
81	**82**	**83**	**84**	**85**	**86**	**87**	**88**	**89**	**90**
B	A	A	B	C	C	C	B	B	C
91	**92**	**93**	**94**	**95**	**96**	**97**	**98**	**99**	**100**
A	B	C	C	A	C	A	C	A	A

* *Error in Questions/Options.*

EXPLANATORY ANSWERS

1. In perfect competition prices is always equal to the marginal cost of production. But under monopoly or imperfect competition, price is always higher than MC. It is because MR = MC at the equilibrium level of output. At this level of output the AR curve lies above the MR curve. So P = AR is greater than MR. Therefore, P > MC. On this point there is hardly any difference between monopoly and imperfect competition. In fact, many economists treat monopoly as an extreme form of imperfect competition.

2. Nash Equilibrium: All games do not have a dominant strategy for every player. In case of payoff matrix of Table below, Firm A has no dominant strategy. Its best decision depends on what Firm B does: if B advertises A must advertise, while if B decides not to advertise, A benefits by not advertising.

		Firm B	
		Advertise	Don't Advertise
Firm A	Advertise	11, 6	16, 0
	Don't Advertise	7, 9	20, 2

Now suppose both firms must make decisions at the same time, then what should Firm A do? The answer is: Firm A must try to determine what action Firm B is likely to take. In other words, Firm A must put itself in Firm B's place, and see what is best from B's point of view: advertising or not advertising. In the above Table, if Firm A advertises, B earns 6 by advertising and 0 by not advertising. If Firm A does not advertise, B gets 9 by advertising and 2 by not advertising. Thus, Firm B has a dominant strategy—advertises (irrespective of what A does). Now, given that Firm B is rational, Firm A knows that Firm B will advertise and, therefore, Firm A should choose the best strategy from column 1. Obviously, now A will choose to advertise as it gains 11 against 7 if it does not advertise. This is Nash Equilibrium for this game. A Nash equilibrium is a set of strategies such that each player believes (correctly) that it is doing the best it can, given the strategy of the opponents. Since player is satisfied that it has made the best decision possible, he has no incentive to deviate from the chosen strategy. Thus, the Nash strategies are stable.

The distinction between Nash equilibrium and the dominant-strategy equilibrium may be well understood. In dominant strategy case, each player chooses his best strategy, irrespective of the strategies of other players. While in case of Nash equilibrium each player chooses a strategy that is his best choice, subject to what strategies the opponent chooses.

As is obvious from the discussion so far, Nash equilibrium is possible only if we assume that all players understand the game and are rational. This may not be true always. If you are cautious and are also concerned that your opponent may not be fully knowing the game or is likely to be irrational then you may choose a strategy which maximizes the minimum gain that can be earned, known as maximin strategy.

3. **Equilibrium in an Oligopolistic Market**

When a market is in equilibrium, firms are doing the best they can and have no reason to change their price or output.

Nash Equilibrium: Equilibrium in oligopoly markets means that each firm will want to do the best it can given what its competitors are doing, and these competitors will do the best they can given what that firm is doing.

Cournot's equilibrium is Nash equilibrium. This particular equilibrium is reached by the assumption of zero conjectural variation.

5. The intersection of average and marginal cost at minimum average cost may be shown by noting that the slops of the average cost curve is equal to zero at its minimum; that is, its first derivative is equal to zero at its minimum. For the average variable cost curve.

$$\frac{dAVC}{dQ} = \frac{d(TVC/Q)}{dQ} = 0$$

$$= \frac{Q(dTVC/dQ) - TVC(dQ/dQ)}{Q^2} = 0$$

Dividing both terms in the numerator and factoring out 1/Q results in

$$\frac{1}{Q}[MC - AVC] = 0$$

For the right side of the expression to equal zero, MC – AVC, or marginal cost equals average variable cost when the slope of average variable cost equals zero (when AVC has reached its minimum).

6. The idea of Cobb-Douglas production function is that output is determined by capital input, labour input and technological progress. The form of the Cobb-Douglas production function is:

$$Y = AK^{\alpha}L^{\beta}.$$

Here, Y is output, K is capital input, L is labour input, α and β are output elasticity of capital and output elasticity of labour, respectively.

7. Asymmetric information usually leads to the following two problems:

1. *Adverse selection:* Behaviour that takes advantage of asymmetric information before a transaction. For example, a person who is not in good health may be more inclined to purchase life insurance than someone who feels good.
2. *Moral Hazard:* Behaviour that takes advantage of asymmetric information after a transaction. For example, if someone has fire insurance they may be more likely to commit arson to reap the benefits of the insurance.

Most commonly, asymmetric information is studied in the context of the *principal-agent problem.* The principal-agent problem is about the difficulties that arise under conditions of asymmetric information when a principal hires an agent. Such situation usually causes the problem of potential moral hazard and conflict of interest since the principal hires the agent to pursue the principal's interests. The principal-agent problem arises when a principal compensates an agent for performing certain acts that are useful to the principal and costly to the agent, and where there are elements of the performance that are costly to observe.

Asymmetric information in general and principle-agent problem in particular are very important in any bargaining process. They are especially important in any contract negotiations.

There are some methods to address information asymmetry. *Signaling* and *screening* are the most popular. Michael Spence (1973) originally proposed the idea of signaling. He proposed that in a situation with information asymmetry, it is possible for people to signal their type, thus believably transferring information to the other party and resolving the asymmetry. Joseph Stiglitz pioneered the theory of screening. In this way the under-informed party can induce the other party to reveal their information. They can provide a set of choices in such a way that the choice depends on the private information of the other party.

8. **Giffen good case:** A Giffen good is special category among inferior goods. It means that not all inferior goods are Giffen goods. Which inferior good is also a Giffen good is determined by the effect of change in its price on its demand. If, with the fall in price of an inferior good its demand also falls, it is called Giffen good. It means that change in price and change in demand of a Giffen good move in the same direction.

9. **Inverse demand function:** The demand function when price is expressed as a function of quantity demanded: $P = f(Q_d)$.

10. In the 1950s, Arrow (1951) and Debreu (1959) formalized Adam Smith's insight in what are now known as the two fundamental theorems of welfare economics. The first theorem says that under certain conditions every competitive equilibrium is Pareto-efficient; that is, in an economy that reaches a competitive equilibrium, no one can be made better-off without making someone else worse-off. The second theorem says that under certain conditions one can obtain every Pareto-efficient allocation of resources through a decentralized market mechanism. These theorems are relevant to any discussion of the government's role in resource allocation. They imply that under the conditions assumed by Arrow and Debreu, no government or central planner, however omniscient and well intentioned, can improve on the results obtained by the free market system. The best of all possible planners might do as well as competitive firms attempting to maximize their own profits, but they would never do better.

If the real word fulfilled the assumptions of the fundamental theorems of welfare economics, the market would produce every good in demand. Governments would not need to provide any good or service. In that case, equity considerations would be the only economic justification for government intervention.

13. Menu costs, a form of transaction costs, refer to the cost of updating menus, price lists, brochures, etc. by firms when prices change in an economy.

14. Keynes gave a lot of importance to the relationship between the demand for money and the rate of interest. This is consistent with his liquidity preference theory of interest. The result was that the relationship between the price-level and the demand for money was completely over-looked by the people. In fact, the influence of the Keynesian analysis was so overwhelming that people have practically forgotten the quantity theory of money. But in 1956, Prof. Milton Friedman restated the quantity theory of money and published an article on it.

According to Friedman, the quantity theory of money is not a theory stating anything about price-level or production. It is a theory about the demand for money. Broadly speaking, this means that the meaning conveyed by the equation $M = \frac{PT}{V}$, is acceptable to Friedman. This equation tries to state that the demand for money changes in the same direction and proportion as the price-level. Similarly, the real income, *i.e.*, T, is also a factor determining the demand for money. This is also acceptable to Friedman. But, the old belief that a change in income brings about a change in the demand for money in the same direction and proportion, is not acceptable to Friedman. Friedman thinks that an increase in income brings about an over-proportionate increase in the demand for money.

15. The Indian capital market is broadly divided as the gilt-edged market and the industrial securities market. The gilt-edged market refers to the market for government and semi-government securities, backed by the RBI. The securities traded in this market are stable in value and are much sought after by banks and other institutions.

The industrial securities market refers to the market for shares and debentures of old and new companies. This market is further divided as the new-issue market and the old capital market meaning "the stock exchange". The new-issue market–often referred to primary market, denotes the raising of new capital in the form of shares and debentures, whereas the old-issue market deals with securities already issued by companies. The old-issue market or the stock market exchange is also known as the secondary market. Both markets are equally important, but often, the new-issue market is much more important from the point of economic growth. However, the functioning of the new-issue market will be facilitated only when there are abundant facilities for transfer of existing securities. Besides the gilt-edged market and variable-yield industrial securities, the Indian capital market includes development financial institutions and financial intermediaries.

17. **Marginal Standing Facility (MSF)** is the rate at which RBI lends funds overnight to the banks, which are included in the Second Schedule of Reserve Bank of India Act, 1934, against government securities. The Reserve Bank of India has come up with this borrowing scheme to regulate the mismatch in short-term asset liability more effectively.

Repo rate vs MSF: Differences

1. Repo Rate is the rate at which the money is lent by Reserve Bank of India to commercial bank on the other hand MSF is a rate at which RBI lends money only to scheduled banks.
2. Repo rate is applicable to loans provided to banks, who are applying to meet short-term financial needs. MSF is meant for lending overnight to banks.
3. Lending money at repo rates is done in lieu of selling bank's securities as collateral to RBI along with the agreement of repurchase. Loans given at MSF rates involve providing government securities as collateral.
4. MSF banks are allowed to use the securities that come under Statutory Liquidity Ratio in the process of availing loans from RBI. And therefore, MSF is 1% more than repo rate.

18. The absorption approach is the Keynesian current account model of the open economy. This approach is historically due to the work of Alexander (1952), who coined the word absorption, as well as Meade (1951); and further elaborated in Harberger (1950) and Johnson (1958). It is also the first macroeconomic approach to the balance of payments, supplanting the earlier partial equilibrium approach, the elasticities approach, examining the relative price responses of imports and exports to devaluation. The absorption approach described the balance of payments as the difference in *aggregate* between income and absorption (or expenditure). If the former exceeded the latter there would be a trade (balance of payments) surplus and vice versa. The intuition is straightforward; if income exceeds spending (absorption or expenditure) then there is a trade balance surplus. This also implies a balance of payments surplus as the capital account is ignored, as are any other service account elements of the current account. Thus the balance of trade and the balance of payments are equivalent in this approach or model.

20. Economists like Gunnar Myrdal, Raul Prebisch and Hans Singer have argued that the primary exporting countries, particularly those of the Third World, have been experiencing a secular (*i.e.,* long-term) deterioration in the terms of trade. The implications of this argument, which is often referred to as the Prebisch-Singer thesis, is that less developed countries had to export increasing amounts of their primary products in exchange for imports of manufactured goods from the industrially advanced countries. The secular deterioration in the terms of trade was considered as one of the important reasons for these countries' economic backwardness. This deterioration in the terms of trade causes large transfer of income from developing to developed countries, as indicated towards the end of this section.

22. The elasticity approach to balance of payments adjustment focuses on the current account of the balance of payments. On the assumption that there may be distortion in relative prices in the international market, it explores the question: what conditions must prevail in the foreign exchange market for a devaluation or depreciation of the currency to improve the balance of payments starting from equilibrium, with the balance of payments measured either in foreign or domestic currency? It is basically a partial equilibrium analysis—holding constant everything else that may affect the supply of and demand for foreign or domestic currency, except the change in the relative price of foreign and domestic goods arising from the change in the exchange rate itself. It also assumes that the supply elasticity of all goods are infinite. It implies that the domestic price of exports, the foreign price of imports, and the prices of import and export substitutes are constant. Also autonomous expenditure in money terms is held constant.

Under these assumptions, the condition for a devaluation to improve the balance of payments is known as the Marshall-Lerner condition, which states that devaluation will improve the balance of payments on current account, if the sum of the price elasticity of demand for exports (e_x) and imports (e_m) exceeds unity in absolute value *i.e.,* if:

$$| e_x + e_m | > 1.$$

24. The theory of mercantilism originated in England during the sixteenth century. The main emphasis of mercantilism was on encouragement of exports and discouragement of imports. The mercantilist view held that the well-being of a nation depends on the gold and silver reserves which it holds. According to mercantilists, this reserve could be increased by exporting more than the imports as exports will result in inflow of gold and silver; and imports will result in outflow of gold and silver.

The mercantilist view dominated the economic thought during the seventeenth and eighteenth century. Nations, in order to export more than the imports, imposed restrictions on the imports and promoted the exports by way of subsidizing the production. The mercantilism was an erroneous theory which regard the trade as a zero-sum game, (*i.e.,* a game in which one nation gains at the expense of other nation).

25. The standard model of comparative cost advantage brings out a very significant and a more realistic aspect of trade between nations. The standard model of foreign trade is, of course, a significant improvement of the comparative advantage theories of trade. The comparative advantage theories of trade end up with the conclusion that trading partners go for complete specialization in the production of goods in which they have a comparative advantage. In contrast, the standard model of the comparative advantage theory reveals that trading partners go for only partial specialization or incomplete specialization.

According to the comparative advantage and the opportunity cost theories of trade, nations tend to have complete specialization in the production of a commodity in which they have a comparative cost advantage.

In contrast, the standard model of comparative advantage concludes that trading partners go for incomplete specialization or for partial specialization under the condition of increasing opportunity cost–not for complete or full specialization.

26. Tax Elasticity and Tax Buoyancy

The tax elasticity and tax buoyancy concepts measure the response of tax revenue to changes in income. These concepts are important in developing countries where considerable lags exist in tax collection and where it is possible for many individuals to evade taxes. The distinction between tax elasticity and tax buoyancy was developed by Mansfield (1972). Tax elasticity measures the automatic response of tax revenue to income changes. Revenue increases under the elasticity concept exclude the effects of discretionary or legal changes in tax rates or in the tax base, as well as the introduction of new taxes. Tax buoyancy measures the total response of revenue changes (including discretionary adjustments) to changes in income. High tax elasticities are considered good for a country since government can pursue expenditure policies without the need for increasing tax rates and bases frequently. The elasticity of total tax revenue is given by:

$$E_T = \frac{\Delta T^b}{\Delta Y}\frac{Y}{T^b}$$

where, T = adjusted total tax revenue

Y = income.

27. The ability-to-pay principle, states that taxes should be levied on a person according to how well that person can shoulder the burden. This principle is sometimes justified by the claim that all citizens should make an 'equal sacrifice' to support the government. The magnitude of a person's sacrifice, however, depends not only on the size of his tax payment but also on his income and other circumstances.

The ability-to-pay principle leads to two corollary notions of equity: vertical equity and horizontal equity. Vertical equity states that taxpayers with a greater ability to pay taxes should contribute a larger amount. Horizontal equity states that taxpayers with similar abilities to pay should contribute the same amount.

28. The economic problem created by externalities is the classic divergence between private cost and social cost. The usual prescription for nonmonetary externalities is to assign property rights, bargain, or apply a dynamic Pigovian tax on the perpetrator or emissions source, with no direct compensation of the victim.

Environmental economists propose two variants to the neoclassical approach. The first is the Pigouvian taxes approach, which controls pollution with taxes; the second is the property rights approach, which offers a market solution to externalities. This second approach maintains that, by redefining property rights, pollution problems can be solved by polluters and sufferers through bargaining; no state intervention should be necessary.

31. Public finance assumes a great importance in every economy. Its chief objective is to gain maximum social advantage. It is on the basis of this objective of public finance that Dr. Dalton has propounded the Doctrine of Maximum Social Advantage. This doctrine is based on the assumption that (*i*) taxes are the major source of government revenue and (*ii*) the law of diminishing marginal social advantage applies to the public expenditure.

Explanation: The doctrine of Maximum Social Advantage in public finance has been propounded mainly by economists like Dalton and Pigou. That is why this doctrine is also called as the Doctrine of Dalton or Pigou. According to this doctrine, *"The best system of public finance is that which secures the maximum social advantage from the operation it conducts."* In all the activities related to public finance, transfer of wealth takes place. Government collects revenue from the public largely in the form of taxes and other forms, and transfers that revenue to the public in the form of public expenditure. The sacrifice that society has to make by paying taxes, is called social sacrifice. Similarly, the gain which society makes by government expenditure on education, health care, etc., is called social satisfaction. According to this doctrine, the government should strike a balance between the public revenue and public expenditure in such a way as could yield maximum satisfaction.

Diminishing Marginal Utility or Equi-Marginal Utility is the under-current of the doctrine of maximum social satisfaction. When a tax is imposed upon a person, he has to make a monetary sacrifice. The utility of money for the people goes on increasing as they have less and less. Every increase in taxes reduces the amount of money with the public. So that, every additional dose of taxation imposes a greater burden on the society than the preceding one. In other words increasing tax-burden causes increase in marginal social sacrifice MSS. Contrary to it, by way of public expenditure, society gets utility or benefits, but due to each extra unit of public expenditure, the society gets diminishing marginal utility. In other words, the marginal social benefit or MSB goes on decreasing. So, the government goes on comparing marginal social sacrifice with marginal social benefit, while it imposes taxes or makes public expenditure. Society will get maximum welfare only when marginal social sacrifice is equal to marginal social benefit (MSS = MSB). In brief, Pigou stated that *"Expenditure should be pushed in a direction up to the point at which satisfaction obtained from the last shilling spent is equal to the satisfaction lost in respect of the last shilling paid as taxes to the government."*

32. There are two types of tax incidence. One is statutory incidence, which refers to who is legally responsible for transmitting tax payments to the government. The other is economic incidence, which refers to the manner in which incomes are redistributed within the marketplace as a result of a tax. In the case of a sales tax, the statutory incidence of the tax falls upon firms responsible for tabulating sales data and transferring required tax payments to state and local governments. This does not necessarily mean that the economic incidence of a sales tax falls upon firms, however. If firms are able to raise prices in equal proportion to the tax, then consumers will bear the full burden of the tax. Only if firms are unable to pass some of the tax along via higher prices do firms bear any burden of the tax.

33.

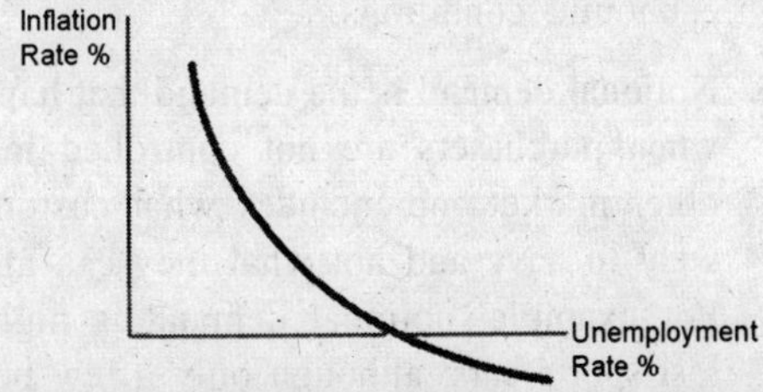

The Phillips curve shows the relationship between inflation and unemployment.

The curve was originally produced by A.W. Phillips in 1958, and suggested a trade off between inflation and unemployment, *i.e.,* if unemployment fell, inflation would rise and vice-versa. This fitted in with thinking at the time, *i.e.,* to reduce inflation the Government had to spend more money to boost aggregate demand, and this would probably cause some inflation; the higher levels of demand would pull up prices. Workers would become more confident because the economy was doing well and because it was not as easy for employers to find new employees, and so wages would be pushed up causing cost push inflation. The model suggested that the Government simply had to pick which point on the Phillips curve it wanted the economy to be at and then introduce the appropriate policies.

However, in the 1970s there were high levels of inflation and high unemployment (called stagflation) which did not seem to fit with the original Phillips curve. The new situation was explained by an expectations augmented Phillips curve (Friedman). This model introduced short and long run Phillips curves and suggested that there was a short run trade off between inflation and unemployment but no long run trade off.

34. Structural unemployment is the rate of unemployment consistent with constant wage inflation (non-accelerating wage rate of unemployment (NAWRU)), or constant price inflation (non-accelerating inflation rate of unemployment (NAIRU)), given current economic conditions.

36. Notional demand is the demand that happens when purchasers are not controlled in any other market and includes what customers' want to have and not what they can afford. For example, notional demand is high for fast sports cars, although only a few people can afford this sort of high price purchase.

Effective demand is the demand for a product or service which occurs when purchasers are constrained by financial capability, government regulation etc. Thus, in the case of the sports car, effective demand might be measured by the actual number of sports cars sold at a certain price during a particular period.

39. Real GDP Growth = Nominal GDP Growth + Inflation

Here, Deflator is 110 *i.e.,* Inflation is 10%

Real GDP Growth = 15 – 10 = 5%.

40. The LM curve represents a *stock equilibrium,* also called *beginning of period equilibrium.* Those stocks of money and bonds that are given at the beginning of a certain period must be held voluntarily—if this is not the case, the rate of interest will adjust until they are.

The IS curve represents a *flow equilibrium,* also called *end of period equilibrium.* The flows 'savings' and 'investment' must match; and real income will adjust if they do not.

41. Income Multiplier

$$= \frac{1}{1 - MPC + MPI}$$

$$= \frac{1}{1 - 0.7 + 0.1}$$

$$= \frac{1}{1 - 0.6} = \frac{1}{0.4}$$

$$= 2.5.$$

42. The extent to which relative factor shares in income are affected by the change in relative factor prices depends on the *elasticity of factor substitution.* The concept of the elasticity of factor substitution was developed by J.R. Hicks. It is regarded as the foundation of the modern neo-classical theory of distribution and relative factor shares. Ferguson remarks that the concept of *elasticity of substitution* lies at the heart of the neoclassical theory of distribution. The *elasticity of substitution* (σ) is defined as:

$$\sigma = \frac{\partial(K/L)/(K/L)}{\partial(MRTS)/(MRTS)}$$

In a perfectly competitive input market, a firm is in equilibrium when it chooses a labour-capital combination at which MRTS is equal to the ratio of factor prices (*w*/*r*).

That is, under perfectly competitive conditions, a firm is in equilibrium when

$$MRTS_{l,\,k} = \frac{w}{r}$$

where w = price of labour (wage rate) and r = price of capital (interest). Thus, in a perfectly competitive factor market, the firm's equilibrium condition given in Eq., may also be written as:

$$\sigma = \frac{\partial(K/L)/(K/L)}{\partial(w/r)/(w/r)}$$

The elasticity of substitution (*i.e.,* the value of σ) is always positive, though in some cases, σ = 0.

Thus, the value of σ ranges from zero to infinity. The value of σ yields useful information regarding the degree of substitutability between the factors. If σ = 0, it means that substitution between factors, say labour and capital, is impossible; the two factors can be used only in a fixed proportion; and that isoquant is L-shaped.

The positive range of σ may be classified and interpreted as under:

- $\sigma < 1$: Inelastic substitutability. The degree of substitutability between the two factors is very low.
- $\sigma = 1$: Unit elasticity of substitution. The two factors can be proportionately substituted for one another.
- $\sigma > 1$: Highly elastic substitutability. One factor can substitute another to a large extent.
- $\sigma = \infty$: Perfect substitutability. One factor can substitute another to any extent.

46. A central concept in neoclassical growth theory is convergence. The Solow model (1956) has provided the basis for examining convergence. Absolute convergence means that different countries with the same population growth rate, the same savings propensity, access to the same technology but different capital–labour ratios will converge to the same growth rate, steady-state capital-labour ratio, output per capita, and consumption per capita. Conditional convergence means that countries which differ in savings propensities and capital–labour ratio, will converge to the same growth rate but not necessarily to the same capital–labour ratio and output per capita. The lack of convergence has been explained theoretically by invoking notions of technological and population induced poverty traps (a vicious circle of low savings and few investment opportunities). In this sense, the (Malthusian) demographic transition is also relevant: as income per capita rises, the population growth rate rises.

47. In his pioneering contribution to modern (neo-classical) growth theory, Solow uses the letter A to represent technology. Specifically, in Solow-type growth models the letter A symbolizes the stock of technology, which for convenience is assumed to increase with time at a fixed rate. The exogenous increase in A is assumed to be labour saving, which means that technical change makes it possible to produce a given level of output by using fewer labour units than before and the same amount of capital. In equation (*i*) *y*, average output per capita for an economy, is a function of the state of technology, A, and the ratio of capital to labour, *k*:

$$y_t = A_t;\ k_t^{\alpha} \qquad (i),$$

In any time period, *t*, output per unit of labour, y_t, is determined by the value of the capital-labour ratio, k_t, Note that A_t is fixed as well as the technical parameter α, which is a positive fraction. With A_t and α given, there exists an optimal value for k_t that maximizes output per unit of labour (or income per capita). In a competitive economy with flawless market institutions, the forces of supply and demand spontaneously establish global equilibrium involving optimal value for *k*. If for some reason the autonomous increase in A would come to an end, in Solow growth models the assumption of sharply diminishing marginal product of capital takes away the possibility of propelling long-term growth of y via capital accumulation (by steadily raising k).

Finally, Solow's growth theory is admired for its formal elegance and bold predictions, particularly the famous convergence hypothesis, which states that in the long-run, regardless of their starting points, all economies will converge on the same per-capita income, y, and realize the same steady-state rate of growth.

49. The Critical Minimum Effort Thesis was developed by *Harvey Leibenstein* in his book "Economic Backwardness and Economic Growth," 1957. This thesis supported the Theory of Balanced Growth and the Theory of 'Big Push'.

Prof. Harvey Leienstein has propounded his thesis of critical minimum effort, as an attempt to provide a lasting solution to the problems of development, faced by underdeveloped countries. The most pressing problem of underdeveloped countries is the vicious circle of poverty, which is an atmosphere of inertia in the economy. Because of such an atmosphere, the development variables (income, employment, saving, investment, etc.) move in the backward direction and thus reverse the process of development. Hence, a minimum effort is needed to overcome the original inertia of the underdeveloped economics.

In other words, critical minimum effort is necessary to achieve a steady, secular growth, raising per capita income in the long period. Leibenstein has expressed the idea in these words. "In order to achieve the transition from the state of backwardness to the more developed state, where, we can expect steady secular growth, it is necessary, though not always a sufficient condition, that at the same point or during the same period, the economy should receive a stimulus to growth that is greater than a certain minimum size."

Thus, critical minimum effort is the only way to break the vicious circle of poverty and to release the force of growth.

According to Leibenstein, there are income-depressing factors like population growth and also income-stimulating factors in underdeveloped countries. There is a biologically determined maximum rate of population growth between 3 and 4%. The rate of population growth is relevant to the level of per capita income. It is related to the various stages of economic development. The rate of population growth is an increasing function of income up to a certain level of income and beyond that it is decreasing function of income.

50. Pasinetti (1962) argues that Kaldor had neglected to take into account the fact that wage earners who saved did not receive a return on their wealth. Accordingly, he modifies Kaldor's approach to take into account two sources of workers' income—from wages and from returns to wealth.

Pasinetti's criticism of Kaldor is unwarranted, since Kaldor does not distinguish between capitalists and workers but between profit and wage income (so that differential saving rates in his model can arise due to savings by firms, and not due to class differences in savings behaviour). However, Pasinetti's model has attracted a great deal of attention because it addresses the important question of how the distribution of assets (between capitalists and workers) evolves in a capitalist economy and implies that the rate of profit, when the economy grows at the natural rate, is given by

$$r \equiv P/K = n/s_c$$

This result has been dubbed the Pasinetti paradox or the Cambridge Theorem, which states that in steady state full employment conditions income distribution depends only on the saving rate of capitalists (and the natural rate of growth), and not on the saving rate of workers, and has been taken to demonstrate the inability of workers to influence the distribution of income in the long run (except by affecting the rate of population growth).

53. The RBI set up a committee to review arrangements for institutional credit for agriculture and rural development under the Chairmanship of Shri B. Sivaraman. The Committee, after reviewing the arrangements, recommended that there was a need for the integration of credit activities for integrated rural development. Truly speaking, there was a massive credit need of benefitting the weaker sections of society in rural areas. At the same time, the RBI was not in a position to perform its role actively in fulfilling such credit needs as it had tremendous responsibilities regarding the many basic functions of central banking in monetary and credit regulations. The Shivaraman Committee submitted its report to the Governor, RBI on November 28, 1979 and recommended the establishment of NABARD.

NABARD was established on the recommendations of the Shivaraman Committee by an act of Parliament on July 12, 1982.

The National Bank for Agriculture and Rural Development Act was passed in 1981. The Agricultural Credit Department (ACD); Rural Planning and Credit Cell (RPCC) of RBI; and the Agricultural Re-finance and Development Corporation (ARDC) were replaced by the NABARD Act 1981. NABARD, as an apex development bank in India, soon became one of the most premier agencies to provide credit in rural areas. It has headquarters in Mumbai and has other branches located all over the country.

57. The logistic growth curve shows a population that increases sharply at first and then levels off as it is affected by limiting factors.

59. The theoretical framework for hedonic pricing was established by Rosen (1974). He applied this method in the area of property price. He derives price equations from property sales data by regression and thereby allows valuation of different exogenous attributes of the property itself and its vicinity. The prices of two houses may differ considerably, even with the same facilities like size, structure etc. The prices may reflect the difference of access to the workplace, commercial amenities, environmental facilities such as parks and the environmental qualities of the neighbourhoods. Such differences may imply that people are, to some extent, making a judgement on how much (more) they will spend for the quality of environment.

64. Article 280 provides for constituting a Finance Commission at the expiration of every fifth year or at such earlier time, as the President of India considers necessary. Even after accepting the necessary principles of interpretation of the statute, it cannot mean that a particular Commission would be given a short tenure of 1½ or 2 years for delineating certain fixed principles for 5 years in advance.

Article 275 speaks of sumes to be charged on Consolidated Fund of India in each year for the purpose of grants-in-aid to the States in need thereof. The question that arises then is, year by year tax and non-tax revenues of the States may not remain static or normatively progressive and may be illusory. Constitutional provisions have been made to solve practical problems and not illusions or hypothetical and astrological calculations, since imaginary and not real needs have been considered.

72. (*a*) First phase of nationalisation of 14 Banks - 1969

(*b*) Establishment of EXIM Bank of India - 1982

(*c*) Establishment of Narshimhan Committee I on Banking system - 1991

(*d*) Enactment of FEMA Act - 1999

76. (*a*) The General Theory of Employment, Interest and Money - 1936
(*b*) The Affluent Society - 1958
(*c*) Asian Drama - 1968
(*d*) Development as Freedom - 1999

77. Market Failures: The reasons of Market failures are imperfect competition, externalities, and imperfect information.

Imperfect Competition: When a firm has market power in a particular market (say it has a monopoly because of a patented drug or a local electricity franchise), the firm can raise the price of its product above its marginal cost. Consumers buy less of such goods than they would under perfect competition, and consumer satisfaction is reduced. This kind of reduction of consumer satisfaction is typical of the inefficiencies created by imperfect competition.

Externalities: Externalities are another important market failure. Recall that externalities arise when some of the side effects of production or consumption are not included in market prices.

For example, a power company might pump sulphurous fumes into the air, causing damage to neighbouring homes and to people's health. If the power company does not pay for the harmful impacts, pollution will be inefficiently high and consumer welfare will suffer.

Not all externalities are harmful. Some are beneficial, such as the externalities that come from knowledge-generating activities. For example, when Chester Carlson invented xerography, he became a millionaire; but he still received only a tiny fraction of the benefits when the world's secretaries and students were relieved of billions of hours of drudgery. Another positive externality arises from public-health programs, such as inoculation against smallpox, cholera, or typhoid; an inoculation protects not only the inoculated person but also others whom that person might otherwise have infected.

Imperfect Information: A third important market failure is imperfect information. The invisible-hand theory assumes that buyers and sellers have complete information about the goods and services they buy and sell. Firms are assumed to know about all the production functions for operating in their industry. Consumers are presumed to know about the quality and prices of goods—such as whether the financial statements of firms are accurate and whether the drugs they use are safe and efficacious.

79. The Palma ratio is the recent invention of Cambridge University economist Gabriel Palma. It consists of the ratio of the income share of the top decile to that of the bottom two quintiles. The intuition behind choosing this ratio is that the excluded upper-middle, from the third quintile through the ninth decile, seems (according to Palma's research) to maintain a fairly stable share of total income in many countries. Thus changing inequality is substantially a shift from the poorest 40 per cent to the top 10 per cent, or vice versa.

85. ∵ Here, $x = 10 - 2p$

$$2p = 10 - x$$

$$p = \frac{10-x}{2}$$

$$\int_0^6 \left[\left(\frac{10-x}{2}\right) - 2\right] dx$$

$$= \int_0^6 \left(\frac{10-x-4}{2}\right) dx = \int_0^6 \left(\frac{6-x}{2}\right) dx$$

$$= \frac{1}{2}\left[6x - \frac{x^2}{2}\right]_0^6 = \frac{1}{2}\left[6 \times 6 - \frac{6 \times 6}{2}\right]$$

$$= \frac{1}{2}[36-18] = \frac{18}{2} = 9.$$

86. Conditions of Producers' Equilibrium

Under MR – MC approach, a producer is in equilibrium, (*i.e.,* maximises profits) at that level of output where (*i*) MR = MC and (*ii*) MC is rising.

Conditions of Producer's Equilibrium under Perfect Competition and Monopoly or Monopolistic Competition

1. In a perfectly competitive market, the marginal revenue and average revenue of a producer coincide and is equal to market price, *i.e.,* AR = MR = P. A competitive producer's equilibrium is established at that level of output where,

   (*i*) P = MC, (*ii*) MC is rising and (*iii*) P ≥ AVC in short-run and P ≥ AC in the long-run. In a situation of equilibrium, a producer may be earning maximum profit, break-even or shut-down.

   A competitive producer always choose that level of output which lies on the rising portion of the MC curve. He will never produce on the decreasing portion of the MC curve. MC curve gives the supply curve of the firm.

2. Under monopoly or monopolistic competition, conditions of producer's equilibrium are MR = MC and slope of MC > slope of MR.

89. Total balls = 5 + 7 + 3 = 15

$$P(\text{green}) = \frac{3}{15} = \frac{1}{5}$$

Hence, required probability = $\frac{1}{5}$.

91. Here, Mean = 40

Mode = 60

Standard deviation = 10

We have, $$S_k = \frac{M - M_O}{\sigma}$$

Where, M = Mean

M_O = Mode

σ = Standard deviation

S_k = Skewness co-efficient

$$S_k = \frac{40 - 60}{10}$$

$$= \frac{-20}{10} = -2.$$

99. Economic profit can be positive, zero or negative. Positive economic profit is also known as supernormal profit, or abnormal profit, because it involves profit over and above normal profit. If economic profit is zero, the firm is earning normal profit. And if economic profit is negative, the firm is making a loss.

To summarise:

Economic profit can be positive, zero or negative.

Positive economic profit: TR > economic cost; the firm earns supernormal profit (or abnormal profit).

Zero economic profit: TR = economic cost; the firm earns normal profit.

Negative economic profit: TR < economic cost; the firm makes a loss.

Previous Paper (Solved)

UGC-NET-Junior Research Fellowship & Assistant Professor Exam

ECONOMICS, November-2017*

PAPER-II

Note: *This paper contains fifty (50) objective type questions of* ***two (2)*** *marks each.* ***All*** *questions are* ***compulsory***.

1. Consider the following diagram with two parallel demand curves AB and CD:

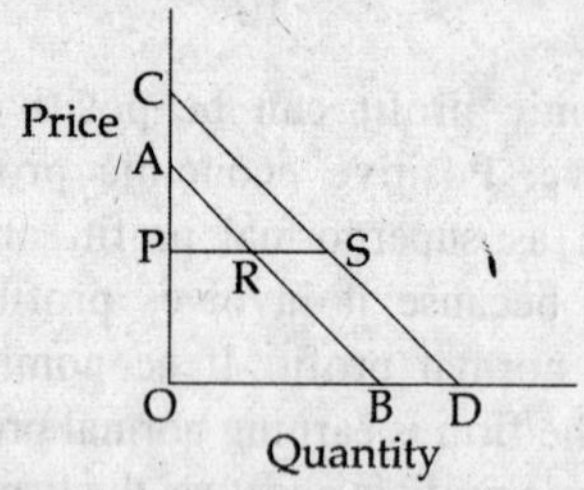

The price elasticity of demand at:

A. points R and S is equal

B. point R is greater than that at point S

C. point R is less than that at point S

D. points R and S is infinity

2. In 2016, the Nobel prize in Economics was awarded for:

A. analysis of trade pattern and location of economic activity

B. analysis of asset prices

C. analysis of globalization

D. contributions to contract theory

3. Which of the following is **not** true for perfect competition?

A. Price = LAC

B. Market demand curve for a commodity is horizontal to X-axis

C. Firms earn normal profits

D. In the long run firms operate at the minimum point of average cost

4. Which amongst the following statements is **correct**?

A. The minimum point of AVC and MC are at the same level of output

B. Minimum of AVC is at lesser output than the minimum of MC

C. Minimum of AVC is at larger output than the minimum of MC

D. Any of the above is possible depending upon operating of the law of returns

5. A firm in monopolistic competition advertises in order to:

A. make its product more similar to its competitors'

B. shift the demand curve for its product to the left

C. make the demand for its product less price elastic

D. reduce the industry's price

6. For an increase in the effective minimum wage to have less of an impact on employment, which of the following is **correct**?

(*a*) The demand for labour is relatively inelastic

(*b*) The demand for labour is relatively elastic

(*c*) The demand for labour is a derived demand

Choose the **correct** answer from the code given below:

A. (*a*) only B. (*c*) only

C. (*a*) and (*b*) D. (*a*) and (*c*)

7. Assume that people like onions on their hamburgers. If the supply of hamburgers decreases, the demand for onions will most likely:

* *Exam held on 05 November 2017.*

A. remain unchanged because hamburgers and onions are different goods
B. increase because hamburgers and onions are substitutes
C. increase because hamburgers and onions are complements
D. decrease because hamburgers and onions are complements

8. In the shortrun, which of the following costs must continuously decrease as output increases?
A. Total variable cost
B. Total fixed cost
C. Average variable cost
D. Average fixed cost

9. If export price increases by 5 per cent and import price by 20 per cent, the commodity terms of trade is:
A. 0.91 B. 0.87
C. 0.25 D. 4

10. If economic agents perfectly anticipate policy changes and if all prices, including wages, are completely flexible, which of the following will be true in the long run?
A. There will be no trade - off between inflation and unemployment
B. The unemployment rate will be less than the natural rate of unemployment
C. The price level will be constant
D. Changes in the money supply will not lead to changes in the price level

11. Who made the statement, "Inflation is everywhere and always a monetary phenomenon"?
A. Milton Friedman B. James Tobin
C. T.W. Swan D. A.W. Phillips

12. Which amongst the following is not correctly matched ?

Concept	Economists
A. New classical economics	Robert Lucas
B. Multiple effects of Balanced Budget	T.H. Haavelmo
C. New Keynssian economics	Paul Romer
D. Permanent income hypothesis	M. Friedman

13. Who argued that Keynes's theory of equilibrium with involuntary unemployment is a special case of the general equilibrium model, augmented to include money?
A. W. Leontief B. J.R Hicks
C. M. Friedman D. D. Patinkin

14. Adam Smith advocated which of the following?
(*a*) laissez faire
(*b*) the invisible hand
(*c*) free trade policy
(*d*) competitive markets

Choose the **correct** answer from the code given below:
A. (*a*) and (*b*) B. (*b*) and (*c*)
C. (*a*), (*b*) and (*c*) D. (*a*), (*b*), (*c*) and (*d*)

15. Indicate the sequence of the following in terms of their implementation with reference to India:
(*a*) Income tax
(*b*) Expenditure tax
(*c*) Value - added tax at the state level
(*d*) Service tax

Choose the **correct** answer from the code given below:
A. (*a*), (*c*), (*b*), (*d*) B. (*a*), (*b*), (*d*), (*c*)
C. (*b*), (*c*), (*d*), (*a*) D. (*c*), (*d*), (*a*), (*b*)

16. Arrange the following grouping of the nations from lower to higher order of integration.
(*a*) F.T.A
(*b*) Economic Union
(*c*) Common Market
(*d*) Custom Union

Choose the **correct** answer from the code given below:
A. (*a*), (*d*), (*c*), (*b*) B. (*a*), (*c*), (*b*), (*d*)
C. (*b*), (*a*), (*d*), (*c*) D. (*b*), (*c*), (*d*), (*a*)

17. A Country can have an increased surplus in its balance of trade as a result of:
A. declining imports and rising exports
B. higher tariffs imposed by its trading partners
C. an increase in domestic inflation
D. an increase in capital inflow

18. Which of the following statements is/are true for the current account of a country?

(*a*) It shows the net income generated in the foreign trade sector

(*b*) It relates to claims and liabilities of financial nature

Choose the **correct** answer from the code given below:

A. Only (*a*) is true
B. Only (*b*) is true
C. Both (*a*) and (*b*) are true
D. Neither (*a*) nor (*b*) is true

19. Which amongst the following economists can be classified as strong advocate of protectionist policy of trade?

A. F. List and A. Hamilton
B. Adam Smith and David Ricardo
C. J.S. Mill and P. Krugman
D. A. Hamilton and J.S. Mill

20. An increase in which of the following would be most likely to increase Long - run growth in developing countries?

A. Tariffs on imported capital goods
B. Subsidies to business for purchases of capital goods
C. Unemployment compensations
D. Pension payments

21. What is Baran's explanation for under development in Asia, Africa and Latin America?

A. Monopolistic business from abroad
B. Conservative ruling coalitions
C. Weak domestic middle class
D. All of the above

22. The Benefit Theory of allocation of tax burden was given by:

A. Seligman B. Lindhal
C. Dalton D. Pigou

23. Consider the following:

(*a*) Oligopolistic market structure

(*b*) Economics of scale

of the above, which are the essential feature of Rosenstein Rodan's approach to development?

Answer from the code below:

A. Both (*a*) and (*b*) above
B. Neither (*a*) nor (*b*) above
C. Only (*a*)
D. Only (*b*)

24. If marginal propensity to consume (m.p.c) = average propensity to consume (a.p.c) for all levels of income (Y) then the corresponding consumption function will be:

A. $C = a + bY$ B. $C = bY$
C. $C = bY^2$ D. $C = a + bY^2$

25. Which of the following goods is covered under GST as on 1st July, 2017?

A. Electricity
B. Liquified Petroleum Gas
C. High Speed Diesel
D. Petroleum Crude

26. The greater the elasticity of supply, the greater is:

A. Incidence of tax on buyers
B. Incidence of tax on sellers
C. Impact of tax on sellers
D. Impact of tax on buyers

27. The ability to pay principle of taxation is logically most consistent with the normative notion of:

A. tax neutrality
B. horizontal equity
C. value - added taxation
D. vertical equity

28. Principle of maximum social advantage is concerned with:

A. Taxation only
B. Public expenditure only
C. Public debt only
D. Both taxation and public expenditure

29. Consider the following statements about optimal tariff:

(*a*) The beneficiary country is a large country in the world market for a particular good.

(*b*) A deviation from optimal tariff will lead to fall in welfare.

Of the above, which statement is correct? Choose the answer from the code below:

A. Both (*a*) and (*b*) are correct
B. Neither (*a*) nor (*b*) is correct

C. Only (*a*) is correct
D. Only (*b*) is correct

30. Which of the following is a distinctive implication of the New Trade Theory developed by Melitz as different from the New Trade Theory?
A. Trade increases the average productivity as more productive firms expand
B. Helpful state intervention
C. Trade encourage R & D and lead to new products
D. A country may both export and import the goods from the same industry

31. The conjecture that inequalities of income first increase with development and then decrease with further development also known as 'Inverted U' hypothesis has been:
A. Supported by all empirical studies
B. Supported mainly by cross section studies and not by time series studies
C. Supported by time series and not by cross section studies
D. Generally repudiated by empirical studies

32. The ultimate effect of the 'invisible hand' of Adam Smith is that in a competitive economy everyone:
A. benefits if each acts in his/her own interest
B. will increase their profits in a free market
C. should act to maximise economic growth
D. should act to promote the public interest

33. Match List-I with List-II and select the **correct** answers from the code given below:

List-I (Investment criteria)	List-II (Economists)
(*a*) The time series criterion	(*i*) Otto Eckstein
(*b*) The social marginal productivity criterion	(*ii*) A.K. Sen
(*c*) The marginal growth contribution criterion	(*iii*) A.E. Kahn
(*d*) The marginal per capita reinvestment criterion	(*iv*) Galenstein - Leibenstein

Code:

	(*a*)	(*b*)	(*c*)	(*d*)
A.	(*ii*)	(*i*)	(*iv*)	(*iii*)
B.	(*iv*)	(*iii*)	(*i*)	(*ii*)
C.	(*ii*)	(*iii*)	(*i*)	(*iv*)
D.	(*iii*)	(*ii*)	(*iv*)	(*i*)

34. If the central prediction of the growth model of Solow is valid then:
A. Per capita real GDP difference among nations will increase
B. Per capita real GDP difference among the nations will diminish
C. Economic freedom as measured by Heritage Foundation Index will decrease
D. Population growth rate in rich countries will increase

35. Given the consumption function, C = 0.75 Y and the investment function, I = 110 – 0.25 i, then the equation of the IS function will be:
A. Y = 110 – 0.75 i B. Y = 440 – i
C. Y = 500 – 0.25 i D. Y = 400 – 0.75 i

36. In which of the following sectors, the employment elasticity has been estimated to be greater than one during the period (2004 – 05 to 2009 – 10):
A. Agriculture
B. Construction
C. Manufacturing
D. Mining and Quarrying

37. Arrange the following in the chronological order:
(*a*) Mahalnobis model
(*b*) Introduction of rolling plan
(*c*) Declaration of plan holiday
(*d*) Inclusive growth strategy

Select the answer from the code below:
A. (*b*), (*a*), (*c*), (*d*)
B. (*a*), (*c*), (*b*), (*d*)
C. (*c*), (*a*), (*b*), (*d*)
D. (*a*), (*c*), (*d*), (*b*)

38. Which amongst the following statements are true in relation to Indian economy during the period 2014-16?
A. Exports have been buoyant

B. Private capital investment happened at brisk pace
C. Both A and B are true
D. Neither A nor B is true

39. The code used under GST for classification of goods is called:
A. NIC B. HSN
C. GSTN D. ITC

40. If CPI based inflation rate in a country is given as:

Year :	2017	2016	2015	2014	2013
Inflation rate (%) :	2	5	6	7	9

This trends will be described as:
A. Disinflation B. Deflation
C. Creeping inflation D. Stagflation

41. Which among the following states has the smallest % of urban population as per census 2011?
A. Bihar B. Odisha
C. Himachal Pradesh D. Meghalaya

42. If the price data for 1980 and 2000 are given and quantity data are given only for the year 2000 then which type of index number, taking 1980 as the base can be constructed?
A. Laspeyre's Index B. Paasche Index
C. Fisher Index D. Kelly Index

43. If two events A and B are mutually exclusive then which one of the following is **correct**?
A. $P(A + B) = P(A) + P(B)$
B. $P(AB) = P(A) \cdot P(B)$
C. $P(AB) = P(A)/P(B)$
D. $P(A/B) = P(A) - P(B)$

44. If a sample of 100 is to be taken from a population of 1,000 farmers consisting of marginal, small and large farmers, which of the following will be the most appropriate sampling method?
A. Simple random sampling
B. Cluster sampling
C. Stratified random sampling
D. Systematic sampling

45. The sum of squares of deviations of a set of values is minimum when deviations are taken about:
A. Arithmetic mean B. Harmonic mean
C. Median D. Geometric Mean

46. Match the following in List-I and List-II and answer from the code given below:

List-I	List-II
(*a*) Sampling distribution	(*i*) Poisson distribution
(*b*) Discrete distribution	(*ii*) Chi-Square (χ^2) distribution
(*c*) Measures of central tendency	(*iii*) Non-probability based sampling
(*d*) Purposive sampling	(*iv*) Mode

Code:

	(*a*)	(*b*)	(*c*)	(*d*)
A.	(*i*)	(*ii*)	(*iii*)	(*iv*)
B.	(*iii*)	(*i*)	(*ii*)	(*iv*)
C.	(*ii*)	(*i*)	(*iv*)	(*iii*)
D.	(*iv*)	(*iii*)	(*i*)	(*ii*)

Note: Questions 47 to 50 are Assertion (A) and Reason (R) type. Key to these questions is as follows:
A. Both (A) and (R) are true and (R) is the correct explanation of (A).
B. Both (A) and (R) are true, but (R) is not the correct explanation of (A).
C. (A) is true, but (R) is false.
D. (A) is false, but (R) is true.

47. **Assertion (A):** Many developing countries demand that movement of natural persons across countries should be promoted.
Reasons (R): The developing countries have comparative advantage in labour intensive services.

48. **Assertion (A):** Revealed preference theory excludes the explanation of Giffen good.
Reasons (R): Revealed preference theory considers only negative income elasticity of demand

49. **Assertion (A):** Indian agriculture still absorbs a major part of workforce.
Reasons (R): Employment elasticity in agricultural sector is high.

50. **Assertion (A):** Friedman argues that money demand function is a stable function.
Reasons (R): Friedman treats money as one type of asset in which wealth holders can keep a part of their wealth

ANSWERS

1	2	3	4	5	6	7	8	9	10
B	D	B	C	C	D	D	D	B	A
11	12	13	14	15	16	17	18	19	20
A	C	D	D	B	A	A	A	A	B
21	22	23	24	25	26	27	28	29	30
D	B	A	B	B	A	D	D	A	A
31	32	33	34	35	36	37	38	39	40
B	A	C	B	B	B	B	D	B	A
41	42	43	44	45	46	47	48	49	50
C	B	A	C	A	C	A	C	C	B

EXPLANATORY ANSWERS

1. **Point Elasticity Method:** Marshall also suggested another method called the point elasticity method or geometrical method for measuring price elasticity at a point on the demand curve. This method tells us to measure elasticity of demand at any point on a demand curve. The demand curve is shown in Figure. When a point is plotted on the demand curve like point P in the figure below, it divides the curve into two segments. The point elasticity is thus measured by the ratio of the lower segment of the curve below the given point to the upper segment of the curve above the point.

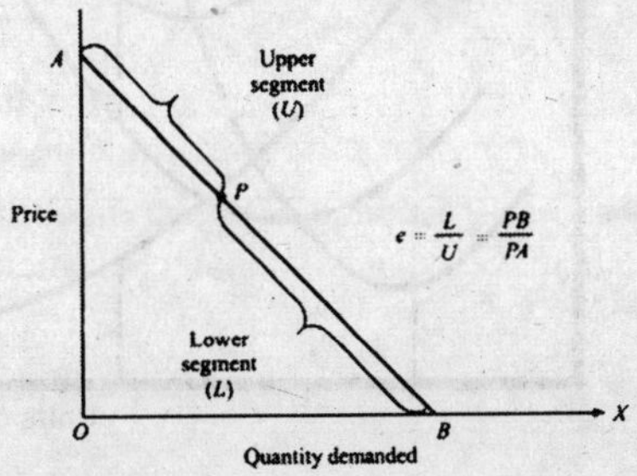

Fig.: *Demand curve in geometrical method*

In other words,

$$\text{Point elasticity} = \frac{\text{Lower segment of demand curve}}{\text{Upper segment of demand curve}}$$

$$\text{Point elasticity} = \frac{\text{Lower portion of tangent}}{\text{Upper portion of tangent}}.$$

2. Oliver Hart and Bengt Holmström from the Massachusetts Institute of Technology have won the Nobel Prize for economics 2016 for their research into contract theory.

3. A market is said to be *perfectly competitive* if (1) there are a great number of sellers and buyers of the commodity, so that the actions of an individual cannot affect the price of the commodity; (2) the products of all firms in the market are homogeneous; (3) there is perfect mobility of resources; and (4) consumers, resource owners, and firms in the market have perfect knowledge of present and future prices and costs.

In a perfectly competitive market, the price of the commodity is determined exclusively by the intersection of the market demand curve and the market supply curve for the commodity. The perfectly competitive firm is then a "price taker" and can sell any amount of the commodity at the established price.

Market demand and supply curves in a perfectly competitive market are shown in Figure (*a*). The demand curve of a single firm is shown in Figure (*b*). The market demand and supply curves are the result of adding all the individual firms' demand and supply curves. The horizontal line at the market price is the demand curve faced by an individual firm in a perfectly competitive market structure. It shows that the individual firm is a price taker—that the demand curve is perfectly elastic.

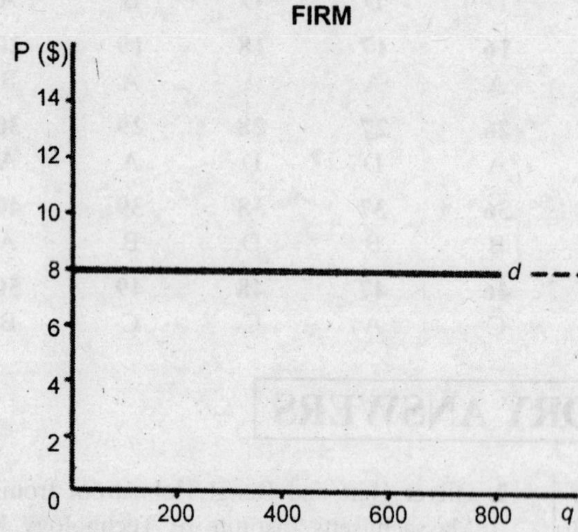

Fig. (b)

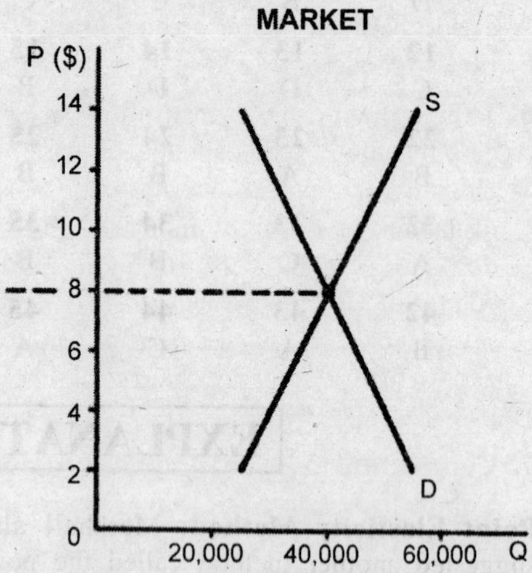

Fig. (a)

4. The output at which MC is minimum (Q_1) is less than the output at which AVC is minimum (Q_2), which in turn, is less than the output at which AC is the least (Q_3).

We know that ATC always exceeds AVC. This is because ATC is the sum of AVC and AFC. Furthermore, since AFC falls as output increases, AVC and ATC get closer as output rises.

Our now familiar relationships between marginals and averages hold for both ATC and AVC. That is, if MC < ATC, then ATC is falling; if MC > ATC, then ATC is rising. And if MC < AVC, then AVC is falling, whereas if MC > AVC, then AVC is rising. This implies that MC must intersect ATC at its minimum point and that MC must also intersect AVC at its minimum point (see Fig.).

Note also that ATC will reach its minimum at an output larger than that at which AVC reaches its minimum. This is because ATC = AVC + AFC. And even though AVC has begun to rise, AFC is still declining, pulling ATC down. Eventually, the increase in AVC will offset the decrease in AFC and ATC, too, will begin to increase.

The relationships between the various average and marginal curves are illustrated in Figure.

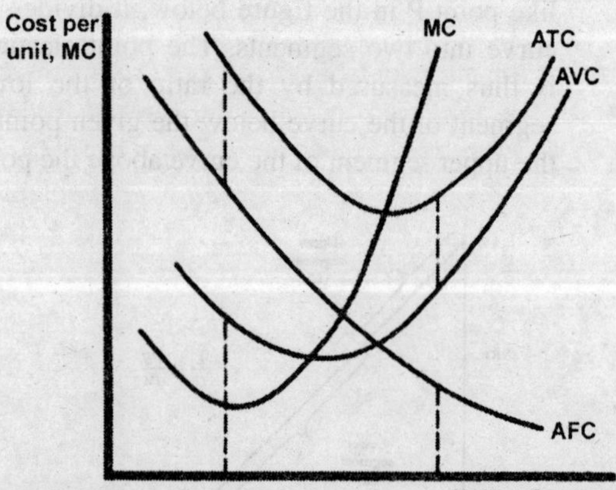

5. The expense and effort involved in product differentiation would be wasted if consumers were not made aware of product differences. Thus, monopolistic competitors advertise their products, often heavily. The goal of product differentiation and advertising—so-called non-price competition—is to make price less of a factor in consumer purchases and make product differences a greater factor. If successful, the demand for the firm's product will increase. The firm's demand may also become less elastic because of the greater loyalty to the firm's product.

6. The impact of a minimum wage on employment levels depends in part on the elasticity of demand and elasticity of supply of labour in different industries. If labour demand is relatively inelastic then the contraction in employment is likely to be less severe than if employers' demand for labour is elastic with respect to changes in the wage level.

7. **Complements:** Some goods, known as Complements, are in Joint Demand. This means that, in demanding one good, a consumer will also be likely to demand another good. Examples of complements are:
   - Tennis rackets and tennis balls
   - Washing machines and soap powder
   - Strawberries and cream
   - Video tapes and video recorders.

   Economic theory suggests that a rise in the quantity demanded of one complement will lead to an increase in the demand for another, resulting in an increase in the price and quantity bought of the other complement.

8. In the short-run, there will be both variable and fixed components of total cost. The total fixed cost does not change with output. The average fixed cost will however decline continuously as output increases making a rectangular hyperbola which joins the output axis at infinity. The total variable cost increases as output increases. The economic theory however postulates that this component of the short-run total cost increases at decreasing rate up to certain level of output; after remaining constant for some time, it increases with increasing rate as output increases. This implies that the marginal cost of production and average variable cost decrease continuously and then rise with the level of output forming familiar U-shape curves. The lowest dip for these costs will be at different levels of output as can be seen in Fig.

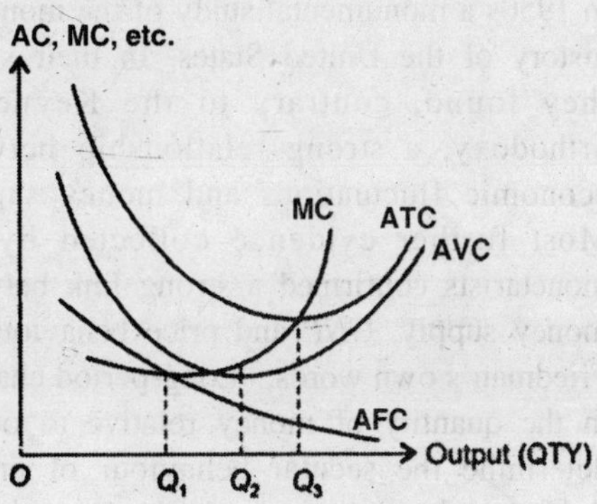

Fig.: *Short-run cost curves*

9. **Commodity Terms of Trade:** The commodity or net barter terms of trade is the ratio between the prices of a country's export goods and import goods. Symbolically, it can be expressed as $Tc = \frac{Px}{Pm}$. Where T*c* stands for the commodity terms of trade, P for Price, the subscript *x* for export and *m* for imports.

$$Tc = \frac{\text{Price of Export}}{\text{Price of Import}} = \frac{105}{120} = 0.87.$$

10. The *Phillips curve* is an empirical relationship found by A.W. Phillips that shows the relationship between the unemployment rate and the rate at which wages change. He discovered that changes in wages were inversely related to the unemployment rate. Subsequent research established the same relationship between inflation and unemployment. During the 1960s, many economists and policy makers thought there was a consistent trade-off between price changes and unemployment. However, the trade-off is a short-run phenomenon, and inflationary expectations can shift the short-run Phillips curve. The long-run Phillips curve is a vertical line at the long-run aggregate supply curve.

11. It was Milton Friedman of Chicago University who revived the classical quantity theory of money. Milton Friedman, a Nobel Laureate, and his associate Anna Schwartz carried out in 1950s a monumental study of the monetary history of the United States. In their study, they found, contrary to the Keynesian orthodoxy, a strong relationship between economic fluctuations and money supply. Most further evidence collected by the monetarists confirmed a strong link between money supply, *GNP* and price behaviour. In Friedman's own words, "Long-period changes in the quantity of money relative to output determine the secular behaviour of prices. Substantial expansions in the quantity of money over short periods have been a major *proximate* source for the accompanying inflation in prices." Friedman is more dogmatic on the relationship between price rise and money supply. He says, "Inflation is always and everywhere a monetary phenomenon in the sense that it is and can be produced only by a more rapid increase in the quantity of money than in output."

15. Income tax – 1961
Expenditure tax – 1987
Value-added tax at the state level – 2005
Service tax – 1994

16. Regional economic integration refers to a group of nation-states in a region who embark on a gradual process by which they eliminate barriers to trade among one another. The purposes of regional economic integration are both economic (increase human welfare by achieving higher levels of growth) and political (cultivate peace, stability, and cooperation). There are four types of regional economic integration: free trade area, customs union, common market, and economic and monetary union.

In a free trade area (FTA), states in a region eliminate tariffs and other restrictions, such as quantitative restrictions (quotas), among themselves but retain their own external tariffs with the outside world. The European Free Trade Association (EFTA) and the North American Free Trade Agreement (NAFTA) are two examples. Although FTA members eliminate internal tariffs and thus relinquish one element of state sovereignty, no other transfer of sovereignty is involved–in contrast to higher forms of regional economic integration.

In a customs union, states not only eliminate tariffs and other trade barriers among themselves but establish a Common External Tariff (CET) with the rest of the world and common institutions that manage the union. The CET is the main feature of a customs union. Without it, a non-member exporter who enters a union at its least taxed entry point could re-export products anywhere within the union duty free. Such action would undermine the purpose of a customs union—that is, to give internal producers preferential access to union markets. Producers within the union would be disadvantaged if their goods were to be underpriced by unwanted imported competition. A customs union represents a major leap in economic integration for its member states. They cede sovereignty to the union to set external tariffs and establish common regulatory, legal, and political bodies. Examples of customs unions include the Zollverein of Germanic states in the nineteenth century and the Belgium-Luxembourg Economic Union of 1921.

A common market, such as the EEC, is a customs union that establishes and regulates an internal market that has free internal movement of goods, services, labour, and capital/investment (production factors). A common market provides for monetary cooperation and the creation of competition, industrial, regional, environmental, and other common policies. The EEC established a common market for all sectors of the member states' economies by the 1970s, with the exception of the defense industry, which falls outside the Treaty purview. However, the EU continues to struggle to ensure free movement of labour and trade in services. Since the 1990s, the EU refers to its common market as the internal market.

An economic and monetary union (EMU) is the highest form of regional economic integration.

17. The difference between the value of a country's exports and the value of its imports during a specific time is the country's balance of trade. A country that exports more than it imports is said to have a *favourable* balance of trade, called a trade surplus. A country that imports more than it exports is said to have an *unfavourable* balance of trade, or trade deficit. When imports exceed exports, more money from trade flows out of the country than flows into it.

18. Balance of payments consists of current account (CA), which includes goods and services, net income from foreign investment, and unilateral transfers.

In addition, it includes capital account (KA), which consists of purchase/sale of real assets; financial account (FA), which consists of purchase/sale of financial assets along with their lending and repayments; net errors and omissions (ER), which defines statistical and other mistakes; reserves and related items (RES), which refers to official means of payment; and overall balance (BAL), which is the reverse of the previous final component as to sign, all expressed as percentage of GDP.

19. The basis of the protectionist argument is to be found in Alexander Hamilton's famous *Report on Manufactures (1791)*, which remains one of the most elaborate general arguments for protection ever written. In his report to the American Congress, Hamilton stressed both the desirability of national self-sufficiency in manufacturing, and the importance of a sizeable non-agricultural consuming class for a stable and prosperous agriculture. Manufacturing industry, he argued, should be encouraged to grow by the use of a system of bounties and subsidies, and behind a protective tariff, which would free domestic manufacturers from foreign competition, and thus enable them to expand the scale of their operations, thereby achieving economies comparable to those enjoyed by foreign competitors. In this way, the 'infant industries' would quickly attain maturity, and would then be able to produce at least as cheaply as foreign manufacturers.

Strongly influenced by Hamilton, the German. Friedrich List *(The National System of Political Economy,* 1841) was highly critical of the classical theory of free trade. In particular, he reproached the classical economists with having purposely ignored the differences in economic strength between the nations which they had invited to trade freely with one another on an equal footing. A country's commercial policy, List argued, was related to its level of economic development and it was therefore wrong to advocate one policy as being universally applicable. He concluded that while free trade is beneficial during the early and later (commercial-industrial) stages of development, the transition from an agricultural to an industrial society could be achieved only through a policy of protection.

21. Baran first outlined his theory of underdevelopment in an article 'On the Political Economy of Backwardness'. which was published in 1952, having been presented as a paper to the American Economic Association two years earlier. This was followed by a more extended account in *The Political Economy of Growth* in 1957, the main ideas of which had been the subject of a lecture series delivered in 1953. During the 1950s and 1960s Baran also wrote articles on various aspects of underdevelopment, some of which were collected together in *The Longer View,* published (posthumously) in 1970. At the same time he was cooperating with Paul Sweezy in writing *Monopoly Capital*. This text was almost wholly concerned with the economic structure of advanced capitalism, but, given the nature of Baran's thesis on backwardness, it formed an integral part of his theory of underdevelopment.

The central idea in Baran's treatment of imperialism is more classical than Marxian. Economic growth is the result of the size and utilisation of the surplus product.

According to Baran the divergence originated in the sixteenth century, when Western European countries began a process of colonial expansion and primitive accumulation. While the domestic surplus was also increasingly being invested at home, it was supplemented by using the surplus of other economies outside Europe. This transfer of surplus undermined the economic development of Latin America. Africa and most of South East Asia. Baran claimed that the seeds of autonomous capitalist development could be discerned everywhere (or, at least, everywhere in Asia) in the sixteenth century, when it had been feasible for accumulation to have occurred over the whole globe. In the event it was concentrated in Western Europe only because European domination of other areas thwarted incipient bourgeois revolutions there, and restructured their economies in the interests of the imperial centres. A small initial advantage possessed by Western Europe at the dawn of modern history was thereby turned into an enduring benefit and gave rise to cumulative divergence.

To support this thesis Baran pointed to the industrial development of India prior to its conquest, and showed how the Indian economy was then distorted by colonial administrations for the benefit of British manufacturers. Established industry was undermined and the surplus produced by the Indian economy was siphoned off by the imperial power. Baran also contrasted Indian experience with the fate of Japan, which had successfully escaped colonisation and consequently preserved its industry intact, carried out its own bourgeois revolution, and used the surplus for its own productive investments. More generally, according to Baran, what determined whether a country developed or became underdeveloped was its incorporation into an imperial economy or the retention of independence.

22. The Benefit Theory: According to this theory, citizens should pay in accordance with the benefits they enjoy from public services financed by taxes. It does not necessarily imply, however, that taxes should be progressive. One could argue, for instance, that all persons enjoy the same protection under the state, so equity requires that all should pay equally. On the other hand, one could just as easily argue that everyone does *not* enjoy the same degree of protection by the state. And even if they did, the cost of protection varies depending on who is being protected. The rich enjoy the protection of their property as well as their persons, which suggests that they should pay more. This "payment for protection" argument suggests a two-part tax in which there is a head tax on individuals and a flat tax on real property. Indeed, both were prominent features of the tax system before the income tax was introduced.

The limitation of this argument is that it takes too narrow a view of the services provided by the state. What about education, transportation, parks, police, law courts, and the myriad of other services that are offered by the modern state? One approach to this problem is simply to ask individuals how much they value these publicly financed activities and then tax them accordingly. This approach to taxation was first suggested by the Swedish economist Erik Lindahl.

23. Rosenstein-Rodan identifies three different kinds of indivisibilities, which may be considered the main obstacles to the development of developing countries. They are:

- Indivisibility in the supply of social overhead capital (lumpiness of capital);
- Indivisibility of demand (complementarity of demand)
- Indivisibility (kink) in the supply of savings.

He argues that a big push in terms of a high quantum of investment is required to scale the economic obstacles to development created by these three kinds of indivisibilities, and the external economies to which they give rise. This implies that the development process is a series of discontinuous jumps, and each jump requires a big push. Besides, there may finally be a phenomenon of indivisibility in the vigour and drive required for successful development policy. Isolated and small efforts may not add up to a sufficient impact on growth. An atmosphere of development may arise only after a critical minimum level of investment has been reached.

24. The short-run Keynesian Function is:

$$C = a + bY,$$

where 'C' stands for consumption, 'a' for autonomous consumption, 'b' for marginal propensity to consume, and 'Y' for income. Now divide it by 'Y' throughout. You get:

$$\frac{C}{Y} = \frac{a}{Y} + b$$

We know that $\frac{C}{Y}$ = average propensity to consume.

So, the function can be rewritten as:

$$APC = \frac{a}{Y} + MPC$$

However in the long run, the consumption function doesn't take into account autonomous consumption, that is, 'a' = 0.

$$\therefore \quad C = bY$$

26. Incidence of taxation shifting also depends upon the elasticity of the supply of the commodity. The elasticity of supply shows the extent to which the change in prices induces the change in the supply of a commodity. The more elastic the supply of commodity, the more burden of the tax will have to be borne by the buyers. So, more shifting will be possible. Contrary to it, if the supply is inelastic, more burden of taxation will fall on the sellers, and the shifting of taxation will be less. In the long run, normally, the supply of a commodity is perfectly elastic because the producers generally get only the normal profits over a long period. Taxation increases the cost of supply. The producers do not get even the normal profits. They reduce the production. Low production results in low supply. Low supply causes an increase in price, and a new equilibrium is established. In such a situation the seller or the producer is successful in shifting the whole of the tax on to the buyer. Contrary to it, the supply of a commodity over a short period is inelastic. The producers are getting abnormal profits. So, they themselves bear the burden of tax. In such a state, less shifting of taxation takes place. So, if the supply of a commodity is more elastic, the burden of taxation can easily be shifted to the buyers. Contrary to it, it is not possible to shift the burden of taxation to the buyers in case the supply is inelastic.

27. The ability-to-pay principle states that taxes should be levied on a person according to how well that person can shoulder the burden. This principle is sometimes justified by the claim that all citizens should make an "equal sacrifice" to support the government. The magnitude of a person's sacrifice, however, depends not only on the size of his tax payment but also on his income and other circumstances.

The ability-to-pay principle lends to two corollary notions of equity: vertical equity and horizontal equity. Vertical equity states that taxpayers with a greater ability to pay should contribute a larger amount. Horizontal equity states that taxpayers with similar abilities to pay should contribute the same amount. These notions of equity are widely accepted, but applying them to evaluate a tax system is rarely straightforward.

28. According to Dalton, the chief objective of public finance is the maximisation of social advantage and the guiding principle of state policy technically described by him is the principle of maximum social advantage. He regards this principle as the most fundamental and extols that system of public finance which secures the maximum social advantage from its fiscal operations. He has also exploded the misconceived notions of some of the earlier writers that "every tax is an evil" and "all public expenditure is unproductive". This principle states that incomes and expenditures of the government should be so managed that after comparing the social burden of taxation and social benefit of public expenditure, the net advantage accruing to the society is the greatest. It is obvious that, like the individual, the state must balance its revenues and expenditures.

30. The Melitz model (first presented in Melitz 2003) is the starting point for most theoretical approaches to trade that incorporate heterogeneous firms. Like Krugman (1980), who introduced product differentiation to a single industry, Melitz models intra-industry dynamics in a monopolistic competition framework. Unlike previous models, Melitz's model accounts for empirically observed asymmetries in firm productivity and size, rather than dismissing them by assumption. These dissimilarities in firms' characteristics drive variations in their market behaviours.

The Melitz model introduced "new new trade theory", which deals explicitly with these intra-industry features by incorporating heterogeneous firms into a trade model based on monopolistic competition. According to Melitz's model and others like it, firm heterogeneity occurs because, prior to entering the domestic production market, firms face uncertainty over both their immediate and future levels of productivity. Immediate productivity is only revealed if the firm chooses to pay the fixed (then sunk) cost of entry to enter the market.

At this point, if productivity is revealed to be at the low end of the distribution, a firm may never realize any profits and will choose to exit without producing anything, in order to avoid incurring further costs (this point is often referred to as the zero-profit productivity cutoff). Where production is profitable, firms do not exit the market, and they incur variable costs of production. In the face of increased exposure to trade, an industry becomes more productive on average. This happens as inter-firm reallocations lead to the most productive firms gaining in market share and factors of production, while the least productive firms exit.

32. "Invisible Hand" was a term coined by Adam Smith to express the idea that though each individual in his/her economic activities acts in his/her own interest such actions are guided by a sort of 'invisible hand' which ensures that they are also to the advantage of the community as a whole. Each individual by pursuing his own self-interest promotes the interest of the society more efficiently than when he really intends to promote it (Adam Smith). Such being the case, it is unwarranted to expect businesses to act directly to promote the common good. Therefore, there is no justification to make a claim that businesses "have any social responsibilities other than to legally and honestly maximise the profits of the firm".

34. The Solow growth model, first introduced in 1956, shows that as countries become more mature, their growth rate will decline even if the ratio of capital spending to GDP remains steady, because more investment will be used for replacement purposes and less for expansion. In a similar vein, it can be argued that when countries are poor, they can make great strides by quickly adopting new methods of technology and shifting workers from agriculture to manufacturing; but as they approach the leading edge of technology, growth will diminish.

35. Equation of the IS function

$$Y = 0.75Y + 110 - 0.25\,i$$
$$\Rightarrow \quad 0.25\,Y = 110 - 0.25\,i$$
$$\Rightarrow \quad Y = 440 - i.$$

37.

Mahalnobis model	—	1953
Introduction of rolling plan	—	1978
Declaration of plan holiday	—	1966
Inclusive growth strategy	—	11th Five Year Plan

39. Harmonized Commodity Description and Coding System, also known as the Harmonized System (HS) of tariff nomenclature is an internationally standardised system of names and numbers to classify traded products. These codes are basically used to fix a rate of tax on various products at the time of export and import. In the Indian context, under GST regime, HSN codes will be used to classify goods in an invoice to make taxation system uniform. Under GST supply invoices will be made by capturing HSN codes in case of goods and service accounting codes in case of services.

42. The Paasche Index: This index uses the quantities *bought in the current year* for the typical basket and is called a Paasche index. This current year weighting compares what a basket of goods bought now (in the current year) would cost, with cost of the same basket of goods in the base year.

This index is calculated as

$$\frac{\Sigma P_n Q_n}{\Sigma P_0 Q_n} \times 100$$

where $\Sigma P_n Q_n$ is the cost of the basket of goods bought in the year *n* at prices and $\Sigma P_0 Q_n$ is the cost of the year *n* basket of goods at base year prices.

43. If two events A and B are mutually exclusive (*i.e.,* only one of them can occur at a time) and P(A) and P (B) are the probabilities of occurrence of A and B, respectively; then

$$P(A \cup B) = P(A) + P(B)$$

44. Stratified Random Sampling: In stratified random sampling, the population is first divided into two or more strata. As with quota sampling, the aim of stratified sampling is to enhance representativeness. Stratified sampling designs subdivide the population into subsets from which elements are selected at random. Stratification is often based on such demographic attributes as age or gender.

Stratifying variables usually divide the population into unequal subpopulations. Researchers may sample either proportionately (in relation to the size of the stratum) or disproportionately.

45. Mathematical Properties of Arithmetic Mean: The arithmetic mean is based on all the observations and is capable of further mathematical treatment. It has some very important mathematical properties:

1. The sum of the deviations of the items from the arithmetic mean is always zero, that is, $\Sigma(x_i - \bar{x}) = 0$.
2. The sum of the squares of the deviation of a set of values is minimum when taken from the mean.

PAPER-III

Note: *This paper contains* ***seventy five (75)*** *objective type questions of* ***two (2)*** *marks each.* ***All*** *questions are* ***compulsory.***

1. Consider the following diagram showing the market demand and supply curves for a commodity. If the government fixes the price P_1 above the market clearing price P_0, then the dead-weight loss is represented by:

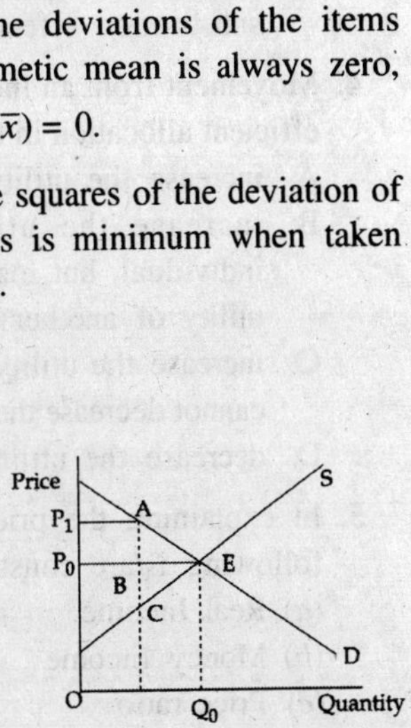

A. Area of triangle ABE
B. Area of triangle EBC
C. Area of triangle ABE + area of triangle EBC
D. Area of rectangle P_1ABP_0

2. Which of the following features belong to Cournots' model of duopoly?

(*a*) It yields determinate and stable equilibrium for the duopolists

(*b*) It is an adequate representation of Nash equilibrium

(*c*) If the duopolists combine to form a monopoly, the price changed by them will be less than the equilibrium price without their combining together.

Of the above which statements are true? Choose from the code below:

A. All the above are correct
B. (*a*) and (*c*) are correct
C. (*a*) and (*b*) are correct
D. (*b*) and (*c*) are correct

3. A good is called a 'Giffen good' when the income effect is:

A. positive and is greater than the substitution effect
B. Equal to substitution effect
C. Less than the substitution effect
D. Negative and is greater than the substitution effect

4. Movement from an inefficient allocation to an efficient allocation in the Edgeworth Box will:

A. increase the utility of all individuals
B. increase the utility of at least one individual, but may decrease the level of utility of another person
C. increase the utility of one individual, but cannot decrease the utility of any individual
D. decrease the utility of all individuals

5. In explaining the price effect, which of the following is/are constant?

(*a*) Real Income

(*b*) Money Income

(*c*) Price ratio

Choose the **correct** answer from the code given below:

Code:

A. Only (*a*)
B. Only (*b*)
C. Both (*b*) and (*c*)
D. Both (*a*) and (*c*)

6. Which of the following is a problem connected with general equilibrium analysis?

A. Existence problem
B. Uniqueness problem
C. Stability problem
D. All of the above

7. In the adjacent Figures 1 and 2, the demand curve DD and supply curve SS are shown. Point E and F represent the equilibrium points. Then which of the following is correct?

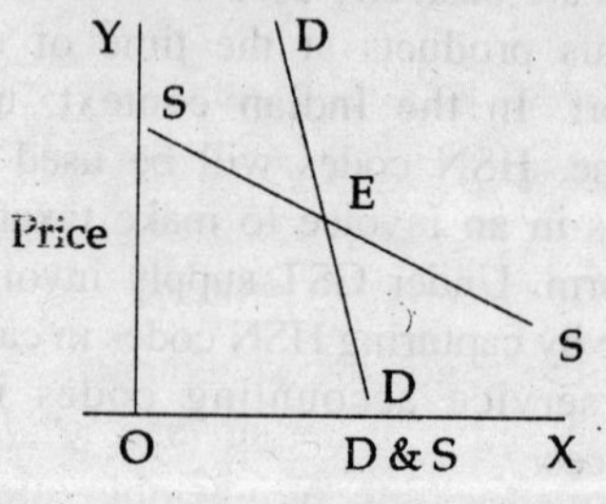

Fig. 1

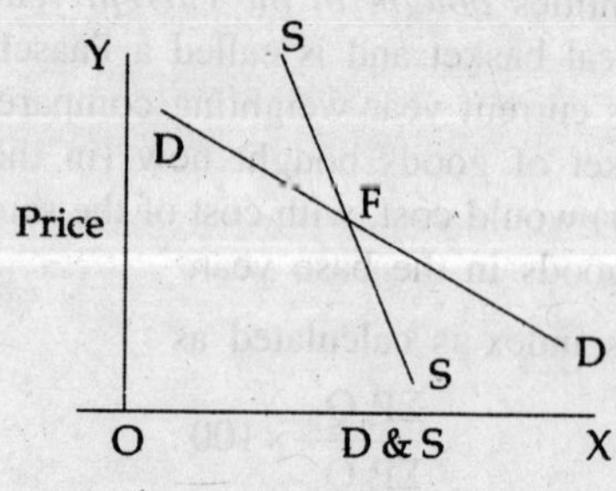

Fig. 2

A. Both points E and F are the points of stable equilibrium
B. Both points E and F are points of unstable equilibrium
C. Equilibrium is stable at point E and unstable at point F
D. Equilibrium is unstable at point E and stable at point F

8. Which of the following statements about Pareto Optimum are **correct**?

(*a*) It changes with changes in the distribution of income

(*b*) At the Pareto optimum, MRS in consumption = MRT in production

(*c*) It is not unique

(*d*) It is obtained under perfect competition

Code:

A. (*a*), (*c*) and (*d*) B. (*b*) and (*c*)

C. (*a*), (*b*) and (*d*) D. (*a*) and (*b*)

9. Market prices adjusted to consider differences between social cost-benefit and private cost-benefit calculations are:

A. Consumer Surplus B. Price distribution

C. Exchange rate D. Shadow prices

10. 'Bandwagon Effect' is found in which of the following?

A. Life cycle hypothesis

B. Permanent income hypothesis

C. Absolute income hypothesis

D. Relative income hypothesis

11. Consider the following statements:

(*a*) Phillips curve is an inverse relationship between the rate of unemployment and the rate of inflation in an economy

(*b*) Engel's Law observes that as income rises the proportion of income spent on food falls even if the actual expenditure on food rises

Which of the above statement(s) is/are correct?

A. Only (*a*)

B. Only (*b*)

C. Both (*a*) and (*b*)

D. Neither (*a*) nor (*b*)

12. Which amongst the following is **not** well matched?

Concept	Economists
A. Dual decision hypothesis	R.W. Clower
B. Natural rate of unemployment	E. Phelps and M. Friedman
C. Limit Price Theory	J. Bhagwati
D. Planned sales curve	Mrs. J. Robinson

13. Which amongst the following is **correct** for the aggregate demand function shown in the diagram?

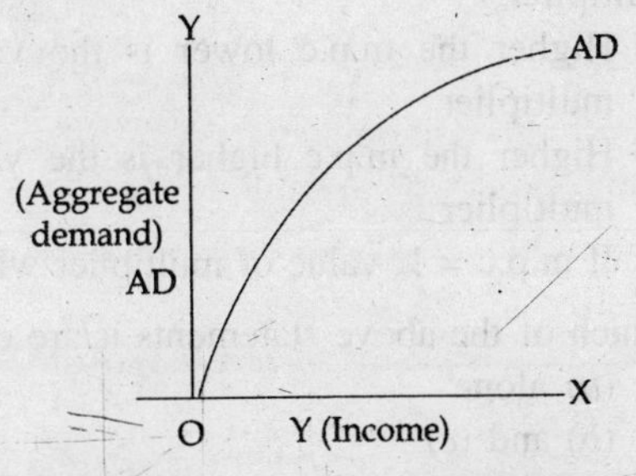

(*a*) $\frac{d(\text{AD})}{d\text{Y}} > 0$ (*b*) $\frac{d(\text{AD})}{d\text{Y}} < 0$

(*c*) $\frac{d^2(\text{AD})}{d\text{Y}^2} > 0$ (*d*) $\frac{d^2(\text{AD})}{d\text{Y}^2} < 0$

Choose the answer from the code below:

A. (*a*) and (*d*) are correct

B. (*a*) and (*c*) are correct

C. (*b*) and (*c*) are correct

D. (*b*) and (*d*) are correct

14. Permanent income hypothesis assumes positive correlation between which of the following pairs of variables?

A. Permanent income and transitory income

B. Permanent income and transitory consumption

C. Permanent income and permanent consumption

D. Transitory income and transitory consumption

15. Which of the following would be the initial impact on an economy if wages were to increase more than workers productivity?

A. Employment would increase, causing a rightward shift in the aggregate demand curve

B. The aggregate demand curve would shift to the left, increasing the price level

C. The short - run aggregate supply curve would shift to the left, increasing the price level

D. Employment would decrease, causing a rightward shift in the aggregate demand curve

16. Consider the following statements describing the relationship between marginal propensity to consume (m.p.c) and the value of the multiplier:

(*a*) Higher the m.p.c lower is the value of multiplier

(*b*) Higher the m.p.c higher is the value of multiplier

(*c*) If m.p.c = 1, value of multiplier will be ∞

Which of the above statements is/are correct?

A. (*b*) alone
B. (*b*) and (*c*)
C. (*c*) alone
D. (*a*) alonc

17. Match List-I and List-II and select the correct answer from the code given below:

List-I (Curve)	List-II (Relationship)
(*a*) Engel curve	(*i*) Tax Revenue - Tax rate
(*b*) Rahn curve	(*ii*) Income - consumption
(*c*) Laffer curve	(*iii*) Environment - Per capita Income
(*d*) Kuznets curve	(*iv*) Govt. Expenditure - per capita Income

Code:

	(*a*)	(*b*)	(*c*)	(*d*)
A.	(*iv*)	(*ii*)	(*i*)	(*iii*)
B.	(*i*)	(*iii*)	(*iv*)	(*ii*)
C.	(*ii*)	(*iv*)	(*i*)	(*iii*)
D.	(*iii*)	(*i*)	(*ii*)	(*iv*)

18. 'Golden rule of accumulation' refers to the savings rate that:

A. maximises the growth rate of output
B. optimises the investment in the economy
C. maximises the growing per capita consumption
D. None of the above

19. Which amongst the following statements are **true** for Schumpeter model of development?

(*a*) Development is possible because of credit creation by Banks

(*b*) Development flourishes in democracy

(*c*) Capitalist economy develops through trade cycles

Of the above which statements are **correct**? Answer from the code below:

A. All the above are true
B. (*a*) and (*b*) are true
C. (*b*) and (*c*) are true
D. (*a*) and (*c*) are true

20. In Marxian model, the rate of profit on capital is:

A. Directly proportional to rate of exploitation as well as organic composition of capital
B. Inversely proportional to rate of exploitation and organic composition of capital
C. Inversely proportional to rate of exploitation and directly proportional to organic composition of capital
D. Directly proportional to rate of exploitation and inversely proportional to organic composition of capital

21. Which of the following is/are true for AK model of growth?

(*a*) It assumes constant savings rate

(*b*) This savings rate is exogeneously determined

(*c*) The marginal product of capital is diminishing as output expands

Of the above which statements are **correct**?

A. All the three above are correct
B. Only (*a*) and (*b*) are correct
C. (*a*) and (*c*) are correct
D. Only (*b*) and (*c*) are correct

22. According to Fisher - Clark thesis which one of the following is the correct sequence of structural shift in the process of development?

A. Agriculture, Services, Industry
B. Agriculture, Industry, Services
C. Agriculture, Industry, Foreign trade
D. Agriculture, Foreign trade, Services

23. Hagen's theory of social change uses psychology, sociology and anthropology to explain how a traditional agricultural society:

A. attains continuing technical progress
B. learns to accept its fate

C. has a social structure where high status is maintained
D. produces an accommodating personality with a high need for achievement

24. According to Lewis model, the dual economy grows. only when:
A. Modern sector increases its output share relative to the traditional sector
B. agriculture sector uses modern equipment
C. agriculture sector hires labour economically
D. modern manufacturing sector is capital intensive

25. One of the dependency theorists, Andre Gunder Frank suggests that the following economic activities have contributed to under development:
(*a*) Workers migrating from villages to foreign - dominated urban complexes
(*b*) Forming an unskilled labour force to work in factories and mines and on plantations
(*c*) Replacing indigenous entreprises with technologically more advanced, global, subsidiary companies
(*d*) Closing the economy to trade with and investment from developed countries

Choose the answer from the code given below:
A. (*a*) and (*b*)
B. (*b*) and (*c*)
C. (*a*), (*b*) and (*c*)
D. (*a*), (*b*), (*c*) and (*d*)

26. If in a Harrodian economy, Ga = 10% and Gw = 8%, this will lead to :
A. Inflation
B. Unemployment
C. Deflation
D. Stagflation

27. Match List-I and List-II and select the correct answer from the code given below:

List-I (Author)	**List-II (Book)**
(*a*) Gunnar Myrdal	(*i*) The rise and fall of nations
(*b*) Ruchir Sharma	(*ii*) In Defence of Globalisation
(*c*) Jagdish Bhagwati	(*iii*) Capitalism, Socialism and Democracy
(*d*) Joseph Schumpeter	(*iv*) Asian Drama

Code:

	(*a*)	(*b*)	(*c*)	(*d*)
A.	(*ii*)	(*i*)	(*iii*)	(*iv*)
B.	(*iv*)	(*i*)	(*ii*)	(*iii*)
C.	(*iv*)	(*ii*)	(*i*)	(*iii*)
D.	(*i*)	(*iii*)	(*ii*)	(*iv*)

28. The 'twin deficit' problem means a country having:
A. High fiscal deficit and high current account deficit
B. High fiscal deficit and high revenue deficit
C. High fiscal deficit and high governance deficit
D. High fiscal deficit and high primary deficit

29. MNCs can help the developing countries to:
(*a*) Obtain foreign technology and innovative methods of increasing productivity
(*b*) Employ rural unemployed labour
(*c*) Finance a savings gap or balance of payments deficit
(*d*) Generate appropriate technology by adapting existing processes

Choose the **correct** answer from the code given below:
A. (*a*) and (*c*) only
B. (*b*) and (*c*) only
C. (*a*), (*c*) and (*d*) only
D. (*a*), (*b*), (*c*) and (*d*)

30. Which of the following is **not** part of the W.T.O. Agreement On Agriculture (AOA)?
A. Input subsidies
B. Export subsidies
C. Domestic support
D. Market Access

31. In the context of US economy, which one of the following is **true** for 'Triffin dilemma'?
(*a*) US has to support a large supply of dollars to act as an internationally accepted currency.

(*b*) There is a conflict in the short run domestic and long run objective of US trade policy resulting in trade deficit.

Which of the above statements are **true**? Choose from the code given below:

A. Both (*a*) and (*b*) are true
B. Neither (*a*) nor (*b*) are true
C. Only (*a*) is true
D. Only (*b*) is true

32. Which of the following does not form part of the foreign exchange reserves of India?

A. Gold
B. SDRs
C. Foreign currency assets
D. Foreign currency and securities held by the banks and corporate bodies

33. The Regional Comprehensive Economic Partnership (RCEP) is a proposed free trade agreement between the members of:

A. SAARC
B. ASEAN
C. BRICS
D. EUROPEAN UNION

34. Match List-I (Concepts) and List-II (Economists) and select the correct answer using the code given below:

List-I (Concepts)	List-II (Economists)
(*a*) Gross Barter terms of trade	(*i*) Jacob Viner
(*b*) Single factoral terms of trade	(*ii*) Dorrance
(*c*) Income terms of trade	(*iii*) F.W. Taussig
(*d*) Secular deterioration in terms of trade of developing countries	(*iv*) Prebisch - Singer

Code:

	(*a*)	(*b*)	(*c*)	(*d*)
A.	(*i*)	(*ii*)	(*iii*)	(*iv*)
B.	(*ii*)	(*i*)	(*iv*)	(*iii*)
C.	(*iii*)	(*i*)	(*ii*)	(*iv*)
D.	(*iv*)	(*iii*)	(*i*)	(*ii*)

35. The presence of increasing returns to scale in an industry leads to:

A. discouraging producers from exporting
B. give a comparative advantage in that industry to large countries
C. make that industry perfectly competitive
D. cause price in that industry to rise with output

36. Hedging in the foreign exchange market refers to:

A. An act of devaluation
B. Covering a risk of fluctuations in the foreign exchange rates in future
C. Not covering a risk of fluctuations in the foreign exchange rates in future
D. An act of revaluation

37. Arrange the following acts in the order in which they came into force:

(*a*) Competition Act
(*b*) Foreign Exchange Management Act
(*c*) Consumer Protection Act
(*d*) The Factories Act

Choose the answer from the code below:

A. (*b*), (*a*), (*d*), (*c*) B. (*d*), (*b*), (*c*), (*a*)
C. (*d*), (*c*), (*b*), (*a*) D. (*c*), (*d*), (*b*), (*a*)

38. Match the following lists:

List-I (Committees)	List-II (Chairperson)
(*a*) Industrial Sickness	(*i*) Abid Hussain
(*b*) Public sector enterprise autonomy	(*ii*) Onkar Goswami
(*c*) Small Scale industry	(*iii*) Rakesh Mohan
(*d*) Infrastructure development	(*iv*) Arjun Sen Gupta

Code:

	(*a*)	(*b*)	(*c*)	(*d*)
A.	(*iii*)	(*ii*)	(*i*)	(*iv*)
B.	(*ii*)	(*iv*)	(*i*)	(*iii*)
C.	(*iv*)	(*i*)	(*iii*)	(*ii*)
D.	(*i*)	(*iii*)	(*ii*)	(*iv*)

39. Arrange the following sectors in the ascending order on the basis of their weight in the Index of Industrial production (IIP) with base year 2011-12. Answer from the code below:

(*a*) Electricity
(*b*) Manufacturing
(*c*) Mining

Code:

A. (*c*), (*b*) and (*a*)
B. (*a*), (*c*) and (*b*)
C. (*b*), (*a*) and (*c*)
D. (*a*), (*b*) and (*c*)

40. For a financial asset, which of the following is/are correct in relation to rate of return and the yield from it?

(*a*) Rate of return is retrospective while the yield is prospective
(*b*) Rate of return does not include capital gains while the yield includes capital gains.

Choose the answer from the code below:

A. Both (*a*) and (*b*) are correct
B. Neither (*a*) nor (*b*) is correct
C. Only (*a*) is correct
D. Only (*b*) is correct

41. When the Reserve Bank of India announces an increase of the Cash Reserve Ratio, what does it mean?

A. The commercial Banks will have less money to lend
B. The Reserve Bank of India will have less money to lend
C. The Union Government will have less money to lend
D. The commercial Banks will have more money to lend

42. Core inflation has been described as:

A. Headline inflation – food inflation
B. Headline inflation – (food inflation + fuel inflation)
C. Headline inflation – fuel inflation
D. Food inflation + Fuel inflation

43. According to T.W. Schultz, which of the following statements is/are true?

(*a*) Farmers in developing countries are unresponsive to government set agricultural prices
(*b*) Farmers in developing countries are willing to innovate and adopt new methods of cultivation

Choose the **correct** answer from the code given below:

A. Both (*a*) and (*b*) are true
B. Neither (*a*) nor (*b*) is true
C. Only (*a*) is true
D. Only (*b*) is true

44. The government levying taxes on Polluters or charging a surcharge for pesticide use means:

A. Internalization of negative spill over effects
B. Marginal abatement cost
C. Examples of a free rider
D. Examples of Coase's theorem

45. Assuming an agricultural growth rate of 4% per annum in India, what will be its contribution to the country's GDP growth rate with a 20% contribution of the agricultural sector to GDP?

A. 8% B. 5%
C. 2 % D. 0.8 %

46. Optimum population will be at a point where:

A. National income is maximum
B. Per capita income is maximum
C. Population is maximum
D. Per capita consumption is maximum

47. Who amongst the following made the following statement?

"The Table of nature is laid for the few. Those who come uninvited will starve".

A. Julius Simon
B. E. Boserup
C. T.W. Malthus
D. H. Dalton

48. Which of the following is **not** part of a life - table?

A. It shows age - specific death rate
B. Age - specific life expectancy can be estimated
C. Probability of surviving at particular year of age can be estimated
D. Age - specific birth rate can be estimated

49. Consider the following data pertaining to India as per NFHS-4 and Match List-I with List-II. Select the correct answer from the code given below:

List-I (Indicator)	List-II (Value)
(*a*) TFR	(*i*) 2.2
(*b*) IMR	(*ii*) 50
(*c*) U - 5 MR	(*iii*) 79
(*d*) Institutional Births	(*iv*) 41

Code:

	(*a*)	(*b*)	(*c*)	(*d*)
A.	(*i*)	(*iii*)	(*ii*)	(*iv*)
B.	(*i*)	(*iv*)	(*ii*)	(*iii*)
C.	(*iv*)	(*i*)	(*iii*)	(*ii*)
D.	(*i*)	(*ii*)	(*iii*)	(*iv*)

50. Rank the following states in descending order according to sex ratio as per census 2011:

(*a*) Madhya Pradesh (*b*) Punjab
(*c*) U.P (*d*) Bihar

Code:

A. (*a*), (*c*), (*d*), (*b*)
B. (*b*), (*a*), (*c*), (*d*)
C. (*a*), (*b*), (*c*), (*d*)
D. (*c*), (*d*), (*b*), (*a*)

51. Pollution is an example of Market failure because:

A. The market price is less than the efficient price
B. The market price is higher than the efficient price
C. Property rights are poorly distributed
D. Those who suffer from pollution are compensated outside the market

52. "For goods that are unrelated in consumption, efficiency requires that tax rates be inversely proportional to elasticity of demand". This is the definition of:

A. The benefits - received principle
B. The second best principle
C. The inverse elasticity rule
D. The Ramsey Rule

53. A forward - shifted tax will affect:

A. Buyers and Sellers equally
B. Sellers more than buyers
C. government revenue negatively
D. Buyers more than sellers

54. The case for progressive tax rates rests on:

A. Benefits received
B. Cost of service
C. Ability to pay
D. None of the above

55. Primary deficit is measured by:

A. Fiscal deficit – interest payments
B. Budget deficit – interest payments
C. Budget deficit + total borrowings
D. Total Revenue expenditure – total revenue receipts

56. Which one of the following is **not** correctly matched?

	Plan	Strategy of Plan
A.	11th Plan	Inclusive growth
B.	2nd Plan	Heavy industry investment
C.	3rd Plan	Balanced growth
D.	8th Plan	Basic Needs

57. Who amongst the following economists have majorly contributed to TFP studies in Indian Context?

(*a*) B.N. Golder
(*b*) A. Virmani
(*c*) D.K. Das
(*d*) A. Sen

Choose the **correct** answer from the code below:

A. All of the above
B. (*c*) and (*d*)
C. (*a*), (*b*) and (*c*)
D. (*b*) and (*d*)

58. Consider the following statements in relation to Gender Budgeting and answer from the code given below:

(*a*) 'Gender analysis' of the budget
(*b*) Preparing a separate budget for women
(*c*) Government of India adopted gender budgeting in 2005-06

Code:

A. (*a*) and (*b*) are correct
B. (*a*) and (*c*) are correct
C. (*b*) and (*c*) are correct
D. (*a*), (*b*) and (*c*) are correct

59. Arrange the following indices in the chronological order and answer from the code given below:

(*a*) Multi Dimension Poverty Index
(*b*) Human Poverty Index
(*c*) Capability Poverty Measure
(*d*) Human Development Index

Code:

A. (*d*), (*c*), (*b*), (*a*)
B. (*d*), (*b*), (*c*), (*a*)
C. (*b*), (*a*), (*d*), (*c*)
D. (*a*), (*b*), (*c*), (*d*)

60. Which organisation in India has been given the responsibility to monitor the progress of sustainable development goals?

A. Reserve Bank of India
B. Central Statistical Office
C. NITI Aayog
D. National Sample Survey office

61. Which of the following does **not** come under Small Savings Schemes as per Government of India?

A. Post office deposits
B. Public Provident Fund
C. Jan Dhan Accounts
D. Sukanya Samridhi Yojana

62. Which one of the following schemes provide upto ₹ 2 lacs accidental death Insurance to the people in the age group of 18 - 70 years?

A. Atal Pension Yojna
B. Pradhan Mantri Jeevan Jyoti Bima Yojna
C. Pradhan Mantri Suraksha Bima Yojna
D. Atal Jeevan Beema Yojna

Directions (Q. Nos. 63-66): *Assertion (A) and Reason (R) type. Key to these questions is as follows:*

A. Both (A) and (R) are true and (R) is the correct explanation of (A).
B. Both (A) and (R) are true, but (R) is not the correct explanation of (A).
C. (A) is true, but (R) is false.
D. (a) is false, but (R) is true.

63. Assertion (A): Public utilities do not opt for profit maximisation policy.

Reason (R): It would lead to under utilization of capacity.

64. Assertion (A): The existence of industries with increasing returns to scale create an additional opportunity to gain from trade.

Reason (R): By specializing in a smaller number of industries, countries can produce more in each industry and the costs of production will, therefore, fall.

65. Assertion (A): Recursive models can be suitably estimated by OLS method.

Reason (R): Recursive models satisfy Identification conditions.

66. Assertion (A): Classical macro model is decomposable into real and monetary sectors.

Reason (R): Money affects both income and employment.

67. An entrepreneur's short - run total cost function is $C = q^3 - 10q^2 + 17q + 66$. If $p = 5$ the output at which profit is maximised by this entrepreneur is:

A. 7 B. 6
C. 5 D. 2/3

68. Given the Market model with Demand and supply functions as under:

$D_t = ap_t + b \qquad a < 0$
$S_t = Ap_{t-1} + B \qquad A > 0$

The condition for stable equilibrium here will be:

A. $a < A$ B. $|a| < \left|\frac{1}{A}\right|$
C. $\left|\frac{1}{a}\right| < \left|\frac{1}{A}\right|$ D. $\left|\frac{1}{a}\right| > \left|\frac{1}{A}\right|$

69. The production function in Input - Output Analysis propounded by W.W. Leontief has implied the value of elasticity of substitution between inputs as:

A. One
B. Zero
C. Constant
D. Infinity

70. For a Demand Function $p = 16 - q - 0.5q^2$ the price elasticity of demand at $q = 4$ is:

A. + 0.5 B. + 0.2
C. + 0.7 D. + 0.3

71. Cobb - Douglas production function $Q = AL^aK^{1-a} (a > 0)$ is **not** characterised by:

A. Constant returns to scale
B. Unit elasticity of substitution
C. Variable elasticity of substitution
D. Linear homogeneity

72. For samples of size greater than 30, the sampling distribution of the rank correlation coefficient is approximately which distribution:

A. *t*
B. Binomial
C. Chi - square
D. Normal

73. If a Durbin - Watson statistics takes value close to zero, what will be the value of first order autocorrelation coefficient?

A. Close to zero
B. Close to plus one
C. Close to minus one
D. Close to either minus or plus one

74. What would be consequences for the OLS estimator if heteroscedasticity is present in a regression model but ignored?

A. it will be biased
B. it will be inconsistent
C. it will be inefficient
D. All A, B and C will be true

75. Match the following and select proper code:

List-I	List-II
(*a*) Koyck	(*i*) Autocorrelated disturbances
(*b*) Durbin - Watson	(*ii*) Lagged variables
(*c*) Fisher's F Test	(*iii*) Causality
(*d*) Granger	(*iv*) Test of significance of overall regression

Code:

	(*a*)	(*b*)	(*c*)	(*d*)
A.	(*i*)	(*ii*)	(*iii*)	(*iv*)
B.	(*ii*)	(*i*)	(*iv*)	(*iii*)
C.	(*iii*)	(*iv*)	(*i*)	(*ii*)
D.	(*i*)	(*iii*)	(*iv*)	(*ii*)

ANSWERS

1	2	3	4	5	6	7	8	9	10
C	C	D	C	A	D	D	C	D	D
11	**12**	**13**	**14**	**15**	**16**	**17**	**18**	**19**	**20**
C	D	A	C	C	B	C	C	D	D
21	**22**	**23**	**24**	**25**	**26**	**27**	**28**	**29**	**30**
B	B	A	A	C	A	B	A	A	A
31	**32**	**33**	**34**	**35**	**36**	**37**	**38**	**39**	**40**
A	D	B	C	B	B	C	B	B	C
41	**42**	**43**	**44**	**45**	**46**	**47**	**48**	**49**	**50**
A	B	D	A	D	B	C	D	B	*
51	**52**	**53**	**54**	**55**	**56**	**57**	**58**	**59**	**60**
A	D	D	C	A	D	C	B	A	C
61	**62**	**63**	**64**	**65**	**66**	**67**	**68**	**69**	**70**
C	C	B	B	A	B	B	C	B	B
71	**72**	**73**	**74**	**75**					
C	D	B	C	B					

EXPLANATORY ANSWERS

1. 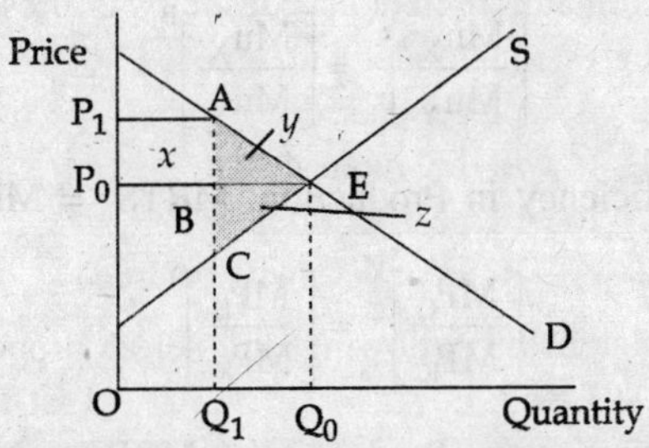

Deadweight Loss: The shaded rectangle and triangles show changes in consumer and producer surplus when moving from competitive price and quantity, P_0 and Q_0 to a monopolist's price and quantity, P_1 and Q_1. Because of the higher price, consumers lose $x + y$ and producer gains $x - z$. The deadweight loss is $y + z$.

2. *Features of Cournot's model*

1. Cournot's equilibrium is Nash equilibrium. This particular equilibrium is reached by the assumption of zero conjectural variation.
2. Cournot's equilibrium is stable.
3. Cournot's model assumes autonomous behaviour. There is however the scope for any firm to improve its position by strategic behaviour. A strategic behaviour here is to observe the other firm's behaviour pattern and determine output accordingly. This behaviour is known as leadership behaviour, which we consider in Stackelberg model in the following section.
4. Cournot's equilibrium is not joint profit maximizing. There is scope for improvement for both firms by joint profit maximization through collusion and formulation of cartel.

3. In case of an inferior good, income and substitution effects of a price change work in opposite directions and that substitution effect outweighs the income effect so that there is net increase in the quantity demanded of and inferior good when its price falls. It means that *the law of demand applies to an 'inferior good' as it applies to a 'normal good'.*

However, there are certain cases of inferior goods to which the law of demand does not apply. Such goods are known as Giffen goods. *In case of Giffen goods, substitution effect is positive and income effective is negative but negative income effect is so powerful that it outweighs the positive substitution effect.* Therefore, when price of an inferior good of Giffen type decreases, its demand decreases and *vice versa.* This phenomenon shows a paradoxical situation, *i.e.*, when the price of an inferior good increases, its quantity demanded increases. This paradox is known as Giffen paradox. *Giffen's paradox is a very strong exception to the law of demand.*

4. The Edgeworth Box diagram is a conceptual device often used in economics to show how a given basket of goods can be efficiently (and also inefficiently) distributed among a set of individuals. The basic idea of an efficient distribution is that of Pareto-optimality: the goods must be allocated in such a way that no redistribution is possible so that one individual increases his/her utility without someone else decreasing his/hers.

5. Price effect and its components: The total effect on the quantity demanded of a commodity of a change in its price is called price effect. It can be divided into two parts: the substitution effect and income effect.

Substitution effect: The substitution effect of a change is measured by holding real income constant on a single indifference curve and examining the effect of changing the ratio of the two prices by altering the slope of the budget line. Substitution effect refers to the change in the consumption of a commodity that occurs when the consumer moves along the same indifference curve, after a change in relative has occurred. It is the same for all commodities.

Income effect: The income of a price change is the difference between price effect and income effect. It is found by holding relative prices constant and varying the position of the budget line with its slope remaining constant.

6. Three problems arise in connection with a general equilibrium:

1. Does a general equilibrium solution exist? (Existence problem).
2. If an equilibrium solution exists, is it unique? (Uniqueness problem.)
3. If an equilibrium solution exists, is it stable? (Stability problem.)

8. A resource allocation is efficient if it is impossible to make one or more persons better off in terms of welfare without making at least one other person worse off. Conversely, an allocation is inefficient, if it is possible to improve someone's position without worsening the position of any other individual. The Italian Economist Vilfredo Pareto has specified a condition of optimal or efficient allocation referred to as *Pareto Optimality Condition.* An allocation is Pareto optimal or Pareto efficient, if it is impossible to make changes in production and consumption activities of firms and households to increase the welfare of at least one individual without affecting the welfare of at least another individual.

There are three conditions that must be satisfied for the allocation to be Pareto optimal or Pareto efficient. They are:

1. Efficiency in consumption.
2. Efficiency in production.
3. Efficiency in product mix.

Conditions for Pareto Efficiency

Efficiency in Consumption: $MRS^A = MRS^B$

$$\left[\frac{Mu_X}{Mu_Y}\right]^A = \left[\frac{Mu_X}{Mu_Y}\right]^B$$

Efficiency in Production: $MRTS^x = MRTS^y$

$$\left[\frac{MP_L}{MP_K}\right]^X = \left[\frac{MP_L}{MP_K}\right]^Y$$

Efficiency in Product Mix: MRPT = MRS

$$MC_X/MC_Y = MU_X/MU_Y$$

9. Shadow Prices: For social cost-benefit analysis, the market prices of both inputs and outputs of a project are required to be corrected suitably if they do not represent the 'real' prices of inputs/outputs. Such corrected price of inputs/outputs is known as shadow price. Hence, the shadow price takes care of the distortions in the market price by suitably adjusting the market price.

For example, newly set up Small Scale Industries in India are granted subsidy on electricity charges by the Government, for the initial few years. The State Electricity Boards (SEB) may produce electricity at a cost of, say ₹ 2.50 per unit. A newly set up Small Scale Industry may be charged at a rate of say ₹ 1.50 per unit of electric power consumed in its first year of operation. ₹ 1.75 per unit, in its second year of operation, ₹ 2.00 per unit in its third year of operation etc., In such a situation, the cost of electric power for the Small Scale Industry is ₹ 1.50 per unit, ₹ 1.75 per unit and ₹ 2.00 per unit for the first, second and third year of operation respectively. However, the cost for the SEB is ₹ 2.50 per unit which is the actual cost, though the SEB charges a lower price. The price of electric power to be used for social cost-benefit analysis is only ₹ 2.50 per unit which is the shadow price of electric power.

10. In micro-economics demonstrative effects are typically studied under the name of "Veblen". "Snob" and "Bandwagon" effects as proposed by Leibeinstein. Although hardly central to the mainstream, "Veblen", "Bandwagon" and "Snob" effects, rely on the acceptance that an individual's consumption of goods is affected by the behaviour of other consumers. "Veblen's" effect is at work when the function of consumption is to manifest pecuniary strength, and the demand of a good may increase with price, the latter being an index of the scarce commodity of status. With "Bandwagon" and "Snob" effects an individual's demand for goods or services is either increased or decreased by the fact that others are seen consuming them.

14. The *absolute income hypothesis* relates household consumption to the *current absolute income* and the *relative income hypothesis* relates it to the *current relative income.* Both these hypotheses relate consumption to *current income*—absolute or relative. Milton Friedman rejected the 'current income hypotheses' and developed another theory of consumption, popularly known as *permanent income hypothesis.* According to the permanent income hypothesis, it is the *permanent income,* not the current income, which determines the level of current consumption expenditure.

Friedman's theory postulates that consumption is the function of permanent income, *i.e.*,

$$C = f(Y_p),$$

and that C is proportional to Y_p, *i.e.*,

$$C = kY_p$$

Permanent income, defined broadly, is the mean of all the incomes anticipated by the households in the long run. The method of estimating permanent income, as described below, is an approximation of incomes anticipated from all human and non-human wealth (or capital). In simple words, it means labour income *plus* capital incomes. If all material, financial and human sources of income are treated as *wealth,* then the permanent income of the current year can be defined as

$$Y_p = rW$$

where Y_p is the permanent disposable income with reference to the current year, W represents overall wealth and *r* is the rate of return.

16. There is direct relationship between investment multiplier and marginal propensity to consume. Higher the marginal propensity to consume, greater is the size of multiplier. On the contrary, lower the marginal propensity to consume, smaller is the size of multiplier. In fact, the value of multiplier is determined by the value of marginal propensity to consume. *i.e.*,

$$K = \frac{1}{1 - MPC}$$

Where, K = Multiplier and MPC = Marginal propensity to consume.

18. For each savings rate, there is a unique steady state per capita capital stock, given the production function, the growth rate of labour and depreciation. As per capita consumption in the steady state depends on the savings rate, one can calculate which savings rate maximises per capita consumption. This savings rate is known as the *golden rule* savings rate. The steady state per capita consumption is maximised when the marginal product of capital equals the growth rate of labour plus the depreciation rate. This is known as the *golden rule of capital accumulation,* as it defines the capital stock that maximises the steady state per capita consumption level.

19. In Schumpeter's theory of economic development, three key words concern economic development. The first is *innovation,* the cause of economic development. Innovation covers the introduction of a new product or a new method of production, the opening of a new market, the acquisition of a new source of supply, and the reorganization of an existing industry. With the introduction of these new elements into an economy, the traditional channels of the economy have to be changed. Innovation destroys old things and creates new ones and is thus called creative destruction.

The second key word is *entrepreneur,* the subject of economic development or the agent of innovation. Schumpeter's entrepreneur is not a business manager himself. In contrast to a manager, who depends on existing goods and existing methods of production, the entrepreneur carries out new and creative projects. When one attempts to initiate new things, he is confronted with various kinds of risk, resistance, and hesitation. Those who are able to prevail are scarce, for innovation requires foresight and originality, resolution and action. If one succeeds in introducing a change, he can get entrepreneurial profits.

The third element is *bank credit,* the means by which the entrepreneur accomplishes innovation. If one wants to undertake innovative activities, one must have control over productive resources. When an economy is in a static state with full employment, the utilization of productive resources for new activities requires the forced withdrawal of the resources from existing uses. The entrepreneur acquires new credit from capitalists or banks and by means of the newly created purchasing power, pays higher prices than before for the needed resources. He is typically a debtor and repays what he owes out of entrepreneurial profits.

As the implementation of new combinations — defined by innovation (cause), entrepreneur (subject), and bank credit (means) — proceeds, a series of changes including those in the business cycle will occur in the economic process; in its totality such transformation is called *economic development.* Economic development pre-supposes capitalism as an institution. Although capitalism is ordinarily defined in terms of private ownership and profit incentives through market mechanisms, Schumpeter stipulated bank credit as essential to the functioning of capitalism.

20. The rate of profit is the relationship of profit and investment or of the monetary expression of surplus-value and the value of the means of production and labour-power (constant and variable capital).

$$\text{ROP} = \frac{s}{c+v}$$

If we divide the numerator and the denominator by v, then we get the following:

$$\text{ROP} = \frac{\frac{s}{v}}{\frac{c}{v}+1}$$

This formula shows that the rate of profit depends (*a*) on the rate of surplus-value, which Marx also calls the rate of exploitation because it described the relationship of unpaid and paid labour, and (*b*) the organic composition of capital, which represents the relationship of dead and living labour, constant and variable capital, the value of machinery/resources and labour-power. The rate of profit is directly proportional to the rate of surplus-value and indirectly proportional to the organic composition of capital.

21. The early mathematical expression of neoclassical growth models show that the long-run rate of growth is exogenously determined by either the rate of savings (Harrod-Domar model) or the rate of technical progress (Solow-Swan model). In reality, if a country demonstrates higher per capita growth, then it means that the country devotes large shares of its output to saving and investment, and this is not reflected in the neoclassical growth model.

In the 1980s, it was realized that the neoclassical framework was not adequate for the analysis of actual growth experience. As a result of this, the endogenous growth model start taking shape building macroeconomic models out of microeconomic fundamentals. The microeconomic groundwork starts at the household level where households maximize utility subject to budget constraints and firms are projected to maximize profits with the production of new technologies and human capital. Based on the above microeconomic groundwork, the AK model is the starting version of endogenous growth model which assumes a constant exogenous saving rate and a fixed level of technology. The AK model is a distinct case of the Cobb-Douglas function and holds constant return to scale as the key assumption, and is presented as:

$$Y = AK^{a}L^{1-a}$$

Where Y = the total production, A = the total factor productivity, K = capital, K (K embodies both physical capital and human capital), L = labour, and the parameter a = the output elasticity of capital. As a special case when $a = 1$ = the production function is linear and the property of constant returns to scale in the capital stock hold. This will prevail for any other value of the capital intensity between 0 and 1. An endogenous growth model can be constructed by having or relaxing the perfect competition assumption.

Technological development is the key component of an endogenous growth model and investment in research will enhance technological enhancements and generate a predictable rate of economic growth. The endogenous growth theory perceives foreign investors as promoters of domestic firms in terms of technical, marketing, and managerial know-how.

22. **Theories of Social Transformation:** The historical development of capitalism has been widely presented as a linear progression. This perception was codified by authors like Fisher and Clark, who presented the trajectory of capitalist development as one based upon sectoral change in which employment moved from a primary sector (agriculture) to a secondary sector (manufacturing) and then on to a tertiary or service sector. The Fisher/Clark 'thesis' emerged in the 1930s and 1940s. This influential analysis defined manufacturing as the making of tangible goods and commodities, while services were associated with the provision of the intangible or non-material. This 'thesis' was subsequently reworked in the post-1945 period by authors like Bell (1973), for whom the shift to the post-industrial society was characterized by the replacement of goods-producing activities by those concerned with the provision of services. Service work involved all those employed in activities such as information handling and the knowledge-based industries.

23. **Hagen's Theory:** *On the Theory of Social Change* (1962), by the economist Everett E Hagen, uses psychology, sociology, and anthropology to explain how a traditional agricultural society (with a hierarchical and authoritarian social structure where status is inherited) becomes one in which continuing technical progress occurs. Because the industrial and cultural complex of low-income societies is unique, they cannot merely imitate Western techniques. Thus, economic growth requires widespread adaptation, creativity, and problem solving, in addition to positive attitudes toward manual labour.

24. In 1954, Lewis produced a seminal paper on a dual economy model. In this model, there are two sectors: a modern capitalist (industrial) sector and a traditional subsistence (agricultural) sector. The traditional sector has "unlimited" supplies of labour (a very large population) where wages are at subsistence. Agricultural production remains unchanged as workers move out to the industrial sector, there is surplus labour (disguised unemployment)" in agriculture. Capitalists in the modern sector reinvest all their profits and hence in the next period they can increase production, employment increases, profits increase, reinvestment takes place and the system continues to grow.

This was a very attractive model for a long time as it appears that we can have something for nothing: agricultural production remains constant as workers move out to the modern sector, while industrial production increases with increased employment and investment.

In many of these models agriculture is simply treated as a sector that is there to produce goods and provide labour for the dominant sector, the industrial sector. Eventually, when the unlimited supply of labour is exhausted wages in the industrial sector would rise, hence slowing down employment and profits. Subsequently, capitalists would continue to reinvest profits and the economy would continue to grow. For Lewis the economy switches from a classical model to a neoclassical one.

Of course, what happened in many developing countries is that there was a mass movement of labour from the agricultural sector to the urban industrial areas that created unemployment, homelessness, slums, and poverty. The industrial sector could not absorb the large number of migrants.

26. Harrod-Domar Growth Model: A model in growth theory developed independently by Roy Harrod and E.D. Domar. The model works on the basis of three growth rates, the actual rate of growth, the warranted rate of growth and the natural rate of growth. As the name implies, the actual rate of growth is the growth path actually followed by the economy. The warranted rate of growth is derived from a savings function and the accelerator principle. It can be shown that the warranted rate of growth (g_w) is given by the expression, $g_w = s/c$, where s is the savings propensity and c is the capital-output ratio. The natural rate of growth is determined by the rate of growth of the labour force and the rate of growth in labour productivity. In equilibrium, all three growth rates will have to be identical. One of the highlights of the Harrod-Domar growth model is the fact that if there is a divergence between the three growth rates, the divergence will not be reduced so that the economy moves towards the equilibrium path. Instead, there will be a cumulative divergence away from the equilibrium path.

If all firms expect demand to grow at the warranted rate and invest appropriately to meet that demand, then their expectations will be fulfilled. If, however, they expect demand to grow more quickly than the warranted rate, the actual *rate of growth* will be greater than the expected rate and there will be excess demand. By contrast, if expectations are pessimistic, the actual rate of growth will be less than the expected rate and there will be excess supply. This is the essence of *Harrod's instability*, which can be considered a statement of the implausibility of a market economy ensuring dynamically stable conditions of equal supply and demand.

28. The *twin deficits hypothesis* refers to the belief that changes in fiscal policy that increase the budget deficit will also increase the current account deficit. The term gained popularity in the 1980s, when tax cuts that caused the U.S. budget deficit to increase by 3 per cent of gross domestic product (GDP) between 1980 and 1985 were followed by trade deficits exceeding 3 per cent of GDP in 1985 and 1986. The concept received renewed attention in the first decade of the 21st century, when a deterioration of the U.S. long-term or structural budget balance of 6 per cent of GDP between 2000 and 2004 was accompanied by current account deficits of 5 per cent of GDP in 2004 and 6.5 per cent of GDP in 2005.

30. Agreement on Agriculture: The Agreement on Agriculture is an international treaty of the World Trade Organization. It was negotiated during the Uruguay Round of the General Agreement on Tariffs and Trade, and entered into force with the establishment of the WTO on January 1, 1995.

Three Pillars: The AoA has three central concepts, or "pillars": domestic support, market access and export subsidies.

31. In 1960, Belgian-American economist Robert Triffin first identified the Triffin dilemma (or Triffin paradox), that is, when a national currency also serves as an international reserve currency, there can be conflicts of interest between short-term domestic and long-term international economic objectives.

33. The Regional Comprehensive Economic Partnership (RCEP) negotiations commenced in late 2012 among 16 countries (that is, the 10-member Association of Southeast Asian Nations (ASEAN) plus the six countries with existing PTAs with ASEAN). The goal of the RCEP negotiations is 'to achieve a modern, comprehensive, high-quality and mutually beneficial economic partnership agreement among the ASEAN Member States and ASEAN's FTA Partners', covering a broad range of areas including trade in goods and services, investment, technical cooperation, intellectual property, competition and dispute settlement.

35. The new trade theory came into existence during 1970s. It held that with the presence of substantial economies of scale there can be increasing returns to specialisation rather then decreasing returns. The economies of scale refers to the reduction in the unit cost due to large scale production. These are derived by spreading the fixed input over a large output.

The new trade theorists believe that due to the presence of substantial economies of scale in many industries, the world market may be able to support only a limited number of firms based in a limited number of countries producing that product. Those countries where the product was first produced will predominate in the export of that product. The producing firms of that product in the concerned country may gain economies of scale and early training in the handling of things. These advantages accruing to a firm for entering early in a particular industry are called first mover advantages. These advantages create barriers for new entrants into the market.

36. Hedging: An important feature of the forward exchange market is *hedging* (or covering). Hedging is settling the exchange rate in advance for future transactions with a view to avoiding loss due to exchanges depreciation in future. Hedging is essentialy covering the risk of exchange rate fluctuations.

37. Competition Act — 2002
Foreign Exchange Management Act — 1999
Consumer Protection Act — 1986
The Factories Act — 1948

39.

Sector	Base year 2011-12		Base year 2004-05	
	Weights (%)	Item groups	Weights (%)	Item groups
Mining	14.373	1	14.157	1
Manufacturing	77.633	405	75.527	397
Electricity	7.994	1	10.316	1
Total	**100**	**407**	**100**	**399**

42. In theory, core inflation is defined as the underlying, or persistent, part of inflation that provides an indication of future inflation, although precise definitions vary. In practice, core inflation is commonly measured using the CPI that excludes food and energy prices, or their most volatile components, but these measures differ across countries. The variation in measurements of core inflation tends to be especially significant among emerging and developing economies, for which inferences about the underlying inflation need to be made with caution.

Otto Eckstein (1981), is considered the originator of the term "Core Inflation". Eckstein defined it as "the trend increase of the cost of factors of production" and observed that this notion of core inflation ... originates in the long-term expectation of inflation in minds of households and business, in the contractual arrangements which sustain the wage-price momentum, and in the tax system." Eckstein definition divides core inflation into demand, supply shock and production cost.

44. The Coase Theorem: The modern analysis of neighbourhood effects or externalities has been strongly influenced by the work of Ronald Coase. Coase wrote a pathbreaking article in 1960 that focused on simple negative spillovers, such as a confectioner whose machinery causes vibrations that disrupt a doctor's examining room next door, or a rancher whose cattle wander onto a farmer's land and trample the crops.

45. % Growth in GDP $= \frac{4}{100} \times 20 = \frac{4}{5}\% = 0.8\%$.

46. Theory of Optimum Population: The theory of optimum population was first formulated by Prof. Sidwick and later developed by **Prof. Dalton and Prof. Carr Saunders**. They developed the concept of *optimum population, i.e.,* that size of population which is the best for a country at a particular time. At this level of optimum population, per capita income would be maximum.

In other words, it is that level of population which enables an economy to produce with given natural resources, technology and capital stock, the highest per capita income. **According to Prof. Carr Saunders,** optimum population is that which produces maximum economic welfare. The concept of economic welfare includes environmental maintenance, pollution check, ecological balance, etc. A country would then said to be under populated if its population is less than the optimum and over populated if its population is more than the optimum.

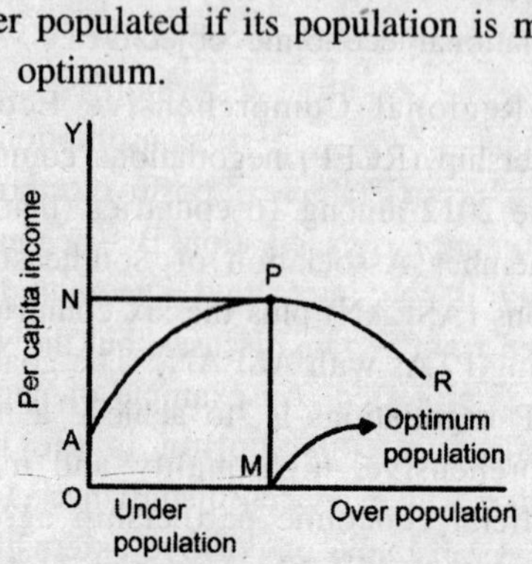

Fig.: *Optimum Population*

Accordingly, three concepts of population are:

1. **Optimum Population:** It is that level of population at which per capita income is the highest, This level of population is changeable with changes in resources and technology.
2. **Over Population:** It is that level of a population where per capita income falls with rise in population. It leads to food shortage, unemployment, poverty and low standard of living.
3. **Under Population:** It is that level of population where per capita income rises with rise in population. It occurs due to underutilisation of resources.

51. Externality is an influence that does not come from the institution of market but affects the welfare of a person either adversely or favourably. Externalities adversely affect the economic efficiency.

Externalities can be positive or negative. Air pollution is an example of negative externality. A negative externality is a cost which is not reflected in the market place. A positive externality is a benefit accruing to a person without his own effort and it is not generated from market transaction. Education is a good example of a positive externality. An educated person is likely to produce many benefits to the society as a better citizen, as a source of information, advice, and so on.

Positive and negative externalities can be found both in the case of consumption and production. An example of positive externality in consumption is vaccination. By vaccination, not only is the individual vaccinated and protected from certain diseases, but the whole society is protected. An example of negative externality in consumption is the noisy motorbike which creates disturbances to the others. An example of positive externality in production is the beehive which not only produces honey for the owner but also help in the pollination of plants. Another example of negative externality in production is the riverside chemical factory which dumps its chemical wastes in the river and pollutes its water.

Negative Externality and Market Failure: In the case of negative externality, the social cost is higher than the private cost. To be more precise, the marginal social cost is higher than the marginal private cost, and the actual output produced by the negative externality creating industry (or film) does not take into account the social cost that it creates. Thus, the competitive equilibrium will result in, (*i*) more than the efficient output and (*ii*) less than the efficient price. The market price falls short of the actual marginal social cost of the product. Under such a situation, an excessive amount of resources is allocated to produce the output which involves externality. The market fails to achieve allocative efficiency.

52. The literature on optimal taxation is highly technical. Contributions have been made by Ramsey (1927), Mirrlees (1971) and Auerbach (1985).

The basic problem of optimal taxation is to choose tax rates to minimize the loss of an individual's utility, that is, minimize excess burden, subject to a required amount of tax revenue to be raised by the government. The theory derives rules of efficient taxation providing a solution to this problem. These rules are the Ramsey rule, the inverse elasticity rule, and the Corlett-Hague rule.

The Ramsey rule states that in order to minimize excess burden "the proportional reduction in compensated demand as a result of the imposition of the set of taxes should be the same for all goods". There are two important aspects of the Ramsey rule. The first is that it is stated in quantity terms and not prices. This is so because it is the reduction in quantity which leads to a loss in excess burden. Changes in relative prices merely induce quantity changes. Second, it is the compensated or Hicksian demand change that matters. The Hicksian demand curve depends only on the substitution effect. This is important because excess burden relates to the distortion in consumer preferences due to the substitution effect.

The second rule is the inverse elasticity rule which states that tax rates should be inversely related to elasticities of demand. The rule implies that since excess burden varies directly with elasticities, this means that high tax rates should be imposed on inelastic goods, a policy which would lead to less distortion in consumer preferences. According to Stern, the inverse elasticity rule appears to be inegalitarian. To the extent that Ramsey formulated the problem in terms of one consumer the rule ignores distributional questions.

57. There are a large number of studies (Ahluwalia, 1991; Dholakia, and Dholakia, 1994; Pradhan and Barik, 1999; *Balakrishnan et.al,* 2000; Goldar and Kumari, 2003; Goldar, 2004; Unel, 2003; TSL, 2003 and Reddy, 2005) on total TFP for India's registered manufacturing sector. However, there is no conclusive agreement among the scholars regarding the trends of TFP neither for Indian manufacturing industries nor about the appropriate methodology for calculating TFP. There are only a few studies (Sivasubramonian, 2001; Virmani, 2004; Pallikata (2004); Bosworth and Virmani, 2007; Gupta, 2008 and *Das et.al,* 2010) which have made an attempt to estimate the TFP at the aggregate level.

58. Gender budgeting (GB) is a practice that accounts-budgetary measures to support gender commitments. According to the Ministry of Women and Child Development, "It is a powerful tool for achieving gender mainstreaming so as to ensure that benefits of development reach women as much as men." It is not just an accounting exercise but an ongoing process of keeping a gender perspective in policy/ programme formulation, its implementation and review. Budget 2016-17 mention that "Gender Budgeting in its simplest connotation is 'Gender Analysis' of the budget aimed at examining the budgetary allocation through a gender lens." The budget accepts that gender budgeting is an evolving area in India. More and more ministries and departments are contributing to the development of the practice in the country.

GB requires Government budgets to establish its gender specific impacts and to ensure that gender commitments are translated into budgetary commitments.

Budgetary resource allocation and the specific expenditure amount for women specific programmes are separately mentioned as part of gender specific budgeting in India.

The central government introduced gender budgeting in 2005-06 as a budgetary practice. It has institutionalized Gender Budgeting by introducing a Gender Budget Statement (GBS) since 2005-06. The GBS captures the total quantum of resources earmarked for women in a financial year.

59. Multi Dimension Poverty Index — 2010
Human Poverty Index — 1997
Capability Poverty Measure — 1996
Human Development Index — 1990

67. Here, Total cost function is

$$TC = q^3 - 10q^2 + 17q + 66$$

∴ Total profit

$$\Pi = TR - TC$$
$$= q.5 - (q^3 - 10q^2 + 17q + 66)$$
$$= 5q - q^3 + 10q^2 - 17q - 66$$

For Maximum Profit

$$\frac{d\Pi}{dq} = 5 - 3q^2 + 20q - 17 = 0$$

$\Rightarrow \quad 3q^2 - 20q + 12 = 0$

$\Rightarrow \quad 3q^2 - 18q - 2q + 12 = 0$

$\Rightarrow \quad 3q(q - 6) - 2(q - 6) = 0$

$(q - 6)(3q - 2) = 0$

$\therefore \quad q = 6$ or $q = 2/3$

For maximum,

$$\frac{d^2\Pi}{dq^2} = -6q + 20 < 0$$

At $q = 6$, This condition is satisfied.

68. Supply response: $S_t = Ap_{t-1} + B$

Consumer demand: $D_t = ap_t + b$

Market equilibrium: $S_t = D_t$

This is the famous cobweb model developed by Ezekiel (1938) and Waugh (1964), which they used to explain the unstable performance of many agricultural commodity markets. The solution to this model, assuming that $p = p_0$ at $t = 0$, is (Henderson and Quandt, 1971):

$$p_t = \left(p_0 - \frac{B - b}{a - A}\right)\left(\frac{A}{a}\right)^t + \frac{B - b}{a - A},$$

which gives the time path of p_t as a function of t. A dynamic market equilibrium is achieved if prices stabilize, *i.e.*, if $p_t = p_{t-1}$ as $t \to \infty$. This requires that $p_t = (B - b)/(a - A)$. For this to occur, the first right hand term in the p_t equation must tend to zero as $t \to \infty$, which will be the case if A/a = slope S/slope D < 1, assuming normal slopes for supply and demand, *i.e.*, A > 0 and a < 0. Thus:

if A/a < 1, the market oscillates toward a stable equilibrium price and quantity;

if A/a > 1, the market oscillates toward unstable and explosive equilibrium.

70. Price Elasticity

$$E_d = -\frac{dq}{dp}\cdot\frac{p}{q}$$

Here, $q = 4$

$\therefore \quad p = 16 - q - 0.5q^2$

$= 16 - 4 - 0.5\,(4)^2$

$= 16 - 4 - 0.5 \times 16$

$= 16 - 4 - 8 = 4$

Here, $p = 16 - q - 0.5q^2$

$$\therefore \frac{dp}{dq} = -1 - 1.0q$$

Give $q = 4$

$$\therefore \frac{dp}{dq} = -1 - 4 = -5$$

$$\Rightarrow \frac{dq}{dp} = -\frac{1}{5}$$

$$\therefore \quad E_d = -\left(-\frac{1}{5}\right)\frac{4}{4} = 0.2.$$

71. Cobb-Douglas Production Function: The American economists like Charles W. Cobb and Paul H. Douglas have studied the relationship between physical input and physical output and formed an empirical production function, popularly known as 'Cobb-Douglas Production Function.'

Given a specific production function Q = f(L, K), Cobb–Douglas production function is of the form:

$$Q = A.L^a.K^b \; [a + b = 1]$$

Where,

Q = the rate of output (or total production)

L = the quantity of labour employed

K = the quantity of capital employed

A, a, b = the positive constants

a = the elasticity of output with respect to labour

b = the elasticity of output with respect to capital.

This function can also be written as:

$$Q = A.L^{a}.K^{1-a} \; [\because \; b = 1 - a]$$

It is noted here that the value of *a* is greater than zero ($a > 0$) but less than one ($a < 1$).

In their research, Cobb and Douglas estimated the function from time series data between 1899 and 1992. The result was that labour's share in national income of the USA is about 3/4 or 0.75 and that of capital share is about 1/4 or 0.25. The estimated value of efficiency parameter A is 1.01 (*i.e.*, $e > 1$). Hence, the result of their research studies was of the form

$$Q = 1 - 01.L^{0.75}.\ K^{0.25}$$

Properties: The following are the important properties of Cobb-Douglas production function:

1. The general form of Cobb-Douglas production function is homogenous of degree one, *i.e.*, $a + b = 1$.
2. If $a + b = 1$, then the production is operating under constant returns to scale.
3. If the inputs—labour and capital—are increased by *m* times, the total output will also be increased by *m* times.
4. The elasticity of substitution between labour and capital is equal to one.
5. The marginal product of labour is equal to the increase in output when labour input is increased by one unit. That is,

$$\frac{\partial Q}{\partial L} = \frac{a}{LQ}$$

6. The marginal product of capital is equal to the increase *e* in output when capital input is increased by one unit. That is,

$$\frac{\partial Q}{\partial K} = \frac{b}{K} \cdot Q$$

7. The average product of labour is equal to the ratio between output and labour input. That is,

$$\frac{Q}{L} = A \cdot L^{a-1} \cdot K^{b}$$

8. The average product of capital is equal to the ratio between output and capital input. That is,

$$\frac{Q}{K} = A \cdot L^{a} \cdot K^{b-1}$$

9. If one of the inputs is zero, the output will also be zero.
10. The 'expansion path' generated by this function is linear homogeneous and it passes through the origin.
11. It satisfies the Euler's theorem. That is,

$$MP_{L}.\ L + MP_{K}.K = Q$$

12. *a* and *b* represent elasticities of output with respect to labour and capital respectively.
13. The multiplicative form of the function can be changed into a log-linear form as:

$$\log Q = \log A + a \log L + b \log K$$

73. The Durbin-Watson Test: The Durbin-Watson test (DW) is may be the most common test for autocorrelation and is based on the assumption that the structure is of first order. Since first order autocorrelation is most likely to appear in time series data, the test is very relevant, and all statistical software has the option of calculating it automatically for you.

The Durbin-Watson test statistic for first order autocorrelation is given by:

$$DW = \frac{\sum_{t=2}^{T} (e_t - e_{t-1})^2}{\sum_{t=1}^{T} (e_t)^2} \qquad ...(1)$$

with e being the estimated residual from a sample regression model. To see that this test statistic is related to the first order autocorrelation case we may rewrite (1) in the following way:

$$DW = \frac{\sum_{t=2}^{T}(e_t - e_{t-1})^2}{\sum^{T}(e_t)^2}$$

$$= \frac{\sum_{t=2}^{T} e_t^2}{\sum^{T}(e_t)^2} + \frac{\sum_{t=2}^{T} e_{t-1}^2}{\sum^{T}(e_t)^2} - \frac{2\sum_{t=2}^{T} e_t e_{t-1}}{\sum^{T}(e_t)^2}$$

$$\approx 1 + 1 + 2\hat{p} = 2(1-\hat{p}) \qquad ...(2)$$

Where $\hat{p}$ on the right hand side is the autocorrelation coefficient from an first order autoregression scheme.

However, it is only an approximation since the expressions in the numerator sum from 2 to T instead of 1 to T as is the case in the denominator. The larger the value of T the better is the approximation.

From (2) it is possible to see that the DW test statistic only takes values between 0 and 4 since the autocorrelation coefficient only takes values between –1 and 1. Hence, when the autocorrelation coefficient equals 0, the DW test statistics equals 2. If DW > 2 we have an indication of a negative autocorrelation, and if DW < 2 we would have an indication of a positive autocorrelation.

YOUR SPACE

Previous Paper (Solved)

UGC-NET-Junior Research Fellowship & Assistant Professor Exam

ECONOMICS, January-2017*

PAPER-II

Note: *This paper contains **fifty (50)** objective type questions of **two (2)** marks each. **All** questions are compulsory.*

1. Marginal rate of transformation between two goods X and Y is defined as

A. $MRT_{X,Y} = \frac{MC_X}{MC_Y}$

B. $MRT_{X,Y} = MRS_{X,Y}$

C. $MRT_{X,Y} = MRS_{X,Y} = \frac{P_X}{P_Y}$

D. None of the above.

2. Consider the following statements regarding the expansion path of a firm:

I. It shows least cost combination for producing different level of outputs.

II. The input prices remain constant.

Of the above which statement is/are true? Answer from the codes given below:

Codes:

A. Both I and II are true.

B. Only I is true.

C. Only II is true.

D. Neither I nor II is true.

3. The First Fundamental Theorem of Welfare Economics requires

A. producers and consumers to be price takers

B. that the economy operate at some point on the utility possibility curve

C. that there be an efficient market for every commodity

D. All of the above

4. Which among the following allocation/ distribution corresponds to Rawlsian concept of equity?

A. All members of the society receive equal amount of goods.

B. Maximise the utility of the least well off people.

C. Market outcomes are most equitable.

D. Maximise the total utility of all members of the society.

5. Under discriminating monopoly, if the elasticity of demand in market I is 2 and in market II, it is 1, (elasticities being in absolute terms) then the price behaviour of the monopolist will be:

A. To charge a higher price in market I

B. To charge a higher price in market II

C. To charge the same price in both the markets

D. In market I, charge double the price of that is charged in market II

6. Given the demand function:

$Q = \frac{20}{P}$, where symbols have their usual meaning, at which price, the elasticity of demand would be unity?

A. 20 B. 10

C. 5 D. All of the above

7. The idea of indicative planning was first adopted in which Five year Plan of India?

A. Second Plan B. Fifth Plan

C. Seventh Plan D. Eighth Plan

---

* *Exam held on 22 January 2017*

8. Consider the following statements about Rashtriya Swasthya Bima Yojana (RSBY) :

(*a*) Under RSBY the premium is shared on 85:15 basis by the centre and state governments.

(*b*) In the case of the North-Eastern States and Jammu & Kashmir, under RSBY the premium is shared in a 90 : 10 ratio.

Which of the statement(s) given above is/are correct?

A. Only (*b*) B. Only (*a*)
C. Both (*a*) & (*b*) D. Neither (*a*) nor (*b*)

9. Match the following from the lists given below:

	List-I	**List-II**
(*a*)	National Rural Employment Programme (NREP)	(*i*) 2001
(*b*)	Sukanya Samridhi Yojana (SSY)	(*ii*) 1980
(*c*)	Food for Work Programme (FWP)	(*iii*) 1983
(*d*)	Rural Landless Employment Guarantee Programme (RLEGP)	(*iv*) 2015

Select the correct codes:

Codes:

	(*a*)	(*b*)	(*c*)	(*d*)
A.	(*iv*)	(*iii*)	(*ii*)	(*i*)
B.	(*i*)	(*ii*)	(*iv*)	(*iii*)
C.	(*ii*)	(*iv*)	(*i*)	(*iii*)
D.	(*iii*)	(*ii*)	(*iv*)	(*i*)

10. Which of the following has the highest share in India's external debt at the end of March 2015?

A. Rupee debt
B. NRI deposits
C. Commercial Borrowings
D. Export credit

11. R.B.I. can print currency notes upto the value of:

A. ₹ 25,000 B. ₹ 10,000
C. ₹ 5,000 D. ₹ 1,000

12. Union Budget 2016-17 imposed a 15% surcharge on the income exceeding

A. ₹ 2 crore B. ₹ 75 lakh
C. ₹ 10 lakh D. ₹ 1 crore

13. 'Paramparagat Krishi Vikas Yojana' aims to boost:

A. Drip Irrigation
B. Organic Farming
C. Horticulture Crops
D. Vegetable Production

14. Classical dichotomy refers to which one of the following?

A. There are two sectors of the economy, namely, agriculture and industry.
B. Influence of money is not on the real variables like employment and output but on price level.
C. Savings come only from profits and not from the wages.
D. All of the above

15. The basic rationale of the theory of 'Big-Push' is based upon the idea of

A. size of population
B. external economies
C. internal economies
D. None of the above

16. "Central problem in the theory of economic development is to understand the process by which a community which was previously saving 4 to 5 per cent or less of its national income, converts itself into an economy where voluntary savings is running about 12 to 15 of national income or more." Who among the following economists is attributed with this view?

A. Ragner Nurkse
B. P.N. Rogenstein-Rodan
C. Gunnar Myrdal
D. W. Arthur Lewis

17. In the Harrod-Domar equation $g = s/v$, where v is defined as:

A. The value of country's capital stock
B. Incremental capital output ratio
C. The change in country's capital stock
D. None of the above

18. Leibenstein in his critical minimum effort thesis treats population as a factor that is

A. investment – inducing
B. income – generating

C. market – expanding
D. income – depressing

19. Who among the following economists was not associated with the Dependency Theory of Development?
A. Raul Prebisch
B. T.D. Santos
C. Andre Gunder Frank
D. Gunnar Myrdal

20. The saving function used in the neo-classical growth model is a:
A. Classical saving function
B. Proportional saving function
C. Differential saving function
D. Constant saving function

21. Consider the following items in the balance of payment in India
I. NRI deposits
II. Remittances

Which among the above is/are part of the capital account of balance of payments? Answer from the codes below:
Codes:
A. Only I above
B. Only II above
C. Both I and II above
D. Neither I nor II above

22. Which of the following pairs is not correctly matched?
A. Taussig : Barter Terms of Trade
B. Prebisch : Deteriorating Terms of Trade
C. Marshal : Offer Curves
D. Walras : Dumping Conditions

23. Which among the following is correct for the discretionary fiscal action?
A. Payment of Unemployment insurance.
B. Payment of Social Security to the retired individuals.
C. A managed change in level of Government spending and/or net tax revenues.
D. Automatic changes in net tax revenues that result from income tax structure.

24. Who among the following called trade as the 'hand maiden' of growth?
A. J. Viner
B. Irwing B. Kravis
C. Anne Kruger
D. J. Bhagwati

25. For the import substitution policy of Latin American countries in 1950's which of the following is/are true?
I. It resulted in overvalued exchange rate.
II. It treated development as a natural process.

Answer from the codes below:
Codes:
A. Both I and II are true.
B. Only I is true.
C. Only II is true.
D. Neither I nor II is true.

26. Consider the following concepts:
I. Leontief Paradox
II. Linder Hypothesis

Which among the following can be treated as exception to the conclusions of the Heckscher-Ohlin theory? Answer from the codes below:
Codes:
A. Both I and II are exception.
B. Neither I nor II is an exception.
C. Only I is an exception.
D. Only II is an exception.

27. Which among the following statements are true for the proposed GST arrangements in India?
I. Both Centre and State taxes will be collected at the point of sale.
II. The Centre and State GST will be charged on the manufacturing cost.

Of the above, which statement/s is/are true? Answer from the code below:
Codes:
A. Neither I nor II is true.
B. Only I is true.
C. Only II is true.
D. Both I and II are true.

28. Economists refer to an unanticipated inflation that reduces the real value of outstanding government debt as:
A. Burden of inflation
B. Unanticipated default
C. Seigniorage
D. The inflation tax

29. A public good is
(*i*) non-excludable in nature.
(*ii*) non-rival in consumption.
(*iii*) excludable in nature.
(*iv*) a good that public must possess.

Select the correct answer using the codes given below:

A. Both (*i*) and (*ii*) B. Only (*iii*)
C. Both (*iii*) and (*iv*) D. Only (*iv*)

30. A forward-shifted tax will affect
A. buyers more than sellers
B. sellers more than buyers
C. buyers and sellers equally
D. government revenues negatively

31. Assume B is social benefits, C is social costs, *r* is the social discount rate, *t* is the time and T is the life of the investment project. The Net Present Value (NPV) of a project is

A. $NPV = \sum_{t=0}^{T} \frac{B_t - C_t}{(1+r)^t}$

B. $NPV = \sum_{t=0}^{T} \frac{C_t - B_t}{(1+r)^t}$

C. $NPV = \sum_{t=0}^{T} \frac{(1+r)^t}{B_t - C_t}$

D. $NPV = \sum_{t=0}^{T} \frac{B_t - C_t}{(C_t)^t}$

32. With reference to the characteristics of 'non-excludability' and 'non-rivalry', "Law and Order" is a classic example of
A. a negative externality
B. a positive externality
C. increasing returns
D. a public good

33. In the trade cycle theory of J.R. Hicks, long run equilibrium growth is determined by
A. Technology
B. Population
C. Autonomous investment
D. Both A and B above

34. Which among the following is not a characteristic of stagflation?
A. High inflation
B. High unemployment
C. Low growth
D. High employment

35. Consider the following statements regarding the consumption function fitted by Simon Kutznets to US economic data for the period 1869 to 1929:

I. There appeared no constant terms in the linear consumption function so fitted.
II. The APC and MPC were not significantly different.

Which of the above statement/s is/are true? Answer from the codes below:

Codes:

A. Both statements are not true.
B. Only I is true.
C. Only II is true.
D. Both statements I and II are true.

36. Which among the following theory/approach does not treat consumption to depend upon expected income?
A. Keynes' approach
B. Friedman's approach
C. Life cycle approach
D. Both B and C above

37. In an economy, the saving and investment functions are given as:

$S = -100 + 0.2y$
$I = -30 + 0.1y$

What will be equilibrium level of income?
A. 1000 B. 900
C. 600 D. 700

38. For the set of observations : 0, 4, 5, 7, 100, which one of the following is the most suitable average?
A. Arithmetic Mean B. Geometric Mean
C. Median D. Harmonic Mean

39. Which is a random sampling method?
A. Quota Sampling
B. Purposive Sampling
C. Systematic Sampling
D. Cluster Sampling

40. The area between – 3σ and + 3σ under standard normal curve is

A. 1 B. 0.9973
C. 0.95 D. 0.6826

41. For a symmetrical distribution skewness is

A. 3 B. 0
C. 1 D. 2

42. Given the following data:

Number of observations = 100
Arithmetic Mean = 180
Variance = 324

The coefficient of variation will be

A. 32.4% B. 10%
C. 18% D. 1.8%

43. Which of the following satisfies time reversal test but not factor reversal test?

A. Lespeyres
B. Marshall-Edgeworth
C. Fisher
D. Paasche

44. For testing the association of attributes which of the following tests is suitable?

A. *t* test B. F test
C. χ^2 test D. Z test

Directions (Q. Nos. 45 to 50): Assertion (A) and Reason (R) type. Key to these questions is as follows:

A. Both (A) and (R) are true and (R) is the correct explanation of (A).
B. Both (A) and (R) are true, but (R) is not the correct explanation of (A).
C. (A) is true, but (R) is false.
D. (A) is false but (R) is true.

45. Assertion (A): In the long period and in perfect competition, a firm earns only normal profit.

Reason (R): There are no transport costs in the system.

46. Assertion (A): Labour becomes ready to work overtime.

Reason (R): Industry pays its employees efficiency wage.

47. Assertion (A): The principle of progressive taxation is a generally accepted state policy.

Reason (R): Progressive taxation does not affect distribution of income and wealth.

48. Assertion (A): Stagflation can develop due to market imperfections.

Reason (R): Wage flexibility can cause stagflation.

49. Assertion (A): Friedman treats money as, one of Luxury goods.

Reason (R): It serves as a medium of exchange.

50. Assertion (A): Moving average method is a method of trend estimation.

Reason (R): Regression method is used to estimate fluctuations in time series.

ANSWERS

1	2	3	4	5	6	7	8	9	10
A	A	D	B	B	D	D	A	C	C
11	**12**	**13**	**14**	**15**	**16**	**17**	**18**	**19**	**20**
B	D	B	B	B	D	B	D	D	B
21	**22**	**23**	**24**	**25**	**26**	**27**	**28**	**29**	**30**
A	D	C	B	B	A	D	D	A	A
31	**32**	**33**	**34**	**35**	**36**	**37**	**38**	**39**	**40**
A	D	C	D	D	A	D	C	C	B
41	**42**	**43**	**44**	**45**	**46**	**47**	**48**	**49**	**50**
B	B	B	C	B	B	C	B	B	C

EXPLANATORY ANSWERS

1. Marginal rate of transformation: The marginal rate of transformation for two products is defined as the ratio of the marginal cost of producing these products. With two products, the marginal rate of transformation is the slope of the economy's production possibility frontier. With a allocation of inputs, the marginal rate of transformation shows how the economy efficiently replace the production of one product by another. Resource allocation is optimal when, for each pair of products, the marginal rate of transformation is equal to the price ratio of the two products.

2. The equilibrium path along which production expands as the outlay increases is called the expansion path. The expansion path is also known as a 'Scale Line' or 'Ray'.

1. In the words of Professor Robert Y. Ahw, "*An expansion path shows the locus of best cost input combinations for producing various levels of output assuming that input prices remain constant.*"
2. According to Stonier and Hague, "*Expansion path is that line which reflects least cost method of producing different levels of output, when factor prices remain constant.*"

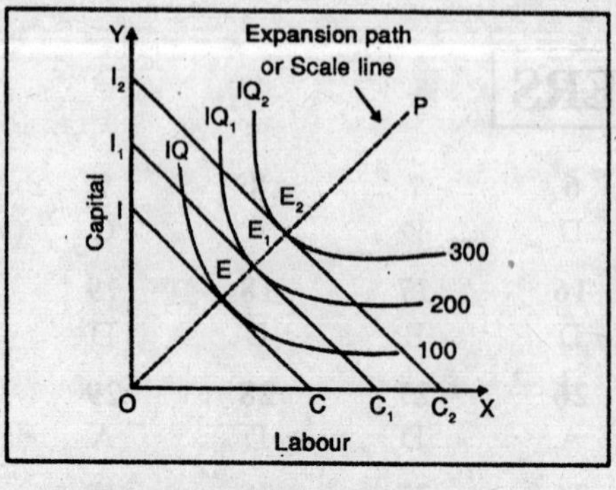

Fig.: *Expansion Path*

3. The First Fundamental Theorem of Welfare Economics: As long as producers and consumers act as price takers and there is a market for every commodity, the equilibrium allocation of resources is Pareto efficient. That is, the economy operates at some point on the utility possibilities frontier.

Intuition behind the First Welfare Theorem:

1. Consumption efficiency: If all people pay the same prices, then every person's marginal rate of substitution (MRS) is equal to the price ratio. Thus, their MRSs must also be equal to each other. This is the requirement for consumption efficiency.

2. Production efficiency: If firms are price-takers in factor markets and output markets, then they all face the same price of labour (w) and price of capital (c). To minimize costs, the firm must set its marginal rate of technical substitution (MRTS) equal to the ratio of the prices of labour and capital. The same is true for any commodity. Therefore, every firm must have the same MRTS, which is the necessary condition for production efficiency.

3. Allocation efficiency: We know that the marginal rate of transformation between two commodities equals the marginal rate of substitution. We also know that a profit-maximizing competitive firm produces output up to the point at which marginal cost is equal to price. Thus the marginal cost ratio of the firms is equal to the price ratio. The MRS of every person is also equal to the price ratio, so the MRS of every person is also equal to the marginal cost ratio of the two firms. Therefore, the MRS for each person is equal to the MRT for the two commodities.

6. We know that

$$e_p = -\frac{P}{Q}\cdot\frac{dQ}{dP}$$

⇒ Given that

$$Q = \frac{20}{P}$$

$$\therefore \quad \frac{dQ}{dP} = \frac{-20}{P^2}$$

$$\therefore \quad e_p = \frac{-P}{Q} \cdot \frac{-20}{P^2}$$

$$= \frac{-P}{20/P} \cdot \frac{-20}{P^2} \quad \left(\because Q = \frac{20}{P}\right)$$

$$= \frac{-P^2}{20} \cdot \frac{-20}{P^2} = -(-1) = 1$$

Hence at each price elasticity of demand would be unity.

7. **Imperative Planning:** In this type of planning, the Central Planning authority decides upon every aspect of the economy, and the targets set, and the processes delineated to achieve them are to be strictly followed. This type of planning is mainly practised in the socialist economies.

   Indicative Planning: In this type of planning, the State sets broad parameters and goals for the economy. It was adopted in our country since the 8th Five-year Plan, as practised in many developed countries.

8. The Rashtriya Swasthya Bima Yojana (RSBY), providing for smart card based cashless health insurance cover of ₹ 30000/- per annum per family (a unit of five) to BPL families in the unorganized sector, has been extended to such Mahatma Gandhi National Rural Employment Guarantee Scheme (MGNREGS) beneficiaries who have worked more than 15 days during the preceding financial year.

   The premium is shared between Central and State Government in the ratio of 75:25 and in case of States in North Eastern Region and Jammu & Kashmir, the ratio of sharing of premium is 90:10. The beneficiaries are required to pay registration/renewal fee of ₹ 30 per annum only.

11. **Issuer of Currency:** The RBI has the sole right to issue bank notes of all denominations as per Section 22 of the Reserve Bank of India Act. The RBI, as the sole note issuing authority in India, is empowered to issue notes up to the value of ₹ 10,000. The RBI is responsible for the design and production and overall management of currency. The department of currency management in Mumbai is required to supervise the production and distribution of currency with the assistance of the issue departments in the Reserve Bank's regional offices. The denominations of coins and notes, in circulation of RBI, are: 25 paise, 50 paise, ₹ 1, ₹ 2, ₹ 5 and ₹ 10. Notes in circulation are: ₹ 5, ₹ 10, ₹ 20, ₹ 50, ₹ 100, ₹ 500 and ₹ 2000.

13. In the union budget 2015 a new programme Paramparagat Krishi Vikas Yojana was announced to boost organic farming. An initial allocation of ₹ 300 crore has been made for the scheme.

    Government is implementing a cluster based programme to encourage the farmers for promoting organic farming called Paramparagat Krishi Vikas Yojana (PKVY). Under this programme, group of farmers would be motivated to take up organic farming.

    Organic farming will be promoted by using traditional resources and the organic products will be linked with the market. It will increase domestic production and certification of organic produce by involving farmers. In order to implement the PKVY in the year 2015-16, an amount of ₹ 300 crore has been allocated.

14. The *classical model* assumes free competition in markets: A large number of buyers and sellers participate in the markets for products and factors of production, and no market participant will dominate the market (*e.g.*, monopoly); all prices are flexible, and adjustment to changing demand and supply takes place immediately. Because aggregate expenditure equals output, the markets will adjust to full-employment levels, as if guided by an "invisible" or "hidden" hand. This leads to two major classical economic conclusions:

    - The price level is fully flexible; real GDP is determined independent from the price level ("money is neutral").
    - The economy will operate at a full- (or natural) employment level.

The first conclusion is described as the classic dichotomy of real and nominal variables (also known as the *neutrality of money*). *Real variables* in the economy (*e.g.*, real GDP, unemployment, and consumption) are the effective indicators of economic performance. *Nominal variables* (*e.g.*, nominal GDP, price level, and inflation rate) are indicators of dollar values and the cost of living in the economy.

The *classical dichotomy* states that at full employment, the forces that determine real variables are independent of the forces that determine nominal variables. The flexibility of prices and wages implies that markets will automatically correct to achieve full employment. For example, if products are not selling and employees are laid off, the market self-corrects to full employment because firms will lower prices to sell off inventory and because workers will accept lower wages and firms will rehire them at those wages. Price and wage levels may change values, but these will be nominal changes. The nominal changes will offset each other, and purchasing power will remain the same.

According to the classical view of macroeconomic equilibrium, there is no need to analyze factors influencing nominal variables, but only those that have an impact on real variables.

15. The 'Big Push' Theory: The therory of the "big push" is associated with the name of *Professor Paul N. Rosenstein-Rodan.* The thesis is that a "big push" or a large comprehensive programme is needed in the form of a high minimum amount of investment to over come the obstacles to development in an under-developed economy and to launch it on the path to progress.

The theory states that proceeding "bit by bit" will not launch the economy successfully on the development path; rather a minimum amount of investment is a necessary condition for this. It necessitates the obtaining of external economies that arise from the simultaneous establishment of technically interdependent industries. Thus, indivisibilities and external economies flowing from a minimum quantum of investment are a prerequisite for launching economic development successfully.

Rosenstein-Rodan distinguishes between three different kinds of indivisibilities and external economies.

1. Indivisibilities in the production function, especially the indivisibility of the supply of social overhead capital;
2. Indivisibilities of demand;
3. Indivisibilities in the supply of savings.

Given these three indivisibilities and the external economies to which they give rise, a "big push" or a minimum quantum of investment is required to overcome the obstacles to development in under-developed countries. "There may be finally a phenomenon of indivisibility in the vigour and drive required for a successful development policy," writes Rodan. But proceeding bit by bit in an isolated and small way does not lead to a sufficient impact on growth. A climate for development is only created when investment of a minimum speed or size is made within an underdeveloped economy.

16. In the early post-Second World War development literature, increased savings were viewed as a major means to increase rate of growth. In the simplest Harrod–Domar model, for example, the equilibrium growth rate that equals the growth in production capacity with the growth in demand is equal to the savings rate divided by the incremental capital output ratio. In a well-known analogy in his influential "Stages of Economic Growth", Rostow (1960) suggested that "take-off" to self-sustained growth occurred when an economy increased its savings rate above 10 per cent. Sir Arthur Lewis, in his celebrated paper on economic development with unlimited supplies of labour, argued that the "central problem of economic development is to understand the process by which a community which was previously saving and investing 4 or 5 per cent of its national income or less converts itself into an economy where voluntary saving is running at about 12 to 15 per cent of national income or more. This is the central problem because the central fact of economic development is rapid capital accumulation (including knowledge and skills with capital)" (Lewis, 1954).

17. The Harrod-Domar equation is

$$g = s/v$$

where g is the growth rate,
s the savings ratio, and
v the incremental capital output ratio.

18. Leibenstein's (1957) critical minimum effort thesis classifies population growth as an income-depressing force. To get development going it is necessary to overcome the low-level equilibrium of a stagnant society where income-raising forces were kept at bay. If developmental stimulants are not strong enough, GDP/head would be raised shortly and fall back to the relatively stable stagnant equilibrium. Therefore a critical minimum effort, comparable to the big push, is mandatory. This minimum increases with population, more people demanding more effort.

The theory given by *Harvey Leibenstein* is based upon the relationship between three factors — per capita income, population growth and investment. Population is an income-depressing factor while investment is an income generating factor. Growth is possible when the latter is more powerful. A small investment would be creating small income which would be eaten away by the rising population and hence many fail to generate growth. So a substantial investment is required to start growth. Not all efforts lead to economic development. Some are too small to do so. A critical minimum effort is necessary to overcome the draf of population, because of the indivisibilities and the existence of interdependence in the economy.

19. Explaining low levels of development in Latin America, Asia, and Africa has been an enduring concern for scholars and policymakers. In very broad terms, two types of explanation have been put forward. The first type – encapsulated in modernisation theory – focuses on factors internal to countries in the Third World. According to modernisation theorists, they lack certain qualities that are necessary for development, which itself should be measured as economic growth. Such qualities include access to capital, high rates of saving, an industrial infrastructure, and technical expertise. The second type of explanation – which includes dependency theory – not only rejects the orthodox focus on development as economic growth in favour of a much greater emphasis on equality and the fulfilment of basic needs, but also focuses on power asymmetries between the First World and the Third World. In other words, underdevelopment is a consequence of factors external to Third World countries.

The concept of dependency was developed in the 1960s and 1970s to account for these structural inequalities in global wealth and power. Dependency theory draws on the work of the structural school of international political economy developed in the 1930s by the Latin American economist Raul Prebisch. The foremost exponent of dependency theory in North America is Andre Gunder Frank, although others such as Fernando Cardozo and Theotonio Dos Santos were important in Latin America.

The dependency theorists not only rejected modernisation theory but also radically undermined Karl Marx's view that capitalism is able to promote development everywhere. Dependency refers to exogenously imposed conditions whereby the exposure of Third World states to foreign direct investment (FDI), unequal trade agreements, interest payments on debt, and the exchange of raw materials for higher-priced manufactured goods creates structurally unequal relations between the core and the periphery.

20. The neoclassical growth theory was developed by Solow in response to the seminal works of Harrod (1939) and Domar (1946). In fact it is these two studies that aroused tremendous interest in growth theory and started an avalanche of research in the area. Neoclassical growth theory was one major output of this massive research effort.

Merits

(*a*) As a pioneer of neo-classical model Solow retains the main features of Harrod-Domar model like homogenous capital, proportional saving function and a given growth rate in the labour force.

(*b*) He takes a continuous production function in analyzing the process of growth.

(*c*) The assumption of substitutability between labour and capital gives the growth process an adjustability and gives a touch of realism.

(*d*) He demonstrates steady state growth paths.

(*e*) The long run rate of growth is determined by an expanding labour force and technical process.

(*f*) He successfully shunted aside all the difficulties and rigidities which go into modern Keynesian income analysis.

(*g*) His purpose was to examine what might be called the lightrope view of economic growth and see where more flexible assumptions about production would lead a simple model.

Demerits

Professor Amartya Sen points out some of his model's demerits:

(*a*) The Solow model takes up only the *problem of balance* between Harrod's Gw and Gn and leaves out the problem of balance between G and Gw.

(*b*) There is absence of an investment function in his model and once it is introduced, Harrod's problem of instability arrives by Solow model.

23. Discretionary fiscal policy involves intentional changes in government spending and/or net tax revenues in order to alter the level of aggregate spending. As we know it an increase in government spending and/or a decrease in lump-sum taxes shifts the aggregate spending line upward and raises the equilibrium level of output, while a decrease in government spending and/or an increase in lump-sum taxes shifts the aggregate spending line downward and lowers the equilibrium level of output. The government can use discretionary fiscal actions to eliminate an inflationary or recessionary gap.

24. The phrase 'trade as handmaiden of growth' is taken from the title of an article by Kravis (1970). He writes (1970),

The term 'engine of growth' is not generally descriptive and involves expectations which cannot be fulfilled by trade alone; the term 'handmaiden of growth' better conveys the notion of the role that trade can play. One of the most important parts of this handmaiden role for today's developing countries may be to serve as a check on the appropriateness of new industries by keeping the price and cost structures in touch with external prices and costs.

25. Much of Latin American economic policymaking from the 1950s until the 1980s was based on the concept of industrialization through import substitution, *i.e.*, the development of domestic industries to produce manufactured goods that were previously imported. This policy was rooted in Latin America's experience of the Great Depression and World War II when world demand for the region's traditional commodity exports fell sharply and imported manufactured goods remained relatively expensive of unavailable. Buttressed by the ideas of Argentine economist Raul Prebisch, Latin American countries drew from this experience the lesson that they should pursue economic independence. Latin American countries pursued this strategy by imposing substantial tariff and nontariff import barriers, regulating foreign investment, restricting currency exchange, maintaining high-valued exchange rates to keep prices of imported inputs low, and by using subsidies and other incentives to encourage domestic manufacturing.

Import-substitution policies failed to free Latin America from dependence on commodity exports, because earnings from these exports were needed to pay for imports of inputs and advanced-technology products that the countries could not produce domestically. Furthermore, these policies often resulted in industries that were inefficient by world standards and unable to compete in world markets. This happened both because the industries were shielded from world competition and because domestic markets were generally too small to achieve efficient scales of production. Some Brazilian industries were an exception to this rule, partly because of the relatively large size of the domestic market and partly because of efforts since the 1970s to make some industries competitive in export markets (*e.g.*, sheet and semi-finished steel, aircraft, and footwear).

In addition to uncompetitive industries, the import-substitution policies, among other factors, contributed to massive, unprofitable state enterprises, distorted capital markets, and substantial public debt. These policy shortcomings contributed to Latin America's being unprepared to respond effectively to the two major changes in its economic environment in the 1980s: the decline in world demand for the region's export commodities and the reduction in lending by foreign banks.

27. GST (goods and services tax) is a comprehensive tax levy on manufacture, sale and consumption of goods and services at a national level.

'G' – Goods

'S' – Services

'T' – Tax

GST is a tax on goods and services with value addition at each stage having comprehensive and continuous chain of set-of benefits from the producer's/service provider's point up to the retailer's level where only the final consumer should bear the tax. Through a tax credit mechanism, GST is collected on value-added goods and services at each stage of sale or purchase in the supply chain.

In the GST system, both Central and State taxes will be collected at the point of sale. Both components (the Central and State GST) will be charged on the manufacturing cost. This will benefit individuals as prices are likely to come down. Lower prices will lead to more consumption, thereby helping companies.

28. The inflation tax is defined as the reduction in the real value of the monetary base due to increases in the price level. Inflation tax revenues are the proportionate rate of increase in the price level times the real monetary base.

The inflation tax is more accurately described as the *anticipated* inflation tax. *Unanticipated* inflation reduces the real value of outstanding nominally indexed fixed rate public debt. The longer the maturity of a given quantity of debt, the larger is this effect for a given increase in current and future inflation. The rate of interest on new public debt issues will take account of expected inflation and may include a risk premium reflecting possible unanticipated inflation. Countries with histories of low inflation tend to be most able to use unanticipated inflation tax levies to reduce the real burden of their national debts. A reputation for low inflation allows a government to issue longer maturity fixed interest rate debt on more favourable interest terms to a larger number of creditors. Unanticipated inflation tax levies on the national debt have been the primary means used by the governments of the United States and the United Kingdom to appropriate real resources through inflation. An unanticipated increase in the price level, in contrast to an increase in the rate of change of the price level, will reduce the real value of both fixed and variable rate debt denominated in national currency. This can be achieved by an unanticipated discrete devaluation.

29. Public goods are defined as being non-excludable and non-rival:

- *Non-excludable* – once provided, individuals cannot be excluded from consuming the goods.
- *Non-rival* – consumption of the goods by one person does not prevent someone else from consuming the goods.

To see what makes a good a *public* good, we must distinguish two features of all goods: the extent to which people can be *excluded* from consuming them and the extent to which one person's consumption *rivals* the consumption of others. A good or service is excludable if it is possible to prevent someone from enjoying its benefits.

A good or service is nonexcludable if it is impossible (or extremely costly) to prevent someone from benefiting from it.

A good or service or a resource is rival if its use by one person decreases the quantity available for someone else.

A good or service or a resource is nonrival if its use by one person does not decrease the quantity available for someone else.

Street lights are perhaps the most famous example of public goods. Once provided, it would be very difficult, if not impossible, to stop anyone benefiting from their consumption – anyone walking down the street would benefit from their presence. Moreover, the ability for an individual to benefit from the light is not affected by the number of other individuals who have previously benefited from the light by walking down the street.

Public goods create a free-rider problem. Because of the non-rival and non-excludable nature of the goods, individuals will not be willing to pay for them, knowing they can 'free-ride' and enjoy the benefits of consumption without paying. This can therefore result in a situation of what is known as 'missing markets' – because individuals have no incentive to pay for the goods, there is a risk that they will not be provided in a free market.

30. The shifting of a tax is the transfer of the burden of paying a tax from those who are legally liable for it to others. When a tax is shifted, those liable for its payment succeed in recouping some of the reduction in their income caused by tax payments through changes in the prices of items that they either buy or sell.

Forward shifting of a tax is a transfer of its burden from sellers who are liable for its payment to buyers as a result of an increase in the price of the taxed good. For example, the price of gasoline increases as a result of a tax levied on sellers, thereby shifting part of the burden to buyers. Backward shifting of a tax is a transfer of its burden from buyers who are liable for its payment to sellers through a decrease in the market price of the taxed goods. For example, if employers are liable for payroll taxes on wages paid to workers, they will succeed in shifting part of the burden of the tax to sellers of labour services (workers) if wages decline as a result of the tax.

31. To enhance efficiency we want to compare the benefits and costs of any action or potential policy change. Therefore, we need to add up all the present and future discounted benefits and subtract the sum of the present and future discounted costs to obtain the net present value (NPV) of the policy change. Let B_t represent the benefits received in period t and let C_t represent the costs incurred in period t. The net present value of a project that lasts T years is

$$NPV = \sum_{t=0}^{T} \frac{B_t - C_t}{(1+R)^t}$$

If a project or policy action results in a positive net present value then it is efficient to use society's resources to implement the policy. Alternatively, if the policy action results in a negative net present value, the resources that would be needed to implement the policy have more value to society in some alternative use.

33. Hicks has developed his theory of trade cycle by combining interaction between multiplier and accelerator with Harrod-Domer growth model. In other words, Hicks combines Samuelson's multiplier-accelerator *interaction* model and Harrod-Domar growth model to expound his own theory of trade cycle. He combines multiplier-accelerator interaction with growth theory since, in his opinion, business cycles have historically taken place against the background of income growth, and therefore, the trade cycle theory should be linked with growth theory.

In his theory, Hicks uses (*i*) Keynesian concept of saving-investment relationship and the multiplier, (*ii*) Clark's acceleration principle, (*iii*) Samuelson's multiplier-accelerator interaction, and (*iv*) Harrod-Domar growth model. These are the main ingredients of Hicks' theory of trade cycle.

In his model, Hicks assumes an equilibrium rate of growth in the model economy. The equilibrium growth rate is defined as the rate at which *realised growth rate* (G_r) equals the *natural growth rate* (G_n). He assumes also that the autonomous investment increases at a constant rate which always equals the rate of increase in voluntary savings. The equilibrium growth rate is determined by the rate of autonomous investment and saving. This is the Keynesian part of his theory.

Besides, Hicks assumes a Samuelson–type of consumption function, $C_t = aY_{t-1}$ (with one-year lag between income and consumption). He gives two reasons for the lagged consumption function: (*i*) lag of consumption expenditure behind income; and (*ii*) lag in non-wage income behind the change in GDP. The saving function naturally becomes the function of the past-year's income. Given these assumptions, Hicks' multiplier becomes a mathematical truism. With the lagged relationship between income and saving-investment, the multiplier process has a dampening effect on the fluctuation. The lagged multiplier "acts as a depressant on upswing and a counterforce on the downswing."

Another important ingredient of Hicks' model is Clark's acceleration principle. In this regard, Hicks distinguishes between *autonomous* and *induced* investment functions. He assumes that *autonomous* investment is a function of current output and is undertaken to replace the wornout capital. The *induced* investment, in his model, is a fuction of change in output. The change in output generates *induced* investment which brings the accelerator in action. It may be noted here that this accelerator interacts with multiplier effect upon income and consumption.

34. Stagflation occurs whenever the aggregate supply curve shifts to the left. Since both inflation and unemployment are rising, this defies the Phillips relationship, which concludes that unemployment and inflation move in opposite directions.

Before 1970, the American economy seemed to be characterized by a stable trade-off between unemployment and inflation. This relationship (described by the Phillips curve) held for most of the 1950s and 1960s.

During the 1970 recession, policymakers appeared surprised to see the rate of inflation rise to 5.7 per cent. Economist Paul Samuelson dubbed this *stagflation* (high unemployment combined with high inflation and stagnant economic growth).

Thus, stagflation occurred in the 1970s in the United States when the supply of a very important resource, oil, was curtailed by the formation of an oil cartel. Notice that stagflation poses a special problem for fiscal policy. If both inflation and unemployment are high, should fiscal policy be used to fight the high unemployment or the high inflation? It cannot remedy both at the same time.

36. The Keynesian consumption function posits a stable relationship between consumption and current income, with average and marginal propensities to consume assumed to be roughly constant. These relationships form the basis of the multiplier and thus of Keynesian fine-tuning.

However, this simple theory of consumption has been criticised on the grounds that it lacks adequate microeconomic foundations (*i.e.*, it represents a macroeconomic theory which is not based on the behaviour of rational individuals at a microeconomic level). Furthermore, the results of numerous empirical studies were found to be at variance with predictions of Keynesian theory; in particular, average propensities to consume were found to vary inversely with disposable income.

Such deficiencies led Milton Friedman to propound the permanent income hypothesis (PIH) in his 1957 work, *A Theory of the Consumption Function*. He argued that individuals would base their consumption decisions not on current income, but rather on expected income over a suitably long period, if not a lifetime (hence *permanent* income). Households with identical permanent incomes and tastes would consume identical bundles of goods and services, regardless of their levels of current income. If individuals experienced an increase in current income, this would only affect consumption plans to the extent that permanent income was raised. If the increase in current income is expected to be temporary, the effect on permanent income, and hence consumption, would be slight.

37. At equilibrium

$$S = I$$

$$\Rightarrow \quad -100 + 0.2y = -30 + 0.1y$$

$$\Rightarrow \quad 0.2y - 0.1y = -30 + 100$$

$$\Rightarrow \quad 0.1y = 70$$

$$\therefore \quad y = \frac{70}{0.1} = 700$$

38. Advantages of Median

1. Unlike arithmetic mean, median is not affected at all by extreme values as it is a positional average. As such, median is particularly very useful when a distribution happens to be skewed.
2. Another point that goes in favour of median is that it can be computed when a distribution has open-end classes.
3. Another merit of median is that when a distribution contains qualitative data, it is the only average that can be used. No other average is suitable in case of such a distribution.

39. Systematic sampling is often used as an alternative to simple random sampling or stratified random sampling for two reasons. First, the process of selecting sample units is simpler for systematic sampling. Second, under certain circumstances, estimates can be expected to be more precise for systematic sampling because the population is covered more evenly.

40. The area between ordinates at $x = \mu - 3\sigma$ and $x = \mu + 3\sigma$ is 0.9973, *i.e.*, the area under the normal curve beyond these ordinates is only 1 − 0.9973 = .0027 which is very small. *Thus, practically, we can say that the whole area under the normal curve lies within $\mu \pm 3\sigma$ limits which are also called 3-sigma limits.* In probability terms, these areas can be summarised as:

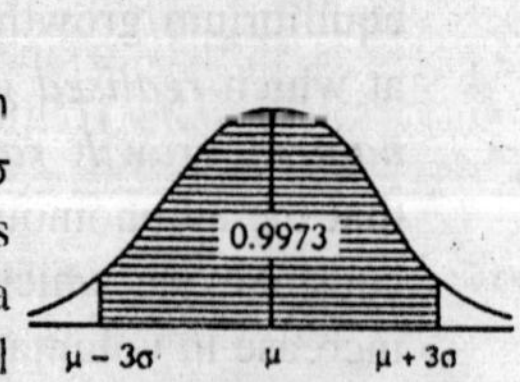

Fig.: *Area between 3σ limits (99.73)*

(*i*) Area within 1σ limits = $P[\mu - \sigma < x < \mu + \sigma] = 0.6827$

(*ii*) Area within 2σ limits = P $[\mu - 2\sigma < x < \mu + 2\sigma]$ = 0.9545

(*iii*) Area within 3σ limits = P $[\mu - 3\sigma < x < \mu + 3\sigma]$ = 0.9973.

41. The term skewness means "lack of symmetry", *i.e.*, if the distribution of data is not symmetrical, it is called asymmetrical or skewed. A distribution is said to be symmetrical when the frequencies are symmetrically distributed about mean, *i.e.*, values of the variable are equidistant from the mean. In other words, a frequency curve is said to be symmetrical if it can be folded along a vertical line at centre (mean) so that two halves of the figure coincide. On the other hand, in a distribution, if the frequencies equidistant from the mean are not equal, the distribution is said to be asymmetrical or skewed. Symmetrical distribution is a bell-shaped curve. In the words of Blair, "*Skewness is the tendency of a distribution to depart from normal in the balance of the two sides*". In simple words, skewness is that type of statistical measure which describes the asymmetrical nature and its limits of a frequency distribution. In a symmetrical distribution the values of mean median and mode are alike. In a skewed distribution these values (Mean, Median and Mode) differ and therefore, the balance of the centre of gravity is shifted to one side or the other, to the left or to the right. The figures on next page illustrate the concept of skewness:

When the distribution has longer tail on the left side, it is said to be negatively skewed and if the distribution has longer tail on the right hand side, it is said to be positively skewed. In a negatively skewed distribution mode is greater than the mean and the median lies in between mean and mode.

In a positively skewed distribution mean is greater than the mode and the median lies somewhere in between mean and mode.

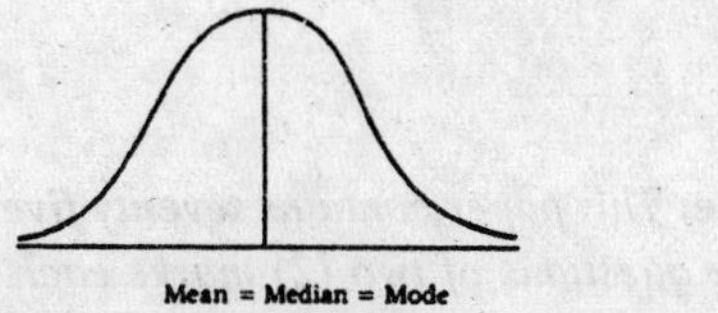

Mean = Median = Mode
Symmetrical Distribution
Skewness = 0

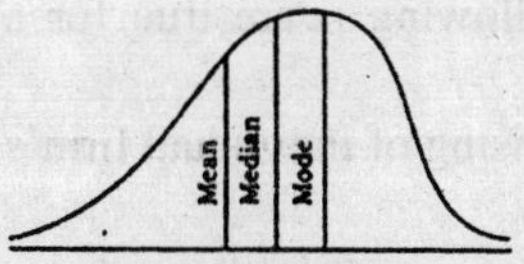

Negatively Skewed
Mean < Median < Mode

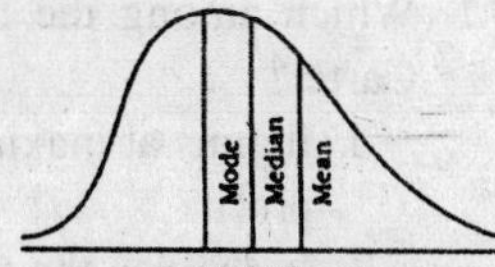

Positively Skewed
Mean > Median > Mode

42. **Coefficient of variation:** It is sometimes useful to describe variability by expressing the standard deviation as a proportion of mean, usually a percentage. The formula for it as a percentage is:

$$\text{Coefficient of variance} = \frac{\text{Standard deviation}}{\text{Mean}} \times 100$$

$$\because \quad \text{Variance} = (\text{SD})^2$$

$$\Rightarrow \quad \text{SD} = \sqrt{\text{Variance}}$$

$$\text{SD} = \sqrt{324} = 18$$

Hence, Coefficient of variance

$$= \frac{18}{180} \times 100 = 10\%$$

44. The chi-square is denoted by the symbol χ^2. It was discovered by Helmert in 1875 and was rediscovered by Karl Pearson in 1900. Chisquare is always positive. The value of χ^2 lies between 0 and ∞.

Since χ^2 is not derived from the observations in a population, it is not a parameter.

Chi-square test is not a parametric test.

The χ^2 distribution is used for testing the goodness of fit. It is used for finding association and relation between attributes. It is also used to test the homogeneity of independent estimates of population. Chi-square is computed on the basis of frequencies in a sample and the value of χ^2 so obtained is a statistic.

PAPER-III

Note: *This paper contains* ***seventy five (75)*** *objective type questions of* ***two (2)*** *marks each.* ***All*** *questions are compulsory.*

1. Which among the following is/are true for a Cartel?

I. It aims at maximising of individual firm's profit.

II. It decides the total output in the industry to which Cartel represents.

III. It does not fix the price at which members sell their output.

Answer from the code below:

A. All are true.
B. I and II are true.
C. Only II is true.
D. Only I and III are true.

2. Why does demand curve have a negative slope?

I. Due to income effect only

II. Due to substitution effect

Answer from the code below:

A. Both I and II B. Only I
C. Only II D. Neither I nor II

3. In the entry prevention model of Bain, firms charge premium over

A. Long period competitive price
B. Short period competitive price
C. Lowest average cost
D. None of the above

4. Which among the following is not well matched?

	Goods		Nature
A.	Fishing in the large lake	–	Non-exclusive but rival
B.	Air	–	Non-exclusive and non-rival
C.	Use of a light house	–	Rival
D.	Stock of washing machines	–	Exclusive

5. The slope of the production possibility curve is the

A. marginal rate of exchange
B. marginal rate of substitution
C. average rate of transformation
D. marginal rate of transformation

6.

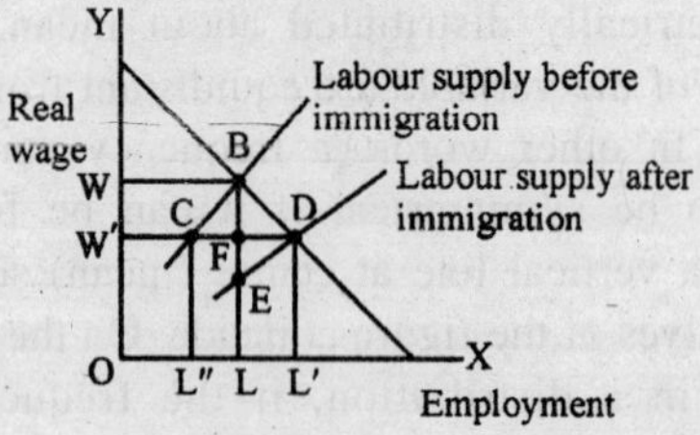

The gain in profit income from an increase in immigration according to this diagram is:

A. the area BDL′L
B. the area of WBDW′
C. the areas WBFW′ and FDL′L together
D. the areas WBDW′ and FDL′L together

7. The demand for rare paintings, and rare stamps, etc., is explained by which among the following effect?

A. Snob effect
B. Bandwagon effect
C. Veblen effect
D. None of the above

8. A market is said to be economically efficient if it maximises

A. consumer surplus
B. producer surplus
C. aggregate of consumer and producer surplus
D. None of the above

9. Who among the following economists are associated with the concept of Quasi rent?

I. A. Marshal

II. J. Robinson

III. D. Ricardo

Answer from the code below:

A. Only I and III B. I and II
C. All the three D. Only III

10. In the adjoining diagram, which of the lines represents law of returns?

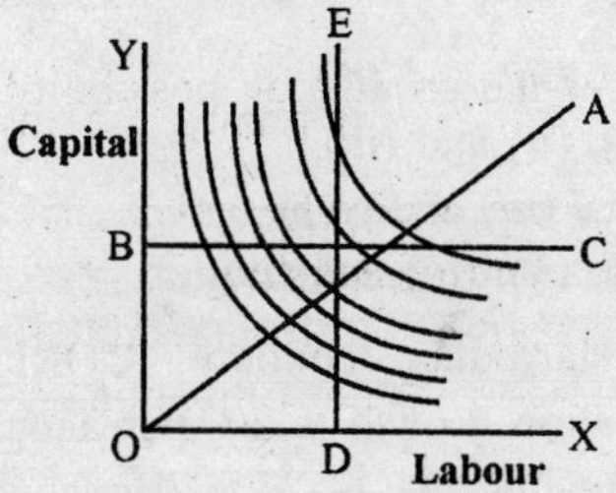

A. OA
B. BC
C. DE
D. Both B and C above

11. In the adjacent diagram, which of the following effects will alter the Aggregate Demand Curve AD?

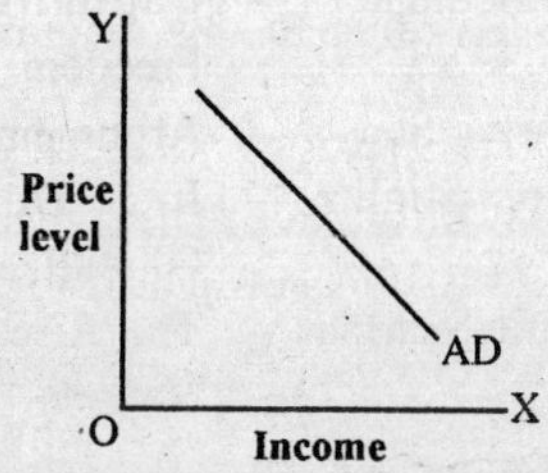

A. Trade effect B. Liquidity effect
C. Wealth effect D. All of the above

12. Match List-I with List-II:

List-I	List-II
(*a*) Keynes	(*i*) Interest is real phenomenon.
(*b*) Irving Fisher	(*ii*) Interest is non-monetary phenomenon.
(*c*) Wicksell	(*iii*) Interest is both monetary and nonmonetary phenomenon.
(*d*) Classical Economist	(*iv*) Interest is monetary phenomenon.

Select the correct answer from the codes given below:

Codes:

	(*a*)	(*b*)	(*c*)	(*d*)
A.	(*iv*)	(*ii*)	(*iii*)	(*i*)
B.	(*i*)	(*ii*)	(*iii*)	(*iv*)
C.	(*iv*)	(*iii*)	(*ii*)	(*i*)
D.	(*ii*)	(*i*)	(*iv*)	(*iii*)

13. 1973 oil crisis also triggered a wide spread economic crisis in USA and some European nations. In this context which statements are true?

A. It led to disillusionment with established policies based on Keynesian economics.
B. There emerged a malady known as stagflation.
C. New classical economics emerged as a challenge to Keynesian economic ideas.
D. All of the above are true.

14. As per IS-LM framework, an increase in government expenditure will result in:

A. increase in income and interest rate both.
B. increase in income only.
C. decrease in investment and interest rate both.
D. decrease in income and interest rate both.

15. Which of the following can be considered as leakages in the force of the multiplier?

A. Higher propensity to import
B. Higher marginal propensity to save
C. Both A and B above
D. Neither A nor B above

16. According to Robinson-Uzawa theorem, steady state growth is possible if the technical progress is:

A. only Hicks neutral
B. only Harrod neutral
C. only Solow neutral
D. Both Hicks and Harrod neutral

17. Which one of the following is not an assumption of permanent income hypothesis?

A. Transitory income can be both positive and negative.
B. Permanent income depends on human and non-human wealth.
C. Transitory consumption can be both positive and negative.
D. Average propensity to consume is greater than marginal propensity to consume.

18. The Accelerator model predicts that changes in investment are determined by the changes in:

A. Interest B. Output
C. Capital D. Inventory

19. Which among the following statements are true for Schumpeter's theory of economic development?
   I. Development is evolutionary.
   II. Development is financed by real savings.
   III. Capitalism keeps its character intact overtime.

   Of the above which statement(s) is/are true? Answer from the code below:

   Codes:
   A. Only I B. Only I and II
   C. All the above D. None of the above

20. Who among the following has not given his model based on the concept of unlimited supply of labour?
   A. D.W. Jorgenson B. Ranis-Fei
   C. W.A. Lewis D. Gunnar Myrdal

21. Which aspect of economic development did Gunnar Myrdal concentrate upon?
   A. Capital scarcity
   B. Human resource scarcity
   C. Regional inequalities
   D. Population exploitation

22. Fei-Ranis's theory of economic development is based on
   A. dualistic approach to development
   B. presence of disguised unemployment
   C. importance of agricultural development
   D. All of the above

23. Andre Gunder Frank, a major dependency theorist suggests that the following economic activities have contributed to underdevelopment :
   (*i*) Replacing indigenous enterprises with technologically more advanced, global, subsidiary companies.
   (*ii*) Closing the economy to trade with, and investment from, developed countries.
   (*iii*) Workers migrating from villages to foreign dominated urban complexes.
   (*iv*) Forming an unskilled labour force to work in factories and mines and on plantations.

   Choose the correct answer from the codes given below:

   Codes:
   A. (*i*), (*iii*) and (*iv*)
   B. (*i*), (*ii*) and (*iii*)
   C. (*ii*), (*iii*) and (*iv*)
   D. (*i*), (*ii*), (*iii*) and (*iv*)

24. In a Harrodian economy, ICOR is 4.5 : 1, population growth is 2% per annum, and the investment rate is 27%. Hence the annual growth of per capita will be:
   A. 2.5% B. 9%
   C. 6% D. 4%

25. Which among the following is not correctly matched?

	Author		**Book**
A.	M. Friedman	–	Capitalism and Freedom
B.	Amartya Sen	–	Argumentative Indian
C.	Joseph Stiglitz	–	In Defense of Globalization
D.	Ruchir Sharma	–	The Rise and Fall of Nations

26. Which among the following statements is not true for the Golden Age equilibrium in the growth model of Mrs. Joan Robinson?
   A. Rate of profit tends to rising.
   B. Level of real wages rises with output per worker.
   C. Technical progress is neutral.
   D. Population is growing at a steady rate.

27. For the Union Budget of 2015-16, arrange the following in the ascending order of their percentage in GDP:
   (*i*) Revenue deficit (*ii*) Effective deficit
   (*iii*) Primary deficit (*iv*) Fiscal deficit

   Choose the correct answer from the codes given below:

   Codes:
   A. (*iii*), (*ii*), (*i*), (*iv*)
   B. (*ii*), (*iii*), (*iv*), (*i*)
   C. (*i*), (*iv*), (*iii*), (*ii*)
   D. (*iv*), (*i*), (*ii*), (*iii*)

28. While recommending horizontal distribution, which of the following criteria got the least weightage by the 14th Finance Commission?

A. Demographic change
B. Area
C. Population
D. Income distance

29. If in a year, the gross fiscal deficit of Government is ₹ 3,00,000 crores, revenue deficit is ₹ 1,50,000 crores and interest payments are ₹ 80,000 crores, which of the following is the primary deficit of the Government in the year?

A. ₹ 70,000 crores B. ₹ 23,000 crores
C. ₹ 2,20,000 crores D. ₹ 1,50,000 crores

30. As per proposals of Union Budget of 2016-17, which of the following tax contributes maximum share out of total tax revenue collection?

A. Corporation tax B. Union Excise Duty
C. Custom D. Income Tax

31. Concepts of concentration and displacement effect in public expenditure are attributed to

A. Allen T. Peacock and Jack Wiseman
B. A.R. Prest and I.M.D. Little
C. A.C. Pigou and J.K. Mehta
D. Kenneth Arrow and Paul A. Samuelson

32. Which one of the following statements is true for the Verdoon's law?

A. Long run productivity generally grows proportionally to the square root of output growth.
B. Short run productivity generally grows proportionally to the growth of output.
C. The value of Verdoon's coefficient is nearly equal to 1.
D. Verdoon's law is quite in consonance with Solow model's functioning.

33. Which among the following can contribute to improvement in industrial climate of the region?

A. Development banks
B. Trade unions
C. Natural resources
D. All of the above

34. Researchers indicate that income velocity of money is falling overtime due to

A. income elasticity of demand for money is greater than unity.
B. income elasticity of demand for money is less than unity.
C. income elasticity of demand for money is equal to unity.
D. All of the above

35. According to Monetarists, demand for money function is

A. stable and interest inelastic
B. constant and interest elastic
C. stable and interest elastic
D. unstable and interest inelastic

36. Arrange the following liquid assets in decreasing order

(*a*) Time deposits (*b*) Saving deposits
(*c*) Currency (*d*) Demand deposits

Select the answer from the codes given below:

A. (*d*), (*a*), (*b*), (*c*) B. (*c*), (*d*), (*b*), (*a*)
C. (*a*), (*b*), (*d*), (*c*) D. (*b*), (*a*), (*c*), (*d*)

37. Match the following:

List-I	List-II
(*a*) Alfred Marshall	(*i*) M = PKT
(*b*) Irving Fisher	(*ii*) M = PKY
(*c*) Robertson	(*iii*) N = PK
(*d*) Keynes	(*iv*) MV = PT

Select the correct codes given below:

Codes:

	(*a*)	(*b*)	(*c*)	(*d*)
A.	(*iv*)	(*iii*)	(*ii*)	(*i*)
B.	(*ii*)	(*iv*)	(*i*)	(*iii*)
C.	(*i*)	(*ii*)	(*iii*)	(*iv*)
D.	(*iii*)	(*i*)	(*iv*)	(*ii*)

38. In his theory of money, James Tobin did **not** agree with which of the following inferences/ assumptions of the demand for money for liquidity preference enunciated by Lord Keynes?

I. Elasticity of expectations of future interest rates
II. Individuals hold either money or bonds

Of the above which are correct? Answers from the codes below:

Codes:

A. Only I
B. Only II
C. Both I and II
D. Neither I nor II

39. A population pyramid of a country shows the:
A. age structure of male and female population
B. age structure of male population
C. age structure of female population
D. age structure of rural and urban population

40. If the actual unemployment rate is below the natural rate of unemployment, it would be expected that
A. the rate of inflation would increase.
B. wages would fall.
C. the Phillips curve would shift to the right.
D. the natural rate of unemployment would fall.

41. Demographic transition means:
A. Shift from the condition of low birth and high death rates to high birth and high death rates.
B. Shift from the condition of high birth and high death rates to low birth and low death rates.
C. Shift from the condition of high death and low birth rates to high death and high birth rates.
D. None of the above

42. In the context of International Trade dumping refers to
A. Free distribution of used products by developed countries in developing countries.
B. Selling a commodity cheaper in foreign market and costly in domestic market.
C. Sending cheap goods to developing countries by developed countries.
D. None of the above

43. Match List-I with List-II and select correct answer from the codes given below:

List-I	List-II
(*a*) International Monetary Fund	(*i*) Lending to private sector
(*b*) International Bank for Reconstruction and Development	(*ii*) Balance of Payments problems
(*c*) International Development Association	(*iii*) Soft Loan to poor countries
(*d*) International Finance Corporation	(*iv*) Socio-economic infrastructure

Codes:

	(*a*)	(*b*)	(*c*)	(*d*)
A.	(*ii*)	(*i*)	(*iii*)	(*iv*)
B.	(*i*)	(*ii*)	(*iv*)	(*iii*)
C.	(*iii*)	(*iv*)	(*i*)	(*ii*)
D.	(*ii*)	(*iv*)	(*iii*)	(*i*)

44. A deficit in balance of payments can be corrected by:
A. a reduction in interest rate
B. discouraging capital inflows
C. an increase in interest rate
D. restricting remittances

45. In the terminology of WTO, which among the following is not an amber box subsidy?
A. Minimum support price of cereals
B. Subsidy on seeds
C. Subsidy on irrigation rates
D. Cost of government pest control and management

46. The weight of manufacturing in old IIP (base 1993-94) was 76.36% which has now been changed in the new IIP (base 2004-05) at
A. 75.53%
B. Unchanged at 76.36%
C. 78.22%
D. 79.39%

47. Which of the following agricultural holdings have largest percentage in India?
A. Marginal Holdings
B. Small Holdings
C. Large Holdings
D. Semi-Medium Holdings

48. First two States/Regions in India having highest yield of rice in 2013-14 were

A. National Capital Territory of Delhi and Punjab
B. Punjab and West-Bengal
C. Andhra Pradesh and Haryana
D. Punjab and Uttar Pradesh

49. Which among the following rates is independently determined in India?

A. Repo rate   B. Reverse repo rate
C. Both A and B   D. Neither A nor B

50. The main objectives of the 12th Five Year Plan are

A. inclusive growth and poverty reduction
B. inclusive and sustainable growth
C. Faster, sustainable and more inclusive growth
D. Sustainable and inclusive growth to reduce poverty and unemployment

51. Match List-I and List-II and select the correct answer from the codes given below:

List-I (Index)	List-II (Base Year)
(*a*) BSE Sensex	(*i*) 2012
(*b*) NIFTY	(*ii*) 2011-12
(*c*) CPI	(*iii*) 1978-79
(*b*) GDP	(*iv*) 1995

Codes:

	(*a*)	(*b*)	(*c*)	(*d*)
A.	(*iii*)	(*iv*)	(*i*)	(*ii*)
B.	(*iv*)	(*iii*)	(*i*)	(*ii*)
C.	(*iv*)	(*i*)	(*ii*)	(*iii*)
D.	(*iii*)	(*ii*)	(*iv*)	(*i*)

52. As per 2013 information, arrange the following States in the decreasing order of infant mortality rate:

I. Uttar Pradesh   II. Rajasthan
III. Madhya Pradesh   IV. Odisha

Answer from the code below:

A. III, IV, I, II   B. IV, III, II, I
C. I, II, III, IV   D. III, I, II, IV

53. Which of the following are not considered as flow variables in economic analysis?

A. Supply and demand
B. Saving and investment
C. Money supply and public debt
D. Exports and imports

54. If the Reserve Bank of India wishes to decrease the money supply, it should

A. raise statutory liquidity ratio
B. buy treasury bills in the open market
C. raise the discount rate
D. lower the reserve requirements

55. Which of the following is included in M_1?

A. Savings deposits
B. Demand deposits
C. Gold stock
D. Assets under money market mutual funds

56. Arrange the following committees appointed in India in the chronological order:

I. Urjit Patel Committee
II. Goipuria Committee
III. Narsimhan Committee
IV. Chakravarti Committee

Answer from the codes given below:

Codes:

A. I, II, III, IV   B. IV, II, III, I
C. III, I, II, IV   D. II, IV, I, III

57. For the following policy rates (as on 30.9.2016) of the RBI, arrange them in the descending order of their magnitude and select the answer from the codes given below:

I. Bank rate   II. Repo rate
III. SLR   IV. Reverse Repo rate

Codes:

A. III, II, IV, I   B. III, I, IV, II
C. I, II, III, IV   D. III, I, II, IV

58. Arrange the following climate events in chronological order:

I. Kyoto Protocol
II. Earth Summit
III. Bali Summit

Answer from the codes below:

Codes:

A. II, I, III   B. II, III, I
C. III, I, II   D. I, II, III

59. The single window system in the Cooperative Sector coordinates

(*a*) Supply of rural credit
(*b*) Supply of agricultural inputs

(*c*) Extension of marketing facilities
(*d*) Creation of warehousing facilities

Select the correct answer from the codes given below:

Codes:

A. (*a*) & (*b*) B. (*a*), (*b*), (*c*) & (*d*)
C. (*a*), (*b*) & (*c*) D. (*c*) & (*d*)

60. Consider the following reasons of continuous decline in average land holding size in India:
(*a*) Farm mechanisation
(*b*) Consolidation
(*c*) Desire of land ownership
(*d*) Law of inheritance

Select the correct answer from the codes given below:

Codes:

A. (*a*), (*b*), (*c*) B. (*a*), (*b*), (*c*) & (*d*)
C. (*b*), (*c*) & (*d*) D. (*c*) & (*d*)

Directions (Q. Nos. 61-65): *The questions given below are two statements labelled as Assertion (A) and Reason (R). Select your answer to these questions using the codes given below:*

A. Both (A) and (R) are true and (R) is the correct explanation of (A).
B. Both (A) and (R) are true, but (R) is not the correct explanation of (A).
C. (A) is true, but (R) is false.
D. (A) is false, but (R) is true.

61. Assertion (A): An improvement in the income terms of trade is an indicator of increase in capacity to import.

Reason (R): Income terms of trade can be computed by multiplying net barter terms of trade by the quantity of imports.

62. Assertion (A): Industrial development strategy in India is faced with the choice of scale, size and intensity of factor use.

Reason (R): Factor imbalances and resource flows are not favourable to sustainable industrial development in India.

63. Assertion (A): Agricultural production is characterised by growth and instability in India.

Reason (R): There are marked inter-regional and inter-crop variations in farm production in India.

64. Assertion (A): Regional Trade blocks hinder free international trade.

Reason (R): They discriminate against non-member countries.

65. Assertion (A): A progressive income tax is based on equimarginal sacrifice.

Reason (R): Higher the income, lower will be the marginal utility of money for the tax payers.

66. The production function $Q = 150\ L^{0.7}\ K^{0.5}$, exhibits the returns to scale as:

A. Constant B. Increasing
C. Decreasing D. Fluctuating

67. In an open economy Input-Output model, A is the input-coefficients matrix, the viability condition to be satisfied is

A. $|I - A| \neq 0$
B. $|I - A| > 0$
C. $|I - A| < 0$
D. All principal minors of the matrix (I – A) must be positive.

68. Match the following:

List-I	List-II
(*a*) Granger Test	(*i*) Auto-correlation
(*b*) Dicky-Fuller Test	(*ii*) Causality
(*c*) F-test	(*iii*) Stationarity
(*d*) Durbin-Watson 'd' test	(*iv*) Overall significance of regression

Codes:

	(*a*)	(*b*)	(*c*)	(*d*)
A.	(*iii*)	(*i*)	(*iv*)	(*ii*)
B.	(*iv*)	(*ii*)	(*iii*)	(*i*)
C.	(*i*)	(*iii*)	(*ii*)	(*iv*)
D.	(*ii*)	(*iii*)	(*iv*)	(*i*)

69. Indirect least squares method of estimation is applied to equations of a simultaneous equation system. The estimates so obtained will be

A. Unbiased and consistent
B. Biased and consistent
C. Biased and inconsistent
D. Unbiased and inconsistent

70. Given the following total cost and demand functions of a firm, find the price at which profits would be maximised :

$C = 5Q^2 + 20Q + 10$

$P = 100 - 3Q$

Where C = Total cost

Q = Output

P = Price

A. 95 B. 85

C. 100 D. 5

71.

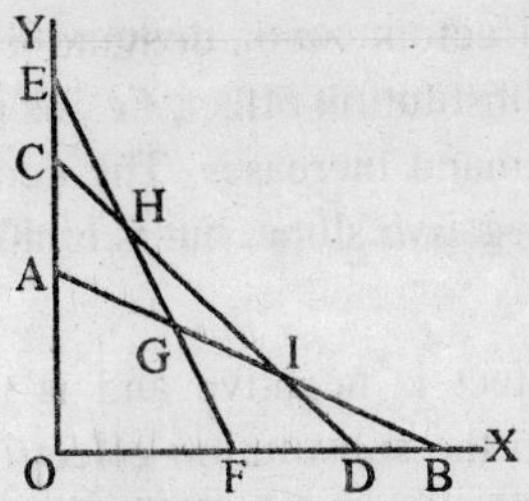

Consider the above diagram of a linear programming problem. If the optimum solution is at point A, then the slack variable(s) corresponding to which constraint(s) is/are non-zero?

A. AB only B. AB and CD

C. EF only D. CD and EF

72. In a two-variable regression Y is dependent variable and X is independent variable. If the correlation coefficient between Y and X is 0.7, then which one of the following result is correct?

A. 7% variations in Y are explained by X.

B. 70% variations in Y are explained by X.

C. 49% variation in Y are explained by X.

D. 0.7% variations in Y are explained by X.

73. Koyck's approach to econometric analysis deals with relationships involving:

A. Lagged explanatory variables

B. Qualitative explanatory variables

C. Exponential explanatory variables

D. None of the above

74. For the demand function $P = 10 - 2x - 0.5\,x^2$, what is price elasticity of demand at $x = 2$?

A. Zero B. 0.5

C. 1 D. 1.5

75. In a regression with 3 independent variables and 20 observations F value calculated is to be tested. What will be degrees of freedom for numerator and denominator in testing procedure?

A. 2, 18 B. 3, 17

C. 3, 16 D. 3, 20

ANSWERS

1 C	2 C	3 A	4 C	5 D	6 B	7 A	8 C	9 A	10 D
11 D	12 A	13 D	14 A	15 C	16 B	17 D	18 B	19 D	20 D
21 C	22 D	23 A	24 D	25 C	26 A	27 A	28 A	29 C	30 A
31 A	32 A	33 A	34 A	35 A	36 B	37 B	38 C	39 A	40 A
41 B	42 B	43 D	44 C	45 D	46 A	47 A	48 A	49 A	50 C
51 A	52 A	53 C	54 *	55 B	56 B	57 D	58 A	59 B	60 D
61 C	62 A	63 A	64 A	65 A	66 B	67 D	68 D	69 *	70 B
71 D	72 C	73 A	74 B	75 C					

EXPLANATORY ANSWERS

1. A Cartel is a formal organisation of the oligopoly firms in an industry. Cartels are the perfect form of collusion. A general purpose of cartels is to centralise certain managerial decisions and functions of individual firm in the industry with a view to promoting common benefits. Cartels may be in the form of *open collusion* or *secret collusion.* Whether open or secret, cartel agreements are *explicit* and *formal* in the sense that agreements are enforceable on member firms trying to pursue an independent pricing policy. Cartels are therefore regarded as the perfect form of collusion. Cartels and cartel type agreements between the firms in manufacturing and trade are illegal in most countries. Yet, cartels in the broader sense of the term exist in the form of trade associations, professional organisations and the like.

A cartel performs a variety of services for its members. The two typical services of central importance are (*i*) fixing price for joint maximisation of industry profits; and (*ii*) market sharing between it members. In this section, we will examine, these two activities of cartels.

2. The shape and slope of the demand curve depends, on the direction in which income and substitution effects of the fall in the price work. In fact, the substitution effect is positive in case of normal goods, but income effect is uncertain. Therefore, given the negative substitution effect, the shape of demand curve depends on the direction and magnitude of the positive income effect. The four possible combinations of substitution and income effects of a fall in the price of a commodity and the corresponding nature of the demand curve may be summarised as follows.

1. When substitution and income effects are positive, quantity demanded of X increases as P_x decreases. The demand curve therefore slopes downward to the right. This is a case of 'normal' goods.
2. If income effect is negative but less than the substitution effect (as it happens in case of inferior goods) the demand curve slopes downward to the right more steeply than usual.
3. If income effect is zero, demand curve follows the substitution effect, *i.e.*, as price decreases, demand increases. The demand curve has a negative slope, but is relatively flatter.
4. If income effect is negative and is more powerful than the substitution effect (as it happens in the case of Giffen goods) demand curve becomes backward bending, similar to Engel curve. But it is most unlikely that any demand curve will slope downward to the left throughout its whole length. It will be so only over that range of price changes over which negative income effect is stronger than the substitution. This aspect of demand curve will be discussed in detail when we take up the case of inferior goods.

3. Bain introduced the concept of *'the condition of entry'*, which he defined as the margin by which established firms can raise their price above the competitive price level *persistently* without attracting entry. Symbolically we have

$$E = \frac{P_L - P_C}{P_C}$$

where E = 'condition of entry'

P_L = limit price

P_C = competitive price, that is, price under pure competition in the long run (P_C = LAC).

Solving for P_L we find

$$P_L = P_C(1 + E)$$

Thus the condition of entry, E, is in fact the premium accruing to the established firms in an industry from charging a price, P_L, higher than the pure competitive price, P_C, without attracting entry.

5. An *important feature* of the production possibility frontier (PPF) is that it is *concave to origin.* Concavity implies that its *slope* goes on increasing as one moves down or up along the production possibility frontier. The slope of the production possibility frontier gives the rate at which one commodity (say, food) can be transformed into another (clothings) at different levels of production. This rate is called, in economic jargon, *the marginal rate of transformation* (MRT). The MRT can be defined as the *rate at which one commodity can be transformed into another.* The increasing slope of the PPF means increasing MRT. The slope of the PPF gives the measure of MRT. In terms of cost,

$$\text{MRT} = \frac{MC_x}{MC_y}$$

Thus, increasing *slope* of PPF means increasing MRT and therefore increasing marginal cost. That is why PPF is concave to origin.

6. See figure in question Before immigration profits were the area of the triangle ABW (= total output ABL0 less wage bill WBL0). After immigration profits are the triangle ADW′ (= new total output ADL′0 less new wage bill W′DL′0).

7. The introduction of the role of external effects on demand is attributed to Harvey Leibenstein (1950). In particular, three external effects were identified, namely, the Bandwagon, Snob and Veblen effects.

These effects are called 'external' since they refer to effects on demand outside of the intrinsic value (or the characteristics) of the good to the consumers. According to Leibenstein, consumers may purchase goods because others are buying them (bandwagon effect), because of the desire to be exclusive (snob effect) or because of the high showroom or conspicuous price (Veblen effect). Because they affect the elasticity of the demand curve and even the sign (Veblen effect), it is useful for suppliers to be aware of these effects in the market. These effects are considered *seriatim.*

The Bandwagon effect: The case where a consumer's desire for a good is positively influenced by the purchases of others represents the Bandwagon effect. In this case, as consumers buy more of the good, other consumers' taste or preference for the good is increased. This is due to the consumers' desire to 'jump on the bandwagon' and be 'in fashion' to fit in with their peers. The more consumers buy these goods, the more other consumers want to buy them as well. Some examples observed over time have been the wearing of blue jeans, brand name shoes and clothes and the toting around of various electronic gadgets including cellular phones and music players.

The Bandwagon effect therefore manifests itself as a shift factor in the demand for the good. Moreover, it feeds on itself since, as more persons acquire the good, this further influences others and keeps shifting the demand curve outwards. Leibenstein recognized that increased demand (shifts) based on increased purchases by others cannot continue indefinitely, and identified a *diminishing marginal external effect,* due to income limitations.

The Snob effect: The Snob effect is the desire for exclusivity by the consumer. It is a negative shift effect in response to quantity bought by others and is opposite to the bandwagon effect. As the price of a snob good falls and others come into the market (movement along the demand curve), the preference (taste) for the good by the 'snobs' in the market diminishes. This leads to an inward shift in the demand curve in response to the belief or actual knowledge of quantity being demanded in the market.

The Veblen effect: The Veblen effect, unlike the other two effects, is a response by consumers to the ostentatious price of the good rather than to the quantity others are buying. It is the effect generally known as conspicuous consumption. An example may be a Ferrari car which may be purchased by many in the market, not specifically for its performance record on the car racing circuit but because it carries a higher rather than a lower price.

In this case the demand curves are drawn with respect to consumers' demands in response to the 'showroom' price of the good. A lower showroom price leads to an inward shift in the demand curve for the good. In this case the Veblen effect completely overwhelms the price effect leading to a positively sloped Veblen demand curve.

8. Economic efficiency takes account of both technical efficiency, which requires least-cost production, and allocative efficiency, which requires that scarce outputs from scarce resources are distributed efficiently among consumers. Achieving economic efficiency is often termed a Pareto optimum, after the Italian economist Vilfredo Pareto (1848-1923). The prime principle of such an optimum is that no agent, consumer or producer can be made better off without making another agent worse off.

In these terms, economic efficiency is achieved through the operation of perfect competition. Perfect competition maximizes the aggregate of *consumer* and *producer surplus* by requiring price (P) to equal marginal cost (MC). P = MC is one of the key rules in Economics. From the consumer's side, the price paid reflects the marginal utility of the good purchased. Rational consumers will equate marginal utility across all goods purchased, so as to maximize their overall utility. At the same time, the marginal rate of substitution between any two goods will be the same for all consumers, because otherwise the utility of one consumer could be improved by reallocation without diminishing the utility of another.

From the producer's side, the price obtained by the sale of the last unit of the good produced matches the marginal cost of production. Here the producer is earning a normal profit and must be producing at least the cost, otherwise competition would drive the firm out of the market.

9. Quasi Rent: Marshall extended the concept of rent to cover the earnings of fixed capital equipment like machines in short run. The distinguishing characteristic of land is the fact that its supply is perfectly inelastic in short runs, and therefore its earning depends mainly upon the demand for it.

In short run the fixed capital equipment like machines are also perfectly inelastic in supply and cost of its production is not relevant once it has been produced. Thus, in short run, the earning of fixed capital equipment depend mainly upon the demand conditions and are thus similar to land rent and have therefore called rent by Marshall.

Since these capital equipments are not permanently in fixed supply like land, and instead their supply is very much elastic in long run. Marshall preferred to call their earning in short run as quasi rent rather than rent.

11. The Aggregate Demand Curve: The aggregate demand curve shows, at various price levels, the quantity of goods and services produced domestically that consumers, businesses, governments and foreigners (net exports) are willing to purchase during the period of concern. The curve slopes downward to the right, indicating that as price levels decrease (increase), more (less) goods and services are demanded.

Factors that can shift an aggregate demand curve include:

- **Real Interest Rate Changes:** Such changes will impact capital goods decisions made by individual consumers and by businesses. Lower real interest rates will lower the costs of major products such as cars, large appliances and houses; they will increase business capital project spending because long-term costs of investment projects are reduced. The aggregate demand curve will shift down and to the right. Higher real interest rates will make capital goods relatively more expensive and cause the aggregate demand curve to shift up and to the left.

- **Changes in Expectations:** If businesses and households are more optimistic about the future of the economy, they are more likely to buy large items and make new investments; this will increase aggregate demand.
- **The Wealth Effect:** If real household wealth increases (decreases), then aggregate demand will increase (decrease).
- **Changes in Income of Foreigners (Trade Effect):** If the income of foreigners increases (decreases), then aggregate demand for domestically-produced goods and services should increase (decrease).
- **Changes in Currency Exchange Rates (Liquidity Effect):** From the viewpoint of the U.S., if the value of the U.S. dollar falls (rises), foreign goods will become more (less) expensive, while goods produced in the U.S. will become cheaper (more expensive) to foreigners. The net result will be an increase (decrease) in aggregate demand.
- **Inflation Expectation Changes:** If consumers expect inflation to go up in the future, they will tend to buy now causing aggregate demand to increase. If consumers' expectations shift so that they expect prices to decline in the future, the aggregate demand will decline and the aggregate demand curve will shift up and to the left.

13. The Oil crisis, which came in the aftermath of the fourth Arab-Israeli war of October 1973, was an important turning point in the post-war international relations in general, and the economic history of many developed and developing countries in particular. It signified, for the first time, the emerging role of the Middle East region and the growing influence of oil in world politics. The crisis not only alerted the industrial world of the vulnerability of its oil-based industrial development, but also created the need for developing alternative energy sources and a policy to deal with such crises in future. It showed that in addition to economic strength or military might, the possession of precious natural resources like oil could also be used to influence the course of international relations.

14. The IS–LM model has a number of well-known implications with respect to the effects of changes in government policy. Increases in government spending G increase the equilibrium levels of *r* and Y and decrease the equilibrium level of I. The reduction in investment induced by an increase in government spending is known as crowding out. When money demand does not depend on the nominal interest rate, there is complete crowding out in the sense that the increase in G is completely offset by a decrease in I, so that aggregate demand is unaffected; the independence of money demand from the nominal interest rate has often been treated as a hallmark of monetarism, since in this case changes in fiscal policy have no real effects. Similar results occur when one considers tax changes; a reduction in either lump sum taxes or the income tax rate increases both Y and *r*. With respect to monetary policy, an increase in M leads to an increase in Y, a decrease in *r* and an increase in I. Hence, unlike expansionary fiscal policy, expansionary monetary policy increases investment, and so causes crowding in. The exception to this result is a liquidity trap in which changes in the supply of money are accepted by the public at the initial nominal interest rate.

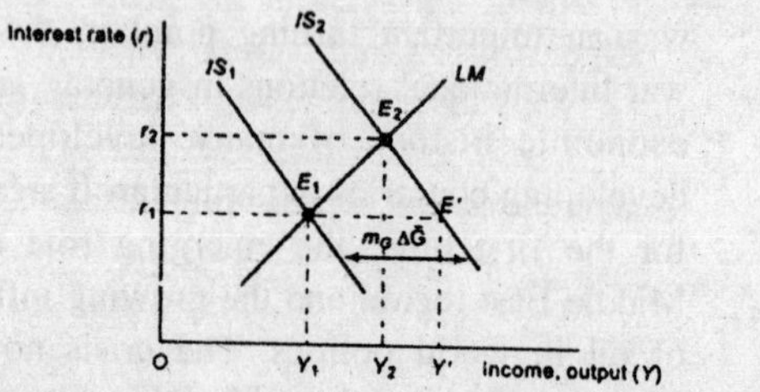

Fig.: *Effects of an increase in Government Purchases*

15. In a closed economy, there is only one leakage, which is saving. The size of a multiplier depends, among other things, on the marginal propensity to consume. Higher the marginal propensity to consume (lower the marginal propensity to save), larger will be the multiplier. An open economy there are two leakages, saving and imports. Imports are also a leakage because money spent on imported goods does not increase our income. Because of two leakages, the size of multiplier of an open economy is always smaller than that of a closed economy.

$$\text{Multipliers} = \frac{1}{\text{MPS} + \text{MPI}}$$

$$= \frac{1}{\text{Leakage}}$$

MPS = Marginal Propensity to Save

The marginal propensity to save (MPS) refers to the increase in saving amount. This increase in savings amount results from an increase in income and not spending some relatively greater proportion, *i.e.*, the marginal propensity to save might be defined as the proportion saving from each additional rupee earned as household income. This is represented by the slope of the saving line. For example, if a household earns one extra rupee, and the marginal propensity to save is 0.25, then 0.25 will be saved from INR 1 and rest 0.75 will be spent. This saving amount will be blocked and will not be available for further multiplication.

MPI = Marginal Propensity to Import

The marginal propensity to import (MPI) refers to the changes in import expenditure that occurs with a change in disposable income (income after taxes and transfers). For example, if a household is now earning one extra rupee of disposable income, and the marginal propensity to import is 0.1, then of that money, the household will spend 10 paise of that rupee on import services and goods. As this increased amount in income will be used for importing goods and services from the originating countries, this money will travel back to the originating country.

The MPS and MPI are collectively known as leakage.

17. Friedman's basic argument is that permanent consumption depends on permanent income. The basic relationship of PIH is that permanent consumption is proportional to permanent income that exhibits a fairly constant APC. That is, $C = kY_p$, where k is constant and equal to APC and MPC.

18. The **Accelerator Theory** of investment suggests that the level of planned investment varies with the rate of change of income or output rather than with the rate of interest.

The simplest form of the accelerator theory can be expressed as:

$$I_t = a(Y_t - Y_{t-1})$$

where I_t is investment in time period t, $Y_t - Y_{t-1}$ is the change in real income during year t and a is the accelerator coefficient or CAPITAL-OUTPUT RATIO. The capital-output ratio is the amount of capital needed in the economy to produce a given quantity of goods. The theory therefore predicts that changes in the level of investment are related to past changes in income.

20. The major consequence of labour market dualism for Lewis is reflected in the title of his 1954 paper: "Economic Development with Unlimited Supplies of Labour." The novel feature of Lewis's framework was that the modern sector faces an unlimited supply of labour at wages only somewhat higher than subsistence levels. It is this that makes the

Lewis model "classical," in contrast to a "neoclassical" model in which labour is scarce and has to be bid away from other uses. This feature was later elaborated by Ranis and Fei (1961), Fei and Ranis (1964), and Jorgenson (1967).

21. When Gunnar Myrdal was Executive Secretary of the United Nations Economic Commission for Europe, he organized a study of regional development and underdevelopment in Europe. The results, which were published in the *Economic Survey of Europe in* 1954, were very interesting: (1) regional gaps were large in the poorer countries, small in the richer ones; (2) regional gaps are increasing in the poorer countries, diminishing in the richer ones. In those days Italy, Turkey, and Spain, along with Greece, Yugoslavia, and Portugal, were still regarded as underdeveloped countries. In such countries, with regional inequality defined as the proportion of the population living in regions where the average income was less than two thirds of the national average, the gap was about 33 per cent, compared to some 10 per cent in such countries as Norway and France, and only "a few per cent" in Great Britain and Switzerland. Moreover, in countries where regional gaps were large they were also increasing; where gaps were small they were diminishing.

22. John Fei and Gustav Ranis in an article entitled "A Theory of Economic Development" analyse "the transition process through which an under-developed, economy hopes to move from a condition of stagnation to one of self-sustained growth". Their theory is an improvement over Lewis's theory of Unlimites Supplies of Labour because Lewis failed to present a satisfactory analysis of the growth of the agricultural sector.

Fei-Ranis theory relates to an underdeveloped labour-surplus and resource-poor economy in which the vast majority of the population is engaged in agriculture amidst widespread unemployment and high rates of population growth. The agrarian economy is stagnant. People are engaged in traditional agricultural pursuits. Non-agricultural pursuits exist but they are characterized by a modest use of capital. There is also an active and dynamic industrial sector. Development consists of the re-allocation of surplus agricultural workers, whose contribution to output is zero or negligible, to the industrial sector where they become productive at a wage equal to the institutional wage equal to the institutional wage in agriculture.

Assumptions: In presenting their theory of economy development, Fei and Ranis make the following assumptions:

1. There is a dual economy divided into a traditional and stagnant agricultural sector and an active industrial sector.
2. The output of the agricultural sector is a function of land and labour alone.
3. There is no accumulation of capital in agriculture except in the form of land reclamation.

23. Andre Gunder Frank (1969), a major dependency theorist argued that under-development does not mean traditional economic, political, and social institutions but the subjection of Third World nations to colonial rule and imperial domination. In essence Gunder Frank sees underdevelopment as the effect of the penetration of modern capitalism into the archaic economic structures of the Third World. More plainly stated, the economic development of the rich countries contributes to the underdevelopment of African nations. Gunder Frank suggests that, the following economic activities have contributed to underdevelopment, not development of Third World nations: (1) Replacing indigenous enterprises with technologically more advanced, global subsidiary companies; (2) Opening the economy to trade with, and investment from developed countries; (3) Workers migrating from villages to foreign-dominated urban complexes; (4) Recruiting highly educated youths for junior posts in the colonial administrative service; and (5) Forming an unskilled labour force to work in factories and mines and on plantations. He feels that the development of the underdeveloped countries will be stimulated by indiscriminately transferring capital institutions and values from developed countries.

24. ∵ Growth rate per capita

$$= \frac{\text{Investment Rate}}{\text{ICOR}} - \text{population growth}$$

$$\text{Growth rate of per capita} = \frac{27}{4.5} - 2$$

$$= 6 - 2 = 4\%.$$

26. Joan Robinson considers an economy in the golden age when 'potential growth ratio' is being realized. The potential growth ratio is the highest rate of capital accumulation which can be permanently maintained at a constant rate of profit. The conditions of a golden age require the growth ratio to be steady because frequent change in the growth ratio disturb the tranquility of a golden age. This tranquility, however, may not be possible even when the growth ratio is stable. An increase in the total stock of capital is likely to slacken the urge to accumulate so that a stage of stagnation starts and the economy deviates from the part of golden age. The golden age is not an ideal. It only represents a state of equilibrium growth at any conceivable rate so that each rate of growth will have its appropriate golden age.

28. Article 280 of the Constitution of India requires the constitution of a Finance Commission every five years, or earlier. For the period 1st April, 2015 to 31st March, 2020 the 14th Finance Commission (FFC) was constituted by the orders of President on 2nd January, 2013 and submitted its report on 15-12-2014. The FFC was constituted under the chairmanship of Dr. Y.V. Reddy, former Governor of RBI.

The Finance Commission was required to recommend the distribution of the net proceeds of taxes of the Union between the Union and the States (commonly referred to as vertical devolution); and the allocation between the States of the respective shares of such proceeds (commonly known as horizontal devolution).

In recommending horizontal distribution, the FFC has used broad parameters of population (1971) and changes of population since, income distance, forest cover and area.

Criteria and Weights for Horizontal Distribution

Criteria	Weight (per cent)
Population	17.5
Demographic Change	10
Income Distance	50
Area	15
Forest Cover	7.5

29. Primary Deficit = Gross fiscal dificit – interest payment

= 3,00,000 – 80,000

= 2,20,000.

31. In order to explain Wagner's Law, Peacock and Wiseman (1961) developed the so-called displacement effect hypothesis. According to this theory, crises such as world wars help to overcome taxpayer resistance to higher taxes, and politicians can therefore raise the public sector's share of GDP. However, once a crisis has been resolved, people become used to a high level of taxation, and the public sector's share of GDP continues to rise instead of falling to the original level. This phenomenon is known as the displacement effect.

32. Verdoorn's law states that in the long run there is a linear relationship between the growth in output and the growth in productivity. This relationship can be explained by the theory of cumulative causation. In this theory it is primarily the growth in effective demand that stimulates technological growth, through a larger potential for division of labour and through learning-by-doing. The resulting productivity increase stimulates higher outputs through the extension of existing markets and the opening up of new markets. This suggests that productivity gains and growth in output are mutually reinforcing mechanisms. Following this line of reasoning, Verdoorn's law has been empirically observed across nations, regions and industries using country-level, region-level and industry-level data.

34. Income velocity is the ratio of the level of real income to the demand for real balances.

Velocity is a function of real income and the interest rate. An increase in the interest rate reduces the demand for real balances and therefore increases velocity: when the cost of holding money increases, money holders make their money do more work and thus turn it over more often. The way in which changes in real income affect velocity depends on the income elasticity of the demand for money. If the income elasticity of the demand for real balances were 1, then the demand for real balances would change in the same proportion as income. In that case, changes in real income would not affect velocity. If income elasticity of demand for money is greater than unity then velocity will decrease with increase in real income.

35. Comparison of 'Keynesian' and 'monetarist' views

Variable, function or prediction	'Keynesian' position	'Monetarist' position
M^S (= nominal money supply)	Primarily endogenous	Primarily exogenous Controllable within workably narrow limits
M^D (= money demand function)	Relatively interest elastic Interest elasticity an inverse function of *r*. Not very stable in the short run	Relatively interest inelastic Usually regarded as a constant Stable
Investment function	Relatively interest inelastic Unstable	Relatively interest elastic Stable
Consumption function	Relatively interest inelastic Stable	Relatively interest elastic (via wealth) cash-balance effect Relatively stable
Money wages	Relatively inflexible	Flexible
Prices	Mark-up on wage costs	Flexible
Output (short run)	Variation in Y primarily explained by shifts in investment function	Variation in Y primarily due to variation in M^S
Output (long run)	—	Unaffected by fiscal policy or money stock
Fiscal policy	Effective in influencing Y	Ineffective in influencing Y
Long run	Too long in calendar time for propositions of 'neutrality' of money to be important	May be quite short, i.e., less than 5 years
Labour market	Involuntary unemployment consistent with equilibrium	Involuntary unemployment zero in equilibrium.

38. According to Tobin, Keynes theory suffers from two major defects: one, it points out that liquidity preference is determined by the inelasticity of expectations of future interest rates and two, that individuals hold either money or bonds. Tobin's analysis removes both these defects. His analysis is based on the assumption that the expected value of capital gain or loss from holding interest-bearing assets is always zero. It also explains that the individual's portfolio contains both money as well as bonds and not either of these at a time. He, therefore, starts his analysis with this assumption. According to him, money neither brings any income nor does it impose any risk on the individual asset holder. Bonds do yield interest and bring about income. It is, however, uncertain and involves a risk of loss or gain. The greater the investment in bonds, the higher is the risk of capital loss. An individual investor can court this risk provided he gets an adequate return from bonds.

39. A population pyramid consists of a bar graph showing the age distribution of both men and women, presented together in a particular way. The age categories proceed from the bottom to the top. The male bars proceed from a vertical center line leftward; the female bars proceed from a vertical center line rightward. Pyramids can be constructed from either frequency distributions or from percentage distributions.

The change in the inflation rate depends on the difference between the actual and the natural unemployment rates. When the actual unemployment rate is higher than the natural unemployment rate, the inflation rate decreases: when the actual unemployment rate is lower than the natural unemployment rate, the inflation rate increases.

The natural rate of unemployment is the rate of unemployment required to keep the inflation rate constant. This is why the natural rate is also called the nonaccelerating inflation rate of unemployment, or NAIRU.

41. The demographic transition occurs when countries change from high birth rates and death rates to low birth rates and death rates. The demographic transition has three phases, as shown in figure:

(*i*) High birth rates and death rates, with little population growth.

(*ii*) Declining death rates due largely to reductions in infant mortality, with little or no reduction in birth rates, resulting in high population growth.

(*iii*) Low birth rates and death rates, with little population growth.

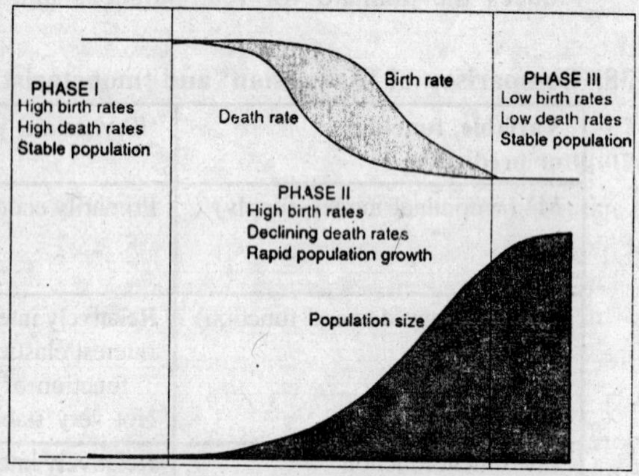

Fig.: *The demographic transition*

42. Dumping is usually defined as selling below cost. In foreign trade, dumping is also defined simply as selling in a foreign market at a lower price than the identical good sells for in the producer's home market. These two either/or criteria were adopted by negotiators of the General Agreement on Tariffs and Trade (GATT) back in 1947 at the insistence of the United States; the definition carried over to the WTO's rules when it superseded the GATT in 1994. Article VI (Part 1) of the GATT says dumping occurs when:

(1) the price of the foreign product is less than the comparable price, in the ordinary course of trade, for the like product when destined for consumption in the exporting country, or

(2) in the absence of such domestic price, the price of the foreign product is less

than either the highest comparable price for the like product for export to any third country in the ordinary course of trade, or the cost of production of the product in the country of origin plus a reasonable addition for selling costs and profit.

The *margin of dumping* is defined as (1) the difference between the selling price in the foreign market and the average production cost plus transport, selling costs, and "reasonable" profit, or (2) the difference between the foreign price and a home price or third-country market price. If either definition of dumping is satisfied, countries are permitted to levy a tariff to exactly offset the alleged dumping.

44. A nation could correct a deficit in its balance of payments by devaluing its currency, by holding its inflation rate lower than abroad, by increasing its short-term interest rates or by direct controls on trade and payments.

A devaluation will make the nation's imports more expensive to domestic buyers and its exports cheaper to foreigners. This usually improves the balance of trade and payments of the nation. The same results could be achieved by holding the domestic rate of inflation lower than that abroad. On the other hand, an increase in the nation's short-term interest rate usually reduces short-term capital outflows from the nation or increases inflows, thus improving its balance on capital account and payments.

45. The agricultural subsidies, in the WTO terminology have in general been identified by 'boxes' which have been given the colours of the traffic lights—*green* (means permitted), *amber* (means slow down *i.e.,* to be reduced) and *red* (means forbidden).

In the agriculture sector, as usual, things are more complicated. The WTO provisions on agriculture has nothing like *red box* subsidies, although subsidies exceeding the reduction commitment levels is prohibited in the '*amber box*'. The '*blue box*' subsidies are tied to programmes that limit the level of production. There is also a provision of some exemptions for the developing countries sometimes called the 'S & D box'.

Amber Box: All subsidies which are supposed to distort production and trade fall into the amber box *i.e.*, all agricultural subsidies except those which fall into the blue and green boxes. These include government policies of *minimum support prices* (as MSP in India) for agricultural products or any help directly related to production quantities (as power, fertilisers, pesticides, irrigation, etc).

Under the WTO provisions, these subsidies are subject to reduction commitment to their minimum level—to 5 per cent and 10 per cent for the developed and the developing countries, respectively, of their total value of agricultural outputs, per annum accordingly. It means, the subsidies *directly related* to production promotion above the allowed level (which fall in either blue box or green box) must be reduced by the countries to the prescribed levels.

Blue Box: This is the *amber box with conditions.* The conditions are designed to reduce distortions. Any subsidy that would normally be in the amber box, is placed in the blue box if it requires farmers to go for a certain production level. These subsidies are nothing but certain direct payments (*i.e.*, direct set-aside payments) made to farmers by the government in the form of assistance programmes to encourage agriculture, rural development, etc.

At present there are no limits on spending on the blue box subsidies. In the current negotiations, some countries want to keep blue box as it is because they see it as a crucial means of moving away from distorting the amber box subsidies without causing too much hardship. Others want to set limits or reduction commitments on it while some advocate moving these subsidies into the amber box.

Green Box: The agricultural subsidies which cause minimal or no distortions to trade are put under the green box. They must not involve price support.

This box basically includes all forms of government expenses which are not targeted at a particular product and all direct income support programmes to farmers which are not related to current levels of production or prices. This is a *very wide box* and includes all government subsidies like—public storage for food security, pest and disease control, research and extension, and some direct payments to farmers that do not stimulate production like restructuring of agriculture, environmental protection, regional development, crop and income insurance, etc.

The green box subsidies are allowed without limits provided they comply with the policy-specific criteria. It means, this box is exempt from the calculation under subsidies under the WTO provisions because the subsidies under it are not meant to promote production thus do not distort trade. That is why this box is called *'production-neutral box'*.

S & D Box: Other than the above-discussed highly controversial boxes of agricultural subsidies, the WTO provisions have defined yet another box *i.e.*, the S & D Box. The Social and Development Box (S & D Box) allows the developing countries for some subsidies to the agriculture sector under certain conditions. These conditions revolve around *human development issues* such as poverty, minimum social welfare, health support etc., specially for the segment of population living below the poverty line. Developing countries can forward such subsidies to the extent of less than 5 per cent of their total agricultural output.

49. Repo/Reverse Repo

In India, two types of repo are in operation: inter-bank repo and RBI repo. The inter-bank repos are permitted under regulated conditions and used for raising funds to meet short-term mismatches between the demand for and the supply of funds. Besides banks, primary dealers are allowed to undertake both repo/reverse repo transactions. Non-bank participants are allowed in the repo market only as lenders. They can lend funds to other eligible participants. All government securities are eligible for repo. Repos have also been permitted in PSU bonds and private corporate securities provided they are held in the dematerialized form in a depository and the transactions are done in the recognized stock exchanges.

All Scheduled Commercial Banks (excluding the Regional Rural Banks (RRBs)) and Primary Dealers (PDs) having current account and SGL account with the RBI, Mumbai, are eligible to participate in the repo and reverse repo auctions.

As the tenure of repo/reverse repo in India is 1 to 14 days, this instrument has been used by the RBI for managing day-to-day or short-term liquidity. Over a period of time, the repo/reverse repo rates, set by the RBI, have become a sort of signalling rates along with the bank rate. These rates provide a corridor for the call money market. The quantity and the rate reflect the liquidity conditions prevailing in the market. Repo and reverse repo rates are also used as a part of the Liquidity Adjustment Facility (LAF) operations, which reflect the day-to-day pressure of marginal liquidity in the system. These rates constitute the interest rate corridor under the LAF. Any variation in these rates, hence, is perceived by the market as short-term interest rate signal arising from a change in the stance of the RBI. Since the implementation of the new operating system, the RBI sets only repo rate independently. The reverse repo rate is aligned to it, and maintained 100 basis point below the repo rate.

53. Macroeconomics uses certain economic aggregates, called macroeconomic variables to assess the performance of an economy.

These variables are grouped under stock variables and flow variables, which may increase or decrease over time.

The distinction between the two variables is that a stock is a quantity measurable at a specific point of time, whereas a flow is a quantity measurable over a specified period of time.

Stock Variables	Flow Variables
1. Total stock or Amount of capital	1. Investment
2. Supply of money	2. Change in money supply
3. Inventories	3. Change in inventories
4. Savings	4. Saving and investment
5. Foreign exchange reserve	5. Balance of payment
6. Number of unemployed people	6. Number of people losing their jobs
7. Government debt	7. Government tax revenue, Government expenditure, Budget deficit or surplus
8. Wealth	8. Income and expenditure

56. I. Urjit Patel Committee : 2014

II. Goipuria Committee : 1990

III. Narsimha Committee : 1991

IV. Chakravarti Committee : 1982

58. I. Kyoto Protocol : 1997 – held at Kyoto (Japan)

II. Earth Summit : 1992 – held at Riode Janario (Brazil)

III. Bali Summit : 2007 – held at Bali (Indonesia)

66. Here, the exponent $\alpha = 0.7$ and exponent $\beta = 0.5$.

The sum of exponents $(\alpha + \beta) = 0.7 + 0.5 = 1.2$

Since $\alpha + \beta > 1$, this production function shows increasing returns to scale.

67. The Hawkins-Simon conditions

It is possible that when trying to compute industry outputs in an input-output model:

(*i*) no solution is possible because the I - A matrix is singular and cannot be inverted,

(*ii*) industry output quantities are computed but have negative values.

Either (or both) these situations would mean that the input-output model could not be used. Situation (*i*) would be akin to trying to divide by zero and situation (*ii*) would mean that the input-output model has no practical use because real industries obviously cannot produce negative outputs.

The Hawkins-Simons conditions state the constraints which must be put on the parameters of an input-output model to prevent such situations arising and for the model to compute non-negative outputs for all industries. The Hawkins-Simons conditions basically require that all the leading principal minors of the (I – A) matrix are strictly positive. This will ensure that the inverse matrix $(I - A)^{-1}$ exists and all elements of $(I - A)^{-1}$ are non-negative.

70. $$C = 5Q^2 + 20Q + 10$$

$$\Rightarrow \quad MC = \frac{dC}{dQ} = 10Q + 20$$

$$\because \quad P = 100 - 3Q$$

$$\therefore \quad TR = P.Q$$

$$= (100 - 3Q)Q$$

$$= 100Q - 3Q^2$$

$$\Rightarrow \quad MR = \frac{d(TR)}{dQ} = 100 - 6Q$$

For maximum profit MR = MC

$$\therefore \quad 100 - 6Q = 10Q + 20$$

$$\Rightarrow \quad 80 = 16Q$$

$$Q = 5$$

$$\therefore \quad P = 100 - 3 \times 5$$

$$= 100 - 15 = 85.$$

72. Here, coefficient of determination

$$r^2 = (0.7)^2$$
$$= 0.49 = 49\%$$

So, 49% variation in Y are explained by X.

74.
$$e_P = -\frac{dx}{dP}\cdot\frac{P}{x}$$

Here, $P = 10 - 2x - 0.5x^2$

Differentiate with respect to P, we get

$$1 = (-2 - 1.0x)\frac{dx}{dP}$$

$$\Rightarrow \quad \frac{dx}{dP} = \frac{-1}{(2+x)}$$

$$\therefore \quad e_p = -\left(\frac{-1}{2+x}\right)\cdot\frac{(10-2x-0.5x^2)}{x}$$
$$= -\frac{-1}{4}\cdot\frac{4}{2}$$
$$= \frac{1}{2} = 0.5.$$

75. Degree of freedom for Numerator

= Number of Independent variables

= 3

and Degree of freedom for denominator

= No. of observation – Independent variables – 1

= 20 – 3 – 1 = 16

Thus, D.F. = (3, 16).

Previous Paper (Solved)

UGC-NET-Junior Research Fellowship & Assistant Professor Exam

Economics, July-2016*

PAPER-II

Note: *This paper contains **fifty (50)** objective type questions of **two (2)** marks each. **All** questions are compulsory.*

1. In the standard adjoining diagram, the measure of consumer surplus is:

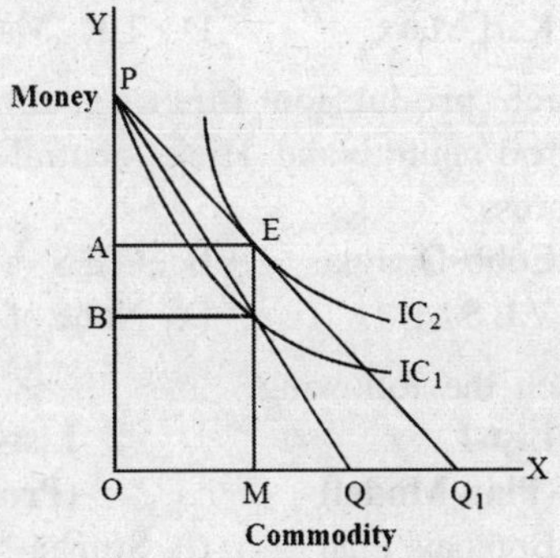

A. PA B. OB
C. AO D. AB

2. A cartel aims at maximising:
A. individual profits
B. industry profits
C. share of output of members
D. goodwill of the members

3. The statement that, "no one can be made better off without making someone worse off" describes which of the following?
A. Pareto Optimum
B. Nash Equilibrium
C. Low level Equilibrium Trap
D. Cournot's Equilibrium

4. Slutsky equation explains the:
A. Demand for durable goods
B. Supply of durable goods
C. Split between price, income and substitution effects
D. Demand for rare or non-reproducible goods

5. L shaped average cost curve is witnessed in the large firms because:
A. Only the law of increasing returns operates
B. The law of constant returns to scale operates
C. Only the law of constant return operates
D. The operation of law of decreasing returns is continuously postponed

6. Consider the following statements regarding the long run equilibrium in the monopolistic market.
I. Firms are in no profit no loss situation.
II. There is no entry or exit of the firms.
Which among the above statements are true? Answer from the code below:
Codes:
A. Only I is true
B. Only II is true
C. Both I and II are true
D. Neither I nor II are true

7. Which of the following is ***not*** a problem of Insurance Markets?
A. Adverse selection
B. Moral Hazard
C. Asymmetric Information
D. Principal-agent problem

8. In consumption, inferior goods have:
A. Negative income effect
B. Positive income effect
C. Zero income effect
D. Infinite income effect

* *Exam held on 10 July 2016.*

9. Consider the following statements:

I. Inflation is advantageous to debtors.

II. Inflation is advantageous to the bond-holders.

Which of the statements given above is/are correct?

Codes:

A. I only B. II only

C. Both I and II D. Neither I nor II

10. 'Near money' is correctly defined as an:

A. asset which has 100% liquidity

B. asset which has no store of value function

C. asset which is a medium of exchange

D. asset which fulfils the store of value function and can be converted into a medium of exchange at a short notice

11. Match the following:

List-I	**List-II (Multiplier)**
(*a*) MPC = 0.2	(*i*) K = 2
(*b*) MPS = 0.5	(*ii*) K = 1.66
(*c*) MPS = 0.75	(*iii*) K = 1.33
(*d*) MPC = 0.4	(*iv*) K = 1.25

Select the correct answer from the codes given below:

Codes:

	(*a*)	(*b*)	(*c*)	(*d*)
A.	(*i*)	(*ii*)	(*iii*)	(*iv*)
B.	(*ii*)	(*iv*)	(*i*)	(*iii*)
C.	(*iv*)	(*i*)	(*iii*)	(*ii*)
D.	(*iii*)	(*i*)	(*iv*)	(*ii*)

12. In the context of steady state growth in Solow's model, the output growth rate overtime will be:

A. increasing B. decreasing

C. constant D. fluctuating

13. Who among the following economists assume dualism in the economy?

I. Ranis and Fei II. D. Ricardo

III. Robert Solow IV. R. Harrod

Answer from the codes given below:

Codes:

A. All the four above

B. Only I and II

C. Only IV

D. I, II and III

14. Who among the following, originally, formulated the 'Turnpike Theorem'?

A. Dorfman, Samuelson and Solow

B. Radner

C. Koopmans

D. Von Neumann and Morgenstern

15. Backward and forward linkages are relevant for which kind of growth strategy?

A. Unbalanced growth

B. Trickle down growth

C. Balanced growth

D. Equilibrium growth

16. 'Reserve Army of labour' term was used by who among the following economists?

A. J. Schumpeter B. J.R. Hicks

C. Karl Marx D. T.R. Malthus

17. Which production function admits both Harrod-neutral and Hicks-neutral technical progress?

A. Cobb-Douglas B. C.E.S.

C. V.E.S. D. None of the above

18. Match the following:

List-I (Plan Model)	**List-II (Proposer)**
(*a*) Bombay Plan	(*i*) Sriman Narayan
(*b*) Gandhian Plan	(*ii*) M.N. Roy
(*c*) People's Plan	(*iii*) Jai Prakash Narain
(*d*) Sarvodaya Approach	(*iv*) Birla and Tata Group

Select the correct answer from the codes given below:

Codes:

	(*a*)	(*b*)	(*c*)	(*d*)
A.	(*iv*)	(*i*)	(*ii*)	(*iii*)
B.	(*i*)	(*ii*)	(*iii*)	(*iv*)
C.	(*iii*)	(*ii*)	(*iv*)	(*i*)
D.	(*i*)	(*iv*)	(*ii*)	(*iii*)

19. Which among the following is ***not*** a criterion for declaring special category state?

A. Over population

B. Poor infrastructure

C. Hilly and difficult terrain

D. Non-viable state finances

20. For the testing of consistency and viability of a planning project, which of the prices are used?

A. Market Price
B. Shadow Price
C. Administered Price
D. Controlled Price

21. In which of the Five Year Plans in India, for the first time an extensive input-output model was used?

A. First Plan B. Second Plan
C. Third Plan D. Seventh Plan

22. Who among the following economists developed the Reinvestment-Criterion?

A. Walter Galenson and Harvey Leibenstein
B. A.K. Sen
C. Maurice Dobb
D. None of the above

23. Area approach to decentralised planning in India was advocated by who among thc following?

A. D.R. Gadgil B. K.N. Raj
C. Raj Krishna D. Pranav Mukherjee

24. Which amongst the following is included in the Capital account of the Balance of payments?

I. Foreign loans
II. Foreign Direct Investment
III. Private Remittances

Choose the correct answer from the codes below:

Codes:

A. All the three B. I and III
C. II and III D. I and II

25. Which amongst the following options is correct for a teaser loan?

A. It is an introductory rate of interest
B. This rate is permanent in nature
C. Both (A) and (B) are correct
D. Neither (A) nor (B) are correct

26. The movement of free international trade is most likely to generate short-term unemployment in which of the following industries?

A. Industries in which there are neither imports nor exports
B. Import competing industries
C. Industries that sell to domestic and foreign buyers
D. Industries that sell to only foreign buyers

27. Which among the following will be classified as non-tariff barrier?

I. Phyto-sanitary measures
II. Import and export licensing
III. Countervailing duty
IV. Environmental standards

Select the answer from the code given below.

Codes:

A. All the four above
B. I and II
C. I and IV
D. III and IV

28. Who developed the use of trade indifference curves in the analysis of trade theory?

A. J.E. Meade B. A. Marshall
C. A.P. Lerner D. B. Ohlin

29. Which among the following is ***not*** the main areas of BASEL III norms?

A. Risk Coverage
B. Bank branch expansion
C. Adequate capital provision
D. Adequate liquidity

30. Which among the following is most volatile flow of foreign exchange?

A. Foreign Direct Investment
B. External Commercial borrowings
C. Foreign Portfolio investment
D. Foreign aid by IMF and World Bank

31. State Governments in India finance their Gross fiscal deficit by:

I. Loans from the Central Government.
II. Market Borrowings.
III External Borrowings.

Select the correct answer from the codes given below:

Codes:

A. I and II B. II and III
C. II only D. I only

32. 'Make in India' campaign aimed at attracting industrialists to make India a Global Manufacturing Hub was launched on:
A. September 25, 2014
B. March 20, 2015
C. February 25, 2016
D. December 30, 2015

33. The Second Green Revolution in India is necessiated by:
I. Productivity in agriculture is stagnating.
II. Diversification of agriculture has not progressed much.
III. Exports of agricultural commodities have declined.
Select the correct answer from the codes given below:
Codes:
A. I and II — B. II and III
C. I and III — D. I only

34. Which among the following is ***not*** included in the Small Savings Scheme?
A. Unit Trust of India
B. National Savings Certificate
C. Kisan Vikas Patra
D. Sukanya Samridhi Accounts Yojana

35. In which of the following year, all tax revenues of Centre have become shareable among the Centre and States?
A. 2000 AD — B. 2003 AD
C. 2007 AD — D. 1998 AD

36. Which arrangement of following would show the correct sequence of demographic transition as typically associated with economic development?
I. High birth rate with high death rate.
II. High birth rate with low death rate.
III. Low birth rate with low death rate.
Select the correct answer from the codes given below:
Codes:
A. I, II and III — B. II, I and III
C. III, II and I — D. I, III and II

37. If with the increase in income, the percentage of income collected as tax remains constant, tax will be called:
A. regressive — B. progressive
C. proportional — D. neutral

38. Consider the following liquid assets:
I. Demand deposits with the banks.
II. Time deposits with the banks.
III. Saving deposits with the banks.
IV. Currency
The correct sequence of these in the ascending order of liquidity is:
Codes:
A. IV, III, II, I — B. I, IV, III, II
C. II, III, I, IV — D. IV, I, III, II

39. Given the budgetary parameters including public expenditure remaining the same, then as a result of imposition of a tax, if the pattern of distribution of income changes, then such an incidence is called:
A. Effective incidence
B. Monetary incidence
C. Relative incidence
D. Specific tax incidence

40. Assertion (A) : The sale of T-bills is conducted through an auction.
Reason (R) : The method helps in price discovery.
Select the answer from the code below:
Codes:
A. (A) is true, but (R) is false
B. Both (A) and (R) are true
C. (A) is false, but (R) is true
D. Both (A) and (R) are false

41. The social cost curve lies above the private cost curve for the producer in case of which of the following?
A. Positive externalities
B. Negative externalities
C. Public goods
D. Near-public goods

42. Which one of the following is true in case of Performance and Programme Budgeting System?
A. Its emphasis is on outcome only
B. Its emphasis is more on outcome and less on expenditure allocation
C. Its emphasis is on expenditure allocation only
D. Its emphasis is more on expenditure allocation and less on outcome

43. Who among the following has developed the concept of 'Effective incidence' of a tax?
A. Ursula K. Hicks B. J.R. Hicks
C. H. Dalton D. A.C. Pigou

44. Voting fails to generate the efficient quantity of a public good because:
A. Lobbying groups use bribes to change people's votes
B. Public goods are not depleted by consumption
C. Public goods cannot be withheld from consumption
D. Voting does not accurately reflect the magnitude of benefits from public goods

45. Which of the following item of expenditure is not a part of the plan expenditure?
A. Agriculture B. Defence
C. Industry D. Social Services

46. The Time Series of production yielded following Trend equation:
$Y = 136\ e^{0.021}\ T.$
Where Y = Production, T = Time
From this equation it can be inferred that growth rate of Y in per cent terms is:
A. 0.021 B. 2.1
C. 21 D. 0.21

47. Which is not a sampling distribution?
A. Student's 't' distribution
B. Fisher's 'F' distribution
C. Poisson distribution
D. χ^2 (chi square) distribution

48. Co-efficient of correlation is independent of which of the following?
A. Change of origin only
B. Change of scale only
C. Change of origin and scale
D. None of these

49. Which of the following is not satisfied for independence of two events A and B?
A. $P(A/B) = P(A)$
B. $P(B/A) = P(B)$
C. $P(A, B) = P(A)\ P(B)$
D. $P(A, B) = P(A) + P(B)$

50. Match the items in List-I and List-II and answer from the codes given below:

List-I	List-II
(*a*) Standard Deviation	(*i*) Positively skewed distribution
(*b*) Stratified Random Sampling	(*ii*) Analysis of attributes
(*c*) Coefficient of Association	(*iii*) Measure of dispersion
(*d*) Mean > Mode	(*iv*) Probability based sampling

Codes:

	(*a*)	(*b*)	(*c*)	(*d*)
A.	(*iv*)	(*ii*)	(*iii*)	(*i*)
B.	(*i*)	(*ii*)	(*iii*)	(*iv*)
C.	(*iv*)	(*iii*)	(*ii*)	(*i*)
D.	(*iii*)	(*iv*)	(*ii*)	(*i*)

ANSWERS

1	2	3	4	5	6	7	8	9	10
D	B	A	C	D	C	D	A	A	D
11	**12**	**13**	**14**	**15**	**16**	**17**	**18**	**19**	**20**
C	C	B	A	A	C	A	A	A	B
21	**22**	**23**	**24**	**25**	**26**	**27**	**28**	**29**	**30**
C	A	A	D	A	B	C	A	B	C
31	**32**	**33**	**34**	**35**	**36**	**37**	**38**	**39**	**40**
C	A	A	A	A	A	C	C	D	B
41	**42**	**43**	**44**	**45**	**46**	**47**	**48**	**49**	**50**
B	B	A	D	B	B	C	C	D	D

EXPLANATORY ANSWERS

1. 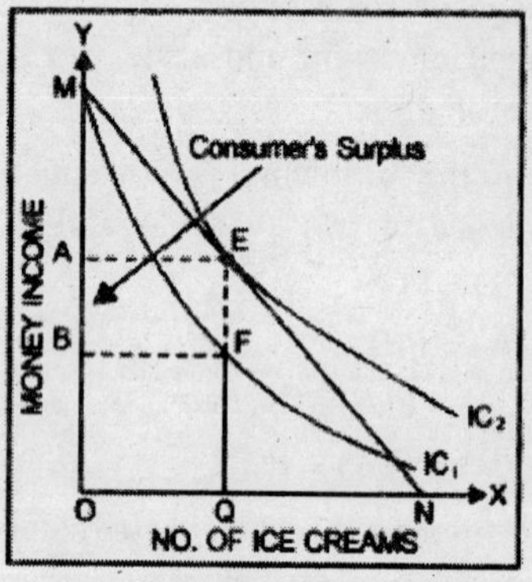

Fig. : *Consumer Surplus*

2. A cartel refers to the group of firms that enter into the agreement regarding uniform price-output policies to be pursued by them. Firms jointly fix the prices to be charged and output to be sold in the market. Since, all the firms in the group implement the joint decisions, cartels are regarded as a perfect form of collusion. Two typical forms of cartels are:
   - Cartels aiming at joint-profit maximization *i.e.*, maximization of industry profits.
   - Cartels aiming at sharing of the market

3. A *Pareto optimum* is defined as a state of affairs such that no one can be made better off without at least one other person being made worse off. A change in the allocation of resources or goods is said to constitute a *Pareto improvement* if at least one person is made better off without anyone being made worse off. Thus, a Pareto optimum is a situation from which no Pareto improvement is possible. Also, according to Pareto, a policy is said to improve economic welfare only if it results in a Pareto improvement, that is, at least one person is made better off without anyone else being made worse off. A study of economic welfare based on Pareto's conditions is known as *Paretian welfare economics.*

4. Prof. Slutsky has presented the relationship between the price effect, the substitution effect (direct price effect) and the income effect in an equation which is called the *Slutsky Equation.* The equation can be written in the following manner:

$$\frac{\partial X}{\partial P_X} = \left(\frac{\partial X}{\partial P_X}\right)_u = \text{constant} + X\left(\frac{\partial X}{\partial I}\right)\frac{P_X}{P_Y} = \text{constant}$$

↓	↓	↓
Total Price Effect	Substitution Effect	Income Effect

5. Modern theory of cost curves has been propounded by economists like *Stigler, Andrews, Sargent Florence* and *Friedman,* etc. According to traditional theory of cost curves, long-run cost curves are U-shaped. But according to modern theory, in real life long-run cost curves are L-shaped. The L-shaped cost curve implies that the production costs fall continuously with increases in output. According to modern theory long-run costs are mainly of two types: (1) Production Cost and (2) Managerial Cost. On account of increase in production, production cost goes on falling continuously due to technical economies of scale. On the contrary, as the scale of production is enlarged managerial costs may rise. Since fall in production-cost is more than rise in managerial-cost, long-run average cost curve falls smoothly or remains constant at very large scales of output.

8. An inferior good is that good whose income effect is negative and substitution effect is also negative. Negative income effect means, a fall in the price of a commodity leads to an increase in real income which results in a fall in quantity demanded. Since consumers react to an increase in income by demanding less of an inferior good. Thus, negative substitution effect implies that a fall in price results in a rise in quantity demanded while negative income effect of change in price implies that

as a result of fall in price the quantity demanded decreases. Negative substitution effect and negative income effect work in opposite directions. Thus, while negative substitution effect leads to an increase in the quantity demanded, the negative income effect leads to a reduction in quantity demanded. However negative income effect of inferior goods, may not be as powerful as the negative substitution effect. In such cases negative substitution effect would dominate and eclipse the income effect. Accordingly quantity demanded should increase with a fall in price and decrease with a rise in price even when the commodity happens to be inferior.

9. Bond holders get a fixed amount of money as interest and this interest is unrelated to inflation and is declared at the time of issuing the bond. A 8% bond implies ₹ 8 as interest each year. If there is inflation then the value of ₹ 8 will fall—the bond holder can buy lesser goods with ₹ 8 than before, so that real value/ purchasing power is lowered. This hurts bond holders as they are unable to use ₹ 8 as they had imagined/wanted to at the time of buying the bond. They are negatively hit by inflation.

10. The term NEAR MONEY refers to assets that fulfil some of the functions of money but not all of them. Specifically, near money is anything that fulfils the store-of-value function, and is readily *convertible* into a medium of exchange, but is *not* itself a medium of exchange. Near monies are highly, but not perfectly, liquid financial assets.

11. $$K = \frac{1}{1 - MPC} = \frac{1}{MPS}$$

$\Rightarrow$ If MPC = 0.2

then $$K = \frac{1}{1 - 0.2}$$

$$= \frac{1}{1.25}$$

$\Rightarrow$ If MPS = 0.5

then $$K = \frac{1}{MPS}$$

$$= \frac{1}{0.5} = 2$$

$\Rightarrow$ If MPS = 0.75

then $$K = \frac{1}{0.75} = 1.33$$

$\Rightarrow$ If MPC = 0.4

then $$K = \frac{1}{1 - 0.4}$$

$$= \frac{1}{0.6} = 1.66.$$

12. The Solow-model economy tends to converge over time towards the steady state in which the output growth is constant (and the per capita output level is constant). First note that all variations in output growth are due to variations in the growth rate of capital input:

$$\frac{\dot{Y}(t)}{Y(t)} = \alpha\left(\frac{\dot{K}(t)}{K(t)}\right) + (1 - \alpha)n.$$

Hence, for output growth to be constant, capital growth should also be constant. That is, the growth rates for capital and output must be the same, and the capital–output ratio is constant along with constant growth.

14. **Turnpike Theorems :** A class of propositions in *growth theory* concerned with the closeness of optimal growth paths to balanced growth at the highest rate. The name 'turnpike theorem' was given by R. Dorfman, P. Samuelson and R. Solow in LINEAR PROGRAMMING AND ECONOMIC ANALYSIS (McGraw Hill, 1958).

15. One of Hirschman's best-known and most creative ideas was that of industrial linkages. When one industry expands, it requires inputs from other industries to be able to produce.

These are called backward linkages, that is, they are induced effects on the output of supplying industries. For example, coal mining and iron ore mining constitute backward linkages from a steel mill. On the other hand, when an industry sells and transports its production to other firms and sectors in the economy, these are the forward linkages of the original producer, that is, the induced effects of the output of the first industry in the direction of the final consumer.

The metal fabrication industry and the chemical and paint manufacturing industry which use the output of the steel industry as their inputs would be forward linkages to the steel industry, and these industries might have further forward linkages to, say, the production of household stoves. Railroads or alternative forms of transport would enter the example as both backward and forward linkages to steel production and at each stage of production.

Thus, the production of one firm in one industry has a multiplicity of backward and forward the steel industry, and these industries might have further forward linkages to, say, the production of household stoves. Railroads or alternative forms of transport would enter the example as both backward and forward linkages to steel production and at each stage of production.

Thus, the production of one firm in one industry has a multiplicity of backward and forward linkages with firms in other industries in the domestic economy and, perhaps, abroad as well. In communicating the induced effects from one sector of the economy to another via shortages and excess capacity in Hirschman's unbalanced growth process, the size of potential backward and forward linkages was of paramount importance in evaluating where to locate the initial investment. Development strategies could be built around the maximization of the estimated stimulus of promoted industries in generating domestic backward and forward linkages.

16. **Reserve army of labour :** Reserve army of labour is a concept in Karl Marx's critique of political economy. It refers to the unemployed and under-employed in capitalist society. It is synonymous with 'industrial reserve army' or 'relative surplus population', except that the unemployed can be defined as those actually looking for work and that the relative surplus population also includes people unable to work.

17. Harrod-neutral technical change in the Cobb-Douglas production function is described by the equation:

$$X = AK^{\alpha}((1+\hat{\gamma})^{t}N)^{1-\alpha}$$

In the Cobb-Douglas case, Harrod-neutral technical change is also Hicks-neutral. We can see this since:

$$X = AK^{\alpha}((1+\hat{\gamma})^{t}N)^{1-\alpha}$$

$$= \left((1+\hat{\gamma})^{1-\alpha}\right)^{t}(AK^{\alpha}N^{1-\alpha})$$

This equivalence between Hicks and Harrod neutrality holds only for the Cobb-Douglas family of production functions.

18. In January 1944 a comprehensive document entitled, "A Plan of Economic Development for India" was published, under the signatures of five eminent industrialists and three technocrats.

The industrialists were: J.R.D. Tata; G.D. Birla; Kasturbhai Lalbhai, the textile millowner from Ahmedabad; Sir Purshotamdas Thakurdas from Bombay and Sir Shri Ram from Delhi. The technocrats were all from Tatas—Sir Ardeshir Dalal; A.D. Shroff; Dr John Matthai. The plan came to be known as the Bombay Plan or the Tata-Birla Plan.

Thereafter, in the same year, 'Gandhian Plan' by Mr. Mannaragan, in 1945 the 'People's Plan' by labour leader M.N. Rai and in 1950 the 'Sarvodaya Plan' by Mr. Jai Prakash Narayan were presented.

19. The concept of a special category state was first introduced in 1969 when the 5th Finance Commission sought to provide certain disadvantaged states with preferential treatment in the form of central assistance and tax breaks. Initially three states Assam, Nagaland and Jammu & Kashmir were granted special status but since then eight more have been included (Arunachal Pradesh, Himachal Pradesh, Manipur, Meghalaya, Mizoram, Sikkim, Tripura and Uttarakhand). The rationale for special status is that certain states, because of inherent features, have a low resource base and cannot mobilize resources for development.

Some of the features required for special status are:

(*i*) hilly and difficult terrain;

(*ii*) low population density or sizeable share of tribal population;

(*iii*) strategic location along borders with neighbouring countries;

(*iv*) economic and infrastructural backwardness; and

(*v*) non-viable nature of state finances.

21. Input-output models of different variants, basically belonging to the Leontief group, have come into increasing use in India's five year plans, since the third plan. These models focused on the need for establishing inter-sectorial consistencies in building the production targets, mainly estimated from the demand side.

In the earlier models, supply side was rather neglected in the sense that no sectorial supply constraints were formulated. However, the models were increasingly articulated by making them 'closed', *i.e.,* by endogenising imports and consumption in the final demand vector. Since the sixth plan (Government of India, Planning Commission, 1980, attempt has been made to integrate Harrod-Domar and input-output approaches in a demand-supply framework.

22. Walter Galenson and Harvey Leibenstein suggested the 'marginal per capita reinvestment quotient' criterion. They aimed at maximising the per capita output potential at some future point of time. According to this criterion, the allocation of resources will be optimum when the marginal per capita reinvestment quotient of capital is equalised in its various alternative uses. Marginal per capita investment quotient is determined by the following basic factors:

1. gross productivity per worker;
2. "wage" goods consumed per worker;
3. replacement and repair of capital;
4. increments in output as a result of non-capital using innovations, such as improvements in skills, health, energy, discipline and malleability of the labour force;
5. decline in mortality;
6. decline in fertility; and
7. direction of investment.

The first six factors determine the per capita investment available period after period and the seventh factor concerns its allocation.

24. The capital account of BOP reflects the capital inflows and outflows of the country. The purchases of real assets (physical assets like lands, buildings, and equipment) located abroad and financial securities (*e.g.,* stocks and bonds) issued by foreign governments or foreign companies are called capital transactions. The difference between such purchases made by the residents of one country (say, India) in all other countries, and such purchases by residents of all other countries in India, is called the balance on capital account.

The capital account includes foreign equity investments, loans, and other foreign investments. Foreign equity investments may take the form of either portfolio investments or direct investments. *Portfolio investments* are cross-border transactions associated with changes in ownership of financial assets and liabilities. *Direct investment* occurs when there are cross-border outflows and inflows of equity capital. Such ownership of a foreign operating business gives a measure of control to the investors. An example of direct investment is an Indian firm promoting business in a foreign country.

When a foreign institutional investor buys the equity stock of an Indian company, it is an instance of portfolio investment. Note that portfolio investment involves the buying of foreign financial assets (*e.g.,* shares and bonds) without any change in the control of the concerned company, whereas foreign direct investments may result in the transfer of control of the company.

25. **Teaser rate :** A teaser rate is a low, adjustable introductory interest rate advertised for a loan, credit card, or deposit account in order to attract potential customers to obtain the service. The teaser rates are normally too good to be true for the long term, and are far below the common realistic rate for the service. In a competitive market, many companies will compete with each other for the lower teaser rate.

27. In trade parlance, the term "non-tariff barriers" (NTBs) refers to a wide range of border and behind-the-border measures that may slow or inhibit trade. The UNCTAD Secretariat (UNCTAD, 2005) has produced a classification scheme for NTBs that defines the following categories:

- Government participation in trade and restrictive practices tolerated by governments;
- Customs and administrative entry procedures;
- Technical barriers to trade;
- Sanitary and phyto-sanitary measures;
- Specific limitations (such as quantitative restrictions);
- Charges on imports (other than tariffs, such as surcharges or port taxes).

Many non-tariff barriers, such as regulations relating to public health and safety, are recognized by the trade-policy community as essential. Other barriers, such as long delays in clearing customs because of over-bureaucratic customs and administrative-entry procedures, are regarded as generally worth streamlining.

28. Trade-indifference curves are used extensively in the geometric analysis of gains from trade, in considerations of optimal tariff under monopoly power in trade and in related discussions.

29. BASEL III which is formally known as the '3rd BASEL Accord' – was released in December, 2010 after being ratified in November 2010 by G20 summit in Seoul – with a view to upgrade the existing norms, *i.e.,* that of Basel II.

BASEL III is the result of the financial crisis of 2007-2008, which made the BCBS feel that a more stringent supervisory guidelines were required to prevent such mishaps from happening in the future.

Its aim, among other things, is to strengthen the banking sector to be able to withstand such severe financial crisis without crumbling. According to BCBS "Basel III is a comprehensive set of reform measures, developed by the Basel Committee on Banking Supervision, to strengthen the regulation, supervision and risk management of the banking sector".

30. Portfolio flows are more volatile than direct investment flows and are of short-term nature. They can cause uneven expansion and contraction in domestic liquidity and thus have a greater impact upon stock markets and expansion in money supply and domestic credit. Direct investment flows on the other hand are long-term nature and for that reason less volatile. Being visibly embedded in investment in plant and equipment, foreign direct investment is less susceptible to sudden withdrawals out of the country and leads to productive uses of capital and consequent economic growth.

32. Prime Minister Narendra Modi on September 25, 2014 launched the NDA Government's 'Make in India' campaign for attracting industrialists to make India a global manufacturing hub, to help in creating additional job opportunities and providing a boost to economic growth in the country. The basic philosophy behind this campaign is to establish India a manufacturing hub for domestic and foreign companies. Prime Minister promised to create and ensure 'business-friendly environment' for making this campaign. Besides, Prime Minister assured that the investor facilitation cell will provide assistance to the foreign investors from the time of their arrival in the country to the time of their departure, with focus on green and advanced manufacturing and helping these companies to become an important part of the global value chain.

The strategical components behind the 'Make in India' campaign are—

- Stress on skill development
- Develop world level infrastructural facilities.
- Making India manufacturing hub for domestic as well as foreign companies.
- Reducing import dependence and promoting exports.
- Creating more employment opportunities for the youth in the country.
- Addition in individual's income and purchasing power in the hands of people.

33. The current crisis in agriculture is in the form of virtual stagnation in productivity, the shrinking area under cultivation raising concern about food security, and the adverse impact of the earlier agricultural strategy that had given rise to an urgent need of a follow-up of the Green Revolution, similar to the one of the mid-60s, which led to major break-throughs in wheat and rice production. This would be known as India's 'Second Green Revolution'. It would chase the twin goal of food security and nutritional diet. Without the second revolution, supply side to growing demand for food will be weak, leading to disturbing price hikes. To achieve the objectives of food security and nutritional diet for its increasing population, a growth rate of 5-6 per cent in the agricultural sector has to be maintained over 15 years or so in the Second Green Revolution. It is also suggested that if the gains of First Green Revolution are to be strengthened, then second Green Revolution is to be initiated.

34. Small savings schemes are designed to provide safe and attractive investment options with fixed returns to people who want to stay away from the uncertainties of the capital markets. These schemes are operated through the large number of post offices and public sector banks throughout the country and have been a great mode of savings for lot of people.

The tax savings and investment instruments available under the small savings scheme are:

- Public Provident Fund National Savings Certificate
- Kisan Vikas Patra (discontinued from December 2011)
- National Savings Scheme, 1992/Indira Vikas Patra (now discontinued)
- Relief Bonds
- Post Office Monthly Income Scheme
- Post Office Time Deposits
- Sukanya Samridhi Accounts Yojana.

36. Demographic Transition: The theory of demographic transition consists of three stages of population growth, namely:

(*a*) The high birth rate and the high death rate;

(*b*) The high birth rate and the low death rate; and

(*c*) The low birth rate and the low death rate.

The first and third stages do not face the problem of population, the birth and death rates both being either high or low. The resultant increase in population is a balanced one. It is due to the second stage, where an imbalance is caused in the population growth due to a high birth rate and a low death rate. Such an imbalance results in an explosive growth of population.

37. Tax incidence indicates who actually bears the burden of the tax. One way to evaluate tax incidence is by measuring the tax as a percentage of income. Under proportional taxation, taxpayers at all income levels pay the same percentage of their income toward that tax. A proportional income tax is also called a *flat tax,* because the tax as a percentage of income remains constant, or flat, as income increases.

39. Specific Tax Incidence : Public expenditure remaining constant, changes or modifications may be introduced in a tax. For example, income tax rates may be reduced or increased. The resulting change in distribution is called specific tax incidence.

For example, if income tax rates are reduced, this will increase the disposable income of the people. Assuming full employment, this will generate inflationary pressures which will transfer resources from the poor to the rich. Likewise if income tax rates are increased, deflationary impact will be generated and resources will be transferred from the rich to the poor.

41. Because of the externality, the cost to *society* of producing aluminum is larger than the cost to the aluminum producers. For each unit of aluminum produced, the *social cost* includes the private costs of the aluminum producers plus the costs to those bystanders affected adversely by the pollution.

Figure shows the social cost of producing aluminum. The social-cost curve is above the supply curve because it takes into account the external costs imposed on society by aluminum producers. The difference between these two curves reflects the cost of the pollution emitted.

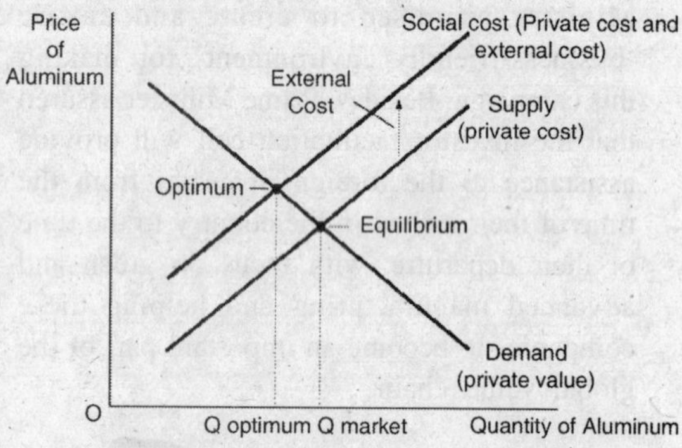

Fig. : *Negative Externalities*

42. Performance Budgeting : The system of performance budgeting (earlier called as functional budgeting of activity budgeting) originated in the USA. The term 'performance budget' was coined by the First Hoover Commission (1949). This commission recommended the adoption of performance budgeting in the USA to make effective management approach to budgeting. Accordingly, it was introduced in 1950 by President Truman.

Unlike the line-item budgeting, the performance budgeting emphasises on the purpose of expenditure rather than the expenditure itself. It presents budget in terms of functions, programmes, activities and projects.

It establishes a correlation between the physical (performance or output) and financial (input) aspects of each programme and activity.

Hence, it necessitates a functional classification of the budget.

In India, the adoption of performance budget was recommended first by the Estimates Committee of Parliament in 1956. In 1964, the Government invited Frank W. Krause, an American expert, to study the suitability and feasibility of this system of budgeting in India. Finally the Central Government introduced performance budgeting in 1968 on the recommendation of the Administrative Reforms Commission. According to this commission, the advantages (benefits/ objectives) of the performance budgeting are as follows:

(*i*) It presents more clearly, the purposes and objectives for which the funds are sought by the executive from the Parliament

(*ii*) It brings out the programmes and accomplishments in financial and physical terms.

(*iii*) It facilitates a better understanding and better review of the budget by the Parliament.

(*iv*) It improves the formulation of the budget.

(*v*) It facilitates the process of decision-making at all levels of government.

(*vi*) It increases the accountability of the management.

(*vii*) It provides an extra tool of management control of financial operations.

(*viii*) It renders performance audit more purposeful and effective.

43. Mrs. Ursula Hicks Concept of Incidence

In 1940, Mrs. Ursula Hicks used the following two concepts of incidence of taxes: (1) Formal Incidence (2) Effective Incidence.

1. Formal Incidence : According to Mrs. Hicks formal incidence of a tax means the money burden of a tax or its money incidence. Formal incidence refers to the proportion of tax payer's income that has been paid over to the government. This amount is used by the government to provide collective goods, without direct benefits to the actual tax payers. Conceptually, the formal incidence refers to the statistical measurement of the mode of distribution of actual tax burden between different income groups during a financial year. The formal incidence of a tax is equal to the amount of that tax collected by the government and the formal incidence of the tax system as a whole is equal to the total tax revenue of the authorities.

2. Effective Incidence : Effective Incidence refers to the effects of taxation on the economy. It will include all the advantages and disadvantages which an economy derives from a tax system. It may be noted that effective incidence of taxation cannot be measured statistically.

45. In the Budget 1987-88 the Government of India adopted a new classification under which public expenditure was classified into: Plan expenditure and Non-Plan expenditure. Plan expenditure includes expenditure on; (*a*) Central plans, such as development of agriculture, rural development, irrigation and flood control, energy, industry and minerals, transport, communications, science and technology and environment, social services and others, and (*b*) Central Assistance for the Plans of the States and Union Territories.

Non-Plan expenditure comprises of:

(*i*) Expenditure on Revenue Account, and

(*ii*) Expenditure on Capital Account.

47. Sampling distribution constitutes the theoretical basis of statistical inference and is of considerable importance in business decision making. Sampling distribution of a statistic is the frequency distribution which is formed with various values of a statistic computed from different samples of the same size drawn from the same population.

Suppose we draw all possible samples of size n from the population (N) with or without replacement. For each possible sample drawn from the population, we compute a statistic such as mean, median, standard deviation, variance, etc. The set of all possible values of a statistic is then classified and grouped into a frequency distribution (or probability distribution).

The distribution so obtained is called the sampling distribution of a statistic. We could have various sampling distribution depending upon the nature of the statistic we have computed.

If, for instance, the particular statistic computed is the sample mean, the distribution is called sampling distribution of mean. If, we compute variance of each sample, then it is called the sampling distribution of variance. Similarly, we could have sampling distributions of proportion, median, standard deviation, etc.

Some Sampling Distributions: Sampling distributions include the sampling distribution of mean, sampling distribution of proportions, t-distribution, F-distribution, and X^2-distribution.

48. Properties of the Coefficient of Correlation

The following are the important properties of the correlation coefficient (r):

1. **Limits of Coefficient of Correlation:** Karl Pearson's coefficient of correlation lies between –1 and +1.

   Symbolically:

   $$-1 \leq r \leq +1$$

   This implies r can never exceed +1 and never becomes less than –1. It always lies between –1 and +1.

2. **Change of Origin and Scale :** Shifting the origin or scale does not affect in any way the value of correlation coefficient. Coefficient of correlation is independent of the change of origin and scale. If the scale of a series is changed or the origin is shifted, then correlation coefficient remains unchanged.

3. **Geometric Mean of Regression Coefficients :** Correlation coefficient is the geometric mean of the regression coefficients *byx* and *bxy*.

   Symbolically:

   $$r = \sqrt{bxy.byx}$$

4. If X and Y are independent variables, then coefficient of correlation is zero but the converse is not necessarily true.

5. **Pure Number :** 'r' is a pure number and is independent of the units of measurements. This implies that even if the two variables are expressed in two different units of measurements *viz.;* rainfall in inches, and yields of crops in quintals, the value of correlation coefficient comes out with a pure number. Thus, it does not require that the units of both the variables should be the same.

6. **Symmetric :** The coefficient of correlation between the two variables x and y is symmetric *i.e.*, $r_{xy} = r_{yx}$. It means that either we compute the value of correlation coefficient between x and y or between y and x, the coefficient of correlation remains the same.

49. Independence : To show that A and B are independent it suffices to prove just one of the following:

$$P(A \mid B) = P(A),$$

$$P(B \mid A) = P(B),$$

$$P(A \cap B) = P(A)\, P(B),$$

Where A may be replaced by A^c and B replaced by B^c, or both. If one of these statements holds, all of them are true. If two events are not independent, they are called dependent.

PAPER-III

Note: *This paper contains* ***seventy five (75)*** *objective type questions of* ***two (2)*** *marks each.* ***All*** *questions are compulsory.*

1. Full demographic dividend will be realised when government promotes:
A. more social security
B. more intensive growth
C. more skill development
D. more capital market

2. Which one of the following is true for the General Fertility Rate?
A. It is an actual measure of fertility
B. It is a potential measure of fertility
C. It is an actual measure of female population composition
D. It is based on hypothetical age specific birth rate profile

3. Which among the following curves is used to depict the long run behaviour of population growth?
A. Normal Curve
B. Logistic Curve
C. Exponential Curve
D. Ogive

4. Among the socio-economic factors responsible for high birth rate in India, we may include:
I. Large scale poverty
II. High mortality rate of children of poor parents
III. Prevalence of under-age marriage
IV. Adverse sex-ratio
A. I and II B. I, II and IV
C. I, III and IV D. I, II and III

5. Match the items in List-I with List-II and give the correct answer from the codes given below:

List-I (Event)	List-II (Date)
(*a*) World Environment Day	(*i*) 11th July
(*b*) World Wildlife Day	(*ii*) 5th June
(*c*) World Water Day	(*iii*) 3rd March
(*d*) World Population Day	(*iv*) 22nd March

Select the correct answer from the codes given below:

Codes:

	(*a*)	(*b*)	(*c*)	(*d*)
A.	(*i*)	(*ii*)	(*iii*)	(*iv*)
B.	(*iii*)	(*i*)	(*iv*)	(*ii*)
C.	(*iv*)	(*iii*)	(*ii*)	(*i*)
D.	(*ii*)	(*iii*)	(*iv*)	(*i*)

6. The coase theorem suggests that private negotiation will lead to the correction of market failure when:
I. Only a few people are involved.
II. Property rights are clearly recognised.
III. Negotiation costs are low.
IV. People are having asymmetric information.
Select the correct answer from the codes given below:

Codes:
A. I, II and III must hold true
B. I and IV must hold true
C. I, II and IV must hold true
D. IV and III must hold true

7. Infrastructure cess is a levy/tax on:
A. Builders B. Railways
C. Motor vehicles D. Public Transport

8. SLR can be defined as:

A. $SLR = \frac{ER + I - CB}{L}$

B. $SLR = \frac{ER - IS + CAB}{L}$

C. $SLR = \frac{ER + IS + CAB}{L}$

D. $SLR = \frac{L + CB + ER}{IS}$

Where ER = Excess Reserve; 1S = Investment in Government and other approved Securities, CAB = Current Account Balances, L = Total demand & Time deposits. CB = Current Balances, I = Investment, SLR = Statutory Liquidity Ratio

9. Which among the following measures would result in an increase in the money supply in the economy?

I. Purchase of Government Securities from the Public by the Central Bank.

II. Deposit of currency in Commercial Banks by the Public.

III. Borrowings by the Government from the Central Bank.

IV. Sale of Government securities to the public by the Central Government.

Select the correct answer from the codes below:

Codes:

A. I only B. II and IV
C. I and III D. II, III and IV

10. The banks which are implementing the Micro Finance Programme linked with Self Help Groups (SHGs) are:

A. Commercial Banks and Co-operative Banks, only
B. Regional Rural Banks and Commercial Banks, only
C. Co-operative Banks and Regional Rural Banks, only
D. Commercial Banks, Regional Rural Banks and Co-operative Banks

11. Which of the following is generally called as Aggregate monetary measure of money supply?

A. M_4 B. M_1
C. M_2 D. M_3

12. The traders reduce the risk of loss in currency fluctuations through which of the following?

A. Speculations
B. Arbitrage
C. Hedging
D. None of the above

13. Among the reasons responsible for the high inflation rate in India in 2015, which of the following is/are true?

I. Rise in prices of petroleum products.

II. Rise in food prices.

III. Rise in domestic consumption demand.

IV. Rise in Indian Exports during the year 2015-16.

Select the correct answer from the codes given below:

Codes:

A. I, II and IV B. I, II and III
C. III and IV D. II and III

14. Originally, the maximum and minimum limits of the Statutory Liquidity ratio prescribed in India was:

A. 40 per cent and 20 per cent
B. 40 per cent and 25 per cent
C. 30 per cent and 25 per cent
D. 30 per cent and 20 per cent

15. Which among the following are the recommendations of the Urjit Patel Committee report of on monetary policy?

I. Curtailment of the fiscal deficit.

II. Inflation anchor at four per cent.

III. Providing adequate liquidity in the money and capital market.

IV. Pegging the exchange value of Indian Currency.

Select the answer from the code below:

Codes:

A. I, II and III B. II and IV
C. III and IV D. I, II and IV

16. **Assertion (A):** Monetarists disagreed with the Phillips curve analysis.

Reason (R): There are no unique correspondence of % inflation rate with % unemployment rate.

Answer from the codes below:

Codes:

A. Both (A) and (R) are true and (R) is the correct explanation of (A)
B. Both (A) and (R) are true and (R) is not the correct explanation of (A)
C. (A) is true and (R) is false
D. (A) is false and (R) is true

17. Who among the following economists considered the rate of interest to influence the transaction demand for money?

A. P. Samuelson
B. W.J. Baumol
C. Keynes
D. I. Fisher

18. Consider the following statements about rising NPAs of banks in India:

I. Rising NPAs are due to slow down in the world economy.

II. Private Sector banks have lower NPAs in comparison Public Sector Banks.

III. Rising NPAs are due to droughts in India.

Which of the statements given above is/are correct?

Codes:

A. Only I B. I and III

C. I and II D. I, II and III

19. Among other things, which one of the following was the purpose for which Deepak Parekh Committee was constituted?

A. To study the socio-economic conditions of minority communities

B. To suggest the measures for financing the development of infrastructure

C. To frame the policies on genetically modified seeds

D. To suggest measures to reduce the fiscal deficit in the Union Budget

20. Consider the following statements.

I. Sick Company is defined as one whose accumulated losses in any financial year are equal to or more than 50% of its average net worth during previous four financial years.

II. The Government set-up Board of Industrial and Financial Reconstruction in 1987.

Which of the statement given above is/are correct? Select the answer from the codes given below:

Codes:

A. Only I

B. Only II

C. Both I and II

D. Neither I nor II

21. Consider the following taxes:

I. Corporation tax

II. Income tax

III. Service tax

IV. Union Excise Duties

Which of the following correctly describes their contribution, in descending order of importance, to the Central Government's Gross Tax Revenue?

A. I, II, IV, III B. II, I, III, IV

C. III, II, I, IV D. IV, I, II, III

22. Which Finance Commission has used forest cover as a criterion for horizontal distribution of resources in India?

A. 10th Finance Commission

B. 12th Finance Commission

C. 13th Finance Commission

D. 14th Finance Commission

23. Consider the following:

Assertion (A) : According to Peacock-Wiseman hypothesis, public expenditure increases overtime in a step by step manner.

Reason (R) : This hypothesis is based on the displacement effect, concentration effect and inspection effect.

Select the correct answer from the codes given below:

Codes:

A. (A) is true, but (R) is false

B. (A) is false, but (R) is true

C. Both (A) and (R) are true, but (R) is not the correct explanation of (A)

D. Both (A) and (R) are true and (R) is the correct explanation of (A)

24. In the Indian context, the studies of poverty were made by:

I. Dandekar and Rath

II. P.K. Bardhan

III. B.S. Minhas

IV. I.J. Ahluwalia

Select the correct answer from the codes given below:

Codes:

A. I and II B. II and III

C. I, II and III D. I, II, III and IV

25. Who among of the following is associated with the theory of optimal taxation?

A. H. Dalton B. R.A. Musgrave

C. U.K. Hicks D. G. Mankiw

26. To reach an economically efficient output level, the size of an excise tax imposed on a firm generating negative externality should be:

A. the firm's marginal cost
B. the social marginal cost
C. the difference between the social marginal cost and the firm's marginal cost
D. the sum of the social marginal cost and the firm's marginal cost

27. Which among the following is the reason for Convergence exhibited by the Solow growth model?

A. Static capital-labour ratio
B. Declining marginal productivity of capital
C. Neutral technical progress
D. Constant rate of growth of population

28. Who among the following economists was not concerned with the problem of Surplus Labour?

A. W.A. Lewis
B. Gustav Renis and Fei
C. R. Nurkse
D. J.S. Mill

29. Match the following lists:

List-I	**List-II**
(*a*) Aggregate demand	(*i*) –a + by
(*b*) Consumption function	(*ii*) C + I
(*c*) Aggregate supply	(*iii*) a + by
(*d*) Saving function	(*iv*) C + S

Select the correct answer from the codes given below:

Codes:

	(*a*)	(*b*)	(*c*)	(*d*)
A.	(*ii*)	(*i*)	(*iii*)	(*iv*)
B.	(*ii*)	(*iv*)	(*iii*)	(*i*)
C.	(*ii*)	(*iv*)	(*i*)	(*iii*)
D.	(*ii*)	(*iii*)	(*iv*)	(*i*)

30. Who is the author of the book, 'Capital in the Twenty First Century'?

A. Thomas Piketty
B. Joseph Stiglitz
C. A.K. Sen
D. Jagdish Bhagwati

31. Match the following lists:

List-I (Economic Idea)	**List-II (Economist)**
(*a*) Life Cycle Hypothesis	(*i*) Karl Marx
(*b*) Tableau Economique	(*ii*) Alfred Marshall
(*c*) Cash Balance Approach	(*iii*) Francois Quesnay
(*d*) Organic Composition of Capital	(*iv*) F. Modigliani

Select the correct answer from the codes given below:

Codes:

	(*a*)	(*b*)	(*c*)	(*d*)
A.	(*i*)	(*ii*)	(*iii*)	(*iv*)
B.	(*iv*)	(*iii*)	(*ii*)	(*i*)
C.	(*iv*)	(*iii*)	(*i*)	(*ii*)
D.	(*ii*)	(*iv*)	(*i*)	(*iii*)

32. In the adjoining standard diagram to explain Hicks' trade cycle theory; which of the following are true, when the actual value of mpc and accelerator fall in the region C?

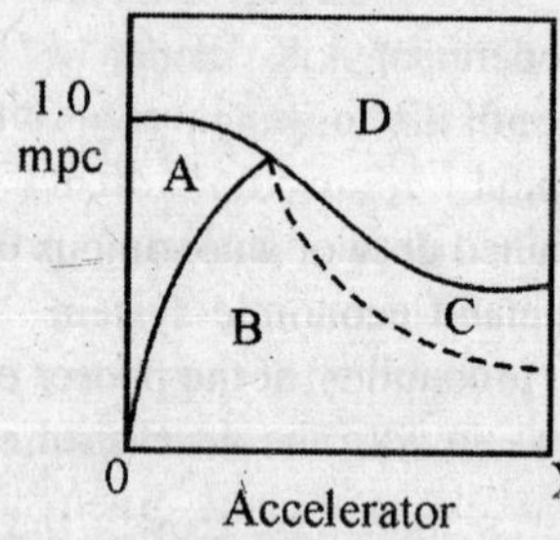

A. There will be oscillations (Cyclical fluctuations)
B. There will be explosive upward movement
C. There will be Steady growth
D. Both (B) and (C) are possible

33. For the Harrod's model of growth, which among the following production functions best matches with the assumptions of the model?

A. Leontief production function
B. Homogeneous production function
C. C.E.S. production function
D. Well-behaved production function

34. In the following Cobb-Douglas production function $Q = AL^{\alpha} K^{\beta}$, if $\alpha + \beta > 1$, then the share of labour would be:

A. α

B. $\frac{\beta}{\alpha+\beta}$

C. $\frac{\alpha}{\alpha+\beta}$

D. $\frac{\alpha.\beta}{\alpha+\beta}$

35. New Keynesian economics challenges which among the following schools of thought regarding the full adaptability of a policy change on the part of economic agents?

A. New classical economics
B. Neo Keynesians
C. Monetarists
D. Both (A) and (B) above

36. Who among the following developed the 'Wage-goods model' of planning?

A. A.K. Sen
B. P.C. Mahalanobis
C. R. Nurkse
D. C.N. Vakil and P.R. Brahmanand

37. A key property of A.K. model is:

A. absence of diminishing returns with respect to capital
B. a sustained dose of autonomous investment
C. a command economic system
D. a high probability of the poorer economies to catch up with the developed economies

38. In Pasinetti's model of growth the interplay among which variables is crucial?

A. Profit rate, Economic growth, Savings
B. Profit rate, Distribution of income and economic growth
C. Profit rate, autonomous investment and economic growth
D. Savings, Investment and technology

39. Consider the following statements in relation to Karl Marx's theory of profit rate:

I. Profit rate depends directly on the value of organic composition of capital.
II. Profit rate depends directly on the value of rate of exploitation.

Which of the above statements are correct? Answer from the codes below:

Codes:

A. Both I and II are true
B. Neither I nor II are true
C. Only I is correct
D. Only II is correct

40. Which among the following is not correctly matched?

	Economist		**Theme**
A.	Adam Smith	–	Extent of Market
B.	J.B. Say	–	Balance in Supply and Demand
C.	T.R. Malthus	–	State of over production
D.	D. Ricardo	–	Modernization of Agriculture

41. Which of the following statements are true for the Triangle model?

I. It is a model developed by New Keynesian economists.
II. It includes built-in inflation in the analysis.

Which of the above statement(s) is/are true? Answer from the codes below:

Codes:

A. I and II
B. None
C. Only I
D. Only II

42. With reference to Asian Development Bank, consider the following statements:

I. United States has the largest proportion of shares in the voting system.
II. China and India have the same percentage of shares for the voting system.

Which of the statement(s) given above is/are correct?

Codes:

A. Only I
B. Only II
C. Both I and II
D. Neither I nor II

43. Which among the following will constitute Foreign Direct Investment (FDI)?

A. Buying a company in the target country
B. Expanding operations of an existing business in that country
C. Investing in the shares and stocks of companies in the capital market
D. Both (A) and (B)

44. Which of the areas given below is/are mainly funded by the International Development Agency in the developing countries?

I. Infrastructure
II. Education
III. Environment friendly projects
IV. Health care

Select the correct answer using the codes given below:

Codes:

A. I, II and IV
B. I, II and III
C. I, III and IV
D. All of the above

45. When two or more countries enter into an agreement to eliminate import quota and tariffs and promote trade among themselves, such a group of countries are said to form a:

A. Free Trade Area
B. Custom Union
C. A Common Market
D. Both B and C

46. Which among the following is/are true for Real Effective Exchange Rate of the currency of a country?

A. It is weighted average of the value of traded currencies
B. It is adjusted for inflation rate of prices
C. It is not adjusted for inflation of prices
D. Both (A) and (B) are true

47. During the episode of sustained fall in crude oil prices during the year 2015, which among the following best describes the pricing strategy of the OPEC countries?

A. Transfer pricing
B. Predatory pricing
C. Defensive pricing
D. Profit maximising prices

48. Which of the following statement(s) is/are true for the gravity model to explain trade?

I. It is used in the bilateral context
II. It was developed by Jan Tinbergen in 1962.
III. It takes into account the distance among the trading nations.

Select the correct answer from the code below:

Codes:

A. II and III are true
B. Only I and III are true
C. Only II is true
D. All the three above are true

49. If the offer curves of the trading countries have constant slope, the terms of trade among them will be:

A. constant
B. decreasing
C. increasing
D. indeterminate

50. In the context of the Indian economy, which of the following options correctly describe the composition of the foreign exchange resources?

A. Foreign currency + loans from the World Bank + SDRs + Gold holdings of R.B.I.
B. Foreign Currency Assets + Gold holdings of R.B.I. + F.D.I.
C. SDRs + Gold holdings of the R.B.I. + Foreign Currency Assets
D. Remittances of NRIs + Exports earnings in a year + loans from the IMF

51. Which among the following are true for excess demand function for an individual?

A. Homogenous of degree zero in all prices
B. These obey Walra's law
C. Both (A) and (B) are true
D. Neither (A) nor (B) are true

52. Which of the following measures the dgree of monopoly power? Here symbols have their usual meaning.

A. $\frac{AR - MR}{AR}$ B. $\frac{AR}{AR - MR}$

C. $\frac{MR}{AR - MR}$ D. $\frac{AR - MR}{MR}$

53. A firm will be of optimum size when:

A. Marginal cost is at a minimum
B. Average cost is at a minimum
C. Marginal cost is equal to marginal revenue
D. The firm maximises its output

54. The time preference theory of interest was developed by:
A. Wicksell B. Böhm-Bawerk
C. Irving Fisher D. J.M. Keynes

55. Which of the following statements is/are true for Arrow-Debreu model of general equilibrium?
A. Goods are identified where they are to be delivered
B. Goods are identified when they are to be delivered
C. Both (A) and (B)
D. None of these

56. If Sales tax on a commodity is raised, but the revenue earned through its sale decreases sharply, which one of the following statements about the nature of this commodity would be correct?
A. Price elasticity of demand for it is unity
B. It must be an essential goods
C. Price elasticity of demand for it is high
D. Price elasticity of demand for it is low

57. The below diagrams show the risk aversion of two individuals with the help of indifference curves. Choose the correct answer from the following by studying the diagrams.

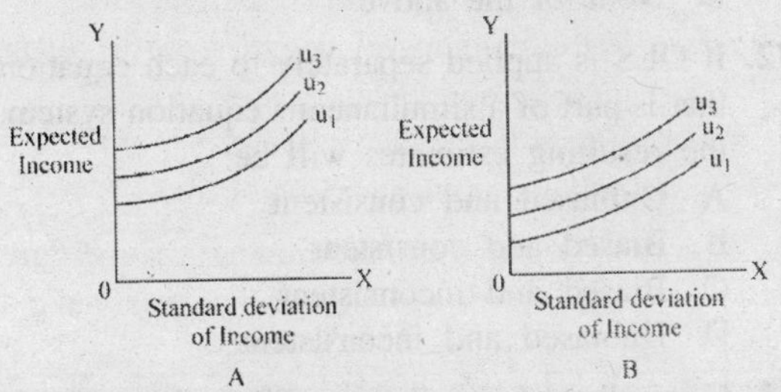

A. A is highly risk averse
B. B is highly risk averse
C. A's and B's risk aversion is identical
D. Degree of risk aversion is indeterminate

58. One of the essential conditions of monopolistic competition is:
A. Homogeneous product
B. Product differentiation
C. Price discrimination
D. Many buyers but one seller

59. Logical extension of Cournot model is:
A. Bertrand model B. Stackelberg model
C. Sweezy model D. None of the above.

60. Minimum support prices for Agricultural Commodities are fixed after taking into account the recommendations of which of the following bodies?
A. Ministry of Agriculture
B. Ministry of Food Processing
C. NITI Aayog
D. Commission for Agricultural Costs & Prices (CACP)

61. Diversification of agriculture implies:
A. Increase in the cropping intensity
B. Shifting labour from agriculture to other areas
C. Promoting cottage and village industries
D. Changing the cropping pattern in favour of horticulture and floriculture crops

62. Which one of the following schemes is not included in the Rashtriya Krishi Vikas Yojna (RKVY)?
A. National Mission for Protein Supplements
B. Saffron Mission
C. Accelerated Fodder Development Programme
D. All of the above

63. **Assertion (A) :** Agricultural Productivity is very low in India.
Reason (R) : Rate of growth of population is high in India.
Select the correct answer from the codes given below:
Codes:
A. Both (A) and (R) are true and (R) is the correct explanation of (A).
B. Both (A) and (R) are true, but (R) is not correct explanation of (A).
C. (A) is true, but (R) is false.
D. (A) is false, but (R) is true.

64. The Agricultural Census is done at which one of the following intervals?
A. Every year B. Once in 3 years
C. Once in 5 years D. Once in 10 years

65. The share of food expenditure in total expenditure for Urban consumer and Rural consumer in India was 56% and 64% respectively in (1987-88) and which changed to 41% and 54% in (2009-10). This is appropriately explained by which of the following?

A. Decline in food production
B. Decline in purchasing power of consumers
C. Operation of Engel's Law
D. Operation of law of diminishing marginal utility

66. For demand function $P = 15 - 2X - X^2$, what is consumer's surplus at X = 2?

A. 6 B. 28/3
C. 7/4 D. 11/3

67. Given the CES production function as:

$$y = \left[a_1 x_1^{\rho} + a_2 x_2^{\rho}\right]^{\frac{1}{\rho}}$$

the elasticity of substitution between factors is:

A. 1 B. ρ
C. $\frac{1}{\rho}$ D. $\frac{1}{1-\rho}$

68. For the diagram below, which of the following is a correct description in terms of derivatives:

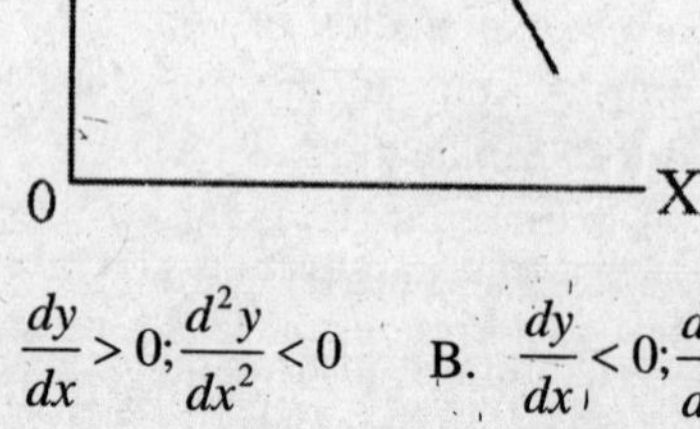

A. $\frac{dy}{dx} > 0; \frac{d^2y}{dx^2} < 0$ B. $\frac{dy}{dx} < 0; \frac{d^2y}{dx^2} < 0$
C. $\frac{dy}{dx} > 0; \frac{d^2y}{dx^2} > 0$ D. $\frac{dy}{dx} < 0; \frac{d^2y}{dx^2} > 0$

69. Which of the following is true for an optimum solution of a linear programming problem?

A. Number of non-zero valued slack variables is equal to the number of constraints
B. Number of non-zero valued variables (including slack) is exactly equal to the number of constraints
C. Number of non-zero valued slack variables is equal to the number of binding constraints
D. Number of non-zero valued variables is equal to the number of non-binding constraints

70. If the targets for an economy are fixed in terms of final demand vector F, then the compatible levels of output vector X, in terms of input-output analysis will be determined according to which of the following?

A. A + F = X B. AX – F = X
C. $(I - A)^{-1} F = X$ D. (1 – A) F = X

71. In a two-variable regression, Y is dependent variable and X is independent variable. The correlation coefficient between Y and X is 0.8. For this, which of the following is correct?

A. 8% variations in Y are explained by X
B. 64% variations in Y are explained by X
C. 0.8% variations in Y are explained by X
D. None of the above

72. If OLS is applied separately to each equation that is part of a simultaneous equation system, the resulting estimates will be:

A. Unbiased and consistent
B. Biased and consistent
C. Biased and inconsistent
D. Unbiased and inconsistent

73. Generalized Least Squares Method is suitable for estimation of parameters in a General Linear Model for dealing with problem of:

(*i*) Measurement Errors
(*ii*) Autocorrelated Disturbances
(*iii*) Multi collinearity
(*iv*) Heteroscelasticity

Select the correct answer from codes given below:

Codes:

A. (*i*), (*ii*), (*iii*), (*iv*) B. (*i*), (*iii*), (*iv*)
C. (*ii*), (*iv*) D. (*i*), (*iii*)

74. Match the following and select the correct answer from codes given below:

List-I	List-II
(*a*) Goldfield–Quandt Test	(*i*) Errors in variables
(*b*) Durbin-Watson Test	(*ii*) Heteroscelasticity
(*c*) Farrar-Glauber Test	(*iii*) Autocorrelation
(*d*) Wald-Bartlett Method	(*iv*) Multicollinearity

Codes:

	(*a*)	(*b*)	(*c*)	(*d*)
A.	(*iv*)	(*ii*)	(*iii*)	(*i*)
B.	(*iii*)	(*i*)	(*ii*)	(*iv*)
C.	(*i*)	(*iii*)	(*iv*)	(*ii*)
D.	(*ii*)	(*iii*)	(*iv*)	(*i*)

75. Consider the following system of equations, using standard notations:

$$Y_1 = \alpha_0 + \alpha_1 Y_2 + \alpha_3 Y_3 + \alpha_4 X_1 + \alpha_5 X_2 + u_1$$
$$Y_2 = \beta_0 + \beta_1 Y_3 + \beta_2 Y_1 + \beta_3 X_2 + u_2$$
$$Y_3 = \gamma_0 + \gamma_1 X_1 + \gamma_2 X_2 + \gamma_3 X_3 + u_3$$

According to order condition, the second equation is:

A. Unidentified
B. Just identified
C. Over-identified
D. Not possible to infer identification due to incomplete information

ANSWERS

1	2	3	4	5	6	7	8	9	10
C	B	B	D	D	A	C	C	C	D
11	**12**	**13**	**14**	**15**	**16**	**17**	**18**	**19**	**20**
D	C	D	B	A	A	B	C	B	C
21	**22**	**23**	**24**	**25**	**26**	**27**	**28**	**29**	**30**
A	D	D	C	D	C	B	D	D	A
31	**32**	**33**	**34**	**35**	**36**	**37**	**38**	**39**	**40**
B	A	A	A	A	D	A	B	D	D
41	**42**	**43**	**44**	**45**	**46**	**47**	**48**	**49**	**50**
A	D	D	A	A	D	C	D	D	C
51	**52**	**53**	**54**	**55**	**56**	**57**	**58**	**59**	**60**
C	A	B	C	C	C	A	B	B	D
61	**62**	**63**	**64**	**65**	**66**	**67**	**68**	**69**	**70**
D	D	B	C	C	B	D	B	B	C
71	**72**	**73**	**74**	**75**					
B	C	C	D	B					

EXPLANATORY ANSWERS

1. The concept of demographic dividend basically connotes the gains in economic growth as a result of the increase in the share of working-age people in the population in relation to the children and the aged, who are considered a part of the non-working population. Such a situation emerges when a country experiences a rapid reduction in fertility leading to a decline in the child population. Put simply, a demographic dividend occurs when a falling birth rate changes the age distribution, so that the needs of the youngest age groups are met through employment and resources that are released for investment in economic development and family welfare. There has been a decline in fertility, indicating that the country is experiencing a demographic dividend.

The demographic dividend relates to India having the world's youngest workforce. Thus, the demographic dividend in India needs to be exploited not only to expand the production possibility frontier, but also to meet the skilled manpower requirements of India and world.

2. General fertility rate is the number of births per 1000 women of reproductive ages. The number of women of childbearing age is taken as a base for calculating the birth rate, instead of the total population.

This method is an improvement over CBR, as it takes into account only the population in the reproductive age group, *i.e.,* only the females in the age group 15-49, since it is only these females who can bear children. Bogue (1969) has defined general fertility rate as the 'number of births in a year per 1000 women of child bearing age'. Barclay states, General Fertility Rate or General Fertility Ratio is the ratio of total yearly registered births to the population of women of childbearing age.

3. The first major scientific challenge to Malthusian doctrine as a pattern of population growth appeared in the 1830's in the work of Pierre Verhulst. In 1839 Verhulst proposed that population normally grow in a much more orderly fashion than that proposed by Malthus, describing in their growth a curve of S-shaped proportion. This became known as the Logistic Theory of population growth. The logistic theory asserted that population have a slow initial growth rate, which increases exponentially until it reaches a maximum, and then becomes progressively less as the population approaches an upper limit of its growth. The upper limit is approached gradually and in an orderly, predictable manner. The resulting curve is the familiar S-shaped of population growth.

It should be noted that the logistic curve and the Malthusian or irrupting curve do not differ in the early stages of population growth—both show a slow start followed by a period of exponential or geometric growth but they do differ fundamentally in the upper or controlling stages of growth. The Malthusian curve is characterized by an erratic, often catastrophic, pattern of limiting growth, whereas the logistic curve characterized by a smooth, orderly and gradual pattern.

6. The Coase Theorem : Coase's argument that private solutions to the problem of externalities are possible is summed up in the Coase theorem: If transactions costs are low, private bargaining will result in an efficient solution to the problem of externalities. In addition to low transactions costs, private solutions to the problem of externalities will occur only if all parties to the agreement have full information about the costs and benefits associated with the externality, and all parties must be willing to accept a reasonable agreement. For example, if those suffering from the effects of pollution do not have information on the costs of reducing pollution, it is unlikely the parties can reach an agreement. Unreasonable demands can also hinder an agreement.

8. Statutory Liquidity Ratio (SLR): The statutory liquidity ratio (SLR) is one of the non-traditional methods of monetary control used by the RBI in addition to the cash reserve ratio. The objective of SLR is to allocate the total bank credit between the government and the business sector. The SLR is a double-edged weapon. On the one hand, it controls the central government borrowings from the RBI, and on the other, it restricts the freedom of the banks to sell the government securities or to borrow against them from the RBI. Under this method of monetary control, banks are required by the statute to maintain a certain minimum proportion of their daily demand and time liabilities (DTL) in the forin of certain *designated liquid assets.* The designated liquid assets include (*a*) excess reserves (ER)—defined as total reserves less cash in hand and balances with RBI, (*b*) investment in unencumbered government (IGS) and other approved securities, and (*c*) current account balances with other banks (CAOB), Thus,

$$SLR = \frac{ER + IGS + CAOB}{DTL}.$$

11. M_3 is a broad concepts of money supply. It includes net time deposits of banks addition to the money supply, M_1.

$M_3 = M_1 + TD$ (Net)

where TD = Time deposits with banks.

This measure use time deposits because although time deposits cannot be withdraw through writing cheques but loans from banks can easily be obtained against such deposits. Further, they can be withdrawn any time by foregoing some interest earned on them. M_3 has become a popular measure of money supply. It is also known as 'aggregate monetary resources of the society'.

12. A hedge is a contract that provides protection against the risk of loss from a change in foreign exchange rates.

14. Statutory Liquidity Ratio: SLR is that proportion of a bank's Net Demand and Time Liabilities (NDTL) that it has to maintain as investments in certain specified assets (cash, precious metals, and govt. approved securities like bonds). SLR is governed by the provisions of Section 24 of the Banking Regulation Act.

There is no minimum stipulation on SLR (earlier there used to be a minimum stipulated SLR of 25% – but this was removed with an amendment to the Banking Regulation Act in 2007). However, SLR cannot exceed 40%.

15. The committee was headed by Dr. Urjit R Patel, the Deputy Governor of RBI and was constituted on 12 September 2013 by the Governor Dr. Raghuram G. Rajan. The committee in its suggestion has recommended that a new Consumer Price Index (CPI) should be adopted by Reserve Bank of India (RBI) to anchor the monetary policy has been recommended on 21 January 2014 by an expert panel set by the central bank. The committee has also set an inflation target at 4 per cent with a band of plus/minus 2 per cent around it. The panel in its recommendation has also suggested that the monetary policy decision should be vested in the hands of the Monetary Policy Committee (MPC) that will be headed by the Governor.

17. Unlike Keynes, Baumol has established that transactions demand for money also depends on the rate of interest, *i.e.,* he has established the interest-elasticity of the transactions demand for money. Keynes considered transactions demand for money as a function of the level of income and the relationship between the two as linear and proportional. Baumol maintains that the relationship between these two is neither linear nor proportional.

According to Baumol, the holding of cash involves two types of costs: (*a*) interest costs, and (*b*) non-interest costs. Holding cash balances mean that the individual forgoes interest income by not investing into other interest yielding assets. This is the interest cost to the individual money holder. When bonds are converted into cash the investors have to meet certain costs like brokerage fee, postal charges, etc. These are known as non-interest costs.

According to Baumol the demand for real balances "is proportional to the square root of the volume of transactions and inversely proportional to the square root of the rate of interest". Hence, the relationship between price level and the transactions demand for money is direct and proportional If the price level doubles, the money value of the transactions will also be doubled. When all prices double, brokerage fees will also be doubled. So people would like to hold high cash balances and avoid investments and withdrawals and the brokerage costs which they would otherwise incur. Hence, the increase in the money value of transactions and in brokerage fees brings about a rise in the optimal demand for money in exactly the same proportion as the change in the price level.

19. Infrastructure bottlenecks have been hampering the Indian economy in realising its real growth potential—pointed out by experts time and again and felt by the governments, too. The heavy investment requirement to support the development of infrastructure for the present time as well as for the future have always been a tough task. Keeping in view the need for financing infrastructure, the Ministry of Finance in December 2006 constituted a Committee under the Chairmanship of Deepak Parekh to identify and suggest measures for financing infrastructure. The Committee submitted its report in May 2007. The major recommendations of the committee are as follows;

(*i*) Improving intermediation of domestic savings towards infrastructure investment (such as risk, tenor and scale).

(*ii*) Facilitating targeted access to foreign savings.

20. Board of Industrial and Financial Reconstruction (BIFR) : In January 1987 this Board (BIFR) was set up under the Sick Industrial Companies (Special Provision) Act., 1985. The Board became operational on May 15,1987. The Board consists of seven members. At the end of 1991, public sector enterprises were brought within its purview.

It is obligatory on the part of management of a sick unit to inform the BIFR about sickness. The Board will then enquiry. If found sick, it will—

(*a*) Change management or sale or leasing out of a part or the entire unit.

(*b*) Take measures for merger or amalgamation with sound unit.

(*c*) Give the sick unit time for overcoming the problem on its own.

22. The 14th FC has given due consideration to the need to balance management of ecology, environment and climate change consistent with sustainable economic development. Thus, Forest Cover has been incorporated as a factor to decide horizontal transfers.

23. Wiseman and Peacock undertook a study of public expenditure in U.K. for the period from 1880-1955, according to which public expenditure does not increase in a smooth and continuous fashion but in jerks or step like fashion.

This is because of the fact that the need for public expenditure increases due to some social or other disturbance, which cannot be met by the existing public revenue. Consequently, the expenditure as well as taxation move to a new higher level which according to the authors is the *displacement effect.* Since the existing revenue falls short of the required public expenditure it creates an *inspection effect.*

The position is reviewed by the government and the people and with a view to finding out a solution of some of the important problems, they agree to finance the increased expenditure. As a result, the people attain a new level of 'tax tolerance', which means that people are willing to bear a higher burden of taxation. This means that the general level of expenditure and revenue goes up and so both public expenditure as well as revenue get settled at a new level until another disturbance occurs leading to a *displacement effect* with each major disturbance.

The government's sphere of economic activity goes on extending and the consequence is the *concentration effect* which implies that the economic activity of the central government tends to grow faster than the governments at the state and local levels.

24. To measure the extent of poverty in India, several studies and estimations have been made by different economists and institutions. Earlier estimates were made by **P.D. Ojha, M.S. Ahuluwalia, B.S. Minhas, P.K. Bardhan, Dandekar** and **Rath,** etc., for different time periods spanning across 1956-57 to 1973-74. The percentage of poor in India differs from estimate to estimate. B.S. Minhas' estimate during 1956-57–1964-65 shows higher percentage of the poor than of M.S. Ahuluwalia's estimate for same period. It is because of different methodology and a different sample used in the estimation.

26. An important public solution for the problem of externalities is the use of a Pigouvian tax or subsidy. Originally suggested by the British economist A.C. Pigou, the idea is to tax a firm producing a negative externality or subsidize a firm producing a positive externality in order to correct for the effects of the externality. In the case of a negative externality, Pigou suggested applying a tax on the firm's output equal to the amount of the marginal damage: t = MD. The firm would then face a private marginal cost curve that would shift up by the amount of the tax. Because the tax is equal to the marginal damage at the socially efficient output level, t = MD(x_s), the firm's private marginal cost curve including the tax, MPC + t, would be the same as the marginal social cost curve at x_s. As a result, the firm would select x_s output, which is exactly the output that is efficient socially. The Pigouvian tax leads the firm to make a private decision that is socially efficient. Figure illustrates the application of a Pigouvian tax to correct for a negative externality.

If the tax can be set equal to the marginal damage (MD), the firm will voluntarily change to the socially efficient output rate. This is one of the strengths of the Pigouvian tax solution. Government action is limited to setting the tax. Once the government sets the tax equal to the marginal damage, market forces solve the problem. No government agency tells the firms what to do. They simply react to the tax, seeking their own best interest, and in the process they are led by market forces to the socially optimal solution. In addition, the tax generates revenue equal to the area *abcd.* The practical difficulty with implementing this solution, however, is determining an accurate estimate of the marginal damage at the socially efficient output rate in order to set the tax at the appropriate level.

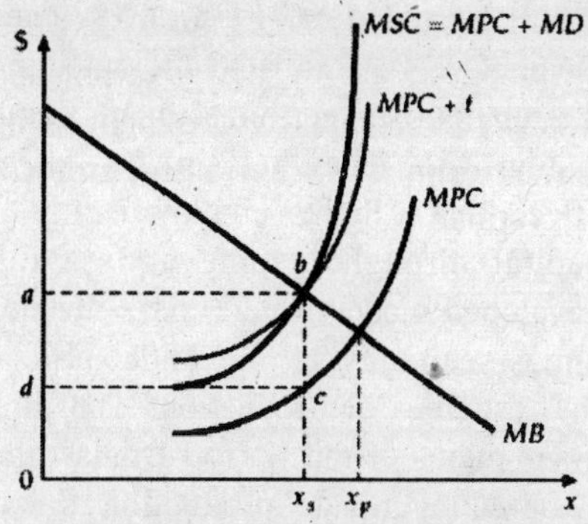

Fig. : *Pigouvian Tax Corrects Negative Externality*

27. The convergence of rich and poor countries is central to Solow's (1956) iconic neoclassical growth model, in which the central mechanism is the declining marginal returns to capital.

The mechanism behind Solow's growth model is diminishing returns to reproducible capital. A poor country characterized by a low capital/labour ratio has a higher marginal productivity of capital and thereby tends to grow at a higher rate than a rich country with a higher intensity and lower marginal productivity of capital. Furthermore, there is a tendency for capital to move from rich to poor and thereby accelerating the convergence process.

30. Capital in the Twenty-First Century is a book by French economist Thomas Piketty. It focuses on wealth and income inequality in Europe and the United States since the 18th century. It was initially published in French in August 2013; an English translation by Arthur Goldhammer followed in April 2014.

The book's central thesis is that when the rate of return on capital (r) is greater than the rate of economic growth (g) over the long term, the result is concentration of wealth, and this unequal distribution of wealth causes social and economic instability. Piketty proposes a global system of progressive wealth taxes to help reduce inequality and avoid the vast majority of wealth coming under the control of a tiny minority.

33. Roy F. Harrod (1900-1978) in 1939 and Evsey Domar (1914-97) in 1946 attempted to analyze the relation between investment, employment and growth. They recognized the dynamic effects that a higher employment rate has on capital through income and savings, and developed models where these dynamics lead almost certainly to the under-utilization of the resources of production. The three basic assumptions of the Harrod-Domar model are: Leontief aggregate production function, no technological progress, and a constant savings rate.

34. In the Cobb-Douglas production function, the parameters α and β also measure the labour share and capital share in total output if the marginal productivity conditions holds.

36. The Wage Goods Model was initially propounded by Dr. P.R. Brahmananda and the late professor C.N. Vakil in 1955-56 to the Planning Commission at the time of the formulation of the second five year plan. It was given as a viable alternative to the heavy industry strategy given by Prof. Mahalanobis. Dr. Brahmananda and late Prof. C.N. Vakil failed to achieve and the second five year plan was based on two sector model and the four sector models.

37. The AK Model : The key property of this class of endogenous-growth models is the absence of diminishing returns to capital. The simplest version of a production function without diminishing returns is the AK function:

$$Y = AK$$

where A is a positive constant that reflects the level of the technology. The global absence of diminishing returns may seem unrealistic, but the idea becomes more plausible if we think of K in a broad sense to include human capital.

38. A specialist in the theory of growth and of distribution, Pasinetti corrected and generalized Kaldor's model by showing that, even in the presence of saving by workers, the profit rate in the economy depends only on the growth rate and the capitalists' propensity to save (1962): what was described as Pasinetti's theorem, or the new Cambridge equation. Thus Pasinetti formulated rigorously the link, brought to light by the classics, between capital accumulation, profit rate and income distribution. In his later works, he also enlarged his analysis of growth by combining it with the study of the structural change in the economy (1981). It is in order to do so that he developed new techniques of analysis, such as that of vertical integration (1973).

39. According to Karl Marx, the Rate of Profit (ROP)

$$\text{ROP} = \frac{\frac{s}{v}}{\frac{c}{v}+1}$$

where c = constant capital, s/v = rate of exploitation (rate of surplus-value) and C/v = organic composition of capital.

This formula shows that the rate of profit depends (*a*) on the rate of surplus-value, which Marx also calls the rate of exploitation because it describes the relationship of unpaid and paid labour, and (*b*) the organic composition of capital, which represents the relationship of dead and living labour, constant and variable capital, and the value of machinery/resources and labour-power. The rate of profit is directly proportional to the rate of surplus-value and inversely proportional to the organic composition of capital.

41. Developed principally by Robert Gordon of North Western University, the triangle model takes its name from the specified dependence of the inflation rate on a set of three determinants: inertia, demand and supply.

The **Neo-Keynesian** economic theory presents three types of inflation, as part of what Robert J. Gordon calls the "triangle model".

- **Demand Pull Inflation—**Inflation due to high demand for goods/services and low unemployment, also known as Phillips Curve inflation.
- **Cost-Push Inflation—**Currently termed "supply shock inflation", due to an event such as a sudden increase in the price of oil from global market forces. Producers for whom oil is part of their cost are very likely to increase the prices of their Outputs. Cost-push can also come for labour demand for increased wages and salaries.
- **Built-in Inflation—**This is induced by adaptive expectations. Often linked to the "price/wage spiral" because it involves workers trying to keep their wages up with prices and then employers passing higher costs on to consumers as higher prices as part of a "vicious circle".

  Built-in inflation reflects events in the past, and so might be seen as hangover inflation. It is also known as "inertial" inflation, "inflationary momentum", and "structural inflation".

These three types of inflation can be added up at any time to get an explanation of the current inflation rate.

However, over time, the first two (and the actual inflation rate) affect the amount of built-in inflation: persistently high (or low) actual inflation leads to higher (lower) built-in inflation.

The neo-classical use the Phillips curve to explain the relationship between inflation and employment. This means some amount of inflation is needed to increase employment or reduce unemployment.

43. Foreign direct investment is investment directly into production in a country by a company located in another country, either by buying a company in the target country or by expanding operations of an existing business in that country. Foreign direct investment is done for many reasons including to take advantage of cheaper wages in the country, special investment privileges such as tax exemptions offered by the country as an incentive to gain tariff-free access to the markets of the country or the region. Foreign direct investment is in contrast to portfolio investment which is a passive investment in the securities of another country such as stocks and bonds.

45. Free Trade Agreement/Free Trade Area (FTA): Whenever some countries sit together and decide to eliminate tariffs, import quotas, and preferences on most (if not all) goods and services traded between them, they are creating a FTA.

- The aim of a free-trade area is to reduce barriers to exchange so that trade can grow as a result of specialization, division of labour, and most importantly via comparative advantage.
- A Free trade agreement can be an agreement between two countries (bilateral) or many countries (multilateral). For example, Canada – United States Free Trade Agreement between the U.S. and Canada was signed in 1988.

46. The nominal and real effective exchange rates are more meaningful for empirical analysis than bilateral exchange rates. The nominal effective exchange rate is the weighted average of a country's exchange rates against other major currencies. International competitiveness is affected not only by the exchange rate, but also by fluctuations in domestic and foreign prices. Thus, the nominal effective exchange rate is adjusted to incorporate inflation rate differences. This type of indicator is called the real effective exchange rate.

50. Generally the foreign exchange reserves comprises of three items: gold, SDRs and foreign currency assets.

51. The excess demand function satisfies the following properties.

1. It is homogeneous of degree zero, $\lambda > 0$.
2. It is continuous.
3. It satisfies Walras' Law.

53. The Optimum Firm : That size of the firm at which the net economy is maximum, is its optimum size. If an organisation in given circumstances of technology and the market for its product can produce its goods at the lowest average cost, then it has achieved maximisation of economy, which is the optimum size. The optimum size varies from industry to industry and from time to time. The optimum point tends to grow with technological development and advance in management science.

54. The time preference theory of interest is associated with Irving Fisher who defined interest as an "index of the community's preference for a dollar of present over a dollar of future income." Time preference, thus is preference of having a certain amount today rather than having it at a point of time in future. Interest is thus price paid for enjoying future income at present. It is determined by the rates of "marginal time preference" and "marginal return over cost." Marginal rate of time preference, also known as the rate of willingness, refers to willingness to borrow. If the rate of willingness is higher than the rate of interest, the individual would borrow, and if it is lower than the rate of interest, the individual will lend. The rate of return over cost is the discount rate at which the net present values of the alternative investment opportunities get equalized. If the rate of return over cost is higher for an investment opportunity than the market rale of interest, the individual would prefer to invest rather than lend at the market rate of interest. In the opposite case, when the rate of return over cost is lower than the market rate of interest, the individual would prefer to lend for the interest rather than go for low return investment.

55. The modern conception of general equilibrium is provided by a model developed jointly by Kenneth Arrow, Gerard Debreu and Lionel W. McKenzie in the 1950s.

Gerard Debreu presents this model in *Theory of Value* (1959) as an axiomatic model, following the style of mathematics promoted by Bourbaki.

Three important interpretations of the terms of the theory have been often cited. First, suppose commodities are distinguished by the location where they are delivered. Then the Arrow-Debreu model is a spatial model of, for example, international trade.

Second, suppose commodities are distinguished by when they are delivered. That is, suppose all markets equilibrate at some initial instant of time. Agents in the model purchase and sell contracts, where a contract specifies, for example, a good to be delivered and the date at which it is to be delivered. The Arrow-Debreu model of intertemporal equilibrium contains forward markets for all goods at all dates. No markets exist at any future dates.

Third, suppose contracts specify states of nature which affect whether a commodity is to be delivered: "A contract for the transfer of a commodity now specifies, in addition to its physical properties, its location and its date, an event on the occurrence of which the transfer is conditional. This new definition of a commodity allows one to obtain a theory of risk free from any probability concept..."

These interpretations can be combined. So the complete Arrow-Debreu model can be said to apply when goods are identified by when they are to be delivered, where they are to be delivered and under what circumstances they are to be delivered, as well as their intrinsic nature.

57. Indifference curves for various types of individuals

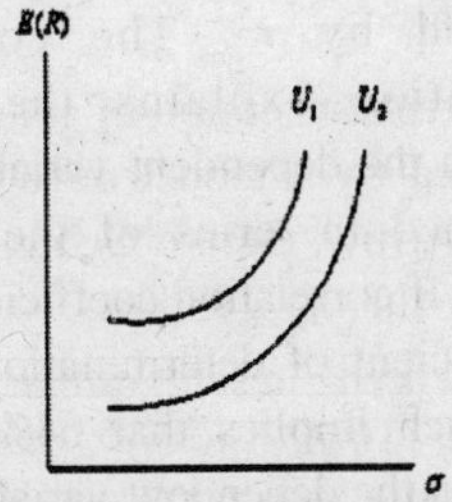

Fig. A : *Risk-Averse Investor*

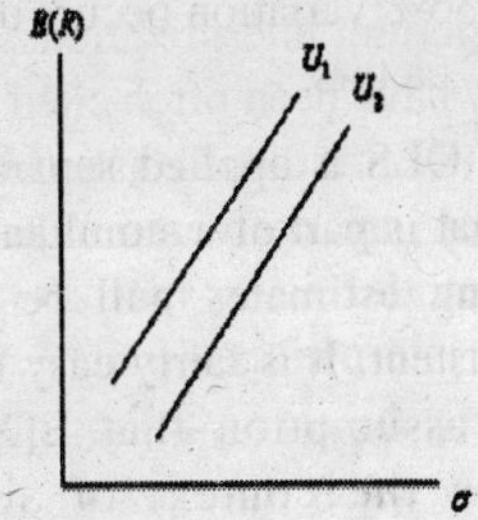

Fig. B : *Risk-Neutral Investor*

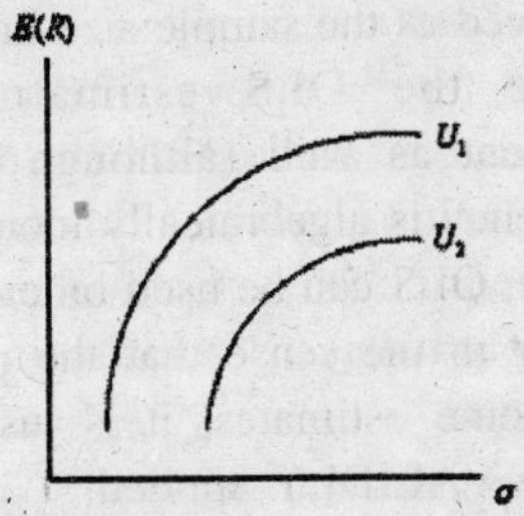

Fig. C : *Risk-Seeking Investor*

Various types of investor's indifference curves are shown in Fig.

In the same level of satisfication, the risk-averse investor requires more return for an extra unit of risk than the return he asks for previous one unit increase of risk. Therefore, the indifference curve is convex. Figure A presents two indifference curves that are risk-averse and $U_1 > U_2$ (higher return and lower risk).

For a risk-neutral investor, the indifference curve is a straight line. In the same level of satisfaction, the investor requires the same return for an extra unit of risk as the return he asks for previous one unit increase of risk. Figure B presents two indifference curves that are risk-neutral, and $U_1 > U_2$. For a risk-seeking investor, the indifference curve is a concave function. In the same level of satisfaction, the investor requires less return for an extra unit of risk than the return he asks for previous one unit increase of risk. Figure C presents two indifference curves that are risk-seeking and $U_1 > U_2$.

59. Stackelberg, a German economist, developed his leadership model of duopoly in 1930. His model is an extension of Cournot's mode. Stackelberg assumes that one of the duopolist (say, firm A) is sophisticated enough to play the role of a leader and the other (say, firm B) acts as a follower. The leading duopolist firm A recognizes that its rival firm B has a definite reaction function which firm A uses for its his own profit function and maximizes its profits.

60. The Minimum Support Prices (MSP) for major agricultural products announced each year are fixed taking into account the recommendations of the Commission for Agricultural Costs and Prices (CACP). The CACP recommends MSPs for 24 important crops. Apart from taking into account the cost of production, the CACP considers other factors such as demand-supply gap, price situation, global availability, intercrop price parity and terms of trade between agriculture and non-agriculture sector.

61. Agricultural diversification is determined by change in cropping pattern as an integral part. The process of agricultural diversification reduces the risk and increases the returns to farms.

64. The Agricultural Census takes place after every five years—the first Agricultural Census in the country was conducted with reference year 1970-71. Agricultural Census is carried out as a Central Sector Scheme under which 100 per cent financial assistance is provided to States/Union Territories. Agricultural Census operation is carried out in three phases. During Phase-I, a list of all holdings with data on area, gender and social group of the holder is prepared with the help of listing schedule. During Phase-II detailed data on tenancy, land use, irrigation status, area under different crops (irrigated and un-irrigated) are collected in holding schedule. Phase-III, which is called Input Survey, relates to collection of data of input use across various crops, States and size groups of holdings, in addition to data on agriculture credit, implements and machinery, livestock and seeds.

66. Given demand function

$$P = 15 - 2X - X^2$$

when, $X = 2$

then, $P = 15 - 2 \times 2 - 2^2$

$$= 15 - 4 - 4$$

$$= 7$$

$$\therefore \quad CS = \int_0^2 (15 - 2x - x^2)dx - 14$$

$$\int_0^2 15dx - \int_0^2 2xdx - \int_0^2 x^2 dx - 14$$

$$= \int_0^2 15x - \int_0^2 \frac{2x^2}{2} - \int_0^2 \frac{x^3}{3} - 14$$

$$= 30 - 4 - \frac{8}{3} - 14$$

$$= \frac{90 - 12 - 8}{3} - 14$$

$$= \frac{70}{3} - 14$$

$$= \frac{70 - 42}{3}$$

$$= \frac{28}{3}.$$

71. The coefficient of determination is defined as the square of the coefficient of correlation. It is denoted by r^2. The coefficient of determination explains the percentage variation in the dependent variable Y that can be explained in terms of the independent variable X. If correlation coefficient (r) is 0.8% then coefficient of determination (r^2) will be 0.64% which implies that 64% of the total variations in the dependent variable (Y) occurs due to the independent variable (X). The remaining 36% variation occurs due to outside or external factors.

72. In fact, if OLS is applied separately to each equation that is part of a simultaneous system, the resulting estimates will be both biased and inconsistent. It is fairly easy to show that, since the assumption that E[X'u] = 0 is violated in the context of simultaneous equations, OLS will lead to biased coefficient estimates. However, nothing in this bias will be improved as the sample size increases, and therefore the OLS estimator will be inconsistent as well (although proving its inconsistency is algebraically more complex). Of course, OLS can be used on each equation separately in the sense that the method will lead to some estimates, it is just that OLS cannot be VALIDLY applied.

75. There are 3 equations in this system, so for an equation to be just identified would require there to be 2 variables absent from a given equation. If there are more than 2 variables absent from a given equation, it would be classed as over-identified, while if less than 2 variables are absent, it would be under-identified. The variables in the system in total are Y_1, Y_2, Y_3, X_1, X_2, and X_3.

Previous Paper (Solved)

UGC-NET Economics

Jr. Research Fellowship & Asstt. Professor Exam, December 2015

PAPER–II

Note: *This paper contains **fifty (50)** objective type questions of **two (2)** marks each. **All** questions are compulsory.*

1. Consider the following statements:

I. According to Keynes, as income rises, lower proportion of income is spent on consumption.

II. According Kuznets, as incomes rise, the average propensity to save remains fairly stable and constant.

Of the above which statement(s) are **correct**.

A. Both I and II are true
B. Neither I nor II are correct
C. Only I is true
D. Only II is true

2. If Marginal Propensity to Consume (MPC) is equal to Average Propensity to Consume (APC) for all levels of income (Y), the correct corresponding consumption (C) function will be:

A. $C = a + bY$ B. $C = a + \frac{b}{Y}$
C. $C = bY$ D. $C = bY^2$

3. Transfer payments by the government are not included in the net domestic product because:

A. These are gifts from the government to the recipients
B. They are not counted as commodities
C. No corresponding production of goods and services has taken place to match such payments
D. There may be leakages in such payments

4. Phillips curve sets up a relation between:

A. Taxes and inflation
B. Inflation and unemployment
C. Money supply and aggregate demand
D. Price and cost of production

5. If economy is operating at potential GDP, an increase in money supply will lead to:

A. Stagflation
B. Structural inflation
C. Demand-pull inflation
D. Cost-push inflation

6. In the long run, the transitory consumption will:

A. Be infinity
B. Remain unchanged
C. Decline but will remain positive
D. Be zero

7. According to Keynes, investment demand depends on which of the following two factors?

(a) Rate of interest
(b) Income of the consumer
(c) Marginal efficiency of capital
(d) Marginal propensity to consume

Answer from the codes below:

A. (a) and (d) B. (b) and (d)
C. (a) and (c) D. (c) and (d)

8. For the demand function $D = D(p)$ and supply function $S = S(p)$, the excess demand brings about market equilibrium in which of the following situations?

A. $\frac{dE(p)}{dp} > 0$ B. $\frac{dE(p)}{dp} < 0$
C. $\frac{dE(p)}{dp} = 0$ D. $\frac{dE(p)}{dp} = \infty$

9. Consider the following statements.

(a) Profit maximization by a producer.
(b) Cournots' duopoly equilibrium.

Which of these are appropriate examples of Nash equilibrium? Answer from the code below:

A. Only (a) B. Only (b)
C. Both (a) and (b) D. Neither (a) nor (b)

10. In which of the following market situations/ forms, firms are able to maximise profits?

A. Price leadership
B. Cartel
C. At the kink point
D. Monopolistic competition

11. Consider the following factors in determination of wage:

(a) Demand for and supply of labour
(b) MRP of labour = Marginal wage
(c) MRP of labour = Average productivity of labour
(d) MRP = Average wage

Which of the above are true? Answer from the code below:

A. (a) and (b) B. (c) and (d)
C. (a) and (c) D. (a) and (d)

12. In the context of a straight line demand curve touching both the axes, which one of the following is **correct**? The demand is elastic:

A. below the mid-point
B. above the mid-point
C. at the mid-point of the curve
D. throughout the length of the demand curve

13. Slutsky equation deals with decomposition of:

A. price effect into substitution and income effects
B. goods into superior and inferior goods
C. goods into necessities and luxuries
D. consumer and producer surplus

14. A discriminating monopolist will charge a higher price in the market in which the price elasticity of:

A. demand is greater B. supply is smaller
C. supply is greater D. demand is smaller

15. Inclusive growth objective was given for the first time in which Plan of India?

A. 9th Five Year Plan
B. 10th Five Year Plan
C. 11th Five Year Plan
D. 12th Five Year Plan

16. Match List-I with List-II and select the **correct** answer from the codes given below:

List-I	List-II
(a) Backward and Forward linkages	(i) Von Neumann model
(b) Turnpike theorem	(ii) Unbalanced growth
(c) Organic composition of capital	(iii) Marxian model
(d) A.K. Production Function	(iv) Endogenous growth model

Codes:

	(a)	(b)	(c)	(d)
A.	(i)	(ii)	(iii)	(iv)
B.	(iii)	(iv)	(ii)	(i)
C.	(ii)	(i)	(iii)	(iv)
D.	(ii)	(iv)	(iii)	(i)

17. Which among the following variables/factors are used in Constructing Human Development Index of India?

(a) Life expectancy at birth
(b) Real GDP per capita
(c) Morbidity

Select the **correct** answer from the codes given below:

A. All the three above
B. Both (a) and (b)
C. Both (b) and (c)
D. Both (a) and (c)

18. Which of the following is credited with introduction of LPG model of economic development in India?

A. Dr. C. Rangarajan
B. Dr. Montek Singh Ahluwalia
C. Dr. Amartya Sen
D. Dr. Manmohan Singh

19. Which one of the following models explains the paradox pertaining to rural-urban migration in the context of rising urban employment?

A. Solow model

B. Lewis model
C. Vakil and Brahmanand model
D. Todaro model

20. In Harrod model of growth, if warranted rate of growth is below the natural rate of growth then it is possible to maintain steady state growth with:
A. Continuously increasing unemployment
B. A constant rate of unemployment
C. Continuously decreasing unemployment
D. None of the above

21. Report of Task Force on the Implementation of Fiscal Responsibility and Budget Management Act, headed by Kelkar Committee suggests some points given below:
I. Fiscal deficit to be abolished by 2008-09.
II. Revenue deficit should be 3 per cent of GDP.

Which of the above statements given above is/are **correct**?
A. Only I B. Only II
C. Both I and II D. Neither I nor II

22. Tobin tax is a tax on:
A. transactions in the share market
B. transactions in the money market
C. transactions in the commodity market
D. transactions in the foreign exchange market

23. Budget incidence refers to:
A. The effect of both government expenditure and tax policies on the distribution of income.
B. The effect of government expenditure on the allocation of resources.
C. The effect of tax policies on the distribution of income and wealth in the private sector.
D. None of the above

24. In case of deficit budget, when the deficits are covered through taxes, that budget is called:
A. unbalanced budget
B. surplus budget
C. balanced budget
D. None of these

25. Match the following:

List-I	List-II
(a) Fiscal deficit	(i) Revenue and interest receipt minus revenue expenditure
(b) Revenue deficit	(ii) Revenue receipts and recovery of loans and other receipt minus total expenditure plus total borrowings
(c) Budgets of deficit	(iii) Receipts minus disbursement in capital account
(d) Capital deficit	(iv) Total receipts and total disbursements

Codes:

	(a)	(b)	(c)	(d)
A.	(i)	(ii)	(iii)	(iv)
B.	(ii)	(i)	(iv)	(iii)
C.	(iii)	(ii)	(iv)	(i)
D.	(iv)	(iii)	(i)	(ii)

26. Efficiency requires that the production of pure public goods be undertaken to the point where?
A. the sum of the marginal private benefits is exactly equal to the marginal social cost of production.
B. the marginal private benefit is exactly equal to the marginal social cost of production.
C. the marginal social cost exceeds the sum of the marginal private benefits.
D. None of the above.

27. Which of the following pairs is **not** correctly matched:
A. Rekhi Committee : Simplification of export and import procedures
B. Nanmjundappa Committee : Railway fare
C. Rangarajan Committee : Balance of payments
D. Goiporia Committee : Banking service improvements

28. Consider the following statements:
I. The Repo rate is the rate at which other banks borrow from the Reserve Bank of India.

II. A value of 1 for Gini Coefficient in a country implies that there is perfectly equality in income distribution.

Which among the above are **correct**?

A. II only B. I only

C. Both I and II D. Neither I nor II

29. Retail Banking is to provide banking services:

A. only to individual customers in an integrated manner

B. entirely to agriculture sector only

C. only to self-help group for their survival

D. None of the above

30. Labour market reforms aim at:

A. Job security

B. Minimum wage

C. Labour market flexibility

D. Employment insurance

31. Jan Dhan Yojana Concerns:

A. Credit

B. Tax payment

C. Bank deposit

D. Insurance premium

32. Which of the following sets does not represent the features of Indian labour market?

A. disguised unemployment; lack of skills; lack of mobility.

B. disguised unemployment; perfect mobility; lack of skills.

C. disguised unemployment; migratory labour; perfect mobility.

D. poverty; illiteracy; Homogeneity

33. The Geometric mean of four numbers 2, X, 16, 32 is 8. What is the value of X?

A. 2 B. 4

C. 6 D. 8

34. If mean = 28 and mode = 25, the value of median will be:

A. 27 B. 29

C. 24 D. 25

35. If the probability of solving a statistical problem by A is $\frac{1}{4}$ and by B is $\frac{1}{3}$; when a problem is given to them, probability that the problem will be solved is?

A. $\frac{1}{2}$ B. $\frac{7}{12}$

C. $\frac{1}{12}$ D. $\frac{2}{3}$

36. Type-I error is defined as:

A. Reject Null-hypothesis when it is false.

B. Reject Null-hypothesis when it is true.

C. Accept Null-hypothesis when it is true.

D. Accept Null-hypothesis when it is false.

37. Given that $\sqrt{xy} = 0.6$, $\sigma_Y = 50$, $\sigma_X = 10$, $\bar{X} = 30$ and $\bar{Y} = 140$; the **correct** regression of Y on X is given by:

A. Y = 50 + 3X B. Y = 110 + 0.6X

C. Y = 140 + 3X D. Y = 140 – 3X

38. Which one of the following is **not** a method of sampling?

A. Systematic sampling

B. Quota sampling

C. Snowball sampling

D. Large sampling

39. Growth in software industry in India can be best explained by:

A. Porter's approach

B. Ricardo's approach

C. Vernon's approach

D. Bella Balassa's approach

40. The form of multi commodity terms of trade is most closely related to:

A. Laspeyre's index number

B. Paasche's index number

C. Edgworth - Marshall index number

D. Fisher's index number

41. If the foreign offer curve has an unitary elasticity, then the optimum tariff will be:

A. unity B. infinity

C. zero D. – 1

42. An overvalued Indian rupee in the foreign exchange market will have which one of the following consequence?

A. Make imports cheaper and exports costlier
B. Make imports costlier and exports cheaper
C. Give protection to domestic industry against foreign competition
D. Will improve balance of payments

43. Which of the following issues were not addressed in Urugvay Round?
A. Migration B. IPRs
C. Services D. Tariff

44. The terms of trade refer to:
A. The excess of import expenditure over export earnings
B. Trade agrument between two nations
C. The ratio between export and import prices
D. The terms and conditions on which a country is offered loan in the event of BOP difficulties

45. 'Plan Holiday' in Indian planning is identified with the period:
A. 1966-69 B. 1979-81
C. 1985-87 D. 1991-93

Introductions : In the question number **46** to **50**, two statements are labelled as **Assertion (A)** and **Reason (R)**. In the context of two statements, which one of the following is **correct**:
A. Both (A) and (R) are true and (R) is the correct explanation of (A).
B. Both (A) and (R) are true and (R) is not the correct explanation of (A).
C. (A) is true, (R) is false.
D. (R) is true, (A) is false.

46. Assertion (A) : Pareto optimality criterion cannot be used alone to measure welfare level of the people.
Reason (R) : The concept Pareto optimality fails in case of externalities, public goods and missing markets.

47. Assertion (A) : APC can never be zero while it can be greater than 1.
Reason (R) : Consumption expenditure is always positive even if income is zero.

48. Assertion (A) : The endogenous growth theory examines production function that shows increasing returns.
Reason (R) : There is specialization and investment in knowledge capital.

49. Assertion (A) : On a bell shaped curve; the value of mean, median and mode would be identical.
Reason (R) : There is no skewness in such a curve.

50. Assertion (A) : Competition Act of 2002 came into force and MRTP Act was repealed.
Reason (R) : MRTP Act was too restrictive and curtailed fair competition in the market.

ANSWERS

1	2	3	4	5	6	7	8	9	10
A	C	C	B	C	D	C	B	B	D
11	**12**	**13**	**14**	**15**	**16**	**17**	**18**	**19**	**20**
A	B	A	D	C	C	B	D	D	A
21	**22**	**23**	**24**	**25**	**26**	**27**	**28**	**29**	**30**
C	D	A	C	B	A	A	C	A	C
31	**32**	**33**	**34**	**35**	**36**	**37**	**38**	**39**	**40**
C	A	D	A	A	B	A	D	A	A
41	**42**	**43**	**44**	**45**	**46**	**47**	**48**	**49**	**50**
C	A	A	C	A	B	A	A	B	A

SOME SELECTED EXPLANATORY ANSWERS

1. According to Keynes, consumers tend to spend a smaller percentage of their disposable income as it rises. In other words, Keynes proposed that *mpc* declines as income rises. Mathematically, $1 > dC/dY > 0$. Keynesian consumption function can be depicted in the following Figure.

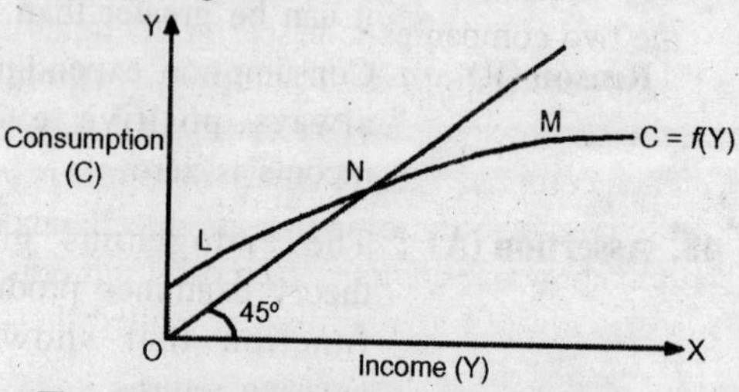

Fig. ***Keynesian Consumption Function***

Data collected and axamined in the post-Second World War period (1945) confirmed the Keynesian consumption function.

Time series data collected over long periods showed that the relation between income and consumption was different from what cross-section data revealed. In the short run, there was a non-proportional relation between income and consumption. But in the long run the relation was proportional. By constructing new aggregate data on consumption and income from 1869 and examining the same, Simon Kuznets discovered that the ratio of consumption to income was fairly stable from decade to decade, despite large increases in income over the period he studied.

This contradicted Keynes' conjecture that the average propensity to consume would fall with increases in income. Kuznets' findings indicated that the APC is fairly constant over long periods of time.

2. In the short period, when $C = C_0 + bY$ average propensity to consume goes on falling but marginal propensity to consume remains constant. So that in the short period APC tends to be more than MPC or APC > MPC.

In the long-run when, $C = bY$, both average propensity to consume and marginal propensity to consume tend to remain constant and average propensity to consume tends to be equal to marginal propensity to consume (APC = MPC).

3. There is a significant exception when accounting for government expenditures. The government may spend money for which it does not receive any good or service in return. Transfer payments, such as social security benefits, unemployment compensation, and various welfare benefits, are excluded from government spending in GDP accounting because they do not reflect productive activity in the period in which they occur. Similarly, interest payments on the national debt are not counted as part of government spending in the GDP accounts. In other words, transfer payment is a payment made for which no goods or services are provided in return. Transfer payments are excluded from GDP.

4. In 1958, Phillips showed the statistical relationship between wage inflation and unemployment in the UK from 1861 to 1957. With wage inflation (ω) on the vertical axis and the unemployment rate (U) on the horizontal axis, a scatter of points was obtained. Each point represented the observation for a particular year. The curve that best fitted the scatter has become known as the 'Phillips curve'. It is illustrated in the Figure and shows an inverse relationship between inflation and unemployment.

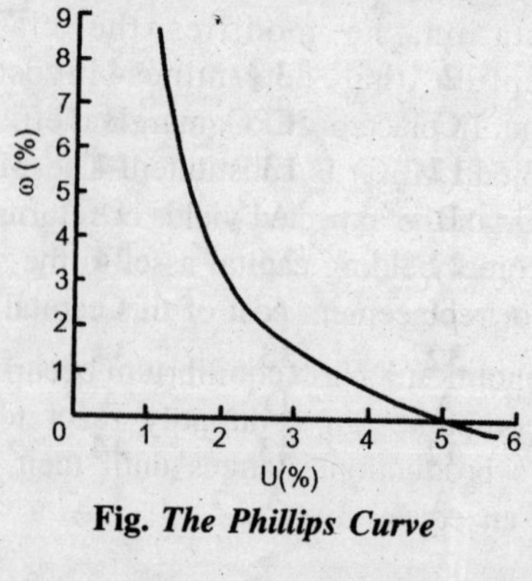

Fig. ***The Phillips Curve***

The curve has often been used to illustrate the effects of changes in aggregate demand. When aggregate demand rose (relative to potential output), inflation rose and unemployment fell; there was an upward movement along the curve. When aggregate demand fell, there was a downward movement along the curve.

6. The permanent income hypothesis states that the transitory components (gains and losses) are expected to cancel out each other over a long period of time.)

7. Income and employment in the Keynesian world are determined by mainly two factors: Consumption and Investment. By investment Keynes means new investment. When price of shares, capital, stocks, etc. are rising, original investment may show a higher monetary value— this should not be taken as additional investment. To the classical economist, investment is determined by two factors: marginal productivity of capital (MPC) and interest rate.

MPC is the actual marginal yield of investment. But Keynes is rightly of the view that the actual yield of investment takes place only when investment has been made and it has started yielding productivity. So MPC cannot determine factor of investment. The investment decision is based not on actual yield of investment but on the expected yield and the market rate of interest.

Keynes is right from the beginning of the view that expectation plays a major role in the case of investment decision. Based upon expectation, he modifies the classical conception that determines investment demand. In place of MPC, marginal efficiency of capital (MEC) is substituted. The MEC is the ratio of the expected yields or returns from an income-yielding capital asset to the supply price or replacement cost of this capital asset.

9. In economics, a Nash equilibrium occurs when two companies in a duopoly react to each other's production changes until their prices reach an equilibrium.

The term is named after John Nash, who is an American mathematician who won the Nobel Prize in Economics in 1994.

How it Works (Example)

A duopoly is a form of oligopoly occurring when two companies (or countries) control all or most of the market for a product or service.

There are two kinds of duopoly. In the first, the Cournot duopoly, competition between the two companies is based on the quantity of products supplied. The duopoly members essentially agree to split the market. The price each company receives for the product is based on the quantity of items produced, and the two companies react to each other's production changes until an equilibrium (called the Nash equilibrium) is achieved.

Nash equilibria do not occur in a Bertrand duopoly, in which two companies compete on price. Because consumers will generally purchase the cheaper of two identical products, this eventually leads to a zero-profit price as the two competitors attempt to attract more customers (and thus more profit) through price cuts. The threat of price undercutting means that Bertrand equilibrium prices and profits are generally lower (and quantities higher) than the Nash equilibrium in Cournot duopolies.

11. Firm employs labour upto the point where its marginal revenue productivity (MRP) is equal to its marginal wage rate (MW). Since wage rate is determined by the demand for and supply of labour in the market, an individual employer accepts this wage rate and seeks to equal MRP of labour with the marginal wage rate. As in the perfect competition in the labour market, the wage rate having been decided by the industry, the employing firm faces a horizontal labour supply curve which shows both the average and the marginal wage rate (i.e., AW = MW). If there is a monopoly in the product market, firm's MR is less than AR (price) and hence the marginal revenue product (MRP) of labour is less than the average revenue product (ARP) of labour and both the curves are downward sloping.

12. 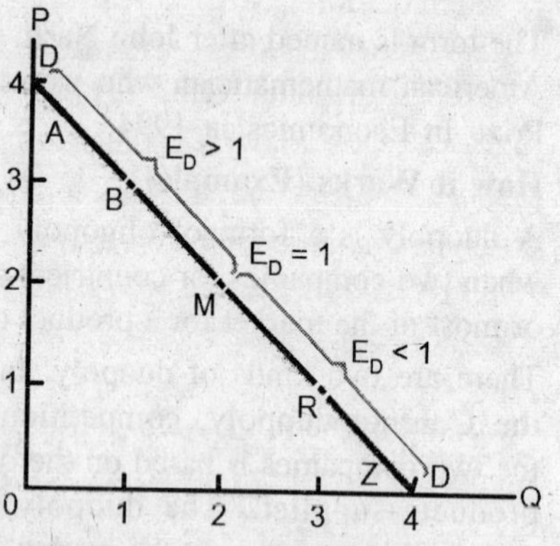

Fig. ***Elasticity of Straight Line***

All points on the straight-line demand curve have the same slope. But above the midpoint, demand is elastic, below it, demand is inelastic; at the midpoint, demand is unit-elastic.

Above the midpoint M of any straight line, demand is elastic, with $E_D > 1$. At the midpoint, demand is unit-elastic, with $E_D = 1$. Below the midpoint, demand is inelastic, with $E_D < 1$.

13. The decomposition of price effect into substitution and income effects is generally expressed through the following mathematical relationship:

$$\frac{\partial q_1}{\partial p_1} = \left(\frac{\partial q_1}{\partial p_1}\right)_{u=u^0} + (-)\left(q_1\frac{\partial q_1}{\partial y}\right)$$

Price effect = Substitution effect + Income effect.

This is known as Slutsky equation in the literature. This relationship is very useful for studying relationships between demand elasticities.

14. Price discrimination is possible when elasticity of demand will be different in different markets. The monopolist will fix higher price per unit in the market where demand is inelastic and lower price per unit in the market where demand is elastic.

17. Human Development Index (HDI) is estimated by taking simple average of three indices.

Human Development Index

$$(\text{HDI}) = \frac{\text{Index of Life Expectancy + Index of Educational Attainment + Per Capita Real GDP Index}}{3}$$

18. **LPG Model of Development:** The LPG model of development was introduced in 1991 by the then Finance Minister, Dr Manmohan Singh with emphasis on liberalisation, privatisation and globalisation.

19. Todaro (1969) explains this paradoxical relationship of accelerated rural-urban migration in the context of rising urban unemployment in developing countries postulating that 'migration proceeds in response to urban-rural differences in expected rather than actual earnings'. It is, therefore, necessary to identify the key factors that are responsible for migration of people from rural areas to urban areas. People migrate from rural to urban areas due to various factors. These factors are generally classified as 'Push' and 'pull' factors. Push factors are those factors which force the people to leave their places. High intensity of poverty & unemployment, in rural areas, lack of basic amenities, displacement due to development projects, natural calamities, social and religious conflicts may be the main push factors. Similarly, better income & employment opportunities, better health & education facilities, better infra-structure and amenities in the urban areas, are the key pull factors in the rural-urban migration.

20. If Natural Rate of Growth is Greater than Warranted Rate of Growth

$$G_n > G_w$$

and the economy is growing at the desired rate

$$G_w = G$$

This rate of growth would fail to provide employment to all. So that there would be unemployment in the economy. In such a situation rate of capital formation would be

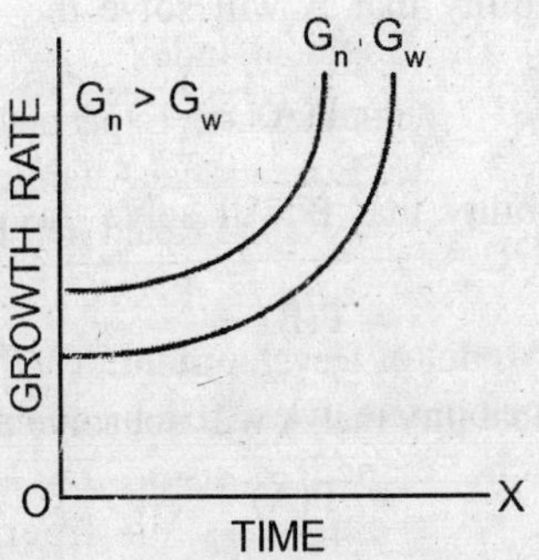

less than the growth rate of population. Capital becomes insufficient to generate employment opportunities for all. Consequently unemployment occurs. Figure shows this situation of imbalance. G_w and G_n curves in the diagram show warranted rate of growth and natural rate of growth respectively. G_n curve is above G_w curve indicating that natural growth rate is higher than the warranted rate of growth. Hence, the growth rate of labour supply is higher than the growth rate of capital. Imbalance and unemployment are the net consequences.

22. The proposal for taxing foreign exchange transactions to hamper speculative exchange rate movements dates back to 1978. It was formulated for the first time by James Tobin (1978) and is now referred to as *Tobin tax*.

23. Budget incidence evaluates the effects of both government expenditure and tax policies on the distribution of income in the private sector.

24. Types of Government Budget

- **Surplus Budget**

  The situation, wherein the estimated receipts of the government exceed its anticipated expenditure is known as surplus budget. It is non-existing.

  Balanced Budget

  The situation, wherein government estimated expenditures are equal to anticipated revenue is known as Balanced Budget. It is also practically non-existing.

- **Deficit Budget**

  The situation, wherein estimated expenditure exceed the anticipated revenue is known as Deficit Budget. It is practically existing.

26. Efficient Output of a Pure Public Good: Efficiency requires that all economic activities be undertaken up to the point that their marginal social benefit is equated with their marginal social cost. This principle holds for pure public goods as well.

Suppose a person were to attempt to produce or purchase a pure public good for his or her own use. By making a unit of the public good available in the community, this person will generate benefits not only for himself or herself but also for every other member of the community in which she resides. The marginal social benefit of this good will be more than the extra benefit to its purchaser. Additional benefits will accrue to each and every other person who will simultaneously enjoy each unit made available. Summing up these benefits to all people in the community gives the marginal social benefit for each extra unit of output produced. The marginal social benefit of any given amount of a pure public good is the sum of the individual marginal benefits received by all consumers.

The efficient quantity per time period of a pure public good corresponds to the point at which output is increased so that the sum of the marginal benefits of consumers equals the marginal social cost of the good. The efficiency conditions for a pure public good are

$$MSB = \sum MB = MSC.$$

27. K.L. Rekhi Committee was constituted in 1992 for suggesting uniform regulations for indirect taxation (custom duty and excise duty).

29. Retail Banking is about providing banking services to individuals and joint individuals as opposed to wholesale banking, which focuses on industry and institutional clients. The concept of retail banking is not new to the Banks. Retail banking is now being viewed as an attractive market segment, which offers opportunities for growth with profits. It is only in the recent times, when it has attracted special attention of the Banks, as a solution to some of their immediate concerns. The essence of retail banking lies in individual customers. While retail banking and retail lending are often used synonymously, but as a matter of fact, latter is just one side of the retail banking. In retail banking, all the Banking needs of the individual customers are taken care of in an integrated manner. Though retail banking encompasses all types of individual customers, often Banks tend to focus on high net worth individuals. Retail banking portfolio encompasses deposit and asset-linked products as well as other financial services offered to individuals for personal consumption.

31. Pradhan Mantri Jan Dhan Yojana (PMJDY) is the biggest financial inclusion initiative in the world. It was announced by the Prime Minister Narendra Modi on 15th August 2014 and Mega launch was done by him on 28th August 2014 across the country.

The scheme has been started with a target to provide 'universal access to banking facilities' starting with "Basic Saving Bank Account" with an overdraft upto ₹ 5000 subject to satisfactory operation in the account for six months and RuPay Debit card with inbuilt accident insurance cover of ₹ 1 lakh and providing social security schemes i.e., Pradhan Mantri Suraksha Bima Yojana (PMSBY), Pradhan Mantri Jeevan Jyoti Bima Yojana (PMJJBY) & Atal Pension Yojana (APY).

33. $8 = \sqrt[4]{2 \times x \times 16 \times 32} = \sqrt[4]{1024.x}$

$\Rightarrow 8^4 = 1024 \times x \Rightarrow x = \dfrac{4096}{1024} = 4$

34. $\because$ Mode = 3 Median – 2 Mean

$\Rightarrow \quad 25 = 3\text{ Median} - 2 \times 28$

$\Rightarrow \quad 3\text{ Median} = 25 + 56$

$\Rightarrow \quad \text{Median} = \dfrac{81}{3} = 27$

35. Probability that A will solve the problem

$$= P(A) = \frac{1}{4}$$

Probability that B will solve the problem

$$= P(B) = \frac{1}{3}$$

$\therefore$ Probability that A will not solve the problem

$$= P(\bar{A})$$

$$= 1 - \frac{1}{4} = \frac{3}{4}$$

and probability that B will not solve the problem

$$= P(\bar{B})$$

$$= 1 - \frac{1}{3} = \frac{2}{3}$$

Since all the events are independent, so

$\therefore$ P(that none will solve the problem)

$$= P(\bar{A}).P(\bar{B})$$

$$= \frac{3}{4} \times \frac{2}{3}$$

$$= \frac{1}{2}$$

$\therefore$ P(that problem will be solved)

$$= 1 - \text{P(that none will solve)}$$

$$= 1 - \frac{1}{2} = \frac{1}{2}$$

36. Type I Error: If the null hypothesis is true but the sample mean is such that the null hypothesis is rejected, then Type I error occurs. The probability that such an error will occur is referred to as the α-risk.

Type II Error: If the null hypothesis is false but the sample mean is such that the null hypothesis cannot be rejected, then Type II error occurs. The probability that such an error will occur is called the β-risk.

37. The Regression line of Y on X is

$$Y - \bar{Y} = r\frac{\sigma_Y}{\sigma_X}(X - \bar{X})$$

$$Y - 140 = 0.6 \times \frac{50}{10}(X - 30)$$

$$Y - 140 = \frac{6 \times 50}{10 \times 10}(X - 30)$$

$$\Rightarrow \quad Y - 140 = 3X - 90$$

$$\Rightarrow \quad Y = 3X - 90 + 140$$

$$Y = 50 + 3X$$

38. Following are some of the well-known probability sampling techniques:

1. Simple random sampling
2. Stratified random sampling
3. Cluster sampling

The following are the common types of Non-probability or purposive sampling.

1. Accidental sampling
2. Dense sampling
3. Judgemental sampling
4. Quota sampling
5. Saturation sampling
6. Snowball sampling
7. Systematic sampling

40. Multi-Commodity Multi-Country Model

In the more realistic case of many products exchanged between many countries, terms of trade can be calculated using a Laspeyres index. In this case, a nation's terms of trade is the ratio of the Laspeyre price index of exports to the Laspeyre price index of imports. The Laspeyre export index is the current value of the base period exports divided by the base period value of the base period exports. Similarly, the Laspeyre import index is the current value of the base period imports divided by the base period value of the base period imports.

41. The optimum tariff for country I involves the intersection of I's offer curve with country II's offer curve in the *elastic* portion of II's curve. If country I's offer curve with a tariff intersected in the inelastic portion of the foreign offer curve, the tariff rate could not be "optimum" for I because an even higher tariff would improve country I's terms of trade and increase I's quantity of imports. (Remember that the inelastic portion of country II's offer curve is downward sloping.) If country I's offer curve with a tariff intersected in the unit-elastic portion of II's curve, the tariff rate also could not be "optimum" because an even higher tariff would improve I's terms of trade and still yield the same quantity of I's imports. (Remember that a unit-elastic portion of II's offer curve would be horizontal.)

44. The terms of trade refer to the rate at which the goods of one country are exchanged for the goods of another country. It is a measure of the purchasing power of exports of a country in terms of its imports and is expressed as the relation between export prices and import prices of its goods. When the export prices of a country rise relatively to its import prices, its terms of trade are said to have improved. On the other hand, when its import prices rise relatively to its export prices, its terms of trade are said to have deteriorated. In case terms of trade deteriorate for a country, its gain from trade is reduced because now it can have a smaller quantity of imports in exchange for a given quantity of exports than before.

When trade takes place between two open economies, certain goods are offered for sale by both the countries. Since many commodities are exported and imported simultaneously from both the sides, we can no longer use the physical quantities (such as kilograms of wheat or metres of cloth). To determine the terms of trade instead, we find the index of export prices and index of import prices and estimate terms of trade using the following equation:

$$T = \frac{P_x}{P_m} \times 100$$

$$\text{Terms of Trade} = \frac{\text{Index of export prices}}{\text{Index of import prices}} \times 100$$

45. A 'Plan Holiday' was announced by the Government of India for the period of three years from 1966 to 1969. The Planning Commission adopted 'Annual Plans' which cover a period from April 1, 1966 to March 31, 1969 in order to maintain continuity in the planning process. Such a situation was due to India's conflicts with China in 1962; and with Pakistan in 1965; temporary suspension of foreign aid; devaluation of Indian rupee in 1966 and the failure of monsoons were some other reasons.

PAPER–III

Note : *This paper contains* ***seventy-five (75)*** *objective type questions of* ***two (2)*** *marks each.* ***All*** *questions are compulsory.*

1. For a linear demand curve, which of the following is **true**?

A. Elasticity of demand is unity at all points.
B. Elasticity of demand is constant at all points.
C. Elasticity increases as one slides down the demand curve.
D. Elasticity declines as one slides down the demand curve.

2. A discriminating monopolist will charge a lower price in the market in which the price elasticity of:

A. demand is greater B. supply is smaller
C. demand is smaller D. supply is greater

3. What is a public limited company?

A. owned by the government
B. owned by shareholders
C. owned by financial institutions
D. owned by MNCs

4. Between the two situations for a firm profit maximization and sales revenue maximization, the equilibrium for a profit maximiser as compared to sales revenue maximiser, takes place at:

A. larger output and lower price
B. lower output and higher price
C. lower output and lower price
D. larger output and larger price

5. Neo-classical production function has which of the following characteristics?

(a) Positive and diminishing marginal productivities of the factors
(b) Constant returns to scale
(c) Satisfies Inada conditions

Choose the **correct** answer from the code below:

A. (a) and (b) B. (a) and (c)
C. (b) and (c) D. (a), (b) and (c)

6. On the given diagram, which of the following segment **correctly** depicts the supply curve of a producer?

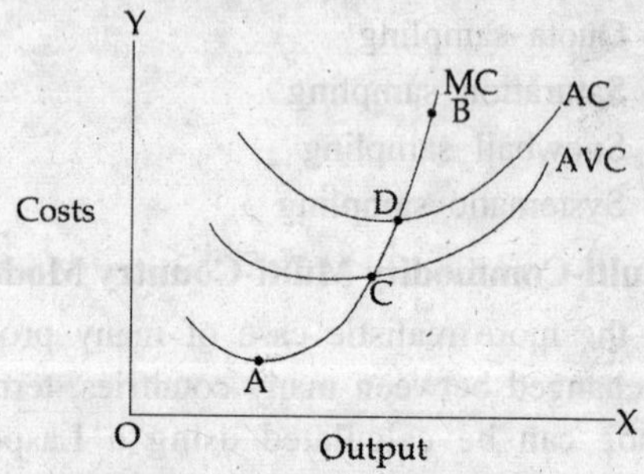

A. DE B. CB
C. AB D. DB

7. Product differentiation is relevant to which set of the following market forms?

A. Monopoly, Monopolistic Competition, Oligopoly.
B. Perfect Competition, Monopoly, Oligopoly.
C. Monopolistic Competition, Oligopoly and Oligopsony.
D. Perfect Competition, Monopoly and Bilateral monopoly

8. In imperfect factor and product markets, labour exploitation is represented by:

(a) When ARP is > Average wage.
(b) When ARP is > Marginal wage
(c) When ARP is < MRP
(d) When ARP is < Marginal wage

Select the **correct** answer from the codes given below:

A. (a), (d) B. (a), (c)
C. (a), (b) D. (d), (c)

9. Who among the following economists emphasized the role of non-economic factors in explaining growth?

A. R.M. Solow B. Roy Harrod
C. N. Kaldor D. E. Domar

10. Which one of the following is **not** an Hirofumi Uzawa condition for a well behaved production function?

A. Continuously differentiable
B. When $x = 0, f(x) = 0$
C. The second derivative of the function is negative
D. The function is concave

11. Exponents of the Cobb-Douglas production represent:

A. Output elasticity of factors
B. Share of factor income in total income
C. Both A and B of the above
D. Neither A nor B of the above

12. Concept of scale economies applies in:

A. Long-run with constant technical coefficients.
B. Long-run with variable technology.
C. Short-run with constant technology.
D. Short-run with variable technical coefficient.

13. Consider an economy with a Cobb-Douglas type of production function with two inputs - capital and labour. The share of capital and labour in total output are, respectively $\frac{1}{4}$ and $\frac{3}{4}$. The rates of growth of capital and labour are, respectively 8% and 4% per annum. Neutral technical progress takes place at the rate of 3% per annum. What will be the rate of growth of output per annum in this economy?

A. 5% B. 7%
C. 9% D. 8%

14. Which of the following conditions is most likely to benefit a debtor under new classical economic framework?

A. Anticipated deflation
B. Anticipated inflation
C. Unanticipated deflation
D. Unanticipated inflation

15. Which theory assumes that increase in stock of money is directly spent on goods?

A. Quantity theory of money
B. IS-LM theory
C. Keynes
D. None of the above

16. In Harrod's model of economic growth, if warranted rate is below the natural rate of growth then it is possible to maintain steady state growth at warranted rate with:

A. Continually increasing unemployment
B. A constant rate of unemployment
C. Continually decreasing unemployment
D. None of the above

17. Wage is determined where:

(a) Demand for labour = supply of labour
(b) MRP of labour = marginal wage
(c) MRP of labour = ARP
(d) MRP of labour = Average wage

Select the **correct** combination from above:

A. (a) and (b) B. (c) and (d)
C. (a) and (c) D. (a) and (d)

18. According to Harrod, neutral technical progress is characterised as:

A. Capital augmenting
B. Labour augmenting
C. Both labour and capital augmenting
D. Productivity increasing

19. The capacity creating aspect of investment in growth theory was explained by:

A. R.F. Harrod B. E.D. Domar
C. R.M. Solow D. P.A. Samuelson

20. The rate at which banks lend to RBI is known as:

A. Bank Rate B. Repo Rate
C. Reverse Repo Rate D. Interest Rate

21. Assertion (A) : AK model is an endogenous model.

Reason (R) : This is due to absence of diminishing returns to scale with respect to capital.

Then which of the following options is **correct**?

A. Both (A) and (R) are true and (R) is the correct explanation of (A).
B. Both (A) and (R) are true and (R) is not the correct explanation of (A).
C. (A) is true but (R) is false.
D. (A) is false but (R) is true.

22. Assertion (A) : According to Marx in a capitalist society organic composition of capital increases with time.

Reason (R) : Technological progress is continuously more capital intensive.

Select the answer from the code given below:

Codes:

A. Both (A) and (R) are true and (R) is the correct explanation of (A).
B. Both (A) and (R) are true and (R) is not the correct explanation of (A).
C. (A) is true but (R) is false.
D. (A) is false but (R) is true.

23. A less elastic IS curve means that:

A. Monetary policy is more effective
B. Monetary policy is less effective
C. Fiscal policy is less effective
D. Both A and C are true

24. Consider the following:

(a) Nominal GDP
(b) Price level
(c) The rate of interest

In monetarism, money supply determines which of the above? Answer from the code given below:

Codes:

A. All the above B. Only (c)
C. (a) and (b) D. (b) and (c)

25. In Keynesian framework, at full employment, which of the following is/are **true**?

(a) Supply curve in the short period is inelastic.
(b) The supply is influenced by the increase in the quantity of money.

Select the answer from the code given below:

Codes:

A. Both (a) and (b) are true
B. Neither (a) nor (b) are true
C. Only (a) is true
D. Only (b) is true

26. Who among the following economists considered the portfolio approach to demand for money?

(a) J.M. Keynes
(b) M. Friedman
(c) James Tobin

Select the **correct** answer from the code given below:

Codes:

A. All the above B. Only (b) and (c)
C. Only (b) D. Only (a)

27. When LM curve is vertical, which one of the following is **correct**? An increase in money supply will lead to:

A. Fall in interest rate
B. Fall in the level of income
C. Rise in the rate of interest
D. No change in the level of income

28. Who among the following believe the velocity of money to be constant?

A. Classicals
B. Keynesians
C. Monetarists
D. Both A and C above

29. Which one of the following is **not** correctly matched?

A. Long-run consumption function : Permanent Income Hypothesis
B. Demand for money balances to be held : Fisher's equation

C. Real balance effect : Tobin's portfolio theory

D. Labour theory of value : Ricardo's theory of distribution

30. For Keynesian demand for money, which of the following is **correct**? People wish to hold money in the form of:

A. Cash

B. Bonds

C. Both Cash and Bonds

D. Neither Cash nor Bonds

31. Crowding out will emerge in the economy, if:

A. Government spending is on the rise

B. Deficit financing is in control

C. Both A. and B. are relevant

D. Neither A. nor B. are relevant

32. Which one of the following is/are **not** true for a simple Y = AK model?

(a) Constant exogenous savings rate

(b) Non-operation of diminishing returns to scale

(c) Constant endogenous savings rate

Choose the answer from the code given below:

Codes:

A. (a) and (b) are true

B. (b) and (c) are true

C. Only (c) is true

D. Only (b) is true

33. Consider the following statements with regard to "Make in India" programme:

(a) It concentrates on 25 industries/sectors.

(b) 100 per cent FDI has been allowed in railway infrastructure projects.

Of the above, which is/are **correct**? Answer from the codes given below:

Codes :

A. Both (a) and (b) are correct

B. Neither (a) nor (b) are correct

C. Only (a) is correct

D. Only (b) is correct

34. Population replacement level of total fertility rate is:

A. 2.1 B. 1.0

C. 2.5 D. 4.0

35. Consider the following regarding shadow banking:

(a) NBFC facilitating credit spread across the global financial system.

(b) These institutions are subject to supervisory control of central banks.

Of the above, which statement/s is/are **true**? Select the answer from the codes given below:

Codes :

A. Both (a) and (b) are true

B. Neither (a) nor (b) are true

C. Only (a) is true

D. Only (b) is true

36. Consider the following statements:

(a) India is one of the first in Asia to recognise the effectiveness of the Export Processing Zone.

(b) Asia's First Export Processing Zone was set-up in Kandla, India in 1965.

Which of the statement/s given above is/are **correct**?

A. Only (a) B. Only (b)

C. Both (a) and (b) D. Neither (a) nor (b)

37. Value of the Marginal Product (VMP) is:

A. MPP × MR B. MPP × AR

C. APP × MR D. APP × AR

38. Which of the following is **not** a part of Bharat Nirman?

A. Rural Housing

B. Agro-based Industries

C. Rural Electrification

D. Rural Telephony

39. The relevant age group for computation of child sex-ratio:

A. 0–1 years B. 0–4 years

C. 0–6 years D. 0–7 years

40. Which committee recommended abolition of tax rebates under Section 88 of the Income Tax Act?

A. Chellaiah Committee

B. Kelkar Committee

C. Shome Committee

D. None of the above

41. As per the UN Report on the convention between Poverty and Environment, which one of the following is **incorrect**:

A. Natural calamities always hit the poor more severely.

B. Poverty escalation leads to environmental degradation.

C. Environmental degradation adversely affects livelihood.

D. Environmental degradation reduces poverty.

42. Which of the following is **not** related to 'empowerment of women'?

A. Gender Development Index

B. Gender Empowerment Measure

C. Gender Budgeting

D. Gender Discrimination

43. The Phenomenon of 'demographic dividend' of a country is related to:

A. A sharp decline in the total population

B. A decline in the Infant Mortality Rate

C. An increase in the sex ratio

D. An increase in the population in the working age group

44. The agricultural census is done at which one of the following intervals?

A. Every year

B. Once in three years

C. Once in five years

D. Once in ten years

45. The 2015, Nobel Prize in Economics has been given to Angus Deaton for his work on:

A. Consumption, Poverty and Welfare

B. Population, Poverty and Development

C. Consumption, Saving and Welfare

D. Consumption, Human Development and Education

46. A tax is said to be buoyant if tax revenue is proportionally:

A. More responsive to changes in output

B. Less responsive to changes in output

C. Equally responsive to changes in tax base

D. Less responsive to changes in tax base

47. Report by Task Force on the implementation of Fiscal Responsibility and Budget Management Act, headed by Kelkar suggests some points:

(a) Primary deficit to be abolished by 2008-09.

(b) Fiscal deficit should be brought down to 3% of GDP.

Which of the above statement/s is/are **correct**? Select from the codes given below:

Codes:

A. Only (a) B. Only (b)

C. Both (a) and (b) D. Neither (a) nor (b)

48. Who was the Chairman of the high powered committee for measurement of poverty in 2013?

A. Suresh Tendulkar B. C. Rangarajan

C. D.T. Lakadawala D. Y.K. Alagh

49. Segmented labour markets imply:

A. Labour discrimination.

B. Labour paid wage less than MRP.

C. MP theory of wage fails to determine market outcomes.

D. Equality of wages of different types of labour.

Which of the above is **incorrect**?

50. In India those farmers are called 'Marginal Farmers' who hold land upto:

A. 1 hectare B. 2 hectares

C. 3 hectares D. 4 hectares

51. Assertion (A) : Indian development programmes are oriented towards growth with social justice.

Reason (R) : Indian economy is afflicted with poverty and income inequalities.

Codes:

A. Both (A) and (R) are true and (R) is the correct explanation of (A).

B. Both (A) and (R) are true but (R) is not the correct explanation of (A).

C. (A) is true but (R) is false.

D. (A) is false but (R) is true.

52. If there is a balance of payments deficit then in a floating exchange rate system:
A. the external value of the currency would tend to fall.
B. the external value of the currency would tend to rise.
C. the injections from trade are greater than the withdrawals.
D. aggregate demand is increasing.

53. Devaluation, will improve the balance of payment deficit, if sum of elasticity of exports and imports of the devaluing country is:
A. greater than unity B. less than one
C. equal to zero D. negative

54. Examples of economic integration are:
(a) Free Trade Area (b) Customs Union
(c) Common Market (d) Cartel
Select the **correct** answer from the given codes.
A. (a) and (b) B. (b) and (c)
C. (a), (b) and (d) D. (a), (b) and (c)

55. Consider the following statements:
(a) India's Trade Policy Review (TPR) is carried out every four years.
(b) WTO has a mechanism for regular review of the trade policies of member countries.
Which of the statement/s given above is/are **correct**?
A. Only (a) B. Only (b)
C. Both (a) and (b) D. Neither (a) nor (b)

56. Which among the following countries was the largest trading partner of India in 2013-14?
A. UAE B. China
C. USA D. Japan

57. New Trade Policy 2015-20 has introduced a new scheme which is called:
A. Merchandise Export from India Scheme
B. Export from India Scheme
C. Merchandise Trade from India Scheme
D. Trade from India Scheme

58. What does 'Price Scissors' refer to?
A. Marshall's example of forces of supply and demand.
B. Exports of two strategic raw materials from a country.
C. A sharp fall in price of a major export item accompanied by a sharp rise in price of a major import.
D. Export basket of competitive local manufactures.

59. Hedging in the foreign exchange market refers to:
A. An act of devaluation.
B. Not covering a risk of foreign exchange in future.
C. Covering a risk of foreign exchange in future.
D. None of the above.

60. For Real Effective Exchange Rate consider the following statements and select the **correct** answer from the codes given below:
(a) It refers to average of value of country's, currency in relation to an index of basket of values major countries' currencies.
(b) It refers to nominal ratio of a country's currency value to average value of a basket of currency.

Codes :
A. Only (a) is true
B. Only (b) is true
C. Both (a) and (b) are true
D. Neither (a) nor (b) are true

61. Consider the following statements:
(a) In the context of the classical model, loan finance may be a means of transferring the burden to the future generation.
(b) Foreign borrowing permits financing public programmes without placing burden on the present generation.
(c) Foreign borrowing is not burden some to the future generations even if the funds are used unproductively.
Which of the statement/s given above is/are **correct**?
A. Only (a) B. (a) and (b)
C. (b) and (c) D. (a) and (c)

62. Tax incidence refers to:
A. Whether a tax is progressive, proportional or regressive.

B. How often a tax is collected.
C. The person or group who ends up paying a tax.
D. How a tax is collected.

63. Assertion (A) : A progressive income tax is based on equi-marginal sacrifice.

Reason (R) : Higher the income, lower will be the marginal utility of money for the tax Payers.

Codes :
A. Both (A) and (R) are true and (R) is the correct explanation of (A).
B. (A) is true, but (R) is not the correct explanation of (A).
C. (A) is true, but (R) is false.
D. (A) is false, but (R) is true.

64. Which one of the following taxes is within the jurisdiction of the State Governments as enumerated in List-II of the Indian Constitution?
A. Taxes other than stamp duties on transactions in stock exchanges and future markets.
B. Taxes on Railway freight and fares.
C. Taxes on mineral rights subject to any limitation imposed by the parliament.
D. Rate of stamp duty in respect of certain financial documents.

65.

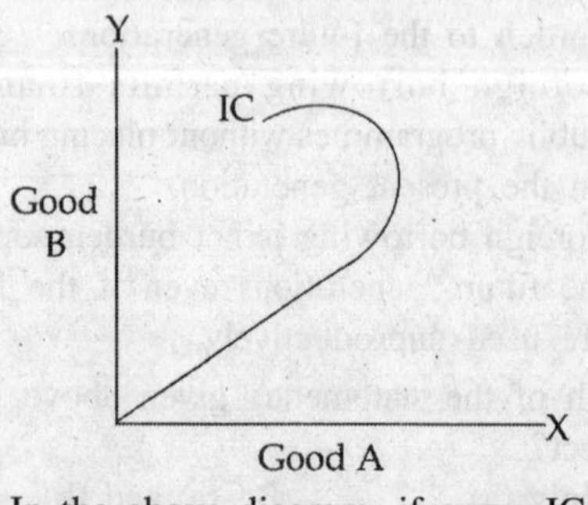

In the above diagram, if curve IC represents income-consumption curve, then it means that:
A. Only (A) is an inferior good.
B. Only (B) is an inferior good.
C. Both (A) and (B) are inferior goods.
D. (A) is a normal good.

66.

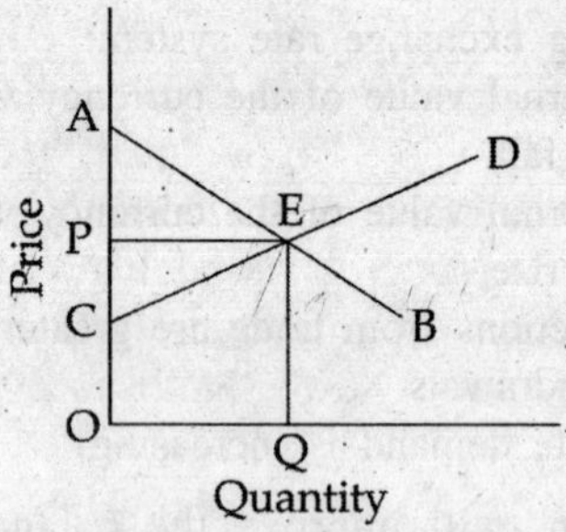

In the above diagram, the consumer surplus is represented by the area of:

A. Δ PCE B. Δ APE
C. Δ ACE D. Rectangle OPEQ

67. Simon-Hawkins conditions relate to which of the following?
(a) Static Leontief model
(b) Dynamic Leontief model
(c) These are necessary and sufficient conditions for the solution of the model.

Choose the **correct** answer from the codes given below:

Codes :
A. (a) and (b) B. (b) and (c)
C. (a), (b) and (c) D. (a) and (c)

68. Given the production function $Q = 2.K^{1/3}.L^{2/3}$, find the output level when 8 units of capital and 27 units of labour are used.
A. 36 B. 54
C. 18 D. 24

69. A consumer spends ₹ 240 when the price of the commodity is ₹ 15 and ₹ 300 when the price rises to ₹ 20. The elasticity of demand is:
A. $\frac{2}{3}$ B. 1
C. $\frac{3}{20}$ D. $\frac{1}{30}$

70. For a regression model
$Y = \beta_0 + \beta_1 X_1 + \beta_2 X_2 + ... + \beta_* X_k + u$,
the degrees of freedom of test statistics $|t|$, with '*n*' observations is:
A. $n - k$ B. $n - k + 1$
C. $n - k - 1$ D. $n + k + 1$

71. Match the following and answer from the codes given below:

List-I	**List-II**
(a) Wald test	(i) Stationarity
(b) Unit root test	(ii) Errors in Variables Model
(c) Student's *t*-test	(iii) Causality
(d) Granger test	(iv) Significance of Regression Coefficients

Codes:

	(a)	*(b)*	*(c)*	*(d)*
A.	(ii)	(i)	(iv)	(iii)
B.	(i)	(ii)	(iv)	(iii)
C.	(iii)	(iv)	(i)	(ii)
D.	(iv)	(iii)	(ii)	(i)

72. Which of the following model/s can be estimated using OLS, following suitable transformations if necessary? Note that '*e*' denotes the exponential.

(a) $Y_t = \alpha + \beta X_t + u_t$

(b) $Y_t = \alpha + \beta e X_t + u_t$

(c) $Y_t = \alpha + \beta \ln(X_t) + u_t$

(d) $Y_t = \alpha + \beta X_t^2 + u_t$

Codes :

A. (a) only

B. (b) and (c) only

C. (a), (c) and (d) only

D. (a), (b), (c) and (d)

73. If OLS is applied separately to each equation that is part of a simultaneous interdependent system, the resulting estimates will be:

A. Unbiased and consistent

B. Biased and consistent

C. Biased and inconsistent

D. It is impossible to apply OLS to the equations that are part of a simultaneous system

74. Which one of the following is **not** a plausible remedy for multicollinearity?

A. Use principal components analysis

B. Drop one of the collinear variables

C. Use a longer-run of data

D. Take logarithm of each of the variables

75. Consider the two regression models:

Model 1: $Y_t = \beta_1 + \beta_2 X_{2t} + u_t$

Model 2: $Y_t = \alpha_1 + \alpha_2 X_{2t} + \alpha_3 X_{3t} + u_t$

Which of the following statements are **true**?

(a) **Model 2** must have an R^2 at least as high as that of **Model 1**.

(b) **Model 2** must have an adjusted R^2 at least as high as that of **Model 1**.

(c) **Models 1** and **2** would have identical values of R^2 if estimated coefficient of α_3 is zero.

(d) **Models 1** and **2** would have identical values of adjusted R^2 if the estimated coefficient of α_3 is zero.

Codes :

A. (b) and (d) only

B. (a) and (c) only

C. (a), (b) and (c) only

D. (a), (b), (c) and (d)

ANSWERS

1	2	3	4	5	6	7	8	9	10
D	A	B	B	D	B	C	C	C	D
11	**12**	**13**	**14**	**15**	**16**	**17**	**18**	**19**	**20**
C	A	D	D	A	A	A	B	B	C
21	**22**	**23**	**24**	**25**	**26**	**27**	**28**	**29**	**30**
A	A	B	C	C	B	A	D	B	*
31	**32**	**33**	**34**	**35**	**36**	**37**	**38**	**39**	**40**
A	B	A	A	C	C	B	B	C	B

41	42	43	44	45	46	47	48	49	50
D	D	D	C	A	A	C	B	D	A
51	**52**	**53**	**54**	**55**	**56**	**57**	**58**	**59**	**60**
A	A	A	D	C	B	A	C	C	A
61	**62**	**63**	**64**	**65**	**66**	**67**	**68**	**69**	**70**
B	C	A	C	A	B	D	A	*	C
71	**72**	**73**	**74**	**75**					
A	D	C	D	B					

SOME SELECTED EXPLANATORY ANSWERS

1. Elasticity measures the responsiveness of quantity to changes in some other variable. Price elasticity of demand is defined as the ratio of percentage change in quantity demanded to percentage change in price. It is given by

$$\eta = \left|\frac{\Delta Q/Q}{\Delta P/P}\right| = \left|\frac{\Delta Q}{\Delta P}.\frac{P}{Q}\right| = \left|\frac{1}{\text{slope}}.\frac{P}{Q}\right|$$

Point elasticity measures the elasticity at a given point on the demand curve, or equivalently, at a given price. Arc elasticity is an approximate average of the elasticities at two points on the demand curve.

For a linear demand curve the slope is constant, and since P/Q falls as we move down the demand curve, price elasticity declines as we move down the demand curve.

2. Price discrimination is possible when elasticity of demand will be different in different markets. The monopolist will fix higher price per unit in the market where demand is inelastic and lower price per unit in the market where demand is elastic. In this way alone he can increase his total revenue. There will be no fear of any change in demand. If elasticity of demand is the same in different markets then price discrimination will just not be possible.

3. The Indian Companies Act of 1956 recognises two forms of companies— private limited company and public limited company. The differences between these two forms are: (i) The formation of private limited company requires a minimum of two shareholders while formation of public limited company requires a minimum of seven shareholders. (ii) The shareholder's right of a public limited company to transfer his shares is restricted while shareholder's right of a public limited company to transfer his shares is not restricted. (iii) The maximum number of shareholders in a private limited company cannot be more than fifty while maximum number of shareholders in a public limited company is not restricted.

In a public limited company, the owners of the company are different from those who manage the firm. The owners of a public limited company are called shareholders; the liability of a shareholder is limited to the value of the shares he/she owns. The management is responsible for the agreements made by the public limited company.

5. The Neo-classical Production Function: The production function satisfies the following three properties (the time notation is suppressed):

1. Positive and diminishing marginal products

$$\frac{\partial F}{\partial K} > 0 \quad \frac{\partial^2 F}{\partial K^2} < 0$$

$$\frac{\partial F}{\partial L} > 0 \quad \frac{\partial^2 F}{\partial L^2} < 0$$

2. Constant returns to scale (CRS)

$$F(cK, cL) = cF(K, L), \text{ for all } c \geq 0$$

3. The Inada conditions:

$$\lim_{K\to 0} F_K = \lim_{L\to 0} F_L = \infty$$

$$\lim_{K\to\infty} F_K = \lim_{L\to\infty} F_L = 0$$

where $F_K = \dfrac{\partial F}{\partial K}$ and $F_L = \dfrac{\partial F}{\partial L}$

6. A perfectly competitive firm maximizes profit by producing the quantity of output that equates marginal revenue and marginal cost. In that price equals marginal revenue for a perfectly competitive firm, price is also equal to marginal cost. In other words, the firm produces by moving up and down along its marginal cost curve. The marginal cost curve is thus the perfectly competitive firm's supply curve.

Because the marginal cost curve is positively sloped due to the law of diminishing marginal returns, so too is the firm's supply curve. And because all firm's in a perfectly competitive industry have positively-sloped marginal cost curves, the market supply curve for the entire industry is also positively sloped.

8. Exploitation of a factor refers to a situation in which it is employed at a price that is less than its marginal productivity. The extent of exploitation depends upon the difference between marginal wage or marginal revenue productivity and average wage or factor price. It is explained diagrammatically in Fig. In this figure units of labour are shown on OX-axis and wages rate/productivity on OY-axis. MW is marginal wage (or MFC) curve and AW is average wage (or AFC) curve. MRP represents marginal revenue productivity curve.

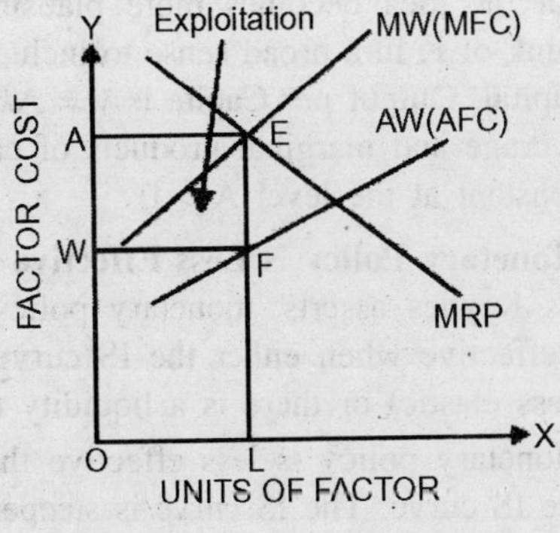

A monopsony firm will employ that number of labourers at which their marginal wage (MW) is equal to their marginal revenue productivity (MRP). In this figure, firm is in equilibrium at point E where MW = MRP. Consequently, firm will employ OL units of labour. Labour will be paid OW wage-rate, as indicated by point F on AW curve. It is because FL is the corresponding average wage (AW) to EL marginal wage (MW). This is less than the marginal revenue productivity of labour (MRP = OA). Monopsony firm will thus earn AW profit per unit of labour. This profit to the firm arises on account of exploitation of labourers. Total profit would be equal to the area AWFE.

In short, price of a factor of production under perfect competition will be equal to marginal revenue productivity (MRP) but under imperfect competition it will be less than marginal revenue productivity. Accordingly, there will be exploitation of the factor under imperfect competition.

9. In 1960, eminent economist Nicholas Kaldor presented a model of growth in his book title "*Essays on Economic Stability and Growth*". Prior to it, he had already published his "Income Distribution Model" in an article 'Alternative Theories of Distribution'. The main objective of Kaldor's Growth model is to analyse the tendency of those non-economic factors which determine long-term rate of equilibrium growth. In this model, Kaldor has attempted to relate technical progress to capital accumulation in order to explain the growth process. Kaldor's model tells that even in the state of rising population the economy can be in a state of long-period stable growth and it need not be in a state of instability.

11. The Cobb-Douglas production function is defined in terms of the flow of services provided by the factors labour (L) and capital (Z). Formally:

$$Y = AL^{\alpha}Z^{\beta}$$

where, Y is output, and A is TFP. When the factors of production are properly measured, A represents technical progress, including the level of efficiency in the utilization of the factors of production. In a competitive equilibrium, the exponents α and β represent the output elasticities of labour services and capital services, respectively. In the special case where, α + β = L, the production function exhibits constant returns to scale, with α and β representing the income shares of labour and capital services, respectively.

13. Rate of growth of output

$$= 3\% + \frac{1}{4} \times 8\% + \frac{3}{4} \times 4\%$$

$$= 3\% + 2\% + 3\%$$

$$= 8\%$$

14. Unanticipated inflation is an inflation rate that the public does not correctly forecast.

Anticipated inflation is an inflation rate that the public correctly forecasts.

15. Quantity Theory of Money: The foundation stone of Monetarism. The theory says that the quantity of Money available in an economy determines the value of money. Increases in the Money Supply are the main cause of Inflation. This is why Milton Friedman claimed "inflation is always and everywhere a monetary phenomenon".

The theory is built on the Fisher equation, MV = PT, named after Irving Fisher (1867-1947). M is the stock of money, V is the Velocity of Circulation, P is the average Price level and T is the number of transactions in the economy. The equation says, simply and obviously, that the quantity of money spent equals the quantity of money used. The quantity theory, in its purest form, assumes that V and T are both constant, at least in the short-run. Thus any change in M leads directly to a change in P. In other words, increase the money supply and you simply cause inflation.

17. With a view to earning maximum profit, a firm will make demand for labourers upto that point where the marginal productivity of labourers is equal to their wage-rate. In other words, firm will be in equilibrium at the point where marginal productivity (MRP) is equal to marginal wage (MW), i.e., MRP = MW and at the point of equilibrium marginal productivity curve (MRP curve) should cut marginal wage curve (MW curve) from above.

18. Harrod neutral technical progress recognizes technical progress as being labour augmenting, i.e. with the passage of time the productivity of any worker increases. The production function in this case can be written as

$$y_t = F\left(K_t, e^{\lambda_1 t} L_t\right)$$

where λ_1 is the rate of labour augmenting technical progress.

19. Domar builds his model around the following question: since investment generates income on the one hand and increases productive capacity on the other at what rate investment should increase in order to make the increase in income equal to the increase in productive capacity, so that full employment is maintained.

21. The AK Model: The key property of this class of endogenous-growth models is the absence of diminishing returns to capital. The simplest version of a production function without diminishing returns is the AK function:

$$Y = AK$$

where A is a positive constant that reflects the level of the technology. The global absence of diminishing returns may seem unrealistic, but the idea becomes more plausible if we think of K in a broad sense to include human capital. Output per Capita is $y = Ak$, and the average and marginal products of capital are constant at the level A > 0.

23. Monetary Policy is Less Effective When ... As Keynes asserts, monetary policy will be ineffective when either the IS curve is steep (less elastic) or there is a liquidity trap.

Monetary policy is less effective the steeper the IS curve. The IS curve is steeper the less interest-elastic is investment, that is, the less responsive investment is to the rate of interest. When the IS curve is steep, loose monetary policy shifts LM right, the rate of interest falls but investment only rises a little bit so income only rises by a small extent.

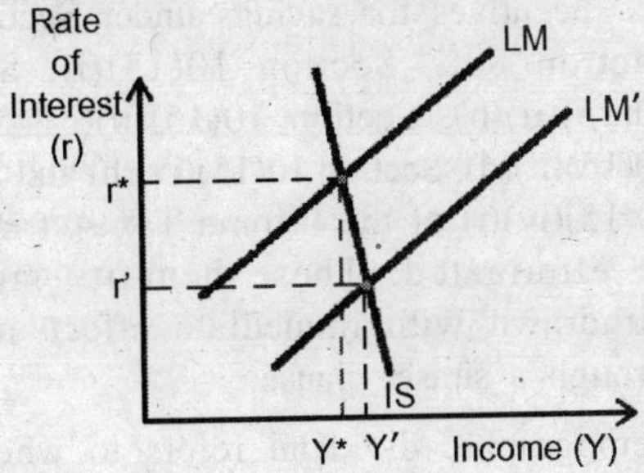

Fig. *Inelastic IS Curve*

24. **Monetarism** is a school of thought in economics that, emphasizes the importance of changes in the nominal money supply as a cause of fluctuations in prices, employment, and output. Leading monetarists include Milton Friedman (who received the Nobel Prize in economics in 1976), Karl Brunner, and Allan Meltzer. Monetarist analysis of the role of money usually begins with the equation of exchange, which can be written as:

$$M \times V = GDP = P \times Y$$

This equation is really an identity – that is, it is true by definition. It says that the nation's nominal GDP (the overall price level, P, multiplied by the real level of output, Y) is equal to the money supply, M, multiplied by velocity, V, which is the number of times the money supply must "turn over" during a year to "mediate" all purchases of goods and services comprising GDP.

26. James Tobin (1958) and Milton Friedman (1956) have imparted money demand a portfolio theory approach. According to them, money is one of the assets in the form of which the people could hold their portfolios of assets. The size of this portfolio depends positively on the wealth of the people. The more wealth a person has, the more he/she would save, and the larger would be the size of his/her portfolio. Thus, wealth is a positive factor in the money demand function. However, since income includes the income from wealth, it is often taken as a '*surrogate*' measure of the asset holding power of individuals. Also, if wealth was used along with income in the function, there could be an econometric problem, called multicollinearity, in the estimation of the function. Due to these factors, wealth is often ignored as a determinant in the money demand function.

27. When the LM curve is vertical, an increase in the money supply increases income and decreases rate of interest.

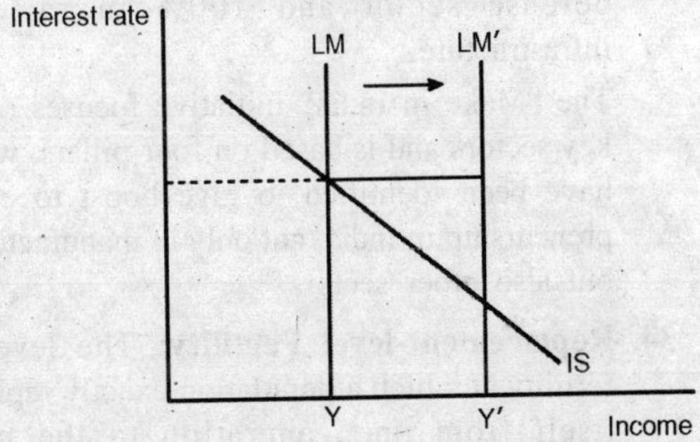

28. Economists hold different views concerning the velocity of money. Classical economists believe velocity is constant; monetarists believe it is not constant but stable and predictable; and Keynesians believe it is neither constant, stable, nor predictable.

30. Keynes in his General 'Theory used a new term "liquidity preference" for the demand for money. Keynes suggested three motives which led to the demand for money in' an economy: (1) The transactions demand, (2) The precautionary demand, and (3) The speculative demand.

31. The crowding-out effect arises when the government engages in deficit spending (government spending exceeds tax revenue), increasing the demand for funds, thereby driving up interest rates. This can reduce consumer spending on durable goods and business investment. Deficit spending has an

expansionary effect on the economy, but this effect can be diminished when the economy approaches full employment by offsetting reductions in private spending.

33. Make in India was launched by Prime Minister, Narendra Modi on 25 September 2014, to encourage companies to manufacture their products in India. He has launched this ambitious campaign with an aim to turn the country into a global manufacturing hub. This study focuses on the changes in FDI rate after introduction of Make in India by Modi and growth due to increase in the FDI rate. In August 2014, the Cabinet of India allowed 49% foreign direct investment (FDI) in the defense sector and 100% in railways infrastructure.

The "Make in India" initiative focuses on 25 key sectors and is based on four pillars, which have been identified to give boost to entrepreneurship in India, not only in manufacturing but also other sectors.

34. **Replacement-level Fertility:** The level of fertility at which a population exactly replaces itself from one generation to the next; currently, the number is 2.1 births per woman (slightly more than 2 because not all female children will live long enough to reach their reproductive years).

37. The Value of Marginal Productivity (VMP) of a factor is derived by multiplying the marginal physical productivity (MPP) of the factor with the price (AR) of the product. According to Prof. Ferguson, "*The value of marginal productivity of a variable factor is equal to its marginal product being multiplied by the market price of the commodity in question.*" Therefore,

$$VMP = MPP \times AR$$

38. Bharat Nirman is a time-bound business plan for action in rural infrastructure. Under Bharat Nirman, action is proposed in the areas of irrigation, rural housing, rural water supply, rural electrification and rural telecommunication connectivity.

39. Child sex ratio measures the number of female children per 1000 male children. In India this is usually estimated for the 0-6 year age group following the data published by the Census of India.

40. Kelkar committee has recommended that the tax incentives for savings under Section 88, Section 80L, Section 10(15)(i), Section 10(15)(ii)(b), Section 10(15)(ii)(c), Section 10(15)(ii)(d), Section 10(15)(iv)(h) and Section 10(15)(iv)(i) of the Income Tax Act must all be eliminated. These benefits must be withdrawn with immediate effect and not through a sunset clause.

43. Demographic dividend refers to where the labour force grows faster than the population dependent on it. A majority of the population, thus, falls under the working age group, thus leading to economic development.

45. The Nobel Prize Committee has awarded the 2015 Nobel in Economic Sciences to Angus Deaton of Princeton University, "for his analysis of consumption, poverty, and welfare." Deaton, 69, was born in 1945 in Edinburgh, Scotland. He holds both U.S. and British citizenship.

46. Taxes are said to be buoyant if the tax revenues increase more than proportionately in response to a rise in national income or output.

48. The Rangarajan Committee, which was set up in 2013 to review the Tendulkar Committee methodology for estimating poverty and clear the ambiguity over the number of poor in the country, submitted its report to the Minister of State for Planning Rao Inderjit Singh. The Rangarajan Committee has estimated that one third of India's population is below the poverty line, *i.e.*, three out of 10 persons in India are poor. As per the Rangarajan panel estimates, poverty stood at 38.2 per cent in 2009-10 and slid to 29.5 per cent in 2011-12. This is at variance with the Tendulkar methodology under which poverty was estimated at 29.8 per cent in 2009-10 and declined to 21.9 per cent in 2011-12. Dismissing Tendulkar

Committee report on estimating poverty, the report claimed that the number of poor in India was much higher. The decline according to Tendulkar in poverty came on account of an increase in per capita consumption.

49. A labour market is seen as segmented if it "consists of various sub-groups with little or no crossover capability". Segmentation can result in different groups, for example men and women, receiving different wages.

50. Government of India categorized the different size classes of landholdings as:

Large	10 hectares and above
Medium	4 to 10 hectares
Semi-medium	2 to 4 hectares
Small	1 to 2 hectares
Marginal	Less than 1 hectare

52. Under the flexible exchange rate system, the first impact of any tendency toward a surplus or deficit in the balance of payments is on the exchange rate. Surplus in the balance of payments will create an excess demand for the country's currency and the exchange rate will tend to rise. On the other hand, deficit in the balance of payments will give rise to an excess supply of the country's currency and the exchange rate will, hence, tend to fall.

53. Results of devaluation or exchange depreciation depends on the following conditions: (i) the most important condition in this regard is the Marshall Lerner condition. The Marshall-Lerner condition states that devaluation will improve the balance of payments only if the sum of elasticities of home demand for imports and that of foreign demand for its exports is greater than unity. If the sum of elasticities is less than unity, the balance of payments can be improved through revaluation instead of devaluation; (ii) devaluation can be successful only if the affected countries do not devalue their currency in retaliation; (iii) devaluation must not change the cost-price structure in favour of imports; and (iv) the government ensures that inflation, which may be the result of devaluation, is kept under control, so that the effect of devaluation is not counter-balanced by the effect of inflation.

54. Economic integration means that two or more nations obtained the advantages of tree trade by minimizing trade restrictions.

There are several levels or degrees of economic integration: free trade areas, custom unions, and common markets. In a free trade area, member countries remove all barriers to trade among them so that they can freely trade goods and services among member countries. A customs union is the next higher level of economic integration. Here, members dismantle trade barriers among themselves while establishing a common trade policy with respect to nonmembers. In a common market, no barriers to trade exist among members, and a common external trade policy is in force.

55. In order to promote transparency and provide better understanding of the trade policies and practices of its members, the WTO has a mechanism for regular review of their trade pólicies. Depending upon its share in world trade, each member's trade policy is reviewed by the WTO at fixed periodic intervals. India's TPR is carried out every *four* years.

The TPR offers an opportunity to other WTO members to ask questions and raise concerns on different aspects of policies and practices of the country under review.

57. New Foreign Trade Policy: The GoI announced the new Foreign Trade Policy 2015-20 on April 1, 2015. The new five year Foreign Trade Policy, 2015-20 provides a framework for increasing exports of goods and services as well as generation of employment and increasing value addition in the country, in keeping with the Make in India. The focus of the new policy is to support both the manufacturing and services sectors, with a special emphasis on improving the 'ease of doing business'. The special features of the

FTP 2015-20 are as follows:

1. Two new schemes have been introduced, namely—
   (i) Merchandise Exports from India Scheme (MEIS) for export of specified goods to specified markets.
   (ii) Services Exports from India Scheme (SEIS) for increasing exports of notified services, in place of a plethora of schemes earlier, with different conditions for eligibility and usage.

58. The price scissors is an economic phenomenon when for a certain group or sector of productive population the overall valuation from their production for sale outside this group drops below the valuation of the demand of this group for goods produced outside the group after a period of reasonable equilibrium. A typical example is when changing world price levels cause a country's exports to plummet in value, while the valuation of its imports remains relatively stable.

59. Hedging refers to the act of avoiding or covering a foreign exchange risk. The need for hedging arises because (spot) exchange rates fluctuate continuously through time. As a result, people who expect to make or receive payments in terms of a foreign currency at a future date face the risk that they will have to pay more or will receive less in terms of the domestic currency than they anticipated. Except for foreign exchange speculators who actually seek foreign exchange risks, everyone else with foreign exchange payables or receivables at a future date should (and usually does) hedge these foreign exchange risks.

62. Tax burden is defined as the total tax payment as a proportion of the total income in a given period. Thus, an imposition of a tax by a government imposes some tax burden on taxpayers or persons on whom it is legally levied.

The burden of a tax can be shifted by the person who is legally responsible for paying the tax to another party who is not legally subject to the tax. Tax incidence indicates the person who actually bears the burden of a tax. The person who ultimately pays for a tax, or put alternately, the person who bears the incidence of a tax, is determined by the market place, specifically by the elasticities of demand and supply. Depending on the values of the elasticities of supply and demand, tax burden can be absorbed by sellers (in the form of lower post-tax prices), or by buyers (in the form of higher post-tax prices). If the elasticity of supply is high (low), less (more) of the tax burden is borne by sellers or suppliers. Conversely, if the elasticity of demand is high (low), less (more) of the tax burden is borne by consumers.

63. Principle of equi-marginal sacrifice or minimum aggregate sacrifice is achieved through progressive taxes.

Following are the important advantages of progressive tax:

1. **Progressive Tax is Based on the Ability to Pay Principle:** A very strong case for progressive tax exists in terms of the ability to pay and the corresponding sacrifice which taxation involves. This argument is based on the assumption that the marginal utility of income falls as income rises. Since the ability to pay increases in direct proportion to the increase in income, the rate of tax increases with every increase in the level of income.

2. **Progressive Tax Promotes Equality of Income and Wealth:** The distribution of income and wealth in society can be made more equitable under progressive taxation because the richer persons are required to pay the tax at a higher rate than the poorer persons.

66. Marshall defines the consumer's surplus in the following words: "*Excess of the price which a consumer would be willing to pay rather than go without a thing over that which he* *actually does pay, is the economic measure of this surplus satisfaction...it may be called consumer's surplus."*

The amount of money which a person is willing to pay for a good indicates the amount of utility he derives from that good; the greater the amount of money he is willing to pay, the greater the utility he will obtain from it. Therefore, the marginal utility of a unit of a good determines the price a consumer will be prepared to pay for that unit. The total utility which a person will get from a good will be given by the sum of marginal utilities (ΣMI) of the units of a good purchased and the total price which he actually pays is equal to the price per unit of the good multiplied by the number of units it purchased. Thus:

Consumer's surplus = What a consumer is willing to pay minus what he actually pays.

= Σ Marginal utility – (Price × Number of units of a commodity purchased)

67. Hawkins-Simon conditions have been developed to ensure that the solution of the input-output model does not contain negative output. Negative output means that more quantity is used as input than what is got as output. For example, if more than one quintal of seed is required to produce one quintal of wheat, then we get negative output and clearly such a situation is economically non-viable. Hawkins-Simon conditions are developed to ensure that the system is economically viable. Hawkins and Simon prescribe two conditions for viability of the system. These are:

(i) Determinant of (l – A) *i.e.* $|l - A|$ is positive, and

(ii) The diagonal elements of [l – A] matrix should all be positive, *i.e.* $(1 - a_{11}) > 0$, $(1 - a_{22}) > 0$, ... $(1 - a_{nn}) > 0$. When translated in term of technology matrix, it would mean that $a_{11} < 1$, $a_{22} < 1$,..., $a_{nn} < 1$. It implies that 1 unit of output of any sector should not use more than 1 unit of its own output as input. (The condition of economic viability).

68.
$$Q = 2 \times 8^{\frac{1}{3}} \times 27^{\frac{2}{3}}$$
$$= 2 \times (2^3)^{\frac{1}{3}} \times (3^3)^{\frac{2}{3}}$$
$$= 2 \times 2 \times 3^2$$
$$= 4 \times 9$$
$$= 36$$

70. The degrees of freedom for error in the multiple regression model are: $n - (k + 1)$.

72. In fact, all of models (*a*) to (*d*) can be estimated using OLS, following suitable transformations where necessary. Clearly (*a*) is simply the standard model. For (*b*), creating a new variable (call it z) as $z = e^x$, would give the standard model as a regression of y on a constant and z. In (*c*), substituting Y = ln(y) and X = ln(x) and regressing Y on a constant and X would again give the standard model. Finally, to estimate (*d*), set $z = x^2$, and regress y on a constant and z.

73. In fact, if OLS is applied separately to each equation that is part of a simultaneous system, the resulting estimates will be both biased and inconsistent. It is fairly easy to show that, since the assumption that E[X'u] = 0 is violated in the context of simultaneous equations, OLS will lead to biased coefficient estimates. However, nothing in this bias will be improved as the sample size increases, and therefore the OLS estimator will be inconsistent as well (although proving its inconsistency is algebraically more complex). Of course, OLS can be used on each equation separately in the sense that the method will lead to some estimates, it is just that OLS cannot be VALIDLY applied.

74. Principal components analysis (PCA) is a plausible response to a finding of near multicollinearity. This technique works by transforming the original explanatory variables into a new set of explanatory variables that are constructed to be orthogonal to one another. The regression is then one of y on a constant and the new explanatory variables.

Another possible approach would be to drop one of the collinear variables, which will clearly solve the multicollinearity problem, although there may be other objections to doing this. Another approach would involve using a longer run of data. Such an approach would involve increasing the size of the sample, which would imply more information upon which to base the parameter estimates, and therefore a reduction in the coefficient standard errors, thus counteracting the effect of the multicollinearity. Finally, taking logarithms of the variables will not remove any near multicollinearity.

75. It is true that model 2 must have an R^2 at least as high as that of model 1 since the former contains an additional variable, and R^2 can never fall when an extra variable is added. The value of the adjusted R^2, however, could rise or fall. If the additional variable x_3 is does not have significant explanatory power for *y*, the adjusted R^2 will fall since the increasé in *k* by one will work to reduce the adjusted R^2 and will more than offset the increase in R^2. Adjusted R^2 thus incorporates a penalty term that penalises large models with insignificant variables. If the estimated value of α_3 were exactly zero, if would be as if the variable x_3 were not included the second model. Therefore, in that case, the two values of R^2 would be equal. Applying the same logic as above, if the estimated value of α_3 were exactly zero, even though the R^2 values were equal for the two models, the adjusted R^2 would be lower for model 2 since the number of explanatory variables has still been increased by one.

Previous Paper (Solved)

UGC–NET Economics, June-2015

PAPER-II

Note : *This paper contains fifty (50) objective type questions of two (2) marks each. All questions are compulsory.*

1. In which one of the following market situations are the firms mutually interdependent in pricing and output decisions?
A. Oligopoly
B. Monopsony
C. Monopoly
D. Monopolistic Competition

2. "Value and Capital" is written by who among the following economists?
A. Hanson B. Philipes
C. Ursula D. J.R. Hicks

3. Giffen paradox occurs when income effect is:
A. Greater than the substitution effect
B. Equal to the substitution effect
C. Less than the substitution effect
D. Negative and is greater than the substitution effect

4. Which one of the following curves will respond the supply curve of labour?
A. Marginal product curve of labour
B. Marginal revenue product curve of labour
C. Value of marginal product curve of labour
D. Average product curve of labour

5. Limit price refers to the:
A. Price which maximizes the profits of the firm
B. Price which prevents entry of new firms
C. Price at which firm just starts earning a surplus over cost
D. Maximum price which the firm is allowed to charge

6. General Pareto Optimality exists where:
A. $MRTS^{X}_{LK} = MRTS^{Y}_{LK}$
B. $MRT_{XY} = MRS^{A}_{XY} = MRS^{B}_{XY}$
C. $MRTS^{L}_{XY} = MRTS^{K}_{XY}$
D. $\frac{MP_L}{MP_K} = \frac{P_L}{P_K}$

7. Advertisement is common in which of the following markets?
(*i*) Oligopoly
(*ii*) Perfect Competition
(*iii*) Monopolistic Competition
(*iv*) Monopoly
Choose from the codes below:
A. (*i*) and (*iii*) B. (*ii*) and (*iii*)
C. Only (*i*) D. Only (*iii*)

8. Intellectual property rights regime is managed by:
A. IMF B. W.T.O.
C. European Union D. SAARC

9. Which of the following statements are **true** for a Euro currency market ? Answer from the codes below:
(*i*) Its existence affects the effective conduct of monetary policy.
(*ii*) It is a highly regulated market.
Codes:
A. Both (*i*) and (*ii*) are true
B. Neither (*i*) nor (*ii*) is true
C. Only (*i*) is true
D. Only (*ii*) is true

10. According to Heckscher-Ohlin theorem, a nation will export a commodity which is:
A. Intensive in its relatively abundant factor
B. Intensive in its relatively cheap factor
C. Both A and B are necessary
D. Neither A nor B in necessary

11. Customs union always leads to:
A. Trade diversion effect alone
B. Trade creation effect alone
C. Both trade creation and trade diversion effects
D. Neither trade diversion nor trade creation effect

12. Which one of the following assumptions is the most important assumption in the Heckscher-Ohlin theorem of international trade?
A. Two-factor model
B. Two commodities
C. No tariff
D. Constant tariff

13. In dual gap model, the two gaps refer to:
A. Inflationary gap and investment gap
B. Saving gap and deflationary gap
C. Savings constraint and foreign exchange constraint
D. Investment gap and savings gap

14. What is the value of the Gini coefficient for an income distribution characterised by complete equality incomes?
A. Zero B. 0.5
C. 1 D. ∞ (infinity)

15. Which of the following has not been identified as a potential consequence of global warming?
A. A fall in agricultural yields
B. The spread of disease
C. The use of nuclear energy
D. A rise in sea levels

16. **Assertion (A):** One of the characteristics of many underdeveloped countries is that they have a low saving rate and low capital formulation.
Reason (R): In underdeveloped countries this is mainly due to high level of consumption.
Codes:
A. Both **(A)** and **(R)** are true and **(R)** is the correct explanation of **(A)**
B. Both **(A)** and **(R)** are true but **(R)** is not the correct explanation of **(A)**
C. **(A)** is true but **(R)** is false
D. **(A)** is false but **(R)** is true

17. Concept of 'surplus value' is developed by who among the following economists?
A. J. Schumpeter B. Karl Marx
C. J.R. Hicks D. R.A. Fisher

18. Monetary policy is most effective when investment spending is:
A. Interest elastic and demand for money is also interest elastic
B. Interest inelastic and demand for money is also interest inelastic
C. Interest inelastic and demand for money is interest elastic
D. Interest elastic and the demand for money is interest inelastic

19. Slope of the LM curve depends upon which of the following?
A. Interest elasticity of investment
B. Interest elasticity of income
C. Interest elasticity of demand for money
D. None of the above

20. In a closed economy and three sector model which of the following is true?
A. Household savings equal net investment
B. Household savings equal gross investment
C. Household savings plus depreciation equals gross investment plus government spending
D. Household savings plus taxes plus depreciation equals gross investment plus government spending

21. According to Keynes, the marginal efficiency of capital is the expected:
A. Rate of return on financial assets
B. Profit from real investment
C. Profit from financial investment
D. Rate of return on real investment

22. In the classical macro system, money determines:

A. Employment B. Real output
C. Both A and B D. Neither A nor B

23.

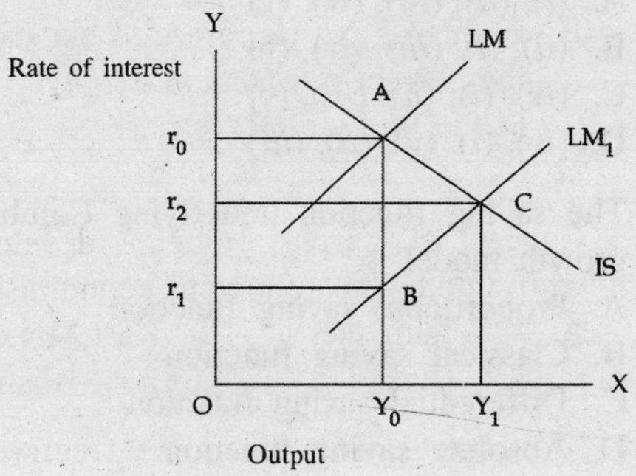

On the conventional IS - LM diagram, LM curve shifts to LM_1. Then which of the following statements are true?

A. Liquidity effect is r_0 r_1
B. Liquidity effect is r_0 r_2
C. Liquidity effect is r_2 r_1
D. None of the above

24. Consider the following statements about Phillips curve:

(*i*) There is inverse relationship between rate of inflation and rate of unemployment.
(*ii*) Economic behaviour is a function of nominal returns.
(*iii*) Economic behaviour is a function of real returns.

Of these statements which are true from the Monetarists point of view?

A. All the above are true
B. Only (*i*) and (*ii*) are true
C. Only (*ii*) is true
D. Only (*iii*) is true

25. An interest rate risk means:

A. When borrowers fail to fulfil the terms of the loan contract
B. A rise in interest rate will mean a fall in the value of security in the secondary market
C. A rise in interest rate will raise the value of financial security in the secondary market
D. When unintended inflation arises

26. In the classical macro system money determines which of the following?

A. Output and Prices
B. Employment and Prices
C. Output and Employment
D. Prices

27. When nominal GDP is ₹ 11,000 crores and real GDP is ₹ 10,000 crores, GDP deflator is:

A. 9.09 B. 90.91
C. 1.11 D. 110

28. **Assertion (A):** India has a big potential demographic dividend.

Reason (R): India's population growth rate is declining.

Codes:

A. Both **(A)** and **(R)** are correct and **(R)** is the correct explanation of **(A)**
B. **(A)** is correct but **(R)** is not correct
C. Both **(A)** and **(R)** are correct but **(R)** is not the correct explanation of **(A)**
D. **(R)** is correct but **(A)** is incorrect

29. Recently the base year for calculating GDP in India has been changed to:

A. 2009-10 B. 2011-12
C. 2014-15 D. 2004-05

30. Which of the following states has the largest share in the total food grains produced in India?

A. Punjab B. U.P.
C. Haryana D. M.P.

31. JAM trinity means:

A. Jan-Dhan Account Money
B. Jan, Awas, Money
C. Jan-Dhan Yojana, Aadhar, Mobile Numbers
D. Jyoti, Aadhar, Mobile

32. Who is the originator of 'Buddhist Economics'?

A. Lee Kuan Yew B. Dalai Lama
C. E.F. Schumacher D. Shinzo Abe

33. Which of the following is **not** a credit rating agency?

A. Moody B. Standard and Poor
C. Fitch D. Nasdaq

34. Which of the following is **not** used to measure inflation?
A. Whole Sale Price Index Number
B. Consumer Price Index Number
C. Purchasing Power Parity Prices
D. GDP Deflator

35. Which one of the following pairs is **not** correctly matched?
A. Similarly placed persons should be taxed similarly – Horizontal equity
B. Interest payments are deducted from fiscal deficit – Primary deficit
C. Goods which are divisible and principle of exclusion applies in full measure – Pure private goods
D. Tax on goods and services is levied according to item's value – State excise duties

36. During the year 2012-13, which one of the following was the largest item of expenditure of the central government?
A. Major subsidies
B. Defence expenditure
C. Interest payment
D. Capital expenditure

37. 14th Finance Commission recommended funds as:
A. Central Assistance to States (CAS)
B. States Development Funds
C. States Share in Sales Taxes
D. States Contributions to Centre

38. FRBM Act 2012 put a ceiling to fiscal deficit of GDP is:
A. 6 per cent B. 5 per cent
C. 4 per cent D. 3 per cent

39. Rostow distinguishes five different stages of economic growth which are:
(*i*) Pre-conditions for take-off
(*ii*) Drive to maturity
(*iii*) Stage of high mass consumption
(*iv*) Traditional society
(*v*) Take-off

Which one of the following is the **correct** sequence of stages of growth?
A. (*i*), (*ii*), (*iii*), (*iv*), (*v*)
B. (*ii*), (*i*), (*iii*), (*iv*), (*v*)
C. (*iv*), (*i*), (*ii*), (*iii*), (*v*)
D. (*iv*), (*i*), (*v*), (*ii*), (*iii*)

40. The saving function underlying Cambridge growth model is:
A. Proportional saving function
B. Classical saving function
C. Differential saving function
D. Absolute saving function

41. According to Keynesions, creeping inflation will help in:
A. Minimising unemployment
B. Maximising real output
C. None of A or B above
D. Both A and B above

42. In the famous equation M = P K Y, K stands for:
A. Fraction of real output held for transaction
B. Fraction of money supply held by persons
C. Fraction of money value of output (transactions) held by public
D. None of the above

43. Geometric mean of 2, 6 and x is equal to 6. What is the value of x?
A. 2 B. 18
C. 9 D. 3

44. Standard Error (S.E.) of a large sample of size n from a population whose variance is σ^2 is:
A. $SE = \frac{\sigma^2}{n}$ B. $SE = \frac{\sigma}{n}$
C. $SE = \frac{\sigma^2}{\sqrt{n}}$ D. $SE = \frac{\sigma}{\sqrt{n}}$

45. What is the probability of throwing a total of 8 from a single throw of two dice?
A. $\frac{1}{8}$ B $\frac{2}{9}$
C $\frac{5}{36}$ D. $\frac{3}{36}$

46. The estimated regression lines are given as follows:

Y = 10 + 0.4 X

X = –4 + 1.6 Y

Then the coefficient of correlation between X and Y is:

A. 0.64 B. 0.40

C. 0.20 D. 0.80

47. For a distribution, Mean = 26, Median = 14, and Mode = 7, the distribution would be:

A. Positively skewed

B. Negatively skewed

C. Symmetrical

D. None of the above

48. For a normal distribution, consider the following statements:

(*i*) It has two points of inflexion.

(*ii*) The distance from the mean zero of these inflexion points is ± σ.

Answer from the codes below:

Codes:

A. Both (*i*) and (*ii*) are true

B. Neither (*i*) nor (*ii*) are true

C. Only (*i*) is true

D. Only (*ii*) is true

49. Match the items in **List-I** and **List-II** and answer from the codes given below:

List-I	**List-II**
(*a*) Simple random sampling	(*i*) Non-probability sampling
(*b*) Systematic sampling	(*ii*) Random-choice of all items from each stratum
(*c*) Quota sampling	(*iii*) Random selection of first and systematic of the rest
(*d*) Stratified random sampling	(*iv*) Equal probability of each item in all trials

Codes:

	(*a*)	(*b*)	(*c*)	(*d*)
A.	(*i*)	(*ii*)	(*iii*)	(*iv*)
B.	(*ii*)	(*iv*)	(*i*)	(*iii*)
C.	(*iv*)	(*iii*)	(*i*)	(*ii*)
D.	(*iii*)	(*i*)	(*ii*)	(*iv*)

50. If in a village all the farmers are divided into three categories-marginal, small and large, and then a sample of 20 farmers is taken randomly from each category, this could be called:

A. Systematic sampling

B. Stratified sampling

C. Cluster sampling

D. Multi-stage sampling

ANSWERS

1	**2**	**3**	**4**	**5**	**6**	**7**	**8**	**9**	**10**
A	D	D	B	B	B	A	B	C	C
11	**12**	**13**	**14**	**15**	**16**	**17**	**18**	**19**	**20**
C	C	C	A	C	B	B	D	A	D
21	**22**	**23**	**24**	**25**	**26**	**27**	**28**	**29**	**30**
D	D	A	D	B	D	D	C	B	B
31	**32**	**33**	**34**	**35**	**36**	**37**	**38**	**39**	**40**
C	C	D	C	D	C	A	D	D	C
41	**42**	**43**	**44**	**45**	**46**	**47**	**48**	**49**	**50**
D	C	B	D	C	D	A	A	C	B

SOME SELECTED EXPLANATORY ANSWERS

1. A very important feature of oligopoly is mutual interdependence of the firms. Mutual interdependence means that firms are significantly affected by each other's price and output decisions. In monopoly and competition, firms make their independent decisions without considering how these will affect other firms and how, in turn, other firms' reactions will affect them. But an oligopolistic firm cannot take independent decisions. Since in oligopoly, a small number of firms compete with each other the sales of one firm depend upon that firm's price and the price charged by other firms. If one firm lowers the price, its own sales will increase, but the sales of other firms in the industry decrease. In such a situation, the other firms will, most likely, lower their prices, too. Then the price cuts of the other firms will lower the profits of the first firm. So, before deciding to cut its prices, the first firm tries to predict how other firms will react and attempts to calculate the effects of their reactions on its own profits. In oligopoly, the cross elasticity of demand is very high between the products of the oligopolists firms because the products are close substitutes. In short the oligopoly firm has to take into consideration the actions and reactions of his rivals while determining its price and output policies. This mutual interdependence of firms distinguishes oligopolistic markets from monopolistic, perfectly competitive and monopolistically competitive markets.

3. **Income and Substitution Effects in case of Giffen Goods**

   Substitution effect is always negative in case of all goods–normal goods, inferior goods and giffen goods. Negative substitution effect implies that, more of X must be purchased in place of Y when X becomes cheaper or X be substituted for Y.

   In the case of inferior goods, income effect is negative. Negative income effect implies that quantity demanded of a commodity is reduced when owing to fall in the price of the commodity, real income of the consumer rises. Increased real income induces the consumer to shift on to the consumption of superior substitutes.

   However, while income effect is negative in the case of inferior goods it need not necessarily be stronger than the substitution effect, so that the net effect or price effect (substitution effect — income effect) continues to be dominated by substitution effect. In such a case, the law of demand is not violated. It continues to hold good, despite the fact that income effect is negative.

   However in the case of Giffen-Goods:

   (a) Income effect is negative and (b) Negative income effect is stronger than the substitution effect.

   So that the net effect (substitution effect (–) income effect) is dominated by negative income effect which implies positive relationship between price of the commodity and its quantity demanded.

   It is only when the net effect is dominated by negative income effect (–ve income effect is stronger than substitution effect) that the law of demand breaks down.

4. The demand for labour is a derived demand because it depends on the demand consumers have for goods and services. The additional output produced by a firm as a result of hiring another worker is called the marginal product of labour. The amount by which the firm's revenue will increase as a result of hiring one more worker is called the *marginal revenue product of labour*. A firm's marginal revenue product of labour curve is its demand curve for labour. Firms maximise profit by hiring workers up to the point where the wage is

equal to the marginal revenue product of labour. The market demand curve for labour is determined by adding up the quantity of labour demanded by each firm at each wage, holding constant all other variables that might affect the willingness of firms to hire workers. The most important variables that shift the labour demand curve are changes in human capital, technology, the price of the product, the quantity of other inputs and the number of firms in the market.

5. Limit pricing occurs when a firm or firms choose to set price below the profit-maximising level in order to prevent entry. The limit price is the highest price that an existing firm can set without allowing entry.

7. Under perfect competition, consumers purchase products at the lowest possible price; there is no advertising, no excessive overhead, and no warranties or guarantees. Under monopoly, people purchase a single product and advertising is virtually nonexistent. With monopolistic competition and oligopoly, advertising commonly plays an important role.

10. The Heckscher–Ohlin, or factor-endowment, theory can be expressed in tems of two theorems. According to the Heckscher–Ohlin (H–O) theorem, a nation will export the commodity intensive in its relatively abundant and cheap factor and import the commodity intensive in its relatively scarce and expensive factor. According to the factor–price equalization (H–O–S) theorem, international trade will bring about equalization of relative and absolute returns to homogeneous factors across nations. If some factors are specific (i.e., can only be used in some industries), the specific-factors model postulates that trade will have an ambiguous effect on the nation's mobile factors: It will benefit the immobile factors that are specific to the nation's export commodities or sectors, and harm the immobile factors that are specific to the nation's import-competing commodities or sectors.

11. The movement towards free trade under a customs union affects world welfare in two opposing ways: a welfare increasing trade creation effect and a welfare reducing trade diversion effect. The overall consequence of a customs union on the welfare of its members, as well as on the world as a whole, depends on the relative strengths of these two opposing forces.

Trade creation occurs when a domestic production of one customs union member is replaced by another member's lower cost imports. The welfare of the member countries is increased by trade creation because it leads to increased production specialization according to the principle of comparative advantage. The trade creation effect consists of a *consumption effect* and a *production effect.*

Although a customs union may add to world welfare by way of trade creation, its trade diversion effect generally implies a welfare loss. Trade diversion occurs when imports from a low-cost supplier outside the union are replaced by purchases from a higher cost supplier within the union.

13. Chenery and Bruno (1962) developed a two-gap (savings/investment and foreign exchange) model in which they relate economic growth to the resources needed for investment, as external capital flows permit developing countries to invest more than their domestic savings. According to the two-gap model, there is an interaction between the "savings constraint" and the "foreign exchange constraint" in the determination of developing countries' long-run economic growth rates. Economic growth and investment of developing countries usually depend on imported intermediate goods. Under these conditions, even if there is no gap between savings and investment, inadequate foreign exchange can become a constraint for the country.

14. The Gini coefficient is defined as a ratio with a range from 0 and 1 (or 0% to 100%). A low Gini coefficient indicates more equal income or wealth distribution, with zero corresponding to perfect equality while higher Gini coefficients indicate more unequal distribution, with 1 corresponding to perfect inequality.

17. In Marxist theory surplus value is the value created by individual labour which is left over, or remains in the product or services produced, after the employer has paid the costs of hiring the worker. Surplus value is the additional value or surplus value which the worker produces but does not get paid for, allowing the capitalist owner to expand their capital.

18. Monetary policy is more successful when:

- Investment is interest elastic: the IS curve is flatter because any change in interest rates generates a proportionally greater change in investment.
- The demand for money is interest inelastic. This means that the LM curve is steeper. Here, any change in the money supply has greater effects on the equilibrium interest rates, i.e., a change in the money supply generates a larger vertical shift in the LM schedule.
- The higher the multiplier, the flatter the IS curve. This implies that the response of output to any change in investment induced by a change in interest rates will be greater.

21. **Marginal Efficiency of Capital:** It refers to the rate of discount which equates the supply price of a capital asset with its propective yields. It is also called expected rate of return on a newly contemplated investment project.

Determinants of Marginal Efficiency of Capital: (*i*) Prospective yields (*ii*) Supply price of the capital asset.

27. The GDP deflator is calculated as follows:

$$\text{GDP deflator} = \frac{\text{Nominal GDP}}{\text{Real GDP}} \times 100$$

Because nominal GDP and real GDP must be the same in the base year, the GDP deflator for the base year always equals 100. The GDP deflator for subsequent years measures the change in nominal GDP from the base year that cannot be attributable to a change in real GDP.

The GDP deflator measures the current level of prices relative to the level of prices in the base year.

$$\text{GDP deflator} = \frac{\text{Nominal GDP}}{\text{Real GDP}} \times 100$$

$$= \frac{11000}{10000} \times 100 = 110.$$

29. The Ministry of Statistics & Programme Implementation has released the new series of national accounts. Two major changes characterize the new series:

- The base year has been revised from 2004-05 to 2011-12.
- The series refers to Gross Domestic Price at Market Prices; earlier Gross Domestic Product at factor cost used to be considered.
- GDP (Market Prices) = GDP (Factor Cost) + Indirect Taxes – Subsidies
- GDP (Market Prices) calculated GDP at the end of consumer, rather than at the end of producer. The difference arises between the two because the price paid by consumers for many goods and services is not the same as the sales revenue received by the producer. There are indirect taxes paid by consumers that are accounted; subsidies attached to factors of production granted to producers, are subtracted.

31. A new jargon – JAM Trinity – has become the buzzword in the Narendra Modi Government. The jargon, coined by Chief Economic Advisor Arvind Subramanian, was first used in the Economic Survey 2014-15.

The Economic Survey for 2014-2015 states that the JAM Number Trinity - Jan Dhan Yojana, Aadhaar and Mobile numbers - allows the state to offer support to poor households in a targeted and less distorted way.

32. Buddist economics is the study of maximizing well-being while minimizing consumption. This goal of Buddhist economics seems contradictory to modern Western economics, where increased consumption is perceived as analogous to improved well-being.

The German-born British economist E.F. Schumacher popularized Buddhist economics in the 1970s. In his classic book *Small Is Beautiful: Economics As If People Mattered* (1973). Schumacher challenged standard assumptions of modern economic systems regarding labour, consumption, technology, peace, and the environment.

33. Origin of the Concept of Credit Rating

This concept originated in the US in 1909 AD when the founder of Moody's Investor Service, John Moody, rated the US Rail Road Bonds. However, the relevance of this concept was realised only after the great depression when investors lost all their money. Lack of symmetric information and high costs of collecting information increased the popularity of credit rating agencies. The world's biggest rating agencies are Moody's Investors Service and Standard and Poor's (S&P). They have been into the rating business for decades. Both Moody's and S&P have been rating bonds since 1916 and have captured the lion's share. The nearest competitor of Moody's and S&P is Fitch Investors Service, which does not even share one-fifth of the business. These three rating agencies are given official recognition by the Securities and Exchange Commission (SEC). These agencies have grown so powerful that even sovereign governments are wary of getting a poor rating from them. Journalist Thomas Friedman once said, 'There are two superpowers in the world today. There is the United States and there is Moody's Bond Rating Service. The US can destroy by dropping bombs and Moody's can destroy you by downgrading your bonds.

34. Purchasing power parity (PPP) is a theory that states that exchange rates between currencies are in equilibrium when their purchasing power is the same in each of the two countries. This means that the exchange rate between two countries should equal the ratio of the two countries' price level of a fixed basket of goods and services. When a country's domestic price level is increasing (i.e., a country experiences inflation), that country's exchange rate must depreciate in order to return to PPP.

39. In his *Stages of Economic Growth* (1960), W.W. Rostow put forward the first important systematic theorization of economic history. His 'theory of stages' suggested there was a growth process based on five stages which each country went through before it achieved complete economic development. The five stages were the traditional society, the development of pre-conditions for take-off, take-off, a drive to maturity, and finally the era of mass consumption.

41. Creeping inflation is a slow upward movement in prices over a period of several years. Creeping inflation is usually defined as a 1%, 2% or 3% increase in the general price level each year. Creeping inflation generally accompanies growth and full employment. Many economists prefer creeping inflation to price stability accompanied by unemployment and lack of economic growth.

43.
$$GM = \sqrt[3]{2\times 6\times x}$$
$$\Rightarrow \quad 6 = \sqrt[3]{12x}$$
$$\Rightarrow \quad (6)^3 = 12x$$
$$\Rightarrow \quad 12x = 216$$
$$\Rightarrow \quad x = \frac{216}{12} = 18.$$

44. The Standard Error (SE) can be calculated dividing the standard deviation (σ) by the square root of *n*.

$$\text{SE of } \bar{x} = \frac{\sigma}{\sqrt{n}}$$

45. In a throw of 2 dice, there are $6 \times 6 = 36$ possible outcomes as follows:

(1, 1)	(1, 2)	(1, 3)	(1, 4)	(1, 5)	(1, 6)
(2, 1)	(2, 2)	(2, 3)	(2, 4)	(2, 5)	(2, 6)
(3, 1)	(3, 2)	(3, 3)	(3, 4)	(3, 5)	(3, 6)
(4, 1)	(4, 2)	(4, 3)	(4, 4)	(4, 5)	(4, 6)
(5, 1)	(5, 2)	(5, 3)	(5, 4)	(5, 5)	(5, 6)
(6, 1)	(6, 2)	(6, 3)	(6, 4)	(6, 5)	(6, 6)

$6 \times 6 = 36$

A total of 8 can come in the following 5 way (6, 2) (5, 3) (4, 4) (3, 5) (2, 6)

∴ The probability of getting a total of 8 is

$$P(A) = \frac{5}{36}$$

46. $b_{YX} = 0.4$, $b_{XY} = 1.6$

$$\text{Coefficient of correlation} = \sqrt{b_{YX} \cdot b_{XY}} = \sqrt{0.4 \times 1.6} = \sqrt{0.64} = 0.80.$$

47. For positively skewed distribution the mean will always be the highest estimate of central tendency and mode will always the lowest estimate of central tendency i.e.

For positive skewed distribution

mean > median > mode

here, mean (26) > median (14) > mode (7)

PAPER-III

Note: *This paper contains **seventy five (75)** objective type questions of **two (2)** marks each. **All questions are compulsory.***

1. A recessionary gap measures the:

A. amount by which autonomous spending is below to that needed to achieve a full employment equillibrium

B. amount by which aggrigate spending exceeds to that needed to achieve full employment

C. difference in real output between the classical model and the Keynesian depression model.

D. extent of paradox of thrift

2. How many countries are the members of European Union?

A. 25 B. 28

C. 26 D. 15

3. Identify the factors which are likely to pose risk to India's external economic situation:

(*a*) U.S. Federal Reserve monetory tightening expected later this year (2015).

(*b*) Viability of the Eurozone in the event of a Greek exit

(*c*) Spike in oil prices

(*d*) Increase in India's share in global exports.

Find the correct combination from the given codes:

A. (*a*) and (*b*) B. (*a*), (*b*) and (*c*)

C. (*b*) (*c*) and (*d*) D. (*a*) and (*d*)

4. Monetary policy in India now aims at targeting:

A. Growth of money supply

B. Consumer price inflation

C. Neither A nor B

D. Both A and B

5. Match **List-I** with **List-II** and show the relation between trade cycle and profit by selecting correct codes given below:

List-I	**List-II**
(*a*) Recession	(*i*) Low
(*b*) Boom	(*ii*) Positive
(*c*) Recovery	(*iii*) Highest level
(*d*) Depression	(*iv*) Negative

Codes:

	(*a*)	(*b*)	(*c*)	(*d*)
A.	(*iii*)	(*iv*)	(*i*)	(*ii*)
B.	(*i*)	(*iii*)	(*ii*)	(*iv*)
C.	(*iv*)	(*iii*)	(*ii*)	(*i*)
D.	(*i*)	(*ii*)	(*iii*)	(*iv*)

6. In relative income hypothesis consumption is related to:

A. Peak past consumptions
B. Median current consumption of peer group
C. Neither A nor B
D. Both A and B

7. Monetary expansion can still be effective in getting out of liquidity trap if it's combined with:
A. Restrictions on bank loans
B. Increased taxes
C. Contractionary fiscal policy
D. Expansionary fiscal policy

8. If a linear consumption function passes through the origin it means:
A. APC > MPC B. APC < MPC
C. APC = MPC D. APC = MPC = 0

9. According to Keynes the Aggregate supply curve during depression :
A. is horizontal
B. is vertical
C. tilts downward to the right
D. tilts upward to the right

10. Identify the transfer payments in the following and answer from the codes below:
(*a*) Annual increment in salary
(*b*) Payment of bonus to employees
(*c*) Interest payment on public debt
(*d*) Pension payment
Codes:
A. (*c*) and (*d*) B. (*b*), (*c*) and (*d*)
C. (*a*) and (*b*) D. (*a*) and (*c*)

11. Technical progress is said to be Hicks Capital intensive if at constant capital labour ratio $MRTS_{L,K}$:
A. remains constant
B. decreases
C. increases
D. none of A, B and C are relevant

12. In the theory of investment decisions, the most appropriate rate of return is the one which makes the:
A. net present value the maximum
B. gross present value the maximum
C. net present value zero
D. gross present value zero

13. Correct statement of cob-web model is:
A. $S_t = a_0 + b_0p_t$; $D_t = -c_0 - d_0p_t$
B. $S_t = a_0 + b_0p_{t-1}$; $D_t = c_0 - d_0p_t$
C. $S_t = a_0 - b_0p_{t-1}$; $D_t = c_0 + d_0p_t$
D. $S_t = a_0 - b_0p_{t-1}$; $D_t = c_0 - d_0p_{t-1}$

14. 'Adverse selection' arises because of:
A. Lack of information
B. Wrong information
C. Asymmetrical information
D. Uncertainty of future

15. Shadow prices can be called:
A. Imputed cost B. Opportunity cost
C. both A and B D. neither A or B

16. Walra's general equilibrium model uses a:
A. system of equations
B. system of simultaneous linear equations
C. system of simultaneous equations
D. system of linear equations

17. Which of the following is an inferior good?
A. Kerosine
B. Cooking gas
C. Electricity
D. Chemical fertilizers

18. Pareto optimality in production is gained in which of the following conditions?
A. $MRTS^X_{LK} = MRTS^Y_{LK}$
B. $MRS^A_{XY} = MRS^B_{XY}$
C. $MRS^K_{XY} = MRT^L_{XY}$
D. $\frac{MP_L}{P_L} = \frac{MP_K}{P_K}$

19. Match **List-I** (Consumer behaviour approach) with **List-II** (Economist with whom it is associated) and select the correct answer using the codes given below:

List-I	List-II
(*a*) Cardinal Approach	(*i*) Von Newman Morgenstein
(*b*) Indifference curve	(*ii*) Alfred Marshell

(*c*) Revealed Preference Approach — (*iii*) J. K. Hicks

(*d*) Neo-utility theory of risky choices — (*iv*) P. A. Samuelson

Codes:

	(*a*)	(*b*)	(*c*)	(*d*)
A.	(*ii*)	(*iii*)	(*i*)	(*iv*)
B.	(*iii*)	(*ii*)	(*i*)	(*iv*)
C.	(*ii*)	(*iii*)	(*iv*)	(*i*)
D.	(*iii*)	(*ii*)	(*iv*)	(*i*)

20. Which one of the following is the correct concept of Natural rating unemployment?

A. Frictionally and structurally unemployed
B. Frictionally and cyclically unemployed
C. Structurally and cyclically unemployed
D. Frictionally, cyclically and structurally unemployed

21. Consider the following statements:

(*a*) Points to the left of the IS curve indicate excess supply of goods.
(*b*) Points to the right of the LM curve indicate excess demand for money.
(*c*) Points to the right of the IS curve indicate excess supply of money.
(*d*) Points to the right of the IS curve indicate excess supply of goods.

Of these statements:

A. (*b*) and (*d*) are correct
B. (*a*) and (*c*) are correct
C. (*b*) and (*c*) are correct
D. (*c*) and (*d*) are correct

22. Match **List-I** with **List-II** and select the correct answer from the codes given below:

List-I	**List-II**
(*a*) $C = 40 + 0.7y$	(*i*) LM function
(*b*) $I = 90 - 6i$	(*ii*) IS function
(*c*) $0.3y - 20i - 160 = 0$	(*iii*) Consumption function
(*d*) $0.3y + 20i - 150 = 0$	(*iv*) Investment function

Codes:

	(*a*)	(*b*)	(*c*)	(*d*)
A.	(*iii*)	(*iv*)	(*i*)	(*ii*)
B.	(*iv*)	(*iii*)	(*ii*)	(*i*)
C.	(*iv*)	(*i*)	(*ii*)	(*iii*)
D.	(*iii*)	(*iv*)	(*ii*)	(*i*)

23. In a linear programming problem, an optimum solution will be:

A. One of the basic solutions
B. One of the feasible solutions
C. One of the basic feasible solutions
D. One of the non-basic solutions

24. Human capital formation can be accelerated by:

A. Promoting skill development programmes
B. Providing medical and health facilities in both rural and urban areas.
C. Strengthening hardware and software industry.
D. A and B above

25. What is the correct sequence for the evolution of society according to Karl Marx?

(*a*) Socialism (*b*) Slavery
(*c*) Feudalism (*d*) Capitalism

Codes:

A. (*a*), (*b*), (*c*) and (*d*)
B. (*d*), (*c*), (*b*) and (*a*)
C. (*b*), (*c*), (*d*) and (*a*)
D. (*c*), (*d*), (*b*) and (*a*)

26. The unbalanced growth strategy is based on:

A. External and Internal economies
B. Spread and backwash effects
C. Increasing and constant returns to scale
D. Backward and forward linkages

27. Financial dualism theory was developed by:

A. B. Higgins B. H. Myint
C. W. A. Lewis D. R. Nurkse

28. Which among the following production function will exhibit both Hicks and Harrod technical progress?

A. Leontieff production functions
B. Cobb-Douglas production functions
C. ACMS production functions
D. None of the above

29. The concept of X-efficiency was formulated by:

A. H. Singer B. H. Leibenstein
C. R. Rodan D. C. Kindleberger

30. Which among the following items has the largest value of exports in India during 2013-15?
A. Engineering goods
B. Garments
C. Gems and Jewellary
D. Agro-processing exports.

31. Which among the following is not correctly matched?
A. Golden age : Mrs. Joan Robinson
B. Golden rule of accumulation : Edmund Phelfs
C. Steady state growth : Robert Solow
D. Low income equilibrium trap : T. R. Malthus

32. Who among the following economists is not associated with the Dependency Theory?
A. S. Amin B. P. Baron
C. Raul Prebisch D. A. G. Frank

33. Which one of the following is **not** a feature of neoclassical economics?
A. Flexible wages and interest rates
B. Capital in physical and financial form
C. Perfect competition
D. Neutrality of money

34. Renewed focus to control increasing population is required from the viewpoint of women because:
A. Family planning programme needs to be reoriented keeping in view the reproductive health rights of women.
B. Increased budget needed to provide quality services to women.
C. Increased number of women councellers needed for health and youth friendly services.
D. All of the above

35. Match **List-I** with **List-II** and select the correct answer:

List-I	**List-II**
(*a*) Supply side of international trade	(*i*) David Ricardo
(*b*) Demand side of international trade	(*ii*) Bastable and Alfred Marshall
(*c*) Opportunity cost of international trade	(*iii*) G. Haberler
(*d*) Real cost theory of International trade	(*iv*) Alfred Marshall and Edgeworth

Codes :

	(*a*)	(*b*)	(*c*)	(*d*)
A.	(*i*)	(*iv*)	(*ii*)	(*iii*)
B.	(*i*)	(*iv*)	(*iii*)	(*ii*)
C.	(*iv*)	(*i*)	(*ii*)	(*iii*)
D.	(*iv*)	(*i*)	(*iii*)	(*ii*)

36. Justice in taxation is best ensured by applying the principle of:
A. Equal marginal sacrifice
B. Equal proportional sacrifice
C. Equal absolute sacrifice
D. None of the above

37. All the funds which belong to Government go to:
A. Public Account
B. Consolidated Fund
C. Contigency Fund
D. Revenue Account

38. During the period 2004 and 2013, India's share in global exports increased from:
A. 0.8 per cent to 1.7 per cent
B. 1.0 per cent to 2.5 per cent
C. 1.0 per cent to 1.5 per cent
D. 1.2 per cent to 2.1 per cent

39. 'Gender budgeting' means:
A. a separate budget for women
B. a tool for gender empowerment
C. a tool for gender discrimination
D. a separate budget for men and women

40. Which sector in India has developed breaking the Colin Clark sequence of development?
A. Export Sector
B. Primary Sector
C. Secondary Sector
D. Service Sector

41. Match **List-I** with **List-II** by selecting correct codes given below:

List-I	List-II
(*a*) Liquidity trap	(*i*) M. Friedman
(*b*) Demonstration effect	(*ii*) A. C. Pigou
(*c*) Permanent Income Hypothesis	(*iv*) J. Duesenberry
(*d*) Wealth Effect	(*iv*) J. M. Keynes

Codes:

	(*a*)	(*b*)	(*c*)	(*d*)
A.	(*iv*)	(*iii*)	(*i*)	(*ii*)
B.	(*i*)	(*ii*)	(*iv*)	(*iii*)
C.	(*iv*)	(*ii*)	(*i*)	(*iii*)
D.	(*i*)	(*iii*)	(*iv*)	(*ii*)

42. An over-valued currency will have which of the following effects:

A. Make exports and imports equally costly
B. Make exports and imports equally cheaper
C. Make imports relatively more costly
D. Make imports relatively cheaper

43. According to Pribisch-Singer thesis which of the following is true?

(*a*) International trade has increased international inequalities and has retarded the development of developing countries.
(*b*) The strategy of import substitution has resulted in misallocation of resources within a developing country.

Codes:

A. Both (*a*) and (*b*) are true
B. Only (*a*) is true
C. Only (*b*) is true
D. Both (*a*) and (*b*) are not true

44. Assertion (A): Marshall-Lerner condition should be fulfilled if devaluation is to be successful.

Reason (R): Devaluation makes exports costly and imports cheaper.

Codes:

A. Both **(A)** and **(R)** are correct
B. Both **(A)** and **(R)** are not correct
C. **(A)** is correct but **(R)** is not correct explanation of **(A)**
D. **(A)** is correct and **(R)** is the correct reason of **(A)**

45. Productivity changes in domestic export industry are incorporated in which types of terms of trade?

A. Income terms of trade
B. Single factoral terms of trade
C. Gross barter terms of trade
D. None of the above

46. The proposed GST bill will subsume:

A. Entertainment tax
B. Value-added tax
C. Union excise duty
D. All of the above

47. Select the pair of economists, who first gave the canons of taxation and public expenditure:

A. R. N. Bhargav and R. A. Musgrave
B. Adam Smith and Findlay Shirras
C. A. C. Pigou and David Ricardo
D. A. R. Prest and Ursula K Hicks

48. Following are some of the effects of parallel economy in India:

(*a*) Loss of revenue to the Government
(*b*) Greater burden on honest tax-payers
(*c*) Results in equitable distribution of wealth and income
(*d*) Encouragement to non-essential items of conspicuous consumption.

Find the correct combination from the codes given below:

A. (*a*), (*b*) and (*c*) B. (*a*), (*b*) and (*d*)
C. (*b*), (*c*) and (*d*) D. (*a*) and (*d*)

49. Reference period for the Neonatal Mortality Rate in India is:

A. Three months after birth
B. One month after birth
C. 28 days after birth
D. None of the above

50. Recently launched "Indradhanush" programme is related with:

A. Production of medicines
B. Vaccination against fatal diseases
C. Multivocational training for adolescent girls
D. None of the above

51. Who suggested to Government of India to introduce expenditure tax?
A. N. Kalder B. J. R. Hicks
C. B Hanson D. Ursula Hicks

52. Which of the following new financing agency provide finance to micro and small business?
A. S I D B I B. M U D R A
C. N A B A R D D. K C C

53. Who said, "Inflation is unjust and deflation is inexpedient"?
A. A. K. Sen B. J. R. Hicks
C. A. C. Pigou D. J. M. Keynes

54. Consider the following reasons of continuous decline in average land holding rise in India. Answer from the code given below:
(*a*) Law of Inheritance
(*b*) Consolidation
(*c*) Farm Mechanization
(*d*) Desire for land ownership
Codes:
A. (*a*) and (*b*) B. (*a*) and (*d*)
C. (*a*), (*b*), (*c*) and (*d*) D. (*a*), (*c*) and (*d*)

55. Central Governments' situation is likely to be stressed because of:
A. Implementation of the recommendations of the Seventh Central Pay Commission
B. Larger devolution to the states arising out of recommendations of the Fourteenth Finance Commission.
C. Compensation to the states on implementation of GST
D. All of the above

56. Which tax is imposed solely by the Government of India?
A. Sales Tax B. Excise Tax
C. Custom duty D. Octroi duty

57. GST in India will be characterised by which of the following features?
Choose the correct answer from the codes given below:
(*a*) There will be a dual GST with Centre and the state.
(*b*) It would be a destination based tax as against the origin based tax.
(*c*) It would apply to all goods and services excluding alcohol for human consumption.
Codes:
A. All the above are correct
B. Only (*a*) is true
C. Both (*a*) and (*b*) are true
D. Only (*b*) and (*c*) are true

58. Consider the following:
(*a*) Interest rate on bonds
(*b*) Rate of inflation
(*c*) Ratio of savings to investment
The velocity of money according to Friedman depends upon which of the above factors?
Choose the code to answer.
Codes:
A. (*a*), (*b*) and (*c*) B. (*b*) and (*c*)
C. (*a*) and (*b*) D. Only (*c*)

59. Which country introduced paper currency system first in World?
A. England B. USA
C. India D. Sweden

60. The 2014 Nobel Prize in Economics was awarded to:
A. Lars Peter Hansen B. Jean Tirole
C. Alvin E. Roth D. Paul Krugman

61. In environmental economics Herman Daly has formulated:
A. Step up approach
B. Space utilisation approach
C. Ecological approach
D. Steady-state approach

62. High powered panel to select the non-executive chairman of public sector banks has been constituted by Government under the chairmanship of:
A. C. Rangarajan B. Raghuram Rajan
C. Bimal Jalan D. Y. V. Reddy

63. **Assertion:** The share of women in decision making process is gradually increasing.
Reasoning: Greater inclusion of women involves greater share of gender budget in general budget.

Of the above statements, which one is correct:
A. Both **(A)** and **(R)** are correct and **(R)** is correct explanation of **(A)**
B. Both **(A)** and **(R)** are correct and **(R)** is not the correct explanation of **(A)**
C. **(A)** is true but **(R)** is false
D. **(R)** is true but **(A)** is false

64. India's 'Green Actions' can be made effective by:
A. Increase in excise duty on petrol and diesel
B. Translating coal cess into a 'carbon tax'
C. Significantly promoting the renewable sources of energy
D. All of the above

65. Which of the following are the conditions of economic viability and technological feasibility of Leontief's static model?
A. Kuhn-Tucker conditions
B. Hawkins-Simon conditions
C. Klein-Rubin conditions
D. Von Neumann-Mogenstern conditions

66. Given the demand function as $p = \frac{1}{4}q^{-\frac{1}{2}}$, consumer's surplus at $q = 25$ is:
A. 1.12 B. 1.25
C. 1 D. 0.5

67. Given the demand function as $p = 20 - 2q$, the average and marginal revenue at $q = 3$ are respectively:
A. 6 and 12 B. 7 and 12
C. 8 and 14 D. 11 and 15

68. Which of the following is true in the context of statistical tests of hypotheses for two variable linear regression model:
A. $t^2 > F$ B. $t^2 < F$
C. $t^2 = F$ D. $t = F$

69. Which is the correct form of model to test the stationarity of a time series through Dicky-Fuller test?
A. $Y_t = \lambda Y_{t-1} + \mu_t$ B. $Y_t = Y_{t-1} + \lambda\mu_t$
C. $Y_t = \lambda_{t+1} + \mu_t$ D. $\Delta Y_t = \lambda Y_{t-1} + \mu_t$

70. The term 'best' in the best linear unbiased estimators (BLUE) implies:
A. Maximum variance of the estimators
B. Minimum variance of the estimators
C. Average variance of the estimators
D. Unbiased variance of the estimators

71. Match the following and answer from codes given below:

List-I	List-II
(a) Durbin's *h*-test	*(i)* Heteroscedasticity
(b) Goldfeld-Quandt test	*(ii)* Overall significance of a regression
(c) F-test	*(iii)* Stationarity of a series
(d) Dicky-Fuller test	*(iv)* Auto-correlation in auto-regressive models

Codes:

	(a)	*(b)*	*(c)*	*(d)*
A.	*(i)*	*(iii)*	*(iv)*	*(ii)*
B.	*(ii)*	*(iv)*	*(i)*	*(iii)*
C.	*(iv)*	*(i)*	*(ii)*	*(iii)*
D.	*(iii)*	*(iv)*	*(ii)*	*(i)*

72. In a simultaneous equations system for an over-identified equation the appropriate method of estimation is:
A. Ordinary Least Squares Method
B. Indirect Least Squares Method
C. Two-stage Least Squares Method
D. Limited information maximum Likelyhood Method

73. Which of the following statements are true concerning a recursive system?
(a) The parameters can be validly estimated using separate application of OLS to each equation
(b) The independent variables may be correlated with the error terms in other equations.
(c) An application of 2SLS would lead to unbiased but unefficient parameter estimates.
(d) The independent variables may be correlated with error terms in the equations in which they appear as independent variables.

A. (*b*) and (*d*) only
B. (*a*) and (*c*) only
C. (*a*), (*b*) and (*c*) only
D. (*a*), (*b*), (*c*) and (*d*)

74. In a multiple regression the regression coefficients are to be tested. Which test would be used?

A. F-test B. χ^2-(Chi-square) test
C. *d*-test D. *t*-test

75. In CES production function

$$Q = A\left[\alpha X_1^{-\rho} + (1-\alpha) X_2^{-\rho}\right]^{-\frac{\mu}{\rho}}$$

Where Q is output and X_1 and X_2 are labour and capital, choose the correct alternative from given codes.

(*a*) Efficiency Parameter (*i*) μ
(*b*) Distribution Parameter (*ii*) ρ
(*c*) Substitution Parameter (*iii*) α
(*d*) Returns to scale parameter (*iv*) A

Codes:

	(*a*)	(*b*)	(*c*)	(*d*)
A.	(*i*)	(*ii*)	(*iv*)	(*iii*)
B.	(*i*)	(*iii*)	(*ii*)	(*iv*)
C.	(*iv*)	(*iii*)	(*ii*)	(*i*)
D.	(*ii*)	(*iii*)	(*iv*)	(*i*)

ANSWERS

1	2	3	4	5	6	7	8	9	10
A	B	B	B	C	D	D	C	A	A
11	**12**	**13**	**14**	**15**	**16**	**17**	**18**	**19**	**20**
B	C	B	C	C	B	A	A	C	A
21	**22**	**23**	**24**	**25**	**26**	**27**	**28**	**29**	**30**
A	D	C	D	C	D	B	B	B	A
31	**32**	**33**	**34**	**35**	**36**	**37**	**38**	**39**	**40**
D	C	B	D	D	A	B	A	B	D
41	**42**	**43**	**44**	**45**	**46**	**47**	**48**	**49**	**50**
A	D	B	C	B	D	B	B	C	B
51	**52**	**53**	**54**	**55**	**56**	**57**	**58**	**59**	**60**
A	B	D	B	D	C	A	C	D	B
61	**62**	**63**	**64**	**65**	**66**	**67**	**68**	**69**	**70**
D	B	A	D	B	B	C	C	A	B
71	**72**	**73**	**74**	**75**					
C	C	C	D	C					

SOME SELECTED EXPLANATORY ANSWERS

1. A recessionary gap exists when the equilibrium level of national income is below the full-employment level. The amount by which aggregate expenditure must increase to achieve full employment is the recessionary gap. An inflationary gap exists when the equilibrium level of national income is above the full-employment level. The inflationary gap is the amount by which aggregate expenditure must decrease to achieve full-employment level. The inflationary gap is the amount by which aggregate expenditure must decrease to achieve full employment.

A recessionary gap can be closed by government spending. When the government spends, a multiple expansion in national income arises. Government spending is not without its problems. It may raise the deficit.

5. Business Cycle (also known as trade cycle) are species of fluctuations in the economic activities of organised communities. It is composed of period of good trade characterised by rising prices and low unemployment, alternating with period of bad trade characterised by falling prices and high unemployment. Every trade cycle has five different subphases—Depression, Recovery, Full Employment, Prosperity (Boom) and Recession.

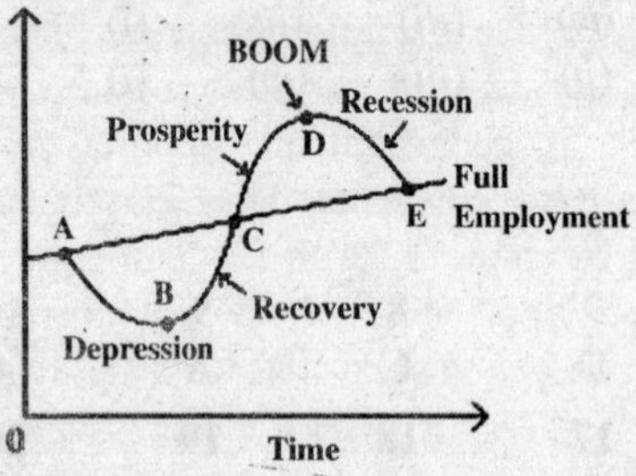

6. Two types of relative income may exert influence on consumption expenditure:
   - Current income relative to the past peak income
   - Own income relative to the average income in the neighbourhood/nation.

   Consumption determines the standard of living and by habit people enjoy raising their standard but hate letting it slide downwards. This implies a somewhat asymmetric behaviour of consumers. When their incomes rise, they raise their consumption but they refuse to reduce their consumption in the face of falling incomes. This behaviour suggests that the ratio of the household's current income to its peak income achieved in the past acts as an additional determinant of its current consumption. If this ratio falls, *ceteris paribus,* the current consumption goes up, and *vice-versa.*

8. When the consumption function intersects the vertical axis below the point of origin of the axes although the APC will be less than the constant MPC but it will be approaching the value of the MPC. When the consumption function passes through the point of origin of the axes, the APC equals MPC. From this it follows that linearity of the consumption function always gives constant MPC because the slope of such a function will always be constant. But it does not always mean a constant APC. Only a proportional income-consumption relationship represented by the special case of linear consumption function passing through the point of origin of the axes will give a constant APC.

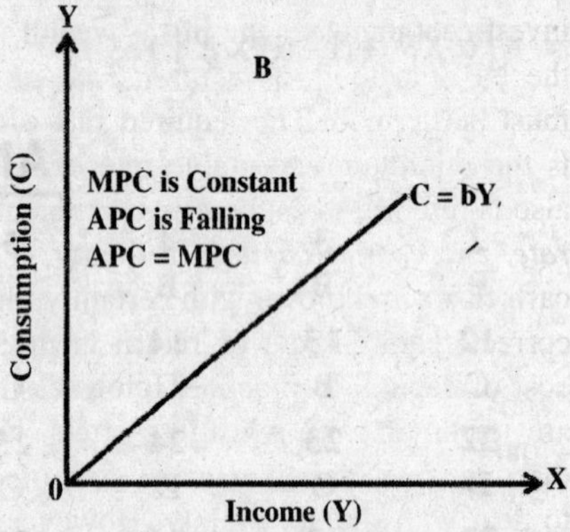

9. The *Keynesian aggregate supply curve* is horizontal, indicating that firms will supply whatever amount of goods is demanded at the existing price level. The idea underlying the Keynesian aggregate supply curve is that because there is unemployment, firms can obtain as much labour as they want at the current wage. Their average costs of production therefore are assumed not to change as their output levels change. They are accordingly willing to supply as much as is demanded at the existing price level. The intellectual genesis of the Keynesian aggregate supply curve lay in the Great Depression, when it seemed that output could expand endlessly without increasing prices by putting idle capital and labour to work.

11. Technological progress is capital-deepening if at a constant K/L ratio the $MRTS_{L,k}$ declines. This implies that at equilibrium the *w*/*r* ratio declines, that is, *r* increases relative to *w*, while K/L remains constant.

Consequently the ratio of factor shares declines:

$$\begin{pmatrix} \text{new} \\ \text{factor-share} \\ \text{ratio} \end{pmatrix} = \frac{(w/r)}{(K/L)} < \begin{pmatrix} \text{initial} \\ \text{factor-share} \\ \text{ratio} \end{pmatrix}$$

This is tantamount to saying that the share of labour decreases and the share of capital increases.

12. NPV measures the profitability of an investment. A positive NPV indicates that the investment increases the firm's wealth. To use the NPV method, a *required rate of return* must be defined. The required rate of return is the minimum acceptable rate of return. It also is referred to as the *discount rate, burdle rate,* and *cost of capital.* In theory, if future cash flows are known with certainty, then the correct required rate of return is the firm's cost of capital. In practice, future cash flows are uncertain, and managers often choose a discount rate higher than the cost of capital to deal with the uncertainty. However, if the rate chosen is excessively high, it will bias the selection process toward short-term investments. Because of the risk of being overly conservative, it may be better to use the cost of capital as the discount rate and find other approaches to deal with uncertainty.

Once the NPV for a project is computed, it can be used to determine whether or not to accept and investment:

- If the NPV is greater than zero the investment is profitable and, therefore, acceptable. A positive NPV signals that (1) the initial investment has been recovered, (2) the required rate of return has been recovered, and (3) a return in excess of (1) and (2) has been received.
- If the NPV equals zero, the decision maker will find acceptance or rejection of the investment equal.
- If the NPV is less than zero, the investment should be rejected. In this case, it is earning less than the required rate of return.

14. Adverse selection arises because buyers and sellers possess different information—what is called asymmetrical information. When asymmetrical information exists, the market may not efficiently allocate goods and services to their highest valued use.

15. Shadow prices reflect intrinsic or true values for factors or products. J. Tinbergen defined them for the first time in 1954 in these words: "Shadow prices are prices indicating the intrinsic or true value of a factor or product in the sense of equilibrium prices. These prices may be different for different time periods as well as geographically separate areas and various occupations. They may deviate from market prices." In 1958, Tinbergen defined shadow prices as those that correspond to intrinsic value and that would prevail if: "(i) the investment pattern under discussion were actually carried out; and (ii) equilibrium existed on the markets just mentioned (*i.e.* labour, capital, foreign exchange markets)."

A UN Report defines shadow prices in terms of the opportunity cost of the factor or product. The shadow price of an output such as capital, labour or foreign exchange represents its "opportunity cost" or the loss to the economy that would result from a reduction in its supply by one unit.

16. Leon Walras (1834-1910) was the first economist to put the neoclassical theory in a formal *general equilibrium* setting. Walras tried to demonstrate how an economy with many goods fits together and reaches equilibrium. For this purpose Walras (1896) built a system of simultaneous linear equations to describe an economic equilibrium model. Walras showed that the whole system is solvable because the number of equations equals the number of unknowns.

20. Natural Unemployment: Adding the frictional unemployment rate and the structural unemployment rate gives the natural unemployment rate (or natural rate of unemployment). We use the symbol U_N to designate the natural unemployment rate. Currently, most economists estimate the natural unemployment rate at between 4 and 6.5 per cent.

Natural unemployment rate (U_N) = Frictional unemployment rate (U_F) + Structural unemployment rate (U_S).

21. Regarding the *IS* curve any combination of income and interest that lies on the *IS* curve represents a goods market equilibrium. However, at all other points, there exists goods market disequilibrium.

(*i*) All combinations of income and interest that lie above and towards the right of the *IS* curve indicate a situation, where Y > C + I or saving is greater than planned investment. Hence, the level of income will fall.

(*ii*) All combinations of income and interest that lie below and towards the left of the *IS* curve indicate a situation, where Y < C + I or saving is less than planned investment. Hence, the level of income will rise.

Regarding the *LM* curve, any combination of income and interest that lies on the *LM* curve represents money market equilibrium. However, at all other points, there exists money market disequilibrium.

(*i*) All combinations of income and interest that lie below and towards the right of the *LM* curve indicate a situation, where the demand for money is greater than the supply of money or there is an excess demand for money. Hence, the rate of interest will rise.

(*ii*) All combinations of income and interest that lie above and towards the left of the LM curve indicate a situation, where the demand for money is less than the supply of money or there is an excess supply of money. Hence, the rate of interest will fall.

23. Basic feasible solution: A feasible solution to an LP problem which is also the basic solution is called the basic feasible solution. That is, all basic variables assume non-negative values. Basic feasible solutions are of two types:

(*a*) **Degenerate:** A basic feasible solution is called degenerate if value of at least one basic variable is zero.

(*b*) **Non-degenerate:** A basic feasible solution is called non-degenerate if value all *m* basic variables are non-zero and positive.

Optimum basic feasible solution: A basic feasible solution which optimizes (maximizes or minimizes) the objective function value of the given LP problem is called an optimum basic feasible solution.

26. Some economists advocate unbalanced growth, like Albert O. Hirschman in his 1958 book *The Strategy of Economic Development.* The advantage of unbalanced growth, argued Hirschman, is linkage. If one or more leading sectors grow, then these sectors will create both backward and forward linkages in the economy.

A backward linkage exists when an industry buys inputs from other industries. A forward linkage exists when the output of an industry is purchased by other industries, aside from the final consumer. Both linkages may be measured by the percentage of inputs purchased. For example, in the manufacture of flat screens for computers, a backward linkage would be the purchase of the display panel, and a forward linkage would be the sale of the finished screen to a company assembling laptops (which ultimately sells the laptops to retail customers).

27. Important feature of the money market of developing countries is what Myint called the 'financial dualism' (Myint, 1971). This implies the coexistence of heterogeneous interest rates in the organized and unorganized money markets. The former market is quite sophisticated, and one expects the speculative demand for money to vary with interest rates. In the latter, that is, the unorganized market (usually dominated by the shopkeepers, moneylenders, landlords, merchants or a combination of some of these which may ultimately create a monopoly situation), the interest rates are expected to change with the risks and returns on real assets. Under such circumstances, the supply of money may not affect the rates of interest significantly. Hence the Keynesian theory may not be very applicable to developing countries.

28. **Cobb-Douglas Production Function:** It is possible for technical progress to be both Hicks-neutral and Harrod-neutral. This can only happen if the elasticity of substitution between capital and labour is one. The only production function with this characteristic is known as the Cobb-Douglas production function.

29. In 1966, Harvey Leibenstein published an article in the *American Economic Review* entitled 'Allocative efficiency vs X-efficiency'. In the article, he develops a very simple but resonant idea. According to Leibenstein, traditional microeconomic theory emphasizes allocative efficiency (that is efficiency in the allocation of resources) to the detriment of other sources of efficiency, which he regards as much more important and in which motivation and incentive occupy a central position.

X-efficiency is a reflection of managerial quality (good or bad). Managers, after all, determine not only their own productivity but also that of the production units for which they are responsible, since effort, which is an *a priori* variable in neoclassical theory, becomes a discretionary variable in X-efficiency theory.

Leibenstein provides a number of examples that tend to support the existence of X-efficiency.

32. Dependency theory originated in Latin America in the 1960s to explain the economic and political backwardness of Latin American countries and particularly in the wake of these countries' subservient relationship to American imperialism. Some of the founding theorists of dependency theory are Andre Gunder Frank, *Dependent Accumulation and Underdevelopment* (New York: Monthly Review Press, 1979), and Samir Amin, *Accumulation on a World Scale: A Critique of the Theory of Underdevelopment* (New York: Monthly Review Press, 1974).

36. **Equal marginal sacrifice:** According to this principle, the sacrifice made by all the taxpayers should be the same. When marginal sacrifice is equal for all taxpayers, total sacrifice will be maximum. Hence, this principle is also known as the least aggregate sacrifice principle of taxation. This was supported by Edgeworth and Pigou.

Edgeworth and Pigou discarded the absolute and proportional sacrifice criterion considering that there was no logical or intuitive choice between them. They advocated the principle of equal marginal sacrifice in taxation as it satisfied the welfare goal by the least aggregate sacrifice.

The relative tax liability and the relative progressiveness of the tax structure under the different sacrifice principles are summarised in Table.

Table: ***Tax liability and structure under different sacrifice principles***

Criterion of sacrifice	*Relative tax liability of the*		*Nature of the tax structure*
	Rice	*Poor*	
1. Equal absolute sacrifice	Least	More	Least progressiveness (proportional taxation)
2. Equal proportional sacrifice	More	Less	Reasonably progressive taxation
3. Equal marginal sacrifice	Maximum	Minimum	Steeply progressive taxation

Of the three versions, equal total sacrifice, equal proportional sacrifice and equal marginal sacrifice, the last one is regarded as the ultimate, the best and generally accepted principle of taxation by modern economists.

39. The concept of "Gender Budgeting" has becoming more and more popular day-by-day. The federal country of Australia, is the first country who introduced gender sensitive budget in 1984.

The term "gender budgeting" has become a catch all phrase to describe various government initiatives that seek to address gender issues in the domain of public expenditure and policy.

'Gender-sensitive budgets', 'gender budgets', and 'women's budgets' refer to a variety of process and tools aimed at facilitating an assessment of the gendered impacts of government budgets.

"Gender budget initiatives analyze how governments raise and spend public money, with the aim of securing gender equality in decision-making about public resource allocation; and gender equality in the distribution of the impact of government budgets, both in their benefits and in their burdens. The impact of government budget on the most disadvantaged groups of women's is a focus of special attention." (IDRC, 2001)

40. Colin Clark viewed economic development through three occupational stages. Nations beginning as initial primary goods producers (agriculture and fishing) move on to a higher level of development with the production of manufactured goods. The secondary stage comes through advancement in knowledge and skill. With the concomitant material accumulation, nations then seek greater welfare through higher forms of culture and labour and moves from a goods-orientation to a service-orientation. Representative of the tertiary stage is the growth in the transport, distribution and public administration sector. The highest levels of income are attained through non-material output.

43. The thesis propounded by Raul Prebisch and H. Singer states that in the long-run, the terms of trade move against the primary producing countries. The thesis has prognosticated a secular deterioration of the terms of trade between the centre and the periphery. This is the principal factor retarding the growth of LDCs. According to them, the terms of trade had shifted in favour of DCs. Prebisch generalised that a long term decline in the terms of trade of LDCs is an essential consequence of growth and trade between the centre and the periphery. H. Singer in 1950 propounded his thesis that opening of LDCs to trade and investment has tended to inhibit their growth. Raul Prebisch's thesis came in 1950 and then 1959. The views of Prebisch and Singer are almost similar: their major conclusions and findings are the same. This is the reason why the thesis is proposed in joint names of Prebisch and Singer.

46. GST will replace central taxes like excise duty and service tax and state levies such as sales, value-added, entertainment and purchase taxes. All entry taxes like octroi will also be subsumed under GST. The Bill tries to balance the concerns of states on loss of revenue and autonomy and the need for a tax structure that will remove barriers across states and ensure seamless flow of goods and services across the country.

49. **Neonatal Mortality Rate:** The *neonatal mortality rate* measures risk of dying among newborn infants who are under the age of 28 days (0–27 days) for a given year. The formula is as follows:

$$\text{Neonatal mortality rate} = \frac{\text{Number of infant deaths under 28 days of age}}{\text{Number of live births}} \times 1000 \text{ live births (during a year)}$$

Postneonatal Mortality Rate: A statistic that is related to the neonatal mortality rate is the *postneonatal mortality rate*. The postneonatal mortality rate measures risk of dying among older infants during a given year.

Postneonatal mortality rate

$$= \frac{\text{Number of infant deaths from 28 days to 365 days after birth}}{\text{Number of live births – neonatal deaths}} \times 1000 \text{ live births}$$

50. Mission Indradhanush is launched by government for children who are partially vaccinated or unvaccinated.

Mission Indradhanush depicts 7 colours of the rainbow which aims to cover all those children by 2020.

This will mostly focus on around 200 districts. Mission Indradhanush will provide protection against seven life-threatening diseases (diphtheria, whooping cough, tetanus, polio, tuberculosis, measles and hepatitis B). In addition, vaccination against Japanese Encephalitis and Haemophilus influenza type B will be provided in selected districts of the country. Vaccination against tetanus will be provided to the pregnant women.

This missions main objective is to raise the immunization coverage annually and to expand its reach to cover most of the children of the country.

52. Prime Minister Narendra Modi on 8 April 2015 launched the Micro Units Development and Refinance Agency Ltd. (MUDRA) Bank to fund the small entrepreneurs.

The Bank was launched under the ambitious Pradhan Mantri Jan Dhan Yojana (PMJDY). The bank will provide credit of up to 10 lakh rupees to small entrepreneurs and act as a regulator for Micro-Finance institutions (MFIs).

53. Some economists like Keynes regard deflation as more harmful than inflation. In the words of Keynes. "Inflation is unjust, deflation is inexpedient, of the two perhaps deflation is worse."

59. The first European bank to print its own paper money was the Stockholm Bank, Sweden, in 1661.

60. French economist Jean Tirole on 13 October 2014 won the 2014 Nobel Prize for Economics. Jean Tirole was awarded for his analysis of market power and regulation.

61. A stationary or steady state economy was a subject discussed by most of the classical economists (e.g. Adam Smith, Thomas Malthus, and John Stuart Mill) and some important contemporary economists (e.g. John Maynard Keynes and Joseph Schumpeter). For Mill, Keynes and Schumpeter the stationary state was something desirable, whereas for others such as Smith it was an inevitable tragedy.

Following on from the classical economists, Herman Daly largely developed the idea of a 'steady state economy' as an alternative to the growth economy in the 1970s (Daly, 1977, 1973). Daly defines a steady state economy (SSE) as:

"An economy with constant population and constant stock of capital, maintained by a low rate of throughput that is within the regenerative and assimilative capacities of the ecosystem..... Alternatively, and more operationally, we might define the SSE in terms of a constant flow of throughput at a sustainable (low) level, with population and capital stock free to adjust to whatever size can be maintained by the constant throughput beginning with depletion and ending with pollution."

64. India has taken a number of green actions, including imposing significantly higher taxation of petroleum products and reenergizing the renewable energy sector.

Unlike some countries, it has taken substantial actions to eliminate petroleum subsidies and gone beyond to impose substantial taxes on these products. These actions have taken India from a carbon subsidization regime to one of significant carbon taxation regime—from a negative price to an implicit positive price on carbon emissions.

66. Demand function, $p = \frac{1}{4}q^{-\frac{1}{2}}$

when $q = 25$, $p = \frac{1}{4}(25)^{-\frac{1}{2}}$

$= \frac{1}{4}(5)^{-1} = \frac{1}{4\times5}$

$= 0.05.$

$$\text{C.S.} = \int_0^q p\cdot dq - 0.05\times q$$

$$= \int_0^{25} \frac{1}{4}(q)^{-\frac{1}{2}}\cdot dq - 0.05q$$

$$= \frac{2}{4}\left[q^{\frac{1}{2}}\right]_0^{25} - 0.05\times25$$

$$= \frac{1}{2}\times5 - 1.25$$

$$= 2.5 - 1.25 = 1.25.$$

67. Demand function $p = 20 - 2q$

$= 20 - 2\times3$

$= 14$

Total revenue $= p.q = 14\times3 = 42$

Marginal revenue $= \frac{42}{3} = 14$

Average revenue $= \frac{d(\text{T.R.})}{dq}$

$= \frac{d}{dq}(20q - 2q^2)$

$= 20 - 4q$

$= 20 - 4\times3$

$= 20 - 12$

$= 8.$

70. It has been known that sample mean is an unbiased estimate of population mean in case of finite as well as infinite populations. Also the sample mean is a linear function $a_1x_1 + a_2x_2 + ... + a_nx_n$ of the sample values $x_1, x_2, ..., x_n$ subject to the condition $\Sigma a_i = 1$ for $i = 1, 2, ..., n$. Linear functions of the sample values with known a_i's represented as Σa_ix_i, such that $\Sigma a_i = 1$, are called *unbiased linear estimators.*

If one is to select an unbiased linear estimator from amongst the class of such estimators, some criteria have to be fixed. One widely accepted criterion to select one linear unbiased estimator out of all available linear unbiased estimators is to select one which has the smallest possible variance. Such a linear estimator is called *minimum variance linear unbiased estimator.* It is generally called the *best linear unbiased estimator* (BLUE). The adjective 'best' refers to minimum variance.

If a unbiased quadratic estimator of the variance σ^2 exists and it possesses the minimum variance out of the class of available unbiased quadratic estimators, it is known as *minimum variance quadratic estimator.*

72. In general, identification basically determines the choice of the econometric method to be used for estimation. In the first place, when an equation is under-identified, it cannot be estimated and therefore the question of choice of appropriate estimation technique does not arise. If, on the other hand, an equation is exactly identified, the ILS (Indirect Least Squares) is most appropriate. In the case of over-identified equations, the 2SLS is popularly used for estimation.

Previous Paper (Solved)

UGC–NET Economics, December-2014

PAPER-II

Note : *This paper contains **fifty (50)** objective type questions of **two (2)** marks each. **All** questions are compulsory.*

1. Which is called Gossen's second law?
A. Law of Equi-marginal Utility
B. Law of Diminishing Marginal Utility
C. Revealed Preference Theory
D. Indifference Curve Approach

2. When a consumer is in equilibrium, MRS_{XY} is 2.5. If the price of commodity Y is 16, then what will be the price of commodity X?
A. 40 B. 6.4
C. 23.2 D. 24

3. Which of the conditions support long run equilibrium in monopolistic competition?
A. MR = MC, AR = AC
B. P = MC, AR = AC
C. MR = MC = AR = AC
D. AR = MC = AC

4. Who explained importance of time element in price determination, for the first time?
A. Chamberlin
B. Stigler
C. Mrs. Joan Robinson
D. Marshall

5. Law of diminishing returns begins to operate when:
A. Total product begins to rise
B. Total product begins to fall
C. Marginal product begins to rise
D. Marginal product begins to fall

6. Consider the following statements regarding Edgeworth Duopoly model:
I. It takes as given output decision of rival.
II. It takes as given price decision of rival.
III. It is an explanation of price rigidity.
Of these, the correct answer is:
A. Only Statement I is true
B. Both I and II are true
C. Both II and III are true
D. Only III is true

7. Public goods are characterised by
1. Collective consumption
2. Divisibility
3. Non-exclusion
4. Rival consumption
Select the correct answer from the code given below:
Codes:
A. 1 and 2 are correct
B. 1 and 3 are correct
C. 1 and 4 are correct
D. 2 and 4 are correct

8. Among the following what causes market failure?
1. Externality
2. Asymmetry of information
3. Perfect competition
Choose the correct answer from the code given below:
Codes:
A. 1, 2 and 3 are correct
B. Only 1 is correct
C. 1 and 2 are correct
D. 2 and 3 are correct

9. Assuming wage-price flexibility, the classical economists asserted that a decline in money wages and price would lead to
A. Unemployment
B. Deflation
C. High level of employment and output
D. Unemployment and decline in output

10. The classical theory of interest postulates that both savings and investments are a function of

A. the level of National income
B. the level of employment and output
C. monetary and fiscal policy
D. rate of interest

11. The relative income hypothesis of Duesenberry suggests that as income increases, consumption function curve shifts above and therefore,

A. Average propensity to consume rises.
B. Average propensity to consume falls.
C. Average propensity to consume remains constant.
D. Average propensity to consume is equal to 1.

12. Who among the following said, "Inflation is everywhere and always a monetary phenomenon"?

A. James Tobin
B. John M. Keynes
C. Milton Friedman
D. Anna J. Schwartz

13. Accelerator is most closely related to

A. interest rate
B. inventories
C. idle capacity
D. induced investment

14. Match List-I and List-II and select the correct answer from the codes given below:

List-I *Concept*	List-II *Economist*
(*a*) Liquidity trap	1. Milton Friedman
(*b*) Demonstration Effect	2. A.C. Pigou
(*c*) Permanent Income Hypothesis	3. J. Duesenberry
(*d*) Wealth Effect	4. J.M. Keynes

Codes:

	(*a*)	(*b*)	(*c*)	(*d*)
A.	4	3	1	2
B.	1	2	4	3
C.	4	2	1	3
D.	1	3	4	2

15. Which one of the following would be inconsistent with the Keynesian view about the effectiveness of monetary policy?

A. Velocity of money is relatively stable.
B. The demand for money is unstable.
C. The demand for money is interest sensitive.
D. Investment demand is unstable.

16. Which of the following statement is true?

A. Sporadic dumping is selling of goods at a low price in the foreign market to get rid of the inventory stocks.
B. Predatory dumping is destroying of competitors even at a loss initially and then, after eliminating of competitors, selling product at a high price.
C. Persistent dumping is selling a product at a lower price in foreign markets due to differences in elasticity of demand at home and in the foreign market.
D. All the above

17. According to Comparative Advantage Theory, International Trade will not take place if

A. one country is efficient in the production of both the products.
B. one country is inefficient in the production of both the products.
C. opportunity costs of the two products are same in both the countries.
D. None of the above

18. Imposition of tariff will lead to

A. Deterioration in terms of trade
B. Improvement in terms of trade
C. No effect on terms of trade
D. None of the above

19. Under a freely exchange rate system, a deficit in a Nation's Balance of Payments Account is automatically corrected by

A. a depreciation of its currency
B. an appreciation of its currency
C. domestic inflation
D. deflation and rise in National income

20. Maastricht Treaty led to the creation of which one of the following?

A. European Parliament
B. Euro
C. European Court of Justice
D. European Union

21. Assertion (A): According to Mundell, "Imbalances in the balance of payments is caused by initial differences in unit factor costs."

Reason (R): Free movement of goods will correct the imbalance in the balance of payments of two countries.

In the context of the two statements, which one of the following is correct?

Codes:

A. Both (A) and (R) are true and (R) is the correct explanation of (A).
B. Both (A) and (R) are true and (R) is not the correct explanation of (A).
C. (A) is true, but (R) is false.
D. (A) is false, but (R) is true.

22. The Stolper-Samuelson theorem postulates that the imposition of a tariff by a nation causes the real income of the nation's

A. abundant factor to rise
B. scarce factor to rise
C. scarce factor to fall
D. Both A and B are possible

23. What is perspective planning?

A. Overall appraisal of planning.
B. Review of planning in different fields.
C. Taking up past experience and reviewing the future in that light.
D. Planning for future so as to meet the long term requirement of development in the country.

24. Who formulated the 'People's Plan' for India in 1944?

A. J.L. Nehru
B. M.N. Roy
C. Subhas Chandra Bose
D. Mahatma Gandhi

25. "Trickle down" strategy implies

A. growing GNP taking care of poverty.
B. reduction in the income of the upper class by deliberate redistribution.
C. direct achievement of better nourishment, health, education, etc. instead of growth of GNP first.
D. to target a particular sector of economy for betterment.

26. What is the correct sequence of the following approaches to development in terms of their chronological emergency?

1. Basic needs approach
2. Per capita income approach
3. Human Development Index approach

Choose the correct answer from the codes given below:

Codes:

A. 1, 2, 3
B. 2, 1, 3
C. 2, 3, 1
D. 1, 3, 2

27. Choose the correct statements for economic development and answer from the code below:

Statements : I. Continuous process
II. Short-term process
III. Long-term process

Codes:

A. II only   B. I and III
C. III only   D. I and II

28. Which of the following economists are proponents of dependency theory of development?

Choose from the code below:

I. Ragnar Nurkse
II. Andre Gunther Frank
III. Raul Prebisch
IV. John Kenneth Galbraith

Codes:

A. I, II and III are correct
B. II and III are correct
C. II, III and IV are correct
D. III and IV are correct

29. What is true for neo-classical growth models?
I. Rate of interest and profit are flexible.
II. Capital is heterogeneous.
III. Perfect competition prevails.
IV. Capital and labour are substitutable.
Choose the correct answer from the codes given below:
Codes:
A. Only I, II and III are true
B. Only II and III are true
C. Only I, III and IV are true
D. All the above are true

30. Choose the top three trading partners of India in 2013-14:
I. UAE II. Korea
III. China IV. USA
Choose the correct answer from codes given below:
Codes:
A. I, II, III B. II, III, IV
C. I. III, IV D. II, I, IV

31. Of the following, which combination of two deficits is most significant for the Indian economy?
A. Fiscal deficit and Revenue deficit
B. Revenue deficit and Primary deficit
C. Budget deficit and Fiscal deficit
D. Current Account deficit and Fiscal deficit

32. Of the following, which sector witnessed the highest growth rate in year 2013-14?
A. Agriculture, forestry and fishery
B. Mining and quarrying
C. Manufacturing
D. Construction

33. Who has advocated the concept of PURA (Providing Urban Amenities in Rural Areas) for our country?
A. A.P.J. Abdul Kalam
B. Manmohan Singh
C. Charan Singh
D. None of the above

34. ECOMARK is a symbol related to
A. Export Goods
B. Import Goods
C. Goods Safe for Environment
D. Best Quality Goods

35. Arrange following countries as per their HDI rank in the descending order (on the basis of 2013, UNDP Report on Human Development):
1. Vietnam 2. China
3. India 4. Sri Lanka
Choose the correct answer from the codes given below:
Codes:
A. 4, 2, 1, 3 B. 2, 1, 4, 3
C. 2, 4, 3, 1 D. 1, 2, 3, 4

36. Consider the following export groups from India for the year 2013-14:
1. Agri. and allied products
2. Engineering goods
3. Gems and Jewellery
4. Textile and Readymade Garments
Arrange them in descending order of magnitude as a per cent to total exports.
A. 2, 1, 4, 3 B. 2, 1, 3, 4
C. 4, 2, 1, 3 D. 3, 4, 2, 1

37. Techniques used to encourage the production and consumption of goods that generate positive externalities are referred to as
A. Tax incentives and vouchers
B. Fees and fines
C. Taxes and charges
D. Special assessment

38. Which of the canons of taxations have been propounded by Adam Smith?
A. Economy, Elasticity, Simplicity and Sufficiency
B. Equity, Certainty, Convenience and Economy
C. Certainty, Convenience, Economy and Elasticity
D. Economy, Coordination, Convenience and Expediency

39. Displacement effect explained in Peacock-Wiseman hypothesis implies:
A. An upward displacement of public expenditure according to higher economic growth

B. The movement from older level of public expenditure and taxation to a newer and higher level

C. Public expenditure increases at steady rate and reaches higher level

D. Government undertakes more and more newer activities and hence public expenditure rises steeply upwards

40. The most important characteristic of a federation is:

A. Perfect match between the functions and resources of the Central and State Governments

B. Non-correspondence between the functions and resources of the Central and State Governments

C. Centre's supremacy over the States

D. None of the above

41. Fiscal consolidation at the Centre can be achieved by:

A. Rationalization of major subsidies alone

B. Reducing the defence expenditure only

C. Raising the tax-GDP ratio and rationalisation of subsidies

D. Minimising the Central assistance to the States

42. Arrange the following Reports in chronological order:

I. Direct Taxes Enquiry Committee, Final Report

II. Final Report on Rationalising and Simplifications of the Tax Structure

III. Indian Tax Reforms – Report of a Survey

IV. Taxation Enquiry Commission

Choose the correct answer from the codes given below:

Codes:

A. IV, III, II, I

B. I, II, III, IV

C. III, I, IV, II

D. II, III, I, IV

43. Identify correctly the taxes in State List (List-II) of the Constitution of India:

I. Taxes on mineral rights

II. Taxes on luxuries

III. Rates of stamp duty in respect of bills of exchange, cheques and promissory notes

IV. Excise duties on tobacco

Choose the right answer from the codes given below:

Codes:

A. I and III are correct

B. I and II are correct

C. I, III and IV are correct

D. II, III and IV are correct

44. Lump sum grant means:

A. A grant whose amount is sufficient to meet the expenditure.

B. A matching and conditional grant.

C. Grant given for a special purpose and it can be utilised only for that purpose.

D. A grant whose amount is not dependent on any matching effort of the recipient.

45. Geometric mean of Laspeyre's and Paasche's indices provides:

A. Marshall-Edgeworth Index

B. Bowley's Index

C. Fisher's Index

D. Kelley's Index

46. **Assertion (A):** Moving averages method can be used to estimate trend in time series.

Reason (R): Moving averages is a device to smoothen the fluctuations in time series.

Choose the correct answer from the codes given below:

Codes:

A. Both (A) and (R) are correct and (R) is a correct explanation of (A).

B. Both (A) and (R) are correct, but (R) is not a correct explanation of (A).

C. (A) is correct, but (R) is incorrect.

D. (R) is correct, but (A) is incorrect.

47. Which one of the following denotes the power of the Test? [α is probability of Type I error and β is probability of Type II error]

A. α B. β

C. $1 - \alpha$ D. $1 - \beta$

48. In a frequency distribution the standard deviation of which is 15.8, the value of median is more than mean by 4, what will be its coefficient of skewness?

A. – 0.76
B. + 0.76
C. – 0.86
D. + 0.86

49. Three coins are tossed simultaneously. What is the probability that they will fall 2 heads and 1 tail?

A. $\frac{1}{2}$ B. $\frac{1}{4}$
C. $\frac{3}{4}$ D. $\frac{3}{8}$

50. In a frequency distribution if each item is multiplied by 5, the coefficient of variation will remain

A. unchanged
B. will be multiplied by 5
C. will be multiplied by 25
D. will be multiplied by 1/5

ANSWERS

1	2	3	4	5	6	7	8	9	10
A	A	A	D	D	A	B	C	C	D
11	**12**	**13**	**14**	**15**	**16**	**17**	**18**	**19**	**20**
C	C	D	A	A	D	C	B	A	D
21	**22**	**23**	**24**	**25**	**26**	**27**	**28**	**29**	**30**
C	B	D	B	A	B	B	B	C	C
31	**32**	**33**	**34**	**35**	**36**	**37**	**38**	**39**	**40**
D	A	A	C	A	B	A	B	B	B
41	**42**	**43**	**44**	**45**	**46**	**47**	**48**	**49**	**50**
C	A	B	D	C	A	D	A	D	A

SOME SELECTED EXPLANATORY ANSWERS

1. Law of Diminishing Marginal Utility (LDMU) : The Law of Diminishing Marginal Utility is one of the very important and fundamental laws of consumption. This is also known as "Gossen's 1st Law of Consumption", named after an Austrian economist Gossen, who introduced it.

The Law of Equi-Marginal Utility (LEMU): The idea of equi-marginal utility was first mentioned by H.H. Gossen (1810-1858) of Germany. Hence, it is called Gossen's second Law of consumption. Alfred Marshall made significant refinements to this law in his 'Principles of Economics'.

According to this law, the consumer will try to maximize his satisfaction when there are substitutes available in the market. So, he will substitute one item in place of the other such that his Marginal Utility is proportional to the price. The law of equi-marginal utility explains the behaviour of a consumer when he consumes more than one commodity. Wants are unlimited, but the income which is available to the consumer to satisfy all his wants is limited. This law explains how the consumer spends his limited income on various commodities to get maximum satisfaction.

2. $\because$ $MRS_{xy} = \frac{P_x}{P_y}$

Here, $MRS_{xy} = 2.5$

$P_y = 16$

$$\Rightarrow \qquad 2.5 = \frac{P_x}{P_y}$$

$$\Rightarrow \qquad P_x = 2.5 \times 16 = 40.$$

3. In the long-run, every firm in the monopolistic competitive industry will earn only normal profits, which are just sufficient to stay in the business. It is to be noted that normal profits are part of average costs.

   In the long-run, in order to achieve equilibrium position in monopolistic competition, the firm has to fulfil the following two conditions:

   (*a*) MR = MC (*b*) AR = AC

   Thus, the firm has to fulfil dual equilibrium conditions as mentioned above. But when compared to long-run equilibrium position of a perfectly competitive firm, even though AR = AC, AC will not be at its minimum point at equilibrium level of output. And also, MR is not equal to either AR or AC, MR is well below AR in the case of monopolistic competitive firm.

4. Marshall explained the role of time element in the determination of price because supply conditions vary with the length of period under consideration. On the basis of response of supply overtime to a given and permanent change in demand, Marshall suggested three periods of time, viz., market period, short period and long period.

5. The law of diminishing marginal returns states that at some points, as the firm hires more of a variable input while other inputs stay unchanged, the variable input's marginal product will begin to fall, such that successive units add less to output than did the previous units. *Marginal returns* is an old term for marginal product. This law applies only in the short run and only when some inputs remain unchanged. It need not apply in the long run.

7. A pure public good is defined as one whose benefits are consumed by all members of a community as soon as it is produced for, or by, any one member. More appropriately, a pure public good can be defined as one which is *consumed jointly* by all the members of a society even if it is produced by an individual, and no one can be *excluded* from its consumption even if one does not pay for the good. Production of a *pure public good* generates external benefits and costs which go to all the members of a society whether intended or not. National defence, law and order system, flood control, control of epidemics and pollution-free atmosphere are some of the classic examples of *pure public goods.*

   There are three basic characteristics of public goods, viz. (*i*) collective consumption, (*ii*) non-rival consumption and (*iii*) non-exclusion. These three characteristics stem from the other features of pure public goods, *i.e.*, its indivisibility forcing their *joint consumption.*

8. *Market failure* means the inability of a system to provide certain goods etiher at all or at the most desirable or 'optimal' level. In general, market failure arises because of four main causes. The *first* is market imperfection, which means deviations from the conditions necessary for perfect competition in the product and factor markets. Thus, if there is monopoly power in the commodity market or if labour is unionized in the labour market, the result is market failure. The *second* cause of market failure is asymmetric (imperfect) information, which means difference in information possessed by the parties to a market transaction. The *third* is the presence of externalities in the production or consumption of goods and services. Externalities are the side effects that can be harmful (known as external cost or external diseconomy) or beneficial (known as external benefit or external economy) for the members of the society. Externalities lead to overproduction or under production of goods and services and the result is economy loss and market failure.

9. Classical economists believed in free markets. They believed that the economy would always achieve full employment through forces of supply and demand. So, if there were more people looking for work than the number of jobs available, the wages would fall until all those seeking work were employed. Thus, market forces guaranteed full employment. The full employment level of employment resulted in a fixed aggregate output/income. The price level (and thus the inflation rate) was determined by the supply of money in the economy. Since, the output level was fixed, a 10 per cent increase in money supply would lead to a 10 per cent increase in the price level—too many dollars chasing too few goods. The real interest rate was also determined by forces of supply and demand in the market for funds that could be loaned out. The nominal interest rate was then simply the sum of the real interest rate and the prevailing inflation rate. Classical economists thus had an unwavering faith in the self-adjusting market mechanism. However, it was crucial for the working of the market mechanism that there was perfect competition in the market, and that wages and prices were fully flexible.

10. Classical Theory of Interest was propounded by economists like J.S. Mill, Walras, Marshall, Pigou etc. According to this theory, interest arises because of such real factors as productivity, thrift, abstinence etc. As such, classical theory regards interest as a real phenomenon. According to this theory, rate of interest is determined by the supply of capital (Savings) and demand for capital (Investment).

11. **The Relative Income Hypothesis :** This hypothesis was first put forward by Dorothy Brady and Rose Friedman. Later on, it was developed by James Duesenberry, in 1952. Duesenberry's theory is referred to as the relative income hypothesis and his theory seems more psychological than economic in nature.

Duesenberry's theory assumes that:

(*i*) One person's consumption is dependent on other people's consumption (Demonstration effect) and

(*ii*) Consumption relations are irreversible over time (Ratchet effect).

This theory states that, if the current and peak incomes grow together, changes in consumption are always proportional to changes in income. In this case, the Average Propensity to Consume (APC) remains constant.

With the help of the above two effects, Duesenberry reformulated the consumption function as follows:

$$C = f(Y_c, Y_{pp})$$

where, Y_c = Current income

Y_{pp} = Previous peak income

(*i*) If $Y_c > Y_{pp}$ consumption is related to one's relative income within the community (demonstration effect)

(*ii*) If $Y_c < Y_{pp}$ consumption is related to previous peak income (Ratchet effect).

12. *Milton Friedman* said, "Inflation is always and everywhere a monetary phenomenon." What exactly does that mean? It essentially means that inflation is always caused because of too much money in the system. In other words, inflation in a country is always caused because the supply of money is much greater than the demand for it. However, *Prof. Friedman* later changed that to: "Substantial inflation is always and everywhere a monetary phenomenon," meaning that hyperinflation (a monthly inflation rate of 50 per cent or more) is caused because of too much money in the system and is usually the result of the Central Bank printing too much money to finance government operations.

13. The famous economist J.R. Hicks has formulated an important theory of trade cycles in his book, *"Contribution to the Theory of Trade Cycles."* According to this theory due to change in investment, interaction between multiplier and accelerator takes place which results in cyclical fluctuations.

According to Prof. Hicks, suppose there is equilibrium in an economy. In this economy autonomous investment is being undertaken. Investment is of two types: firstly, Autonomous Investment and secondly, Induced Investment. Autonomous investment is not related to the changes in income or output. Contray to it, induced investment responds to changes in income or output. Autonomous investment is the core of multiplier while induced investment is the basis of the principle of acceleration.

17. The Theory of Comparative Advantage states that countries will find it mutually advantageous to trade if comparative costs of production differ. If, however, comparative costs are identical, there can be no gains from trade. Table shows the maximum output of two countries, A and B of two products, X and Y. The Table shows that country A, for instance, can either proudce 20 units of good X or 40 units of good Y or some combination of both. The comparative costs or the opportunity cost of production is identical in both countries: one unit of X costs two units of Y. Hence, there can be no gains from trade.

Table

	Output		
	Good X		Good Y
Country A	20	OR	40
Country B	50	OR	100

18. The imposition of a tariff by a large nation improves its terms of trade, reduces the volume of trade and may improve the nation's welfare. However, since the improvement in the nation's position comes at the expense of its trade partner, the trade partner is likely to retaliate and, in the end, both nations usually lose. These effects are best analyzed with offer curves.

19. A deficit in a nation's balance of payments means that at a given rate of exchange, there is a shortage (an excess of quantity demanded over quantity supplied) of the foreign currency. If the exchange rate is freely flexible or floating, the exchange rate will rise until the quantity demanded of the foreign currency equals the quantity supplied and the deficit is completely eliminated. This rise in the exchange rate means that the relative value of the domestic currency is falling or depreciating. The exact opposite occurs when there is a surplus and the nation's currency appreciates (or increases) in relative value.

20. Maastricht Treaty (signed in February 1992, in force November 1993): created a European Union composed of three pillars. The first pillar (the European Community) contained amendments to the EC treaties: it expanded the EP's powers and the use of QMV, extended the possibility for common policies in more areas, and created a single currency. The other two pillars institutionalized cooperation in foreign and security policy, and justice and home affairs.

23. Perspective Planning: It refers to long-term planning based on the existing and short-term economic conditions and requirements. Draft of perspective planning is prepared keeping in view the future economic conditions and requirements. Long-term targets and programmes are parceled out in short-run programmes and their details are worked out. These details are so arranged in the short run that each successive short-term plan results in preparing the ground for long-term targets.

In the words of **J. Tinbergen,** *"The main purpose of a perspective plan is to provide a background of the shorter-term plans, so that the problems that have to be solved over a very long period can be taken into account in planning over short-term."* **Prof. Mahalanobis** is of the view that perspective planning is necessarily a continuous process..

24. **People's Plan-1944:**
"In April 1944 the People's Plan was drafted by the Post-war Reconstruction Committee of Indian Federation of Labour (released by MN Roy, General Secretary, Indian Federation of Labour). The aim of the plan was to provide for the satisfaction of immediate basic needs of the Indian people within a period of 10 years in respect to food, clothing, shelter, health and education.

25. *Trickle-down* is a political-economic term used to describe certain economic theories and policies. It implies that policies to help the wealthy directly will also have a positive impact on the middle and lower classes and the poor, with a trickle of the original largesse.

27. Economic development, is a continuous increase in net national income. If national income increases for a short-time, it may not be called economic development. For instance, if there is a bumber crop in a given year and as a result national income increases, then this temporary increase in national income will not be treated as economic development. Economic development refers to that state in which national income increases continuously for a period of at least 25 years.

28. The "Dependency Theory" has been one of the major products of what may be broadly termed neo-Marxist thought, or radical political economy, since World War II. Much of it has been generated in Latin America, and the dependency school is associated with the United Nations Economic Commission for Latin America, and with the names of economists who have written in and about Latin America: Raul Prebisch, Osvaldo Sunkel, Fernando Cardoso, Celso Furtado, André Gunder Frank. However, the school has by no means been confined to Latin America, but include Africans like Samir Amin and Europeans like Johan Galtung, Stuart Holland, and Frances Saunders. Like many of the theories, the dependency theory is concerned with underdevelopment in general, with poverty, and with disparities among social groups. It has been applied more frequently to differences among nations than to regional gaps; but, like other theories, it has been extended to the explanation or regional disparities.

29. **Prof. Robert M. Solow** is an eminent neo-classical growth economist. This noted M.I.T. Professor has contributed in the Quarterly Journal of Economics, LXX (February 1956) a model of long-run economic growth. His model is an alternative of Harrod-Domar growth model. He has incorpórated in his model the possibilities of factor substitutions and diminishing returns to a factor. According to **Prof. Solow,** *"Harrod-Domar model is based on unrealistic assumptions like fixed factor proportions and constant capital-output ratio."*

As per Solow model, economies will conditionally converge to the same level of income, given that they have the same rates of savings, depreciation, labour force growth and productivity growth. Thus, the Solow model is the basic framework for the study of convergence across countries.

Assumptions: Growth model of Robert Solow is based on the following assumptions:

1. Only a single composite commodity, *i.e.*, national output is produced.
2. There are only two factors of production, labour and capital.
3. State of full employment is found in the economy.
4. Labour supply is exogenously determined and Labour grows exponentially at constant rate so that, $L(t) = L_0e^{nt}$.
5. Labour and capital can be substituted for each other.
6. It assumes that diminishing returns apply to labour and capital separately.
7. There is constant returns to scale in the production. Production function is a linear homogeneous production function of the first degree.

8. Propensity to save (sy) is constant and all saving is transformed into investment. There is no hoarding.
9. Production refers to net production. It is the difference between gross production (output) and depreciation.
10. Prices and wages are flexible.
11. There is perfect competition in the economy.
12. Technological improvement is neutral.

33. In his address to the Food Security Summit in February 2004, President A.P.J. Abdul Kalam outlined the concept of PURA (Providing Urban Amenities in Rural Areas) as the harbinger of economic upliftment of the villages. The model advocates integrated action in the following five areas:

(*i*) The country should target food and agricultural production of 360 million tonnes by the year 2020. Allied activities in agriculture and agro-food processing should be given due focus to bring prosperity to rural people and speed up economic growth.

(*ii*) Reliable and electric power should be supplied in all parts of the country.

(*iii*) Education and health care should be ensured for all.

(*iv*) Information and communication technology should be expanded to rural areas to promote education and create national wealth.

(*v*) Growth in nuclear energy, space technology and defence technology should be given more attention.

34. The Government of India instituted a scheme known as ECOMARK in February, 1991 for labelling environment friendly products. This scheme is administered by the Bureau of Indian Standards (BIS). The scheme provides for labelling of household and other consumer products which meet certain environmental criteria alongwith quality requirements prescribed in relevant Indian Standards. For a product to be eligible for ECOMARK, the product shall confirm to the relevant Indian Standards as well as additional requirement incorporated for ensuring environment friendly nature of the product. The mark is a combination of BIS Standards Mark (ISI) and the Eco logo.

37. Tax incentives (deductions, exclusions or credits, usually on the income tax) and vouchers are two techniques used to encourage the production and consumption of goods that generate positive externalities. In both cases, these instruments are intended to roughly approximate the value of the marginal social benefits in order to increase consumption of such desirable goods and services as education, beautification, energy-efficient housing, and private social welfare agencies (through the charitable deduction). The value of the tax revenue forgone in order to promote certain kinds of production or consumption is known as a tax expenditure. Vouchers (typically for housing, education, or health care services) allow individuals to purchase those goods or services free or at a reduced price. The service provider redeems the vouchers for payment from the government that issued them.

38. Adam Smith, father of the modern economics, presented for principles of a good taxation system, called Adam Smith's Canons of Taxation.

Canons of taxation : Name given to the four principles of taxation propounded by Adam Smith:

1. *Equity:* The tax payable should accord with ability to pay or taxable capacity.
2. *Certainty:* The taxpayer should know exactly what is being taxed, how much he has to pay, and how and when he has to pay it, meaning that the law should be clear and unambiguous and the tax authorities' interpretation of it should be readily available.

3. *Convenience:* The tax should be payable in a manner and at a time convenient to the taxpayer.
4. *Economy:* Enforcement and collection costs should be reasonably proportionate to the receipts. This concept is also referred to as administrative efficiency.

39. According to Wiseman and Peacock Public Expenditure does not increase in a smooth and continuous manner. The increasing public expenditure over time has occurred in a step-like manner. They studied the experience of the United Kingdom for a secular period (1890-1955). Instead of studying the trend of public expenditure, they studied the fluctuations in government expenditure over time. The general approach to the hypothesis refers to the three related concepts:

1. Displacement effect
2. Inspection effect
3. Concentration effect.

The movement from older level of expenditure and taxation to a new and higher level is called the displacement effect.

War and other social disturbances force the people and governments to find solutions of important problems, which had been neglected earlier. This is called the inspection effect. That is, new obligations imposed on state, in the form of increased debt interest and war pensions etc.

The concentration effect refers to the apparent tendency for the central govt. economic activities to become an increasing proportion of the total public sector economic activity when the society is experiencing economic growth.

40. According to Robert Garran, "A federation is a form of government in which sovereignty or political power is divided between Central and Local Governments, so that each of them within its own sphere is independent of the other". Thus, in a federation, there is constitutional division of powers, functions and resources between the Central and the State Governments. In the words of R.N. Bhargava, "The term federal finance refers to the finance of the Federal as well as of the State governments and the relationship between the two". Federal governments such as the U.S.A., Canada, Australia and Switzerland are the older federations, while federal governments in India, Pakistan, Malaysia and Nigeria have slightly different form of federations to suit their own environment.

42.
- Taxation Enquiry Commission (1953-54)
- Indian Tax Reforms—Report of a Survey (1956)
- Final Report on Rationalising and Simplification of the Tax Structure (1967)
- Direct Taxes Enquiry Committee, Final Report (1971)

44. A grant earmarked for a specific program is the most prevalent type offered by the federal and state governments. The dominant state categorical program provides grants for local education. There are several types of categorical grants. A grant is lump sum, or nonmatching, if the amount does not change as a recipient government changes its taxes or expenditures. Matching grants, in contrast, require recipient government taxes or spending, with the size of the grant dependent on the recipient government's response. Typically, a specific matching grant offers to match each dollar of recipient tax or expenditure on the target service (*e.g.*, education) with R grant dollars, to be spent on that service. R is the grant's matching rate. Generally, the share financed by the grant (M) is $M = R/(1 + R)$, and the local marginal tax price (P) of an additional dollar of service is $P = 1 - M = 1 - [R/(1 + R)] = 1/(1 + R)$. Both matching and non-matching categorical grants may be allocated either by formula or on a project basis and may be either open-ended (*i.e.,* no limit on the grant amount) or closed-ended (*i.e.,* grant amount is limited).

Project categorical grants are more prevalent than formula grants, while open-ended categorical grants are relatively rare.

45. Fisher's index number is the geometric mean of the Laspeyres and Paasche indices. Fisher's index can be calculated using the formula:

$$P_{01} = \sqrt{L \times P}$$

$$= \sqrt{\frac{\Sigma P_1 Q_0}{\Sigma P_0 Q_0} \times \frac{\Sigma P_1 Q_1}{\Sigma P_0 Q_1}} \times 100$$

It is considered to be an ideal index number because:

- Theoretically, geometric mean is considered the best average for the construction of index number and Fisher's index uses geometric mean.
- It is free from bias as the upward bias of Laspeyres index and downward bias of Paasche's index are balanced to a great extend.
- Both the quantities of base period and current period are considered in the formula.
- It satisfies the tests of consistency which we shall discuss later.

47. The probability of rejecting a false null hypothesis is called *Power of the test.* Therefore, Power is the probability of drawing a correct conclusion by the test, when the null hypothesis is false. For a specified value of the parameter consistent with the alternative hypothesis.

Power = 1 – Probability of Type II error.

It the power is graphically plotted against all specified alternatives, the curve obtained is known as *Power Curve.* The power of a test determines the extent to which a test can discriminate between true and false null hypothesis.

The quantity $1-\alpha$ is known as the confidence level of the test and $1-\beta$ is called the power of the test. The power of the test denotes the ability of the test statistic to reject a false hypothesis.

48. **Karl Pearson's Coefficient of Skewness.** Karl Pearson's relative measures of Skewness is based on the difference between Mean and Mode is given by

Coefficient of Skewness (Sk_p)

$$= \frac{\text{Mean} - \text{Mode}}{\text{Standard Deviation}}$$

It is a pure number. This formula cannot, however, be used when the mode is ill-defined. In such case median is used because of their following relationship existing in a moderately asymmetrical distribution

Mean – Mode = 3 (Mean – Median)

Thus, the formula becomes

Coefficient of Skewness (Sk_p),

$$= \frac{3(\text{Mean} - \text{Median})}{\text{Standard Deviation}}$$

Standard Deviation = 15.8

and (Mean – Median) = –4

$$\therefore \text{ Coefficient of Skewness} = \frac{3 \times (-4)}{15.8}$$

$$= \frac{-12}{15.8}$$

$$= -0.76.$$

49. The chance that a coin falls or p is $\frac{1}{2}$ and the chance that if it falls tails or q is also $\frac{1}{2}$. The probability that out of 3 coins there will be exactly two heads and one tail.

Meaning and Definition of Probability,

$$= {}^3C_2 p^2 q = 3 \times \frac{1}{2} \times \frac{1}{2} \times \frac{1}{2} = \frac{3}{8}$$

$$= \frac{3}{8}.$$

PAPER-III

Note: *This paper contains* ***seventy five (75)*** *objective type questions of* ***two (2)*** *marks each.* ***All*** *questions are compulsory.*

1. Which among the following statements are true for the Revealed Preference Theory?

Choose the correct answer from the code given below:

Statement:

I. Income elasticity of demand should be positive.

II. Consumers Preferences satisfy strong ordering.

Codes:

A. Both are true

B. None are true

C. Only I is true

D. Only II is true

2. Demand for foodstuff is income inelastic. This is explained by

A. Giffen's Paradox

B. Engel's Law

C. Gossen's Law

D. Ricardo's Law

3. Consider the following factors:

I. Free entry

II. Advertising

III. Goal of satisfactory profits

Which of these are part of Chamberlin's Monopolistic Competition?

Codes:

A. All the three

B. Only I and II

C. Only II and III

D. Only III

4. Non-symmetric risk means:

A. A risk that can be eliminated by diversifying.

B. A risk that cannot be eliminated by diversifying.

C. A risk that can be eliminated without diversifying.

D. A risk that cannot be eliminated.

5. Who among the following economists developed the concept of 'Barriers to Entry' of firms?

A. J.S. Bain

B. W.J. Baumol

C. Alfred Marshall

D. W.S. Jevons

6. Even as fixed average cost continues to fall, the average variable cost begins to rise because

A. returns to factors start diminishing

B. returns to factors start rising

C. input prices start rising

D. producers budget starts shrinking

7. Consider the following statements:

I. The lowest point on the long run average cost curve is known as minimum efficient scale.

II. It is the output at which long run average cost curve stops falling.

Choose the correct option from the code given below:

Codes:

A. Both I and II are correct

B. Both are wrong

C. Only I is correct

D. Only II is correct

8. Which among the following is not a characteristic of Imperfect Competition?

A. Perfect knowledge

B. Free transport

C. Free Entry of firms

D. Homogeneous product

9. Which among the following conditions are true for Golden Rule of Accumulation of Edmund Phelps for optimum capital accumulation?

Choose from the code below:

I. Savings rate is unique.

II. Marginal productivity of capital be equal to capital depreciation.

Codes:
A. Both are true
B. None of these are true
C. Only I is true
D. Only II is true

10. Which among the following were neglected by Keynes in his theory of employment?
A. Role of expectations
B. Role of capital stock
C. Role of consumption
D. Role of government

11. Which of the propositions of the past income hypothesis of Duesenberry are correct?

Choose from the code below:

Statements :

I. The current consumption is a function of not only current income, but also the past income.
II. There is asymmetrical relationship between income and consumption during contraction and expansion.
III. Consumption income relationship is irreversible.
IV. Consumption falls less than income during depression, but the rise in consumption is much more during expansion.

Codes:
A. I and III
B. I, II and III
C. I, II and IV
D. All the above statements are true

12. An increase in the quantity of money in the classical macro system will result in:

I. Increase in price level
II. No change in price level
III. Level of output and employment do not change
IV. An increase in employment and output

Select the answer from the codes given below:

Codes:
A. II and IV
B. I and II
C. I and IV
D. I and III only

13. Given below is the well-known LM Curve and its range is marked in three parts. In which of the marked range Keynes effect does not operate?

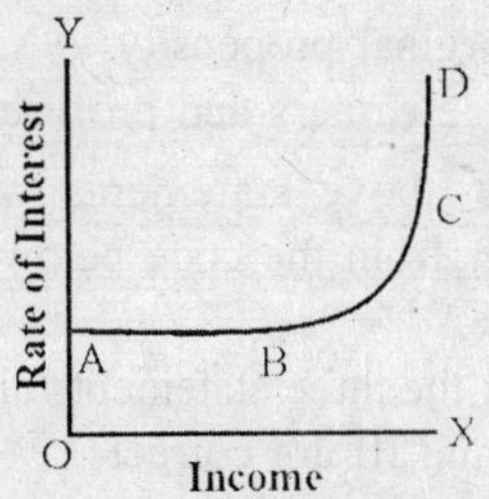

A. In the range AB
B. In the range BC
C. In the range CD
D. In the range AB and BC

14. The theoretical proposition of stable velocity of money is being weakened by the recent researchers. This has the effect of weakening the position of
A. Keynesians
B. Monetarists
C. New Classicals
D. Utopians

15. Which of the following is the correct assumption for the Lewis two sector model?
A. High unemployment in urban sector
B. Rising real wages
C. High marginal productivity in the rural sector
D. Surplus labour in the rural sector

16. Which of the following is a major indivisibility of Rosenstein-Rodan Model of development?
A. Services
B. Agriculture
C. Infrastructure
D. Supply

17. Which among the following statement is true for Marxian model of development?
A. Change in Mode of production and Relations in production happen simultaneously.
B. Change in Mode of production follows change in Relations in production.
C. Change in Mode of production precedes the change in Relations in production.
D. Relations in production are not important.

18. Consider the following statements about the Kaldor's model of economic growth:

I. Investment is a function of profit rate.

II. Capital is homogeneous.

III. Marginal propensity to save is same for wage earners and profit earners.

Of the above statements which are true? Answer from the code below:

Codes:

A. All the three statements above are correct
B. II and III are correct
C. Only I is correct
D. I and III are correct

19. Which one of the following is true for disguised unemployment?

A. It has savings potential
B. It has investment potential
C. It is a source of expanding production
D. It is a source of social unrest

20. In the steady state growth situation in the Solow's model of growth, the upper limit to growth would be determined by the growth rate of

A. Population (Labour supply)
B. Capital
C. Output
D. Capital and output

21. Which one of the following pairs is not well matched?

Concept	*Economist*
(*a*) Learning by Doing	I. B.S. Minhas
(*b*) Disembodied Technical Progress	II. Joan Robinson
(*c*) Golden Age	III. Kenneth Arrow
(*d*) CES Production Function	IV. R.M. Solow

Codes:

	(*a*)	(*b*)	(*c*)	(*d*)
A.	I	II	III	IV
B.	IV	I	II	III
C.	II	III	I	II
D.	III	IV	II	I

22. A tax is said to be progressive, when the marginal rate of tax is

A. greater than the average rate
B. less than the average rate
C. equal to the average rate
D. equal to the marginal sacrifice

23. Assertion (A): Relatively few private goods are totally rival and excludable.

Reason (R) : Most consumption (and production) has at least some shared aspects.

Codes:

A. Both (A) and (R) are correct.
B. Both (A) and (R) are not correct.
C. (A) is correct, but (R) is not the correct reason of (A).
D. (A) is correct and (R) is the correct reason for (A).

24. Methods of debt-redemption include

A. Capital levy B. Sinking fund
C. Debt repudiation D. All the above

25. Assertion (A): For fiscal discipline, expenditure cap is quite desirable.

Reason (R) : A widening fiscal deficit adversely impacts finances of the Central Government.

Codes:

A. Both (A) and (R) are correct, but (R) is not the correct explanation of (A).
B. Both (A) and (R) are correct and (R) is the correct explanation of (A).
C. (A) is true, but (R) is false.
D. (R) is true, but (A) is false.

26. Assertion (A): The debt-GDP ratio of the State Governments witnessed a decline after reaching the peak level in 2004.

Reason (R): 'Debt swap' scheme was introduced and interest rates were reduced.

Codes:

A. Both (A) and (R) are correct and (R) is the correct explanation of (A).
B. (A) is true, but (R) is not the correct explanation of (A).
C. (A) is false, but (R) is true.
D. (R) is true, but (A) is false.

27. Taxes in List-I of the Union Government as per the Constitution of India include:

I. Taxes on consumption and sale of electricity

II. Taxes on sale or purchase of newspapers and on advertisements published therein

III. Taxes on capital value of assets

IV. Duties in respect of succession to property

Codes:

A. I, II and IV are correct

B. I, II and III are correct

C. II, III and IV are correct

D. II and III are correct

28. Assertion (A): There is automatic change in net tax revenue when level of output changes.

Reason (R): Automatic stabilizers moderate aggregate spending in times of boom and slow down.

Codes:

A. Both (A) and (R) are correct and (R) is the correct explanation of (A).

B. Both (A) and (R) are true, but (R) is not the correct explanation of (A).

C. (A) is true, but (R) is false.

D. (A) is false, but (R) is true.

29. Match the following:

List-I	List-II
(*a*) Sum of price elasticity of demand for exports and imports greater than unity.	1. J-curve effect
(*b*) Balance of Payments is the difference between National Income and expenditure	2. Import quota systems
(*c*) Empirical evidence showing lower short run price elasticities of exports and imports.	3. Marshall-Lerner condition
(*d*) Method to cut down imports	4. Absorption approach

Select correct code:

Codes:

	(*a*)	(*b*)	(*c*)	(*d*)
A.	4	3	1	2
B.	4	1	3	2
C.	3	1	4	2
D.	3	4	1	2

30. Which of the following is related with optimum currency area?

A. Optimal geographical area for a single currency.

B. Optimal geographical area for several currencies whose exchange rates are relatively pegged.

C. Single currency or the pegged currencies fluctuate jointly vis-à-vis other currencies.

D. All the above

31. Which one of the following is not included under WTO regulations?

A. Removal of industrial licenses

B. Removal of import tariffs

C. Removal of foreign portfolio investments

D. Removal of price controls

32. Which of the following statements is true?

A. Asian financial crisis is generally considered to have started on July 2, 1997 with the devaluation of the Thai Baht.

B. Asian financial crisis is generally considered to have started on 2nd August, 1998 with the Russian's crisis.

C. Brazil's 1999 crisis is generally considered to be the main cause of Asian financial crisis.

D. All the above are true

33. Match the following:

List-I	List-II
(*a*) Banks that conduct trading in market for Euro currencies	1. Euro currencies
(*b*) Deposits denominated and payable in dollars and other foreign currencies in banks outside USA	2. SDRs
(*c*) Dollar deposits located in banks outside US	3. Euro banks
(*d*) Currency baskets composed of five currencies of IMF members	4. Euro dollars

Codes:

	(*a*)	(*b*)	(*c*)	(*d*)
A.	3	4	1	2
B.	3	1	4	2
C.	3	4	2	1
D.	1	3	4	2

34. Which of the following is true for European Union?

A. All member countries have the Euro currency.
B. All member countries have the same defence policy.
C. There are no tariffs between member countries.
D. All member countries have the same taxation policy.

35. When a nation imposes an import tariffs, the nation's offer curve will

A. shift away from the axis measuring exports
B. move closer to the axis measuring exports
C. no shift will take place
D. None of the above

36. Market at which transaction will be consummated at some specified time in future is called

A. Spot market
B. Current market
C. Capital market
D. Forward market

37. Capital adequacy ratio of all commercial banks in India is

A. below the required rate of 9%
B. equal to the required rate of 9%
C. well above the required rate of 9%
D. far below the required rate of 9%

38. Which of the following are liabilities of commercial banks?

I. Capital and reserves
II. Cash and balances with RBI
III. Investments
IV. Borrowings

Codes:

A. I and III B. I and IV
C. I, II and III D. II, III and IV

39. **Assertion (A):** There was remarkable acceleration in deposit mobilisation of commercial banks after the nationalisation of 14 commercial banks in 1969.

Reason (R): There was tremendous branch expansion, rise in interest rates and introduction of myriad innovative deposit scheme.

Choose the correct answer from the codes given below:

Codes:

A. (A) is correct, but (R) is not correct.
B. Both (A) and (R) are not correct.
C. Both (A) and (R) are correct, but (R) is not the correct explanation.
D. Both (A) and (R) are correct and (R) is the correct explanation of (A).

40. Arrange in chronological order, the establishment of the following in India :

I. Industrial Investment Bank of India
II. R.B.I. working group on Development Financial Institutions
III. Small Industrial Development Bank of India
IV. Insurance Regulatory and Development Authority (IRDA)

A. I, IV, III, II B. III, I, IV, II
C. III, IV, I, II D. IV, I, III, II

41. Which of the following are term lending institutions in India?

I. Industrial Development Bank of India
II. EXIM Bank
III. Small Industrial Development Bank of India
IV. NABARD

Codes:

A. I and III B. I, III and IV
C. I and II D. I, II and III

42. Which of the following are included in broad money (M_3) in India?

1. Currency with the public
2. Demand deposits with Bank
3. Time deposits with Banks
4. 'Other deposits' with RBI

Codes:

A. 1, 2 and 3
B. 1 and 2
C. 3 and 4
D. 1, 2, 3 and 4

43. **Assertion (A):** The minimum rate at which the Central Bank is ready to lend is bank rate.

Reason (R) : The bank rate is determined by demand and supply of money.

Codes:

A. Both (A) and (R) are individually true and (R) is correct explanation of (A).
B. Both (A) and (R) are individually true, but (R) is not the correct explanation of (A).
C. (A) is true, but (R) is false.
D. (A) is false, but (R) is true.

44. **Assertion (A):** Delhi has very high density of population.

Reason (R): People from rural areas are migrating to Delhi.

Choose the correct answer from the code given below:

Codes:

A. Both (A) and (R) are false.
B. Both (A) and (R) are correct and (R) is correct reason for (A).
C. (A) is true, but (R) is false.
D. Both (A) and (R) are true, but (R) is not an adequate reason for (A).

45. An stable population is characterised by

A. Constant birth rate
B. Unchanging age structure
C. None of the above are true
D. Both the above are true

46. Which of the following is true for Net Reproduction Rate?

A. It relates to average number of daughters born to a female.
B. It relates to the life span of a female.
C. Both A and B are true.
D. None of A or B are true.

47. Which option is true for population dividend to manifest?

A. Population in the age group between 0-7 years is likely to increase.
B. Population in the age group between 8-15 years is likely to increase.
C. Population in the age group between 15-64 years is likely to increase.
D. Population in the age group above 65 years is likely to increase.

48. Which one of the following is the correct sequence of development of sectors in India post-independence?

A. Agriculture, Industry, Service
B. Service, Agriculture, Industry
C. Industry, Agriculture, Service
D. Agriculture, Service, Industry

49. The term HYVP in new agriculture strategy stands for

A. High Yielding Variety Pesticides
B. High Yielding Volume Production
C. High Yielding Varieties Programme
D. High Yielding Volume Programme

50. If more & more capital and labour are applied to a fixed piece of land, the system of cultivation of farming is known as

A. Intensive cultivation
B. Extensive cultivation
C. Cooperative farming
D. Double cropping

51. Mention the crop where Green Revolution is the most successful one

A. Tea & Coffee
B. Wheat & Rice
C. Wheat & Pulses
D. Jowar & Oilseeds

52. Which of the following is not an item of social security of labour?

A. Wage
B. Maternity benefits
C. Pensions
D. Industrial Injury Compensation

53. Which of the following is correct about the Contingent Valuation Method (CVM) used in Environmental Economics?

A. It is used only for pollutants.
B. It is used only for items with positive utilities.
C. It is used for items under market failures.
D. It is used only for natural resources.

54. Which among the following is not a cause of sickness of industrial units in India?

A. Obsolescent technology
B. Lack of capital account convertibility
C. Labour problems
D. Faulty location

55. Assertion (A): In India, the traditional small scale industries have greater employment potential than the modern small scale industries.

Reason (R) : The value of capital per worker in traditional small scale industries is small than the value of capital per worker in modern small scale industries.

Codes:

A. Both (A) and (R) are true and (R) is the correct explanation of (A).
B. Both (A) and (R) are true, but (R) is not the correct explanation of (A).
C. (A) is true, but (R) is false.
D. (A) is false, but (R) is true.

56. For the year 2012-13 procurement of wheat has been largest in which of the following States?

A. Punjab and U.P.
B. U.P. and M.P.
C. U.P. and Haryana
D. Punjab and Haryana

57. For the year 2013-14 arrange in descending order, the contribution of following taxes as percentage of G.D.P.:

1. Income Tax
2. Service Tax
3. Corporation Tax
4. Excise Duty

Codes:

A. 4, 2, 3, 1 B. 3, 1, 4, 2
C. 2, 3, 1, 4 D. 1, 2, 3, 4

58. Which of the following facts are correct about the Competition Commission of India?

I. It was established in 2003.
II. It was established on the recommendations of Raghavan Committee.

Codes:

A. Both I and II are true
B. Both I and II are not true
C. Only I is true
D. Only II is true

59. The base year for newly developed All India Consumer Price Index Number – Rural C.P.I. and Urban C.P.I. is

A. 2004–05 B. 2006–07
C. 2009–10 D. 2010

60. On the basis of 10 parameters for the 'ease of doing business', World Bank's latest report, during the period July 2013 to May 2014, India has come to which of the following position?

A. 138 B. 142
C. 144 D. 146

61. Which is false in following?

A. The duration of Tenth Five Year Plan was 2002-2007.
B. Ryotwari tenure has been the intermediary in Indian land system.
C. Zamindari system was introduced by Lord Dalhousie.
D. Mahalwari land tenure system was introduced in Agra and Oudh.

62. The Financial Sector Legislative Reforms Commission 2013 submitted its recommendations on the following aspects:

I. Legislative
II. Non-legislative
III. Marketing
IV. Advertising

Codes:

A. I, II, IV B. I, II, III
C. II, III, IV D. I, II

63. Which of the following States had the lowest women employment percentage under MNREGA programme during 2013-14?
A. U.P. and Rajasthan
B. Odisha and M.P.
C. U.P. and Odisha
D. Rajasthan and West Bengal

64. In a growth model given below:
$S_t = \alpha Y_t \qquad 0 < \alpha < 1$
$I_t = \beta[Y_t - Y_{t-1}] \qquad \beta > 0$
$S_t \equiv I_t$
Growth requires the condition:

A. $\dfrac{\beta}{\beta - \alpha} > 0$ B. $\dfrac{\beta}{\beta - \alpha} < 0$

C. $\dfrac{\alpha}{\beta - \alpha} > 0$ D. $\dfrac{\alpha}{\beta - \alpha} < 0$

65. Given total cost function $C = 5Q^2 + 20Q + 5$, at price = ₹ 5, marginal cost is
A. 100 B. 200
C. 85 D. 70

66. For testing the significance of overall regression the test to be used is
A. *t* Test B. F Test
C. χ^2 Test D. *d* Test

67. Including relevant lagged values of the dependent variable on the right hand side of a regression equation could lead to which one of the following?
A. Biased but consistent coefficients' estimates
B. Biased and inconsistent coefficients' estimates
C. Unbiased and inconsistent coefficients' estimates
D. Unbiased and consistent coefficients' estimates

68. In the production function $Q = AL^aK^b$ match the following:

List-I	List-II
(*a*) $a + b = 1$	(*i*) *a*
(*b*) Elasticity of substitution	(*ii*) *b*
(*c*) Labour elasticity of output	(*iii*) Constant Returns to Scale
(*d*) Capital elasticity of output	(*iv*) One

Codes:

	(*a*)	(*b*)	(*c*)	(*d*)
A.	(*i*)	(*ii*)	(*iii*)	(*iv*)
B.	(*i*)	(*iii*)	(*ii*)	(*iv*)
C.	(*iii*)	(*iv*)	(*i*)	(*ii*)
D.	(*ii*)	(*iii*)	(*iv*)	(*i*)

69. Match the following:

List-I	List-II
(*a*) Box-Jenkins	(*i*) Causality Method
(*b*) Unit-root test	(*ii*) Forecasting
(*c*) Durbin-Watson '*d*' statistics	(*iii*) Stationarity
(*d*) Granger Test	(*iv*) Auto-correlation

Codes:

	(*a*)	(*b*)	(*c*)	(*d*)
A.	(*iii*)	(*i*)	(*ii*)	(*iv*)
B.	(*ii*)	(*iii*)	(*iv*)	(*i*)
C.	(*i*)	(*ii*)	(*iii*)	(*iv*)
D.	(*iv*)	(*i*)	(*ii*)	(*iii*)

70. If OLS is used in the presence of auto-correlation, which of the following will be likely consequences?
(*i*) Coefficients estimates may be misleading.
(*ii*) Hypothesis tests could reach the wrong conclusions.
(*iii*) Forecasts made from the model could be biased.
(*iv*) Standard errors may be inappropriate.
A. (*ii*) and (*iv*) only
B. (*i*) and (*iii*) only
C. (*i*), (*ii*) and (*iii*) only
D. (*i*), (*ii*), (*iii*) and (*iv*)

71. In the context of simultaneous equations econometric models, consider the following statements:
(*i*) Identification is a problem to be dealt with before estimation.
(*ii*) Order condition is necessary but not a sufficient condition of identification.
(*iii*) Two-stage least squares method of estimation gives consistent estimators if the equation is under-identified.

(*iv*) Under indirect least squares method, least squares method is applied to reduced form equations.

Which of the following is correct?

A. (*i*) and (*ii*)

B. (*i*), (*ii*), (*iii*) and (*iv*)

C. (*i*), (*ii*) and (*iii*)

D. (*i*), (*ii*) and (*iv*)

72. Simplex method is used for solving the problems of

A. Linear Programming

B. Input Output Analysis

C. Regression

D. Correlation

73. Which statement is false in following?

A. *t*-distribution was given by W. Gosset.

B. Tippet's Tables are used for random sampling.

C. Binomial distribution is symmetrical if $p = q$.

D. The regression coefficient of y on x is equal to $r\dfrac{\sigma_x}{\sigma_y}$.

74. Given that LM function is Y = 100 + 10i and the IS function is Y = 160 − 20i, find the correct value of equilibrium level of income and rate of interest from the given options.

A. 120 and 2

B. 90 and 3

C. 150 and 2

D. 120 and 3

75. In a two industry case, for the Simon Hawkins viability condition which statement is correct (a_{ij}; i = 1, 2 and j = 1, 2)?

A. $\begin{bmatrix} 1-a_{11} & -a_{12} \\ -a_{21} & 1-a_{22} \end{bmatrix} < 0$

B. $\begin{bmatrix} 1-a_{11} & -a_{12} \\ -a_{21} & 1-a_{22} \end{bmatrix} > 0$

C. $\begin{bmatrix} a_{11} & -a_{12} \\ -a_{21} & a_{22} \end{bmatrix} > 0$

D. $(1 - a_{11})(1 - a_{22}) - a_{12}.a_{21} < 0$

ANSWERS

1	2	3	4	5	6	7	8	9	10
A	B	B	A	A	A	A	A	A	B
11	12	13	14	15	16	17	18	19	20
D	D	A	B	D	D	C	C	A	A
21	22	23	24	25	26	27	28	29	30
D	A	A	D	A	A	C	A	D	D
31	32	33	34	35	36	37	38	39	40
C	A	B	C	B	D	C	B	D	B
41	42	43	44	45	46	47	48	49	50
C	D	C	A	D	A	C	D	C	A
51	52	53	54	55	56	57	58	59	60
B	A	C	B	A	D	B	A	D	B
61	62	63	64	65	66	67	68	69	70
C	D	C	A	D	B	A	C	B	A
71	72	73	74	75					
D	A	D	A	B					

SOME SELECTED EXPLANATORY ANSWERS

2. The nineteenth-century German statistician Engel established an inverse relationship between the level of household income and the proportion of income spent on foodstuffs. This implied that the demand for foodstuffs was income inelastic, so that the share of food production in total industrial production would fall, ceteris paribus, as average income rose.

3. E.H. Chamberlin and J. Robinson are associated with the monopolisitc competition. In 1933, Chamberlin published the book, *Theory of Monopolistic Competition* and J. Robinson published *The Economics of Imperfect Competition.* This led to the monopolistic competition revolution. Also factors such as product differentiation, advertising and brand preference gained importance with the coming of monopolistic competition.

   Monopolistic competition is a market structure with large number of buyers and sellers dealing with externally differentiated close substitutes. Each seller acts like a monopoly to his loyalist buyers. Product differentiated being generally external—caused by packaging, external looks, or simply by brand positioning. Products are close substitutes of each other internally. Firms in monopolistic competition incur huge advertising or selling costs in order to position their products vis-à-vis other competing brands. The basic purpose of such advertising is to lure the consumers away from the competing brands by making them believe that the brand used by them is superior to other brands.

   Another feature of the monopolistically competitive market is the existence of free entry and free exit which ensure only normal profits to the firms in this type of market in the long-run. The abnormal profits of the short-run are driven to zero due to free entry. Likewise, short-run loss is also driven to zero due to free exit of firms. Price is greater than LMC but equal to LAC in the long-run.

4. Every investor has to face two types of risk: (*i*) Systematic Risk and (*ii*) Unsystematic Risk. Systematic Risk arises by dint of the economy-wide uncertainties and the tendency of individual securities to move together with the changes in the market. Investors are exposed to face such market risk even when they hold well-diversified portfolio of securities. Unsystematic risk arises due to the unique uncertainties of individual securities. These uncertainties are diversifiable if a large number of securities are combined to form well-diversified portfolio. Uncertainties of individual securities in a portfolio cancel out each other. Unsystematic risk can be totally reduced through diversification. Systematic and unsystematic risks together make total risk. Total risk of an individual security is the variance of its return. It consists of two parts: Total risk of a security = Systematic risk + Unsystematic risk.

   Systematic risk is the covariance of the individual securities in the portfolio. An investor has to suffer the systematic risk, as it cannot be diversified. The difference between variance and covariance is the diversifiable or unsystematic risk. The systematic risk cannot be diversified, and therefore, one will expect a compensation for bearing this risk.

5. An economics and business term, *barriers to entry* is based on the theory of competition in which the tendency of competitors in the market is to limit competition in an effort to raise profits to a maximum. The first thorough study of the nature and extent of barriers to entry was conducted by Joe S. Bain in his 1956 book titled *Barriers to New Competition,* in which he defined an entry barrier as the set of technology or product

conditions that allows incumbent firms to earn economic profits in the long run. Bain identifies three sets of conditions in which barriers to entry are evident: economies of scale, product differentiation, and absolute cost advantages.

6. The average-total-cost curve is U-shaped because at low levels of output, average total costs are high due to high average fixed costs. As output increases, average total costs fall because fixed costs are spread across additional units of output. However, at some point, diminishing returns cause an increase in average variable costs, which in turn begins to increase average costs. The efficient scale of the firm is the quantity of output that minimizes average total cost. Whenever marginal cost is less than average total cost, average total cost is falling. Whenever marginal cost is greater than average total cost, average total cost is rising. Therefore, the marginal-cost curve crosses the average-total-cost curve at the efficient scale.

7. The minimum efficient scale (MES) is the scale of production where the internal economies of scale have been fully exploited. It corresponds to the lowest point on the long run average cost curve and the output that achieves productive efficiency. The MES usually covers a range of output levels where the firm achieves constant returns to scale and has reached the lowest feasible cost per unit in the long run. The Minimum Efficient Scale (MES) of plant is that beyond which long-run costs stop falling, *i.e.*, stay constant, or start to rise.

9. The term "golden rule", originated by Phelps (1961), derives from neoclassical growth theory where it is used to describe the optimal growth path that provides the maximum level of sustainable per capita consumption.

11. Reconciliation of the short-run and long-run consumption functions was first attempted by James S. Duesenberry in his work entitled *Income, Saving and the Theory of Consumer Behaviour* published in 1949. His theory, known as the *relative income hypothesis,* is based on the assumptions that (1) the consumption behaviour of individuals is interdependent and not independent; and (2) consumption relations are irreversible over time. On the basis of the first assumption, Duesenberry developed the proposition that the ratio of income consumed by an individual does not depend on his absolute income; instead, it depends on his relative income—on his percentile position in the total income distribution. In any given year, an individual will consume a smaller percentage of his income as his absolute income increases if his percentile position in the income distribution improves and *vice versa.* This is supported by evidence from the cross-section data. If, however, an individual's percentile position in the income distribution remains unchanged over time, he will continue to spend the same percentage of his income on consumption as his absolute income increases. In other words, if a family's relative position on the income scale remains unchanged when its absolute income has increased, the fraction of income spent on consumption and the fraction of income saved will remain unchanged—the division of income between consumption and saving will not change. For all individuals remaining in the same percentile position over time, the rise in their disposable personal incomes over the long period will cause an equal percentage increase in their consumption spending. Although the relative income position of some individuals may change, these changes will balance in the aggregate with the result that the long-run aggregate C/Y ratio will remain constant.

The second assumption of this hypothesis explains the fluctuations in the aggregate consumption-income ratio C/Y during a trade cycle. Given the irreversible consumer standards, a fall in income during the cyclical downswing will cause a less than proportionate fall in the consumption because individuals base their current consumption partially on the previous higher levels of income and consumption represented by the previous peak income and consumption. This means that during a recession the ratio of consumption to income (APC) increases and the saving-income ratio (APS) falls because consumers try to maintain their previous high level of consumption.

12. In the classical system, the quantity of money determines the price level and, for a given real income, the level of *nominal* income. In this sense, monetary policy was quite important to classical economists. Stable money was a requirement for stable prices. In another sense, money was not important. The quantity of money did not affect the equilibrium values of the real variables in the system: output, employment, and the interest rate.

To classical economists, money was a 'veil' that determined the nominal values in which we measure such variables as the level of economic activity, but had no effect on real quantities.

15. The initial economic model for migration is known to be the one developed by Lewis (1954) which was modified and enriched later by Fei and Ranis (1961) and then by Harris and Todaro (1970). In Lewis (1954) model of rural-urban migration, the economy is composed of two sectors: one is a traditional, rural subsistence sector held in extremely low marginal labour product, and the other is a modern urban industrial sector with high marginal labour product. People move from the subsistence sector to the industrial sector. Migration takes place because of the expansion of the capitalistic industrial sector and the earnings gaps between the two sectors. The process continues until the re-allocation of surplus labour of the subsistence sector to industry is complete.

16. Rosenstein-Rodan identifies three different kinds of indivisiblities, which may be considered the main obstacles to the development of developing countries. They are:

- Indivisibility in the supply of social overhead capital (lumpiness of capital);
- Indivisibility of demand (complementarity of demand); and
- Indivisibility (kink) in the supply of savings.

18. In 1960, eminent economist **Nicholas Kaldor** presented a model of growth in his book title *"Essays on Economic Stability and Growth"*. Prior to it, he had already published his **"Income Distribution Model"** in an article 'Alternative Theories of Distribution'. The main objective of Kaldor's Growth model is to analyse the tendency of those non-economic factors which determine long-term rate of equilibrium growth. In this model, Kaldor has attempted to relate technical progress to capital accumulation in order to explain the growth process. Kaldor's model tells that even in the state of rising population the economy can be in a state of long-period stable growth and it need not be in a state of instability.

Assumptions: Main assumptions of Kaldor's Model of Growth are as under:

1. There is full employment in the economy.
2. Income is distributed in the form of wage and profit.
3. Labourers and profit-earners both affect saving but as against labourers, the saving capacity of profit-earners is more. Investment decisions of the entrepreneurs depend on two factors: (a) Rate of profit and (b) Level of output in the last year.
4. Role of monetary policy is passive or the rates of interest have no role in the determination of investment.
5. A fixed proportion of the total capital goes waste in the form of depreciation every year.

20. In the 1950s neoclassical economics gave rise to celebrated long-run, supply-driven, growth models such as Solow (1956). In this model, the rate of technical change, the savings ratio and the rate of population growth are the three parameters that determine the rate of growth of the economy in a steady state. In this model, the investment ratio plays a role only in the transition between steady states (in practice that transition may take a few decades), but not in the configuration of long-run growth equilibrium of the economy.

22. Taxation is progressive when the marginal tax rate is higher than the average rate: the amount of tax paid increases more than proportionally with income. Taxes are regressive when the amount of tax paid increases less than proportionally with income.

24. **Debt Redemption :** Repayment of public debt. Debt repayment maintains and strengthens the national credit and releases funds for trade and industry as well. The following are some of the methods of debt redemption:

1. Repudiation of debt (*i.e.,* refusal to pay the interest as well as the principal).
2. Conversion of loans (*i.e.,* conversion of an old loan into a new loan).
3. Serial bond redemption (*i.e.,* paying every year a certain portion of the bonds issued previously).
4. Buying up loans (*i.e.,* spending the amount to pay off government loan bonds from the market where they are bought and sold).
5. Sinking fund (*i.e.,* the creation and the gradual accumulation of a fund sufficient to pay off public debt).
6. Capital levy (*i.e.,* once-for-all tax).

30. Optimum currency area (OCA) theory originates from two seminal articles in the early 1960s by the economists Mundell (1961) and McKinnon (1963). An optimum currency area theory is a branch or an extension of the *fixed versus flexible exchange rate* debate. A currency area is defined either as a common currency area or an area within which rigidly fixed exchange rates operate.

In the words of **Carbaugh,** *An optimum currency area is a region in which it is economically preferable to have a single official currency rather than multiple official currencies.* It has fixed exchange rates within the area, but flexible exchange rates with trading partners outside the area.

It is believed that a common currency area may provide the best long-term solution for the balance of payments problems of the countries in the world. A currency may be linked through a common currency such as the Euro of the European Economic Community (EEC).

According to the theory of optimum currency area, the common currency provides multiple benefits. These gains include more uniform prices, lower transaction costs, greater certainty for investors and enhanced competition.

32. The Asian currency crisis started with a drastic devaluation of Thai Baht on July 2, 1997, quickly followed by devaluations of the Philippine peso, the Malaysian ringgit, the Indonesian rupiah, and the Singaporean dollar. After the first round of currency attacks took place between July and October of 1997, the second round started in October of 1998, when the Hong Kong stock market lost 40 per cent of value and ended with the South Korean won's dramatic devaluation in less than two months.

After frantic attempts to protect their currencies, many countries gave up and let their currencies go into a free fall. Only Hong Kong managed to maintain the peg, but at a cost of more than US $1 billion to defend its currency. Steep devaluations of local currencies increased debt burdens in Asia, since most existing borrowings were made in foreign currencies. As a result, there were massive numbers of bankrupticies.

34. After the Second World War (1939-45), European countries were determined not to see their continent torn apart by further wars so the Council of Europe was formed. It committed itself to the Convention of Human Rights in 1951 and by the end of the 1950s six counties had formed the Common Market, which the UK joined in 1971. This is now the European Union.

The EU is a strong trading bloc with no tariffs operating between member countries, and it has strong social and political objectives as well.

36. There are the spot rate of foreign exchange and the forward rate of foreign exchange ruling in the foreign exchange markets. The spot rate of foreign exchange is the rate or price expressed in terms of the home currency which is payable for spot delivery of specified type of foreign exchange. The forward rate of foreign exchange is the rate or price at which a transaction will be consummated at some specified time in future.

The spot transactions in foreign exchange in which the buyer buys and seller sells 'on the spot' are conducted in the spot foreign exchange market. In the spot transaction, the seller of foreign exchange has to deliver the foreign exchange sold by him 'on the spot' (within two days). Likewise, a buyer of foreign exchange will immediately receive the foreign exchange bought by him. In the forward foreign exchange market the seller agrees to sell and the buyer agrees to buy a certain stated amount of foreign exchange at some specified future date at a price agreed upon in advance. Usually the forward contracts are made on the three-month basis. The spot and forward foreign exchange markets are intimately linked through interest arbitrage, hedging and speculation.

37. Capital Adequacy Norms: Capital adequacy ratio is the ratio of paid-up capital and reserves (after write off bad debts) as a percentage of the banks assets. Weights are first given to different items based on their prescribed risks and then the capital adequacy ratio is calculated.

The Reserve Bank of India introduced a risk weighted ratio system for banks based on the reports of Basle Committee and Narasimhan Committee. This was done in order to strengthen the capital base of the banks. The provisions are also applicable to foreign banks operating in India.

38. Liabilities of A Commercial Bank: It includes all those items which the bank owes to others. It shows the various sources through which the bank raises funds for its business. They are classified into:

1. Paid Up Capital
2. Reserves and Surplus
3. Deposits
4. Borrowings
5. Other Liabilities: These are incurred by the bank during the course of business. They include bills payables such as drafts, travellers, cheques, pay slips, bankers, cheques etc. They also include provision for income tax.

Assets of A Commercial Bank: 1. Cash Balance, 2. Money at Call and Short Notice, 3. Investments, 4. Loans and Advances, 5. Other Assets.

42. The measures of money supply used by the Reserve Bank of India (RBI) have been changing depending on the recommendations of its *Working Group*. The First Working Group was appointed in 1961, the Second in 1977 and the Third in 1998. Different Working Groups have recommended different measures of money supply. We give here the details of the measures of money supply recommended by the *Third Working Group* and currently being used by the RBI. However, RBI uses a somewhat modified version of measures of money supply. The following measures of money supply are used by the RBI.

1. M_0 (Reserve Money) = Currency in Circulation + Bankers' Deposit with the RBI + Other Deposits with the RBI.
2. M_1 (Narrow Money) = Currency with the Public + Demand Deposits with Banks + Other Deposits with the RBI.
3. $M_2 = M_1$ + Time Liabilities of the Saving Deposits with banks + Certificate of Deposits issued by Banks + Term Deposits (excluding FCNR(B) Deposits) with Banks
4. M_3 (Broad Money) = Currrency with the Public + Demand Deposits with Banks + Time Deposits with Banks + Other Deposits with the RBI.

Or, $M_3 = M_1$ + Time Deposits with Banks.

43. Bank rate is the minimum rate at which the Central Bank provides loans to the commercial banks. It is also called the discount rate. Usually, an increment in bank rate results in commerical banks increasing their lending rates. Changes in bank rate affect credit creation by banks through altering the cost of credit.

45. The population that is established by a prolonged regime of unchanging fertility and mortality schedules is called the stable population; it is characterized, by a fixed age composition, constant birth and death rates, and a constant rate of increase.

46. **Total marital fertility rate:** Average number of children born per married female in the reproductive age group.

Gross reproduction rate: Number of daughters born to a woman who survives through the reproductive age and reproduces at current fertility rate.

Net reproduction rate: Average number of daughters that would be born to a woman if she experiences the current fertility and mortality patterns throughout her reproductive span (15-44 years).

47. According to the Technical Group on Population Projections constituted by the National Commission on Population, May 2006, annual population growth is expected to gradually decelerate from 1.6 per cent in the five years ending in 2006 to 0.9 per cent in the five years ending in 2026, India's population, which is estimated to have gone up from the Census 2001 figure of 1029 million to 1112 million in 2006, is projected to increase to 1400 million by 2026.

The well-known 'demographic dividend' will manifest in the proportion of population in the working age group of 15-64 years increasing steadily from 62.9 per cent in 2006 to 68.4 per cent in 2026. The actual tapping of this demographic dividend will, however, depend a lot on ensuring proper healthcare and other human resource development such as education.

49. The New Agricultural Strategy (NAS) was initiated in 1966. Under it, policies were formulated to utilise and promote high-yielding varieties of foodgrains in all districts selected under the IADP and IAAP schemes. The NAS was first introduced in the Kharif season of 1966. It also came to be known as the High-Yielding Varieties Programme (HYVP).

50. **Intensive Cultivation:** This is the system under which small farms are used intensively with large input of manual labour and manures and fertilisers, etc. This system, being labour-intensive, is practised in those areas where the density of population is high. Emphasis is laid on increasing the per hectare production and the practice of more than one crop in a year is followed wherever possible.

Extensive Cultivation: Just the opposite of intensive cultivation, this type of farming is practised on farms of large size with the help of machines and the input of labour per unit of area is low. This type of farming is highly capital-intensive and is practised in sparsely populated areas. The emphasis is laid on the increased production irrespective of production per hectare. Crop specialisation is one of the major characteristics of this type of farming.

52. Social security legislation in India in the industrial field consists of the following enactments:

1. the Workman's Compensation Act, 1923;
2. the Employees' State Insurance Act, 1948;
3. the Coal Mines Provident Funds and Miscellaneous Provisions Act, 1948;
4. the Employees' Provident Funds and Miscellaneous Provisions Act, 1952; and Employees' Pension Scheme, 1995 and the Employees' Deposit Linked Insurance Scheme, 1976;
5. the Maternity Benefit Act, 1961; and
6. the Payment of Gratuity Act, 1972.

53. The contingent valuation method is the non-market valuation method used in environmental economics. Contingent valuation is the name given to a collection of methods used in welfare analysis to value goods that are not traded in markets.

The concept of willingness-to-pay (WTP) for valuing environmental goods is one of the core issues in environmental economics. Environmental goods such as clean air, biodiversity or environmentally sound products are normally not traded in markets. Theory of market failure explains why they cannot, in general, be traded like consumer goods because there are no prices assigned to them. In these cases, non-market valuation techniques such as 'hedonic pricing' or 'contingent valuation' are employed to clarify consumers' preferences in monetary value. By means of hedonic pricing methods, the demand for environmental goods (*e.g.* clean air) is derived by the market demand for complementary consumers goods *e.g.*, housing prices. While these methods are indirect methods, contingent valuation directly tries to investigate consumers' preferences by asking them about their willingness-to-pay for ecological goods.

58. Competition Commission of India is a body of the Government of India responsible for enforcing The Competition Act, 2002 throughout India and to prevent activities that have an adverse effect on competition in India. It was established on 14 Ocotober 2003. It became fully functional in May 2009.

59. CSO has started compiling a new series of CPIs for the entire population, viz. CPI-Rural, CPI-Urban and CPI-Combined (Rural + Urban) since January 2011 with 2010 as the base year.

62. FSLRC, set up in March 2011 for rewriting financial-sector laws to bring them in harmony with the current requirements, had submitted its report to the government on March 22, 2013. It had recommended a non-sectoral, principle-based, legislative architecture for the financial sector by restructuring or upgrading existing regulatory agencies and creating new ones wherever needed for better governance and accountability.

66. In multiple regression, the t test and the F test have different purposes.

1. The F test is used to determine whether a siginificant relationship exists between the dependent variable and the set of all the independent variables: we will refer to the F test as the test for overall significance.
2. If the F test shows an overall significance, the t test is used to determine whether each of the individual independent variables is significant. A separate t test is conducted for each of the independent variables in the model: we refer to each of these t tests as a test for individual significance.

67. Including lagged values of the dependent variable y will cause the assumption of the CLRM that the explanatory variables are non-stochastic to be violated. This arises since the lagged value of y is now being used as an explanatory variable and, since y at time t-1 will depend on the value of u at time t-1, it must be the case that lagged values of y are stochastic (*i.e.* they have some random influences and are not fixed in repeated samples). The result of this is that the OLS estimator in the presence of lags of the dependent variable will produce biased but consistent coefficient estimates. Thus, as the sample size increases towards infinity, we will still obtain the optimal parameter estimates, although these estimates could be biased in small samples. Note that no problem of this kind arises whatever the sample size when using only lags of the explanatory variables in the regression equation.

70. The consequences of autocorrelation are similar to those of heteroscedasticity. Thus the coefficient estimates will still be okay (*i.e.* they will be consistently and unbiasedly estimated) provided that the other assumptions of the classical linear regression model are valid. The OLS estimator will be inefficient in the presence of autocorrelation, which implies that the standard errors could be sub-optimal. Since the standard errors may be inappropriate in the presence of auto-correlation, it is true that hypothesis tests could reach the wrong conclusion, since the t-test statistic contains the coefficient standard error in it. As the parameter estimates should still be correct, forecasts obtained from the model will only use the coefficients and not the standard errors, so the forecasts should be unbiased. Therefore (*ii*) and (*iv*) are likely consequences and so option (A) is correct.

72. All linear programming problems are concerned with maximization (or minimization) of a linear function subject to a set of linear constraints. The linear constraints governing the problem may be of the ≤, = or ≥ forms.

The simplex method of linear programming was developed by Prof. G.B. Dantzig in 1947, then working for the U.S. Airforce. He demonstrated how to use an objective function to find the optimum solution from amongst the several feasible solutions to a linear programming problem.

74. In equilibrium,

LM and IS interest each other so,

$$100 + 10i = 160 - 20i$$

$$30i = 60 \Rightarrow i = 2$$

if $i = 2$,

$$y = 100 + 10 \times 2 = 120.$$

Previous Paper (Solved)

UGC–NET Economics, June-2014

PAPER-II

Note : *This paper contains* ***fifty (50)*** *objective type questions, each question carrying* ***two (2)*** *marks. All questions are compulsory.*

1. Who distinguished between value in use and value in exchange and gave the famous example of diamonds and water?

A. Adam Smith B. David Ricardo
C. Alfred Marshall D. Karl Marx

2. In an economy of two individuals A and B and two commodities X and Y, general equilibrium of production and exchange occurs when

A. $MRT_{XY} = \left(\frac{P_X}{P_Y}\right)$

B. MRS_{XY} for A and B $= \left(\frac{P_X}{P_Y}\right)$

C. $MRS^{A}_{XY} = MRS^{B}_{XY}$

D. $MRT_{XY} = MRS^{A}_{XY} = MRS^{B}_{XY}$

3. When income effect becomes stronger than substitution effect, the labour supply curve will

A. Slope positively B. Negatively sloped
C. Bend backward D. Slope upwards

4. Assertion (A) : The concept of supply curve is meaningless for the monopolist.

Reason (R) : Monopolists are price setters; it does not make reuse to ask what output they will produce at various prices.

Codes :

A. Both (A) and (R) are correct and (R) is the correct explanation of (A).
B. (A) is correct, but (R) is not correct.
C. Both (A) and (R) are correct, but (R) is not the correct explanation of (A).
D. (R) is correct, but (A) is incorrect.

5. Predatory pricing policy is designed to

A. drive competitors out of business
B. maximise profits
C. encourage entrants into the market
D. attain least cost output

6. Match items in List–I with items in List–II and select the correct answer from the code given below :

List–I	*List–II*
(*a*) The Screening Hypothesis	1. George A. Akerlof
(*b*) Job Market Signalling	2. K.J. Arrow
(*c*) The problem of moral hazard in the case of medical insurance	3. M. Spencer
(*d*) The market for lemons	4. Paul W. Miller and Paul A. Volcker

Codes :

	(*a*)	(*b*)	(*c*)	(*d*)
A.	3	2	4	1
B.	2	3	4	1
C.	4	3	2	1
D.	2	4	3	1

7. An industry whose long run supply curve is horizontal is called

A. Constant Cost Industry
B. Increasing Cost Industry
C. Decreasing Cost Industry
D. Efficient Industry

8. The practice of charging each consumer the reservation price is called

A. Peak load pricing
B. Inter-temporal price discrimination
C. First degree price discrimination
D. Third degree price discrimination

9. Frictional unemployment is also known as

A. Disguised unemployment
B. Turnover unemployment
C. Cyclical unemployment
D. Structural unemployment

10. Arrange in ascending chronological order the following consumption hypotheses in which they appeared in the economics literature :

1. Absolute increase hypothesis
2. Permanent increase hypothesis
3. Life cycle hypothesis
4. Relative increase hypothesis

Codes :

A. 1, 3, 4, 2
B. 1, 2, 4, 3
C. 1, 4, 3, 2
D. 1, 3, 2, 4

11. Assume a model of income determination of the following type :

$$C = a + b \bullet Y^d$$
$$Y^d = Y - T$$
$$T = T_0 + t_1 \bullet Y$$
$$I = \overline{I}$$
$$G = \overline{G}$$
$$Y = C + I + G$$

Where C = Consumption expenditure; Y = income; Y^d = disposable income; T = taxes; T_0 = Tan, when Y = 0; t_1 = marginal tax rate; I = investment expenditure; G = Government expenditure; and bar '–' as the variable indicates that these autonomous variables. Then the tax multiples with respect to T_0 is:

A. $\dfrac{1}{1-b+bt_1}$ B. $\dfrac{-b}{1-b+bt_1}$

C. $\dfrac{1-b}{1-b-bt_1}$ D. $\dfrac{1}{1-b-bt_1}$

12. Which of the following components of aggregate demand is self-terminating and self-financing?

A. Investment expenditure
B. Durable consumption expenditure
C. Non-durable consumption expenditure
D. Government expenditure

13. Arrange all the four concepts of money supply M_1, M_2, M_3 and M_4 in the ascending order in terms of their liquidity :

A. M_3, M_2, M_1 and M_4
B. M_1, M_2, M_3 and M_4
C. M_4, M_2, M_3 and M_1
D. M_4, M_3, M_2 and M_1

14. Who amongst the following economists imparted money demand of a portfolio theory approach?

1. J.M. Keynes 2. Baumol
3. James Tobin 4. Milton Friedman

Codes :

A. 1, 2 B. 3, 4
C. 1, 2, 3 D. 2, 3, 4

15. Which of the following is not a characteristic feature of the Phillips curve?

A. The Price expectations are adaptive
B. The unemployment rate, when money wage stabilises, is 5½ per cent
C. The price expectations are static
D. There is a loop around Phillips curve

16. The crowding out effect is zero when

A. there is liquidity trap, or investment is perfectly interest inelastic
B. money demand is perfectly interest inelastic, or investment is perfectly interest elastic
C. IS curve is falling and LM curve is rising
D. None of the above

17. Meeting the needs of present generation without compromising the needs of future generation is

A. Economic Development
B. Social Development
C. Sustainable Development
D. Economic Growth

18. The full capacity growth rate in Harrod-Domar Model is also known as
A. Actual growth rate
B. Warranted growth rate
C. Natural growth rate
D. Expected growth rate

19. Inventors of HDI are
I. Harris-Todaro
II. Megnad Desai
III. Robert Solow
IV. Amartya Sen
Codes :
A. I and II are correct
B. I and III are correct
C. III and IV are correct
D. II and IV are correct

20. Components of PQLI
I. Morbidity
II. Infant mortality
III. Life expectancy at age one
IV. Basic literacy at age 15
Codes :
A. I, III and IV are correct
B. III, II and IV are correct
C. I, II and III are correct
D. IV, I and II are correct

21. Assertion (A) : All historical events are the results of continuous economic struggle between different classes and groups in society.
Reason (R) : The main cause of this struggle is the conflict between the 'mode of production' and the 'relations of production'.
Codes :
A. (A) is correct, but (R) is wrong
B. (A) is wrong, but (R) is correct
C. Both (A) and (R) are wrong
D. Both (A) and (R) are correct

22. Match the items given in List–I with those in List–II :

List–I	*List–II*
(*a*) Swarm-like clusters	1. Brundtland Report
(*b*) Organic composition of capital	2. Ragner Nurkse
(*c*) Sustainable Development	3. Schumpeter
(*d*) Vicious circle of poverty	4. Karl Marx

Codes :

	(*a*)	(*b*)	(*c*)	(*d*)
A.	4	2	3	1
B.	3	4	1	2
C.	1	3	2	4
D.	2	1	4	3

23. Match the items given in List–I with those in List–II :

List–I	*List–II*
(*a*) Low level equilibrium trap	1. Simon Kuznets
(*b*) Inverted 'V' shaped income distribution hypothesis	2. Nelson
(*c*) Endogenous growth theory	3. Arthur Lewis
(*d*) Unlimited supplies of labour	4. Robert Solow

Codes :

	(*a*)	(*b*)	(*c*)	(*d*)
A.	2	1	4	3
B.	3	2	1	4
C.	4	3	2	1
D.	1	4	3	2

24. Which of the following is correct about the 'Hindu Growth Rate'?
A. This is about economic growth of the Hindu population.
B. Shows economic disparities among different social groups in India.
C. Reflects low growth performance of the Indian economy during 1950-80.
D. Hints at accelerated growth in India since 1980

25. Find out the incorrect statement about the success of economic reforms in India.
A. Benefits of demographic dividends
B. Increased share of the corporate sector in Gross Domestic Savings
C. Narrowing down of the current account deficit
D. Slow down of population growth rate

26. Single out the activity that is not included in the Industrial Production Index of India :
A. Manufacturing
B. Construction
C. Mining
D. Electricity

27. High growth of which industry provides a positive signal for industrial growth in future?
A. Capital goods industries
B. Basic goods industries
C. Durable consumer goods industries
D. Intermediate goods industries

28. Identify the method not being used for unemployment estimation by the NSSO in India.
A. Current monthly status
B. Current daily status
C. Current weekly status
D. Usual principal and subsidiary status

29. The process of budget making after reevaluating every item of expenditure in every financial year is known as
A. Performance Budgeting
B. Fresh Budgeting
C. Debit Budgeting
D. Zero Based Budgeting

30. Rank the states in terms of ascending Human Development Index (HDI) as per India Human Development Report 2011 :
I. Bihar
II. Gujarat
III. Odisha
IV. Tamil Nadu

Codes :

A.	I, II, III, IV	B.	III, I, II, IV
C.	I, III, IV, II	D.	III, II, I, IV

31. A difference in relative commodity prices between two nations can be based upon a difference in
A. factor endowment
B. technology
C. tastes
D. All of the above

32. Which type of trade is not explained by the Heckscher-Ohlin model?
A. Trade based on economies of scale
B. Intra industry trade
C. Trade based on imitation gaps and product cycles
D. All of the above

33. An example of a Euro currency is
A. a dollar deposit outside the U.S.
B. a pound sterling deposit within UK
C. a mark deposit with Germany
D. All of the above

34. A deficit or surplus in the India's balance of payments is measured by the net balance of
A. the current account
B. the capital account
C. allocation of SDRs and the statistical discrepancy
D. All of the above

35. If the demand of the domestic consumers is infinitely elastic and the supply of the foreign producer is perfectly inelastic, then the whole of the tariff will
A. be paid by the domestic consumers
B. be paid by the foreign producer
C. be equally shared by the domestic consumers and the foreign producer
D. yield neither revenue nor protection to either of them

36. The RBI made Indian Rupee fully convertible in current account transactions related to goods and services in the year
A. 1985
B. 2002
C. 1994
D. 2011

37. According to the monetary approach, a revaluation of a nation's currency
A. increases the nation's demand for money
B. increases the nation's supply of money
C. reduces the nation's demand for money
D. reduces the nation's supply of money

38. Arrange the following in chronological order:

I. Sarkar Award
II. Niemeyer Award
III. Deshmukh Award
IV. Meston Award

Codes :

A. II, IV, III, I
B. IV, III, II, I
C. III, II, IV, I
D. IV, II, I, III

39. In which of the following, Zero Based Budgeting is difficult to introduce?

I. Establishment charges
II. Public works
III. Irrigation Projects
IV. Federal fiscal transfers

Codes :

A. I, III and IV are correct
B. II, III and IV are correct
C. I and IV are correct
D. II and III are correct

40. Match the items given in List–I with those in List–II :

List–I	*List–II*
(*a*) Theory of Clubs	1. Anthony Downs
(*b*) Impossibility theorem	2. Charles Tiebout
(*c*) Political of Decision Making Model	3. James Buchanan
(*d*) Optimum provision of local public goods	4. Kenneth Arrow

Codes :

	(*a*)	(*b*)	(*c*)	(*d*)
A.	3	1	2	4
B.	3	4	2	1
C.	2	3	4	1
D.	3	4	1	2

41. Which of the following tax has 'announcement effect'?

A. Income tax
B. Property tax
C. Excise Duties
D. Capital gains taxation

42. Which of the following tax is within the jurisdiction of Union or Central Government as enumerated in List–I of Schedule VII of the India Constitution?

A. Taxes on the consumption and sale of electricity.
B. Taxes on goods and passengers carried by road.
C. Taxes on luxuries, including entertainments.
D. Taxes on Sales and purchase of newspapers and on advertisement therein.

43. A tax imposed on a commodity according to its weight, size or measurement is called

A. Advalorem tax
B. Specific tax
C. Single tax
D. Double taxation

44. Which of the following is Musgrave's views on incidence of taxation?

A. Settlement of tax on ultimate tax payer.
B. Formal and effective incidence of taxation.
C. Changes in the distribution of income for private use arising from changes in budget policy.
D. The final direct money burden of a tax.

45. Given arithmetic mean = 45, mode = 48, then median =

A. 46 B. 45
C. 48 D. 49

46. If two events A and B are mutually inclusive, then P(A or B) is

A. P(A) + P(B) – P(AB)
B. P(A) + P(B) + P(AB)
C. P(A) + P(B)
D. P(A) P(B)

47. The analysis of variance is carried out by using

A. *t*-test
B. Z-test
C. χ^2-test
D. F-test

48. Systematic sampling implies that the first item is selected randomly and

A. the other items are selected by lottery method

B. the other items are selected purposively

C. then every *k*th item is selected

D. the other items are selected at the will of the investigator

49. Given the following information match the item in List–I with List–II :

List–I	*List–II*
(*a*) Rejecting H_0, if it is true	1. β error
(*b*) Accepting H_0, if it is false	2. Standard error
(*c*) Probability of rejecting H_0, when it is false	3. α error
(*d*) Measuring sampling variability due to random force	4. 1 – β error

Codes :

	(*a*)	(*b*)	(*c*)	(*d*)
A.	3	1	2	4
B.	2	1	4	3
C.	2	4	1	3
D.	3	1	4	2

50. Assertion (A) : Geometric mean is theoretically considered as the best average to construct index numbers.

Reason (R) : Geometric mean is used if the range of observations is extremely large.

Codes :

A. Both (A) and (R) are true and (R) is the correct explanation of (A).

B. Both (A) and (R) are true, but (R) is not the correct explanation of (A).

C. (A) is true, but (R) is false.

D. (A) is false, but (R) is true.

ANSWERS

1	2	3	4	5	6	7	8	9	10
A	D	C	A	A	C	A	C	B	C
11	**12**	**13**	**14**	**15**	**16**	**17**	**18**	**19**	**20**
B	B	D	B	A	A	C	C	*	B
21	**22**	**23**	**24**	**25**	**26**	**27**	**28**	**29**	**30**
D	B	A	C	D	B	A	A	D	B
31	**32**	**33**	**34**	**35**	**36**	**37**	**38**	**39**	**40**
D	D	A	D	B	C	C	D	C	D
41	**42**	**43**	**44**	**45**	**46**	**47**	**48**	**49**	**50**
C	D	B	C	A	*	D	C	D	A

SOME SELECTED EXPLANATORY ANSWERS

1. The term "utility" is associated with the British philosopher Jeremy Bentham (1748-1832). However, neither he nor the economists of the time understood the relationship between the value of goods and the utility derived from their consumption. Adam Smith (1723–1790) distinguished between *value in use* and *value in exchange* and gave the famous example of diamonds and water. Diamonds have a high price (value in exchange), but they are unnecessary for life (a low value in use). Water has a low price (value in exchange) but is necessary for life (a high value in use).

2. General equilibrium of exchange : The condition when the marginal rate of substitution (MRS) in consumption for the two commodities is the same for both individuals.

General equilibrium of production : The condition when the marginal rate of technical substitution (MRTS) of one factor for another is the same in the production of both commodities.

General equilibrium of production and exchange : The condition when the marginal rate of transformation between two commodities is equal to the marginal rate of substitution consumption between the two commodities for each individual.

4. Under monopoly, shape of different cost curves is exactly like that under perfect competition. Fixed cost (FC) curve is parallel to OX-axis and average fixed cost (AFC) curve is rectangular hyperbola. Average Variable Cost (AVC) curve, marginal cost (MC) curve and average cost (AC) curve are U-shaped. Whereas, marginal cost curve is the supply curve of the firm under perfect competition and marginal cost is equal to price (average revenue) in long-run equilibrium under perfect competition, but under monopoly marginal cost curve is not the supply curve and price (average revenue) is higher than marginal cost. It may also be noted that a monopolist is not obliged to sell a given amount of the commodity at a given price. If he fixes the price, then how much quantity he will have to supply at that price, will be left to the decision of the buyers. If buyers demand more, he will have to supply more. If buyers demand less, he will have to supply less. Accordingly, under monopoly, the concept of supply curve becomes meaningless.

5. Predatory pricing occurs, where a dominant enterprise charges low prices over a long enough period of time so as to drive a competitor from the market or deter others from entering the market and then raises prices to recoup its losses. The greater the diversification of the activities of the enterprise in terms of products and markets and the greater its financial resources, the greater is its ability to engage in predatory behaviour.

8. First-degree price discrimination is a situation in which the monopolist firm, if it could, would charge each customer the maximum price that the customer is willing to pay for each unit bought. This maximum price is called the customer's demand or reservation price. Therefore, the practice of charging each customer his or her reservation price is called perfect price discrimination or first-degree price discrimination.

9. *Frictional unemployment* refers to people who choose to leave their jobs in search of other opportunities. Sometimes referred to as turnover unemployment.

10. Absolute increase hypothesis – 1935
Permanent increase hypothesis – 1975
Life cycle hypothesis – 1963
Relative increase hypothesis – 1949

13. In India there are 4 alternative measures of money supply—M_1, M_2, M_3 and M_4

M_1 = CC + OD + DD

M_2 = M_1 + Post office savings deposits

M_3 = M_1 + Time deposits with banks

M_4 = M_3 + Total Post office deposits.

These 4 concepts of money supply indicate varying degrees of liquidity. M_1 is most liquid. M_2, M_3, M_4 follow it in descending order in terms of liquidity.

14. James Tobin (1958) and Milton Friedman (1956) have imparted money demand a portfolio theory approach. According to them, money is one of the assets in the form of which the people could hold their portfolios of assets. The size of this portfolio depends positively on the wealth of the people. The more wealth a person has, the more he/she would save, and the larger would be the size of his/her portfolio. Thus, wealth is a positive factor in the money demand function. However, since income includes the income from wealth, it is often taken as a *'surrogate'* measure of the asset holding power of individuals. Also, if wealth was used along with income in the function, there could be an econometric problem, called multicollinearity, in the estimation of the function. Due to these factors, wealth is often ignored as a determinant in the money demand function.

16. The crowding out is zero when:
(*a*) There is liquidity trap (LM curve is horizontal), or
(*b*) Investment is perfectly interest inelastic (IS curve is vertical).
The crowding out is full (= increase in government expenditure) when :
(*c*) Money demand is perfectly interest inelastic (LM curve is vertical), or
(*d*) Investment is perfectly interest elastic (IS curve is horizontal)
The crowding out is only partial under:
(*e*) Intermediate situations (when the IS curve is falling and the LM curve is rising).

21. Karl Marx (1818–1883) was developed a comprehensive theory of economic growth based on "materialistic interpretation of history". Karl Marx, while analysing the various stages of growth, tried to show that all historical events are formed as a result of a continuous struggle between various groups and classes in society. The struggle itself is caused by the conflict between the mode of production and the relations of production. The mode of production refers to the type of arrangement of production in a society which determines the manner in which its social, political and religious way of living is moulded. People enter into mutual relations for using the mode of production which keeps changing continuously. The relations of production, on the other hand, refer to the class structure of society.

24. Raj Krishna popularised the phrase 'Hindu rate of growth' during the 1970s, a period characterised by increasing controls and a slowing growth rate.

28. The NSSO has given four definitions of unemployment, viz, (1) usual principal activity status, (2) usual principal and subsidiary status (ps + ss), (3) current weekly status, and (4) current daily status. Among the four definitions, the usual principal and subsidiary status definition is the most suitable one in the Indian conditions due to the informal nature of employment. This definition covers all workers, viz, the workers who worked for a relatively longer part of the 365 days preceding the date of survey and also those who worked at least 30 days during the reference period of one year. To get the overall position of the regional as well as the national situation of employment, this definition is a better one.

29. Zero-based budget means that an organization while preparing budget for the current financial year should not take the expenditure of earlier years for granted but should start afresh. The traditional budget is based in 'incremental budgeting', i.e., it takes the current expenditure level as fixed and analyses the desired increases from this fixed point, and it examines only a fraction of the total budget. But in Zero-based budgeting the existing programmes and activities have to be examined in the same manner as the newly proposed ones. The old programmes, which have lost their utility and become ineffective, are shelved to be replaced by new programme.

31. Trade can be based on a difference in factor endowments, technology or tastes between two nations. A difference either in factor endowments or technology results in a different production possibilities curve for each nation, which, unless neutralized by a difference in tastes, leads to a difference in relative commodity price and mutually beneficial trade. If two nations face increasing costs and have identical production possibilities curves but different tastes, there will also be a difference in relative commodity prices and the basis for mutually beneficial trade between the two nations. The difference in relative commodity prices is then translated into a difference in absolute commodity prices between the two nations, which is the *immediate* cause of trade.

38. Sarkar Award – 1948

Niemeyer Award – 1936

Deshmukh Award – 1950

Meston Award – 1920

43. **Specific Tax :** When a tax is imposed on a commodity according to its weight, size or measurement, it is called a specific tax. For instance, when the excise duty is imposed on sugar on the basis of its weight or the cloth is taxed according to its length or a tax on a picture is levied on the basis of its size, it is known as a specific tax. The main advantage of specific tax is that it is easy to levy and more convenient to collect because it is collected either according to the weight of the commodity or according to the size of the unit of the commodity. The main disadvantage of this tax is that it imposes a greater burden on the poor people than on the rich people. The reason is that the marginal utility of money for the rich people is lower than that for the poor people.

44. According to Musgrave incidence of taxation refers to the changes in the distribution of income available for private uses. These changes are caused by changes in budgeting policy that involve resource transfer. Musgrave is of the view that distributional changes may be caused either due to change in tax policy or expenditure policy or in both. He mentioned five forms of incidence relating to different type of changes.

1. Specific Tax Incidence.
2. Differential Tax Incidence.
3. Specific Expenditure Incidence.
4. Differential Expenditure Incidence.
5. Balanced Budget Incidence.

45. Mode = 3 Median – 2 Mean

From question,

$$48 = 3 \text{ Median} - 2 \times 45$$

$$\Rightarrow \quad 3 \text{ Median} = 90 + 48 = 138$$

$$\therefore \quad \text{Median} = \frac{138}{3} = 46.$$

47. The F distribution is introduced as used in a test to compare the variances of two independent samples. The more common use of the F test is in *analysis of variance* (ANOVA).

48. In systematic sampling, sample elements are selected from the population at uniform intervals in terms of time, order, or space. For obtaining samples in systematic sampling, first of all, a sampling fraction is calculated. For example, a researcher wants to take a sample of size 30 from a population of size 900 and he has decided to use systematic sampling for this purpose. As the first step, he has to calculate a sample fraction k, which is equal to $\frac{N}{n}$, where, N is the total number of units in the population and n is the sample size.

So, in this case, sample fraction will be $\frac{900}{30} = 30.$

For obtaining the sample, the first member can be selected randomly and after that every 30th member of the population is included in the sample. Suppose the first element 3 is selected randomly and after this, every 30th element, that is, 33rd, 63rd, ... element up to a sample size of 30 are included in the sample. For obtaining starting point or the beginning point of the sampling process, a random number table can also be used. In our example k = 30, so a researcher can use a random number table to get the first element between 1 and 30.

PAPER-III

Note : *This paper contains* ***seventy five (75)*** *objective type questions, each question carrying* ***two (2)*** *marks. All questions are compulsory.*

1. Which of the following are the basic assumptions of cardinal utility analysis?
I. Utility is a measurable and quantifiable entity.
II. Marginal utility of money changes with changes in real income.
III. Utilities derived from various goods are inter-dependent.
IV. The use of introspective method in judging the behaviour of marginal utility.
Codes :
A. I and II are correct
B. I and III are correct
C. I and IV are correct
D. I, III and IV are correct

2. Engel Curve denotes
A. various amounts of a good which a consumer would be willing to purchase at various price levels.
B. various amounts of a good which a consumer would be willing to purchase at various income levels.
C. various amounts of a good purchased when the price of its substitutes tend to rise.
D. the relationship between income effect and substitution effect.

3. A producer is said to be operating with excess capacity
A. when he produces an output greater than that given by the Minimum Average Total Cost
B. when he produces an output greater than at given by the Maximum Average Total Cost
C. When he produces an output equal to that given by the Minimum Average Total Cost
D. When he produces an output smaller than that given by the Minimum Average Total Cost

4. Assertion (A) : Harvey Leibenstein asserted that marginal conditions required for economic efficiency are not usually satisfied in practice.
Reason (R) : People are not fully motivated towards maximization or minimization.
Codes :
A. Both (A) and (R) are correct and (R) is the correct explanation of (A).
B. (A) is correct, but (R) is not correct.
C. Both (A) and (R) are correct, but (R) is incorrect explanation of (A).
D. (R) is correct, but (A) is incorrect.

5. A graphical illustration used to explain efficiency conditions and demonstrates how the allocations of some goods and resources can be improved through exchange is called
A. production possibility curves
B. social indifference curves
C. Edgeworth box diagram
D. Phillips curve

6. Match the following :

List–I	***List–II***
(a) A double Kaldor-Hicks Test	1. A. Bergson
(b) Compensation Principle	2. K.J. Arrow
(c) Social Welfare function	3. T. Scitovsky
(d) Impossibility theorem	4. Kaldor-Hicks

Codes :

	(a)	*(b)*	*(c)*	*(d)*
A.	4	1	3	2
B.	3	4	1	2
C.	3	4	2	1
D.	4	3	2	1

7. The oligopoly model in which the businessman assumes that his competitors output are fixed and simultaneously decide how much to produce is
A. Cournot oligopoly model
B. Stackelberg oligopoly model
C. Chamberlin's oligopoly model
D. Bertrand oligopoly model

8. According to Game Theory, if increased advertising, raises costs more than revenues and the profits of both firms decline, we have a

A. Positive-sum game
B. Non zero-sum game
C. Zero-sum game
D. Negative-sum game

9. Arrows impossibility theorem implies

A. Any social decision rule should not violates the requirements of rational choice.
B. Any social decision rule must violate atleast one of the requirements of rational choice.
C. Any social decision rule must violate all the requirements of rational choice.
D. It is impossible to violate social decision rules.

10. 'Bandwagon effect' is found in

A. Relative income hypothesis
B. Permanent income hypothesis
C. Life cycle hypothesis
D. Absolute income hypothesis

11. Let the consumption function in life cycle hypothesis be represented as

$$C = \left(\frac{w}{w+e}\right)\bar{y}$$

where e = number of post retirement years of living.

$\bar{y}$ = average annual income during the working period

Then Marginal Propensity to Consume (MPC) is represented by the equation :

A. $\frac{1}{w+e}(\Sigma y)$

B. $\left(\frac{w}{w+e}\right)\left(\frac{\partial \bar{y}}{\partial y}\right)$

C. $\left(\frac{w}{w+e}\right)\left(\frac{\bar{y}}{y}\right)$

D. None of the above

12. Complete the statements given in List–I with there given in List–II :

List–I	List–II
(*a*) Instantaneous adjustment of income with investment spending occurs in	1. MPC is smaller
(*b*) Consumption lags income by one period in	2. increase in investment expenditure is once-for-all
(*c*) Value of investment multiplier is zero when	3. state multiplier
(*d*) Major portion of multiplier is realized in fewer periods when	4. dynamic multiplier

Codes :

	(*a*)	(*b*)	(*c*)	(*d*)
A.	3	4	1	2
B.	3	4	2	1
C.	4	3	1	2
D.	2	3	1	4

13. Assertion (A) : The individual speculative demand for money is a discontinuous one.

Reason (R) : Because the aggregate speculative demand for money function is smooth downward sloping with liquidity trap at extremely low interest rates.

Codes :

A. Both (A) and (R) are correct and (R) is the correct explanation of (A).
B. Both (A) and (R) are correct but (R) is not the correct explanation of (A).
C. (A) is correct, but (R) is incorrect.
D. (A) is incorrect, but (R) is correct.

14. Transaction Cost is also called

A. Shoe Leather Cost
B. Menu Cost
C. Opportunity Cost of holding cash
D. All of the above

15. Given the consumption function, C = 0.8Y, and the investment function I = 102 – 0.2i, then the IS-curve is

A. Y = 500 – 10i B. Y = 450 – i
C. Y = 510 – i D. Y = 505 – 2i

16. Match the premise given in List–I with that in List–II :

List–I	*List–II*
(*a*) Price expectations are static	1. Okun's law
(*b*) Price expectations are adaptive	2. Phillips Curve
(*c*) People do not make systematic errors	3. Natural Rate of unemployment hypothesis
(*d*) Deviations of output from its natural rate is inversely related to the deviation of unemployment rate from its natural level	4. Rational expectations hypothesis

Codes **:**

	(*a*)	(*b*)	(*c*)	(*d*)
A.	2	3	4	1
B.	4	3	2	1
C.	1	3	4	2
D.	4	2	1	3

17. Given that the increment in aggregate demand (Y) per unit of time, *t*, is given by the equation

$$\left[\frac{\partial Y}{\partial t}\right]_d = \frac{1}{1-MPC}\left[\frac{\partial I}{\partial t}\right]$$

and the increment in supply of output is represented by the equation

$$\left[\frac{\partial Y}{\partial t}\right]_S = \sigma\frac{\partial k}{\partial t}$$

Where MPC = Marginal Propensity to Consume, $\frac{\partial I}{\partial t}$ & $\frac{\partial k}{\partial t}$ are change in investment & capital stock respectively, per unit of time, then the capacity creating effect or Domar effect of investment following goods market equilibrium equals

A. σ (1 – MPC) B. $\sigma\left(\frac{1}{1-MPC}\right)$

C. $\frac{1}{\sigma}(1-MPC)$ D. $\frac{1}{\sigma}.\frac{1}{1-MPC}$

18. When the aggregate supply schedule is positively sloped, continuous increases in the nominal money supply, ceteris parilus, result in

A. No change in the price level and proportional increases in real output.

B. No change in real output and proportional increases in the price level.

C. An increase in the price level and real output.

D. An increase in the price level and a decrease in real output.

19. "Golden Age" as per Mrs. Joan Robinson is (where $\frac{\Delta N}{N}$ is growth rate of population and $\frac{\Delta K}{K}$ is growth rate of capital)

A. $\frac{\Delta N}{N} = \frac{\Delta K}{K}$ B. $\frac{\Delta N}{N} > \frac{\Delta K}{K}$

C. $\frac{\Delta N}{N} < \frac{\Delta K}{K}$ D. None of these

20. A technical change is neutral if $\frac{MP_K}{MP_L}$ remains unchanged at constant $\frac{K}{L}$ ratio :

A. Harrod B. Hicks

C. Solow D. Kaldor

21. Concept of disembodied technical change is associated with

I. Abramovitz

II. Kaldor

III. Kendrick

IV. Solow

A. I and II B. III and IV

C. I, III and IV D. II, III and IV

22. Joan Robinson's growth model deals with

I. Desired growth rate

II. Possible growth rate

III. Natural growth rate

IV. Warranted growth rate

Codes **:**

A. I and III B. II and IV

C. I and II D. III and IV

23. Assertion (A) : To Marx, it is surplus labour that lead to capital accumulation.

Reason (R) : The difference between actual labour and subsistence labour that a labourer puts in for which he receives nothing is surplus labour.

Codes :

A. (A) is correct, but (R) is not the correct reason for (A).

B. (A) is correct and (R) is incorrect.

C. Both (A) and (R) are correct.

D. Both (A) and (R) are incorrect.

24. Arrange the "Structural Development Processes" in a sequential order :

I. Resource Allocation Processes

II. Accumulation Process

III. Distributional Processes

IV. Demographic Processes

Codes :

A. I, IV, II, III B. II, I, IV, III

C. III, II, I, IV D. IV, III, I, II

25. Match the items in List–I with List–II :

List–I	*List–II*
(*a*) MP_L is zero in overpopulated economies	1. Gunnar Myrdal
(*b*) Two gap model	2. J.E. Mead
(*c*) Critical growth rate	3. Arthur Lewis
(*d*) Backwash effects	4. Hollis Chenery & others

Codes :

	(*a*)	(*b*)	(*c*)	(*d*)
A.	1	3	4	2
B.	3	4	2	1
C.	2	1	3	4
D.	4	2	1	3

26. Match the items in List–I with List–II :

List–I	*List–II*
(*a*) Learning by doing	1. Kaldor
(*b*) Biased Technical Progress	2. Karl Sax
(*c*) Co-efficient of sensitivity of income distribution	3. Kenneth J. Arrow
(*d*) Theory of Demographic Transition : Four stages of Population growth	4. Joan Robinson

Codes :

	(*a*)	(*b*)	(*c*)	(*d*)
A.	3	4	1	2
B.	1	3	2	4
C.	2	1	4	3
D.	4	2	3	1

27. Assertion (A) : Solow model is a major improvement over Harrod-Domar Model.

Reason (R) : Solow built a model of long run growth without the assumption of fixed proportion in production.

Codes :

A. (A) is correct, but (R) is not the correct reason of (A).

B. (A) is not correct, but (R) is correct.

C. Both (A) and (R) are correct.

D. Both (A) and (R) are not correct.

28. The concentrations effect explained in Peacock-Wiseman hypothesis implies

A. public expenditure does not increase in smooth and continuous manner

B. public expenditure increases the necessity of increased revenue

C. the Central Government's economic activity to grow faster than that of subnational Governments

D. absolute level of public expenditure increases

29. A tax imposed upon monopoly profits

A. can be shifted forward

B. can be shifted backward

C. can be shifted both forward and backward

D. cannot be shifted

30. The plan expenditure on Revenue Account of the Union Government includes

I. Economic Services

II. Social and Community Services

III. Grants-in-aid to States and Union Territories

IV. Loans and Advances to Finance Public Enterprises

Codes :

A. I and II are correct

B. I, II and III are correct

C. I, II and IV are correct

D. I, II, III and IV are correct

31. Debt obligations of Government of India (Government liabilities)

I. State Provident Funds

II. Small Savings

III. Reserve Funds and Deposits

IV. Consolidated Fund of India

Codes :

A. II and III are correct.

B. I, II and III are correct.

C. II, III and IV are correct.

D. I, III and IV are correct.

32. Identify the chronology of the following Committees on tax reforms in India :

I. Committee on Taxation of Agricultural Income and Wealth

II. Kaldor Proposal for Tax Reform in India

III. Taskforces on Direct and Indirect Taxes

IV. Direct Taxes Administration Enquiry Committee

Codes :

A. II, I, IV, III   B. II, IV, I, III

C. II, III, I, IV   D. I, III, IV, II

33. Which of the following are the role of Finance Commissions in India?

I. To make recommendations on the distribution of tax proceeds between Centre and States.

II. To make Recommendations on levying, removing or restructuring of taxes.

III. To recommend Grants-in-aid under Article 275 of the Constitution

IV. To recommend plan and other grants under Article 282 of the Constitution

Codes :

A. I and II are correct.

B. I and III are correct.

C. I, III and IV are correct.

D. All are correct.

34. Under a managed floating exchange rate system, the nation's monetary authorities intervene in foreign exchange markets to

A. smooth out short-run and long-run fluctuations in exchange rates

B. keep exchange rates fixed among a group of nations

C. smooth out short-run fluctuations in exchange rates

D. keep exchange rates flexible

35. Euro currency market is a part of a larger global market known as Eurodollar market.

A. Above statement is correct.

B. Above statement is not correct.

C. Above statement is partially correct.

D. Above statement is partially incorrect.

36. Match the following :

List–I	*List–II*
(*a*) WTO	1. Provide finance to correct disequilibrium in balance of payments.
(*b*) IMF	2. Generally forbids the use of quantitative restrictions in trade.
(*c*) SAARC	3. Sanction of soft loans
(*d*) IDA	4. Promotes trade among South Asian Countries

Codes :

	(*a*)	(*b*)	(*c*)	(*d*)
A.	1	2	3	4
B.	2	3	4	1
C.	2	1	4	3
D.	3	2	4	1

37. A sudden shift from import tariffs to free trade may induce short term unemployment in

A. import competing industries

B. industries that are only exporters

C. industries that sell domestically as well as export

D. industries that neither import nor export

38. The immediate cause for the collapse of the Bretton woods system was

A. the expectation that the U.S.A. would soon be forced to devalue the dollar

B. the massive flight of liquid capital from the U.S.A.

C. the attempt by three small European Central Banks to convert part of their dollar holding into gold at the Federal Reserve Bank.

D. All of the above

39. A feasible effect of international trade is that
A. a monopoly in the home market becomes an oligopoly in the world market
B. an oligopoly in the home market becomes a monopoly in the world market
C. a purely competitive firm in the home market becomes an oligopolist
D. a purely competitive firm in the home market becomes a monopolist

40. The European Union has achieved all of the following, except
A. adopted a common fiscal policy for member nations
B. established a common system of agricultural price supports
C. disbanded all tariffs between its member countries
D. levied common tariffs on products imported from non-members

41. A Foreign Trade Zone (FTZ) is
A. a regional area within which trade with foreign nations is allowed
B. a free trade agreement among several nations
C. designed to promote exports by deferring import duties on intermediate inputs and waving such duties if the final product is re-exported rather than sold domestically
D. designed to limit exports of manufactured goods by placing import taxes on goods made within the zone

42. The formula that shows the correct relationship between
I. The supply of high powered money (H)
II. The currency (C)
III. The money supply (M)
IV. Required Reserves (RR)
V. Excess Reserves (ER)
VI. Demand deposits (D), is

A. $\frac{M}{H} = \frac{D+C}{C+RR+ER}$

B. $\frac{H}{M} = \frac{D+C}{C+RR+ER}$

C. $\frac{M}{D+C} = \frac{C+RR+ER}{H}$

D. $\frac{H}{M} = \frac{C+RR+ER}{D}$

43. Which of the following will act as the 'lender of intermediate resort'?
A. RBI
B. NABARD
C. SBI
D. None of the above

44. According to Gurley and Shaw, the various substitutes of currency and commercial bank demand deposits should be assigned different weights according to
A. their degree of replacement
B. their degree of substitutability
C. their share in the money market
D. their share in money supply

45. **Assertion (A) :** Primary financial markets deals in new financial claims.
Reason (R) : It mobilises savings and supplies new capital to the business units.
Codes :
A. Both (A) and (R) are correct and (R) is the correct explanation of (A).
B. Both (A) and (R) are correct and (R) is not a correct explanation of (A).
C. (A) is true, but (R) is false.
D. (A) is false, but (R) is true.

46. Margin requirement specified under which instruments of monetary policy?
A. Variable Reserve Requirement
B. Statutory Liquidity Requirement
C. Selective Credit Controls
D. Open Market Operations

47. As per Micro, Small and Medium Enterprise Development Act, 2006, Medium Enterprises are defined as those with investments :
A. < 25 lakhs
B. 25 lakhs to 5 crores
C. 5 crores to 10 crores
D. > 10 crores

48. Theory of Industrial Location is associated with the names of

I. Losch
II. Weber
III. Christaller
IV. Lerner

Codes :

A. I & II   B. I only
C. I, II and III   D. I, II, III and IV

49. The Committees related to industrial licensing policy are

I. Arjun Sengupta Committee
II. D.G. Karve Committee
III. Subimal Dutt Committee
IV. R.K. Hazari Committee

Codes :

A. I and II   B. II and III
C. III and IV   D. I, II and III

50. Which Industrial Policy Resolution gave the public sector a strategic role in the Indian Economy?

A. 1948   B. 1956
C. 1977   D. 1980

51. Average industrial growth rate during Tenth Plan period was

A. 5.3%   B. 8.8%
C. 10.2%   D. 15.3%

52. Suggest the correct choices about the nature of the Environmental Economics :

I. Nature of Market failure is similar to public goods under public finance.
II. Willingness to pay can be negative.
III. It deals for items which are not used.
IV. It deals for items which are used.

Codes :

A. I, II, III & IV   B. I, II & III
C. II, III & IV   D. II & IV

53. Which of the following methods would be used for estimation of price change of a house due to either pollution or good environment like existence of park and scenic beauty?

A. Hedonic Method
B. Contingent Valuation Method
C. Externality Effects
D. All of the above

54. In a life table which of the following does not fit?

A. There are eight columns in a life table.
B. It tells the age-specific mortality rate.
C. Age-specific birth rate can be derived from a life table.
D. Age-specific life expectancy can be estimated

55. Optimum theory of population tells about the relationship between

A. Population and food supply
B. Population and overall resources
C. Dependent population and working population
D. Present population and growth rate of population

56. What is meant by 'population neutralism'?

A. Impact of population growth on economic growth is negligible.
B. Growth rate of population is hovering around stationary population.
C. Impact of population growth on food supply is neutral.
D. Due to population growth, change in age structure is almost neutral.

57. What is the essence of wage goods model explained by Professor P.R. Brahmananda in the Indian economy context?

A. It tells about low wage rate in the agriculture.
B. It tells about low wage rate for labour in the economy.
C. It tells about shift of labour from agriculture to industry.
D. It tells about the impact of the shortage of food items on the wage rate and growth rate of the economy.

58. Match the highest crop production state given in List–I with List–II from the given code :

List–I (States)	***List–II (Highest crop production)***
(*a*) West Bengal	1. Total course cereal

(*b*) Uttar Pradesh	2. Rice
(*c*) Maharashtra	3. Potato
(*d*) Gujarat	4. Groundnut

Codes :

	(*a*)	(*b*)	(*c*)	(*d*)
A.	2	3	1	4
B.	3	2	1	4
C.	4	2	3	1
D.	1	3	4	2

59. About minimum support price, find out the correct combinations :

I. If market price is higher, farmers will sell to the government.

II. It ensures minimum assured price for the produce of the farmers.

III. It helps in food security mission.

IV. This is highly rewarding to farmers because they earn huge profits on their produce.

Codes :

A. I, II & IV
B. II, III & IV
C. II & III
D. II & IV

60. Which of the followings have been important in growth of rice and wheat output in India after initiating green revolution programme?

I. Changes in cropping pattern
II. Improved yields
III. Crop insurance
IV. Increased area under cultivation

Codes :

A. II, III & IV B. I, II & IV
C. I, II & III D. I, III & IV

61. 'Green agriculture' involves

A. organic farming and emphasis on horticulture
B. avoiding pesticides, chemical fertilizers while focussing on horticulture and floriculture
C. integrated pest management, integrated nutrient supply and integrated natural resource management
D. emphasis on food crops, horticulture and floriculture

62. The average cost function is given as $AC = \frac{1}{3}x^2 - 10x + 9$. The level of output at which average cost is equal to marginal cost is :

A. 18 B. 12
C. 15 D. 21

63. The demand and supply functions are given as : $P_\alpha = 30 - 5x$ and $P_s = 3x - 10$ respectively (x = quantity). The consumer surplus is

A. 125 B. −62.5
C. 62.5 D. −125

64. The linear programming problem specified as

$$\text{Max} \quad : Z = 3x_1 + 5x_2 + 10x_3$$

$$\text{Sub to} : x_1 + x_2 + x_3 \le 100$$
$$9x_1 + x_2 + 8x_3 \le 95$$
$$x_1 + 8x_2 + 3x_3 \le 60$$
$$2x_1 + 7x_2 + x_3 \le 150$$

and $x_1 \ge 0$, $x_2 < 0$ and $x_3 > 0$ has

A. a feasible solution
B. an optimal solution
C. multiple solutions
D. no solutions

65. The estimated regression equation of a firm producing scooter tyres is :

$\ln y = -3.56 + 0.31 \ln X_1 - 0.05 \ln X_2 + 0.53 \ln X_3 + 0.37 \ln X_4$,

$\bar{R}^2 = 0.89$ (Y = output and X_1 to X_4 are factor inputs).

Assuming that all the estimated parameters are statistically significant from zero, the firm has

A. constant returns to scale
B. decreasing returns to scale
C. increasing returns to scale
D. neutral returns to scale

66. The test statistic used to test the significance of the adjusted coefficient of multiple determination ($\bar{R}^2$) is :

A. t–test B. Z–test
C. χ^2–test D. F–test

67. Given that the CES production function as :

$$Y = A\left[\alpha L^{-\beta} + (1-\alpha)K^{-\beta}\right]^{-\frac{\gamma}{\beta}}$$

Match List–I with List–II and select the answer from the codes given below :

List–I	*List–II*
(*a*) A	1. Factor intensity
(*b*) α	2. Elasticity of substitution
(*c*) β	3. Factor homogeneity
(*d*) γ	4. Efficiency parameter

Codes :

	(*a*)	(*b*)	(*c*)	(*d*)
A.	1	4	2	3
B.	2	4	1	3
C.	1	2	3	4
D.	1	4	3	2

68. The technique used to estimate the over-identified system of simultaneous equations is

A. ordinary least squares

B. maximum likelihood

C. limited information maximum likelihood

D. two stage least squares

69. Which of the following assumptions are required to show the consistency, unbiasedness and efficiency of the OLS estimates

I. $E(\nu_t) = 0$

II. $Var(\nu_t) = \sigma^2$

III. $cov(\nu_t, \nu_{t-j}) = 0$ for all values of $j \neq 0$

IV. $\nu_t \sim N(0, \sigma^2)$

Codes :

A. II and IV only. B. I and III only.

C. I, II and III only. D. All the above four

70. The sources of auto correlation among the following are :

I. Omitted explanatory variables

II. Interpolation in the statistical observation

III. Mis-specification of the true random term 'v'

IV. Economic variables to move together over time

Codes :

A. I and II only B. I, II and III only

C. I, III and IV only D. All of the above

71. Arrange the following sub-sectors of the services sector of the Indian economy in ascending order of their contributions to the GDP in recent years :

I. Trade, hotels and restaurants

II. Transport, storage and communication

III. Financing, insurance, real estate and business services

IV. Community, social and personal services

Codes :

A. I, II, III, IV B. II, IV, III, I

C. II, I, III, IV D. I, III, IV, II

72. Which of the following can be linked with those providing method for estimating black money in India?

I. Kaldor's approach

II. NIPFP method

III. O.P. Chopra's method

IV. Arjun Sengupta

Codes :

A. I, II & III B. II, III & IV

C. I, III & IV D. I & II

73. What is the share of single lane/intermediate lane in the total length of National Highways?

A. 12 per cent B. 15 per cent

C. 22 per cent D. 29 per cent

74. During which year, gross domestic savings of the public sector turned negative in the Indian economy?

I. 1990 – 91

II. 1995 – 96

III. 1999 – 2000

IV. 2002 – 2003

Codes :

A. I and II

B. II and III

C. III and IV

D. I and IV

75. What has been the projected investment ratio for the infrastructure development for the Eleventh Five Year Plan of India?

A. 5.43 per cent

B. 6.53 per cent

C. 7.60 per cent

D. 9.34 per cent

ANSWERS

1	2	3	4	5	6	7	8	9	10
C	B	D	A	C	B	A	D	B	A
11	**12**	**13**	**14**	**15**	**16**	**17**	**18**	**19**	**20**
B	B	B	A	C	A	A	C	A	B
21	**22**	**23**	**24**	**25**	**26**	**27**	**28**	**29**	**30**
C	C	C	B	B	A	C	C	D	B
31	**32**	**33**	**34**	**35**	**36**	**37**	**38**	**39**	**40**
B	B	B	C	B	C	A	D	A	A
41	**42**	**43**	**44**	**45**	**46**	**47**	**48**	**49**	**50**
C	A	C	B	A	C	C	*	C	B
51	**52**	**53**	**54**	**55**	**56**	**57**	**58**	**59**	**60**
B	C	A	C	B	A	D	A	C	B
61	**62**	**63**	**64**	**65**	**66**	**67**	**68**	**69**	**70**
C	C	C	D	C	D	*	D	C	B
71	**72**	**73**	**74**	**75**					
B	A	C	C	C					

SOME SELECTED EXPLANATORY ANSWERS

2. An Engel curve, named after Ernest Engel, the propounder of the *Law of Family Expenditure,* shows variations of quantities of a good (say *X*) consumed with variation in consumer's income, given his tastes, preferences, fashions, product prices and prices of the related goods.

3. The output that corresponds to the minimum average total cost is often called by economists and business people, the *capacity* of the plant. Capacity is *not* the maximum possible output. Instead, by this definition, it is the largest output that can be produced without encountering rising average or per-unit costs.

A producer producing an output smaller than that given by the minimum average total cost is said to be operating with *excess capacity.* A producer may also be producing an output greater than that corresponding to the minimum average total cost. In this case the producer is said to be operating *above capacity.*

5. The Edgeworth box diagram is a graphic way of describing the efficiency conditions discussed in the previous sections and showing how the allocations of some goods and resources can be improved upon by exchange. The box diagram is named after a famous British economist Francis Y. Edgeworth (1845-1926). Although named after him, this box diagram does not appear in any of Edgeworth's writings and apparently was first used by Pareto in 1893.

7. The Cournot Model (Simultaneous Quantity Setting Model)

The assumptions : The model was developed in the year 1838. It is based on the following assumptions:

1. *All firms make the output decision at the same time :* No firm is a leader and no firm is a follower. All the firms are on the same footing.
2. *Each firm treats the output level of its rival fixed :* In deciding how much to produce, the firm makes this assumption.

9. Arrow's Impossibility Theorem : This is the most famous theorem in welfare economics, named after Kenneth Arrow's famous contribution in 1951. It states that, given certain conditions (described below), it is not possible to choose a social welfare function that will optimize society's welfare and that is unambiguous.

The criteria are the following :

1. The Pareto criteria should be fulfilled.
2. There should be no dictatorship.
3. There should be independence of irrelevant alternatives.
4. There should be an unrestricted domain.

10. Under the "bandwagon effect," the demand for a good can increase because of its popularity (as, for example, the demand for a movie that people are already talking about). Under the "snob effect," declining prices can lower the perceived value of a good because lower prices lower the value of the good as a status symbol. It is well known that if a person's neighbour has a car and he does not have one, his children will pursued him to buy one. This is called the bandwagon effect in economics.

14. Shoe-leather costs refer to the costs of engaging in more financial transactions as the cost of holding less money. Since money loses value during inflation, people economize on their holdings of money. Instead they hold mutual fund shares, or equities, or bonds that offer higher rates of return than money. But to carry out transactions they need money. Thus, they must engage in an endless series of financial transactions, transferring funds from illiquid accounts to liquid accounts to make payments. This takes time and effort and often involves some monetary cost.

15. For equilibrium

$\because \quad Y = C + I$

$\therefore \quad Y = 0.8y + 102 - 0.2i$

$\Rightarrow \quad 0.2y = 102 - 0.2i$

$\Rightarrow \quad Y = \frac{102}{0.2} - i$

$\therefore \quad Y = 510 - i.$

19. If desired (warranted) and possible (natural) growth rates are equal, there will be steady equilibrium marked by full employment of labour and full utilisation of capital. Such a situation, according to Joan Robinson, is called *Golden Age.* The balance between the two is expressed as under :

$$\frac{\Delta K}{K} = \frac{\Delta N}{N}$$

When the growth rates of labour and capital are equal to each other, there would be no possibility of involuntary unemployment and excess capacity of capital stock.

21. Technical change, disembodied : Disembodied technical change is the shift in the production function (production frontier) over time. Disembodied technical change is not incorporated in a specific factor of production.

Technical change, embodied : Embodied technical change refers to improvements in the design or quality of new capital goods or intermediate inputs.

28. Wiseman and Peacock Hypothesis : Wiseman and Peacock undertook a study of public expenditure in U.K. for the period from 1880-1955, according to which public expenditure does not increase in a smooth and continuous fashion but in jerks or step like fashion.

At times, some social or other disturbance takes place, creating a need for increased public expenditure which the existing public revenue cannot meet. While earlier, due to an insufficient pressure for public expenditure, the revenue constraint was dominating and restraining an expansion in public expenditure, now under changed requirements such a restraint gives way. The public expenditure increases and makes the inadequacy of the present revenue quite clear to every one. The movement from the older level of expenditure and taxation to a new and higher level is the *displacement effect.* This inadequacy of the revenue as compared with the required public expenditure creates an *inspection effect.* The government and the people review the revenue position and the need to find a solution of the important problems that have come up and agree to the required adjustments to finance the increased expenditure. They attain a new level of *tax tolerance.* They are now ready to tolerate a greater burden of taxation and as a result the general level of expenditure and revenue goes up. In this way, the public expenditure and revenue get agree to the required adjustments to finance the increased expenditure. They attain a new level of *tax tolerance.* They are now ready to tolerate a greater burden of taxation and as a result the general level of expenditure and revenue goes up. In this way, the public expenditure and revenue get stabilised at a new level till another disturbance occurs to cause a displacement effect. *Thus each major disturbance leads to the government assuming a larger proportion of the total national economic activity.* In other words, there is a *concentration effect.* The concentration effect also refers to the apparent tendency for central government economic activity to grow faster than that of the state and local level governments.

29. A monopolist, by definition, fixes the output and supply price of his product so as to get the maximum possible profits, which in turn are given by a position where marginal cost equals the marginal revenue (MC = MR). Now, if a tax is imposed upon monopoly profits, the monopolist cannot choose a better position of supply and price so as to increase his profits out of which to pay the tax. Actually he is supposed to have chosen the maximum profit position even if no tax on monopoly profits is imposed. This conclusion remains valid whether the tax on monopoly profit is a lump sum or a proportionate tax. We can also say that imposition of such a tax does not shift the demand or supply curve and so the sale price of the commodity does not change.

34. Managed Floating Exchange Rate System : Managed floating exchange rate systems require monetary authorities to intervene in foreign exchange markets to smooth short-run fluctuations and prevent their currencies from moving too far from a perceived fundamental value. Under this system, monetary authorities can moderate the tendency for the nation's currency to depreciate by selling or buying to change the volume of foreign currency reserves. The feasibility of this system rests on the fact that it does not require the monetary authorities to know the long-run trend in exchange rates. However, the effectiveness of official intervention in foreign exchange markets is limited because official foreign currency reserves are much smaller than international capital flows.

37. The reason of this is that when production shifts from import to export goods, workers must move out of industries that produce the imported goods. In general, it seems likely that they will eventually be reemployed in other industries, but they may have to learn new skills to get those jobs and the process of doing so may take some time. Many nations offer "trade-adjustment" policies that seek to mitigate the costs involved in such transitions by offering worker training or extra unemployment benefits.

42. The money supply (M) consists of deposits of commercial banks (D) and currency (C) held by the public. Thus supply of money M = D + C. High powered money (H) (or monetary base) consists of currency held by the public (C) plus required reserves (RR) and excess reserves of commercial banks. Thus high-powered money H = C + RR + ER. The relation between M and H can be expressed as the ratio of M to H, *i.e.*, by dividing the equation M by H, *i.e.*, M/H.

43. Lender of the Intermediate Resort : Among banks, the State Bank of India, because of its formidable liquid position is always on the lenders' side of the market. It acts as the lender of the intermediate resort in the sense that the banks may approach the SBI for accommodation before going to the RBI, who is the lender of the last resort.

44. The Gurley and Shaw approach is superior to the Chicago approach because unlike the Chicago approach in which currency, demand deposits and time deposits all have been lumped together, the Gurley and Shaw approach refuses to lump the currency, bank deposits and close substitutes together; instead, it circumvents the problem of making arbitrary assumptions regarding the degree of substitutability by assigning the weights to different assets on the basis of their closeness to means of payment.

46. The selective credit controls are used to regulate credit for specific purposes. These controls operate on the distribution of total credit by encouraging the flow of credit into certain sectors and discouraging its flow into certain other sectors of economy. The important selective credit controls include credit rationing, direction against the erring banks, changes in margin requirements, differential rate of interest and moral suasion.

48. Central Place Theory : The classical theory of market-sensitive activities is central place theory, formulated by Christaller (1966) and Losch (1954). Central place theory gives rise to a hierarchical pattern of market centers. The distribution and size of markets are functions of consumer range and market threshold requirements.

Industrial Location Theory : Industrial location theory focuses on the transport or shipping costs of product inputs and outputs. Often termed the "classical model" of industrial location, the theory was first formulated by Weber (1928), and later developed by Hoover (1948), Isard (1956), and Moses (1958). It applies primarily to manufacturing activities. Location choice depends on the relative costs of shipping inputs and outputs, as well as economies of scale in production.

49. Dr. R.K. Hazari was appointed to review the working of industrial licensing in 1966 who submitted his report in 1967 and made several sensational disclosures of bungling by big houses.

Following a discussion of the Hazari Report in Parliament, the Government of India appointed a Committee in July 1967—known as the Industrial Licensing Policy Inquiry Committee—to enquire into the working of the licensing system during the past 10 years under the chairmanship of Subimal Dutt. The Committee submitted its report in July 1969. The Dutt Committee Report indicated the working of licensing system which had led to the growth of monopoly capital and economic concentration in the hands of a few business houses.

53. Environmental Valuation techniques

Valuation Technique	Ways to value environment	Applications
Monetary Valuation Techniques:		
1. Market Price Method (MPM)	Estimates economic values from the economic benefits and costs arising from changes in environmental quality.	Can be applied to estimate the economic value of ecosystem products or services that are bought and sold in commercial markets.
2. Hedonic Pricing Method (HPM)	Estimates economic values for ecosystem or environmental services	Most commonly applied to variations in housing prices that reflect the value

	that directly affect market prices of some other goods. Most commonly applied to variations in housing prices that reflect the value of local environmental attributes.	of local environmental attributes.
3. Travel Cost Method (TCM)	Estimates economic values by assuming that the value of an eco-system or recreation site is reflected in how much people are willing to pay to travel to visit the site.	Often applied to value recreation sites, which have zero or nominal admission price.
4. Contingent Valuation Method (CVM)	Estimates economic values by asking people to directly state their willingness to pay for specific environmental services, based on a hypothetical scenario.	Can be applied to estimate economic values for all kinds of ecosystem and environmental services and most widely used method for estimating non-use values.
5. Contingent Choice Method (CCM)	Estimates economic values by asking people to make tradeoffs among sets of ecosystem or environmental services or characteristics. Does not directly ask for willingness to pay–this is inferred from tradeoffs that includes cost as an attribute.	Can be used to estimate economic value for virtually any ecosystem or environmental service, and can be used to estimate non-use as well as use values.

55. **Theory of Optimum Population :** The theory of optimum population was first formulated by **Prof. Sidwick** and later developed by **Prof. Dalton** and **Prof. Carr Saunders.** They developed the concept of optimum population, *i.e.,* that size of population which is the best for a country at a particular time. At this level of optimum population, per capita income would be maximum.

56. The economic consequences of population growth have long been the subject of debate. Early views on the topic, pioneered by Thomas Malthus, held that population growth would lead to the exhaustion of resources. In the 1960s, it was proposed that population growth aided economic development by spurring technological and institutional innovation and increasing the supply of human ingenuity. Toward the end of the 1960s, a neo-Malthusian view, focusing again on the dangers of population growth, became popular. Population control policies in China and India, while differing greatly from each other, can be seen in this light. Population neutralism, a middle-ground view, based on empirical analysis of the link between population growth and economic performance, has held sway for the past two decades. According to this view, the net impact of population growth on economic growth is negligible.

61. **Organic Agriculture :** cultivation without any use of chemical inputs like mineral fertilizers and chemical pesticides.

Green Agriculture : cultivation with the help of integrated pest management, integrated nutrient supply and integrated natural resource management systems.

Ecoagriculture : based on conservation of soil, water and biodiversity and the application of traditional knowledge and ecological prudence.

EM Agriculture : system of farming using effective microorganisms (EM).

White Agriculture : system of agriculture based on substantial use of microorganisms, particularly fungi.

62. $\because$ $\text{AC} = \frac{1}{3}x^2 - 10x + 9$

$\therefore$ $\text{TC} = \frac{1}{3}x^3 - 10x^2 + 9x$

$\therefore$ $\text{MC} = \frac{d(\text{TC})}{dx}$

$= \frac{d}{dx}\left(\frac{1}{3}x^3 - 10x^2 + 9x\right)$

$= x^2 - 20x + 9$

For AC = MC

$\therefore \frac{1}{3}x^2 - 10x + 9 = x^2 - 20x + 9$

$\Rightarrow -10x + 20x = x^2 - \frac{1}{3}x^2$

$\Rightarrow 10x = x^2\left(\frac{2}{3}\right)$

$\Rightarrow \frac{2x}{3} = 10$

$\Rightarrow x = \frac{10 \times 3}{2} = 15.$

63. For equilibrium

$P_\alpha = P_s$

$30 - 5x = 3x - 10$

$\Rightarrow 8x = 40$

$\Rightarrow x = 5$

$\because P_\alpha = 30 - 5x$

$= 30 - 25 = 5$

$\therefore P_\alpha = 5$

and $P_\alpha x = 5 \times 5 = 25$

$\therefore$ Consumes Surplus

$= \int_0^5 f(x)dx - P_\alpha x$

$= \int_0^5 (30 - 5x)dx - 25$

$= \left[30x - \frac{5x^2}{2}\right]_0^5 - 25$

$= \left(30 \times 5 - \frac{5 \times 25}{2}\right) - 25$

$= \left(150 - \frac{125}{2}\right) - 25$

$= (150 - 62.5) - 25$

$= 87.5 - 25 = 62.5.$

68. ***Estimation of just identified and overidentified systems using 2SLS :*** This technique is applicable for the estimation of overidentified systems, where ILS cannot be used. In fact, it can also be employed for estimating the coefficients of just identified systems, in which case the method would yield asymptotically equivalent estimates to those obtained from ILS. Two-stage least squares (2SLS or TSLS) is done in two stages:

- **Stage 1 :** Obtain and estimate the reduced form equations using OLS. Save the fitted values for the dependent variables.
- **Stage 2 :** Estimate the structural equations using OLS, but replace any RHS endogenous variables with their stage 1 fitted values.

69. All of the assumptions listed in (*i*) to (*iii*) are required to show that the OLS estimator has the desirable properties of consistency, unbiasedness and efficiency. However, it is not necessary to assume normality (*iv*) to derive the above results for the coefficient estimates. This assumption is only required in order to construct test statistics that follow the standard statistical distributions—in other words, it is only required for hypothesis testing and not for coefficient estimation.

72. Estimates of Black Money in India : Several attempts have been made to quantify black money in India since Second World War.

1. Estimates of Black Money based on Kaldor's Method : Kaldor's Estimate-1956
2. Wanchoo Committee's Estimate 1953
3. Chopra's Estimate
4. NIPFP Study on Black Money in India
5. Suraj B. Gupta's Study of Black Money

Previous Papers (Solved)

UGC-NET ECONOMICS, DECEMBER 2013

PAPER–II

Note: *This paper contains **fifty (50)** objective type questions of **two (2)** marks each. **All** questions are compulsory.*

1. The cost incurred by the firm in hiring labour is called as

A. Explicit Cost B. Implicit Cost

C. Marginal Cost D. Total Cost

2. The locus of Pareto Optimality in Production and Consumption is given by

A. The Social Welfare Function

B. The Utility Possibility Curve

C. The Transformation Curve

D. The Grand Utility Possibility Curve

3.

List-I	**List-II**
(*a*) Tea and Coffee	1. Veblen goods
(*b*) Car and Petrol	2. Substitutes
(*c*) Gold and Diamonds	3. Giffen goods
(*d*) Ragi and Bajra	4. Complementary

Codes:

	(*a*)	(*b*)	(*c*)	(*d*)
A.	2	1	3	4
B.	2	4	1	3
C.	4	1	2	3
D.	4	3	1	2

4. Assertion (A): In the short run under perfect competition, given the market demand and market supply the industry is in equilibrium at that price which clears the market.

Reason (R): In the long run all the firms in the industry earn profit.

Codes:

A. Both (A) and (R) are true and (R) is the correct explanation of (A).

B. Both (A) and (R) are true, but (R) is not the correct explanation of (A).

C. (A) is true, but (R) is false.

D. (A) is false, but (R) is true.

5. Put the following in chronological order on the basis of development:

(*i*) Law of Demand

(*ii*) Revealed Preference Analysis

(*iii*) Indifference Curve Analysis

(*iv*) Law of Diminishing Marginal Utility

A.	(*i*)	(*iii*)	(*ii*)	(*iv*)
B.	(*i*)	(*iv*)	(*iii*)	(*ii*)
C.	(*i*)	(*ii*)	(*iv*)	(*iii*)
D.	(*i*)	(*iii*)	(*iv*)	(*ii*)

6. If the monopolist incurs loss in the short run, then in the long run

(*a*) he will go out of business

(*b*) he will stay in business

(*c*) he will break even

(*d*) any of the above is possible

A. (*a*) and (*b*) B. (*a*) and (*c*)

C. (*a*) only D. (*d*) only

7. The condition of Pareto Optimality holds correct under

A. Perfect Competition

B. Monopolistic Competition

C. Oligopoly

D. Monopoly

8. Assertion (A): Compared to the individual supply curve, the aggregate supply curve is more elastic.

Reason (R): There is the possibility of moving between being out of the labour force and being in the labour force.

Choose amongst the following the correct answer.

Codes:

A. (A) is correct, but (R) is not the correct explanation of (A).
B. (A) is correct and (R) is the correct explanation of (A).
C. (A) is correct, but (R) is incorrect.
D. (A) is incorrect, but (R) is correct.

9. Assuming life cycle hypothesis, let a person starts working when he is 20 years old, works until the age of 60 and expects to die at the age of 70. If this person earns, say ₹ 1.50 lac annually when he is 20-30 years, ₹ 2 lac annually when he is 30-40 years, and ₹ 3 lac annually when he is 40-60 years, then his life time average propensity to consume is

A. 0.60 B. 0.70
C. 0.80 D. 0.90

10. With reference to demand for money, match List-I with List-II:

List-I	List-II
(*a*) Demand for money is stable	1. J.M. Keynes
(*b*) Liquidity Preference as behaviour towards risk	2. W. Baumol
(*c*) Inventory Theoretic Approach	3. James Tobin
(*d*) No portfolio diversification	4. Milton Friedman

Codes:

	(*a*)	(*b*)	(*c*)	(*d*)
A.	4	3	1	2
B.	3	4	1	2
C.	2	1	3	4
D.	4	3	2	1

11. The negative relationship between the gap between actual GDP and its trend value and the difference between actual unemployment rate and its equilibrium value is called

A. The Aggregate Supply Curve
B. The Phillips Curve
C. The Natural Rate of Unemployment Hypothesis
D. Okun's Law

12. It is often true that as the economy begins to recover from a recession, the unemployment rate rises because

A. as the economy initially recovers from a recession the demand for goods and services falls, so the demand for workers falls.
B. as the economy begins to recover from a recession, workers who were previously discouraged about their chances of finding a job begin to look for work again.
C. as the economy begins to recover from a recession because of the errors in the way the data are collected.
D. as the economy initially recovers from a recession, firms do not immediately increase the number of workers they hire. Firms wait to hire more individuals until they are convinced that the recovery is strong.

13. When additional government expenditure is financed by selling government securities, then what will be the nature of crowding out effect, given in List-I in the context of the situation given in List-II?

List-I Crowding out effect	List-II Situation
(*a*) Full	1. Keynesian Range
(*b*) Partial	2. Classical Range
(*c*) Nil	3. Intermediate Range

Codes:

	(*a*)	(*b*)	(*c*)
A.	2	3	1
B.	3	1	2
C.	1	3	2
D.	1	2	3

14. Match items given in List-I with those in List-II:

List-I	List-II
(*a*) Equation of Exchange	1. J.M. Keynes
(*b*) Cash Balances Approach	2. Irving Fisher

(*c*) Regressive Expectation model of Demand for Money	3.	W.J. Baumol
(*d*) Square Root Formula of Demand for Money	4.	A.C. Pigou and Alfred Marshall

Codes:

	(*a*)	(*b*)	(*c*)	(*d*)
A.	2	4	1	3
B.	3	2	4	1
C.	4	3	1	2
D.	1	3	2	4

15. The premise, that benefit of economic growth will reach all sections of population is called

A. Trickle up effect
B. Trickle down effect
C. Take-off effect
D. Backlash effect

16. In whose growth model, entrepreneur's significance is pivotal?

A. Keynes B. Schumpeter
C. Harrod D. Domar

17. The classical model of economic development emphasises

A. Laissez-Faire Policy
B. Capital Accumulation
C. Both A and B
D. None of these

18. Which one of the following pairs is not correctly matched?

	Author	**Book**
A.	Simon Kuznets	Asian Drama
B.	J. Robinson	Essays in the Theory of Economic Growth
C.	Karl Marx	Das Kapital
D.	A.W. Lewis	Theory of Economic Growth

19. What does change in economic growth?

A. Structure of economy
B. Mindsets of people
C. National Income
D. None of these

20. Which States/U.Ts. have been placed at first three places in Gender Development Index List 2006 made by the Government of India?

A. Kerala, Chandigarh, Goa
B. Kerala, Goa, Chandigarh
C. Chandigarh, Goa, Kerala
D. Goa, Kerala, Chandigarh

21. Assertion (A): There is no incentive for a profit maximizing producer to supply the public goods.

Reason (R): If he produces it he is unable to exclude people from consuming it and hence he cannot charge a price.

Codes:

A. (A) is true, but (R) is false.
B. Both (A) and (R) are false.
C. (A) is not correct, but (R) is correct
D. Both (A) and (R) are correct and (R) is the correct explanation of (A).

22. The distribution of the burden of paying a tax is called

A. Sharing of tax burden
B. Shifting of the tax
C. Incidence of a tax
D. Tax capitalization

23. Which one of the following is short period debt meant to meet current needs, that is filling temporary gap in budgets?

A. Funded debt B. Unfunded debt
C. Redeemable debt D. Irredeemable debt

24. Monetised deficit means

A. Fiscal deficit less interest payments
B. Government expenditure which is financed through the sale of adhoc treasury bills.
C. Increase in RBI credit to Central Government.
D. Fiscal deficit less loans and advances.

25. A proportionate increase in tax revenue to a proportionate increase in the tax base is called

A. Elasticity of a tax
B. Buoyancy of a tax
C. Neutrality of a tax
D. None of the above

26. 'Vent for surplus approach' is applicable to
A. Rich countries
B. Underdeveloped countries
C. Oil exporting countries
D. None of the above

27. According to monetary approach, a revaluation of a nation's currency
A. increases the nation's demand for money
B. increases the nation's supply of money
C. reduces the nation's demand for money
D. reduces the nation's supply of money

28. The Bretton Woods System was based on
A. a gold standard
B. a flexible exchange rate system
C. a gold exchange standard
D. None of the above

29. The imposition of an import tariff by a large nation
A. usually improves the nation's terms of trade and increases the volume of trade.
B. worsens the nation's terms of trade but increases the volume of trade
C. worsens the nation's terms of trade and reduces the volume of trade.
D. usually improves the nation's terms of trade but reduces the volume of trade.

30. The value of foreign trade multiplier will be high under the condition when
A. marginal propensity to save is high
B. marginal propensity to import is high
C. there is increase in exports
D. marginal propensity to consume domestic goods is high

31. Match the weight of different industry groups between List-I & List-II:

List-I	**List-II**
(*a*) Basic goods industries	1. 45.7
(*b*) Capital goods industries	2. 8.8
(*c*) Intermediate goods industries	3. 15.7
(*d*) Consumer goods industries	4. 29.8

Codes:

	(*a*)	(*b*)	(*c*)	(*d*)
A.	1	2	3	4
B.	2	4	3	1
C.	3	2	1	4
D.	1	3	4	2

32. Plant load factor of thermal power stations in India in recent years has been around
A. 50 per cent B. 60 per cent
C. 70 per cent D. 80 per cent

33. Which of the following is not the part of National Telecom Policy (NTP) 2012 in India?
A. Strive to create One-Nation-One License across services and service areas.
B. Achieve One Nation – Full Mobile number portability
C. To work towards 'Right to Broadband'
D. Recognize telecom as basic goods industry

34. Percentage share of the manufacturing output of India in the world total is now
A. 2.2 per cent B. 3.9 per cent
C. 6.2 per cent D. 7.5 per cent

35. India's current account deficit in Balance of Trade is mainly due to
(*a*) Increasing imports of oil and petroleum
(*b*) Increasing imports of gold and silver
(*c*) Increasing imports of foodgrains
(*d*) Increasing imports of iron and steel

Codes:
A. (*a*), (*b*) and (*c*) B. (*a*) and (*c*)
C. (*a*) and (*b*) D. (*a*) and (*d*)

36. The MRTP Act of 1969 has been
A. replaced by Competition Act, 2002
B. merged in Industrial Policy Act of 1978
C. replaced by Trade Union (Amendment) Act, 2001
D. merged in Industrial Policy Act of 1991

37. In the context of agricultural development the trickle down theory has been interpreted to suggest that
(*a*) Growth in agriculture output without radical institutional reforms will reduce the incidence of poverty.

(*b*) Growth in agriculture output with radical institutional reforms will reduce the incidence of poverty.
(*c*) Only radical institutional reforms can reduce the incidence of poverty.
(*d*) Only growth in agriculture output will reduce incidence of poverty.

A. Both (*a*) and (*b*) B. Both (*a*) and (*c*)
C. (*b*) only D. (*d*) only

38. As per the latest figures of the Ministry of Agriculture the per capita per day foodgrains availability is

A. 280 gm B. 440 gm
C. 580 gm D. 900 gm

39. In which year the Kissan Credit Card System was introduced?

A. 1978 B. 1998
C. 1988 D. 2008

40. Assertion (A): PL-480 grants was used to import foodgrains.

Reason (R): PL-480 grants facility was granted by Japan.

Codes:

A. Both (A) and (R) are true and (R) is the correct explanation of (A).
B. Both (A) and (R) are true and (R) is not the correct explanation of (A).
C. (A) is true, but (R) is false.
D. (A) is false, but (R) is true.

41. Productivity of groundnut is highest in

A. U.S.A. B. Mexico
C. India D. China

42. NAFED is a

A. Company
B. Non-Government Organisation
C. Government Body
D. Cooperative Organisation

43. Based on the SRS data for 2010 in India, which of the following seems to be incorrect?

A. TFR = 2.5 B. CDR = 7.2
C. IMR = 48.9 D. CBR = 24.2

44. Upto which census, synchronous *de facto* method was adopted in India wherein the census was conducted throughout the country in a single night?

A. 1901 B. 1931
C. 1951 D. 1971

45. Match the following:

Group – I	Group – II
(*a*) Type II error	1. $P_{01} \times P_{10} = 1$
(*b*) Mean > Mode	2. Probability of not rejecting H_0 when it was not true
(*c*) Population is homogenous	3. Positively skewed distribution
(*d*) Time Reversal Test	4. Simple random sampling

Codes:

	(*a*)	(*b*)	(*c*)	(*d*)
A.	2	3	4	1
B.	3	1	2	4
C.	4	2	3	1
D.	1	2	3	4

46. Assertion (A) : For normal distribution Mean = Median = Mode.

Reason (R): Normal distribution is mesokurtic.

Codes :

A. Both (A) and (R) are correct and (R) is the correct explanation of (A).
B. Both (A) and (R) are correct but (R) is not the correct explanation of (A).
C. (A) is correct, but (R) is incorrect.
D. (A) is incorrect, but (R) is correct.

47. Given the two regression lines estimated from given data as under:

$Y = 4 + 0.4X$
$X = -2 + 0.9Y$

Then coefficient of correlation between X and Y will be

A. 0.4 B. 0.5
C. 0.6 D. 0.8

48. Which of the following satisfy time reversal test but not factor reversal test?

A. Laspeyre's Index No.
B. Fisher's Index No.
C. Paasche's Index No.
D. Marshall-Edgeworth Index No.

49. The value of χ^2 in a 3 × 5 contingency table is computed as 8.0. The Null hypothesis of no association will be tested at 5% level of significance, if this value is less than or equal to the value of χ^2 from the table at degrees of freedom:

A. 8 B. 6

C. 4 D. 3

50. Which is a non-probability based sampling method?

A. Systematic Sampling

B. Stratified Random Sampling

C. Quota Sampling

D. Simple Random Sampling

ANSWERS

1	2	3	4	5	6	7	8	9	10
A	B	B	C	B	D	A	B	C	D
11	**12**	**13**	**14**	**15**	**16**	**17**	**18**	**19**	**20**
D	B	A	A	B	B	C	A	C	A
21	**22**	**23**	**24**	**25**	**26**	**27**	**28**	**29**	**30**
D	B	B	C	B	B	C	C	D	C
31	**32**	**33**	**34**	**35**	**36**	**37**	**38**	**39**	**40**
A	C	D	A	C	A	C	B	B	C
41	**42**	**43**	**44**	**45**	**46**	**47**	**48**	**49**	**50**
A	D	D	B	A	A	C	D	A	C

SOME SELECTED EXPLANATORY ANSWERS

1. Explicit Cost: Many inputs are bought or hired by the firm. The monetary payments which a firm makes to those outsiders who supply labour services, material, fuel, transportation services, power and so forth are called explicit costs.

In the words **Leftwitch**, *"Explicit costs are those cash payments which firms make to outsiders for their services and goods."* Wages to the labourers, cost of raw-material or semi-finished goods, interest on loans, depreciation charges, etc; are the examples of explicit costs of a firm. *These costs are also called "absolute costs" or "outlay costs" or "actual costs."*

2. The utility possibility curve, giving the maximum possible utility for one household for the given utility of the other, represents the set of economic optimum points or Pareto optimal points. Underlying any point on this curve are the efficiency and Pareto optimality conditions. Moving along this curve generally requires a change in the output mix and a reallocation of scarce resources in the economy.

4. In the long-run, firms earn only normal profits due to free entry and exit. Conditions of equilibrium of the firm are: 1. AR(P) = LAC; 2. MC = MR, with MC curve cutting MR curve from below.

7. Perfect competition and Pareto optimality: A necessary condition for the Pareto optimality is the existence of perfect competition in both product and factor markets. This is, in fact, one the basic assumptions of Pareto optimality.

9. Here, Working Life

$$WL = 60 - 20 = 40$$

Number of years of life

$$NL = 70 - 20 = 50$$

$$\therefore \quad \frac{WL}{NL} = APC$$

$$\Rightarrow \quad APC = \frac{40}{50} = 0.8.$$

11. Okun's law: The generally observed relationship between the output gap and the unemployment rate, whereby each additional percentage point of output gap reduces the unemployment rate by less than 1 percentage point.

15. Trickle-down theory of development: The notion that *development* is purely an economic phenomenon in which rapid gains from the overall growth of *gross national product* and *income per capita* would automatically bring benefits (trickle down) to the masses in the form of jobs and other economic opportunities. The main preoccupation is therefore to get the growth job done while problems of *poverty*, unemployment, and *income distribution* are perceived to be of secondary importance.

16. Joseph Schumpeter (1883–1950) has an enduring reputation for his theory of the entrepreneur and the entrepreneur's role on the process of creative destruction. To Schumpeter, the entrepreneur was the pivotal figure in capitalist development; the entrepreneur was the person with the drive to get new products and production processes introduced, thereby making capitalism the dynamic economic system that it was. Whenever an entrepreneur introduced a new product or production process, the economic world turned upside down and everyone in the economy had to change what they did. In the process, new industries were created that destroyed old ones – think of how much the internet has changed the way businesses must now operate – but the overall outcome was better and cheaper products for consumers. As a reward, the entrepreneur earned high profits, but these lasted only until the next entrepreneur came along and destroyed what the previous entrepreneurs had created.

17. The classical economists believe in the existence of an automatic free market, perfectly competitive economy which is free from any government interference. *Laissez-faire* policy was supported and it is the 'invisible hand' which maximizes the national income. Profits induce investment. The larger the profits, greater the accumulation and investment. Capital accumulation is key to economic progress. But profits do not increase continuously. They tend to decline when competition increases for larger capital accumulation among the capitalists. All the classicists visualize the stationary state as the end of the process of capital accumulation. In the classical model, the end result of capitalist development is stagnation. This stagnation resulted from the natural tendency of profit to fall and the consequent choking of capital accumulation. When this happens, capital accumulation ceases, population becomes constant and stationary state sets in.

22. Shifting of Taxation: It studies the intricate questions of how much of a tax burden is actually borne by the tax-payer, and how much of it is shifted on to others. The term 'shifting' refers to transfer of some or the entire burden of the tax by the one on whom tax is imposed to another person. The burden of taxation is to be shifted through exchange. Exchange of goods is an essential condition for the shifting of taxation. For example, the government imposes excise duty on the manufacture of cloth and collects the tax-amount from the manufacturer. The manufacturer will add the tax-amount to the cost of production and will fix price of the cloth accordingly. By fixing price of the cloth inclusive of taxation, the producer shifts the burden of excise duty on to the consumers.

23. Funded and Unfunded: Funded debt is a long-term debt, payable after a year, while unfunded debt is a short-term debt, payable within a year. The former is incurred to create a permanent asset, whereas the latter is incurred to meet temporary gap in budget. Unfunded debt is also known as floating debt and includes treasury bills, ways and means advances from central bank and so on.

Redeemable and Irredeemable: When the government borrows money with a promise to pay off in future at a specified date, it is known as redeemable debt. When the government, on the other hand, borrows without any intention to repay the same in future, it is known as irredeemable debt. However, the government continues to pay the interest on such loans. The redeemable and irredeemable debts are also known as terminable and perpetual debts.

24. **Monetized Deficit:** It refers to the increase in net RBI credit to the government. It is the sum of net increase in holding of Treasury bill of central bank and its contribution to the market borrowing of the government.

    It gives rise to the expansion of new money of currency is called Monetizing the deficit. Hence it leads to the creation of reserve money or high powered money by the RBI. When the government is monetizing the fiscal deficit, it shows the extent of deficit financing in India. Thus monetized deficit is responsible for directly raising the general price level.

25. The tax buoyancy is defined as the percentage change in tax collection caused by a given percentage change in the tax base *i.e.*,

$$\theta_b = \frac{\text{\% change in tax revenue}}{\text{\% change in tax base}}$$

    Thus, it is a measure of increase in the actual tax revenue from a given change in the tax base. The tax base in an amount on which a taxpayer pays taxes. It varies with the type of tax. For example, in the case of personal income tax the base is income of individuals or households; for the corporate tax it is carporate profits, for the custom duty the tax base is the amount of imports; for the excise it is manufacturing output and for an overall tax buoyancy the tax base is the GDP.

    The tax buoyancy is adversely affected by various exemptions available in the tax base. Exemptions narrow the tax base, and therefore, the tax revenue may not increase proportionately with an increase in the GDP. The value of less than one for the tax buoyancy implies that the GDP is growing at a faster rate than the growth in the tax revenue. This suggests that the tax structure needs a reform. On the other hand, the value of greater than 1 implies that tax structure or discretionary tax policies of the government affecting the tax structure is supportive of the growing expenditure requirement of the government.

26. **Vent (Outlet) for Surplus:** The vent or outlet for surplus approach assumes that a country has 'free' or surplus commodity or some unused resources which it can use to generate the export earnings. This approach is specially applicable to developing countries. It states that a less developed country often has some good for which the domestic demand is already satisfied and which it can easily export. Central to this approach, is the idea that in autarky the country is producing well inside her production possibilities curve.

27. **Policy implications of the monetary approach under fixed exchange rates:** According to the monetary approach, a policy can affect a nation's balance of payments only through its effect on the demand for and supply of money in the nation. Any policy that increases a nation's demand for money relative to its supply leads to an inflow of money or reserves from abroad (an improvement in the nation's balance of payments) under a fixed exchange rate system. On the other hand, an increase in the nation's money supply relative to its demand results in an outflow of money or reserves, which worsens the nation's balance of payments. However, the effect of these policies is only temporary because of the monetarists' belief that there is an automatic tendency toward equilibrium in the balance of payments in the long run.

    Example: A devaluation of its currency by a deficit nation increases domestic prices and results in an increased demand for money in the nation. This helps absorb the excess supply of money causing the deficit. However, according to the monetary approach, the devaluation does no more than speed the adjustment process in the short run and is entirely unnecessary in the long run because of the automatic tendency toward equilibrium in the balance of payments in the long run. If the nation's monetary authorities meet the increased demand for money resulting from the devaluation with an equal increase in the supply of money, the devaluation is completely ineffective, even in the short run. With a larger increase in the supply of money, the nation's balance of payments deficit will actually increase.

28. Bretton woods system of exchange rates: In view of the unstable exchange rates during the 1930s and early 1940s, various moves were afoot to create an orderly international monetary system. Finally, at the Bretton Woods Conference, it was resolved to create the International Monetary Fund. The IMF, that evolved a novel exchange rate system was established in 1945. Since the new system was the outcome of the Bretton Woods Conference, it is often termed as the *Bretton Woods System.*

An important aspect of the Bretton Woods exchange rate system was that the US dollar was convertible into gold at a fixed rate of $ 35 per troy ounce of gold. The other currencies were convertible into gold via the US dollar. This currency was given the position of intervention currency in the system in view of the fact that in the immediate post-War period, it was the strongest currency. This system was, therefore, likened with the gold exchange standard where countries redeemed their currency into gold-convertible currency and not necessarily into gold directly.

29. The imposition of a tariff by a large nation improves its terms of trade, reduces the volume of trade and may improve the nation's welfare. However, since the improvement in the nation's position comes at the expense of its trade partner, the trade partner is likely to retaliate and, in the end, both nations usually lose.

30. The foreign trade multiplier also known as export multiplier operates like the investment multiplier of Keynes. It may be defined as the amount by which national income of a nation will be raised by a unit increase in domestic investment on exports. As exports increase there is an increase in the income of all persons associated with the exports industries. These in turn create demand for goods. But this is dependent upon their marginal propensity to save (MPS) and marginal propensity to import (MPM). The smaller these two propensities are, the larger will be the value of multiplier and vice versa. The foreign trade multiplier can be obtained by using the formula

$$\frac{\Delta Y}{\Delta X} = \frac{1}{1-(MPC - MPI)}$$

where MPI denotes the marginal propensity to import. The value of foreign trade multiplier depends on MPC and MPI. The higher the value of MPC, the larger will be the value of the foreign trade multiplier; and the higher the value of MPI, the lower will be the value of the foreign trade multiplier.

36. Competition Act, 2002 has been framed to replace MRTP Act, 1969. With the enactment of this Act, MRTP Act has been repealed. Keeping in view the widespread economic reforms and rapid economic development of the nation, the focus of the government was shifted from curbing monopolies to promoting competition in line with the international environment. In 1999, government of India appointed a committee on 'Competition Policy and Law' under the chairmanship of Sh. S.V.S. Raghavan. This committee submitted its report in year 2000. On the basis of recommendations of this committee, the Competition Act, 2002 was passed. The Act was enforced on 13th January 2003. The Competition Act extends to whole of India except the state of Jammu and Kashmir. This Act has replaced the Monopolies and Restrictive Trade Practices Act, 1969 (MRTP Act).

39. Kisan credit card (KCC) scheme was introduced in August 1998 by the Government to facilitate short-term credit to farmers. This scheme provides adequate and timely support from the banking system to the farmers for their cultivation needs, as it enables the purchase of all inputs in a flexible and cost effective manner.

The Kisan Credit scheme is a revolving cash credit facility with unlimited withdrawals and repayments, with the credit limit based on operational landholding, cropping pattern and scale of finance. The average limit is ₹ 50,000. Developed by NABARD, KCC is issued by the rural branches of commercial banks, cooperative banks and RRBs. NABARD refinances the banks for all credit extended by them.

42. National Agricultural Cooperative Marketing Federation of India Ltd. (NAFED) is the apex Cooperative Organisation. It works at the national level to coordinate the activities of various state marketing societies in India, as well as to stimulate domestic and international trade related to agricultural products.

Established in the year 1958, the National Agricultural Cooperative Marketing Federation is the apex and federal organisation for all the state level marketing federations. The main objective of NAFED is to co-ordinate the activities of the state federations and guide them with technical and infrastructural support, in order to serve the primary and district co-operative societies better.

It also plays a major role in stabilising the prices of agricultural goods and carries out various activities to regulate the market.

47. $b_{yx} = 0.4$

$b_{xy} = 0.9$

Co-efficient of correlation

$$= \sqrt{b_{yx} \cdot b_{xy}} = \sqrt{0.4 \times 0.9}$$

$$= \sqrt{0.36} = 0.6.$$

48. Marshall-Edgeworth Formula: According to Marshall-Edgeworth Formula:

$$P_{01} = \frac{\Sigma p_1 q_0 + \Sigma p_1 q_1}{\Sigma p_0 q_0 + \Sigma p_0 q_1}$$

Interchanging 0 to 1 and 1 to 0

$$P_{10} = \frac{\Sigma p_0 q_1 + \Sigma p_0 q_0}{\Sigma p_1 q_1 + \Sigma p_1 q_0}$$

$$\therefore P_{01} \times P_{10} = \frac{\Sigma p_1 q_0 + \Sigma p_1 q_1}{\Sigma p_0 q_0 + \Sigma p_0 q_1} \times \frac{\Sigma p_0 q_1 + \Sigma p_0 q_0}{\Sigma p_1 q_1 + \Sigma p_1 q_0} = 1$$

Since $P_{01} \times P_{10} = 1$, Marshall-Edgeworth satisfies time reversal test.

Marshall-Edgeworth's formula does not satisfy factor reversal test. Factor reversal test is satisfied only by Fisher's Ideal formula. This is shown below:

Marshall-Edgeworth Formula: According to Marshall-Edgeworth Formula:

$$P_{01} = \frac{\Sigma p_1 q_0 + \Sigma p_1 q_1}{\Sigma p_0 q_0 + \Sigma p_0 q_1};$$

$$Q_{01} = \frac{\Sigma q_1 p_0 + \Sigma q_1 p_1}{\Sigma q_0 p_0 + \Sigma q_0 p_1}$$

$$\therefore P_{01} \times Q_{01} = \frac{\Sigma p_1 q_0 + \Sigma p_1 q_1}{\Sigma p_0 q_0 + \Sigma p_0 q_1} \times \frac{\Sigma q_1 p_0 + \Sigma q_1 p_1}{\Sigma q_0 p_0 + \Sigma q_0 p_1} \neq \frac{\Sigma p_1 q_1}{\Sigma p_0 q_0}$$

Since, $P_{01} \times Q_{01} \neq \frac{\Sigma p_1 q_1}{\Sigma p_0 q_0}$, the test is not satisfied by Marshall-Edgeworth formula.

50. Samples can be either probability samples or non-probability samples. With probability samples each element has a known probability of being included in the sample but the non-probability samples do not allow the researcher to determine this probability. Probability samples are those based on simple random sampling, systematic sampling, stratified sampling, cluster/area sampling whereas non-probability samples are those based on convenience sampling, judgement sampling and quota sampling techniques.

PAPER–III

Note : *This paper contains* ***seventy five (75)*** *objective type questions of* ***two (2)*** *marks each.* ***All*** *questions are compulsory.*

1. The Model of Managerial Enterprise is associated with

A. R.A. Gordan B. R. Marris
C. Baumol D. Scitorsky

2. Which one of the following is not an assumption of linear programming?

A. Constant output prices
B. Constant input prices
C. Increasing returns to scale
D. Technologically fixed factor proportion

3. In the Paul Sweezy Model of Oligopoly in the Kinked Demand Curve, the point of kink represents

A. Quantity Rigidity
B. Price Rigidity
C. Both the Price and Quantity Rigidity
D. Only Price Rigidity

4. Match List-I with List-II:

	List-I		**List-II**
(*a*)	Offer Curves	1.	Public Revenue
(*b*)	Laffer Curves	2.	Sticky Price
(*c*)	Lorenz Curve	3.	Reciprocal demand
(*d*)	Kinked Demand Curve	4.	Inequalities

Codes:

	(*a*)	(*b*)	(*c*)	(*d*)
A.	3	1	4	2
B.	1	3	2	4
C.	3	4	1	2
D.	4	1	2	3

5. Match the items in List-I with items in List-II:

	List-I		**List-II**
(*a*)	Technical Monopoly	1.	Gold and Silver
(*b*)	Global Market	2.	Cartel
(*c*)	Legal Monopoly	3.	Coca Cola
(*d*)	Oligopoly	4.	Patent Rights

Codes:

	(*a*)	(*b*)	(*c*)	(*d*)
A.	3	1	4	2
B.	3	2	1	4
C.	4	3	1	2
D.	4	1	2	3

6. Assertion (A): Consumer Surplus is the difference between the potential price and actual price.

Reason (R): There exists an inverse relationship between the price and consumer surplus.

Codes:

A. Both (A) and (R) are true and (R) is the correct explanation of (A).
B. Both (A) and (R) are true, but (R) is not the correct explanation of (A).
C. (A) is true, but (R) is false.
D. (A) is false, but (R) is true.

7. Assertion (A): The long run cost curve is L shaped rather than U shaped.

Reason (R): The new technique of production of large plants reduce the total cost per unit of output in the long run.

Codes:

A. Both (A) and (R) are true and (R) is the correct explanation of (A).
B. Both (A) and (R) are true, but (R) is not the correct explanation of (A).
C. (A) is false, but (R) is true.
D. (R) is false, but (A) is true.

8. Which of the following is true?

(*a*) Indifference curves slope downward from left to right.
(*b*) Indifference curves slope downward from right to left.
(*c*) Indifference curves are convex to the point of origin of the two axes.
(*d*) Indifference curves never intersect each other.

A. (*a*), (*b*) and (*c*) are true.
B. (*b*), (*c*) and (*d*) are true.
C. (*a*), (*c*) and (*d*) are true.
D. (*a*) and (*d*) are true.

9. A major portion of the multiplier effect is realized in fewer periods when marginal propensity to consume is

A. unity B. larger
C. smaller D. None of the above

10. The optimum capital stock is achieved when the user cost of capital is equal to

A. the interest rate
B. the depreciation rate
C. the marginal product of capital
D. Tobin's Q

11. If the economy is operating at potential GDP, an increase in money supply will lead to

A. Stagflation
B. Structural inflation
C. Demand-side inflation
D. Supply-side inflation

12. Which of the following is true in case of the orthodox (early) Keynesians?

1. Interest elasticity of demand for money is extremely high.
2. Interest elasticity of demand for money is low.
3. Changes in the quantity of money do not have important predictable effects on the level of economic activity.
4. Demand for money is unstable.

A. 1, 2, 3 B. 1, 3, 4
C. 1, 2, 4 D. 2, 3, 4

13. Which of the following statement is false?

A. The IS curve is flatter, lower the value of the Keynesian multiplier and lower the interest resistiveness of investment.
B. The IS curve is steeper lower the value of the Keynesian multiplier and lower the interest resistiveness of investment.
C. The position of LM curve depends negatively on the price level and the resistiveness of the money demand to the changes in income.
D. The LM curve is flatter, the larger the interest resistiveness of the money demand and the lower the income resistiveness of the money demand.

14. Which of the following statements are true?

1. Increased government spending affects aggregate spending more quickly than does an increase in money supply.
2. An increase in aggregate demand has no effect upon real output when aggregate supply is vertical.
3. An increase in government spending always crowds out an equal amount of private sector interest sensitive spending.
4. Increased government spending affects aggregate supply less quickly than does an increase in money supply.

Codes:

A. 1 and 2 B. 1 and 3
C. 1 and 4 D. 3 and 4

15. In the context of the theory of economic growth, match the theory/facts given in List-I with their propounders given in List-II:

List-I	***List-II***
(*a*) Stylised facts of economic growth	1. R.M. Solow
(*b*) Exogenous growth theory	2. N. Kaldor
(*c*) Golden rule of accumulation	3. Radner & Samuelson
(*d*) Optimal growth turnpikes	4. E.S. Phelps

Codes:

	(*a*)	(*b*)	(*c*)	(*d*)
A.	2	1	3	4
B.	3	2	1	4
C.	2	1	4	3
D.	2	4	3	1

16. The endogeneous growth theory seeks to provide explanation for which of the following determinants of growth that the Solow's model did not explain?

A. Technical Progress
B. Labour Growth
C. Role of the government in promoting growth
D. All of the above

17. 'Multi-dimensional Poverty Index' (MPI) is a new index to be included in

A. World Human Report
B. Human Development Report
C. World Development Report
D. India's Human Development Report

18. Which is the better measure of welfare?
A. National Income
B. Per Capita Income
C. Per Capita Disposable Income
D. Gross National Product

19. Which of the following year of the 11th Five Year Plan registered the highest GDP growth rate?
A. 2007-08 B. 2008-09
C. 2009-10 D. 2010-11

20. What is the main purpose of U.N.E.P.?
A. Equal development
B. Economic development
C. Reduction in temperature
D. Sustainable development

21. Foodgrains in India are canalized by
A. ONGC B. OIL
C. FCI D. MMTC

22. As per provisional data released by C.S.O. for Q1 of 2012-13, the GDP growth has been estimated at
A. 5.1% B. 5.5%
C. 5.9% D. 6.2%

23. In whose economic theories, Malthus' theories are in the base?
A. Adam Smith B. Ricardo
C. Keynes D. Robins

24. There are four phases of a business cycle. Identify the correct sequence of the occurrence of these phases:
A. Recovery, Recession, Expansion, Depression
B. Recovery, Expansion, Depression, Recession
C. Depression, Expansion, Recession, Recovery
D. Recovery, Expansion, Recession, Depression

25. The Total Factor Productivity (TFP) in agriculture during the 11th plan in India
A. Increased
B. Declined
C. Remain unchanged
D. Had no specific pattern

26. Income elasticity of demand for food in developed countries is less than
A. zero B. 1
C. 2 D. 3

27. 'Apna Khet, Apna Kaam' (*i.e.* own field, own work) is a new scheme under MNREGA and it was initiated in the State
A. Punjab B. Gujarat
C. Rajasthan D. Madhya Pradesh

28. 'Price Scissors' refer to
A. Relative price of fuel and industrial goods
B. Relative price of industrial goods in terms of agricultural goods
C. Relative price of imported goods in terms of the exported goods
D. None of the above

29. **Assertion (A):** Yellow Revolution increased the production of seeds.

Reason (R) : White Revolution increased the production of milk.

Codes:
A. Both (A) and (R) are true and (R) is the correct explanation of (A).
B. Both (A) and (R) are true, but (R) is not the correct explanation of (A).
C. (A) is true, but (R) is false.
D. (A) is false, but (R) is true.

30. The immediate cause for the collapse of the Bretton Woods system was
A. the expectation that the U.S. would soon be forced to devalue the dollar.
B. the massive flight of liquid capital from the U.S.
C. the attempt by three small European Central Banks to convert part of their dollar holdings into gold at the Fed.
D. All of the above

31. In case of Fixed Exchange Rate regime adjustment in Balance of Payments takes place through
A. changes in price level
B. changes in exchange rate
C. changes in interest rate
D. None of the above

32. A spot Foreign Exchange Transaction refers to

A. the purchase or sale of foreign exchange for delivery within two business days.
B. the sale of foreign exchange for delivery.
C. the purchase of foreign exchange for delivery.
D. None of the above.

33. Regarding M.F.N. (Most Favoured Nation) clause, find out the correct statement:

A. It guarantees special privilege to the contracting parties.
B. It guarantees only equal treatment.
C. The unconditional M.F.N. clause seems to be more equitable than the conditional one.
D. The conditional M.F.N. clause confers significant rights on the contracting party.

34. Match List-I with List-II:

List-I	List-II
(*a*) Hamilton List	1. Trade creation and Trade diversion effects
(*b*) Marshall-Learner	2. Indian Industry
(*c*) F.Y. Edgeworth	3. Elasticity approach
(*d*) Jacob Viner	4. Impoverishing growth

Codes:

	(*a*)	(*b*)	(*c*)	(*d*)
A.	2	3	1	4
B.	2	3	4	1
C.	3	2	4	1
D.	3	2	1	4

35. Under a managed floating exchange rate system, the Nation's monetary authorities intervene in Foreign Exchange Markets to

A. smooth out short-run fluctuations in exchange rates
B. smooth out long-run fluctuations in exchange rates
C. smooth out short-run and long-run fluctuations in exchange rates
D. keep exchange rates fixed among a group of nations

36. Which of the following is related with optimum currency area?

A. Optimal geographical area for a single currency
B. Optimal geographical area for several currencies whose exchange rates are relatively pegged
C. Single currency or the pegged currencies fluctuate jointly *vis-à-vis* other currencies
D. All of the above

37. Which of the following is true with respect to the monetary approach to the balance of payments?

A. A balance of payments deficit results from an excess supply of money in the nation.
B. A balance of payments surplus results from an excess demand for money.
C. Balance of payments disequilibrium are automatically corrected in the long-run.
D. All of the above

38. Which one of the following tax is within the jurisdiction of the Central Government as enumerated in List-I of Seventh Schedule of the Constitution of India?

A. Taxes on mineral rights subject to any limitation imposed by the Parliament
B. Taxes on the consumption and sale of electricity
C. Taxes on sale and purchase of newspapers and on advertisements therein
D. Excise on alcoholic liquors for human consumption, opium, Indian hemp and other narcotics

39. Grants from the Centre to the States under the recommendations of Finance Commission are known as

A. Plan grants
B. Development assistance
C. Statutory grants
D. Discretionary grants

40. Match the items given in List-I with those in List-II:

List-I	List-II
(*a*) Committee on Taxation of Agricultural Wealth and Income, 1972	1. Raja J. Chelliah
(*b*) Direct Taxes Enquiry Committee, 1970	2. L.K. Jha

(*c*) Tax Reform Committee, 1991 — 3. K.N. Wanchoo

(*d*) Indirect Tax Enquiry Committee, 1976 — 4. K.N. Raj

Codes:

	(*a*)	(*b*)	(*c*)	(*d*)
A.	4	1	2	3
B.	4	3	1	2
C.	3	2	1	4
D.	2	3	1	4

41. The biggest holder of Government of India dated securities:

A. Reserve Bank of India
B. Life Insurance Corporation of India
C. Employees Provident Fund
D. Commercial Banks

42. Arrange the introduction of the following taxes in India in chronological order:

I. Service tax
II. Income tax
III. Banking cash transaction tax
IV. Gift tax

Codes:

A. II, IV, I, III B. II, I, III, IV
C. II, III, I, IV D. IV, II, I, III

43. Who amongst the following has not worked for estimation of Black Money in India?

A. N. Kaldor
B. Dr. D.K. Rangnekar
C. O.P. Chopra
D. Sukhamoy Chakravarthy

44. For which of the following items of household consumption expenditures in India, NSSO takes the reference period as 365 days?

A. Clothing, footwear, bedding, education etc.
B. Edible oil, fish & meat, egg
C. Vegetables, fruits, spices, beverages & processed food
D. All other food, fuel & light, misc. goods & services

45. What is the average monthly per capita expenditure (modified mixed recall period) for rural India in 2009-10?

A. ₹ 845.54 B. ₹ 1053.64
C. ₹ 1322.25 D. ₹ 1984.46

46. What is the target for total outstanding liabilities at the end of 2015-16 as per medium term Fiscal Policy Statement of the Union Budget 2013-14 (Per cent of GDP)?

A. 42.3 B. 44.5
C. 41.1 D. 47.8

47. Which of the following years recorded growth rate of agriculture-GDP (at constant prices) more than 5 per cent?

(*i*) 2006-07 (*ii*) 2007-08
(*iii*) 2010-11 (*iv*) 2011-12

Codes:

A. (*i*) and (*iii*) B. (*i*), (*ii*) and (*iii*)
C. (*ii*) and (*iii*) D. (*i*) and (*iv*)

48. Which of the following items of private final consumption expenditure has the largest share (in the PFCE) in recent years in the Indian Economy?

A. Clothing & Footwear
B. Gross rent, Fuel & Power
C. Transport & Communication
D. Furniture, Furnishings, etc.

49. Which of the following has not been one of the terms of reference of the Thirteenth Finance Commission of India?

A. The distribution between the Union and the States of the net proceeds of taxes which are to be, or may be, divided between them.
B. The principles which should govern the grants-in-aid of the revenues of the States out of the Consolidated Fund of India.
C. The measures needed to augment the Consolidated Fund of a State to supplement the resources of the Panchayats and Municipalities in the State.
D. The method of rescheduling the debt burdens of the States in view of their growing deficits.

50. Match price indices in India given in List-I with their latest base year in List-II:

List-I	List-II
(*a*) Wholesale Price Index	1. 2001 = 100
(*b*) Industrial Workers (CPIIW)	2. 2010 = 100

(*c*) Consumer Price Index (New Series) — 3. 2004-05 = 100

(*d*) Agricultural Labourers (CPIAL) — 4. 1986-87 = 100

Codes:

	(*a*)	(*b*)	(*c*)	(*d*)
A.	3	1	2	4
B.	3	2	4	1
C.	2	1	4	3
D.	2	4	1	3

51. Which of the following does not hold correct about the Demsetz view of concentration and monopoly power?

A. Superior efficiency produces both increased concentration and more profits.
B. The causal link is from concentration to profitability.
C. The causal link is from efficiency to concentration.
D. The causal link is from efficiency to profit.

52. Find out the value of Gini coefficient for estimating the industrial concentration for the following industry using the formula

$G = \frac{1}{N}\sum_{i=1}^{N}(N-2i+1)S_i$ (Where N is the number of firms and S_i is the share of *i*th firm in terms of sales of the industry.)

Firm 1	Firm 2	Firm 3	Firm 4	Industry
70	10	10	10	100

A. 25 B. 35
C. 45 D. 65

53. Relate the items given in List-I with the List-II with regard to Wage Theory:

List-I	**List-II**
(*a*) Iron law of wages	1. J.S. Mill
(*b*) Wage-funds theory	2. John R. Hicks
(*c*) Surplus-value theory	3. David Ricardo
(*d*) Marginal productivity theory	4. Karl Marx

Codes:

	(*a*)	(*b*)	(*c*)	(*d*)
A.	1	3	4	2
B.	2	1	3	4
C.	3	4	2	1
D.	3	1	4	2

54. Which of the following is not an item of social security of labour?

A. Wage
B. Maternity benefits
C. Pensions
D. Industrial injury

55. Which of the following has not been suggested as the features of informal sector endorsed by the UN Statistical Commission (July, 1993)?

A. Private un-incorporated Enterprises
B. No complete accounts are available that would permit a financial separation of the production activities of the Enterprise
C. Casual jobs or jobs of a limited short duration
D. The employment size of the enterprise is below a certain threshold

56. Which of the following constitutes the intermediate layer in the three-tier co-operative credit structure?

A. State Co-operative Banks
B. Central Co-operative Banks
C. Primary Agricultural Credit Societies
D. NABARD

57. High powered money is

A. Banks' reserves at Central Bank
B. Money held by the Banks
C. All loans and advances of Banks
D. Currency held by Public and cash reserves of the Banks

58. **Assertion (A):** Investment companies have not been able to attract much public savings in India.

Reason (R): Investment companies are pure financial intermediaries and they specialise in the mobilisation of public saving for investment in corporate securities.

Codes:

A. (A) is true, but (R) is false.
B. Both (A) and (R) are correct, but (R) is not the correct explanation of (A).

C. (A) is not correct, but (R) is correct.
D. Both (A) and (R) are correct and (R) is the correct explanation of (A).

59. Find out the correct answer from the code given below:

Main features of Regional Rural Banks (RRBs)

I. RRBs have been established by 'sponsor bank' usually a public sector commercial bank.
II. RRBs grant direct loans and advances only to small and marginal farmers, rural artisans and agricultural labourers.
III. The area of RRB is limited to a specified region comprising one or more districts of a State.
IV. The lending rates of RRBs are not higher than the prevailing lending rates of co-operative societies.

Codes:

A. II and III are correct.
B. I and III are correct.
C. I, II and IV are correct.
D. I, II and III are correct.

60. Find out the correct answer from the codes given below:

Technique of selective credit control of RBI.

I. Determination of margin requirement for loans against certain securities.
II. Determination of maximum amount of advances or other financial accommodation.
III. Changing of discretionary interest rates on certain type of advances.
IV. Changing the cash reserve requirements of commercial banks.

Codes:

A. I and II are correct.
B. I, II and III are correct.
C. I, II and IV are correct.
D. I and IV are correct.

61. In a two variable regression Y is dependent variable and X is independent variable. The correlation coefficient between Y and X is 0.6. For this which of the following result is correct?

A. 36% variations in Y are explained by X.
B. 60% variations in Y are explained by X.
C. 6% variations in Y are explained by X.
D. None of the above.

62. In a multiple regression with three independent variables, the regression coefficients are to be tested. Which test would be used?

A. Z-test B. F-test
C. χ^2-test D. t-test

63. Input-Output Technique was invented by

A. Gunnar Myrdal B. Wassily Leontief
C. Hollis B. Chenery D. Robert Solow

64. The Linear Cobweb model is given as

Supply : $q_t = \alpha + \beta p_t - 1$
Demand : $p_t = \gamma + \delta q_t$
Where $q(0) = q_0$ is initial condition.

For this model stability of market requires the condition

A. $|\delta| < |\beta|$ B. $|\delta| < |\frac{1}{\beta}|$
C. $|\delta| > |\beta|$ D. $|\delta| = |\frac{1}{\beta}|$

65. Which of the following statements is true concerning the optimal solution of linear program with two decision variables?

A. There is only one solution to a linear program.
B. The optimal solution is either an extreme point or is on a line connecting extreme points.
C. All resources must be used up by an optimal solution.
D. All of the above

66. Given a production function $Q = AL^{\alpha} K^{\beta}$; $\alpha, \beta > 0$, increasing returns to scale requires that

A. $\alpha + \beta = 1$ B. $\alpha + \beta = 0$
C. $\alpha + \beta > 0$ D. $\alpha + \beta > 1$

67. For the demand function $P = 10 - 3x - x^2$, what is consumer's surplus at $x = 3$?

A. 16.25 B. 20.50
C. 07.50 D. 12.50

68. From the following life-table, find out the value of life expectancy at age 4(e_4).

Age	q_x	l_x	d_x	L_x	T_x	e_x
4	0.000194	99208	19	99,199	?	?
5	0.000177	99189	18	?	7,246,663	73.1

A. 72.0 B. 73.0
C. 74.0 D. 75.0

69. Match List-I with List-II for a hypothetical population fertility estimates:

List-I	List-II
(*a*) Total marital fertility rate	1. 4.0
(*b*) General fertility rate	2. 1.3
(*c*) Gross reproduction rate	3. 39.1
(*d*) Total fertility rate	4. 0.7

Codes:

	(*a*)	(*b*)	(*c*)	(*d*)
A.	1	2	3	4
B.	4	2	3	1
C.	2	4	3	1
D.	1	3	4	2

70. Verdoon's law is about the
A. positive relation between the growth of population, employment and output with the growth of production per head.
B. negative relation between the growth of population, employment and output with the growth of production per head.
C. positive relation between population growth and employment.
D. negative relation between population growth and employment.

71. Which of the following statements is true concerning standard regression model?
A. Y has a probability distribution
B. X has a probability distribution
C. The disturbance term is assumed to be correlated with X
D. For an adequate model the residual (û) will be zero for all sample data points

72. Which of the following statements are true concerning a triangular or recursive system?
(*i*) The parameters can be validly estimated using separate applications of OLS to each equation.
(*ii*) The independent variables may be correlated with the error terms in other equations
(*iii*) An application of 2 SLS would lead to unbiased but inefficient parameter estimates
(*iv*) The independent variables may be correlated with error terms in the equations in which they appear as independent variables.
A. (*ii*) and (*iv*) only
B. (*i*) and (*iii*) only
C. (*i*), (*ii*) and (*iii*) only
D. (*i*), (*ii*), (*iii*) and (*iv*)

73. What would be the consequences for the OLS estimator if heteroscedasticity is present in a regression model but ignored?
A. It will be biased.
B. It will be inconsistent.
C. It will be inefficient.
D. All A, B and C will be true.

74. Match the following

List-I	List-II
(*a*) Unit Root Test	1. Durbin-Watson Test
(*b*) Contingency Table	2. Student's *t*-test
(*c*) Regression Coefficient	3. Stationarity
(*d*) Auto-correlation	4. χ^2-test

Codes:

	(*a*)	(*b*)	(*c*)	(*d*)
A.	2	3	1	4
B.	4	2	3	1
C.	3	4	2	1
D.	3	2	1	4

75. Consider the following system of equations, using standard notations:

$$Y_1 = \alpha_0 + \alpha_1 Y_2 + \alpha_3 Y_3 + \alpha_4 X_1 + \alpha_5 X_2 + u_1$$
$$Y_2 = \beta_0 + \beta_1 Y_3 + \beta_2 Y_1 + \beta_3 X_2 + u_2$$
$$Y_3 = \gamma_0 + \gamma_1 X_1 + \gamma_2 X_2 + \gamma_3 X_3 + u_3$$

According to the order condition, the first equation is
A. Unidentified
B. Just identified
C. Over-identified
D. Not possible to tell whether the equation identified or not because reduced form of the model is not given.

ANSWERS

1	2	3	4	5	6	7	8	9	10
B	C	C	A	A	B	A	C	C	C
11	**12**	**13**	**14**	**15**	**16**	**17**	**18**	**19**	**20**
C	B	A	A	C	C	B	C	A	D
21	**22**	**23**	**24**	**25**	**26**	**27**	**28**	**29**	**30**
C	B	C	D	A	B	A	B	B	D
31	**32**	**33**	**34**	**35**	**36**	**37**	**38**	**39**	**40**
A	A	B	B	A	D	D	C	C	B
41	**42**	**43**	**44**	**45**	**46**	**47**	**48**	**49**	**50**
D	A	D	A	B	A	C	B	D	A
51	**52**	**53**	**54**	**55**	**56**	**57**	**58**	**59**	**60**
B	C	D	A	C	B	D	B	D	B
61	**62**	**63**	**64**	**65**	**66**	**67**	**68**	**69**	**70**
A	D	B	B	B	D	*	C	D	A
71	**72**	**73**	**74**	**75**					
A	C	C	C	A					

SOME SELECTED EXPLANATORY ANSWERS

1. Marris's Model of Managerial Enterprise: This model explains the "growth" of the firm under managerial constraints. Growth of the firm's size can be measured in different terms such as capital, output, revenue, market share, and so on. Marris believes that the maximization of any one of these can be reasonably assumed to maximize the other under a "steady rate of growth" of the firm in the long run. The theory is built on the tenets of the "separation of ownership and management" and the conflict of the interests of owners and managers. But Marris's managers do not simply aim at the maximization of their own 'utility' but also that of the owners as they pursue the approach of the 'balanced growth'.

Balanced growth is achieved when the growth of demand for a firm's product is equal to the growth of supply of capital. Since the growth of demand maximizes managerial utility and the growth of supply of capital maximizes entrepreneurial utility, their equilibrium equally satisfies both. Marris's managers are, however, not interested in the absolute growth of the size of the firm. They try to maximize the rate of growth. The model should have been classified under growth theories but for the dominating role assigned to the managers in the firm's operations.

2. Linear programming is a mathematical technique for solving maximization or minimization problems when more than one constraint exists. Its main advantage is computational and is based on the utilization of computers. Linear programming is based on the following assumptions:

1. There is more than one constraint (otherwise the problem could be easily solved by traditional methods).
2. Output and factor prices are constant (so that the budget and isocost lines, as well as any other constraint, can be represented by straight lines).
3. There are constant returns to scale and technologically fixed input or factor proportions (so that the expansion paths are straight lines through the origin).

6. The concept of consumer's surplus was originated by Dupuit, a French engineer-economist in 1844. The concept was further developed and popularized by Alfred Marshall.

Prof. Kenneth E. Boulding has renamed it as 'Buyer's Surplus'. The concept of consumer's surplus has been defined by Alfred Marshall as follows:

"The excess of the price which a person would be willing to pay rather than go without the thing, over that which he actually does pay, is the economic measure of this surplus satisfaction. It may be called 'consumer's surplus".

In the words of Prof. Taussig, consumer surplus is the difference between the 'potential price' and the 'actual price'. The potential price means the total amount of money the consumer would be willing to pay for the product while the actual price is the amount he actually does pay for the product.

The concept of consumer's surplus in based on the law of diminishing marginal utility. If the marginal utility of a product is higher than its actual market price, the consumer derives excess satisfaction. This excess satisfaction is referred to as consumer surplus. Therefore, consumer surplus can be measured as the difference between the maximum price the consumer is willing to pay for product and the actual market price changed for it.

7. Modern theory of cost curves has been propounded by economists like **Stigler, Andrews, Sargent Florence** and **Friedman,** etc. According to traditional theory of cost curves, long-run cost curves are U-shaped. But according to modern theory, In real life long-run cost curves are L-shaped. The L-shaped cost curve implies that the production costs fall continuously with increases in output. According to modern theory long-run costs are mainly of two types : 1. Production Cost and 2. Managerial Cost. On account of increase in production, production cost goes on falling continuously due to technical economies of scale. On the contrary, as the scale of production is enlarged managerial costs may rise. Since fall in production-cost is more than rise in managerial-cost, long-run average cost curve falls smoothly or remains constant at very large scales of output.

10. Firms use capital, along with labour, to produce goods and services for sale. Their goal is, of course, to maximize profits. In deciding how much capital to use in production, firms have to balance the contribution that more capital makes to their revenues against the cost of using more capital. The *marginal product of capital* is the increase in output produced by using 1 more unit of capital in production. The *rental (user) cost of capital* is the cost of using 1 more unit of capital in production. (Note that both concepts are *flows*). Whether a firm actually buys its own capital or leases it, the rental cost is the right measure of the *opportunity cost.* As long as the value of the marginal product of capital is above the rental cost, it pays the firm to add to its capital stock. Thus, the firm will keep investing until the value of the output produced by adding 1 more unit of capital is equal to the cost of using that capital–the rental cost of capital.

11. **Demand-Pull Inflation:** The demand-pull inflation occurs when the aggregate demand increase much more rapidly than the aggregate supply. The demand-pull inflation caused by monetary and real factors.

Demand-Pull Inflation due to Monetary Factors: An important reason for demand-pull inflation is increase in money supply in excess of increase in potential output.

Demand-Pull Inflation due to Real Factors: The real factors that cause demand-pull inflation are those that cause upward shift in the IS curve. The factors that cause upward shift in the IS curve is:

(*i*) Increase in government spending given the tax revenue.
(*ii*) Cut in tax rates without change in the government expenditure.
(*iii*) Upward shift in the investment function.
(*iv*) Downward shift in the saving function.
(*v*) Upward shift in export function.
(*vi*) Downward shift in the import function.

16. **Endogenous Growth Theory**

The Solow model of economic growth has proved inadequate to explain the actual rates of growth across countries and over time. This has inspired new research, both theoretical and empirical, to look into its assumptions and to identify the additional or other determinants (called the fourth wheel) of output and growth. Under the Solow model, the saving rate affects the growth rate only up to the steady state position, beyond which technology and population growth alone determine the growth rate in real GDP. Further, both technical progress (the crucial determinant of growth) and growth rate in population (which affects positively the growth rate in the total income and not in per capita income) are treated as exogenous variables in the model and, accordingly, the model is branded as an exogenous growth theory. Accordingly, the growth rate beyond the steady state becomes exogenous in any economy and the Solow model leaves little scope for the government to influence the growth rate. Such a scenario is incompatible with the significant roles policy makers have been making across the world in improving their growths. The pleasant experiences of China and the tiger economies of South East Asia (Singapore, Taiwan and South Korea), among others, on the one hand; and the not so good experiences of the countries like those in Africa and Latin America and Russian Federation etc. on the other hand, points out that economic policies do matter in economic growth. To incorporate such factors, the alternative growth model has been advanced. The said model—which tries to explain technical progress, labour growth and the role of the government in promoting growth besides discovering the 'other' determinants—is termed as the endogenous growth theory. The endogenous growth model is an extension of the exogenous growth model as it goes deeper in the question of the ultimate sources of growth and provides a better explanation of growth over space and time. Though the alternative model of economic growth is not in a neat form as the Solow model, it is free from the faulty assumptions of the latter model and it gives due recognition to 'other factors' of growth.

17. Multi-dimenstional Poverty Index (MPI): Launched in July 2010, the MPI provides multi-dimensional picture of people living in poverty (and is to replace the 'Human Poverty Index' in the UN's Human Development reports). Ten indicators across the three HDI dimensions of human development are used to complement money-based indicators. They are: nutrition and child mortality (health), years of schooling and children enrolled in school (education) and type of cooking fuel, toilet, water, electricity, type of floor and assets (living standard).

20. United Nations Environment Programme: The United Nations Environment Programme (UNEP) was established in 1972 with its headquarters at Nairobi, Kenya. UNEP works to encourage sustainable development through sound environmental practices everywhere. Its activities cover a wide range of issues: from the promotion of environmental science and information, to an early warning and emergency response capacity to deal with environmental disasters and emergencies.

21. The Food Corporation of India was setup under the Food Corporation Act 1964, in order to fulfil following objectives of the Food Policy:

⇒ Effective price support operations for safeguarding the interests of the farmers.

⇒ Distribution of foodgrains throughout the country for public distribution system.

⇒ Maintaining satisfactory level of operational and buffer stocks of foodgrains to ensure National Food Security. FCI has played a significant role in India's success in transforming the crisis management oriented food security into a stable security system. FCI's Objectives are:

⇒ To provide farmers remunerative prices.

⇒ To make foodgrains available at reasonable prices, particularly to vulnerable section of the society.

⇒ To maintain buffer stocks as measure of Food Security.

⇒ To intervene in market for price stabilization.

23. Prior to Keynes, noted classical economist R.T. Malthus had also expressed similar opinion that deficiency of effective demand was the main cause of fall in employment. But Malthus could not explain the reason for fall in effective demand.

24. Phases of Business Cycles

According to **Prof. Schumpeter,** a trade cycle can have four phases:

1. Expansion or Boom
2. Recession
3. Depression or Trough or Contraction
4. Recovery

The following figure illustrates all the four phases or stages of trade cycles:

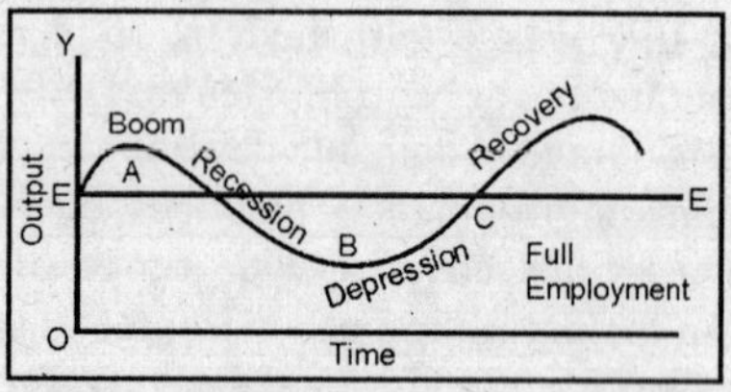

28. The price scissors refers to the phenomenon that the price of industrial products is higher than their value while the price of agricultural products is lower than their value for a long period in the exchange of industrial products for agricultural products.

32. A spot foreign exchange transaction refers to the purchase or sale of foreign exchange for delivery within two business days. The exchange rate at which this occurs is called the spot rate. For example, £100 could be obtained immediately by paying $2.00 per pound for a total of $200.

A forward foreign exchange transaction involves an agreement today to buy or sell a specific amount of foreign exchange at a specified future date and at a rate agreed upon today (the forward exchange rate). For example, I could enter into an agreement today to purchase £100 3 months from today at $2.02 = £1. After 3 months, I get the £100 for $202, regardless of what the spot rate is at that time.

33. Most Favoured Nation: In international economic relations and international politics, most favoured nation (MFN) is a status or level treatment accorded by one state to another in international trade. The term means the country which is the recipient of this treatment must, nominally, receive equal trade advantages as the "most favoured nation" by the country granting such treatment. (Trade advantages include low tariffs or high import quotas). In effect, a country that has been accorded MFN status may not be treated less advantageously than any other country with MFN status by the promising country.

The members of the World Trade Organization (WTO) agree to accord MFN status to each other. Exceptions allow for preferential treatment of developing countries, regional free trade areas and customs unions. Together with the principle of national treatment, MFN is one of the cornerstones of WTO trade law.

35. Managed floating exchange rate systems require monetary authorities to intervene in foreign exchange markets to smooth short-run fluctuations and prevent their currencies from moving too far from a perceived fundamental value. Under this system, monetary authorities can moderate the tendency for the nation's currency to depreciate by selling or buying to change the volume of foreign currency reserves. The feasibility of this system rests on the fact that it does not require the monetary authorities to know the long-run trend in exchange rates. However, the effectiveness of official intervention in foreign exchange markets is limited because official foreign currency reserves are much smaller than international capital flows.

37. The *monetary approach to the balance of payments* views the balance of payments as an essentially monetary phenomenon, with money playing the key role in the long run both as a disturbance and an adjustment in the nation's balance of payments. According to the monetary approach, a deficit in a nation's balance of payments results from an excess in the stock of money supplied that is not eliminated or corrected by the nation's monetary authorities. A surplus results from an uncorrected excess demand for money in the nation. Under a fixed exchange rate system, the deficit or surplus is automatically corrected in the long run by an outflow or inflow of money (international reserves) that eliminates the excess supply of or demand for money.

39. Statutory Grants : Article 275 empowers the Parliament to make grants to the states which are in need of financial assistance and not to every state. Also, different sums may be fixed for different states. These sums are charged on the Consolidated Fund of India every year. Apart from this general provision, the Constitution also provides for specific grants for promoting the welfare of the scheduled tribes in a state or for raising the level of administration of the scheduled areas in a state including the State of Assam.
The statutory grants under Article 275 (both general and specific) are given to the states on the recommendation of the Finance Commission.

42. Service Tax – 1994
Income Tax – 1860
Banking Cash transaction tax – 2005
Gift tax – 1958

44. Reference periods used for collection of consumption data in Schedule 1.0 Type 1 and Type 2

Category	*Item groups*	*Reference period for*	
		Schedule Type 1	*Schedule Type 2*
I	Clothing, bedding, footwear, education, medical (institutional), durable goods	'Last 30 days' and 'Last 365 days'	Last 365 days
II	Edible oil; egg, fish & meat; vegetables, fruits, spices, beverages and processed foods; pan, tobacco & intoxicants	Last 30 days	Last 7 days
III	All other food, fuel and light, miscellaneous goods and services including non-institutional medical; rents and taxes	Last 30 days	Last 30 days

51. Harold Demsetz in 1973 pointed out that if an industry has some superior firms, these firms will increase their shares and their profits, hence industry concentration will rise and industry profits will rise. Demsetz's "superior efficiency hypothesis" is sometimes called the "efficiency hypothesis."

52. $G = \frac{1}{4}[(4 - 2 \times 1 + 1)70 + (4 - 2 \times 2 + 1)10 + (4 - 2 \times 3 + 1)10 + (4 - 2 \times 4 + 1)10]$

$= \frac{1}{4}[210 + 10 + (-10) + (-30)]$

$= \frac{1}{4}[210 + 10 - 10 - 30]$

$= \frac{1}{4} \times 180 = 45.$

54. Social Security : Social Security for employees is a concept which overtime has gained importance in the industrialized countries. Broadly, it can be defined as measures providing protection to working class against contingencies like retirement, resignation, retrenchment, maternity, old age, unemployment, death, disablement and other similiar conditions.

Social Security for employees in India: With reference to India, the Constitution levies responsibility on the State to provide social security to citizens of the country. The State, here, discharges duty as an agent of the society in order to help those who are in adverse situations or otherwise needs protection owing to above mentioned contingencies. Article 41, 42 and 43 of the Constitution do talk about the same. Also, the Concurrent List of the Constitution of India mentions issues like-Social Security and insurance, employment and unemployment. Welfare of Labour including conditions of work, provident funds, employers' liability, workmen's compensation, invalidity and old age pension and maternity benefits.

56. In India, the cooperative credit structure usually followed a three-tier arrangement, with an apex co-operative bank at the top of the pyramid in each state. The intermediate level of the structure was made up of district or central cooperative banks, while primary credit societies reached out to villages and individual members.

61. Coefficient of determination: The use of *coefficient of determination,* which is the square of coefficient of correlation, is perhaps a more convenient and useful way for interpreting the dependence between the variables. This is because the coefficient of determination gives the per cent of variation explained by one variable in the other.

$$\left.\begin{matrix}\text{coefficient of}\\ \text{determination}\end{matrix}\right\} = r^2 = \frac{\text{Variance explained by X in Y}}{\text{Variance in Y}}$$

Thus if $r = 0.6$, then $r^2 = 0.36$. Then it would mean 36% of the variance in variable Y is explained by the variable X due to linear dependence between them.

62. Multiple regression models are traditional predicting models that are used to identify independent variables and their relationships with the dependent variable, and predict the independent variables for their future. In multiple regression modelling, three evaluation measures are used: t-Test and F-Test. t-Test is used to test the significance of regression coefficients and F-Test the significance of the sum of the estimated coefficients.

68. *Parameter*	*Symbol*
• Probability of dying within age x to $x + 1$	$[q(x)]$
• Number surviving to age x	$[l(x)]$
• Number dying between ages x to $x + l$	$[d(x)]$
• Person years lived between ages x to $x + l$	$[L(x)]$
• Total number of person years lived above age x	$[T(x)]$
• Expectation of life at age x	$[e(x)]$

The following formulas apply to the data:

- $d(x) = q(x) \times l(x)$
- $L(x) = l(x) - (d(x)/2)$
- $T(x) = \text{Sum } (L(x))$
- $e(x) = T(x)/L(x)$

Age	q_x	l_x	d_x	L_x	T_x	e_x
4	0.000194	99208	19	99,199	73,45,861	74.0
5	0.000177	99189	18	99,180	72,46,663	73.1

70. The empirical relation between productivity growth and output growth in manufacturing is known as Verdoorn's Law; following Verdoorn's (1949) paper published in Italian, entitled 'Fattori che Regolano lo Sviluppo della Produttivita del Lavoro'. Interestingly, at the time of publication, Verdoorn was working for Kaldor in the Research and Planning Division of the Economic Commission for Europe in Geneva, of which Kaldor was Director. It was Kaldor who revived Verdoorn's Law in 1966, and it is also known as Kaldor's second law; that is, there is a strong positive causal relation between the growth of manufacturing output and the growth of productivity in manufacturing.

72. (*i*), (*ii*) and (*iii*) are all correct. A triangular system is one where the causality between the 'endogenous variables' all goes in one direction. Thus, such a system is not a simultaneous system at all, and hence OLS can validly be applied separately to each equation in the system. It thus follows that if a systems technique such as 2SLS is used, this would have been done unnecessarily, and hence an efficiency loss would occur when the reduced-form fitted values are used instead of the actual values.

73. Under heteroscedasticity, provided that all of the other assumptions of the classical linear regression model are adhered to, the coefficient estimates will still be consistent and unbiased, but they will be inefficient. Thus (*c*) is correct. The upshot is that whilst this would not result in wrong coefficient estimates, our measure of the sampling variability of the coefficients, the standard errors, would probably be wrong. The stronger the degree of heteroscedasticity (*i.e.* the more the variance of the errors changed over the sample), the more inefficient the OLS estimator would be.

75. There are 3 equations in this system, so, for an equation to be just identified would require there to be 2 variables absent from a given equation. If there are more than 2 variables absent from a given equation, it would be classed as over-identified, while if less than 2 variables are absent, it would be under-identified. The variables in the system in total are Y_1, Y_2, Y_3, X_1, X_2, and X_3. The only variable missing from the first equation is X_3, so this equation is not identified (unidentified).

Previous Papers (Solved)

UGC-NET ECONOMICS, JUNE 2013*

PAPER–II

Note: *This paper contains **fifty (50)** objective type questions of **two (2)** marks each. **All** questions are compulsory.*

1. Under Cournot Model of Duopoly, each duopolist will produce

A. half the output
B. one-fourth of the output
C. one-sixth of the output
D. one-third of the total output

2. As long as the substitution effect dominates the income effect, the labour supply curve is

A. negatively sloped
B. positively sloped
C. bend backward
D. shifting towards left

3. The distinguishing characteristics of monopolistic competition are

I. Product differentiation
II. Non-price competition
III. Large number of firms and freedom to entry and exit
IV. Firms are interdependent

Codes:

A. I and III are correct.
B. I, II and IV are correct.
C. I, II and III are correct.
D. I, III and IV are correct.

4. Assertion (A) : Monopoly is Pareto inefficient.

Reason (R) : It would be possible to change the allocation of resources to make the amount of income he would be prepared to pay in exchange of the reduction in price.

Codes:

A. Both (A) and (R) are correct and (R) is the correct explanation of (A).
B. (A) is correct, but (R) is not correct.
C. Both (A) and (R) are correct, but (R) is incorrect explanation of (A).
D. (R) is correct, but (A) is incorrect.

5. If MP_L/MP_K does not change with any proportionate change in labour and capital then the production function is

A. Linear B. Non-linear
C. Homogeneous D. Homothetic

6. Match the items in the List-I with items in List-II. Select the correct answer from the code given below :

List-I	*List-II*
I. Agency Theory of Firm	1. O.E. Williamson
II. X-inefficiency	2. M.C. Jensen and W.J. Meckling
III. The Utility Maximisation Model	3. Wilfredo Pareto
IV. Edgeworth box diagram first used by	4. Harvey Leibenstein

Codes:

	I	II	III	IV
A.	3	2	1	4
B.	2	4	1	3
C.	2	3	4	1
D.	3	4	1	2

7. At the point of tangency between short-run average total cost and long-run average cost, the short-run marginal cost

A. greater than long-run marginal cost
B. less than long-run marginal cost
C. is far above long-run marginal cost
D. equals long-run marginal cost

* Exam held on 30-06-2013

8. The equilibrium in a market is incomplete with increasing returns to scale only in the case of

A. imperfectly competitive market
B. monopolistic market
C. perfectly competitive market
D. none of the above

9. If 1 = Involuntary unemployment;
2 = Disguised unemployment;
3 = Frictional unemployment; and
4 = Structural unemployment, then full employment is consistent with

A. 1 and 2 B. 2 and 3
C. 3 and 4 D. 1 and 4

10. In Keynes' equation of absolute income hypothesis, $C = \alpha_0 + by$, where C = Consumption expenditure; α_0 = Consumption expenditure when income (y) is zero; and b = Marginal Propensity to Consume (MPC), then which of the following statements is false?

A. MPC is independent of the level of income.
B. MPC is dependent on the level of income.
C. APC falls as income rises.
D. APC > MPC.

11. Which of the following statements is false?

A. The balanced budget multiplier is unity when taxes are lump sum taxes.
B. The balanced budget multiplier is less than unity when taxes are ad valorem taxes.
C. Tax multiplier is less than government expenditure multiplier.
D. Tax multiplier is more than government expenditure multiplier.

12. Match the theory/criterion of investment determination as given below in List-II with their propounders given below in List-I:

List-I	*List-II*
I. Dale Jorgenson	a. Q-Theory
II. J.M. Keynes	b. Neo-classical Theory
III. James Cohin	c. Accelerator Theory
IV. James Clark	d. Present Value Criterion

Codes:

	I	II	III	IV
A.	a	d	b	c
B.	b	d	a	c
C.	c	d	a	b
D.	c	a	d	b

13. **Assertion (A):** In liquidity trap, the demand for money is perfectly interest elastic.

Reason (R): Because in this situation, all the investors expect the market rate of interest to rise towards the natural rate of interest.

Codes:

A. (A) and (R) both are correct and (R) is the correct explanation of (A).
B. (A) and (R) both are correct, but (R) is not the correct explanation of (A).
C. (A) is correct, but (R) is incorrect.
D. Both (A) and (R) are incorrect.

14. The rate of net investment spending per time period depends on steepness of the downword slope of

A. Marginal efficiency of Investment Schedule
B. Marginal efficiency of Capital Schedule
C. LM-Schedule
D. IS-Schedule

15. Which of the following is not specifically mentioned as a determinant of the demand for money?

A. Wealth
B. Nominal yield on alternative assets
C. Inflation rate
D. Real rate of interest

16. Whose model of the following economists makes use of the stock adjustment principle to explain business cycles?

A. N. Kaldor B. J.R. Hicks
C. P. Samuelson D. J.M. Keynes

17. The concept of vicious circle of poverty is associated with

A. J.M. Keynes B. Ragner Nurkse
C. Karl Marx D. J.S. Mill

18. Inverted 'U' shaped income distribution hypothesis is associated with

A. J.B. Clark B. David Ricardo
C. Simon Kuznets D. Adam Smith

19. Components of HDI are
I. Longevity
II. Infant mortality
III. Educational attainment
IV. Decent standard of living

Codes:
A. I, II and III are correct.
B. II, III and IV are correct.
C. II, I, and IV are correct.
D. I, III and IV are correct.

20. Arrange the proponents of classical theory of development in a sequential order:
I. David Ricardo II. Adam Smith
III. J.S. Mill IV. Robert Malthus

Codes:

A.	II	IV	III	I
B.	IV	III	I	II
C.	III	II	IV	I
D.	I	II	III	IV

21. Assertion (A): In Marxian scheme of things, $M \rightarrow C \rightarrow M'$, where $M' > M$ and $M' - M$ is surplus value.

Reason (R) : The main cause of this surplus value is raw materials, machines, etc.

Codes:
A. (A) is wrong but (R) is correct.
B. (A) is correct but (R) is wrong.
C. Both (A) and (R) are correct.
D. Both (A) and (R) are wrong.

22. Match the items in the List-I with items in List-II :

List-I	*List-II*
I. Structural view of Underdevelopment	1. Classical Economists
II. Laissez-faire Policy	2. Hollis Chenery
III. Departmental Scheme of Expanded Reproduction	3. Steady State Growth
IV. Golden Age of Accumulation	4. Karl Marx

Codes:

	I	II	III	IV
A.	2	1	4	3
B.	4	2	3	1
C.	1	4	2	3
D.	3	4	1	2

23. Match the items in the List-I with items in List-II :

List-I	*List-II*
I. Critical Minimum Effort Thesis	1. R.F. Kahn
II. Knife-edge Equilibrium	2. Rosentein-Rodan
III. Bastard Golden Age	3. Leibenstein
IV. Big Push Theory	4. Harrod

Codes:

	I	II	III	IV
A.	3	4	1	2
B.	1	3	4	2
C.	2	1	3	4
D.	4	2	1	3

24. Which years in India have been the best and the worst in terms of growth rate of national income?
A. 2007-08 and 1997-98
B. 2006-07 and 1966-67
C. 1988-89 and 1979-80
D. 2003-04 and 1957-58

25. Rank the States in ascending order of the crude birth rate in the recent years:
I. Andhra Pradesh
II. Karnataka
III. Madhya Pradesh
IV. Uttar Pradesh

Codes:
A. I, II, III, IV B. II, III, I, IV
C. I, II, IV, III D. II, I, IV, III

26. Which five year plan of India has recorded the largest gap in terms of growth rate between the services sector and the industrial sector?
A. Seventh Plan B. Eighth Plan
C. Ninth Plan D. Tenth Plan

27. Provide the correct answer about the desired growth target of the manufacturing sector in the medium term as per the National Manufacturing Policy of India.
A. 6–8 per cent B. 8–10 per cent
C. 10–12 per cent D. 12–14 per cent

28. Which of the following countries have better Human Development Index (HDI) as per the HDR 2011?

I. Sri Lanka　　II. Pakistan
III. Kenya　　IV. Egypt

Codes:

A. Sri Lanka and Egypt
B. Sri Lanka and Kenya
C. Pakistan and Sri Lanka
D. Pakistan and Kenya

29. What was the amount of outlay under MGNREGA in 2011-12 by the Government of India?

A. ₹ 25,000 crore　　B. ₹ 30,000 crore
C. ₹ 40,000 crore　　D. ₹ 55,000 crore

30. Provide correct answer about the share of India in the world merchandize exports in 2010:

A. 0.5 per cent　　B. 0.9 per cent
C. 1.1 per cent　　D. 1.5 per cent

31. If the cost of transporting a goods between two nations exceeds the pretrade difference for the goods between two nations, then trade in that goods is

A. possible　　B. impossible
C. reversal　　D. cannot say

32. According to the Rybczynski theorem, the growth of only one factor at constant relative commodity prices, leads to an absolute expansion in the output of

A. both commodities
B. the commodity using the growing factor intensively
C. the commodity using the non-growing factor intensively
D. any of the above

33. The exchange rate is kept the same in all parts of the market by

A. exchange arbitrage
B. interest arbitrage
C. hedging
D. speculation

34. Which are relevant conditions assumed by the factor price equalization theorem?

I. The countries are characterised by different factor endowments.
II. The countries are characterised by different production functions.
III. The industries are characterised by different factor intensities.
IV. Each country will export the commodity which uses its abundant factor relatively intensively.

Codes:

A. I, II, III, IV　　B. I, III, IV
C. I, II, IV　　D. I, III, II

35. Which of the following is true with respect to the monetary approach to the balance of payments?

A. It views the balance of payments as an essentially monetary phenomenon.
B. A balance of payments deficit results from an excess demand of money in the nation.
C. A balance of payments surplus results from an excess supply of money.
D. Balance of payments disequilibrium are not automatically corrected in the long run.

36. When a nation imposes an import tariff, the nation's offer curve will

A. shift away from the axis measuring its export commodity.
B. shift away from the axis measuring its import commodity.
C. not shift.
D. any of the above is possible.

37. If the international terms of trade settle at a level that is between each country's opportunity cost then

A. there is no basis for gainful trade for either country.
B. both countries gain from trade.
C. only one country gains from trade.
D. one country gains and the other country loses from trade.

38. Arrange the following in chronological order:

I. The Indirect Tax Enquiry Committee (Jha Committee)

II. Tax Reforms Committee (Chelliah Committee)
III. Taxation Enquiry Commission (Matthur Commission)
IV. The Direct Tax Enquiry Committee (Wanchoo Committee)

Codes:

A. III, II, IV, I　　B. III, I, IV, II
C. II, III, I, IV　　D. III, IV, I, II

39. Which of the following are relevant in Zero Base Budgeting?

I. Each item of expenditure is challenged in pre-budget review.
II. No minimum level of expenditure is allowed to be taken as given.
III. Expenditure of each item is increased marginally.
IV. Most item of expenditure is taken for granted when budget is prepared for the next year.

Codes:

A. I and III are correct.
B. I, II and IV are correct.
C. I and II are correct.
D. I, III and IV are correct.

40. Match the items given in List-I with those in List-II:

List-I	*List-II*
I. Optimal Income Taxation	1. Charles Tiebout
II. An Economic Theory of Politics	2. Peter A. Phyrr
III. Local Public Goods	3. F. Ramsey
IV. Zero Base Budgeting	4. Anthony Downs

Codes:

	I	II	III	IV
A.	3	1	4	2
B.	2	3	1	4
C.	3	2	1	4
D.	3	4	1	2

41. Which of the following is tantamount to absence of taxation?

A. Shifting of the tax
B. Tax transformation
C. Evasion of tax
D. Tax capitalisation

42. Which of the following tax is within the jurisdiction of States as enumerated in List-II of the Schedule VII of the Constitution of India?

A. Taxes on Railway freights and fares.
B. Taxes on sale and purchase of newspapers and on advertisement therein.
C. Rate of stamp duty in respect of certain financial documents.
D. Taxes on luxuries, including entertainments, betting and gambling.

43. Cohin Clark has argued that for most countries of the world, the safe upper limit of taxation is

A. 40 per cent of national income
B. 30 per cent of national income
C. 25 per cent of national income
D. 20 per cent of national income

44. Which of the following tax can be shifted easily?

A. Lump-sum tax imposed on the monopolist
B. Tax imposed on residential house
C. Capital goods meant for sale
D. Succession duty

45. In a binomial distribution, the sum of mean and variance is 15 and the product of mean and variance is 54, then the number of observations (n) is equal to

A. 27　　B. 30
C. 24　　D. 33

46. If 'r' is the correlation coefficient and byx and bxy are the regression coefficients of the regression lines y on x and x on y respectively, then r =

A. $bxy \times byx$　　B. $\sqrt{bxy / byx}$
C. $\sqrt{1 - bxy\, byx}$　　D. $\sqrt{bxy\, byx}$

47. χ^2 (chi-square) test is used to test

A. analysis of variance
B. association between the qualitative variables

C. difference between means of two distributions drawn from the same population.

D. difference between the means of two distributions drawn from different population.

48. Random sampling implies that

A. the observations are selected purposively.

B. the observations are selected in a systemic manner.

C. the observations are selected in an adhoc manner.

D. the observations are selected in clusters.

49. Given the following information, match the item in List-I with List-II:

List-I	*List-II*
I. Coefficient of Variation	1. μ_4/σ^4
II. Coefficient of Correlation	2. μ_3/σ^3
III. Coefficient of Skewness	3. $\sigma/\bar{x}$
IV. Coefficient of Kurtosis	4. $\Sigma xy/\sigma_x\sigma_y$

Codes:

	I	II	III	IV
A.	1	2	3	4
B.	3	2	4	1
C.	3	4	2	1
D.	3	4	1	2

50. **Assertion (A):** Fisher's index is an ideal index.

Reasoning (R): Fisher's index satisfies Time Reversal and Factor Reversal Tests.

Codes:

A. Both (A) and (R) are true and (R) is correct explanation of (A).

B. Both (A) and (R) are true, but (R) is not correct explanation of (A).

C. (A) is true, but (R) is false.

D. (A) is false, but (R) is true.

ANSWERS

1	2	3	4	5	6	7	8	9	10
D	B	C	A	D	B	D	C	C	B
11	**12**	**13**	**14**	**15**	**16**	**17**	**18**	**19**	**20**
D	*	A	A	D	A	B	C	D	A
21	**22**	**23**	**24**	**25**	**26**	**27**	**28**	**29**	**30**
B	A	A	C	A	C	D	A	C	D
31	**32**	**33**	**34**	**35**	**36**	**37**	**38**	**39**	**40**
B	B	A	B	A	A	B	D	C	D
41	**42**	**43**	**44**	**45**	**46**	**47**	**48**	**49**	**50**
C	D	C	C	A	D	B	B	C	A

SOME SELECTED EXPLANATORY ANSWERS

1. Cournot's Duopoly Model

Antoine Augustin Cournot, *a French economist,* developed the earliest duopoly model in 1838. Cournot illustrated his model with the example of two firms selling homogeneous product under zero cost of production.

Assumptions:

1. There are two firms (firm A & firm B) in the market.
2. Both firms are selling homogeneous product *i.e.* mineral water.
3. They sell their output in the market with straight line downward sloping demand curve.

4. Cost of production is zero *i.e.* marginal cost (MC) = 0.
5. The two firms adjust the output and not the prices.
6. Each firm acts on the assumption that its rival holds its output constant (Behavioural assumption).
7. Both firms decide their output in order to maximize their profits.

Cournot solution is stable in which each firm sells **one-third** of the total market demand, at a common price. Cournot's model can be extended beyond duopoly (where there are more than two sellers). Thus if there are three sellers, the total output would be **three-fourth** of the total market demand and each firm will sell one-fourth of the total market demand. When there are 'n' numbers of sellers in the market, then each seller will sell $1/(n + 1)$ of the total market demand and jointly they will sell $n/(n + 1)$ of the market demand. Thus, as the number of firms in the industry is increased, total quantity supplied increases and hence the price is lower.

2. **The Shape of Supply Curves:** Because the substitution effect and the income effect work in opposite directions, the labour supply curve can slope either upward or downward. The supply curve slopes upward if the substitution effect dominates—that is, as the wage rises, individuals work more because the price of leisure (the opportunity cost of not working) rises. The labour supply curve slopes downward if the income effect dominates—as the wage rises, individuals choose to work less because they can earn as much if not more money by working fewer hours. Several possibilities for the shape of a labour supply curve are illustrated in Figure 1.

Moreover, the same supply curve may slope upward for some range of wages and downward for another range. For example, at high wage levels—when people earn enough to take long vacations—the income effect may dominate. At lower wages, the substitution effect may be dominant, which then would result in a **backward-bending labour supply curve,** as shown in Figure 2.

Three Labour Supply Curves

The three curves differ in the relative strength of the income and substitution effects. The labour supply curve on the left slopes upward because the substitution effect is stronger than the income effect. For the curve on the right, the income effect is stronger than the substitution effect. For the vertical curve in the middle, the two effects are the same.

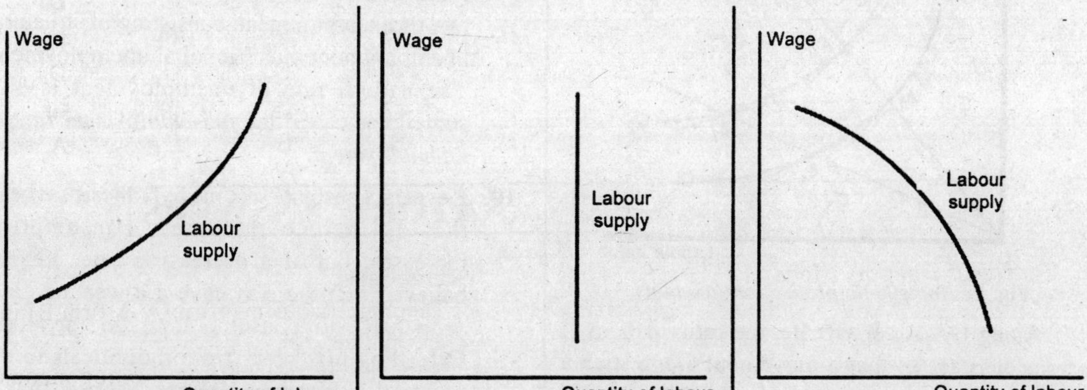

Fig. 1

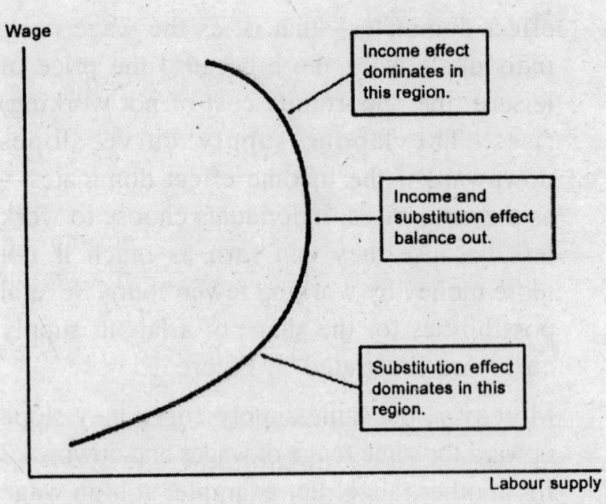

Fig. 2

5. A production function is *homothetic* if MP_L/MP_K does not change with any proportionate change in L and K. We will explain the concept of a homothetic production function in terms of two isoquants. In Figure 1, we have two isoquants. Draw any lines OA_1A_2 and OB_1B_2 through the origin. Then the production function is said to be homothetic if

slope of Q_1 at A_1 = slope of Q_2 at A_2

and

slope of Q_1 at B_1 = slope of Q_2 at B_2

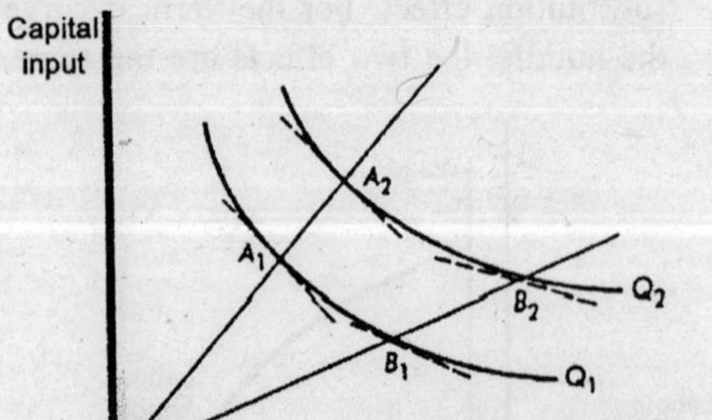

Fig. 1: *Homothetic production functions*

Along OA_1A_2 or OB_1B_2, the ratio of L to K is constant so that a movement along such a ray represents a proportionate change in L and K. If the slope of the isoquants are equal along any ray, then MP_L/MP_K must not change with a proportionate change in L and K. But since the input price ratio is constant, all the isocost lines are parallel. Homotheticity now requires that all tangencies between the isocosts and isoquants lie along a single ray from the origin so that the long-run expansion path coincides with such a ray.

A special case of homothetic production function is the *homogeneous* production function. With reference to Figure 1, the production function is homogeneous if, in addition, $OA_2/OA_1 = OB_2/OB_1$.

7. The long-run average cost curve is the envelope of the short-run average total cost curves. Short-run average total cost is always greater than or equal to long-run average cost.

Plant capacity is defined as the output corresponding to the minimum point on the short-run average total cost curve. At the point of tangency between a short-run average total cost curve and the long-run average cost curve, short-run marginal cost equals long-run marginal cost. Economies of scale cause the *LRAC* curve to slope downward, whereas diseconomies of scale cause the *LRAC* curve to slope upward. External economies of scale cause the *LRAC* curve to shift downward and external diseconomies cause it to shift upward.

9. **Natural rate of unemployment:** The normal rate of unemployment, consisting of structural unemployment plus frictional unemployment. The natural rate of unemployment is also sometimes called the *full-employment rate of unemployment.*

10. Keyners's absolute income hypothesis suggests that as income increases, consumption increases, but at a decreasing rate. Keynes believed that the rich have a lower marginal propensity to consume than do the poor. Extending his theory from individuals to the national economy, Keynes argued that a nation's marginal propensity to consume depends on the absolute level of national income.

13. A special case is where the demand for money demand is perfectly interest elastic. Keynes referred to this situation as the liquidity trap. The argument is that once interest rates reach a certain low level, the opportunity cost of holding cash falls to zero and bonds become unattractive. This does not have to be at a zero interest rate, but just at a rate where the opportunity cost of holding money is below the value of liquidity. This is why it is called the liquidity trap—the interest rare is so low that people are unwilling to forgo the benefits of holding money by investing in bonds.

In this case, the demand for money schedule is completely horizontal. So, when the interest rate has fallen to a sufficiently low level, changes in the real money supply will not change the equilibrium interest rate. The LM curve becomes horizontal and invariant to changes in the money supply. This is when the liquidity trap is reached.

15. Determinants of Money Demand

The demand for money varies directly with scale variables (income and wealth) and negatively with the returns on alternative assets. The alternative assets, which could serve as a store of value, include bonds, equity and even the durable goods. However, durable goods are only a rather poor substitute for money and, thus, the return on them (capital appreciation or inflation) is often ignored. Therefore, the interest rate on bonds (and return on equity), is considered as the negative factor in the money demand function.

It is instructive to note here that the interest rate relevant in the money demand function is the nominal rate (not the real interest rate), as it is the nominal rate alone that clearly measures the yield on bonds.

17. The vicious circle of poverty

The idea of a vicious circle of poverty is closely associated with the work of Ragnar Nurkse who published his influential book *Problems of Capital Formation in Underdeveloped Countries* in 1953.

Nurkse argued that a vicious circle was a 'circular constellation of forces tending to act and react upon one another in such a way as to keep a poor country in a state of poverty'. The most widely quoted example of a vicious circle is with respect to capital accumulation. The low level of real, income in 'underdeveloped areas' resulted in a limited capacity to save and was itself a reflection of low productivity. Low productivity in turn was the result of the lack of capital which was the result of the limited capacity to save. The circle was thus complete (see Figure 1).

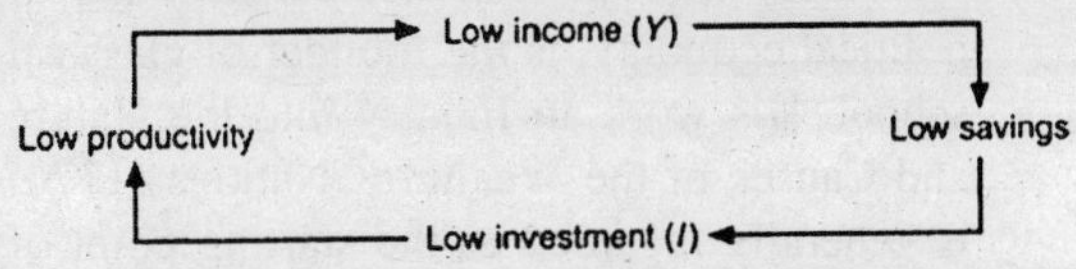

Fig. 1: *Vicious circle - capital accumulation*

On the demand side, the inducement to invest may be low because of the limited size of the market, itself the result of low real income resulting from low productivity. Productivity is low because of the limited use of capital in production which in turn may be at least partly caused by the low inducement to invest (see Figure 2).

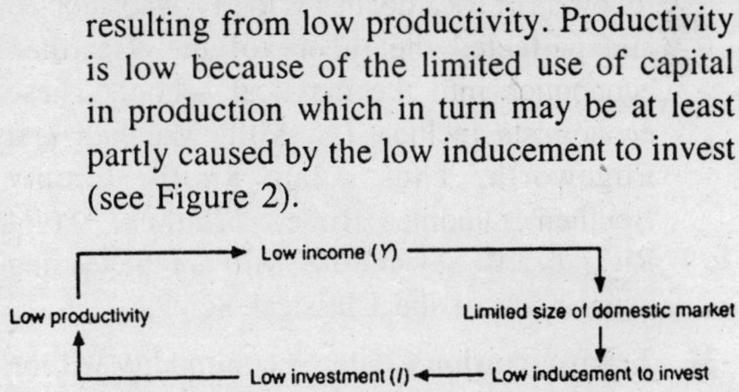

Fig. 2: *Vicious circle - demand side*

18. The Kuznets "Inverted U-Shaped Hypothesis"

Simon Kuznets was one of the first people to explore the relationship between economic growth and income distribution. In a landmark study published in 1955, he formulated the hypothesis that the least developed of the developing countries, that is, those whose economies are mainly in the traditional sector (agriculture), generally will have a more even income distribution than those developing countries that are more advanced in modernizing their economies.

The basic reasoning behind this is that wages in the modern sector will be substantially higher than in the traditional sector, thereby creating greater inequality. However, when the former developing country becomes developed, and the modern sector dominates the economy, most of the population will depend on income from the modern sector and the income distribution will tend toward more equality. This has become the "inverted U-shaped hypothesis".

20. The Classical School

Adam Smith (1723-90), also called father of political economy, is the founder of classical school. His work an Inquiry into the Nature and Causes of the Wealth of Nations (1776) is generally regarded as the starting point of Classical school. According to Keynes, the classical economists was a name invented by Marx to cover Ricardo and James Mill and their predecessors. But Keynes included the followers of Ricardo, that is to say, who adopted and perfected the theory of the Ricardian economics into the classical school. These economists include J.S. Mill, Marshall and Edgeworth. Thus Adam Smith, Jeremy Benthem, Thomas Robert Malthus, David Ricardo, J.B. Say and J.S. Mill are the leading economists of the Classical School.

31. Transportation Costs: A commodity will be traded only if the pretrade price difference between the two nations exceeds the cost of transporting it between them. In addition, when trade is in equilibrium, the price of the traded commodity in the importing nation exceeds the price of the same commodity in the exporting nation by the cost of transportation.

32. Growth in Factor Supplies Through Time: If technology remains the same but the factors of production available to a nation increase, the nation's production possibilities curve shifts outward. This shift is uniform or symmetrical (so that the new production possibilities curve has the same shape as the old one) if labour and capital grow in the same proportion. This is called *balanced growth.* If only the nation's supply of labour increases or if its supply of labour increases proportionately more than its supply of capital, then the nation's production possibilities curve shifts more along the axis measuring the L-intensive commodity than along the axis measuring the K-intensive commodity. The opposite shift occurs if only the nation's supply of capital increases or if its supply of capital increases proportionately more than its supply of labour.

According to the *Rybczynski theorem,* at constant relative commodity prices, the growth of only one factor leads to an absolute expansion in the output of the commodity using the growing factor intensively and to an absolute reduction in the output of the commodity using the nongrowing factor intensively.

33. The Foreign Exchange Rates: The *foreign exchange rate* is the domestic currency price of the foreign currency. This exchange rate is kept the same in all parts of the market by arbitrage. *Foreign exchange arbitrage* refers to the purchasing of a foreign currency where its price is low and selling it where the price is high. A rise in the exchange rate refers to a *depreciation* or a reduction in the value of the domestic currency in relation to the foreign currency. A fall in the exchange rate refers to an *appreciation* or an increase in the value of the domestic currency. Since a nation's currency can depreciate against some currencies and appreciate against others, an *effective exchange rate* is usually calculated. This is a weighted average of the nation's exchange rates.

35. The Monetary approach stresses that the balance of payments is essentially a monetary phenomenon. To be specific, it claims that money plays a vital role in determining the balance of payments.

36. General Equilibrium Analysis of a Tariff in a Large Nation

The imposition of a tariff by a large nation improves its terms of trade, reduces the volume of trade and may improve the nation's welfare. However, since the improvement in the nation's position comes at the expense of its trade partner, the trade partner is likely to retaliate and, in the end, both nations usually lose. These effects are best analyzed with offer curves (see Example). In the vast majority of cases the Stolper-Samuelson theorem also holds for large nations.

Example: Assume that both the U.S. and the U.K. are now large nations and affect world prices. Under free trade, offer curves U.S. and U.K. in Fig. 1 cross at point E giving the equilibrium $P_C/P_W = P_E = 1$, at which 60C are exchanged for 60W. If the U.S. now imposes a 100% import tariff on cloth, offer curve U.S. rotates down to offer curve U.S.′, which is at all points twice as distant from the wheat axis as offer curve U.S. This happens because with a 100% tariff on cloth imports, the U.S. now wants 100% more, or twice as much, cloth as before for each quantity of wheat exported. With offer curve U.S.′, the terms of trade of the U.S. improve to $P_W/P_C = 1/P_{E'} = ¼ = 1.25$, but the volume of trade declines to 40W for 50C. If the positive effect on the U.S.'s welfare resulting from the better terms of trade exceeds the negative effect from the reduced volume of trade, the U.S.'s welfare will also be greater. Starting from the free-trade position as the U.S. imposes higher tariffs, the U.S.'s welfare will increase up to a point (the *optimum tariff*) and decline thereafter. However, since the improved position of the U.S. comes at the expense of the U.K., the U.K. is likely to retaliate. If the U.K. imposed a 100% import tariff on wheat, the offer curve of the U.K. would rotate up and cross offer curve U.S. at point E″. Then both nations would be worse off than under free trade.

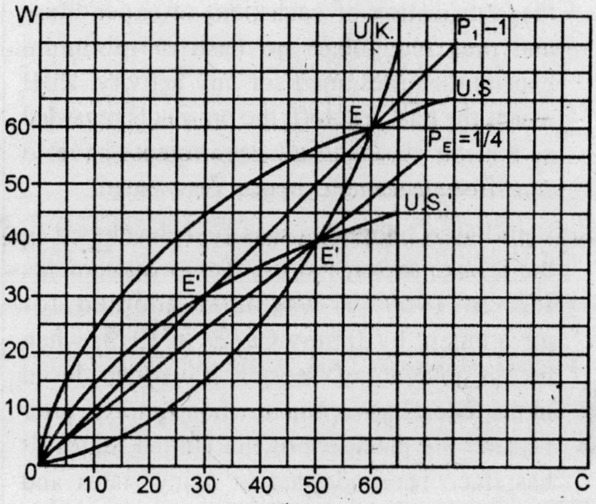

Fig. 1

38. Taxation is one of the oldest sources of revenue of government. In India, since independence, tax revenue has remained amongst the chief sources of finances of the federal government. The government, from time to time, appointed committees/commissions to mobilize more and more resources through taxes by introducing new taxes and restructuring the existing ones. During pre-reform period, the commissions/committees include Taxation Enquiry Commission of 1953-54 (chaired by Dr. John Mathai); Nicholas Kaldor Committee (1956); Bhuthalingam Committee (1967); Direct Taxes Enquiry Committee (Chaired by Dr. Wanchoo, 1971); Committee on Taxation of Agricultural Wealth and Income (1972) chaired by Dr. K.N. Raj; Indirect Taxation Enquiry Committee (1978), under the chairmanship of Dr. L.K. Jha. The Committee on Tax Reform (1991) under the chairmanship of Raja J. Chelliah; Advisory Group on Tax Policy and Tax Administration for the Tenth Plan constituted by the Planning Commission in 2000; Task Forces on Direct and Indirect Taxes (2002) under the chairmanship of Vijay L. Kelkar, are important committees constituted by the Central government for reforming tax administration during post-reform period.

39. Peter A. Pyhrr was the father of the concept 'Zero Based Budget'(ZBB). ZBB insists for the justification of each item of expenditure and thus recognizes no base or minimum expenditure presumed for any activity. ZBB means the past is cutoff; the present is regarded as a clean state and all departments have to start from a scratch (hence Zero-base).

Zero-based budgeting was first developed in the private sector, namely Texas Instruments Inc. in 1969. It was later adopted for government by Jimmy Carter in 1973, when he was governor of Georgia. It was introduced in the federal government when Jimmy Carter became the president of the United States. It has since been adopted in many states and local governments in the U.S.A.

43. Colin Clark has suggested that the safe upper limit of taxation is 25 per cent of the national production. The reasons for this limit are; When taxes rise too high, many people do not work efficiently. Production is therefore affected and the shortage of goods tends to lead to inflationary rise in prices. Thus, inflation and depreciation of the value of currency would take place, if inflation crosses the limit of 25 per cent.

45. Mean $\mu = np$

Variance $\sigma^2 = npq$

According to the question,

$$np + npq = 15 \quad ...(i)$$

and $$np \times npq = 54 \quad ...(ii)$$

From equation (*i*) and (*ii*)

$$(np - npq)^2 = (np + npq)^2 - 4n^2p^2q$$
$$= (15)^2 - 4 \times 54$$
$$= 225 - 216$$
$$= 9$$

$$\therefore \quad np - npq = 3 \quad (iii)$$

{As mean > variance, so –3 is neglected}

Now, from (*i*) and (*iii*), we get

$$np = 9 \text{ and } npq = 6$$

$$q = \frac{6}{9} = \frac{2}{3},$$

$$p = 1 - q = 1 - \frac{2}{3} = \frac{1}{3}$$

from $$np = 9$$

$$n \times \frac{1}{3} = 9$$

$$n = 27.$$

46. Properties of Regression Coefficients

The main properties of the regression coefficients are as follows:

1. **Coefficient of correlation is the geometric mean of the regression coefficients, *i.e.*,**

$$r = \sqrt{bxy \times byx}$$

2. **Both the regression coefficients must have the same algebraic signs:** The means either both regression coefficients will be either positive or negative. In other words, when one regression coefficient is negative, the other would be also negative. It is never possible that one regression coefficient is negative while the other is positive.

3. **The coefficient of correlation will have the same sign as that of regression coefficients:** If both regression coefficient are negative, then the correlation coefficient would be negative. And if *byx* and *bxy* have positive signs, then *r* will also take plus sign.

4. **Both the regression coefficients cannot be greater than unity:** If one regression coefficient of *y* on *x* is greater than unity, then the regression coefficient of *x* on *y* must be less than unity. This is because

$$r = \sqrt{byx \cdot bxy} = \pm 1$$

and never greater than one. If both the regression coefficients happen to be more than 1 then their geometric mean will exceed 1 which will not give the correlation coefficients whose value never exceeds 1.

5. **Arithmetic mean of two regression coefficients is either equal to or greater than the correlation coefficient:** In terms of the formula:

$$\frac{byx + bxy}{2} \geq r$$

6. **Change of origin does not affect regression coefficients but change in scale does affect regression coefficients.**

47. The χ^2 test is widely used by social scientists to examine the relationship between two qualitative variables. The test is performed under the assumption that there is no association between the variables concerned. A high value of χ^2 shows the presence of association between the variables and a low value shows absence of association.

48. Random and non-random Sampling

There are two categories of sampling: *random (probability) and non-random (non-probability) sampling,* with a number of sampling techniques contained within the two categories.

In a probability sample, each member in the population has a known probability of being selected. Probability sampling methods include *simple random sampling, systematic random sampling, stratified random sampling* and *cluster sampling.* If random sampling method is used, an investigator can use a relatively small sample to make inferences about an arbitrarily large population. Randomness is an essential part of the protection against selection bias. To ensure true randomness, the method of selection must be independent of human judgement.

In non-probability sampling, members are selected from the population in some non-random manner. These include *convenience sampling, judgement sampling* and *quota sampling.*

50. Fisher's Ideal Index Number

The Geometric mean of Laspeyre's Index number and Paasche's Index number is known as Fisher's Ideal Index number after the name of Irving Fisher.

Fisher's Ideal Index Number (I_{01})

$$= \sqrt{\text{Laspeyre's Index number} \times \text{Paasche's Index number}}$$

$$= 100\sqrt{\frac{\Sigma p_1 q_0}{\Sigma p_0 q_0} \times \frac{\Sigma p_1 q_1}{\Sigma p_0 q_1}}$$

Fisher's ideal quantity index number

$$= Q_{10} = 100 \times \sqrt{\frac{\Sigma q_1 p_0}{\Sigma q_0 p_0} \times \frac{\Sigma q_1 p_1}{\Sigma q_0 p_1}}$$

Fisher's Index Number is Called Ideal–Why

Fisher's index number is called ideal because of the following reasons:

1. Geometric mean is useful in averaging percentages and ratios. Index numbers indicate percentage changes and Fisher's ideal index number is a Geometric mean between Laspeyre's and Passche's index numbers.
2. It takes into account both Current Year as well as Base Year quantities.
3. It satisfies certain mathematical tests such as time reversal and factor reversal tests.
4. It is free from bias upwards as well as downwards (Please note that Laspeyre's index numbers suffer from upward bias whereas Paasche's index suffer from downward bias.

PAPER–III

Note: *This paper contains seventy five (75) objective type questions of two (2) marks each. All questions are compulsory.*

1. Who is widely known as the founder of Austrian School?

A. W.S. Jevons B. Leon Walras

C. Knut Wicksell D. Karl Menger

2. For substitutes, cross elasticity of demand is

A. Positive

B. Negative

C. Zero

D. Always less than one

3. Reservation wage means

A. Fair wage at which workers are willing to work

B. Subsistence wage at which an individual is willing to work

C. Minimum wage at which an individual is willing to work

D. Maximum wage at which an individual is willing to work

4. An economic region of production consists of

A. The positively sloped portions of all isoquants

B. The negatively sloped portions of all isoquants

C. The middle of all isoquants

D. The highest points of all isoquants

5. Elasticity of substitution is

A. The substitution of cheaper inputs for dearer inputs.

B. The rate at which the inputs (labour and capital) are substituted.

C. A measure of the responsiveness of input ratio to a change in input-price ratio.

D. A measure of the responsiveness of input prices and the substitution of the cheaper inputs.

6. In game theory model, strategies include

I. The potential choices to change the price

II. To develop new or differentiated products

III. To introduce a new or different advertisement campaign

IV. To build excess capacity

Codes:

A. II and III are correct.

B. I and II are correct.

C. I, II and III are correct.

D. All are correct.

7. Pareto optimum implies

A. A resource allocation for which a Pareto improvement is possible.

B. A resource allocation in which social improvement is possible.

C. A resource allocation for which atleast one is better off and no body is worse off.

D. A resource allocation for which there are no Pareto improvements.

8. A model of oligopoly in which one business sets output before the other business do is

A. Cournot oligopoly model

B. Bertrand oligopoly model

C. Stackelberg oligopoly model

D. Chamberlin oligopoly model

9. Assertion (A): Sunk costs are not relevant to economic decisions.

Reason (R): The opportunity cost of such resources is zero.

Codes:

A. Both (A) and (R) are correct and (R) is the correct explanation of (A).

B. (A) is correct, but (R) is not correct.

C. Both (A) and (R) are correct, but (R) is incorrect explanation of (A).

D. (R) is correct, but (A) is incorrect.

10. Match the statement given in List-I with that given in List-II and choose the correct code:

List-I	*List-II*
I. Employment and output are determined solely by the factors operating on the supply side of the labour market, according to	a. Karl Marx
II. The term 'classical' was coined by	b. Classical economists
III. The classical production function was used to derive the aggregate supply function by	c. J.M. Keynes
IV. A linear aggregate consumption function was used by	d. Keynesian economists

Select correct code for the correct answer from the following:

Codes:

	I	II	III	IV
A.	b	c	a	d
B.	d	a	b	c
C.	a	c	d	b
D.	b	a	c	d

11. The permanent income hypothesis is consistent with cross-section and time-series data because

A. Higher-income households are savers since their current income includes positive transitory components.

B. Higher-income households are savers since their current income includes negative transitory components.

C. Lower-income households are savers since their current income includes negative transitory components.

D. Lower-income households are savers since their current income includes positive transitory components.

12. Which of the following statements is true?

A. Net investment is more stable than gross investment when replacement investment is constant over time.

B. Gross investment is more stable than net investment when replacement investment is constant over time.

C. Replacement investment equals capital-output ratio times the expected increase in output ($v - \Delta_y$).

D. Net investment is greater than $v - \Delta_y$ when the capital-output ratio (v) decreases.

13. Match the demand for money approach given in List-I with their propounders given in List-II and choose the correct code:

List-I	*List-II*
I. Inventory Theoretic Approach	a. Milton Friedman
II. Cash Balance Approach	b. James Cohin
III. Portfolio Optimization Approach	c. W.J. Baumol
IV. Quantity Theory of Money	d. Cambridge Economists

Codes:

	I	II	III	IV
A.	d	b	c	a
B.	d	a	c	b
C.	c	d	b	a
D.	b	d	c	a

14. Assertion (A): According to Keynes, individuals hold either cash or all bonds.

Reasoning (R): Because, according to him, the speculative demand for money is associated with uncertainty.

Codes:

A. Both (A) and (R) are correct and (R) is the correct explanation of (A).

B. Both (A) and (R) are correct, but (R) is not the correct explanation of (A).

C. (A) is correct, but (R) is incorrect.

D. Both (A) and (R) are incorrect.

15. Which one of the following is not a correct interpretation of the Golden Rule of Accumulation?

It is that capital per person at which

A. Savings per person and investment per person are maximum.

B. Marginal productivity of capital is equal to the rate of growth of population.

C. Marginal productivity of capital is equal to saving ratio.

D. Elasticity of output with respect to capital is equal to saving ratio.

16. For particular high values of marginal propensity to consume and the accelerator coefficient, explosive non-oscillatory cycles will occur in the model of the business cycles propounded by

A. Paul A. Samuelson

B. J.R. Hicks

C. Nicholas Kaldor

D. All of the above

17. In the context of IS-LM framework, which of the following statements is false?

A. IS curve is steeper, the lower the value of the Keynesian multiplier and the lower the interest sensitiveness of investment demand.

B. Crowding out is effective when money demand is perfectly interest inelastic and investment is perfectly interest elastic.

C. The fiscal policy is least effective and the monetary policy is most effective, the higher the interest sensitiveness of money demand and the lower the interest sensitiveness of investment demand.

D. The Pigou effect restores the effectiveness of monetary policy even under the liquidity trap.

18. Assertion (A): The fiscal policy is less effective in an open economy than in a closed economy.

Reasoning (R): Because the value of the multiplier in an open economy is less than that in a closed economy.

Codes:

A. Both (A) and (R) are correct and (R) is the correct explanation of (A).
B. Both (A) and (R) are correct, but (R) is not the correct explanation of (A).
C. (A) is correct, but (R) is incorrect.
D. Both (A) and (R) are incorrect.

19. Embodied technical change model is based on which production function?

A. CES B. Cobb-Douglas
C. Translog D. VES

20. "A technical change is neutral if at a constant rate of profit or interest, the capital output ratio also remains constant." This concept was propounded by

A. Kaldor B. Hicks
C. Solow D. Harrod

21. Endogenous growth models have been developed by

I. Kenneth J. Arrow
II. Paul M. Romer
III. Robert E. Lucas
IV. R.M. Solow

Codes:

A. I and II B. III and IV
C. I, II and III D. II, III and IV

22. Kaldor's growth model is based on the following assumptions :

I. Output consists of wages and profits only.
II. Investment output ratio is an independent variable.
III. MP_S and MP_C are constant.
IV. There is less than full employment.

Codes:

A. I and IV B. II and III
C. III and IV D. I and II

23. Assertion (A): Innovations in one field rarely induce innovations in related fields.

Reason (R): Once an innovation becomes profitable, other entrepreneurs follow it in "Swarm like clusters".

Codes:

A. (A) is not correct and (R) is correct.
B. (A) is correct and (R) is not correct.
C. Both (A) and (B) are not correct.
D. Both (A) and (R) are correct.

24. Arrange the concepts of Endogenous growth model in a sequential order :

I. Production of ideas by research.
II. Learning by doing.
III. Learning by investment.
IV. Learning by watching.

Codes:

A. III, I, II, IV B. IV, III, I, II
C. I, II, IV, III D. II, IV, III, I

25. Match the items in List-I with List-II:

List-I	*List-II*
I. Increasing outlay on education leads to rapid Economic Growth	a. C.P. Blacker
II. Spread Effects	b. Kaldor
III. Theory of Demographic Transition : Five Stages of Population Growth	c. T.W. Schultz & others
IV. Widows Curse	d. Gunnar Myrdal

Codes:

	I	II	III	IV
A.	a	b	d	c
B.	b	a	c	d
C.	d	c	b	a
D.	c	d	a	b

26. Match the items in List-I with List-II :

List-I	*List-II*
I. Capitalist rules of the game	a. Karl Marx
II. Embodied Technical Change	b. UNDP
III. Industrial Reserve Army	c. Robert Solow
IV. Human Development Report	d. Joan Robinson

Codes:

	I	II	III	IV
A.	c	d	b	a
B.	a	b	d	c
C.	b	a	c	d
D.	d	c	a	b

27. **Assertion (A):** Dependence of Less Developed Countries (LDCs) on Developed Countries (DCs) is the main cause for the underdevelopment of the former.

Reason (R): "This is because of historical evolution of a highly unequal international capitalist system of rich-poor country relationships."

Codes:

A. (A) is correct and (R) is the correct reason for (A).
B. (A) is incorrect, but (R) is correct.
C. Both (A) and (R) are incorrect.
D. Both (A) and (R) are correct.

28. Which of the following is relevant for Wagner's Law of Increasing State Activities?

A. Public expenditure does not increase in a smooth and continuous manner.
B. Public expenditure increases in step like fashion.
C. There are inherent tendencies for the activities of the Government to increase both intensively and extensively.
D. Economy grows faster than the governmental sector.

29. The share of the tax borne by the seller will be larger

A. if the demand for the product is less elastic.
B. if the demand for the product is inelastic.
C. if the demand for the product has greater elasticity.
D. if the elasticity of supply of the product is larger.

30. The non-plan revenue expenditure of Central Government on Revenue Account include:

I. Interest payments
II. Subsidies
III. Grants-in-aid
IV. Loans to Public Enterprises

Codes:

A. I and II are correct.
B. I, II and III are correct.
C. I, II and IV are correct.
D. I, II, III and IV are correct.

31. The Constitution of India provides for transfer of resources from Centre to States in the form of

I. Tax sharing
II. Loans
III. Grants-in-aid
IV. Grants for implementation of Five Year Plans

Codes:

A. I, II and III are correct.
B. I and III are correct.
C. I, III and IV are correct.
D. All are correct.

32. Identify the correct chronology of implementation of the following taxes in India:

I. Service taxes
II. Fringe benefits tax
III. Personal income-tax
IV. Expenditure tax

Codes:

A. III, I, II, IV B. III, II, I, IV
C. III, IV, I, II D. IV, III, II, I

33. The taxes which Kaldor proposed for India in 1956 to check tax evasion, supplementing income tax are

I. Capital gains tax
II. Annual tax on wealth
III. Personal expenditure tax
IV. Gift tax

Codes:

A. II and III are correct.
B. I, II and III are correct.
C. II, III and IV are correct.
D. All are correct.

34. According to the cost based definition of dumping, dumping occurs when a firm sells a product abroad at a price that is less than

A. Average Total Cost
B. Average Variable Cost

C. Marginal Cost
D. Average Fixed Cost

35. Select the correct statement out of the following:
A. Multilateral Trade Negotiations are a process of increasing tariffs to trade among member countries.
B. Multilateral Trade Negotiations are a process of increasing non-tariff barriers to trade.
C. Multilateral Trade Negotiations are a process of increasing tariffs but decreasing non-tariff barriers to trade.
D. Multilateral Trade Negotiations are a process of reducing tariff and non-tariff barriers to trade among member countries of GATT or WTO.

36. Consider the following statements: As per the Trade Related Investment Measures (TRIMs)
1. all restrictions on foreign capital companies are to be scrapped.
2. no restrictions will be imposed on any area of investment.
3. imports of raw materials are to be allowed freely.
4. export of part of the output will be mandatory.

Which of the above statements are correct?

Codes:
A. 1, 3 and 4 B. 1, 2 and 3
C. 1, 2 and 4 D. 2, 3 and 4

37. The fundamental cause for the collapse of the Brettonwoods System was
A. the liquidity problem
B. the adjustment problem
C. the confidence problem
D. all of the above

38. Match List-I with List-II and select the correct answer using the codes given below the lists:

List-I	*List-II*
I. Forward exchange	a. A device of covering exchange risk against the price rise of foreign currency.
II. Hedging	b. A contract to buy and sell foreign exchange against another currency at some fixed rate in the future at a price agreed upon now.
III. Arbitrage	c. The movement of exchange rate between two limits set by the cost of moving gold from one country to another.
IV. Specie points	d. A mechanism which merges two separate physical markets into a single market in economic sense.

Codes:

	I	II	III	IV
A.	d	c	b	a
B.	b	a	d	c
C.	d	a	b	c
D.	b	c	d	a

39. Arrange the following WTO ministerials in the chronological order:
I. Seattle II. Cancun
III. Singapore IV. Hong-Kong

Codes:
A. III, IV, I, II B. III, I, II, IV
C. II, III, IV, I D. II, IV, I, III

40. If Hong-Kong and Taiwan have identical production possibility curves that are subject to increasing opportunity costs, then
A. trade would depend on differences in demand conditions.
B. trade would depend on economies of large scale production.
C. trade would depend on the use of different currencies.
D. there would be no basis for gainful trade.

41. Trade deflection is the diversion of exports to a country within a free trade area that has
A. higher tariffs on goods

B. highest tariffs on exports
C. lower tariffs on goods
D. none of the above

42. The formula that shows the correct relationship between:
(*i*) Total demand and time liabilities (L)
(*ii*) Excess Reserves (ER)
(*iii*) Current-account balances with other banks (CB)
(*iv*) Investment in unencumbered government and other approved securities (I*)
(*v*) Statutory Liquidity Ratio (SLR) is

Codes:

A. $SLR = \frac{EL + I^* - CB}{L}$

B. $SLR = \frac{ER + I^*}{L + CB}$

C. $SLR = \frac{L + CB + ER}{I^*}$

D. $SLR = \frac{ER + I^* + CB}{L}$

43. Consider the following:
I. RBI II. SBI
III. NABARD IV. LIC

The financial intermediaries among the above are:

Codes:
A. All the four B. II, III, IV
C. II, III D. II, IV

44. Real balance effect relates to
A. the effect which a change in value of the real cash balances held by the public produces in the economy.
B. the effect which a change in value of the real cash balances held by the commercial banks produces in the economy.
C. the effect which a change in value of the real cash balances held by the multi-national banks produces in the economy.
D. the effect which a change in value of the real cash balances held by the NBFIs produces in the economy.

45. Assertion (A): Reserve Bank of India raises money supply through purchase of securities in the money market.

Reason (R) : Increase in money supply may result in the expansion of investment and employment.

Codes:
A. Both (A) and (R) are correct and (R) is the correct explanation of (A).
B. Both (A) and (R) are correct, but (R) is not the correct explanation of (A).
C. Both (A) and (R) are incorrect.
D. (A) is correct, but (R) is incorrect.

46. Match the items in List-I against the items in List-II and select the answer from the codes given below:

List-I	*List-II*
I. Simple Deposit System	a. 100% backing of metallic reserves
II. Maximum Fiduciary System	b. Certain percentage of total notes is kept in specific reserves.
III. Percentage Deposit System	c. Maximum note issuing is statutorily fixed.
IV. Bonus Deposit System	d. Reserves of IOUs and short period loans.

Codes:

	I	II	III	IV
A.	c	d	b	a
B.	a	b	c	d
C.	b	a	d	c
D.	a	c	b	d

47. As per Micro, Small and Medium Enterprises Development Act, 2006, micro enterprises are those with investments:
A. < ₹ 25 lakhs
B. ₹ 25 lakhs to ₹ 5 crores
C. ₹ 5 crores to ₹ 10 crores
D. > ₹ 10 crores

48. Match the items given in List-I with those in List-II:

List-I	*List-II*
I. Rangrajan Committee	a. Report on small Industries
II. Karve Committee	b. Disinvestment of shares in PSE's
III. Dr. R.K. Hazari Committee	c. Review of the Policy for Public Enterprises
IV. Arjun Sengupta Committee	d. Industrial Licensing

Codes:

	I	II	III	IV
A.	a	c	d	b
B.	c	b	d	a
C.	b	a	d	c
D.	b	d	a	c

49. The Eleventh Five Year Plan aimed at generating

A. 15 million work opportunities
B. 35 million work opportunities
C. 58 million work opportunities
D. 100 million work opportunities

50. The Unorganised Workers Social Security Act came in existence in the year

A. 2001 B. 2005
C. 2008 D. 2012

51. The share of industry in India's GDP in the year 2006-07 is estimated at

A. 20 % B. 15 %
C. 45 % D. 26 %

52. According to Hotelling rule about the exhaustible natural resources, which of the following is used for price variation of the exhaustible natural resources:

A. Rate of interest
B. Labour cost
C. Rent and royalties of mines
D. Production cost and royalty of mines

53. Suggest the correct answer about the 'Pigovian Tax':

I. Provides solution in order to 'internalize' the total costs of an activity into the market.
II. Provides solution to reduce the production of pollutants through public policy.
III. It helps in increasing the factor productivity in the real sector.
IV. It acts like a severance tax.

Codes:

A. I & II B. III & IV
C. I, II & IV D. I, II, III & IV

54. Which of the following is correct about the Contingent Valuation Method (CVM) used in Environmental Economics?

A. It is used only for pollutants.
B. It is used only for items with positive utilities.
C. It is used for items under market failures.
D. It is used only for natural resources.

55. Natural growth of population is the outcome of the following:

I. Crude Birth Rate
II. Crude Death Rate
III. Migration
IV. Marriages

Codes:

A. Only I B. Only III
C. II & IV D. I & II

56. Identify the correct statement about the relationship between total fertility rate and gross-reproduction rate:

A. TFR > GRR is possible.
B. TFR = GRR is possible.
C. TFR < GRR is possible.
D. All the above is possible.

57. Why does the share of agriculture in developing economies decline when national economy is growing rapidly?

I. Food becomes like inferior commodity.
II. Growth of agriculture cannot be very fast.
III. Industrial sector grows faster.
IV. Public spending on the farm factor is not enough.

Codes:

A. I, II, III & IV B. II, III & IV
C. II & III D. I, II & IV

58. Share of fishing in the GDP of India in recent years has been around

A. 0.8 per cent B. 1.2 per cent
C. 1.7 per cent D. 2.1 per cent

59. What is the economic cost of foodgrains to the Food Corporation of India?

A. Minimum support price and bonus paid to farmers + transportation costs.
B. Minimum support price + bonus + interest cost.
C. Minimum support price + bonus + procurement incidentals + charges for godowns.
D. Minimum support price (including bonus, if any) + procurement incidentals + distribution cost.

60. What is meant by farm mechanization?

A. Using only machines for farm operations.
B. Replacement of biological sources of energy by the mechanical sources of energy for farm operations.
C. Using machines, tractors, tube wells, etc. for agricultural production.
D. Using machines, tractors, tube wells, fertilizers, etc. besides soil testing and certified seeds for agricultural production.

61. Inter-sectoral terms of trade in an economy refers to

A. ratio of prices received and paid by the farmers.
B. ratio of domestic and international price of farm commodities.
C. terms at which government purchases farm produce.
D. trade of industrial products in the foreign markets.

62. The utility function is given as U = $f(x, y)$, where U = total utility and x & y are two goods consumed. The budget constraint is given as C = $p_x x + p_y y$, where p_x and p_y are the prices of 'x' and 'y' respectively. The condition for maximisation of utility is

A. $\frac{\partial f}{\partial x} / \frac{\partial f}{\partial y} = \frac{p_y}{p_x}$ B. $\frac{\partial f}{\partial x} / \frac{\partial f}{\partial y} = \frac{p_x}{p_y}$

C. $\frac{\partial f}{\partial x} = \frac{\partial f}{\partial y} = \frac{p_x}{p_y}$ D. $\frac{\partial f}{\partial x} = \frac{\partial f}{\partial y} = \frac{p_y}{p_x}$

63. The total cost function and the market demand function of a competitive firm are C = $\frac{1}{3}x^3 - 10x^2 + 9x + 1000$ and $x = (12 - p)/9$ respectively. The level of output at which profits will be maximised?

A. 1 B. 2
C. 3 D. 4

64. An input-output model which has endogenous final demand vector is known as

A. Open Input-Output Model
B. Closed Input-Output Model
C. Static Input-Output Model
D. Dynamic Input-Output Model

65. Let the two regression lines be given as: $3x = 10 + 5y$ and $4y = 5 + 15x$. Then the correlation coefficient between x and y is

A. – 0.40 B. 0.40
C. 0.89 D. ± 1.05

66. The estimated regression equation of the form $y = \alpha_0 + \alpha_1 x_1 + \alpha_2 x_2 + e$ is $y = -6.79 + 1.79(x_1) + 0.97\, x_2$ and SE $(\alpha_0) = 1.32$, SE $(\alpha_1) = 0.41$ and SE $(\alpha_2) = 0.53$. To test $H_0 : \alpha_1 \neq 0$, the test statistic $| t |$ is equal to

A. 5.144 B. 4.366
C. 1.830 D. 3.377

67. Given that the Cobb-Douglas production function is:

$y = AL^{\alpha} K^{\beta}, \alpha, \beta > 0$

Match List-I with List-II and select the answer from the codes given below:

List-I	*List-II*
I. Increasing returns to scale	a. $\alpha + \beta = 1$
II. Decreasing returns to scale	b. $\alpha + \beta > 1$
III. Constant returns to scale	c. $\alpha + \beta < 1$
IV. Diminishing returns to factors	d. $\alpha, \beta < 1$

Codes:

	I	II	III	IV
A.	a	b	c	d
B.	a	c	d	b
C.	b	c	a	d
D.	d	b	c	a

68. In the presence of heteroscedasticity, the best linear unbiased estimators are provided by the method of

A. Ordinary Least Squares
B. Indirect Least Squares
C. Weighted Least Squares
D. Instrumental Variables

69. To test the stationarity of the series in time series analysis, the following test will be used:

A. Unit Root Test
B. Random Walk Test
C. Cochrane-Orcutt Iterative Procedure Test
D. Durbin-Watson Statistic Test

70. Match List-I with List-II and select the answer from the codes given below:

List-I	*List-II*
I. Koyck's Lagged Model	a. Adjustment Equation
II. Almon's Lagged Model	b. Geometric Progression
III. Nerlov's Model	c. Adaptative Expectation
IV. Cogan's Model	d. Approximation Polynomial

Codes:

	I	II	III	IV
A.	d	a	b	c
B.	b	c	d	a
C.	b	d	a	c
D.	d	a	c	b

71. Identify the Five Year Plans when actual growth realisation has been higher than the growth target:

I. Fifth Plan
II. Seventh Plan
III. Ninth Plan
IV. Tenth Plan

Codes:

A. I, II & III B. II, III & IV
C. I & II D. III & IV

72. Which of the following development programmes is receiving 100 per cent funding as centrally sponsored scheme from the Government of India?

I. Accelerated Power Development & Reform Programme (APDRM)
II. Rashtriya Krishi Vikas Yojana
III. National Social Assistance Programme (NSAP)
IV. Women & Child Development Programme

Codes:

A. I, II, III & IV B. I & II
C. III & IV D. I, II & III

73. Rank the States in descending order of their size of State Domestic Product at current prices in the recent years:

I. Karnataka II. Maharashtra
III. Uttar Pradesh IV. Tamil Nadu

Codes:

A. I, IV, III & II B. III, IV, I & II
C. II, IV, I & III D. II, III, IV & I

74. What has been the share of the 'food, beverages and tobacco' in the private final consumption expenditure in India in the recent years?

A. 25 per cent B. 33 per cent
C. 45 per cent D. 56 per cent

75. Find out the incorrect statements from the following statements:

I. Savings, credits and insurance are the parts of microfinance.
II. Share of agriculture in the GDP has come down to below 11 per cent in India recently.
III. CSO has revised the consumer price index series on new base 2011 = 100.
IV. Poverty estimation in India is done on NSSO data.

Codes:

A. I & IV B. I & II
C. I & III D. II & III

ANSWERS

1	2	3	4	5	6	7	8	9	10
D	A	C	B	C	D	D	C	A	D
11	**12**	**13**	**14**	**15**	**16**	**17**	**18**	**19**	**20**
A	B	*	C	A	A	C	B	B	D
21	**22**	**23**	**24**	**25**	**26**	**27**	**28**	**29**	**30**
C	D	A	D	D	D	C	C	C	B
31	**32**	**33**	**34**	**35**	**36**	**37**	**38**	**39**	**40**
A	C	D	A	D	B	D	B	B	A
41	**42**	**43**	**44**	**45**	**46**	**47**	**48**	**49**	**50**
C	D	D	A	B	D	A	C	C	C
51	**52**	**53**	**54**	**55**	**56**	**57**	**58**	**59**	**60**
D	A	C	C	D	A	A	A	D	B
61	**62**	**63**	**64**	**65**	**66**	**67**	**68**	**69**	**70**
A	A	C	B	B	B	C	C	A	C
71	**72**	**73**	**74**	**75**					
C	D	D	B	D					

SOME SELECTED EXPLANATORY ANSWERS

1. Austrian School of Economics

The Austrian School of economics was a name given to the group that formed around the leadership of Carl Menger at the University of Vienna, beginning in the 1870s. Menger's pre-eminence was established as a consequence of his publishing *Principles of Economics* in 1871. In this book Menger demonstrated, in contradiction to the British Classical School, that value was a relationship between the needs of individuals and the importance that they attached to the goods they believed would satisfy those needs. Value originated not in the good itself but in the subjective assessments of human beings. This insight, combined with his development of the notion that the value of an individual unit of a good declined as more units were acquired, led to Menger's being hailed, along with Jevons and Walras, as instigators of the marginal revolution.

Menger's initial subjectivist and marginalist perspective led him to develop theories of value, exchange and prices that seemed eminently compatible with similar developments in England and at Lausanne. It also inspired his two most famous associates, Friedrich von Wieser and Eugén von Böhm-Bawerk, to further develop aspects hinted at in Menger's work. Wieser developed the notion of opportunity cost, and extended marginalism to include a notion of diminishing marginal product of factors of production. Böhm-Bawerk is most noted for his development of a theory of capital that argued for the superior productivity of time-consuming methods of production, an approach inspired by Menger's discussion of capital as 'goods of a higher order'. Böhm-Bawerk's theory of capital later became the cornerstone of the Austrian theory of the business cycle as developed by a later generation of Austrian economists, Ludwig von Mises and Friedrich von Hayek.

The Austrian School has undergone significant evolution since the early days of Meneger, Wieser and Böhm-Bawerk. During the 1920s the dominant figure in Vienna was Ludwig von Mises, whose early work on money and credit established him as a rising star of the Austrian School. For more than a decade, Mises conducted a regular seminar from his offices at the Austrian Chamber of Commerce, which attracted virtually all of the important economists in Vienna at One time or another. Among the regular participants were Fritz Machlup, Oscar Morgenstern, Gottfried Haberler and Friedrich von Hayek. While Machlup, Morgenstern and Haberler all acknowledged their ties to Austrian ideas, it was Hayek who emerged in the 1930s, on his move to the London School of Economics, as the major representative of the Austrian School to the English-speaking world.

Hayek's move to England was precipitated by interest in his work on capital theory and his 'Austrian' theory of the trade cycle. Hayek's capital theory builds on Böhm-Bawerk to explain production as a series of time-consuming states that are at various distances from final production, His trade cycle theory explains booms and busts as the consequences of artificially low interest rates, brought about by excessive money expansion, that distort the structure of production and make current investment projects unsustainable in the long run. Until the publication of *The General Theory of Employment, Interest and Money* in 1936, Hayek was regarded as Keynes's major, rival in macroeconomic matters.

The Austrian School went into eclipse after 1945. By the end of the 1930s, most Austrian economists of a liberal persuasion left Austria to avoid Nazi persecution. Mises migrated first to Geneva and then to the United States in 1940. He settled in New York, where he began a weekly economics seminar at New York University that was to last two decades. Hayek left England in 1950 and moved to the University of Chicago, where he devoted his time to philosophy, political and social theory and psychology rather than economics.

3. In the economics-literature, the term "reservation-wage" has been used with two different meanings. In the job search literature, the term refers to the lowest wage a person would accept if the person has to pay a positive sum to gain another job offer from a wage distribution. In the labor supply literature, it has been used as the lowest wage at which a person will work, which has also been referred to as the "asking-wage."

4. **Economic region of production:** Though on an isoquant one input can be substituted in place of another input, there is a range within which this substitution can take place. Within this range the isoquants are negatively sloped.

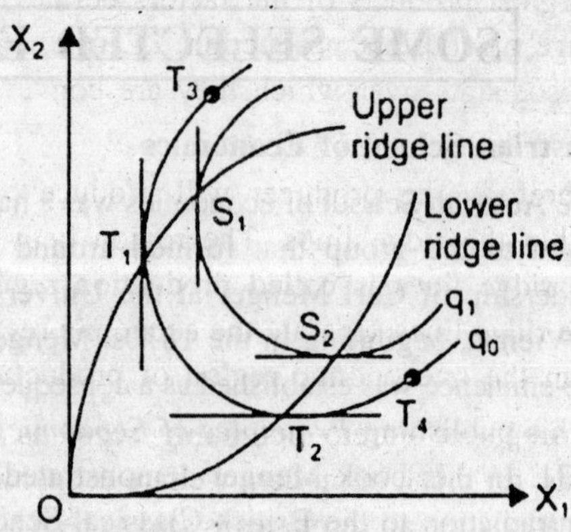

Fig. 1

In Fig. 1, let q_0 and q_1 are the two isoquants. On q_0, T_1 be the point where a tangent to the isoquant, q_0 is parallel to the vertical axis and T_2 be the point where a tangent to the isoquant, q_0 is parallel to the horizontal axis. This portion of the isoquant which lies between T_1 and T_2 is the portion over which the marginal products of factors are diminishing but positive, At T_1 on q_0 and S_1 on q_1,

$MPx_2 = 0$ and at T_2 on q_0 and S_2 on q_1, $MPx_1 = 0$. The locus of points of isoquants where the marginal products of the factors are zero form the ridge lines. The upper ridge line implies that the MP of factor x_2 is zero. The lower ridge line implies that the MP of factor x_1 is zero. Production techniques are only efficient inside the ridge line. Outside the ridge lines the marginal products of factors are negative and the methods of production are inefficient since they require more quantity of both factors for producing same level of output, Here at any point in between T_1 and T_3 or T_2 and T_4 on isoquant q_0 more of both the factors are required to produce the same level of output. Such inefficient methods are not considered by the theory of production, since they imply irrational behaviour of the firm. The condition of positive but declining, marginal products of the factors defines the range of efficient production, *i.e.*, the range of isoquants over which they are convex to the origin.

Therefore, the producer will produce only within the ridge lines. The region between the ridge lines is called production region. The ridge lines separate the economic region from the uneconomic region of production.

7. Concepts of Pareto optimality serve as the basis, for much of modern welfare economics. An allocation all resources is said to be *Pareto optimal* if there is reallocation of production or distribution of the products of production that will increase the economic utility of one or more households without decreasing the economic utility of other households. We may also define a non-Paretian allocation of resources as one in which it is possible to increase the utility of one household without reducing the utility of any other.

8. **The Stackelberg model**

The Cournot model assumes that each firm sets its output simultaneously, not knowing what the other will do. The German economist Heinrich von Stackelberg put forward a modified model in 1934. The Stackelberg model supposes that one firm is a leader, and sets its output first, and then the other firm reacts and sets its output. The model assumes that the leader expects the follower to react on the basis of its Cournot reaction curve.

9. *Sunk costs* are costs only in the accounting sense. These are costs that the producer cannot recover by renting or selling the productive resource. Suppose that a firm purchases a custom-designed piece of specialized machinery with no alternative use. Once purchased, the price of the machine is a sunk cost. The concept of sunk cost is generally related to equipment (or even some labour) that is already in place and that has no alternative use. The opportunity cost of such resources is 0 and, hence, sunk costs are net relevant to economic decisions.

11. Cross-section data is that data which represents values of consumption and income for several different individuals or groups during a given year. Time-series data is that data which represents values of aggregate consumption and income over several different years.

Friedman's hypothesis makes the simplifying assumption that life is indefinitely long and chat consumers base their expenditures on their perceptions of expected or "permanent" income. A constant fraction of permanent income is consumed. The difference between actual and permanent income is called "transitory" income. Aggregate permanent income is based on a moving average of actual aggregate income over a number of years. The marginal propensity to consume out of permanent income is high; but the marginal propensity to consume out of transitory income is low and very little is consumed.

Friedman's first serious attack on the Keynesian theoretical framework came with his work on the theory of the consumption function, which was one of the most important components of Keynesian macroeconomics. Keynes had assumed that aggregate consumption demand was a function of total income in society, but he had presented no theoretical justification for this hypothesis, nor had he discussed what precise definitions of income and consumption one ought to use in attempts to confront the hypothesis with statistical data. The postwar development did not seem to be in accordance with Keynes's hypothesis of decreasing average propensity to consume, and Friedman became convinced that both the theoretical and empirical research that were inspired by Keynes's work rested on much too weak foundations. This conviction motivated him to develop a new theory of the consumption function, the so-called permanent income hypothesis (Friedman 1957).

The basic theoretical hypothesis was based on an analysis inspired by the work of Irving Fisher (1930) who had assumed that consumers maximize utility over time subject to a given level of lifetime income. Friedman pointed out that an implication of this view was that consumption was related to permanent income—a long-run expected normal level of income—and not to current income, which may deviate from permanent income both in positive and negative directions. He went on to demonstrate that this theory was able to reconcile two apparently conflicting sets of empirical observations. The first is that in a cross-section of the population at a given time one observes a relationship between consumption and saving that fits with the Keynesian hypothesis: the rich consume a smaller share of their income than the poor. The second is that in time series data for the long run there is proportionality between consumption and income. Friedman's hypothesis was that the time series data reflected the relationship between consumption and permanent income, The cross-section data, on the other hand, contained components of so-caned transitory income (positive or negative) that would not have appreciable effects on consumption.

In the short run, therefore, the average propensity to consume is decreasing while in the long run it is constant. This has an important implication for economic policy: attempts to stabilize the economy through short-run fiscal policy measures like variations in public spending and the tax level will be ineffective or at least off target. In order to influence consumption demand, the government must be able to influence permanent income, while short run increases or decreases of taxes that are expected to be reversed when the business cycle turns will have little effect.

15. *Optimal growth theory* analyzes the level of economic growth required to maximize GDP per capita. The *golden rule of capital accumulation* suggests that the optimal growth path is the one that maximizes consumption per worker over time. The key to finding this maximum is finding a level of capital per worker such that the marginal productivity of capital (equals profitability in a perfectly competitive economy) equals the growth rate of the population.

"Golden Rule" of Accumulation: In neoclassical growth models, a commonly cited criterion for choosing among saving rate is the golden rule, which maximizes per capita consumption through time. The golden-rule criterion suggests that the highest sustainable level of per capita consumption is attained when the net rate of return on capital equals the sum of the population growth rate and the rate of technological progress. If allowance is made for time preference, then a modified golden-rule proposition emerges under which the welfare-maximizing steady-state path is characterized by the condition that the rate of return on capital minus the rate of pure time preference equals the sum of the population growth rate and the rate of technological progress. In the steady state, a saving rate above or below this welfare-maximizing rate will be suboptimal.

18. Because the multiplier is smaller in an open economy, fiscal policy is less effective (at stimulating output) in an open economy with flexible exchange rates than in a closed economy.

19. Embodied technical change results from the efficient use of new and better types of capital and is considered endogenous. It captures the effects of learning by doing (experience), advances in applied technology, managerial efficiency and industrial organization which transform into better methods and organization that improve the efficiency of both new and old factor inputs. With embodied technical change, more output is obtained with a given quantity of inputs, or the same output can be produced with lesser inputs at the same cost, and this results in movements towards known production boundaries. Disembodies technical change, on the other hand, is not embodied in factor inputs and refers to technology as useful knowledge pertaining to the art of production where concern is with the knowledge-creating activities of research, invention and development, thereby resulting in the expansion of production boundaries themselves due to increases in knowledge.

21. The research on economic growth falls into three chronologically and methodologically different streams. The first is the *classical* stream that started with David Hume and Adam Smith in the eighteenth century and ended with John Stuart Mill and Karl Marx in the mid-nineteenth century. The second is the *neoclassical* stream that reinvigorated growth research with the new statistical data that became available after the Second World War. The seminal works in this stream belong *inter alia* to Robert Solow, Simon Kuznets, Moses Abramovitz, Hollis Chenery and Edward Denison. The third, and most recent, is the *endogenous* stream which rejects the classical and neoclassical assumptions of perfect markets and diminishing returns to productive factors (particularly capital). The endogenous growth theories focus on increasing returns, research and development (R&D) and knowledge spillovers, learning-by-doing and technology diffusion. Key figures in this stream are *inter alia* Kenneth Arrow, Paul Romer, Robert Lucas, Gene Grossman and Elhanan Helpman.

28. Various economists have given explanation for the growth of public expenditure. Among the various theories of public expenditure, the following are the important theories.

1. Wagner's law of public expenditure
2. Peacock-Wiseman hypothesis
3. Colin Clark hypothesis

Wagner's law of public expenditure: Adolph Wagner (1835–1917), the famous German political economist based his Law of Increasing State Activities on historical facts, primarily of Germany. According to Wagner, there are inherent tendencies for the activities of different layers of a government (such as central and state governments) to increase both intensively and extensively. Wagner believed that a functional 'cause-and-effect' relationship exists between the growth of an economy and the relative growth of the public sector and the governmental sector grows faster than the economy.

29. If a per-unit tax is placed on the seller of a good, both the buyer and the seller will pay part of the tax if the demand curve is downward-sloping and the supply curve is upward-sloping. The more inelastic the demand, the larger the percentage of the tax paid by the buyer. The more elastic the demand, the smaller the percentage of the tax paid by the buyer. When demand is perfectly inelastic, buyers pay the full tax. When demand is perfectly elastic, sellers pay the full tax. Also, when supply in perfectly elastic, buyers pay the full tax. When supply is perfectly inelastic, sellers pay the full tax.

34. Dumping is selling exports at a price that is too low—less than normal value (or "fair market value," as it is often called in the United States). There are two legal definitions of *normal value:*

The long-standing definition of *normal value* is the price charged to comparable domestic buyers in the home market (or to comparable buyers in other markets). Under this traditional definition, dumping is international price discrimination favoring buyers of experts.

The second definition of *normal value* arose in the 1970s. It is cost-based—the average cost of producing the product, including overhead costs and profit. Under this second standard, dumping is selling exports at a price that is less than the full average cost of the product.

41. Rules of origin (preference) are the basis of a free trade agreement, as well as other preferential trade deals with the exception of a customs union. These rules prevent geographical *trade deflection.* This effect of a free trade area refers to the import of goods from third countries into the area by country A (which has a relatively lower tariff than the partner country B) in order to re-export the goods in question to country B. These speculations depend not only on the difference in the level of tariffs, but also on transport, storage and insurance costs, as well as on the quality (perishability) of goods. Without rules of origin in a free trade area, only the lowest tariffs would be effective. In fact, a free trade area would be equal to a customs union in which the lowest tariffs of a member country would apply, Trade deflection problems do not exist in customs unions because of the existence of the common external tariff.

42. The Banks in India are required statutorily to maintain a prescribed minimum proportion of their total demand and time liabilities (L) in the form of liquid assets. These liquid assets consists of excess reserves (ER), unencumbered government and other approved securities (I) and other current account balances with other banks (CB)

$$\text{Thus, SLR} = \frac{ER + I + CB}{L}$$

SLR operates as an instrument of monetary control by affecting the freedom of the banks to sell government securities and borrow against these from RBI.

44. The term 'real balance effect' was coined by Don Patinkin. It is an important discovery in monetary economics.

Real balace effect means the real purchasing power of the stock of cash balances held by the public. When the price level changes, it affects the purchasing power of people's cash balances which, in turn, affects the supply of and demand for goods. This is 'real balance effect'. It affects both monetary and real sectors. It is a part of dynamic analysis. Real balance effect is the combination of both 'Pigou Effect' and 'Keynes Effect'.

Pigou effect indicates permanent changes in the consumption-saving ratio. It is the effect of wage-price reduction on consumption, stock of money (outside money) being constant and given. It affects only the real sector. It is a part of static analysis.

Keynes' effect shows that when the real value of cash balance increases owing to wage-price reduction, smaller transaction balaces are required. This creates higher demand for securities. As a result, secuity prices rise and the rate of interest falls at each level of income.

Don Patinkin has used the concept of real balance effect to integrate the monetary sector and the real sector and also to rehabilitate the classical quantity theory of money.

The classical quantity theory of money maintains a dichotomy between the monetary sector and the real sector. It assumes that money is neutral and has no influence on output which is governed by real factors like labour, capital and technology. An increase in money supply raises the 'absolute' price level without affecting 'relative' prices which are determined in the real sector.

Patinkin rejected the classical dichotomy between the monetary sector and the real sector in his book *Money, Interest and Prices* published in 1965. He argues that this dichotomy is neither necessary nor valid. According to him, an increase in the quantity of money first of all incluences the demand for goods and their relative prices through real balance effect and then the absolute price level. Thus, Don Patinkin has tattempted to integrate the monetary sector with the real sector through the real balance effect.

47. The Micro, Small and Medium Enterprises Development Act 2006, which came into force with effect from 02/10/2006, gives the technical definition of the Micro, Small, and Medium Enterprises. As per the Act, the activities are classified into *manufacturing* and *service* Category. Initially, the MSMED Act 2006 had not defined the 'Services Sector' and RBI's guidelines were awaited. However, subsequently RBI defined the services sector and the activities that can be covered under the SME sector.

Table indicates the the threshold investment levels for both manufacturing sector (investment in plant and machinery) and services sector (investment in equipment) for the following three categories of manufacturing and services enterprises:

Table: Investment levels for MSMEs vide MSMED Act

Enterprise	*Investment levels for manufacturing units*	*Investment levels for services sector*
Micro Enterprise	Up to ₹ 2.5 million (25 lakh)	Up to ₹ 1 million (10) lakh)
Small Enterprise	More than ₹ 2.5 (25 lakh) million but up to ₹ 50 million (5 crore)	More than ₹ 1 million (10 lakh) up to ₹ 20 million (2 crore)
Medium Enterprise	More than ₹ 50 million (5 crore) but up to ₹ 100 million (10 crore)	More than ₹ 20 million up to ₹ 50 million (5 crore)

53. Pigovian tax is a kind of tax, which is levied to correct a negative cost that is created by the actions of any business firm, but that is not considered in a firm's private costs or profits. Also known as 'sin tax', it is a tax placed on an action with a negative externality, to correct market failure. In the presence of negative externalities, the social cost of a market activity is not covered by the private cost of the activity. In such a case, the market outcome is not efficient and may lead to over-consumption of the product. A Pigovian tax equal to the negative externality is thought to correct the market outcome back to the level of efficiency.

For example, a factory does not financially take into consideration the damages caused to the environment by their emissions. By imposing Pigovian Tax, the government can artificially make the firms bear the cost of the damages, which will ideally be equal to what the price would have been if a market for such an activity existed. In a country like Canada with a publicly funded health care system, that is, where the medical service of every patient is funded from government revenues, the cigarette tax acts as a Pigovian tax — it raises the revenue necessary to offset the expenses towards the health care system, as a consequence of smoking.

54. Contingent Valuation Method

The Contingent Valuation Method (CVM) is a survey-based technique for the valuation of non-market resources. The method involves surveying to assess how much people would be willing to pay for specific environmental services (willingness to pay—WTP). In other cases, people are asked for the amount of compensation they would be wining to accept in order to give up specific environmental services (willingness to accept—WTA). It is caned "contingent" valuation, because people are asked to state their willingness to pay, *contingent* on a particular hypothetical scenario and description of the environmental service.

The CVM is an important valuation tool and has been widely applied by resources economists, following a great deal of empirical and theoretical refinements in the 1970s and 1980s. The contingent valuation survey was originally proposed by Ciriacy-Wantrup (1947) as a method of eliciting market values of non-market goods. It was first applied by Davis in 1963 to estimate the place of value hunters, and tourists in a specific wilderness area (Davis 1963). Since then, the CVM has been widely applied in various fields, such as air quality, biodiversity and recreation, wildlife, forest and wilderness areas, ecosystem services, sewerage and waste management.

60. Meaning of Mechanization

According to Bhattacharjee, "mechanization of agriculture and farming process connotes application of machine power to work on land, usually performed by bullocks, horses and other draught animals or by human labour." This definition calls substitution of biological sources of energy by mechanical sources as mechanization. But this definition visualizes a very limited scope of mechanization in agricultural sector. To this, mechanization means use of machines on land alone, which means application of machines for tilling, harrowing, harvesting, threshing, etc. In fact, at the initial stage of mechanization machines are used on land alone but ultimately it covers all the processes connected with farming and allied activities such as irrigation, hauling, storage, dairy operations, etc. Therefore, mechanization stands for the use of mechanical power driven implements for the various operations of an agriculturist. Thus, "complete mechanization would mean the application of machines even in the domestic affairs and operations of a farmer." Indian Society of Agricultural Economics views that it is a system of land utilization in which cultivation rests on a different and infinitely more complex basis than is found in the local self-sufficient economy.

63. Cost function: $C = \dfrac{x^3}{3} - 10x^2 + 9x + 1000$

Demand function : $x = \dfrac{(12-p)}{9}$

$\because$ Total revenue $= p \times (x)$

$\therefore \qquad \text{T.R.} = \dfrac{p(12-p)}{9}$

Total cost function in terms of p

$$\text{T.C.} = \frac{1}{3}\left(\frac{12-p}{9}\right)^3 - 10\left(\frac{12-p}{9}\right)^2 + 9\left(\frac{12-p}{9}\right) + 1000$$

Profit π = T.R. − T.C.

$$= \frac{p(12-p)}{9} - \frac{1}{3}\left(\frac{12-p}{9}\right)^3 + 10\left(\frac{12-p}{9}\right)^2 - 12 + p - 1000$$

For maximum profit, $\frac{d\pi}{dp} = 0$

$$\frac{d\pi}{dp} = \frac{12-2p}{9} + \frac{1}{9}\left(\frac{12-p}{9}\right)^2 - \frac{20}{9}\left(\frac{12-p}{9}\right) + 1$$

$$= \frac{(12-p)^2 - 180(12-p) + 81(12-2p) + 729}{729}$$

$$= \frac{144 + p^2 - 24p - 2160 + 180p + 972 - 162p + 729}{729}$$

$$= \frac{p^2 - 6p - 315}{729}$$

when $\frac{d\pi}{dp} = 0$

$$p^2 - 6p - 315 = 0$$
$$p^2 - 21p + 15p - 315 = 0$$
$$(p - 21)(p + 15) = 0$$

$\therefore$ either $p = 21$ or -15

at $p = 21$, $x = \frac{12-21}{9} = -1$

which is not a permissible value.

at $p = -15$

$$x = \frac{12-(-15)}{9} = 3$$

which is the required level of output.

65. $\sigma_{xy} = \frac{5}{3}$ and $\sigma_{yx} = \frac{15}{4}$

Correlation coefficient

$$= \frac{1}{\sqrt{\sigma_{xy} \cdot \sigma_{yx}}}$$

$$= \frac{1}{\sqrt{\frac{5}{3} \times \frac{15}{4}}} = \frac{1}{\sqrt{\frac{25}{4}}}$$

$$= \frac{2}{5} = 0.4.$$

66. Test on individual Regression co-efficient (t test)

$$T_0 = \frac{\hat{\alpha}_j}{SE(\alpha_j)}$$

$$= \frac{1.79}{0.41}$$

$$= 4.3658 = 4.366.$$

Previous Paper's (Solved)

UGC-NET ECONOMICS, DECEMBER 2012

PAPER–II

Note: *This paper contains* ***fifty (50)*** *objective type questions, each question carrying* ***two (2)*** *marks. Attempt* ***all*** *the questions.*

Directions (Qs. 1 to 10): *Read the following questions and choose the correct answer from the options given below these questions.*

1. For downward movement along the iso-quant, MRTS of Labour per unit of capital ($MRTS_{L,K}$) is given by

A. – dK/dL B. dK/dL

C. dL/dK D. – dL/dK

2. Charging a different price in different markets is called

A. price discrimination

B. second degree price discrimination

C. third degree price discrimination

D. perfect price discrimination

3. Which of the following is the most significant in stabilization policy?

A. Private investment

B. Inventory investment

C. Autonomous investment

D. Public investment

4. The concept of vicious circle of poverty is associated with

A. Kindleberger B. Schumpeter

C. Ragnar Nurkse D. Gunnar Myrdal

5. Solow built his model as an alternative to

A. Kaldor's model of growth

B. Ranis-Fei model of growth

C. Harrod-Domar model of growth

D. Meade's model of growth

6. If interest payments are subtracted from gross fiscal deficit, the remainder will be

A. revenue deficit

B. gross primary deficit

C. capital deficit

D. budgetary deficit

7. Which of the following measures of central tendency will be the most appropriate to use if the data relate to rates, proportions and ratios?

A. Arithmetic mean B. Median

C. Harmonic mean D. Geometric mean

8. Opportunity cost version of comparative cost advantage doctrine was introduced by

A. J.M. Keynes B. Kindleberger

C. Haberler D. Karl Marx

9. The most popular definition of sustainable development is given by

A. World Development Report

B. UNDP Report

C. Brundtland

D. IMF Report

10. During the planning period, highest growth rate was achieved during

A. eighth plan B. tenth plan

C. ninth plan D. seventh plan

Directions (Qs. 11 to 20): *Read the questions and select the correct option for the answer from the list given below:*

11. Labour theory of value was propounded by

a. Adam Smith

b. David Ricardo

c. Ragnar Nurkse, Gunnar Myrdal, R.M. Solow

d. Fei-Rani's, Ragnar Nurkse

Codes:

A. a and b B. a and c

C. a, b and c D. a, b, c and d

12. The features of the classical system are

a. Monetary factors determine output and employment.

b. Self adjusting mechanism of the economy.

c. State action to direct development.

d. Optimization through market in the absence of state control.

Codes:

A. a and b B. a, b and c

C. b and d D. a, b and d

13. Concepts of displacement and concentration effect in public expenditure are attributed to

a. A.C. Pigou and J.K. Mehta

b. Alan T. Peacock and Jack Wiseman

c. Kenneth Arrow and Paul A. Samuelson

d. A.R. Prest and I.M.D. Little

Codes:

A. a and b B. only b

C. a, b and c D. a, b, c and d

14. Human Development Index (HDI) is constructed with reference to

a. Life expectancy at birth, real GDP per capita, gross enrolment ratio, adult literacy rate.

b. Life expectancy at birth, real GDP per capita, combined gross enrolment ratio, adult literacy rate.

c. Life expectancy, GDP per capita, infant mortality rate, literacy rate.

d. GDP per capita, infant mortality rate, literacy rate.

Codes:

A. a and b B. a and c

C. only c D. a, b and d

15. The unbalanced growth model was propounded first by

a. Albert O. Hirschman

b. H.S. Singer and Raul Prebisch

c. Kindelberger and Ragnar Nurkse

d. W.W. Rostow and Paul Streeten

Codes:

A. a and b B. a and c

C. a and d D. only a

16. Harrod-Domar model of growth is based on the concepts of and their equality

a. Population and productivity growth.

b. Investment and average growth rate of income.

c. Actual, warranted and natural growth rate.

d. Productivity growth and investment growth.

Codes:

A. a and c B. a and d

C. only c D. a, b and c

17. Factor endowment theory is also known as

a. Modern theory of international trade.

b. Classical theory of international trade.

c. Reciprocal demand theory.

d. Factor proportions theory of international trade.

Codes:

A. a and b B. b and c

C. a and d D. c and d

18. Most important theory of increasing public expenditure is associated with

a. Adolph Wagner's hypothesis

b. Critical limit hypothesis

c. Administrative efficiency hypothesis

d. Stability of income hypothesis

Codes:

A. a and b B. a and c

C. only a D. c and d

19. Under the Brettonwood system, the long term development assistance was to be provided by

a. IBRD b. IDA

c. IMF d. All of the above

Codes:

A. a and b B. a, b and c

C. b and c D. only d

20. The Planning Commission of India has recently announced the poverty line as

a. ₹ 42 per day per person for urban area.

b. ₹ 26 per person per day for rural areas.

c. ₹ 32 per person per day for urban areas.
d. ₹ 32 per day per person for rural areas.

Codes:
A. a and b   B. a and c
C. b and c   D. c and d

Directions (Qs. 21 to 30): *Read the following questions and select the right combination of Assertion (A) and Reason (R) from the codes given below:*

21. Assertion (A): There is a natural tendency to collude under oligopoly.
Reason (R): Interdependence of firms in oligopolistic markets.

Codes:
A. Both (A) and (R) are correct but (R) is not the correct explanation of (A).
B. Both (A) and (R) are correct, and (R) is the correct explanation of (A).
C. (A) is correct but (R) is incorrect.
D. (A) is incorrect but (R) is correct.

22. Assertion (A): In short run, the marginal cost of output is the cost of additional labour and materials used in production.
Reason (R): Materials and labour used in production alone vary in short run.

Codes:
A. (A) is correct but (R) is incorrect.
B. (A) is incorrect but (R) is correct.
C. Both (A) and (R) are correct, and (R) is the correct explanation of (A).
D. Both (A) and (R) are incorrect.

23. Assertion (A): Post reform liberal trade policies have stimulated India's growth.
Reason (R): Private enterprise got opportunities to contribute to growth of Indian manufacturing industries.

Codes:
A. Both (A) and (R) are correct, and (R) is the correct explanation of (A).
B. Both (A) and (R) are correct but (R) is not the correct explanation of (A).
C. Both (A) and (R) are incorrect.
D. (A) is incorrect but (R) is correct.

24. Assertion (A): Use of goods and services from which one can be excluded are pure private goods.
Reason (R): Such goods and services are not provided free by the State.

Codes:
A. Both (A) and (R) are correct, and (R) is the correct explanation of (A).
B. Both (A) and (R) are correct but (R) is not the correct explanation of (A).
C. (A) is correct but (R) is incorrect.
D. (A) is incorrect but (R) is correct.

25. Assertion (A): 'A country is poor because it is poor'.
Reason (R): Income of a poor country is low, so its savings and investment are low. Low investment limits its productive capacity which leads to low output and income.

Codes:
A. Both (A) and (R) are correct, but (R) is not the correct explanation of (A).
B. Both (A) and (R) are correct, and (R) is the correct explanation of (A).
C. (A) is correct but (R) is incorrect.
D. (A) is incorrect but (R) is correct.

26. Assertion (A): All historical events are the result of a continuous economic struggle between different classes and groups in a society.
Reason (R): This struggle is because of the conflict between the mode of production and the value attached to the roles of different agents of production.

Codes:
A. Both (A) and (R) are correct but (R) is not the correct explanation of (A).

B. Both (A) and (R) are correct, and (R) is the correct explanation of (A).
C. (A) is correct but (R) is incorrect.
D. (A) is incorrect but (R) is correct.

27. Assertion (A): K/L will adjust through time to the equilibrium value of the ratio.

Reason (R): Technical coefficients of production are fixed.

Codes:
A. Both (A) and (R) are correct but (R) is not the correct explanation of (A).
B. Both (A) and (R) are correct, and (R) is the correct explanation of (A).
C. (A) is correct but (R) is incorrect.
D. (A) is incorrect but (R) is correct.

28. Assertion (A): Investment has a demand effect.

Reason (R): Investment augments the productivity and income in the economy.

Codes :
A. Both (A) and (R) are correct, and (R) is the correct explanation of (A).
B. Both (A) and (R) are correct but (R) is not the correct explanation of (A).
C. (A) is correct but (R) is incorrect.
D. (A) is incorrect but (R) is correct.

29. Assertion (A): Agriculture is the main source of livelihood of people in India.

Reason (R): Measures for agricultural development should be undertaken.

Codes:
A. Both (A) and (R) are correct, and (R) is the correct explanation of (A).
B. Both (A) and (R) are correct but (R) is incorrect explanation of (A).
C. (A) is correct but (R) is incorrect.
D. (A) is incorrect and (R) is correct.

30. Assertion (A): In the following regression equation $Y = a + bX$, 'a' shows the autonomous value of Y.

Reason (R): If $X = 0$, $Y = a$ holds. Hence, a is the minimum value of Y which is independent of any influence of X on Y.

Codes:
A. Both (A) and (R) are correct, and (R) is the correct explanation of (A).
B. (A) is correct but (R) is not the correct explanation of (A).
C. (A) is correct but (R) is incorrect.
D. (A) is incorrect but (R) is correct.

Directions (Qs. 31 to 40): *Read the questions and select the correct sequence from the codes given below:*

31. Identify the order of chronological development of the theory of demand.
a. Marshall's theory of demand
b. Indifference curves
c. Revealed preference theory
d. Weak Preference ordering theory of demand

Codes:
A. a, c, d, b B. d, b, a, c
C. a, c, b, d D. a, b, c, d

32. Identify the correct chronological order of the following theories:
a. Cambridge version of quantity theory of money.
b. Fisher's version of quantity theory of money.
c. Tobin's theory of demand for money.
d. Baumol's theory of demand for inventory.

Codes:
A. c, d, a, b B. b, a, d, c
C. d, a, b, c D. a, b, c, d

33. Identify the correct chronological order of the following:
a. Keynes' consumption function
b. Life Cycle hypothesis
c. Relative income hypothesis
d. Friedman's permanent income hypothesis

Codes:
A. d, b, a, c B. b, a, c, d
C. a, c, d, b D. c, d, b, a

34. Identify the correct chronology of stages of Marxian model of economic development.

a. Capitalist crisis
b. Capital accumulation
c. Surplus value
d. Materialistic interpretation of history

Codes:

A. b, a, c, d B. c, d, b, a
C. d, c, b, a D. c, b, a, d

35. The sequencing process of Harrod's model of development is

a. Natural growth rate
b. Warranted growth rate
c. Actual growth rate
d. Divergence

Codes:

A. d, c, b, a B. c, b, a, d
C. b, a, d, c D. a, d, c, b

36. Arrange the following summits of SAARC members in order in which these were organized:

a. New Delhi
b. Bangalore (Bengaluru)
c. Islamabad
d. Kathmandu

Codes:

A. a, c, d, b B. a, b, c, d
C. b, d, c, a D. c, b, a, d

37. Arrange the structure of balance of payments accounts in which these items appear:

a. Capital account
b. Errors and omissions
c. Current account
d. Official settlements account

Codes:

A. a, b, c, d B. c, a, d, b
C. d, c, b, a D. c, d, a, b

38. State the order of the appointment of the following as chairman of Finance Commission:

a. K.C. Neogy
b. K. Brahamanand Reddy
c. N.K.P. Salve
d. A.K. Chanda

Codes:

A. a, c, b, d B. a, d, b, c
C. a, c, d, b D. a, b, d, c

39. Indicate the sequence of the following in terms of the implementation.

a. Income Tax
b. Expenditure Tax
c. Value Added Tax
d. Fringe Benefits Tax

Codes:

A. a, c, b, d B. a, b, c, d
C. b, c, d, a D. c, d, a, b

40. Determine the order in which the following were developed.

a. Fisher's F test of significance of differences between the means of more than two samples.
b. Gosset's t-test of difference between the means of two samples.
c. Pearson's correlation coefficient.
d. Spearman's rank correlation coefficient.

Codes:

A. a, b, c, d B. b, a, c, d
C. c, b, a, d D. d, a, b, c

Directions (Qs. 41 to 50): *Read the following questions and match the correct pair from List-I and List-II. Use the codes given below for answering:*

41.

List-I	*List-II*
(*a*) Kinked demand curve hypothesis	1. William Baumol
(*b*) Sales maximization model of oligopoly	2. Paul Sweezy
(*c*) Social Welfare Criterion	3. Adam Smith
(*d*) Law of Invisible hand	4. Bergson

Codes:

	(*a*)	(*b*)	(*c*)	(*d*)
A.	4	3	1	2
B.	2	1	4	3
C.	2	3	1	4
D.	1	4	3	2

42. *List-I* | *List-II*

(*a*) Psychological Law of Consumption — 1. Irving Fisher
(*b*) Time preference theory of interest — 2. J.M. Keynes
(*c*) Public Choice View — 3. Mundell and Fleming
(*d*) Open Economy IS-LM model — 4. Gorden Tullock

Codes:

	(*a*)	(*b*)	(*c*)	(*d*)
A.	3	2	4	1
B.	4	1	3	2
C.	2	1	4	3
D.	1	3	4	2

43. *List-I* | *List-II*

a. Mid-day meal scheme — 1. 2006
b. Implementation of M-NREGA — 2. 1995
c. Cash Reserve Ratio — 3. Finance Commission
d. Divisible Taxes — 4. Reserve Bank of India

Codes:

	(*a*)	(*b*)	(*c*)	(*d*)
A.	1	2	3	4
B.	2	1	4	3
C.	4	2	3	1
D.	3	4	1	2

44. *List-I* | *List-II*

(*a*) Monetary Policy — 1. Tax Rate
(*b*) Trade Policy — 2. Margin Money
(*c*) Credit Policy — 3. Imports and Exports
(*d*) Fiscal Policy — 4. Bank Rate

Codes:

	(*a*)	(*b*)	(*c*)	(*d*)
A.	4	3	2	1
B.	4	2	3	1
C.	3	2	1	4
D.	2	1	4	3

45. *List-I* | *List-II*

(*a*) J.M. Buchanan — 1. Canons of Public Expenditure
(*b*) Findlay Shirras — 2. Functional Finance
(*c*) R.N. Bhargava — 3. Public-Choice Theory
(*d*) A.P. Lerner — 4. Federal Finance

Codes:

	(*a*)	(*b*)	(*c*)	(*d*)
A.	3	2	1	4
B.	3	1	4	2
C.	2	3	1	4
D.	1	4	3	2

46. *List-I* | *List-II*

(*a*) Organic Composition of Capital — 1. Hirschman
(*b*) Doctrine of Natural Law — 2. Schumpeter
(*c*) Innovation — 3. Marx
(*d*) Doctrine of Unbalanced Growth — 4. Adam Smith

Codes:

	(*a*)	(*b*)	(*c*)	(*d*)
A.	3	4	2	1
B.	4	3	1	2
C.	2	1	3	4
D.	1	2	4	3

47. *List-I* | *List-II*

(*a*) Low Income Equilibrium Trap — 1. Karl Marx
(*b*) Poverty Measurement — 2. Adam Smith
(*c*) Laissezfair — 3. Nelson
(*d*) Industrial Reserve Army — 4. Suresh Tendulkar

Codes:

	(*a*)	(*b*)	(*c*)	(*d*)
A.	1	2	4	3
B.	3	4	2	1
C.	4	3	1	2
D.	2	1	3	4

48. *List-I* | *List-II*

(*a*) Law of Absolute Cost Advantage — 1. Haberler
(*b*) Doctrine of Comparative Cost Advantage — 2. Hescher-Ohlin
(*c*) Modern Theory of International Trade — 3. Adam Smith
(*d*) Opportunity Cost Principle — 4. Ricardo

Codes:

	(a)	(b)	(c)	(d)
A.	4	2	1	3
B.	3	4	2	1
C.	2	3	4	1
D.	1	4	3	2

49. **List-I** **List-II**

(*a*) Monetarism 1. R.F. Kahn

(*b*) Employment multiplier 2. T. Havelmo

(*c*) Multiplier effect of balanced budget 3. John Muth

(*d*) Rational expectation hypothesis 4. Milton Friedman

Codes:

	(a)	(b)	(c)	(d)
A.	2	4	3	1
B.	4	1	2	3
C.	1	3	4	2
D.	3	2	1	4

50. ***List-I*** ***List-II***

a. Theory of Probability 1. Single value to represent distribution

b. Mean 2. Uncertain events

c. Normal Distribution 3. Mini replica of of population

d. Sample 4. Symmetrical with almost total area within M(mean) ± 30(sigma)

Codes:

	(a)	(b)	(c)	(d)
A.	1	2	3	4
B.	4	3	2	1
C.	2	1	4	3
D.	4	1	2	3

ANSWERS

1	2	3	4	5	6	7	8	9	10
A	A	C	C	C	B	D	C	C	B
11	**12**	**13**	**14**	**15**	**16**	**17**	**18**	**19**	**20**
A	C	B	C	A	C	C	C	A	B
21	**22**	**23**	**24**	**25**	**26**	**27**	**28**	**29**	**30**
B	C	A	A	B	B	B	A	A	A
31	**32**	**33**	**34**	**35**	**36**	**37**	**38**	**39**	**40**
D	B	C	D	B	C	B	B	D	B
41	**42**	**43**	**44**	**45**	**46**	**47**	**48**	**49**	**50**
B	C	B	A	B	A	B	B	B	C

SOME SELECTED EXPLANATORY ANSWERS

2. Price discrimination is the practice of charging different prices from different consumers for the same good or service at the same time. When the monopoly firm practices price discrimination, it is called discriminating monopoly. The other words for price discrimination are 'selective pricing' or 'pricing by market segmentation' or 'charging what the traffic will bear'. The cost of production is either the same or it differs by a small margin. Products are basically the same but the producers convince the consumers that the products are different on the basis of different brand name, different packaging, different advertising, etc. We will deal with identical products, produced under same cost and sold at different prices to different consumers.

Conditions for Price Discrimination

The conditions which are essential for the implementation of price discrimination are:

1. There should be monopoly or other forms of imperfect competition present in the market. Price discrimination cannot be implemented under perfect competition.
2. There should be two or more markets which can be separated and can be kept separate. If they cannot be kept separate then the consumer can resell the monopoly product in the high priced market.
3. The elasticity of demand in these two or more markets must be different. If coefficient of price elasticity of demand is same in all markets, then price discrimination cannot be implemented.
4. There should be no contact among buyers.
5. The monopolist must have complete control over the supply of the commodity.

4. The idea of a vicious circle of poverty is closely associated with the work of Ragnar Nurkse who published his influential book *Problems of Capital Formation in Underdeveloped Countries* in 1953.

Nurkse argued that a vicious circle was a 'circular constellation of forces tending to act and react upon one another in such a way as to keep a poor country in a state of poverty'. The most widely quoted example of a vicious circle is with respect to capital accumulation. The low level of real income in 'underdeveloped areas' resulted in a limited capacity to save and was itself a reflection of low productivity. Low productivity in turn was the result of the lack of capital which was the result of the limited capacity to save. The circle was thus complete (see Figure 1).

On the demand side, the inducement to invest may be low because of the limited size of the market, itself the result of low real income resulting from low productivity. Productivity is low because of the limited use of capital in production which in turn may be at least partly caused by the low inducement to invest (see Figure 2).

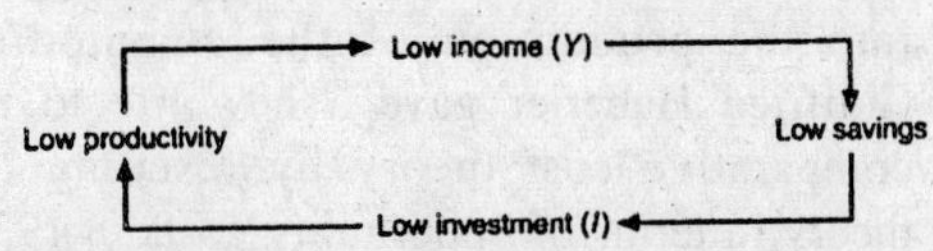

Figure 1 Vicious circle – capital accumulation

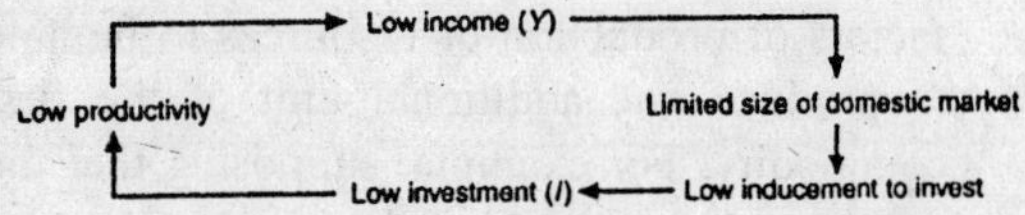

Figure 2 Vicious circle – demand side

5. The Harrod-Domar model said that if demand conditions were made right, the only bottleneck to growth was a lack of physical capital. In this sense, physical capital was the only ultimate source of economic growth. This line of thought left little scope (really none at all) for other factors and forces in the growth process. Population or labour-force growth is absent in the Harrod-Domar formula, which explains output growth solely by saving and efficiency. Robert Solow, therefore, developed an alternative model, that gave birth to the neo-classical model, to explain the growth process. The basic neo-classical model expanded on the Harrod-independent variable technology, to the growth equation (Todaro, 1997). Unlike the fixed coefficients, constant-returns-to-scale assumption of the Harrod-Domar model, Solow's neo-classical growth model exhibited diminishing returns to labour capital separately and constant returns to both factors jointly. Technological progress became the residual factor explaining long-term growth, and its level was assumed by Solow and other new-classical growth theorists to be determined exogenously, that is, independently of all other factors (Todaro, 1997: 88).

8. One of the main drawbacks of the Ricardian comparative cost theory was that it was based on the labour theory of value which stated that the value or price of a commodity was equal to the amount of labour time going into the production of the commodity. Gottfried Haberler gave a new life to the comparative cost theory by restating the theory in terms of opportunity costs in 1933.

The opportunity cost of a commodity is the amount of a second commodity that must be given up in order to release just enough factors of production or resources to be able to produce one additional unit of the first commodity. For example, supposing that the resources required to produce one unit of commodity X are equivalent to the resources required to produce two units of commodity Y. Then, the opportunity cost of one unit of X is two units of Y.

According to the opportunity cost theory, a nation with a lower opportunity cost for a commodity has a comparative advantage in that commodity and a comparative disadvantage in the other commodity. If the opportunity cost of one unit of X is two units of Y in Country A and 1.5 unit of Y in Country B, then Country A must specialise in production of Y and import its requirements of X from B, and B should specialise in the production of X and import Y from A rather than producing it at home.

9. The concept of sustainable development emerged in the 1980s in an attempt to explore the relationship between development and the environment. Eagerly embraced by policy makers, governments, corporations, global organizations, NGOs and local and regional councils, sustainable development soon became the buzzword of the 1990s. The problem with buzzwords is they tend to become disengaged from their original context and their meanings become discursively contested and deployed by a variety of agents, institutions and texts. In 1992, there were more than 100 definitions of sustainable development (Holmberg and Sandbrook, 1992) and a few more have probably been invented since then. The most widely accepted definition is from the Brundtland Commission, which defines sustainable development as 'a process of change in which the exploitation of resources, direction of investments, orientation of technological development, and institutional change are made consistent with future as well as present needs'.

11. Adam Smith and David Ricardo had put forward a theory of value which took the position that commodities are valuable because of the labour that goes into them. For the most part, Smith and Ricardo focused their arguments on the idea that labour was the sole source of all value, stating that 'it was the real measure of the exchange value of all commodities'. Ricardo, for his part, refined the theory by stating that the measurable quantities of labour time that went into the production of the commodity created all value, and went on to say that these 'quantities' could be calculated in units of labour time. Thus, where Smith tended to locate value in labour generally. Ricardo focused on specific 'units of labour time' that produced amounts or quantities of value. This view is called the labour theory of value and essentially it holds that the value of a commodity is created by labour and that value inheres in a commodity as a thing or substance by virtue of the labour applied to it.

15. The Unbalanced Growth Strategy is the opposite of the Balanced Growth Strategy. According to this concept investment should be made in selected sectors rather than simultaneously in all sectors of the economy. By making such type of investment it is possible to develop a few industries and the economies accruing from them can be utilized for the development of other sector. Economists like Singer, Kindelberger, Streeten, etc. have expressed their views in favour of this concept.

17. The Modern Theory of International Trade was propounded by the Swedish economist Heckscher in an article published in 1919. It was further improved upon by his student

Bertil Ohlin in a research paper published in 1924 and later in his book *"International and Inter-regional Trade"* published in 1933. This theory does not contradict Comparative Cost Theory of International Trade, rather supports it. According to Comparative Cost Theory, international trade takes place because of difference in comparative costs. But it throws little light on the factors accounting for the difference in comparative costs. On the contrary, modern theory of international trade reveals the causes responsible for difference in the international trade.

18. Adolph Wagner (1835–1917), the famous German political economist based his Law of Increasing State Activities on historical facts, primarily of Germany. According to Wagner, there are inherent tendencies for the activities of different layers of a government (such as central and state governments) to increase both intensively and extensively. Wagner believed that a functional 'cause-and-effect' relationship exists between the growth of an economy and the relative growth of the public sector and the governmental sector grows faster than the economy.

38.

Finance Commission	*Chairman*	*Operational Duration*
I	K.C. Neogy	1952-57
II	K. Santhanam	1957-62
III	A.K. Chanda	1962-66
IV	P.V. Rajamannar	1966-69
V	Mahaveer Tyagi	1969-74
VI	Brahamanand Reddy	1974-79
VII	J.M. Shellet	1979-84
VIII	Y.B. Chawan	1984-89
IX	N.K.P. Salve	1989-95
X	K.C. Pant	1995-00
XI	A.M. Khusro	2000-05
XII	Dr. C. Rangrajan	2005-10
XIII	V.L. Kelkar	2010-15

PAPER–III

Note: *This paper contains* ***seventy five (75)*** *objective type questions of* ***two (2)*** *marks each.* ***All*** *questions are compulsory.*

1. A demand curve, which is parallel to the horizontal axis, showing quantity, has the price elasticity equal to

A. Zero B. Infinity

C. Less than one D. One

2. Although a monopolist can charge any price he likes, but does not charge a higher price than his equilibrium price because

A. higher price means fall in total revenue

B. higher price can be charged only on that segment of firm's demand curve which is price inelastic implying that the marginal revenue will be negative

C. it is inconsistent with profit maximization goal under monopoly

D. marginal cost will be negative over the relevant range of output

3. Which of the following conditions specify the least cost-output combination?

A. P_L/P_k = MRTS

B. $P_L/P_k = MP_L/MP_k$

C. $MP_k/MP_L = dL/dK$

D. All the above

4. Which of the following is not relevant in case of Sweezy's oligopoly model?

A. A price cut by a firm is followed by the price cut by the rival firms

B. Price hike is not followed by the rival firms

C. Firms do not react to price change made by one of the firms

D. Firms react to all kinds of price changes made by the rival

5. Quasi rent is the reward to a factor of production which is
A. Economic rent in the short run but transfer earnings in the long run
B. Transfer earnings in the short run
C. Transfer earnings both in the short and long run
D. Economic rent both in the short and long run

6. According to the Loanable Funds Theory, the rate of interest is a function of
A. Investment
B. Desire to hoard money
C. Quantity of money
D. All the above

7. While analyzing the marginal productivity theory of distribution, Clark gave more emphasis on
A. Demand for Labour
B. Supply of Labour
C. Both Demand as well as Supply of Labour
D. Profit Maximization

8. A general equilibrium is defined as a state in which all economic units maximize their respective objective functions, all prices are simultaneously in equilibrium and all markets are cleared. The statement is
A. Correct B. Incorrect
C. Perfectly correct D. None of these

9. According to Mundell in an optimum currency area, the achievement of internal and external balance is possible through
A. Capital flows
B. Inflow of funds from abroad
C. Official development assistance
D. The mobility of factors

10. An agreement between two countries to maintain a free trade area, a common external tariff, free mobility of capital and labour and degree of unification in government policies and monetary policy is called
A. Common market B. Free trade area
C. Economic union D. Customs union

11. The core principles of multi lateral trading system are
I. Non-discrimination
II. Reciprocity
III. Protectionism
IV. Domestic Safeguards
Select the right code from the list given below:
A. I, II and IV are correct
B. II and III are correct
C. II, III and IV are correct
D. I and II are correct

12. **Assertion (A):** Many developing countries contend that labour standards constitute a barrier to free trade.
Reason (R): Their competitive advantage in the global economy is cheap labour.
A. Both (A) and (R) are correct but (R) is not the correct explanation of (A)
B. Both (A) and (R) are correct and (R) is the correct explanation of (A)
C. (A) is incorrect but (R) is correct
D. (A) is correct but (R) is incorrect

13. Arrange in order the WTO ministerials:
I. Geneva II. Doha
III. Hong Kong IV. Seattle
A. II, IV, III, I B. III, IV, I, II
C. IV, II, III, I D. I, IV, II, III

14. What does Hedging mean?
A. The acceptance of a foreign exchange risk
B. The covering of a foreign exchange risk
C. Foreign exchange speculation
D. Foreign exchange arbitrage

15. In which terms a unit of SDR was originally denominated?
A. The world marked value of U.S. Dollar
B. The gold value equivalent of one US Dollar
C. The Pound-Sterling
D. The German Mark

16. Which of the following is an adverse effect of Euro Currency Market?
A. International Capital Market
B. Decrease in World's Nominal Money Supply

C. Integration of International Capital Markets
D. Meeting BOP Deficit

17. Employment Guarantee Scheme was first introduced in
A. Gujarat B. Madhya Pradesh
C. Maharashtra D. Tamil Nadu

18. According to Weber's Theory of Location, the important factors influencing location are
I. Transport Cost II. Land Cost
III. Labour Cost IV. Innovation Cost
Choose the correct code:
A. I and II B. II and III
C. I and III D. I and IV

19. Given below are two statements, one labelled as assertion (A) and the other labelled as Reason (R).
Assertion (A): India's Public sector helped in the development of a sound industrial base.
Reason (R): Public sector is under State control. The role of State in formulating appropriate policies and providing financial and other support has helped the public sector.
A. (A) is correct but (R) is wrong
B. Both (A) and (R) are correct
C. (A) is wrong but (R) is correct
D. Both (A) and (R) are wrong

20. Match 'labour force' with the appropriate item from amongst the following:
A. Workforce
B. All educated
C. Employed + Unemployed
D. All rural workers

21. There are four phases of a business cycle. Identify the correct sequence of the occurrence of these phases:
A. Recovery, Recession, Expansion, Depression
B. Recovery, Expansion, Depression, Recession
C. Depression, Expansion, Recession, Recovery
D. Recovery, Expansion, Recession, Depression

22. The production of 'finished steel' in India, since independence, has increased over
A. 10 times B. 20 times
C. 30 times D. 50 times

23. The concept of 'Effective Revenue Deficit' has been used for the first time in the Union Budget for
A. 2009–10 B. 2010–11
C. 2011–12 D. 2008–09

24. Which tax is likely to contribute maximum to the Central Government tax revenue during the year 2011–12?
A. Central Excise Duty
B. Customs Duties
C. Income Tax
D. Corporate Tax

25. Gross fiscal deficit of the State Governments is financed by
I. Market Borrowings
II. Printing of Currency
III. Loans from the Central Government
IV. External Borrowings
Find the correct answer from the given code:
Codes:
A. I, II and III are correct.
B. II, III and IV are correct.
C. I and III are correct.
D. II and IV are correct.

26. Match the items of List-I with the items of List-II from the given code:

List-I	*List-II*
(*a*) Canons of Taxation	1. U.K. Hicks
(*b*) Canons of Public Expenditure	2. Adam Smith
(*c*) Effective incidence of Tax	3. Findlay Shirras
(*d*) Benefits received approach of Public Expenditure	4. Erik Lindahl

Codes :

	(a)	(b)	(c)	(d)
A.	2	3	1	4
B.	1	2	3	4
C.	2	3	4	1
D.	4	1	2	3

27. Assertion (A): During the financial year 2011–12, the Central Government is not likely to achieve the target of raising ₹ 40,000 crores through disinvestment policy.

Reason (R): Policy of increased public borrowings to bridge the fiscal gap is justified.

In the context of the above two statements, which one is correct from the given?

Codes:

A. Both (A) and (R) are correct and (R) is the correct explanation of (A)
B. Both (A) and (R) are correct but (R) is not the correct explanation of (A)
C. (A) is correct but (R) is incorrect
D. (R) is correct but (A) is incorrect

28. Arrange the following Reports in chronological order from the given codes:

I. Direct taxes Enquiry Committee Final Report
II. Final Report on Rationalizing and Simplification of the Tax Structure
III. Indian Tax Reforms-Report of a Survey
IV. Taxation Enquiry Commission

Codes:

A. IV, III, II, I B. I, II, III, IV
C. III, I, IV, II D. II, III, I, IV

29. The most important characteristics of a federation is

A. Centre's Supremacy over States
B. Non-correspondence between the functions and resources of the Centre and State Governments
C. Perfect match between the functions and resources of the Central and State Governments
D. None of the above

30. In the equation $C = C_0 + C_1 Y_d$, where C is planned consumption expenditure, Y_d is disposable income, C_0 is intercept or autonomous consumption (value of C when disposable income is zero), and C_1 is marginal propensity to consume; which of the following is the endogenous variable?

A. C_0 B. C_1
C. $C_1 Y_d$ D. None of the above

31. Which of the following statement is false?

A. In dynamic multiplier, there is lagged relationship between consumption and disposable income
B. The dynamic multiplier process can be presented as a decreasing geometric series of change in income in the following period
C. A major portion of the multiplier effect is realized in fewer periods when the marginal propensity to consume is smaller
D. A major portion of the multiplier effect is realized in fewer periods when the marginal propensity to consume is larger

32. According to which of the following hypotheses, consumption is irreversible?

A. Absolute Income Hypothesis
B. Relative Income Hypothesis
C. Permanent Income Hypothesis
D. Life Cycle Hypothesis

33. Which of the following models of business cycle generates constrained cycles?

A. Samuelson's model
B. Hick's model
C. Kaldor's model
D. All of the above

34. Which of the following is not an assumption of Harrod's model of growth?

A. The desired capital output ratio is constant
B. Savings are a constant proportion of real income in the economy
C. The labour force grows at some exogenously determined constant exponential rate
D. Factor prices are flexible in the long run

35. Match the statements given in List-I with their propounders in List-II:

List-I (Statements)	*List-II (Propounders)*
(*a*) Velocity of money is a stable function of its determinants	1. Keynesians
(*b*) Velocity of money is an unstable function of its determinants	2. Monetarists
(*c*) Velocity of money is a constant, and does not depend on income and interest rate	3. Classicals

Choose the correct code:

Codes:

	(*a*)	(*b*)	(*c*)
A.	2	3	1
B.	1	2	3
C.	2	1	3
D.	3	2	1

36. A.W. Phillips' wage-inflation unemployment trade off is based on

A. Static expectations hypothesis
B. Adaptive expectations hypothesis
C. Extrapolative expectations hypothesis
D. Rational expectations hypothesis

37. Suppose the money supply and the price level are constant, and the demand for money is a function of income and interest rate. When the income level increases, there is

A. an increase in the quantity of money demanded and an increase in the rate of interest
B. an increase in the quantity of money demanded and a decrease in the rate of interest
C. a decrease in the quantity of money demanded and a decrease in the rate of interest
D. a decrease in the quantity of money demanded and an increase in the rate of interest

38. Fiscal reform measures in India included

I. Increasing Tax-GDP ratio
II. Expenditure Management
III. Managing revenue deficit and fiscal deficit
IV. Increasing liquidity in the economy

Find the correct combination from the given codes.

A. I, II and III are correct.
B. I and IV are correct.
C. II, III and IV are correct.
D. III and IV are correct.

39. During the Tenth Five Year Plan, some of the following things were experienced:

I. Services sector witnessed the highest growth rate.
II. Agriculture experienced the lowest growth rate.
III. Rate of growth in the industrial sector was negative.

Which of the aforesaid statements are correct?

A. I, II and III are correct
B. I and II are correct
C. I and III are correct
D. II and III are correct

40. Assertion (A): Employment growth in the organized sector (both public and private combined) has increased during the period 1994–2008.

Reason (R): There has been relatively faster employment growth in the private sector.

Codes:

A. Both (A) and (R) are correct and (R) is the correct explanation of (A)
B. Both (A) and (R) are correct but (R) is not the correct explanation of (A)
C. (A) is correct but (R) is incorrect
D. (A) is incorrect but (R) is correct

41. According to the provisional figures for 2011 census, which of the following States has the lowest child sex ratio both in rural and urban areas?

A. Uttar Pradesh

B. Kerala
C. Jammu and Kashmir
D. Haryana

42. Of the following, which sector experienced maximum growth rate at 2004–05 prices in India during 2009–10?
A. Trade, hotels, transport and communication
B. Manufacturing, construction, electricity, gas and water supply
C. Financing, insurance, real estate and business services
D. Agriculture, forestry, fishing, mining and quarrying

43. In which of the following years, gross domestic savings as a percentage of GDP was the highest?
A. 2009–10 B. 2008–09
C. 2007–08 D. 2006–07

44. Growth process resulting into broad based benefits and providing equality of opportunity to all is referred to as
A. Faster growth B. Inclusive growth
C. Exclusive growth D. Sustained growth

45. Which of the following plans witnessed the highest growth rate in India?
A. Ninth Plan B. Eighth Plan
C. Tenth Plan D. Seventh Plan

46. For any pair of variables X and Y, two regression equations-one regression of Y on X and other regression of X on Y exist because
I. Tangent of the angle made by two regression equations with each other determines the coefficient of correlation.
II. Regression model does not help in the identification of dependent and independent variables of the equation.
III. Regression and correlation coefficients represent the co-variation of the two variables.
IV. Regression equation represents jointly the value of X and Y.

Select the right code from the following as the answer to the question:

Codes:
A. I and II are correct
B. I and III are correct
C. I and IV are correct
D. III and IV are correct

47. Which of the following are not associated with the Leontief's Static Model?
I. Final demand is a stochastic vector.
II. Reciprocal of the Perron-Frobinius root is the maximum growth rate.
III. Input coefficients are the fixed technological parameters.
IV. $(I - A - RB)^{-1}\ WL = P$

Select the correct code from the following:
A. I, II, III
B. I, III, IV
C. I, III
D. I, II, IV

48. If $X_1 = f(P_1, P_2)$ and $X_2 = \phi(P_1, P_2)$, then the two commodities are substitutes if
A. $(\delta X_1 / \delta P_2) < 0, (\delta X_2 / \delta P_1) > 0$
B. $(\delta X_1 / \delta P_2) > 0, (\delta X_2 / \delta P_1) < 0$
C. $(\delta X_1 / \delta P_2) > 0, (\delta X_2 / \delta P_1) > 0$
D. $(\delta X_1 / \delta P_2) < 0, (\delta X_2 / \delta P_1) < 0$

49. In the context of simultaneous equations econometric models, consider the following statements.
I. Identification is a problem to be dealt with before estimation.
II. Order condition is necessary but not a sufficient condition of identification.
III. Two stage least squares method of estimation gives consistent estimators if the equation is under identified.
IV. Under indirect least squares method, least squares method is applied to the reduced form equations.

Use the following code to answer the question.
A. I and II are correct but III and IV are incorrect
B. I, II, III and IV are correct
C. I, II and III are correct but IV is incorrect
D. I, II and IV are correct but III is incorrect

50. If $r_{xy} = 0.3$, match the items in List-I with the items in List-II :

List-I	List-II
(*a*) –1 to +1	1. 0.3
(*b*) Correlation coefficient between –X and Y	2. Limits of correlation coefficient
(*c*) The square of correlation coefficient	3. –0.3
(*d*) Coefficient of correlation between –X and –Y	4. Coefficient of determination

Codes:

	(*a*)	(*b*)	(*c*)	(*d*)
A.	1	2	3	4
B.	2	3	4	1
C.	3	1	2	4
D.	4	1	2	3

51. Match List-I and List-II:

List-I	*List-II*
(*a*) Durbin-Watson '*d*' Statistics	1. Stationarity
(*b*) R^2	2. Qualitative Effects
(*c*) Dickey-Fuller test	3. Serial Correlation
(*d*) Dummy Variable	4. Goodness of fit of regression function

Codes:

	(*a*)	(*b*)	(*c*)	(*d*)
A.	1	2	4	3
B.	2	1	3	4
C.	4	3	2	1
D.	3	4	1	2

52. In CES production function,

$$Q = M\left[\alpha X^{-p} + (1-\alpha)X_2^{-p}\right]^{-\frac{1}{p}}$$

Where Q is output and X_1 and X_2 are labour and capital. Elasticity of substitution is given by

A. $-p$ B. $\frac{-1}{p}$

C. $\frac{1}{(1+p)}$ D. M

53. In Linear Programming problem involving two variables, multiple optimal solutions are obtained when one of the constraints is

A. The objective function should be parallel to a constraint that forms boundary of the feasible region

B. The objective function should be perpendicular to a constraint that forms the boundary of the feasible region

C. Neither (A) nor (B)

D. Two constraints should be parallel to each other

54. In an open economy model of input output analysis, if A is the input coefficients matrix and (I – A) is technology matrix, the following is the viability condition to be satisfied.

A. $|I - A| \neq 0$

B. $|I - A| > 0$

C. $|I - A| < 0$

D. All principal minors of the (I – A) matrix must be positive

55. For the Cobb-Douglas Production function $Q = A L^{\alpha} K^{1-\alpha}$

The elasticity of substitution is

A. Zero B. Infinity

C. One D. A

56. Coefficient of determination of a regression model

I. Explains the proportion of total variation in the values of the dependent variable.

II. It can be used to derive the estimate of the extent of variation in the value of Y that is explained by the random factors.

III. Direction of interrelation between the dependent and independent variables.

IV. It explains the influence of the intercept on the dependent variable.

Select the correct code from the list given below:

A. I, II, III B. I, II

C. II, III, IV D. IV, I

57. The input coefficients/elements of which of the following matrices are interpreted as inputs required directly and indirectly per unit of final demand.

A. A B. (I – A)

C. $(I - A)^{-1}$ D. All of these

58. Total food grains production target for the year 2010–11 has been placed at

A. 250 million tonnes
B. 240 million tonnes
C. 244 million tonnes
D. 234 million tonnes

59. Indicate the year in which National Food Security Mission (NFSM) was launched

A. 2001–02 B. 2004–05
C. 2010–11 D. 2007–08

60. Identify sources of agricultural credit in India from the code given below:

1. Commercial Banks
2. Money Lender
3. Regional Rural Bank
4. Small Industries Development Bank of India

Codes:

A. 1, 2 and 3 B. 2, 3 and 4
C. 3, 4 and 1 D. 1, 2, 3 and 4

61. Low productivity for agriculture in India is attributed to

A. Poor irrigation facilities
B. Heavy dependence on monsoon
C. Absence of new technology
D. All the above

62. Quantum of food subsidy was highest in the year

A. 2009–10 B. 2008–09
C. 2004–05 D. 2001–02

63. Productivity of Indian agriculture can be enhanced by

I. Increased public investment
II. Increased irrigation facilities
III. Higher support price to the farmers
IV. Shifting workers from industry to agriculture

Select the correct answer from the given codes.

Codes:

A. I, II and IV B. I, II and III
C. II, III and IV D. III, IV and I

64. High powered money comprises

A. Currency held by the public + Cash reserves of banks
B. Currency held by the public + Demand and time deposits + Cash reserves of banks
C. Currency held by the public + Cash reserves of banks + Other deposits of RBI
D. Currency held by the public + other deposits of RBI

65. Capital to risk-weighted asset ratio of all scheduled commercial banks in India under the Basel–I framework is stipulated at the minimum of

A. 7% B. 9%
C. 12% D. 14%

66. Which of the following financial institutions are operating in the money market?

I. Non-banking financial institutions
II. Acceptance Houses
III. Central Bank
IV. Stock Exchanges

Select the correct answer from the given codes:

Codes:

A. II and III B. I and III
C. I, II and IV D. I, II and III

67. Assertion (A): The capital base of regional rural banks (RRBs) is found to be weak.

Reason (R): Deposit mobilization of RRBs has been inadequate.

From the above two statements, select the correct answer from the given codes.

Codes:

A. Both (A) and (R) are correct and (R) is the correct explanation of (A).
B. Both (A) and (R) are correct but (R) is not the correct explanation of (A).
C. (A) is incorrect but (R) is correct.
D. (A) is correct but (R) is incorrect.

68. Which of the following is broad money (M_3) in India?

A. Currency with public + demand deposits in the banks
B. Currency + demand deposits + other deposits with RBI
C. Currency + demand deposits + time deposits
D. Currency + demand deposits + time deposits + other deposits with RBI

69. Which of the following did not contribute significantly to inflationary pressure in Indian economy in 2010–11?
A. Food prices
B. Prices of manufactured prices
C. Fuel prices
D. Metal and mineral prices

70. In Joan Robinson's growth model, capital accumulation depends on
A. Saving-income ratio
B. Profit-wage relation and labour productivity
C. Profit-income ratio and capital productivity
D. Saving-investment ratio

71. In Hicks' neutral technical progress, the technical progress is
A. Capital augmenting
B. Labour augmenting
C. Both Labour and Capital augmenting
D. Change in the efficiency and productivity of labour

72. In dual gap model, the gap can be filled up by
A. Raising the level of saving
B. Export promotion
C. Steady rate of growth
D. Foreign aid

73. The concept of 'learning by doing' was given by
A. J.R. Hicks
B. Kenneth Arrow
C. Joan Robinson
D. Nicholas Kaldor

74. Which of the following represents the concept of human capital?
A. Total human resources
B. Total population
C. Human resources gainfully employed in productive activities
D. All of the above

75. Which of the following is disadvantageous to developing countries' international trade?
A. Protection
B. Free trade
C. Exports of primary and import of manufactured goods
D. None of the above

ANSWERS

1	2	3	4	5	6	7	8	9	10
B	A	D	D	A	D	A	A	D	C
11	**12**	**13**	**14**	**15**	**16**	**17**	**18**	**19**	**20**
A	B	D	B	C	B	C	C	B	C
21	**22**	**23**	**24**	**25**	**26**	**27**	**28**	**29**	**30**
D	D	C	D	C	A	A	A	B	C
31	**32**	**33**	**34**	**35**	**36**	**37**	**38**	**39**	**40**
C	B	B	D	C	A	A	A	B	A
41	**42**	**43**	**44**	**45**	**46**	**47**	**48**	**49**	**50**
D	A	C	B	C	A	D	C	D	B
51	**52**	**53**	**54**	**55**	**56**	**57**	**58**	**59**	**60**
D	C	A	D	C	B	C	C	D	A
61	**62**	**63**	**64**	**65**	**66**	**67**	**68**	**69**	**70**
D	A	B	C	B	D	B	D	B	B
71	**72**	**73**	**74**	**75**					
C	D	B	C	C					

SOME SELECTED EXPLANATORY ANSWERS

1. Perfectly elastic demand ($E_d = \infty$): When the demand for a commodity rises or falls to any extent without any change in price, demand for the commodity is said to be perfectly elastic. It can be shown graphically in the given figure. It is an imaginary situation. Perfectly elastic demand curve is a horizontal line parallel to the *x*-axis. It means that at price OP, demand can be OQ or OQ_1 or OQ_2.

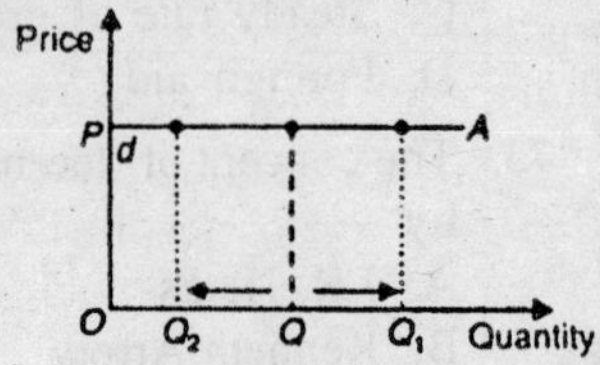

Fig. *Perfectly Elastic Demand Curve*

2. A monopolist can control either price or quantity, though not both at the same time. It may be assumed that the monopolist can charge any price it likes since it is the only supplier of a commodity. This is not true because the monopolist has little, if any, control over consumers' demand (although it has complete control over the supply of a commodity). Since the demand curve the monopolist faces is also the market demand curve for the product, it is always downward sloping. The implication is obvious. The monopolist is faced with two options: (*i*) if the objective is to sell more, price cut is essential; (*ii*) if the objective is to raise price, output restriction (or creation of an artificial shortage) is vital. But the monopolist can never raise the price and force buyers to buy more at this price. As R.G. Lipsey and C. Harbury have rightly commented: "If it (the monopolist) chooses to set price, the quantity it will be able to sell is fixed by the demand curve. If it choose to set output, the price at which that output can be disposed of, is also fixed by the demand curve. The monopolist cannot set both price and output."

4. Various models have been suggested to demonstrate the equilibrium and price-and-output determination under oligopoly. Prof. Paul Sweezy's model is perhaps the most popular one and hence we shall consider that one model only. This model provides an explanation of price-rigidity, *i.e.,* why price is not changed. The individual oligopolist sees the situation somewhat like this. If he raises the price his rivals would not follow suit and hence he is likely to lose his customers to his rivals. But if he reduces his price, others would do the same thing quickly. As a result, at a price higher than the customary one, demand is seen to be highly elastic; while at a price lower than the ruling one, the demand is seen to be highly inelastic.

5. The term 'Quasi' comes from the Latin language, which means 'as if'. Thus, 'quasi-rent' means 'as if rent'. Alfred Marshall introduced the concept of quasi rent in the economic theory.

   Factors like land (and other gift of nature) have inelastic supply in short run as well as long run. Thus, land earns rent in both the short run and long run. There are some factors like man-made machines, buildings, which have inelastic supply in the short run but have elastic supply in the long run. The supply of these factors cannot be increased or decreased in the short run with the change in demand because it takes time to make it. But the supply can be changed with the change in demand conditions in the long run. In the short run, when the demand of these factors increases, it earns income over and above the normal price. Marshall called this extra income of the factors as 'quasi-rent.' Thus, "quasi-rent" can be defined as "Extra payment made to those factors of production whose supply is fixed in short run but variable in long run."

   The quasi-rent is a short run phenomenon *i.e.,* it is earned in short run only. This is because, in the long run, the supply of these factors can be changed according to their demand and they will not earn any surplus income. Thus, quasi rent disappears in the long run.

In the long run also, quasi-rent is equal to zero. All factors are variable in the long run and hence all costs are variable. Each firm earns normal profits in the long run and there are no excess earnings over and above the costs. Therefore, no quasi-rent is earned by the factors in the long run.

6. The Loanable Funds Theory was developed by Knut Wicksell, Dennis Robertson and others. The loanable funds theory is wider in its scope than the classical theory of interest. The term "loanable funds" includes not only saving out of current income but also bank credit, dish hoarding and disinvestments. But by saving, the classical economists referred only to saving out of current income.

We know now that bank credit is an important source of funds for investment. In the classical theory, saving was demanded only for investment. But according to loanable funds theory, the demand for funds arose, not only for investment but also for hoarding wealth. The classical theory regarded interest as a function of saving and investment, $r = f$ (S.I.). But, according to loanable funds theory, the rate of interest is a function of four variables, *i.e.*, $r = f$ (I, S M.L.) where r is the rate of interest, I = investment, S = saving, M = bank credit (Quantity of money) and L = desire to hoard or the desire for liquidity.

7. At the end of the 19th century, J.B. Clark the famous neo-classical economist developed the marginal productivity theory of distribution. This theory is used to explain factor pricing from the point of view of an individual firm. According to this theory, each factor is paid on the basis of its marginal product, *i.e.*, by the addition made to the total product of the firm by the last unit of the factor. The marginal productivity theory is essentially a theory of demand for factors of production and the marginal product curve of a factor is its demand curve. The theory does not explain the supply side of the factor market.

9. The concept of optimum currency area to do away with the imbalances in the balance of payments of a country was first advocated by Meade in 1957–58. It was formalized in a theoretical shape by Mundell in 1961.

According to Mundell internal and external balance in a country can be achieved under optimal currency area. He further held that the countries of optimal currency area must allow free mobility of labour and capital and other factors of production among themselves.

13. **Ministerial Conferences**

#	Date	Host City
1st	9–13 December 1996	Singapore
2nd	18–20 May 1998	Geneva, Switzerland
3rd	30 November–3 December 1999	Seattle, United States
4th	10–14 November 2001	Doha, Qatar
5th	10–14 September 2003	Cancun, Mexico
6th	13–18 December 2005	Hong Kong
7th	30 November–3 December 2009	Geneva, Switzerland
8th	15 December–17 December 2011	Geneva, Switzerland
9th	December 2013 (expected)	Bali, Indonesia

14. Since foreign exchange rates usually fluctuate through time, anyone who has to make or receive a payment in a foreign currency at a future date runs the risk of having to pay more or receiving less in terms of the domestic currency than originally anticipated. These foreign exchange risks can be avoided or "covered" by hedging. This usually involves

an agreement today to buy or sell a certain amount of foreign exchange at some future date (usually 3 months hence) at a rate agreed upon today (the forward exchange rate).

15. With a view to increasing international liquidity, on 28th July, 1969, IMF initiated a new scheme called **Special Drawing Rights** (SDR) or Paper Gold. It is a novel method of obtaining adequate amount of foreign exchange for international payments. Price of one unit of SDR was equal to gold worth one dollar. In other words, gold value of SDR was 0.88867 gram of gold. Consequent upon the devaluation of dollar in February, 1973, value of SDR was revised to 0.20635 dollar. According to a decision on 14th June, 1974, it has been delinked from gold. **The SDR is a currency basket composed of the U.S. Dollar, the Euro, German Mark, the Japanese Yen and the U.K. pound sterling.**

17. Employment Guarantee Scheme of Maharashtra: In 1972–73, the Maharashtra Government introduced this novel scheme for the first time to give recognition to the 'right to work' included in the Constitution. The scheme was just a reflection of the commitment by the State to provide work to a person who was ready to offer his service. The basic objectives of the scheme was to provide gainful and productive employment.

18. Weber's theory of location is purely deductive in its approach. It says the differences of production costs due to differences in regions is the main reason for industrial location—Weber's analysis is based on general principles which are having an influential bearing on the location of industries and to pull their location to different geographical regions and factors that decide thet actual setting up of an industry in a particular locality.

Weber showed two causes for industrial location. They are:

Primary Causes

These are regional factors to establish industries at a particular region. Other factors like land and buildings, plant and machinery, depreciation, interest etc., does not show influence in industrial location. Industries are pulled towards centres of least transport costs. Lowest transportation costs show influence both on place of consumption and the place of deposits of materials.

Regional Factors

It is natural to change the costs depending on the region. In view of industrial location, difference in different regions can be found. Preference should be given to those costs which can change according to change in region. After careful consideration, Weber identified transportation costs and labour costs.

Secondary Causes

Weber gave less preference to secondary causes. He divided then into agglomerative and deglomerative factors. An agglomerative factor is an advantage or a cheapening of production or marketing which results from the fact that production is carried on to some considerable extent at one place. Deglomerative factor is a cheapening of production which results from the decentralisation of production.

32. James Duesenberry propounded the Relative Income Hypothesis. He was of the opinion that the basic relation between consumption and income was one of proportionality. The relative income hypothesis lays down that consumption is a function of relative income and not of absolute income. According to this hypothesis, household consumption is based on its relative position in the distribution of income among other households.

Duesenberry argues that the fraction of a family's income devoted to consumption depends on the level of its income relative to the income of the neighbouring family or families with which it identifies and not on the absolute level of the family's income. Thus, if the family's income rises but its relative position on the income scale remains unchanged because the incomes of other families, with whom it identifies, have risen at the same rate. If revision of income between consumption and saving will remain unchanged, the family's absolute income has risen so its absolute consumption and absolute saving will also rise. But the fraction of income devoted to consumption will be the same at the higher level of absolute income as it was at the lower level.

Criticism

(1) The Relative income hypothesis focuses on the individual family's current income as the income concept relevant to its spending. However, according to Friedman it is the permanent income which can appropriately explain the proportionality of consumption function.

(2) This hypothesis considers consumption behaviour to be irreversible. It means that if a fall in income should prevail for a long period of time, the consumption will continue to be determined by the short-run consumption function and people will continue to dissave forever. And it is more reasonable to assume that eventually household will return to long-run consumption function.

(3) According to this hypothesis recessions must be accompanied by a decline in consumption function but during the recession of 1944–45 the consumption has increased.

(4) It has been found that a large increase in income causes generally a less than proportionate increase in consumption.

(5) Demonstration effect may not always be true. An increase in income may lead to an increase in saving. Consumption may be based on preference rather than in imitation.

(6) It is not yet fully proved that consumers of lower income group will emulate the consumption pattern of higher income group.

34. Sir Roy Harrod has shown in his model how steady growth may occur in an economy. He is the path-finder of the trend of macro-economic single sector dynamic models of economic growth. His seminal paper on An Essay in Dynamic Theory, was later illustrated in a book called Towards Dynamic Economics (1939). His model deals with developed countries, which have already attained full employment. Harrod model explains the way to maintain full employment. In this model, the theory of "multiplier" has been integrated with the theory of the "accelerator".

Assumptions

Harrod model is based on the following assumptions:

1. Constant returns to scale holds.
2. The level of ex-ante aggregate saving is a constant proportion of aggregate income.
3. Capital output and labour output ratios are assumed to be constant.
4. The overall effect of technical progress is neutral.
5. The entrepreneurs wish to undertake investment which in turn depends on the pace of increase in output.

The Harrod model is based on three distinct rates of growth:

Firstly, there is actual growth rate represented by G which is determined by the saving ratio and the capital output ratio.

Secondly, there is warranted growth rate expressed by G_w which is the full capacity growth rate of income of an economy.

Thirdly, there is the natural growth rate expressed by G_n, which according to Harrod is the 'welfare optimum'. It can also be regarded as the potential or full employment rate of the growth.

46. A regression line is a straight line which indicates the best probable average value of one variable corresponding to the average value of another variable.

A line which represents the average relationship between two variables is called regression line. It is used to show the functional relationship between two variables, say, X and Y. It is also called as the estimating line since it is used to estimate the value of dependent variable from the given value of independent variable.

In the case of two variables X and Y, there are two regression lines. One regression line is as the regression of X and Y and the other is as the regression of Y and X. The regression line X on Y is used for estimating the most probable value of X for the given value of Y and the regression line Y on X is used for estimating the most probable value of Y for given values of X.

55. The Cobb-Douglas production function was proposed by Wicksell and tested against statistical evidence by Charles W. Cobb and Paul H. Douglas in 1928. It is one of the most popular and commonly used production functions. It has been widely used in large number of cases worldwide. The Cobb-Douglas production function is represented as:

$$Q = AL^{\alpha} K^{1-\alpha}$$

where α, β are constants. A is the technological parameter, α is the elasticity of output with respect to labour and (1 – α) is the elasticity of output with respect to capital.

Let us now move on to the properties of this production function.

(*a*) Cobb Douglas production function is a homogeneous production function: You should know that a homogeneous function is one in which if each input is multiplied by λ, then λ is factored out of the function. The power of λ is known as the degree of homogeneity and is a measure of returns to scale. A homogeneous function of degree *v* is one in which if each independent variable is multiplied by a given factor λ, then the dependent variable is multiplied by the same factor raised to the power of *v*.

Cobb Douglas production function is a homogeneous of degree (α + β).

- If (α + β) = 1 the production function exhibits constant returns to scale; increasing both inputs by a factor λ raises output by exactly the same factor. It is linearly homogeneous.
- If (α + β) > 1 the production function exhibits increasing returns to scale.
- If (α + β) < 1 the production function exhibits decreasing returns to scale.

So a Cobb-Douglas production function has the property that the returns to scale is immediately revealed by the sum of the two parameters α and β.

(*b*) Isoquants are negatively sloped and convex to the origin.

(*c*) The marginal products of the factors are given by:

$$MP_L = AK^{\alpha}\beta L^{\beta-1} = \frac{\beta}{L}AK^{\alpha}L^{\beta}$$

$$= \beta\frac{Q}{L} = \beta.AP_L$$

$$MP_K = A\alpha K^{\alpha-1}L^{\beta} = \frac{\alpha}{K}AK^{\alpha}L^{\beta}$$

$$= \alpha\frac{Q}{K} = \alpha.AP_K$$

(*d*) The $MRTS_{LK}$ of the Cobb Douglas production function is:

$$MRTS_{LK} = \frac{MP_L}{MP_K} = \left(\frac{\beta Q/L}{\alpha Q/K}\right) = \frac{\beta}{\alpha}.\frac{K}{L}$$

(*e*) Elasticity of substitution is equal to 1.

(*f*) Elasticity of output with respect to labour (e_L) shows the response in output with respect to one unit change in labour input.

64. High-powered money is the money, which is produced by the government and the central bank and held in the hands of the public and the banks. It can be defined as:

H = C + R + OD

where, H = High-powered money
C = Currency held by the public
R = Cash reserves held by banks
OD = Other deposits of RBI

70. The neo-classical economists have presented the classical ideas of economic growth (regarding population, savings and technology etc.) in the form of growth models by applying Keynesian and Harrod-Domar terminology. These models are known as neo-classical growth models. Mrs. Joan Robinson has also developed a similar type of growth models in her book, "The Accumulation of Capital" published in 1956. It is a simple model of economic growth, based on the "Capitalist Rules of the Game". This growth model clearly incorporates the problem of population growth in a developing economy and analysis its effects upon the capital accumulation and growth of output.

Assumption of the Model

The model is based upon the following assumptions.

1. The economy is a closed one and capital (K) and labour (L) are the only factors of production.
2. Capital and labour are combined in fixed proportions for production.
3. Production technology is unchanged (or fixed).
4. Total income (Y) of the economy is divided between the wage earners (labourers) and profit earners (entrepreneurs).
5. The wage earners spend their entire income on consumption (*i.e.,* no saving of wage-earners), while profit-earners spend their entire income (profits) on investment or capital formation and consume nothing.
6. Total wage-bill is the real wage rate multiplied by the number of workers.
7. Total profits are calculated by multiplying the profit-rate by the amount of capital.
8. The total natural income is the sum of the total wage share and the total profit share.
9. Price level is constant.

Now the equation of total income may be written as:

$$Y = w.L + \pi.K \qquad ...(1)$$

where Y = Total Income (output)

w = Real Wage Rate

L = Labour

π = Profit Rate

K = Capital

Mrs. Robinson states that profit rate (π) is an important factor in the theory of capital accumulation (growth). We may get this profit rate from equation:

$$\pi = \frac{Y - w.L}{K} \qquad ...(2)$$

Equation (2) states that the profit rate can be expressed as the ratio of total income (Y) minus total wage bill (W.= w.L) to the amount of capital (K). In other words, profit per labour employed (or per capita profit) is the difference between the output per labourer and the real wage. Hence,

$$\pi = \frac{Y - w.L}{K}$$

or $$= \frac{Y/L}{K/L} - w \cdot \frac{L}{K} = \frac{y}{k} - \frac{w}{k}$$

or $$\pi = \frac{1}{k}(y - w)$$

or $$k\pi = y - w \qquad ...(3)$$

where $y = \frac{Y}{L}$ (per capita output)

$k = \frac{K}{L}$ (per capita capital)

or $$\pi = f(k, y, w) \qquad ...(4)$$

where $y = f(k)$

This means that the rate of profit (π) would depend on labour productivity (y), the real wage rate (w) and the amount of capital per labour (k). Hence, profit can increase if wage-rate (w) decreases or y (labour productivity) increases or (capital labour ratio) decreases while at the same time other variables are held constant.

71. Hicks neutral technical progress occurs when technical progress augments both labour and capital. In other words, the productivity of capital and that of labour are enhanced with the passage of time.

73. Learning-by-doing is a concept of economic theory. It refers to the capability of workers to improve their productivity by regularly repeating the same type of action. The increased productivity is achieved through practice, self-perfection and minor innovations.

The concept of learning-by-doing has been used by Kenneth Arrow in his design of endogenous growth theory to explain effects of innovation and technical change. Robert Lucas, Jr. (1988) adopted the concept to explain increasing returns to embodied human capital. Yang and Borland (1991) have shown learning-by-doing plays a role in the evolution of countries to greater specialisation in production. In both these cases, learning-by-doing and increasing returns provide an engine for long run growth.

Previous Papers (Solved)

UGC-NET ECONOMICS, JUNE – 2012

PAPER-II

Note : *This paper contains* ***fifty (50)*** *objective type questions, each question carrying* ***two (2)*** *marks. Attempt* ***all*** *the questions.*

Directions (Qs. 1 to 10): *Read the following questions and find correct answer from the choices given below these questions.*

1. Marginal Revenue of a Monopoly firm is less than the price. Because
   A. Demand curve has a positive slope.
   B. Demand curve has a negative slope.
   C. Monopolist incurs losses.
   D. Monopolist is in equilibrium.
2. For an inferior goods, income consumption curve and Engles curves are
   A. Positively sloped
   B. Negatively sloped
   C. Are the same
   D. Income consumption curve positively sloped and the Engles curve is negatively sloped
3. The classical economists focussed on the role of money as
   A. medium of exchange
   B. medium of distribution
   C. wealth
   D. link between present and future
4. If the demand for money is perfectly interest inelastic, the LM schedule will be
   A. Upward sloping
   B. Downward sloping
   C. Horizontal line
   D. Vertical line
5. Harrod-Domar model of economic growth is based on the equilibrium between
   A. Income generation and productive capacity creation
   B. Equilibrium between income and consumption
   C. Equilibrium between savings and investment
   D. None of the above
6. In calculating the buoyancy of a tax, we consider
   A. Only discretionary changes
   B. Only automatic changes
   C. Both A and B
   D. Neither A nor B
7. Which of the following measures of the central tendency suits the data best if the objective is to assess the distribution of values?
   A. Arithmetic mean B. Mode
   C. Median D. Kurtosis
8. Comparative cost advantage in Ricardo's international trade theory arises due to
   A. Labour cost differences
   B. Differences in factor endowment
   C. Factor abundance defined in terms of factor prices
   D. All of the above
9. In India, in 2004-05 the number of poor persons below poverty line was the highest in the State of
   A. Bihar B. Uttar Pradesh
   C. Madhya Pradesh D. Rajasthan
10. Which of the following is not a component of Bharat Nirman?
    A. Rural housing
    B. Rural electrification
    C. Agro-based industries
    D. Rural telephony

Directions (Qs. 11 to 20): *Read the following questions and find out correct answer from the codes given below these questions.*

11. A point of 'Kink" in the kinked demand curve indicates
I. Price rigidity
II. Quantity rigidity
III. Price flexibility
IV. Quantity flexibility
Codes :
A. I and II are correct
B. II and III are correct
C. III and IV are correct
D. I and IV are correct

12. Improvement in the BOP deficit may be effected through
I. Import control
II. Export promotion
III. Foreign exchange control
IV. Devaluation
Codes :
A. I and II are correct
B. I, II, III and IV are correct
C. II and III are correct
D. I, II and III are correct

13. The problem relating to burden of public debt has been dealt by
I. A.P. Learner
II. E.D. Domar
III. A.C. Pigou
IV. A.H. Henson
Codes :
A. I and II are correct
B. II and III are correct
C. I and IV are correct
D. II and III are correct

14. Fiscal policy relates to the Government decision in respect of
I. Taxation
II. Government spending
III. Government borrowing
IV. Public Debt
Codes :
A. III and IV are correct
B. II, III and IV are correct
C. I and II are correct
D. All the above are correct

15. HDI is entrusted with reference to :
I. Life expectancy at birth
II. Real GDP/per capita
III. Infant mortality
IV. Morbidity
Codes :
A. I and II are correct
B. II and III are correct
C. III and IV are correct
D. All of the above

16. The doctrine of unbalanced growth was propounded by
I. Hirschman
II. Robert Solow
III. Singer
IV. Ragnar Nurkse
Codes :
A. I and II are correct
B. II and III are correct
C. III and IV are correct
D. I and III are correct

17. Harrod-Domar model of economic growth is based upon
I. Warranted growth rate
II. Investment growth rate
III. Productivity growth rate
IV. Natural growth rate
Codes :
A. I and II are correct
B. II and III are correct
C. III and IV are correct
D. I and IV are correct

18. In Keynesian system speculative demand for money arises because of
I. Uncertainty of future interest rates
II. Unexpected expenditures
III. To bridge the gap between income and eventual expenditure
IV. Relationship between changes in the interest rates and bond prices
Codes :
A. I and III are correct
B. I and IV are correct

C. II and III are correct
D. III and IV are correct

19. According to Milton Friedman Theory of permanent component of consumption-expenditure depends on
I. Transitory income alone
II. Transitory and permanent income
III. Permanent income alone
IV. Windfall gains
Codes :
A. I and II are correct
B. I and III are correct
C. II and IV are correct
D. Only III is correct

20. The Planning Commission of India has recently made announcement regarding Poverty Line :
I. ₹ 42 per capita per day in urban area
II. ₹ 26 per capita per day in rural area
III. ₹ 32 per capita per day in urban area
IV. ₹ 32 per capita per day in rural area
Codes :
A. I and II are correct
B. I and III are correct
C. II and III are correct
D. III and IV are correct

Directions (Qs. 21 to 30): *Read the following questions of given Assertions with their Reasoning and find correct answer from the codes given below these questions.*

21. Assertion (A): Giffin's paradox rarely occurs in the real world.
Reason (R): Inferior goods are narrowly defined for which suitable substitutes are available.
Codes :
A. Both (A) and (R) are correct and (R) is the correct explanation of (A).
B. Both (A) and (R) are correct and (R) is not the correct explanation of (A).
C. (A) is correct, but (R) is incorrect.
D. (A) is incorrect, but (R) is correct.

22. Assertion (A): According to the Life Cycle Theory of consumption, an individual level of consumption depends not just on current income but also on long run expected earnings.
Reason (R): Individuals are assumed to plan a pattern of expenditure based on expected earnings over life time.
Codes :
A. (A) is true, but (R) is false.
B. Both (A) and (R) are false.
C. (A) is not correct, but (R) is correct.
D. Both (A) and (R) are correct and (R) is correct explanation of (A).

23. Assertion (A): Effective demand can be increased by more equitable distribution of wealth.
Reason (R): Thirty or forty entities with income averaging between 1 lakh and 5 lakhs would create much more effective demand than a single entity having income of 10 lakhs a year.
Codes :
A. Both (A) and (R) are correct and (R) is not the correct explanation of (A).
B. Both (A) and (R) are correct and (R) is the correct explanation of (A).
C. (A) is correct, but (R) is incorrect.
D. (A) is incorrect, but (R) is correct.

24. Assertion (A): During the period 2004-05 to 2007-08 fiscal consolidation process was witnessed in India.
Reason (R) : There was buoyancy in tax revenue during this period.
Codes :
A. Both (A) and (R) are correct and (R) is the correct explanation of (A).
B. Both (A) and (R) are correct and (R) is not the correct explanation of (A).
C. (A) is correct, but (R) is incorrect.
D. (A) is incorrect, but (R) is correct.

25. Assertion (A): K/L ratio will adjust through time in the direction of equilibrium ratio.

Reason (R): Because the technical coefficient of production are variable.

Codes :

A. Both (A) and (R) are correct and (R) is not the correct explanation of (A).
B. Both (A) and (R) are correct and (R) is the correct explanation of (A).
C. (A) is correct, but (R) is incorrect.
D. (A) is incorrect, but (R) is correct.

26. Assertion (A): Financial inclusion is desirable to help weaker sections of society in the country.

Reason (R): Investment activity needs to be promoted to facilitate access to development benefits to masses.

Codes :

A. Both (A) and (R) are correct and (R) is not the correct explanation of (A).
B. Both (A) and (R) are correct and (R) is the correct explanation of (A).
C. (A) is not correct, but (R) is correct.
D. (A) is correct, but (R) is not correct.

27. Assertion (A): Stationary state is the end of the process of capital formation.

Reason (R): Scarcity of natural resources as also capital leads the economy to the stationary state.

Codes:

A. Both (A) and (R) are correct and (R) is not the correct explanation of (A).
B. Both (A) and (R) are correct and (R) is the correct explanation of (A).
C. (A) is correct, but (R) is not correct.
D. (A) is not correct, but (R) is correct.

28. Assertion (A): Investment has also a supply effect.

Reason (R): Because it raises capacity to produce.

Codes:

A. Both (A) and (R) are correct and (R) is not the correct explanation of (A).
B. Both (A) and (R) are correct and (R) is the correct explanation of (A).
C. (A) is correct, but (R) is not correct.
D. (A) is not correct, but (R) is correct.

29. Assertion (A): Gold standard was finally given up after the Second World War.

Reason (R): Countries had different rates of inflation.

Codes:

A. Both (A) and (R) are correct and (R) is the correct explanation of (A).
B. Both (A) and (R) are correct and (R) is not correct explanation of (A).
C. (A) is correct, but (R) is not correct.
D. (A) is not correct, but (R) is correct.

30. Assertion (A): Disguised unemployment is present in Indian agriculture.

Reason (R): Marginal productivity of agriculture is close to zero.

Codes:

A. Both (A) and (R) are correct and (R) is the correct explanation of (A).
B. Both (A) and (R) are correct and (R) is not the correct explanation of (A).
C. (A) is correct, but (R) is not correct.
D. (A) is not correct, but (R) is correct.

Directions (Qs. 31 to 40): *Read the following questions and find the correct sequence from the codes given below these questions.*

31. Arrange the following in chronological order:

I. CES production function
II. Cobb-Douglas production function
III. Tronslog production function
IV. The law of variable proportions

Codes :

A. III, I, IV, II
B. I, IV, II, III
C. IV, II, I, III
D. II, III, I, IV

32. Consider the following schemes :

I. EAS II. TRYSEM
III. JRY IV. RLEGP

The correct chronological sequence of the launching of these schemes are :

Codes:

A. II, IV, I, III B. IV, II, III, I

C. IV, III, I, II D. II, IV, III, I

33. Arrange the origin of money in a sequential order

I. Cheque

II. Metallic money

III. Commodity money

IV. Paper money

Codes:

A. IV, I, III, II B. I, III, II, IV

C. III, II, IV, I D. II, IV, I, III

34. Arrange the following theories in the chronological order :

I. Restatement of Quantity Theory

II. Income Theory

III. Quantity Theory

IV. Cash Balance Approach

Select the correct answer from the given codes:

Codes:

A. I, II, IV, III B. III, I, II, IV

C. IV, III, I, II D. III, IV, II, I

35. Identify the correct chronological order of the following classical economists :

A. Adam Smith, Malthus, Ricardo, J.S. Mill

B. Adam Smith, Ricardo, Malthus, J.S. Mill

C. Adam Smith, J.S. Mill, Ricardo, Malthus

D. Adam Smith, Malthus, J.S. Mill, Ricardo

36. The sequencing process of Schumpeter model of development is

A. Swarm like Clusters, Innovation, Bank credit, Breaking circular flow

B. Breaking circular flow, Innovation, Bank credit, Swarm like Clusters

C. Innovation, Bank credit, Breaking circular flow, Swarm like Clusters

D. Bank credit, Innovation, Swarm like Clusters, Breaking circular flow

37. Arrange the following theories in order in which they appeared :

I. Comparative Cost Advantage Theory

II. Absolute Cost Advantage Theory

III. Leontief Paradox

IV. Factor Endowment Theory

Codes:

A. I, III, II, IV B. II, III, IV, I

C. II, I, IV, III D. I, IV, II, III

38. Arrange the stages of economic growth in a sequential order :

I. The age of high mass consumption

II. The traditional society

III. The take-off stage

IV. The drive to maturity

Codes:

A. I, III, IV, II B. II, IV, I, III

C. III, I, II, IV D. II, III, IV, I

39. Identify the sequence of implementation of the following taxes.

Select the correct answer from the given codes:

I. Land Revenue II. Sales tax

III. MODVAT IV. Service tax

Codes:

A. I, II, III, IV B. II, IV, I, III

C. III, II, IV, I D. IV, II, I, III

40. Identify the correct chronology of the following :

I. Fisher's test of significance of differences between means of three or more samples.

II. Kendal's partial rank correlation.

III. Gosset's T test of significance between means of two samples.

IV. χ^2 test of goodness of fit of the curve and randomness of the sample values.

Codes:

A. III, I, II, IV

B. I, II, III, IV

C. IV, III, II, I

D. I, II, IV, III

Directions (Qs. 41 to 50): *Match the items given in **List-I** with those in **List-II** and answer the correct matching option from the codes given below these questions.*

41.	**List-I**	**List-II**
	I. Behavioural theory of the firm	1. J.B. Clark

II. Marginal productivity theory of distribution — 2. Cyert and Mark

III. Double criterion of welfare — 3. Kenneth Arrow

IV. Impossibility Theorem — 4. Scitovosky

Codes:

	I	II	III	IV
A.	2	1	4	3
B.	3	2	4	1
C.	1	4	3	2
D.	2	1	3	4

42.

List-I	List-II
I. New Classical Economics	1. T.H. Haavelmo
II. Permanent Income Hypothesis	2. Robert Lucas
III. Multiple effect of Balanced Budget	3. N. Gregory Mankiw
IV. New Keynesian Economics	4. Milton Friedman

Codes:

	I	II	III	IV
A.	3	4	1	2
B.	4	3	2	1
C.	2	4	1	3
D.	1	2	4	3

43.

List-I	List-II
I. Invisible Hand	1. Karl Marx
II. Warrier Knight	2. Adam Smith
III. PQLI	3. Schumpeter
IV. Surplus Value	4. Morris D. Morris

Codes:

	I	II	III	IV
A.	1	4	2	3
B.	2	3	4	1
C.	1	2	3	4
D.	4	3	2	1

44.

List-I	List-II
I. Four Sector Model	1. Rosestein-Rodan
II. Critical Minimum Effort Thesis	2. Arthur Lewis
III. Big Push Theory	3. Mahalanobis
IV. Theory of Unlimited Supply of Labour	4. Leibeistein

Codes:

	I	II	III	IV
A.	4	3	2	1
B.	3	4	1	2
C.	4	1	3	2
D.	1	2	4	3

45.

List-I	List-II
I. Food-grains Production	1. Industrial Sector
II. Level of Prices	2. Revenue deficit
III. Industrial Growth	3. Agricultural Sector
IV. Fiscal Indicators	4. Wholesale Price Index

Codes:

	I	II	III	IV
A.	4	2	1	3
B.	3	4	2	1
C.	3	4	1	2
D.	2	3	4	1

46.

List-I	List-II
I. National Agricultural Policy	1. 2004
II. Marine Fishing Policy	2. 1978
III. New Foreign Trade Policy	3. 2000
IV. Seventh Finance Commission	4. 2004

Codes:

	I	II	III	IV
A.	2	1	3	4
B.	4	3	1	2
C.	1	4	2	3
D.	3	1	4	2

47.

List-I	List-II
I. GATT	1. Managing balance of payments
II. IMF	2. Developmental Finance

III. IBRD — 3. Free Trade

IV. UNO — 4. Maintenance of peace among nations

Codes:

	I	II	III	IV
A.	2	1	4	3
B.	3	1	2	4
C.	2	3	1	4
D.	4	1	3	2

48.

List-I	List-II
I. Adam Smith	1. Availability doctrine
II. David Ricardo	2. Factors endowment
III. Ohlin	3. Absolute advantage
IV. I.B. Kravis	4. Comparative advantage

Codes:

	I	II	III	IV
A.	1	2	3	4
B.	3	4	2	1
C.	2	4	3	1
D.	4	3	1	2

49.

List-I	List-II
I. Simple Random Sampling	1. Equal probability of selection of an item in a trial
II. Random Sampling	2. Equal probability of each item in all trials
III. Stratified Random Sampling	3. Random selection of first and systematic of the rest
IV. Stratified Systematic Random Sampling	4. Random choice of all items from each stratum

Codes:

	I	II	III	IV
A.	1	2	3	4
B.	3	1	4	2
C.	4	3	1	2
D.	2	1	4	3

50.

List-I	List-II
I. IS-LM Theory	1. Franko Modigliani & Richard Brumberg
II. Consumption Ratchet	2. Lucas & Sargent
III. Life Cycle Hypothesis	3. Hicks and Hanson
IV. Critics of Keynesian Economics	4. James Dussenbery

Codes:

	I	II	III	IV
A.	3	4	1	2
B.	3	2	1	4
C.	4	3	1	2
D.	1	3	4	2

ANSWERS

1	2	3	4	5	6	7	8	9	10
B	B	A	D	C	C	C	A	B	C
11	12	13	14	15	16	17	18	19	20
A	B	C	D	A	D	D	B	D	C
21	22	23	24	25	26	27	28	29	30
C	D	B	A	B	B	B	B	B	A
31	32	33	34	35	36	37	38	39	40
C	A	C	D	B	B	C	D	A	A
41	42	43	44	45	46	47	48	49	50
A	C	B	B	C	D	B	B	D	A

PAPER–III

Note : *This paper contains* ***seventy five (75)*** *objective type questions of* ***two (2)*** *marks each.* ***All*** *questions are compulsory.*

1. A solution of Walrasian general equilibrium will exist if and only if;

A. Condition of fixed point theorem is satisfied.

B. Pareto's condition of optimality is satisfied.

C. Hick's stability conditions are satisfied.

D. The condition of Pareto's law of income distribution is satisfied.

2. Select the correct statement of Adding up Theorem.

A. If income generated by the given output produced during the given period is distributed according to average productivity of all factors, total income will be exhausted.

B. Total income derived from the output will be exhausted if all factors are paid according to their marginal productivity.

C. Total income derived from the output will be exhausted if all factors are paid at the same rate.

D. Total income will be exhausted if all factor rewards are proportional to commodity prices.

3. The producer will substitute capital for labour till he reaches that point of isoquant at which.

A. The price of the good he produces equals wage rate.

B. Marginal rate of technical substitution equals interest rate.

C. Marginal rate of technical substitution equals marginal revenue.

D. Marginal rate of technical substitution equals the ratio of marginal productivity of labour and capital.

4. Match the items from the **List-I** with items in **List-II** :

List-I	List-II
I. Sales maximization as the objective of the firm	1. Morris
II. Growth maximization as objective of the firm	2. Baumol
III. Managerial Utility Function Maximization as objective of the firm	3. Williamson
IV. Sales, profit & growth maximization as objective of the firm	4. Kaldor

Select the correct answer from the following codes :

Codes:

	I	II	III	IV
A.	2	1	3	None
B.	1	2	3	4
C.	2	1	4	3
D.	4	3	2	1

5. Match the items in List-I with items in List-II:

List-I	List-II
I. Cardinal Utility Theory of Demand	1. Hicks
II. Revealed Preference Theory of Demand	2. A. Marshall
III. Indifference Preference Theory of Demand	3. Neuman & Morgenstern
IV. Utility Index under uncertainty	4. Samuelson

Select the correct answer from the following codes :

Codes:

	I	II	III	IV
A.	1	2	3	4
B.	4	3	2	1
C.	2	4	1	3
D.	4	1	3	2

6. Arrange the proponents of the marginal productivity theory of factor reward in chronological order :

1. J.B. Clark
2. Marshall
3. Walras
4. Jevons

Select the correct code for correct answer :

Codes:

A. 1, 4, 2, 3 B. 4, 3, 1, 2
C. 1, 3, 4, 2 D. 2, 1, 4, 3

7. **Assertion (A) :** Non-collusive model of Chamberlin asserts that a stable equilibrium can be reached if each firm charges Monopoly price and equally shares the market demand for their products.

Reason (R) : Reasoning is that the firms recognize mutual interdependence in terms of action and reaction with regard to price decision with the objective of profit maximization which will be realized if prices are determined at a level which equals marginal cost.

Codes:

A. Both (A) & (R) are correct and (R) is the correct explanation of (A).
B. (A) is correct, but (R) is not correct.
C. Both (A) & (R) are correct but (R) is not the correct explanation of (A).
D. (R) is correct, but (A) is incorrect.

8. The revealed preference approach to the derivation of indifference curve
A. Assumes stability over time of an observed person's tastes.
B. Assumes that all people have identical tastes.
C. Relies on repeated observations of the market behaviour of a single person.
D. Is correctly described by both A and C.

9. Which of the following statements does not hold true in case of the Keynesian Economics?
A. Velocity of money is an unstable function of its determinants.
B. Labour is subject to money illusion.
C. Aggregate supply function tends to become flat at levels of output well below full employment and to become steeper as full capacity is reached.
D. Aggregate supply schedule is vertical, and output and employment are completely supply determined.

10. Tobin's q-theory of investment indicates that firms add to their stock of capital when
A. the replacement value of their real assets exceeds the market value of their financial assets.
B. the market value of their financial assets exceeds the replacement value of their real assets.
C. the market value of their real assets exceeds the book value of their financial assets.
D. the market value of their financial assets exceeds the book value of their real assets.

11. When current income includes negative transitory component, relating consumption with current income will produce
A. an average propensity to consume that is lower than the long run average propensity to consume.
B. an average propensity to consume that is higher than the average long run propensity to consume.
C. an average propensity to consume that equals the long run average propensity to consume.
D. None of the above

12. Liquidity trap is a situation when
A. all potential investors expect the rate of interest to rise in future
B. all potential investors expect the rate of interest to fall in future
C. natural rate of interest is above the critical rate of interest
D. demand for money for speculative purpose is interest-inelastic

13. In Harrod's model of economic growth, if warranted rate is below the natural rate of growth then it is possible to maintain steady state growth at the warranted rate with
A. continually increasing unemployment
B. a constant rate of unemployment
C. continually decreasing unemployment
D. None of the above

14. Which of the following is not a feature of the A.W. Phillip's inflation-unemployment trade-off relation?

A. A non-linear inverse relationship between unemployment rate and the rate of exchange in wage rate.

B. There is a loop in the anticlockwise around the Phillip's curve.

C. The wage-inflation unemployment relationship is predictable.

D. Philip's curve shifts when expected rate of inflation shifts.

15. Suppose there is full employment and vertical aggregate supply schedule. An increase in the nominal money supply

A. reduces the rate of interest and changes the composition of output

B. causes a proportional increase in real output

C. has no effect on the real money supply or the composition of output

D. causes the real money supply to increase, which changes composition of output

16. In the context of the Mundell-Fleming model of open economy, consider the following variables that shift the IS function.

1. a rise in the exchange rate
2. an increase in foreign income
3. a cut in taxes
4. a fall in exchange rate

Which of the following combinations of these factors shift the IS function upwards towards the right?

A. 1, 2, 4 B. 2, 3, 4

C. 1, 2, 3 D. 3, 4, 1

17. Since March 2010, how many times the Reserve Bank of India has increased the repo rate?

A. Eleven times

B. Thirteen times

C. Ten times

D. Twelve times

18. Which of the following Committees has been set up in India for identification of BPL families in urban areas?

A. Tendulkar Committee

B. Saxena Committee

C. Lakdawala Committee

D. Hashim Committee

19. A major financial inclusion initiative named 'Swabhiman' was formally launched on__

A. February 2010

B. February 2011

C. February 2009

D. February 2008

20. Which of the Five Year Plans has laid emphasis on 'faster, sustainable and inclusive growth'?

A. Eleventh Five Year Plan

B. Twelfth Five Year Plan

C. Tenth Five Year Plan

D. Ninth Five Year Plan

21. Under the revised Index of Industrial Production (IIP) series, with 2004-05 as the base, the total number of items covered has increased from 538 to

A. 682 B. 662

C. 652 D. 642

22. Which one of the following States had the highest per capita income in 2009-10?

A. Punjab

B. Haryana

C. Madhya Pradesh

D. Delhi

23. Which one of the following States had the highest number of branches of Regional Rural Branches (RRBs) in 2010?

A. Bihar

B. Haryana

C. Madhya Pradesh

D. Punjab

24. Growth of Indian agriculture has been slowed down since the adoption of new economic policy due to

1. low increase in crop yield
2. low or no public investment
3. stagnant green revolution technology
4. low retail market prices of agricultural produce

Answer this question by selecting the correct combination of codes given below :

Codes:

A. 1, 2, 3, 4 B. 2, 3

C. 1, 2, 3 D. 1, 4

25. According to the monetarists, money supply constitutes

A. Currency + demand deposits

B. Currency + demand deposits + time deposits

C. Currency + demand deposits + time deposits + equity shares

D. Currency + all kinds of bank deposits + deposits with other institutions + borrowing

26. Which of the following is not a specialized sub market of the money market?

A. Collateral loan market

B. Discount market

C. Bond market

D. Acceptance market

27. Arrange the following Committees in chronological order from the given codes

I. Khusro Committee

II. Dantewala Committee

III. Narasimham Committee

IV. Kelkar Committee

Codes :

A. I, II, III, IV B. II, IV, I, III

C. II, I, IV, III D. II, III, I, IV

28. Assertion (A) : The working of Regional Rural Banks (RRBs) revealed that they eroded their capital base.

Reason (R) : Many RRBs are non-viable and having high operating costs.

Of the above two statements, give the correct answer from the given codes :

Codes:

A. Both (A) and (R) are correct and (R) is the correct explanation of (A).

B. Both (A) and (R) are correct, but (R) is not the correct explanation of (A).

C. (A) is true, but (R) is false.

D. (A) is false, but (R) is true.

29. Which of the following institutions are regulated by the RBI as All India Financial Institution?

I. Export Import Bank of India

II. National Housing Bank

III. State Bank of India

IV. Small Industries Development Bank of India

Select the correct answer from the given codes :

Codes:

A. I, II and IV B. II, III, IV

C. I & II D. III & IV

30. Core inflation is a measure of inflation

A. that is based only on food and energy prices

B. that includes items that face volatile price movements, notably food and energy

C. that excludes items that face volatile price movements, notably food and energy

D. None of the above

31. First Green Revolution was primarily concerned with the production and productivity of

A. Pulses

B. Oilseeds

C. Wheat

D. Fruits & vegetables

32. During the period from 2004-05 to 2010-11, agricultural sector GDP

A. witnessed a higher growth rate than the overall GDP

B. witnessed a lower growth rate than the overall GDP

C. witnessed a stagnant growth rate as compared to the overall growth rate

D. witnessed a similar growth rate as that of the overall GDP.

33. The main objectives of food management are

A. Procurement of food grains from farmers at remunerative prices

B. Distribution of food grains to consumers at affordable prices.

C. Maintenance of food buffers for food security and price stability

D. All of the above

34. Which one of the following States contributed maximum to the production of pulses in the year 2009-10?

A. Uttar Pradesh

B. Madhya Pradesh

C. Rajasthan

D. Punjab

35. A Kisan Credit Card (KCC) Scheme was introduced in the year

A. 2001 B. 2005
C. 1998 D. 1999

36. Increase in agricultural production and productivity is a pre-condition

A. to raise the share of agriculture in GDP
B. to ensure national food security
C. to provide livelihood and nutritional security
D. All of the above

37. Select the year in which the gross fiscal deficit, revenue deficit and primary deficit of the Central Government as per cent of GDP were the highest?

A. 2008-09 B. 2006-07
C. 2007-08 D. 2005-06

38. Which item is likely to be the most significant item of expenditure of the Central Government during 2011-12?

A. Subsidies
B. Defence
C. Interest
D. Share of States in Central taxes

39. Items of social sector expenditure of the State Governments include

I. Education and sports
II. Energy and transport
III. Medical and public health
IV. Water supply and sanitation

Find correct answer from given codes :

Codes:

A. I, II and III are correct.
B. I, III and IV are correct.
C. II, III and IV are correct.
D. I and III are correct.

40. Match the items of **List-I** with items of **List-II** from the given code :

List-I	List-II
I. Law of increasing State activities	1. R.N. Bhargava
II. Displacement effect	2. Adolph Wagner
III. Federal Finance	3. Weisman and Peacock
IV. Functional Finance	4. A.P. Lerner

Codes:

	I	II	III	IV
A.	1	2	3	4
B.	2	3	1	4
C.	3	4	2	1
D.	4	1	3	2

41. Assertion (A) : The Union Budget for 2010-11 had begun the process of fiscal consolidation with a partial withdrawal of the stimulus measures.

Reason (R) : There was a clear evidence of economic recovery in the economy.

In the context of the above two statements, which one is correct from the given codes?

Codes:

A. Both (A) and (R) are correct and (R) is the correct explanation of (A).
B. Both (A) and (R) are correct and (R) is not the correct explanation of (A).
C. (A) is correct, but (R) is incorrect.
D. (R) is correct, but (A) is incorrect.

42. Arrange the following Reports in chronological order from the given codes :

I. Committee on Taxation of Agricultural wealth and income
II. Report of the task force on direct taxes
III. Thirteenth Finance Commission : 2010-15
IV. Indian Tax Reforms–Report of a survey

Codes:

A. III, II, IV, I B. IV, I, II, III
C. II, III, I, IV D. I, IV, III, II

43. In a competitive market, a tax on wage income falls wholly on labour if :

A. Labour supply is inelastic
B. Labour supply is elastic
C. Labour supply is highly elastic
D. Demand for products has infinite elasticity

44. The apex financial institution responsible for the development of small and micro industries in India is

A. IDBI B. SIDBI
C. NABARD D. None of the above

45. The general methods used to solve industrial disputes in India are

1. Collective bargaining
2. Compulsory arbitration
3. Adjudication
4. Decision by trade unions

Choose the correct combination of methods from this following :

A. 1 and 2 B. 2 and 3
C. 2 and 4 D. 1 and 3

46. Given below are two statements, one labelled as Assertion (A) and other labelled as Reason (R):

Assertion (A): Information Technology (IT) industry is a 'high knowledge" based industry that has developed rapidly, mainly on its own merits in India.

Reason (R): Industry that is based on high knowledge does not need any significant support from the Government nor there is much scope for outside interference.

Choose the correct combination of codes given below :

Codes:

A. (A) is correct, but (R) is wrong.
B. Both (A) and (R) are correct.
C. (A) is wrong, but (R) is correct.
D. Both (A) and (R) are wrong.

47. Match 'SEBI' with the appropriate item among the following :

A. Regulation of Money market
B. Regulation of Capital market
C. Regulation of Commodity market
D. All of the above

48. Given below are the various combinations giving the steps of industrial development. Select the correct sequential combination of steps.

A. Monetary expansion; industrial development; fall of interest; investment is stimulated.
B. Industrial development; fall of interest; monetary expansion; investment is stimulated.
C. Monetary expansion; fall of interest; investment is stimulated; industrial development.
D. Industrial development; fall of interest; monetary expansion; investment is stimulated.

49. Under the post 1991 economic policies, the Government of India supports

A. Private manufacturing sector
B. Export industries
C. Small industries
D. All of the above

50. Which of the following is the condition(s) of economic viability and technological feasibility of Leontief's static model?

A. Perron-Frobinius root
B. Value of the objective function of the primal should equal the value of the objective function of the dual of the primal
C. Kuhn-Tucker conditions
D. Hawkins-Simon conditions

51. Given the following production function, match the items in **List-I** and **List-II** :

$Y = A L^{\beta} K^{\alpha}$ $\alpha, \beta > 0$

List-I	**List-II**
I. Decreasing returns to scale	1. $\alpha + \beta > 1$
II. Increasing returns of scale	2. α
III. Output elasticity with respect to L	3. $\alpha + \beta < 1$
IV. Output elasticity with respect to K	4. β

Codes:

	I	II	III	IV
A.	3	1	2	4
B.	1	2	4	3
C.	4	1	3	2
D.	2	3	4	1

52. Match the following :

List-I	**List-II**
I. Box-Jenkins Method	1. Causality
II. Unit-root test	2. Forecasting
III. Durbin-Watson 'd' statistic	3. Stationarity
IV. Granger test	4. Auto correlation

Codes:

	I	II	III	IV
A.	3	1	2	4
B.	2	3	4	1
C.	1	2	3	4
D.	4	1	2	3

53. Which of the following hypotheses are tested by a regression function?

A. Interrelation between two or more variables is significantly different from Zero.
B. The degree and direction of interrelations between two or more variables are non-zero and goodness of fit of the regression function is satisfactory.
C. Degree of influence exercised by systematic explanatory factors is greater/lesser/equal to the influence exercised by random factors.
D. All of the above

54. In the presence of Heteroscedasticity, which of the following is not a correct statement?

A. Heteroscedasticity does not alter the unbiasedness and consistency properties of OLS estimators.

B. OLS estimators are of minimum variance or efficient.
C. BLUE estimators are provided by the method of weighted least squares.
D. 't' and 'F' tests based on standard assumptions of classical linear regression model may not be reliable.

55. Correlation coefficient between X and Y is 0.3 and correlation coefficient between P and Q is 0.6, then the strength of correlation between P and Q is higher than between X and Y by
A. two times B. three times
C. four times D. five times

56. Which of the following are conditions of consumer's equilibrium in a two commodity case where U = utility and P_1 and P_2 are prices of two goods?
A. $\delta U/\delta X = 0$ B. $\delta U_1/\delta U_2 = 0$
C. $\delta^2 U/\delta X^2 < 0$ D. None of the above

57. The production function
$Q = A\,[\beta K^{-a} + \alpha L^{-a}]^{-1/a}$ is homogeneous of degree
A. zero B. one
C. Infinity D. a

58. Given the total cost function
$C = 7Q^2 + 26Q + 5$, MC at Q = ₹ 5 is
A. ₹ 100 B. ₹ 200
C. ₹ 85 D. ₹ 96

59. Match the following :
List-I
I. Acceptance of H_0 when it is false
II. Mean is equal to degrees of freedom
III. Population is homogeneous
IV. Mean > Mode
List-II
1. Simple random sampling
2. Type II error
3. Positively skewed distribution
4. χ^2 Distribution
Codes:

	I	II	III	IV
A.	2	4	3	1
B.	1	2	3	4
C.	2	4	1	3
D.	4	1	2	3

60. For the regression model given below
$Y = \beta_0 + \beta_1 X + U$
$Y = 20 + 2X$
SE : 0.46
To test $H_0 : \beta_1 = 2.1$ against $H_1 : \beta_1 \neq 2.1$ (not equal to 2.1), test statistic $|t|$ is equal to
A. 4.609 B. 0.217
C. 4.34 D. 0.33

61. For the regression model
$Y = \beta_0 + \beta_1 X_1 + \beta_2 X_2 + ... + \beta_k X_k + e$
The degrees of freedom of test statistic $|t|$, with n observations is
A. n – k B. n – k + 1
C. n – k – 1 D. n + k – 1

62. The act of simultaneously buying a currency in one market and selling in another market is called
A. Speculation B. Spotting
C. Forwarding D. Arbitrage

63. All internationally traded services are covered under which of the following WTO agreements?
A. GATS B. TRIPS
C. TRIMS D. PTA

64. The Bretton-Woods system
A. set up a code of rules for nations to follow their conduct of international trade
B. set up borrowing facilities for nation's temporary balance of payments problems
C. Evolved over the years in several important ways
D. All of the above

65. Full employment and balance of payments equilibrium will be automatically achieved in an optimum currency area
A. if exchange rates are flexible
B. foreign capital flows into the country
C. if labour and capital move freely
D. if trade is liberalized

66. Examples of economic integration
I. Free trade area II. Customs union
III. Common market IV. Cartel
A. I and II are correct
B. II and III are correct
C. I, II and IV are correct
D. I, II and III are correct

67. Arrange the order of WTO ministerial
I. Seattle II. Cancun
III. Singapore IV. Doha
A. II, I, III, IV B. III, II, I, IV
C. III, I, IV, II D. II, III, I, IV

68. Maximum rate of tariff India can levy on edible oil under WTO Agreement on Agriculture is

A. 100% B. 150%
C. 200% D. 300%

69. WTO Agreement on Agriculture consists of
I. Domestic support II. Export subsidies
III. Market access IV. Input subsidies
A. I and IV are correct
B. II and IV are correct
C. I, II and III are correct
D. I, II and IV are correct

70. In Harrod's growth model, neutral technical progress implies technical progress as
A. Capital augmenting
B. Labour augmenting
C. Both labour and capital augmenting
D. Productivity increasing

71. Which are the two gaps affecting growth process of an economic system in the two gap model of growth?
A. Saving gap and investment gap
B. Income gap and consumption gap
C. Foreign exchange gap and domestic saving gap
D. Export gap and import gap

72. **Assertion (A) :** The new endogeneous growth theory examines production function that shows increasing returns.
Reason (R) : Because of specialization and investment in knowledge capital.
A. (A) is true, but (R) is false.
B. (R) is true, but (A) is false.
C. Both (A) and (R) are correct, but (R) is not the correct explanation of (A).
D. Both (A) and (R) are correct and (R) is the correct explanation of (A).

73. The 'Golden Age' model was developed by
A. Nicholas Kaldor B. Joan Robinson
C. J.R. Hicks D. R.F. Harrod

74. Terms of Trade of the developing countries are unfavourable due to the fact that whenever income in developed countries increases the demand for primary goods reduces because
A. Income elasticity of demand for primary goods is high.
B. Income elasticity of demand for primary goods is low.
C. Income elasticity of demand is neutral towards primary goods.
D. None of the above

75. T.W. Schultz has given the following ratios in relation to education for economic growth :
A. Education capital and labour ratio
B. Education labour ratio
C. Education-income ratio
D. Education labour ratio, education income ratio and education investment ratio

ANSWERS

1	2	3	4	5	6	7	8	9	10
B	B	D	A	C	*	A	D	D	B
11	12	13	14	15	16	17	18	19	20
B	A	A	D	C	C	B	D	B	B
21	22	23	24	25	26	27	28	29	30
A	D	A	C	B	C	B	B	A	C
31	32	33	34	35	36	37	38	39	40
C	B	D	B	C	D	A	C	B	B
41	42	43	44	45	46	47	48	49	50
A	B	A	B	D	B	B	C	D	D
51	52	53	54	55	56	57	58	59	60
A	B	D	B	C	D	B	D	C	B
61	62	63	64	65	66	67	68	69	70
C	D	A	D	C	D	C	D	C	B
71	72	73	74	75					
C	D	B	B	D					

* None of the given option is correct.